DRAMA
CRITICISM

Guide to Gale Literary Criticism Series

For criticism on	Consult these Gale series
Authors now living or who died after December 31, 1959	*CONTEMPORARY LITERARY CRITICISM (CLC)*
Authors who died between 1900 and 1959	*TWENTIETH-CENTURY LITERARY CRITICISM (TCLC)*
Authors who died between 1800 and 1899	*NINETEENTH-CENTURY LITERATURE CRITICISM (NCLC)*
Authors who died between 1400 and 1799	*LITERATURE CRITICISM FROM 1400 TO 1800 (LC)* *SHAKESPEAREAN CRITICISM (SC)*
Authors who died before 1400	*CLASSICAL AND MEDIEVAL LITERATURE CRITICISM (CMLC)*
Black writers of the past two hundred years	*BLACK LITERATURE CRITICISM (BLC)*
Authors of books for children and young adults	*CHILDREN'S LITERATURE REVIEW (CLR)*
Dramatists	*DRAMA CRITICISM (DC)*
Hispanic writers of the late nineteenth and twentieth centuries	*HISPANIC LITERATURE CRITICISM (HLC)*
Native North American writers and orators of the eighteenth, nineteenth, and twentieth centuries	*NATIVE NORTH AMERICAN LITERATURE (NNAL)*
Poets	*POETRY CRITICISM (PC)*
Short story writers	*SHORT STORY CRITICISM (SSC)*
Major authors from the Renaissance to the present	*WORLD LITERATURE CRITICISM, 1500 TO THE PRESENT (WLC)*

ISSN 1056-4349

DRAMA
CRITICISM

Criticism of the Most Significant and Widely Studied
Dramatic Works from All the World's Literatures

VOLUME 5

Lawrence J. Trudeau, Editor

Margaret Anne Haerens, Jeff Hill, Drew Kalasky, Jane Kelly Kosek,
Associate Editors

≋ Gale Research Inc.

An International Thomson Publishing Company

I(T)P

NEW YORK • LONDON • BONN • BOSTON • DETROIT • MADRID
MELBOURNE • MEXICO CITY • PARIS • SINGAPORE • TOKYO
TORONTO • WASHINGTON • ALBANY NY • BELMONT CA • CINCINNATI OH

STAFF

Lawrence J. Trudeau, *Editor*

Margaret Anne Haerens, Jeff Hill, Drew Kalasky, Jane Kelly Kosek, *Associate Editors*

Martha Bommarito, Debra A. Wells, *Assistant Editors*

Marlene H. Lasky *Permissions Manager*
Margaret A. Chamberlain, Linda M. Pugliese, *Permissions Specialists*

Susan Brohman, Diane Cooper, Maria L. Franklin, Arlene Johnson, Josephine M. Keene, Michele Lonoconus,
Maureen Puhl, Shalice Shah, Kimberly F. Smilay, Barbara A. Wallace, *Permissions Associates*

Edna Hedblad, Tyra Y. Phillips, *Permissions Assistants*

Victoria B. Cariappa, *Research Manager*
Andrew Guy Malonis, *Research Specialist*
Eva M. Felts, Donna Melnychenko, Tamara C. Nott,
Tracie A. Richardson, Norma Sawaya, *Research Associates*

Maria E. Bryson, *Research Assistants*

Mary Beth Trimper, *Production Director*
Mary Kelly, *Production Associate*

Cynthia Baldwin, *Product Design Manager*
Barbara J. Yarrow, *Graphic Services Supervisor*
C.J. Jonick, *Desktop Publisher*
Willie F. Mathis, *Camera Operator*
Pamela A. Hayes, *Photography Coordinator*

Library of Congress Catalog Card Number 92-648805
ISBN 0-8103-8941-X
ISSN 1056-4349

Printed in the United States of America
Published simultaneously in the United Kingdom
by Gale Research International Limited
(An affiliated company of Gale Research Inc.)
10 9 8 7 6 5 4 3 2 1

I(T)P™ Gale Research Inc., an International Thomson Publishing Company.
ITP logo is a trademark under license.

Contents

Preface vii

Acknowledgments xi

List of Authors xv

Preface

*D*rama Criticism (*DC*) is principally intended for beginning students of literature and theater as well as the average playgoer. The series is therefore designed to introduce readers to the most frequently studied playwrights of all time periods and nationalities and to present discerning commentary on dramatic works of enduring interest. Furthermore, *DC* seeks to acquaint the reader with the uses and functions of criticism itself. Selected from a diverse body of commentary, the essays in *DC* offer insights into the authors and their works but do not require that the reader possess a wide background in literary studies. Where appropriate, reviews of important productions of the plays discussed are also included to give students a heightened awareness of drama as a dynamic art form, one that many claim is fully realized only in performance.

DC was created in response to suggestions by the staffs of high school, college, and public libraries. These librarians observed a need for a series that assembles critical commentary on the world's most renowned dramatists in the same manner as Gale's *Short Story Criticism* (*SSC*) and *Poetry Criticism* (*PC*), which present material on writers of short fiction and poetry. Although playwrights are covered in such Gale literary criticism series as *Contemporary Literary Criticism* (CLC), *Twentieth-Century Literary Criticism* (*TCLC*), *Nineteenth-Century Literature Criticism* (*NCLC*), *Literature Criticism from 1400 to 1800* (*LC*), and *Classical and Medieval Literature Criticism* (*CMLC*), *Drama Criticism* directs more concentrated attention on individual dramatists than is possible in the broader, survey-oriented entries in these Gale series. Commentary on the works of William Shakespeare may be found in *Shakespearean Criticism* (*SC*).

Scope of the Series

By collecting and organizing commentary on dramatists, *DC* assists students in their efforts to gain insight into literature, achieve better understanding of the texts, and formulate ideas for papers and assignments. A variety of interpretations and assessments is offered, allowing students to pursue their own interests and promoting awareness that literature is dynamic and responsive to many different opinions.

Each volume of *DC* presents:

- 8-10 entries

- authors and works representing a wide range of nationalities and time periods

- a diversity of viewpoints and critical opinions.

Organization of an Author Entry

Each author entry consists of some or all of the following elements, depending on the scope and complexity of the criticism:

- The **author heading** consists of the playwright's most commonly used name, followed by birth and death dates. If an author consistently wrote under a pseudonym, the pseudonym is listed in the author heading and the real name given in parentheses on the first line of the introduction. Also located at the beginning of the introduction are any name variations under which the dramatist wrote, including transliterated forms of the names of authors whose languages use nonroman alphabets.

- A **portrait** of the author is included when available. Most entries also feature illustrations of people, places, and events pertinent to a study of the playwright and his or her works. When appropriate, photographs of the plays in performance are also presented.

- The **biographical and critical introduction** contains background information that familiarizes the reader with the author and the critical debates surrounding his or her works.

- The list of **principal works** is divided into two sections, each of which is organized chronologically by date of first performance. If this has not been conclusively determined, the composition or publication date is used. The first section of the principal works list contains the author's dramatic pieces. The second section provides information on the author's major works in other genres.

- Whenever available, **author commentary** is provided. This section consists of essays or interviews in which the dramatist discusses his or her own work or the art of playwriting in general.

- Essays offering **overviews and general studies of the dramatist's entire literary career** give the student broad perspectives on the writer's artistic development, themes and concerns that recur in several of his or her works, the author's place in literary history, and other wide-ranging topics.

- **Criticism of individual plays** offers the reader in-depth discussions of a select number of the author's most important works. In some cases, the criticism is divided into two sections, each arranged chronologically. When a significant performance of a play can be identified (typically, the premier of a twentieth-century work), the first section of criticism will feature **production reviews** of this staging. Most entries include sections devoted to **critical commentary** that assesses the literary merit of the selected plays. When necessary, essays are carefully excerpted to focus on the work under consideration; often, however, essays and reviews are reprinted in their entirety.

- As an additional aid to students, the critical essays and excerpts are often prefaced by **explanatory annotations**. These notes provide several types of useful information, including the critic's reputation and approach to literary studies as well as the scope and significance of the criticism that follows.

- A complete **bibliographic citation**, designed to help the interested reader locate the original essay or book, precedes each piece of criticism.

- The **further reading list** at the end of each entry comprises additional studies of the dramatist. It is divided into sections that help students quickly locate the specific information they need.

Other Features

- A **cumulative author index** lists all the authors who have appeared in *DC* and Gale's other Literature Criticism Series, as well as cross-references to related titles published by Gale, including *Contemporary Authors* and *Dictionary of Literary Biography*. A complete listing of the series included appears at the beginning of the index.

- A **cumulative nationality index** lists each author featured in *DC* by nationality, followed by the number of the *DC* volume in which the author appears.

- A **cumulative title index** lists in alphabetical order the individual plays discussed in the criticism contained in *DC*. Each title is followed by the author's name and the corresponding volume and page number(s) where commentary on the work may be located. Translations and variant titles are cross-referenced to the title of the play in its original language so that all references to the work are combined in one listing.

A Note to the Reader

When writing papers, students who quote directly from any volume in *Drama Criticism* may use the following general formats to footnote reprinted criticism. The first example pertains to material drawn from periodicals, the second to materials reprinted from books.

[1]Susan Sontag, "Going to the Theater, Etc.," *Partisan Review* XXXI, No. 3 (Summer 1964), 389-94; excerpted and reprinted in *Drama Criticism,* Vol. 1, ed. Lawrence J. Trudeau (Detroit: Gale Research, 1991), pp. 17-20.

[2]Eugene M. Waith, *The Herculean Hero in Marlowe, Chapman, Shakespeare and Dryden* (Chatto & Windus, 1962); excerpted and reprinted in *Drama Criticism,* Vol. 1, ed. Lawrence J. Trudeau (Detroit: Gale Research, 1991), pp. 237-47.

Suggestions are Welcome

Readers who wish to suggest authors to appear in future volumes of *DC,* or who have other suggestions, are cordially invited to contact the editor.

Acknowledgments

The editors wish to thank the copyright holders of the excerpted criticism included in this volume and the permissions managers of many book and magazine publishing companies for assisting us in securing reprint rights. We are also grateful to the staffs of the Detroit Public Library, the Library of Congress, the University of Detroit Mercy Library, Wayne State University Purdy/Kresge Library Complex, and the University of Michigan Libraries for making their resources available to us. Following is a list of the copyright holders who have granted us permission to reprint material in this volume of *DC*. Every effort has been made to trace copyright, but if omissions have been made, please let us know.

COPYRIGHTED EXCERPTS IN *DC*, VOLUME 5, WERE REPRINTED FROM THE FOLLOWING PERIODICALS:

Monographs, v. 42, March, 1975 for "Plays: Well Complicated" by Patti Gillespie. Copyright 1975 by the Speech Association of America. Reprinted by permission of Speech Communication Association and the author.—*Studies in American Drama, 1945-Present,* v. 6, 1991. Copyright 1991 by the Ohio State University Press. All rights reserved. Reprinted by permission of the publisher.—*Text & Performance Quarterly,* v. 9, October, 1989. Copyright 1989 by the Speech Communication Association. Reprinted by permission of the publisher.—*Theater,* v. 12, Spring, 1981 for "Witches, Ranters and the Middle Class: The Plays of Caryl Churchill" by Alisa Solomon; v. XIV, Summer-Fall, 1983 for "Sam Shepard's Free-For-All: 'Fool for Love' at the Magic Theatre" by William Kleb; " 'Fen' and the Production of a Feminist Ecotheater" by Sheila Rabillard. Copyright © by *Theater,* formerly *yale/theater* 1981, 1983, 1994. All reprinted by permission of the publisher and the respective authors.—*Theater Week,* v. 2, April 24, 1989 for "The Effects of Staten Island on a Pulitzer Prize-Winning Playwright" by Gerard Raymond. Copyright © 1989 by That New Magazine, Inc. Reprinted by permission of the author.—*Theatre Journal,* v. 36, March, 1984. © 1984, University and College Theatre Association of the American Theatre Association. Reprinted by permission of the publisher.—*Theatre Quarterly,* v. IV, August-October, 1974. Copyright © 1974 TQ Publications Ltd. —*Time,* New York, v. 121, June 13, 1983. Copyright 1983 Time Warner Inc. All rights reserved. Reprinted by permission from *Time.*—*The Times Literary Supplement,* n. 1326, June 30, 1927. Copyright The Times Supplements Limited 1927, renewed 1955. Reproduced from *The Times Literary Supplement* by permission.—*The Village Voice,* v. X, October 22, 1964 for a review of 'Cowboys' and 'The Rock Garden' by Michael Smith. Copyright © The Village Voice, Inc., 1964. Reprinted by permission of the author.—*The Virginia Quarterly Review,* v. 1, April, 1925. Copyright, 1925, renewed 1953, by *The Virginia Quarterly Review,* The University of Virginia. Reprinted by permission of the publisher.—*The Wall Street Journal,* June 24, 1983; April 12, 1989. © 1983, 1989 Dow Jones & Company, Inc. All rights reserved Worldwide. Both reprinted by permission of *The Wall Street Journal.*—*World Literature Written in English,* v. 15, November, 1976 for "J. P. Clark's 'The Raft': The Tragedy of Economic Impotence" by R. N. Egudu. © copyright 1976 *WLWE-World Literature Written in English.* Reprinted by permission of the publisher and the author./ v. 18, November, 1979; v. 28, Spring, 1988. © copyright 1979, 1988 *WLWE-World Literature Written in English.* Both reprinted by permission of the publisher.

COPYRIGHTED EXCERPTS IN *DC,* VOLUME 5, WERE REPRINTED FROM THE FOLLOWING BOOKS:

Adler, Thomas P. From *Mirror on the Stage: The Pulitzer Plays as an Approach to American Drama.* Purdue University Press, 1987. Copyright © 1987 by Purdue Research Foundation, West Lafayette, Indiana 47907. All rights reserved. Reprinted by permission of the publisher.—Auerbach, Doris. From *Sam Shepard, Arthur Kopit, and the Off Broadway Theatre.* Twayne, 1982. Copyright © 1982 by G. K. Hall & Company. All rights reserved. Reprinted with the permission of Simon & Schuster Macmillan from the Twayne Publishers book.—Baines, Barbara Joan. From *The Lust Motif in the Plays of Thomas Middleton.* Institut für Englische Sprache und Literatur, 1973. Reprinted by permission of the publisher.—Balakian, Anna. From "Pirandello's 'Six Characters' and Surrealism," in *A Companion to Pirandello Studies.* Edited by John Louis DiGaetani. Greenwood Press, 1991. Copyright © 1991 by John Louis DiGaetani. All rights reserved. Reprinted by permission of Greenwood Publishing Group, Inc., Westport, CT.—Bassnett, Susan. From "Henry IV—The Tragic Humorist," in *A Companion to Pirandello Studies.* Edited by John Louis DiGaetani. Greenwood Press, 1991. Copyright © 1991 by John Louis DiGaetani. All rights reserved. Reprinted by permission of Greenwood Publishing Group, Inc., Westport, CT.—Bentley, Eric. From *The Playwright as Thinker: A Study of Drama in Modern Times.* Reynal & Hitchcock, 1946. Copyright 1946, renewed 1973 by Eric Bentley. Reprinted by permission of Harcourt Brace & Company.—Betsko, Kathleen, and Rachel Koenig. From an interview in *Interviews with Contemporary Women Playwrights.* Morrow, 1987. Copyright © 1987 by Kathleen Betsko and Rachel Koenig. All rights reserved. Reprinted by permission of William Morrow and Company, Inc. In the British Commonwealth by Rachel Koenig.—Bloom, Michael. From "Visions of the End: The Early Plays," in *American Dreams: The Imagination of Sam Shepard.* Edited by Bonnie Marranca. Performing Arts Journal Publication, 1981. Copyright © 1981 by Performing Arts Journal Publications. All rights reserved. Reprinted by permission of the publisher.—Brown, Janet. From *Taking Center Stage: Feminism in Contemporary U.S. Drama.* The Scarecrow Press, Inc., 1991.

xiii

List of Playwrights Covered in *DC*

Caryl Churchill
1938-

INTRODUCTION

Churchill is one of Britain's foremost female playwrights. Her works are distinguished by unconventional dramatic methods, such as the manipulation of time sequence, a flexible approach to characterization, and the incorporation of elements of prominent literary works or historical events. Acknowledging herself to be both a socialist and feminist, Churchill illustrates the hypocrisy and conflicts inherent within society and culture in works that analyze conventions of behavior and gender roles, the capitalist and class system, the institution of the nuclear family, and most prominently, the status of women in a patriarchal society.

BIOGRAPHICAL INFORMATION

Churchill was born in London, the only child of a political cartoonist and an actress. In the late 1940s her family emigrated to Canada, where Churchill completed her primary and secondary education. Returning to England after high school, she attended college at Oxford where she received a bachelor's degree in English literature in 1960. While at Oxford, Churchill's first play, the one-act *Downstairs*, was produced at the National Union of Students Drama Festival. She subsequently married and began to raise a family, but she found the role of suburban wife and mother restrictive. Although she continued writing—mainly radio plays—Churchill has described this period as a frustrating one: "During that time I felt isolated. I had small children and was having miscarriages. It was an extremely solitary life. What politicized me was being discontent with my own way of life—with being a barrister's wife and just being at home with small children." Churchill's first major stage play, *Owners*, reflects some of the author's growing political and feminist concerns in its examination of both material and sexual "ownership." The success of this play led to Churchill's appointment in 1974 as the first-ever woman playwright-in-residence at the Royal Court Theatre. In 1976 Churchill began working with the feminist theater company Monstrous Regiment, a collaboration which was to permanently influence the content and method of her writing. That same year Churchill commenced an association with another alternative company, Joint Stock, with which she produced a number of her most successful works, including *Light Shining in Buckinghamshire,* the Obie award-winning *Cloud Nine, Fen,* and *A Mouthful of Birds.* A prolific writer, Churchill has consistently published and produced at least one play per year since the early 1970s. In 1987, she won a second Obie for *Serious Money.*

MAJOR WORKS

Churchill's body of work represents the evolution of the author's own personal and political awareness. Her early

radio plays, as she herself has described them, "tended to be about bourgeois middle-class life and the destruction of it." Churchill's emerging feminism is evident in her plays of the 1970s, such as *Objections to Sex and Violence, Vinegar Tom* (produced with Monstrous Regiment), and *Cloud Nine.* This last work examines the interconnectedness of sexual, racial, and political repression. The first act presents a Victorian family in colonial Africa; the second act takes place a century later but features the same characters, who have aged only twenty-five years. Actors from the first act assume new roles in the second, crossing racial and gender lines. In the 1980s, Churchill continued to focus on women's issues with works such as *Top Girls* and *Fen,* but also began to address other social and political issues. *Top Girls* employs mythical, historical, and contemporary female characters to examine the loss of feminine identity that women suffer as they strive for economic, social, or professional status. *Fen,* described by Sheila Rabillard as a study in "ecofeminism," is comprised of a series of vignettes focusing on the lives of poor women sharecroppers. Exploring other issues, Churchill offered a seriocomic investigation of crime, punishment, and social responsibility in *Softcops,* in which the characters represent various approaches to the deterrence of crime. *Serious Money*, patterned after

Thomas Shadwell's 1662 play *The Stockjobbers*, satirizes the London stock exchange and involves murder, drug smuggling, and greed. *The Skriker*, Churchill's most recent work, is a multi-media production incorporating dance, music, and elaborate sets. In this work she returns to the theme of witchcraft and female persecution—also addressed in *Vinegar Tom*—as a skriker haunts the lives of two women who are social outcasts in medieval England.

CRITICAL RECEPTION

Response to Churchill's works has been largely mixed, and Churchill herself has observed the sometimes contradictory interpretations of her plays: "I'm accused of being both too optimistic and too pessimistic . . . and of being too philosophical and aesthetic and not sufficiently political." Initial reactions to her plays have at times been negative, with reviewers judging the disjointed time sequences, reversals of gender roles, and abrupt shifts in tone to be pointless and confusing. Later critics, however, have been able to discover underlying connections and congruences among the seemingly disparate elements in the plays. They have noted provocative juxtapositions, which may be ironic or poignant or both. For example, as Austin E. Quigley has observed regarding the unconventional role changing in *Cloud Nine*, "the double approach to character . . . opens up a realm in which not just double, but multiple, options are available. The performers and the audience, not just the dramatist, must make choices among them."

PRINCIPAL WORKS

STAGE PLAYS

Downstairs 1958
Owners 1972
Objections to Sex and Violence 1975
Vinegar Tom 1976
Light Shining in Buckinghamshire 1976
Traps 1977
Cloud Nine 1979; revised with the subtitle *A Comedy of Multiple Organisms* 1984
Top Girls 1982; revised 1984
Fen 1983
Softcops 1984
A Mouthful of Birds [with David Lan] 1986
Serious Money 1987; revised with the subtitle *A City Comedy* 1990
Lives of the Great Poisoners 1991
The Skriker 1994

RADIO PLAYS

The Ants 1962
Lovesick 1967
Identical Twins 1968
Abortive 1971

Not, Not, Not, Not, Not Enough Oxygen 1971
Henry's Past 1972
Schreber's Nervous Illness 1972
Perfect Happiness 1973
Crimes 1982

TELEVISION PLAYS

The Judge's Wife 1972
Turkish Delight 1974
The After Dinner Joke 1978
The Legion Hall Bombing 1978

COLLECTIONS

Plays 1 [includes *Owners, Vinegar Tom, Traps, Light Shining in Buckinghamshire, Cloud Nine*] 1985
Plays 2 [includes *Top Girls, Fen, Softcops, Serious Money*] 1990
Shorts [includes *Lovesick; Abortive; Not, Not, Not, Not, Not Enough Oxygen; Schreber's Nervous Illness; The Hospital at the Time of the Revolution; The Judge's Wife; The After Dinner Joke; Seagulls; Three More Sleepless Nights; Hot Fudge*] 1991

AUTHOR COMMENTARY

Interview with Churchill (1984)

SOURCE: *Interviews with Contemporary Women Playwrights*, by Kathleen Betsko and Rachel Koenig, Beech Tree Books, 1987, pp. 75-84.

[*The interviewers Kathleen Betsko and Rachel Koenig are both American drama critics; Emily Mann is an American playwright. The following is taken from a two-part interview, first with Betsko and Koenig in February 1984, and then with Mann in November of that year. Churchill discusses her association with Joint Stock Theatre in London, her politics, and her writing career.*]

[Interviewer]: *Is there a female aesthetic? And we'd like you to wrap this question up once and for all. [Laughter]*

[Churchill]: I don't see how you can tell until there are so many plays by women that you can begin to see what they have in common that's different from the way men have written, and there are still relatively so few. And we have things in common with male playwrights who are worried about similar things in their particular country and who have worked in the same theaters with the same directors. So it's hard to separate out and think of "women playwrights" rather than just "playwrights." Though I do remember before I wrote **Top Girls** thinking about women barristers—how they were in a minority and had to imitate men to succeed—and I was thinking of them as different from me. And then I thought, "Wait a minute, my whole concept of what plays might be is from plays written by men. I don't have to put on a wig, speak in a special voice, but how far do I assume things that have been defined by men?" There isn't a simple answer to that. And I remember long before that thinking of the "maleness" of the traditional structure of plays, with conflict and building in a certain way to a climax. But it's not something I think about very often. Playwriting will change not just because more women are doing it but because more women are doing other things as well. And of course men will be influenced by that too. So maybe you'll still be no nearer to defining a female aesthetic.

Some of the playwrights we've interviewed suggest there are no "lost masterpieces" and that "the cream will rise to the top" in terms of women's writing for the stage.

Most theaters are still controlled by men and people do tend to be able to see promise in people who are like themselves. Women directors have pointed out to me how established men tend to take a young male director under their wing, and seem to feel more uncomfortable with a woman director because they can't quite see where she is, because they weren't like that at her age. I think the same thing can happen with writers: If you're at the stage where you are promising but not doing it all that well yet, it's perhaps easier for a man choosing plays to see the potential in a man writer. I don't know about "lost masterpieces" but people don't usually start out writing masterpieces and women may have less chance of getting started. Having productions does seem to make people write better.

Has the political climate for women dramatists changed drastically since you began writing plays?

I began writing plays in 1958, and I don't think I knew of any other women playwrights then. Luckily, I didn't think about it. Do you know Tillie Olsen's book *Silences?* She says that at different times, whole categories of people are enabled to write. You tend to think of your own development only having to do with yourself and it's exciting to discover it in a historical context. When I began it was quite hard for any playwrights to get started in London. The English Stage Company had just started a policy of doing new writing at the Royal Court, but that was almost the only place. I had student productions at first, and then wrote for radio. In the late sixties and early seventies there was a surge of fringe theaters and interest in new writing, starting with the Theatre Upstairs and the Royal Court, and that was the first place to do a professional stage production of one of my plays, ***Owners,*** in 1972. For a while, a lot of writers were getting produced for the first time, though far fewer women than men. Gradually during the seventies the number of women increased, coming partly through fringe theaters and partly through women's theater groups. In the last five years there seem to be far more women playwrights and some theaters are more open to them, though others still aren't. At the moment, because of the financial cuts, it's again become quite hard for all playwrights. Theaters are having to do co-productions with other theaters because they haven't enough money to do a whole year's work on

their grants, so it means one new play gets done instead of two. The Royal Court, for instance, can now only afford to do four new plays in the main house instead of eight. But I get the impression life is even harder for playwrights in the United States than in England because of there not being a subsidized theater.

In Laurie Stone's Village Voice *interview [March 1, 1983], you talked about women becoming Coca-Cola executives and you said, "Well, that's not what I mean by feminism." What exactly do you mean by feminism?*

When I was in the States in '79 I talked to some women who were saying how well things were going for women in America now with far more top executives being women, and I was struck by the difference between that and the feminism I was used to in England, which is far more closely connected with socialism. And that was one of the ideas behind writing ***Top Girls,*** that achieving things isn't necessarily good; it matters *what* you achieve.

Thatcher had just become prime minister; there was talk about whether it was an advance to have a woman prime minister if it was someone with policies like hers: She may be a woman but she isn't a sister, she may be a sister but she isn't a comrade. And, in fact, things have got much worse for women under Thatcher. So that's the context of that remark. I do find it hard to conceive of a right-wing feminism. Of course, socialism and feminism aren't synonymous, but I feel strongly about both and wouldn't be interested in a form of one that didn't include the other.

Do you think it's odd, given the fact that there is at best indifference, at worst hostility, [to] political plays in America, that your works are so popular here?

Is it true that on the whole plays here tend to be more family-centered, personal, individual-centered?

Yes, more psychological.

Whereas I've been quite heavily exposed to a tradition of looking at the larger context of groups of people. It doesn't mean you don't look at families or individuals within that, but you are also looking at bigger things. Like with the kind of work Joint Stock Theatre Group has done, where you go and research a subject and where you have a lot of characters, even if played by only a few people. It tends to open things out.

The critics do ask, "Where are the American plays with the larger social issues?" Unfortunately, when one comes along our own critics usually turn thumbs down if the politics are overt. An overt political position is considered poor craft or preaching.

When I was in San Francisco I was talking to the people at the Eureka Theatre [where Richard Seyd directed a production of ***Cloud Nine*** in 1983] and they were talking about developing a school of playwriting which would break away from family-centered plays, and write about other issues.

Could you talk a little about working with Joint Stock?

I've worked with them three times, on *Light Shining in Buckinghamshire* [1976], *Cloud Nine* [1979] and *Fen* [1983]. The company was started in 1974 by several people, including Max Stafford-Clark, who directed *Light Shining* and *Cloud Nine.* There's usually a workshop of three or four weeks when the writer, director and actors research a subject, then about ten weeks when the writer goes off and writes the play, then a six-week rehearsal when you're usually finishing writing the play. Everyone's paid the same wage each week they're working and everyone makes decisions about the budget and the affairs of the company, and because of that responsibility and the workshop everyone is much more involved than usual in the final play. It's not perfect, but it is good, and I do notice the contrast with more hierarchical organizations and feel uncomfortable in them. Because everyone is involved it's taken for granted that everyone will have good parts, so you can't write a couple of main characters and give everyone else very little to do. And usually because of the subject matter, the plays tend to have a large cast of characters, although the company is about six or eight, and the actors double. It's very pressured because the tour's booked and the posters printed long before the play is finished. It's a very intense way of working.

Do you find collaboration difficult?

No, I like it. I'd always been very solitary as a writer before and I like working that closely with other people. You don't collaborate on writing the play, you still go away and write it yourself, so to that extent it's the same as usual. What's different is that you've had a period of researching something together, not just information, but your attitudes to it, and possible ways of showing things, which means that when you come back with the writing you're much more open to suggestions.

Do you feel subordinate to the director in rehearsal? One writer we interviewed was actually ejected from her rehearsals by a well-known director.

No, I've always got on well with directors. But it depends on having someone with roughly the same ideas as you so you trust each other, and if you do work well together you keep on with the same people, as I have with Max Stafford-Clark and Les Waters. It's one of the things the Theatre Writers' Union has put in contracts, the writer's right to attend rehearsals, and it's very important. Though, of course, if you're having to invoke the contract you're already in trouble.

Does the playwright have an obligation to take a moral and political stance?

It's almost impossible not to take one, whether you intend to or not. Most plays can be looked at from a political perspective and have said something, even if it isn't what you set out to say. If you wrote a West End comedy relying on conventional sexist jokes, that's taking a moral and political stance, though the person who wrote it might say,

"I was just writing an entertaining show." Whatever you do your point of view is going to show somewhere. It usually only gets noticed and called "political" if it's against the status quo. There are times when I feel I want to deal with immediate issues and times when I don't. I do like the stuff of theater, in the same way people who are painting like paint; and of course when you say "moral and political" that doesn't have to imply reaching people logically or overtly, because theater can reach people on all kinds of other levels too. Sometimes one side or the other is going to have more weight. Sometimes it's going to be about images, more like a dream to people, and sometimes it's going to be more like reading an article. And there's room for all that. But either way, the issues you feel strongly about are going to come through, and they're going to be a moral and political stance in some form. Sometimes more explicitly, sometimes less.

[Mann]: *How do you go about gathering research?*

[Churchill]: *Fen* is the most documentary of the plays, I suppose. We didn't use tape recorders. We went off to stay in a village and everyone would go out each day and talk to people and make notes or remember. The actors in the group would report back by becoming the person they met and saying the things the person had said; you could ask more questions and the actor would start to improvise and develop the character. Those of us who weren't actors simply described what had happened. So I was left with a lot of notes and quotes and things different people had said. But never a whole speech, just lines here and there. And I didn't make any characters who were based on a single person. For example, the old great-grandmother's speech on her birthday, practically every line is something that somebody actually said to us, but it's a composite of many different people. We met a woman who had been the secretary of the agricultural union, and the murder story, the Frank and Val story, was a newspaper cutting about someone she knew. A lot of the union references in the play were hers. There were a lot of things from one particular woman that went into the character Shirley, who's always working, about pride in working hard and not giving up, lines like "I didn't want my mother to think she'd bred a gibber."

You and the company started out with subject matter, an idea?

We started out very open—we were going to do a workshop in the Fens. But before we went, Les Waters, the director, and I had talked a lot about people having a bad time in the country; that's where the original sense of direction came from. We made a company of more women than men, so that was a decision affecting the subject of the play that was taken before we began the workshop. We read the book *Fen Women* by Mary Chamberlain before we went and during the workshop. And by the end of the workshop we had all focused on women land workers and knew the kind of issues it might be about.

But the difference between that way of working and what you've done, Emily, is that mine is an invented play, whereas you've written documentary things drawing on tapes.

You were making a completely fictional play, based on what you learned, from your response to being in the Fens and meeting all those people. In Execution of Justice *I was working with the Eureka Theatre Company, and we talked and talked and talked and batted ideas around, then they gathered research for me, and I went out to San Francisco and did field work in the Castro district, and so on. The play is documentary, yes; that was a choice I made.*

The only documentary play I've done was a television play about Northern Ireland, about a trial in the Diplock courts, which were introduced in 1973 because the government felt it was too hard to get convictions otherwise. There's no jury and only one judge. I had the transcript of a trial of a boy who was given sixteen years. A bomb had been planted in a British Legion Hall where some people were playing cards, and a boy walked in, put the thing down, and said, "Clear the hall" and they all went out. Half an hour later, a small bomb went off and nobody was hurt. The trial was extraordinary because there was no evidence to say the boy who was accused did it, except the police saying he'd confessed, which he denied. There was no signed statement by him. And there was an old man who'd been in the hall who said, "I don't know what boy it was but it was definitely not *that* boy." There was no positive identification at all, and it was hard to believe you would get a conviction in a normal court. So I did a play for television with Roland Joffe; it meant reducing the nine and a half hours of trial transcript. We put on a voice-over at the beginning and end of the program that explained the Diplock courts, and the BBC took it off because they said it was political comment, and put one of their own in different words, which they said was objective. We took our names off the credits as a protest. That was the only documentary I've ever done, and again it's different from what you've done because it was more specific and didn't involve so much research or so much material. Most of the plays I've written have been without any research, from what I already knew or what I imagined.

Let's talk about your play Top Girls.

When I wrote *Top Girls* I was writing it by myself and not for a company. I wanted to write about women doing different kinds of work and didn't feel I knew enough about it. Then I thought, this is ridiculous, if you were with a company you'd go out and talk to people, so I did. Which is how I came up with the employment agency in the second act.

Are there specific characters in Top Girls *that have their real life counterparts?*

Quite a few of the things Win tells Angie about her life are things different people said to me. And of course the dead women at the dinner are all based on someone [from art, literature or history]. But apart from that, it's imaginary.

Tell me about the ways in which Top Girls *has been misunderstood.*

What I was intending to do was make it first look as though it was celebrating the achievements of women and then—

by showing the main character, Marlene, being successful in a very competitive, destructive, capitalist way—ask, what kind of achievement is that? The idea was that it would start out looking like a feminist play and turn into a socialist one, as well. And I think on the whole it's mostly been understood like that. A lot of people have latched on to Marlene leaving her child, which interestingly was something that came very late. Originally the idea was just that Marlene was "writing off" her niece, Angie, because she'd never make it; I didn't yet have the plot idea that Angie was actually Marlene's own child. Of course women are pressured to make choices between working and having children in a way that men aren't, so it *is* relevant, but it isn't the main point of it.

There's another thing that I've recently discovered with other productions of *Top Girls.* In Greece, for example, where fewer women go out to work, the attitude from some men seeing it was, apparently, that the women in the play who'd gone out to work weren't very nice, weren't happy, and they abandoned their children. They felt the play was obviously saying women *shouldn't* go out to work—they took it to mean what they were wanting to say about women themselves, which is depressing. Highly depressing. [Laughter] Another example of its being open to misunderstanding was a production in Cologne, Germany, where the women characters were played as miserable and quarrelsome and competitive at the dinner, and the women in the office were neurotic and incapable. The waitress slunk about in a catsuit like a bunnygirl and Win changed her clothes on stage in the office. It just turned into a complete travesty of what it was supposed to be. So that's the sort of moment when you think you'd rather write novels, because the productions can't be changed.

I don't know whether we're safer in the theater or not. . .

With a play you do leave more room for other things and that's one of the attractions, that people can keep coming to it fresh and doing it differently. Lots of times I've liked foreign productions. I liked *Cloud Nine* in New York [at Lucille Lortel's Theater De Lys, directed by Tommy Tune, 1981], and it was very different, though in many ways it wasn't as different as you might have expected. I was at rehearsals and Tommy Tune had seen Max Stafford-Clark's production in London. But still it was different.

What were the big differences?

Two main differences. It was broader, so it was more farcical in the first act and more emotional in the second. Tommy [Tune] talked about "permission to laugh" and thought the American audience might not realize at the beginning of the play that it was meant to be funny if the colonial thing was played as straight as it had been in England. And the other difference—which ties in with the more emotional feeling of the second half—is the moving of Betty's monologue and the song to the end of the play, to make more of a climax. It was sort of wonderful—the emotion of the end of the play in the American production—but I didn't really like it as much because it threw so much emphasis onto Betty as an individual, while the other

A scene from Owners, *Churchill's first professional production, which opened at the Royal Court Theatre Upstairs on 6 December 1972.*

way seemed to be more about the development of a group of people, in the same way as the first act. The New York version also meant that it ended with her very solitary, having the self-discovery that she enjoys sex in masturbation, but without taking her on from that to anything else. Whereas that monologue originally came earlier in the scene so you know from that that she's a sexual person and then you see her make her first move out toward someone else, even though it's a completely ridiculous and wrong move, trying to pick up her son's gay lover, but you know she'll have another go another time and it will work.

This is incredible, how much this changes what the play is about. Was it Tommy Tune who changed it? Or did you agree to it?

Moving the monologue was an idea of Tommy's that he had when I wasn't there, but I was quite glad and interested to try it. And I knew he wanted very strongly to make more of a climax at the end of the play. In the original production there's a song before the last scene of the second act and it's as if during it things change, because in the last scene everyone has moved on a bit and things have got better. But Tommy felt having the music there would make people

think that was the ending, because we had a sort of climax with the music and then the last scene where people had changed and it ended more levelly and coolly. He wanted a different song, more uplifting, whereas the original one was a bit more ironical, and he wanted the music and climax right at the end. So it had quite a different shape and feeling to it.

So the difference for you is Tommy Tune changed your structure and in so doing changed the broader-based contextual look at the whole society.

Yes, they took it more to an emotional, personal point. And I suppose we could then launch off into the idea that this is one of the differences between the kind of work that comes out of a company like Joint Stock, which tends to deal more with groups of people and society as opposed to the personal. . . .

Yes.

You find lots of works which are just about people and their feelings in England, too. It isn't as if everything here was socially based. But there is a stronger vein of that, in this country, I think.

OVERVIEWS AND GENERAL STUDIES

Alisa Solomon (essay date 1981)

SOURCE: "Witches, Ranters and the Middle Class: The Plays of Caryl Churchill," in *Theater,* Vol. 12, No. 2, Spring, 1981, pp. 49-55.

[*Below, Solomon provides an overview of Churchill's writing career, her dramatic technique, and her incorporation of socialist-feminist politics into her works.*]

Whether Caryl Churchill writes about frighteningly familiar middle-class life, 17th Century witches, Levellers and Ranters of the 1640's, or 1960's burnouts, her plays challenge our most basic assumptions, those that make it possible for us to function in the most mundane and necessary ways. Forcing us to take a second look at our usually unshaken premises, Churchill's plays won't allow us the regular comfort of supposed truths about human nature, Western values, social organization, or historical progress.

But Churchill's plays do not occupy a safely distant metaphysical stratosphere. Their issues confront us in terms of human, earthly existence. Churchill's questionings insinuate themselves into our experiences of her plays. Her plays do not assault their audiences, affording us the chance to erect barriers against their thorny uncertainties. They facinate and entertain; their challenges are sneaky.

Churchill is one of those British playwrights categorized as leftist or political writers, who are beginning to achieve recognition in this country. This group includes Edward Bond, Howard Brenton, David Edgar, Steve Gooch, David Hare, Snoo Wilson, and others. There are difficulties in assuming any consensus among these leftist writers, even though they do comprise a distinct group. John McGrath, the founder of the 7:84 Theater Company, for instance, strongly opposes David Edgar's belief that the way to socialist theater lies through the Royal Court and Royal Shakespeare Company, England's largest and most established theaters. Churchill's identification within this group is even more complicated since, as she stated in an interview, "if pushed to labels, I would be prepared to take on both socialist and feminist."

Churchill is one of several women who have been making significant contributions to the body of political playwriting in England. With the exception of Pam Gems, whose play *Piaf,* about the mythology of the star performer, opened on Broadway after a long success in England, these women receive fewer productions on the main stages of England's most exposed theaters than their male colleagues. Their work often addresses feminist issues related to the lack of regard, fearful misunderstanding, and condescending wonder with which their work is received. But just as there is no single party line shared by leftist writers, it would be a mistake to lump these women together as representing the unified feminist voice of England. There are disagreements among feminist writers over purpose, procedure, and places of work. Margaretta D'Arcy, for example, believes that current political theater is obliged to engage the issue of British imperialism and involvement in Ireland. Michelene Wandor, perhaps the most militant feminist among these writers opposes D'Arcy. She is more interested in examining specific social issues, particularly those involving:

> the relationship between the material exploitation and ideological oppression of women, the way their function in the family is used as an excuse to limit their activities outside the family, and the way the ideology of the nuclear heterosexual family constrains sexual choice and sexual practice in general.
>
> ("Sexual Politics and the Strategy of Socialist Theater" [*Theatre Quarterly* 36])

Churchill takes a broader approach than D'Arcy and Wandor. She wants to expose the interrelatedness of particular social issues, and their effect on individuals' lives. At a symposium on political writing she stated:

> If people come to a play completely non-political and they go out opened up to the feeling that socialism is a good idea, that would be much more than most plays achieve.

Clearly, there is a danger in treating these female writers as a homogeneous unit, as if they converge into some kind of literary and politicized hydra. Another common and misleading error in approaching women writers is criticism's affirmative action: the benevolent embrace and praise of a mediocre writer simply on the basis of gender. Churchill's fascinating work, however, does not succumb to such patronization. Her plays are respectable when judged by the most critical of standards, and offer one of the best instances of how a body of drama with political biases can succeed. With no claim to being exhaustive, I want to introduce Churchill's work by examining four of her plays. Soon, perhaps Churchill's plays will be published and produced here. Until then, American readers will have to content themselves with imported copies or the summaries that follow.

Churchill began writing when she was an undergraduate at Oxford with some "broadly groping towards anti-capitalist plays" (Churchill quoted by Katherine Itzin in *Stages of Revolution* [1980]). During the sixties she wrote some radio plays which she describes as generally about the destruction of bourgeois middle-class life. They include: *The Ants,* (1963); *Lovesick,* (1967); *Identical Twins,* (1968); *Abortive,* (1971); *Not, Not, Not, Not, Not Enough Oxygen,* (1971); *Schreber's Nervous Illness,* (1972); *Henry's Past,* (1972); and *Perfect Happiness,* (1973).

Her professional stage plays, beginning with *Owners* in 1972 also question the values of bourgeois life and the conditions necessary for few to enjoy it. When Churchill focuses on society's oppression of women, she is not engaging in any single issue sloganeering. She explores this situation as one example of the oppression and alienation of people that she sees as an unavoidable effect of capitalism.

Churchill's characters' psychic, emotional and ethical experience are the inexorable result of their socio-political organization—their social being determines their thought. Churchill questions that organization and reveals our tendency to mistake the systematic structures that determine our thought for the necessities of human nature. And she asks us to question the mechanisms by which we apply our schematized thinking to experience. But Churchill is not presenting treatises scrambling to disguise themselves as drama. She has no *a priori* ideological tenets to drape like plastic furniture covers over her art. Rather, the political values she examines are intrinsic to the writing. Perhaps this harmony is a result of her gradual and personal development of political consciousness:

> What politicized me was being discontent with my own way of life, of being a barrister's wife and just being at home with small children . . . My attitude then was entirely to do with self-expression of my own personal pain and anger. It wasn't thought out . . . (But now) if pushed to labels, I would be prepared to take on both socialist and feminist . . .

Owners, first produced at the Royal Court Theater Upstairs, provides Churchill's most naked and lean dramatic treatment of her socialist and feminist concern. As her first play, it is the most schematic and conventional. But it exhibits the clear starting point of Churchill's search for a style that will embody her vision. Though the play has formal characteristics of a naturalistic melodrama, these conventions are stretched and tested—as if they can't quite contain Churchill's unconventional ideas—with macabre comic elements and a subtle grotesqueness of characters. The play also demonstrates Churchill's ability—sometimes unexpected in one with so extensive a background in radio drama—to make use of the visual richness possible on the stage.

As its title suggests, *Owners* concerns the proprietary impulse of Western society. As the desire to possess includes other people, sexism is shown to be a consequence of the obsession to own. Clegg, a butcher whose coarseness is tersely established as he hacks chickens while making inane small talk with his housewife customers, cannot tolerate the professional success of his wife Marion, a shrewd property speculator. Unable to accept the possibility of not having absolute control over her—"She can stand on her own two feet which is something I abominate in a woman"—Clegg plans to murder her and enlists Worsley, Marion's office assistant, in this plot. But Worsley is so preoccupied with trying to kill himself that he never manages to do Marion in. Yet each of his suicide attempts is unsuccessful, repeatedly interrupted, he says, by a good samaritan who represents one perverse extreme of materialistic life. "Life is a leasehold. It belongs to God the almighty landlord. You musn't take your life because its God's property, not yours," he argues. As a running gag, Worsley appears progressively more bandaged and bedraggled with each entrance.

Churchill does not stack the deck to support her feminist concerns. The need to own and control is not exclusive to the male characters. Marion wants to have and keep others too—a former lover, and a child. In order to regain control over the lover, Alec's, affections, Marion buys the house where he is a tenant and threatens to raise the rent exorbitantly. Unlike all the other characters, Alec has become completely passive. "He just wants nothing," his wife Lisa complains. Thus, Lisa is the one who must take action if they are to keep their apartment. Marion, infertile, names the price: Lisa's new baby.

Thus, Churchill is proposing that even the most basic of human actions can be overcome by capitalistic preoccupations. This relation of sexism to sexuality is most vividly suggested in a scene at a strip joint. Marion and Worsley discuss business as Clegg, droolingly intent on the stripper and her pistol, murmurs crassly, gasps, moans, and shouts. Continuing to consider women as objects, Clegg persuades Lisa to sleep with him, promising that he will then help her retrieve her child. While "possessing" her in bed, Clegg exclaims, "Vengeance is mine . . . this is his chattle. I've got it." But Clegg isn't satisfied with this retaliation, and he employs Worsley to kill Alec. This time Worsley succeeds by setting their building on fire. We learn from Worsley's report (despite the wicked landlord, there is no melodrama of flames blazing on stage) that Lisa escapes with the baby Worsley had secretly returned to her. Alec leaves the apartment "walking quite calmly considering the heat." But when he remembers the neighbors' baby and returns for it "He rose as if climbing the stairs. Turning into flames quite silently."

In an interview printed along with *Owners* in *Plays and Players* (January 1973), Churchill discusses this image of Alec, and his contrast to the other characters who have not overcome the will to possess:

> The thing of a man being totally passive and walking through fire and jumping into water and not being affected because he doesn't expect to be. Just going with things. Going with the fire and the water. And then people say afterwards "How did you walk through fire?" he says, "What fire?" Then of course he knows, he can't go back without burning himself. The complete opposite of the feeling of tremendous striving and getting and owning, and feeling one must be in control of one's property, one's family, one's life.

Alec embodies this opposition to materialism and underscores the play's question about what might be left to life once the urge to get and keep is recognized as empty.

While *Owners* is not totally free of the tendency for characters to exemplify philosophical stances, it is not a flat tract that celebrates passivity. Churchill doesn't really side with Alec. Even as the only presented alternative to the challenged attitudes, Alec is not very attractive. We are not meant to tolerate, any more than Lisa can, Alec's lack of desire, ambition, or self-expression. Churchill does not offer any simple moral even though the emblematic characters suggest that she might. This play contains the seeds of Churchill's grappling with interconnected and complicated issues. Summing up some of these issues, Churchill states in the *Plays and Players* interview:

it has to do with the whole thing of western capitalistic individualism, puritanism, and everything which came out of Christianity.

In two later plays, Churchill further explores the relationship of Christianity and puritanism to capitalism, and its human consequences. In *Vinegar Tom* this notion is considered in terms of sexual politics and the oppression of women.

With *Vinegar Tom* Churchill begins to find an innovative style that is more suited to her thematic concerns. Her ideas also become more sophisticated in this play. Instead of presenting exemplars of various facets of materialistic thinking in an individualistic drama as in *Owners, Vinegar Tom* offers complex characters whose personal lives are foregrounded in a socio-political context. The characters' social being is brought into the action, and their behavior is the dramatically linked product of that being. Part of this development may be a result of her method of creating the play. In 1976 she collaborated with the feminist theater company, the Monstrous Regiment. Their influence on her was significant, as she remarks:

> Discussing with Monstrous Regiment helped me towards a more objective and analytical way of looking at things. Their attitude toward witches was in terms of economic pressure and the role of women in that society . . . I was more aware than I had been before of what I was doing.
>
> (Quoted by K. Itzin)

Set in the 17th Century, and made up of about twenty-two episodic scenes with seven interspersed contemporary songs, *Vinegar Tom* concerns the violent expulsion from a repressed society of women who will not conform to acceptable social patterns. Those women who do not fit into the expected female roles are declared witches. They are condemned to torture and hanging because of their rejection of the society's values through their lower class lifestyle, and their acknowledged sexuality.

In a rapid succession of short scenes, the play economically introduces the characters. Only one of the six women, Margery, is clear of the community's admonishing scrutiny. A model citizen, Margery is an automaton of puritan values who has been so reduced by her cold self-righteousness that she can no longer fulfill her "womanly" duties and chores. In the most visually expressive scene of the first half of the play, and an example of its abundant sexual imagery, Margery can't churn cream into butter despite her coaxing chant:

> Come butter come, come butter come. Johnny's standing at the gate waiting for a butter cake. Come butter come, come butter come. Johnny's standing at the gate waiting for a butter cake. Come butter come, . . .

Nor can Margery arouse her husband Jack. He is, however, passionately attracted to Alice Noakes, a poor and suspicious neighbor with an even more suspicious, impious and vagrant mother, Joan. As more and more things go wrong in Jack and Margery's narrow life, they look for a cause and conclude that Noakes women have cursed them. They recite a litany of accusations when the travelling witch hunter, Packer, arrives in town:

Margery: Stopped the butter.

Jack: Killed the calves.

Margery: Struck me in the head.

Jack: Lamed my hand.

Margery: Struck me in the stomach.

Jack: Bewitched my organ.

Margery: When I boiled my urine she came.

Jack: Blooded her and made my hand well.

Margery: Burnt her thatch.

Jack: And Susan, her friend, is like possessed screaming and crying and lay two days without speaking.

Margery: Susan's baby turned blue and its limbs twisted and it died.

Jack: Boy threw stones and called them witch, and after, he vomited pins and straw.

Margery: Big nasty cat she has in her bed and sends it to people's dairies.

Jack: A rat's her imp.

Margery: And the great storm last night brought a tree down in the lane, who make that out of a clear sky?

Two other women are victims of the witch hunt. Susan, a pregnant and poor woman who accepts that God sent pain to women as a punishment for their sins, lets Alice take her to the cunning woman, Ellen, where she receives a potion to cause an abortion. Guilt-ridden into derangement, Susan blames Alice's witchery on the loss of the baby. But the witch hunters do not accept this excuse, arguing that any woman who does not want her child might be a witch. Ellen too is tried for practicing witchcraft since she is not a licensed doctor.

The play comes most alive after Packer's arrival. By this point all of the characters have been introduced and *Vinegar Tom* proceeds with brutal and powerful events. Packer and his assistant Goody, a woman who is happy to have a job that helps humanity, especially one that is so lucrative, have a horrifying and degrading method for determining whether or not a woman is a witch. Searching for a spot impervious to pain, and therefore protected by the devil, they jab the accused under her skirt until there is no more blood or screaming. Churchill graphically presents these bloody examinations:

(Packer and Goody take Joan, and Goody holds her, while Packer pulls up her skirts and pricks her legs. Joan curses and screams throughout. Packer and Goody abuse her: a short sharp moment of great noise and confusion . . . Goody takes Alice. Packer helps, and her skirts are thrown over her head while he pricks her. She tries not to cry out and her cries are muffled by the skirt but slight whimpers are heard.) . . . Packer: Have I the spot though? Which is the spot? There. There. There. No, I haven't the spot. Oh, its, tiring work.

Beginning with these torturing tests, the most violent of Churchill's images, the play accelerates to its end with a succession of scenes that comprise a dynamic architecture of images. With the bodies of Joan Noakes and Ellen hanging in the background, Alice and Susan take account of the events, Susan accepts that Joan and Ellen were guilty, sliding into common belief as easily as she had accepted an abnegating religious faith:

> I was a witch and never knew it. I killed my babies. I never meant it. I didn't know I was so wicked. I didn't know I had the mark on me. I'm so wicked. Alice, let's pray to God we won't be damned. If we're hanged, we're saved Alice, so we mustn't be frightened. It's done to help us. Oh God, I know now I'm loathsome and a sinner and Mr. Packer has shown me how bad I am and I repent I never knew that but now I know and please forgive me and don't make me go to hell and be burnt forever.

But Alice remains adamant and opposed:

> I'm not a witch. But I wish I was. If I could live I'd be a witch now after what they've done. I'd make wax men and melt them on a slow fire. I'd kill their animals and blast their crops and make such storms, I'd wreck their ships all over the world. I shouldn't have been frightened of Ellen, I should have learnt. Oh if I could meet with the devil now I'd give him anything if he'd give me power. There's no way for us except by the devil. If I only did have magic I'd make them feel it.

From the jolt of bloody tortures and dangling corpses, the play abruptly shifts theatrical worlds. Bursting onto the stage, Kramer and Spengler, two vaudevillian professors, "inquisitors of heretical pravities . . . we must fill those moral cavities," plug their book on witches and enumerate the many flaws and inferior qualities of women, from which they conclude "It is no wonder there are more women than men found infected with the heresy of witchcraft." But Churchill concludes with a contrary point of view in the final song: if women are perceived as evil, nasty, and the embodiments of destructive lust, then it is because the dominant male of Western society has made them so:

> Evil women
> Is that what you want?
> Is that what you want to see?
> On the movie screen of your own wet dream
> Evil women.
>
> Do you ever get afraid
> You don't do it right?
> Does your lady demand it

> Three times a night?
> If we don't say you're big
> Do you start to shrink?
> We earn our own money
> And buy our own drink.
>
> Did you learn you were dirty boys, did you learn
> Women were wicked to make you burn?
> Satan's lady, Satan's pride
> Satan's baby, Satan's bride
> Witches were wicked and had to burn.

The juxtaposition of these incongruous scenes bludgeons and then cajoles the audience into considering the perhaps more subtle, but equally destructive, ways in which contemporary society restricts women. Churchill's use of songs throughout the play is not entirely successful, however. Following Brecht's example, perhaps, the contemporary songs that are interspersed throughout the narrative are meant to make the audience think about the action. But here they are not essential to the association of the play's scapegoating of women with the plight of contemporary women. Their inclusion seems to suggest that Churchill does not yet trust her new and developing style.

In her next play, *Light Shining in Buckinghamshire*, Churchill reaches the fullness of her powers. Where *Vinegar Tom* relied on the device of songs for its contemporary implications, *Light Shining* is a self-contained and cohesive work. Though it is also set in the 17th Century, its contemporaneity evolves vividly out of its imaginative world. Again working with a group of actors, Churchill wrote *Light Shining* with the Joint Stock company who performed it in Edinburgh in 1976 before moving it to the Royal Court Theater Upstairs. With this play, Churchill continues to develop both her style and her thought, and makes them converge into an artistic whole; Churchill explores the relations among puritanism, Christianity, capitalism, and ownership in a thoroughly dramatic manner and with larger scope than in her earlier plays.

Combining documentary material such as newspapers and the Putney debates of 1647, and Churchill's own fiction, *Light Shining in Buckinghamshire* centers on England's almost-but-not-quite revolution of the mid 1600's. The play does not follow the development or psychological life of any specific character or group of characters. If there is any single hero or main character, it is an attitude—the play follows the birth of class consciousness. The unfulfilled revolution began not as a Marxist upheaval, but as a crusade against the anti-Christ, led fervently by the Church. Historical and fictional characters whose paths intersect, run parallel, and circumscribe each other like a freeway system, are all looking for a way to freedom and power of some degree, and all eventually learn that property ultimately rules.

At the beginning of the play, 1647, the poor are enlisted by the Church to challenge the monarchy and fight for the creation of Parliament. In one of the twenty-five episodic scenes, the preacher encourages the common people to join the fight:

It is no sin to take up arms against the king. It is no sin if we fight singing praises to God, if we fight to bind an unjust king with chains . . . for it is written: "The saints of the most High shall take the kingdom and possess the kingdom forever, even forever and ever."

Taking advantage of the Church's new liberal policy to allow questions in church, Hoskins reveals that the church mirrors the hierarchical structure that it is opposing. She wants to know who the saints are. The preacher forbids her to speak in church because she is a woman, and she outdoes him in a scripture quoting debate. When she is thrown out, she exposes the hypocrisy of the Church stance:

Not just a few elect go to heaven. He thinks most people are bad. The king thinks most people are bad. He's against the king but he's saying the same. In his kingdom of heaven there's going to be a few in bliss and the rest of us in hell. What's the difference from what we've got not? You are all saved. Yes, you are all saved. Not one of you is damned.

The common people fighting on the side of the Church soon discover the wisdom of Hoskin's angry words. They begin to perceive the revolution as an intensification of the status quo rather than as liberation. Consequently the Levellers rise up and try to claim what is rightfully theirs without waiting for Parliament to bestow it benevolently. The opening scene of the second act represents an exemplary event of 1649. Three men began to dig and sow the ground of a city commons. Within a few days their number has increased to thirty. Winstanley, one of the leaders of these Diggers, recites:

A declaration to the powers of England and to all the powers of the world, showing the cause why the common people of England have begun to dig up, manure and sow corn upon George Hill in Surrey. Take notice that England is not a free people till the poor that have no land have a free allowance to dig and labour the commons. It is the sword that brought in property and holds it up, and everyone upon recovery of the conquest ought to return into freedom again, or what benefit have the common people got by the victory over the king? . . . There can be no universal liberty until this universal community be established.

After this pronouncement (derived from an original document) six actors directly report—as actors, but in first-person accounts—of the arrests, beatings, and jailings that befell the Diggers, and of the ruin of the land. This scene exemplifies one of Churchill's most interesting dramatic procedures, that draws its effect from the interweaving of historical data, dramatic representation, and the non-illusionistic theatricality of that representation. This technique de-emphasizes the particularity of this event and its participants in the historical and dramatic plot. Thus she is not presenting an aestheticized analogue of historical events, but creating an imaginative world from which her vision of history, that focusses on collective experiences, emerges.

Adopting a telescopic rather than a traditional microscopic approach to dramatic characters, Churchill commingles imagined and historical people in a web of fictional and real events to provide the foundation for her view of history. Churchill emphasizes this point in the staging of her play with this note on production:

The characters are not played by the same actors each time they appear. The audience should not have to worry exactly which character they are seeing. Each scene can be taken as a separate event rather than part of a story. This seems to reflect better the reality of large events like war and revolution where many people share the same kind of experience.

The conclusions afforded by these experiences obtain an ironically optimistic expression in the final scene. The revolution has fizzled out. In a prayer meeting that takes place in a bar, the common people find solidarity in their mutual feelings of betrayal, disillusionment, and emptiness, together with serious questioning of the fixed social and ecclesiastical hierarchies. Their emphasis on collective identity, their dreams of a communal life-style, and the language with which they express their ideals, convey the play into the 1960's without making it budge from its historical setting.

Each person in the bar is given an equal voice as they concur that God speaks through everyone equally, and they proclaim an ideal of the commonness of property that justifies stealing from the exploiting rich. —"What's it mean 'Thou shalt not steal?' Not steal stolen goods?" Hoskins asks as she presents an apple she has liberated. Passing through everyone's hands, it at once implicates and exonerates each person from a notion of sin that is no longer valid. Claxton gives voice to the common lesson:

while I was waiting for God, he was here already. So God was first in the king. Then in parliament. Then in the army. And now he has left all government. And shows himself naked. In us.

But these burned out revolutionaries, like their counter-culture counterparts of the 1960's have not come close to effecting a warless, classless, unrepressed society. As Churchill points out in an interview:

Soldiers fought the king in the belief that Christ would come and establish heaven on earth. What was established instead was an authoritarian partliament, the massacre of the Irish, the development of capitalism.

(Quoted by Itzin)

Having followed a circuitous path, history in **Light Shining** turns back on itself as if it has gone nowhere, like a mobius strip.

With this bizarre and twisted figure as its thematic and structural image, Churchill takes up counter-culture contemporaries who seek an alternative to typical bourgeois life-styles in her next play, **Traps,** first performed at the Royal Court Theater Upstairs in 1977. This play is reminiscent of **Owners** since it is a return to a more personal drama, centering on relationships among individuals. But in

Traps, Churchill has learned to give her ideas dramatic extension.

In her earlier plays, Churchill is suspicious of the structures of thought that seep insidiously into consciousness through socialization and political and economic organization. In *Traps* she places in doubt the absolute and natural stability of the most basic categories of human thought—space and time. The play concerns three men and one woman who live together in a run-down house, and the visiting sister and brother-in-law of one of the housemates. These characters replace each other's traditional roles without losing their distinct identities. At one point, for instance, it seems that Albert is Syl's lover and the father of her unborn child. Later Jack is so identified, not only in terms of a functional role, but in terms that help constitute his very identity. Thus Churchill is giving intimate application to her notion in *Light Shining* where different actors play the same roles.

The characters pass time laboring over a jigsaw puzzle, demonstrating card tricks, watching sunsets, completing household chores, and harassing each other. But the nature of time's passage is corrupt. Events happen in the play and are later retracted casually. One character disappears, and the others discuss his suicide. Later he reappears without shocking anyone. Space is similarly mysterious and estranging. This group has moved, in the second act, from the city to the country. Nonetheless, the set, a cluttered room with one floor and window, remains the same.

The idea that the movements of space and time are functions of the human mind is reflected in Jack's belief that he is a clairvoyant who can will the accomplishment of events, including conjuring people to appear when and where he wants them. He discusses his notions with his housemate Del:

> *Jack:* I believe everything.
>
> *Del:* Ghosts?
>
> *Jack:* Don't you?
>
> *Del:* I tried very hard one time to believe in Father Christmas.
>
> *Jack:* I believe all world religions and minor sects before I even start. All science and superscience. And that every vision can be made real. Before breakfast. That's all possible things. I spend the morning believing impossible things.
>
> *Del:* Like?
>
> *Jack:* That you love me.
>
> *Del:* And afternoon?
>
> *Jack:* Being impossible things.
>
> *Del:* Like?
>
> *Jack:* Here. Now.

Where Churchill questioned social organization in her earlier plays, in *Traps* she questions reality itself. In *Traps* she extends her earlier depiction of social being determining thought, and investigates the mechanisms of thought itself. With such unwieldy and ambitious themes, it is no wonder that the play is not entirely successful. Certainly it is provocative though it sometimes seems to bog down into a superannuated Absurdism. But perhaps those aspects of the play that remain obscure; for instance the abundance of specific stage directions whose execution go without motivation, comment or consequence are part of the play's traps, traps for the audience who will strain to find Significance where there isn't any. *Traps* experiments with theatrical realities that are real life impossibilities with its disregard for our laws of time and space. This suggests that Churchill will continue to stretch our notions of drama.

Clearly, Churchill is still searching. And if her strength so far seems to lie in her political passions, as she expands these concerns, no doubt her artistic expression will continue to enlarge to accomodate her broadening perspectives. I expect that her future plays will combine her interest in the influence of political structures, with her exploration of the most basic, intimate aspects of human experience in space, time, and consciousness.

CLOUD NINE

PRODUCTION REVIEWS

Peter Jenkins (review date 7 April 1979)

SOURCE: "Sex Puzzle," in *The Spectator,* Vol. 242, No. 7865, 7 April 1979, pp. 25-6.

[Cloud Nine *was a collaborative effort between Churchill and the Joint Stock Company, whose director was Max Stafford-Clark. It received its first performances in the English provinces before moving to London's Royal Court Theatre; later, a slightly revised version of the play was presented in a New York production directed by Tommy Tune. In the following evaluation of a London performance, Jenkins offers a mixed opinion of the play, finding it moving at times but obscure in its overall meaning.*]

Joint Stock starts with the acting. The style has become established, almost stylised, but is still quite different to what most theatre goers are used to seeing. The actors have helped to shape the characters they are acting, from outside as well as from the inside; in effect they have helped to write the play. In part the inspiration was Brechtian, the actor stepping back from the part and helping the audience to break the spell of theatrical illusion; partly it derived from an American fashion for acting out everyday experiences and partly also from a British desire to be topical and political.

Cloud Nine by Caryl Churchill brings out the virtues and exposes the vices of the Joint Stock technique. Its most constant danger is degeneration into a mere sequence of acting exercises, or cabaret turns, loosely plotted together. The element of improvisation is liable to take on an air of school-play larkishness unless the proceedings are structured with a good deal more art than meets the eye. Another trouble is that however perceptive and sensitive the performers may be for the purpose of capturing daily experience or speech they can not be guaranteed to rise above a portentous banality of social, political and philosophic comment—but then some of our theatre writers have no need of the assistance of actors to that end.

Caryl Churchill's play is her second for Joint Stock and is heavily contrived as a vehicle for the company's and Max Stafford-Clark's talents. The theme is sex—sex of all manner and variety—and the perennial hypocrisy towards it. Part One of the play takes place in Africa at the time of Livingstone and Stanley and Part Two in Britain following the publication of the Hite report. We see the same people, in the form of their descendants, repeating themselves; two generations are missed out. Not only do they exchange roles generationally, however, but also sexually: that is the central device of the play, a man (Jim Cooper) playing the pedestalled Victorian wife, Betty, and a woman (Julie Covington) playing Edward, turned prematurely queer by the prospect of Victorian manhood. When we meet them again, a century later, Julie Covington has become Betty, now a grandmother, while Antony Sher, the male pillar of the empire in Part One has moved down in age and sideways in sex to become Cathy, a pig-tailed horror armed with war toys by a man-hating Lesbian mother.

This may sound preposterously complicated and much sillier than it is on the stage for it is the strength of Joint Stock that seven distinctive and highly versatile performers can engage an audience in their role-playing, not just in the narrow theatrical sense. A man playing the unliberated Victorian wife is a powerful device and adults acting out childhood—as Dennis Potter proved recently on television—is more disturbing than it is comic. The point which seemed to be running through the whole had to do with the ambivalence of sexuality: like poles repel and unlike poles attract; everything is in danger of becoming its opposite— boys of turning into girls and girls into boys, homosexual liaisons into Victorian marriages, and so on.

However, you will be better employed not trying to puzzle out a total meaning from *Cloud Nine* which has a jingle-like title song with a refrain about being 'upside down when you reach Cloud Nine'. Instead, enjoy the moments when it flies high or reaches deep. The best of these are Julie Covington's soliloquy about the rediscovered joys of masturbation, an embarrassing subject on which she completely vindicates the Joint Stock method. Tony Rohr delivers two monologues on promiscuous homosexual loneliness which are beautifully truthful in hearing and observation, and William Hoyland is doubly excellent as the Victorian explorer of orifices and rivers and as the quintessential post-Hite husband. That formidable actor Antony Sher, whom I admired so greatly in the American play, *A Prayer*

For My Daughter, last year, is splendid both as the ideal Victorian husband and male chauvinist pig-sticker, and as the ghastly child of liberated woman.

There were some wincing moments too: the appearance of the ghost of the dead soldier from Belfast, the sentimentality of the liberated gay wife who used to like doing the cooking and like being paid, and the over-indulgent (theatrically) orgy in the park. On balance, however, the audience was correct in its warm enthusiasm for an evening, which when awful was very, very awful but when good was marvellous.

Hugh Rorrison (review date May 1979)

SOURCE: A review of *Cloud Nine*, in *Plays and Players* Vol. 26, No. 308, May, 1979, p. 23.

[*In the following assessment of* Cloud Nine *during its London run, Rorrison judges the plot confused, with no clear relation between the two parts of the play.*]

What the Boy Saw, a Victorian colonial farce, that is the first half of Joint Stock's new collaborative play [*Cloud Nine*]. It starts in Africa where the local commissioner's family, complete with resident mother-in-law, is visited by Harry Bagley, explorer and bounder, and Mrs. Saunders, a widow of amazing spirit. This cast of *Boy's Own Paper* caricatures is then permutated in pairs to show what a variety of passions throbbed behind the Imperial façade. Clive's wife Betty (She's everything he hoped a wife would be) melts into the arms of Harry, who has already bestowed his favours on her adolescent son, Edward, and on Clive's African boy, Joshua, though he ends up, for decency's sake, marrying the governess Ellen, who for her part loves Betty. Cross-casting of Jim Hooper as Betty and Julie Covington as Edward underlines the artificiality of the characters who are crisply sent up by their own clichés. Clive extolling male comradeship, feels a hand on his bottom. 'I didn't know you felt like that,' says Harry who has misunderstood. 'I feel contaminated', expostulates Clive, 'rivers will be named after you, Harry. It's unthinkable!' In the wings villages burn and natives are flogged, for we are to understand, Victorian morality marches with Imperialism.

The second half of the play is set in present-day England and confronts roughly the same set of characters (now played by different members of the cast however) with the problem of finding their own sexual level in a world with few taboos and no fixed standards. Victoria's marriage is in the sexual doldrums and she slides with gently amused curiosity into an affair with Lin, the lesbian mother of Cathy, a tomboy played as a grotesque, scintillating child-impersonation by Anthony Sher. Victoria's husband is trying too hard not to be chauvinstic, while her brother Edward is smothering his lover Gerry with an excess of wifeliness. The alternative society has its own hang-ups. Against this background Julie Covington weighs in with a character which is new to her range, a middle-aged grandmother. (The play skips about 80 years to make us the immediate inheritors of Victorian England.) Her Betty starts

A rehearsal photograph from the 1979 production of Cloud Nine *at the Royal Court Theatre, London.*

as a gushing, fussing grandmother, about to leave her husband. On her own she struggles to find herself. With Clive she felt she didn't exist if he wasn't looking at her, but masturbation, timidly resorted to, proves to her that she has been there as a person all the time. An interesting twist, since masturbation has of late mostly been a symbol of isolation or inadequacy, as in Franz Xaver Kroetz. She goes on to accept her children's bisexuality without flinching and even to make a tentative, light-hearted pass at Edward's lover, Gerry, who consoles her with the observation that not everyone's gay, to which she replies, 'That's lucky, isn't it.' How true. The unassuming warmth with which Julie Covington invests her as she probes to find the personality which Victorian marriage denied her is the strongest plea for liberal attitudes in the play. What the other characters communicate is mainly insecurity, or in the case of Gerry, ironic egotism.

Spectres from the first part of the play appear in the second, to no clear purpose, and the ghost of Lin's brother, shot in Belfast, appears to remind us that for some, imperialism survives.

The general drift of the production is clear enough. Victorian morality was a sham and nourished secret aberrations. We can laugh at that, and Caryl Churchill's script has plen-

ty of witty lines to help us. Today's alternative society has scrapped the rules and everyone can do his own thing, but their own things turn out to be exactly what the Victorians got up to in secret. Does this mean that the Victorians intuitively got the practice right though they got the rules wrong? Or are we not free from the Victorians yet, just on the other swing of their pendulum? The latter seems more likely.

A roughly staged touring performance I saw at the Humberside Theatre in Hull went with more of a swing than the stuttering final version at the Royal Court, possibly because up there the second half seemed no less exotic than the first.

Anthony Curtis (review date Summer 1979)

SOURCE: A review of *Cloud Nine,* in *Drama,* London, No. 133, Summer, 1979, p. 57.

[*In this review of the London production, Curtis applauds the way in which Churchill offered an "adroit and amusing exposure of what goes on behind the masks of conventional behaviour" in* Cloud Nine.]

Caryl Churchill's **Cloud Nine** [was] directed by Max Stafford-Clark. This play was written for the Joint Stock Company of which he is a director. It is a comedy, first seen at Dartington earlier this year, that takes a leaf or two out of what used to be called our island's story and tears them up into shreds. We begin on an outpost of empire in the African jungle *circa* 1900; we end in a London park and a recreation hut *circa* 1979. To highlight the caricature a black is played by a white, a woman by a man, an infant by a grown person. The result is a little bit like an extended Farjeon revue sketch.

The whole cast attacked the role-switching which the text requires with relish. Julie Covington for instance made a most convincing small boy, incipiently gay, in the colonial section of the first half of the show, and then a tired matriarch who, failing to pick up a young man in the modern permissive playground of the second, turns for the first time in her life to erotic self-satisfaction. Her account of this was really rather moving.

Meanwhile Jim Hooper, another fine actor, who played the randy mother on whom the sun never sets in part one, turned into the park attendant, that same Edward no less, played earlier by Ms. Covington, now a fully-fledged homosexual. Ms. Churchill gives an adroit and amusing exposure of what goes on behind the masks of conventional behaviour. Playwrights who readily avail themselves of the freedom to show things that used to be regarded as disgusting and to mention things that used to be regarded as unmentionable are nearly always utterly humourless about it; or else they have a 'black' sense of humour that leaves me white with boredom. It is refreshing to find in **Cloud Nine** a genuinely funny play arising out of this freedom.

Douglas Watt (review date 19 May 1981)

SOURCE: "With Patience, *Cloud 9* Develops a Silver Lining," in *Daily News,* New York, 19 May 1981.

[*In the following review of the New York production of* Cloud 9, *Watt considers the play "ill-balanced," faulting the startling shift in scene and tone between the two acts.*]

The first of the two long acts of **Cloud 9,** a British comedy concerned mainly with perversions and particularly those of a homosexual nature, is so insistently and tediously campy that one returns for the second act with considerable reluctance. But although the last half of Caryl Churchill's play also has its fair share of outrageous moments, it has touching ones, too, and the acting and direction are so telling here that one leaves the theater not sorry to have stayed to the end.

At the risk of confusing you as much as I was, I must state that while some of the same characters are observed in both halves, 100 years separate the two, yet the characters have aged only 25 years. No, it's not the *Brigadoon* spell at work again, it's just that of the author who may be trying to tell us something about the decay of English society stemming

from past abnormalities, or who may just have outsmarted herself by trying to outdo her countryman Alan Ayckbourn in cleverness.

Act One has us in a British settlement in Africa in 1880, and while there is much flag-waving and stout-fella talk of queen and empire, much more time is devoted to adultery, homosexual behavior and permutations on the sexual act. In addition, the teenage son of the household, who has been seduced by a valiant explorer, is played by an actress, while a male actor impersonates the wife of the household's master.

In the second act, set in one of present-day London's larger parks, the roles have been distributed correctly among men and women, except for that of a tubby girl child played by the round actor who portrays a native servant who turns on his "betters" in the first act. And while homosexuality and sex in general, including a night-time orgy, are even more rampant in this half, there are some affecting, pathetic, and well-written scenes involving married couples, lesbian attachments, gay males, and even widowhood. They are too often marred for the sake of a gag, but they are there, nevertheless.

The performances are of a high grade for this sort of thing. For example, the actor Zeljko Ivanek, who plays the master's submissive, though flirtatious, wife in the first half (only his voice gives him away now and then), is startlingly in contrast as a rough-trade Cockney loner in the second half. Concetta Tomei, first seen as a shy but knowing 1880 son, is a moving Victoria, the troubled young wife (the character is represented by a rag doll in Act One) won over by a Cockney lesbian named Lin, very well played by Veronica Castang (she is Grandmother Maud in the earlier piece).

And so it goes. Jeffrey Jones, switching from an imperious, pious-sounding womanizer of a husband early in the evening, turns into a timid homosexual later. E. Katherine Kerr, who doubles as a lesbian maid and a whip-wielding horsewoman in 1880 Africa, moves us (until the part is joked up) as the widowed Betty in Part Two. Nicolas Surovy is impressively disoriented both as the famous explorer and, later, as Victoria's puzzled husband, and Don Amendolia makes the most of the native servant and obnoxious little girl roles in addition to appearing as the ghost of Lin's British soldier brother killed in Belfast.

It's when the ghosts of the first act begin to appear toward the end of the second that the playwright's notion starts to come into some sort of focus, ending with a sentimental embrace by the two Bettys—in clouds of dry-ice vapor, of course.

Tommy Tune has staged all this exceedingly well according to its peculiar demands; that is, extremely campy at times and compassionately at others. A very effective scenic device, green louvered panels for the first act and rows of green benches for the second, has been created by Lawrence Miller, and the two halves are considerably enhanced by the costuming and lighting.

A very odd, overly tricky and ill-balanced play; but one, at least in the second half, with revealing glimpses and an interesting sense of theater.

Frank Rich (review date 20 May 1981)

SOURCE: "Sexual Confusion on *Cloud 9*," in *The New York Times,* 20 May 1981, p. C30.

[*In the following review, Rich provides a mixed assessment of* Cloud 9, *stating that "the acting buttresses the writing considerably."*]

Cloud 9, a new comedy by a British writer named Caryl Churchill, may not transport the audience all the way to Cloud 9 but it surely keeps us on our toes. The evening's subject is sexual confusion, and Miss Churchill has found a theatrical method that is easily as dizzying as her theme. Not only does she examine a cornucopia of sexual permutations—from heterosexual adultery right up to bisexual incest—but she does so with a wild array of dramatic styles and tricks.

Her first act, which is part bedroom farce and part Waughian satire, unfolds in the darkest colonial Africa of 1880. Act II, a foray into sometimes sentimental agitprop, takes place in a London park of the present day. Though a few characters appear in both halves, the holdovers age only 25 years during intermission, rather than a full century. As if this weren't mad enough, the seven actors change roles for Act II—and don't necessarily play characters of their own age or gender.

Miss Churchill, as you might gather, is one daft writer. *Cloud 9,* now at the De Lys, has real failings, but intelligence and inventiveness aren't among them; we're always interested in what the playwright is up to, no matter what the outcome. And in her director, Tommy Tune, she has found the most helpful possible ally. Working with just the right, delicate balance of rowdiness and sensitivity—as well as with an unusually good cast—Mr. Tune often succeeds in giving a seriously overlong evening the illusion of flight.

In Act I, the director sends his company dashing about the sliding doors of Lawrence Miller's clever set to create a nonstop round-robin of sexual liaisons. This half of *Cloud 9* is about what happens when a very proper colonial British family receives a visit from a pith-helmeted explorer named Harry Bagley (Nicholas Surovy). While the natives outside the camp are getting restless, they have nothing on the rakish Harry. He's *really* been too long in the bush. Grabbing every clandestine opportunity he can, this explorer seduces the household's wife (played by a man), schoolboy son (played by a woman) and obsequious black servant (played by a white)—all before getting married to the governess, a lesbian.

What makes this carnal circus funny is the contrast between the characters' manners and deeds. No matter what they do, Miss Churchill's colonials act and talk like true-blue, gen-

teel Victorians. When Harry is caught in a homosexual act, he apologizes by explaining that he is merely the helpless victim of "a disease worse than diphtheria." When his host engages in his own dalliance with a local widow, the fully clothed couple reach orgasm with a stiff-upper-lip reticence worthy of a Westminster debate.

The joke does wear thin too quickly. Once we understand that Miss Churchill is stripping bare the hypocrisies of an oversatirized era, Act I becomes stalled. The transsexual casting is also problematic: though the male and female impersonations are amusing, not smirky, they nonetheless serve the unwanted function of announcing the jokes. Nor is the story's farcical structure so strong that it pulls up the slack. Instead of the ingenious clockwork of, say, an Alan Ayckbourn play, Miss Churchill provides a progression of overly similar scenes that steadily reveal each character's particular proclivity.

Act II has its own problems—and pleasures. We re-encounter three members of the 1880 family, as well as four new characters, and find that, in 1980, they are as liberated as their predecessors were repressed. But progress presents its own difficulties. The homosexual schoolboy of 1880, now hitting middle age, is so confused by his love for both his sister and an insolent young male lover that he worries that he might be a lesbian. His sister, meanwhile, is torn between her ostensibly enlightened husband (a writer at work on "a novel about women from the woman's point of view") and a woman who propositions her in the park.

Miss Churchill covers this and much more territory by relying on tender monologues. The speeches are very well written, but one hungers for stronger interchanges between the characters. An element of ideological Polyanna-ism also creeps in, for the playwright provides most of her lost souls with happy endings. Is everyone really so much better off in the swinging 1980's? It seems a waste that Act II's wittiest conceit—the ghostly return of characters from Act I—is mainly used to draw mawkish parallels between now and then.

Yet the acting buttresses the writing considerably. Despite the cast's showy sex changes, Mr. Tune keeps the performances at a realistic level: he goes for the heart of Miss Churchill's play even as he gives full polish to its surface pranks. Some actors are best in Act I (Mr. Surovy, Don Amendolia) and some in Act II (Veronica Castang, Concetta Tomei). Others shine throughout. Zeljko Ivanek does a fine transformation from fluttery colonial wife to wary young street hustler. Jeffrey Jones, a pompous twit of a father in Africa, is sad and sweet when he turns up in London as the forlorn homosexual son.

Perhaps the stand-out performance comes from E. Katherine Kerr, who in Act II inherits the mother's role. Looking and sounding not unlike England's present Queen, Miss Kerr delivers a beautiful closing speech in which she graphically describes how she overcame her sheltered 1880 upbringing to take her rightful place in a modern, feminist world of infinite possibilities. "If there isn't a right way to do things," she explains, "you just have to invent one."

By the end, we're terribly moved by this middle-aged woman's brave attempt to reinvent herself—just as we're moved by Caryl Churchill's attempt to reinvent the comedy of manners so that it might do such a heroine justice.

TOP GIRLS

PRODUCTION REVIEWS

Bryan Robertson (review date 11 September 1982)

SOURCE: "Top-Notch Churchill," in *The Spectator,* Vol. 249, No. 8044, 11 September 1982, p. 25.

[Top Girls *premiered in London at the Royal Court Theatre, transferred to New York for a run at the Newman Theatre, and then returned to London for further performances. In the following review of a performance during the first London run, Robertson extols the play as "brilliantly conceived with considerable wit to illuminate the underlying deep human seriousness of [Churchill's] theme."*]

When the curtain rises on the first of Peter Hartwell's resourceful and elegant sets for Caryl Churchill's new play—and remember its title, *Top Girls*—we find ourselves in a restaurant, and rather a good one from the style of the lettering on the window which spells out La Prima Donna. A smartly dressed woman, the hostess, soon identified as Marlene, is giving final instructions to a young waitress dressed in that Grecian-tunic-and-sandals outfit worn sometimes by waiters in our sillier looking expense account restaurants. Almost at once a woman enters, the first of the guests, looking like a Victorian missionary in long black coat and dismal black hat. She congratulates Marlene on some unknown achievement which later on turns out to be arrival at managerial status and in her broad Scottish accent starts talking about her travels in foreign parts, her concern for the natives and her love for her sister Hennie back in Tobermory. She is Isabella Bird, a 19th-century traveller. A few seconds later a blond woman arrives dressed in Japanese robes and with unconvincingly made-up slit eyes and slanting eyebrows. Lady Nijo, it seems, sometime concubine of the Emperor and full of talk about a woman's role in court life before she became a Buddhist nun . . . Then a shaggy-looking woman in breastplate, bloodstained ragged tunic, leather cap and wild haircut comes in, looking a bit like that other no-nonsense head-girl, Shirley Williams, and we're off.

This latest guest is identified in the programme as Dull Gret, a mythical freedom fighter with other women against devils in a painting by Brueghel. The gathering is completed by Pope Joan, no less, reminiscing about her acceptance among the clergy when she more or less behaved like a man, and her death at the hands of an angry mob when her baby, bewilderedly greeted as the anti-Christ, is born, and

'Patient Griselda', a self-destructively obedient wife whose story appears in Bocaccio and Chaucer. The dialogues, feminist dialectic and recitals of experience among these five contrasting personages on stage, conducted by Marlene, are vivid and funny, establish the common theme of self-abasement, destruction or grim survival in a male-dominated world and the bond of abandoned, forbidden or murdered babies. The talk becomes increasingly dramatic, action freezes, there is a blackout and then the brightly lit office of the Top Girls employment agency emerges, where Marlene as newly elevated manager is interviewing a cautious Jeanine, a few seconds earlier seen as the over-obedient Griselda, who wants to change her job and whose efforts to improve her lot are suavely dispersed by Marlene-the-manager coming on rather like a role-imposing husband—not sexually, but cutting the applicant's dim efforts down to a stereotype as imposed by generally accepted male decree.

Other quick scenes in the Top Girls agency establish a series of themes and predicaments among the staff and their clients—the actress, Selina Cadell, who played Pope Joan reappears, for instance, as an executive in early middle age eager for a change of job to escape the maddening sight of younger women 'getting away' with attitudes to work and male officialdom which are impossible for her generation. The focus narrows to Marlene, the supreme Top Girl, and the price she pays for her career in her relationship with her sister Joyce, who has brought up Marlene's mentally retarded daughter and coped with their ageing parents. This is really the play, the contrasting lives and attitudes of two sisters with the Top Girls agency both real in the issues acted out in its office and an obviously symbolic device which mirrors and distorts the opening dinner table extravaganza of historical stereotypes.

Ms Churchill is one of our best writers and apart from an irritating conceit in the first scene of forcing her characters to sometimes talk simultaneously, which serves no purpose, real or symbolic, her play is brilliantly conceived with considerable wit to illuminate the underlying deep human seriousness of her theme. The play is feminist, all right, but it is an entertaining, sometimes painful and often funny play and not a mere tract. She is magnificently served by her cast who offer the sharpest and most intelligent display of acting to be seen in London right now. Deborah Findlay as Joyce, the shrewd, wryly self-sacrificing sister, builds up a performance which establishes her as a great actress, alive, sensitive and deeply felt in every detail, and Carole Hayman playing the difficult part of the slow-witted and loving daughter is funny and touching.

John Russell Taylor (review date November 1982)

SOURCE: A review of *Top Girls,* in *Plays & Players,* No. 350, November, 1982, pp. 22-3.

[*Taylor offers a very mixed assessment of a London performance of* Top Girls. *He finds both the theme and structure poorly delineated and considers much of the piece "fundamentally . . . old-fashioned."*]

In *Cloud Nine* you could not always quite produce a logical reason why one thing followed another, but somehow you never doubted that it did. *Top Girls,* Caryl Churchill's new play at the Royal Court, progresses in a similar zigzag way between present and past, realism and outrageous fantasy. The connections are just as much (and just as little) there for the reason to apprehend. And yet, to me at least, the pieces in the puzzle remain determinedly separate, never quite adding up to more than, well, so many fascinating pieces in a fascinating puzzle.

One thing about Caryl Churchill, you are never bored. Or hardly ever. Even the scene that sets the attention drifting here, the short glimpse of a present day rustic childhood which concludes a first half primarily taken up with very different things, is not so much boring in itself as too much of a let down after the long first scene, a real virtuoso piece if ever there was one. If this were—perish the thought in 1982—a three-act play instead of a two, we would no doubt accept it quite happily as a slight prologue to other things. But really it just cannot be tagged on to the end of the mad dinner party in which Pope Joan, Patient Griselda, the thirteenth-century Japanese Lady Nijo, the Victorian traveller Isabella Bird and Dull Gret out of a Breughel painting are all gathered together into a Buñuelian dinner party to celebrate the promotion of our heroine (?) Marlene to directorship of the chic employment agency Top Girls.

This scene is, to begin with, very funny. It also rehearses, directly and indirectly, the themes which will run through the rest of the play: woman's role in relation to men, children lost, stolen or strayed, the question of whether equal is the same as the same in the balance of the sexes. The whole discussion is so bizarre that you actually want to hear all of it—something which the structure of the play's overlapping dialogue effectually prevents. (This aspect is in fact sometimes irritating, since director Max Stafford-Clark and his cast have not quite yet hit on the correct emotional level—or perhaps just sound level—to make this device work smoothly.) Churchill manages particularly well the sudden transition of tone, as when Joan concludes an hilarious account of how she was caught short in childbirth during a papal procession with the bland observation that of course then she was dragged off into the country and stoned to death: yes indeed, things like that can put a damper on a jolly social evening.

At least, for all its oddity and obscurity, we know what this scene is about. It is difficult to be so sure about the rest. Like most of Churchill's work, it is about nothing simple and easily capsulated. It is not even plugging a simple feminist line. Clearly she must be on the side of women, and all for their escaping from the ridiculous position of total dependency in which Griselda and Nijo in particular are trapped. But her modern career-girls seem to have settled instead for what Osborne calls 'the Brave-New-Nothing-very-much-thank-you'. They have, in a very real sense, taken the place of men, but only so that they can ape men's least appealing traits, ogling the pretty fellows and competing for the flashiest cars, the cushiest fringe benefits. Is that what it was all for? Even the examples of subject females who come into the office are not subject so much to the

hegemony of men as to their own limitations of intelligence (the first interviewee is really just too dopey to get anywhere) or generation (the second has made a god of unobtrusive service and now resents being taken for granted), just like men.

And as for Marlene—well, is she a heroine or isn't she? She seems to start as the model of a woman who can handle herself in a man's world, but gradually, as revelation follows revelation, we begin to wonder. So she has made it, but at what human price? And revelation does follow revelation: the rest of the play after the first scene proves to be fundamentally a good, old-fashioned piece with clues planted and secrets kept and revealed, climaxing in a splendidly sustained session of kitchen-sink drama which puts a situation like that in Catherine Hayes's *Skirmishes* (one sister stayed, one sister went; which was right?) into Wesker country (literally rustic East Anglia) and lets it rip until we find out all there is to know. The result is achieved, in typical Churchill fashion, by putting the chronolgically earliest scene at the end, but otherwise it could be Pinero.

And why not, after all? All is fair in love, war and drama. And it certainly puts Gwen Taylor (Marlene), Deborah Findlay (her sister Joyce) and Carole Hayman (Angie, the backward child of the family) through their paces to excellent effect. I'm not sure that the current Royal Court thing of cross-casting quite works in the case of Angie, since it is distracting that Carole Hayman never looks any younger than her mother—whoever that is—though on the other hand Lindsay Duncan's defiantly tall, blonde Lady Nijo comes off perfectly. Anyway, it is a play which sends you out asking questions and trying to work out, not disagreeably, just what it is you have been watching. Not quite *Cloud Nine,* but it leaves no doubt that Caryl Churchill is a big talent, still developing.

Clive Barnes (review date 29 December 1982)

SOURCE: "Wry *Top Girls* Is Hard to Top." in *New York Post,* 29 December 1982.

[*In the following review, Barnes deems the acting superb in the New York production and considers Churchill a "playwright to cherish and explore."*]

Caryl Churchill's new play *Top Girls* starts with a strange meeting and ends with an odd encounter. It is a social comedy about women and politics, chiefly politics, and is as unexpected as you would expect from the author of *Cloud Nine.* It opened last night at the Newman Theater of Joseph Papp's Public Theater.

It is a production that has been bodily transported from London's Royal Court, where it was first staged last August. The original cast and staging are intact, and the production marks the beginning of an exchange arrangement between the Royal Court and the New York Shakespeare Theater. This seems a great idea.

Miss Churchill's very funny and densely provocative play is about winners and losers and the dangers of winning and losing, all from a woman's standpoint in the Britain of the '80s. The case history of half a nation.

The piece opens at a chic Chelsea restaurant, called with good reason La Prima Donna. Marlene is celebrating her appointment as managing director of the Top Girls employment agency. She is, as she would put it, "a very high-flying lady."

Her friends assemble—but it turns out to be a kind of come-as-you-were party. The friends have all time-traveled back in history and taken on the being of their prototype.

One is a Japanese courtesan who became a Buddhist nun, another is a Scottish traveler. There is Pope Joan, and Patient Griselda, and even an earthy, rebellious character from a Bruegel painting. They have something in common—they have all suffered the loss of children and lovers, have all known a kind of success and paid its dues.

This mad-milliner's lunch party over, the play having stated its theme, Miss Churchill shows us Marlene's life as a contemporary example of woman in her social landscape.

The drama centers around Marlene, her sister Joyce, who has never left the Suffolk village where they both grew up, and Angle, Joyce's child, accurately enough described as "stupid, lazy and frightened." She is also slightly mentally disturbed and, in every way, a lump.

On the day Marlene lands her great job, Angie comes up to London and dumps herself down in Marlene's office. She has clearly come to stay. And with an aunt she has only seen once—"the happiest day of her life"—in eight years.

Marlene, the ultimate in haves, meets Angie, who is in training to be the ultimate in have-nots. But that is not the odd encounter that ends the play. This is a meeting that in real time took place a year earlier—indeed on Angie's "happiest day"—and it was between Marlene and Joyce, facing the previously unspoken realities of their missing relationship.

The work is oddly constructed—the time switch at the end demands from the audience the hindsight of foresight, and the play's momentum never catches again the originality of its opening *coup de theatre*. Nothing after that quite matches that first big bang.

Yet if difficult in its structure, it is marvelously easy in its texture, which is rich, creamy, and rewarding. It is a play to dig your mind into.

The production was exemplary in London and is even better in New York, after the cast has had weeks of playing together.

Max Stafford-Clark, artistic director of the Royal Court, has staged the play with the utmost economy and elegance, never wasting an inflection. The acting is superb. Top ladies doing top jobs.

Apart from Gwen Taylor's successful super-executive, played with just the right combination of brass and flounce, all the others have two—or in the case of Deborah Findlay, wonderfully wary as Joyce—even three parts.

All of them are truthful and accurate to play and life alike. Carole Hayman's lumpen Angie, Selina Cadel's philosophically urbane Pope Joan, Lou Wakefild's bright urchin of a kid-next-door, Lindsay Duncan's Japanese courtesan, and Lesley Manville as an offbeat Patient Griselda, are all beautifully in key.

Miss Churchill has a strange dramatic imagination. She is a playwright to cherish and explore.

Douglas Watt (review date 29 December 1982)

SOURCE: "British *Top Girls* Not for U.S." in *Daily News*, New York, 29 December 1982.

[*Below, Watt censures the poor integration of the three scenes in* Top Girls *and judges the play of little interest to American audiences.*]

The story of an ugly duckling whose destiny is to remain an ugly duckling, and just possibly a convicted murderer at 16, has been tricked up and implanted in a study of career women in *Top Girls,* a confused play by Caryl Churchill that Joseph Papp brought to the Public's Newman unit last night in a British production imported in toto from London's Royal Court Theater. The English equivalent of an Off Broadway production, it is a very professional piece of work, but of such limited interest that it should never have ventured this far from Sloane Square.

The first item in an exchange program between Papp's outfit and the Royal Court (the Festival will ship over a new Thomas Babe comedy in the spring), *Top Girls* is named after a London employment agency (for men and women alike, actually) with an office manager named Marlene (Gwen Taylor), who is about to be promoted to a higher executive post supposedly earmarked for a veteran male employe. But I'm getting ahead, or behind (that really doesn't matter much in a play by Churchill, who also wrote the long-running *Cloud Nine*), of the story.

The Play opens today in a London restaurant at a table set for six. Marlene's guests include a strange assortment of women, mainly mythical or fictional, from the past: Pope Joan, a woman thought to have been a disguised 9th century Pope; Lady Nijo, a 13th century emperor's courtesan who became a Buddhist nun; Patient Griselda, the Chaucerian character; Dull Gret, the aggressive subject of a Brueghel painting, and Isabella Bird, an independent 19th century Scottish traveler. As a young waitress serves the various courses, the women relate their histories, often interrupting one another so that at times the conversation rises to the level of a squabble of overlapping chatter.

This long, exotic and exceedingly arch opening scene has nothing to do with the remainder of the play other than to emphasize the supposedly unhappy fate down through the years of adventurous women, leading up to Marlene. For in leaving a drab family life in Suffolk, the sleek and hard-nosed Marlene has also left behind an illegitimate child, Angie, who has been raised by Marlene's dull sister, Joyce, in the belief that she is her mother.

Scenes in the Top Girls' Employment Agency (in which the actresses who portray those exotic ladies of the first scene appear either as employes or job-seekers) are followed by ones in Joyce's Suffolk backyard and a closing scene, which takes place a year earlier and after Angie has declared her intention of killing her "mother" and after we've seen her show up at the employe agency managed by her "aunt," in Joyce's kitchen where Marlene has appeared on a visit.

As she demonstrated in *Cloud Nine* following an unbearable first act, Churchill can write touchingly and with a good ear for everyday speech about middle-class Londoners today. But while concern for ugly ducklings may be universal (this one, by the way, has no real future, as Marlene confides sadly to an associate), *Top Girls* is a genre piece likely to arouse even less interest here than Alan Ayckbourn's equally tricky, but infinitely more amusing, works about the English middle class.

CRITICAL COMMENTARY

Joseph Marohl (essay date 1987)

SOURCE: "De-realised Women: Performance and Identity in *Top Girls*," in *Modern Drama,* Vol. XXX, No. 3, September, 1987, pp. 376-88.

[*In the following essay, Marohl demonstrates how* Top Girls *succeeds in debunking the myth of the feminist hero whose achievements are gained through her imitation of powerful men rather than through the avenues of a "socially conscious feminism."*]

For a decade now, deliberate confusion of dramatic roles and playfulness about otherwise serious concepts of gender and history have distinguished Caryl Churchill's plays from the work of mainstream playwrights in Great Britain and the United States. For instance, six performers in *Light Shining in Buckinghamshire* play twenty-four different *dramatis personae* with individual role assignments which vary from scene to scene and are unrelated to the performers' actual sexes. In the finale of *Vinegar Tom,* her "sequel" to *Light Shining,* two female performers portray two seventeenth-century theologians in the top hat and tails of music hall entertainers, singing with great irony the song "Evil Women." In a prefatory note to *Traps* [in her *Plays: One* (1985)], Churchill describes the play as an "impossible object," like an Escher drawing: "In the play, the time, the place, the characters' motives and relationships cannot all be reconciled—they can happen on stage, but there is no other reality for them. . . . The characters can be thought of as living many of their possibilities at once." The cast of

seven performers in *Cloud Nine,* Churchill's first *bona-fide* commercial hit, play thirteen roles of varying age, gender, and race. In Act One, a white performer plays a black servant, a male performer plays the role of a woman, a female performer plays a boy, and a small dummy represents an infant girl. Act Two brings a degree of naturalism as women play women and men play men, with the exception of Cathy, a five-year-old girl played by a man. A stage note explains that "Act One takes place in a British colony in Africa in Victorian times. Act Two takes place in London in 1979. But for the characters it is twenty-five years later." Only three characters appear in both acts, and in all three instances the actors portraying them in the second act are not the same persons portraying them in the first. In *Top Girls,* an all-female cast of seven play a total of sixteen different characters, five of whom do not exist in the present. Even more recently, in *Fen* five women and one man play twenty-two characters in an ambiguous setting which is simultaneously interior and exterior: in Annie Smart's 1983 stage design, "a field in a room."

Multiple casting and transvestite role-playing, which modern directors of the 1940s and 1950s practiced deliberately in several experimental productions of Shakespeare and other standard dramatists, reflect the many possibilities inherent in the real world and subvert conventional ideas about the individuality or integrity of character. The theatrical inventiveness of Churchill's comedies suggests, in particular, that the individual self, as the audience recognizes it, is an ideological construct and the "real world," the world as it is recast by the performers, klieg lights, and chicken wire on the stage, consists of people and events which are individual only in so far as they are rhetorically defined in contrast to others. Her plays conceive character and event as paradoxes. People in her plays are not whole, though sometimes they are ignorant of their own fragmentation; they exist only in tension with their environment (time and space), the other people in the environment, and with the "others" who they themselves used to be at an earlier age (their former "selves"). Churchill describes the condition more vividly in dramatic terms in the closing image of *Cloud Nine,* when a character in Act Two confronts the version of herself from Act One: "BETTY *and* BETTY *embrace.*"

In performance, the plays assume obvious political importance, espousing the social concerns of contemporary feminism: gender stereotyping, the division of labor according to sex, the proprietary family, the oppression of sexual variety through compulsory heterosexuality, class struggle, ageism, and ethnocentrism. The dramatic events raise the audience's consciousness about social principles through the actions depicted and, more importantly, through the actual events of the performance: woman playing man, man playing woman, one person playing two (or more) persons, two persons playing one, the deconstruction of history and geography (and the related unities of time, place, and action) in order to dramatize the cyclical progress of political and social events in history. What the audience experiences during the performance, then, is defamiliarization of the ordinary (alienation effect) and the subversion of positive ideologies about gender, social hierarchies, and chronology.

The comedies are parodic enactments and satires of prevalent, middle-class belief-systems and values, i.e., mythologies.

In *Top Girls,* the one continuous character, Marlene, embodies the characteristics of the popular myth of career woman as castrating female and barren mother. The play uses the myth in order to undermine it, to supplant radical and bourgeois feminist styles with a socially conscious feminism, to "trick" the audience into condemning the "feminist hero" for, in the end, practicing a too-conventional role in the existing power structure. In this, the play succeeds brilliantly and unconsciously. The purpose of the present reading is to discover the political practice of the play as it works through the performance, particularly of the first scene, but a summary of the play's successive parts is necessary first.

Top Girls begins at a restaurant, with a dinner party celebrating the protagonist Marlene's promotion to managing director of the "Top Girls" Employment Agency. Joining her at the party are five ghost characters drawn from history, painting, and fiction: the nineteenth-century Scottish lady-traveler Isabella Bird; the thirteenth-century Japanese courtesan-turned-nun Lady Nijo; Dull Gret, whom Bruegel pictured storming hell in apron and armor; the legendary Pope Joan, who, disguised as a man, headed the Church in the ninth century; and Patient Griselda, ironically arriving late and last, the incredibly long-suffering hero of Chaucer's Clerk's Tale. The group ostensibly represents women of outstanding courage and achievement, but the dialogue, often cast as a series of overlapping narrative monologues, reveals pointed differences in ideology and practice. The scene is unique in that it is the only scene in which the play's seven actors appear together and the only scene which does not portray a naturalistic event. It is also the longest scene of the play. The women playing the ghost characters and the waitress appear in subsequent scenes as Marlene's clients, fellow workers, sister, and daughter.

Immediately following the dinner party scene is a brief scene at the employment agency, where Marlene interviews a secretary who aspires to a better position with a new company. There follows a long scene at Marlene's sister Joyce's back yard, where Marlene's sixteen-year-old daughter Angie, whom Joyce has raised as her own daughter, and Angie's younger friend Kit discuss violence on television, money, matricide, death in general, and menstruation, with Angie announcing at the end her intent to visit Marlene in London. The scene sets up the argument for the play's final scene, in which Marlene and Joyce quarrel about politics and family. More important, the scene reveals the complex disturbed psychology of the slow-witted Angie, whose sex, class, appearance, and low intelligence present a multiple threat to her eventual employability and welfare. The girl's resolution to travel to London to her successful "aunt" hints of Sophoclean tragedy. But her threats of matricide and her Oedipal attachment to Marlene do not effect catastrophe or catharsis in the end; Churchill's play is neither tragic nor obvious. The tragic implications of the scene are not, however, wasted, for, as subsequent events prove, Angie, like Oedipus or Antigone, is a victim of history and fate.

Act Two opens at an office of the "Top Girls" Employment Agency. In the first scene, Win and Nell, two employment agents with the firm, arrive for work and discuss Marlene's promotion, aware that now, as one of them remarks, "There's not a lot of room upward." To which the other one responds, "Marlene's filled it up." Both women agree, nevertheless, that they had rather see a woman promoted than Howard Kidd, a male employee at the agency. Between interviews conducted by Win and Nell, Marlene receives two unexpected visitors at work: Angie, whose surprise visit is treated less than enthusiastically by her mother, and Mrs Kidd, Howard's wife, who asks Marlene to turn down the promotion so that her husband will not be reduced to "working for a woman." The scene ends with news that Howard is in the hospital after a heart attack. The women in the office greet the news with deadpan irony, remarking, "Lucky he didn't get the job if that's what his health's like." Marlene then turns towards her daughter, who has fallen asleep at Win's desk, and prophesies: "She's not going to make it." The line is the end of the story but not the end of the play.

The last scene occurs one year before the scenes preceding it in the play. Once again, the scene is Joyce's house, the kitchen this time. The use of flashback allows the audience to observe a number of changes that will occur over the year in Marlene's character. In the last scene, Marlene, drunk and guiltily maudlin, argues that Angie will "be all right" someday. She regards her career advancement as beneficial to women everywhere and herself as an independent, self-made person, in the same mold as Margaret Thatcher, much to the annoyance of her sister, who reminds her that she could have accomplished nothing had not Joyce been willing years before to take the burden of Angie off her hands. Marlene asserts her belief in middle-class individualism; she is, she says, "an original," a supporter of Ronald Reagan and a "free world." Joyce, whose politics are Marxist and pro-Labour, criticizes her successful sister's priggishness and egotism. She reminds Marlene about her parents, common workers who lived wasted lives and died without happiness or meaningful employment, and about their daughter Angie, who will also be a victim of monetarism and class prejudice. Nevertheless, Marlene persists blindly to endorse a system that values profits over the needs of people, and in the end she seems to accept that Angie, Joyce, and her mother are reasonable sacrifices to make in order to realize her own success in the business world. Abandoned by Joyce, Marlene sits alone in the kitchen until Angie stumbles in, half-awake after a nightmare, and utters the last line of the play, the single word "Frightening," an unknowing indictment of her mother's self-interested individualism or perhaps an apprehension of her own miserable future.

Taken as a whole, the play demonstrates several larger formal devices which appear immediately to be significant. The central image of the story related to Marlene is the employment agency, a company which locates meaningful and profitable work for its clients. Employment is likewise the central action of the play. All the characters are involved in the assessment of their own work and the division of labor in general: Marlene's promotion to managing director, Angie's unsuitability for the work force, Joyce's unpaid labor as wife and mother, and, of course, the employees and clients of the agency. Work, promotion, money, and success are topics of conversation among the characters throughout the play. The three interviews conducted in turn by Marlene, Win, and Nell in the course of the performance do not, however, indicate that much real change is possible for the status of women in the existing labor system. For Jeanine, the secretary looking for "better prospects" in Act One, Marlene is able to suggest only other secretarial positions. Jeanine wants more money and prestige, a job like Marlene's, for instance, but Marlene urges her to lower her sights. In the end, Marlene convinces Jeanine to interview for a secretarial position with a lampshade company, which pays no better than the job she already has. Marlene attempts to make the new job more enticing by assuring the client that "the job's going to grow with the concern and then you'll be in at the top with new girls coming in underneath you." In a small firm operated by a man and his two sons, Jeanine's chances for a real promotion to the "top" are practically non-existent; her best bets are longevity and the chance someday to manage new girls in even more subordinate positions. Louise, an older client looking for a change from her middle-management position of twenty years, succeeds only in stirring up the ire of Win, her interviewer. Louise complains that newer male employees move up the ranks much more speedily than her, but admits that she has difficulty with other female employees. Win develops an instant dislike for the client, who in some respects represents her own limitations in advancing at "Top Girls." She tells Louise that in most situations she will be forced into competition with younger men and en-

courages her to accept a position with a cosmetics company, a field that is "easier for a woman," but probably with a reduction in salary. The most pathetic case of all, however, is Shona, whom Nell interviews. She aspires to employment in a "top field" such as computers but seems willing to settle for a lesser position at the "Top Girls" agency. For all her ambition and energy, Shona cannot conceal the disadvantages of her class: poor education, an unrealistic and naive concept of the business world, and lack of connections or experience. She fails in her attempt to bluff Nell into placing her in a position with management status. Together, the three interviews challenge the idea of individual achievement, so important in Marlene's ideology and in the ideology of the English middle-classes who deny the existence of class. The three interviews depict the world of business as a vertical progress from bottom to top, hence "Top Girls," which, intentionally or not, affirms the class distinctions which Marlene ignores: "I don't believe in class. Anyone can do anything if they've got what it takes." The changes Jeanine, Louise, and Shona attempt to make in their social situations, in which the "Top Girls" agency professes to give assistance, prove to be impossible within the establishment. Despite all the talk of advancement, *Top Girls* dramatizes the economic stasis of women in business and, more important, the impossibility of genuine social reform of any kind within a system maintaining vertical class distinctions.

The same circular, self-consuming logic can be traced in other parts of the play. The audience's attention is drawn towards a particular line of discourse only to see it totter and collapse anticlimactically later on, its premises shattered. The play moves backwards, negating its "arguments" as it proceeds. It begins in a place of consumption (a restaurant) and ends in a place of production (a kitchen). It begins with a celebration for a promotion and ends antichronologically with a drunken reunion which occurred one year before the promotion. The progress of the principal character Marlene proves to be illusory, and, in the end, she is no more morally advanced than the other characters and seems unusually dependent upon the sacrifices of others. Marlene's solicitousness about Angie in Act Two, Scene Two, which initially resembles "womb envy" (before the audience is aware that Angie is Marlene's daughter), ends up being little more than feelings of guilt for having abandoned her, years before. Contrary to one's usual sense of dramatic cause and effect, Marlene's guilty conscience is not redemptive; she repeats the abandonment of her daughter at the end of the scene and resumes her original course. The first scene, moreover, celebrates a promotion which the audience comes to realize was achieved at the high cost of the displacement of a number of other women of equal worth. In the end, Marlene lacks the transcendent quality of heroism the audience had come to expect of her at the beginning. Neither is she as reprehensible as her antagonists Mrs Kidd and Joyce (both played by the same actor) would have the audience believe. Marlene, too, is a victim of the hierarchy in which she operates. Even though *Top Girls* lacks faith in individualism as a vehicle for social reform, it is not entirely pessimistic in its outlook. Its faith resides in the revolutionary processes of history, which a theatrical performance can duplicate.

The most obvious device of the play, that the performers are all women, allows the drama to take a number of directions which would otherwise have been impossible. Playwright and theater analyst Micheline Wandor says [in her *Carry On, Understudies: Theatre and Sexual Politics* (1986)] that the "single-gendered play may be 'unrealistic' in the sense that we all inhabit a world which consists of men and women, but it does provide an imaginative opportunity to explore the nature of the gendered perspective (male or female) without the complexities and displacements of the 'mixed' play." Ironically, by the exclusion of active male characters, *Top Girls* manages to escape the pitfall of sexism, that is, allowing the audience to mistake the class struggle which is the basis of the dramatic plot for a "battle of the sexes," which is exactly the mistake Marlene, Win, Nell, Mrs Kidd, and Angie make, Joyce being exceptional. The action of the play indicates that the female perspective is capable, too, of drawing class distinctions and enforcing a patriarch-like matriarchy based on tyranny and division. The issue of plural feminisms as opposed to homogeneous (i.e., authoritarian) Feminism emerges in the play through the demonstration of differences of class and history among members of the same sex, a demonstration which begins in the opening scene.

Before moving to a more particular reading of the play, it is important to recognize the multiple natures of the women in the play. They are first of all, obviously, real women—actors performing roles. They are also female characters—fictions and *dramatis personae*. On yet another level, they enact roles of gender—cultural codes by which "female/feminine" defines itself as different from "male/masculine" codes. The absence of male characters on stage diminishes the obvious importance of this third level of significance, even though it plays a major part in the discourse of some of the characters. The play in performance de-realizes the women in two ways: one, by being "framed" or abstracted by the theatrical event, their sex becomes a signifier within the dramatic discourse; and two, by performing assigned roles in the drama, their characters contribute to the dramatic discourse through action and dialogue. Thus, one can call *Top Girls* a "women's play" because all of its actors and characters are women, and, at least initially, gender appears to be the dramatic focal point. Gender, however, is de-centered as the real subject of the play almost as soon as the performance begins. The first scene, in which women of different historical periods and different cultures convene to celebrate Marlene's promotion, dramatizes the lack of unity among persons of the same sex, effected by the lack of ideological unity. The six women at the dinner party represent diverse cultural attitudes towards class, religion, family, ethics, and gender; gender is given only an equal footing with other matters of cultural identity. Apart from its definition in the context of a specific culture, male or female gender does not exist. Only by the reformation of entire social systems, then, can gender roles be changed (or dispensed with) and authentic liberation of the sexes occur. Marlene's bourgeois style of feminism is proved in the course of the play to be culturally conditioned, for her success does not really challenge patriarchal authority but appropriates it, conforming, as it does, to the existing hierarchy. Joyce's argument with Marlene in the last scene makes this criticism explicit:

MARLENE: And for the country, come to that. Get the economy back on its feet and whoosh. She's a tough lady, Maggie. I'd give her a job. / She just needs to hang in there. This country

JOYCE: You voted for them, did you?

MARLENE: needs to stop whining. Monetarism is not stupid.

JOYCE: Drink your tea and shut up, pet.

MARLENE: It takes time, determination. No more slop. And

JOYCE: Well I think they're filthy bastards.

MARLENE: who's got to drive it on? First woman prime minister. Terrifico. Aces. Right on. / You must admit. Certainly gets my vote.

JOYCE: What good's first woman if it's her? I suppose you'd have liked Hitler if he was a woman. Ms Hitler. Got a lot done, Hitlerina. / Great adventures.

MARLENE: Bosses still walking on the workers' faces? Still Dadda's little parrot? Haven't you learned to think for yourself? I believe in the individual. Look at me.

JOYCE: I am looking at you.

It is our cultural prejudice, perhaps, that women should be political only about "women's issues," and *Top Girls* uses the prejudice against its audience by deceptively foregrounding gender in order to displace it with Joyce's class-conscious politics in the last scene. Marlene's mistaken concept of female homogeneity in the first scenes, then, parallels the mistake the audience makes about the play's message: to overestimate the importance of sex in feminist politics.

The writing of the French semiotician Julia Kristeva has done much to demonstrate how the opposition of male and female, upon which much of Western thought rides, is constructed by the social hierarchy which it supports. It is ideologically circular; patriarchy invents a myth to justify and perpetuate its own existence. A concept of feminism, like Marlene's, which defines itself in the context of a polarity of the sexes (i.e., female *versus* male/male *versus* female) cannot transcend the inherently man-centered or phallocentric assumptions of the ruling power system. (The problem is portrayed imaginatively in the "Top Girls" Employment Agency, which cannot place women into high levels of corporations which are designed especially to exclude women.) *Top Girls* circumvents the cultural polarity with its single sex cast. The dramatic conflict arises not out of a battle of the sexes but out of class struggle as it persists through many generations of history. The first scene functions as the medium whereby certain lines are drawn so that the subsequent political discourse will be clear and understandable.

The play opens with a simple and familiar theatrical image, a table set for six. Marlene and the waitress enter or are discovered as the lights go up. They are costumed in familiar contemporary dress befitting their status and occupation. Enter Isabella Bird in Victorian blouse and skirt. Immediately, Isabella's appearance estranges the setting. As each successive character enters in costume (Lady Nijo in kimono and geta, Dull Gret in apron and armor, Pope Joan in cassock and cope, and later Patient Griselda in medieval dress), the audience becomes aware, perhaps only dimly, of the process of history the costumes represent. Given the new context, what Marlene and the waitress wear is peculiarly historical and cultural, too. Modern dress is another form of period costume. The visual lesson of the opening scene, if taken, is to recognize the cultural relativity of certain norms.

Little is learned about Marlene in the first scene except that she has received a promotion at the employment agency where she works. Her function at the beginning is to serve as interviewer and interlocutor for the five ghost characters. Each of the characters delivers a personal narrative which, like her costume, distinguishes her from the others in the group by identifying her with the ideology of her culture. Each woman, moreover, has a distinctive manner of speaking appropriate to her class, the more extreme examples being Isabella's chatty and anecdotal monologues and Gret's monosyllabic grunts. Despite Marlene's frequent affirmation of a unity based on gender, the ghost characters do not discover much common ground among themselves. For Isabella, the others seem to lack civilization and education. Nijo perceives the others as barbarians, and Joan sees them as heretics and pagans. In fact, the common denominator of the group, besides sex, is zealous regard for their distinct cultural identities. Only Marlene perceives herself primarily as an individual apart and as a woman; the others view themselves as members of other collective enterprises: for Gret, it is a battle with her townspeople against the devils; for Griselda, it is her marriage to the Marquis; for Joan, it is the Church of Rome; for Nijo, it is her father's household and the Emperor's court; and for Isabella, it is the British Empire. Only Marlene feels a bond with the others based on sexual identity. Only she senses an allegiance to a subculture contradistinctive to the dominant culture in which she lives.

Parallels of situation do exist between the ghost characters' narratives, but the differences are more significant. Most of the women have survived tragic love affairs with weaker men. At one point, Joan asks rather unemotionally, "Have we all got dead lovers?" Nijo lost her lover, the poet-priest Ariake, before she bore their son. Isabella's American lover, the mountain man Jim Nugent, died of a gun-shot wound to the head. In later life, Isabella married John Bishop, because of his resemblance and devotion to her beloved sister Hennie, but he died shortly after the marriage. Joan's lover died in the midst of a debate with her over the theology of John the Scot.

Their narratives reveal also that many of them have borne children. Gret had ten children, whom either war or pestilence killed. Nijo gave birth to children by the Emperor and her lovers Akebono and Ariake. Griselda bore the Marquis a daughter and a son, which he removed from her in order to test her allegiance to him. Pope Joan narrates the grotesque nativity of her baby in the middle of a papal procession and their joint executions at the hands of the Roman cardinals. Only Isabella is childless, which she compensated for, she claims, by a fondness for horses. Marlene does not mention her daughter.

All the women left home, several at an early age, but for different purposes. Isabella traveled the world in search of adventure and a variety of experiences. Nijo wandered as a vagabond nun in Japan in obedience to her father's wishes and in penance for losing the Emperor's favor. At age twelve, Joan went with her comrade and lover to Athens to study theology. Gret made an epic descent into hell to avenge the death of her family and to rob the devil's storehouses. And Griselda was carried away, in fairytale fashion, to marry the Marquis, Walter.

Although, as Marlene says of them, the ghost characters are women distinguished by their courage and accomplishments, they have made obvious and often extreme concessions to their various patriarchies, against which they utter no word of condemnation or complaint. In order to study science and philosophy in the library, Joan disguised herself as a boy and continued to pass for male for the rest of her life. She moved to Italy because Italian men were beardless and became Pope after Pope Leo died. So strong was her identification with the male sex that she was unable to interpret obvious signs that she was pregnant, which failure led to her downfall and death. By way of explanation, she says she "wasn't used to having a woman's body." There is a hint of irony, perhaps, when later in the play Louise (whom the same actor plays) remarks during her interview with Win, "I don't care greatly for working with women; I think I pass as a man at work." What is more remarkable is Joan's lack of outrage against the vicious hegemony of the man-centered government of the Church. She even joins in the condemnation of herself and her sex, saying, "I'm a heresy myself" and "I shouldn't have been a woman. Woman, children and lunatics can't be Pope."

Griselda submitted to paternal oppression in a different fashion. As part of a marriage contract, she agreed to obey her husband unconditionally. She then "patiently" allowed her husband to separate her from her own daughter and son and later to send her back barefoot to her father's house so that he could marry another woman. At the end of the story, the Marquis revealed that all this was only a test of her love and loyalty towards him, welcomed her back to his house, and reunited her with their children. All the women, except Nijo, seem shocked at the Marquis's tyrannical treatment of her, but like Joan, Griselda defends the hand that oppresses her. Explaining her own reluctance to interfere when the daughter was taken from her, ostensibly to be killed, she says, "It was Walter's child to do what he liked with."

Nijo's accomplishments in life were the result of strict adherence to the wishes first of her father and then of the Emperor of Japan. In every respect, she judges herself and the other women at the dinner party according to man-imposed standards, especially those of her father, even her decision to wander Japan as a penitent nun:

> NIJO: Oh, my father was a very religious man. Just before he died he said to me, "Serve His Majesty, be respectful, if you lose his favour enter holy orders."
>
> MARLENE: But he meant stay in a convent, not go wandering round the country.
>
> NIJO: Priests were often vagrants, so why not a nun? You think I shouldn't? / I still did what my father wanted.

Isabella Bird's concern to be known as a "lady," despite her wanderlust and sense of adventure, is a milder, less obvious form of submission to male authority. Only Gret, who remains silent for most of the scene, gives less evidence of paternal domination. Isabella is less successful in her acquiescence to the standards nineteenth-century English society had set down for women, but her spirit was nevertheless willing. "I tried to do what my father wanted," she laments shortly after Nijo's speech above. And later in response to Griselda's strange tale of marital perseverance, she says, "I swore to obey dear John, of course, but it didn't seem to arise. Naturally I wouldn't have wanted to go abroad while I was married." Of all the characters present at the party, Isabella most closely resembles Marlene, an effect, no doubt, of their relative closeness in history and culture.

All the women at the dinner party are able to detect areas of intolerance and sexual tyranny in the cultures of the other women present; their blind spots are the inequities of their own cultures. Joan expresses shock and disgust at Griselda's servile obedience of the Marquis: "I never obeyed anyone. They all obeyed me"; but she does not comprehend how her own denial of her sex was also a concession to anti-feminist hegemony. Isabella decries the "superstition" of the Church during Joan's lifetime, but she is ignorant that the Victorian woman's obsession with being a proper lady was another form of female subjugation. Marlene does not approve of Nijo's acquiescence to her rape in the Emperor's palace, but later in the play she encourages a client to adapt herself to a certain professional image to please male employers. Only near the end of the scene, after the women have begun to be drunkenly boisterous, do some of them guardedly criticize their cultures. "How can people live in this dim pale island and wear our hideous clothes?" Isabella wonders. "I cannot and will not live the life of a lady." Nijo complains about the Emperor's granting permission to his attendants to flog his concubines. Patient Griselda ventures to comment aloud, "I do think—I do wonder—it would have been nicer if Walter hadn't had to." Marlene's awakening comes much later, when she sees

her daughter sleeping in the office and acknowledges, after everything, very little has really changed in the world: "She's not going to make it."

The first scene prepares the audience to perceive the play's subsequent scenes in the light of culturally-conditioned ideology. Like the ghost characters, Marlene has accomplished much in her life, and like them too, she has done so by making concessions to a phallocentric system oppressive to women. Although she expresses disapproval of the extreme, vicious acts of Griselda's Marquis, for instance, or the more intolerant doctrines of the medieval Church, she often praises the ghost characters for their pragmatic manipulation of the patriarchy to further their own ends, a compliment which, needless to say, baffles its recipients. Unwilling to be tyrannized herself, Marlene has joined the powers-that-be and, like Pope Joan, seeks to be obeyed rather than to obey. Nijo perceptively uncovers the secret significance of the promotion to managing director when she adds the phrase "Over all the women you work with. And the men" to Marlene's new title. Marlene's advancement helps no one but herself, however much she would like to believe in a right-wing feminism, and, as the following scenes reveal, she endorses a hierarchical system oppressive to the less fortunate women and men in her society.

Gender fails to be a rallying point in Act One, Scene One, because it is a signifier distinctive to the ideologies which encode it. The conceptions of gender differ culturally and historically as do the costumes. When Marlene proposes a toast "to you all," Isabella responds, "To yourself surely, we're here to celebrate your success." Pleased at the compliment to her promotion, Marlene nevertheless attempts to turn around Isabella's toast, "To Marlene," by adding, "And all of us." She says, "*We*'ve *all* come a long way. To *our* courage and the way *we* changed *our* lives and *our* extraordinary achievements" (italics mine). Marlene wants her promotion to be a sign of progress for women collectively, but the others perceive her success as peculiarly Marlene's own. Because of her blindness to class and ideology, Marlene persists in her naive belief that what she individually accomplishes for herself will automatically redound to the common good. Her separation from her sister Joyce in the last scene duplicates her separation from the five ghost characters in the first. In the quarrel which marks the end of the drama, the use of pronouns to demarcate the characters' opposing points of view becomes an explicit element of the discourse:

> MARLENE: *Them, them. / Us and them?*
>
> JOYCE: And *you're one of them.*
>
> MARLENE: And *you're us,* wonderful *us,* and Angie's *us* / and Mum and Dad's *us.*
>
> JOYCE: Yes, that's right, and *you're them.*
>   (italics mine)

Whereas the cultural divisions of the dinner party scene are somewhat blurred by the amicable situation, the bluntness of the sibling quarrel at the end of the play effectively splits Marlene and Joyce into separate classes, in spite of apparent shared features such as sex, family, and a common interest in the well-being of their daughter Angie. Gender fails to be a rallying point in Act Two, Scene Two, because Joyce, unlike Marlene, does not see the perpetuation of class differences within a hegemonic patriarchy (or matriarchy) as an acceptable feminist model for society. Joyce's argumentative point, which in effect is the political statement of the play, is that Marlene has misperceived the lines of conflict. Inadvertently, Marlene has become "them," the tyrants, even as she endeavors, on the basis of gender, to identify herself with "us" (a sisterhood of all women) in the first and last scenes.

The play in performance moves the audience from the apparent dichotomy of "female/male," which Marlene's discourse asserts, to the underlying dichotomy of "oppressor/oppressed" which is the effect of phallocentric hierarchism and which operates outside of the classifications of sex and gender. Within the society of the play, which includes only women, hegemony continues to exist even as women gain token power within the system. Given the context of the whole play, the expression "top girls" becomes, of course, ironic in as much as it implies a middle and a bottom, that is, hierarchy and class tyranny. The drama which the process of scenes enacts is the decentering of Marlene as "top girl" and the deconstruction of the ideology encoding the expression.

Churchill's comedy is disloyal to the historical process of civilization it chronicles in the opening scene. The apparent feminist front at the dinner party proves to be neither unified nor really feminist in any social or political sense. The five women present are as unconscious of Marlene's concept of sisterhood as they are of her concept of the individual. In their own ways, they endorse the several tyrannies under which they lived: Joan, Isabella, and Marlene by emulating the oppressor; Nijo and Griselda by conceding to him. Dull Gret's naive assault upon hell and its he-devils in an attempt to steal infernal wealth parodies radical and bourgeois forms of feminism, which either reverse or capitalize on existing inequalities rather than remove them. In Gret's army, the women-invaders stop to gather the money that the "big devil" shits upon their heads and bludgeon the "little devils, our size," an action which offers the satisfaction of victimization to those who themselves once suffered as victims. The ideology of these actions is not explicitly challenged until Joyce pronounces her judgment on it in the final scene: "Nothing's changed for most people / has it?" Marlene's feminism, defined by paternal models for dominating the weak, fails to envision "alternative, non-oppressive ways of living" [Rosemary K. Curb, "Re/cognition, Re/presentation, Re/creation in Woman-Conscious Drama: The Seer, The Seen, The Scene, The Obscene," *Theatre Journal*, 37 (1985)]. It is the presence of "stupid, lazy, and frightened" Angie, however, who disturbs Marlene's ideology from the beginning. Angie, whose presence once posed a threat to Marlene's career, threatens at the end her sense of moral equilibrium—Marlene's world cannot account for or accommodate her. The world continuing to be what it is, Angie, like most women, can never be a "top girl."

Janet Brown (essay date 1991)

SOURCE: *"Top Girls,"* in *Taking Center Stage: Feminism in Contemporary U.S. Drama,* The Scarecrow Press, Inc., 1991, pp. 101-15.

[*Brown is an American educator and critic who specializes in feminist critical theory, concentrating on the relationship between gender and class. In the excerpted essay below, she argues that* Top Girls *is not, as many critics believe, a purely "feminist" drama, but rather a critical examination of the limitations of the women's movement and a call for the audience "to move beyond individual solutions to confront the larger contradictions created by a capitalistic patriarchy."*]

Caryl Churchill's play ***Top Girls*** opens with a feminist fantasy of the past, a dinner party for extraordinary women from history and fiction, and ends with a young girl's nightmare of the future. The dream of the past reminds us of the historical weight of women's oppression, but also of the futility of individual solutions. The child's nightmare of the future reminds us what is at stake in the contemporary feminist struggle for societal transformation.

Between these two dreams lies a realistic drama that forms a critique of Marlene, a woman executive. Alternating scenes depict life at the Top Girls Employment Agency, of which Marlene is the new director, and in a working-class family in the country eventually revealed as Marlene's sister Joyce, her adopted daughter Angie, and Angie's friend, Kit. Angie, the slow-witted, overweight daughter, runs away from home to see Marlene, who is clearly nonplussed by her presence and explains to her colleagues that Angie's "a bit thick. . . . She's not going to make it." The last scene of the play, a year earlier, shows Marlene in a rare visit to Joyce's home. An argument between the sisters ranging from their own life choices to Margaret Thatcher's government (supported by Marlene, opposed by Joyce) awakens Angie, who realizes vaguely that Marlene must be her mother. In the play's final moments, Angie stumbles into the living room half-awake, crying, "Frightening. Frightening."

Top Girls opened at the Royal Court Theatre in London in the fall of 1982. After a successful London run, the production was brought to the Public Theatre in New York in December 1982, and it later received another production with a New York cast. *New York Times* reviewer Frank Rich praised the play's "brave gambles" and "angry wit" [New York Times (29 December 1982)]. His review recognized that to Marlene, "the ability to make it by male success standards is the only criterion of female worth," making her "figuratively speaking, a male oppressor." His only quarrel with the argument of the play was the "absence of the middle range—of women who achieve without imitating power-crazed men and denying their own humanity." Walter Kerr echoed Rich's objection in his *Times* column a few weeks later headed, "Are These Feminists Too Hard on Women?" [*New York Times* (23 January 1983)]. He enjoyed the first scene of ***Top Girls*** the most, "because at this juncture no one was yet trying to put anyone else down," and he questioned whether a play that shows a woman as

A scene from the 1982 London production of Top Girls *at the Royal Court Theatre.*

unfeeling as Marlene is toward Angie "should be called feminist at all."

Nor was Kerr alone in his discomfort at labeling *Top Girls* a feminist drama. Even the actresses in the original cast, interviewed in the *New York Times,* differed on this point. Carole Hayman, who played Angie and Dull Gret, said, "It's been called a feminist play, but I would say it is a socialist play first, and a feminist play second." Lou Wakefield, who played the waitress at the dinner party, Kit, and a Top Girls client, put it differently [in the *New York Times* (6 January 1983)]:

> This is a feminist play in that it's self-criticism of the women's movement. The big popular wave of the women's movement was geared toward women being successful and equal. What Caryl Churchill is doing is asking you to reassess what is happening to the popular women's movement, not necessarily the intellectual feminist. Some women are succeeding and getting on very well, but it's no good if feminism means that women get on and tread on men's heads, or other women's heads, as hard as men ever tread on theirs. If women do get the top jobs, there's also a job to be done in reassessing that job in feminist or humanitarian terms.

Churchill addresses an audience that already accepts the feminist struggle for individual autonomy and asks them to criticize its limitations as many contemporary theorists have begun to do.

Bell Hooks points out that the modern feminist movement in the United States began with Betty Friedan, who addressed the problem of the white, middle-class housewife as if it were the problem of all women—ignoring the poor, the nonwhite, and the unmarried. The demands of these women for meaningful work with equal pay and social equality with white middle-class men were easily co-opted by the capitalist patriarchy. The underlying "ideology of domination" remains untouched by these women's individual gains, however, while they themselves may assume that the feminist struggle is over, or may even join the ranks of the oppressors [Bell Hooks, *Feminist Theory: From Margin to Center,* 1984].

Jean Baker Miller [in *Toward a New Psychology of Women,* 1986] asserts that "even in their traditional roles, women, by *their very existence,* confront and challenge men because they have been made *the embodiment of the dominant culture's unsolved* [psychological] *problems.*" In response

27

to this threat, and as a fundamental step in the male maturation process of separation from mother, many men have denied the female in themselves. This denial has created the patriarchal culture of constant wars, imperialism, and technological destruction of the environment. Women, raised by women, have tended to remain in connection, first with their mothers and later with the larger community. Because women have traditionally experienced political oppression and assignment to the domestic sphere, they have tended to develop an alternative culture and ethic [see Josephine Donovan, *Feminist Theory: The Intellectual Tradition of American Feminism* (1985)]. As other options develop for middle-class women, however, the likelihood that they will continue to unthinkingly adopt an alternative female ethic fades. Instead, they may conclude that success in a patriarchal system demands the adoption of patriarchal values. Only by conscious moral choice can the "ethic of care" described by [Carol] Gilligan be retained in a changing society [cited by Jean Bethke Elshtain in *Public Man, Private Woman: Women in Social and Political Thought* (1981)]. It is by this standard of conscious moral choice that Marlene and the other "top girls" in Churchill's play are tried and found wanting.

In the opening scene of *Top Girls,* Marlene hosts a dinner to celebrate her promotion to managing director of the Top Girls Employment Agency. The guests are all extraordinary women drawn from history, art, or literature—a group of characters who had haunted Churchill for years. They include the Victorian adventurer and travel writer, Isabella Bird; Lady Nijo, a medieval concubine who became a wandering Buddhist nun; Pope Joan, who may have passed as a man to become pope for a brief period in the ninth century, and Dull Gret, who leads a charge of peasant women through hell in a Brueghel painting. In a long, chatty scene that is funny and touching by turns, these women relate their life stories. . . .

Churchill's dinner party . . . offers no explanation for the women selected, relates their lives in continually overlapping and interrupted dialogue, and presents the women with a lively irreverence that is often very funny. Isabella Bird, a courageous traveler and a best-selling author of her time, is full of hypocritical regrets and psychosomatic symptoms that provided her with excellent excuses for further travel. Lady Nijo confesses that she never enjoyed the "rough life" of a Buddhist nun. "What I enjoyed most was being the Emperor's favorite and wearing thin silk."

Although their conversation is informal supper talk interrupted by food and drink orders (Pope Joan orders canelloni and a salad), they are searching for commonalities, giving the scene the intellectual cast of a Women's Studies seminar on exceptional women. "Have we all got dead lovers?" Joan asks, and only Marlene responds, "Not me, sorry." In fact, despite the wildly and sometimes hilariously disparate circumstances of their lives, commonalities among the diners quickly emerge. Isabella Bird, Pope Joan, and Lady Nijo were all adventurous women who in some sense "passed" as men. All three had lovers who died, and Nijo and Joan both lost children to the patriarchy—Nijo because her children were by lovers and not by the Emperor, Joan's

baby being the cause of her own discovery and death by stoning. Isabella, though briefly married, never had children, and seems to have felt affection only for her sister, whom she nevertheless seldom saw because of her extensive travels. Thus isolated from other women and from family life, they are all terrible egotists who interrupt one another continually—less a community than a group of competitors. They either browbeat or ignore the young, unnamed waitress who never speaks. Of the diners, only Dull Gret is similarly silent, eating her way through the breadbasket and the scene, revealing only in response to the others' questions that she raised ten children and a pig.

Chaucer's Patient Griselda arrives late, and seems at first to present a contrast to the other, more active women. As Marlene draws out her story, however, points of agreement begin to emerge. Like Griselda, Isabella and Nijo felt most closely identified with their fathers to whom they offered perfect obedience. Griselda was not reluctant to swear the same obedience to her husband because "I'd rather obey the Marquis than a boy from the village," she says, and Marlene responds, "Yes, that's a point." When the Marquis takes her children from her one by one, Lady Nijo agrees that "of course you had to [accept it], he was your life. And were you in favour after that?" Griselda's uncritical acceptance of the patriarchy ultimately elevates her to a position of the highest status, far above the peasant class into which she was born—much like Marlene.

In fact, the apparently autonomous lives of all the diners have been predicated on a patriarchal system that simply co-opted them, and at a high price in isolation and suffering. Toward the end of the scene, Marlene begins to wonder, "Oh God, why are we all so miserable?" Despite their adventures, their privilege, and their visibility to history, these women are miserable because they are the lonely and powerless pawns of the patriarchy. Their similarities despite the separation of their lives by hundreds of years suggest a complete lack of historical progress. Each had great adventures; nevertheless, as Isabella Bird says in the closing lines of the scene, the adventure was "only temporary."

At the end of the scene, Dull Gret finally breaks her silence, revealing herself as the true exception to the group. She begins by describing Hell, a place "like the village where I come from." She says she rallied the other women around her for her fight against the devils. They were unafraid: "Well we'd had worse, you see, we'd had the Spanish. We'd all had family killed. Men on wheels. Babies on swords. I'd had enough, I was mad, I hate the bastards." Unlike the other "top girls," Gret remains a member of the lowest class and leader of her community. She identifies herself with other women, does not give up her children for her own advancement, and in fact is moved to fight not only for herself but for the children and the men as well. . . .

Act 1 of *Top Girls* jumps from the dinner party in scene 1 to Marlene interviewing a client at the Top Girls Employment Agency in scene 2, to Angie and Kit hiding from Joyce in the backyard in scene 3. No explanation is offered of the relationship among the scenes, and only Marlene appears in more than one of them. Although Angie refers to an aunt whom she suspects may be her real mother, she never mentions Marlene by name. Thus the audience is forced to imagine their own connections among the three scenes that comprise act 1.

These sudden shifts in scene and style, criticized by some reviewers, can also be viewed as a deliberately jarring use of Brechtian alienation technique. Janelle Reinelt points out that British feminists including Churchill have often adopted Brechtian techniques in an effort to "make ideology visible" ["Beyond Brecht: Britain's New Feminist Drama," *Theatre Journal* (May 1986)]. Significantly, the stage directions offer no time, only a place for each of the first three scenes. All three seem meant to occur in an eternal present time. Certainly this is true of the dinner party, in which much of the humor arises from bringing together women from such widely varied time periods. The dinner party also serves to "historicize" the contemporary scene that follows, making Marlene's achievement less a sign of progress. Instead, she is categorized as one of that group of anomalous women throughout history who escaped the fate of invisibility but whose lives have failed nevertheless to alter the patriarchal system.

In scene 2, Marlene's advice to her young client suggests that she not only is no reformer of the present capitalistic patriarchy, she actually helps to promulgate it. She coolly

---

Churchill on the formation of her political views:

Like many women Caryl Churchill's political consciousness came slowly and subjectively, and grew out of her own personal experience rather than as a response to public political events. Churchill [stated during an interview]: "I didn't really feel a part of what was happening in the sixties. During that time I felt isolated. I had small children and was having miscarriages. It was an extremely solitary life. What politicised me was being discontent with my own way of life—of being a barrister's wife and just being at home with small children." And the most politicising event was—with her husband—changing her life-style, when her husband left the bar and started working for a law centre: "We did not want to shore up a capitalist system we didn't like." And there was "that decision of having no more children," when, after another miscarriage, her husband had a vasectomy. And there was the packing up lock, stock and barrel for six months, three in Africa and three on Dartmoor, where she wrote *Objections to Sex and Violence*: "me living with David and coping with things so that he could work for ten years, so why didn't he take time off to do what I wanted to do?" Like Edward Bond, Churchill came only gradually to be able to intellectualise what was always an intuitive socialist (and feminist) perspective—to analyse and to understand her own personal experience in terms of class society. Churchill: "My attitude then was entirely to do with self-expression of my own personal pain and anger. It wasn't thought out."

Catherine Itzin, in her Stages in the Revolution: Political Theatre in Britain since 1968, *Eyre Methuen, 1980.*

---

assesses twenty-year-old Jeanine on the basis of her scores at school and her "presentation" of herself, advises her not to mention marriage plans to any potential employers, and recommends a job prospect that will "grow with the concern and then you'll be in at the top with new girls coming in underneath you." She teaches Jeanine, in other words, to be competitive, isolated, and totally achievement oriented—like herself and the other "top girls" at the dinner party in scene 1. When Jeanine asks wistfully about travel prospects, Marlene inquires, "Does your fiancé want to travel?" Clearly, the sacrifices Isabella Bird and Lady Nijo made for their freedom are still required to some extent today.

Scene 3, like scenes 1 and 2, presents a community of females. Although this one is the more traditionally domestic group of mother and children, the characters seem no less alienated from one another. As the scene opens, Angie and Kit are hiding from Joyce in a shelter made from junk. When Joyce stops calling to Angie and goes inside, Angie remarks, "Wish she was dead." Here a depressing alternative to the top girls' adventures is presented as Joyce nags endlessly at the sullen Angie, first to come inside, then to clean her room, while Kit and Angie struggle for money and permission to go to the cinema to see *The Exterminator*.

The two children, Kit and Angie, are as intensely close now as only adolescents can be, but it is clear that the hierarchical system will soon separate them. Already Kit, three years younger than Angie, has continued longer in school and is in a higher "track" than Angie was. Kit's dream of becoming a nuclear physicist may be possible; as she points out to Joyce, "I'm clever." Angie, on the other hand, is "not going to get a job when jobs are hard to get," according to Joyce. "She'd better get married. I don't know who'd have her, mind. She's one of those girls might never leave home." Although Kit is clearly the luckier of the two, her choice of career is based on her fear of nuclear war. She confides that she lies awake at night wondering whether she would be safer if she moved to New Zealand, or if she should "find out where they were going to drop it and stand right in the place." Angie is less interested, but only because she is focused on fantasies of killing Joyce and running off to join her glamorous "aunt," Marlene.

It is not until act 2 that the story reenters chronological time with a long series of consecutive encounters on "a Monday morning" at the Top Girls Employment Agency. In these scenes we begin to see Marlene's adoption of patriarchal values not as exceptional, but merely as unusually thorough and successful. In one interview the Top Girls representative, Win, forces a middle-aged woman to realize that she has given her life to her company but will never receive further advancement, and now is in competition with younger, more stylish women for positions in other firms. In another, Shona, a young woman in sales, is urged to present herself as having "the guts to push through to a closing situation. They think we're too nice. They think we listen to the buyer's doubts. They think we consider his needs and his feelings." Shona assures her interviewer, Nell, that "I never consider people's feelings." Then, when urged to describe her present job, she is reduced to detailing what she would order for dinner on the road, revealing her resumé as a fraud. Nell responds with simple exasperation, "Christ what a waste of time." Nell, like Shona, Win, and Marlene, seems without ethical concerns of any kind. All are simply the heartless representatives of the heartless business world.

At one level, then, the play is a critique of the individual woman who achieves equality in the work world without regard for her sisters (literal or figurative), and even at their expense. Marlene and her associates are not simply oppressors, however, as some reviewers suggested; they are victims of the system as well. Just as the dinner party ends in drunken mourning over the lost children, the loneliness, and the violent endings to which the diners came, so the present-day female executives feel the loss of family and friends. It is only in fantasy that Marlene could celebrate her promotion with a dinner party; in reality, she says, she fell asleep in front of the television. She sees her mother, sister, and daughter perhaps once in three years; she has never married, but has had two abortions. Win, whose very name suggests her competitive nature, describes her idea of a wonderful weekend: sneaking into her married lover's house with him while his wife is away. She admits that she has had a drinking problem, that her second husband has been in prison for three years, and that she "went bonkers for a bit, thought I was five different people."

Nor is the traditional upper-middle-class couple in a better situation, as represented by Howard Kidd, who lost his anticipated promotion to Marlene. According to Mrs. Kidd, who comes into the office on this same Monday morning to confront Marlene, Howard is devastated by losing his promotion, and worse, losing it to a woman who will now be his supervisor. "It's me that bears the brunt," says Mrs. Kidd. "I'm not the one that's been promoted. He's not being dominated by me, I've been right behind him, I put him first every inch of the way. And now what do I get? You women this, you women that. It's not my fault." Marlene says she is sorry that Howard's been taking it out on Mrs. Kidd, but adds, "He really is a shit, Howard." an opinion the audience is likely to share. Still, when Mrs. Kidd is called away by the news that Howard has had a heart attack, it's difficult to share the cool reaction of the women executives who point out, "Lucky he didn't get the job if that's what his health's like."

Mr. and Mrs. Kidd represent the traditional dichotomy described by Miller [in *Toward a New Psychology*], in which the man defines himself as isolated, autonomous, and aggressive, while the woman carries the emotional, expressive burden for both husband and wife. Thus they remind the audience, who by now have seen plenty of unlikable behavior from the "top girls" that traditional sex roles are as much a dead end as their imitations of male selfishness. "We all need *both* ourselves *and* each other. Our troubles seem to come from an attempt to divide ourselves so that we force men to center around themselves and women to center around 'the other.' From this division both groups suffer." In the case of the Kidds (whose name suggests their immaturity), the same pressure to compete in a capitalistic patriarchy that drives Kidd to abuse his wife cuts him down

with a heart attack and hardens the hearts of (even) his female colleagues against him. Mrs. Kidd, by staking her ego entirely on her husband, sets herself in isolated opposition to other women.

Her tirade against Marlene is witnessed by Angie, who has just "run away" to Marlene. While Angie is full of admiration for Marlene's aggressive handling of Mrs. Kidd, Marlene is clearly baffled and repelled by Angie. When Win asks about Angie, Marlene can only assess her as she would an unsuccessful Top Girls client, speculating that she will grow up to be a grocery store packer. "She's a bit thick. She's a bit funny," Marlene tells Win. In the final scene of the play, these closing words of scene 1 achieve their full resonance with the disclosure that Marlene is Angie's mother.

Act 2, scene 2 takes place "a year earlier. Sunday evening." Thus, while time is specific in act 2, chronology is reversed. Just as the opening scene of the play denies historical progress in the condition of women, the structure of the play itself moves from a vague, eternal present in act 1 to a regression into the past in act 2. This spiraling or circular structure, characteristic of women's writing, seems here to say that human society is "going in circles"; no progress is being made.

The roots of Marlene's present circumstances are finally revealed in this scene, while her life choices are contrasted with her sister's. Marlene's struggle as an adolescent was for a personal, isolated autonomy more typical of masculine psychological development. A working-class girl with an illegitimate child, she abandoned her daughter to be raised by her married sister and sought a career in the city. Since then, she has found opportunities to travel (she worked in America for a time) and is clearly on the "fast track" in her career. Though Marlene elicits sympathy when she describes fleeing the "dead end" life she saw their mother live with their crude, violent father, her abandonment of her daughter and her rejection of the working class, including her own family, can scarcely be construed as admirable. Marlene, whose rise to the executive suite many middle-class feminists might unthinkingly admire, is, like her ghostly dinner companions, a selfish, isolated snob.

Joyce, in contrast, still lives in the community where she grew up and supports herself and her adopted daughter by cleaning houses. She has retained strong family ties to Angie and to her own mother, whom she now visits weekly in a nursing home. She defends their father to Marlene despite his violent behavior, saying that he worked "in the fields like an animal." She has maintained her self-respect by breaking off her marriage after her husband's repeated infidelities, by fending off the husbands of friends after her divorce, and by supporting herself and Angie without financial help from Marlene. If Joyce represents the more traditional female development in her commitment to family and community, she also demonstrates the powerless position in which this commitment places her.

In the play's final scene, Joyce and Marlene spell out their differences. Marlene declares she favors Margaret Thatcher's government, believes in the individual, and doesn't "believe in class. Anyone can do anything if they've got what it takes," she says. Of course, "If they're stupid or lazy or frightened, I'm not going to help them get a job, why should I?" she adds. In one of the play's most telling moments, Joyce responds, "What about Angie? . . . She's stupid, lazy and frightened. What about her?"

Angie's "frightening" dream a few minutes later concludes the play. Although she consciously admires Marlene, her unconscious, dreaming response tells a deeper truth. If Angie, representing those children who will never be at the "top" of any hierarchy, has only Marlene to depend upon, then she and the society have every reason to fear. Marlene has practiced denial of the female to such an extreme that she brushes off her abortions as "boring . . . messy talk about blood" and avoids visiting her mother because it makes Marlene "feel better" to stay away. The impact of her individualistic politics on the rest of society—even on her own family—escapes her entirely. She predicts that "the eighties are going to be stupendous" and misses the irony in Joyce's response: "Who for?"

Top Girls draws on the strategies of radical feminist theatre groups of the sixties and early seventies. As in many of those productions, there is no clear protagonist in the play; while Marlene is a central figure, she is by no means the active, sympathetic protagonist of traditional drama. The cast is entirely female, and each cast member with the exception of Marlene takes on two and sometimes three roles. (The characteristic Churchill touch comes with the choices of characters to be double-cast. Pope Joan, for instance, reappears as the older executive who "passed as a man at work," she felt, but now finds herself stuck in middle management.) The final scene's debate between the two sisters typifies the direct didacticism of the early works. The centrality of women characters, the satiric commentary on contemporary women's experience in the work world, and the extended reference to heroic women of the past are all characteristic of the work of these groups.

At the same time, the play is typical of feminist drama of the eighties in its concern with silenced women, its reflection on women's community, and its depiction of female psychological and moral development. Marlene, who keeps her illegitimate daughter and her two abortions secret, is forced to silence her female experience in order to "pass" in the patriarchal business world. The silent peasant Gret, whose sole speech forms the climax of the dinner party, foreshadows the silent Angie, whose anguished cry closes the play.

The issue of women's community is raised in the tension between an all-female cast and the lack of communal feeling that pervades the dinner party, the employment agency, and even the home. Of all the characters in the play, only Angie and Kit show any warmth for one another, and their relationship is not destined to outlast childhood. The two sisters, Joyce and Marlene, illustrate the traditional female psychological development and its contemporary variant: the attempt to deny the female and adopt masculine attitudes and behavior. Joyce's relative passivity and her com-

mitment to her mother and her niece form a contrast with Marlene's isolation and constant quest for "adventures." Joyce makes ethical decisions based on empathic concern for those around her; Marlene feels no responsibility other than to play by the cut-throat rules of the business world. If the self-centered Marlene with her complete lack of maternal concern represents the final triumph of feminism in our society, then the future is indeed "frightening."

Clearly, *Top Girls* is directed at an audience that is both sympathetic and conversant with feminist views. The 1986 Gallup Poll showing that 56 percent of all American women identify themselves as feminist, and only 4 percent "anti-feminist" [cited by Barbara Ehrenrich in "The Next Wave," *Ms.* (August 1987)], no less than the mainstream press coverage and the box office appeal of Churchill's plays, confirm the existence of such an audience. Churchill, however, does not offer this audience a comfortable reinforcement of their beliefs. Instead, she challenges them to move beyond individual solutions to confront the larger contradictions created by a capitalistic patriarchy. In fact, the play demands nothing less than a feminist transformation of society. As Jean Baker Miller writes, "It now seems clear we have arrived at a point from which we must seek a basis of faith in connection—and not only faith but recognition that it is a requirement for the existence of human beings." Frank Rich misses the point when he defends women who achieve without "losing their humanity" against *Top Girls'* indictment. It is not only the individuals but the patriarchal system itself that is being indicted, and the loss of humanity is everyone's loss.

FEN

PRODUCTION REVIEWS

Frank Rich   (review date 31 May 1983)

SOURCE: *"Fen,* New Work By Caryl Churchill," in *The New York Times,* 31 May 1983, p. 10.

[*The Joint Stock production of* Fen *debuted in London in February 1983 and played at the Almeida Theatre until March, when it began a tour that included a run at New York's Public Theatre. In the following New York production review, Rich asserts that although the play is "at times the most off-putting" of Churchill's works, it is nevertheless "another confirmation that its author possesses one of the boldest theatrical imaginations to emerge in this decade."*]

Fen, the new Caryl Churchill play at the Public, could well be called *Bottom Girls.* As the author's *Top Girls* told of Marlene, a self-made businesswoman who sells out her provincial working-class roots and humanity for corporate success in London, so the new one examines the less privileged sisters such top girls leave behind. The characters of

Fen are downtrodden farmworkers in the Fens of East Anglia. Marlene would dismissively claim that these women deserve their fate because they're too "lazy and stupid" to claw their way up the economic ladder as she did. But in Miss Churchill's view, it's the Marlenes of contemporary England who callously keep the benighted poor in their lowly place.

As befits the shift in focus, the new play contains little of its predecessor's laughter: even as the audience enters the Public's LuEsther Hall, it is swept up in a gloomy mist that pours out from the stage. *Fen* is dour, difficult and, unlike either *Top Girls* or *Cloud 9,* never coy about its rather stridently doctrinaire socialism: it's the most stylistically consistent of Miss Churchill's plays and at times the most off-putting. It is also yet another confirmation that its author possesses one of the boldest theatrical imaginations to emerge in this decade.

Fen was created by Miss Churchill with the Joint Stock Theater Group, the communal London fringe company whose actors conduct their own documentary research into the characters they portray.

As an impressionistic, class-conscious portrait of an agrarian community, the play recalls David Hare's Joint Stock piece about a similar village in nascent revolutionary China, *Fanshen*: a few actors—five women, one man—play more than 20 roles in a mosaic of Brechtian vignettes. But unlike *Fanshen,* which was seen here this year in a weak local staging, *Fen* has been brought intact from London as part of the Britain Salutes New York festival. It's a high-powered production, faultlessly directed by Les Waters with an acting ensemble as accomplished as the imported Royal Court cast of *Top Girls.* . . .

The action unfolds on a stunning set designed by Annie Smart: the stage floor is carpeted with the dirt of the potato fields and surrealistically bordered by walls and furnishings suggesting the women's dreary homes. In Tom Donnellan's eerie lighting—all shades of Thomas Hardy dankness, no sunlight—the 90 minutes of scenes loom in the icy dark like fragmented nightmares. One minute the women are picking potatoes in a thunderstorm; then, through startlingly sharp transitions, that dominant image gives way to the sight of two illicit lovers dancing in moonlight or a madonna-like portrait of mother and child or a forlorn Baptist revival meeting.

"We're all rubbish," says one of the suffering Baptists, "but Jesus still loves us, so it's all right." As in *Top Girls,* Miss Churchill sees one and all as helpless, exploited victims of a dehumanizing capitalistic system. She further feels that women can only escape its clutches, as Marlene did, by adopting that system's most selfish, ruthless traits.

There are two top girls in *Fen*—as unfeeling workers' overlord and a slick real-estate entrepreneur—and even their power doesn't give them freedom from top guys. They must answer to the countryside's real barons—a faceless multinational conglomerate, which, as a prologue implies, is or will be owned by the Japanese.

Most of the women in *Fen,* however, are laborers, bound to the land by an age-old, oppressive tradition that enslaves them from birth to grave. As Miss Churchill presents these sad serfs, they can only ameliorate their misery in self-destructive ways: by drinking in a pub or gossiping or taking Valium or betraying one another or going mad. Yet it the playwright's definition of these women's choices is rigidly deterministic, her concentrated dramatization of their lives has an open, poetic intensity that transcends the flat tendentiousness of mere agitprop.

Shadowy and spare as the brief scenes are, luminous individual characters gradually emerge. Chief among them is Val (Jennie Stoller), who leaves her daughters for a new lover (Bernard Strother)—only to discover, to her eternal torment, that she can't live either without her children or without her man. Angela (Amelda Brown) is a sexually frustrated woman who lets out her anger by torturing her stepdaughter Becky (Tricia Kelly), a teen-age misfit not unlike the "dim" daughter Marlene disowns in *Top Girls.* In one grotesquely disturbing scene, Angela and Becky wound one another by composing limericks that are alternately sadistic and suicidal. The self-hating stepmother explains that only by hurting her ward can she "feel something."

Other characters waft in and out like plumes of smoke. We meet a male oligarch who sells off his estate, thereby becoming a tenant on his own grandfather's land; a spectral 150-year-old peasant woman stalking a despised landowner for eternity; a hermaphrodite taunted by neighborhood kids; a trio of schoolgirls singing a cappella of their circumscribed futures as housewives, hairdressers and nurses; a 32-year-old grandmother caring for a baby and a senescent 90-year-old grandmother lost in reveries of coffins and long-ago union strife.

Eventually, there is a tragic climax—a death as ritualized as an act of hara-kiri. Depending on whether or not you buy the author's position that her women have only no-win alternatives, you'll either be moved by this gruesome catharsis or left cold.

After that comes the evening's somewhat sentimental but striking coda, in which the characters all haunt the Fens as ghosts: they drift through the suffocating green mist, soliloquizing like Dylan Thomas phantoms radicalized by the playwright Edward Bond. "The earth's awake!," says one of them—and it's Miss Churchill who has awakened it. Here's a writer, amazingly enough, who is plowing new ground in the theater with every new play.

T. E. Kalem   (review date 13 June 1983)

SOURCE: "Tragedy in an Aching Stoop," in *Time,* New York, Vol. 121, No. 24, 13 June 1983, p. 64.

[*Below, Kalem offers a laudatory assessment of* Fen*'s New York production, concluding: "The unifying element is a love story played out against a landscape of doom."*]

Tiny spires of smoke rise from the stage as if the earth were releasing noxious fumes. In the brooding mist on this blasted brown heath, we almost expect *Macbeth*'s three witches to materialize.

The women who do appear are simple farm laborers gathering up a potato crop. In rigid lines and soulless silence, they move forward, whisking loose dirt from the potatoes and tossing them into baskets. They are harrowing illustrations from Edwin Markham's *The Man with the Hoe:* "Time's tragedy is in that aching stoop."

Currently at Joseph Papp's Public Theater, *Fen* is the third of British Playwright Caryl Churchill's plays to be presented in New York. "Infinitely distantly" related to Winston, Churchill, 44, is a no-nonsense feminist whose convictions are firm without being strident. She is the mother of three boys, ages 20, 18 and 13, and her barrister husband tended them for stretches so that she could write. She possesses a startling imagination, and her way with words ranges from the stark to the lyrical.

Fen is quite unlike **Cloud Nine,** Churchill's wickedly ambisextrous foray into the man-woman relationship in the heyday of Victoria's imperial sway, updated in Act II to contemporary Britain. Nor does it remotely resemble **Top Girls,** her study of the modern career woman's adaptive skills at the Big Business pastime of cat-kills-mouse. The women of *Fen* seem primordially immune to change, though Churchill would doubtless argue that they have been ensnared in a capitalistic slave pen.

In the east of England, less than 100 miles north of London, the Fens draws its name from the fact that it was swampland reclaimed for farming beginning in the 17th century. This rich earth is gradually falling into the hands of interlocking conglomerates, and the play implies that the Japanese may eventually own it. Against this backdrop Churchill fashions a kind of *Under Milk Wood* as it might have been seen through the bleak, baleful eyes of Thomas Hardy.

The unifying element is a love story played out against a landscape of doom. Val (Jennie Stoller) falls in love with Frank (Bernard Strother), a farm laborer separated from his wife and children. She leaves her husband and two young daughters. But Val is soon torn by anguish. She cannot live without her children and would die without her man. The lovers are both earthbound and star-crossed.

In between, we meet the villagers: cantankerous, narrowly provincial, soaked in religious zeal and, occasionally, intoxicated with a bizarre humor. The desire to escape a barren, futile existence is grimly repressed. It translates into a lurking violence. Three children taunt a woman said to be a hermaphrodite (Cecily Hobbs) and try to impale her on a hoe as if it were a pitchfork. A sadistic step-mother (Amelda Brown) torments her placidly submissive stepdaughter (Tricia Kelly) in order to "feel something." At one point, Val asks Frank: "What are you frightened of?" Frank replies: "Going mad. Heights. Beauty." Says Val: "Lucky we live in a flat country." Churchill interprets the flat country

to be the death of the heart, and with the aid of an absolutely superb cast, she has composed a moving requiem.

Sylviane Gold (review date 24 June 1983)

SOURCE: "Bottom Girls: Love Among the Potato Fields," *The Wall Street Journal,* 24 June 1983, p. 24.

[*Below, Gold asserts that the atmosphere overwhelms the message in* Fen.]

A particular way of life, a distinct sense of place—these aren't the things we usually expect to discover at the theater. Movies and books seem better equipped to reveal the inner workings of a village or a landscape; we look at plays to learn the inner workings of a soul.

So to say that British playwright Caryl Churchill succeeds, in *Fen,* in rendering the texture of life in the rich agricultural flatlands of England's Fens district is to credit her with something of a feat. And to add that, in the end, *Fen* is less satisfying than the previous Churchill efforts seen in New York, **Cloud 9** and **Top Girls,** is merely to add that, in the end, we want more of theater than merely a portrait of a place—however fine.

The atmosphere of *Fen* hits you in the face in a quite literal way: A thick, wet mist fills the Public Theater's LuEsther Hall as you walk in. And before your lungs and eyes have adjusted, your ears are assaulted by the angry clack of a wooden rattle for frightening crows. This, Churchill and her director, Les Waters, seem to imply, is life in a Fens village, a dull haze pierced occasionally by fierce alarms.

The villager whose panic we will come to know most intimately is Val, played with a mopey kind of grit by Jennie Stoller. . . . Val has left her husband for another farm laborer, but their passionate affair cannot erase her longing for the two children she has left behind.

As she bounces back and forth between her lover (Bernard Strother, who, as the one man in the cast, gets to play *nearly* all the male roles) and her family, we find ourselves comparing her with her daughters, her mother, her mother's mother, and her neighbors. And we begin to feel the weight of the past on these women of the Fens. Caught in the age-old rural antagonism between landowner and landworker, and bound by fear and custom to the village they were born in, they live with the same dark legends and bizarre folk remedies, the same resignation as the tenants who worked the land when it was reclaimed from swamp in the 16th century. They know how to cure warts, but despair is beyond their remedy.

"I've been unhappy as long as I can remember," says one woman. And, she confesses, so were her parents and her grandparents before that. She takes first to drink, then to Jesus. Another woman finds a way out in a species of willed madness. Still another visits her frustrations on her pathetic stepdaughter. Even Val's love affair can be seen as a desperate attempt to break the mold that holds then all so fast. The most modest hopes—to become a hair-dresser or a housewife or a nurse—will, we know, be buried in the potato fields.

Our sense of the omnipresence of the fields—and, of course, the field work—is not simply the result of Churchill's writing. Annie Smart's set *is* a field: neat furrows serve as ground for both exterior and interior scenes. They dirty the boots of the laborers, of course; but they also soil a dropped teacup, or the clothing of embracing lovers. You can almost smell the country. In fact, you do smell the country, when the women bag onions.

Abetted by Tom Donnellan's evocative lighting, the sights and smells and sounds of this production give *Fen* a physicality that would be hard to match in a book or movie. It is undoubtedly the result of the way in which the play was created. The Joint Stock Theater Group, whose production this is, spent time living in a Fens village, and the play is based in large part on the stories they heard there.

Nevertheless, facts haven't prevented Churchill from taking those free-flights through time and space that marked her earlier plays. When a landowner challenges a strange woman grubbing in his field, and she responds in a weird way, he says matter-of-factly, "My *father* saw you!" She is, we're delighted to discover, a ghost. Churchill can map the imaginative life of a community as accurately as she renders its gossipy backchat. Her sociology has four dimensions.

The Churchill technique of making a play, however, could use another dimension. Becoming familiar now, it owes much to the Impressionist way of making a painting: a daub here, a daub there—it's when you step back that the picture emerges. In *Cloud 9,* the sex-farce underpinning kept her scatter-shot scenes in focus. In *Top Girls,* she had no ready-made structure to fall back on, and she never quite managed to integrate the play's fantasy history of women's roles with its here-and-now plot about a woman who sacrifices her emotional life to her career.

Fen is not without the wit that shone in *Cloud 9.* Nor does it lack the narrative monologues that gave *Top Girls* its spin. But it lacks both the sparkle of the first and the punch of the second: Its brief scenes must, for the most part, do without both humor and history, and they suffer for it.

The problem, of course, is that *Fen* is neither a comedy nor a meditation. It delineates a landscape, a mind-set. And while its cumulative power is considerable, the fragments from which it is pieced together can't stand as easily on their own. Before they all fall into place, the audience has spent a lot of time wondering if they ever will. That discomfort, present to some extent in all the Churchill I've seen so far, is prolonged in *Fen* nearly beyond forgiveness. But forgive we do. Because *Fen* persuades us, finally, that we have glimpsed not just the contours of the geographical fen, but a dim swamp encircling human hearts.

CRITICAL COMMENTARY

Sheila Rabillard   (essay date 1994)

SOURCE: *"Fen* and the Production of Feminist Ecotheater," in *Theater,* Vol. 25, No. 1, Spring-Summer, 1994, pp. 62-71.

[*Rabillard is a Canadian educator and author of works on modern drama. In the following essay, she examines* Fen *within the context of "ecofeminism"—Churchill's attempt to "merge ecological and socialist-feminist concerns."*]

I

Caryl Churchill is, in the best sense, a playwright of ideas. In her early works, she took inspiration from the theories of such writers as Sigmund Freud (*Schreber's Nervous Illness*), Frantz Fanon and R. D. Laing (*The Hospital at the Time of the Revolution*), and Michel Foucault (*Softcops*). Speaking of one of the dramas that made her name [in the introduction to her *Churchill: Shorts* (1990)], she remarked that "Fanon's *Black Faces, White Masks* was one of the things (along with Genet) that led to Joshua, the black servant, being played by a white in *Cloud Nine.*" Moreover, Churchill's eclectic reading in philosophy, psychology, and politics informs the structure and production process of her drama, as well as its content. *Softcops* is not just a witty dramatization of ideas from *Discipline and Punish;* the play presents itself as a species of enacted theatrical theory, a series of elegant, Foucauldian inquiries into the politics of performance: Can punishment be adequately staged? Can theater function viscerally to arouse and quell the spectator when it exposes the workings of its own controlling mechanisms? In short, Churchill's work is not merely drama concerned with particular intellectual trends, but a linked theatrical practice and poetics—in a sense, a drama that attempts to stage the radical implications of theory. This claim allies Churchill with predecessors as disparate as Gertrude Stein, whose theatrical art constitutes a highly intellectualized criticism of theatrical art, and [Bertolt] Brecht, whose alienating dramaturgy exposes the workings of ideology, giving "what is 'natural' the force of what is startling" ["Theater for Pleasure or Theater for Instruction," in *Brecht on Theater: The Development of an Aesthetic,* edited and translated by John Willett (1964)]. The analogy between Brecht's techniques and those of dramatists strongly influenced by socialism, like Churchill, has often been remarked; what I want to emphasize, however, is not continuity of form, or shared political lineage, but a common philosophical interrogation of the theatrical process. Churchill, like Stein, invigorates potentially abstract intellectual discourse by putting it into play.

In certain crucial respects, *Fen* is typical of Churchill's dramatic practice. *Fen* engages an emerging body of theory that links a socialist-feminist critique with ecological politics—what has come to be called "ecofeminism." Churchill strives to bind the theatrical practice of her drama to the theory in which the play is grounded, and this effort lends

A scene from the 1983 New York production of Fen. *Annie Smart's set design featured a potato field for both interior and exterior scenes.*

Fen much of its complexity and interest. The project is far from straightforward, however. For when Churchill attempts, by disclosing the means and methods of dramatic production, to reshape the relation between aesthetic and material culture—to create, figuratively speaking, an ecologically sound process of theatrical production—the inadequacies and inherent contradictions of this processual resolution are exposed by the premises of materialist analysis itself. Moreover, *Fen* stages a brief but canny critique of its own processes that hints at a broader potential interrogation of socialist-feminist dramatic practice.

The work of a founding practitioner, Vendana Shiva, may help to clarify what I mean by ecofeminism. In *Staying Alive,* and more recently in *The Violence of the Green Revolution,* Shiva argues that the productive powers of both nature and women have been devalued and destroyed by the transformation from self-sustaining commons to privatized, revenue-generating land dependent on monoculture, technocracy, and debt. This "maldevelopment" (ongoing since the 17th century in Europe, and increasingly now in the "developing" countries) leaches away the essential wealth of the land—its capacity to renew itself—and destroys the basis of women's productivity, their role in drawing the elements of human subsistence from the land, as resources are removed from their control and incorporated into a patriarchal, capitalist system of ownership and production. As Shiva explains, destruction and devaluation are profoundly linked: "Patriarchal categories which understand destruction as 'production' and regeneration of life as 'passivity' have generated a crisis of survival. Passivity, as an assumed category of the 'nature' of nature and of women, denies the activity of nature and life" [*Staying Alive: Women, Ecology, and Development* (1989)]. Historically, the work of women generated much of the commons' sustaining and sustainable wealth. Shiva terms this mode of intimate and subtly responsive engagement with the natural world "the feminine principle," which "dies simultaneously in women, men, and nature when violence and aggression become the masculine model of activity, and women and nature are turned into passive objects of violence."

Shiva's work helps to illuminate the general praxis of ecofeminist theater and in particular the problematic attempt in Churchill's *Fen* to merge ecological and socialist-feminist concerns. Ecofeminist theater is a growing body of plays and performance pieces that work to expose the cracks in the apparently seamless, and distinctly gendered, ideological structures governing our relationship to the environment. Such theater strives to disentangle an ideological complex in which masculinist values render "natural" a capitalist approach to the "development" of the worlds' resources, and capitalism—with its valorization of aggression, competition, possession—in turn reinforces a particular construction of the dominant gender. While ecofeminist theater does not yet constitute a concerted movement, a variety of recent plays employ such strategies: Rona Munro's exploration of gender, violence, and mythic constructions of the Scottish seashore in *Piper's Cave;* Margaret Hollingsworth's *The House That Jack Built,* with its slyly comic treatment of the gender stereotypes driving Toronto's suburban sprawl; Monique Mojica's *Princess Poca-*

hontas and the Blue Spots, a cabaret-style performance satirizing white conquest of the hearts of Indian Maidens and their land.

While Shiva's work was not a specific source for *Fen,* it provides a paradigm of the ecofeminist thought that shapes Churchill's play because of the clarity (and poetic vigor) with which Shiva deploys Marxist and feminist critiques in her analysis of environmental use. Churchill clearly shares her commitment to socialism as well as feminism, and has stated [in *Interviews with Contemporary Women Playwrights,* edited by Kathleen Betsko and Rachel Koenig (1987)] that she "wouldn't be interested in a form of one that didn't include the other." The play's provisional title revealed her fundamental concern with the economic basis of women's lives—*Strong Girls Always Hoeing,* taken from an 1842 agricultural report [quoted in *Churchill the Playwright* by Geraldine Cousin (1989)] advising employers that "strong girls who are always hoeing can do the work better than men and they cost only 1/6 instead of 2/." Churchill's final choice of title, however, locates her drama in the land itself; as Shiva does, she strives to place feminist and Marxist concerns within a larger, more elemental frame.

Fen's sequence of 21 scenes offers a series of images that associate exploited land with oppressed women workers, a baseline of misery figured in the conjunction of the bare horizontal line of the fields and the bodies of women literally bent to the earth in toil. Annie Smart, the designer for the original production, created a single set: a surface of furrowed earth bounded on three sides by rough board walls that was at once a field and a domestic interior. As Sylviane Gold commented in her *Wall Street Journal* review of the 1983 New York production, the furrows "dirty the boots of the laborers, of course; but they also soil a dropped teacup, or the clothing of embracing lovers." The bond between the lives of the women and the fate of the land is inescapable; in the closing scene Churchill reemphasizes the implications of the set—the women's constant labor, domestic and agricultural, sustaining the agribusiness of the fens—as Shirley irons the field.

The earth that clings to their garments and marks their every move is also a reminder that the lives of these women, vividly characterized though they are, cannot be understood solely in terms of individual choice and psychology; or, rather, that their psyches are themselves touched by the earth. Thus, the close of the play confronts the audience with images of cruelty, rebellion, and pain, with the possibility that to follow one's desires in this flat, limited world is a form of "madness": Val, who sought romantic love, persuades her lover to kill her; Nell, who intransigently protests exploitation, stalks crazily through the scene on stilts, claiming the sun spoke to her. One grim note of hope is sounded by Shirley—a woman habitually encased in a stoic pride in her own capacity for endurance—who for an instant realizes that it is a greater madness still to accept such a world: "I'd forgotten what it was like to be unhappy. I don't want to."

At the same time as the stage set linked the women and the land they worked, it created a spatial hierarchy, a visual language that lifted some into power and bent others towards the soil that carpeted the stage. It is hard to imagine a more visceral demonstration of the twinned devaluation of woman and natural world. There are few men in the piece (only one male actor in the original cast of six), and each of them is in some way, if only slightly, elevated above the women (with the exception of Miss Cade, supervisor of the field gang, and the bird-scaring boy, played by a woman). Wilson, a boy of 16 who works the potato fields with them, separates himself from the crew of women by begging to pick Val's rows for her pay when she walks off the job; Frank, though tormented by his affair with Val, rides above the fields on a tractor (composed of chairs); Towson, bought out by a syndicate, still lives a farm owners' comfortable life and influences the economic fate of the farm employees; and the Japanese businessman, Mr. Takai, reflects the divorce from the true nature of the land brought about by ownership, capital investment, "development." Virtually all the males enjoy a higher status than the women; in terms of the visual economy, likewise, they rise above the lowest common denominator, the rows of dirt—and the greater the power, the more instruments (mechanical and financial) intervene between them and the earth that generates their wealth. Towson, the farmer, is insulated from the land by technological comforts ("You never see a farmer on a bike," Nell says sarcastically) and by a financing scheme through which he relinquishes ownership and renounces a large degree of responsibility for the fate of the land and its workers in order to avoid death duties. As Nell says, his workers don't know who the boss is: "Who do you have a go at? Acton's was Ross, Ross is Imperial Foods, Imperial Foods is Imperial Tobacco, so where does that stop?"

The greatest distance from the soil, and hence the greatest power, is embodied in Mr. Takai, executive of the vast international corporation that, at many removes, owns the land. It is he, therefore, who addresses the audience in the first speech of the play and welcomes us in a fashion that suggests the land has been transformed utterly into a mere representation, both theatrical and monetary: "Mr. Takai, Tokyo Company, welcomes you to the fen. Most expensive earth in England. Two thousand pounds acre." There is more than a hint, here, of what Terry Eagleton, in *The Ideology of the Aesthetic,* has called the Marxist sublime—a linking of representation and exchange value, as in the *Eighteenth Brumaire,* that implies representation itself must be broken and exceeded. For Mr. Takai, the fens are so foreign as to be realized only in the aesthetic realm: "How beautiful English countryside. I think it is too foggy to take pictures. Now I find teashop, warm fire, old countryman to tell tales."

Mr. Takai's tourist itinerary evokes something of the vexed relationship between Churchill's critique of production and her own artistic modes of production; but most plainly, his monologue is a history of the destruction of the fenland commons:

> Long time ago, under water. Fishes and eels swimming here. Not true people had webbed feet but did walk on stilts. Wild people, fen tigers. In 1630 rich lords planned

to drain fen, change swamp into grazing land, far thinking men, brave investors. Fen people wanted to keep fishes and eels to live on, no vision. Refuse work on drainage, smash dikes, broke sluices. Many problems. But in the end we have this beautiful earth. Very efficient, flat land, plough right up to edge, no waste. This farm, one of our twenty-five farms, very good investment. Belongs to Baxter Nolesford Ltd., which belongs to Reindorp Smith Farm Land trust, which belongs 65% to our company.

An initial positive image of the "wild people, fen tigers" hovers behind the historic layers of suffering that are shaded into the play by reminiscences, gruesome old tales, and fleeting appearances of figures from the past. As Mr. Takai identifies with the "far thinking men, brave investors" of 17th-century venture-capital development, Churchill provides the opposing images that determine the interpretive frame of the play: commons and capitalism, what Shiva calls the feminine and the masculine principles in human relations to nature and society.

If the majority of the play that follows evokes the ethos of the commons by its absence, the closing scene presents one figure reminiscent of the wild marsh, as if inspired by Mr. Takai's opening history: Nell, walking on stilts across the earth-strewn stage. Churchill employs a structural symmetry here that emphasizes the importance of both "masculine" and "feminine" principles to our understanding of the play: where Mr. Takai's monologue brought the lost commons before the mind's eye inadvertently, as it were, by praising its destruction and rationally advocating the virtues of capitalist development, the closing scene also offers a monologue, though one that strikingly evades the structures of rationality and allows the voices of those who have suffered under "development" to speak through the character of Val.

Val has begged Frank to kill her; finally, he picks up an axe, murders her, puts her body in a wardrobe, and sits on the floor with his back against the wardrobe door. As he sits there, Val comes in through the door on the opposite side of the stage. She now utters a series of dream-like, subtly connected fragments that express her own misery but also describe the lives and fates of suffering figures from the past and present who seem to be pressing themselves on her consciousness:

> There's so many of them all at once. He drowned in the river carrying his torch and they saw the light shining up through the water.

> There's the girl again, a long time ago when they believed in boggarts.

> The boy died of measles in the first war.

After some struggle, Val focuses on one figure—"the girl"—and recites the story of a weak, white child who, in a hard winter when many people died, spoke a wish to see the spring again even if she lived no longer than the cowslips at her gate. ("The mother says, 'Hush, the boggarts'll hear you.'") The green mist of spring comes, and with it her strength, but a boy picks the flowers and she dies. "She's a wrinkled white dead thing like the cowslips." This uncanny folk tale, echoing something of Val's own death-wish, seems to arise from a collective memory of deprivation and speaks of a suffering so cruel that the fenlanders imagined malevolent spirits at work. But Val, who says she has come "back in" from death, is open to the experience of the living as well—especially, it seems, their terrors. The next section of her monologue describes young Becky's mind as she sleeps: "She's having a nightmare. She's running downstairs away from Angela. She's out on the road but she can't run fast enough." Val's monologue conjures up all that is omitted from Mr. Takai's tidy history of economic conquest, and suggests by its structure—which evokes the upwelling powers of repressed anger, fear, and desire—not simply lives and facts forgotten in his account, but a radically different understanding of the world.

Indeed, even the boundaries of the monologue form, and the subjecthood it implies, become blurred. Val's ability to describe a nightmare as it is being dreamed by another character suggests a strangely permeable, though still tenable, subjectivity; however, when the words of the monologue suddenly conjure Becky herself onto the stage and the girl's own speech takes up the thread of Val's description, divisions between dialogue and monologue, separations on which conventional characterization are based, grow indistinct.

> VAL: Instead of waking up in bed she's falling into another dream and she's here. BECKY *is there.*
>
> BECKY: I want to wake up.

Within the destabilizing context created by Val's monologue, Nell makes her appearance too, as do Angela, Shirley, and Meg, in a setting freed from the usual temporal restrictions: dramatic chronology has been disrupted by Val's return; historic past and present mingle in the same stage space; and Meg's "song"—she does not open her lips—disturbs performance time and seems to belong to the time of what might have been and cannot quite be represented (VAL: My mother wanted to be a singer. That's why she'd never sing). The audience may read Nell's stilt-walk in a number of ways: as if she is a historic figure from the lost marshes; as a present-day fenlander with an odd and nonconformist streak (the village children call her a hermaphrodite) that makes her a virtual anachronism in a capitalist system designed to render each worker exchangeable for any other; or, in this temporally fluid context, as part of a past that could have been and a future that might be. Nell's elevation above the dirt plane of the stage might seem to disrupt the visual hierarchy established earlier in the play, but the ambiguity of her position in space (as well as time) again allows us to read her figure in multiple fashion: as elevated into power, and yet (unlike Frank, Towson, or Mr. Takai) as vitally connected with the soil. The people who walked the marshes on their stilts gathering fish and wild plants walked *through* the watery meadows, not above them, stepping delicately into the yielding, saturated earth like great wading birds. While Nell's action, like that of the silent/singing Meg, makes us aware of the limits of systems

of representation by breaching familiar conventions, it suggests, as well, an alternative to the limitations of a "masculine" power identified with distance from the earth—with the physical and monetary transformation of the natural world into commodity for exchange.

II

One of the most complex links between *Fen* and ecofeminist theory lies in the process of the play's composition. As a Joint Stock production, *Fen* may be said to constitute a kind of creative "commons"—like a great deal of contemporary feminist drama, *Fen* was created in part collaboratively. Moreover, both on the page and in program notes, the play has been framed in such a way as to make the audience aware of the collective nature of its creation. Foregrounding of the production process has come to mark the practice of feminist theater for a variety of reasons. In much radical feminist theater, such gestures may invoke solidarity between audience and actors, and assert a new valuation of the work of women. More generally, the uncovering of the processes of production and performance, including the mutual construction of meaning by stage and audience, serves to expose and render non-natural the performance of gender. As we interrogate the significance of the gesture *Fen* makes in disclosing its process of production, however, we find a situation made more complex by Churchill's own self-conscious attempt to enact an alternative to the capitalist model of the production and ownership of aesthetic goods—an effort to construct in the aesthetic realm not simply a critique of the capitalist economy but a commons that somehow escapes it. A review of the remarkable process of bringing *Fen* into being may be helpful here.

Though the Joint Stock company was made up of a constantly changing membership, old hands tried to communicate the values of the group to newcomers, and these values had been shaped by the development and production of David Hare's *Fanshen* (1975), a play based on William Hinton's sympathetic study of communist land reform in a Chinese village during the 1940s. Joint Stock strove to incorporate democratic and collaborative methods into every stage of the productive process, though various members admitted that the directors still retained a degree of authority and the writers—after a collective workshop period—did retreat into privacy for nine weeks or so in order to produce the dramatic text, which would then be modified to varying degrees during rehearsal.

While Churchill has produced other dramas by means of the company's characteristic process of isolated writing combined with collaborative research, rehearsal, and revision, she has commented [in Betsko and Koenig] that "*Fen* is the most documentary of the plays," growing not merely from collaboration among company members, and the influence of Mary Chamberlain's oral history, *Fenwomen,* but through a direct encounter with the people and the land. The company lived for two weeks in a cottage in Upwell, in the heart of the fens. Jennie Stoller, one of the actors, reports in *The Joint Stock Book:* "Unlike other workshops we did not go our separate ways at the end of the day so there was an added intensity to the work. We cooked together, read together, combed the village for people, stories, ideas, images—and fought like mad to get into the bathroom." Four of the company spent a day fruit-picking for a local farmer.

As the company tried to organize its work on the model of the communal labor and collective decision-making in the communist village of Fanshen, it also attempted—at least in some degree—to write both *from* and *for* the experience of Upwell. Acting exercises included the movements of stoop labor; one of the actors reported she would never eat "crisps" again without thinking of the toil of potato growing. Although they could not perform *Fen* in Upwell because there was no suitable venue, when one of the villagers they had interviewed, a Mrs. Parrish, traveled to a nearby town with her husband to see the show, the company made certain to ask them what they thought of it. Mr. Parrish informed one of the actors that he had had his hoe the wrong way round. What's important here is not that the production fell short of accuracy in some minor details or that the actors strove to immerse themselves in the arduous experience of Upwell life, but rather that in the company's attempt to enact the rigors of agricultural labor there was a kind of ingenuous desire to elide the gap between production and artistic reproduction, between quotidian existence and representation. Yet at the same time Churchill's feminist socialism provides a frame in which such efforts, which risk being perceived as naive, become cannily ironized.

While Marxist theory taught us that the tangled processes of cultural production are always inscribed unconsciously in the literary text, Churchill deliberately marks the published text of her play with evidence of a collective creativity, eschewing artistic ownership—or what one might call the capitalist model of aesthetic production. Churchill's introduction to *Plays: Two* announces that *"Fen* is a play with more direct quotes of things people said to us than any other I've written"; five quotations from fenland villagers are used as epigraphs to the play-text; a note acknowledges the brilliant contribution of the set designer Annie Smart to the effect of the original production. It is this highly self-conscious effort to impose an alternative economy—a species of literary commons—upon the artistic process that generates much of *Fen*'s instructive tension. For Churchill proposes, it would seem, to evade the inescapable, to make conscious the unconscious reproduction of ideology.

There are problems with Churchill's attempt to engage directly with material production both in the subject and the mode of creation of her play. Her rejection of Romantic notions of authorship and private artistic possession in favor of an aesthetic commons may in fact constitute a new leftist romanticization of the author. But more disturbingly, the classic Marxist critique that underlies Churchill's approach as well as Shiva's theory suggests that the relationship between literary "superstructure" and economic "base" is far more subtle and complex than this simple collective transformation may allow. By joining a company that organizes its aesthetic labor in such a fashion, and representing this as a means of transforming the nature of the relation between the literary artifact and its subject, Churchill implies that her collaborative creation can somehow establish

a critical position detached from the unconscious, profoundly wedded, economic and cultural processes of her capitalist society. Churchill proposes a restructuring of the bond between aesthetic and material production characteristic of a familiar brand of feminist literary praxis, yet the very self-consciousness with which she pursues this identification between modes of production is potentially subversive of her effort. Churchill here struggles to accomplish a radical rethinking of the processes of ideology. Ironically, it may be her failure that is in the end of most interest, her effort to register the complex ecology of life producing aesthetic consciousness.

Churchill herself seems to acknowledge the difficulty of making overt the workings of the political unconscious. Some of her earlier works have taken for their subject precisely the inescapable and complicated relation of "base" to "superstructure." (As Raymond Williams reminds us in *Marxism and Literature,* the metaphor of base and superstructure itself, suggesting the spatial separation of a structure laid atop a foundation, falsifies by dividing what is intrinsically bonded.) *Not . . . not . . . not . . . not . . . not enough oxygen,* a vision of the future in which the earth's ecosystem has been destroyed by pollution, incorporates within its dystopia the notion of nature technologized *and* aestheticized. Both science and art are part of the systems of control: oxygen is purchased and sprayed from a bottle when needed; a park provides a glimpse of the "natural" world like an exhibition in a museum. *The After Dinner Joke* explores in broad, satiric fashion the difficulties of a young woman trying to escape from participation in politics and business as usual. Though she has quit her job to work for an international relief organization, she finds that everything she does in the end contributes to the well-being of established governments and global capitalism. She rejoins her old firm with a valuable line added to her resume: "It's what I like to see, Miss Selby, a young person spending a year or two working for charity," says her boss. "I'll be able to bring you in at the management level."

One self-reflexive moment in *Fen,* in particular, invites a meditation on the complexities of the production of aesthetic consciousness. It is a moment that evokes the various and perhaps contradictory uses that her play might serve for different audiences—rural and urban, bourgeois and working class—as well as the subtlety and indirectness of the nevertheless indissoluble connections between material production, political and cultural institutions and activity, and consciousness. Angela, flirting unsuccessfully with Frank in the pub, complains that he is dull and flat like the fen landscape around them and announces that she wants to live "in the country." When Frank asks, "What's this then?" she replies "I like more scenery. The Lake District's got scenery. We went there on our honeymoon. He said we were going to live in the country. I wouldn't have come. Real country is romantic. Away from it all. Makes you feel better." This exchange alludes to a pastoral image of English rural life that Churchill is in the process of destroying for her mostly bourgeois audiences. The persistence of that aesthetic here among the fen dwellers she depicts reminds us that it is her art, her distanced perspective, not deep 'white knight'; Allan Corduner in a series of finely-tuned experience of the material "facts" of fen life, that destroys an ideal still held by some who live in the countryside; and that the art itself uneasily aspires both to express and transform the desires of a deeply divided culture. The moment discloses a disjunction between the material life of the fens and the creative process that Churchill elsewhere attempts to bind to it. In the end, such disjunctions evoke an absent solidarity, a perfect congruence between an ideal material and aesthetic production, a missing commons that escapes the systems of representation.

To return to Mr. Takai, the emblem for Churchill's uneasy and fascinating negotiations may well be this slightly embarrassing stereotype whose single speech yokes a paradigm of capitalist development, the historical memory of a lost commons, and—within the context of the businessman's own production of an aesthetic picturesque—a peculiarly self-conscious allusion to Churchill's creative method of gathering from the common mind of the people: "Now I find teashop, warm fire, old countryman to tell tales."

SERIOUS MONEY

PRODUCTION REVIEWS

Victoria Radin (review date 3 April 1987)

SOURCE: "Cash, Bang, Wallop," in *New Statesman,* Vol. 113, No. 2923, 3 April 1987, pp. 25-6.

[*As with many other Churchill plays,* Serious Money *was first staged at the Royal Court Theatre. It later moved to Wyndham's in London's West End theater district and then, with some cast changes, to New York's Public Theatre. Early in 1988, a Broadway production was mounted with an entirely American cast. In the following review of a Royal Court performance, Radin maintains that* Serious Money *is not* "a lasting work, but its quality of cheap immediacy, an inky newness like this morning's tabloid, gives it a freshness one rarely sees in the theatre."]

Coming Into the Royal Court to see **Serious Money** I was crushed against a wall by a large gentleman who evidently saw no reason why my presence should impede his progress towards his chosen destination. The episode served as a fitting introduction to Caryl Churchill's new comedy, whose subject is the Big Bang in the City but whose real theme is the naked ruthlessness and greed that characterises much of life in Britain in the late 1980s. The 20 characters (played by eight actors) steal, cheat, lie and vigorously trample down anyone who stands in their way. 'Greed has been good to me,' enthuses a young whizzkid. The tone is hectic and exuberant, and the audience responds in kind. At the end of the first half, when the cast hissed out a rapping song whose words, written by Ian Dury, were largely a list

of expletives, we all reacted as if we'd heard music from paradise.

Churchill is not out to instruct. The terms 'corporate raider' 'leveraged buy-out' and 'junk bond', despite the fact that I've now watched people being, doing or buying these things for two hours, remain as gnomic as ever; and I wouldn't be able to explain the finer points of such plot as there is. Basically there are two of them. One concerns the death of Jake who has been amassing a fortune, or what I do now understand to be 'serious' money, by shopping inside information to a very hard lady in New York called Mary-Lou. His sister embarks on a mission to discover the real facts behind his death—though much more from desire to lay hands on his money than out of feelings of family piety, which the play reveals to be universally extinct. At the same time, this Scilla, daughter of a stockbroker, is involved in a conspiracy to buy up a 'good, old-fashioned' Northern firm called Albion, no less. This scam is masterminded by Billy Corman, a drop-out from a CSE metalwork course whom Scilla's father describes as an 'Oik', or 'one of those barrow boys you expect to see on a street corner selling cheap watches.' Gary Oldman, sporting greasy hair and a shady moustache, plays him with a limp arm that hints at Richard III.

Churchill doesn't make the mistake of thinking Corman is any worse than the representatives of older money, whom she shows to be every bit as ruthless; nor of believing that integrity ruled before the Bang released naked greed in its most incontrovertible forms. Her curtain-raising scene lifted from Thomas Shadwell shows Restoration pillars of the establishment merrily dreaming up trading chicaneries and a playwright rejoicing in it. Churchill rejoices in it too; and has a good time at peppering her play with awful puns, rhyming couplets and theatrical in-jokes. I could have done without some of these sallies, and with more of the rhyming, which tends, like the dynamic of the piece, to die out in the second half. And the couplets, which seemed so marvellous when they were flying at one like the bubbles in a glass of champagne (a drink that Corman calls 'poo', as in 'a glass of poo') look fairly dismal when one reads over one's notes the next day. I don't think this is a lasting work, but its quality of cheap immediacy, an inky newness like this morning's tabloid, gives it a freshness one rarely sees in the theatre: it feels as if it had been written today.

Max Stafford-Clark does wonders with the directing: a riding scene and the two songs which end each half are beautifully choreographed, and the whole evening proceeds—on Peter Harwell's two-levelled set which suggests Rome, Egypt and the Globe Theatre all at once—with maximum speed and efficiency. The acting—from Linda Bassett in her dual roles as a devious English stockbroker and an outfront ruthless American arbitrageur (whatever that is, though it's clear that the Americans are better at it); Alfred Molina as a New York-Jewish banker who casually orders a flock of tropical birds from Harrods to clinch a friendship; Meera Syal as a be-furred Peruvian lady prepared to dump her copper mines and get into cocaine ('Pictures of starving babies are misleading. Only the masses are poor.'); Lesley Manville as both the Sloaney Scilla and a brisk Northern 'white knight'; Allan Corduner in a series of finely tuned portraits of bastards ranging from a smoothy Cabinet Minister to the semi-wicked Chairman of the threatened Albion; Burt Caesar as a fake African prince and an American personal assistant and Julian Wadham as both the murdered wheeler-dealer and the tweedier double who informs on him—all give perfectly balanced and intensely attractive performances in one of the most enjoyable evenings I've spent at the Court in some time. Greed has been good to the whole company.

Christopher Edwards (review date 11 April 1987)

SOURCE: "A Piece of Self-Indulgence," in *The Spectator* Vol. 258, No. 8283, 11 April 1987, p. 47.

[*In this evaluation of a Royal Court performance, Edwards detects some "predictable moralising" in* Serious Money, *but finds that the production was "driven by a convincing, crude energy."*]

Caryl Churchill's new comedy is in the best Royal Court tradition of vital, anti-establishment work. It is a tendentious, up-to-the-minute satire about corruption and insider dealing in the City. By way of historical colour, and to show that City speculators have been seen as ever thus, the evening opens with an extract from Shadwell's *The Stock-jobbers.* Four characters anxiously plan a deal involving patents for mousetraps, but the objective, naturally enough, is to 'turn a penny'. We then switch to a frenetic trading floor in the City, post Big Bang, complete with blinking screens, banks of telephones and, set into the back of the stage, a large wine rack full of champagne.

The well-researched world recreated by Caryl Churchill comes complete with transatlantic arbitrageurs in the Boesky mould (Alfred Molina), public school boy operators (Julian Wadham) and working-class oiks made good (Gary Oldman). It is full of 'corporate raiders', 'white knights', 'fan clubs', 'concert parties' and (without the jargon) conmen. Styles of dealing may differ between the characters but the playwright succeeds in convincing us, in her own terms, that their greatest talents are unscrupulousness and an instinct for street trading.

The plot turns upon a takeover bid for a company called, coincidentally, Albion. Jake Todd, an upper-class paper dealer and social linkman for the investing jet set, dies in suspicious circumstances. Jake's sister, Scilla, vows to investigate his connections. We never learn who, if anyone, actually 'did it' but this hardly matters. The main interest for us and for Caryl Churchill is a vision of the City motivated by fear and greed. It is, needless to say, a highly-coloured vision which also contains some predictable moralising. But the production is driven by a convincing, crude, energy which fairly represents the real City. Perhaps the best compliment one can pay both cast and playwright is to say that as well as making fun of that world (often wittily), as well as judging it by exaggerating its more grotesque aspects, they also manage to do justice to its quality of awful exhiliration. This is a production to be recommended.

Frank Rich (review date 4 December 1987)

SOURCE: A review of *Serious Money*, in *The New York Times,* 4 December 1987, p. D4.

[*In the following New York production review, Rich provides a stylistic and comparative analysis of* Serious Money, *characterizing it as a play in which "the heartlessness of the late 80s finds its raucous voice."*]

When the antiquated London stock market finally cast off tradition and plugged into the deregulated frenzy of modern Wall Street in 1986, the phenomenon was heralded as the Big Bang. In **Serious Money,** a ferocious new satire about the financial wheeler-dealers born in the ensuing boom, Caryl Churchill takes the term literally.

The play at the Public Theater travels to the trading pits and board rooms of London's financial district, the City, to find the precise pitch of the arena of arbitrage, inside trading, greenmail, corporate raiding and leveraged buyouts. *Serious Money* wants us to hear the very sound of megascale greed as it is practiced on that circuit of telephone wires and computer screens blinking 24 hours a day from Tokyo to New York.

That sound is not the sound of music. It is not the polite ringing of a cash register. It is not even the insistent chatter of a ticker tape. The noise, emanating from the brokers and bankers and dealers in **Serious Money** is a cacophonous, feverish screech of numbers and obscenities that builds into a mad roar. It is, indeed, a big bang, and it rivals other apocalyptic explosions of our nuclear age in its potential for devastation. As Ms. Churchill and the recent crash both demonstrate, the bursting financial bubble can leave small investors, large corporations, third world countries and Western economies shattered in its wake.

Yet in the theater, the noise creates a strange, if chilling, exhilaration. If **Serious Money** is an angry, leftist political work about ruthlessness and venality, about plundering and piggishness, it is also vivid entertainment. The fun comes in part from the vicarious pleasure always to be had in watching the flimflams of others. Ms. Churchill opens her play with an excerpt from a 1692 Thomas Shadwell comedy about stock jobbers—and a bit of *The Solid Gold Cadillac* could have made the same plus ça change point. But even more of the evening's lift can be attributed to Ms. Churchill's own inventive approach to her enduring subject. As her characters have rewritten the rules of the marketplace to create a new order of Darwinist capitalism, so she rewrites the rules of the theater expressly to capture that bizarre world on stage.

Such daring is typical of this playwright, who in her previous **Cloud Nine** and **Top Girls** has sent characters floating between historical periods and genders to make trenchant points about sexual and economic oppression. While **Serious Money** is well aware of Ben Jonson, Restoration comedy and Brecht, it has been written in its own outrageous style. The script is almost entirely composed of rhymed couplets, many of them juvenile and scatological, some of them clever ("If it was just inside dealing / It's not a proper crime like stealing.") The action is fast and confusing—intentionally so, given all the overlapping dialogue—and the people are no more than cartoons. The closest thing *Serious Money* has to a plot—the mysterious death of a commercial paper dealer—is never even resolved.

The overall result, repetitive and unruly as it sometimes may be, is wholly theatrical. Though based on up-to-the-minute research and clearly inspired in part by the actual Guinness and Boesky scandals in London and New York, *Serious Money* is not a *Nightline*-style documentary. Nor is it a work of satirical narrative fiction, like *The Bonfire of the Vanities,* Tom Wolfe's thematically related novel about a high-rolling Wall Street bond trader. Ms. Churchill valiantly makes the case, as so very few playwrights do these days, that the stage can still play its own unique role, distinct from that of journalism or television or movies, in dramatizing the big, immediate stories of our day.

Only in a theater could we watch a Peruvian businesswoman (Meera Syal) deliver a long, rhymed soliloquy that captures the fashions, ethos and economic basis of a cocaine-fueled branch of the OPEC jet set. Or watch the traders on the floor of Liffe—the London International Financial Futures Exchange, and pronounced like "life"—transform their hand signals and brokerage jargon into a rap number (with lyrics by Ian Dury) that really makes their business seem, as one character describes it, "a cross between roulette and Space Invaders." While Ms. Churchill does periodically send her players forward to explain terminology and history, one need not be able to define "junk bonds" or know the real-life basis of a scene inspired by the fall of Lehman Brothers to grasp her polemical drift. Visceral theater, not didactic sermonizing, is the medium of her message.

Nor is that message as simplistic as one might think. To be sure, Ms. Churchill is tough on red-suspendered, champagne-guzzling hustlers who speed down the fast lane in BMW's and Lamborghinis on their way to the scrap heap at age 35. She is also tough on the paternalistic, old-style businessmen overturned (and often taken over) by the new deal-makers and on African and black American entrepreneurs who sell out their own for a share of the spoils. But *Serious Money* is more an indictment of a system than of specific sharks and crooks. When money—not even land or widgets or pork bellies—is the main commodity traded on the floor of Liffe, the game loses all connection to life. Real lives are soon cold-bloodedly crunched along with the fast-flying abstract numbers.

When *Serious Money* falters—and it does, notably after intermission—the problem is only partly Ms. Churchill's refusal to engineer her story as niftily as Mr. Wolfe or a Restoration playwright might. The principal actors, all English but only some of them from the first Royal Court Theater cast, too frequently fail to etch firmly the writer's caricatures. In addition to laughable American accents, we get a corporate raider (Daniel Webb, in a role originated in London by Gary Oldman), who rants like a George Raft impersonator, and a narrating banker (Paul Moriarty) of no

discernible personality whatsoever. Much better are Ms. Syal's smooth Peruvian cut-throat, Joanne Pearce as the yuppiest of female traders, Allan Corduner as several impressively different representatives of a dying old-boy establishment, and especially Linda Bassett as three of those hatefully hard Thatcher-era "top girls" Ms. Churchill loves to skewer. Among Ms. Bassett's roles is a public-relations expert who advises the Boesky-like raider to sweeten his image by sponsoring London's National Theater—a particularly rude joke, given the real Mr. Boesky's onetime service on the board of the theater in which the New York audience of *Serious Money* sits.

Working on a smart Peter Hartwell set that vandalizes London's classical architectural past with the flickering electronic hardware of the financial bullring, Max Stafford-Clark stages the play at a fittingly breakneck pace. "Sexy greed *is* the late 80's," says Ms. Bassett's P.R. woman, and the director does not ignore the racy pull of "massive sums of money being passed around the world." In concert with the slangy, punchy script, he gives the show the overheated tone of the raunchy London gutter press. But on the one occasion when two of the characters actually try to arrange a romantic tryst, they fail to find a free hour in common in their Filofax diaries. The Big Bang leaves no time for that kind of orgasm; Ms. Churchill's traders regard even AIDS as just another "great market opportunity." In *Serious Money,* the heartlessness of the late 80's finds its raucous voice in comedy that is, as it must be, hilariously, gravely sick.

CRITICAL COMMENTARY

Patricia M. Troxel (essay date 1989)

SOURCE: "Making Serious Money: Caryl Churchill and Post-Modernist Comedy," in *Text and Presentation,* edited by Karelisa Hartigan, University Press of America, 1989, pp. 149-59.

[*Below, Troxel examines* Serious Money *as a "post-modern comedy of manners."*]

Big Bang! Marzipan set! Ivan the Terrible! OIKS! DINKS! OINKS! All terms from the newest Orwellian world—The City, London's financial trading center. The artistic attraction to this staccato, acronymistic, elliptical Cityspeak is matched only by our society's fascination with the crimes of insider dealing, share price manipulation and fraud. From paperback bestsellers on Boeksy and Guinness to Oliver Stone's film *Wall Street* to recent episodes of Steven Bochco's *LA Law,* literary and dramatic representations of this financial circus abound. But among such works, Caryl Churchill's play, *Serious Money,* offers the most provocative, creative, and devastating portrait of high finance.

Much critical interest in this play stems directly from Churchill's staging of the financial world. However, her subtitle, "A City Comedy," indicates that she is equally concerned with the genre context of her work. *Serious Money* succeeds as a drama that expands our understanding of the genre of post-modernist comedy; a simple story of crime is transformed by inversions and subversions of time, character, and language into an elaborate post-modernist exposé of duplicity and corruption among the international financial elite.

Serious Money offers murder, mystery, and mayhem during Scilla Todd's pursuit of the murderers of her brother, Jake Todd. Scilla "works on the floor of LIFFE, the London International Financial Futures Exchange" where "trading options and futures looks tricky if you don't understand it. But if you're good at market timing you can make out like a bandit." Despite her aristocratic background Scilla is one of the new breed, an OINK (one income no kids) concerned with the passion and excitement of making "serious money".

> I found O levels weren't much use, the best qualified people are street traders.
> But I love it because it's like playing a cross between roulette and space invaders.

While Scilla has been enjoying her pit work, her brother Jake, a commercial paper dealer, has entangled himself in the insider trading schemes of MaryLou Baines, an American arbitrageur. Jake is further enmeshed in the machinations of Zac Zackerman (an American banker with the firm of Klein Merrick), Billy Corman (a corporate raider whose newest target is the British firm, Albion), and Jacinta Condor (a Peruvian businesswoman, looking for new ways to improve on her Eurobond investments). Unfortunately for Jake, the Department of British Trade and Industry (DTI) has begun an investigation of these dealings at the behest of Frosby, a disenfranchised old-school jobber bent on revenge against the entire Todd family.

While the play rejects any formal chronology and plotting, the two principal schemes—Jake's murder and Corman's takeover of Albion—provide the mystery. As the DTI investigation proceeds, Jake's greed and nervousness increases until the government arranges his demise: the Tories simply cannot afford to have their involvement in insider trading schemes revealed. Jake's partners in these schemes, Jacinta Condor, MaryLou Baines, and Zac Zackerman are also involved in Billy Corman's takeover of Albion Enterprises. Despite elaborate maneuvering on the Paper and the Commodities exchanges, blackmail attempts, and a glitzy media campaign, Corman's takeover bid is rejected by the government and the conspirators are forced to pursue other projects. At the play's conclusion, Scilla has given up on the quest for her brother's killer, and moved to New York where "she has been named by *Business Week* as Wall Street's rising star." Zac and Jacinta have married and are pursuing projects in Shanghai; Corman joins the Peerage and organizes the "Channel tunnel campaign"; and Mary-Lou Baines runs for US President in 1996. The play ends with the promise of "five more glorious years" hailed by the entire cast rockin' to the beat of Ian Drury.

As an exposé of corruption in the financial and political world, Churchill's drama owes less to the Jacobean tradition of mercantile comedy set within the geographical boundaries of the City of London and more to the post-Restoration comedy of manners. As David Hirst has indicated [in his *Comedy of Manners* (1979)], comedy of manners centers on "sexual and monetary acquisitiveness tempered by a refined yet subtle wit and a flair for intrigue." It is also the genre most likely to "subordinate the artificiality of conventional moral standards to a re-establishment of decorum and propriety, and to an astute and agile dissection of each society's rules of the game."

This is not to suggest that Churchill's comedy of manners favors game over earnestness, style over truthful expression. Quite the contrary. In a playworld where insider trading is practiced by regulatory bodies such as the DTI and the Cabinet, the rules of the game are that there are no rules, only the game. Churchill frequently argues that only in comedy of manners does one find the appropriate blend of humor and suffering, experience and instinct, necessary for dramatic creation. In a recent interview focusing on her play, *Softcops,* Churchill spoke directly to this issue:

> I don't think I set out to be funny. Things that end up being serious or being funny I set about in exactly the same way. . . . We rehearsed the seriousness of the relationships and it all became terribly sad . . . and the whole thing became quite painful. Then we put together the sequence of truthfully played love stories and it all became very funny again and the more funny for being done for real.

Serious Money displays this intersection of humor and pain in its integration of Jake's murder-suicide and the financial machinations of the dealers, raiders and arbitrageurs of High City finance.

If Churchill draws on the "serious fun" possible in this comic genre, she also acknowledges that genre's traditions in the opening sequence of *Serious Money.* Here, in this 1987 drama, we encounter a scene from Thomas Shadwell's 1662 play, *The Stockjobbers.* As with *Cloud Nine, Top Girls,* and *Softcops, Serious Money*'s first illusions are created by historical allusion. Shadwell's comedy of manners explored the newest Restoration obsession—the buying and selling of patent shares. It offered its period audience a glimpse of the power to be had in the financial institutions of the seventeenth-century City. *Serious Money* picks up on this theme. With the completion of *The Stockjobber*'s scene, played on the apron in front of the main curtain, that curtain opens to reveal the trading floors, phones and computer terminals of a contemporary London financial center. Here the power introduced in a seventeenth-century playworld is reenacted in a modern one.

By transforming a Restoration comedy of manners to a post-modernist comedy of manners, Churchill places her own work in the theatrical tradition which examines the codes and games of society. In *Serious Money,* she reinforces the importance of the financial world to our contemporary society. It is not by chance that the protagonist of *Serious Money* works as a dealer on the floor of LIFFE.

It is also true that in selecting a Restoration model that calls attention to a group, a gestalt of stockjobbers, rather than a

The cast of Serious Money, *Royal Court Theatre, London, 1987.*

specific character, Churchill establishes a dramatic precedent which emphasizes the dynamics of group behavior over that of selected individuals. In her study of feminist theatre [*Feminist Theater* (1984)], Helene Keyssar points out that Churchill's predilection for workshopped productions stems from a concern for the history of the many, the ordinary citizenry. Drawing on this community of experience, Churchill strives to "revise the history of the past and the present, to make a new kind of history—of both theatre and society—appear not just possible, but necessary."

Written for production during an election year that saw Maggie Thatcher succeed to a third term as Prime Minister, **Serious Money** explores the relationship between the Big Bang power of the City's financial institutions and the Conservative Party platform. From the "Futures Song" of Act One to "Five More Glorious Years" which ends the play, Churchill presents a conservative government up to its eyeballs in insider deals and financial trading schemes. The DTI investigates Corman's takeover of Albion because such "raiding" of a traditional British firm looks bad on election eve.

> The game must be protected.
> You can go on playing after we're elected.
> Five more glorious years free enterprise
> And your services to industry will be recognized.

And in a clever exchange between Corman and Gleason, a Cabinet minister, (during the interval at a National Theatre production of *King Lear*), we learn that the government will forbid Corman's takeover of Albion.

> A takeover like this in the present climate
> Makes you, and the City, and us look greedy.
> Help us be seen to care abut the needy.

> . . . . .

> Mr. Corman, I'll be brutally frank.
> A scandal would not be welcomed by the Bank.
> Nor will it be tolerated by the Tories.

Corman accepts the minister's plan and ends the play with a peerage and a seat on the National Theatre's Board.

This alliance of economics and politics is seen in the government's involvement in Jake Todd's murder and in the takeover war between Albion and Corman Enterprises. But Churchill's interest in the dominance of this alliance doesn't stop here. The play's one sexual scene, between Zackerman, and Peruvian businesswoman, Jacinta Condor, shows the two characters, filofaxes in hand unable to arrange a rendezvous because of their crowded business calendars. By the time they are finally able to connect, the financial schemes with Corman have soured and Zackerman has lost serious money. In the following exchange, the two indicate the relative value of money and sex.

> ZAC: Jacinta, I still can't forgive you for going to
> Biddulph, the whole deal could have been wrecked.

> JAC: But I get more money that way, Zac, really what
> do you expect?
> I can't do bad business just because I feel romantic.

ZAC: The way you do business, Jacinta, drives me
    completely frantic.

      . . . . .

ZAC: I thought we'd never manage to make a date.
    You're more of a thrill than a changing interest rate.

JAC: I am very happy. My feeling for you is deep.
    But will you mind very much if we go to sleep?

In this modern high stakes world, sexual interest and ability
are subordinate to financial acumen. Gamesmanship in a
modern comedy of manners is of the boardroom, not the
bedroom.

For all characters in **Serious Money,** financial activities
take precedence. Unable, or unwilling to separate other
desires and experience from financial concerns, each character judges the world in financial equivalents. Terry
equates hitmen with corporate raiders. Jacinta equates hos-
pitals for the poor with under-the-table payments. And
Greville Todd, Jake's father, sees world events in terms of
financial success or failure.

    When an oil tanker sank with a hundred men, the
      lads cheered because they'd made a million.
    When Sadat was shot I was rather cuffed because
      I was long on gold bullion.

To emphasize the dominance of economic concerns,
Churchill changes our understanding and expectations regarding time, character, and language in favor of the new
forms she offers in her comedy of manners. She begins
Serious Money by conflating 1662 and 1987 London. Each
setting contains appropriate costumes and languages, yet
Churchill offers no explanation for a shift from one scene
to the next. No logic can account for this three-century
shift, and there is no internal acknowledgement that such a
shift has occurred. Time ceases to be order or progression.
In place of chronology and "fact", we are offered repetition
and what Roger Caillois has defined as the fantastic—"A
break in the acknowledged order, an irruption of the inad-
missible with changeless everyday legality" [quoted by
Tzvetan Todorov in *The Fantastic: A Structural Approach
to a Literary Genre* (1975)].

This new illegality of time is accentuated by the play's
second scene which calls for "three different dealing rooms
simultaneously. All have screens and phones." For ten minutes of stage time, we watch the Paper, Shares, and Commodities exchanges erupt in a fast-paced bombardment of
action and sound. There is neither conventional chronology
nor formal plot. There is only a mass of color, linguistic
bedlam, and flying paper note-cards. The NOW of history is
expanded to a universal—all times enacted altogether in an
ever present moment—a perverse form of realism. At this
point, the audience often feels dislocated.

Having dislocated our concept of the present, Churchill
moves on to completely disrupt all standard notions of time.
For the remainder of the play, the chronological sequence
of cause and effect will be shattered by an interplay of past,

present, and future events. For example, the scene in which
Scilla, Jake, their father and Zackerman meet for a horse-
back-riding party is quickly followed by a scene in which
Scilla reveals her shock at Jake's death. Both scenes are
preceded by Jake's negotiations with MaryLou Baines and
the three scenes are immediately followed by Jake and
Scilla's meeting for coffee before the New York deal is set.
The "when," just like the "how," of Jake's death is omitted.
Only events of financial wheeling and dealing become focal
points in this play's plotline. Since each deal is a repetition
of every other, *when* one occurs is of little consequence.
Jake's death, rather than functioning as a major plot component, becomes only an element of yet another deal.
"When" and "if" are only important in a playworld which
anticipates a future. Here, Futures are traded like anything
else.

Besides shattering our perception of time, Churchill revises
our expectation of character. As with all her recent plays,
from **Cloud Nine** to **Serious Money,** Churchill creates a
fluidity and flexibility in character. In the course of each
drama, every actor plays a number of roles so that multiplicity in identity is enhanced. In **Serious Money,** this character variety shows us the depth of financial corruption and
gamesplaying—the duplicity in the City is mirrored in the
duplicity of character.

The same actress plays both Scilla Todd and Ms. Biddulph,
the White Knight savior of Albion. Both characters begin as
liberated women and able professionals. Yet both are quickly corrupted by the system—Scilla sells out for a position
in the New York firm of Marylou Baines and Biddulph
sells out for control of Albion and profits in ITV. Similar
duplicity is revealed in other character combinations—
Grimes, a streetsmart gilt trader, gets to wheel and deal as
Corman, the corporate raider. Jake Todd, the victim and
highstakes player, reappears as Grevett, the DTI inspector
responsible for Todd's murder. Only Zackerman remains a
single role; he is the only player in this financial game who
has actively participated in machinations from the beginning of the play. He is the only character who has nothing
to learn about the game.

Finally, in her treatment of language, Churchill demonstrates the range of her transformed comedy of manners.
Serious Money is composed entirely of verse. Yet while the
tradition of linguistic decorum appears to surrender to the
diction—slang, profanity, ellipsis—it is re-established by
the verse structure and end-rhyme. The rhyming slang is
brought to full power in the "Futures Song" and "Five More
Glorious Years," in which the driving rock-and-roll beat
enhances the monosyllabic exclamatory chorus. "Out you
cunt! Out in! Oh fuck it!" It also has a tendency to make the
audience think twice about the lines just heard.

When employed at a more sophisticated diction level, this
recalls the "wit" which constituted an essential element in
traditional comedies of manners. Such wit, [according to
Hirst], frequently relies on sexual innuendo, rapid-fire
stychymythic exchanges, puns, and specialized vocabulary.
Serious Money's wit displays similar components. In fact,
the compact, quick-tempoed codified language of City-

speak presents numerous difficulties for the audience. The tempo Churchill creates in her works—a sort of punching bag, cartoonesque delivery—when coupled with British slang or dialect makes the playworld's language hard to follow. With an added dimension of Cityspeak vocabulary, one can find it difficult to understand this play, even text in hand.

In addition to such linguistic stylization and complication, Churchill employs overlapping dialogue. Throughout *Serious Money,* characters engage in simultaneous speech, interruptive speech and intersecting speech. In the first instance, characters begin to speak at precisely the same moment, and continue on with their lines despite other speakers. Thus, the following exchange occurs as if it were a single line.

> DAVE: I've got a certain winner for the 3:30 if anyone is interested.
>
> BRIAN: You haven't paid us yesterday's winnings yet.
>
> KATHY: Come on gilts. 2 at 4, the gilts.

In the second case one character begins a new line before another character had finished speaking (/), and again both continue without an increase in volume or tempo.

> JAKE: No it's just . . . I'm in a spot of brother with the authorities / but it's no problem, I'm sorting it out.
>
> SCILLA: What have you done?

And in the final instance, characters begin one conversation which is then interrupted by another exchange. Despite that interruption, when the character's conversation resumes, s/he picks up the idea where s/he left off (*), as if the intermittent dialogue had never ocurred.

> BRIAN: How much would it cost to shoot her through the head?*
>
> TERRY: You can't get rid of your money in Crete hire every speedboat, drink till you pass out, eat
>
> Till you puke and you're still loaded with drachs.
>
> BRIAN: *And he says five grand.

By subverting the traditional theatrical conventions of logical dialogue, Churchill forces the audience to be an active participant in her post-modern comedy of manners. The audience must make its own choice—selecting one exchange over another, questioning each character as s/he questions every other. Through disruptive yet intriguing linguistic constructs, Churchill forces the text and the performance to assault what Julia Kristeva calls "reason's archaic and repressive structures which include order, normalcy, normative classical psychological-tending discourse." Kristeva goes on to refer to this form of postmodern art as attacking the fascist ideology of traditional

western discourse ["The Speaking Subject," in *On Signs,* edited by Marshall Blonsky (1985)]. By denying us the stability, the clarity, and the directed vision of a traditional text and performance, Churchill forces us to examine our assumptions and attitudes about political and economic behavior within our culture.

FURTHER READING

AUTHOR COMMENTARY

Cousin, Geraldine. "The Common Imagination and the Individual Voice." *New Theatre Quarterly* IV, No. 13 (February 1988): 3-16.

> Interview in which Churchill discusses the genesis and development of her writing career. She also elaborates on the making of *Serious Money* and audience responses to her work.

Truss, Lynn. "A Fair Cop." *Plays & Players* No. 364, (January 1984): 8-10.

> Interview in which Churchill recounts the conception, themes, and technique of such works as *Top Girls, Cloud Nine,* and *Softcops.*

OVERVIEWS AND GENERAL STUDIES

Chambers, Colin, and Prior, Mike. "Caryl Churchill: Women and the Jigsaw of Time." In their *Playwrights' Progress: Patterns of Postwar British Drama,* pp. 189-98. London: Amber Lane Press, 1987.

> Examination of Churchill's unique position in the male-dominated postwar British theater.

Cousin, Geraldine. *Churchill: The Playwright.* London: Methuen, 1989, 135 p.

> Reveals the development of Churchill's work, drawing thematic, technical, and stylistic parallels between various plays. Cousin's study also includes a chronology of Churchill's career and a bibliography of works published by and about the author.

Fitzsimmons, Linda. "'I won't turn back for you or anyone': Caryl Churchill's Socialist-Feminist Theatre." *Essays in Theatre* 6, No. 1 (November 1987): 19-29.

> Critical essay on *Top Girls* and *Fen.* Disputing various critical readings of the plays that emphasize their aesthetic and philosophical value rather than their political scope, Fitzsimmons argues that these two works are on the contrary "political texts, specifically. . . socialist-feminist texts."

Itzin, Catherine. "Caryl Churchill." In her *Stages in the Revolution: Political Theatre in Britain Since 1968,* pp. 279-87. London: Eyre Methuen, 1980.

> Explains Churchill's "politicization" and discusses the issues Churchill addresses in each of her works, their impact on the public, and the responses of the media and the government.

Keyssar, Helene. "The Dramas of Caryl Churchill: The Politics of Possibility." *The Massachusetts Review* XXIV, No. 1 (Spring 1993): 198-216.

> Biographical examination of the personal and political views that inform Churchill's work.

Swanson, Michael. "Mother/Daughter Relationships in Three Plays by Caryl Churchill." *Theatre Studies* Nos. 31/32 (1984-85/1985-86): 49-66.

> Essay exploring the nature of relationships between mothers and daughters in *Cloud Nine*, *Top Girls*, and *Fen*. Swanson maintains that Churchill's focus on the dynamics between mothers and daughters is a way "to advocate the improvement of the status of women through societal change."

Thomsen, Christian W. "Three Socialist Playwrights: John McGrath, Caryl Churchill, Trevor Griffiths." In *Contemporary English Drama*, edited by C. W. E. Bigsby, pp. 157-75. London: Edward Arnold, 1981.

> Examines the central image or metaphor in several of Churchill's plays in order to elucidate their presentations of individuals in conflict with capitalist society.

Wandor, Michelene. "The Fourth Phase: Women Playwrights in the 1970s and Early 1980s." In her *Carry on, Understudies: Theatre and Sexual Politics*, Second Edition, pp. 161-91. London: Routledge & Kegan Paul, 1986.

> Discusses prominent socialist-feminist themes in Churchill's works produced for the stage.

————. "Existential Women: *Owners* and *Top Girls* by Caryl Churchill." In her *Look Back in Gender: Sexuality and the Family in Post-War British Drama*, pp. 119-25. New York: Methuen, 1987.

> Considers Churchill's exploration of women's roles as presented in *Owners* and *Top Girls* as "the existential choice" between public and private worlds, between career and motherhood.

CLOUD NINE

Cohn, Ruby. "Modest Proposals of Modern Socialists." *Modern Drama* XXV, No. 4 (December 1982): 457-68.

> Includes a consideration of Churchill in an essay on several British socialist playwrights and their use of comedy and satire as vehicles to entertain bourgeois audiences.

Lange, Bernd-Peter. "*Cloud Nine* by Caryl Churchill." In *Contemporary Women Dramatists*, edited by K. A. Berney, pp. 282-83. London: St. James Press, 1994.

> Brief explication of *Cloud Nine* in which Lange states: "The play's major innovative device of syncopating individual and historical time inscribes political themes into personal development."

Worthen, W. B. "Political Theater: Staging the Spectator." In her *Modern Drama and the Rhetoric of Theater*, pp. 143-81. Berkeley: University of California Press, 1992.

> Demonstrates how in *Cloud Nine* Churchill "makes use of cabaret, stand-up comedy, and variety-show routines to evoke a collusion between stage and audience."

A MOUTHFUL OF BIRDS

Hersh, Allison. "'How Sweet the Kill': Orgiastic Female Violence in Contemporary Re-visions of Euripides *The Bacchae*." *Modern Drama* XXXV, No. 3 (September 1992): 409-23.

> Demonstrates how Maureen Duffy's *Rites* and Churchill's *A Mouthful of Birds* reenact Euripides' drama *The Bacchae*. States Hersh: "Duffy and Churchill's revisions of *The Bacchae* implicitly deconstruct the oppositional tension between the representation of murder as a gendered phenomenon both by thematizing the plight of the feminist murderer and by foregrounding issues of patriarchal repression, female transgression and ritualistic violence."

Reinelt, Janelle. "Feminist Theory and the Problem of Performance." *Modern Drama* XXXII, No. 1 (March 1989): 48-57.

> Examines *A Mouthful of Birds* as an example of what Reinelt terms the third, or "reconstructive phase of feminist theatre."

SERIOUS MONEY

Barnes, Clive. "A Nasty Business." *New York Post* (10 February 1988).

> Mixed review of the American version of *Serious Money*.

Gussow, Mel. Review of *Serious Money*. *The New York Times* (10 February 1988).

> Positive review of the American production of *Serious Money* in which Gussow claims that the play "is a new-Restoration comedy crossed with a Jacobean revenger's tale."

Henderson, Liza. "Serious Money and Critical Cost: Language in the Material World." In *Theater* XIX, No. 3, (Summer/Fall 1988): 87-8.

> Argues that the failure of *Serious Money* in New York testifies to "mainstream theater's inability to contend with the challenge of independent thought."

Wallach Allan. "Arbitrage, Outrage in *Serious Money*." *New York Newsday* (4 December 1987).

> Mixed review of *Serious Money* in which Wallach characterizes the play as "offputting comedy."

Additional coverage of Churchill's life and career is contained in the following sources published by Gale Research: *Contemporary Authors*, **Vol. 102;** *Contemporary Authors New Revision Series*, **Vol. 22;** *Contemporary Literary Criticism*, **Vols. 31 and 55;** *Dictionary of Literary Biography*, **Vol. 13; and** *Major 20th-Century Writers.*

John Pepper Clark
1935-

Born Johnson Pepper Clark Bekederemo.

INTRODUCTION

Clark is one of Nigeria's foremost anglophone dramatists and poets. In his plays he unites Western literary techniques with themes, images, and speech patterns drawn from traditional African theater. He also incorporates elements of the myths, religion, and folklore of his people, the Ijaw, and utilizes masks, drum rhythms, and dance. By integrating aspects of both African and Western cultures in his plays, Clark comments on the effects of English colonization on Ijaw society and the consequences of eroding cultural traditions.

BIOGRAPHICAL INFORMATION

Clark was raised in a fishing village located in the Delta region of Eastern Nigeria. The son of an Ijaw tribal leader, Clark was among a minority of children to attend elementary school, and as a young boy he decided to become a writer. He later attended the Government College in Ughelli and later earned a bachelor's degree in English at University College Ibadan, a branch of the University of London. While in school, Clark and a group of fellow students founded the *Horn*, a publication for which Clark served as editor and where he began to publish his poetry. In 1960 Clark wrote his first dramatic work, *Song of a Goat*, which was staged in Ibadan the following year. After graduation, Clark worked as a journalist, editor, and feature writer in Lagos for *Express* newspapers. His success as a journalist resulted in his being awarded a fellowship to study at Princeton University in the United States. Clark did not complete the program but returned to Nigeria, whereupon he accepted a position teaching English at the University of Lagos. In 1964 he published *America, Their America*, which chronicles his experiences and impressions of American society. Clark served as the Department Head of English at the University of Lagos until his retirement in 1980. He is currently the director of the PEC Repertory Theatre in Lagos.

MAJOR WORKS

Clark's first four plays are verse dramas, and they demonstrate the influence of William Shakespeare and T. S. Eliot, as well as Ijaw folk literature. *Song of a Goat* has often been compared to both classical Greek drama and Shakespearean tragedy. Set among the Ijaw, the play tells the story of a fisherman whose impotence leads his frustrated wife to consult a masseur. The masseur advises the wife to conceive a child with her husband's brother. After the affair

has been consummated, both the husband and his brother commit suicide. *The Masquerade* continues the story, focusing on Tufa, the child born of the taboo union in *Song of a Goat*. Grown to manhood, he becomes engaged to a beautiful, strong-willed woman. When the circumstances of Tufa's birth become known to the family of his betrothed, her father forbids the marriage, but she refuses to abide by his decision. In a violent conclusion, all die. *Song of a Goat* and *The Masquerade* share a relentless aura of gloom; and in both neighbors function as a chorus, commenting on the tragic happenings.

Clark's third play, *The Raft*, traces the misadventures of four men on a raft who attempt to bring logs downstream to be sold. Unlike the plots of his first two dramas, which focus on Nigerian folklore and sexual mores, *The Raft* has often been interpreted as a critique of economic determinism or as an allegory of the political situation in Nigeria. Clark's first full-length play, *Ozidi*, was adapted from an Ijaw saga in which two feuding families seek revenge upon each other. The saga traditionally uses mime, music, and dance in its performance, and Clark retains some of these elements in his version. After *Ozidi* Clark did not write for the theater for more than ten years; but in 1981 he produced

The Boat at the University of Lagos and in 1985 staged both *The Return Home* and *Full Circle*. These three short plays were performed together as a trilogy in 1985 and subsequently published as *The Bikoroa Plays*.

CRITICAL RECEPTION

Clark's dramatic works have generally garnered mixed reviews. While often admired for their rich poetic imagery, Clark's plays have also been criticized for employing cliched situations and florid rhetoric. As Margaret Laurence has contended, the language in *Song of a Goat* is "effective when it is simplest and most unadorned, but [Clark] frequently gives way to the urge to be grandiose." Some commentators have regarded the construction of his plays as faulty, judging the perceived flaws to be the result of Clark's lack of experience as a dramatist. Critics have continually debated the extent to which Clark patterns his dramatic works upon Greek tragedy, in which the characters are controlled by external forces beyond their control. While some stress the influence of Western classical models, others argue Clark's plays owe more to the folklore, imagery, and customs of the Ijaw people, which have furnished the playwright powerful symbolic representations of the human condition.

PRINCIPAL WORKS

PLAYS

Song of a Goat 1961
The Masquerade 1964
The Raft 1964
Ozidi 1966
*The Boat 1981
The Wives' Revolt 1984
*The Return Home 1985
*Full Circle 1985

OTHER MAJOR WORKS

Poems (poetry) 1961
America, Their America (autobiography) 1964
A Reed in the Tide (poetry) 1965
Casualties: Poems, 1966-68 (poetry) 1970
The Example of Shakespeare: Critical Essays on African Literature (essays) 1970
The Ozidi Saga [with Okabou Ojobolo] (translation) 1977
A Decade of Tongues: Selected Poems, 1958-1968 (poetry) 1981
State of the Union (poetry) 1985
Mandela and Other Poems (poetry) 1988
Collected Plays and Poems, 1958-1988 (drama and poetry) 1991

*These three plays were published together in 1985 as *The Bikoroa Plays*.

AUTHOR COMMENTARY

Interview with Clark (1970)

SOURCE: *Palaver: Interviews with Five African Writers in Texas,* edited by Bernth Lindfors and others, The University of Texas at Austin, 1972, pp. 15-22.

[*In the following interview, conducted by faculty and students at the University of Texas at Austin in 1970, Clark responds to questions regarding the political themes in several of his plays and offers his thoughts on the role and responsibilities of the writer.*]

[Students and faculty at the University of Texas]: *You have written all your plays in English, a non-African language. Did you write* **Ozidi,** *a play based on indigenous theatrical traditions, with an African or non-African audience in mind?*

[John Pepper Clark]: In a new nation like Nigeria which cuts across several groups of people, or rather which brings together several peoples speaking different languages, you've got to have a *lingua franca,* and this is the role that English is playing in the absence of one widely-spoken Nigerian language.

So a play like *Ozidi* has several audiences and communicates at several different levels. It is true that my father and mother would not be able to follow the dialogue in the play because it is written in English. But at the same time, my brothers and sisters, who are part of the growing English-speaking community in Nigeria, can understand what I have written. I can communicate with them at two levels—one, at the level of the cultural heritage which they share with me and with my parents, and the other at the new linguistic level and overall culture uniting all the different peoples of Nigeria. And of course we also have a third audience, which is you people outside. So there are different audiences one has in mind, and one hopes to reach as many people as possible.

I will not pretend for one moment that I enjoy the same kind of local audience which, say, Hubert Ogunde enjoys in and outside Western Nigeria. This dramatist and his numerous imitators in what we may call the Yoruba dramatic movement write in Yoruba, act with Yoruba companies, and play mostly to Yoruba-speaking audiences. When their plays are running in Lagos, Ibadan or Ife, the audience, players, and playwright are of one community. This kind of instant union which they achieve with their public is not available to one who writes in English. I belong to the new community of Nigerians who have undergone a new system of education and therefore share a new kind of culture, a synthetic one which exists alongside the traditional one to which fortunately I also belong. Since the function of a play—like the function of any other work of art—is a social one, I write in order to speak to my own kind of people.

How much were you influenced by Greek tragedies in writing **Song of a Goat**?

It's quite possible that Sophocles or Euripides are in that play. It's quite possible that the Elizabethans are there too. But this business of looking for sources can be misleading. I remember that one of the first persons who saw the play in manuscript said, "Oh, J.P., you've been reading Lorca." I said, "Who is he?" So he lent me his volume of Lorca's tragedies, and there I read for the first time *Yerma, The House of Bernarda Alba,* and *Blood Wedding,* but, you see, by that time I had already written my play. What I am trying to say is that the influences may be there, but there are coincidences, too, because we are all human beings with the same basic emotions and experiences.

There are some differences, some regional variations, of course. The Ijo man who comes to this play will probably recognize things the Greeks never dreamt of. The idea of sacrifice is a universal one, but the theme of impotence is something that doesn't have the same kind of cultural significance for you as it has for me. The business of reproduction, of fertility, is a life and death matter in my home area. If a man doesn't bear, he has not lived. And when he is dead, nobody will think of him. Whereas here, you have other interests and preoccupations which have made you less concerned with the issue of procreation, and the sense of survival after death that we derive from it. Of course there are several aspects to any work, and certain of the ideas in **Song of a Goat** may have come from places other than the Niger Delta. I suppose one is doing a sort of synthesis, marrying lots of things one knows in the course of producing. But it takes the courage of an old John Bull like Gerald Moore, alias Mr. I-know-my-Africa, to pontificate that in Ijo the sins of the father are not visited upon his children, sometimes to the last generation, by a particular god invoked to determine a dispute between two parties. Naturally, it's the guilty ones who get the punishment but so do the innocent if they fail to acknowledge the decision and sentence awarded.

Are any of the Shakespearean echoes in **The Masquerade** *deliberate?*

Yes. I would say that the Bard was very much in my mind in *The Masquerade.* When I made one of the neighbors cry in admiration that the bride, a shrew of a girl, "walked afloat, doing the last of her pageants," I wasn't unmindful of Enobarbus eulogizing Cleopatra, or of T. S. Eliot's parody of her in "The Waste Land." There are times when you are well aware you're doing a double-take, and it doesn't take a very clever critic to detect that.

Does your play **The Raft** *contain a political message?*

I was at Princeton in 1962-63 when I wrote **The Raft** soon after seeing Edward Albee's *Who's Afraid of Virginia Woolf?* It is a play which has been seen by some critics as being an allegory of the Nigerian situation—one of the four old regions breaking away, seceding, when the raft breaks up. I tell them that I wrote it in 1963, and don't remember trying to write a political thesis. But then they insist that the

seeds were already there by 1963, that there were signs and symptoms of distress that were to lead to the threatened break-up of the nation. So maybe subconsciously I was thinking about all this. But essentially I was trying to create a human condition which I knew existed not only in Nigeria but elsewhere. The play may, however, have at the same time some remote or close connection with the political reality in Nigeria at one time, though basically it's an invention, a work of my imagination.

Why has the philosophy of negritude had little impact on English-speaking African authors?

I don't consider negritude a philosophy as such but a natural reaction, a movement which was necessary at one time for a number of Africans who were living abroad in Paris and found themselves too assimilated, found themselves too submerged in French civilization for their own comfort. Negritude was a cry that they wanted to surface and be themselves. They didn't want to be drowned by European culture; they wanted to swim in their own stream, as it were. A good number of us in English-speaking Africa didn't find it necessary to shout our identity because we were not culturally submerged by the British in the same manner as was Senghor or the West Indian Aimé Césaire. This is not to say we've all stayed outside the broad current and sweep of negritude, our protests and criticisms notwithstanding. What is more important, perhaps, is that we who employ English in our works have tended to operate more as individuals than as parts of any movement such as Senghor and his French African contemporaries have had to do.

Senghor has claimed that intuition and emotion are innate qualities of the African. What do you think of this?

To say that some group of people have all heart and no head is, I think, one of those things you say to make a special point. I'm sure that Senghor is a very intelligent man, and knows fully well that Africans are not all music, all soul, and no brains, no technology. Science is acquired, after all, it's not genetic. You acquire it over a period of time. I think he felt music and dance and art were the things we had to offer Europe at that time. He was a good salesman, but he said those things then to counteract certain prevailing forces. It's like that in any war—you overstate most of the time to survive. Everything on this side is virtue, everything on the other, vice. Otherwise you wouldn't be able to kick the other man really hard to win.

Do you think negritude has a viable future?

No, I think it a temporary kind of achievement. Negritude was a useful movement at the time that it came, but to want to use it to apply to all life at all times is falsifying life and falsifying the movement as a useful measure. It served a useful purpose once, but no movement can be static. If negritude were to grow, it would have to grow into something else in a scene no longer the same. It would have to go forward or decay and die. I think part of the crisis of negritude today is that Senghor is trying to pump fresh blood into the heart of a body now grown old.

How would you define an African writer?

That's a question that frequently comes up in my own literature classes at home when discussing topics like the "African novel." Is there any literary genre that could be called African, and if so, are we talking about subject matter, language, ideas, forms, settings, or nationalities of authors? Because all these problems arise, and where do you draw the line? If you delimit it by subject matter and setting, *Heart of Darkness* by Conrad, which is about colonialism and right in the heart of the Congo, could it be called an African novel? Graham Greene of *The Heart of the Matter* or *A Burnt-Out Case* and Joyce Cary with his Nigerian tales—are they African writers then? Are the white South Africans African writers? And is there a new African form of the novel, or is it merely a rehash, a poor imitation of models within the great tradition of the English novel and the larger European context? Have African writers actually taken this and turned it into something which you can say is distinctively African in form or in spirit? These are some of the questions we are asking ourselves right now, and until we find the right answers, we cannot really arrive at any definite kind of statement of whether there is an African novel or an African writer. I don't know that nationality is enough. Think of an African who is living in the United States and writing about apple-picking, for instance, and writing in some so-called cosmopolitan language like English, French or some other European language. What would you call his piece? Are we actually producing African works of art with recognizable African qualities out of our experience of a European culture with language as its vehicle? These are complex questions calling for no cut-and-dried answers.

But what would you say the African writer's role in society should be?

I think that the writer—whether African, European or American—is just like a lawyer, a doctor, a carpenter, a janitor, one type of citizen within society. He has his work as has everyone with a job to do. I don't think that any one role—not even that of the highest elective political office of the land—is so special that it should subsume the others. This is where I find it personally disturbing that some of my friends—some of my own kind—do not seem to be satisfied with their own role of writing and would rather become soldiers and politicians, preferring to play roles other than the one that they are good at and recognized for. If you are a poet and write songs for soldiers to march to, to fight to, I suppose you would be well within your field of militancy. If you write a play like any of Brecht's to propound and push an ideology, a way of life, you would be well within your field. But to be an artist while doing all this, you must at the same time create a work of art, carve a figure which, when all capital has been made of it in the interest of whatever ideology that is attached to it, retains its hold upon us principally as an object of beauty.

Another thing, the artist, we accept, is a social person. What he is creating is for consumption by a living group of people, and if it is anything valid it will have as long a tenure as the collective life of the people into the future. He may create his work for worship, he may direct it to an audience that is political, and he may direct it to audiences that are not political or religious-minded. It depends on where his talents really lie; he tries to create a work that is of interest to his public, and this may or may not address itself to any kind of topical issue. To that extent of his being a communicating citizen, I feel he is engaged and committed. But when as a writer he puts pen aside to take up sword, gun and hand grenade, or when he mounts a soapbox to spit slogans chosen for him by others, then I think he has left one role for another.

So you believe he should pick his line, mind his own business, and just write things down?

A lawyer practices his trade; so does a doctor. That does not mean either will not vote. And let's get this straight, a creative writer is not a scribe, just writing things down.

But that is what you were implying.

No, no, it's you who aren't listening in your zest to make me say the unpopular thing in these critical times that will have the artist "committed" to a cause. I didn't say the writer or artist should go and live out in a secluded place. He is a citizen like all the other citizens who make up the Republic.

And should he fight in a war?

Oh, yes, the professional man can give up his practice, but when a lawyer gives up his wig and gown and volunteers to go and fight as a combat soldier, that's that; he is no longer operating in a law court. And nobody remembers afterwards that he is a lawyer. But the glamor of the writer is such that even when he has left his position as a writer and taken on the newer duty of a soldier, there is a carry-over still from the old role to the new one, so that when he gets killed, everybody says, "What a waste!" whereas you don't hear that kind of cry when a lawyer, a doctor is shot down fighting. You may find it odd coming from me, but it seems to me that people are creating for the writer an almost superstitious role which I find unbearable, as if he were a special kind of human being who has certain duties, functions, privileges mystically set apart from other human beings. I don't at all assume that kind of romantic position. I'm not impressed with the social or political life a poet leads outside of his profession if he doesn't produce poems. He is a poet because he composes poetry; he is a playwright because he writes plays, not because he is out killing people or getting himself killed. That is a different role entirely, one for another type of citizen, I mean, the soldier. It may be a role that is open to every able-bodied man in society— taking up a gun in defence of the fatherland—but even in such an extreme circumstance not every draftee or volunteer can shoot or should be allowed to shoot.

Isn't it possible to think of fighting as an extension of one's writing career?

How many great poems have come out of men going to fight? How many plays? Do you think you have to see how people are killed before you can go and write about them? Did Homer, did Virgil, did Shakespeare for all their carnage? The writer, they say, is protean in his imagination: that is why he is able, without ever living a part, without actually acting out a part in life, to enter into it. This is what Keats called "negative capability." You are a chameleon, an actor assuming many roles, because you are able to experience something without ever going into it. I don't believe a writer has to be actively engaged in battles for his vision of them to be valid. I think that is a dangerous way of looking for experience, and mankind must be thankful indeed that the great majority of its artists through the ages have not resorted to that method of chasing after metaphors and images.

You seem to be saying there is no relationship between the writing you do as a profession and the kind of life you lead as an individual. In other words, you could completely turn your back on whatever is happening in society in order to keep your art clear.

There you go again. No, these are not the options. One does not write in outer space. All art is a product of life, and nobody can create art out of void. This is no Miltonic heresy! But when you say a writer should be socially committed, it all depends on what you are talking about. There are many kinds of functions he can perform in society. The very business of giving pleasure is a social function. The business of urging people to go and die is another function. The point is that in producing art you are ordering material and creating something new which you hope will not just show life, not just help to interpret life, but also probably help to direct life. This is where the commitment is. I am saying that it is the quality of the work, it is what you do with your talent, that matters. It is what you create that matters, not any extra duties you take on as a politician, priest, prophet, or bomber-pilot.

Now don't get me wrong. Of course there have been men like Sir Philip Sidney who was a courtier, soldier, poet, critic—the kind of dashing hero that many of us would like to play. But we must not confuse the various roles of the man. His *Defence of Poesie* is not read today because he was a courtier and soldier at the same time. It is read because it is the work of a scholar and poet. I'm only saying that you must separate his talents. When you get the life of the artist mixed up with the work of the artist, then I think you are entering a new realm. Except of course you are dealing with autobiographical work in which case there is obviously a direct link between the life and the work of the artist as in the middle and later Yeats, or old man Donne. But even here, we've to be on the look-out for the theatrical and dramatized version of reality.

The commitment you seem to be insisting upon is the commitment to put words on paper.

No, not to put down empty words on paper, if you please. The commitment to produce something beautiful, and perhaps functional as well—this is the business of the artist as an interpreter, as a maker, as a creator, as a constant renewer of life.

And you insist that he write even when caught up in a compelling personal situation?

Oh, yes, just like Wilfred Owen, unless he has reached his menopause. When Owen was in the trench, he was writing poems. But he has survived as a poet because he was writing poetry, not because he was in the trench. I repeat, the role of the poet is to create poems, and you don't have to go and carry a gun to create a poem about war. There are some times when a man finds himself fighting and comes out of it with new material to write about. I am therefore not trying to limit his subject matter or the area of his experience. And he can use his art in the service of whatever he believes. Like Shelley, he can, and run the risk of having it vitiated or strengthened. This is what a number of artists do all the time anyway. All I am disputing is that it is necessary for you to go some place like Vietnam and fight because you want to extend your art.

OVERVIEWS AND GENERAL STUDIES

T. O. McLoughlin (essay date March 1975)

SOURCE: "The Plays of John Pepper Clark," in *English Studies in Africa,* Vol. 18, No. 1, March, 1975, pp. 31-40.

[*In the following essay, McLaughlin examines the role of the hero in* Song of a Goat, The Masquerade, The Raft, *and* Ozidi *and compares and contrasts these plays with Greek myth and Shakespearean drama.*]

John Pepper Clark's early plays show the influence of established European literary forms, yet Nigerian myths and cultural attitudes have so asserted themselves in his most recent play, *Ozidi,* that his artistic manner has changed considerably. His fascination for the Ijaw saga of Ozidi has an odd sense of culmination for a writer who has spent his dramatic career turning back to his cultural roots: odd because he has integrated his formal educational influences with his more local traditional influences at a comparatively early age, *Ozidi* having been published when he was only 31.

The interesting point about John Pepper Clark is that his awareness of what he calls "traditional" and "native" influences has come to dominate what he has learned from western literature. He is conscious of the two cultures in tension. On the one hand he gives convincing proof that the springs of drama in Nigeria are [as he states in *The Example of Shakespeare* (1970)] "in the early religious and magical ceremonies and festivals of the peoples of this country". Nigeria's drama, in other words, did not start at the University of Ibadan. Yet without that institution the flowering might have been a lot slower, and Clark acknowledges that the imported skills learned at that kind of institution have helped to generate the new writers. "The new playwright in Africa", he says, "though employing a European idiom and technique, plies a traditional art form."

His own progress from Warri to schools in Okrika and Jeremi, to Warri Government College and to the University of Ibadan to read English Honours is a typical enough cursus through local and more sophisticated education. Until he went to Ibadan he grew up in the midst of local Warri influences. He comes, as he puts it [in *A Reed in the Tide* (1965)], from "ancient multiple stock in the Niger Delta area of Nigeria from which I have never quite felt myself severed". The repeated locale of his plays, the river delta area, confirms this sense of rootedness in the sensuous, social, cultural and mythological character of a particular place. Most of his characters take their livelihood from the river and the sea. In his work the tides, the creeks, the ships, ports, fog have a teasing fascination: sometimes they are symbolic of loneliness, chaos and death, but always they are firm images of a particular people and their way of life.

The sea itself is referred to as a metaphoric presence early in *The Masquerade* and at the end of *The Raft*. Clark's poem addressed to Olokun, goddess of the sea, concludes with this obeisance:

> So drunken, like ancient walls
> We crumble in heaps at your feet;
> And as the good maid of the sea,
> Full of rich bounties for men,
> You lift us all beggars to your breast.
>
> ["**Olokun**"]

The strongly felt emotional flux from ruin to hope, and the ritual action of falling down and being raised up captures the movement of the sea, with the control and subtlety of an artist working with immediate and felt experiences. It typifies the relation of Clark to his local surrounds.

It is not surprising then that his main themes in the first two plays, *Song of a Goat* (1962) and *The Masquerade* (1964), have local pertinence: fertility, respectable family lineage, a husband thwarted by forces outside his control, families feuding. These themes are worked out within the ambience of the Masseur, a crippled itinerant who is doctor and oracle, and Orukorere, a half-possessed aunt. The language is laced with an animalistic imagery of goats, leopards, hens, cocks, lizards, snakes, all of which evoke a local rather than a Beckett-like universal setting.

But Clark's protagonists do struggle with broader situations than their context might suggest. They are caught in the frustrations of failure. In the opening scenes of *Song of a Goat* in which Zifa's wife consults the Masseur because she is now barren, her language has the suppressed, controlled despair of a wife who wants to remain loyal to her husband yet realizes that he is impotent, that "there isn't just a pith to the stout staff". Zifa knows she is anxious and hopes against hope that he will not be permanently impotent, declaring "the thing / May come back any day, who knows? The rains / Come when they will." But the natural imagery of water, fertility, seasons, all part of what Clark calls the language of "indirection", works against Zifa's hopes. His

own and his wife's conversation with the Masseur is courteous, sensitive, respectful of intimate feelings of shame and pride; but the accumulation of images of fecundity— bringing forth fruit, raising green thatch, tilling the fertile soil—stands in contradistinction to imagery of death, as in the comment "they have picked my flesh / To the bones like fish a floating corpse". This latter imagery makes it clear that because Zifa is impotent he will wither and die. In an imagistic context of fertility he is doomed to a passionate but fruitless isolation. Clark says of Zifa that he is

> an Ijaw fisherman who loses the will to live when he loses potency and all hope of further procreation. His surely is a tragic passion as the Greeks knew it, and as only primitive people today, like Garcia Lorca's and mine, may know it.
>
> [*The Example of Shakespeare*]

It is helpful to recognize constructional and thematic ties between these first two plays and Greek tragedy, but to dwell on them any more than Clark does is an injustice to what the plays offer. *Song of a Goat* is not a Greek tragedy that fails to come off. Certain aspects of Greek drama which critics have overlooked give the play a universal pathos; but because these aspects are in the service of plays as patently rooted in the particular traditions and mores of Nigeria as Greek tragedy was in those of Greece they should not be considered as imitated but as adapted.

Clark suggests that there is a similar handling of tragic passion in his and in the Greek plays. This passion is fanned by the older women, particularly Orukorere in *Song of a Goat* and Oreame in *Ozidi*. Worn by time and experience their words have a prophetic sadness. Thus, when Zifa's wife Ebiere dies, his aunt Orukorere wearily foresees the death of the whole family:

> There, another blow
> Has been dealt the tree of our house, and see
> How the sap pours out to spread our death. I
> Believe it, now I believe it. White ants
> Have passed their dung on our roof-top.
> Like a tree rotten in the rain, it
> Topples. What totem is there left now
> For the tribe to hold on to for support?
>
> [*Song of a Goat*]

The images of collapse are permeated with a sense of inevitability: the life has already gone out of the wood, and this in spite of Ebiere's good intentions and the Masseur's kindly advice. Good motives in a complex situation have brought nothing but disaster. Likewise in *The Masquerade* the father, Diribi, has traditional honour on his side to justify his anger. He is "lashed by forces fit / To confound forests" because his daughter wants to marry a bastard, a "cur without pedigree", and he cries out:

> Must I kill her, too, this witch and bitch
> Who has quite infected her breed and
> Now makes corruption of all that is
> Sacred?
>
> [*The Masquerade*]

The passion is justified, but its consequences are pitiable. In both plays the parent generation finds itself inextricably involved in turbulent emotions which their children have brought upon them.

The protagonists are not, however, akin to traditional Greek tragic heroes: they are not "wanton boys" struggling against the gods. The imagery, a factor which Clark repeatedly stresses in his criticism, never suggests those proportions. Zifa, Tufa and Kengide have nothing of the stature of Ozidi, but are more like anti-heroes, playing out their difficulties in a limited metaphoric arena. They suffer or survive, not according to fate, but as a result of their own resources to resist the pressures that isolate them from their society. Death is the defeat of self. It does not purge. If we regard *The Raft* as a development of Clark's concern in the previous plays with the dramatic function of death, we see that he is working at something other than a Greek tragic model.

The problems he tackles in the first two plays—fertility, family lineage, infidelity—are played out in a context similar to that in Greek tragedy and among people with similar attitudes to the family; but Clark's explorations are not into heroism or avenging fate. At the end of the two plays less attractive features of his society stick in the mind. The legend surrounding Tufa in *The Masquerade,* the bogus suitor from another village come to entice away a local belle, gives no room for heroism or even sympathy for Tufa, for he and Titi are presented as victims of social traditions embodied in the fiery prejudices of Titi's father Diribi. The latter is a Brabantio figure whose daughter has been "corrupted / By spells and medicines bought of mountebanks" [from Shakespeare's *Othello*]. Like Brabantio, Diribi is covetous of his daughter, which would be no fault if he were not also so pretentiously moralistic and intolerant of youthful romance. Moreover, local convention, the priests, and legend are against Titi. The priests contemptuously relate her death: "Now she lies squashed / Like a lizard in the sand." Yet, as the priests acknowledge, she had "the dream of all girls" in wanting to love and be loved. Social pressures had militated against her in the mind of her father, as they had done against Zifa in the mind of Ebiere. In *The Masquerade* Diribi feels his family lineage has been insulted. No less does Tufa feel that his rights as a husband to Titi have been violated. From that tension between a husband's rights and a society's traditions comes the pathos, for neither wins in any meaningful sense, and there is no victorious passion or feeling of vindication. Neither the survivors nor the dead have won anything.

We have to wait for *The Raft* to see what positive values Clark means to assert. Here the same sense of unmitigated waste is countered by something more positive. Again, people die, victims of their own failings. Unlike Orestes or Agamemnon or Macbeth or Hamlet the main characters hold no prominent position in society; nor do the survivors. All are local Ijaw, unknown and unsung even within their own community, men doing a job of work. Of them, two prove foolish, two wise, and whereas wisdom in the previous plays was not an issue, in *The Raft* it is in the limited sense that survival is affirmed to be better than death.

The point is made in *The Raft* by Kengide, an old lumberman. At times he is cynical, testy, cantankerous, but always a realist. Moreover, he is no passive sufferer like old Orukorere. He repeatedly sees the journey on the raft as symbolic of his people's aimlessness; and in his affirmation, "Truly / We are a castaway people", he states more positively what was latent in the earlier plays.

But Kengide is not a romantic either, and herein lies Clark's second positive assertion. He is the first to say that the raft is caught in "the great Osikoboro whirlpool", admitting the truth so frightening to the others. Only by facing reality does he keep sane. The immediate details and pressures of being adrift are a challenge to reasonableness which each of his companions tries to avoid. Afraid to admit their plight and to allow that there is no escape from fear except in the mind, they try to change their predicament. Olotu and Ogro do get away, but it is to their deaths. Only Kengide accepts the finality of being a castaway, and he alone is able to live with the situation. In knowing danger when he sees it and in recognizing the deceitful hopes of those who run in the face of it, he accepts his limitations and thus retains his judgement.

It is important to see the differences between Kengide and the others because his realistic appraisals, his refusal to put up with the anxieties and romantic illusions of his companions protect him against a tragic death. He watches the loss of Olotu and Ogro with a cynical acceptance. When at the end Ibobo's fears make him frantic to go ashore and he gradually cracks under the strain of admitting that the raft is helplessly adrift, Kengide remains assertive of initiative, sanity and the need for company. Life may be bitter, sordid and corrupt, but the altruism of Ogro and the hopes of Ibobo are dangerous and foolish compared with the assurance of someone else's company in the darkness and uncertainty of not knowing where you are or where you are going.

Kengide is something of a watershed character for Clark. He stands between the sufferers in the first two plays and Ozidi in the latest play. He is a workman exploited by his employers. As a victim he sees the need to scorn heroic gestures of protest: victims need one another if they are to survive. Thus, when at the end Kengide and Ibobo go on down to the sea shouting out at the dark, it is a dismal predicament; but the spirit of Kengide is demonstrative of life for if it were not for Kengide, Ibobo would succumb to death by throwing himself into the river teeming with sharks. In neither of the previous two plays do we find such resistance to death or the forces that control man's future. Zifa in *Song of a Goat* gives himself to the sea as Ibobo would like to, Tufa in *The Masquerade* dies asking, "how is it they left me loose / To litter such destruction?" Kengide would never have let him reach so vulnerable a stage. If we see Kengide in these terms, *Ozidi* is less of a break from Clark's previous writing than it may at first appear.

As Clark tells us in a prefatory note [to *Ozidi,*], the play is based on an Ijaw saga. Not unexpectedly Kengide [in *The Raft*] dismissed the Ozidi story as "mere mud", but for

Two scenes from a 1981 performance of The Boat *at the University of Lagos.*

Clark the saga provides a framework of epic proportions. The play is almost as long as the first three put together, with a cast of well over fifty. The action is at times reminiscent of the *Iliad*, the *Aeneid*, and Shakespeare's *Julius Caesar*. Ozidi the father, a warrior-like figure, and his elder but idiot brother Temugedege are rivals for the throne of Orea. The family situation of the earlier plays has been broadened on a much wider social and political scale. The division within the family—Ozidi has locked up his brother because he thinks him incapable of the job—is reflected in the public sphere where Ofe, the popular leader, plans to kill Ozidi knowing that he and his group can control Temugedege. Ozidi goes to his death through a sequence of bad omens strongly reminiscent of the Caesar story in Shakespeare. The consequent disorder, the offence to Ozidi's family and the corruption in Orea under the ineffectual Temugedege, must wait for their reform by Ozidi's son who, like many a hero in classical epics, will have to assert himself by his own prowess in single combat. Moreover he is assured of victory by the help of supernatural powers, in particular his grandmother-witch, Oreame. The climax (a four-day fight with Ofe his chief enemy and leader of the murderers of his father), the saving intervention of Oreame and the stakes themselves echo the great contests of Achilles and Hector, of Aeneas and Turnus in classical literature, indeed epic fights in many literatures.

The fight is played out at levels other than the physical and ritual. Just as *The Raft* succeeds dramatically because of its sustained tensions (those between Kengide's cynical realism and the wilful individualism of his companions, and in the last scene between Ibobo's fear and Kengide's defiance), so in *Ozidi* there is a similar opposition of sentiment at the thematic level. The play is a celebration of Ozidi the warrior, but there is much within it reminiscent of the depressing end to *The Masquerade*. For example, Ozidi is never liberated from anxiety. Bad dreams of vengeance haunt him and he seems doomed to live in a perpetual state of fear. Like Macbeth he wants to protect himself against his enemies only to find that he is threatened, as was Macbeth by Fleance, by the next generation, the sister and son of Tebesonoma:

> . . . Take it from me, Ozidi, except you murder them
> too,
> Twenty years from now, as you did
> With your father's assassins, you shall be called to
> account . . .
>
> *[Ozidi]*

The struggle is reinforced by further echoes of epic and tragic literature. Ozidi's son, like Orestes, returns from exile to avenge his father's murder and is thrown into a dramatic situation which he does not fully understand. His own mother, Orea, who nevertheless wants him to renounce his role of public valour, complains:

> I have only this one child and I do
> All I can to keep him under cover of
> My roof. But you always incite him to fly out
> Among black-kites.
>
> *[Ozidi]*

Yet like Achilles he has an invulnerable protection in battle, and like so many heroes of saga literature he has a sword "not seen before by eyes of man". Thus equipped and sustained, Ozidi the younger is the invincible harbinger of revenge for his family. But when he dies we are not at all assured that the whole cycle will not repeat itself, perhaps in favour of the other side.

It is difficult to see what are the rewards of the struggle for vengeance. An uncomfortable feature of Clark's plays is the lack of a redemptive theme, the want of any adequate consolation for the waste of human life and suffering. There is a Senecan justice in Ozidi's son revenging the murder of his father, but in this Ijaw saga justice does not work on a *quid pro quo* basis. It does not bring order or hope or peace to the external world. Society remains vulnerable. Suspicion, fear, malevolence and corruption are not reduced by feuds and death. These are not the cost of a better world. Family honour is set right, a point is made, but that is all and only for the moment. The society is forever at war with itself.

Furthermore Ozidi learns little from the experience. The supernatural powers of the opposing witches, Oreame and Azema, the spell of the old wizard of the forest and the whole backdrop of magic reduce his final significance. The decisions in his world are made and worked out on a level at which he is powerless. Like Orestes he will have blood for blood; but his grandmother's lust for vengeance, like Clytemnestra's, colours the entire play, and Ozidi is never anything more than an actor in her revenge drama. As the Story-Teller says of the fight between Ozidi and Odogu whose wife Ozidi means to abduct:

> . . . For as the bowels of Ozidi
> Boil over in rage from the mortar-and-pestle charm
> So the bowels of Odogu. Unknown to either,
> The old wizard of the forest Bouakarakarabiri
> Or Tebekawene, as some call him after
> His habit of walking on his head, has invested
> The other with his celebrated master charm,
> Thus creating our deadlock.
>
> *[Ozidi]*

Not only are Ozidi and his protagonists ignorant of certain forces within their situation, they are powerless to curb or excite them. The element of tragedy does not develop to the horrifying proportions of the *Oresteia* largely because Ozidi, unlike his father, is never asked to make a fateful decision. Nor does Clark intend him to be concerned with such choices. More important is the climate and significance of magic.

Ozidi's future is foretold, approved and worked out by characters like the Old Woman, the Old Man of the Forest, and the witch Oreame. His reaction to them is never critical or anything but responsive. Only at the end does he cut down Oreame, a mistake it seems, and in so doing reduces himself to a more human level. The relation is a passive one and differs in its dramatic possibilities from that between, say, Macbeth and his witches. *The Tempest, Friar Bacon and Friar Bungay* and *Dr. Faustus* rely on magic for much of their dramatic impact but where this is meant to be taken seriously, as in Faustus's conjuring, the audience's belief in the supernatural is not challenged so much as its critical ability to see the action as a dramatic metaphor of the tensions between intellectual pride and spiritual fear. It is feasible that the principal characters can renounce their involvement in the magic at any time: Faustus [in Christopher Marlowe's *Dr. Faustus*] has the chance to repent, Prospero [in Shakespeare's *The Tempest*] is able to say at the end, "I'll break my staff . . . I'll drown my book." Ozidi, however, is powerless in this respect. As a boy he is taunted by his playmates for not knowing who he is. His mother and grandmother exacerbate his curiosity by not telling him. From first to last he is provoked by and entangled in the unknown. In the scene in which the Old Man of the forest goes through his ritual with Oreame and the boy Ozidi to ensure that "No sword wielded by man may cut through / His skin nor any spear or bullet wound pass / Beyond a bump", Ozidi has no foreknowledge of the ceremony or of what the wizard will do or why. The forces of magic are protective, as are the gods of Aeneas, but never problematical as they are to Faustus.

But the play is no worse because it is not concerned with free will or choice. In **The Raft** Ogro dies because he chooses a certain course of action and it can be argued that his character is such that his choice is predictable. Nevertheless he does choose and, by contrast, Kengide is too wise to the world to do otherwise than choose to run no risks. Ozidi's role, however, is much more a predetermined one. Past events in the family history, the memory and spirit of his grandmother give him no chance other than to play the role of expiator.

This mechanistic trait and the absence of human choice could be expected to reduce the dramatic tension. Even in the bleaker drama of Samuel Beckett and in certain plays of Athol Fugard there is still the freedom to choose how to cope with despair or nihilism or social and political rejection. But the nature of the Ozidi saga is such that Clark does not dwell on Ozidi's relations to a society or even to a particular person. Ozidi seldom questions or retaliates against the people closest to him. Like many characters in Homer's epics his character does not change or develop as a result of his experience; he simply grows physically stronger and acquires the skills and accoutrements necessary to his role. We may talk of his development only in this very limited sense.

All of this raises the question of the kind of drama we are dealing with in *Ozidi*. Again one might ask whether it is a tragedy in the Greek mould that fails, or something else. The answer depends on seeing the role of Ozidi the younger in the right light. He is a hero only in the sense of being the warrior who defeats all his enemies. But to say even this is to give him more credit than is his due. Tebesonoma, like most of Ozidi's opponents, realizes that Ozidi has supernatural powers on his side. Having tied up Ozidi, he taunts him:

> Call for her, poor suckling boy, call for
> Your mother and let's see whether she can hear
> And get you out of this.
>
> [*Ozidi*]

Tebesonoma has taken on much more than Ozidi, for the powers that protect and guide Ozidi are his real opponents. Rather than trying to see Ozidi as a hero we should recognize that what the plot and characters might lose by simplification, the drama gains by admitting layers of spiritual and miraculous influence. We have to accept Ozidi as a character within this genre together with the peculiarities of the genre.

Do we have then the exciting and frightening world of, say, Tolkien in which all kinds of magic and strange mythologies are admitted, serious in their own terms, but tenuously related to a realistic or historical truth? Or do we have the expression of a local African saga through recognizable literary conventions, serious in itself and a significant comment on life as lived in Nigeria, and possibly on that lived elsewhere?

An audience unfamiliar with Ijaw rituals and mythology can respond only in much the same sort of way as they would to Tolkien but they will still inevitably go on to place the experience of the play into a recognizable relation with the broader body of their own experience and reading. This is certainly possible if, as Auerbach says of the concept of God, one regards the magical element not as a cause but a symptom of Clark's way of comprehending and representing things [see Eric Auerbach's *Mimesis* (1946)]. In short, *Ozidi* takes its interest and dramatic impact from a mimesis not of historical but of spiritual experience.

In **The Raft** the actual and real world provides a dramatic basis for the spiritual: the physical isolation of the four men on the raft and the dangers of the river gradually pale against the spiritual struggle between Ibobo and Kengide, between fear and defiance. In *Ozidi* metaphors of spiritual struggle exert a central force on the direction of the play. In the dénouement scene (IV. v) where Ozidi kills his *deus ex machina*, Oreame, and in so doing loses his powers, the dramatic contest is between the two zombie-like witches haggling over their price and their power. Ozidi is not important. He says nothing during the scene, then falls victim to the smallpox. The figures Cold, Headache, Spots, Fever, crowd in on him gloating at his vulnerability and his final sickness is appropriate to his lack of merely personal achievement in the play. Whereas he was a strong and peaceable man on his own, his dramatic context has singled him out to fulfil an almost impersonal role, that of the archetypal avenger of family honour. His grandmother tells the Old Man of the Forest that Ozidi

> Must go forth and scatter death among
> His father's enemies.

To this the Old Man replies:

> It's a good son; for how else can
> His father come home from company of the
>   castaway?
>
> [*Ozidi*]

What emerges is that the play has a strong celebratory and ritual air. The younger Ozidi is the god's favourite. He is chosen for an honourable task, "a son who Oyin Almighty /

Herself is sending forth to put to right / This terrible wrong done to his father". He is "a good son" not because he chooses, like Hamlet, to avenge, but because he is chosen.

What pathos there is surrounds his mother, Orea, who insists on a lesser role for him and in doing so is guilty of self-pity. Her final plea, "you cannot / Let this happen to me", breaks into an accusation of Ozidi's failure in familial duty, and her words are full of both love and self-love:

> I am only a poor hen roosting
> Here in a hut by a hearth at which only one chicken
> Nestles—my one child bigger than a crowd!
> A child sees home his parents in the dusk
> Of their lives: so should his in his own turn.
> No such duties has my boy done.
>
> [*Ozidi*]

She is asking for customary familial affection. What she fails to see, and this points up her self-pity and the honourable role her son has been chosen for, is that private affection has to be sublimated into something more public. It is easy to mistake her for a typical bereaved woman of Greek tragedy, but her egoism makes her far less noble, and is implicitly criticized by the celebratory air at the end.

It is important to note that the audience, who may or may not be the people of Warri, are asked to partake in the "festival" of Ozidi. The ritual at the start and end is an explicit movement into and out of an area of "play" coloured by singing, music, procession, and dance. The recognizable world of Nigeria, explicitly referred to by the Story-Teller, has something to celebrate in the saga of Ozidi. And as the play progresses from the scenes of treachery and death in Act One to the promise of a son and his fashioning in Act Two, there is little doubt that the young Ozidi is destined to play a victorious role. When he provokes his enemies' wives (III. iii), he has a confident ritual deliberateness that is amusing rather than frightening because his final victory is assumed. The speeches of Oreame as she prepares Ozidi for his fight with Azezabife are counterpointed by the sounds of an orchestra "beating in the event of the day".

Her prayer at the shrine followed by her ritual light beating of Ozidi with her fan are all part of the atmosphere of the deliberateness of success when Ozidi wins his first victory over Azezabife. A "great spontaneous cheer fills the air and the people pour into the square cheering and beside themselves with excitement".

Just as Kengide in *The Raft* asserts himself over the unknown by shouting at it, so the Story-Teller and the audience in *Ozidi* assert that the tragic overtones and possibilities count for nothing in comparison to the heroic example of Ozidi. Heroic is perhaps the wrong word, because Ozidi, unlike Kengide, fights against nothing and risks nothing. He is the elected one. The audience rejoice that his example exists; and they ritualize it.

In the final analysis, the acting out of the various ritual scenes stamps the play with the awesome and joyous char-

acter of a ceremonial. It is Clark's first success in what he regards as the most promising area for dramatic writing in Nigeria, "this composite art of the folk theatre", the combination of dance, music, ritual, and poetry [*The Example of Shakespeare*]. The shift from the first two plays is remarkable but not inconsistent. The lonely role of Ozidi, often facing the same chaos as Ibobo and Kengide on their raft, is finally ameliorated. His cause is noble in the eyes of the audience and the audience share in its celebratory quality. It is no answer for an individual like Zifa to walk away into the sea, or for the audience simply to watch Kengide's stirring defiance of the unknown. *Ozidi* is a play in which the audience must share. The dramatist foregoes an individualistic interpretation of life for something more public: a dramatic manifestation of the community to itself. Clark acknowledges this when he writes [in *The Example of Shakespeare*], "the very myths upon which many of these dramas are based, so beautiful in themselves, serve to record the origins and *raison d'etre* of the institutions and peoples who own them". It would be intolerable if these were tragic. To respond to the role of Ozidi is to confirm the worth of his ordeal and to make of his example a living and joyous defiance of the spirit of evil.

SONG OF A GOAT

Wole Soyinka (essay date 1976)

SOURCE: "Drama and the African World-View," in *Exile and Tradition: Studies in African and Caribbean Literature,* edited by Rowland Smith, Longman Group Ltd, 1976, pp. 173-89.

[*Soyinka is a Nigerian novelist and dramatist, and he was the recipient of the 1986 Nobel Prize in literature. In the following excerpt, he discusses* Song of a Goat *within the context of the "matrical consciousness of the African world."*]

Song of a Goat, a play by J. P. Clark, has the advantage . . . of fitting into the neat category of tragedy in the European definition of this genre. It was first performed in Europe at the 1965 Commonwealth Festival of the Arts, London; its reception was not of the best, and for very good reasons. First, the production was weak and amateurish. An inexperienced group playing on a London stage for the first time in their lives found that they could not match the emotions of the play with the technical demands of the stage and auditorium. The staging of the play was not particularly sensitive, in addition to which there were the usual unscripted happenings which seem to plague amateur productions everywhere. A rather lively goat (another practical mistake) tended to punctuate passages of intended solemnity with bleats from one end and something else from the other. The text itself—we may as well get over the critical carps at once—the text, written in verse, betrays a self-conscious straining for poetic effect, leading to inflated phrasing and

Clark at a 1973 lecture.

the play—and tries to kill Tonye. He escapes, but only to hang himself in the loft. Zifa walks out to sea and the house of Zifa is left to the bats and goats.

I have touched on some of the technical reasons why, unlike some African audiences before whom this play has since been staged, the European audience found itself estranged from its tragic statement. One other reason, however, was voiced by the newspaper critics and this had nothing to do with the fortuitous events of stage presentation but rather chose to limit, in far more general terms, what areas of human unhappiness may contain the tragic potential. It underlined yet another aspect of the essential divergencies of the European cast of mind from the African: that, on the one hand, which sees the cause of human anguish as viable only within strictly temporal capsules and, on the other, whose tragic understanding transcends the causes of individual disjunction and recognises them as reflections of a far greater disharmony in the communal psyche. The objection was this: sexual impotence was a curable condition in modern medicine (or psychiatry). In addition, child adoption provided one remedy, among others, for sterility; therefore sexual impotence or sterility were outside the range of tragic dimensions for a European audience.

There was something familiar in that plaint. I had heard it some years before after a London production of Ibsen's *Ghosts.* Syphilis, asserted a critic or two, was no longer an incurable disease. Ibsen's play had consequently lost any tragic rationale it might have had in the mercury days of venereal science. I could not help recalling this particular critical thesis when I found myself in Sydney a year or two later and encountered an Australian poet who, with his wife cheerfully supplying the details, boasted that he had caught a completely new mutation of the syphilitic virus which had the entire Australian medical profession stumped. Nicknamed the Golden Staphylococcus because of its appearance under the microscope, it had developed powerful resistance to all known antibiotics. Research and consultations with international laboratories would shortly, I was relieved to learn, put an end to the reign of the Golden Staphylococcus, but I could not help wondering aloud if Ibsen's *Ghosts* should not quickly be declared the definitive antipodeal tragedy of the sixties. . . .

In relating ***Song of a Goat*** to such drama, I make no exaggerated claims for its actual achievement. It remains, however, excellent premises from which to enter the matrical consciousness of the African world. The play is contained within a microcosmic completeness . . . with especially strong affinities—again for ease of reference—to the world of Lorca. A play of brooding violence, its central motif, the symbolic design may be described as one of contained, poetic violence. We encounter human beings whose occupation and environment are elemental and visceral. Flood and ebb affect their daily existence, their language, their spectrum of perception. Mists and marsh colour their mood. Within this claustrophobia of threatening metaphors, existence is economic and intense; its expansion into an awareness of immediately exterior forces merely reinforces their circumscribed intensity of being. From this closed relationship a thread of potential violence is gradually drawn, con-

clotted passages. For a company which was not wholly at home in the English language, the difficulties were insurmountable. In an English audience it created resistance, even hostility.

The drama takes place in a fishing village. The characters are Ijaw, a riverine people on the Niger delta. Two brothers, Zifa and Tonye, Ebiere, the wife of the elder Zifa, and Orukorere, a scatty old aunt of the two brothers, are the central characters. The old lady provides a Cassandra presence throughout the unfolding of the tragedy which is centred on the sexual impotence of Zifa.

At first Zifa sends his wife to consult the Masseur, a doctor-cum-seer who diagnoses the real problem without difficulty, recognising that it is the husband not the wife who is the real patient. He suggests that the younger brother, Tonye, take up the marital duties of the elder, an idea which is violently rejected by Zifa (who later consults him) just as Ebiere indignantly spurned it in her turn. But the inevitable does happen. In one of the most credibly sexual scenes of progressive frustration Ebiere goads the brother into taking her. Zifa suspects, manoeuvres the guilty pair into a revelatory ritual—this ritual is made the climactic moment of sistently prepared through metaphors within the dialogue of action. Until we are brought at last, bound to the protagonists, to the climactic image which, for the principal sufferer, is also the image of revelation—a sacrificial pot and the ram's head within it, a precariously contained force, barely held, barely restrained. It parallels that core of sexual frustration, that damming up of natural continuity and beneficent release by sterile opposition compounded with individual pride, self-deception, a code of morality which presupposes normal circumstances.

The whole point, however, is that the circumstances are abnormal, even unnatural. The interaction of man and nature so pervasively rendered in the play demands a drastic redress of these abnormal circumstances and it is a demand which cannot be pushed aside by the pride of one man. The poetic containment of violence is very much the environmental reality of *Song of a Goat.* Storms do not occur every day nor are fishermen washed off their canoes on every fishing-trip. But the hovering claims of this natural cycle dominate the natives' daily awareness, giving to rituals of appeasement an integrated essentiality for every event. Thus the death of an individual is not seen as an isolated incident in the life of one man. Nor is individual fertility separable from the regenerative promise of earth and sea. The sickness of one individual is a sign of, or may portend, the sickness of the world around him. Something has occurred to disrupt the natural rhythms and the cosmic balances of what is the total community.

> There, another blow
> Has been dealt the tree of our house, and see
> How the sap pours out to spread our death. I
> Believe it, now I believe it. White ants
> Have passed their dung on our roof-top.
> Like a tree rotten in the rain, it
> Topples. What totem is there left now
> For the tribe to hold on to for support.

Passages like this, displaying little of the lapses of language which mar a good portion of the play, convey an unselfconscious conjunction of the circumcentric worlds of man, social community and Nature in the minds of each character, irrespective of role. And one important, even vital element in the composition of the elaborate interiority of such tragic drama is of course its moral order. This must not be understood in any narrow sense of the ethical code which society develops to regulate the conduct of its members. A breakdown in moral order implies, in the African worldview, a rupture in the body of Nature just as the physical malfunctioning of one man. And the literature of this viewpoint is not to be found in the ruminative asides or debates among principals but in the metaphor of existence in the most mundane or in the most exalted circumstances. We find, to revert to J. P. Clark's play, that moral disorder is not simply a matter of sleeping with another man's wife, especially if that man is your brother. This is of course an anti-social act and is recognised as such. It is neither desirable nor is it condoned. Deviations from harmonious conduct such as this are dealt with by set processes which vary from society to society. But this anti-social act can be— depending on circumstances—a far less dangerous threat to

communal well-being than, for instance, Zifa's self-delusion and sterile pride.

Where society lives in a close inter-relation with Nature, regulates its existence by nature phenomena within the observable processes of continuity—ebb and tide, waxing and waning of the moon, rain and drought, planting and harvest—the highest moral order is seen as one which guarantees a parallel continuity of the species. We must try to understand this as operating within a framework which can conveniently be termed the metaphysics of the irreducible: knowledge of birth and death as the human cycle, the wind as a moving, felling, cleansing, destroying, winnowing force, the duality of the knife as blood-letter and creative implement, earth and sun as life-sustaining verities, etc., etc. These serve as matrices within which mores, personal relationships, even communal economics are formulated and reviewed. Other 'irreducible' acceptances may evolve from this; for instance, the laws of hospitality or taboo on incest, but they do not possess the same strength and compulsion as the fundamental matrix. They belong to a secondary category and may be reversed by accident or human error.

The profound experience of tragic drama is comprehensive within such irreducible hermeticism. Because of the visceral intertwine of each individual with the fate of the entire community, a rupture in his normal functioning not only endangers this shared reality but threatens existence itself.

LeRoi Jones on Clark's Poetic form:

John Pepper Clark . . . because of his verse play *Song of a Goat,* convinces me that he is one of the most interesting Africans writing, English or French. . . .

[*Song of a Goat*] is English, but it is not. The tone, the references (immediate and accreted) belong to what I must consider an African experience. The English is pushed, as Senghor wished all Africans to do with European languages, past the immaculate boredom of the recent Victorians to a quality of experience that is non-European, though it is the European tongue which seems to shape it, externally. But Clark is after a specific emotional texture nowhere available in European literature or life. . . .

The play is about a traditional West African family split and destroyed by adultery. And the writing moves easily through the myth heart of African life, building a kind of ritual drama that depends as much on the writer's insides for its exactness and strength as it does on the narrating of formal ritualistic acts. The language is gentle and lyrical most of the time, but Clark's images and metaphors are strikingly and, I think, indigenously vivid. . . .

LeRoi Jones, in his "A Dark Bag," in
Poetry CIII, No. 6, March, 1964.

P. Emeka Nwabueze (essay date 1988)

SOURCE: "J. P. Clark's *Song of a Goat:* An Example of Nigerian Bourgeois Drama," in *World Literature Written in English,* Vol. 28, No. 1, Spring, 1988, pp. 35-40.

[In the following essay, Nwabueze argues that classifying Song of a Goat *as a "Greek tragedy" is erroneous, countering that it exemplifies a modern "bourgeois" drama.]*

John Pepper Clark is undoubtedly one of the most talented African writers. His plays, poetry, and critical essays have received serious critical acclaim from many quarters. But unfortunately, his *Song of a Goat* has not been placed in its generic family in dramatic criticism. Dramatic critics are accustomed to classifying plays by generic labels, especially tragedy, comedy and, perhaps, melodrama. This mode of classification creates a generic lacuna in dramatic criticism. Perhaps it was this situation that prompted Northrop Frye to propose five archetypal modes: myth, romance, tragedy, comedy, and satire. One might complain that Frye leaves no middle ground in his classification of literary texts. Since, as John Gassner maintains [in the introduction to *A Treasury of the Theatre: From Henrik Ibsen to Eugene Ionesco* (1962)], "most people are neither comic nor tragic, neither heroes nor villains, they fall into intermediate classifications"; hence they produce drama of intermediate effect and their actions should be discussed under appropriate generic classifications. It is in recognition of this fact that this new look at J.P. Clark's *Song of a Goat* becomes necessary.

Critics are divided in their opinions why *Song of a Goat* is in disharmony with the genre under which it is categorized. For instance, Oyin Ogunba [in "Modern Drama in West Africa," in *Perspectives on African Literature,* edited by Christopher Heywood (1977)] does not consider the handing over of a wife to a virile younger brother by an impotent elder one a theme of tragic proportion. Martin Esslin [in "Two Nigerian Playwrights," in *Introduction to African Literature: An Anthology of Critical Writing,* edited by Ulli Beier (1982)] sees Clark's use of highly stylized free verse as an alibi for the problems of translation posed by the incongruity between his peasant characters and the English language used to depict them. Though Lewis Nkosi talks about the echo of Elizabethan blank verse in the play [in *Tasks and Masks: Themes and Styles in African Literature* (1982)], he presents the play as a real achievement in its evocation of the poetry of village life in a traditional African setting, coupled with its moral strictness, its adherence to a time-tested code of honour and social regularity, and the inevitable punishment that follows. Benham and Wake refer to Clark's plays as being akin to classical Greek drama because of the interwoven actions of gods and man, and curses passing through one generation to another [Martin Benham and Clive Wake, in *African Theatre Today*]. To them this affinity to Greek tragedy is coincidental. Adrian Roscoe, on the other hand, observes [in *Mother is Gold* (1971)] that Clark seems confused about the "advantages which the indigenous tradition had to offer: hence the play bears the marks of indecision and is clearly a work of low voltage." He calls the play a "Graeco-African tragedy" because of the merging of the Greek with African elements.

But to Geoffrey Hill [in "Nigerian Plays," in *Journal of Commonwealth Literature* 1 (1965)], the play confronts the difficult task of combining the tragic theme of guilt with satirical observations of a transitory society.

It is evident, from this brief review, that the problem of these critics is that they have not placed the play in its appropriate generic family, thus seeing it in a completely different, if not confused, manner. A careful reading of the play reveals that its profundity lies in the playwright's employment of the characteristics of bourgeois drama. For a play that ought to go down in history as the first Nigerian bourgeois drama to be totally misinterpreted by critics is disheartening.

To understand Clark's *Song of a Goat* as a Nigerian bourgeois drama, a brief excursion into the concept of this dramatic genre is in order. C. Hugh Holman defines bourgeois drama [in *A Handbook to Literature* (1981)] as "a term applied in plays in which the life of the common folk and the middle class rather than that of the courtly or the rich is depicted." Although Edwin Wilson [in *The Theater Experience* (1980)] traces bourgeois drama's origins to the eighteenth century when societal changes called for serious drama about people with whom audiences could identify, bourgeois drama actually began in the Elizabethan age with the move towards realism in drama. Such plays as the anonymous *Arden of Feversham* (1586), Thomas Heywood's *A Woman Killed With Kindness* (1603) and another anonymous play, *Yorkshire Tragedy,* dramatized actual domestic murders in middle-class families. In the nineteenth century the concept of middle-class tragedy came to be associated with social issues. Twentieth-century bourgeois drama represented in the work of such playwrights as Eugene O'Neill, Arthur Miller and Tennessee Williams frequently portrays middle-class characters as victims of complex social structures or heredity. Because its subject matter is the domestic life of common people, bourgeois tragedy is synonymous with domestic tragedy.

Bourgeois drama owes much of its popularity to characterization. In defiance of the conventional concepts of classical tragedy, this genre deals with the lives of middle class protagonists rather than the noble or the rich. These characters might be victims of their environment, their society, their psychology or their heredity. Characterization, therefore, is the most obvious element that makes *Song of a Goat* bourgeois drama.

The characters in this play are typical bourgeois dramatic characters performing roles that are appropriate to their social status. Zifa is a fisherman and part-time ship pilot in one of the Niger estuaries. His younger brother, Tonye, is his professional assistant, while the crippled Masseur serves as an itinerant family doctor to many homes in this idyllic African community. These are bourgeois characters in a comparatively proletarian society. Clark places these characters side by side with regular neighbours in a realistic setting. The characters are, therefore, neither heroic nor poetic, as Clark himself maintains in his reply to Ben Obumselu's criticism of his dramatic poetry, but are only ordinary Ijaw people enacting their lives on stage. This is in contrast to Greek tragedy, with which the play has been compared, since the most important factor about the classical hero is his superhuman qualities, which set him apart from ordinary men. Zifa's tragic end cannot be blamed on fate since he does not in any way try to ward off that fate. The fact of a curse on the household is not in doubt, as in *Oedipus Rex,* for example, but unlike a classical tragic hero, Zifa does not confront that fate with fortitude.

Zifa is essentially a bourgeois tragic character, not that of classical tragedy, as some critics erroneously maintain. Not only is he a mere fisherman, but in sending his wife to the Masseur, he does not try to confront his fate. This is unlike Oedipus who, immediately after consulting the oracle in his foster father's land, deserts the town and its environs to avert the possibility of killing his "father." Zifa turns deaf ears to the Masseur's advice of giving over his wife to Tonye so that she may become pregnant. Even when it is done and the affair consummated, Zifa drives Tonye to suicide and walks into the sea himself. His actions resemble those of Willy Loman in *Death of a Salesman,* who succumbs to fate and takes his life, or even like Barnwell in Lillo's *The London Merchant,* who walks against all advice and foolishly succumbs to the caprices of a vicious woman.

Where the classical heroes are mainly victims of fate and errors of judgment due to the beliefs of the period, most of the characters in bourgeois drama are victims of society. Instead of fighting against their conditions like the heroes of classical tragedy, bourgeois characters succumb to their fate whimpering in resignation and self-pity. Such characters lack the tragic dimension of characters in modern serious drama who confront their destiny with courage and dignity, as does Zifa.

As in all bourgeois drama, society is a major factor in Clark's *Song of a Goat.* The subject matter of the play is a contemporary issue in a traditional African environment. A curse is placed on a household, and the impotence of a man is blamed on the woman, who has little or nothing to say in an African society. To prove herself guiltless, she takes a lover, her husband's younger brother. Her husband feels slighted and pursues his brother to suicide and drowns himself. As a characteristic bourgeois drama, the issue revolves around domestic problems and the effect of society on those problems. Because he could not produce any more children after the first son, Zifa sees himself losing everything that makes a man in an African society. So, like a typical bourgeois drama, *Song of a Goat* is based on the problems of the middle class people in an African society. The typical African man might decide to marry many wives rather than give one to a younger brother for procreation. His problem becomes more acute if he lacks the wealth to marry another wife. Zifa's problem, therefore, assumes a magnified stance because of his effort to attain the accepted standards of his society. His individuality is thus less significant than his effort to meet societal norms.

In his effort to depict a realistic environment, a feature of bourgeois drama, Clark shows his interest in nature and actuality, and employs descriptions which immediately call the landscape to mind. The open ground found among the creeks of the Niger delta, the usual constant rainfall, and the vast stretches of water are presented by the speeches of the characters in the play, for example:

> Don't you
> See it is raining over the sea tonight?
> On the sands sprawling out to dazzle
> Point till eyes are scales
> This outpouring should be impression
> Indeed. Here only waves pour out
> On waves, only dunes upon dunes.

or the following lines from the Third Neighbour:

> It was a heavy walk, the fishing
> Baskets scattered all about, the new canoes
> Carving on the shore. And the grass was wet
> On our feet. Presently, fording the sands,
> We saw him reach the water's edge.

Song of a Goat, like other bourgeois drama, is serious in intent but lacks the profundity found in tragic plays. When treating this play as a classical tragedy, most critics hold this lack of profundity against Clark, but it is characteristic of bourgeois drama. The seriousness of *Song of a Goat* lies in impotence, the passion of an African man cuckolded, and the suicides in the play. Whereas the lack of profundity could be attributed to the common folk characters, a foreigner who is unfamiliar with the passion of a possessive African man, the seriousness of birthright to the African, and the woman's situation in an African society might consider all these as trivialities. But to Zifa, his position is a very disgraceful one. His predicament is clearly seen in his statements to the Masseur:

> You talk of help. What help can one expect
> That is placed where I stand? People
> Will only be too pleased to pick at me
> As birds at worms squirming in the mud. What,
> Shall I show myself a pond drained dry
> Of water so their laughter will crack up the floor
> Of my being?

In her own predicament, Ebiere prefers death to her position, as exemplified in the following lamentation:

> Oh, how I wish I'd die, to end all
> This shame, all this showing of neighbours my
> Fatness when my flesh is famished!

Admittedly, *Song of a Goat* has a poetic form, while most bourgeois plays, except those written in the fifteenth and sixteenth centuries, take the prose form to effect a realistic tone. However, *The London Merchant,* the first bourgeois drama to employ the prose form, was influenced by the blank verse measure. Clark is emphatic in his belief that the problem of an Ijaw artist or a Nigerian artist generally is one of finding an original and natural language to suit his characters. In an extract from a letter to Gerald Moore, he says that "style, imagery, etc., are what tell one user of a language from another—not grammar or class" ["Aspects of Nigerian Drama," in *Drama and Theatre in Nigeria: A*

Critical Source Book, edited by Yemi Ogunbiyi (1981)]. Thus, his poetic language serves as a vehicle that brings into focus the status of his characters. Matching the language with the status of dramatic characters is an important feature of bourgeois drama.

To achieve this linguistic characterization, Clark depicts African speech patterns through the use of proverbs, imagery, and allusions or ambiguity of phrases by loading simple words with heavy sexual undertones. Ebiere's womb, for instance, is referred to as a room and a house; a male organ is called a "stout staff," the woman's organ is the "gate," "the door," "the thing," and "a piece of land." The woman's reproductive cycle is compared to a planting season, as exemplified in the following statement from the Masseur:

> She has waited too long already,
> Too long in harmattan. The rains
> Are here once more and the forest getting
> Moist. Soon the earth will put on her green
> Skirt, the wind fanning her cheeks flushed
> From the new dawn. Will you let the woman
> Wait still when all the world is astir
> With seed and heady from flow of sap?

Thus, Clark's language in this play is that of commonplace people in their environment; the aphorisms and stock expressions suit the characters and place the play firmly within the convention of bourgeois drama.

It is evident, therefore, that Clark has succeeded in *Song of a Goat* in raising a common people's problem to a tragic level. This is then in contrast to the lack of profundity that Esslin ascribed to the play when he juxtaposed it with conventional classical tragic elements which represent an action that is serious and has magnitude. Apart from observing the classical unities of time, place and action and using few characters, Clark also achieves universality in his subject matter with the fertility theme. Perhaps the classical unities and use of a universal theme is what persuades many critics that the play is a classical work. Sticking to the unities is a dramatic technique which has its roots in ancient dramatic theory but which is not confined to it. On the other hand, the use of fertility theme does not make the play a classical one, but does give it universality, an important feature of dramatic poetry not confined to classical drama. As Esslin rightly points out, "in order to reach truly universal acceptance, a play must fulfil both conditions—it must have a subject-matter that is accessible to the maximum number of different societies, and it must be an example of supreme craftsmanship in construction and language." In using the fertility theme, Clark achieves this universality in *Song of a Goat.*

Characterization, as has been noted, is the "soul" of bourgeois drama and is in fact carefully handled in the play to suit this dramatic genre. Clark's characters are best suited for the common people's subject matter he has chosen. In the character of Zifa, he combines two forces that devise his fall: psychology, an element of pride which prevents him from giving his wife to his virile younger brother for pro-

creation, and fate. The impact they create in us is not the pity and terror necessary for classical catharsis, but the emotional mixture of sympathy and outrage characteristic of bourgeois drama.

In *Song of a Goat,* Clark has succeeded in creating bourgeois dramatic characters and situations which create a close and natural relationship between his commonplace characters and his audience.

THE MASQUERADE

William Connor (essay date 1979)

SOURCE: "Diribi's Incest: The Key to J. P. Clark's *The Masquerade,*" in *World Literature Written in English,* Vol. 18, No. 2, November, 1979, pp. 278-86.

[*In the following essay, Connor contends that critics of* The Masquerade *have misunderstood the play and have neglected the complexity and subtlety of the plot, whose predominant theme is one of incest.*]

John Pepper Clark's second play, *The Masquerade,* has not been a favourite of the critics; I believe they do Clark and his play a great injustice.

The basic plot of *The Masquerade* is deceptively simple: the hand of a village belle, Titi, who has become a local celebrity by refusing all suitors, is finally won by a rich stranger. Tufa, who falls in love with her at first sight, showers her with lavish presents and wins her acceptance on the spot. Titi's father Diribi, one of the outstanding men of his village, is as overwhelmed by the prepossessing stranger as his daughter, but it is plain that much of Diribi's enthusiasm is generated by Tufa's apparent wealth. On the night before the wedding it somehow becomes public knowledge that Tufa, unbeknown even to himself, is the son of his mother's husband's brother, that this resulted in the unnatural deaths of all three members of the triangle, and, moreover, that his family is the object of an hereditary curse. Diribi and his wife Umuko, on learning this, turn against Tufa and forbid the marriage, but Titi refuses to be gainsaid in her desire to marry him and leaves her parent's house. While Tufa, an eminently reasonable man, is trying to find ambassadors through which he may placate Diribi, Diribi in a mad rage shoots Titi to death with a shotgun. This act leads both Diribi and Umuko to mental collapse and causes Tufa to commit what amounts to suicide when he forces the broken Diribi to shoot him.

The main objection taken by critics to the progress of this action is that, while Diribi's hostility toward Tufa is logical enough, the murderous rage in which he kills his daughter seems to lack believeable motivation. Margaret Laurence [in her *Long Drums and Cannons* (1968)] has stated this case effectively:

It is necessary to accept Diribi's strong feelings against Tufa. Where lineage is of the utmost importance, a man such as Tufa, born of an unsanctioned relationship which might have been regarded as incestuous, would have been intolerable to Diribi as son-in-law, especially as the curse on Tufa's family would be regarded as still being potentially dangerous. What is not well enough developed, however, is Diribi's feeling against his daughter. Titi has always been his favourite, and it is understandable that he should be enraged at the thought of her marrying someone whose heritage he regarded as tainted. But as the final scene opens, we discover that Diribi has killed his daughter. There has been no build-up, no conflict, no sense of Diribi's having been torn this way and that, no indication that some final unbearable word on her part bent his mind into madness.

Laurence's apparent confidence in her objections is not justified. A closer reading will reveal that Diribi's rage against his daughter is actually a fit of sexual jealousy coupled with the unbearable self-revulsion attendant upon it, and that there is ample evidence indeed of build-up, conflict and a strong sense of Diribi's having been torn this way and that, as well. While there is no suggestion at all—this should be clearly understood—that any physical act of incest has been committed, indications that Diribi has long harboured a subconscious sexual desire for his daughter are many. And, although it is less vital to understanding the movement of the play, there is good reason to believe that Titi, without really knowing what she was doing, has encouraged him in this.

The opening scene (or "Situation," as Clark chooses to call the divisions of his play) consists of a tryst between Tufa and Titi together with the commentary of a chorus of neighbours who witness it from hiding. Here it is revealed that Diribi is rich and a great hunter and that Titi, whose beauty is as exceptional as her father's ability, has long refused all suitors, even though "the gifts they showered on her" have "quite dammed her path." Where the village beaux failed Tufa has succeeded, and not surprisingly so for in addition to his personal attractions, which are considerable, he is able to offer Titi more than anyone in her village ever could: "The doorways / Through which I shall take my wife / Lead to a greater world."

While it is less clear in this opening scene than later, there are at least strong indications that Titi has rejected her earlier suitors because they could not measure up to the standard set by her father. The peculiar possessiveness of the neighbours with regard to Titi prepares the audience for Diribi's greater possessiveness in the next scene, and the unnatural behaviour of the tides coinciding with the wedding preparations suggests that something is greatly amiss in the relationships of the characters involved. But more pointedly revealing is Titi's tendency to place her father and her lover in similar metaphorical roles in the verbal sparring of this scene:

TITI: I should like to see it! [the greater world]

TUFA: Tomorrow when the passage is complete and
Of course if your father agrees to release
The bird.

TITI: You are unkind to my father
Who is himself a great hunter. He hates
Playing the keeper. It was the bird
Herself that chose indoors. She flies out now
To test if the hunter can jump bramble
And brook. Or is he tripping up as did
The rest?

Considered in retrospect, Titi's statement that her father hates playing the keeper and is himself a great hunter is filled with tragic irony. A little later, when Tufa attempts to take Titi in his arms, she breaks away exclaiming, "Brute, you brute. Oh, my father!" This is, of course, just playful banter, but it shows that Titi's regard for her father's manly attributes and her habit of holding him up as a barrier between herself and potential lovers are both deeply enough ingrained to have survived even her love for Tufa.

Hunting as a metaphor for sexual conquest is not used idly in the passage above. Significantly, it is taken up again in the final scene in connection with Diribi's murder of Titi. Here Titi, who several times in the play has been described as a bird that cannot be caught by hunter-lovers, is described again as a bird when her father hunts her down with his "fowl piece / In hand—" Fowl piece, not fowling piece? Whether this is meant as a pun or not, the shotgun is definitely phallic, and Diribi's murder of Titi has definite overtones of symbolic rape:

FIRST PRIEST: She tried tears, tried prayers and
                    like some bird
Already struck, but still struggling
For sunlight, skipped from one twig
To another, but leaves and boughs shrunk in
                    her path
And none could offer her closet.
Meanwhile, her father with that fowl piece
In hand—

TUFA: Oh, it was the double-barrelled piece I myself
Brought him as gift from son to father!

FIRST PRIEST: With it he chased her like a new-
                    spawned chick to the wall
Oh, is it not indeed a strange tide when cocks
Turn hawk on their own brood? But there she was,
Visibly strung to a thread which the man
Seemed only too daggers-glad to snap
That instant, and break it he did with one burst
Of his gun.

In a variation of the bird metaphor Diribi is described as a cock and Titi as a chick, which suggests a situation in the animal world where incest would be inevitable.

Strong in themselves, the symbolic implications of the final scene are supported by more explicit suggestions of Diribi's suppressed desires for his daughter earlier in the play. At the beginning of Situation Two, even before there is any question about Tufa's background, Diribi is clearly having second thoughts about the marriage, and just as clearly he is jealous of his future son-in-law for trying to rival him:

DIRIBI: Enough, enough, young man, or
Shall I believe the stories you are
In competition with us?

TUFA: How is that, Father?

DIRIBI: You are too precipitate with your
Distribution of bounty. Boy, with right and
Left palm you toss out money and gifts
Among spectators and dancers in more times
Than I have done a single round.

TUFA: That's just not true, Father, the story
That I seek to rival you. . . .

The ostensible point of jealousy here is only a mask for the deeper, more important one, the possession of Titi herself, and Diribi soon brings the argument around to her. Although the nuptial festivities are already well along, Diribi treats the marriage as if it were in serious doubt:

DIRIBI: . . . After tomorrow then if you aren't,
My son, to return home with hands leaky,
We can think about granting to you loan
Of the pet we have all her life held
To breast.

And, while Tufa still seems the perfect suitor, Diribi's reservations about him multiply rapidly:

DIRIBI: . . . They say
I am too possessive with my daughter
Titi to grant her hand all this time
To a husband. But now I begin
To wonder if by marrying you
She is not exchanging the pipe for the ladle!

In this scene the taunts of the neighbours point to the truth: Diribi was temporarily won over to the idea of his daughter's marriage by Tufa's wealth, but his growing irritability at Tufa and at them show that he is having second thoughts as the event becomes imminent. Since Tufa could hardly be more innocent of offence at this point, the logical conclusion is that Diribi finally could not bear to have his favourite daughter marry anyone.

Situations Three A and Three B give a picture of the private life of Diribi, Umuko and Titi that strongly supports the impression given elsewhere that Diribi is unnaturally fond of his daughter. At first in Three A Titi argues her case well, maintaining that since Diribi originally allowed himself to become caught up in the prospect of gaining a rich son-in-law without paying a dowry he has committed himself and has no right to back down at the last minute. Her arguments are bold; she is not afraid of her father, and there is a certain coyness in her manner that suggests a practised effort to manipulate him:

TITI: . . . I
Rather half feared that moment it was
A refusal of me, this great delight and
Haste to endorse the man of my choice.

DIRIBI: You know very well I never
Would deny you, you of all my children. . . .

And Diribi, for all his protests of fatherly solicitude, is a little too insistent on the fact that beauty is now complete between Titi's thighs, as he put it, and, at the same time, he seems strangely anxious about her opinion of his own undiminished potency.

Umuko, although she is not a particularly clever woman, seems to be aware that Titi's influence over her father has in the past been too strong, and relations between her and her daughter are noticeably strained. At one point Titi accuses Umuko of wanting to be rid of her, and by his subsequent actions Diribi illustrates why Umuko might well feel this way:

TITI: . . . It will not be long
Before you have me outside your house. That is
What you have always desired.

DIRIBI: Shall I send you out, Umuko, or are
You going to leave me the ground
I need to pursue this?

UMUKO: All right, all right, it is a matter
Touching the Diribi race, and of course
Only those that belong may open mouth.

DIRIBI: Come this way, my daughter, come sit
By me, I can still carry my child on my laps,
Can't I? There, don't laugh, or do
You honestly think my loins have got the rheums?

Here, as elsewhere, Diribi shows a tendency to neglect his wife in his excessive interest in his daughter.

Throughout Situation Three B Diribi's sexual jealousy becomes progressively more evident. Although it is impossible for him to face the true nature of his emotions, both his anger and his love for Titi have sexual overtones as he speaks of them:

DIRIBI: . . . the one who I took for my heart
Has turned out worse than a harlot . . .

. . . . .

. . . Titi, Titi I loved
To think sat innocent between my laps and
Who I have hugged to myself as
A river laps an island, now seeks
To dam my path, even as I answer
The unavoidable call to sea . . .

His use here of the river metaphor to represent his relationship with Titi is clearly meant to be connected by the audience with his repeated references to the polluted stream of his blood, which he is so obsessed with cleansing. While this pollution is nominally Tufa, it is plain from the above link as well as the general context that the real corruption, the evil Diribi subconsciously fears so much, is his own suppressed sexual desire for his daughter.

Diribi is an interesting psychological study. In him Clark has created an embodiment of the psychological phenomenon usually termed projection, in which a person avoids an unacceptable feeling or compulsion of his own—here illicit sexual passion—by projecting it, seemingly without regard to reason, on someone with whom it is associated. Thus it is that, despite the sensible reassurances of Umuko and the chorus of Women of the House, Diribi is unable to control his obsession with Titi's promiscuity:

> DIRIBI: The bitch was not in her bed, do you
> Get that? She is even now not asleep
> In the bridal bed I myself built for her before
> That mongrel ran in, tongues down, to foul us all.

(This resembles the language of a jealous lover much more than it does that of a concerned parent.) Thus also it is that Diribi's obsession with eradication focuses on Titi rather than Tufa:

> DIRIBI: Must I kill her, too, this witch and bitch
> Who has quite infected her breed and
> Now makes corruption of all that is
> Sacred?

In the end Diribi's fear of having his own suppressed passion surface in his mind is greater than his love—sexual and otherwise—for his daughter.

Apparently *The Masquerade* did not work well in production at the 1965 Commonwealth Arts Festival in London. According to Laurence its "weaknesses . . . were even more apparent on the stage than they are on paper" and "the vast emotions which the play tries to conjure up seemed to collapse flimsily." This is most surprising. The psychological depth and sophistication of Clark's characterization should have made this one of his most successful plays on the stage: the parts of Titi and Umuko hold rich possibilities, and I can think of few roles in a play of this length as challenging or potentially as rewarding for an actor as that of Diribi. Therefore, I can only conclude that the failure of the 1965 production was the fault of the theatre company that performed it. While Clark's treatment of the incest theme in *The Masquerade* is sufficiently subtle that its importance might well be missed in a single reading, a competent director should be able to convey its full impact to an audience in a single performance. And in doing so he would virtually eliminate the problems which flawed the 1965 production.

In addition to being a fine psychological study, *The Masquerade* is an excellent vehicle for the cosmic irony—the irony of fate and coincidence—which is pervasive in Clark's drama. There is, of course, a high degree of ironic coincidence in its basic situation: Diribi, the incestuous father, and Tufa, the cursed son of an incestuous liaison, coming together to their mutual destruction. And so, even if it were not for the obtrusive involvement in the lives of the characters of external forces like the portentous tides, the plot alone would make it plain that fate is an important factor in the world of *The Masquerade*. Furthermore, Clark heightens the inherent irony of the situation by juxtaposing the self-righteousness of Diribi, who is genuinely guilty in his heart, with the self-condemnation of Tufa, who, apart from his inherited guilt, is entirely innocent.

The importance of cosmic irony builds up throughout the play as the true nature of Diribi's problem becomes ever more apparent. In Situation Three B, when Diribi in his efforts to avoid facing his incestuous desires becomes increasingly vehement in his condemnation of Tufa's unfortunate background, the fundamental irony of the situation is continually underlined by the dramatic irony of his speeches. Here and in the final scene, Situation Four, similarities between *The Masquerade* and the story of Tufa's conception in *Song of a Goat* are repeatedly drawn to the attention of the audience. For instance, the use of the sea as a symbol for the destiny to which a man is driven by his lineage and his *teme* (roughly the Ijaw equivalent of the soul, but in many cases a soul with a will contrary to that of the conscious mind) links Diribi with Zifa, Tufa's mother's husband, who, as Diribi relates, "Walked of his own will into the sea." It would be hard not to notice the parallel when Diribi associates his love for his daughter (in the passage already quoted) with his "unavoidable call to sea." And later, when in the final scene the priests tell of Diribi's murder of Titi, the parallel between Diribi's infant son being thrown to safety by Titi at the moment of destruction and Tufa's own birth should be clear. This must almost certainly represent a deliberate effort by Clark to underline Tufa's essential innocence—the innocence which ironically neither he, Diribi, nor the priests who tell the tale can comprehend—as well as to link the two disasters and point to the cyclical nature of destiny. Perhaps the most successful instance of dramatic irony in the play is the long speech delivered by Tufa after he has precipitated his own death as an act of atonement. Here he describes his birth and, unwittingly linking his position to Diribi's by employing the recurring metaphor of the corrupted stream, he takes upon himself the full responsibility for all that has happened. Thus Tufa dies without understanding that the tragedy which has befallen Diribi's house is not a chance misfortune consequent upon his having entered it. He fails to see that he is merely the appropriate agent of the higher "fate" which by merging the corrupted stream of his family with that of Diribi's causes the two to cancel each other out.

The Masquerade is a subtle play, both psychologically and in the complexity of its irony, and without recognition of Diribi's incestuous passion for Titi this subtlety can be neither understood nor appreciated. Unless one accepts this fundamental fact, even the title makes only dubious sense, since Tufa is not really a masquerader: the real masquerade around which the play is constructed is, of course, that of Diribi, ironically Tufa's most determined accuser. Hence, it is little wonder that those who have failed to recognize that incest is a recurrent motif in Clark's unfinished trilogy were disappointed with *The Masquerade*. Yet, on the other hand, considering the amount of evidence Clark supplies, plus the importance of incest in the preceding play, plus the complete failure of **The Masquerade** when Diribi's passion for his daughter is disregarded, it is a great wonder that so many have ignored its presence for so long. By accepting too readily that Clark would write and publish a genuinely bad play, his critics have failed to grasp how successful **The Masquerade** really could be on the stage. Indeed, I can think of no other modern play which in its compactness, the power of its tragic irony and the neatness of its resolution comes as close to duplicating the achievement of Clark's models, the classical Greek tragedies. Considering the injustice done by critics generally to this fine dramatic effort, it is hardly surprising that Clark failed to complete his proposed trilogy.

THE RAFT

R. N. Egudu (essay date 1976)

SOURCE: "J. P. Clark's *The Raft*: The Tragedy of Economic Impotence," in *World Literature Written in English*, Vol. 15, No. 2, November, 1976, pp. 297-304.

[*In the essay below, Egudu characterizes* The Raft *as "an outright indictment on economic cannibalism and a sincere plea for the observance of the Marxist principle of an equitable distribution of the basic means of human existence and survival."*]

The Raft is a tragedy of a group of four economically weak lumbermen who have undertaken a journey by a raft on a river. Their journey is not without cause. The purpose of the journey is to take logs to a rich trader resident in Warri, who will pay them some money for their service. The journey is therefore a deliberate effort on the part of the four men to make a livelihood. This information is given early in the play, where Kengide addresses Olotu:

> . . . You and I
> And every fool that ever set foot on this raft
> Are on the same payroll, and the man
> With the purse is up wining away at Warri.

References to this economic background to the journey on the raft are made here and there in the first three parts of the play; and the whole of the last (i.e. part IV) is almost entirely devoted to it.

It is necessary to make this point early in this paper in order to emphasize the fact that although no definite cause beyond those speculated on by the characters can be attributed to the drifting of the raft, yet it was not blind chance that brought the four men together on the raft and forced the journey on them. The immediate cause of the journey is the four men's need to exchange their services for wages; and

it is this that remotely (albeit) sets the stage for the tragic end of the men. The cause/effect relationship is basic to the structure of the play and indispensable to the full understanding of its "meaning."

However, many critics who have hitherto studied the play seem so engrossed in talking about the role of "fate" or "chance" with regard to the drifting of the raft, that they tend to lose sight of the economic situation which engendered the action of the play. Thus all emphasis has so far been placed on the "effect" with little or no attention paid to the "cause." And to correct this imbalance is the main task of this study.

Wilfred Cartey, one of the most vocal among the critics about the theory of universal "fate" they have discovered in **The Raft,** has this to say [in his *Whispers from a Continent: The Literature of Contemporary Black Africa* (1971)]: "Clark predicts in his play **The Raft** accident and chance (for we do not know how the raft was set adrift), and that man is indeed adrift and his actions to escape the drift are futile. Therefore Clark's vision of history is based on the uninterrupted continuity of man's tragic destiny." Similarly, Adrian Roscoe [in *Mother is Gold: A Study in West African Literature* (1971)] says that the play "has a moral ambiguity which is at once honest and consciously modern. The fearful questions of the four characters—'Who are we?' 'Where are we from?' 'Where are we going?'—have echoes all round the modern world. The play does not pretend to provide answers." He also says that "the predicament of the four men . . . drifting helplessly in the night, is meant to be taken as the predicament of the Nigerian nation as a whole as it looks for directions, searches for a teleology while floating about in the dangerous waters of the modern world"; and that "in an obvious and rather prophetic reference to the divisive forces at work in the ship of state, the raft breaks in half after a sail has been hoisted to help move the vessel out of its becalmed state." Another critic, Dan Izevbaye [in "Poetry and Drama of John Pepper Clark," in *Introduction to Nigerian Literature,* edited by Bruce King (1971)], observes that the events in the play symbolize "the plight of the country"; and that "the writer's intention does not appear to be prophetic or satiric" but "to present in more universal terms the general plight of man."

We may now briefly respond to the issues raised by these critics, and after that pursue our own argument. There is no doubt that what has happened to the lumbermen is an accident, such as could happen to any person in his normal work. But to universalize this incident is tantamount to failure to recognize the social reality that produced the play. For the mental attitudes of the characters are determined all through the play by their ever present consciousness of the fact of their economic inferiority which condemns them to the "payroll" of one rich Chief. Ogro tells us his stake in the venture is greater than that of any of the others (implying of course that each of them has one), for on the "safe arrival of this raft" he would have for wife the Chief's "fairest daughter." And this means that his services on the raft would offset the bride-price and other expenses one normally runs in order to get himself a wife. And Kengide, that mouthpiece of the ugly, economic plight of the men, tells a pathetic personal story, part of which equally applies to all four:

> . . . Now, you didn't know I worked
> For the Niger Company at one time, did you?
> Always
> Making money for some man other
> Than myself, that has been my fortune.

Roscoe's observation imbues the play with the existentialist doctrine of "Angst" or "Dread" which among other things, questions God's guardianship of the world. This seems to be forced on to the play, for the characters have not asked the question "Who are we?" or "Where are we from?" which Roscoe has arbitrarily given them to ask. The questions which two of them (Ogro and Olotu) asked respectively are "Will anyone tell *where* we are?" and " . . . where exactly are we going *now?*" (My italics). These questions are not asked in vacuum by the characters, but in the particular context of their loss of direction while on the river. They are not drifting aimlessly, nor do they not have and know their destination, which is Burutu. And they know why they are on the journey by the raft, as has been shown earlier in this study. Ibobo and Kengide recognize the street lights shining at Burutu even when they are as many as "eight bends of the river" from there. The characters are at no time lost in the sense of cosmic wandering; rather they have lost their sense of direction on a river they have always known and that only for some time, for the two who remained alive after the other two had perished later found their direction even if they never reached their destination.

That Ibobo and Kengide get drowned just at the moment they are almost at the port is one of a number of ironies which help to enhance the dramatic intensity of *The Raft*. There is a similar ironic situation in the second part of the play. After the raft remained stagnant in the whirlpool for some time, the men repaired it, and it started moving. Kengide shouted joyfully: "It's moving! It really is moving"; and Ogro called on all of them saying, "now give a loud shout, boys. Our raft / Is moving again—behind a big bellyful / Of tornado—Oh, shout for joy." But then, quite ironically, this was the time when the raft broke into two. Such an irony is of course not rare in real life.

Also, the political interpretation given to the play appears forced, since it fails to take into account the content of the pages of the play. In the first instance the four men's mission is economic, not political. But they are not asking for aid; they are rendering a service for which they hope to be paid. Secondly, they are not just "floating about" passively; at every turn of events they try to devise some means for solving their problem. And of course Nigeria could not be said to have drifted aimlessly. She has always had set objectives after which she has been striving. And in connection with the notion of the "prophetic" significance of the breaking of the raft, one would like to observe that the breaking of the raft is not the result of any design by the characters to split into two or more camps. Each of the first two to get drowned loses his life in a sincere attempt to save the raft as a whole. The breaking of the raft is a sheer

accident, and this cannot be correctly said of the situation which led to the Nigerian civil was and to which Roscoe is referring.

Finally, and with regard to Izevbaye's comment, it is right to say that the play is concerned with "the plight of the country," but not that it deals with "the general plight of man." Furthermore, it may be true that the play is not "prophetic," but it definitely is "satiric." And it is the presence of satire in it that reflects the "plight of the country" in the play. For the actual "plight" dealt with by the playwright is economic and moral, not political.

The Raft therefore in its last part, at least, is indeed a serious satirical comment on moral turpitude among Nigerians, that is, whether or not the writer's intention is "satiric." (We do not need here to engage in a discussion of "intentional fallacy.") The last part of *The Raft* opens with Ibobo's lamentation over the loss of lives resulting from the men's venture. Kengide then relates the parable of five fingers which naturally leads to the conclusion that money is the root of evil. This dictum has been given by Chaucer in *The Pardoner's Tale,* a story which deals with quest for money by foul, not fair means. According to Kengide's parable, "the small fellow" who "happened one day to cry hunger" is the smallest of the five fingers. And as has been seen earlier "hunger" which is a result of economic impotence is the force behind the journey by the raft. The means suggested by the finger next to the smallest one is grabbing: "Let's / Go out and grab ourselves something." The next two fingers somewhat agree to the proposition. Only the thumb—the slow "Burly being who all the time was drowsing / In the corner"—opposes it, saying "Count me out!" The thumb stands for the few in the society who would not grab. But he is a negligible minority. Thus, as will be confirmed later by Kengide, grabbing is shown to be a way of life in the society.

Through the dialogue that follows between Ibobo and Kengide, we are shown the various shades of corruption among the people. The man for whom the lumbermen are suffering and losing their lives is himself the chief grabber, a "rogue waiting down / At Warri." Kengide hates the evil way people make their wealth. He even regrets his allowing himself to be lured into the "lumber gang" by Olotu's "sweet" talk "about the quick money there is to make / In this log business." And the thought of it is made more of a harangue by the fact that the "sole owner" of the logs "is miles away rolling on laps / Of his innumerable wives." This emphasizes the contrast between the lazy relaxing rich people and the toiling hungry ones who are virtually their slaves. Olotu, though he is poor, is linked with the Chief in Kengide's hatred, because he (Olotu) shares with the Chief the grabbing tendency which is rife in the society. And indeed, Kengide thinks that Olotu is "probably only too glad / That he has been left with his own share / Of the timber."

It is because of Kengide's hatred for the rich rogues dealing in timber that he likes to burn trees down so as to introduce suspicion and confusion among the rival timber capitalists, who are the economic great-grandchildren of Darwinism:

Playwright Wole Soyinka as Kengide (seated) and another actor in The Raft, *at the University of Ibadan Arts Theatre in 1964.*

. . . In this game
Of getting rich, it is eat me or I eat
You, and no man wants to stew in the pot,
Not if he can help it.

Kengide makes this remark to show how much foul play and corruption there is in the timber business. He goes on to prove that one can and does easily steal the logs belonging to another:

. . . A Straight
Bribe of five shillings on every twelve
And the most erect of them in all
The forest will as easy erase as imprint
With that almighty hammer of theirs.

And that is in spite of the fact that, according to Ibobo, "all the logs bear their owner's name and besides / They have all been stamped by the forest guard."

But the forest guards, like some other government officials, are themselves the embodiment of corruption. Ibobo expresses surprise "at the rate / Those forest-guard fellows put up buildings at Warri" in spite of the fact that "government

couldn't be paying them more / Than it does its clerks!" Then Kengide, who knows the society very well, comes up with the following sarcastic explanation:

. . . For all their stiff khaki
And sashes, your green folk don't get paid
One bag of money a month. But who will arrest
Their sway? The police who should apply the rope
Are themselves feeding so fat, their belts and barracks
No longer can hedge in the smallest
Weed. And so with the courts. Man, it is
We ordinary grass and shrubs who get crushed
As the mahoganies fall.

The use of the image of mahoganies to represent the rich but corrupt people, and that of grass the poor but innocent ones, features also in one of Clark's poems, **"Emergency Commission."** And the idea that the poor suffer under the rotten weight of the rich is also expressed in the poem. There is general chaos

. . . When mahoganies
Show a centre too rotten
For rings, and twigs and grass,

Already denied room and sun,
Carry the crush and shock?

That this theme of corruption is handled and expressed in the two works in the same type of imagery is not an accident. The works were written (at least published) about the same time. The play was published in 1964 and the poem in 1965; the poem must have been written in 1964 but not before 1962 since it did not appear in the 1962 Mbari publication of Clark's *Poems.* The time in which the works were written was that in which there was the Western Nigerian election crisis which shook the whole of the country (though it did not split the country into two).

To return to the satirical nature of *The Raft,* we also notice that after Kengide showed how corrupt the forest guards, the police and the others were, he was provoked by Ibobo's remark that they should be in port "before the town goes / To sleep," to make a general attacking comment on town dwellers. He said that "towns don't go to sleep," for "if they did, those who run them / Will have little time to plot their pleasure / And plunder."

The two words "pleasure" and "plunder" summarize the major aspects of corruption as Kengide sees it in towns. Pleasure here is the destructive pleasure of copulation with city whores, which Ibobo incidentally is anxious to enjoy. Kengide reminds him that that would be a desire "to wreck your wretched self / At the feet of some woman," and later that "not all the bedbugs / In this world can suck as one woman / Sharing with you a bed." Besides this, Kengide also lands one of his strokes on the homosexuals (the white ones) that inhabit the city: "Didn't you know one white man / Will go to bed with another—Even / In preference to a woman?" he asks Ibobo who of course thinks that is an abomination.

Kengide ends this dialogue on the corruption in the society with a final indictment on trading companies and government, which, according to him, are the most callous agents of oppressive plundering. As has been noted earlier in this study, Kengide had worked for the Niger company at one time and it totally emasculated him, since he was merely "making money for some man" other than himself. Because he had a family to feed he joined the strike, demanding better pay. But in that he lost too, for the "politicians" and the "papers" "who had promised Jericho itself" and who incited the workers to go on strike, got divided among themselves, and so the strike collapsed. And the consequences were disastrous for the poor people:

. . . So, Government or Niger
Company, two faces to one counterfeit coin,
As usual won the field. Not only that,
They went on to raise taxes and prices on
Everything money could buy in the shop—from
     buckets
To umbrellas—they raised them all, while lowering
Those on our crops.

Here then is the story of Kengide and of all the wretched of the earth like him. It is to make sure we are told this sad story of perpetual economic bondage that Kengide and Ibobo are allowed to live longer than Olotu and Ogro in the play. This done, they can now sing their own *Nunc Dimittis.* All the four have to die because the economic system of their society has not made any provision for their existence. For such people who have known nothing but misery and suffering and slaving for others to end up in such a tragic manner cannot but evoke our deepest sympathy. This, it seems to me, is Clark's main message in the play, and the message is home with us in this country, not on any one unknown planet in the universe. So that if there is any determinism in the play, it is more of the economic than of any other type.

The social relevance of *The Raft* therefore consists in the consequences in the country of this economic determinism. It is this rather than the political implications that has informed it with meaning and social relevance. According to Gerald Moore [in *The Chosen Tongue: English Writing in the Tropical World* (1969)], "Drama is a popular language not simply because it transcends the boundaries of literacy but because it re-unifies its audience by appealing to them at a level which they all recognize." And J. P. Clark himself has said [in his *The Example of Shakespeare* (1970)] that drama means "an elegant imitation of some action significant to the people" and that one of the functions of drama is to be of "spiritual relevance for both actors and spectators."

The Raft adequately performs these functions. It appeals to its audience which is made up of all the people who have experienced or witnessed economic oppression and the effects of corruption in society, because many of them see their counterparts in the characters. The action of the play is therefore significant (in the sense of being relevant) to the audience; and the central action is that of struggle for existence in the face of odds. And finally, it is to be hoped, the play has spiritual relevance in that it is concerned with the attitude of man's heart and soul to man. The inner nature of man is indirectly appealed to by means of satire in the play in order to explore the possibility of producing regenerate man in the society. The play is an outright indictment on economic cannibalism and a sincere plea for the observance of the Marxist principle of an equitable distribution of the basic means of human existence and survival.

OZIDI

Margaret Laurence (essay date 1968)

SOURCE: "Rituals of Destiny: John Pepper Clark," in *Long Drums and Cannons: Nigerian Dramatists and Novelists,* Macmillan, London, 1968, pp. 77-96.

[In the following excerpt, Laurence provides an overview of Ozidi, *with special emphasis on Clark's use of traditional*

*material and the play's relationship to his earlier works,
particularly* Song of a Goat.]

Ozidi is based upon an Ijaw epic, one of the masquerade
serial plays which were told in seven days, accompanied by
dance, music and mime. Clark made tape-recordings of this
masquerade series and also filmed it. He later did a translation of the entire epic into English. His own verison is an
adaptation which nevertheless adheres fairly closely to the
original play cycle, at least in the action.

The series is in five parts, and the masquerade opens with
an invocation to the water spirits. In the first scene, the
elders of the ancient town of Orua are meeting to discuss
choosing a new king. Within recent years, the kings of Orua
have all died after a short reign. An elder suggests that they
must discover the cause of the taint that lies on every oc-
cupant of the throne. But—and in this beginning is the
end—this advice is overruled and ignored. The elders want
Ozidi, the strongest warrior, to become king. Ozidi refuses,
saying that he knows it is the turn of his house to provide
a king, but he is the younger brother, and his elder brother,
Temugedege, is an idiot. He declines on behalf of them
both, but Temugedege suddenly appears and says he will
accept the throne. Temugedege becomes king, but everyone
knows this is a farce. Ozidi is furious that his brother has
accepted the throne, and mocks Temugedege, who sees
rulership only in terms of the slaves and fine women he will
now own. Ozidi's comment carries a distinct ring of Zifa's
words in ***Song of a Goat,*** in the expression of the curse
upon a family:

> They say man is better than goat,
> But having you for brother I can now see
> The curse upon our house.

The villagers discuss the new king, in terms that are reminiscent of Orukorere in ***Song of a Goat*** warning Zifa that
'when the gods ask for blood it is foolish to offer them oil'.

> . . . a god is
> A god once you make him so. After
> The ceremony, he ceases to be mere wood. Give him
> Palm oil then, and he'll insist on blood.

Irresponsibly the people of Orua have made a madman
king. But sacred acts cannot be done lightly, and the gods
are not mocked. The idiot king, having undergone the ceremonies of kingship, has become sacred, something more
than himself.

It was this situation that Ozidi wanted to avoid, and now the
elders are afraid of Ozidi's vengeance.

Constantly, throughout this drama, the imagery of sacrifice—of slayer and victim—is used, the same kind of imagery that is found in ***Song of a Goat.*** Here it is Ozidi who
is described as the leopard.

> How shall we stop the leopard's left paw
> From falling on our necks?

Or,

> He'll tear us to pieces
> Like mere goats unless we do something at once.

Orea, Ozidi's wife, is the daughter of the seer-woman
Oreame, and therefore has something of her mother's second sight. She warns Ozidi not to go out, but Ozidi goes
and is killed. The elders bring his head to the king, as a cup
for him to drink from. Temugedege, upon seeing his brother's head, falls into a fit and later runs away. Orea laments
and tries to commit suicide, but is stopped by an old woman
who says that Orea is carrying Ozidi's child and must live
to bear it, for the son will avenge his father.

As Act Two opens, we learn that Orea has borne a son,
whose birth (in the familiar manner of the heroic child in
the legends of many cultures) was attended by storms and
various upheavals of nature. The boy has been brought up
by his mother and by his grandmother, the witch Oreame.
Orea worries about her son, but Oreame says:

> Shame! Will you tie him
> To the hearth like a goat—my boy
> That is a leopard and must prowl?

Oreame is determined that the boy will avenge his father.
She takes him to the village of Orua, and on the way he
encounters the 'hill' masquerade, which is Oreame in another form, attempting to test his mettle. The boy is frightened, and Oreame, disappointed, assumes her own form
and reassures him. Once again, however, she tests him by
shouting that a leopard has attacked her. The boy flees.
From this time forward, Oreame sets out to harden the
boy's nerve and to prepare him for vengeance.

Ultimately, she takes him to the Old Man of the Forest—
Bouakarakarabiri—who is a 'half human figure', a wizard
who knows all the secrets of 'all life and leaves of the
forest'. Oreame obtains from him a charm for the boy, a
potion made of eagle, hornbill, lizard and monkey, which
will enable him to experience the fury necessary for battle
and will protect him against his enemies. Oreame, as a
character, is very like Orukorere in ***Song of a Goat***—she is
intensely protective of the boy; she is a prophetess and seer.
The difference is that Orukorere is merely a wise-woman,
sometimes possessed but not herself using magic, whereas
Oreame is a full-fledged witch, experienced in the occult.

Ozidi sets off with Orea and Oreame for the town of Orua.
The elders of the town, led by Ofe, are terrified at the return
of the son of Ozidi the First. One by one, the young Ozidi
picks off his enemies until there are only a few left. The
townspeople, like a chorus, beg Ofe to get rid of Ozidi
before he destroys the whole town. They accuse Ofe and
the elders of not having made the proper sacrifices to the
gods and of not having the masquerades performed for the
water spirits. At last Ofe is forced to deal with Ozidi alone.
Ofe's own people are criticising him within the town, and
outside the gates Oreame is taunting and Ozidi is challenging. Ofe meets Ozidi, who finally wins and cuts off Ofe's
head, but after this act falls into a state of possession.

Ozidi's father has been avenged, but the young man cannot settle to a life of fishing and farming. He has been too well prepared to be a warrior and now he cannot lead an ordinary life. He longs for more fights, yet those men whose lives he has taken haunt his memory. He feels that he is cursed for despoiling the land. An old man, Ewiri, tells him that what he needs is a wife. But Ozidi is drawn into battle once more by a challenge from a seven-headed giant. With the help of Oreame's magic, Ozidi slays the giant, but before he dies, the giant says his sister will avenge him.

Here the play becomes truly macabre. Ozidi's fate seems to be forcing him on relentlessly, for Oreame, who more and more becomes a sinister figure, tells the young man to go to the giant's sister and kill her. He does go, accompanied by his grandmother, and finds that the woman is an ordinary decent person who is delighted at having at last borne a child after many years of childlessness. Oreame is not moved at all. She urges Ozidi on, even though he says 'I don't want to kill anybody again', and he kills both the woman and her child. His *teme* is leading him on to fulfil his inevitable and disastrous fate. His grandmother, the witch Oreame, seems like an externalisation of this side of his soul, and Ozidi himself says at one point:

> . . . my grandmother, she is
> The sea that fills my stream.

Several interesting questions arise here. It is impossible to tell exactly how closely Clark has stuck to the Ijaw original, but both an Ijaw view of destiny and an outlook which owes much to contemporary psychology appear to be present. Ozidi longs for a woman, but he is a clumsy and tactless lover. He longs to stop killing, but he goes on killing. He is talented at only one thing—the dealing of death. With his conscious mind he wants to change his life entirely, but subconsciously he is still totally attached to the repetitive acts of death. In Ijaw terms, his personal soul wants peace and a life of work and family, but that part of his soul which decided his fate before he was born urges him irresistibly towards destruction. As with Zifa in *Song of a Goat,* there might be a way out, through the changing of his destiny by the proper ritual, but he does not seek it. Ozidi is terribly bound to his own course through the subtle bondage imposed upon him by his grandmother. The figure of Oreame is a decidedly dual one. She is the ancestress, and she both protects Ozidi and makes it impossible for him to change. He relies upon her, and calls upon her every time he is in trouble. Yet her protection is a deadly one, for it keeps him firmly and even obsessively within his own narrow groove.

This ambiguous nature of the ancestors is brought out in Ozidi's fight with Odogu, the man whose wife Ozidi tried to take. Odogu has a charm from the forest wizard as well, so the battle ends in stalemate. Odogu's mother is also a witch, and she turns up, along with Oreame. The two witches—in a scene of unparalleled grotesquerie—engage in a battle of power, turning themselves into fires and showers of sand. The conflict is broken by the entrance of the wizard, the Old Man of the Forest, who says that the one who wins will be the one who first fetches the magic leaf. It falls

to Oreame to do so, and she rubs the leaf on Ozidi's eyes. Ozidi, strengthened, cuts down Odogu, but, blinded by the herb, he also cuts down his own grandmother. We can see here both the subconscious urge to be rid of her and the horror that such an act must impose upon the conscious mind. Ozidi, realising what he has done, and knowing Oreame is dying, becomes mad.

The ending of the masquerade is in a lower key entirely and is peopled by symbolic figures such as the Smallpox King, attended by his servants Cough, Cold and Fever. In a masked dance of great intricacy, these figures arrive as though on a barge. Ozidi is in a state of high fever. His mother says, 'You'll be the death of us all,' and Ozidi replies:

> There's nothing else
> I know how to do, is there?

He has recognised his own destiny but cannot combat it. He cannot die by war because he has been magically protected, but there is an inevitable flaw in the gods' protection of him. His destiny impelled him to live by the sword, even when with his conscious mind he desired to stop killing, but his death can only be achieved by disease.

In Clark's version of this Ijaw play sequence, the characters are very much more simplified than they are in *Song of a Goat,* but the same elements are present in the drama—the theme of lineage, the concern with blood honour, the curse laid on an entire house, the son obliged to act out a fate begun by his father, the destiny-deciding *teme* catapulting a man into situations not of his conscious choosing, the different parts of the individual soul working in opposition to one another. Clark's rendering of this Ijaw epic shows the complexity of his traditional sources and the ways in which he has drawn—in all his plays—upon forms and concepts of Ekine masquerade drama, extending these and using them as a means of expressing conflicts which are both contemporary and universal.

FURTHER READING

AUTHOR COMMENTARY

Pieterse, Cosmo, and Duerden, Dennis, eds. "J. P. Clark." In *African Writers Talking*, pp. 63-74. New York: Africana Publishing, 1972.

   Compilation of three interviews. In the first interview, dated September 1962, with Lewis Nkosi, Clark discusses cultural influences on his dramatic and poetic works. In the following two interviews with Andrew Salkey, dated January and September 1964, Clark chronicles his reasons for writing in English and describes his role as a poet, playwright, and journalist.

OVERVIEWS AND GENERAL STUDIES

Adejumo, Z. A. "Language in the Plays of J. P. Clark." In *Nigeria Magazine*, Nos. 130-31 (1980): 56-74.

> Examination of Clark's creative use of English to capture the spirit of the African societies he portrays in his dramatic works. Adejumo remarks: "In the process of recreating an authentic Ijaw society he has evolved a technique which could be described as Ijaw traditional conventions of language."

Astrachan, Anthony. "Like Goats to the Slaughter." In *Black Orpheus* 16 (October 1964): 21-4.

> Compares *Song of a Goat*, *The Masquerade*, and *The Raft* to one another and examines how their forms and structures follow or deviate from the canons of Greek tragedy.

Esslin, Martin. "Two African Playwrights." In *Black Orpheus* 19 (March 1966): 33-9.

> Describes the "handicaps and dilemmas inherent" in Wole Soyinka's and Clark's work. Esslin argues that Clark's ability to adapt vernacular language to poetic verse attests to his achievement as a playwright.

Ferguson, John. "Nigerian Drama in English." In *Modern Drama* XI, Nos. 1-4 (May 1968): 16-26.

> Brief synopses and positive reviews of *Song of a Goat*, *The Masquerade*, and *The Raft*.

Nnoka, Barbara Grant. "Authenticity in John Pepper Clark's Early Poems and Plays." In *Literature East and West* XII, No. 1 (March 1968): 56-67.

> Identifies literary and cultural influences on Clark's early works: Clark's education at a British University in Ibadan, Nigeria; his reading of the English poet Gerard Manley Hopkins and playwright T. S. Eliot; and the rhythm, sound, and imagery of Nigerian cultural traditions.

Roscoe, Adrian A. "J. P. Clark." In his *Mother is Gold: A Study in West African Literature*, pp. 200-18. Cambridge: At the University Press, 1971.

> Examines the ways Clark attempts to balance African and Western traditions in his plays. *Ozidi*, he asserts, represents Clark's "wholehearted espousal of the dramatic heritage of his own people. Although written in English, in theme, style, idiom, and inspiration, *Ozidi* is, quite simply, African."

Additional coverage of Clark's life and career is contained in the following sources published by Gale Research: *Black Literature Criticism*, Vol. 1; *Black Writers*; *Contemporary Authors*, Vols. 65-68; *Contemporary Authors New Revision Series*, Vol. 16; *Contemporary Literary Criticism*, Vol. 38; *Dictionary of Literary Biography*, Vol. 117.

Adrienne Kennedy
1931-

Full name Adrienne Lita Kennedy.

INTRODUCTION

Kennedy's controversial, often violent plays symbolically portray African-American characters whose multiple or uncertain identities reflect their struggle for self-knowledge in a white-dominated society. Although some audiences have expressed discomfort with the dark, brutal nature of Kennedy's plays, critics have consistently praised their lyricism and expressionistic structure, frequently comparing them to poetry. Wolfgang Binder observed: "[These] dramas are to some degree exorcizing personal and collective racial traumas and have anger, the urge to communicate and (attempted) liberation as the motivating forces."

BIOGRAPHICAL INFORMATION

Kennedy grew up in a multi-ethnic, middle-class neighborhood in Cleveland, Ohio. She had an early interest in drama, but did not begin writing until she enrolled in a course on twentieth-century literature at Ohio State University. Shortly after graduating, Kennedy married, had her first child, and began writing plays while staying up late with the baby. Although her work was praised by writing instructors, she became discouraged by consistent rejections from publishers. At the age of twenty-nine Kennedy traveled to West Africa and Rome with her family, and the contrast between her African and European experiences provided the background for her first published play, *Funnyhouse of a Negro*. When she returned to the United States, she submitted the drama to a workshop taught by playwright Edward Albee. Soon afterward, the play enjoyed a successful off-Broadway run and won an Obie Award in 1964. Over the past several years, she has taught creative writing at such institutions as Yale University, Princeton University, and the University of California at Berkeley.

MAJOR WORKS

Kennedy is best known for *Funnyhouse of a Negro*, which focuses on a young girl named Sarah whose confusion regarding her identity arises from her mixed heritage: her mother is white and her father is black. Simultaneously obsessed with and alienated from Western culture, she is tormented by visions of figures who her represent the white, Western world, in particular her mother, Queen Victoria, the Duchess of Habsburg, and Jesus Christ.

Kennedy's following work, *Cities in Bezique*, consists of two one-act plays, *The Owl Answers* and *A Beast Story*. Like *Funnyhouse of a Negro*, *The Owl Answers* portrays a African-American woman's quest for self-knowledge in a world dominated by white races. Other critically acclaimed works by Kennedy include the lesser-known *A Rat's Mass* and *A Lesson in Dead Language*, which present surrealistically distorted religions that precipitate the loss of childhood innocence through sexual initiation rites. *Sun: A Poem for Malcolm X Inspired by His Murder*, a short play about creation, is one of Kennedy's few dramas dominated by a male perspective. In 1980 she presented a children's play, *A Lancashire Lad*, a fictionalized version of Charlie Chaplin's childhood in England.

CRITICAL RECEPTION

Kennedy's work is often praised by critics for its innovative and provocative use of poetic language and imagery to convey facets of the African-American experience. Commentators contend that several elements contribute to the highly expressionistic quality of her plays, particularly the lack of plot, rhythmic and repetitious dialogue, and use of characters from the mythical and historical past as well as allusions from her dreams and memory. As Robert L. Tener has asserted: "Set in the surrealistic theatre of the mind, her dramas are rich collages of ambiguities, metaphors, poetic insights, literary references, and mythic associations, all of which provide a dramatic form unique to Miss Kennedy."

PRINCIPAL WORKS

PLAYS

Funnyhouse of a Negro 1962
The Owl Answers 1963
A Rat's Mass 1966
The Lennon Play: In His Own Write [with John Lennon and
    Victor Spinetti] 1967
A Lesson in Dead Language 1968
A Beast Story 1969
Boats 1969
Sun: A Poem for Malcolm X Inspired by His Murder 1970
An Evening with Dead Essex 1973
A Movie Star Has to Star in Black and White 1976
Black Children's Day 1980
A Lancashire Lad 1980
Orestes and Electra 1980
The Ohio State Murders 1990

OTHER MAJOR WORKS

People Who Led to My Plays (memoir) 1987
In One Act (collection of plays) 1989
Deadly Triplets: A Theatre Mystery and Journal (novel
    and journal) 1990

AUTHOR COMMENTARY

Interview with Kennedy (1990)

SOURCE: *Intersecting Boundaries: The Theatre of Adrienne Kennedy*, edited by Paul K. Bryant-Jackson and Lois More Overbeck, University of Minnesota Press, 1992, pp. 3-12.

[*In the following interview, conducted in February 1990, Kennedy discusses the background, influences, and stylistic and thematic aspects of her plays.*]

[Adrienne Kennedy]: Joe [Chaikin] is . . . very important because when people had totally forgotten about me, in the mid-seventies, Joe was one of the people saying quite extravagant things about me, and working on my plays at his workshops. What he did with *Movie Star* [1976] was a

total moving image; it just never stopped moving. It was a masterpiece the way he did it.

[Lois More Overbeck]: *So it was choreography?*

No. It was the process of the Open Theater, Joe's troupe. . . . Joe and Michael Kahn, as far as I'm concerned, played the biggest role in keeping my morale up and for keeping my work in front of people throughout the seventies. Michael interested Juilliard in commissioning me.

What kind of a director was Michael Kahn with your work?

Very painstaking. And even as a very young director, he had phenomenal insight and vision.

Did you talk with him a great deal about the work?

We talked for two years. You know it took Edward Albee two years to produce **Funnyhouse.** So in those two years, Michael and I had plenty of time to discuss the play. There was really a base there.

We were very interested in the dramatization of Sarah, particularly because, in a sense, she stops speaking after the first third of the play, but she is still there, and she "speaks" through the other voices. What is Sarah doing when she is on stage even though she no longer has a speaking part?

Well that was one of the things that Michael worked on: what Sarah was going to be doing when she was not speaking. He anchored Sarah in her room.

In the transition from the Albee workshop production of **Funnyhouse** *to its production on the commercial stage, were you making changes?*

I had a script, an original script of **Funnyhouse.** And then when I went into the workshop at the Circle [in the Square], I (literally) took out the word "niggers." And I gave it to Michael. Then as it got closer to the production, he said, "Albee says you have another script, and that's the one we should do. You know, the script you handed in to get in the class." So I did the first one. After that the script remained exactly the same.

[Paul K. Bryant-Jackson]: *Do you think that . . . the interchange that you were having in the workshops affected the writing of* **The Owl Answers** *that you were doing at the time?*

No, I had already written *Owl Answers.*

[Overbeck]: *You do write about . . . the turning point at which you learned that you could take the many parts of the self and use them as characters. . . . In* **Owl Answers,** *characters are transformed by just stepping out of their costumes. We wanted to ask you more about the transforming of characters and metamorphosis.*

It's back to childhood—people turning into different people, different characters, feeling that you have a lot of characters inside of you, that's just so much a part of me. I've always been like that. I always just could very easily become a character in the movies or in a book.

What about the Duchess of Hapsburg?

You mean how did I choose her?

Is it as parallel to Queen Victoria?

No. Like most people, I have always been fascinated by royalty. Why are people royal? I mean, that just used to drive me out of my mind, you know. It's in **People Who Led to My Plays.** I saw the movie *Juarez*; it's about the Duchess of Hapsburg. Then my husband and I took a trip to Mexico and we saw Chapultepec Castle, where the Hapsburgs lived. Too, probably because Bette Davis had played her, she interested me.

It is interesting, though, that the Duchess of Hapsburg and Queen Victoria did preside with power that was based on colonization.

There are negative qualities about all of Sarah's personas, except Lumumba.

A working title for this collection of essays on your work is Transforming Margins.

Transforming is a great word.

[Bryant-Jackson]: *What about margins?*

Boundaries, I think boundaries is a good word, too. [To Paul:] I don't know what kind of black world you grew up in, . . . the kind I grew up in—I respected. But it really was a very rigid childhood. I wasn't allowed to speak, just arbitrarily; I had to speak when I was spoken to. I wasn't allowed to express what I was thinking. I had to say things that were correct in school and at home. So all these people were burning inside of me.

[Overbeck]: *We read in* **Deadly Triplets** *that you were writing a play called* **Cities in Bezique.** *But the bill done at the Public Theater was another play.*

Joe Papp commissioned me to write [a play]. It was called **Cities in Bezique.** I wrote it when I lived in London. It was horrible. And Joe, a very understanding person said, "Well, I don't really like the play very much. But I'd like to use the title." And he decided to do **The Owl Answers** and **A Beast's Story** and call it **Cities in Bezique.**

So you just abandoned the other play?

I trusted Joe. Joe likes writers. I have abandoned a lot of work: stories, novels, plays. I know that I am in fact working something out. It is not wasted.

The several manuscript versions of **A Beast's Story** *in the Archives of the Public Theater seem radically different from*

the one that was published.

It's because I changed it so. **A Beast's Story** was just a total failure, as far as I'm concerned (the writing, not the production). I just think that I never got the play right. When Samuel French said they wanted to publish it, I just took it and chopped it in two. I am never going to let it get republished.

Can you tell us about the production of **Rat's Mass** *at La Mama?*

It was a very big success. Seth Allen directed and Mary Alice and Gilbert Price were the leads. Then later Ellen Stewart wanted an opera of it.

[Bryant-Jackson]: *What became of the opera?*

It ran for six weeks. It had exquisite music that Cecil Taylor wrote. But it didn't work as an opera. It could have been, what do you call that—a cantata. I was never able to make a book out of it that fit the great music that Cecil composed.

[Overbeck]: *You did the libretto and he did the music?*

Yes.

You loved the music?

Oh, entirely. The guy is a genius.

What about the ballet you did for Jerome Robbins?

Jerome Robbins had something called Theatre Lab. And I was one of the first writers, I think, that he commissioned. He had liked **Funnyhouse.**

What did you write?

That's when I first started to try to write about Malcolm X. I never finished it. Also I went to live in England.

Tell us a bit more about **Sun.**

The Royal Court asked me to write a play. I had been working on some material from drawings of Leonardo da Vinci. And that's how I wrote **Sun.**

Your style is poetic—almost like a concerto, and the visual elements are so complex. Now, under the spell of performance art, perhaps there is a much more ready acceptance of this kind of theatrical performance.

[Bryant-Jackson]: *One of the things I really admire when I look at your work from a theatrical sense [is that] your plays demand a new acting approach. A lot of people are involved with method acting, and with realistic plays the method works very well—allows you time to prepare the necessary emotional transitions. But in your plays, emotional transitions often come back to back, and so you have to go somewhere else in terms of your ability to become that character.*

I see.

And I think, it was really groundbreaking in 1964, in the sense that on many levels, the acting style had to catch up to the form.

You are making me remember what Joe Chaikin used to talk about. He worked with Robbie [McCauley] on the monologues in the Winter Project, to explore them.

[Overbeck]: *Did you see the Paris production of* **Funnyhouse**?

I saw a rehearsal of it.

Was the play quite different in French?

Jean-Marie Serreau put the play in a very small area. Serreau was one of France's great directors. He had a wonderful troupe.

There was a dominating white sculpture of Queen Victoria, and otherwise the set seemed very black. How did he direct "Sarah"?

He wanted her to be still. . . . Serreau loved my writing so much. And he talked about it intensely. And when I met Jean-Louis Barrault, he kissed my hand. [Laughter.]

You must have been pleased. To have your work translated—

Funnyhouse had already been on Radio Denmark and the BBC.

Were you pleased with the BBC production?

Oh sure, because Emlyn Williams narrated it.

How could it be on the radio without the visual elements?

He read the stage directions.

[Bryant-Jackson]: *When you teach playwriting, you have the students keep a journal of their dreams, which is different from a daily journal. May I ask why?*

Oh, I just have the students do things that I did over the years. I kept a dream journal for years.

[Overbeck]: *You have said that* **Rat's Mass** *came out of a dream.*

Definitely. That's in that article, "A Growth of Images." That was one of the strongest dreams I ever had, on a train from Paris to Rome.

[Bryant-Jackson]: *As the world changes, how does it impact upon the vision of writers, the playwriting student, perhaps yourself?*

I have been more haunted and obsessed in recent years with how the media treats blacks. I think I am even more con-

cerned about that than, say, the Berlin Wall. I'm interested in the Berlin Wall, but on a different level. What I am interested in right now is how in the media, blacks have become very much identified with drugs and a lot of negative things, and I don't remember that being [so] in the forties or fifties or the sixties. I am really worried about that. I don't know how that happened. The average black family is hardworking and has a very high morality.

Don't you think that there is an agenda; that is to say, there has to be a relationship between negative portrayal of blacks in the media and how the power structure wants them to be perceived?

I totally agree. Yes, I certainly do.

How then do you look at someone like Spike Lee?

I am glad that Spike Lee was smart enough to make his movies. I am glad that he was smart enough to see a place for himself. I think that as a black person in America, you almost have to force yourself on society.

[Overbeck]: *It is not enough to believe in yourself and what you do?*

I think you have to feel, always, that there is a resistance to you. There is a resistance, and it is never going to let up. It never lets up. I feel that quite strongly. That any black person has to fight twice as hard to achieve anything.

How did you come to write **An Evening with Dead Essex**?

I read about Mark Essex in *Time* magazine, and I just got very interested in this quiet little guy who went berserk and shot those people.

Did you see him as a victim of the culture?

A victim and a hero. . . .

When did you write the play?

About 1973.

You saw that all these feelings were working inside of him, and then he just exploded?

Yes, I feel tremendous rage against American society. I feel like Mark Essex. I *still* feel that.

[Bryant-Jackson]: *I think every African-American person feels like that from time to time.*

[Overbeck]: *Is it a play trying to get at the essence of Essex?*

We only knew him from the newspaper.

The newsclips?

Yes, the news photographs, [interviews with] his mother. A

lot of people liked Mark Essex around that time [1973].

[Bryant-Jackson]: *They knew where he was coming from.*

Yes.

[Overbeck]: *Gaby Rodgers directed the play in New York, and Robert Brustein produced the play at Yale?*

Yes.

[Overbeck]: *What happened with that production?*

It didn't work on a big stage. It had worked down in the bottom of the American Place Theatre because it was a rehearsal hall, and the play took place in a rehearsal hall. But when we put it on at Yale Repertory Theatre, it didn't work.

[Bryant-Jackson]: *In our conversation, you mentioned James Baldwin?*

I liked him a lot. . . . He used his writing like bullets. And his essays meant so much to me when I read them. His essays filled in a lot of gaps . . . issues I was struggling with.

What about **Lancashire Lad***? That seems to be very charming. I would love to see it.*

Oh, that was wonderful. I took sections of Chaplin's autobiography and, made a theatre piece out of it. It was totally charming. But Lady Chaplin didn't want us to continue with the material.

Could you tell us about **Black Children's Day***?*

George Bass asked me to come up and live at Brown for a year to see if I could write a play. That's how ***Black Children's Day*** came about. He wanted me to write about the history of blacks in Rhode Island. The play is about these children on a Sunday in May—Children's Day. It attempts to use the history of Rhode Island. I was told there were slave tunnels under Providence. The children put on a pageant of black history, and, at the same time, . . . there is a bombing that occurs in the city. It's too melodramatic. I'm not sure I'd go back to it. I never quite got the language right. But George liked it.

[Overbeck]: *You don't have an interest yourself in working more on it?*

No.

It seems that you were not completely satisfied with much of the writing that was commissioned.

That's not true. I was happy with ***Electra*** and ***Orestes*** at Juilliard and the Chaplin piece. And I'm happy with ***The Ohio State Murders*** that I am writing for Jerry Freedman at the Great Lakes Theater Festival.

When you work on a commission, do you feel you are writing for someone else instead of yourself?

No. I feel it's a challenge. It's a good discipline to have something finished at a certain time, and I'm often getting into a different world. For example, I lived in Providence for a year.

You are immersing yourself in a different place?

Yes.

In **Deadly Triplets,** *you say that you were always writing sketches. Do you think that the sense of the moment and of the scene is innate to your writing? There seems to be nuance and complexity suggested in a few strokes, always implying that there is more to be seen.*

I think that's the way I see life. I'm just haunted by billions of scenes and they are indelible.

[Bryant-Jackson]: *Do you think that is why, often in your plays, you have the scene go to black so that we might have that focus with the blackout on another scene?*

Maybe, I don't know. That's great. I see, sure. That *is* how I experience it. Yes, that is true.

[Overbeck]: *In cinematographic terms, it would be like the switching of the camera eye.*

That's right. But I *don't* experience things (it took me a long time to understand) like a Victorian novel.

That is very important, the way of seeing—

I do see black things all around scenes. It's true, it's really true. [Laughter.] And we're back to the movies again?

[Bryant-Jackson]: *What about the scenes of childhood that you write about in* **People Who Led to My Plays,** *the* Now, Voyager *home?*

I always saw rooms. My family existed in scenes, very vivid scenes. . . . I often saw our family, [as] if they were in a play. (I wasn't that aware of that until maybe about ten years ago.)

[Overbeck]: *With regard to "scenes," what was the influence of movies, especially French movies?*

I saw French movies when I was a teenager. When I was in high school—a lot of kids took French. I never did. But my friends who took French would take me to these movies. And that is when I first saw *Children of Paradise* and *Devil in the Flesh.*

Because you didn't speak French, do you think that you concentrated on the images in these films?

Perhaps. However, those movies were great. There were subject matters, too, that I had never seen necessarily in American movies. I couldn't articulate it, but they were dealing with things I had never thought of. Later it was Fellini and Bergman.

Which Bergman?

Through a Glass Darkly, Wild Strawberries, . . . Antonioni's *L'Avventura.* They gave a validity to what I thought, because these were people in another country.

You said that you lived in your imagination; did you feel different as a child?

I don't think I felt different from my family at all. I was very proud of my family, because my father was in the newspaper a lot. I was very proud of my mother because she was so pretty. I loved my childhood friends. I never felt different.

. . . My parents were *very* interested in me. Now that I have raised two children, I really see that. They really did *so* many things for me. They were so interested that I did feel sometimes that I was strangled. It was very typical of that time.

[Bryant-Jackson]: *I remember that my sister and I would sort of hide and watch our parents and their friends when they had parties and club meetings. Did you do that too?*

Oh, sure.

That reminds me of Paula Gidding's book [When and Where I Enter], *and that whole club movement that she talks about which is absolutely integral to African-American women's interaction with each other and society.*

Yes, they had so many clubs.

The bridge club was my personal favorite. What was your personal favorite?

I liked the bridge club also. I watched my mother *preparing* for it. I liked the dishes, the bridge club tablecloths, the phone ringing, and what they all wore. What they served. That was thrilling, truly thrilling. There is a trilogy in that somewhere. [Laughter.] Those people truly fascinate me. I've never been able to capture those people. I admire those people very much, that generation. Most of them are dead now. [To Paul] . . . Don't you admire these people? They are fabulous people.

Of course. They were wonderful, with their clubs and their sororities.

And their formal dances. I don't think that's reached literature, yet, do you? I wish I could write a book about those women. They were perfectionists. They were raising children. They seemed to do very well as wives. They played all those roles.

And they even had time for everyone else's kids.

Yes, they had a lot of time for their neighbor's kids. There

was something about the values of that time. It wasn't just middle-class blacks. It was in American society. These people were working all the time . . . my parents' friends. The wife was either a social worker or a teacher, mostly a teacher. She was working. These people were keeping black culture alive. And they were forging ahead financially at the same time. They were doing both. And that is what is so amazing.

[Overbeck]: *Often in looking at your work, people notice the repetition—*

I think that is the spirituals. I love them.

[Bryant-Jackson]: *You have said that your neighborhood was both black and European.*

My piano teacher was from Warsaw. . . . And Mt. Pleasant was mainly Italian and black, but there were people from all the central European countries. Most of the teachers had been born in Europe. I only had one black teacher, Miss Shook.

[Overbeck]: *There was a great sense that education was the way to a better life?*

We all seemed to have that.

Your expectations?

Tremendous expectations.

[Bryant-Jackson]: *Wasn't [it] also a part of the African-American experience (one of the things that you bring out in **People Who Led to My Plays***) that you were "forced" to be bicultural?*

Oh Yes. You were forced, oh, definitely. But there was tremendous respect for DuBois and Langston Hughes. . . . So it wasn't one-sided.

[Overbeck]: *Your culture was rich—*

Yes. My parents went to those southern schools—Morehouse, Atlanta University—these had a tremendous effect. And they took us to the concerts and banquets. They were involved in achievement, black achievement.

As a young woman with two young children, writing as intensely as you were—how did you do this?

As people have remarked over the years, I am a very determined person. And so, I just stayed up late at night, and I was always tired. And the miracle is that my children . . . love my work; they are proud of it. I also feel as if I owe everything to my former husband, Joe Kennedy. He read everything I wrote; he was always encouraging me. He was always talking about the possibilities of things. There is no way I could have done it without him. Because he is the person that released me from this image of myself as simply somebody who might teach the second grade. [Laughter.] It was very important.

How do you see your work changing?

I don't know. I really don't. And I think that's important, that I not know. I always think I am not going to write another word. I don't have anything planned. I don't have any plans at all.

OVERVIEWS AND GENERAL STUDIES

Susan E. Meigs (essay date 1990)

SOURCE: "No Place but the Funnyhouse: The Struggle for Identity in Three Adrienne Kennedy Plays," in *Modern American Drama: The Female Canon,* edited by June Schlueter, Fairleigh Dickinson University Press, 1990, pp. 172-83.

[*In the following essay, Meigs addresses the "damaged social identity" of black Americans as presented in Kennedy's plays* Funnyhouse of a Negro, The Owl Answers, *and* A Movie Star Has to Star in Black and White.]

> I know no places. That is I cannot believe in places. To believe in places is to know hope and to know the emotion of hope is to know beauty. It links us across a horizon and connects us to the world. I find there are no places only my *funnyhouse.*
>
> —Adrienne Kennedy, *Funnyhouse of a Negro*

In 1960, while dramatists were forging a rhetoric of black theater from the emerging black power movement, twenty-nine-year-old Adrienne Kennedy travelled to Africa with her husband and son. The trip would prove to be the catalyst for her career as one of America's most complex contemporary playwrights. At the time of her trip, Kennedy had been writing stories and plays for nearly ten years and had received virtually no public attention. Her failure to establish herself as a writer was made more discouraging by the recognition her husband Joseph Kennedy received for his work in social psychology at Columbia. She felt increasingly that she "was just accompanying another person as he lived out his dreams" and that she had acquiesced "to another person's desires, dreams and hopes." As she struggled to maintain her identity as a black woman author and attempted to invest herself in the Western literary tradition she embraced, Kennedy grew conscious of a buried African heritage. Africa opened to her a world of black artists and leaders, like Congo Prime Minister Patrice Lumumba, to match and challenge the Western literary figures and rulers she admired. The conflict between these two ancestral traditions would become one of the primary themes in Kennedy's complex, surrealistic psychodramas.

Although her rhetoric maintains a political agenda, albeit one aimed more at expressing black women's struggles, Kennedy's method draws from the mythic elements of traditional African ritual drama, particularly the Kuntu form described by Paul Carter Harrison. Ritual drama empowers its participants as they negotiate their roles within its theatrical community. Kennedy discovered, however, that these roles, designated like those in many black protest groups by men, fail to allow female participants self-determination. This dissonance in the fragmented black family/community impedes the collective expression of harmony required of ritual theater. "Having been fractionalized, [the black American's] rituals are often played out in a spiritual vacuum, [her] energies dissipated without the generative feedback of a stable society" [Paul Harrison, in *The Drama of Nommo,* 1972]. Kennedy's plays address the cultural and political fragmentation of black Americans that occurs when a dominant (white) social structure interrupts efforts to construct a black community.

Kennedy uses this damaged social identity in her plays as a symptom of the deeper psychological fragmentation black women suffer. Kennedy particularly uses the mask, a traditional symbol of power and mystery, as a device to develop what Michael Goldman calls "the double movement of dramatic elation—both escape from self and self-discovery" [*The Actor's Freedom: Toward a Theory of Drama,* 1975]. Kennedy undermines this empowerment and elation, however, and transforms the mask into an image of imprisonment and terror. Many of her characters become trapped in the mask's freakish impersonality and are unable either to discover themselves fully or to escape from the horrifying selves they do discover.

In three of Kennedy's plays, *Funnyhouse of a Negro* (1964), *The Owl Answers* (1965), and *A Movie Star Has to Star in Black and White* (1976), the protagonists are black women who fail to unite the fragmented elements of their identities into harmonic, dynamic wholes. Their equally fragmented communities have failed to provide them with the ritual means for locating themselves and have made them feel guilty for recognizing the extra measure of alienation assigned to black women. These characters represent the community of women, largely excluded from the political mechanisms of black protest, who are nonetheless expected to sacrifice gender issues for racial concerns. In these three one-act plays, Kennedy exposes how black Americans, especially women, having been denied a social context and history, are therefore powerless to resolve the chaotic elements of their black female identities.

In *Funnyhouse of a Negro,* Sarah seeks to find herself among four historical figures who share her voice: Queen Victoria, the Duchess of Hapsburg, Jesus, and Patrice Lumumba. Although she lives in a brownstone with her Jewish boyfriend, she mentally inhabits the expressionistic settings suggested by these figures. After her mad mother introduces the play's action, Sarah and her selves confront her fear that her father will find and rape her as he did her mulatto mother. She imagines his various fates, including one in which she bludgeons him with an ebony mask. Herself a mulatto, Sarah's conflicting racial histories are illustrated but never resolved by the figures that serve as her masks. Far from empowering her, these character masks trap Sarah in a role of self-hatred, fear, and the inability to integrate her personality that leads to her suicide.

Kennedy introduces the mask motif in the play's first sequence. Sarah's mad mother passes before the closed curtain wearing an eyeless yellow mask that renders her not only blind but faceless. She gropes across the stage in a dreamlike state we later learn is death, separated from the "life" of the play only by the rat-eaten shroud of a white stage curtain. She carries before her a bald head, an image of weakness that recurs as Sarah's selves lose their wild, kinky hair throughout the play. Although Kennedy later introduces a bald head that drops and hangs from the ceiling to indicate the martyrdom of Christ and Lumumba, the baldness of Victoria and the Duchess is more "hideous" and frightening because it links them to Sarah's dead mother. For Sarah, baldness indicates not only death but also a life of repulsion, vulnerability, and madness. As her female selves lose their hair, the threat of her father's return, of a confrontation with her irreconcilable blackness, grows imminent. Unable to cope with the jungle's darkness, Sarah attempts to hide herself in a white city.

Kennedy's plays address the cultural and political fragmentation of black Americans that occurs when a dominant (white) social structure interrupts efforts to construct a black community.

—Susan E. Meigs

During the course of the play, two historical characters who represent her white heritage assume Sarah's psychological narrative. These alter egos, Queen Victoria and the Duchess of Hapsburg, also wear white, expressionless death masks and are cast in a strong white light that contrasts with the stage's unnatural darkness. These other selves express Sarah's thoughts while the connotations of their historical identities comment on them. The sense of power and authority evoked by the two European rulers cannot be appropriated properly by Sarah, who is neither white nor black. Their imperialistic implications comment on the extent of Sarah's psychological oppression, one history a victim of the other. Nonetheless, she spends her days writing poetry that imitates Edith Sitwell's and dreaming of living in a white, European culture. She attempts to efface her black heritage not only by "killing" her father but by injecting herself into white society. She claims to need these white figures "as an embankment to keep me from reflecting too much upon the fact that I am a Negro. For, like all educated Negroes . . . I find it necessary to maintain a stark fortress against recognition of myself." The expressionless masks of the two rulers serve both to identify an aspect of Sarah's historical identity and to alienate her from it. In the play's final scene, Sarah is discovered hanging from the ceiling of her "funnyhouse" as the lights come up on the white plaster statue of Queen Victoria. Enshrined in Sarah's room, she is finally reduced to a voiceless, immobile image of "astonishing repulsive whiteness." When Sarah dies, the masked figures that have given body to her voice are stripped of their narrative power. They become hollowed references to a history that is finally unavailable to Sarah.

The persona of Patrice Lumumba, whom Sarah both adopts and associates with her father, differs from the first two in that he is black and carries rather than wears his ebony mask. Because Lumumba acts as a bridge between Sarah and her father, he represents both the black man's noble efforts to save his race and her inescapable and damning blackness. Lumumba, murdered by African radicals who smashed his skull, appears in the play with a split and bleeding head. At one point, as Sarah explains how she killed her father, she confuses him with Lumumba: "No, Mrs. Conrad, he did not hang himself, that is only the way they understood it, they do, but the truth is that I bludgeoned his head with an ebony skull that he carries about with him. Wherever he goes, he carries out black masks and heads." Sarah's previous statements about her desires to integrate into white society are repudiated by an unidentified black man who recalls Lumumba because he too carries his mask: "I am a nigger of two generations. I am Patrice Lumumba. . . . I am the black shadow that haunted my mother's conception. . . . It is my vile dream to live in rooms with European antiques and my statue of Queen Victoria."

Because Sarah is a mulatto, she cannot wear the masks of both the Negro and the white woman simultaneously. As the mask signifies the character's fragmented identity, the mulatto bastard becomes a metaphor for the black woman's alienation from her gender and her race. Sarah attempts to reconcile her identity as a mulatto by claiming to have murdered her black father. She is unable to conceal her hatred of him for literally blackening her family. Sarah conflates her story with his story as she recalls how her grandmother encouraged her father to become a black Messiah. Sarah believes he betrayed her wish and his future family by marrying a light-toned woman with "hair as straight as any white woman's." His mother "hoped he would be Christ but he failed. He had married [Sarah's] mother because he could not resist the light. Yet, his mother from the beginning in the kerosene lamp of their dark rooms in Georgia said, 'I want you to be Jesus, to walk in Genesis and save the race, return to Africa, find revelation in the black.'" To fulfill his mother's vision, he takes his white wife to Africa to pursue mission work. There she "falls out of live" with him and slowly goes mad, symbolized by her gradual hair loss. He rapes her when she denies him access to the marriage bed because he is black and creates a legacy of violence, madness, and failure for their daughter Sarah. "Forgiveness for my being black, Sarah. I *know* you are a child of torment. . . . *Forgive my blackness!*" her father pleads. But Sarah can neither accept nor escape her own blackness: "before I was born," she laments, "he haunted my conception, diseased my birth."

Sarah seeks to neutralize her blackness by living with her white boyfriend, Raymond Mann, whom she wishes she could love but doesn't, in an apartment run by a white landlady, Mrs. Conrad. These two white characters in Sarah's "funnyhouse" are modelled after the looming clown-like figures that guard an amusement park in Kennedy's hometown, Cleveland. The set for the scene in which Raymond and the Duchess of Hapsburg engage in a bizarre exchange includes a backdrop of mirrors, revealed only as Raymond alternately opens and closes the blinds that conceal them. The flashing mirrors recall the disorienting nightmare quality of what is ironically called a funnyhouse. Raymond and Mrs. Conrad laugh, in accordance with their roles as funnyhouse guards, at Sarah's bewilderment and failure to distinguish herself from her historical reflections. They mock her attempts to gain self-knowledge and control over the conflicting elements of her persona. When she is unable to do so, Sarah hangs herself. After discovering her body, Mrs. Conrad and Raymond suggest that Sarah's father is not dead but lives in a white suburb with a white prostitute. He and his "whore" join the other white characters in the funnyhouse who, in refusing to understand or sympathize with Sarah's internal struggle, derive ironic amusement from her desperate suicide. "She was a funny little liar," Raymond comments as he observes her hanging figure. Mrs. Conrad can only offer the unsympathetic remark, "The poor bitch has hung herself!" Sarah, ultimately powerless to reconcile and integrate her conflicting selves and incongruent historical narratives, chooses to abandon the white funnyhouse. That Sarah recognizes no escape other than suicide testifies to the insidiousness of her tragedy. Unable to move beyond feebly articulating her oppression, Sarah can neither appropriate the power of her masks, as Harrison might suggest, nor follow the mandate of Amiri Baraka's militant theater to create white-free spaces for blacks. To excise her whiteness would leave Sarah vulnerable to a terrifying blackness she cannot control.

Kennedy continues to explore the fragmented psyche of the female mulatto in *The Owl Answers*. Rather than function as mouthpieces for a single character's states of mind, however, the play's characters are each composed of multiple personae with a common voice. As the stage directions indicate, "The characters change slowly back and forth into and out of themselves, leaving some garment from their previous selves upon them always to remind us of the nature of SHE WHO IS CLARA PASSMORE WHO IS THE VIRGIN MARY WHO IS THE BASTARD WHO IS THE OWL's world."

Like Sarah, Clara Passmore is the bastard product of an illicit relationship between "The Richest White Man in Town" and his black cook. After her mother dies, probably in childbirth, the cold Reverend and Mrs. Passmore adopt her. When her legitimate father dies and Clara is barred from the funeral, she travels instead to England to claim his British heritage. There she confronts three representatives of that heritage, Shakespeare, Chaucer, and William the Conqueror, who deny her access to it. Theirs is a white male tradition that finds little space for black women. Clara envisions her Negro heritage as a father, incarcerated and executed by the three masked figures, whose peeling white skin reveals a deeper, darker skin color. Clara's characterization of herself as "the ancestor of somebody that cooked for somebody and William the Conqueror" further illustrates the conflict between her English heritage and the black ancestry it seeks to suppress. In the course of the play, her Dead Father, the white father who never acknowledged her as his child, encourages her to repudiate her

"blackness": "He came to me in the outhouse . . . He told me you are an owl, ow, oww, I am your beginning, ow. You belong here with us owls in the fig tree, not to somebody that cooks for your Goddam Father."

Goddam Father is concomitantly the Richest White Man in the Town, the Dead White Father, and the Reverend Passmore. Through her association with the Reverend Passmore and his "Holy Baptist church on the top of the hill," She Who is Clara Passmore . . . becomes (the Virgin) Mary, to whom an altar is built in the course of the play. "The Reverend's Wife goes on building the High Altar with owl feathers, prays, builds, prays, stops, holds out her hand to She, puts up candles, puts up owl feathers, laughs, puts more candles on the High Altar." The altar becomes a bed upon which a Negro Man attempts to seduce She. . . . In the final moments of the play, "They are upon the burning High Altar. He tried to force her down, yet at the same time he is frightened by her. The Dead Father who has been holding the candles, smiles." Despite his attempts to "whiten" She. . . , he laughs in cruel recognition of her inability to be completely the mulatto bastard or Clara, the adopted daughter of the Reverend Passmore, the pure Virgin Mary, or the white "owl" of her (fore)fathers. She. . . is all and none of these. She. . . cannot conceal from the Negro Man who seduces her that underneath her clothing her body is black; yet one of the figures with which she is affiliated is Anne Boleyn, a white historical figure imprisoned and executed by a white patriarchy.

Representing that patriarchy, Chaucer, Shakespeare, and William the Conqueror wear masks that not only serve to identify them but allow them to oppress in anonymity. The mystery and power of the Kuntu mask is reserved for members of the white patriarchy and those complicit in it, who use its power to dominate and suppress the black and the woman. She . . . 's vision of a white history imprisoning and dismantling her black identity in the form of her Negro Father shatters her dreams of "love" and freedom from the internal conflict this domination creates.

> They took him away and would not let me see him. They who are my Black Mother and my Goddam Father locked me in the fig tree and took his body away and his white hair hung down.
>
> Now they, my Black Mother and my Goddam Father who pretend to be Chaucer, Shakespeare, and Eliot and all my beloved English, come to my cell and stare and I can see they despise me and I despise them . . .
>
> From my tower I keep calling and the only answer is the Owl, God. I am only yearning for our kingdom, God.

Kennedy's use of bird imagery is most poignant in her characterization of She. . . as the Owl. In contrast to the play's haunting raven and God's white dove, the owl can see through the darkness that empowers it. But for Clara, the silence of the darkness and of the owl's world undermines its power. Although She. . . struggles to define her own historical and psychological space, the play's surrealistic dreamscapes merge. Clara stands at the base of St. Paul's Chapel as she confronts a seducer on the subway platform, as she perches in the fig tree. She rebuffs the Negro Man on the burning high altar/bed with a knife covered in the owl's blood and feathers, which are her own. As she burns on Mary's altar, her feathers fly like the pages of her journal, and her silence is broken only by the echoes of the owl's unanswerable question "Ow . . . oww" whooo?

In *A Movie Star Has to Star in Black and White,* Kennedy complicates the issue of masks and personae by incorporating movie stars who don the masks of film roles. This multiplicity of personae is emphasized and heightened as the film characters become mouthpieces for the protagonist, Clara, at the same time they constitute her personal history for the audience. Clara's characterization occurs through a complex and often ironic system of projections and transferences of voice and symbolic significations. Her internal monologues and dialogues are prompted by her brother Wally's near fatal accident that serves to reunite her with her divorced parents. Clara's own marital conflicts over her desire for a career as a writer and her husband Eddie's desire to pursue his academic career at Columbia while Clara raises their expanding family (she is carrying Eddie's child) are examined in light of her parents' failed marriage.

Clara's concerns are voiced by the movie stars Bette Davis, Jean Peters, and Shelley Winters, whose film characters and narratives in their respective films *Voyage Out, Viva Zapata,* and *A Place in the Sun* are superimposed on Clara's own narrative. The play takes on the dimensions and properties of the "well-made" Hollywood movie in the opening scene, in which the Columbia Pictures Lady appears in a brilliant light to introduce the "film's" stars and sets. The story is Clara's, but she plays only a bit part. Her perceptions and reflections make up the plot, yet the film characters who give them voice separate her from them.

As playwright or, rather, screenplay writer, Clara seeks to write/right the script of her life so that she may play a more active, starring role in it than mere spectator. She works to activate the desires she records in her diary and to construct a unifying narrative from the pieces of her voice that have been distributed among the female movie stars. Clara suppresses her desire to construct a coherent self that can "coexist in a true union" with other selves, however, by casting herself as an "angel of mercy" in her parents' marriage. Displaced from her own narrative and unable to dispel her fear that she will miscarry, as she did in her first pregnancy, Clara projects her despair onto her parents. Blaming herself for not being able to unify them, Clara laments her failure:

> When I came among them it seems to me I did not bring them peace . . . but made them more disconsolate. The crosses they bore always made me sad.

> The one reality I wanted never came true . . . to be their angel of mercy to unite them.

Bette Davis voices these reflections on the ship set of *Voyage Out.* In the film, her character achieves a fulfilling transformation on her voyage, a bleak contrast to Clara's attempt to transform her (family's) life by journeying into her parents' past. As Bette Davis, Clara pores over her father's scrapbook and discovers her parents' journey of transformation. Their trip takes them from the rural, segregated South, where whites live on one side of the town and blacks on the other, to a more "progressive" Cincinnati. There, Clara's father becomes active in community work and receives a commendation from the city's mayor for his seven years of work on the New Settlement for the Negro community. His achievements in the North, like those of Bette Davis's character, however, are fleeting and ultimately unsatisfying. After an unsuccessful suicide attempt, he leaves Clara and her mother, returns to Georgia, and marries "a girl who talked to willow trees." He tells Clara that he left her "yellow bastard" mother because she wouldn't accompany him back to Georgia and because she thought herself superior to him. "You know Mr. Harrison raised her like a white girl, and your mother, mark my word, thinks she's better than me."

Her father's effort to escape the racial oppression of Georgia, like Clara's own attempt to reconstitute her family in her memories, like Bette Davis's character's attempt to maintain her transformed self in the face of her mother's neuroses, fails and leads to greater despair. Not only does Clara fail to unify her parents, she is unsuccessful in redeeming herself as harmonizer in her own marriage. The affirmation of the marriage union in the *Viva Zapata* wedding night scene, which is superimposed on the *Voyage Out* set, is ironically juxtaposed to the confrontations between Clara's parents and between her and Eddie. These marital conflicts are deviations from the Hollywood norm, epitomized in the union of Jean Peters's femininity and Marlon Brando's virility. Neither Clara's parents nor she and Eddie are able to live up to the social roles designated by the masks of Peters and Brando's characters.

While Clara suffers the weight of her own guilt, her mother believes that by failing to please her husband she contributed to the dissolution of her daughter's family. She urges Clara to return to Eddie because she is pregnant, despite Clara's insistence that Eddie does not understand her. Like Eddie, Clara's mother cannot understand how her desire to be a writer can supersede the desire to raise a family:

> MOTHER. Your family's not together and you don't seem happy. . . .

> CLARA. I'm very happy mother. Very. I've just won an award and I'm going to have a play produced. I'm very happy. . . .

> MOTHER. When you grow up in boarding school like I did, the thing you dream of most is to see your children together with their families.

> CLARA. Mother you mustn't think I'm unhappy because I am, I really am, very happy.

> MOTHER. I just pray you'll soon get yourself together and make some decisions about your life. I pray for you every night. Shouldn't you go back to Eddie especially since you're pregnant?

Clara is trapped by social values that prove insufficient for expressing her identity as a black woman author. Because she and her mother cannot live up to white or black social expectations, they suffer for abdicating their designated roles as mother and wife.

Because the only roles that are available to Clara are those fashioned by a white patriarchy in Hollywood or a black patriarchy in New York, she initially accepts Jean Peters's role of self-sacrificing wife. She suppresses her awareness of its repressiveness and berates herself for not properly wearing its mask. Clara is finally unable to justify playing the role that provides her with so little satisfaction when she becomes increasingly aware of its "darkness" and her resulting "floating anxiety." Because he relies on Clara to continue playing her proper role, however, Eddie is suspicious of her "obsession to be a writer" and dismisses it as unrealistic and unnecessary.

Nevertheless, despite her family's objection, Clara shifts the focus of her unifying efforts from her parents and her marriage to herself and works to unite her fractured and diffused self through her writings. Whereas Clara plays only a bit part in the play's narrative, she exerts some of the constructive power of the mask when she exchanges her wifely mask for that of the writer. Although her social environment forces her to choose between the two, she finally attempts to invest herself fully in the role that allows her the most power and fulfillment. Scattered throughout the play are excerpts from the play she is writing, which is Kennedy's play, **The Owl Answers.** As Jean Peters, Clara explains to her film husband Marlon Brando, "It's about a girl who turns into an Owl. Ow. (*Recites from her writings.*) He came to me in the outhouse, in the fig tree. He told me, 'You are an owl, I am your beginning.' I call God and the Owl answers. It haunts my tower, calling." Following this description, Clara's slightly drunk father staggers toward her and her mother and rushes out of the hospital lobby where they have been waiting to see Wally. The image of the owl that represents the protagonist's white ancestry in Kennedy's earlier play is juxtaposed in *A Movie Star* to her black father, her "goddam father," who fails in the white northern city and retreats to the South. Although Clara's family and film stars silence and mask her, she hopes to voice publicly and thus resolve her despair by writing a play about it.

This desire to achieve self-actualization is represented by the character Shelley Winters portrays in *A Place in the Sun.* For Kennedy, Winters's role depicts the "essence of longing," a longing that persists throughout the last third of the play. Clara's desire for fulfillment is transposed onto Shelley Winters's character. None of the actresses takes on the role of Clara, although they voice her thoughts and feelings; the voice is Clara's. Nonetheless, the resonances of their characters and films are superimposed onto Clara's narrative in such a way that they simultaneously comment on it. The stage reflects the layering of characters and plots in that the "fantasy" sets and actors from the three films

Front cover for Kennedy's Obie Award-winning play.

remain on stage alongside the corresponding "realistic" sets of the hospital lobby, Wally's hospital room, and Clara's old room from childhood. Clara's longing to act out her life in these secure movie sets is mirrored in Shelley Winters's obsessive desire for Montgomery Clift in *A Place in the Sun.* In the final moments of the play, a union of character and voice occurs when Clara and Winters speak in harmony about Wally's hopeless prognosis. Almost immediately following this union, however, Shelley Winters falls into the water on which her "dark" boat has been floating and drowns while Montgomery Clift looks helplessly on. That she can only call silently for help signifies the fleeting and precarious power of the theatrical/literary mask through which Clara tries to express her "floating anxiety."

The voicelessness of Montgomery Clift and the other male stars, Paul Henreid and Marlon Brando, indicates their inappropriateness as voices for Clara's identity. She cannot speak through them, and they cannot speak for or with her because she rejects them, finds them inaccessible. In her mental narrative, Clara does attempt to give voice to the play's most significant silent male, her brother Wally, around whom the play's surface action revolves. His silence not only is a result of his paralyzing accident but is noticeable particularly when he returns from duty on the German front in World War II. As Clara recalls,

Once I asked you romantically when you came back to the United States on a short leave, how do you like Europe Wally? You were silent. Finally you said, I get into a lot of fights with the Germans. You stared at me. And got up and went into the dining room to the dark sideboard and got a drink.

Later, in the persona of Jean Peters, Clara reveals that Wally was court-martialed for a crime he committed in the army in Germany. "He won't talk about it," she says. "I went to visit him in the stockade." Her description of his shaven head and "vein that runs down his forehead" recalls his appearance in the hospital bed. She describes his successive failures to become an Olympic athlete: "I'm a failure he said. I can't make it in those schools. I'm tired. He suddenly joined the army." Because of his lack of education, Wally cannot even appropriate the literary tools that represent his sister's hope for self-fulfillment. His wife graduates cum laude while he is a prisoner in the army stockade. Only by being silenced, or rather silencing himself, in an automobile accident, that renders him brain dead does Wally finally avoid the madness of coping not with a surplus of voices and roles but with a lack of viable identities.

In the postscript to her *People Who Led to My Plays,* Kennedy states that "my plays are meant to be states of mind." These states of mind not only are her own but belong to her entire race of "Negroes," whom she characterizes as "underdogs, and underdogs must fight in life." In these plays, Kennedy exposes the barriers black women face in their struggle for power, voice, and unity. The double binds of race and gender produce the black anguish that afflicts the plays' protagonists. The roles that the white and black communities offer these women, like the masks they wear, threaten to silence them and efface their identities in a miasma of conflicting historical connotations.

Written during the black protest movements of the seventies, these plays evolved in the ideological space between the agitprop theater of Amiri Baraka and the ritual drama of Paul Carter Harrison. Although Kennedy recognized the political power of Harrison's theater to revitalize the black community spiritually and of Baraka's to incite it to militant protest, she cut to a deeper level of psychological oppression. Her plays reveal the disorientation and despair of black women who can find no other space for themselves but the funnyhouse.

An excerpt from *Deadly Triplets: A Theatre Mystery and Journal*

When I joined Albee's workshop, January 1962, I submitted my play *Funnyhouse of a Negro* as a writing sample to get into the class. You were to mail or bring your play to the Circle-in-the-Square. My husband took it down to Bleeker Street on his way to work. He relayed a message that a secretary had said that the people who would be selected to be in the class would soon receive a phone call. Finally after several weeks someone called. He said his name was Michael Kahn. "Edward Albee liked your play very much, you have been selected to be in the workshop." There were about thirteen of us that went up the long dark steps to the room above the Circle.

Albee was wearing a tweed suit and seemed shy and frightened. In a muted voice he read from his notes about what our playwriting class was to consist of. Each person was required to have a play done in workshop. Outside the wind blew the Circle-in-the-Square sign which still hangs there today. He invited the class to a rehearsal of the *Sandbox* at the Cherry Lane. During that rehearsal he went up on the stage and quietly spoke to the actors; there was a hole in his sweater, it gave him the air of a struggling writer. Michael Kahn was the Circle's brilliant young director. It was his job to cast the workshop productions. My play was to be in April. Michael had mentioned the possible casting of Diana Sands, Yaphet Kotto, and others. But during the winter, I became frightened. My play seemed far too revealing and much to my own shock, I had used the word "nigger" throughout the text. I decided to drop out of the class.

I arrived early at what I thought would be my last class. Since the workshop productions had started, the class had moved down into the theatre. Edward Albee was in the theatre alone.

"Mr. Albee," I said, "I've decided to drop the class." He stared straight into my face with his exceptional eyes.

"Oh," he said. "It's your decision. But don't you want to see your play performed? It is a chance to see your characters on the stage."

"My play is too revealing," I said. "I'm embarrassed to have it done. The other plays so far are not as revealing."

He stuck his hands into his pockets, came closer to me and stared. His gaze was hypnotic.

"Do you see that stage?" he said, glancing at the Circle's theatre in the round.

"Yes."

"Well, do you know what a playwright is? A playwright is someone who lets his guts out on the stage and that's what you've done in this play." I didn't know what to say. That was the point. I didn't want my guts let out in front of the whole class. I stepped back and started toward the door.

"It's your decision," he said. He didn't smile or move but only continued to look at me with his hypnotic eyes.

Adrienne Kennedy, in Deadly Triplets: A Theatre Mystery and Journal, *University of Minnesota Press, 1990.*

Elinor Fuchs (essay date 1992)

SOURCE: "Adrienne Kennedy and the First Avant-Garde," in *Intersecting Boundaries: The Theatre of Adrienne Kennedy,* edited by Paul K. Bryant-Jackson and Lois More Overbeck, University of Minnesota Press, 1992, pp. 76-84.

[*Fuchs is an American educator and theater critic. In the following essay, she discusses the wide range of influences on Kennedy's work and compares her plays to those identified with the early symbolist movement.*]

There are some writers in the theatre, not many, whose works read as if they were scooped up by radio telescope. One finds the widest range of previous sources, entire traditions, reflected in their intensely concentrated fields. This is the experience of reading Adrienne Kennedy. Whatever angle I engage her from, Kennedy, like Kilroy, has been there. Her echoes and intimations of the European avant-garde alone span nearly a century of that tradition in both theatre and criticism, from the symbolists to (among others) the surrealists, Lorca, Artaud, Genet, and Roland Barthes. This essay will suggest my own sense of Kennedy's strong connection to what John Henderson has called the "first avant-garde," the international symbolist movement inaugurated in theatre with Van Lerberghe's *Les Flaireurs* and Maeterlinck's short plays of the early 1890s.

The early Kennedy plays of the 1960s, *Funnyhouse of a Negro, The Owl Answers,* and *A Rat's Mass,* are mystery or passion plays. They take the form of ritual reenactments, enclose ceremonies and processions, and culminate in dark sacrificial events. Kennedy wrote them in a period when ritual theatre, via Artaud and Genet, was coming into vogue. Yet much of this work (Grotowski, Brook, Serban) became known or was created well after Kennedy found her own way to what I have elsewhere called the modern *mysterium,* a lineage that can be traced to those brief, often terrifying plays written by the symbolists just before the turn of the twentieth century and to Strindberg's post-*Inferno* pilgrimage/dream plays.

Without being religious drama, these plays were steeped in the sense that human beings are exposed without mediation to vast, mysterious forces in the universe. In them, proximate concerns of the social order give way to questions of ultimate destiny—sin, death, and redemption. Playwrights found a dramatic vocabulary, derived in part from allegory, from the moralities, from the passion play, and from the atmospherics of mysticism, to signal the audience that the stage represented not merely a particular time and place, but the universe; and that characters were not only individuals, and sometimes not even individuals, but emblematic figures embodying transcendental human destiny. The *mysterium* evolved past the symbolists to include many expressionists, Artaud (whose *Le jet de sang* is a fractured mystery out of the Book of Revelation), and eventually Beckett. In America the flamboyant symbolist Sadakichi Hartmann, as well as Eugene O'Neill and Percy MacKaye, experimented with mystery plays.

Kennedy's plays of the sixties belong in a general sense to this tradition of the modernist mystery. However, her work has many specific, sometimes uncanny, points of contact with the turn-of-the-century avant-garde.

In the night worlds of Van Lerberghe's *Les Flaireurs,* Maeterlinck's *The Intruder* and *The Death of Tintagiles,* and many other early symbolist plays, the reigning sign is death. The first wave of symbolist plays projected a closed and fatal universe inhabited by abstract, doomed figures. The characters stalked by death are frequently the young, like Hofmannsthal's adolescent aesthete in *Death and the Fool,* the Daughter in *The Intruder,* the child Tintagiles, and a host of others. "The entire corpus of symbolist writing for the theater . . . is haunted by mortality," writes Daniel Gerould [in *Doubles, Demons, and Dreamers: An International Collection of Symbolist Drama,* 1985], "yet filled with a perverse animism—hence the dualistic vision of life in death and death in life that is the central paradox of drama in the symbolist mode." The first generation of symbolists, it is worth noting here, had been inspired by Villiers, whose ideal of death became something of a fashion. Axel's cry, "Live? Our servants will do that for us," resonates with Kennedy's generation of white fifties intellectuals in *Funnyhouse*: "My white friends, like myself, will be shrewd, intellectual and anxious for death."

Kennedy's mystery plays, like Maeterlinck's early plays, take place in a hermetic night world, the time of dreams, madness, and darkness of the soul. In *Funnyhouse,* the playing area is surrounded by "unnatural Blackness"; it is crepuscular and candle-lit in *A Rat's Mass,* and sealed in the prisonlike steel of a subway car in *The Owl Answers.* All three project stifling and fatalistic universes whose central characters are doomed by their own guilt, the crimes of earlier generations, and a sense of extrusion from the normative world. As the doomed center of *Funnyhouse,* Sarah, the generic educated "Negro" with the noose around her neck, is dead even before she hangs herself. Death pervades the setting, whose white curtain resembles "the interior of a cheap casket." Black ravens out of Poe circle the mausoleum room, dominated by a monumental bed "resembling an ebony tomb." Death is not merely atmospheric in *Funnyhouse,* however, but finds a structural equivalent in the paralytic stasis that is at the core of Kennedy's early dramaturgy, reminiscent of the sense of stasis at the heart of Maeterlinckian theatre.

In 1896, Maeterlinck published a seminal essay, "The Tragical in Daily Life," that rejected external action in drama as a noisy distraction. A static theatre, he believed, could be used to put the spectator in touch with the invisible, the unknown, "the ominous silence of the soul and of God." In his early one-act plays, plot and character recede and the sense of dramatic change or dynamism is carried by mood and tone. The rustling of leaves, the groaning of a door, the rising wind, the rising of a cold moon, the gliding of swans, and other effects provide the sense of an alive universe and become a substitute for the gross conflicts of an articulated narrative.

For all their intensity, Kennedy's plays are in this tradition of a static theatre. Something has happened in the past—one is not sure what—that hangs like a shroud over the fraught, yet actionless, stage. To seek to know whether Sarah killed her "black beast" of a father, or Clara (the "Bastard") Passmore's father was actually her mother's white employer, or the Rat children actually committed the crime of incest is to seek a realism that Kennedy does not intend. The guilt of crime and sin, real or imagined, and the torment of unresolvable racial antinomies create a charged environment in which Kennedy's essentially stationary characters obsessively repeat their titanic conflicts. Though Kennedy's conditions of stasis differ from Maeterlinck's, once they are created she, too, rejects progressive narrative for a dramatic texture created through variations in repeating patterns of language and effects. These effects revolve feverishly, yet nothing happens, and nothing *can* happen, except death (suicide in *Funnyhouse,* machine-gun fire in *Rat's Mass*) or the overwrought immolation of *Owl,* hinting of Wagner, whose own techniques of stasis and repetition were a direct influence on symbolist playwriting.

> Whatever angle I engage her from, Kennedy, like Kilroy, has been there. Her echoes and intimations of the European avant-garde alone span nearly a century of that tradition in both theatre and criticism, from the symbolists to (among others) the surrealists, Lorca, Artaud, Genet, and Roland Barthes.
>
> —*Elinor Fuchs*

Accordingly, Kennedy's texts do not so much progress as recircle, proceeding through accreting motifs, not unlike the Wagnerian leitmotiv. "My mother looked like a white woman"; "It begins with the disaster of my hair"; "white stallions roaming under a blue sky"; "photographs of Roman ruins, pianos and oriental carpets" are among the many recurring themes that inhabit Kennedy's *Funnyhouse* text almost like characters. These repetitions, as other commentators on Kennedy's work have noted, endow Kennedy's language with the quality of litany or incantation, repetition in the service of a ritual event.

A consequence of creating a closed and static dramatic world, and the most obvious link between Kennedy and the symbolists, is the necessity of finding a concentrated dramatic form. A dramaturgy that eschews plot and character development tends to reveal itself through sheer density or saturation. Kennedy follows the same dramatic logic that led the symbolists to the one-act form. Maeterlinck was never more successful than in this form, and as symbolism spread outward from Belgium and France, Yeats, Micinski, Briusov, and others discovered its virtues. In *Waiting for Godot* Beckett made a cosmic joke of the static aesthetic by in effect repeating the one-act form twice.

The symbolists swept away the concerns and conflicts of family and society so that the mysterious could penetrate the spectator directly. But Kennedy appears to differ from them definitively in her relationship to culture and history. The death net that traps the figures in symbolist plays is metaphysical and timeless, beyond the social and political order. Kennedy's plays revolve about just those explosions of violence the symbolists detested, festering family crimes like patricide, rape, and incest; political crimes like assassination or tyranny; and most of all the deep cultural crime of racism. And yet in Kennedy's mystery plays, the social/political itself is raised to the power of metaphysics. The signs may be historical, but their power is eternal. Whatever is always was and cannot be altered. The Rat children are forever trapped in crime and guilt, and the Nazis will always punish them. Clara is racially torn on a rack that is built into her flesh. (Her name Passmore is a pun on racial "passing"—will she pass more, or less? Does she believe in the white Virgin, or the African Owl?) And Sarah of *Funnyhouse* is forever ground between the millstones of Europe and Africa, between the hideously white English queen and the black African leader with the mask in his hand. The Negro's white personae cannot for all eternity rid themselves of their black father.

> VICTORIA. Why does he keep returning? He keeps returning forever, coming back ever and keeps coming back forever. He is my father. . . .
>
> DUCHESS. We are tied to him unless, of course, he should die.
>
> VICTORIA. But he is dead.
>
> DUCHESS. And he keeps returning.
>
> (*Funnyhouse*)

Maeterlinck depicted his characters as estranged in a cold, echoing universe. His shivering, puppetlike figures are defenseless against a manipulative fate. Maeterlinck's early plays were, in fact, written to be performed by puppets, an expression of a widely shared symbolist aesthetic of distancing from the human figure. Kennedy's characters are more likely to die of fever than of cold. Her masks and animal costumes are related to the symbolist interest in puppets, marionettes, and mask-work, but she uses them to intensify rather than distance. Similarly, Kennedy's characters are not so much estranged as trapped. Her female protagonists are condemned to retell their stories from the penitentiary of airless distorted funnyhouses, rathouses, and screeching subway cars. Her plays implode. Her stasis has the quality not of the void, but of an impacted wound that can never heal. The pain expressed in them is far more violent and tragic—in the conventional sense that Maeterlinck wanted to avoid—than Maeterlinck's own metaphysical ache. There is, in short, a sharp difference in "feeling tone" between the abstract, universalized cruelty of the symbolist universe and the cruelty concentrated on the dismembered black and female psyche of the Kennedy universe. But even as Kennedy places her characters in a thicket of cultural and historical contradictions and boiling subjectivity, she still continues a fundamental link to the symbolists, for her focus is never social interaction but, like theirs, the mystery of the isolated soul.

Strindberg acknowledged that his later dream and chamber plays owed an immense debt to Maeterlinck, whose work struck him with the force of a "newly discovered country." In a startling shift of focus in the late 1890s, Strindberg took up the symbolist commitment to depicting "structures of the soul" [according to Gerould]. However, Strindberg extended the theatrical viability of symbolist spirituality with two dramatic strategies: the pilgrimage form, taken from medieval station drama, and a transformational dream dramaturgy. The resulting dramatic form has frequently been acknowledged as proto-expressionist, but in the effect that Peter Szondi has described [in *Theory of the Modern Drama,* ed. and trans. by Michael Hays, 1987] as the "static, futureless quality of the scenes," it is strongly linked to symbolist aesthetics.

Kennedy attributes her own discovery of the "greater dream setting" to her reading of Lorca, but her way of writing the dream/nightmare/hallucination feels closer to Strindberg. Her funnyhouse is a descendent of Strindberg's ghost house. Her burning altar as the final image of *Owl* is reminiscent of his burning castle in *A Dream Play.* Her lightning scenic transformation from the Duchess of Hapsburg's palace to the African jungle is as extreme and bizarre as Strindberg's leap from the Lawyer's office to Foulstrand. The very disappearance of linear time into spatial transformation in Kennedy can be traced to Strindberg's discoveries in *A Dream Play.*

Still, it is the quasi-allegorical Strindberg nearer to the symbolists, the Strindberg of *To Damascus, Part I,* with whom I particularly connect Kennedy. It was there that Strindberg first emerged with his new bi-level drama of correspondence. Where older dramatic forms were dialogic and interactional, this drama of correspondence was almost totally subjective, organized around a central character whose interior states are the spectator's principal focus. These internal states assume transcendental importance, however, because all events on the individual plane are mysteriously linked with the operations of cosmic forces. In Strindberg this open horn to the universe both inflates and ironically diminishes his central character's every move. Each quite ordinary event that befalls his Stranger is lit up with supernatural significance. While waiting for a check, the Stranger can become Adam, Cain, Paul, the accursed of Deuteronomy, and Christ. But the same motion undercuts the flight of myth and allegory above his head, for the heroic seeker on the road to Damascus is still merely a down-on-his-luck writer.

This is Strindberg's interchangeable I—now naturalistic and autobiographical, now historical, mythic, and biblical; now many texts within a single character, now broken into separate individuals. Kennedy's prismatic characters, as well as her daring placement of myth and life on the same ontological footing, can be traced to this Strindbergian innovation. Thus Clara Passmore of *Owl* and Sarah of *Funnyhouse* are simultaneously autobiographical and generic figures. While Clara passes through multiple aspects as "the Virgin Mary who is the Bastard who is the Owl,"

Sarah-Negro of *Funnyhouse* is fragmented into freestanding separate bodies sharing a single if divided mind.

The almost casual combination of the painfully autobiographical and the mythic, the quotidian and the typological, invented by Strindberg, was not to my knowledge recreated until Kennedy, but Kennedy extended the Strindbergian drama of correspondence by adding to it a dialectical tension. Kennedy's worlds are not only aligned vertically—between the intimate and the mythic—they are also in dialectical relation horizontally. Sarah's "selves" are black, white, and "high yellow," male and female, and riven by opposed ideologies. Sarah's search for a place to stand or to hide is more complex than Strindberg's Stranger's. She passes through roles the way the Stranger passes through "stations." But all that is required for the Stranger to pass through the Stations of the Cross is a change of heart, whereas Sarah can never resolve the tension between roles. She faces not only spiritual necessity, to which she might rise, but historical necessity, which she is powerless to control. Strindberg's Stranger is willing to walk to the door of the church at the end of his journey through the Dantean inferno, but Kennedy's Negro cannot make the Stranger's leap from Saul to Paul; she can find no religious, cultural, or ideological identity on which to rest. Her tragedy is that "she" can find no cohesive "she" outside the historical contradictions that dismember her. This is the deepest meaning of the multiplicity of Sarah's selves.

The "mysterium" in the modernist sense may not be religious drama, but its chief interests are eschatological, and it frequently avails itself of the vocabulary and imagery traditionally associated with such questions. Religion can function in contradictory ways, often in the same play, as warning or scourge, as model, haven, or trap, but it is never without significance. Without conveying a sense of doctrinal resolution or commitment, Strindberg fills his late plays with the emblems of religion, and with characters who stagger toward and away from those emblems in terrible struggles to come to terms with an oppressive sense of sin. Kennedy similarly creates characters who are tormented by guilt, and this guilt is elevated to the level of metaphysical problem by her inclusion of religious figures and/or ceremonies in all three of the mysteries. At the same time these emblems of religion are often used blankly or ambiguously, and sometimes with hostility.

In *Funnyhouse,* Jesus is one of Sarah's selves, but this Jesus is a hunchbacked, yellow-skinned dwarf, the Jesus that was left after Sarah discovered that her loving relationship with him was a lie. In *The Owl Answers* the High Altar seems the antipode to the harsh subway, but it is also a place of brutal blood sacrifice and agony. The central images of *A Rat's Mass* are a communion mass and religious procession. The procession, with its Holy Family, Wise Men, and Shepherd, seems at first a comforting image from childhood; by the end of the play the procession has turned into brutal Nazis with shotguns. "God is hanging and shooting us," the Rat children cry. Religion waits patiently for Strindberg's Stranger while he rages at it, flirts with it, then backs away again. Kennedy's view of the religious sign is more complex. It can turn punishing and vengeful, or its affirmative power may be exactly balanced by a sign from another culture—the Virgin Mary by the Owl, the pale Jesus by the black Lumumba—leading to spiritual doubt and paralysis.

Modernism in theatre can be traced to the first avant-garde at the turn of the century. It was the symbolists who first rejected realism in both its classical and "romantic" variants, and attempted to create a theater uncompromisingly of the inner world and of the cosmos. The early Kennedy of the mystery plays shares the symbolists' and the late Strindberg's attraction to the absolute. Though history is always recognizable in Kennedy, from the assassination of Patrice Lumumba to the withering depiction of her generation of fifties intellectuals, Kennedy emerges in the early mystery plays as one who asks not, "How can I change the social order?" but "Where do I stand in the universe? What is my destiny? Is there redemption for me?"

After 1970, these questions recede in Kennedy's work in favor of more direct issues of gender and sexuality (*A Lesson in Dead Language*), of race and class (*A Movie Star Has to Star in Black and White* and *An Evening with Dead Essex*). In these plays Kennedy continues to use the transformational dream setting and the technique of corresponding levels, but her theatrical worlds are lighter, more open, more humorous, and more grounded in the immediacy of life. Her symbolist moment had passed.

Lois More Overbeck (essay date 1992)

SOURCE: "The Life of the Work: A Preliminary Sketch," in *Intersecting Boundaries: The Theatre of Adrienne Kennedy,* edited by Paul K. Bryant-Jackson and Lois More Overbeck, University of Minnesota Press, 1992, pp. 21-41.

[*Below, Overbeck offers an overview of Kennedy's career.*]

There are no consolidated archives of Adrienne Kennedy's manuscripts or of the production history of her plays. Many of the plays had their first appearance in workshop productions with brief runs and without critical notice. Experimental theatres seldom had resources to record the development of their productions when funding for their season or even the next play was a priority. When available, programs, reviews, and interviews have been consulted to gain a sense of production values and directorial choices. While these are inadequate resources for a comprehensive stage history, the resulting overview will suggest directions for further research.

Kennedy indicates that both *Funnyhouse of A Negro* and *The Owl Answers* were completed manuscripts when she applied to Edward Albee's Circle in the Square workshop, and that the script of *Funnyhouse* produced in the workshop was the original. In an interview [in *Intersecting Boundaries: The Theatre of Adrienne Kennedy*], performer Billie Allen comments on her sense of Kennedy's writing as "finished": "It is all there, and it is all done." With Kennedy, as with any writer, there are manuscripts that were written and abandoned or not produced, or produced

in workshop but not published (e.g., *Diary of Lights, Boats*), or performed in workshop and then altered by others (e.g., *The Lennon Play: or In His Own Write*). Other works were published initially in a journal or anthology but not republished in the author's collected plays (e.g., *A Beast Story, An Evening with Dead Essex*).

Even if manuscripts and variants of Kennedy's plays were available for study, a script alone would not tell us the nature of the production, because dramaturgical improvisation brings the nuances and the suggestive possibility of images and nonlinear structures to life in performance. Music, though seldom designated in the script, is often integral to production values (*Sun, She Talks to Beethoven,* the adaptation *Solo Voyages*), and musical forms even generate theatrical shape. Visual effects are visceral evocations of subliminal/emotional realities (the massive sculpture of Queen Victoria in *Funnyhouse of a Negro* in the Théâtre Odéon production, the rotating stage of *The Owl Answers* in the 1969 production at the Public Theater, the simultaneous layers of reality expressed by multiple levels of staging in *The Owl Answers,* the projections of *An Evening with Dead Essex,* the dominant color in the set of *Orestes* and *Electra*).

It is clear from interviews with directors and actors that Kennedy's plays are open to a directorial hand, as indicated by Michael Kahn's comment that he did not stage the jungle scene in *Funnyhouse,* though he would today, and in Gerald Freeman's note that Kennedy's plays require "new techniques and new answers." In some cases the final form of the play varies considerably from the original. Differing slightly in title (*A Beast Story*), the published version of *A Beast's Story* is not the same as the one indicated by the prompt books and acting scripts when it was performed as part of *Cities in Bezique* at the Public Theater (1969); in production the number of beasts multiplied, and the beasts' costumes indicated by the text were dropped in favor of rehearsal clothes. There are also changes from script to performance that reflect variations in the playing space, conceptualization of a character, or casting; there were differences between the original production of *An Evening with Dead Essex* in the small rehearsal space of the American Place Theatre and the larger stage at Yale, and differences between the original production of *Funnyhouse of a Negro* and that directed by David Wheeler at the Theater Company, Boston. Complete records of these productions and their variations would be desirable, because they would offer interpretive illuminations of the plays. . . .

Kennedy's early writing is largely unpublished. *Pale Blue Flowers* (1955), a one-act play modeled on Tennessee Williams's *The Glass Menagerie,* has not been published or performed. In an interview with Kathleen Betsko [in *Interviews with Contemporary Women Playwrights* (1987)], Kennedy describes working on it for two years: "I had written the play in a course at the New School taught by Mildred Kunner," who entered it in a play contest in Chapel Hill, North Carolina; it didn't win. She then sent it to Williams's agent, Audrey Wood, "who wrote me a long letter which said she couldn't take me as a client, but that she thought I was very talented. That was a great encouragement to me." Kennedy's first published writing, **"Because of the King of France,"** appeared under the name Adrienne Cornell in *Black Orpheus: A Journal of African and Afro-American Literature* [1963]. The short story about the vicissitudes of Sidney Carter as viewed by a middle-class young woman, the writer, prefigures the themes and narrative shifts of the plays that follow it: racial exclusion and punishment for loving across racial barriers, artistic gifts expressed within the Eurocentric traditions, self-hatred and deformity, class discrimination, and imaginary conversations with historical figures.

In *Deadly Triplets,* Kennedy describes submitting *Funnyhouse of a Negro* to Edward Albee's workshop at the Circle in the Square in application to the workshop; Michael Kahn called her later to say "Edward Albee liked your play very much[;] you have been selected to be in the workshop." Although Kennedy indicates that the play done in the workshop production was the original version, she felt that her play was too revealing and, at one point, had decided to drop out of the class. She reports Albee's response: "A playwright is someone who lets his guts out on the stage and that's what you've done in this play. . . . It's your decision." The play was done first at the Circle in the Square and then again at the Actor's Studio (1964), directed by Michael Kahn, with Diana Sands, Fran Burnett, Lynne Hamilton, Yaphet Kotto, and Andre Gregory in the cast.

Kennedy says that she wrote *Funnyhouse of a Negro* in 1960, "when I was exactly twenty-nine," and that the play reflected fourteen months spent in Europe, Ghana, and Nigeria:

> My writing became sharper, more focused and powerful, and less imitative. It was a tremendous turning point. . . . I would say that almost every image in *Funnyhouse* took form while I was in West Africa where I became aware of masks. . . . I discovered a strength in being a black person and a connection to West Africa.

Funnyhouse of a Negro opened at the East End Theatre on January 14, 1964, produced by Theatre 1964 (Richard Barr, Clinton Wilder, and Edward Albee), with performances twice a night (closing February 9, 1964). The Play was directed by Michael Kahn; settings and lighting were by William Ritman and costumes were by Willa Kim. The role of Sarah was played by Billie Allen; other actors were Cynthia Belgrave, Ellen Holly, Gus Williams, Norman Bush, Ruth Volner, Leonard Frey, and Leslie Rivers. In describing the play as "the hallucinated horrors that torment the last hours of a Negro girl," Howard Taubman acknowledged the power of the play [in the *New York Times,* 15 January 1964], saying that Kennedy "digs unsparingly into Sarah's aching psyche." He also describes the sideshow figures of *Funnyhouse,* positioned on either side of the stage, and the presence of a statue of Queen Victoria, and elaborates: "Her other companions [the Duchess of Hapsburg, Queen Victoria, Jesus, and Patrice Lumumba] are the impalpable figments of her imagination . . . that become corporeal on the stage. She speaks the brief litany of her

fears and hatred and despair and her ghosts often repeat and mock her."

[In the *New Yorker,* 25 January 1964] Edith Oliver sketches the elegance of "elaborate period costumes of white" with "white or gray masklike makeups" worn by the figures of Victoria, Hapsburg, and Jesus; she contrasts the image of Lumumba, black and dressed "in tatters"; she notes that the Funnyhouse man and woman are in "clown makeups" and move with "marionette gestures." Although Sarah's monologue supplies the play's narrative, Oliver notes that "she is in no shape to give it" and that Sarah's "obsession with hair" parallels the "obsession with grief and guilt over her treatment of her father, whom she has driven away because of his blackness." She comments that Kahn's expressionist attempt to "reproduce the girl's madness and anguish . . . seems appropriate" and that *Funnyhouse* is a "strong and original" first play.

Although George Oppenheimer [*Newsday,* 15 January 1964] saw the play as bad theater of the absurd and a dismal "charade," a "non-play" with a "non-plot," Taubman concluded, "If nothing much happens according to conventional theatrical tenets, a relatively unknown territory is explored and exposed." Writing for *Nation* [10 February 1964], Harold Clurman underscores the uniqueness of Kennedy's voice:

> The play . . . embraces far more than plays of similar theme when they are couched in terms of pathetic appeals for "tolerance" and fair play. The torment of the colored girl in *Funny House* [sic] *of a Negro* parallels that of all people who suffer the pathology of minorities. Their number extends far beyond the boundaries of race.

Funnyhouse of a Negro was awarded an Obie for "most distinguished play" in May 1964. The play was produced by the Theater Company of Boston beginning March 11, 1965. Directed by David Wheeler, this production conceptualized Sarah, played by Barbara Ann Teer, as a powerful female; Gustav Johnson enacted the role of Lumumba, with settings by Robert Allen and lighting by Neville Powers. Wheeler's production emphasized the mythic element of the play, building to "an unbearable crescendo"; strips of black muslin were hung at angles, so that props and figures seemed to emerge from the nightmare. [In the *Boston Globe,* 12 March 1965] Kevin Kelly said that Wheeler "captured the focal fear at the heart of the play and exposed it with an unfaltering sense of drama."

Funnyhouse was presented as *Drôle de baraque* on a double bill with Sam Shepard's *Chicago* at the Petit Odéon in Paris under the direction of Jean-Marie Serreau on March 8, 1968. Adapted by Augy Hayter, the play featured Toto Bissainthe, a Haitian, as Sarah and Douta Seck as Lumumba. "The play expresses [Sarah's] dreams, her fantasies, her nightmares brought on by the horror of her estranged condition in a white world" [C. G., "Jeunes Américains," *Les nouvelles literraires,* 7 March 1968]. Central to the production was a huge white bust of Queen Victoria. [In *Le Monde,* 19 March 1968] B. Poirot-Delpech compares Kennedy's work to Genet's *The Blacks* and O'Neill's *Em-*

peror Jones. [In *Le Figaro,* 11 March 1968] Jean-Jacques Gautier emphasized the production's grating music, which underlines the "spasmodic monologue" in which Sarah "kills her father. It is true. It is not true." He finds the production ambiguous—"it is nearly impossible to know who is who and who does what." On the other hand, the review in *Combat* [19 March 1968] is very appreciative: "Showing a young black [woman] imprisoned in the complexes and conditioning that American society has created in her," Kennedy's theatre has "fantastic life (and so real at the same time)"; it is "theatre that has a power to attack that is, finally, as sure as that of LeRoi Jones." Supported by jazz rhythms and physical movement, "the black American problem is evoked in an excruciating way." The review in the *Journal de Genève* [6 April 1968] said of the production, "In a dance macabre rhythm and full of a poignant poetry, the spectacle . . . astonishes with its content and its form, with the ensemble as with the least detail, with its rhythm where the music plays in counterpoint to the role of the broken and cruel world in which we live." And Jacques Lemarchand wrote [in *Figro Litérraire,* 25 March 1968], "Adrienne Kennedy defines an aspect of the American problem with great simplicity in reverie, without proposing solution, without preaching sufferance or reconciliation."

Funnyhouse of a Negro was presented by the English Stage Society at the Royal Court on Sunday, April 28, 1968, with *A Lesson in Dead Language*; there it was directed by Rob Knights with Sheila Wilkinson as Sarah. [In the *Times,* London, 29 April 1968] Michael Billington wrote, "Unfortunately the phantasmagoric nature of the action . . . only serves to confuse. . . . Miss Kennedy's language has a controlled, deliberate rhythm to it but even this suffers from the belief that anything said three times is poetry." Kennedy wrote a filmscript of *Funnyhouse of a Negro* with Pablo Feraro in 1971; it was not produced.

Kennedy had written *The Owl Answers* by the time she submitted *Funnyhouse of a Negro* to the Edward Albee playwriting workshop. The original production by Lucille Lortel was at the White Barn Theater, Westport, Connecticut, on August 29, 1965, as a benefit for the Free Southern Theater; it was also performed at the Theatre de Lys in New York as part of the ANTA Matinee Theater Series on December 14, 1965. Directed by Michael Kahn, the production starred Ellen Holly as "She who is Clara." Like a *Funnyhouse of a Negro, The Owl Answers* "takes place on different levels of consciousness," said Kahn. "She has several father figures . . . and several mothers, . . . and historical figures . . . who appear as passengers on the subway and as jailors." Kennedy points to personal experience as embedded in the play. Living in Ghana, she would hear owls in the trees, and particularly at night "the owls sounded as if they were in the very center of the room"; memory of the owl sounds mingle with fear, as Kennedy recounts listening to them while confined to bed with a difficult pregnancy. "In a few months I would create a character who would turn into an owl."

When produced by the New York Shakespeare Festival (Joseph Papp), *Owl Answers* was paired with Kennedy's *A Beast's Story* under the title, *Cities in Bezique.* Actually,

Cities in Bezique was the title of a play that Adrienne Kennedy had written in 1967-68; it had been commissioned by Joseph Papp for the New York Shakespeare Festival, but Papp found it "too chaotic and abstract" and instead used this title for the two one-act plays, *Owl Answers* and *A Beast's Story.* As Kennedy indicates in the interview [in *Intersecting Boundaries*], Joseph Papp said, "Well, I don't really like the play very much. But I'd like to use the title." Gerald Freedman, who directed the program at the Public Theater, describes the original *Cities in Bezique* in the interview with Paul Bryant-Jackson [in *Intersecting Boundaries*]:

> A lot of it was images. . . . I thought I could do a wonderful piece of it in a darkened room with a slot where one person could look through, and I could change images. . . . [However] it didn't become practical for the Public Theater to do it. It would have been a wonderful performance piece. . . . Bezique is a card game . . . of chance and so her text actually had pictures in it. And cards turned over. . . . I would have loved to do it, but I don't know a theatre company that could afford to do it.

The production of *The Owl Answers* and *A Beast's Story* as *Cities in Bezique* ran for sixty-seven performances at the Public Theater, January 4 to March 2, 1969. Gerald Freedman directed, with settings by Ming Cho Lee, costumes by Theoni V. Aldredge, lighting by Martin Aronstein, and incidental music by John Morris. "She who is Clara Passmore who is the Virgin Mary who is the Bastard who is the Owl" was played by Joan Harris; Cynthia Belgrave played the mother(s); Moses Gunn, the father(s); Henry Baker, the white bird; and Paul Benjamin, the Negro Man in *The Owl Answers.*

Reviewers noted the similarities to *Funnyhouse*: both plays explored a "lightskinned Negro woman's mental anguish and search for a sense of identity" [*Variety,* 29 January 1969]. Although beginning in realism, *The Owl Answers* introduced other dimensions of time and space. [In the *Daily News,* 13 January 1969] Lee Silver wrote of Clara as "a nice student in tweed skirt and sweater, calmly reading through the screeching noises of the underground," and Richard P. Cooke describes transmutation into the surreal: "Through the subway aisles parade creatures of [Clara's] imagination—Shakespeare, Chaucer, William the Conqueror, Anne Boleyn, along with some Negroes in modern dress. White people are represented by masks" [*Wall Street Journal,* 14 January 1969]. As Richard Watts observed [in the *New York Post,* 13 January 1969] "Past and present merge, characters shift from being one person to another, and time is telescoped."

Comparing Kennedy's double bill to "the surrealist school of films of the 30's," George Oppenheimer [*Daily Item* (Port Chester, N.Y.) 13 January 1969] found "kinship in manner and mood," if not symbolic clarity, with Cocteau. [In *New York,* 3 February 1969] John Simon describes the variety of settings: the Tower of London, St. Paul's Cathedral [Chapel], and a Harlem hotel room, noting that place and time shift continually and characters double; he describes "a large white papier-mâché bird, which flaps its wings at arbitrary intervals," hovering above the stage and "a large black man clad in white feathers who occasionally speaks." Labeling *Cities in Bezique* as a "happening," Steve Tennen wrote:

> [Freedman] has molded the plays into nightmarish, almost ritualistic forms. Through precisioned movement of his cast, their vocal quality and facial expressions, he has removed them from the human element and left only the shadow of the supernatural.

> Theoni Aldredge's costumes & masks . . . add to this strange dimension. Ming Cho Lee's set is dark and forbidding, and, combined with John Morris' music and sound, it becomes rattingly eerie [*Show Business,* 25 January 1969].

In what he calls "the female face of tragedy," J. Lance Ermatinger says [in *Off-Off,* April 1969] that Kennedy "aims a poet's eye along a surgeon's scalpel, and she penetrates layer after layer of the white/black protagonist. . . . The birds represent both the Holy Spirit of Christianity and the *coq blanc* of Voodoo that traces its flight back from Harlem to Haiti to Dahomey in West Africa. . . . [*Cities in Bezique*] immolates the white consciousness in a vortex of the Black Context." Ermatinger also offers comment on audience response to the plays at the Public Theater:

> The witnesses are completely involved, although there is no physical invasion of the audience. Neither black nor white can deny the power of Adrienne Kennedy's fierce poetry. . . . Yet both react with confused anger.

> What provokes this anger? I think it is the absence of the doctrinaire in *Bezique.* The White Liberals are offered none of the clichés that bring cold comfort to our day of confrontation. The Black Militants, on the other hand, hear no sizzling slogans. All witness only the story of one human being in a context as richly personal as it is beautifully black.

A Beast's Story (1965) was commissioned by Herbert Blau and Jules Irving for Lincoln Center but was not produced until its performance as a part of *Cities in Bezique,* with Amanda Ambrose as the Woman, Moses Gunn as the Man Beast, and Robbie McCauley, Theta Tucker, and Camilie Yarbrough as the Girl Beasts. The published text indicates a single Girl Beast, whereas the production at the Public Theater had three.

Understood by Clive Barnes as a "word image," the play evokes sexual fear and repression as it enacts the rape of a young girl by a man whom she "identifies with her father," a subsequent stillbirth, and "the murder of the young man with an ax" [*New York Times,* 13 January 1969]. Cooke writes, "[The] young woman's personality is projected by three other women"; they are "painting the colors of the sun, to represent the feelings experienced on the day [the] girl murders the man who violated her."

"Roles seem to be interchangeable between girl beasts,

while woman, human woman beast, man beast and other beasts enact an allegory . . . [with] a haunting quality," wrote George Oppenheimer. Walter Kerr described his impressions:

> All roles blur, blend, divide and recombine while two doves—one white, one black beneath the white—flutter moldy wings overhead and the heavens light up with fingerpainted child's pictures of houses, robins, bloodstains, and ebony suns. Sounds, sights, gestures recur as in a dream that won't move forward . . . back [*New York Times,* 19 January 1969].

[In *Intersecting Boundaries*] Gerald Freedman discusses the evolution of the production he directed, with particular reference to the Beast figures. [In a 1969 radio review] David Marash indicated that the two plays were "worlds apart," citing *The Owl Answers* as "the best play off-. . . or for that matter on Broadway this year" but *A Beast's Story* as "beastly, boring and banal." [In *Women's Wear Daily,* 13 January 1969] Martin Gottfried called the plays "unjustified indulgence," but Richard Watts said, "If what [Kennedy] is saying is at times difficult to decipher, . . . she is giving us important and moving insights into the minds and emotions of deeply tormented people." Although Walter Kerr felt that the spectator was left outside of the plays and that in them "nothing is drawn to a center, distilled, condensed to leave a residue," there was "a spare, unsentimental intensity about the work that promises to drive a dagger home some day." On the other hand, despite their expressionism, Edith Oliver noted [in the *New Yorker,* 25 January 1969] that the plays "command and hold one's unflagging attention." *Cities in Bezique* was published in 1969; only *The Owl Answers* was republished in *Adrienne Kennedy: In One Act.*

A Rat's Mass, written in 1963, was directed by David Wheeler of the Theater Company of Boston (opening April 12, 1966) and was named one of the best plays of the Boston season. The cast included Paul Benedict, Edward Finnegan, Warren Finnerty, Josephine Lane, James Spruill, Nadine Turner, and Blythe Danner. The play was produced by F. Carlton and Ann Colcord at the San Saba Theatre in Rome (opening June 21, 1966) with Ben B. Ardery, Jr., directing it on a program with Ardery's *Beside the Pool* and Sam Shepard's *Icarus.* Joan Sutherland and Nat Bush played Sister and Brother Rat, with Betty Jane Hobbs as Rosemary. [In *Rome Daily American,* 26-27 June 1966] Ann Colcord described the theme and action of the play: "They gnaw and nibble surreptitiously at the very standards of life that Americans use to hold themselves together, individually and as a group." Brother and Sister Rat are unable to expiate their guilt for a childhood incest inspired by playmate Rosemary, a Catholic girl dressed for her first communion, who also refuses to pardon them; the siblings are caught in and alienated by the white/Christian ethos. [In "A Growth of Images," *Drama Review* 21 (December 1977)] Kennedy has said that the images of *A Rat's Mass* were based on a dream she had while traveling by train from Paris to Rome: "I had this dream in which I was being pursued by red, bloodied rats. It was [a] very powerful dream, and when I woke up the train had stopped in the Alps. It was at night. . . . I was just haunted by that image

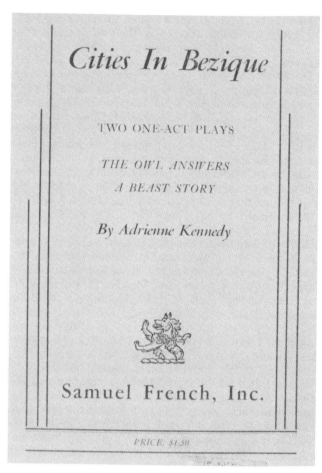

for years, about being pursued by these big, red rats."

Italian response to the play was enthusiastic. *L'Unità*'s reviewer discussed the "archetypal symbolism" that insists on a "historic reality, almost an existential reality": rather than being characteristics of individuals, the segregation and bestial behavior of the characters are the image of a "degrading collective condition." In *Specchio* [3 July 1966] *A Rat's Mass* was described as a "kind of black spiritual," with Kennedy's voice both "lyrical and obsessive"; "instead of the liberation of catharsis . . . we have a regression to the terrible condition of rats." The conviction of the production impressed the reviewer for *Il Messaggero* [23 June 1966]: "Even to people who do not understand the English text, the play speaks with the suggestion of a ballet." *A Rat's Mass* played in the repertory of the New American Theater at the Cultural Union in Turin from October 28, 1966.

It was produced in New York by La Mama E.T.C. (August 17, 1969), directed by Seth Allen, with music by Lamar Alford; Mary Alice played Sister Rat; Robert Robinson, Brother Rat; and Marilyn Roberts, Rosemary. Allen staged the play as a "parody mass" and "illuminate[d] its shadows and heighten[ed] its echoes." [Clive] Barnes continued, "[Kennedy's] plays read like nonsense and yet, when acted, their phrases float accusingly in the mind. . . . Of all our black writers, Miss Kennedy is most concerned with white, with white relationship, with white blood. She thinks black,

but she remembers white" [*New York Times,* 1 November 1969]. La Mama took *A Rat's Mass* to London's Royal Court Theatre; there it was directed by Ching Yeh, with Barbara Montgomery as Sister Rat, Lamar Alford as Brother Rat, and Patricia Gaul as Rosemary. [In the *Times,* London, 27 May 1970] Irving Wardle observes that Kennedy, unlike most black American playwrights, is an experimentalist, and he sees *A Rat's Mass* as a lurid poetic ritual; Rosemary turns into a Medusa head as Brother and Sister Rat become rodents "who infest the beams of the house."

As Kennedy mentions [in her interview in *Intersecting Boundaries*], the La Mama production of *A Rat's Mass* enjoyed great success, and Ellen Stewart proposed to do the play as an opera. In 1976, *A Rat's Mass/Procession in Shout* was performed at the La Mama Annex with music by Cecil Taylor, jazz composer and pianist. Taylor used fragments from the original play in dialogue and lyrics and used orchestrated voices as instruments. Played by the Cecil Taylor Unit, "the plangency of the music echoes the doom-filled sentiments of the text," wrote Mel Gussow [in the *New York Times,* 11 March 1976]. *A Rat's Mass* was published in *New Black Playwrights* (1968).

A Lesson in Dead Language (1964) was presented by the English Stage Society at the Royal Court (London) on a double bill with *Funnyhouse of a Negro* (April 28, 1968). Directed by Rob Knights, the production featured Julia McCarthy as the Teacher and Anne Thompson as the Pupil. [In the *Times,* London, 29 April 1968] Michael Billington called it a "playlet of startling brevity and obscure intent" and mentions engaging music by Ginger Johnson and his African Drummers as part of the program. Gaby Rodgers directed a workshop performance of *A Lesson in Dead Language,* a production of Theatre Genesis, at St. Mark's Church in New York from April 22 to May 2, 1971. In the interview with Howard Stein [in *Intersecting Boundaries*], Rodgers details the process of discovery that was involved in developing her production. As is suggested by the first line of the play, "Lesson I bleed," sexual maturation is treated as trauma. Rodgers recollects that Kennedy had a nun in mind in creating the figure of the teacher, depicted as a white dog teaching a class of adolescent girls, all in white dresses with red stains. In Rodgers's production, the setting included the stations of the cross, and movement included actors as religious sculptures. She also used gospel music played by Lamar Alford. *A Lesson in Dead Language* was published in *Collision Course* (1968).

In the "Theatre Journal" included in *Deadly Triplets,* Kennedy explains that her son had the nonsense books of John Lennon, *A Spaniard in the Works* and *In His Own Write,* and she often "sat among [his] toys" reading them. Interested in doing a play from them, and encouraged by Gillian Walker at the Circle in the Square, Kennedy began writing *The Lennon Play* in a borrowed studio atop the Dakota (ironically, where Lennon later was living at the time he was shot) shortly before she left for England on a Rockefeller Grant. In London she was introduced to Victor Spinetti, who had been in the Beatles movies; he became interested in directing the play and helped Kennedy adapt Lennon's books to the stage. Later, after a single performance of the play for an invited audience (1967), it was decided that the play should be done, but without Kennedy. She asked Lennon to intervene ("After working on this play for almost a year I hear they want me out of it"), and he did by calling Kenneth Tynan, literary manager at the National Theatre. It was announced that Victor Spinetti would direct the "emended production" at the National Theatre in June 1968 and that John Lennon was collaborating with Adrienne Kennedy on the play. Martin Esslin's review [in the *New York Times,* 14 July 1968] notes that the play was "originally devised" by Adrienne Kennedy, but "extensively revised" by Spinetti and Lennon. Under the direction of Victor Spinetti, the play was modified with improvisational work by the cast.

It opened as *The Lennon Play: In His Own Write* as part of *Triple Bill* (with Henry Fielding's *The Covent Garden Tragedy* and a Victorian farce by John Maddison Morton, *A Most Unwarrantable Intrusion*) at the Old Vic of the National Theatre on June 18, 1968. The central figure of the play is "Me" (played by Ronald Pickup), who, as a member of a family of television addicts, invents his own fantasy world out of vignettes of childhood and popular culture. Irving Wardle's review [in the *Times,* London, 19 June 1968] describes "a montage of working-class provincial upbringing" (boys' comics, Sherlock Holmes, "a burlesque *Halmet, . . .* nonsense sermons and launching ceremonies, nightmares, and quarrels"); the production "made elaborate use of side screen and back projections," costume changes, and "spirited" group movement. He found it faithful to the Lennon word games and cartoons, but said, "It leaves you with . . . a soporific flow of mindless punning." In the *New York Times* [10 June 1968], Wardle says that Lennon's books consist of "brief pieces directed against every sacred British cow." He adds, "The books are anything but theatrical, but with the aid of an American adapter, Adrienne Kennedy, and the director, Victor Spinetti, they have been assembled into the loose but workable stage form of a boy's struggle between his fantasies and his environment." [In the *New York Times,* 9 July 1968] Clive Barnes called attention to Lennon's obsession with language, notably "strange surrealistic malapropisms," and called the production "fast, furious and fun." *The Lennon Play* was produced in Albany, New York, by the Arena Summer Theatre in August 1969; it was published as *The Lennon Play: In His Own Write* (1968).

Sun: A Poem for Malcolm X Inspired by His Murder was commissioned by the Royal Court Theatre in 1968 and was produced at the Theatre Upstairs, the Royal Court, in August 1969. It was published in *Scripts* (1971). In her interview [in *Intersecting Boundaries*], Kennedy indicates that she had been commissioned by Jerome Robbins to write something for the Theatre Lab and had begun to write about Malcolm but did not finish it; then, when she was commissioned to write a play by the Royal Court, she was "working on some material from drawings of Leonardo da Vinci." Complemented by sound effects/music, improvisational lighting, and rear-screen projections, movement merges with verbal and visual imagery in a tone poem about a man dismembered among the shattered elements of a cosmos; the only remnant is a "tiny black Sun." Wilfred Leach di-

rected *Sun: A Poem* at La Mama E.T.C. (Cafe La Mama) January 11 to 13, 1974; Andre Mtumi played "The Man." The production was "conceived by The Present Elements"; visuals were done by Karma Stanley, audio by Ancel O'Garro, and lighting by Charles Embry. [In *Black Theatre in the 1960s and 1970s: A Historical-Critical Analysis of the Movement,* 1985] Lance Williams calls *Sun* a choreopoem, precursor to Shange's *For Colored Girls Who Have Considered Suicide When the Rainbow Is Enuf,* because it "combines poetry and body movement to create dramatic intensity"; he particularly notes the improvisational "Free Jazz" accompaniment by the Ornett Coleman Double Quartet in the La Mama production. Director Gaby Rodgers indicates [in an unpublished interview] that she had developed a production of *Sun* "frame by frame, but it was finally too expensive to mount for Off-Off Broadway."

Kennedy's play, *Boats,* was commissioned for "An Omnibus of Short Works," organized by Gordon Davidson and directed by Ed Parone. It was performed at the Mark Taper Forum in Los Angeles as part of the second "Evening of Plays" on October 11 and 12, 1969. The script of this brief play is not available.

Adrienne Kennedy mentions the way that *An Evening with Dead Essex* evolved from a sniper incident in New Orleans that ended with the slaying of James Essex. A departure for Kennedy's dramaturgy, the play uses projections of Vietnam news headlines to counterpoint the story of Essex. Its situation is a rehearsal; the director-producer works with black actors to recreate scenes from the life of the dead Essex. Brechtian projections establish media representation of Essex as a presence in the play (the projectionist, who never speaks, is designated as the only white character). Images of religious comfort, such the Twenty-third Psalm, stand in opposition to Essex's story and war headlines from Vietnam, reports of other assassinations (President Kennedy, Malcolm, Robert Kennedy, Martin Luther King, Kent State), black revolutionary slogans, a tape of "When I've Done the Best I Can," and Nixon's banalities intended to gloss military aggression in Viet Nam.

Both at the American Place Theatre (New York), directed by Gaby Rodgers (November 28, 1973), and at the Yale Repertory Company (New Haven, Connecticut), directed by Andre Mtumi (March 1974), the process of producing the play reflected the volatility of racial tensions at that time. In the interview with Howard Stein [in *Intersecting Boundaries*], Gaby Rodgers elaborates on the improvisations and struggles that took place in rehearsal of this play that is itself a rehearsal—of a life and of a play; its cast included Mary Alice, Bill Cobbs, Sid Morgan, Jr., Andre Mtumi, Fred Seagraves, and Karma Stanley.

When Kennedy was a CBS fellow at the Yale School of Drama (1973-74), *An Evening with Dead Essex* was produced on a program with Sam Shepard's *Geography of a Horse Dreamer* by the Yale Repertory Company (March 1974). Robert Brustein describes the rehearsals and performance of the play in *Making Scenes:* "In her own mind, Adrienne had written not a documentary but an activist piece with revolutionary implications, and the director she selected [Andre Mtumi] wanted to treat **Dead Essex** as a piece of racial propaganda." On the other hand, Brustein had perceived Essex as a "symbol of violence," and he was concerned that the production conferred martyrdom on Essex as "a victim of a repressive white police state." The script has each character leave the theatre for home at the end of the play; however, in rehearsal for the production, Brustein says, "the play ended with everybody passing a gun from hand to hand, the implication that they were preparing to take up Essex's dedication to violence." Brustein asked that the gun be removed from the play, but admits his ambivalence because any act of censorship was troubling and created an impasse for the production. *An Evening with Dead Essex* was published in *Theater* (1978); it was not reprinted in *In One Act.*

Directed by Joseph Chaikin as a work-in-progress in the workshop series of the New York Shakespeare Festival at the Public Theater in New York, *A Movie Star Has to Star in Black and White* was performed in November 1976. Robbie McCauley played Clara, the writer, with Avra Petrides as Bette Davis, Elin Ruskin as Shelley Winters, and Gloria Foster as the mother. Arthur Sainer, in the *Village Voice* [29 November 1976], described the play as the vision of a single character, a writer, "whose life is so tied up with the films that . . . scenes from these films (*Now, Voyager, Viva Zapata!,* and *A Place in the Sun*) . . . become structures within which the events in her life are replayed." Sainer saw the play in the same "confessional" vein as *Funnyhouse of a Negro,* but reported that knowledge about the character was blocked rather than revealed.

According to Eileen Blumenthal [in her *Joseph Chaikin: Exploring the Boundaries of Theater,* 1984], **Movie Star** was the "only new script" that Chaikin had directed that was "not connected to one of his laboratories"; she also indicates that Chaikin worked closely with Kennedy, "condensing, tightening dialogue, and clarifying." He was drawn to her "depiction of direct experience being redigested and reshaped to conform to popular culture models." The play was first published in *Wordplays* 3 (1984). It was produced at the University of Houston (from February 8, 1985), and directed by Ntozake Shange.

Kennedy was commissioned to write **The Lancashire Lad** by the Empire State Youth Theater Institute, where it was performed in May 1980. The play is a fictionalized account of the childhood of Charles Chaplin, based on Chaplin's biography. Produced by Patricia B. Snyder, the play includes musical numbers and "a full-blown Palladium review, complete with fan dancer and low comics." [In the *New York Times,* 21 May 1980] Frank Rich says that Kennedy "tells her central story with such heart-stopping passion that not even a circus could upstage it or blunt it." The boy, here called William Grimby, contends with an alcoholic father, a mentally disturbed mother, and grinding poverty. Although he succeeds as a performer, Kennedy does not "allow her audience to escape her drama's gravest implications." The play was directed by Joseph Balflor, with music by George Harris; John Thomas McGuire III was William Grimby. Rich concludes that "the real star is Miss Kennedy, whose language achieves powerful emo-

tional effects with the sparest of means." The text of the play is not available.

Black Children's Day, a children's play, was commissioned by Brown University while Kennedy was artist-in-residence; it was directed by George Houston Bass and produced by Rites and Reason at Brown University, Providence, Rhode Island (November 1980).

Orestes and **Electra,** adaptations of Euripides' plays, were commissioned by the Juilliard School, where they were directed by Michael Kahn as a performance project (November 5 to 9, 1980) and in repertory (April 11 to 14, 1981). With music and vocal sounds by Kirk Nurock, sets and lights by Loren Sherman, choreography by Randolyn Zinn, and costumes by Mariann Verheyen, the cast included Linda Kozlowski as Electra and Val Kilmer as Orestes. [In *Theatre Crafts* 15 (August-September 1981)] Ronn Smith commented that the plays were "loosely condensed and finely adapted" by Kennedy. Noting the female-dominated chorus and a robust Electra, Robert Massa called it an "Amazon production"—"an interesting approach, since the plays chronicle the re-establishment of the patriarchal order after the Trojan War" [*Village Voice,* 21 April 1981]. Mythic dimensions, heightened by primitive and feathered costumes combined with movement and color ("performers writhing about the burnt-orange bowl-shaped stage"), created a "visceral production of ancient drama."

Kennedy's **Diary of Lights,** a musical without songs, was directed by David Willinger at CitiRep, Davis Hall, City College in New York, from June 5 to 14, 1987. The production of this autobiographical play included a jazz continuo by Gib Veconi and abstract dance movements superimposed on the text; Tracy Hendryx designed the choreography. "The play is concerned with the youthful idealism of a young black [married] couple on the inter-racial Upper West Side of New York City" [an advertisement in *Black Masks,* May/June 1987]. The text is not published.

Solo Voyages, Joseph Chaikin's adaptation of three monologues from the plays of Adrienne Kennedy (**The Owl Answers, A Rat's Mass,** and **A Movie Star Has to Star in Black and White**), was performed by Robbie McCauley. Produced by the Interart Theatre in association with the American National Theatre at Kennedy Center, the adaptation was performed in New York (September 11 to October 20, 1985) and Washington (November 25 to December 14, 1985). The production included music composed and performed by Skip LaPlante and Edwina Lee Tyler, set by Jun Maeda, and puppets by Ronnie Asbell. Alisa Solomon's review in the *Village Voice* [1 October 1985] describes LaPlante's "wispy strains on various string and wind instruments" that play from the shadows, while Tyler's insistent drums establish "a rich dialogue with McCauley . . . suggesting a heritage which Clara barely acknowledges." "Poetic language, music, solo performance and design blend and give a theatrical immediacy to an interior monologue," wrote Mel Gussow [in the *New York Times,* 20 September 1985].

Chaikin chose "excerpts that emphasize the cross-references among Kennedy's works . . . ; the images accrete, referring to and illuminating what came before, eventually converging on the grievous complications of an unfixed black, female identity," wrote Solomon. [According to Gussow, the] voyages are a quest for "ancestry (literary as well as genetic)" through the mind of Clara Passmore, who is both "tourist and refugee" of a Eurocentric/Hollywood culture.

David Willinger, assistant director of *Solo Voyages,* discusses the development of the piece in [*Intersecting Boundaries*], "Developing a Concert for the Spoken Voice," and includes an interview of Robbie McCauley. The collaboration of music, scene, mask, and puppets enrich the varied and expressive performance of Robbie McCauley "on her mystical pilgrimage toward self recognition" [Gussow] in this chamber piece.

Kennedy's *Deadly Triplets: A Theatre Mystery and Journal* (1990) includes a novella based on her experiences in London in the sixties; it is set in the theatre world. "It concerns confused identities and the [narrator's] own search for a clearer sense of self as she considers what she knows about her estranged (and possibly dead) mother" [Jean Keleher, *Library Journal* 115 (1 May 1990)]. The "Theatre Journal" includes Kennedy's memoirs from the same period in London; these vignettes suggest the counterpoint between autobiography and the novella and rehearse important backgrounds for Kennedy the playwright.

The Ohio State Murders was given in a workshop production by the Great Lakes Theater Festival (which commissioned the work) in Cleveland, Ohio, on June 16 and 17, 1990 (three performances), at the Eldred Theatre, Case Western Reserve University, and in Yale University's "Winterfest," January 16 to February 9, 1991 (fifteen performances), at the University Theatre. Both productions were directed by Gerald Freedman. At the Great Lakes Theater Festival, Hazel Medina played the central figure, writer Suzanne Alexander, with Bellary Darden as the younger Suzanne; at Yale, the role of the "present Suzanne" was enacted by Olivia Cole and Simi Junior was "Suzanne in 1949, 1950 and 1951."

Kennedy set her play on the Ohio State University campus, "where Suzanne Alexander, a prominent black writer who attended Ohio State, has been asked back to lecture on the roots of the violent imagery in her work. Told mostly in flashback sequences that recount Alexander's student years in Columbus, *The Ohio State Murders* is a shocking portrait of a young black woman's struggle in the racially torn America of the late 1940's and early 1950's." If, as Kennedy says, her "plays are meant to be states of mind," then this work examines the concourse of social violence and hatred in the life and mind of a sensitive student-become-writer. Although given A's for her brilliant analysis of Hardy's *Tess of the D'Urbevilles,* Suzanne is prevented from becoming an English major because of race; seduced by her white professor, Suzanne and her children become the victims of violence and guilt. The narrative structure allows past and present to merge in a timelessness that permits repressed fears to be a presence on the stage.

Kennedy's *She Talks to Beethoven* was published in *Antaeus* (1991); it was given a staged reading at River Arts (Woodstock, New York) in 1989. Kennedy sees the material in this play as an extension of *The Ohio State Murders.* The central character is also the writer, Suzanne Alexander, who writes about and speaks to Beethoven in a meditation that merges time into presence. It is framed and interrupted by radio broadcasts about Suzanne's husband, David, who is missing under mysterious circumstances; he has received threats and has disappeared to protect his wife from whom he is otherwise inseparable. Although the play is set in Legon near Accra, West Africa, Suzanne's writing concerns Beethoven's life in Vienna; the play becomes a dialogue between writer and composer merging distance and time in a bond of mutual understanding, while music sustains a continuum emphasizing the counterpoint of Eurocentric and African-American culture. Having revealed to Suzanne that her wound is not healing, Beethoven confides his deafness and his need for "conversation books" to her. Imagining this loss through reading the "conversation books," Suzanne also discovers poems and encouragement from the absent David, who left them between the leaves of the books. Finally, as Beethoven's death scene is read from Suzanne's manuscript, David returns to her side, his danger abated. Tonally unlike Kennedy's earlier writing, *She Talks to Beethoven* discovers connections that comfort.

The Film Club conveys the anxiety of Suzanne Alexander awaiting the release of her husband, who is detained in West Africa. Images from Bette Davis movies are counterpointed by scenes from *Dracula;* compulsive walks in Windsor Park near London prefigure dread-become-hysteria when Suzanne returns to Washington. *The Film Club* is published with *She Talks to Beethoven* and *The Ohio State Murders* as *The Alexander Plays.*

Adrienne Kennedy continues to write new plays, and so conclusions about the place(s) of her oeuvre in the context of American theatre are necessarily tentative. As their production history suggests, her plays have intrigued producers and directors of the experimental stage. Among the plays on New York stages in 1964 were Samuel Beckett's *Play,* Harold Pinter's *The Lovers,* Edward Albee's *Who's Afraid of Virginia Woolf,* Eugene Ionesco's *Le Piéton de L'Air,* Pirandello's *Right You Are (If You Think You Are).* Like Kennedy's *Funnyhouse of a Negro,* these plays expressed the problematic of fragmented selves and self-perception; unlike them, Kennedy's materials and dramaturgy reflected a uniquely Afro-American circumstance. Also on stage in New York in 1964 were Amiri Baraka's *Dutchman,* Athol Fugard's *Blood Knot,* James Baldwin's *Blues for Mr. Charlie,* and Lorraine Hansberry's *The Sign in Sidney Brustein's Window,* each bringing voice to racial and social issues. Among them, Kennedy's material and method was an anomaly. Michael Kahn indicates [in an interview in *Intersecting Boundaries*] that Kennedy's early work was ostracized because the plays were "considered neurotic and not supportive of the black movement." When Kennedy turned to a more overtly political event in *An Evening with Dead Essex,* critics saw a new facet in her writing, yet, no matter how deeply they are embedded within the psyche of a character, Kennedy's plays all express cultural conflict and allude to wider events (as in, for example, the Nazis in *A Rat's Mass*, Lumumba in *Funnyhouse*).

The commissioned works of the 1980s (*Black Children's Day, A Lancashire Lad,* and the adaptations of *Orestes* and *Electra*) were based on structures of narrative; perhaps these and the autobiographical writings (*People Who Led to My Plays* and *Deadly Triplets*) have led to the new plays, *The Ohio State Murders* and *She Talks to Beethoven*, which conflate narrator with writer.

Naturally, the reception of Kennedy's works reflected critical expectations and circumstance as much as it did the world and methods of her plays. Audiences have been confused and negative as well as enthusiastic and moved by her writing. European response, particularly in Rome (*A Rat's Mass*, 1966) and in Paris (*Drôle de baraque*, 1968), showed appreciation for Kennedy's plays, recognizing her articulation of racial politics in a personal and intense mythopoetic dramaturgy. Over the thirty years that Kennedy has been writing, American theatre has embraced new forms; the plays that invited excitement because of their challenges seem more accessible.

FURTHER READING

Binder, Wolfgang. "A *MELUS* Interview: Adrienne Kennedy." *MELUS* 12, No. 3 (Fall 1985): 99-108.

> Interview in which Kennedy discusses her artistic career and development.

Blau, Herbert. "The American Dream in American Gothic: The Plays of Sam Shepherd and Adrienne Kennedy." *Modern Drama* XXVII, No. 4 (December 1989): 520-39.

> Discusses the concept of the "American dream" in relation to the plays of Shepherd and Kennedy.

Bryant-Jackson, Paul K., and Overbeck, Lois More, eds. *Intersecting Boundaries: The Theatre of Adrienne Kennedy.* Minneapolis: University of Minnesota Press, 1990, 254 p.

> Collection of critical essays.

Cohn, Ruby. "Black on Black: Baraka, Bullins, Kennedy." In her *New American Dramatists: 1960-1980*, pp. 94-115. New York: Grove Press, 1982.

> Brief survey of Kennedy's work.

Curb, Rosemary K. "Re/cognition, Re/presentation, Re/creation in Woman-Conscious Drama: The Seer, the Seen, the Scene, the Obscene." *Theatre Journal* 37, No. 3 (October 1985): 302-16.

> Interprets *Funnyhouse of a Negro* as a feminist drama,

contending that in the play "a pivotal female character speaks in an intensely private voice of the anguish and paralysis she experiences as her identity is broken into stereotyped roles or alter egos."

Fletcher, Winona L. "Who Put the 'Tragic Mulatto' in the Tragic Mulatto?" In *Women in American Theatre: Revised and Expanded Edition*, edited by Helen Krich Chinoy and Linda Walsh Jenkins, pp. 262-68. New York: Theatre Communications Group, 1987.

> Contends that Kennedy "turns from realism to a surrealist world that can display the tortures and nightmares of her female character—a tragic mulatto searching for an identity that is trapped in conventions and torn by the paradoxes of living in a no man's (nor women's) land."

Kintz, Linda. "The Sanitized Spectacle: What's Birth Got to Do with It? Adrienne Kennedy's *A Movie Star Has to Star in Black and White*." *Theatre Journal* 44, No. 1 (March 1992): 67-86.

> Analyzes Kennedy's play from a feminist perspective, focusing on the concept of birth.

Murray, Timothy. "Facing the Camera's Eye: Black and White Terrain in Women's Drama." In *Reading Black, Reading Feminist: A Critical Anthology*, edited by Henry Louis Gates, Jr., pp. 155-75. New York: Meridian, 1990.

> Includes a brief thematic and stylistic analysis of Kennedy's *An Evening with Dead Essex*.

Oliver, Edith. Review of *Funnyhouse of a Negro*, by Adrienne Kennedy. *The New Yorker* XXXIX, No. 49 (25 January 1964): 76, 78.

> Laudatory review of the New York production.

Sollors, Werner. "Owls and Rats in the American Funnyhouse: Adrienne Kennedy's Drama." *American Literature: A Journal of Literary History, Criticism, and Bibliography* 63, No. 3 (September 1991): 507-32.

> Overview of Kennedy's work. Sollors states: "It is hoped that the following reading of seven of Kennedy's major plays against the background of her autobiography may suggest the unpredictability and open-endedness of literary influences and stimulate further interest in her work."

Tener, Robert L. "Theatre of Identity: Adrienne Kennedy's Portrait of the Black Woman." *Studies in Black Literature* 6, No. 2 (Summer 1975): 1-5.

> Explores the imagery in *The Owl Answers*, maintaining that Kennedy uses "images of historical and religious figures and those of birds and the fig tree to make a bitter and satirical comment on the American black female trapped by the conflict of cultures and sexual roles in twentieth-century America."

Thomas Middleton
1580-1627

INTRODUCTION

Middleton is one of the finest English playwrights of the Jacobean period, ranked by some critics behind only William Shakespeare and Ben Jonson. A productive writer and frequent collaborator, he composed some thirty plays as well as prose pamphlets, masques, and pageants with such contemporaries as Thomas Dekker, John Webster, and William Rowley. Some scholars argue that he even collaborated with Shakespeare on *Timon of Athens* and was the anonymous reviser of *Macbeth*. (Two songs from Middleton's *The Witch* have been incorporated into Shakespeare's tragedy.) Middleton's plays are noted for their intricate plotting and detached, ironic tone. His comedies, such as *The Roaring Girl* and *A Chaste Maid in Cheapside* are admired for their lively depictions of city life in London, while his greatest tragedies—including *The Revenger's Tragedy*, *Women Beware Women*, and *The Changeling*—are heralded for their incisive depictions of corruption and moral depravity.

BIOGRAPHICAL INFORMATION

Middleton was born in London, the son of a prosperous bricklayer. His father died in 1586, leaving a substantial estate, over which the heirs conducted numerous and protracted legal disputes. Middleton entered Queen's College, Oxford, in 1598, but it appears that he did not complete his studies. A legal document from early 1601 records testimony that indicates that Middleton was in London at that time, "accompaninge the players." Evidence of Middleton's earliest theatrical work comes from the *Diary* of Philip Henslowe, joint owner of the Fortune theater and banker for the Lord Admiral's Men, an acting company that played at the Fortune. Henslowe recorded that on 22 May 1602 a payment of five pounds was made to Middleton and others for work on *Caesar's Fall, or The Two Shapes*, a play now lost. In 1603 Middleton married Magdalen Marbecke, whose brother Thomas was a member of the Admiral's Men. Around this time Middleton also began writing for the Boys of St. Paul's, a company of child actors associated with the school at St. Paul's Cathedral. A number of his early successes, including *A Trick to Catch the Old One*, *A Mad World My Masters*, and *Michaelmas Term* were produced by this troupe. Subsequently he was briefly associated with another children's company, the Blackfriars, before beginning a series of tragedies for the King's Men, the foremost company of its time—a group that included Shakespeare among its members. It is during this period that Middleton is thought to have worked on *Timon of Athens*.

In 1613 Middleton was engaged to write a civic pageant for the inauguration of the new Lord Mayor of London. This work, *The New River Entertainment*, was the first in a series

Vera Effigies Tho. Middletoni Gent.

of pageants that eventually led to Middleton's appointment as Chronologer to the City of London in 1620. The duties of this remunerative post, which he held until his death, included the keeping of a journal of civic events and the occasional writing of speeches and public entertainments. Middleton's greatest triumph on the stage came with his last—and most controversial—play, *A Game at Chess* (1624). A biting satire depicting religious and political contentions between Spain and England, the play was a phenomenal success that ran an unprecedented nine days to packed houses until it was suppressed at the command of King James I. The principal actors of the King's Men were questioned, as was Middleton's son Edward. Middleton himself apparently had gone into hiding. There is no firm evidence that he or anyone else was ever punished, though tradition holds that Middleton was imprisoned for a time. The play was soon published and went through three editions within a year. This, then, was Middleton's final artistic achievement of any note; aside from a pair of civic pageants, he wrote nothing more before his death in 1627.

MAJOR WORKS

Proficient in several genres, Middleton produced comedies, satires, tragicomedies, and tragedies. His greatest comedies were his early "citizen comedies" set in contemporary London among the middle class. Constructed around schemes and intrigues typically involving money and marriage, such plays as *A Trick to Catch the Old One*, *A Mad World My Masters*, *A Chaste Maid in Cheapside*, and *Michaelmas Term* are highly theatrical pieces, carefully plotted and suffused with realistic detail. The realism is offset, however, by the frequently farcical action and the numerous outlandish or grotesque characters. The world Middleton depicts in his comedies is one in which there are no moral absolutes; the ostensible heroes are often merely the most effective schemers, the villains may go unpunished, and supposedly virtuous characters are frequently depicted as fools or hypocrites. Middleton's great tragedies are also set in morally ambiguous worlds that corrode the virtue of the principal characters. Vindice in *The Revenger's Tragedy*, Beatrice and De Flores in *The Changeling*, and virtually all of the figures in *Women Beware Women* are depraved by the pervasive corruption of the societies depicted in the play. With penetrating psychological realism, Middleton shows these characters to be fully aware but powerless victims of desires that are unchecked by societal restraints.

CRITICAL RECEPTION

Because he worked so often in collaboration and wrote plays for hire in a variety of styles and genres, Middleton's reputation among critics was for many years that of a theatrical craftsman rather than an artist. Beginning in the nineteenth century, however, his works began to receive scholarly attention. Fundamental studies have since been conducted which have more precisely defined Middleton's canon, establishing which plays were or were not composed by him and determining his share in his numerous collaborations. With the author's overall output at least reasonably well established, subsequent commentators have been able to evaluate the characteristic attributes of Middletonian drama. They have examined and admired the intricate plots, swift pacing, and complex characterizations in his work. Critics have also analyzed the ironic tone, the close correspondence between characters and their speech patterns, and the vivid evocation of place and situation in Middleton's plays. With such investigations has come greater recognition of Middleton's stature as an artist. As T. S. Eliot said simply, "Middleton in the end . . . is a great example of great English drama."

NOTE: The authorship of *The Revenger's Tragedy* has been the subject of much scholarly debate. It is assumed in the following entry that Middleton is the author of the play, though individual critics may attribute it to Cyril Tourneur.

PRINCIPAL WORKS

PLAYS

The Honest Whore, Part 1 [with Thomas Dekker] 1604
The Phoenix c. 1604
A Trick to Catch the Old One c. 1605
Your Five Gallants c. 1605
A Mad World My Masters c. 1606
Michaelmas Term c. 1606
**The Revenger's Tragedy* c. 1606
A Yorkshire Tragedy c. 1606
The Second Maiden's Tragedy 1611
The Roaring Girl, or Moll Cutpurse [with Dekker] 1611
No Wit, No Help Like a Woman's c. 1611
A Chaste Maid in Cheapside c. 1613
The Witch c. 1614
A Fair Quarrel [with William Rowley] c. 1617
The Mayor of Queenborough, or Hengist King of Kent c. 1618
The Old Law, or A New Way to Please You [with Rowley] c. 1618
Anything for a Quiet Life [with John Webster] c. 1621
Women Beware Women c. 1621
The Changeling [with Rowley] 1622
A Game at Chess 1624

OTHER MAJOR WORKS

The Wisdom of Solomon Paraphrased (poem) 1597
The Ghost of Lucrece (poem) 1598-99
The Black Book (pamphlet) 1604
The New River Entertainment (pageant) 1613
The Triumphs of Truth (pageant) 1614
The Triumphs of Honor and Industry (pageant) 1617
The Inner Temple Masque, or Masque of Heroes (masque) 1619
A Courtly Masque; the Device Called the World Tossed at Tennis [with Rowley] (masque) 1620
Honourable Entertainments Composed for the Service of This Noble City (collected pageants) 1621

*This work is sometimes attributed to Cyril Tourneur.

OVERVIEWS AND GENERAL STUDIES

T.S. Eliot (essay date 1927)

SOURCE: An originally unsigned essay entitled "Thomas Middleton," in *The Times Literary Supplement*, No. 1326, 30 June 1927, pp. 445-46.

[*Eliot, a celebrated American-born English poet, essayist, and critic, stressed in his commentary the importance of tradition, religion, and morality in literature. His emphasis on imagery, symbolism, and meaning helped to establish the theories of New Criticism. Eliot's concept of the "objective correlative" is considered a major contribution to literary analysis. In his* Selected Essays *(1932), he defines the objective correlative as "a set of objects, a situation, a chain of events which shall be the formula of [a] particular emotion" and which has the ability to evoke that emotion in the reader. Here, in a very influential and often-cited survey of Middleton and his works, Eliot extols the playwright as one of the greatest writers of the Elizabethan period. For example,* The Changeling, *he asserts, "stands above every tragic play of its time, except those of Shakespeare"; and Moll, the heroine of* The Roaring Girl *is, in his estimation, the most vivid depiction of a woman in any drama of the period.*]

Thomas Middleton, the dramatic writer, was not very highly thought of in his own time; the date of his death is not known; we know only that he was buried on July 4, 1627. He was one of the more voluminous, and one of the best, dramatic writers of his time. But it is easy to understand why he is not better known or more popular. It is difficult to imagine his "personality." Several new personalities have recently been fitted to the name of Shakespeare; Jonson is a real figure—our imagination plays about him discoursing at the Mermaid, or laying down the law to Drummond of Hawthornden; Chapman has become a breezy British character as firm as Nelson or Wellington; Webster and Donne are real people for the more intellectual; even Tourneur (Churton Collins having said the last word about him) is a "personality." But Middleton, who collaborated shamelessly, who is hardly separated from Rowley, Middleton, who wrote plays so diverse as **Women Beware Women** and *A Game at Chesse* and *The Roaring Girl,* Middleton remains merely a collective name for a number of plays—some of which, like **The Spanish Gypsy**, are patently by other people.

If we write about Middleton's plays we must write about Middleton's plays, and not about Middleton's personality. Many of these plays are still in doubt. Of all the Elizabethan dramatists Middleton seems the most impersonal, the most indifferent to personal fame or perpetuity, the readiest, except Rowley, to accept collaboration. Also he is the most various. His greatest tragedies and his greatest comedies are as if written by two different men. Yet there seems no doubt that Middleton was both a great comic writer and a great tragic writer. There are a sufficient number of plays, both tragedies and comedies, in which his hand is so far unquestioned, to establish his greatness. His greatness is not that of a peculiar personality, but of a great artist or artisan of the Elizabethan epoch. We have **The Changeling, Women Beware Women,** and *A Game at Chesse;* and we have **The Roaring Girl** and *A Trick to Catch the Old One.* And that is enough. Between the tragedies and the comedies of Shakespeare, and certainly between the tragedies and the comedies of Jonson, we can establish a relation; we can see, for Shakespeare or Jonson, that each had in the end a personal point of view which can be called neither comic nor tragic. But with Middleton we can establish no such relation. He remains merely a name, a voice, the author of certain plays, which are all of them great plays. He has no point of view, is neither sentimental nor cynical; he is neither resigned, nor disillusioned, nor romantic; he has no message. He is merely the name which associates six or seven great plays.

For there is no doubt about **The Changeling.** Like all of the plays attributed to Middleton, it is long-winded and tiresome; the characters talk too much, and then suddenly they stop talking and act; they are real and impelled irresistibly by the fundamental motions of humanity to good or evil. This mixture of tedious discourse and sudden reality is everywhere in the work of Middleton, in his comedy also. In **The Roaring Girl** we read with toil through a mass of cheap conventional intrigue, and suddenly realize that we are, and have been for some time without knowing it, observing a real and unique human being. In reading **The Changeling** we may think, till almost the end of the play, that we have been concerned merely with a fantastic Elizabethan morality, and then discover that we are looking on at an impassionate exposure of fundamental passions of any time and any place. The conventional opinion remains the just judgment: **The Changeling** is Middleton's greatest play. The morality of the convention seems to us absurd. To many intelligent readers this play has only an historical interest, and only serves to illustrate the moral taboos of the Elizabethans. The heroine is a young woman who, in order to dispose of a *fiancé* to whom she is indifferent, so that she may marry the man she loves, accepts the offer of an adventurer to murder the affianced, at the price of becoming the murderer's mistress. Such a plot is, to a modern mind, absurd; and the consequent tragedy seems a fuss about nothing. But **The Changeling** is not merely contingent for its effect upon our acceptance of Elizabethan good form or convention; it is, in fact, far less dependent upon the convention of its epoch than a play like *A Doll's House.* Underneath the convention there is the stratum of permanent truth to human nature. The tragedy of **The Changeling** is an eternal tragedy, as permanent as *Oedipus* or *Antony and Cleopatra;* it is the tragedy of the not naturally bad but irresponsible and undeveloped nature, suddenly caught in the consequences of its own action. In every age and in every civilization there are instances of the same thing: the unmoral nature, suddenly caught in the inexorable toils of morality—of morality not made by man but by Nature—and forced to take the consequences of an act which it had planned light-heartedly. Beatrice is not a moral creature; she becomes moral only by becoming damned. Our conventions are not the same as those which Middleton assumed for his play. But the possibility of that frightful discovery of morality remains permanent.

The words in which Middleton expresses his tragedy are as great as the tragedy. The process through which Beatrice, having decided that De Flores is the instrument for her purpose, passes from aversion to habituation, remains a permanent commentary on human nature. The directness and precision of De Flores are masterly, as is also the virtuousness of Beatrice on first realizing his motives—

> Why, 'tis impossible thou canst be so wicked,
> Or shelter such a cunning cruelty,
> To make his death the murderer of my honour!
> Thy language is so bold and vicious,
> I cannot see which way I can forgive it
> With any modesty

—a passage which ends with the really great lines, lines of which Shakespeare or Sophocles might have been proud:—

Can you weep Fate from its determined purpose?
So soon may you weep me.

But what constitutes the essence of the tragedy is something which has not been sufficiently remarked; it is the *habituation* of Beatrice to her sin; it becomes no longer sin but merely custom. Such is the essence of the tragedy of *Macbeth*—the habituation to crime, the deadening of all moral sense. And in the end Beatrice, having been so long the enforced conspirator of De Flores, becomes (and this is permanently true to human nature) more *his* partner, *his* mate, than the mate and partner of the man for the love of whom she consented to the crime. Her lover disappears not only from the scene but from her own imagination. When she says of De Flores,

A wondrous necessary man, my lord,

her praise is more than half sincere; and at the end she belongs far more to De Flores—towards whom, at the beginning, she felt such physical repulsion—than to her lover Alsemero. And it is De Flores, in the end, to whom she belongs, as Francesca to Paolo:—

Beneath the stars, upon yon meteor
Ever hung my fate, 'mongst things corruptible;
I ne'er could pluck it from him; my loathing
Was prophet to the rest, but ne'er believed.

And De Flores's cry is perfectly sincere and in character:—

I loved this woman in spite of her heart;
Her love I earned out of Piracquo's murder . . .
Yes, and her honour's prize
Was my reward; I thank life for nothing
But that pleasure; it was so sweet to me,
That I have drunk up all, left none behind
For any man to pledge me.

The tragedy of Beatrice is not that she has lost Alsemero, for whose possession she played; it is that she has won De Flores, that she thereafter belongs to him and he to her. *The Changeling* is one of the great tragedies of character originally neither good nor bad deflected by circumstance (as character neither good nor bad may always be) towards evil. Such tragedies are not limited to Elizabethan times: they happen every day and perpetually. The greatest tragedies are occupied with great and permanent moral conflicts: the great tragedies of Æschylus, of Sophocles, of Corneille, of Racine, of Shakespeare have the same burden. In poetry, in dramatic technique, *The Changeling* is inferior to the best plays of Webster, or even of Tourneur. But in the moral essence of tragedy it is safe to say that in this play Middleton is surpassed by one Elizabethan alone, and that is Shakespeare. In every essential respect in which Elizabethan tragedy can be compared to French or to Greek tragedy *The Changeling* stands above every tragic play of its time, except those of Shakespeare.

The genius which blazed in *The Changeling* was fitful but not accidental. The next tragedy after *The Changeling* is

Women Beware Women. The thesis of the plays, as the title indicates, is more arbitrary and less fundamental. The play itself, although less disfigured by ribaldry or clowning, is more tedious. Middleton sinks himself in conventional moralizing of the epoch; so that, if we are impatient; we decide that he gives merely a document of Elizabethan humbug—and then suddenly a personage will blaze out in genuine fire of vituperation. The wickedness of the personages in *Women Beware Women* is conventional wickedness of the stage of the time; yet slowly the exasperation of Bianca, the wife who married beneath her, beneath the ambitions to which she was entitled, emerges from the negative; slowly the real human passions emerge from the mesh of interest in which they begin. And here again Middleton, in writing what appears on the surface a conventional picture-palace Italian melodrama of the time, has caught permanent human feelings. And in this play Middleton shows his interest—more than any of his contemporaries—in innuendo and double meanings; and makes use of that game of chess, which he was to use more openly and directly for satire in that perfect piece of literary and political art, *A Game at Chesse.* The irony could not be improved upon:—

Did I not say my duke would fetch you o'er, Widow?
I think you spoke in earnest when you said it, madam.
And my black king makes all the haste he can too.
Well, madam, we may meet with him in time yet.
I've given thee blind mate twice.

There is hardly anything truer or more impressive in Elizabethan drama than Bianca's gradual self-will and self-importance in consequence of her courtship by the Duke:—

Troth, you speak wondrous well for your old house here;
'Twill shortly fall down at your feet to thank you,
Or stoop, when you go to bed, like a good child,
To ask you blessing.

In spite of all the long-winded speeches, in spite of all the conventional Italianate horrors, Bianca remains, like Beatrice in *The Changeling,* a real woman; as real, indeed, as any woman of Elizabethan tragedy. Bianca is a type of the woman who is purely moved by vanity.

But if Middleton, this obscure and uninteresting person, understood the female better than any of the Elizabethans—better than the creator of the Duchess of Malfy, better than Marlowe, better than Tourneur, or Shirley, or Fletcher, better than any of them except Shakespeare alone—he was also able, in his comedy, to present a finer woman than any of them. *The Roaring Girl* has no apparent relation to Middleton's tragedies, yet it is agreed to be primarily the work of Middleton. It is typical of the comedies of Middleton, and it is the best. In his tragedies Middleton employs all the Italianate horrors of his time, and obviously for the purpose of pleasing the taste of his time; yet underneath we feel always a quiet and undisturbed vision of things as they are and not "another thing." So in his comedies. The comedies are long-winded; the fathers are heavy fathers, and rant as heavy fathers should; the sons are wild and wanton sons, and perform all the pranks to be expected of them; the machinery is the usual heavy Elizabethan machinery; Middleton is solicitous to please his audience with what they expect; but there is underneath the same steady impersonal passionless observation of human nature. *The Roaring Girl* is as artificial as any comedy of the time; its plot creaks loudly; yet the Girl herself is always real. She may rant, she may behave preposterously, but she remains a type of the sort of woman who has renounced all happiness for herself and who lives only for a principle. Nowhere more than in *The Roaring Girl* can the hand of Middleton be distinguished more clearly from the hand of Dekker. Dekker is all sentiment; and, indeed, in the so admired passages of *A Fair Quarrel,* exploited by Lamb, the mood if not the hand of Dekker seems to the unexpert critic to be more present than Middleton's. *A Fair Quarrel* seems as much, if not more, Dekker's than Middleton's. Similarly with *The Spanish Gypsy,* which can with difficulty be attributed to Middleton. But the feeling about Moll Cut-Purse of *The Roaring Girl* is Middleton's rather than anybody's; and after Miranda, and Dante's Beatrice, there is hardly any heroine of fiction who does more honour to her sex than Moll. In Middleton's tragedy there is a strain of realism underneath which is one with the poetry; and in his comedy we find the same thing.

In her recent book on *The Social Mode of Restoration Comedy . . .* Miss Kathleen Lynch calls attention to the gradual transition from Elizabethan-Jacobean to Restoration comedy. She observes, what is certainly true, that Middleton is the greatest "realist" in Jacobean comedy. Miss Lynch's extremely suggestive thesis is that the transition from Elizabethan-Jacobean to later Caroline comedy is primarily economic: that the interest changes from the bourgeois aping gentry to the bourgeois become gentry and accepting a code of manners. In the comedy of Middleton certainly there is as yet no code of manners; but the merchant of Cheapside is *aiming* at becoming a member of the county gentry. Miss Lynch remarks: "Middleton's keen concentration on the spectacle of the interplay of different social classes marks an important development in realistic comedy." She calls attention to this aspect of Middleton's comedy, that it marks, better than the romantic comedy of Shakespeare, or the comedy of Jonson, occupied with what Jonson thought to be permanent and not transient aspects of human nature, the transition between the aristocratic world which preceded the Tudors and the plutocratic modern world which the Tudors initiated and encouraged. By the time of the return of Charles II., as Miss Lynch points out, society had been reorganized and formed, and social conventions had been created. In the Tudor times birth still counted (though nearly all the great families were extinct); by the time of Charles II. only breeding counted. The comedy of Middleton, and the comedy of Brome, and the comedy of Shirley, is intermediate, as Miss Lynch remarks. Middleton, as she observes, marks the transitional stage in which the London tradesman was anxious to cease to be a tradesman and to become a country gentleman. The words of his City Magnate in *Michaelmas Terme* have not yet lost their point:—

A fine journey in the Whitsun holydays, i'faith, to ride with a number of cittizens and their wives, some upon pillions, some upon side-saddles, I and little Thomasine i' the middle, our son and heir, Sim Quomodo, in a peach-colour taffeta jacket, some horse length, or a long yard before us—there will be a fine show on's I can tell you.

But Middleton's comedy is not, like the comedy of Congreve, the comedy of a set social behaviour; it is still, like the later comedy of Dickens, the comedy of individuals, in spite of the perpetual motions of city merchants towards county gentility. In the comedy of the Restoration a figure such as that of Moll Cutpurse would have been impossible. As a social document the comedy of Middleton illustrates the transition from government by a landed aristocracy to government by a city aristocracy gradually engrossing the land. As such it is of the greatest interest. But as literature, as a dispassionate picture of human nature, Middleton's comedy deserves to be remembered chiefly by its real—perpetually real—and human figure of Moll the Roaring Girl. That Middleton's comedy was "photographic," that it introduces us to the low life of the time far better than anything in the comedy of Shakespeare or the comedy of Jonson, better than anything except the pamphlets of Dekker and Greene and Nashe, there is little doubt. But it produced one great play—*The Roaring Girl*—a great play in spite of the tedious long speeches of some of the principal characters, in spite of the clumsy machinery of the plot: for the reason that Middleton was a great observer of human nature, without fear, without sentiment, without prejudice, without personality.

And Middleton in the end—after criticism has subtracted all that Rowley, all that Dekker, all that others contributed—is a great example of great English drama. He means nothing, he has no message; he is merely a great recorder. Incidentally, in flashes and when the dramatic need comes, he is a great poet, a great master of versification:—

I that am of your blood was taken from you
For your better health; look no more upon 't,
But cast it to the ground regardlessly,
Let the common sewer take it from distinction:
Beneath the stars, upon yon meteor
Ever hung my fate, 'mongst things corruptible;
I ne'er could pluck it from him; my loathing
Was prophet to the rest, but ne'er believed.

The man who wrote these lines remains inscrutable, solitary, unadmired; purely an Elizabethan and not himself; welcoming collaboration, indifferent to fame; dying no one knows when and no one knows how, or with what thoughts, if any; attracting, in three hundred years, no personal admiration. Yet he wrote one tragedy which more than any play except those of Shakespeare has a profound and permanent moral value and horror; and one comedy which more than any Elizabethan comedy realizes a free and noble womanhood; and he remains, inscrutable, unphilosophical, interesting only to those few who care for such things.

L. C. Knights (essay date 1937)

SOURCE: "Middleton and the New Social Classes," in *Drama & Society in the Age of Jonson,* 1937. Reprint by Barnes & Noble, 1962, pp. 256-69.

[*A renowned English Shakespearean and Elizabethan scholar, Knights followed the precepts of I. A. Richards and F. R. Leavis as he attempted to identify an underlying pattern in all of Shakespeare's work. His* How Many Children Had Lady Macbeth? *(1933)—a milestone study in the twentieth-century reaction to the Shakespearean criticism of the previous century—disparages the traditional emphasis on "character" as an approach which inhibits the reader's total response to Shakespeare's plays. The following discussion of Middleton is taken from his highly regarded study* Drama & Society in the Age of Jonson, *which was first published in 1937. Knights examines Middleton's comedies and finds the writer overrated, particularly in respect to his often-admired "realism."*]

The assimilation of what is valuable in the literary past . . . is impossible without the ability to discriminate and to reject. Everyone would admit this, in a general way, but there are few to undertake the essential effort—the redistribution of stress, the attempt to put into currency evaluations based more firmly on living needs than are the conventional judgements. To disestablish certain reputations that have 'stood the test of time', to see to it that the epithet 'great' does not spill over from undeniable achievement to a bulk of inferior matter in the work of any one author, is not incompatible with a proper humility.

Sharp discrimination is nowhere more necessary than in the Elizabethan and post-Elizabethan period. It is not—emphatically—a minor nuisance that young men who are capable of an interest in literature should be stimulated to work up a feeling of enjoyment when reading the plays of Dekker and Heywood, or *A King and No King.* There is of course such a thing as an historical interest, but it is as well we should know when it is that we are pursuing and when we are engaged in a completely different activity. It is as well that we should realize—to come to the subject of this [essay]—that our 'appreciation' of *The Changeling* is something different in kind from our 'appreciation' of *The Roaring Girl, A Trick to Catch the Old One, The Phoenix, Michaelmas Term* and all those plays which have led Mr Eliot to assert that Middleton is 'a great comic writer'.

The reference to Mr Eliot is deliberate. His essay [in the *Times Literary Supplement,* 30 June 1927] on Middleton is, it seems to me, a good deal nearer to Lamb than Mr Eliot would care to admit. It does not of course show the exuberant idolatry of Romantic criticism, but it encourages idolatry (see the unusually generous provision of 'great's' in the final paragraphs) and—what is the same thing—inertia. Now that *The Sacred Wood* and its successors are academically 'safe' it is all the more necessary to suggest that certain of Mr Eliot's Elizabethan Essays (those, I would say, on Middleton, Marston, Heywood and Ford) are in quite a different class from, say, the essay on Massinger, and that to ignore the lapses from that usually taut and

distinguished critical prose is not the best way of registering respect for the critic. Middleton, then, is an interesting case—for various reasons.

As the author of *The Changeling,* perhaps the greatest tragedy of the period outside Shakespeare, Middleton deserves to be approached with respect. It is, however, as a comic writer that I wish to consider him here, and a careful re-reading of the dozen comedies by which he is remembered suggests that the conventional estimate of him—the estimate that Mr Eliot has countenanced—needs to be severely qualified.

In the first place, it is usually held that Middleton is a great realist. 'He is the most absolute realist in the Elizabethan drama, vying with the greatest of his fellows in fidelity to life'—that is the text-book account [Schelling, *Elizabethan Drama*]. Miss Lynch remarks that, 'As the greatest realist in Elizabethan drama, Middleton is a hearty observer of life at first hand' [Kathleen M. Lynch, *The Social Mode of Restoration Comedy*], and Mr Eliot, endorsing her verdict, says: 'There is little doubt . . . that Middleton's comedy was "photographic", that it introduces us to the low life of the time far better than anything in the comedy of Shakespeare or the comedy of Jonson, better than anything except the pamphlets of Dekker and Greene and Nashe'.

'Realist', of course, means many things, but what these critics are asserting is that Middleton accurately reflects the life of a certain section of Jacobean London, of gallants and shopkeepers, of lawyers, brokers, cheats and prostitutes. But, reading his comedies as carefully as we can, we find—exciting discovery!—that gallants are likely to be in debt, that they make love to citizens' wives, that lawyers are concerned more for their profits than for justice, and that cutpurses are thieves. Middleton tells us nothing at all about these *as individuals* in a particular place and period. (Turn up any of his brothel scenes—in *Your Five Gallants,* say—for examples of completely generalized conventionality: *The Honest Whore* does it better.) And the obvious reason, it seems to me, is that he was not interested in doing so.

If we take *A Chaste Maid in Cheapside,* a typical comedy, neither one of Middleton's worst nor his best, we find after a second or third reading that all that remains with us is the plot. That certainly is complicated and ingenious. The only fortune of Sir Walter Whorehound, a decayed Welsh knight, lies in his expectations from his relative, the childless Lady Kix. He plans to better his fortunes by marrying Moll, the daughter of Yellowhammer, a goldsmith, and he brings to town a cast-off mistress whom he represents as an heiress and a fit match for Tim, the goldsmith's son. Moll, however, is in love with Touchwood Junior, whose lusty elder brother has had to part from his wife since he begets more children than he can maintain. In London Sir Walter visits the Allwit household, where the husband, Master Allwit (=Wittol—the joke is characteristic) is well paid to father the illegitimate children of Sir Walter and Mistress Allwit. Alarmed lest the knight's marriage should cut off his livelihood Allwit reveals the existence of Sir Walter's children to Yellowhammer, just as the news arrives that Touchwood Senior has procured an heir for Lady Kix, and

Sir Walter's creditors are ready to foreclose. The true lovers are united by the well-worn device of feigning death and going to church in their coffins, and the only unfortunates are Sir Walter and Tim, now married to the Welsh-woman.

I have summarized the plot since it may be evident even from this where the interest centres; it centres on the intrigue. Swinburne's praise [in his Introduction to *The Best Plays of Middleton*] is significant:

> The merit does not indeed consist in any new or subtle study of character, any Shakespearean creation or Jonsonian invention of humours or of men: the spendthrifts and the misers, the courtesans and the dotards, are figures borrowed from the common stock of stage tradition: it is the vivid variety of incident and intrigue, the freshness and ease and vigour of the style, the clear straightforward energy and vivacity of the action, that the reader finds most praise-worthy.

The style is certainly easy and, for its purpose, vigorous enough, but incident, intrigue and action do not make literature, nor are they capable of presenting a full-bodied, particular impression of any kind. Some of Jonson's comedies are the best of farces, but in each of them it is what is *said* that remains in the memory rather than what is *done*. *A Chaste Maid,* however, is thoroughly representative. Middleton's comedies are comedies of intrigue (in spite of the occasional professions of moral intention), and they yield little more than the pleasure of a well-contrived marionette show. One need hardly say that the charge is not that they fail to present full-bodied, three dimensional 'characters' (neither does *Volpone* or *The Alchemist*), nor that they suffer from the 'invraisemblance choquante' of which M. Castelain once found Jonson guilty (the impressionistic scenes are often very good), it is simply that they present neither thought, nor an emotional attitude to experience, nor vividly realized perceptions. They stake all on the action, and that which made them successful on the stage makes them rank low as literature.

To say this is to suggest their limited usefulness as 'social documents'—and it is as social documents 'introducing us to the low life of the time' that they are often praised. They do not embody the thought and opinion of the time, since that is irrelevant to the intrigue. They do not seize on, clarify and explore particular aspects of the social scene, since general counters are all that the action demands. Their value in this connexion lies almost entirely in what Middleton takes for granted, in the indications provided by the situations—situations to which he thought the audience would respond sufficiently for the action to be got under way.

Indirectly, then, but only indirectly and within these limitations, Middleton does reflect some important aspects of the social scene, and we should be grateful to Miss Lynch for telling us where to look. The background that he implicitly asks his audience to accept is a world of thriving citizens, needy gallants and landed gentlemen, and fortune-hunters of all kinds—a world that had sufficient basis in actuality to provide some theatrical verisimilitude for his thoroughly improbable plots.

His shopkeepers and merchants are all of the kind described in *The Roaring Girl*—'coached velvet caps' and 'tuftaffety jackets' who 'keep a vild swaggering in coaches now-a-days; the highways are stopt with them'; who have 'barns and houses yonder at Hockley-hole', and throughout Surrey, Essex and the neighbouring counties. The gallants, on the other hand,

> are people most uncertain; they use great words, but little sense; great beards, but little wit; great breeches but no money,
>
> [*The Family of Love*]

and most of the country gentlemen in Town are like Laxton of *The Roaring Girl*:

> All my land's sold;
> I praise heav'n for't, 't has rid me of much trouble.

For all of this class a wealthy widow or a citizen's daughter is an irresistible bait, and if they cannot manage a 'good' marriage they intrigue with citizens' wives for maintenance.

The numerous kindred of Sir Walter Whorehound are all fortune hunters, and a good deal of the amusement they provided, when their intrigues were successful, must have been due to their showing the tables turned; the underlying assumption is that as a rule the city preys on the country:

> Alas, poor birds that cannot keep the sweet country, where they fly at pleasure, but must needs come to London to have their wings clipt, and are fain to go hopping home again!
>
> [*Michaelmas Term*]

It is not merely that the city is the home of the usurer, or that individual merchants 'die their conscience in the blood of prodigal heirs' [*A Chaste Maid*], Middleton assumes a major social movement—the transference of land from the older gentry to the citizen middle class.

> You merchants were wont to be merchant staplers; but now gentlemen have gotten up the trade, for there is not one gentlemen amongst twenty but his land be engaged in twenty statutes staple.
>
> [*The Family of Love*]

In *A Trick to Catch the Old One* (c. 1605?) Witgood, having sunk all his 'goodly uplands and downlands . . . into that little pit, lechery', resolves to mend his fortunes. He takes a former mistress to London, introducing her to his uncle, Lucre, as a wealthy widow whom he is about to marry. The trick succeeds as only the tricks of comedy prodigals can. Lucre holds the mortgage of Witgood's lands, and to improve his nephew's prospect's with the 'window' temporarily—as he intends—hands over the papers. Hoard, another usurer and Lucre's lifelong enemy, also pays court to the widow, finally marrying her. Both Lucre and Hoard realize that they have been duped, whilst Witgood, freed from his debts, marries Hoard's niece.

The fun that Middleton gets out of this is dependent upon three assumptions. The first is that a widow reputed to have land worth £400 a year will be 'mightily followed'; the second, that the gulling of usurers, lawyers and creditors is intrisically comic; the third, that the bait of a country estate will catch any citizen.

Michaelmas Term has a similar basis of reference. Easy, a gentleman of Essex, comes to London at the beginning of the Michaelmas Term. Quomodo, a grasping woollendraper, has seen and coveted Easy's lands, and sets one of his 'familiar spirits', Shortyard, to bring about his ruin. Easy is soon gulled; he enters into bond for the disguised Shortyard, standing surety for a supply of cloth worth less than a third of its nominal value, and finally forfeits his estate to Quomodo. The latter, however, overreaches himself. He spreads a false report of his death (so that he can enjoy the spectacle of his sorrowing widow), and so prepares the way for a stage trick by which Easy both regains his estates and marries Quomodo's wife. As usual there are subordinate figures who illustrate various 'foul mysteries'.

Here too the merchants and shopkeepers form part of a flourishing economy:

> You've happened upon the money-men, sir; they and
> some of their brethren, I can tell you, will not stick to
> offer thirty thousand pound to be cursed still: great
> monied men, their stocks lie in the poor's throats.

The source of their gains is indicated—'Gentry is the chief fish we tradesmen catch', 'We undo gentlemen daily'—and Easy, Salewood, Rearage, as their names show, belong to the class whose incomes have failed to rise in proportion to prices.

In both these plays it is the manner in which citizen ambition is presented that is significant. Hoard, rejoicing at having obtained the widow, soliloquizes:

> What a sweet blessing hast thou, Master Hoard, above
> a multitude! . . . Not only a wife large in possessions,
> but spacious in content. . . . When I wake, I think of her
> lands—that revives me; when I go to bed, I dream of
> her beauty. . . . She's worth four hundred a year in her
> very smock. . . . But the journey will be all, in troth,
> into the country; to ride to her lands in state and order
> following: my brother, and other worshipful gentlemen,
> whose companies I ha' sent down for already, to ride
> along with us in their goodly decorum beards, their broad
> velvet cassocks, and chains of gold twice or thrice double;
> against which time I'll entertain some ten men of mine
> own into liveries, all of occupations or qualities; I will
> not keep an idle man about me: the sight of which will
> so vex my adversary Lucre—for we'll pass by his door
> of purpose, make a little stand for the nonce, and have
> our horses curvet before the window—certainly he
> will never endure it, but run up and hang himself
> presently. . . . To see ten men ride after me in watchet
> liveries, with orange-tawny capes,—'twill cut his comb
> i' faith.

> [*A Trick to Catch the Old One*]

Quomodo's ambition is the same as Hoard's; it is 'land, fair neat land' that he desires.

> O that sweet, neat, comely, proper, delicate, parcel of
> land! like a fine gentlewoman i' th' waist, not so great
> as pretty, pretty; the trees in summer whistling, the silver
> waters by the banks harmoniously gliding. I should have
> been a scholar; an excellent place for a student; fit for
> my son that lately commenced at Cambridge, whom
> now I have placed at Inns of Court. Thus we that seldom
> get lands honestly, must leave our heirs to inherit our
> knavery. . . . Now I begin to set one foot upon the land:
> methinks I am felling of trees already; we shall have
> some Essex logs yet to keep Christmas with, and that's
> a comfort. . . .

> Now shall I be divulg'd a landed man
> Throughout the livery: one points, another whispers,
> A third frets inwardly; let him fret and hang! . . .

> . . . Now come my golden days in. Whither is the
> worshipful Master Quomodo and his fair bed-fellow rid
> forth? To his land in Essex. Whence come those goodly
> loads of logs? From his land in Essex. Where grows this
> pleasant fruit, says one citizen's wife in the Row? At
> master Quomodo's orchard in Essex. O, O, does it so?
> I thank you for that good news, i' faith. . . .

> A fine journey in the Whitsun holydays, i' faith, to ride
> down with a number of citizens and their wives, some upon
> pillions, some upon side-saddles, I and little Thomasine i'
> th' middle, our son and heir, Sim Quomodo, in a peach-
> colour taffeta jacket, some horse-length, or a long yard
> before us;—there will be a fine show on's, I can tell you.

> [*Michaelmas Term*]

There is an obvious difference between the tone and manner of these soliloquies and the handling of similar themes by Jonson or Massinger, and it is this difference that places Middleton as a social dramatist. The ambition of Hoard and Quomodo is not set in the light of a positive ideal of citizen conduct (something that we find, though fitfully, in the work of Dekker and Heywood, dramatists inferior to Middleton), its implications are not grasped and presented. (Contrast the way in which we are made to feel the full significance of Volpone's lusts, of the City Madam's ambitions.) Middleton is, I think, relying on what was almost a stock response, making a gesture in the direction of a familiar scene where those goodly decorum beards wagged in real life as their owners journeyed to their newly acquired manors in the country.

To say this is to say that the attitude presented at a given point does not emerge from the interplay of different pressures *within* the drama, and that it does not engage with other elements in the reader's response to form a new whole. In each case it is a purely local effect that is obtained (it is significant that prose, not verse, is the medium), and Hoard's meditation could appear equally well in any one of half a dozen plays. Middleton's satire, in short, is related to the non-dramatic prose satire of the period; more particularly, it has affinities with the 'Character', in which the sole and proposed is the exhibition of witty 'sentences' and ingenious comparisons, of a general self-conscious dexterity.

> How many there be in the world of his fortunes, that prick their own calves with briars, to make an easy passage for others; or, like a toiling usurer, sets his son a-horseback, while he himself goes to the devil a-foot in a pair of old strossers.

> [*No Wit, No Help Like a Woman's*]

> What a fortunate elder brother is he, whose father being a rammish ploughman, himself a perfumed gentleman spending the labouring reek from his father's nostrils in tobacco, the sweat of his father's body in monthly physic for his pretty queasy harlot! he sows apace i' th' country; the tailor o'ertakes him i' th' city, so that oftentimes before the corn comes to earing, 'tis up to the ears in high collars, and so at every harvest the reapers take pains for the mercers: ha! why, this is stirring happiness indeed.

> [*The Phoenix*]

> . . . Then came they [gallants] to their gentility, and swore *as they were gentlemen;* and their gentility they swore away so fast, that they had almost sworn away all the ancient gentry out of the land; which, indeed, are scarce missed, for that yeomen and farmers' sons, with the help of a few Welshmen, have undertook to supply their places.

> [*The Family of Love*]

Middleton constantly gives us such glimpses of a society in the process of rapid reorganization. Most of his characters assume that social advancement is a major preoccupation of the citizen class, and certainly the passages that I have quoted are amongst the most vivid in his plays; but Miss Lynch is, I think, wrong when she says that 'his comic intrigue is directed by the psychology of class relationships'. That would imply a far different distribution of emphasis within the plays themselves, and a far keener penetration; for Middleton only seizes on a few external characteristics—the velvet cassocks and gold chains of the citizens galloping into the country in their holiday clothes—and these, lively as the descriptions sometimes are, are merely incidental to the main intention. It is possible, that is, to assemble 'evidence' of a limited kind from Middleton's plays, but it is no use looking for the more important kind of illustration of the life of the period, for the kind of fact that is inseparable from interpretation and criticism of the fact. The isolated passages are not, in fact, unified by a dominant attitude, and one can only regret that the profound understanding of an essential human morality that one finds in **The Changeling** is nowhere displayed in the comedies.

That Middleton was a 'transitional' writer, not merely because he reflected social change, a single comparison may show. If we read, first, Jonson's satire on 'the godly brethren' in *The Alchemist,* then Dryden's description of Shimei, we shall be in a position to judge the quality of Middleton's satire on 'puritan' hypocrisy.

> *Dryfat.* I do love to stand to anything I do, though I lose by it: in truth, I deal but too truly for this world. You shall hear how far I am entered in the right way already. First, I live in charity, and give small alms to such as be not of the right sect; I take under twenty i' th' hundred, nor no forfeiture of bonds unless the law tell my conscience I may do't; I set no pot on a' Sundays, but feed on cold meat drest a' Saturdays; I keep no holydays nor fasts, but eat most flesh o' Fridays of all days i' th' week; I do use to say inspired graces, able to starve a wicked man with length; I have Aminadabs and Abrahams to my godsons, and I chide them when they ask me blessing: and I do hate the red letter more than I follow the written verity.

> [*The Family of Love*]

The Middleton passage is good fooling, but it has neither the drive and assurance of Jonson, on the one hand, nor of Dryden on the other. I have tried to indicate the source of Jonson's power; he is able to enlist the common interests of a heterogeneous audience, and to build on common attitudes; in the satire directed against Ananias the idiom and the method of caricature are alike 'popular'. Dryden provides an obvious contrast. The tone of the Shimei passage is one of cool superiority, and the manner is, characteristically, urbane. Dryden, that is, is sure of his code; it is the code of a homogeneous, though limited, society—'the Town'. Middleton has neither of these sources of strength. At times he betrays something like a positive animus against the citizens, but he has nothing to set against their standards, neither an aristocratic code nor a popular tradition. That he was an almost exact contemporary of Jonson warns us against a rigid interpretation of any period, and suggests the limits to which an enquiry into the effects of environment on personality can be profitably pursued. And we should do well, I think, to reserve the description 'great comedy' for plays of the quality of *Volpone* and *The Alchemist*—when we can find them.

Ronald Huebert (essay date 1987)

SOURCE: "Middleton's Nameless Art," in *The Sewanee Review,* Vol. XCV, No. 4, Fall, 1987, pp. 591-609.

[*In the following essay, Huebert examines Middleton's depiction of sexuality and the desire for power in* A Chaste Maid in Cheapside, Women Beware Women, *and* The Changeling. *"Middleton's work as a whole," he claims, "is a statement of what happens when you make self-interest (including sexual self-interest) the measure of all things."*]

Thomas Middleton was "but a base fellow," Ben Jonson said to Drummond of Hawthornden [see *Ben Jonson's Conversations with William Drummond of Hawthornden,* ed. R. F. Patterson, 1974]. I'm sure this remark owes more to Jonson's drinking habits than to his critical principles; but it does imply something worth knowing about the distance which separates Middleton from his famous contemporaries. In temperament, connections, and circumstances he was a man apart from the mainstream. Eliot thought Middleton was a playwright without a point of view [*Times*

Literary Supplement, 30 June 1927], and this is a tempting refuge if you've come to him expecting Marlowe's titanic self-assurance or Jonson's bearish conviction or even Fletcher's voluptuous royalism. Middleton had none of these. But I think it's more likely that Middleton had a point of view which Eliot either didn't understand, or perhaps didn't want to understand. If Margot Heinemann is right, in *Puritanism and Theatre: Thomas Middleton and Opposition Drama under the Early Stuarts* (1980), and if Middleton really did see his art as a minority report, as contributing to the cause of parliamentary Puritanism, then his commitment would be outrageously hostile to the program Eliot declared for himself: "The general point of view may be described as classicist in literature, royalist in politics, and anglo-catholic in religion." But like most simple dichotomies this one is too simple. Middleton would have wanted to resist being classified into either of the great seventeenth-century camps that the retrospective eye of history so easily distinguishes. He wouldn't have called himself a puritan. Even Heinemann has to admit, nervously I think, that "Middleton never uses the word 'Puritan' in a favourable sense." He does use it, conspicuously in *A Chaste Maid in Cheapside*, with uninhibited satirical glee. But I don't think that puts him into the King's party or Buckingham's or Archbishop Laud's. Middleton was an ironist. He was skeptical of dogmas, uncomfortable with party-line loyalties, and keenly aware that a political stance that seemed cogent in 1605 might have become absurd by 1624. I'm sure he had a well-trained ear for whatever might sound sanctimonious on either side of the great divide. Where did Middleton stand? It's not a question you can answer by appealing to party loyalties of one kind or another, because Middleton had the courage to stand stubbornly on his own ground.

In his attitude toward women, for example, he seems to have been liberated from many of the stereotypical vices and habits of his contemporaries. He did not believe that women are less intelligent than men, or that they deserve inferior education. I doubt if the passively decorative ideal of femininity could have survived the influence of a mother as enterprising as Middleton's appears to have been. In his comedies the female characters are just as clever and self-interested as the men; the middle-class women in particular don't think of themselves as chattels, and they rebel if their menfolk do. Thomasine, in *Michaelmas Term*, resents being married to a man so enraptured with the prospect of acquiring land that nothing else matters. "Why am I wife to him that is no man?" she asks; her tone of voice makes it certain that she's not satisfied with being called "sweet honey-thigh" and then dismissed with a wave of her husband's hand. The women in Middleton's plays want to be taken seriously—as domestic, economic, conspiratorial, or sexual partners—and if they aren't they raise hell.

Middleton's view of society is a very messy picture on the whole. It includes woolen drapers (Quomodo in *Michaelmas Term*), tobacco-sellers (Vapor in *A Fair Quarrel*), prostitutes (Frank Gullman in *A Mad World, My Masters*), distinguished criminals (Moll Cutpurse in *The Roaring Girl*), lawyers, hair-dressers, country wenches, apothecaries, apprentices, scriveners, bailiffs, midwives, ruined gen-

tlemen, discarded soldiers, merchant adventurers, moneylenders, and the odd wealthy aristocrat. This chaotic material isn't that much different from what Jonson was using in his comedies, but Middleton's way of organizing it is. He resists imposing a ready-made hierarchy onto the social fabric. Many of his characters are either sliding down the social scale or clawing their way up, but the integrity of the scale is itself in doubt; it seems to exist subjectively, in the minds of such middle-class overreachers as Quomodo or Walkadine Hoard (in *A Trick to Catch the Old One*), but it never has the status of divine truth or even social consensus. To call this a democratic attitude would be historically awkward but in many senses true. There's no stuffiness in his view of society—not even the snobbery of the selfmade man—and the judgments he makes or wants others to make are the ones you can't evade by appealing to class prejudice or economic power. Jonson, after having established himself as a major playwright, began to earn big money by devising and writing scripts for the masques performed at court; Middleton, at a comparable point in his career, became the regular inventor of the Lord Mayors' shows. In middle age Jonson was granted a pension by the crown, Middleton became City Chronologer. The difference does imply something about what mattered to each of them.

And while Jonson couldn't stand the Italianate cleverness of his best scenographic collaborator, Inigo Jones, Middleton had no such problems with Gerard Christmas. To the printed text of *The Triumphs of Honour and Virtue*, the Lord Mayor's pageant for Sir Peter Proby (1622), Middleton appends this note: "For the body of the whole triumph, with all the proper graces and ornaments of art and workmanship, the reputation of those rightly appertain to the deserts of Master Garret Chrismas, an exquisite master in his art, and a performer above his promises." It's a generously worded acknowledgment. I've chosen this one (from among the half-dozen similar compliments Middleton paid Christmas) because it says something interesting about Middleton's concept of art. It seems to me exactly right that "art" and "workmanship" should be connected in Middleton's mind. To master an art is to acquire and perfect a particular skill. Used in this way, the term isn't veiled in darkness or overburdened with prestige. Unlike Jonson, Middleton doesn't have to argue about the relative status of pen and pencil (or, in this case, the chisel), because for him status isn't the point. Nor does he have to renounce the metaphysical terrors he can't control, as Prospero does when he remembers the graves that have been opened "by my so potent Art." Middleton's use of the term is more casual, closer to the ordinary usage of his day, and even less ponderous than a synonym such as "craft" would be today. I don't think the difference between an artist and an artisan would have mattered much to him.

To demystify the term in this way needn't (and in Middleton's case doesn't) cleanse it of ambiguities. What counts as craftsmanship in one set of circumstances may be craftiness in another; the close association between "art" and "cunning" in Middleton's day would have ensured a permissive context for this ambiguity. In *The Changeling*, as Beatrice-Joanna pounces on the solution to her problem—to hire De Flores as her hit-man, that is—she's amazed that it's taken her so long to come up with the idea: "Why, men of art make much of poison, / Keep one to expel another; where was my art?" Knowledge, skill, craft, cunning, art: these are morally neutral, in the sense that they are instruments which men and women use for ends both fair and foul. In Middleton's world it's perfectly right that a term such as *art* should remain uncommitted. Verbally he does want to have it both ways. And until you grant him this license (and the responsibility that goes with it), you're unlikely to admire what he does have to offer in his best plays: *A Chaste Maid in Cheapside, Women Beware Women,* and (especially) *The Changeling.*

A Chaste Maid in Cheapside is a play about sexual management. Middleton takes the polymorphous perversity of his Londoners for granted, and poses a series of remarkable scenarios for dealing with it. The need for something more structured than just following your sexual inclinations arises most obviously in the Touchwood Senior plot. Touchwood Senior has a problem: fertility. His wife bears a child every year, and in some years two; his recreations with country wenches result in an epidemic of pregnancies serious enough to disable the labor force in haymaking season. He's cursed with "a fatal finger," as he puts it, the instrument of domestic overpopulation.

Since money is in short supply, something has to be done. The illegitimate children aren't that much of a problem: Touchwood Senior is callous enough by now to disown his bastards and to offer their mothers nothing better than ridicule, threats, denials, or at most a handout of pretty small change. The big problem is the legitimate children, whom Touchwood Senior does undertake to support. He and Mrs. Touchwood agree that it's best to live apart, at least until their economic crisis is over. So she's going to live with her uncle, and he (no doubt) will go back to making hay. He's gratified by his wife's ability to make the required adjustment: "I hold that wife a most unmatched treasure / That can unto her fortunes fix her pleasure / And not unto her blood."

Sir Oliver Kix and his wife have the opposite problem: loads of money, but no children. Because both partners when provoked are in the habit of blaming their mates for infertility, their marriage is, after seven years, under plenty of emotional strain. And without direct heirs they fear that their property will eventually fall into the hands of Sir Walter Whorehound, the next legal claimant. So in this case too sexual management is needed. The laws of comic compensation require only that Lady Kix get access to Touchwood's famous finger, and the miracle unfolds: "Ho, my wife's quicken'd," Sir Oliver chortles; "I am a man for ever! / I think I have bestirr'd my stumps, i' faith." And the fee Touchwood Senior earns as a fertility expert—£400 for administering a "water that he useth"—is going to rescue his marriage too from its double awkwardness of penury and abstinence.

In what you might call the main plot if this were a more conventional play, the goldsmith Yellowhammer and his wife Maudline are trying to control the sexual choices of their children so as to ensure upward social mobility. For their son Tim they've picked out the Welsh Gentlewoman, a redhead whose relationship to Sir Walter Whorehound is decorously covered by the term *niece*, and whose dowry is said to include nineteen mountains in Wales. For their daughter Moll they've settled on Sir Walter Whorehound himself. Tim's Cambridge education has addled his brain to the point where he has no stamina to resist events; at the end of the play he is married to a whore whom he is trying to translate, by means of logic, into an honest woman. But Moll, whose domestic lessons in music, dancing, and deportment have all been directed to the end of making her "fit for a knight's bed," has survived this training with her will intact. Her true lover is Touchwood Junior, brother to Cheapside's pillar of potency. The lovers make repeated attempts to elope, each of which backfires and increases their misfortune; but in the final scene, where everyone except the Yellowhammers has gathered to mourn the death of this star-crossed pair, their coffins burst open at a signal from Touchwood Senior and the "sweet, dear couple" is united at last in a marriage ceremony that must have set the Jacobean record for brevity.

Bizarre as the rest of this play may be, it's the character of Allwit who makes everyone else look almost normal. Allwit's domestic life is perfectly tranquil: he has no quarrels with his wife, his children are models of cleverness and decency, his financial prospects are secure. The reason for all this bliss is the place the Allwits reserve in their family for the "founder," Sir Walter Whorehound. Allwit celebrates his benefactor at length in a brilliant soliloquy:

> The founder's come to town: I am like a man
> Finding a table furnish'd to his hand,
> As mine is still to me, prays for the founder:
> 'Bless the right worshipful, the good founder's life.'
> I thank him, h'as maintained my house this ten years,
> Not only keeps my wife, but a keeps me
> And all my family: I am at his table;
> He gets me all my children, and pays the nurse
> Monthly or weekly; puts me to nothing. . . .
> I may sit still and play; he's jealous for me;
> Watches her steps, sets spies; I live at ease;
> He has both the cost and torment: when the strings
> Of his heart frets, I feed, laugh, or sing.
>
> (1.2.11-55)

At least he's not a hypocrite. Allwit understands his place in this *ménage* with such clarity, and outlines it with such disarming candidness, that you can't fault him for hiding anything. A cuckold he most certainly is: his name is the oral inversion of "wittol," the term for a knowing and contented cuckold. What kind of response is Middleton setting in motion with this amazing creation? Not quite the scornful outrage that Jonson unleashes at Corvino's expense in *Volpone.* I think Allwit triggers a mixed response. It includes a grudging respect for someone who can carry his own system as far as this and way beyond what you thought possible: the kind of respect now reserved for the grasshopper-eating champion of the State of Oregon, or for parents who claim to have created a child prodigy through behavior-modification therapy. But this kind of respect includes loathing as well: loathing of a discipline directed at no other end than proving what the human animal might be capable of if pushed and punished. Allwit is conducting an ugly experiment with human subjects, and it doesn't really exonerate him to say that the principal victim is himself.

The whole play is a send-up of sexual mismanagement, and in Allwit's case this takes the form of grotesque overmanagement. You can't really claim to be controlling your sexual nature if you engage in an act of repression so comprehensively deadening as this. The distortions are bound to show, and they do in Allwit's case. There's a nasty streak of anti-feminism in his casual conversations, where it counts most: when he thinks of his wife awaiting labor he says "she's even upon the point of grunting"; after the christening of his wife's new baby he winces at the atmosphere spread through his house by a female-dominated celebration: "How hot they have made the rooms with their thick bums." This is a man who secretly hates women—for obvious reasons—because the only alternative to doing so would be to hold himself in complete and utter contempt. All this remains laughable, of course, or it should if the part of Allwit is played with the right cynical charm; but I think the laughter should include a nervous awareness that sex education and alternate lifestyles do have their built-in limitations. How much can you achieve by sexual self-management and social engineering? If you're Allwit, almost everything, including complete annihilation of your claim to sexual being.

The setting of *Women Beware Women* is Renaissance Florence, but the forces that drive human action here are the same as they were in Cheapside: sex, money, and social status. The stakes have been raised a bit in each of these categories—enough to ensure that the machine Middleton sets in motion here will be tragic—but the human capacities for corruption are essentially the same. Even the techniques for getting what you want in Florence owe something to the managerial strategies of Cheapside. But in *Women Beware Women* the range of sexual manipulation has been greatly expanded to include Mafia tactics: secrecy, fraud, bribery, intimidation, threats of humiliation or exposure or death.

At the outset it looks as if one intimate couple might be able to survive in this world of sexual politics. Leantio, an ordinary Florentine "factor" (roughly a salesperson or a marketing agent), and his young Venetian bride, Bianca, are settling rapturously into their nest. They have eloped, escaping the social ambitions Bianca's well-to-do parents had in mind for her, and limiting their expectations to whatever Leantio can provide by working hard at his modest but steady job. You can argue that they're too complacent, that she hasn't begun to understand the social sacrifices she's making, that he's being smugly possessive in his every thought and word about her. All of these objections are valid, but for me they don't rob this couple of the one thing they have: they are in love.

And that's exactly why they're so pitifully defenseless in a society where sexual manipulation has the status of an art. To appreciate the sense in which this is true you have to look at Livia: a widow twice over, thirty-nine years old, and utterly bereft of anything but the power to manipulate oth-

ers. When her brother Hippolito tells her he's in love with their niece, Isabella, she pretends to be shocked and then tells him not to worry—she'll arrange his life so that he'll get exactly what he wants. Isabella, genuinely shocked by a declaration Hippolito has just made her, comes running to Livia for help. Within minutes Livia convinces Isabella that (1) her mother years ago had a secret affair with the Marquis of Coria, (2) her father Fabritio isn't really her father, (3) her supposed uncle is therefore a perfectly acceptable lover, (4) the marriage her family is arranging for her to the stupidly boorish Ward would be a perfectly convenient cover, and (5) the details of her parentage have to be kept absolutely secret. When Hippolito confronts his niece again, she's his for the taking: "Pray make your love no stranger, sir, that's all." And he's bewildered, stunned, amazed by his sister's achievement:

> What has she done to her, can any tell?
> 'Tis beyond sorcery this, drugs, or love-powders;
> Some art that has no name, sure; strange to me
> Of all the wonders I e'er met withal
> Throughout my ten years' travels, but I'm thankful for't.
>   (2.1.231-5)

There's nothing all that mysterious about Livia's art—if you assume the right combination of intelligence and cynicism—except perhaps her motivation. What does she stand to gain from this act of matchmaking? Her brother's gratitude, no doubt, and if she's sexually enraptured with him herself, then gratitude perhaps would be at least a weak substitute for what she really wants. But the next transaction to pass through her "shop in cunning," as she terms it, has not even this devious parentage. I think Livia is in love with her own expertise above all; the game has become its own justification for her, the playing a greater joy than any object she might stand to win as a reward.

Livia's kind of expertise is exactly what the Duke needs when, after having singled out Bianca's beautiful face from a crowd of onlookers at an outdoor procession, he determines to make her his own. Word passes quickly along a discreet bureaucratic chain, and Livia is of course brought in to arrange events so that Bianca will be left alone with the Duke. He seduces her with a combination of reassurance, flattery, suggestiveness, bribery, and firmness that she hasn't the wit or the will to resist. "There's nothing but respect and honour near thee," he croons. He finds her as beautiful as "figures that are drawn for goddesses." He likes her resistance—in fact it's a sure sign that she knows how to please him. But she mustn't take it too far: "I can command, / Think upon that." All she needs to do is "trust in our love" and she'll get whatever she wants, including "peace." Does she really want to spend years of her life in marginal economic circumstances and social isolation? "Come play the wise wench, and provide for ever." She's roughly sixteen; he's fifty-five. She knows it's a trap, but it's baited so well that she melts into silent compliance.

Now Middleton's real genius begins to show itself, as he unravels the precise consequences of living in a society such as this. In Bianca's case they are immediate and severe. First is the awareness of how she's been violated:

"I'm made bold now," she says; "sin and I'm acquainted, / No couple greater." The love-nest no longer pleases her. She complains to her mother-in-law that it's devoid of all the luxuries and fashionable furnishings she especially likes. When Leantio comes home from work, she can't welcome him with anything like the loving attentions he's been expecting. At the first invitation she runs back to the Duke, eager to be celebrated and fondled at a banquet which publicly makes her the ruling sex-goddess of Florence. Leantio, who has been summoned so he can watch this occasion, fights back his grief and revulsion just enough to graciously accept his reward for holding his tongue: the captainship of a minor outlying citadel. But even such humiliating prudence won't preserve him. When Bianca finds out what a drag it is to run into Leantio, even occasionally, in her new social world, all she has to do is mention it to the Duke: "The former thing, my lord, to whom you gave / The captainship; he eats his meat with grudging still." Say no more. By sunrise the next morning Leantio lies dead.

I'm not going to follow Middleton's workmanship beyond this point, through the bizarre series of counterthrusts that leads to a stage decorated with corpses at the end. I agree with G. R. Hibbard ("The Tragedies of Thomas Middleton and the Decadence of the Drama," *Renaissance and Modern Studies,* 1957) that the strength of the play is in the subtlety and unflinching honesty of the first three acts, and that in bringing the whole machine to its crashing dead end Middleton made too many concessions to public morality and theatrical taste. Even so, and again for reasons that Hibbard was aware of long ago, *Women Beware Women* is a major point of reckoning in Middleton's career: it's a great failure in the sense that it could have been so much more than it is.

The women in this play are lucidly aware of what is being done to them. Bianca, after rising to the pinnacle of her borrowed power, pauses for a revealing moment to remember how she grew up in Venice:

> 'Tis not good in sadness
> To keep a maid so strict in her young days.
> Restraint breeds wand'ring thoughts, as many fasting
>   days
> A great desire to see flesh stirring again.
> I'll nev'r use any girl of mine so strictly. . . .
>   (4.1.30-34)

Isabella, when faced with the prospect of an abhorrent marriage, knows that she's being abused by a system that even under normal circumstances is a form of "subjection." Livia tells the men it's an "injustice" to coerce a woman into marriage; fidelity to one man is "a hard task" at the best of times, so a woman ought to have at least the right to choose her man. What was Middleton up to when he put these progressive thoughts into the heads of his three principal female characters? Didn't he see the contradiction between these advanced sentiments and the sexual exploitation to which, in their various ways, all three of them submit? I think he did. I think he was aware that Bianca's beauty only increases the likelihood that she'll never make

any real or lasting choices, that Isabella's fondness for her uncle is a misplaced form of trust in patriarchal care, and that Livia's art makes her a collaborator in the injustices she condemns. These ironies, I think, rather than the need for an easy moral, are the real reason for the title of the play.

In *The Changeling* Middleton was able to reach something deeper and more primitive than the sexual networking of *A Chaste Maid in Cheapside* and *Women Beware Women.* What happens between Beatrice-Joanna and De Flores is enough to confer on their relationship a charismatic energy that makes *The Changeling* a disturbing play, even today. You can't explain this power, but you can identify it easily enough. They are a couple apart, both the achievement and the violation of everything their society values, Patti Hearst and her Symbionese Liberation Army captor. They dominate the play because every audience—no matter how timid, ordinary, or sane—will want them to.

The first brilliant scene in *The Changeling* is the encounter between Beatrice-Joanna and De Flores which ensures that everything else will follow: she engages his help to dispose of her unwanted suitor, Alonzo de Piracquo, in order to clear the path (as she thinks) for marriage to the man she now desires, Alsemero. Although Beatrice-Joanna has shown nothing but hostility toward De Flores up to this point, she approaches him now with the "Come hither" tactics of an accomplished flirt. With frightening speed they reach perfect accord: he will do the dirty job for her, and she will make sure he's amply rewarded. But they've reached a perfect misunderstanding too, on the question of how she's going to reward him. This issue is at the center of their next great scene, which I want to turn to at once because it's the best example of what makes Middleton's a distinctive art.

De Flores carries out the murder with chilling efficiency and returns, when Beatrice-Joanna is again alone, to claim his recompense. This time he has the initiative and he knows it. He makes her wait—a little—until she asks: "Is it done then?" There should be a pause now, I think, before he answers: "Piracquo is no more." She weeps with joy at the news, but he brings her back to him by announcing he's got a "token" for her; he produces from a pocket in his costume the piece of flesh he cut from his victim's body and presents it to her by remarking that it came "unwillingly": "I could not get the ring without the finger." She's shocked by this, as he knows she will be and as he wants her to be. The code of good mental grooming has not prepared her for this: "Bless me! What hast thou done?" And when he sees that she's on the defensive he rushes forward, easily making her delicacy seem false and foolish. What's all this fuss about a finger when the real deed has been murder? "A greedy hand thrust in a dish at court, / In a mistake hath had as much as this." He refuses to let her retreat into the self-serving euphemistic dream in which blood and all of its attendant ugliness is somebody else's business.

This tactic of shocking her with sensory overload, and thus shattering the decorum by which she conducts her social life, he will use repeatedly until she is ready to submit.

Concurrently he uses two other strategies: holding his ground and offering comfort. Holding your ground is particularly effective when the other person is improvising a dance from one precarious alternative to another, as it is when Henry Bolingbroke uses this ploy on the King in the deposition scene of *Richard II.* Extending the gratifications of comfort over a history of antagonism or alienation will be possible only when the injured person feels weakest and most exposed, as in Cordelia's treatment of her father near the end of *King Lear.* In both Shakespearean instances, and in *The Changeling,* the result is complete abdication, passive surrender.

De Flores holds his ground without wavering while she offers him 3,000 florins, then doubles the amount, and at last raises the bid to every penny she's worth. He can do so because he's got a carefully arranged scale of values, and as he's already said, he's thought about it "beforehand." While she rummages through her social handbag to find something that will suffice, he merely sticks to his one position; either I get you, he tells her without flinching, or we both get nothing:

> For I place wealth after the heels of pleasure,
> And were I not resolv'd in my belief
> That thy virginity were perfect in thee,
> I should but take my recompense with grudging,
> As if I had but half my hopes I agreed for.
>
> (3.4.115-19)

While he's sure of himself, "resolv'd" in his "belief," intuitively right in every assumption he makes about her, she's coasting without an anchor. "I understand thee not," she says when he refuses her money; "I'm in a labyrinth." She realizes she's getting out of her depth, and urges him to leave at once; then he can "send" his "demand in writing." It's an oddly bureaucratic straw for her to be grasping at; all he needs to do is repeat that he won't go anywhere without her. And again she's at a loss: "What's your meaning?" She tries wagging a prudent finger at him (when he claims the right to kiss her); she tries moral outrage; she tries pulling rank; she tries appealing to his pity. In each case he has a perfectly plausible refutation based on a single principle: "The wealth of all Valencia shall not buy / My pleasure from me."

When he sees her adrift in confusion, he offers her the solace of shared guilt: "we should stick together," he argues. Without me here to protect you, there are going to be questions that you can't answer, suspicions that you can't put to rest. "Nor is it fit we two, engag'd so jointly, / Should part and live asunder." Repeatedly he invites her with the half-cajoling, half-soothing imperative "Come." As each line of defense melts away, as each retreat turns into a cul de sac, her confusion builds into desperation. By the end of the scene she is kneeling to him, begging him for mercy. "I make thee master," she says with greater verbal adroitness than she realizes:

> Of all the wealth I have in gold and jewels;
> Let me go poor unto my bed with honour,

> And I am rich in all things.
>
> (156-9)

He is unrelenting, and she knows he has won. Now he can lift her out of this humiliating mess and into his arms: "Come, rise, and shroud your blushes in my bosom." She will never resist him again.

This is a wonderful scene for many reasons, most of which have been amply celebrated. Its emotional undertow is both threatening and irresistible; its dramatic unfolding is both logically compelling and ironically satisfying; its language both tersely appropriate and loaded with ambiguities that reach into every corner of the play. I think it is also the most frightening exposure in drama of how and why the game of sexual coercion is played. To praise the scene in this way is to emphasize what is psychologically horrible about it, and I think that emphasis is warranted. It is a scene in which one person gains absolute control over another through strategies that exploit and degrade. "Though thou writ'st maid," De Flores says to Beatrice-Joanna, "thou whore in thy affection." He now has the power to make her swallow anything, and he knows it. But even if the relationship is disgusting, it's also in some curious and amazing way exactly right, for both of them. When Beatrice-Joanna defends herself by appealing to the social "distance" between them, to the privilege of caste that ought, she thinks, to make her invulnerable, De Flores makes a counterstatement that both shatters and liberates her:

> Look but into your conscience, read me there,
> 'Tis a true book, you'll find me there your equal:
> Push, fly not to your birth, but settle you
> In what the act has made you, y'are no more now.
> You must forget your parentage to me:
> Y'are the deed's creature. . . .
>
> (132-7)

He is, as always, right about her. They are equal partners in action, in guilt, in desire. The cause of her humiliation is the pain of relinquishing a superior position. I find myself backing De Flores here in the same way as I'm backing Jane Eyre when she challenges Rochester: "I am not talking to you now through the medium of custom, conventionalities, nor even of mortal flesh: it is my spirit that addresses your spirit; just as if both had passed through the grave, and we stood at God's feet, equal—as we are!" And what I find most disturbing about the bond between De Flores and Beatrice-Joanna is not its degrading ugliness but the shock of being forced to acknowledge how perfectly they belong to each other. The deed has made them creatures of a kind.

When you read *The Changeling* or see it performed, a great many questions arise that I've been avoiding here. How did the work of Middleton's collaborator, William Rowley, influence the design of the whole piece? What is the relationship (if any) between the madhouse scenes and the main plot? What kind of society were the authors of *The Changeling* projecting into the castle they prescribe as its principal setting? What is the relationship (if any) between the social environment of *The Changeling* and the behavior of its individual characters? And what kind of response were the authors aiming for at the end of the play, when the castle people link arms and exchange reassurances over the corpses of their disgraced female idol and her unrepentant seducer? I do have opinions on each of these questions— opinions that would add qualifications to my argument but wouldn't change its direction. So I'm going to shelve them for the time being.

That leaves me with [an] unavoidable question. . . . How do you name an art that's both so distinctive and so elusive as Middleton's? In one sense his art is the same as Livia's: sexual manipulation. His characters may be sincerely looking for true love, like everyone else, but if they act on their desires they enter a sexual marketplace in which money, prestige, and power can be exchanged for intimacy and pleasure. Desire has to be nurtured, if at all, among these contaminations. And that means you'll always have plenty of openings for corruption and exploitation, especially if you're one of the professional brokers in this system (like Allwit or Livia) or one of its official sponsors (like Sir Walter Whorehound) or even one of its hungry malcontents (like De Flores). It also means that the sexual choices people make are going to set up traps and create entanglements that may be inescapable, especially since these choices change people, and may change them beyond repair. Nowadays there are plenty of names for the art I'm describing— too many, perhaps—and if Middleton couldn't find a name for it, that's only a measure of how far he had advanced beyond the conventional thinking of his day.

He seems to have been largely untouched by conventional religious attitudes and pieties, or at least to have outgrown them at a very early age. The long religious exercise he composed in his teens, *The Wisdom of Solomon Paraphrased* (1597), doesn't really count as evidence when you're talking about his art. Nobody prays in Middleton's drama; it wouldn't occur to anyone to do so. No matter how bizarre or how basic their moral conundrums or choices, his characters don't look to religion for help. They don't even use theological terms or concepts when they're arguing. Sir Walter Whorehound is a possible exception to this rule, since he does begin to worry about his "adulterous guilt" (after being seriously wounded) and feels sure that his prayers of repentance are beaten back to earth "Ere they be half way up." The Cardinal in *Women Beware Women* is an exception too, in the sense that he browbeats his brother the Duke into the appearance of religious conformity with a rhetorically violent attack on sin. But these are technical rather than fundamental exceptions. I think it's fair to say that when Sir Walter Whorehound and a pasteboard Cardinal are your religious spokesmen, your outlook as a whole is radically secular. Middleton, in fact, is the first great secular playwright in English drama.

The castle people in *The Changeling* go to church, of course, but I can't believe they're doing so out of devotion to anything more elevated than the status quo. The one event that happens in the house of worship is a sexual awakening: "'Twas in the temple where I first beheld her," says Alsemero, and he takes this as a sign of the holiness of his infatuation. There's a vaguely spiritual climate at times. During the ceremony in which Alsemero and Beat-

rice-Joanna are married, the ghost of Alonzo de Piracquo makes a watchdog appearance to De Flores. And when the lovers are arranging their next murder (with Beatrice-Joanna's maid as their victim this time), the ghost appears again, so dimly now that neither of them can be sure what's happening. De Flores does speak to it. "I dread thee not," he says, and while the ghost "slides by" he explains to Beatrice-Joanna that it's "but a mist of conscience." It's a remarkably subservient ghost, this faint echo of a spiritual past in the minds of two people who don't want anything to do with it.

So in a sense *The Changeling* is a critique of what happens when you make man the measure of all things but can't (or won't) abandon the formulas of an obsolete tradition. And Middleton's work as a whole is a statement of what happens when you make self-interest (including sexual self-interest) the measure of all things. When the world is changing faster than might be comfortable for most human beings, when old values are under attack and new ones uncertain, the most disastrous course of all is the decision to simply drift. And this holds true almost equally for the Allwits and Biancas and Beatrice-Joannas of Middleton's imagination. So I think he is serving a warning, not about what will happen to sinners in the hands of an angry God, but about what we are capable of doing to one another and to ourselves.

THE REVENGER'S TRAGEDY

L. G. Salingar (essay date 1938)

SOURCE: "*The Revenger's Tragedy* and the Morality Tradition," in *Scrutiny,* Vol. VI, No. 4, March, 1938, pp. 402-24.

[*In the essay below, Salingar argues that much of the special quality of* The Revenger's Tragedy *is attributable to its grounding in medieval dramatic modes. He stresses that in this play, much as in morality plays, "the physical world is treated, in a peculiarly direct and consistent manner, as emblematic of the moral order, man in relation to divine will." In this essay, Salingar ascribes* The Revenger's Tragedy *to Cyril Tourneur.*]

Tourneur's plays have too often been described as if they were texts for illustration by an Aubrey Beardsley. They have suffered as a result. Symonds read *The Revenger's Tragedy* as a melodrama with agreeable thrills and some needless moralizing; and, on this reading, it was not difficult for William Archer, applying the standards of naturalism, to make the play appear ludicrous. Though Mr. Eliot has supplied a corrective by pointing out that the characters are not to be taken as studies in individual iniquity, but as figures in a pattern with a poetic life of its own, his essay on Tourneur [in the *Times Literary Supplement,* 13 November 1930] again misrepresents him. He is made 'a highly sensitive adolescent with a gift for words . . . '

The cynicism, the loathing and disgust of humanity, expressed consummately in **The Revenger's Tragedy,** are immature in the respect that they exceed the object. Their objective equivalents are characters practising the grossest vices; characters which seem merely to be spectres projected from the poet's inner world of nightmare, some horror beyond words. So the play is a document on humanity chiefly because it is a document on one human being, Tourneur; its motive is truly the death motive, for it is the loathing and horror of life itself.

This is the reading of the 'nineties again. Tourneur's poetry, however, unlike the Romantic poetry of decadence, has a firm grasp on the outer world. Cynicism, loathing, and disgust there are in **The Revenger's Tragedy**; but if Tourneur were merely giving expression to a neurotic state of mind, he could hardly have written successful drama at all. The 'object' of his disgust is not the behaviour of his characters, singly or together, so much as the process they represent, the disintegration of a whole social order. It is this theme, particularized and brought to life by the verse, that shapes the pattern of the play; and it is developed with the coherence, the precise articulation, of a dramatist assured that his symbols are significant for his audience as much as for himself. Tourneur is writing in the contemporary Revenge convention; but behind the Revenge plays is another dramatic influence, working in harmony with Tourneur's narrowly traditionalist outlook, that of the Moralities. **The Revenger's Tragedy** is a logical development from the mediæval drama.

The Moralities had been the staple of popular drama when Marlowe began writing, and their methods were absorbed into the blank verse narrative play. That they were absorbed, not abandoned, is clear from *Faustus*; and Mr. Knights has pointed out [in his *Drama and Society in the Age of Jonson,* 1937] that their influence on Jonson and his contemporaries was considerable and varied. They offered the Elizabethans a group of stock situations, types, and themes which had been utilised for the representation of social and religious problems throughout the changes of a century; and the later drama could rely on their familiarity in presenting fairly complex situations simply and effectively on the stage. The Morality influence makes itself felt, under the Senecanism and the literary satire, through the conventions of the Revenge plays themselves, and in **The Revenger's Tragedy** most strongly of all. The characters in the Moralities are personified abstractions and moral or social types, representing the main forces making for or against the salvation of the individual and social stability; they have no dramatic functions outside the doctrinal scheme. The actions on the stage are symbolic, not realistic, and the incidents are related to each other logically, as parts of an allegory, or as illustrations of the argument. **The Revenger's Tragedy** is constructed on closely similar lines. Miss Bradbrook [in her *Themes* and *Conventions of Elizabethan Tragedy,* 1935] has analysed the narrative into 'a series of peripeteia,' representing 'the contrasts between earthly and heavenly vengeance, and earthly and heavenly justice'—linked as the parts of an allegory rather than as a natural sequence of events. The characters are exclusively the instruments of this movement, and it is from this point

of view that they explain themselves to the audience; their speeches reveal their world, rather than individual minds. The Duke and his court are simply monstrous embodiments of Lust, Pride, and Greed; Vendice and the other revengers, despite the intensely personal tone of their speeches, are portrayed in the same way. The characters' motives are generalized and conventional—Lussurioso, for example, is an extreme case of Pride and Lust—and many of the speeches are general satiric tirades, spoken in half-turn towards the audience. This is a narrower dramatic pattern than Marston's, and more like those of the Moralities; but Tourneur gains in dramatic coherence from the earlier examples. With Jonson, he was the last writer to apply them successfully.

'I see now,' says Ambitioso in the underplot—the traditional comic underplot in which the Vices are confounded—'there's nothing sure in mortality, but mortality.' The contrast between the skeleton and the specious overlay provided by wealth and sensuality is fundamental to Tourneur and the Morality-writers alike. When Pride, in Medwall's *Nature,* leads Man to debauchery, he prepares for him 'a doublet of the new make':

> Under that a shirt as soft as silk,
> And as white as any milk
> To keep the carcase warm.

These lines might have provided Tourneur with his text. Medwall, however, writes with an equanimity, a sense of security in the value of Nature, that Tourneur has lost. His sense of decay, of the skull, is overpowering:

> Advance thee, O thou terror to fat folks,
> To have their costly three-piled flesh worn off
> As bare as this; for banquets, ease, and laughter
> Can make great men, as greatness goes by clay;
> But wise men little are more great than they.

The Stoical conclusion is feeble beside the savage intensity of the first lines. Death has triumphed, and the only course left open to Vendice is to convert a horrified recoil into a grim acceptance, turning the forces of death against themselves. Nevertheless, the fascination of physical decay has not corrupted Tourneur's satiric purpose; there is nothing mechanical in Vendice's wielding of the lash. The changes of tone in this first soliloquy with the skull imply an attitude active and controlled:

> When two heaven-pointed diamonds were set
> In those unsightly rings—then 'twas a face
> So far beyond the artificial shine
> Of any woman's bought complexion,
> That the uprightest man (if such there be
> That sin but seven times a day) broke custom,
> And made up eight with looking after her.
> O, she was able to ha' made a usurer's son
> Melt all his patrimony in a kiss;
> And what his father fifty years told,
> To have consumed, and yet his suit been cold.
> But, O occursed palace!
> Thee, when thou wert apparelled in thy flesh,

The old duke poisoned . . .
O, 'ware an old man hot and vicious!
'Age, as in gold, in lust is covetous.'

(I, i)

The contrasts between life and death, between natural virtue
and the effects of lust and greed, are not merely presented—they are shown as a unified process in Vendice's mind,
a process which extends through the whole world of the
play. The imagery associated with the skull is concrete,
exact, and dramatically useful; Tourneur builds up a system
of relationships between images and situations which gains
in cumulative effect—these lines, for example, have a bearing on the ironic undertones of the scene where the Duchess
tempts Spurio, who is wearing her jewel in his ear (' . . . had
he cut thee a right diamond . . . '), and, again, on the second
appearance of the skull, poisoned with cosmetics. The pun
in the first line is flat, but not extraneous; it emphasizes the
way in which the symbols are to be taken—the physical
world is treated, in a peculiarly direct and consistent manner, as emblematic of the moral order, man in relation to the
divine will. This moral order is rigidly identified with the
traditional social hierarchy of ranks and obligations; but the
narrowness of Tourneur's outlook makes for concentration,
and his poetic material is ranged and ordered by reference
to the experience of society as a whole. In this passage, the
physical contrast between the 'diamonds' and their sockets,
visible on the stage, prepares for, and supports, the crude
cynicism of the parenthesis, which marks the change of
tone. The complete degeneration of virtue is represented by
placing the 'usurer's son' on the same footing of sensuality
as 'the uprightest man,' the mock inflation overturning any
protest from respectability. Here, however, the tone changes again: the 'patrimony,' by implication the ill-gained result of greed, is itself 'melted' away, and, though virtue
cannot be reinstated, divine justice is vindicated in the
rhyme. Vendice's tone mounts again as he reverts to the
palace; but the Duke, with the 'internal fires' burning in his
'spendthrift veins,' has already been paralleled with the
usurer's son—the two types of social disintegration are
juxtaposed throughout the play—so that Vendice's exultant
determination on revenge appears as part of an inevitable
cycle of feelings and events.

The trite 'sentences' at the end of Tourneur's most passionate speeches are meant to enforce this sense of inevitability
by lowering the tension and appealing to the commonplace.
Tourneur himself calls them 'conceits,' and continually
draws attention, in Marston's manner, to his virtuosity in
using them. The resemblance to Marston, however, is only
superficial; they are more closely akin to the popular moralists and the Morality writers. Vendice's emblem is an
example:

A usuring father to be boiling in hell, and his son and
heir with a whore dancing over him:

Again:

O, you must note who 'tis should die,
The duchess' son! she'll look to be a saver:

'Judgment, in this age, is near kin to favour.'

(I, iv)

Could you not stick? See what confession doth!
Who would not lie, when men are hanged for truth?

(V, i)

These popular aphorisms and tags of Seneca Englished
gave Marston and Tourneur a large part of the raw material
from which their more ambitious speeches are developed.
But while Marston works up his material as a self-conscious litterateur, Tourneur adheres to the Morality mode.
The language of the latter is plain and colloquial, but adequate, as a rule, to the simple didactic purpose; a speech to
the audience from Lupton's All for Money is typical:

Is not my grandfather Money think ye of great power
That could save from hanging such abominable whore,
That against all nature her own child did kill?
And yonder poor knave that did steal for his need
A few sort of rags, and not all worth a crown,
Because he lacks money shall be hanged for that deed,
You may see my Grandsire is a man of renown:
It were meet when I named him that you all kneeled
    down.
Nay, make it not so strange, for the best of you all,
Do love him so well, you will come at his call.

The audience is included in the framework of the play, the
function of the speeches being to expound the theme to
them from their own point of view. Marston's sophisticated
railing has quite a different effect; it draws attention to itself:

Pietro: Tell me; indeed I heard thee rail—

Mendoza: At women, true; why, what cold phlegm
    could choose,
Knowing a lord so honest, virtuous,
So boundless loving, bounteous, fair-shaped, sweet,
To be contemn'd, abused, defamed, made cuckold!
Heart, I hate all women for't; sweet sheets, wax lights,
antique bed-posts, cambric smocks, villanous curtains,
arras pictures, oiled hinges, and all the tongue-tied
lascivious witnesses of great creatures' wantonness.

(The Malcontent, I, vii)

The lively phrasing here is at odds with the ostensible moral
purpose—it is true that Mendoza is gulling Pietro, having
cuckolded him himself, but his speech is in the same style
as the Malcontent's own speeches;—the literary exhibitionism accompanies a confusion of dramatic motives. Tourneur's railing is more surely realized; it is presented in the
older and simpler dramatic mode:

Vendice: Now 'tis full sea abed over the world:
There's juggling of all sides; some that were maids
E'en at sunset, are now perhaps i' the toll-book.
This woman in immodest thin apparel
Lets in her friend by water; here a dame
Cunning nails leather hinges to a door,
To avoid proclamation.

THE
REVENGERS
TRAGÆDIE.

*As it hath beene sundry times Acted,
by the Kings Maiesties
Seruants.*

AT LONDON
Printed by G. E ʟ ᴅ, and are to be sold at his
house in Fleete-lane at the signe of the
Printers-Presse.
1 6 0 8.

Title page to a 1608 edition.

Now cuckolds are coining apace, apace, apace, apace!
And careful sisters spin that thread in the night
That does maintain them and their bawds i' the day.

Hippolito: You flow well, brother.

Vendice: Pooh! I'm shallow yet;
Too sparing and too modest; shall I tell thee?
If every trick were told that's dealt by night,
There are few here that would not blush outright.

The direct appeal to the audience, as Miss Bradbrook remarks, is bathetic; but it is significant of the condition of success for the first speech, Tourneur's single-minded attitude towards subject and audience together. The shaping influence is that the Moralities, transmitted directly through Jonson.

It was this influence which enabled him to use the Revenge conventions so successfully. His main preoccupations appear in his first work, *The Transformed Metamorphosis*, clumsily set forth in the form of a vision. The institutions of church and state, and even the objects of the physical world, are perverted from their original and proper func-

tions; Pan, for example, the church, has become a 'hellish ill o're-mask'd with holiness'—'Pan with gold is metamorphosed.' The Prologue describes the poet's bewilderment at the Cimmerian darkness in which he finds himself:

Are not the lights that Jupiter appointed
To grace the heav'ns, and to direct the sight,
Still in that function, which them first anointed,
Is not the world directed by their light?
And is not rest, the exercise of night?
Why is the sky so pitchy then at noon,
As though the day were govern'd by the Moon?

This has the naïvety, the misplacement of emotion, that finds its counterpart in the cynicism of *The Revenger's Tragedy*. The conceits are painstakingly clumsy because Tourneur is genuinely bewildered; he treats them as if they were literal statements of fact. It is evident, however, that they are not affectations of style, as with many of his contemporaries, but organic parts of his thought. The symbolism of the poem reappears in the play, in the pervasive imagery of metamorphosis, falsification, and moral camouflage. It has been thoroughly assimilated to the rhythms of dramatic speech:

Last revelling night,
When torch-light made an artificial noon
About the court, some courtiers in the masque,
Putting on better faces than their own,
Being full of fraud and flattery . . .

(I, iv)

Ha, what news here? is the day out o' the socket,
That it is noon at midnight? the court up?

(II, iv)

The details are worked out in relation to a central group of metaphors, repeated, on the level of action, in the disguises and deceptions which compose the plot. Here again, the method is derived from the Moralities.

These disguises and deceptions are symbolic, not naturalistic—an occasion is even created for making Castiza herself appear in a false character. Vendice is disguised three times—when, as Piato, he enters 'the world' and becomes 'a man o' the time,' a court pander; a second time, when he appears as a fantastic 'character' of himself, a melancholy, litigious scholar; and finally, as a masquer. The disguises are distinguished from the disguiser; what Vendice does in his assumed roles affects his character as Vendice, but the relationship is circumscribed and conventional; no provision is made to render it plausible, realistically, that Vendice would or could have sustained his roles. When he tempts his sister, he is not Vendice in disguise, he is Vendice-become-Piato; Piato and Vendice are sharply distinguished. Nevertheless, Vendice suffers for what Piato has to do; and the separate roles, moreover, are complementary to each other. At first, Vendice is the honest malcontent, the nobleman wronged and depressed by poverty; then he becomes a member of the society that has wronged him. He is sardonically aware of himself in his role, as if necessity, not policy, had changed him, just as it threatens to change his mother—(this is the way in which Flamineo and Bosola fuse the roles of villain and critic [in John Webster's *The White Devil* and *The Duchess of Malfi,* respectively]). He is morally involved in his actions as Piato; and when he appears in the conventional fatal masque, he is justly the victim as well as the instrument of heavenly vengeance. The second disguise is a caricature of his original position. Thus the different roles are not linked together by reference to circumstantial probability, but by reference to the dramatic and social functions of the original character, as with Edgar in *Lear.* The disguisings are related symbols of a transformation within the moral and social order.

Symbolic disguising with a similar dramatic purpose was a stock convention of the Moralities; sometimes there is a change of dress, sometimes only of name. This was not merely a convention of the stage; it embodied popular beliefs about the methods of the Deceiver—'the devil hath power To assume a pleasing shape.' Thus, in Medwall's *Nature,* Pride and Covetise beguile Man under the names of Worship and Worldly Policy, the other Deadly Sins being disguised in the same way. Moreover, the disguisers, besides their attributes as moral types, are usually given, more specifically than any other figures in the play, the attributes of a particular social class. Man, in *Nature,* is a noble, but he is made representative of humanity in general; it is emphasized, on the other hand, that Pride is a knight, and the Deadly Sins only appear as officers of the household. In the later Moralities, social themes, as distinct from theological, become more prominent; and the moral role of the disguisers is often completely merged into their role as the agents of social change. In the Marian play, *Respublica,* for example, the Reformation is engineered by the profiteer Avarice, disguised as Policy; and the characters with aliases in *The Tyde Taryeth No Man* are the broker, Hurtful Help, who operates under the deceptive title of Help, and his accomplices.

The disguisers are contrasted with the other characters in that the latter represent the permanent and unequivocal moral standards which maintain social stability. Even in the middle-class Moralities of the sixteenth century, the disguisers—and the vices in general—frequently stand for 'usury' in its various forms; the other characters, for its opponents and victims. Traditional ethics under the Tudors subsume social and economic questions directly under moral categories; the system rests on the belief that the social order has been established by Nature in accordance with the divine will. This is expounded by Nature herself at the beginning of Medwall's play:

> Th' almighty God that made each creature,
> As well in heaven as other place earthly,
> By His wise ordinance hath purveyed me, Nature,
> To be as minister, under Him immediately,
> For th' enchesoun (*the reason*) that I should, perpetually,
> His creatures in such degree maintain
> As it hath pleased His grace for them to ordain.

This is the ethic of a society predominantly agricultural, in which 'everything . . . seemed to be the gift of nature, the obvious way of life, and thus the result of the Divine order-

ing, whether as a good gift or as a penalty' [E. Troeltsch, *The Social Teaching of the Christian Churches*]. In order to enjoy the divine bounty, to maintain each individual in the sufficiency appropriate to the station in which he was born, it was necessary to observe the conditions on which it was given; and the satisfaction of the profit-motive, of 'greed,' or, equally, the wasteful gratification of selfish pleasure, whether on the part of knight, burgher, or peasant, interfered with this primary necessity. They were 'against nature,' contrary to the obvious expression of the divine will. Opportunities for personal aggrandisement, by means of capital investment, organizing ability, or technical innovation, were, relatively, too few and unimportant, before the sixteenth century, seriously to disturb this traditional order; and it seemed evident that they could only be taken at someone else's expense. By the end of the century, as commercial enterprise, money power, and new industrial techniques began to dominate economic life, they seemed to involve a change in the whole relationship between man and nature, between the individual and his vocation. To conservative minds, it meant the substitution of appearances for realities.

Hence, while the Elizabethans applied the Morality conventions of disguise to a variety of new purposes, the earlier associations were not lost. The tradition of dramatic allegory, with disguising as an essential part, was also maintained by the court masque; and *Cynthia's Revels,* in particular, with its satire on the social climbers and rootless adventurers infesting the court, is avowedly a combination of masque and Morality. 'The night is come,' says one of the Children in the Induction, explaining the plot, 'and Cynthia intends to come forth . . . All the courtiers must provide for revels; they conclude upon a masque, the device of which is . . . that each of these Vices, being to appear before Cynthia, would seem to be other than indeed they are; and therefore assume the most neighbouring Virtues as a masquing habit.' Here Jonson turns the popular ethic against the courtly, the Morality against the masque; for it was the convention of the masques that the courtiers who came to dance as virtues or deities were in fact the incarnations of the qualities they assumed; the masque itself was a social institution, representing the court as the magnificent embodiment of the virtues by right of which it claimed to govern. *The Malcontent,* **Women Beware Women,** and **The Revenger's Tragedy** make ironic use of this function of disguisings in the masque. In Tourneur's case, especially, the masque, as a symbol of courtly riot, is treated from the point of view of the Morality. The courtiers in the masque described by Antonio are Morality Vices—

> Putting on better faces than their own
> Being full of fraud and flattery;

and, throughout the play, descriptions of revels form the nucleus of the satire, leading up to the fatal masque at the end. They are associated with the references to bastardy and prostitution, and to 'patrimonies washed a-pieces,' and with the images of cosmetics and of justice 'gilt o'er' with favour. Against the 'forgetful feasts' is set the image of the skeleton. The corruption of the court by wealth and luxury, and its violation of the moral order which justifies high rank, is set beside the effects of usury, both alike overthrowing the standards of Nature. Virtue and honour, on the other hand, are identified, as in Castiza's first soliloquy, with the norms of the traditional manorial order, which Tourneur makes to stand for social norms in general. Several of his metaphors are taken from the payment of rents—vengeance, for example, is a 'quit-rent.'

Professor Knight's description of the structure of a Shakespearean play, then, is peculiarly appropriate to *The Revenger's Tragedy* also: it is 'an expanded metaphor, by means of which the original vision has been projected into forms roughly correspondent with actuality, conforming thereto . . . according to the demands of its nature.' The central metaphors, and the technique of presentation, are the products of mediæval ways of thought, as they had taken shape on the stage in the conventions of the Moralities. With his narrow and hypersensitive mentality, his imperviousness to the psychological make-up of individuals, and his intense preoccupation with ethics, Tourneur could not have written successful drama except by means of their example.

The total impression created by the development of his plot, by the figures of the lecherous old Duke and his court, by the imagery and rhythms of the verse, is that of a hectic excitement, a perverse and over-ripe vitality on the verge of decay; the themes of the danse macabre, suggested in *Hamlet* and *The Malcontent*, dominate *The Revenger's Tragedy.* But the satire is not hysterical; Tourneur maintains an alert sardonic irony which makes its objects grotesque as well as disgusting. The sense of proportion expressed in the style is not that of the Revenge plays; it comes from the Moralities, and from Jonson. Jonson's influence is most apparent in the scene where Vendice tempts his mother and sister; the subject is from *The Malcontent,* the style from *Volpone:*

> *Vendice:* Would I be poor, dejected, scorned of greatness,
> Swept from the palace, and see others' daughters
> Spring with the dew o' the court, having mine own
> So much desired and loved by the duke's son?
> No, I would raise my state upon her breast;
> And call her eyes my tenants; I would count
> My yearly maintenance upon her cheeks;
> Take coach upon her lip; and all her parts
> Should keep men after men, and I would ride
> In pleasure upon pleasure . . .
>
> *Vendice:* How blessed are you! you have happiness alone;
> Others must fall to thousands, you to one,
> Sufficient in himself to make your forehead
> Dazzle the world with jewels, and petitionary people
> Start at your presence . . .

These passages are not mere echoes of Jonsonian phrasing; they have the energetic hyperbole and the finely measured scorn of Jonson's best manner. The scene continues with a passage of brilliant extravaganza:

> *Vendice:* O, think upon the pleasures of the palace!

> Secured ease and state! the stirring meats,
> Ready to move out of the dishes, that e'en now
> Quicken when they are eaten!
> Banquets abroad by torchlight! music! sports!
> Bareheaded vassals, that had ne'er the fortune
> To keep on their own hats, but let horns wear 'em!
> Nine coaches waiting—hurry, hurry, hurry—
>
> *Castiza:* Ay, to the devil,
>
> *Vendice:* Ay, to the devil! (*Aside*) To the duke, by my faith.
>
> *Gratiana:* Ay, to the duke: daughter, you'd scorn to think o' the devil, an you were there once.
>
> (II, i)

The excitement of these passages is hardly the product of a nightmare vision. On the contrary, it is controlled and directed by a sense of the crude realities underlying the court's fantastic behaviour. The source and character of Tourneur's grotesquerie is indicated, again, by Spurio's soliloquy:

> Faith, if the truth were known, I was begot
> After some gluttonous dinner; some stirring dish
> Was my first father, when deep healths went round,
> And ladies cheeks were painted red with wine,
> Their tongues, as short and nimble as their heels,
> Uttering words sweet and thick; and when they rose,
> Were merrily disposed to fall again.
>
> (I, ii)

The nervous and sinister tones of the mockery are balanced by the 'primitive' realism.

Nevertheless, Tourneur does not escape from his cycle of decay; there is nothing in the play, in its scheme of moral and social values, to compensate for Vendice's fall. In the process of commercial development, which had brought new hopes and possibilities to the middle classes, Tourneur saw only that the court had been uprooted from the people and the soil, while the old-fashioned gentry were left to their honour, their poverty, and their discontent. As, throughout the sixteenth century, landlord and ploughman alike had been submitted to a growing dependence on money, and their customary incomes had proved inadequate to meet rising costs and a rising standard of living, the stability of the old hierarchy had broken down. Many of the nobility and gentry were forced to give up their 'hospitality' or to sell their estates; and their successors and survivors, knowing, with Burghley, that 'gentility is nothing else but ancient riches,' had acted accordingly. The nobility themselves had become enclosers, joint-stock-holders, company-promoters, monopolists; the court, at the turn of the century, was the happy-hunting-ground for adventurers and profiteers. Until the end of Elizabeth's reign, this commercialization of the nobility was in harmony with the main economic and political needs of the middle classes: but when the latter had outgrown their royal tutelage, the powers of the court became obstructive; and when titles were sold and honours conferred on irresponsible favourites, it became clear that the system of court privileges opened the way to the machiavellian and the sycophant. The fount of honour was poisoned at the source. While 'the disproportion between honour and means' became more glaring, large numbers of the lesser gentry, deprived of the security of the old order, found themselves landless men, dependent on an uncertain or an insufficient patronage, men without 'vocations.' Tourneur's Vendice is one of the dramatic spokesmen of these malcontents. His independence belongs to the past; the present is contaminated by the values of 'gold.' On the basis of this contrast, which is extended to society as a whole, Tourneur's poetry formulates an exceptionally coherent response to the life of his time. But the business of buying and selling, the accumulation of wealth without social responsibility, which has hoisted sensuality to its evil eminence in his court, is accepted as normative and final; it becomes a process by which the values of Nature and the impulses which go to maintaining a civilized life are inevitably decomposed into their opposites. This conception forms the organizing principle in Vendice's second speech to the skull, where the complex themes and symbols of the whole play are concentrated into a single magnificent passage.

The irony of this speech is reinforced by the dramatic situation: 'all the betrayed women are in a sense represented by the poisoned skull of Vendice's mistress—not only she herself, but Antonio's wife, Castiza, who would have been betrayed, and the imaginary 'country lady' whom the Duke thought he was about to seduce [Bradbrook]. Similarly, 'yon fellow' is the imaginary profligate turned highwayman, the approaching Duke, and the Duchess's youngest son, who has already appeared under judgment for rape, and is ironically despatched in the next scene. Thus the skull becomes the fitting symbol, as it is the final result, of the process represented by the action and the imagery, by which solid realities are exchanged for treacherous appearances. The metaphor of 'exchange' is important; Vendice's irony turns, in this speech, on the ambiguities of the word 'for,' referring both to equivalence in exchange and to purpose or result. In the first lines, a complex group of relationships are associated in the image contrasting the 'labours' of the worm—physically present in 'expend' and 'undo'—with the silken bedizenment of the lady for whom they are undertaken, a contrast which appears, at the same time, as one between the silk and the skeleton it covers; it is for the skull that the labours are ultimately intended. The 'silkworm' is also the worm of the grave; it suggests, too, the poor weaver, 'undone' for the sake of the wealthy—the contrast between rich and poor is made explicit in the next speech;—and the colours of the silk and of the gold which is paid for it are made flat and wan by the suggested comparison with her 'yellow' face. The speech is developed round a further series of exchanges:

> Does the silkworm expend her yellow labours
> For thee? for thee does she undo herself?
> Are lordships sold to maintain ladyships
> For the poor benefit of a bewitching minute?
> Why does yon fellow falsify highways
> And put his life between the judge's lips,
> To refine such a thing, keeps horse and men
> To beat their valours for her?

> Surely we're all mad people, and they
> Whom we think are, are not; we mistake those,
> 'Tis we are mad in sense, they but in clothes.

>   (III, v)

In the third and fourth lines, the process of commercial exchange is again ironically invoked; the social stability implied by 'lordships' and 'maintained' is undermined in the colloquial sarcasm of 'ladyships,' and the 'bewitching minute' of lust is a 'poor benefit' to exchange for an inherited estate—'poor,' too, in the sense that procreation is made futile. 'Bewitching' recalls the earlier scene in which it was suggested that Gratiana's attempt to prostitute her daughter was due to diabolic possession; it detaches Vendice from the dissolution he contemplates and yet implies that it is inescapable. 'Yon fellow' implicates the Duke and his stepson as well as the broken gallant, so that 'falsify' attaches to the royal justice itself together with the royal highway. There is also a suppressed pun on counterfeit coinage, which, with the corrosive impression of 'falsify,' is carried on in the next lines: by his emphasis on the root senses of the verbs ('maintain,' 'falsify,' 'refine'), Tourneur sets up a characteristic tension between the imagined activities and the ideal relationships to which they ought to conform. In the old dispensation—as in Medwall's play—Nature had appointed Reason to govern Sensuality; here, Reason has been overturned. It takes its revenge, against the irrationality of the 'bewitching minute,' in the contrast between the life and the moment of sentence. The judgment is also the Last Judgment. As before, the mounting rhythm then returns, after a pause, to the slow, heavy syllables referring to the skull, the final cause, it is suggested, as it is the final stage, of the whole movement—'to refine such a thing.' The phrase, coming at this point, implies both that the overlay of 'refinement' on her 'ladyship' is as futile, and as deathly, as the poisoned cosmetic on the skull, and that this comparison actually clarifies a state of affairs present wherever bones are clothed with flesh. The next phrase again catches in its puns the self-destruction of a powerful stimulus; 'keeps' relates it to 'maintains,' four lines above; 'beat their valours' refers primarily to the fierce courage of the highwaymen, but 'beats' also means 'abates,' and 'valors' are 'values'—once again the purchase of death for life. Thus the perversion of the impulses making for life finds its culminating expression in the image of violent action, and the activity is simultaneously nullified by means of the puns. The last three lines generalize what has already been revealed to the senses. Just as the great lady of the first lines has dissolved into her 'ladyship,' so all seeming realities have been reduced to the skull; so that to murder the Duke with the poisoned skull is a fully appropriate revenge.

Tourneur's symbols, then, are organized by applying to the contemporary world the standards of the mediæval social tradition, as it had survived through the sixteenth century. But *The Revenger's Tragedy,* with its alternation between finely wrought passages of high mental and nervous tension and passages of clumsy sententious generalization, represents an emotional equilibrium which Tourneur evidently could not maintain. He had profited by the example of Jonson, who had remodelled the Morality drama, with its barely delineated types and its sparse, loosely connected incidents, into something solid and closely-knit; but Jonson's mind was the more elastic, more confident of the permanent validity of his standards, more independent and detached. His dramatic structures allow of a varied interplay of motives and experiences; Tourneur's do not. In *The Revenger's Tragedy* he succeeded in directing the response to his situation by presenting Morality figures who express, or arouse, acute and powerful, but narrowly restricted emotions. When, instead of dealing with types, he tried to examine individual motives, and to argue out the reasons for his judgments, he failed. By comparison with the earlier play, *The Atheist's Tragedy* is abstract and forced. The best passages, such as the description of Charlemont's supposed death at Ostend, are set speeches, almost independent of their dramatic contexts; the symbolism is mechanical, the poetic theorising lame and unconvincing. Charlemont, who, unlike Vendice, leaves his revenge to heaven, is an uninteresting paragon; and D'Amville's villainy and Castabella's innocence are so naïvely paraded that Tourneur defeats his purpose—if Castiza's shrill chastity were emphasized in the same way, so that the puppet became a person, she would be nauseating. Charlemont and his father have some of the virtues Tourneur attributed to Vere and Salisbury; but when he comes to offer his positive values, they are formal and, dramatically, lifeless.

With Jonson and *The Revenger's Tragedy,* the influence of the mediæval tradition virtually came to an end. None of the Stuart dramatists whose main work came later—with the partial exception of Massinger, in his comedies—attempted to revive it; the trend of dramatic writing was towards semi- or pseudo-naturalism. Webster fumbled with the Revenge conventions in the effort to develop something relatively new to the stage—to excite varied or conflicting sympathies for individuals at odds with their surroundings. His picture of society resembles Tourneur's; but the Morality elements, which had represented for the latter the dramatic equivalents for a central core of judgments and feelings, have disappeared; and Webster, unable to come to rest on any attitude, from which to value his people, more stable or more penetrating than a pose of stoical bravado, could not write coherent drama at all. Where they are not simply melodrama, his plays depend on exploiting immediate sensations, disjointed from their dramatic contexts; and this applies not only to his stagecraft, but to his verse, which works by analogous means, and which gains, as Tourneur's loses, from quotation in short passages. His plays, with their unrealized 'sense of tragic issues' in the individual, point towards a dramatic reorientation, a development from Shakespeare, which they do not themselves achieve. After Shakespeare, the only dramatist to achieve such a reorientation was Middleton.

Samuel Schoenbaum (essay date 1955)

SOURCE: "The Revenger's Tragedy," in *Middleton's Tragedies: A Critical Study,* 1955. Reprint by Gordian Press, 1970, pp. 3-35.

[*In the following excerpt from his influential work, Schoenbaum provides a far-ranging survey of issues related to* The Revenger's Tragedy, *including possible historical influences on the play, Middleton's use of various literary conventions and techniques, and his style of versification.*]

Thomas Middleton began writing for the stage at the turn of the seventeenth century. In 1602 his name is associated with two tragedies which have not survived. According to Henslowe's *Diary,* he wrote *Randal Earl of Chester,* or *The Chester Tragedy,* for the Admiral's Men and collaborated with Munday, Drayton, Webster, and Dekker on *Caesar's Fall* (apparently also called *Two Shapes*), for the same company. But Middleton's creative energies were at this time devoted primarily to a series of comedies, designed to appeal to the fashionable audiences that attended the performances of Paul's Boys and the Children of the Queen's Revels.

In plays which are uneven in quality, occasionally tedious but often brilliant, he analyzes contemporary manners, especially as observed in the seamier side of London life. The mood may vary from the harsh realism of *Your Five Gallants* to the uproarious and fantastic farce of *A Mad World, My Masters*; from the bitter anger of *The Phoenix* to the dispassionate cynicism of *A Trick to Catch the Old One.* But the subject matter remains fairly constant from play to play. Middleton interests himself not so much in folly as in vice, not so much in fopperies and affectations as in impostures and cony-catching. He depicts a world of amoral rogues driven by lust, greed, or desire for social advancement: scapegraces pursuing eagerly a career of sensual indulgence or engaged in a relentless struggle for acquisition or prestige. Wealth, land, and women—the symbols of value—slip quickly from gull to knave, to be wrested away by knaves of superior cunning.

The underworld and Bohemian circles of London and the world of the shopkeeper—the dregs and the middle class—comprise the milieu of these plays. Middleton's underworld is made up of scoundrels who live by their wits and prey upon one another. His middle class consists of incorrigible upstarts and social climbers: toothdrawers' sons infatuated with finery, wives who yearn for recognition at court, merchants who dream of cheating young heirs. The gentry dissipates itself in extravagance; all sense of "degree" has been lost. The view of Jacobean society is not a pleasant one, but the atmosphere is brightened by the dramatist's command of ingeniously ironic effects, by the geniality of some of his sinners, and (in the best plays) by his ability to create as central figure a Witgood or Follywit: the rogue who is clever rather than vicious, who is perhaps even appealing.

Sometime during this period of the City comedies, probably between 1604 and 1607, Middleton's imagination turned away temporarily from the familiar shops and taverns of London to dwell upon the decadent splendor of a nameless Italian court. The conventions of comedy give way to the conventions of revenge tragedy; the extreme violence of the tragedy of blood replaces the essentially trivial reversals of farce. Art based firmly on a realistic appraisal of the social scene is succeeded by the grotesque expression of a view of reality that seems nightmarish and perverse. *The Revenger's Tragedy* is, indeed, a remarkable and complex work—in so many ways unlike the City comedies and yet at the same time akin to them; in some respects very different from any other play produced by the Jacobean age, yet also the culmination of attitudes and conventions long established.

I

Because of its complexity *The Revenger's Tragedy* has stimulated much controversy, and discussion has often obscured rather than illuminated the issues involved. Critics of Elizabethan drama have classified *The Revenger's Tragedy* as genuine tragedy "second only to the masterpieces of Shakespeare and Webster," as the supreme example of "thoroughgoing, unadulterated" melodrama, as "a kind of melodramatic farce." The author has been called humorless; he has been praised for his sense of the comic. One reader criticizes his draftsmanship as "spasmodic and uncertain," the plot having "the air of being fabricated after a recipe." Yet another can say: "It is . . . superlatively well plotted. It vies in this respect with the best of Jonson, with 'The Maid's Tragedy,' and with 'The Traitor.'" The play has been disparaged for relying too heavily upon the conventions of revenge tragedy; it has been commended for departing from the same conventions. Boyer feels that "the separate scenes hold the attention, but are not carefully connected." However, Wells asserts that "the play . . . has never been surpassed for logical consistency." To Oliphant *The Revenger's Tragedy* is the work of "a stern and uncompromising moralist." "Full of thrills and unspeakable juxtapositions," writes Thorndike, "it is governed by a sheer delight in horror and unrelieved by any moral standard." To Vernon Lee the characters are "mere vague spectres"; to Nicoll they are, for the most part, true and living; to Eliot they are "distortions, grotesques, almost childish caricatures of humanity."

When there is so much disagreement concerning the nature of a literary work, it is perhaps not surprising to find differences—extreme differences—about its quality. William Archer, who dislikes Elizabethan drama generally, is entirely revolted: "I will only ask whether such monstrous melodrama as *The Revenger's Tragedy,* with its hideous sexuality and its raging lust for blood, can be said to belong to civilised literature at all? I say it is a product either of sheer barbarism, or of some pitiable psychopathic perversion." Prior's evaluation is more moderate. "After making all allowance for over-simplification," he writes, "it is nonetheless the case that the play gives occasion for the fine and brilliant things in it, though it cannot be said that it is a fine and brilliant play." But to Oliphant *The Revenger's Tragedy* is "one of the literary and dramatic masterpieces of the period. . . . It is . . . one of the most perfect works of art—an art too that is noble in its austerity."

Several of these conflicting statements may, no doubt, be the result of misinterpretation or insensitivity. But the difficulties are perhaps more the result of the complexity of *The Revenger's Tragedy* itself—a play that is at once farcical and tragic, conventional and unique, barbaric and austere, sternly moral and strangely perverse. Although discussed frequently for more than a century, it remains some-

thing of a mystery: its meaning in doubt, its place in the Jacobean drama still not fully explored, its position in the literature of tragedy as yet undetermined.

II

The scene of *The Revenger's Tragedy* is that Italy which Elizabethans regarded with mingled horror and fascination. "O Italie," exclaims Nashe [in *Pierce Penilesse*], "the Academie of man-slaughter, the sporting place of murther, the Apothecary-shop of poyson for all Nations: how many kind of weapons hast thou inuented for malice?" There Robert Greene "sawe and practizde such villainie as is abhominable to declare" [*The Repentence of Robert Greene*]. From Italy, inveighs Marston, the traveler brings cosmetics, paints, and poisoning, "Aretine's pictures, some strange luxury, / And new-found use of Venice venery" [*Satires*].

But if young masters returned with vicious habits, they also brought back gossip: tales of intrigue and duplicity, violence and sensuality; accounts of the atrocities of despots, of incest and the slaughter of kinsmen. Perhaps some had learned of Ezzelino da Romano, who mutilated the entire population of Friola, or of the gracious Gianpaolo Baglioni, who murdered his father and had incestuous relations with his sister, or of Sigismondo Malatesta. Lord of Rimini, who encouraged the arts and slew his three wives. Others may have been told how the *condottiere* Werner von Ürslingen proclaimed himself "the enemy of God, of pity, and of mercy." Still others may have heard the legend of how fifty courtesans and valets gamboled naked after chestnuts on the Vatican floor, then mated before Pope Alexander VI and his offspring, Cesare and Lucrezia Borgia: the same Alexander VI whose corpse was found a blackened and swollen mass, the result, it was rumored, of some dreadful poison intended for two cardinals but through some error taken by the Pope himself.

Through Geoffrey Fenton's translation of Guicciardini's history of the Italian wars, Englishmen could familiarize themselves with the depravity and remorseless ingenuity of Cesare Borgia, who with overtures of peace enticed Vitellozzo Vitelli and De' Ferme to a banquet, where they unsuspectingly met death; who, more terrible yet, had reportedly enjoyed his own sister Lucrezia. Oral and written reports described the impudence of Vittoria Accorombona, who took Bracciano as her mate within a fortnight of her husband's murder—a murder to which she had been accessory. English and French renderings of sensational Italian *novelle* contributed to the general impression of the iniquity of Renaissance Italy. "It is nowe a priuie note amongst the better sort of men," declares Nashe [in his *Unfortunate Traveller*], "when they would set a singular marke or brand on a notorious villaine, to say, he hath beene in *Italy.*" *Inglese Italianato è un diavolo incarnato* runs the Italian proverb which gained currency in England and appeared in the writings of Ascham, Greene, Howell, Parker, and Sidney.

What appalled the Elizabethans particularly, however, was not so much the monstrousness of the crimes themselves, as that curious combination of refinement and bloodlust on the part of the villain: a combination which made for ingenuity rather than passion, for unbridled egotism and a sense of frigid detachment, for a defiance of gods and men. Italy produced the Machiavellian who held religion but a childish toy. "The Italyans," writes Moryson [in his *Shakespeare's Europe*, 1903], " . . . are close, secrett, crafty, and the greatest dissemblers in the world." And Nashe [in *Pierce Penilesse*] enumerates such "Italionate conueyances" as

> to kill a man, and then mourne for him, *quasi vero* it was not by my consent, to be a slaue to him that hath iniur'd me, and kisse his feete for opportunitie of reuenge, to be seuere in punishing offenders, that none might haue the benefite of such meanes but my selfe, to vse men for my purpose and then cast them off, to seeke his destruction that knowes my secrets; and such as I haue imployed in any murther or stratagem, to set them priuilie together by the eares, to stab each other mutually, for feare of bewraying me; or, if that faile, to hire them to humor one another in such courses as may bring them both to the gallowes.

Murder may be a convenient political expedient, but it is also a stimulant for the imagination of an artist, and so the Italian acquired a reputation for his skill in poisoning: his ability to devise envenomed letters, to anoint sedan chairs with deadly poisons, to mix with sweetmeats mysterious white powders which were very pleasant to the taste and quite gradual in their effect. Webster's Lodovico [in *The White Devil*] yearns for no ordinary revenge upon Brachiano:

> T'have poison'd his praier booke, or a paire of
>   beades,
> The pummell of his saddle, his looking-glasse,
> Or th'handle of his racket—ô that, that!
> That while he had bin bandying at Tennis,
> He might have sworne himselfe to hell, and strooke
> His soule into the hazzard! O my Lord!
> I would have our plot bee ingenious,
> And have it hereafter recorded for example
> Rather than borrow example.

Such a disinterested taste for wickedness, along with the sensational consequences of that taste, left a deep impression upon the Elizabethan mind, and especially upon the sensibilities of the dramatists—providing the diverse talents of such playwrights as Marston and Ford, Webster and Shirley, with magnificently lurid material for studies in evil. Renaissance Italy became early the most popular setting for Jacobean tragedies of blood. It is extraordinary when the manners of a foreign nation are able to influence so strongly a literature essentially native in tradition.

III

The Revenger's Tragedy appears to have a basis in actual events, may indeed be derived in part from a notorious episode in Florentine history. Middleton had probably heard or read of the career of Alessandro de' Medici, the cruel and licentious Duke who for more than five years, from 1532 until 1537, controlled the destiny of Florence. His nights were given to profligacy. Attended by his cham-

berlain L'Unghero and his minion Giomo da Carpi, he would appear vizarded at banquets, dances, and revels—orgies where the youth of Florence abandoned themselves to debauchery, suppers costing five hundred to a thousand florins, masques where the most alluring young women were assembled to entice him. Still dissatisfied, the Duke lusted after the beautiful Luisa Strozzi, but his efforts to seduce her were scornfully rejected. A few nights after one such episode Luisa was convulsed with abdominal pains while dining with her sister Maria. She died two hours later—perhaps, as Varchi asserts, sacrificed by her relations to preserve the honor of the family [*Storia Fiorentina*]; perhaps, as Segni believes, poisoned by a hired instrument of Alessandro [*Istorie Fiorentine dall' Anno MDXXVII al MDVL*].

The Duke's favorite and constant companion during the last months of his rule was his cousin, Lorenzo de' Medici, called Lorenzino because of his slightness. Lorenzino had insinuated himself into Alessandro's confidence by affecting effeminacy, by providing new mistresses and proposing newer pleasures. When Alessandro yearned for the attractive and virtuous widow of Alemanno Salviati, a young woman who had previously scorned him, Lorenzino went so far as to promise the Duke that he would persuade her to submit to his lust—even though she was Lorenzino's own sister, Laudomia. On the evening of January 5, 1537, he informed Alessandro that Laudomia had agreed finally to meet him late that night, at Lorenzino's secret chambers adjoining the Medici palace. Stirred by the prospect of pleasure, Alessandro donned his green satin robe lined with sable and his perfumed leather gloves, and accompanied Lorenzino to his quarters. There the Duke unbuckled his sword and reclined on the bed. Lorenzino took his leave, and returned a few minutes later. But, instead of Laudomia, he brought with him the ruffian Scoronconcolo, a devoted follower whom Lorenzino had rescued from the gallows. In a brutal struggle Alessandro was stabbed through with a short sword, slashed across the face and temple, pierced through the throat by Scoronconcolo's knife, which the assassin turned round and round while the Duke in his agony bit down on Lorenzino's thumb. Finally Alessandro expired and Lorenzino fled on horseback to Bologna. The Duke's body was not discovered until the next evening.

In these events may be seen the possible basis for several elements in *The Revenger's Tragedy*. The poisoning of Luisa Strozzi brings to mind the poisoning of Gloriana for refusing to become the Duke's mistress. Lorenzino's efforts on behalf of Alessandro are paralleled by Vindice's attempts to debauch his own sister, Castiza, while acting as pander for Lussurioso. Finally, the circumstances of Alessandro's death bear some resemblance to the murder of the Duke in the secluded lodge to which he had repaired, at Vindice's behest, in expectation of finding there a young woman ready to satisfy his lust. Accounts of Alessandro's rule may also have provided the author with background material for his conception of a Renaissance Italian court, but for this he could just as well have turned to the works of contemporary dramatists, and especially to the plays of John Marston.

IV

The vogue of Italianate tragedies of violence owes much to Marston, whom Swinburne aptly describes as "the most Italian of our dramatists" ["John Marston," in *The Complete Works of Algernon Charles Swinburne,* Vol. XI, 1925-27]. In a series of eccentric plays—harsh, satiric, frequently bloody and as often incoherent—Marston selected Italy as the setting for intrigues concerning deposed dukes and heartless despots, lustful duchesses and child-slaying avengers. Of these dramas *Antonio's Revenge* and *The Malcontent* are perhaps the most significant. In *Antonio's Revenge* Marston first combined an Italian milieu with the theme of vendetta; in *The Malcontent* he emphasized the nastiness of sex, indeed, of life itself. In both plays the background is the court, and Marston created a picture of Italian court life to which the author of *The Revenger's Tragedy* was much indebted. It is a world of parasites and knaves, of cynical jesters and sinister Machiavellians, all engaged in endless machinations and a ruthless struggle for power. But it is also a world of lechers and wittols, luxury and revels: "sweet sheetes, waxe lights, Antique bed-posts, Cambrick smocks, villanous Curtaines, Arras pictures, oyl-de hinges, and all the tong-tide lascivious witnesses of great creatures wantonnesse" [*The Malcontent,* I. vii]. Its viciousness, according to Malevole, exceeds that of a bordello, where sin soon displays her ugly form and surfeit dissipates sensual longings—while "in an *Italian* lascivious Pallace, a Lady gardianlesse,

> Left to the push of all allurement,
> The strongest incitements to immodestie,
> To have her bound, incensed with wanton sweetes,
> Her veines fild hie with heating delicates,

> Soft rest, sweete Musick, amorous Masquerers, / lascivious banquets, sinne it selfe gilt ore, / strong phantasie tricking up strange delights, / presenting it dressed pleasingly to sence, / . . . thus being prepar'd, clap to her easie eare, / youth in good clothes, well shapt, rich, / faire-spoken, promising-noble, ardent bloudfull, / wittie, flattering: *Ulisses* absent, / O *Ithaca,* can chastest *Penelope,* hold out?

> III, ii

It is a world, too, of cruelty and sudden death. "Enter *Piero,* unbrac't," reads the stage direction for the opening scene of *Antonio's Revenge,* "his armes bare, smeer'd in blood, a poniard in one hand bloodie, and a torch in the other, *Strotzo* following him with a corde." Glorious bridal mornings become Stygian nights; poison is slipped into carousing bowls; tongues are plucked out; children are butchered and their severed limbs placed before their fathers' eyes. "Murder and torture," exults Antonio over his helpless opponent: "no prayers, no entreats."

V

Such a milieu forms the background for *The Revenger's Tragedy,* but in Middleton's play the atmosphere is even more heightened. The motifs popularized by such works as *Antonio's Revenge* and *The Malcontent* are, indeed, carried

beyond the limits of Marston's bizarre art to make up a fantastic picture of Mediterranean opulence and decay. *The Revenger's Tragedy* is the most extreme of the Elizabethan portrayals of Italy. It is the result not so much of historical study and contemporary observation as of a vivid and intense imagination operating upon fact and gossip to create a world that is scarcely realistic at all, but rather fantastic and grotesque. The play tells us little about Renaissance Italy, more about the concept of Italy that some Elizabethans shared, and a good deal about the state of mind of the dramatist himself.

The setting is one of dazzling artificial brightness, as night is made noon by the glare of tapers—and also of unnatural darkness, as the light of day is obscured to shroud deeds of evil. Perfumed courtiers parade richly in three-piled velvet and cloth-of-gold; royal mistresses luxuriate in silks and precious jewels and cloth-of-silver trains. Life is a round of sensual delights. "O thinke vpon the pleasure of the Pallace," Vindice urges his sister,

> Secured ease and state; the stirring meates,
> Ready to moue out of the dishes, that e'en now
>   quicken when their eaten,
> Banquets abroad by Torch-light, Musicks, sports,
> Bare-headed vassailes, that had nere the fortune
> To keepe on their owne Hats, but let hornes were em.
> Nine Coaches waiting.

> II, i, 222-28

But no pleasure is sweet unless it has a taste of sin; and so by day the Duke rides privately forth to secret assignations in hidden lodges "guilty / Of his fore-fathers lusts, and great-folkes riots." There music, perfumes, and feasts excite the senses to wantonness. The night is given to revels and lust:

> Now tis full sea a bed ouer the world;
> Theres iugling of all sides; some that were Maides
> E'en at Sun set are now perhaps ith Toale-booke;
> This woman in immodest thin apparell
> Lets in her friend by water, here a Dame
> Cunning, nayles lether-hindges to a dore,
> To auoide proclamation.
> Now Cuckolds are a quoyning, apace, apace, apace,
>   apace.
> And carefull sisters spinne that thread ith night,
> That does maintaine them and their bawdes ith daie!

> II, ii, 152-61

Vizarded masquers dance, healths go round, ladies' cheeks flush with wine. There is whispering and laughter; then lecherous courtiers and their willing partners silently withdraw, while male bawds keep watch at the stairhead. Should persuasion fail, innocence is violated or beauty snuffed out with poison, for impudence is goddess of the palace. Midnight is the Judas of the hours, when chastity is betrayed to sin. A man might be rich if he had "all the fees behind the *Arras;* and all the farthingales that fal plumpe about twelve a clock at night vpon the Rushes" (II, ii, 90-92).

In the "accursed Pallace" there is no remorse for wickedness, no fear of vengeance, no thought of a life after death. The aims of existence have been narrowed to the fulfillment of degraded ambitions and the pursuit of new sensual experiences. Moral restraints have been either perverted or destroyed; romantic love has ceased to be: "All thriues but chastity, she lyes a cold." Apparently Castiza's only suitor is Lussurioso, Italy's "lecherous hope." "Wert not for gold and women," reflects Vindice bitterly,

> there would be no damnation,
> Hell would looke like a Lords Great Kitchin without
>   fire in't.
>
> II, i, 278-79

The scriptures are cited to justify incest; men are hanged for telling the truth; the most upright man sins seven times a day. Flattery and bribes make a mockery of justice. "Fayths are bought and sold, / Oths in these daies are but the skin of gold" (III, i, 6-7). The functioning of the judicial machinery has been reduced to hollow routine, as judges solemnly weigh evidence while the Duke summarily determines the fate of the prisoner. The phraseology at times reflects, as Lockert observes [in his "The Greatest of Elizabethan Melodramas," in *Essays in Dramatic Literature,* ed. Hardin Craig, 1935], the inversion of moral values:

> A man that were for euill only good;
>
> I, i, 88

> My haires are white, and yet my sinnes are Greene.
>
> II, ii, 360

> Best side to vs, is the worst side to heauen.
>
> III, v, 222

And always, in the midst of revels, appears the motif of the skull, mute reminder of evils done and retribution that is to strike. Portents of destruction loom over the riots of the court: blazing stars light up the heavens, thunder crashes. The orgies of the palace provide an ideal setting for the working out of murderous intrigues, for "in this time of Reuells tricks may be set a foote." Lussurioso, newly installed as Duke, basks in the flattery of his obsequious followers. Seated proudly at his banqueting table he calls out for diversions—"We're ready now for sports, let'em set on"—not realizing that he calls for his own death. For Vindice has promised earlier,

> And when they thinke their pleasure sweete and good,
> In midst of all their ioyes, they shall sigh bloud.
>
> V, ii, 23-24

The lecherous old Duke, prepared to meet pleasure in a perfumed mist, kisses the poisoned lips of a skull and brings to himself lingering torment and the terrible revelation of his wife's infamy. In this one dreadful moment lies the essence of *The Revenger's Tragedy*—the union of cruelty and sexuality, the blending of the motif of lust and the motif of death.

VI

If the setting is Italy of the Renaissance, the conventions are those of revenge tragedy, conventions which Thomas Kyd introduced upon the Elizabethan stage and which were modified by the playwrights who came after him. In *The Spanish Tragedy* (*ca.* 1584-*ca.* 1589) Kyd offered, for the first time in English popular drama, revenge as the basic theme of a complex intrigue. The Senecan ghost, the motif of madness, and hesitation on the part of the avenger are his innovations. He exploited the melodramatic effectiveness of bloodshed (there are ten deaths) and made skillful use of irony, especially in the scene where Pedringano goes to his death confident that he will be saved by the man who, in reality, wishes most to have him destroyed. The Kydian formula was repeated in *Titus Andronicus.* In *Hamlet* Shakespeare centered the entire action around the personality of the revenger. Chettle made his central character, Hoffman, the villain, and substituted a skeleton for the ghost. In *Antonio's Revenge* Marston elaborated the intrigue to include a whole series of revenges and counter-revenges, and made disguise an essential part of the avenger's plans.

By the time of *The Revenger's Tragedy* the conventions of the form, essentially a narrow one, had already hardened into tradition, the possibilities for innovation virtually depleted. Yet what Middleton contributed to the pattern is significant. He emphasized savagery, making the play "a distinct forerunner of the new school of true horror tragedies" [Fredson Bowers, *Elizabethan Revenge Tragedy: 1587-1642,* 1940]. He introduced, as Bowers points out, a new type of protagonist: the self-deluded avenger who is not aware that his own character is tainted, who does not foresee that he is destined to perish. Most important, Middleton adapted to the revenge tragedy formula the ironic method that he had perfected in the City comedies.

Irony had from the first been implicit in the situations of the vendetta plays, and ironic twists accompanied naturally the unraveling of the plot; but the role of irony was incidental, a by-product of melodrama. In *The Revenger's Tragedy* irony becomes the aim rather than the means of achieving a particular effect. Almost every scene contains a variation of the biter bit theme. "The narrative illustrates with ingenious variety," Bradbrook notes [in her *Themes and Conventions of Elizabethan Tragedy,* 1935], "in how many ways a villain may be hoist with his own petard."

The result is a tour de force, a work of schematized brilliance, in which the conventions of revenge tragedy are manipulated to form a pattern of the utmost complexity. Vindice, for example, uses disguise not once, but on three separate occasions, appearing as pander, malcontent, and masquer. [Moody E. Prior, in his *Language of Tragedy,* 1947] compares the dramatist's method "to a chess problem posed by an expert who assumes that his audience knows the conventions which govern the restricted movements of individual pieces and the possibilities of the game, and then demonstrates the solution in such a way as to encompass the maximum number of variant situations latent in the problem." Yet the intrigue never collapses into obscurity, the action never falters in its headlong pace. If certain artistic values are of necessity sacrificed, the play remains nevertheless unique among Jacobean dramas. Neither romantic nor realistic, it is formalized and artificial an experiment in technique, an exercise in the stylization of conventions.

VII

Bradbrook counts twenty-two instances of ironic reversals in *The Revenger's Tragedy,* but the use of irony is not limited to situations. It also underlies the wordplay, the juxtaposition of phrases, the reflective asides. Even the title harbors an ironic double meaning: *"The Revenger's Tragedy* is," as Parrott and Ball point out [in their *Short View of Elizabethan Drama,* 1943], "not only the tragedy accomplished by the revenger, but the tragedy which overtakes the revenger in the corruption of his own nature."

Ironic reversals are indeed frequent. Lussurioso, for example, finds himself attracted to the virtuous Castiza and seeks a pander to assist in the intended seduction. Since he has a flair for irony, Lussurioso turns to Hippolito, his mortal enemy and Castiza's brother, asks him to suggest a suitable male bawd. Hippolito recommends his brother Vindice, who appears before Lussurioso disguised as a certain Piato. The Duke's son then naïvely betrays himself by commissioning a brother to ruin his own sister, and basks in his sense of irony in the presence of the very man who plans his ironical undoing:

> LUSSURIOSO: That was her brother
> That did prefer thee to vs.
> VINDICE: My Lord I thinke so,
> I knew I had seene him some where— . . .
> LUSSURIOSO: We may laugh at that simple age within
>   him.
> VINDICE: Ha, ha, ha.
> LUSSURIOSO: Himselfe being made the subtill
>   instrument,
> To winde vp a good fellow.
> VINDICE: That's I my Lord.
> LUSSURIOSO: That's thou.
> To entice and worke his sister.
> VINDICE: A pure nouice!
> LUSSURIOSO: T'was finely manag'd.
>
>   I, iii, 148-51, 155-63

Later "Piato" tells Lussurioso that the Duchess expects to lie with her bastard stepson that night. Enraged by this affront to his father's honor, Lussurioso breaks into the Duchess' chamber. There he finds not Spurio, but the Duke himself, who fears an attempt upon his life. Thus Lussurioso's solicitude for his father's reputation is rewarded by imprisonment.

Ambitioso and Supervacuo (sons to the Duchess by a previous marriage) want Lussurioso executed and their brother Junior, who has been jailed temporarily for rape, freed. They manage to obtain the ducal signet, present it to the prison officers, bid them urge the executioner to hurry—but they forget to indicate whom they wish killed. Thus, Junior,

whose release they so much desire, goes off to his death, the news being brought even as the two brothers quarrel over who deserves credit for the ingenious maneuver:

> AMBITIOSO: Was not this execution rarely plotted?
> We are the Dukes sonnes now.
> SUPERVACUO: I you may thanke my policie for that.
> AMBITIOSO: Your policie, for what?
> SUPERVACUO: Why wast not my inuention brother . . . ?
> AMBITIOSO: Heart, twas a thing I thought on too.
> SUPERVACUO: You thought ont too, sfoote slander not
>   your thoughts
> With glorious vntruth, I know twas from you.
> AMBITIOSO: Sir I say, twas in my head.
> SUPERVACUO: I, like your braines then,
> Nere to come out as long as you liu'd.
> AMBITIOSO: You'd haue the honor on't forsooth, that
>   your wit
> Lead him to the scaffold.
> SUPERVACUO: Since it is my due.
> Ile publisht, but Ile ha't in spite of you.
>
>   III, vi, 1-5, 10-19

Lussurioso realizes eventually that "Piato" is unreliable. Although he should have better sense, he consults Hippolito once more, and this time learns of a discontented brother, Vindice. Lussurioso sends for him; Vindice returns undisguised, posing as a malcontent. Lussurioso informs the two brothers of his pander's treachery, confides in them how the "ingreatfull villayne" proposed the debauching of Castiza, then sought "of his owne free will" the corruption of both mother and daughter. "Oh villaine," cries Hippolito; Vindice remarks, simply, "He shall surely die that did it." Lussurioso defends his unassailable virtue, charges Vindice with the murder of Piato (IV, ii). "Do you marke it," Vindice says later, with obvious relish, "And I must stand ready here to make away my selfe yonder—I must sit to bee kild, and stand to kill my selfe, I could varry it not so little as thrice ouer agen, tas some eight returnes like Michelmas Tearme" (V, i, 5-8).

When Lussurioso finally becomes duke, Vindice and Hippolito see their opportunity to destroy him. They will appear as masquers at the revels that have been proclaimed in celebration of his accession. They will dance their measures and, at the right moment, draw their swords, slay the profligate Duke, purge the court of corruption. But Ambitioso and Supervacuo have devised a similar plan: they too will don vizards and masquing suits, take part in the revels, steal out their swords at the proper instant—and then seize the coronet. But they arrive too late. The rhythm of the second dance is broken by the groans of the dying; Vindice and Hippolito have already accomplished the slaughter. The newly arrived conspirators proclaim themselves dukes, turn their swords against one another, complete the purgation of the court. Thus, those who have come to murder are themselves murdered. It is almost, but not quite, the final irony.

Antonio is now duke. Few others have survived the slaughter, but among these are Vindice and Hippolito. Standing alongside the corpses of their enemies, they enjoy now their moment of triumph. They have avenged a father disgraced, a mistress poisoned, a sister tempted. They have destroyed evil, but in the process they have themselves become evil, stained with a bloodlust exceeding the bloodlust of their opponents: they are destined soon to fall victim to their own cleverness. Pleased with their own wit, appreciative of the "quaintness" of their own devices, they hover near Antonio, their secret bursting within them. Antonio cannot help marveling at how the old Duke came to be murdered:

> Antonio: It was the strangeliest carried, I not hard of
> the like.
> Hippolito: Twas all donne for the best my Lord.
> Vindice: All for your graces good; we may be bould
> to speake it now,
> Twas some-what witty carried tho we say it.
> Twas we two murdered him.
> Antonio: You two?
> Vindice: None else ifaith my Lord nay twas well
> managde.
> Antonio: Lay hands vpon those villaines.
> Vindice: How? on vs?
> Antonio: Beare 'em to speedy execution.
> Vindice: Heart wast not for your good my Lord?
> Antonio: My good! away with 'em; such an ould
> man as he,
> You that would murder him would murder me.
>
> V, iii, 136-48

It is the last, the cosmic, irony.

But the irony of *The Revenger's Tragedy* is, as has been noted, not a matter of situation alone; it permeates the dialogue as well. Irony underscores Vindice's words to the Duke in the trysting lodge:

> Duke: What Lady ist?
> Vindice: Faith my Lord a Country Lady, a little bashfull
> at first as most of them are, but after the first kisse my
> Lord the worst is past with them; your grace knowes
> now what you haue to do; sha's some-what a graue
> looke with her—but—
>
> III, v, 139-43

It lurks in seemingly casual conversation:

> Lussurioso: Thy name, I haue forgot it?
> Vindice: *Vindice* my Lord.
> Lussurioso: Tis a good name that.
> Vindice: I, a Reuenger.
> Lussurioso: It dos betoken courage, thou shouldst be
> valiant,
> And kill thine enemies.
> Vindice: Thats my hope my Lord.
>
> IV, ii, 189-95

It springs from the mistaken words of the bemused characters. "Stay, yonder's the slaue," cries Lussurioso when he comes upon a form that appears to be the drunken "Piato," but which is, in reality, the corpse of his murdered father:

> Vindice: Masse there's the slaue indeed my Lord;
> Tis a good child, he calls his Father slaue.
> Lussurioso: I, thats the villaine, the dambd villaine.
>
> V, i, 37-40

In Vindice's meditations on the skull of Gloriana—his contrast of present luxuries and sensual pleasures with the imminence of death, of life's fleeting physical beauty with the irreparable decay that is to come—we have, as Lockert remarks, "the quintessence of satiric irony." But it would be tedious to include further illustrations of Middleton's irony in this play: *The Revenger's Tragedy* is perhaps the most notable example in Jacobean drama of deliberate and sustained reliance upon the ironic method.

VIII

Although the author calls his play a tragedy, the dramatic types that participate in the ironic reversals are, it would seem, associated more properly with farce. They are not so much living characters as embodiments of abstract qualities, symbols of lust and ambition, chastity and hypocrisy. Even Vindice, the protagonist, is unreal: a fiercely energetic incarnation of the spirit of revenge. The figures who make up the play lack variety and complexity; they have neither nobility nor humanity. Plotting and counterplotting, betraying each other and themselves, they are puppets hurled from one situation to another, automata whose misfortunes stir sardonic mirth rather than terror or compassion. Painted with the broad strokes of caricature, they are fantastic creations: monstrous, it is true, but also amusing.

There is an insistent note of ludicrous exaggeration. The pander "Piato" has "beene witnesse / To the surrenders of a thousand virgins" (I, iii, 54-55). The Duke, "a parcht and iuicelesse luxur," will need not days or weeks, but months to confess his sins. Lussurioso's "heate is such," remarks Vindice,

> Were there as many Concubines as Ladies
> He would not be contaynd, he must flie out:
> I wonder how ill featurde, vilde proportiond
> That one should be: if she were made for woman,
> Whom at the Insurrection of his lust
> He would refuse for once, heart, I thinke none.
>
> I, i, 90-96

"He [the Duke] yeelds small comfort yet," grumbles Spurio during the trial of Junior,

> hope he shall die,
> And if a bastards wish might stand in force,
> Would all the court were turnde into a coarse.
>
> I, ii, 38-40

In death, as in life, these figures are without dignity, evoke no sympathy. Unable to understand why "a man should lie in a whole month for a woman," Junior goes off to his execution complaining,

My fault was sweet sport, which the world approoues,
I dye for that which euery woman loues.

                                        III, iv, 86-87

—and dies "full of rage and spleene." Vindice's final words reflect not pain, but self-satisfaction, perhaps even elation:

Yfaith, we're well, our Mother turnd, our Sister true,
We die after a nest of Dukes, adue.

                                        V, iii, 168-69

Such obstinate good cheer, under such uncomfortable circumstances, does not accord well with a tragic view of life but is entirely compatible with the methods of farce. The laughter of *The Revenger's Tragedy* may be, as Wells suggests, "infernal," but it is laughter nonetheless [Henry W. Wells, *Elizabethan and Jacobean Playwrights,* 1939].

                                IX

If the characters and situations are often broadly comic, the language is not of the kind usually associated with farce. The verse is, indeed, Jacobean blank verse of the great period before the decadence: poetry of an order encountered most frequently in the supreme tragedies of the age. Such is the impression that remains with the reader—in spite of the careless alternating between verse and prose; in spite of the naïvely aphoristic couplets that jingle discordantly in the most splendid passages; in spite of lines that are too long or too short, of syntax that is occasionally awkward, of metre that is at times impossible.
Perhaps Collins was the first to liken the style to flame, when he remarked on the "words which burn like fire," on "the fierce and fiery splendour" of the poet's genius [J. Churton Collins, ed. *The Plays and Poems of Cyril Tourneur,* 1878]. Swinburne, too, was entranced by "the fiery jet of his molten verse, the rush of its radiant and rhythmic lava," and since his time, commentators have almost always made the flame analogy. It remains entirely apt. As in the opening scene the torches illuminate the sin-ravaged faces of the royal house-hold, so too the language, flamelike, flashes through the blackness of human corruption, lighting up folly, searing and lacerating evil. The dialogue smolders and crackles in fierce exchanges:

VINDICE: Shall we kill him now hees drunke?
LUSSURIOSO: I best of all.
VINDICE: Why then hee will nere liue to be sober?
LUSSURIOSO: No matter, let him reele to hell.
VINDICE: But being so full of liquor, I feare hee will
   put out all the fire.
LUSSURIOSO: Thou art a mad beast.
VINDICE: And leaue none to warme your Lordships
   Gols withall;
For he that dyes drunke, falls into hell fire like a
Bucket a water, qush, qush.

                                        V, i, 49-57

It burns in lines of intense metaphorical concentration:

Throwne inck vpon the for-head of our state

                                        I, ii, 7

And fed the rauenous vulture of his lust,

                                        I, iv, 50

CASTIZA: I haue endur'd you with an eare of fire,
Your Tongues have struck hotte yrons on my face;
Mother, come from that poysonous woman there.
MOTHER: Where?
CASTIZA: Do you not see her? shee's too inward then:

                                        II, i, 258-62

My wrath like flaming waxe hath spent it selfe,

                                        II, ii, 315

Nay and you draw teares once, go you to bed,
Wet will make yron blush and change to red:
Brother it raines, twill spoile your dagger, house it.

                                        IV, iv, 51-53

A drab of State, a cloath a siluer slut,
To haue her traine borne vp, and her soule traile i'th
   durt.

                                        IV, iv, 80-81

It blazes in passages of scorching eloquence:

Let blushes dwell i'th Country. Impudence!
Thou Goddesse of the pallace, Mistris of Mistresses
To whom the costly-perfumd people pray,
Strike thou my fore-head into dauntlesse Marble;
Mine eyes to steady Saphires: turne my visage,
And if I must needes glow, let me blush inward
That this immodest season may not spy
That scholler in my cheekes, foole-bashfullnes,
That Maide in the old time, whose flush of *Grace*
Would neuer suffer her to get good cloaths;
Our maides are wiser; and are lesse ashamd,
Saue *Grace* the bawde I seldome heare *Grace* nam'd!

                                        I, iii, 7-18

"It never cools," Barker writes [in his *Thomas Middleton,* 1958], "never burns itself out. It is as though the author had written the whole play at a single sitting as the expression of a single mood."

The effectiveness of the verse may be owing to a bold ellipsis—"for this time wipe your Lady from your eyes," (I, iv, 78)—or to the ingenious figures that suggest the metaphysical poets:

For had hee cut thee a right Diamond,
Thou hadst beene next set in the Duke-doomes Ring,
When his worne selfe like Ages easie slaue,
Had dropt out of the Collet into th' Graue.

                                        I, ii, 169-72

Her honor first drunke poyson, and her life,
Being fellowes in one house did pledge her honour.

                                        I, iv, 15-16

Its strength may derive from the grotesque images:

> If he but winck, not brooking the foule obiect,
> Let our two other hands teare vp his lids,
> And make his eyes like Comets shine through bloud;
>
> III, v, 213-15

> Are you so barbarous to set Iron nipples
> Vpon the brest that gaue you suck?
>
> IV, iv, 9-10

But the verse is always daring, always startles the imagination with its power and originality.

Reference is made again and again to poison and disease, fire and light and darkness, metals and precious stones. This last group of images at times imparts to the verse a kind of hardness: "the unpleasant tang of cold metal on the tongue" [Wells]. But the essence of great dramatic verse can scarcely be isolated and analyzed. One need say only that the poet has succeeded in devising the perfect instrument for expressing the bitterness, the passion, the splendor of his nightmare vision. By so doing he has been able to leave behind one of the most remarkable achievements of the Jacobean stage.

X

This curious fusing of blank verse of tragic grandeur, farcical situations, and melodramatic violence sets the play apart from the rest of Jacobean drama, gives it indeed a status that is unique. *The Revenger's Tragedy* may perhaps be best described as macabre art and, one might add, the sort of macabre art usually associated with the Middle Ages. For, although the background of the play is Renaissance Italy, the point of view suggests more often the medieval heritage. A heritage that was always close to the Elizabethans, it was to exert a profound influence upon the literature of the Jacobean age—a time when many thinking men were given to skepticism, looking back with melancholy to the past rather than hopefully awaiting the future.

Lussurioso, Supervacuo, and the other figures with the oddly descriptive names certainly do not belong to history. The immediate source of several names is Florio's Italian dictionary, but the types themselves have a longer pedigree. They may possibly derive from the classical tradition of satiric comedy; more likely, however, they go back to the medieval tradition of allegory, and especially to the morality plays, with their Wanton, Lust, and Iniquity. The remarkably effective opening tableau of the ducal family and train is little more than a procession of the Seven Deadly Sins in Jacobean trappings. The author's preoccupation with sex in general and woman's frailty in particular stems not, as Marston's does, from the tirades of Juvenal and the Roman satirists, but rather from the Biblical inheritance and the medieval condemnation of the sensual life. There are only two classical references in the play—a mention of the Phoenix and a vague allusion to the sirens—but Middleton repeatedly associates lust with Judas and Lucifer, the breaking of God's commandments, and loss of salvation. Vindice's famous address to his mistress' skull is little more

than a characteristic sermon of the Middle Ages transformed by the magic of Jacobean blank verse:

> here's an eye,
> Able to tempt a greatman—to serue God,
> A pretty hanging lip, that has forgot now to
>   dissemble;
> Me thinkes this mouth should make a swearer
>   tremble,
> A drunckard claspe his teeth, and not vndo e'm,
> To suffer wet damnation to run through e'm.
> Heres a cheeke keepes her colour; let the winde go
>   whistle,
> Spout Raine, we feare thee not, be hot or cold
> Alls one with vs; and is not he absurd,
> Whose fortunes are vpon their faces set,
> That feare no other God but winde and wet?
>
> III, v, 58-68

These lines recall themes dwelt upon by the medieval preacher, who would "point his audience to the skulls and bones of the departed, bidding them reflect how through the mouth once so delectable to kiss, so delicate in its eating and its drinking, through eyes but a short while before so fair to see, worms now crawl in and out. The body or the head, once so richly attired, so proudly displayed, now boasts no covering but the soil, no bed of softness, no proud retinue save worms" [Gerald R. Owst, *Preaching in Medieval England*, 1926].

The dramatist's imagination, it has been said more than once, flourishes in the charnel house. To Spencer *The Revenger's Tragedy* is "the skull's apotheosis" [Theodore Spencer, *Death and Elizabethan Tragedy*, 1936]. "Its motive," Eliot writes, "is truly the death-motive, for it is the loathing and horror of life itself" [*Times Literary Supplement*, 13 November 1930]. Perhaps, however, criticism has gone too far. The insistence upon dissolution is not entirely somber but appears, as has been remarked, in conjunction with broadly comic situations. Even the death scenes themselves are lightened by a note of ghastly merriment. Supervacuo threatens a prison officer with the bleeding head of his youngest, and most cherished, brother. "Villaine," he cries, "Ile braine thee with it" (III, vi, 106). Harsh puns and bitter repartee accompany the whole episode of the Duke's murder. His final words are played upon by Vindice with malicious humor:

> DUKE: I cannot brooke—
> VINDICE: The Brooke is turned to bloud.
>
> III, v, 234-35

This grimly mocking treatment of death contributes to the macabre mood. One may, indeed, say even that *The Revenger's Tragedy* suggests in several ways the *danse macabre,* a theme that captured the imagination of the later Middle Ages.

At first the Dance of Death was impersonal, but it began to reflect personal horror and fascination when the medieval outlook of stoicism mingled with Christian hope gave way to the Renaissance justification of life in terms of this world, when death became more final and immeasurably more terrifying. [Leonard P. Kurtz, in his *Dance of Death and the Macabre Spirit in European Literature,* 1939] describes a late version of the Dance in the church of the commune of Bar. "The dancers," he writes,

> are . . . worldly people clothed in elegant costume, the men in close fitting trousers and jacket and hood in fashion at the end of the XVth century.

> The men and women, holding each other by the hand, dance a sort of farandole to the sound of the tabor-pipe that the musician plays while beating a drum at the same time. Death, an emaciated figure armed with bow and arrow, strikes down the dancers one after the other. One woman has been shot through the breast; her dancing partner is stretched out dead on the ground. Little demons gambol on the heads of the dancers, awaiting the opportunity to take possession of the soul which escapes from the mouth of the dying. . . . On the right the angel of judgment, Saint Michel, weighs the souls of the dead, the book of life in the other balance. A demon puts his fork on the scales in order to overbalance the soul. . . . God appears above hell in his halo and indicates with his hand the balance of justice.

> To the left of this scene are three persons. One, clothed in a long robe with a stick in his hand, is evidently the "Docteur" who speaks the lines written under the picture. He addresses his neighbor, a lay person in elegant costume, who points to the Dance and is inclined to participate. The "Docteur" seems to wish to prevent him from entering the "terribla dansa."

"The meaning of this allegorical tableau," Kurtz goes on to remark, "is clear. Wordly life is a dance, a farandole, which turns the thoughts of man from death, and conceals the sad reality and the terrible consequences of sin, judgment, and the eternal punishments. In the midst of the joy and freedom of the dancers, Death strikes at random noblemen and ladies, and the demons await the passage of the soul of the sinner."

The Revenger's Tragedy has essentially the same message and conveys it in essentially the same terms. Almost all the important elements are here: the macabre atmosphere of mingled mirth and horror; worldly life represented as a revel turning man's thoughts away from the inevitability of death and the consequences of sin; the luxurious exteriors of the courtly revelers; Death, symbolized by the skull of Gloriana, lurking in the background or joining the dance in the masque of revengers. There is but one significant deviation: the deaths in *The Revenger's Tragedy* are not random, but derive inevitably from the irony which constitutes the framework of Middleton's moral order.

The characters who make up the play consider themselves very clever and worldly. They scheme and engage in intrigues; they pride themselves on their superior wit. But, as we have seen, they err quite grossly, quite stupidly—even when Vindice is not at hand to spoil their plans. For their little world is part of a larger universe which they are incapable of understanding. They do not realize that even as they strain eagerly after pleasure they invite disaster, must succumb ultimately to the inexorable moral order. Vindice himself, the cleverest of them all, the instrument of divine vengeance, has been corrupted and must eventually fall. The wheel has to come full circle; an omnipotent God and His angels weigh the souls of the sinners in the scales of judgment and mete out appropriate punishments. Vindice may be regarded as a kind of "docteur," pointing out the moral to the audience, warning all potential sinners.

The movement of a dance is suggested by the technique of the play. The pace never slackens; one startling situation follows another with ever increasing rapidity. The formalized, almost abstract, treatment of conventions contributes to the regularity and artificiality of the dance pattern. The ironic reversals are like variations on a theme; the repeated allusions to luxury and revels, sensuality and death, resemble musical motifs, recurring and blending. But it is in its final scene that *The Revenger's Tragedy* comes closest to being a dramatized Dance of Death. While a comet gleams balefully in the heavens and thunder reverberates, the masked avengers go through their last gyrations, courtly riot gives way to bloodshed, the laughter of the revelers to the moans of the dying.

It is altogether unlikely that Middleton ever visited the commune of Bar and saw there the unknown artist's tableau of the Dance of Death. Rather, because he was deeply attracted to the macabre and molded, perhaps more than he was aware, by the medieval heritage, he turned to a theme at once familiar and unusual—a theme rich in dramatic potentialities, ideally suited to the expression of his own sardonic attitude toward life. He uses the conventions of Elizabethan revenge tragedy as his framework, and Renaissance Italy as his setting. But he appears determined to divest his work of any topical relevance. The background is neither the Venice of *Antonio's Revenge,* the Parma of *'Tis Pity She's a Whore,* nor the Rome and Padua of *The White Devil.* It is merely "Italy," and this we know only from a few casual references. For Middleton is telling a timeless parable of man's wickedness and God's punishment for sin.

XI

The Revenger's Tragedy is a difficult work upon which to pass judgment. One may relate the author's mood to the mood of his age. One may trace the forces that shaped his art: the traditions that he inherited from the past, the attitudes that he shared with his countrymen, the methods that he learned from his fellow playwrights. Yet, when all has been said, the play defies classification. Neither melodrama nor tragedy, neither farce nor satire, it has attributes of all these genres. It is the result not so much of an outer frame of reference as of some inner vision. *The Revenger's Tragedy* anticipates surrealist art, is perhaps essentially less akin to other Jacobean plays than to the grotesque fantasies which haunted the imagination of Hieronymus Bosch when he conceived his *Temptation of Saint Anthony.* The play has the accomplished draftsmanship of a Dali, but unlike Dali's work, it has passion and a message.

The Revenger's Tragedy has all the virtues of fantastic art and its weaknesses as well. It is unusual and effective; it is technically dazzling—perhaps too dazzling. We are aware always of the author's striving after originality, his desire to give a new and more sensational twist to any standard situation. And so we become interested less in what the characters are doing than in what startling interplay the dramatist will provide next for his automata, what new reversal will take place in the ensuing scene. Although the ironic method was essential to Middleton in setting forth his concept of the divine retribution for sin, he perhaps became infatuated with his own technique. The irony usurps the reader's attention; it becomes unintentionally the end, rather than an artistic embellishment, and detracts ultimately from the play's more serious purpose. Such preoccupation with technique is evidence, perhaps, of immaturity, of a precocious delight in displaying virtuosity.

The play suffers also from a narrowness of appeal, owing to the limitations of the author's view of life. It is as if his entire emotional energy were channeled into his loathing for humanity. There is no love, no pity: only anger and disgust and satanic laughter. Now a hatred of life may be, as Eliot believes, a significant phase of life itself, and therefore valid material for creative expression. But there is no reasonable explanation for the hatred in this work: it is a scream that pierces the night, and communicates little more than shrill horror. It appears to be based neither on observation nor experience, but rather on some hidden, inexplicable torment. Other writers have experienced a loathing for mankind, though rarely with such intensity; few have communicated it so well. But the poet has not made it relevant to the relationships into which men enter, to the problems which men face. "[It] is such a vision as might come," remarks Eliot,

> to a highly sensitive adolescent with a gift for words. . . . The cynicism, the loathing and disgust of humanity, expressed consummately in *The Revenger's Tragedy,* are immature in the respect that they exceed the object. Their objective equivalents are characters practising the grossest vices; characters which seem merely to be spectres projected from the poet's inner world of nightmare, some horror beyond words. So the play is a document on humanity chiefly because it is a document on one human being.

The Revenger's Tragedy is a finer work than a *Titus Andronicus,* because it has poetry and a point of view. But the play is inferior to a *Hamlet,* because its point of view is a fragmentary and inadequate one, because it lacks the most compelling type of dramatic interest: a concern for people. *The Revenger's Tragedy* is in its own way very great, but it is not an example of the greatest type of art.

As Middleton goes on to develop his conception of tragedy, he does not revise materially his estimation of humanity nor does he acquire compassion. The figures in his later plays are often weak and contemptible, driven by the baser impulses, devoid of any moral sense. But the author's mood ceases to be one of agonized revulsion. He seems no longer to say, "How revolting life has become, how loathsome are the passions to which men yield," but rather, "This is the way life is, these are the passions that destroy men." The

macabre atmosphere gives way to a realistic atmosphere characterized by an attention to homely detail. If the verse loses concentration and intensity, it gains in subtlety and fluency. Middleton is able now to translate his ironic view of life into terms of character. He probes with infinite delicacy the emotional recesses of men and women, specializing in the psychology of sexual relationships and abnormal states of mind. Although he remains fascinated by the manifold ways in which the sinner may set in motion the forces that destroy him, he never again attempts anything quite like *The Revenger's Tragedy.*

A. L. and M. K. Kistner (essay date 1984)

SOURCE: "*The Revenger's Tragedy,*" in *Middleton's Tragic Themes,* Peter Lang, 1984, pp. 1-11.

[*In the following excerpt, the critics trace Vindice's moral degradation in the course of* The Revenger's Tragedy, *finding his decline representative of the spiritual decay of the entire society depicted in the play.*]

The Revenger's Tragedy, the earliest tragedy that can be assigned to Middleton, already reveals his interest in some of the themes that distinguish his later works and his attempts at the parallel structures that also characterize them. The chief themes of the play develop from the subjects of loss of identity, which appears later in *The Changeling* and *The Spanish Gipsy,* and of moral degradation, also seen in *The Changeling.* In *The Revenger's Tragedy,* Middleton shows the results of immoral action, the loss of one's original guiltless identity, and the moral degradation in which one sin leads to another until the original identity is lost beyond hope of recovery and death is the inevitable and even desirable outcome. The tragicomic *Spanish Gipsy* has world enough and time for repentance, forgiveness, and recovery of the original identity when a person errs and loses his innocence, but in *The Changeling* and *The Revenger's Tragedy,* the addition of the continued moral deterioration of the protagonist creates an ineluctable movement toward his doom. Thus Vindice's death, as we shall see, is the unrelenting culmination of his own personal tragedy.

Middleton brings the necessity of Vindice's death into relief by representing the play's social order in terms of the mythological ages of man—the Iron Age that prevails through the main portion of the play and the Silver Age that is returned with the succession of Antionio. He carefully and elaborately depicts the corruption and cynicism of the Iron Age as the background against which Vindice and his career can be assessed. In the first scene he presents a thoroughly sordid set of villains visually and morally contrasted to the bitter Vindice, who succinctly outlines the evil characters of his opposites, the Duke, Duchess, Lussurioso, and Spurio:

> Duke! royal lecher! Go, gray-hair'd adultery,
> And thou his son, as impious steep'd as he,
> And thou his bastard true-begot in evil,

And thou his duchess that will do with devil:
Four exc'lent characters.

(I.i.1-5)

This scene, with Vindice perhaps positioned on the fore-stage and the others passing in procession behind him on the main stage, symbolizes the initial moral disparity between Vindice and the members of the court. The physical distance suggests the moral gap between Vindice and the others and visually presents the starting point from which Vindice's downward movement can be measured.

After this preliminary introduction to the evil of the Iron Age, Middleton continues his picture of degeneracy with direct pronouncements on its nature. Whether he is commenting on the condition of Italy as conceived by a Renaissance Englishman or on the state of English society itself, within the play's context, decadence is attributed to the Iron Age. For example, Vindice says that his disguise as a pander makes him a "man o'th'time" (I.i.94), and Hippolito echoes that as a pander "This our age swims within him" and that he might be mistaken for Time, "he is so near kin to this present minute" (I.iii.24-25). In other instances, Vindice mentions the moral frailty of women "in these days" (II.ii.26-27) and contrasts "this immodest season" with "the old time" in which virtue was dominant (I.iii.10-14). Lussurioso may seem an unlikely character for commenting on the corruption of the current decline, but nonetheless he refers to "this luxurious day" and asserts that the name bawd "Is so in league with age, that nowadays / It does eclipse three quarters of a mother" (I.iii.110, 154-55). Like Vindice, Lussurioso contrasts the era with other times which were less sinful (I.iii.137). Finally, Antonio and Castiza add their condemnation of the age. Antonio speaks of the perversion of justice "in this age" (I.iv.55), and Castiza laments that "The world's so chang'd, one shape into another, / It is a wise child now that knows her mother" (II.i.162-63). These overt pronouncements on the nature of the Iron Age complement Middleton's characterization of his villains.

In addition, Middleton interweaves Vindice's descriptive examples of moral deterioration in order to complete his picture of a dissolute age. To the examples of lechery, rape, incest, and prostitution depicted in the play's action, he adds Vindice's testimony that

> I have been witness
> To the surrenders of a thousand virgins,
> And not so little;
> I have seen patrimonies wash'd a-pieces,
> Fruit fields turn'd into bastards,
> And in a world of acres,
> Not so much dust due to the heir 'twas left to
> As would well gravel a petition.

(I.iii.47-54)

Vindice's partial intent in this speech is to fool Lussurioso, but in his next, he becomes so impassioned in his moral outbreak against unchastity that he discomfits Lussurioso, who brushes aside such unpleasant thoughts as sin and damnation (I.iii.57-74). The particular sins that interest

Vindice in the second speech are drunkenness, adultery and incest. Other specific details that Vindice later adds to the picture of corruption are the misuse of land to support various vanities (III.v.73-74; II.i.214-21), diverse means to forward adultery (II.ii.138-41), and an example of avarice that defies even death (IV.ii.68-75). Vindice summarizes his view of the Iron Age in the picture he suggests to Lussurioso: *"A usuring father, to be boiling in hell, and his son and heir with a whore dancing over him"* (IV.ii.85-86). The sum effect is to present a period of time set off from other epochs by its over-whelming evil and degeneracy.

The evident source of the corruption of the times is the court. The chief members of the duchy—the Duke, Duchess, Spurio, Lussurioso, Ambitioso, Supervacuo and the Youngest Son—are notably vicious in one way or another. Virtue, in the forms of Castiza, Gratiana and Antonio's wife, dwells away from the Duke's palace. Through its agent, the pander, the court extends outward to reach Castiza and Gratiana and partially succeeds in spreading its corruption; Gratiana is temporarily overcome by the temptation to seek advancement through vice. In addition, the life of Antonio's virtuous wife is ravaged by the court; she is raped by the Duchess' Youngest Son but maintains her honor through suicide.

Vindice's relationship to the court, the source of corruption, grows stronger throughout the play, and as it does, his virtue declines. The relationship can be traced through successive stages from his isolation from the court to his complete unity with it. As the play opens, Vindice is contrasted to the court; watching the royal procession, he stands aloof, bitterly moralizing upon the court's vices. His only contact with the Duke's household is through his brother, Hippolito, who, like Vindice, disapproves of the court and desires revenge upon the Duke. Both Hippolito's and Vindice's wrongs "are for one scabbard fit" (I.i.57). On the other hand, Hippolito's integrity already seems to have suffered somewhat from his proximity to royalty:

> Faith, I have been shov'd at, but 'twas still my hap
> To hold by th' duchess' skirt: you guess at that;
> Whom such a coat keeps up can ne'er fall flat.

(I.i.62-64)

Hippolito provides an opportunity for Vindice to go to court in order to perpetrate his revenge. To do so, however, Vindice must become a "man o' th' time," a pander; he must pretend to be evil even to gain access to the Duke. His acceptance of a guise of evil is his first step downward, and the disguise itself symbolizes his first deviation from his true identity. When he appears in his new form, he asks his brother, "Am I far enough from my self?" and Hippolito assures him, "As if another man had been sent whole / Into the world, and none wist how he came" (I.iii.1-3). Vindice, then, has abandoned his true self and becomes "the child o' th' court" which he despises (I.iii.4).

Vindice reaches another stage in his moral degradation when, in his first contact with the court, Lussurioso confirms the compact between them by giving him gold and seals their pact with the words, "And thus I enter thee," as if he were an evil spirit taking possession of Vindice's body. In addition, he insists that Vindice "swear to be true in all," including an attempt to seduce Vindice's own sister and mother. By his reluctant oath, Vindice thrusts himself into the dilemma of being damned if he does not attempt the seduction and damned if he makes the vicious trial of his mother's and sister's virtues. Vindice rightly declares that Hippolito and he have been made "innocent villains" (I.iii.167)—innocent in intention, but villains in deed. Hippolito likewise exclaims that Lussurioso had made an "unnatural slave" and bawd of him (II.ii.10-11, 16).

To allay curiosity and "for the salvation of my oath" (II.i.49), Vindice decides to "forget my nature" and attempt the seduction. When required to report to Lussurioso, however, he finds himself between the Scylla and Charybdis of damning himself by a lie or by failing to honor his mother (II.ii.36-39). He opts for honesty and reveals his mother's moral weakness to Lussurioso but later accuses himself:

> Forgive me, heaven, to call my mother wicked;
> O lessen not my days upon the earth.
> I cannot honor her; by this, I fear me,
> Her tongue has turn'd my sister into use.
> I was a villain not to be forsworn
> To this our lecherous hope, the duke's son.
>
> (II.ii.94-99)

His self-condemnation marks another stage of degradation; his villainy is no longer innocent. He has placed himself in such a situation and transformed himself into such a character that he must perform evil acts whichever way he turns. Since he does not return to his original identity, each contact with the court further depraves him and narrows the gap between them.

In Vindice's next association with the court, he agrees to be a pander to the Duke, and he is ecstatic over the opportunity for revenge presented to him (III.v.11-30). Here is not the reluctant, tortured decision for revenge and justice that characterizes Othello and Hamlet or even Hieronimo [in Thomas Kyd's *The Spanish Tragedy*], but an eager lust for the enemy's blood. Not content to become pander and murderer himself, Vindice has brought Gloriana to court as prostitute and murderess. Furthermore, his desire to revenge her death is no longer motivated by love for her; lust for revenge alone has become his dominant emotion:

> And now methinks I could e'en chide myself
> For doting on her beauty, though her death
> Shall be reveng'd after no common action.
>
> (III.v.68-70)

Vindice's marked change in feeling toward Gloriana and the change within himself are evident in the contrast between his address to her in the first scene of the play and his words to her as they await the arrival of the Duke. In the first scene, his tone is one of adoration, and his emotion almost a deep despair over her loss:

> Thou sallow picture of my poisoned love,

> My studies' ornament, thou shell of death,
> Once the bright face of my betrothed lady,
> When life and beauty naturally fill'd out
> These ragged imperfections,
> When two heaven-pointed diamonds were set
> In those unsightly rings—then 'twas a face
> So far beyond the artificial shine
> Of any woman's bought complexion
> That the uprightest man (if such there be,
> That sin but seven times a day) broke custom
> And made up eight with looking after her. . . .
> But O accursed palace!
> Thee, when thou wert apparell'd in thy flesh,
> The old duke poison'd,
> Because thy purer part would not consent
> Unto his palsy-lust.
>
> (I.i.14-25, 30-34)

In the later scene, before he kills the Duke, Vindice's tone has degenerated to flippant mockery, his emotion to scorn and contempt:

> Madame, his grace will not be absent long.—
> Secret? ne'er doubt us, madame. 'Twill be worth
> Three velvet gowns to your ladyship.—Known?
> Few ladies respect that disgrace: a poor thin shell!
> 'Tis the best grace you have to do it well. . . .
> . . . Here's an eye,
> Able to tempt a great man—to serve God;
> A pretty hanging lip, that has forgot now to dissemble;
> Methinks this mouth should make a swearer tremble,
> A drunkard clasp his teeth and not undo 'em
> To suffer wet damnation to run through 'em.
> Here's a cheek keeps her color, let the wind go whistle;
> Spout rain, we fear thee not; be hot or cold,
> All's one with us.
>
> (III.v.43-47, 54-62)

When, as they cruelly murder the Duke, Vindice calls Hippolito, Gloriana, and himself knaves and "villains, all three!" (III.v.151, 156), there is little reason to disagree with him.

Now Vindice is sufficiently degraded to cast away the role of Piato and to come to court without a disguise. In his "own shape" and under his own name, he hires out to Lussurioso as a murderer, and as Vindice, he kills his disguise, Piato, his alter ego, the pretended villain. The genuine villain symbolically destroys the make-believe one. Middleton is able to indulge in some meaningful verbal irony as Lussurioso describes his intended victim to Vindice as one "who hath disgrac'd you much," which Vindice in his Piato disguise certainly did; and after hearing the account of Piato's attack on his sister, Vindice vows with more truth than he realizes, "He shall surely die that did it." With ironic accuracy Lussurioso describes Piato as Vindice's enemy, and Vindice replies, "I'll doom him" (IV.ii.119, 132, 172). After the supposed murder, Vindice again rightfully castigates himself as rascal. He condemns the acts of his other self, Piato, and deprecates Piato, Lussurioso, and himself with "O villain! O rogue! O slave! O rascal!" (V.i.65, 95).

Vindice's final step downward makes him a full member of the court. He and Hippolito appear disguised in a revel, taking advantage of their masks to perform murder. They have now equated themselves with the brothers Supervacuo and Ambitioso, who wear the same disguises for the same reason, to murder Lussurioso. Their equality in physical appearance when all don the costumes represents their moral equivalence as well. Moreover, Vindice's desire to murder Lussurioso has not the firm connection with revenge that his lust to kill the duke had. Peter Murray [in his *Study of Cyril Tourneur,* 1964] ingeniously suggests that Vindice must kill Lussurioso "to prevent him from destroying her [Castiza] as the old Duke did Gloriana." Vindice, however, mentions only that he wishes to "blast this villainous dukedom vex'd with sin" and to destroy "those few nobles that have long suppress'd" him and his cohorts (V.ii.6, 11); the plan to assassinate Lussurioso, he assures Hippolito, will "crown our wit" (V.i.158). Furthermore, Lussurioso is actually guilty of less sin against Castiza than Vindice is. Lussurioso may have wished to seduce her, but Vindice attempted it, just as he carried out the murder of Piato which Lussurioso wanted done. Vindice's murder of Lussurioso has more the look of armed rebellion than revenge. Vindice, who once called upon Heaven to protest Lussurioso's villainy and to proclaim vengeance in thunder and lightning (IV.ii.154, 193-94), now ironically interprets thunder as applause for his actions rather than as protestation and proclamation (V.iii.42-43, 48).

A further indication of Vindice's oneness with the villainy that characterizes the court and the Iron Age is the contrast between his attitude toward the age in the early acts of the play and his disposition toward it just before the murder of Lussurioso. In the beginning of the play, Vindice makes bitterly moral judgments on the inferiority of the current age's morality to the virtue of earlier times. For instance, as he dons his disguise as Piato he addresses Impudence, "Thou goddess of the palace":

> Let Blushes dwell i' th' country. Impudence!
> Thou goddess of the palace, mistress of mistresses,
> To whom the costly-perfum'd people pray,
> Strike thou my forehead into dauntless marble,
> Mine eyes to steady sapphires; turn my visage,
> And if I must needs glow, let me blush inward,
> That this immodest season may not spy
> That scholar in my cheeks, fool bashfulness,
> That maid in the old time, whose flush of grace
> Would never suffer her to get good clothes.
>
>   (I.iii.5-14)

Modesty, according to Vindice, is characteristic of a previous era and must not be found in him if he is to perpetrate his disguise as part of the current "immodest season." Late in the play, when Vindice is exhorting Piero and the other lords to join him in the masque and murder Lussurioso, he not only accepts, but also promulgates, the superiority of the current morality:

> Strike old griefs into other countries
> That flow in too much milk and have faint livers,

> Not daring to stab home their discontents.
>
>   (V.ii.2-4)

The double meanings of the three chief nouns in the passage, *countries, milk,* and *livers,* concentrate Vindice's contempt on the more virtuous times in contrast to the present, which he praises as "daring to stab home their discontents." The "other countries" designates (1) another time or place and (2) the inhabitants thereof. The countries "flow in too much milk" characteristic of (1) the Golden Age in which the rivers flowed milk and wine and (2) the inhabitants who possess too much of the milk of human kindness to right their wrongs with murder. And, finally, the countries "have faint livers" or (1) faint, cowardly inhabitants whose (2) livers, the source of violent emotions, are weak and consequently, the inhabitants are not prone to shed blood. In this speech, Vindice's sentiments rest with the vicious rather than the virtuous. Vindice himself admits his oneness with the villainous court when, after hearing his sentence of execution, he asks Hippolito, "May not we set as well as the duke's son?" (V.iii.105).

Having shown Vindice's descent into evil and the need for his removal, Middleton then supplies a moral norm which will provide for the restoration of order. His positive values are embodied in the new duke, Antonio, whose succession commences the new age: His years and wisdom "will make the silver age again" (V.iii.84) in contrast to the Iron Age that has preceded. Antonio's morality, the nature of his outlook on justice, vengeance, honesty, and order, as evidenced by his words and actions, is Middleton's indication of what moral order is possible for the corrupt society he has presented.

Many critics wish to see Antonio's succession as the beginning of ideal order and an ideally moral society. Such a view, however, fails to take into consideration the background of the mythological ages of man and the play's Fourth Lord. First, the Golden Age, not the Silver, is the ideally innocent and happy epoch, and Middleton in no way indicates that Antonio's reign is to bring back the Golden Age, only "the silver age again, / When there was fewer but more honest men" (V.iii.84-85). Yet the Silver is two ages better than the Iron, which prevails through most of the play.

The second consideration which the proponents of Antonio's restoration of Utopian order by-pass is the Fourth Lord, whom Antonio condemns to "bitter execution" for the murder of Lussurioso (V.iii.69-71). Although the removal of the Fourth Lord, who did stab Spurio for stabbing Ambitioso, helps to tidy up the stage by clearing it of a murderer, Antonio's sentencing of him for the wrong crime on insufficient evidence parallels Lussurioso's death sentence for the First Gentleman who, like the Fourth Lord, truthfully explained the extent of his misdoing (V.i.111-23).

Antonio's reign, then, is not heaven on earth, the return of the goddess Astraea, or the Golden Age; nor is it an ironic picture of a simple exchange of politicians. It is the Silver Age, better than the Iron, but not the best. For despite his execution of the Fourth Lord, Antonio is indicated to be superior to the previous old and young Dukes and less corrupt than Vindice. Throughout the play, Antonio has stayed away from court. Unlike Vindice, he has not actively sought vengeance for the death of his lady. To Antonio, the vengeance for her rape is divine justice (V.iii.88-89). In addition, his appeals to Heaven as the ultimate source of all action and authority give hope for a better age (V.iii.87, 127). Vindice and Hippolito, however, have become true sons of the Iron Age; their cruelty and lack of mercy have brought them to the moral level of the Duke and his family whom they sought to destroy, and the Iron Age cannot give way to the Silver until all its members and propagators are removed.

Thus the moral deterioration of Vindice serves both thematic and structural functions. Vindice's degradation exemplifies Middleton's view of the disastrous outcome of sin and the loss of one's identity, and at the same time, it provides the structural outline which the main plot follows in his step-by-step decline from probity to perdition.

In addition to showing Vindice's ultimate viciousness by contrasting it to his original moral righteousness, Middleton emphasizes his final depravity by paralleling it to that of several other revengers. In fact, the play's title has the same ambiguous quality of **The Changeling,** for just as there are multiple changelings, there are nine revengers among the named characters and several more in the miscellaneous lords and gentlemen. Each of the significant revengers is shown to be vile: the Duke, who precipitates Vindice's revenge by his own on Gloriana; the Duchess and Spurio, whose incestuous vengeance against the Duke is only effective because Vindice makes it known to him; Lussurioso, who mixes policy and revenge against the nonexistent Piato; and the brothers Supervacuo and Ambitioso, who most closely resemble the chief revengers, Hippolito and Vindice, and who are characterized, as their names indicate, by stupidity and ambition. The likeness between the two pairs of brothers is conveyed by means of parallel situations: Vindice and Hippolito wish to revenge themselves on the Duke for actual wrong done them, just as Supervacuo and Ambitioso seek revenge on Spurio for the wrong done to their honor by his affair with the Duchess. In contrast, as we have pointed out, Vindice and Hippolito's desire to revenge themselves on Lussurioso is rather weakly motivated; the source of their drive is apparently the fact that they propositioned Castiza and murdered Piato for him. Similarly, Supervacuo and Ambitioso desire to slay Lussurioso because they themselves killed their brother in attempting to execute Lussurioso (III,vi.88-91). Like Vindice's and Hippolito's, their machinations are ruinous for their relatives; Vindice nearly seduces his sister and mother while trying to attack the Duke, and Ambitioso succeeds in executing his brother while trying to murder Lussurioso.

The two sets of brothers are also shown to be similar in their tendencies to self-congratulation. Vindice and the two Duchess' sons are given to gloating over the cleverness of their plots and to taking great delight and satisfaction from their revenges. This parallel is especially pointed when

Vindice, at the beginning of III.v, crows to Hippolito about his plan for murdering the Duke: "O sweet, delectable, rare, happy, ravishing!" and Ambitioso, at the beginning of III.vi, exults over what he thinks has been the clever disposal of Lussurioso: "Was not his execution rarely plotted?" Ambitioso and Supervacuo learn almost immediately that they have undone their brother by their machinations; whereas the final reversal, the comeuppance of the other hubristic overreachers, Vindice and Hippolito, is delayed until the last scene, but it also comes at a moment of smug self-congratulation. The earlier example of Ambitioso and Supervacuo serves as Middleton's dramatic forewarning of the rewards for the viciously over-clever.

Finally, the two pairs meet in their plots against Lussurioso. As we have mentioned, there are no strongly logical motives for revenge against Lussurioso. Vindice's uprising of the lords seems armed rebellion, and Ambitioso and Supervacuo's plan seems spurred more by ambition than vengeance. In fact, Supervacuo comments that "a mask is treason's license" (V.i. 170). As soon as the revels are mentioned, the two pairs seize upon the opportunity for assassination. The parallel is made especially apparent by the juxtaposition of their statements of intent. Vindice and Hippolito reveal their plan to strike during the masque and leave the stage; Spurio indicates a desire to strike at anyone and exits; and Supervacuo and Ambitioso remain long enough to disclose that they too intend to use the masque as cover for their schemes (V.i.158-74). Finally, all four brothers, and Spurio, are made physically identical, as well as spiritually, by their costumes and murderous plans. There is little if any moral distinction to be made between any of these revengers; the only contrast lies between all revengers and Antonio, who alone seeks no vengeance, although given as sufficient a cause as anyone in the play.

By paralleling Vindice's vengeance with the revenges of the subplots, Middleton underscores Vindice's moral degradation, and by comparison to another subplot character, Gratiana, he stresses Vindice's loss of identity, his transformation from his true virtuous self to the vicious murderer. Like Vindice, his mother loses her identity when she slips from virtue. When she succumbs to Piato's arguments for prostituting Castiza to the Duke's son, she is no longer herself. She promises Piato-Vindice, "If she be still chaste, I'll ne'er call her mine," and he draws attention to the double meaning of her words with his aside, "Spoke truer than you meant it" (II.i.132-33). Castiza too remarks her mother's transformation when she evades Gratiana's pressure to convert her with the pretense of not recognizing her own mother:

> I cry you mercy, lady, I mistook you.
> Pray, did you see my mother? Which way went you?
> Pray God I have not lost her.
>
> (II.i.157-59)

Castiza's simulation is perhaps a prelude to Middleton's later presentation of the actual inability of **The Spanish Gipsy**'s characters to recognize one another after sinning.

But Castiza still knows her mother in actuality, and she appeals to Gratiana's dual personality, "Mother, come from that poisonous woman there. . . . Do you not see her? She's too inward then" (II.i.234-35). In this temptation scene, then, both Vindice and Gratiana are divided in nature. Vindice is the would-be moral scourge dressed as a pander, and Gratiana is the loving mother attempting to be her daughter's bawd. Each is sliding from one identity to another.

Later, after Vindice has cast off his Piato disguise and gone to court as himself, he returns home as himself and confronts Gratiana; he accuses her, "Thou dost usurp that title [mother] now by fraud, / For in that shell of mother breeds a bawd" (IV.iv.9-10), and she blatantly denies his allegation and protests her innocence. Vindice reacts to her bare-faced lie with the exclamation, "O I'm in doubt / Whether I'm myself or no!" (IV.iv.24-25). He is confused by and amazed at her impudence, but in addition, he is correct. He is no longer himself, and the bawd that has replaced his mother did so at the instigation of the pander who is Vindice himself. He is perhaps the first of Middleton's many male figures who react with surprise when they have defiled the women they should have protected and have turned the social order and all natural relationships upside down.

Gratiana is soon reformed by her sons' revelation of her sin, and she promises, "To myself I'll prove more true" (IV.iv.38). The emphasis is placed, not on the wrong done to abstract morality or even to Castiza, but to her self, her original, guiltless identity. Gratiana regains her identity, as do many of the erring characters of *The Spanish Gipsy*, through weeping and repentance and the forgiveness of those she wronged (her sons and daughter). She proves her reformation by influencing Castiza to remain virtuous, and she can then respond to Castiza's question,

> Are not you she
> For whose infect persuasions I could scarce
> Kneel out my prayers, and had much ado,
> In three hours' reading, to untwist so much
> Of the black serpent as you wound about me?
> (IV.iv.127-31)

with the assertion, "I'm now your present mother" (IV.iv.133). Gratiana, like the characters in the tragicomedy, can repent and reform and regain her lost identity. Presumably the inference can be drawn that at one point, before he had murdered the Duke, perhaps, Vindice too might have recognized the error of his course, repented, and returned to the original Vindice who started the play viewing the court from an abhorring distance. But no one confronts him with his sins, and he proceeds down the path he elected when he first came to court to seek revenge. The possibility of reform presented by Gratiana's restoration to her true self heightens Vindice's tragedy. His downfall becomes more than justice; it becomes, like Hamlet's, Romeo's and Juliet's, a tragedy of lost potential. His moral rectitude about the court and about his mother and sister reveal his possibility for good. His tragedy is that in order to destroy evil he destroyed the good in himself.

A CHASTE MAID IN CHEAPSIDE

Samuel Schoenbaum   (essay date 1959)

SOURCE: "*A Chaste Maid in Cheapside* and Middleton's City Comedy," in *Shakespeare and Others,* Folger Books, 1985, pp. 203-17.

[*In this essay, which was first published in 1959, Schoenbaum compares* A Chaste Maid in Cheapside *to Middleton's other comedies of urban life and judges this work far superior. A Chaste Maid, he declares, "testifies to the sudden advent of maturity, poetic and dramatic, in a major writer."*]

In his early twenties, the exasperating juvenilia behind him, Thomas Middleton applied himself to a series of comedies portraying the contemporary scene and set, for the most part, against the background of Jacobean London. At first he stumbled. In *The Family of Love* (ca. 1602) he combined satire with romance; but the satire is no more than tedious calumny of an insignificant Puritan sect, and fornication and blackmail—principal ingredients of the main action—perhaps do not afford the most promising basis for romantic comedy. In his next work, *The Phoenix* (1603), the dramatist gave his new monarch unexceptionable advice on the responsibilities of kingship. The play itself is less satisfactory: an odd mixture of allegory, harsh satire, and good-humored farce. Middleton provided it, however, with his earliest distinctive verse—Prince Phoenix's soliloquy on "Reverend and honourable Matrimony"—and for the first time he employed the ironic method that stamps all his characteristic later writing. In *Your Five Gallants* (ca. 1605), he depicted, with unusual concern for detail, life in London's underworld circles; but a series of set scenes, however brilliant their execution, hardly constitutes an animated or cohesive play. These uncertain experiments were followed by three fine comedies, in which realistic settings and the natural rhythms of colloquial speech are united with ingenious, at times extravagant, narratives. With *Michaelmas Term, A Mad World, My Masters,* and *A Trick to Catch the Old One* (all ca. 1606-7), the playwright proved that he had mastered his medium. About 1613 Middleton produced his greatest comic achievement, *A Chaste Maid in Cheapside.*

Among the City comedies (which have on the whole received rather desultory critical attention), the *Chaste Maid* enjoys a somewhat ambiguous status. Anthologists have preferred the less indecent *Trick.* Earlier critics, when not outraged, were pleasantly scandalized to find so little chastity in the *Chaste Maid.* Of the more recent commentators, Miss Ellis-Fermor feels that it is "the finest of all Middleton's comedies" [*The Jacobean Drama*, 1936], but her estimate, although not unique, is scarcely the prevalent one. The play is not mentioned by T. S. Eliot in his essay on Middleton [in the *Times Literary Supplement*, 30 June 1927]; to Frederick S. Boas it is objectionable [*An Introduction to Stuart Drama*, 1946]; to L. C. Knights it is "a typical comedy, neither one of Middleton's worst nor his best" [*Drama & Society in the Age of Jonson*, 1937], and he finds after several readings that "all that remains with us is the plot." Actually, the **Chaste Maid** is the richest, most impressive of Middleton's comedies, the culmination of a decade of creative experimentation and growth. With this play the themes, technique, and point of view of the dramatist's City comedy attain their ultimate form. At the same time, the harsh mood of the **Chaste Maid**—its essential misanthropy—prefigures the somber tragicomedies and tragedies to follow. Written by a great dramatist at the midpoint of his career, the play is a crucial work that demands more searching study than it has received.

Middleton's early comedies, with the exception of the **Family** (possibly written for the Admiral's men) and **Your Five Gallants** (a Blackfriars play), were all produced by Paul's boys. Comedy, rather than tragedy or history, was the dramatic commodity preferred by the sophisticated audiences patronizing the children's theaters, but the first new comedies acquired by Paul's—such ineptitudes as the anonymous *Wisdom of Doctor Dodypoll* and *Maid's Metamorphosis*—could scarcely have been much superior to the "musty fopperies of antiquity" with which the company resumed operation. Seen from this perspective, Middleton's City comedies constitute a singular achievement. For the dramatist created, almost singlehandedly, a repertory of original and distinctive plays for a major theatrical enterprise; apart from *Eastward Ho,* which led to the closing of Paul's, the only truly notable comedies extant from this company belong to the Middleton series. They are quite unlike anything that the age knew. Parrott, almost half a century ago [in his edition of *The Comedies of George Chapman,* 1914], grasped Middleton's significance as an innovator:

> It [Westward Ho] is one of the first specimens of a new fashion in comedy which seems to have come into vogue shortly after the opening of the theatres in the spring of 1604. This new fashion was the realistic comedy of London life. . . . It seems probable that the first deviser of this fashion was Thomas Middleton, who after some years of experimental collaboration, opened in 1604, with **Michaelmas Term,** a vein that he continued to work for nearly a decade. Middleton has been well called 'the most absolute realist' in Elizabethan drama. He paints life as it is, but without the sympathetic interest that marks such work as Dekker's best. . . . His bourgeois comedies are undoubtedly clever, entertaining, and valuable as pictures of contemporary life, but they are anything but edifying. . . . His influence upon his contemporaries, however, is undeniable.

Parrott's remarks are colored by a Victorian sensibility, but the essential point is nonetheless valid.

Even innovations have their origins. For his City comedies Middleton utilized, more adroitly than most of his fellow playwrights, the popular conventions (multiple disguise and the like) that the theater of his time conveniently provided. In the cony-catching pamphlets of Greene, Rowlands, and others, with their sensational revelations of the indignities to which rogues subjected gulls, the dramatist may have found inspiration for scenes of metropolitan low life. No doubt, also, he was familiar with the current town scandal,

heard tavern tales of the fetching over of young heirs and the merry tricks by which gallants cuckolded citizens and outwitted their creditors. More important, he looked about him and caught the accents of Jacobean speech firsthand in Holborn and on Goldsmith's Row, at Puddle-wharf and Cole Harbour, in the lodgings, shops, ordinaries, and playhouses of the great city.

An age in transition provided Middleton with the stuff of realistic comedy. As the traditional social superstructure, with its inherited privileges and obligations, moved rapidly toward dissolution, economic dislocations and shifting class alignments created the semblance, at least, of disorder and accentuated the discrepancy between social appearance and reality. (Thus, in **Your Five Gallants** the "gallants" of the title wear beaver hats, dice at the best ordinaries, and court a rich heiress; but all lack roots or status, and all owe their finery and pretensions to the grossest vices.) At the same time that "housekeeping" decayed, there was emerging, out of the economic ferment of the day, a new order in which "wealth commands all." From the ranks of the citizen class rose the "money-men"—"they and some of their brethren . . . will not stick to offer thirty thousand pound to be cursed still: great monied men, their stocks lie in the poors' throats" [*Michaelmas Term*]. The woollen draper Quomodo, in **Michaelmas Term,** typifies Middleton's conception of these new men: flourishing, unscrupulous, insatiable. The gentry in the play, on the other hand, are more attractive and less affluent, as their names (Easy, Rearage, Salewood) suggest. But their land—"that sweet, neat, comely, proper, delicate land!"—is the citizen's sensual dream: For only by securing the gentry's holdings can tradesmen inspire the envy of the livery and ensure status for their descendants. "Gentry is the chief fish we tradesmen catch," declares Quomodo, and out of the clash between the two classes springs much of the dramatic tension of the City comedies.

The materials—literary, social, and economic—of these plays were equally accessible to Middleton's contemporaries. In the comedies of Jonson, Dekker and Webster, and Massinger, one sees reflections of the same world and manifestations of the same antiacquisitive attitude. But Middleton, more than the others, is concerned with the effects of the competitive struggle on family relationships—on ties of blood or marriage. The variety of relationships treated in his plays is wide, and the results of the ruthless quest for money and land are distinctly unsettling. In **The Phoenix** the Captain sells his own wife for five hundred crowns, and counts his gold as the scrivener reads the inventory of her virtues from the deed of sale. Falso, in the same play, attempts to seduce his niece, and is puzzled that she permits moral scruples to weigh against her obvious material interests:

> A foolish, coy, bashful thing it is; she's afraid to lie with her own uncle: I'd do her no harm, i' faith. I keep myself a widower a' purpose, yet the foolish girl will not look into 't: she should have all, i' faith; she knows I have but a time, cannot hold long.

> (2.3.33-37)

His daughter, the Jeweler's Wife, uses her father's house as a place of assignation with her lover, an impoverished knight who significantly addresses her as his "sweet Revenue." In the *Trick,* Theodorus Witgood uses all his ingenuity to cheat the uncle who has ingeniously cheated him; Dick Follywit, in the *Mad World,* devises elaborate stratagems to rob his rich grandfather of money, jewels, watch—anything of value—and for the old man it is a capital jest to find that his whore has snared his grandson as a husband. In *Michaelmas Term* the Country Wench sets up as a prostitute in London, and takes into service her own father, who fails to recognize his daughter in her rich new satin gown. Her lover Lethe, a toothdrawer's son risen to sudden eminence, is likewise unrecognizable, and so can hire his mother "as a private drudge, / To pass my letters and secure my lust." The point made by the action is suggested as well by snatches of inconsequential dialogue. "Are your fathers dead, gentlemen, you're so merry?" Fitsgrave greets the five gallants, and his sally is applauded as "a good jest." "Is not whole-sale the chiefest merchandise?" asks the Country Wench, "do you think some merchants could keep their wives so brave but for their wholesale? you're foully deceived and you think so." In focusing on marriage and the family, Middleton conveys, perhaps more adequately than any of his contemporaries, the breakdown or corruption of traditional values in the wake of the new materialistic order.

The plays remain comedies, of course, and in them laughter is uppermost. But in spite of the moments of wild hilarity, the apparent detachment of mood, the lightness of touch and incomparable irony, and the last-minute reformations and reconciliations, one senses the dramatist's essential seriousness: his genuine concern with the contemporary scene. It is a seriousness comedy must have if it is to attain, as do the best of these plays, the permanence of art. In his City comedies Middleton in a sense fulfills the high requirements for the artist as expressed by André Gide. "I will maintain," Gide writes in his *Journal,* "that an artist needs this: a special world of which he alone has the key. It is not enough that he should bring *one* new thing, although that is already an achievement; but rather that everything in him should be or seem new, seen through a powerfully coloring idiosyncrasy." Middleton brings the new thing, and also the coloring.

Although the *Chaste Maid* followed the earlier City comedies by over half a decade, it clearly belongs with the group they comprise. "The Eighth Epigram" of Chapter VI of Campion's *Art of English Poesie* may have furnished Middleton with suggestions for the character of Allwit, and from the chapter "The humor of a woman lying in Childbed," in *The Batchelars Banquet,* the dramatist may have taken hints for the festivities at the Allwits' in Act 3, scene 2. Otherwise his precise literary sources, if indeed there were any, have eluded investigation. But the world of the *Chaste Maid* is the familiarly sordid one of mercenaries, fools, religious fanatics, cuckolds, whores, and whoremasters: most of the characters, however animated or fantasticated, derive from stage traditions by then well established. Nor does the play reveal Jacobean society in a new light. Once again we see that the gentry are lecherous and economically precarious, that citizens are prosperous and thirst after social advancement, that the two classes do some brisk

bartering of dowries and titles. The dramatist's astonishing advance over his earlier work lies not in his materials but in his shaping of those materials. The *Chaste Maid* testifies to the sudden advent of maturity, poetic and dramatic, in a major writer.

In his earlier City comedies Middleton preferred prose to verse. The stylistic evolution of the playwright's prose dialogue is yet to receive adequate, or even detailed, analysis; but it may, I believe, be said that what immediately impresses us about Middleton's best and most characteristic prose is that it is at once natural and stylized. It records faithfully, or with apparent faithfulness, the everyday speech of Jacobean London, and at the same time achieves the virtues of ease and buoyancy. In the realistic comedy of Middleton's contemporaries these qualities are rare. One does not seek or find them in such routine works as *Northward Ho* or *Westward Ho,* and one misses them even in the great plays of Jonson. The verse with which Middleton occasionally experimented in his early comedy is, on the other hand, less satisfactory: self-conscious, too much given to rhetoric and rhyme, distinctly immature. The *Chaste Maid* may well be the first of his acknowledged plays to be written almost entirely in verse, and the transformation it reveals is a notable one. For Middleton gains the added dimension that only verse can confer, without sacrificing the qualities that distinguish his prose.

The contrast between Middleton's earlier verse and the mature verse of the *Chaste Maid* is more effectively demonstrated than described. The following passages afford some basis for comparison. Both are of some length and both are representative—neither the poet's best work nor his worst; moreover, they express similar emotions and mark similar turning points for the personages involved. Here is Penitent Brothel as he experiences the reformation his name promises:

> Where were thy nobler meditations busied,
> That they durst trust this body with itself;
> This natural drunkard, that undoes us all,
> And makes our shame apparent in our fall?
> Then let my blood pay for't, and vex and boil!
> My soul, I know, would never grieve to th' death
> Th' eternal spirit, that feeds her with his breath:
> Nay, I that knew the price of life and sin,
> What crown is kept for continence, what for lust,
> The end of man, and glory of that end,
> As endless as the giver,
> To doat on weakness, slime, corruption, woman!
> What is she, took asunder from her clothes?
> Being ready, she consists of an hundred pieces,
> Much like your German clock, and near ally'd;
> Both are so nice, they cannot go for pride:
> Besides a greater fault, but too well known,
> They'll strike to ten, when they should stop at one.
> *(Mad World,* 4.1.7-24)

And here is Sir Walter Whorehound, similarly guilt-struck, as he repudiates his mistress:

> Some good, pitying man,

Remove my sins out of my sight a little;
I tremble to behold her, she keeps back
All comfort while she stays. Is this a time,
Unconscionable woman, to see thee?
Art thou so cruel to the peace of man,
Not to give liberty now? the devil himself
Shows a far fairer reverence and respect
To goodness than thyself; he dares not do this,
But part[s] in time of penitence, hides his face;
When man withdraws from him, he leaves the place:
Hast thou less manners and more impudence
Than thy instructor? prithee, show thy modesty,
If the least grain be left, and get thee from me:
Thou shouldst be rather lock'd many rooms hence
From the poor miserable sight of me,
If either love or grace had part in thee.

(*Chaste Maid*, 5.1.35-51)

The first passage is, like so much of Middleton's earlier verse, stiff and exclamatory. The tone of the second, on the other hand, is intimate; if the poet betrays his occasional tendency to continue a speech after the point has been made, he also shows impressive progress in fluency and naturalness—in awareness of the resources of his medium.

Maturity is evident also in the structure of the play. The *Chaste Maid* is the grandest, most textured of the City comedies. Middleton forges three major actions, with three sets of characters and much incident, into a single dramatic entity, and at the same time is able to include a well-integrated minor intrigue (Tim's courtship of the Welsh courtesan), a topical digression on government informers, and the great naturalistic genre study that is the episode of the christening celebration. Yet the play never sprawls under the weight of its abundance, nor does it lapse into the loose ends that disfigure even the best of the preceding comedies. Indeed, the gusto of the *Chaste Maid* is unparalleled in Middleton's comedy. Perhaps, as Miss Bradbrook suggests, its vitality is due to the fact that the dramatist was writing for the public stage of the Swan and not, as previously, for the less robust audiences of the private houses [*The Growth and Structure of Elizabethan Comedy*, 1955]. Perhaps it is also significant that the *Chaste Maid* was designed for an adult company, the Lady Elizabeth's men, rather than for the boy actors of Paul's. But circumstances alone could hardly account for the play's vigor. The *Chaste Maid* is clearly the work of a writer whose powers are at their height and who knows precisely what he wishes to do with them.

It is a disturbing vitality that informs the play. The "joyous animation" and "good-natured impartiality" which Miss Lynch discerns in Middleton's City comedies are in little evidence here [*The Social Mode of Restoration Comedy*, 1926]: no personable Witgood or "frolic" Sir Bounteous brightens the dramatist's mood. In his earlier plays Middleton sometimes used a spokesman—a Phoenix or Fitsgrave—to serve as an outlet for his moral indignation; but it is the wittol of the *Chaste Maid* who becomes the principal agent of retribution. Never has the playwright envisioned a world of more pervasive squalor.

The London of the *Chaste Maid* is a harsh city. In the streets the abandoned Country Wench searches for a way to dispose of her bastard infant. The season is Lent; at the corners lurk "poisonous officers" who corruptly enforce the new "religious wholesome laws" prohibiting the consumption of flesh. Within doors, degradation and brutality exist on a scale unequaled in Jacobean comedy. At the Allwits', Sir Walter fathers Mistress Allwit's children and provides for the entire household. When the "good founder" arrives, the husband bows and scrapes, whispers "Peace, bastard!" to the boy who innocently addresses him as father, and smiles complacently while wife and lover embrace. At the Yellowhammers', Moll—the chaste maid of the title—tries to elope and in so doing brings down upon herself the wrath of her parents. It is a wrath which reveals the emotional bankruptcy that ensues when the only values recognized are those associated with social and material advancement. Middleton had expressed similar views in the earlier City comedies, but not to such chilling effect as in the scenes concerning Moll Yellowhammer and her family.

Imprisoned by her parents in a tiny room, Moll escapes, only to be overtaken by her mother on a Thames barge and, after a futile suicide attempt, dragged half drowned back to land. At the docks a brief, fierce exchange between the mother, Maudlin, and a bystander permits the dramatist to underscore the ugliness of the episode:

Maudlin [*to* Moll]. I'll tug thee home by the hair.
First Waterman. Good mistress, spare her!
Maudlin. Tend your own business.
First Waterman. You're a cruel mother.

(4.3.45-47)

When afterwards it finally appears that Moll is dead and her presumably lifeless body is carried out, the preoccupations of the household are characteristic. Brother Tim, the Cambridge scholar, busies himself with a Latin epitaph, while Yellowhammer anxiously anticipates the reactions of his neighbors:

All the whole street will hate us, and the world
Point me out cruel: it's our best course, wife,
After we've given order for the funeral,
T' absent ourselves till she be laid in ground.

(5.2.92-95)

His wife is at once consoled by the prospect of her son's marriage. "We'll not lose all at once," she hopefully concludes, "somewhat we'll catch."

Most of the dramatist's personages, major and minor, are involved in some form of duplicity, and most of them are venal; others—a Tim or Sir Oliver—are the necessary gulls. Sir Walter looking forward to his wedding day, when he will receive a dowry of "two thousand pound in gold / And a sweet maidenhead worth forty," is representative. So, likewise, is Touchwood senior, as he cures the sterility of the Kixes. He has Sir Oliver swallow a special potion, jump up and down several times, and then go off on horseback for five hours; meanwhile Lady Kix lies down to receive her potion from Touchwood himself. His therapy (which costs Kix a total of four hundred pounds) proves so effective that she conceives at once, to the indescribable elation of her husband. The notable exception to Middleton's pattern of the dupers and the duped is the virtuous Moll; but, like Castiza in *The Revenger's Tragedy* and Celia in *Volpone,* she seems to exist primarily to throw into relief the depravity around her.

The playwright's mood is mirrored in his language. Figures suggesting contempt and debasement color the verse. A mother about to give birth is "even upon the point of grunting"; a baby is "this half yard of flesh, in which, I think, / It wants a nail or two." Lady Kix refers to her impotent husband as "brevity." Bawds, we are told, will grow so fat that "Their chins will hang like udders by Easter-eve, / And, being stroak'd, will give the milk of witches." The government spies stand

> pricking up their ears
> And snuffing up their noses, like rich men's dogs
> When the first course goes in.
>
> (2.2.55-57)

The idiom even of Middleton's young lovers may reflect the hardness of the world in which they furtively meet. "Turn not to me till thou mayst lawfully," Touchwood junior whispers to Moll in her father's shop, "it but whets my stomach, which is too sharp-set already."

But perversity reaches its ultimate form in the soliloquy Allwit delivers upon learning that Sir Walter has come to town. First the wittol prays for the preservation of the benefactor who has for ten years maintained him and his family, and he then goes on to enumerate the domestic joys he owes to his cuckolder:

> I'm at his table:
> He gets me all my children, and pays the nurse
> Monthly or weekly; puts me to nothing, rent,
> Nor church-duties, not so much as the scavenger:
> The happiest state that ever man was born to!
> I walk out in a morning; come to breakfast,
> Find excellent cheer; a good fire in winter;
> Look in my coal-house about midsummer eve,
> That's full, five or six chaldron new laid up;
> Look in my back-yard, I shall find a steeple
> Made up with Kentish faggots, which o'erlooks
> The water-house and the windmills: I say nothing,
> But smile and pin the door.
>
> (1.2.17-29)

After cataloguing the embossings, embroiderings, and spangles, the restoratives, sugar loaves, and wines that Whorehound provides when his mistress lies in, Allwit turns to the question of jealousy:

> And where some merchants would in soul kiss hell
> To buy a paradise for their wives, and dye
> Their conscience in the bloods of prodigal heirs
> To deck their night-piece, yet all this being done,
> Eaten with jealousy to the inmost bone,—

> As what affliction nature more constrains,
> Then feed the wife plump for another's veins?—
> These torments stand I freed of; I'm as clear
> From jealousy of a wife as from the charge:
> O, two miraculous blessings!
>
> (1.2.41-50)

Allwit's soliloquy is perhaps the most audacious example in Middleton of one of the dramatist's favorite devices: the deliberate inversion of traditional morality and customary emotional responses. Surely Miss Ellis-Fermor errs in seeing affinities between the *Chaste Maid,* with its disquieting cynicism, and *Tom Jones,* with its essential humanity. One hesitates to regard the creator of Allwit in quite the same light as the creator of Allworthy.

To some extent Middleton's cynicism in the *Chaste Maid* is compensated by his irony, which here (as elsewhere in the City comedies) serves as an unobtrusive instrument of ethical comment. As the dramatist develops, his irony becomes deeper and takes more varied forms; in this respect, too, the play marks an advance over his earlier work. Middleton may convey his irony by means of a miniature story embodied in a simile:

> this shows like
> The fruitless sorrow of a careless mother,
> That brings her son with dalliance to the gallows,
> And then stands by and weeps to see him suffer.
>
> (5.1.61-64)

It may reside in the contrast between the Lenten season of self-denial, during which much of the action takes place, and the gross carnal self-indulgence of the participants. The narrative is enriched with ironic detail: Thus Touchwood junior orders his wedding ring, with the inscription "Love that's wise / Blinds parents' eyes," from the father of the very girl with whom he plans to run off, and maintains a discreet silence when the old man winks at him knowingly:

> You'll steal away some man's daughter: am I near you?
> Do you turn aside? you gentlemen are mad wags!
> I wonder things can be so warily carried,
> And parents blinded so: but they're serv'd right,
> That have two eyes and were so dull a' sight.
>
> (1.1.198-202)

"Thy doom take hold of thee!" Touchwood junior prays in an aside; and indeed ultimately it does.

In the larger reversals of the play, the dramatist's personages, vicious or foolish, find themselves unwilling recipients of an ironic dispensation. The Yellowhammers, who have failed with their daughter, succeed only too well with the son. Tim marries the Welsh gentlewoman; but the "heir to some nineteen mountains" is revealed to be Sir Walter's penniless cast mistress, and the Cambridge student is left to make good, as best he can, his previous boast that by logic he could prove a whore an honest woman. Whorehound himself is crushed in the play's supreme moment of irony. As Sir Walter lies bleeding and repentant at the Allwits', the cuckold thrusts wife and children upon him in a desper-

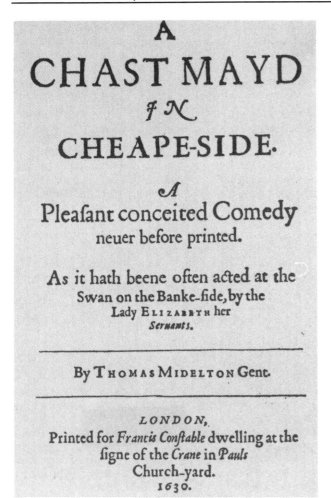

Title page to a 1630 edition.

ate effort to win back his favor. But Allwit's sole reward is a curse upon the entire household. The tide turns, however, when servants rush in to announce that Whorehound has killed a man in a duel and that he has lost his fortune, which he held only so long as the Kixes remained barren. (It is, as Miss Bradbrook observes, a suitable irony that the begetter of bastards should be undone by an equivocal conception.) Sir Walter must now seek refuge with the family he has repudiated. But Allwit, realizing that he can hope for nothing from his ruined patron, turns upon him in a sudden assertion of virtue fully as impudent as his former defense of depravity. "I pray, depart, sirs," he orders the knight's men,

> And take your murderer along with you;
> Good he were apprehended ere he go,
> Has kill'd some honest gentleman; send for officers.

And to Sir Walter:

> I must tell you, sir,
> You have been somewhat bolder in my house
> Than I could well like of; I suffer'd you

Till it stuck here at my heart; I tell you truly
I thought y'had been familiar with my wife once.

(5.1.138-46)

Ironic understatement could scarcely be carried further.

Cruel, perverse, ironic—these qualities suggest the appalling comedy of *Volpone.* But the sinister decadence of Jonson's Venice has little in common with the spirit of the **Chaste Maid.** For Middleton's mood is, paradoxically enough, Rabelaisian as well as sardonic, and great gales of laughter sweep through the play. It is somewhat as though the author of *Gulliver's Travels* has contrived to relate his Fourth Book with uproarious good humor.

Laughter reaches its peak in the christening celebration at the Allwits'. In this, the central episode of the **Chaste Maid,** most of the principal characters—the Allwits, Yellowhammer and Maudlin, Tim and his tutor, Moll, Touchwood junior, Sir Walter, and Lady Kix—gather and mingle with a number of minor figures. At the door Maudlin and a gossip strain courtesies; the wives of an apothecary and a comfit maker clash briefly over precedence; the Puritans enter "in unity, and show the fruits of peace." Within all is movement, as charwomen, nurses, maids, and guests arrive, as Mistress Allwit receives gifts in bed and the midwife displays the "fine plump black-ey'd slut." Allwit, reveling in "recreation" that costs him nothing, modestly puts by compliments on his chopping baby. "They're pretty foolish things, put to making in minutes," he disclaims, "I ne'er stand long about 'em." Chief among the visitors is Sir Walter, who acts as godfather to his own infant to forestall scandal. Entering with his gifts (a silver standing cup and two large apostle spoons), he has a flattering word for the wives who, seated on needlework stools, shuffle up the rushes with their cork heels and heat the room with their thick bums. A nurse passes among the guests with wine and confections. The gossips, their tasseled handkerchiefs spread between their knees, greedily seize upon the sweetmeats with their "long fingers that are wash'd / Some thrice a-day in urine." Again and again the cups go round, and the wives fall into hiccups and intimate confessions. Maudlin thrusts comfits upon her son. "Come I from Cambridge," he protests, "and offer me six plums?" But he finds the kissing even more difficult to endure. "Let me come next," Mistress Underman shrieks, drunk:

> Welcome from the wellspring of discipline,
> That waters all the brethren.

She tries to kiss Tim, but staggers and falls.

> *Tim.* Hoist, I beseech thee!
> *Third Gossip.* O bless the woman!—Mistress
>   Underman— [*They raise her up.*]
> *First Puritan* [*Mistress Underman*]. 'Tis but the
>   common affliction of the faithful;
> We must embrace our falls.

(3.2.161-66)

At last the guests reel off to the conduit, and Allwit and

Davy Dahanna, Sir Walter's attendant, survey the damage:

> *Allwit.* What's here under the stools?
> *Davy.* Nothing but wet, sir;
> Some wine spilt here belike.
> *Allwit.* Is't no worse, think'st thou?
> Fair needlework stools cost nothing with them,
>   Davy. . . .
> Look how they have laid them,
> E'en as they lie themselves, with their heels up!
>   (3.2.184-88)

The festivities are done; the scene closes.

For perhaps the only time in Middleton's career a single theatrical situation called forth simultaneously all his diverse talents as a comic dramatist: his skill at conveying life and movement, his ability to faithfully set down colloquial speech and visual detail, his capacity for ludicrous invention, and his gift for effortlessly blending irony, innuendo, and open bawdry. The playwright's mastery of the Jacobean stage, apparent throughout the christening episode, is notable even in the handling of properties. Stage properties are employed far more extensively than was customary in the open-air houses, and they perform an important role in evoking atmosphere and heightening the audience's sense of familiar reality. Yet some critics are uneasy. Knights feels that "the gathering of city wives . . . is presented with imperfectly controlled disgust," and to Miss Bradbrook the episode stands "among the rankest in all Elizabethan drama." No doubt the Puritans are subjected to merciless ridicule, and certainly the entire scene is quite uninhibited. But "disgust" would appear to be an imperfectly selected term, and those of us who relish cakes and ale will scarcely be deterred from the greatest triumph of Middleton's comic realism.

The *Chaste Maid* is not a simple play, and the powerful impression it leaves is achieved, it seems to me, largely by means of a tension maintained between disparate elements: The essential brutality of the content of the play is counterpoised by the laughter which informs the dramatist's treatment of his chilling material. In effecting and sustaining this recalcitrant balance, Middleton is well served by his irony—an instrument peculiarly fitted to the expression of the cruel and the comic alike. Thus we laugh at what, under other circumstances, might well horrify us.

But there is another factor, as yet unsuggested, that contributes to the complex effect produced by this extraordinary play. As the action unfolds, we gradually perceive that Middleton's realism has taken on an added dimension—a dimension to which the Elizabethan comic dramatist does not often aspire. The life of the play overflows the artificial bounds of stage narrative; becomes, as it were, a fragment out of time. In the London of *Michaelmas Term* Easy meets Quomodo for the first time; Follywit in the *Mad World* and Witgood in the *Trick* set in motion their intrigues in the opening scenes. But situations introduced in

the *Chaste Maid* existed before the play's beginning: Moll and Touchwood junior have already accepted one another, Mistress Allwit has borne Sir Walter six children in the course of a decade. In Elizabethan comedy the dramatist will of course provide necessary background information concerning his principal figures (Witgood's previous dealings with his uncle, for example) but in the *Chaste Maid* the characters' pasts have a concreteness beyond the immediate needs of the action. We learn much, for example, about the Yellowhammers. Maud was "lightsome and quick" two years before her marriage and took dancing lessons from "a pretty brown gentleman"; her husband is descended from the Yellowhammers of Oxfordshire, near Abingdon, and many years back had a child by Mistress Anne ("he's now a jolly fellow, / Has been twice warden"); for eight years Tim stumbled over *as in praesenti* in his grammar, only to go on to impress the gentleman commoners in the hall at Cambridge by eating his broth with a silver spoon. Even minor personages are portrayed with a scrupulous particularity. We are told of the Welsh courtesan's red hair, we hear her speak in her native tongue, we learn that she is from North Wales and lost her maidenhead at Brecknockshire.

As we follow the movement of the play, we are aware—as we were not with the earlier City comedies—of the passage of time and the changes wrought by the succession of events; finally, we can envision a future for some, at least, of Middleton's characters. Sir Walter travels his rake's progress to the Knights' ward. Mistress Allwit, "as great as she can wallow," longs for her lover's return and pickled cucumbers. Time passes: her infant is born and christened; the "good founder" casts her off and is himself cast off; in the end the Allwits look ahead to a different life as they prepare to take a house in the Strand and let out lodgings. The result of the dramatist's consciousness of time is an illusion of reality so persuasive that it is scarcely vitiated by the fantastic elements in plot and characterization.

In the years following the *Chaste Maid,* Middleton occasionally returned to comedy, but he never again attempted anything quite like the fantastic realism of the great earlier plays. In *No Wit, No Help Like a Woman's* (ca. 1615), he relied unimaginatively on his source, Della Porta's *La Sorella;* in *The Widow* (ca. 1616), he modeled himself on the popular Fletcherian formula. Both plays succeed on their own limited terms, but lack the vitality, concreteness, and depth of social implication of Middleton's previous comedies. The most distinctive writings of the dramatist's later years are his tragicomedies and tragedies, in which the corrosive view of humanity underlying the *Chaste Maid* takes disturbing new forms. In these plays Middleton becomes a subtle analyst of the mind—particularly the female mind—and of sexual passion; at the same time he achieves something of that "lofty impersonal power" which the young James Joyce admired as Ibsen's "highest excellence." Perhaps when *A Chaste Maid in Cheapside* was completed, Middleton realized that he had written a masterpiece of City comedy and that his most compelling creative energies must thereafter find quite different expression.

J. R. Mulryne on the ending of *A Chaste Maid*:

The play's fifth act represents something of a theatrical *tour de force,* blending caustic and unexpected reversals with emotionally heightened theatre that reminds one of Fletcher (yet always qualified by Middleton's wit). A sardonic first scene shows Sir Walter, wounded in a skirmish with Touchwood Junior, turning death-bed moralist and heaping abusive strictures on his erstwhile liaison with Mistress Allwit; the Allwits, at first doing everything to repair the relationship, come to recognize that Sir Walter has nothing more to give, and coldly banish him their house, planning instead to set up fashionably in the Strand, surrounded by the furniture derived from years of Sir Walter's bounty. Thus Middleton dramatises the realities underlying the absurdly sunny veneer of the Allwit and Sir Walter menage: conscience and self-interest both declare themselves boldly, as Sir Walter reviews his life, and is seized by the terrors of death and damnation, and Allwit, once a lighthearted *mari complaisant,* is revealed as a Tartuffe, a cold-hearted manipulator. The dramatic tone is subtly and daringly judged, as the audience's mood is suspended between laughter and shock. In another emotionally complicated action, the apparent deaths of Moll and Touchwood Junior lead to a mock funeral, elaborately staged and the occasion of considerable sentiment, both of a lachrimose and, when the young couple revive, a genial character. The threatened sentimentality is qualified not only by the audience's broader knowledge of events, but also by Middleton's quicksilver varying of focus, as the playing touches-in the range of motive and sensibility among all those on stage, and as the complicated plot resolves itself. Such freedom of invention and depth of character-perception, over a range of *dramatis personae,* distinguishes *A Chaste Maid* from the earlier comedies, and ensures its theatrical vitality: a richly conceived and densely particular play, made buoyant by the dramatist's skilled manipulation of audience-response over a wide emotional area.

J. R. Mulryne, in his Thomas Middleton, *Longman Group for The British Council, 1979.*

Richard Levin (essay date 1965)

SOURCE: "The Four Plots of *A Chaste Maid in Cheapside,*" in *The Review of English Studies,* Vol. XVI, 1965, pp. 14-24.

[*Levin uncovers numerous interrelationships among the various plots of* A Chaste Maid, *finding contrasts or correspondences in their actions, themes, tones, and genres.*]

A Chaste Maid in Cheapside is now held to be the last of the plays that Thomas Middleton wrote in that remarkable series known as his 'city comedies', and it is also almost the last of them to win the kind of recognition that it surely deserves. Most of the critics of an earlier generation seem not to have progressed very far beyond the initial shock or titillation they experienced upon discovering that certain of its sexual situations were even more daring than those of the preceding comedies (which were themselves notorious for their 'realism' in this area), so that such favourable comments as they ventured were qualified and defensive.

But in more recent years other readers, including some of the most perceptive students of Middleton and the drama of his day, have come to see that this play is really the culminating achievement of all his efforts in this genre, and one of the great comedies of the age. They also appear to agree, whatever their mode of approach, in locating its distinctive excellence primarily in the marvellous richness and variety of the incidents, characters, and emotional effects that Middleton has been able to combine here into a coherent artistic whole, although I am not aware that anyone has attempted to explain in detail exactly how this complex unity has been attained. In view of this reaction, it is very difficult to accept the judgement of L. C. Knights, one of the few moderns to attack the play, that after several readings 'all that remains with us is the plot' [*Drama & Society in the Age of Jonson,* 1937]. On the contrary, virtually all commentary upon *A Chaste Maid* has been given over to discussions of some of the more striking scenes (usually emphasizing the scene of the promoters and the christening celebration, which are only tenuously connected to the plot), or else to generalizations about Middleton's realism and irony and moral position, or lack of one. Yet, if the play represents such an impressive feat of construction, it should be possible to examine it at a level somewhere between these individual scenes and intellectual abstractions—at the level of plot, since this is what shapes the diverse particulars into an effective structure, and determines their emotional and moral significance. Such an examination, moreover, should prove especially interesting here, since in this play we have one of the most sophisticated and successful examples of that peculiar dramatic institution of the period, the multiple plot, which was the despair of earlier critics and is still too often dismissed as an unhappy burden imposed on these playwrights by the tyranny of convention.

This kind of analysis would have to begin by separating out the distinct plots that are at work here. Although other enumerations have varied from three to five, I find four of these actions, carefully arranged in a descending order of importance, which is also the order of their inception. The main plot, which opens the play, centres in the attempts of Touchwood Junior to win Moll Yellowhammer (the 'chaste maid' of the title) despite the violent opposition of her parents, who want to force her to marry Sir Walter Whorehound. The second plot, beginning in the second scene, deals with the Allwit household, where Sir Walter has for years been carrying on an affair with the wife and supporting the complaisant husband. The third scene (II. i) initiates the third action, the story of the barren couple, Sir Oliver and Lady Kix, who finally acquire a child through the ministrations of Touchwood Senior. And in the fourth plot, which does not get under way until Act IV, Tim Yellowhammer courts and marries a supposed Welsh heiress, who turns out to be Whorehound's former mistress. Actually, the number of plots here is not as unusual as it might at first appear, since the fourth, although it is a complete sequence with its own complication and denouement, is developed much less fully than the others, both in itself and in its relationship to them, and so is really not very different from certain clownish episodes in a number of what we are accustomed to call 'double-plot' plays of this period, which include, in addition to their two main actions, a fool or pair of fools (like Tim and his Tutor) who pursue a more or less independent line that evokes a third level of dramatic response.

In some ways, too, Middleton follows the standard practice of his age in combining these four plots. Thus we find him, like many of his contemporaries, relying upon family ties or even geographic proximity to provide contact between the different plots at various points. The two Touchwoods are brothers, Moll is Tim's sister, the Kixes are related to Whorehound, some members of the Kix, Allwit, and Yellowhammer households seem to be neighbourhood acquaintances—and these connexions are exploited, on the simplest level, to permit the characters of one action to refer to those of another, and to bring almost everyone in the play together in the two great ensemble scenes, the Allwit christening and the mock funeral of Moll and Touchwood Junior. However, Middleton does not rest with perfunctory, external relationships of this kind—sometimes the only kind provided in multiple-plot plays of the period—but makes use of them to establish much more important causal connexions among the different plots. Sir Walter Whorehound is the principal link through which these inter-plot sequences work, since he is actively engaged in plots one, two, and four, and is vitally affected, as a kinsman of the Kixes, by the outcome of plot three, because his inheritance depends upon their remaining childless, and is lost forever when Lady Kix is impregnated by Touchwood Senior. But Touchwood undertakes this task in order to help his brother by impoverishing, and so disqualifying, his rival for Moll's hand (just as he aids him more directly in the planning and execution of each of the three attempts to spirit Moll away). Whorehound's scheme to marry Moll, therefore, links the first plot to the third; moreover, it links the first to the second, for Allwit, unwilling to lose his benefactor, calls on Yellowhammer (in the guise of a distant relative) in order to stop the marriage, and the *ménage à trois* of plot two finally breaks up because of Whorehound's duel with Touchwood Junior in plot one, which leads to his repentance and rejection of the Allwits, and Lady Kix's pregnancy in plot three, which removes any inducement on their part to hold him. Even Tim's relationship to his sister is used to connect his plot to the first, since his marriage to the Welshwoman is a consequence of Whorehound's courtship of Moll, and his parents' discovery that this woman (whom Sir Walter had introduced as his wealthy niece) is really a penniless whore is one of the factors, along with the disinheriting of Sir Walter, that reconciles them to their daughter's marriage to Touchwood Junior. This connexion of plot four to the other action is rather weak, as was pointed out, but in the first three plots these interrelationships are so skilfully arranged that each plot affects, and is affected by, the others, the whole complex system being made to turn upon the efforts of Whorehound and Touchwood, in the main action, to win the 'chaste maid'. This in itself is a very remarkable structural achievement, one of the most remarkable of its kind in the Jacobean drama, and it has not passed unnoticed, several of the commentators having spoken admiringly of at least some aspects of this elaborate causal network that, on this level, combines the disparate actions into a unified whole.

These actions, however, are also unified on another, quite different level that has received relatively little notice—a level of significant comparisons and contrasts which are developed among the four plots and used to relate them to each other in what might be called analogical or 'spatial' terms (as opposed to the temporal cause-effect sequences just discussed). It is evident that these four plots were placed together with a view to exploiting certain symmetrical patterns of character and action. Each of them, for example, is based on a sexual triangle involving two men and a woman; and, in their treatment of this triangle, the first and fourth plots can be seen to form a meaningful pair, as do the second and third. Both plots of the first pair are stories of two young people who get married, conceived in such a way that one story is made to seem the exact opposite of the other. This is certainly true of the relationship of Yellowhammer and his wife to the two marriages, for they do everything they can to prevent the first, but fail, and then come to approve of it, whereas they aggressively promote the second, are successful, and later regret it. Whorehound's roles in the two actions are also contrasted, since in the first he tries to get the girl and fails, while in the second he is trying to get rid of the girl and succeeds. Moreover, as these differences suggest, the difficulties faced by the two couples are directly opposite: the courtship of Moll and Touchwood is over and their only problem is getting married, hence the major scenes of this plot portray their attempts to elope and, finally, the wedding itself; but in the other plot the only problem (and subject of the only big scene) is Tim's courtship, the actual marriage being quickly passed over. But all this simply reflects the much more basic contrast in the nature of the two relationships— the contrast between a couple whose true love eventually triumphs over external pressures, and a couple who have nothing but these external pressures to bring them together. And this, in turn, relates to the contrasting natures of the persons involved. Touchwood is, along with his brother, the chief 'wit' or manipulator in the play, and Moll is the only maid and apparently, except for the wife of Touchwood Senior, the only chaste woman (for even her mother, it is suggested, committed indiscretions in the past); their wedding, therefore, is made to represent the most desirable union possible in this particular world. Tim, on the other hand, though a Cambridge scholar, is the fool of the play, and the Welshwoman, although she passes for a virgin, is the most disreputable woman in it; thus this wedding marks the lowest point in the play's scale of value, the key terms of which are expressed, appropriately enough, in Tim's school logic when he demonstrates by syllogism that *stultus est animal rationale,* and offers to 'prove a whore to be an honest woman'. The other principal value in the world of the play is also at issue here, since Moll has a dowry of 'two thousand pound in gold', while the Welshwoman's 'two thousand runts' turn out to be as illusory as her maidenhead. Therefore, in all significant respects—emotional, intellectual, moral, and financial—the story of Tim and his bride is made to seem a kind of false imitation or parody of the main plot.

A very similar relationship emerges from the juxtaposition of plots two and three, for they, too, share a basic situation which invites comparison between them, but develop it in contrasting ways. These two plots are set apart from the first pair because they are concerned, not with the 'romantic' problems of youth that terminate in wedlock, but with the 'domestic' affairs of older, married people in established households. (A further difference can be seen in the roles played by Whorehound, who is largely a passive character here, acted upon by the course of events that constitute these two plots, whereas in one and four his active intervention was what set both plots in motion.) The central situation in each is a triangle that involves a long-married couple and another man who cuckolds the husband and fathers his children. Indeed, a certain superficial symmetry is produced here by the fact that the second plot opens with the expected birth of the Allwit child, who is really Whorehound's, while the third ends with the anticipated birth of the Kix baby, really sired by Touchwood Senior. Actually, this sort of symmetrical opposition extends throughout the two sequences, which proceed in reverse order. At the beginning of plot two we are shown an apparently stable *ménage à trois* which has been flourishing for many years, but which is destroyed by the subsequent action; the action of plot three, however, brings such a relationship into being, and when Kix in the final scene invites Touchwood to move in with them in order to beget more children, he is creating a kind of replica of the Allwit household that will continue, presumably, well into the future. Another element in this contrast is the happiness of the participants, which seems to depend upon this unusual domestic arrangement. Our first sight of the Allwits shows that they have long been satisfied with it, and their peace is only disturbed when they face the loss of Whorehound; on the other hand, the Kixes are first seen engaged in a squabble, which has obviously been going on for years, and which is only resolved when Touchwood moves in—indeed, Kix is just as elated by this prospect at the very end of his plot as Allwit was by Whorehound's visit as the very beginning of his. Similarly, Whorehound seems to have been quite contented as a member of the Allwit family, and the final blow in his catastrophe (which, of course, includes other factors) comes when they throw him out, while Touchwood Senior is first presented at the bottom of his fortunes, and attains his greatest happiness when he joins the Kixes. However, beneath this reversal in the direction of the two plots lies a much more important contrast in the nature of the human relationship involved, for while Allwit and Kix are both cuckolds, the former is aware of it, which makes him a scoundrel, but the latter is not, and so is only a fool. This crucial difference determines the two financial arrangements—Allwit is well paid by Whorehound to put up with him, and is actually victimizing him, whereas Kix is paying Touchwood Senior, and is to be regarded as his victim. The motives of the two women are likewise contrasted; Lady Kix accepts the situation because she desperately wants a child (although this also has its financial side), and Mistress Allwit, as far as we can tell, because it is so lucrative. But this turns upon the difference between the two marriages. The Kixes, for all their bickering, have a real affection for each other, which is presented comically in the intervals between the fights but is made quite believable and is even commented on, with a certain sympathy, by Touchwood (III. iii. 43-48). The Allwits, on the other hand, never fight, but neither do they feel any emotional attachment; their

marriage is nothing more than an efficient business partnership, as becomes clear (if there were any doubt remaining) in their revealing conversation at the close of V. i. This basic difference between the two couples is also reflected in their attitudes towards the other man—the Allwits, who have been maintained for years by Whorehound, reject his appeal for help without a qualm when they can get no more out of him; but the Kixes, even though they have paid Touchwood, are genuinely grateful and press further rewards upon him beyond their original bargain. And this difference is paralleled, finally, in the motive of the cuckolder, for Whorehound, as his name implies, is simply satisfying his lust, while Touchwood takes on this task (though he certainly enjoys it, and the money) primarily to help his brother. It appears, therefore, that these two plots have been contrasted in the same emotional, intellectual, moral, and financial terms that were found to differentiate the first pair, so that a kind of proportion has been established, the first plot being related to the fourth as the second is to the third.

These symmetrical 'spatial' interrelationships, together with the casual or 'temporal' connexions already discussed, can explain, I believe, how the four plots are combined into a single whole, but they cannot in themselves explain the significance of this combination, since that depends not only upon how the unity is achieved, but also upon what is being unified. Each of these four plots has its own distinctive tone or character which, weighted and brought into proper focus through this cohesive structure, contributes to the total effect of the play. And the arrangement of these plots in terms of their individual tones coincides, as might be expected, with this structure, for the order in which the plots begin, which was shown to be the order of descending importance as determined by the casual system of the play, also turns out to be the order of decreasing seriousness. The first plot is the most serious of all, being pitched at the level of traditional 'romantic' comedy. Its story of two young lovers who eventually overcome the opposition of the anti-romantic, mercenary older generation derives from one of the most venerable comic conventions that goes back at least as far as the Greek stage, and probably beyond that, if we are to believe the anthropologists, to the primitive fertility rituals associated with the cycle of the seasons. Indeed, the plot would almost seem to be a textbook illustration of this theory, with the magical triadic sequence of elopements, each bringing the lovers closer to disaster (the first ends in Moll's imprisonment, the second in a kind of 'death by water', and the third in a counterfeit of death itself, with an elaborately staged funeral), and the final miraculous transcendence when they rise from their coffins to marry, having used death to outwit the 'death-forces' keeping them apart, and taking their winding sheets, as Touchwood Senior suggests, for the bridal bed on which they will create new life. More to the purpose, though, is the fact that this story and this ending belonged to a well-established dramatic convention of the period, for this would immediately enlist the audience's sympathies for the lovers and, to some extent, guide their response. The convention itself, however, does not determine the degree of seriousness; in fact, most of the plots of this general type exhibit much greater comic elaboration, usually in the clever tricks that the lovers play on the parents or the obnoxious suitor favoured by them. Except for that brief first episode where Touchwood buys his wedding ring from Moll's unsuspecting father, there is none of this here; the lovers' first two stratagems are simple, straightforward flights, and the mock funeral is not treated in comic terms. The emphasis throughout is not on the cleverness of Moll and Touchwood at all, but on the cruelty and venality of Moll's parents, who in their basic attitudes, as well as in their unholy alliance with Whorehound, are made to resemble the Allwits. And this emphasis necessarily insures greater sympathy for the lovers, and increases the seriousness of their plot.

The fourth plot, which was seen to be the opposite of the first in its fundamental design, is also at the opposite emotional pole. It is the least serious of the four, conceived from beginning to end at the level of farce, with its one big scene (Tim's wooing of the Welshwoman) relying heavily on a kind of verbal slapstick. Moreover, it involves the complete reversal of the romantic convention, since here the calculating older generation (the Yellowhammers and Whorehound) succeeds in manipulating and bringing together a de-romanticized young couple (a fool and a whore) in what is a travesty of a love-match. But this reversal of the standard romantic formula had itself become a dramatic convention at this time, with its own stock situations and scenes, such as the clown's inept courtship, and the whore's passing herself off as an heiress, which are adopted here. Clearly these two conventions can reinforce each other when they are juxtaposed, as they are in this play, for the marked contrasts between them serve to make the romantic plot seem even more serious and the other even less, and, similarly, to increase our sympathy for the first pair of lovers and our alienation from their debased counterparts, particularly the fool, whose role, as defined both by the tradition and the context of the play, evokes an unsympathetic response. It is true that our feelings are only weakly engaged because of the farcical level of the action, and so never pass over into real antipathy, but they do require his comic discomfiture, which is provided by the marriage to a whore—a 'punishment' appropriate both to the lack of seriousness and lack of sympathy we found here, and one which, for these same reasons, frequently figures in the denouement of plots in this general tradition.

Therefore, these two plots, romance and anti-romance, although they are the furthest apart in the play, actually fit very neatly together because of their conventional nature, and of what might be called the symbiotic relationship that exists between the 'straight' model and the travesty of it. Indeed, it would not be difficult to imagine a comedy composed only of these two plots (both padded out with additional incidents), though it would be difficult to imagine it causing much critical stir. For the special flavour of this play depends to a considerable extent upon the other two plots, whose unique contribution to the total effect lies in their striking unconventionality. That is why the analysis of the contrast between plots two and three could not treat either as a parody of the other, as was done with the first pair, for there is no identifiable norm here that would make parody meaningful. Yet it is possible to locate them in the overall dramatic structure in the same terms that were ap-

plied to plots one and four. It is evident that the second plot is the more serious of the two, because of its treatment of the marital triangle and, particularly, its conclusion, with the near death of Sir Walter and his bitter denunciation of the Allwits (although I would argue that even this moment, which some critics regard as the most profound in the play, does not attain the seriousness of the main action, since Whorehound's violently moral tone is partially undercut by the comic efforts of the Allwits to placate him, and then by their outrageous about-face when they turn to denounce him). On the other hand, the continual quarrels and reconciliations of the Kixes, and the hilarious prescription of Touchwood's 'physic' in III. iii, the major scene of the third plot, approach much closer to the level of plot four. Moreover, these two actions can be differentiated, like the first pair, in terms of our feelings for the characters, since the sordid relationship of Whorehound and the Allwits makes them antipathetic—much more so, certainly, than Tim and the Welshwoman—whereas we are quite sympathetic to Touchwood Senior and even to the Kixes, whose follies are exposed with considerable good humour. The four plots, therefore, seem to have been selected and arranged in a scheme that exhausts the possibilities of comic action defined by these variables (understanding that the term 'serious' here marks only the upper limit of the comic spectrum, without passing over into a different genre): the first action is serious-sympathetic comedy, the second serious-unsympathetic, the third farcical but sympathetic, and the last farcical-unsympathetic. And the outcomes of these plots would appear to confirm this analysis, for both sympathetic actions, one and three, end very happily for all the major characters except Whorehound (even Moll's parents finally welcome her marriage), while in the two unsympathetic actions everyone is forced to accept, more or less grudgingly, some kind of defeat. (Whorehound is a special case since he is affected by all four outcomes and cannot react differently to each, as the Yellowhammers do in plots one and four; but his downfall is associated primarily with plot two, because the scene that portrays it is placed in the Allwits' home, and their rejection of him is made to seem the last, crushing blow.)

The general effect of the play, then, must be in some sense the product of these four levels of comic development, combined by means of the systems of causal and analogical relationships into a single organic whole. Therefore, this effect cannot fit any simple formula, and the critics who attempt to sum up the play as a 'slight farce', or, at the other extreme, as 'cynical' or 'rank' or the like, have been guilty of abstracting certain of the plots (or, in some cases, certain scenes) from the total context. Equally guilty, I think, are those critics who wish to write off the main action as a mere 'neutral frame' on which to 'hang the more interesting comedy of fleshly passions and follies' [Madeleine Doran, *Endeavors of Art,* 1954], for the story of Moll and Touchwood certainly is not neutral, and, even though it is not as intriguing as plots two and three, it is at the structural centre of the play, modifying, and being modified by, these subordinate actions, not only in terms of the causal connexions between them (which were all seen to work through the main action), but also in terms of the emotions they arouse. Actually, the very audacity of these two plots is emphasized, and at the same time kept within appropriate bounds, by their being placed within the frame, as it were, of the two conventional stories. And, conversely, these two unconventional actions serve to create the kind of environment that gives the romantic main plot its special significance. This is particularly evident, I believe, in the scenes of the promoters and the Allwit christening, the two famous 'realistic' studies that are loosely connected to the second and third plots, and that many critics have praised without considering their dramatic relevance. They are included partly, of course, for their independent satirical interest, but they also function (especially the christening celebration) to bring the characters of the various plots together at a moment of stasis, after the exposition has been completed and before the unravelling begins, and, more important, they establish, with marvellous vividness, the identity of 'Cheapside', the district of Goldsmith's Row and centre of the shopkeeper's world—the world of the Yellowhammers and the Allwits—which has a major role in this play, for its sordid sexual and commercial values, that are shown in these two scenes corrupting the 'religious wholesome laws' of Lent and the sacrament of baptism, constitute the real enemy of Moll and Touchwood, and the background against which the triumph of their love and fidelity is made to stand out as something uniquely attractive—as the comic miracle expressed in the title of *A Chaste Maid in Cheapside.*

Barbara Joan Baines (essay date 1973)

SOURCE: "Lust and Avarice in the Comedies: *A Chaste Maid in Cheapside,*" in *The Lust Motif in the Plays of Thomas Middleton,* Institut für Englische Sprache und Literatur, 1973, pp. 45-54.

[*Baines analyzes the characters' "habitual exploitation of sex for financial gain" in* A Chaste Maid in Cheapside.]

I think most critics who have given much thought to *A Chaste Maid in Cheapside* would agree that it is one of the most successful creations of multiple-plot structure in the English language. Because of the complex relationships of characters and their pursuits, there is little agreement as to exactly how many distinct plots and subdivisions of the same plot exist. Richard Levin [in "The Four Plots of *A Chaste Maid in Cheapside,*" *Review of English Studies,* XVI (1965)] presents a good argument for seeing the action of the play as four distinct plots: (1) Moll and Touchwood Jr.'s romance crossed by her parents' efforts to marry her to Sir Walter Whorehoud; (2) Lady and Sir Oliver Kix's need for a child and the appropriate services rendered them by Touchwood Sr.; (3) Walter Whorehound and Mistress Allwit's arrangement complicated by Walter's intentions to marry Moll; (4) Tim Yellowhammer and the Welsh whore's courtship and marriage. The characters are related or associated with each other enough so that all of them may be logically brought together at two points in the play, at a christening (II.iii.iv) and at a funeral (V.iv). All of the plots, however one wishes to divide and count them, are unified by a common subject—man's sexual and financial

pursuits. For every character except the chaste maid, these two pursuits are inextricably linked together. The Yellowhammers intend through marriage to exchange their children for land, cattle, and prestige. Walter Whorehound intends to pay his debts and secure his future by acquiring Moll's dowry. The Allwit household depends financially upon the continued sexual relationship between Sir Walter and Mrs. Allwit. Lady and Sir Oliver Kix must have an heir in order to receive a rich inheritance that otherwise will fall to Sir Walter. Because of financial need, Touchwood Sr. must end his fruitful sexual relationship with his wife and seek an additional income. Even Touchwood Jr., who truly loves Moll, is not indifferent to the financial advantages of marrying her. All of the characters except Moll are clearly aware of—and, in most cases, determined to exploit—the financial possibilities of marriage, sexual desire, and procreation.

The world of the play is Cheapside, the neighborhood of goldsmiths and gamesters—of Yellowhammers and Allwits. This is a place where money is foremost in the mind, and there is little room for sentiment. Even the one romantic relationship, that between Moll and Touchwood Jr., is generally void of the language and manners of romance. Touchwood Jr.'s first private words to Moll are hardly those of the traditional lover: "Turn not to me till thou mayst lawfully; it but whets my stomach, which is too sharp-set already" (I.i.143-4). The harassed lovers are never allowed an intimate scene in this world which comprehends sex only as a means of exploitation. They are forced to scheme and deceive in order to preserve their love relationship. The star-crossed lovers of Cheapside become a parody of the Romeo-and-Juliet pattern as they pretend to die for love. Parody and satire control what in another setting would clearly be sentimentality. The parody becomes quite clear in the last scene of the play when the two coffins of the lovers are brought in and placed side-by-side. Touchwood Sr. (who has successfully fulfilled his contract with Lady and Sir Oliver Kix) begins his solemn elegy,

> Never could death boast of a richer prize
> From the first parent; let the world bring forth
> A pair of truer hearts. . . .
>
> (V.iv.1-3)

Parody of romantic sentiment is appropriate for a world where sex is such a matter-of-fact financial business. The play opens with the Yellowhammers' dehumanizing efforts to present Moll as marketable merchandise. They can afford the luxury of exchanging Moll's dowry for a title, since they expect to exchange their stupid son for land and cattle. Moll's second attempt to escape this marriage arrangement begins with a difficult flight through a primitive sewage system (IV.iii.34) and ends with her being dragged from the river by her hair. Her last and finally successful attempt takes the form of deadly despair. Confronted with Moll's imminent death, the Yellowhammers are still incapable of the proper emotional and moral responses. They worry about what the neighbors will think and about the money they have wasted on medicine for Moll (V.ii). They console themselves with the idea of a lucrative match between Tim and the Welsh lady.

The satire against the cruelty and insensitivity of the Yellowhammers reaches a climax when Allwit, disguised as a Yellowhammer from Oxfordshire, reveals to Moll's father Sir Walter's degenerate relationship with the Allwits. At first old Yellowhammer expresses appropriate moral indignation, but then practicality triumphs:

> The Knight is rich, he shall be my son-in-law;
> No matter, so the whore he keeps be wholesome,
> My daughter takes no hurt then; so let them wed:
> I'll have him sweat well ere they go to bed.

It is, of course, most fitting that Yellowhammer should make these remarks to Allwit and that Allwit should claim to be a Yellowhammer, himself. Allwit, the wittol, embodies the same cynical practicality and the same lack of moral sensibility where sex and money are concerned.

Sir Walter discovers, too late, that the Allwits are in fact "gamesters" (V.ii.150) and that he has lost against them in the game of sexual exploitation. The audience feels no sympathy for him. He, like the Allwits, is a skillful gamester in his dealings with the Yellowhammers. His sudden repentance (V.i) is, in fact, a mock repentance. Sir Walter suffers awareness but not remorse. He is simply a gamester who has lost against the box. The concluding couplet of V.ii explains Allwit's triumph and Sir Walter's defeat:

> There is no gamester like a politic sinner,
> For whoe'er games, the box is sure a winner.

Fear of death after Touchwood wounds him forces an awareness and prudent action upon Sir Walter. He turns against the Allwits in righteous anger, but never for a moment considers his own cruelty in his efforts to marry Moll. Act V, Scene i is a parody of the typical death-bed confession and repentance. Sir Walter goes through all of the right motions:

> O, how my offenses wrestle with my repentance!
> It has scarce breath;
> Still my adulterous guilt hovers aloft,
> And with her black wings beats down all my prayers
> Ere they be half-way up. What's he knows now
> How long I have to live? O, what comes then?
> My taste grows bitter; the round world all gall now;
> Her pleasing pleasures now hath poison'd me,
> Which I exchang'd my soul for
> Make way a hundred sighs at once for me!
>
> (V.i.73-82)

But the conversation surrounding these lines makes it impossible not to laugh at Sir Walter. For example, in an effort to cheer him, Allwit brings in Sir Walter's bastards. Sir Walter looks at them and shrieks, "Wretched, death of seven!" Bullen [in *The Works of Middleton*, V] offers a note explaining that Walter's outburst is directed at the seven children. The point, however, and the humor of the situation lies in the fact that Sir Walter is accusing his children of being the seven deadly sins. To Sir Walter's vituperative attack, Mrs. Allwit answers in the fashion appropriate for a mourning widow: "He's lost for ever!" (V.i.52). Sir Walter

quickly forgets his own sins in order to concentrate on his anger and hatred for the Allwits. Prayers are quickly replaced by curses and accusations. Sir Walter is finally forced to leave the comforts of his death bed and make his way once more in the world.

The amoral, matter-of-fact attitude toward sex which pervades the world of this play is equally clear in the more likeable characters, the Touchwoods. Touchwood Sr.'s first speech (II.i.3-17) declares a domestic problem. He must part with his wife for a while, because he cannot support the children which come each year from their fruitful union. He expresses the same complaint which runs throughout *Michaelmas Term*:

> How adverse runs the destiny of some creatures!
> Some can get riches and no children;
> We only can get children and no riches:
>
> (II.i.10-12)

Touchwood Sr. each year brings into the world "a child and some years two! / Besides drinkings abroad, that's never reckon'd." We discover precisely what is meant by "drinkings abroad" when the country girl appears with one of Touchwood's bastards. With complete honesty, Touchwood explains his poverty, gives the girl his purse, and urges her to get rid of the baby by leaving it on a rich man's porch or by some other device. The girl, responding to this honesty, admits that this is her fifth child and assumes responsibility for it. The conversation between Touchwood and the country girl implies that many women in London and in the country can attest to his procreative powers.

Touchwood Jr. is quick to see a lucrative outlet for his older brother's unusual powers. Sir Oliver Kix and his wife greatly desire and, for financial reasons, need a child. The lady, however, has not managed to conceive. The knight and his lady spend much of their time blaming each other for their fruitless union. Touchwood Jr. tells his brother about Sir Oliver's situation and offers the following practical advice:

> Get but his wife with child, perch at tree top,
> And shake the golden fruit into her lap;
> About it before she weep herself to a dry ground,
> And whine out all her goodness.
>
> (III.iii.11-14)

Clearly this advice is meant to rescue the Kixes as well as the improverished brother. Touchwood Jr. and his brother see no moral complexity in this service which is to be rendered to the Kixes. All that matters is that the business be handled tactfully. Sir Oliver is given a special potion and ordered to ride for five hours. While he is riding, Touchwood approaches the problem more directly with Lady Kix. Touchwood's efforts are a success and the Kixes are completely satisfied. The point here, as elsewhere in the play, is not that this is an amoral play, but that these are characters who, *for a particular reason,* lack moral sensibility. Sir Oliver is concerned solely with the very lucrative business of getting his wife pregnant. This matter is all that the couple can talk about. The description which is worked upon Sir Oliver by Touchwood Sr. is a satirical form of justice.

The same justice is operative in the Allwits' triumph over Sir Walter and in Tim's union with the penniless Welsh whore.

The emotional and moral impoverishment of the characters is a result of their habitual exploitation of sex for financial gain. This impoverishment is expressed most bluntly in Tim Yellowhammer and his courtship of the Welsh whore. The object of his affection is the lady's wealth—her nineteen mountains and her 2000 runts. After Tim's stupid misunderstanding about the lady's nationality, he courts her with an apologetic kiss and declares with consummate coarseness,

> O delicious!
> One may discover her country by her kissing:
> 'Tis a true saying, there's nothing tastes so sweet
> As your Welsh mutton—
>
> (IV.i.153-155)

Tim's inability to make moral distinctions is epitomized by his assertion that he, through logic, can "prove a whore to be an honest woman" (IV.i.42). By marrying Sir Walter's whore he ironically fulfills his ludicrous assertion.

Old Yellowhammer, the spirit of Cheapside, ends the play with one last financial consideration: one feast will serve both weddings. The dinner will be given at a place most appropriate for the society of this play—Goldsmith's Hall. In this world where money has replaced emotional and moral considerations, the chaste maid is, indeed, as Levin puts it, the miracle of Cheapside.

WOMEN BEWARE WOMEN

Inga-Stina Ewbank (essay date 1969)

SOURCE: "Realism and Morality in 'Women Beware Women'," in *Essays and Studies 1969, Vol. 22*, edited by Francis Berry, John Murray, 1969, pp. 56-70.

[*In this essay, Ewbank assesses* Women Beware Women, *paying particular attention to the unity underlying what initially seems to be a loosely constructed mixture of realistic and moralistic elements. She stresses that the highly theatrical nature of Middleton's conception and execution, rather than heightening the unreality of the allegorical masque, actually integrates it into the realistically depicted intrigues of the play.*]

In this essay I wish to examine the unity of Thomas Middleton's **Women Beware Women.** The art of this play is a compound of realism and morality—a compound which has laid the play open to some fundamental criticisms. Middleton has been praised for the naturalism and psychological insight of the first three and a half acts, and reprimanded for (allegedly) betraying his own vision and art by concluding the play in terms of conventional Jacobean morality and

theatrical sensationalism. Recent critics have, on the whole, abandoned T. S. Eliot's view of Middleton as a playwright who 'has no message; he is merely a great recorder' [*Times Literary Supplement,* 30 June 1927]; and at the other extreme we have been given the 'highly moralistic artist who could skilfully pattern his actions in terms of a central theme' [I. Ribner, 'Middleton's *Women Beware Women:* Poetic Imagery and the Moral Vision', *Tulane Studies in English,* IX (1959)]. It seems to me that in **Women Beware Women** realism is not at war with morality; nor is one simply subservient to the other, like the two layers of an allegory. To understand their relationship one should, I think, look at the play through two (necessarily interrelated) questions: is there a unity of viewpoint? and, is there a dramatic unity?

I

'It isn't difficult to be a country gentlemen's wife,' Rebecca thought. 'I think I could be a good woman if I had five thousand a year' . . . And who knows but Rebecca was right in her speculations—and that it was only a question of money and fortune which made the difference between her and an honest woman? . . .

It may, perhaps, have struck her that to have been honest and humble, to have done her duty, and to have marched straightforward on her way, would have brought her as near happiness as that path by which she was striving to attain it. But . . . if ever Becky had these thoughts, she was accustomed to walk round them, and not look in . . .

We grieve at being found out, and at the idea of shame or punishment; but the mere sense of wrong makes very few people unhappy in Vanity Fair.

Middleton has often been seen as a seventeenth-century Ibsen, but it might be more helpful to suggest that, if we were to look for a nineteenth-century equivalent of **Women Beware Women,** we would find it in the social novel. The themes of the play are the favourite domestic and social ones of love, money and class—indeed, G. R. Hibbard has spoken of **Women Beware Women** as 'the most powerful criticism of the education of women and of the *mariage de convenance* in Elizabethan drama' ['The Tragedies of Thomas Middleton and the Decadence of the Drama', *Renaissance and Modern Studies* I (1957)]. The structure is formed not so much by plot and subplot as by interlinked groups of characters, so that the interest is spread over a cross-section of society rather than being centred on the development of a few characters. And, most important, Middleton's handling of the moral perspective is, in its combination of apparent objectivity, implicit evaluation and outright moralizing, curiously like that of some nineteenth-century novelists.

The passage from *Vanity Fair* which I have quoted seems to me in many ways a paradigm of the viewpoint of **Women Beware Women.** Like *Vanity Fair,* **Women Beware Women** is a work without a hero (or heroine). Like Becky Sharp, all the characters in the play confound the relation between money and honesty. But it is the handling of the moral point-of-view which chiefly makes this passage a parallel in narrative form to the dramatic art of *Women Beware Women.* Thackeray has the novelist's advantage—which he uses particularly fully in this novel—of being able to illuminate his work 'by the author's own candles', but he does so in a variety of ways. First, Rebecca is given apparently free rein in the dialogue; then ('And who knows . . . ') the author, with pretended objectivity, explains her in purely social-economic terms; then ('It may, perhaps, have struck her . . . ') the omniscient observer becomes a moral judge of her actions; and finally his focus widens out to a universal moral statement, and to reveal the 'preacher in cap and bells'.

In much the same way Middleton deals with his characters in *Women Beware Women.* For most of the play, their own speeches are remarkably lacking in ethical insight into their own actions. There is a great deal of documentation provided, of a sociological rather than psychological nature, so that we may see how they have become what they are. Who knows but that Bianca and Leantio's marriage would have had a chance if they had been rich? Who knows but that Bianca, as she asks in her soliloquy in IV. i, would have been less easily corrupted, had she had a less restrained upbringing? Who knows but that Isabella would have been saved from incest, adultery and ultimately murder, but for the loveless and mercenary attitude of her father which has thrown her and Hippolito 'whole nights together in discourse' and leads to the miseries of enforced marriage with the Ward? This is not to say that Middleton, while making us ask these questions, remains the clinically detached observer, for throughout the play there is an undertow of reminders of an inexorable moral order. Many commentators have drawn attention to the persistent imagery of love/ money, and love/gluttony, which interprets and judges the corruption of the play's world. But the characters are kept away from comprehension of the moral order, even while referring to it, just as Becky Sharp uses the word 'good' without knowing what it means. Middleton manages this in several different ways. In the opening scene, Leantio delivers a diatribe against adultery:

> Methinks it should strike earthquakes in adulterers,
> When ev'n the very sheets they commit sin in,
> May prove, for aught they know, all their last garments.
> (I.i. 22-4)

which, on the face of it, has a Vendice-like vigour. But it is undercut by his own blatant Pharisaism:

> Now when I go to church, I can pray handsomely,

much as his speech, in III. i, on 'a glorious dangerous strumpet' is undercut by being in praise of this smug youth's sexual self-control. It is undercut, too, by searing irony, for when Leantio self-rightously proclaims

> I find no wish in me bent sinfully
> To this man's sister, or to that man's wife:
> (I.i.28-9)

he is in fact unwittingly telling us exactly what is going to happen to sisters, brothers, men and wives, in the rest of the play. Such counterpointing (of the blindness of a character with generally valid judgments) is, however, dramatically uneconomic—hence the wordiness and drag of the opening scene. More successful is Middleton's technique of making his characters themselves thwart our ethical expectations. Hippolito, for example, first tells of his incestuous desires in a speech which, from its tense beginning, we might have expected to be one of inner struggle:

> I would 'twere fit to speak to her what I would, but
> 'Twas not a thing ordained; Heaven has forbid it.
> (I. ii. 154-5)

But it peters out into a clichéd resolution to stay silent—which he immediately proceeds to break. Finally, there is the technique of making the mercenary imagery invade what should be moral statements: so that in Livia's mock-sermon on incest even religion becomes a matter of economics:

> So he Heaven's bounty seems to scorn and mock,
> That spares free means, and spends of his own stock.
> (II. i. 15-16)

'Spatially', then, the play judges its characters throughout; but in terms of the time-sequence of the plot the Cardinal, with his explicit judgments in scenes i and ii of Act IV, becomes a wondrous necessary man. He is necessary because all the other characters, like Becky Sharp, 'walk round' such thoughts of sin as occur to them. His appearance corresponds to the omniscient judge stance in the Thackeray passage ('It may perhaps have struck her') and represents, to the play audience, a closing-in on the characters of the moral scheme they have ignored. And so, finally, that scheme is made explicit in action, in the moral retributions of the masque.

In terms of viewpoint, the masque corresponds to the generalization that concludes the Thackeray passage: as the characters are made to destroy themselves and each other with fiendish irony, the focus widens and the Cardinal becomes the preacher, left to point out what 'these ruins show too piteously'. The very deliberate contrivance of the ending, the patterning of the ironies:

> vengeance met vengeance
> Like a set match: as if the plagues of sin
> Had been agreed to meet here altogether,
> (V. ii. 155-7)

detach us and put us in the Cardinal's position. We see, too, that the moral view of the play is a question of the movement of the whole: rather than moral confusion, or inconsistency, there is a dynamism of viewpoint. This is where, ultimately, the dramatist scores over the novelist, for, because of the very nature of the form, his art is one of progression. In shaping his viewpoint, and so controlling our reactions, Middleton has used the art of drama to the full.

II

For, of course, *Women Beware Women* is supremely a work of the theatre. The strength of its dramatic poetry lies less in the obviously poetic speeches than in apparently unmemorable lines which are thrust into dramatic life through the context of character and action. Thus Isabella's words,

> In that small distance from you man to me
> Lies sin enough to make a whole world perish,
>
> (IV. ii. 131-2)

which articulate the perverse horror of her situation, combining kinship and theatrical fact (for 'that small distance' is in blood as well as stage area) into what is virtually a metaphysical conceit, are in the theatre a far more powerful evocation of the reality of sin than any of the speeches of the Cardinal. Middleton's poetry is, to use Francis Fergusson's distinction, more *of* the theatre than *in* it. It lies in the texture and the structure of his play, in the way social context is established, in the handling of characters and their relationships, and in the movement of the play as a whole. It is to these aspects of the play that I should now like to turn my attention.

One of the remarkable features of *Women Beware Women* is the realistic density of its *milieu*. Like no playwright outside Shakespeare, Middleton is able to give a solid context to his play world. It is partly a matter of his almost documentary use of objects—like Bianca's list of the furnishings lacking in Leantio's home, or the *two* handkerchiefs which the Mother runs to fetch in order to 'pocket up some sweetmeats' from the banquet. Partly it is a matter of scattering pieces of apparently irrelevant information—like the history of the room 'at the end of the dark parlour' where Leantio wants to immure Bianca, or of the genesis of the masque: prepared for the Duke's first wedding and cancelled because of the death of Isabella's mother (a lady who, like Leantio's father and Bianca's parents, is more present in the play than the cast-list would suggest). These hints create a sense of continuous life. How many husbands Livia has had *matters,* and so does her story about the lady who, at the age of forty-nine, kept a young 'friend'—who, in his turn,

> kept a quean or two with her own money,
> That robbed her of her plate and cut her throat.
>
> (II. ii. 165-6)

It is through carefully planted details like this little tragicomedy, as well as through the action itself, that the quality of life in the play is rendered.

One of the main sources of the density of *Women Beware Women* is a type of metaphorical language which is common throughout the play and used by all the characters, from the Ward to the Cardinal. This is a simile, usually beginning 'as if' or 'as when' and going on to draw an analogy between the dramatic situation and another human situation. Thus, around an already large group of charac-

ters, there is formed a whole background cast, ranging, in the social spectrum, from the country-maid 'dressing her head / By a dish of water' to 'great gallants the next day / After revel'. Genre-paintings like the Ward's reaction to kissing Isabella—'methinks it tasted as if a man had stepped into a comfit-marker's shop to let a cart go by'—are obviously an inheritance from Middleton's city-comedies; but the technique as a whole is put to a specific use in the play. The analogies which the characters are made to make so elaborately tend, on the one hand, to play down and trivialize their emotions, so as to suggest that they are composing satires on their own experiences rather than coming to grips with them. Hippolito's view of himself in the banquet scene,

> Like the mad misery of necessitous man,
> That parts from his good horse with many praises,
> And goes on foot himself,
>
> (III. ii. 199-201)

is an inept version of the emotions he should have—but is structurally apt as an anticipation of the following scene, in which Isabella is literally put through her paces before the Ward and Sordido. Leantio is constantly referring his experiences of love, for good or ill, to events in the life of 'some rich man', thus judging himself by the play's prevailing image-pattern of commercialized relationships. On the other hand, these analogies build up a dramatic metaphor of characters masquerading in other selves: selves which are parodies on human experience. This metaphor, which is a product of the play's realism as well as of its moral commentary, is also structural: it helps to prepare us for the masque which is the greatest masquerading, the climactic 'as if' image, of the play. No wonder, in a world where people so consistently relegate their experiences to some imaginary character, that Fabricio is confused about the identify of Livia's real and her masque self: 'I hope / *My sister Juno* has not served me so'.

Within the social context which Middleton so carefully establishes, the most outstanding 'figure in the carpet' is that of human relationships. For all T. S. Eliot's praise of Middleton's insight into the psychology of a few great individuals, the dramatic impact of *Women Beware Women* is made not so much through single characters—who are often static, or who, when like Bianca they change, are treated very much in dramatic shorthand—as through the dynamism of relationships. It is significant that Leantio, who has more and longer soliloquies than anyone else in the play, gives far less sense of an inner life than many of the other characters; and that he only really comes alive when he and Bianca, in IV. i, are pitted against each other in their new corruption and new finery. From the opening lines, where the Mother (who has no other name than 'Mother', or 'Widow') expounds the most intimate of all ties:

> Welcome, with all the affection of a mother,
> That comfort can express from natural love

to Fabricio's outcry:

Dead? my girl dead? I hope
My sister Juno has not served me so,

(V. ii. 142-3)

the dramatic mechanism is a pattern of family relationships, confounded and criss-crossed by erotic links. The ordinary appellations of kinship are used with more than ordinary care and point—for example in Livia's scenes with her two brothers, or in the Mother's little ritual of the two kisses with which she moves from a 'gentlewoman' to a 'daughter' relationship with Bianca—and as relationships tangle so these words are fed with peculiar significance. There is pathos as well as irony in Isabella's appeals to her 'sweet uncle' when we know that his feeling for her is 'somewhat too unkindly' and that he loves her 'dearlier than an uncle can'; and Guardiano's shrewdness about other relationships makes his words to the Ward doubly ironic when he explains that

he that weds her
Marries her uncle's heart too.

(III. ii. 18-19)

The reverberations of the action can make simple lines extremely sinister, as in Guardiano's gloating, Pandar-like greeting:

How now, ward and nephew,
Gentlewoman and niece! speak, is it so or not?

(III. iii. 130-1)

And in the end, the conjunction of kinship words can produce an effect like oxymoron, as when the Duke asks Hippolito:

How does that lusty widow, thy kind sister?

(IV. i. 141)

The action of the play is a progressive perversion of natural relationships, one violation of a natural bond leading to another—as Leantio sees in a moralistic speech which anticipates the symmetry of retribution in the masque:

Oh equal justice, thou hast met my sin
With a full weight; I'm rightly now oppressed:
All her [Bianca's] friends' heavy hearts lie in my breast.

(III. ii. 97-9)

Livia, the king-pin of the *liaisons dangereuses* in the play, is, of course, the centre of these perversions. She forgets words of kinship when she sees people as touchstones against which to sharpen her wit (then both Fabricio and Hippolito become just 'man'); and she tramples on their meaning when it comes to a game of sexual intrigue:

y'have few sisters
That love their brother's ease 'bove their own honesties.

(II. i. 70-1)

In the scenes where she presides, complete havoc is played with family bonds; and well may she remind Isabella, after she has slandered 'your dead mother, my most loving sis-

ter' and set the niece on the way to an incestuous union:

I pray forget not but to call me aunt still.

(II. i. 167)

There is an ironic echo of this line in Isabella's recognition speech, perhaps the most sinister expression of what relationships have come to mean in the play:

I'ld fain bring
Her name no nearer to my blood than woman,
And 'tis too much of that.

(IV. ii. 127-9)

Under the impact of this pervading dramatic image, the masque at the end becomes an integral part of the figure in the carpet. It has been defended, when at all, as a moral ritual 'utterly without logic in terms of human probability' [Ribner]. Certainly, in real life, no people would plot so heedlessly against each other, or be subject to such coincidences. But within the play's own world, 'human probability' has come to mean the utter perversion of blood relationships; and so it seems logical enough that in conclusion an aunt should kill her niece, a niece her aunt, a sister her brother—and, a fitting irony, that in her own masque Bianca should kill the wrong brother. The context of the play makes us accept it, much as we accept the spontaneous combustion in *Bleak House:* in terms not of realism in the ordinary sense but of the reality of the central image, which is one of self-destructiveness.

Destructiveness, of self and others, is also the ultimate effect of the wit which is such an outstanding feature of the social world of the play—wit in language and in action. 'It's a witty age', Guardiano gloats after he has assisted in the seduction of Bianca; and Livia is forever priding herself on her wit, from the harmless 'I think I am more than witty. How think you, sir?', to the more sinister:

Sir, I could give as shrewd a lift to chastity
As any she that wears a tongue in Florence:
Sh'ad need be a good horsewoman and sit fast
Whom my strong argument could not fling at last.

(II. i. 36-9)

Wit in the play, as in this speech, means control of language as well as situation—that is, of other people. Leantio is bought by Livia, and Livia, who, when she first set eyes on Leantio, declared herself 'dumb to any language now / But love's', finds exactly the right love's language for Leantio. Her analysis of marriage-for-love puts in clear and persuasive terms what was an undertone in Leantio's speeches in Act I:

It brings on want, and want's the key of whoredom.
I think y'had small means with her?

(III. ii. 287-8)

And her direct offer to Leantio picks up his favourite term of reference, the 'rich man':

I have enough, sir,
To make my friend a rich man in my life,

A great man at my death.

                                                    (III. ii. 362-4)

The way in which people's wit in the play is directed to-wards *using* each other is epitomized in the clinching of their bargain:

> *Livia:* Do but you love enough, I'll give enough.
> *Leantio:* Troth then, I'll love enough and take
>   enough.
> *Livia:* Then we are both pleased enough.

                                                    (III. ii. 376-8)

The chess scene is obviously the best example of wit in action and language: double action and double talk. It shows, too, how, as previously innocent characters are drawn into the whirlpool of the play's sex-game, they join, as it were, the group language and the group action. We learn how corruption has affected Bianca through her single speech of outrage—'Now bless me from a blasting!'—but, more sustainedly, through her new use of words. In almost exactly the same terms as she spoke of Guardiano at the outset of the scene, she now, with ironical doubleness, re-fers to him as 'this kind, honest, courteous gentleman'; she makes bawdy, albeit feeble, jokes in the banquet-scene and in the scenes (IV. i) with the court ladies (this functions as an image of court-wit) and with Leantio. And, of course, the ultimate product of her wit is the masque she devises, fatal to the Duke and herself.

It has been well said that, throughout the play, Livia uses other people like pawns in a game of chess; but this is true for all the other characters as well, even if they are not as clever at the game as Livia. Guardiano plays on Fabricio, for Isabella; Fabricio uses Isabella as a pawn in the mone-tary game; Isabella and Hippolito use the Ward as 'the only veil wit can devise / To keep our acts hid from sin-piercing eyes'; the Duke uses Hippolito to rid himself and Bianca of Leantio. By the time death is involved as an element in the game, only one outcome is possible; and, again, there is a particular rightness about the masque, with its doubleness of language and action, as the climactic and fatal game of this society.

This is where, finally, the 'realism' of the masque scene lies. In itself—even if there were not a long tradition of masques in plays to support it—the masque is as natural a form of social occasion in the world of the play as is the ball in *The Cherry Orchard* or the coffee-party in *Pillars of Society.* It is justified, too, by expectancies within the play itself, such as Leantio's image of how the idle rich live: 'Grow fat with ease, banquet, and toy and play.' It is set within a realistic framework of preparation, supplied by the scene between Guardiano and the Ward (V. i) and by Fab-ricio's bustling around with 'the model / Of what's present-ed'. All this, together with Middleton's careful attention to the reaction of the masque audience, makes it a fully real-ized social occasion—as against the very schematic masques of, say, *The Revenger's Tragedy* and *Antonio's Revenge.*

But the 'realism' of the masque is also a matter of the structure of *Women Beware Women* as a whole. Middleton

has a unique power of constructing group scenes, in which a very large number of people—virtually the whole cast—interact, take cues from each other, clash and score off each other. The three such scenes (if we may include the chess-scene, which in fact gradually involves nearly all the char-acters) form nodal points in the structure of the play. They form, too, a progression up the social scale. In the chess scene, Livia presides, and the Duke is hidden 'above'; in the banquet, the Duke presides, but the scene takes place in Livia's house; in the masque scene, the Duke presides, and the location is the Court. The structural irony of the masque is the ultimate involvement of all the characters in the masque. Bianca acts, in her aside, as a Presenter of her own private 'antimasque':

> But I have made surer work; . . .
> Cardinal, you die this night; the plot's laid surely:
> In time of sports death may steal in securely.

                                                    (V. ii. 17-22)

Soon she also has to act as an Epilogue:

> Pride, greatness, honours, beauty, youth, ambition—
> You must all down together; there's no help for't.
> Yet this my gladness is, that I remove,
> Tasting the same death in a cup of love.

                                                    (V. ii. 216-9)

The supposed audience become real masquers, just as in Livia's masque real death hits the masquers proper. The masque scene demonstrates in a stage image how the very ethos of their society has overtaken the characters. And, within this image we are prepared to accept that people speak their last words not as (psychological) characters but as masquers in the masque of retribution:

> *Hippolito:* Lust and forgetfulness has been amongst us,
> And we are brought to nothing.

Critics have spoken of the coolness and detachment of this play which would seem to preclude a tragic vision. It is true that there is an extraordinary precision about the 'puppet show' at the end; but in the theatre, I think, our reaction is not all detachment. The masque scene shows Middleton's peculiar power of combining the ordinary with the horrible. As, in the chess scene, the ordinary surface of the game between Livia and the Mother is counterpointed with the horror of the act 'above', so, in the masque scene, the hor-ror of the surface is placed in relation to the ordinary reac-tions of bystanders like Fabricio. The greatest emotional moments in the play are when a character gives voice to the tension between these two levels: Bianca's outcry at the evil she has seen 'above', or Fabricio's 'Dead? my girl dead? I hope / My sister Juno has not served me so'. Within Middleton's vision, as crystallized in these moments, there was room for a tragedy which not only dealt in convention-al terms of retribution and damnation, but also saw the horror of life precisely in what men will do to men (or women to women). Therein, I think, lies Middleton's par-ticular morality, as well as his realism; and as a theatrical image for this vision *Women Beware Women* has a unity of its own.

Stephen Wigler   (essay date 1983)

SOURCE: "Parent and Child: The Pattern of Love in *Women Beware Women*," in *"Accompaninge the players": Essays Celebrating Thomas Middleton, 1580-1980,* edited by Kenneth Friedenreich, AMS Press, 1983, pp. 183-201.

[*Wigler investigates the three love affairs in* Women Beware Women—*between Bianca and the Duke, Isabella and Hippolito, and Leantio and Livia—in support of his contention that "the pattern of love" in the play "is ultimately something very close to incest."*]

Three romantic intrigues form the subject matter of Middleton's **Women Beware Women.** The first of these is the story of Bianca's love affair with the Duke, their murder of her husband Leantio, and the end of their subsequent marriage in Bianca's mistaken murder of the Duke and her suicide. The second intrigue relates the history of Hippolito's incestuous passion for his niece Isabella, and of the latter's betrayal to Hippolito by Livia, who is Isabella's aunt as well as Hippolito's sister. Livia persuades Isabella that she is illegitimate and, therefore, that Hippolito is not really her uncle. This reduces unthinkable incest to acceptable adultery. The third love affair concerns Livia's intense liaison with Leantio which is cut short by Hippolito's murder of Leantio. The first and second intrigues comprise respectively the main plot and the subplot of **Women Beware Women.** The third affair brings together characters from each plot, but its real structural significance is that it brings both plots together. Livia's love affair with Leantio begins as a consequence of the other intrigues. Livia is the bawd who betrays Bianca to the Duke. Leantio's loss of Bianca is the circumstance which permits the formation of his attachment to Livia. And Livia's relationship with Leantio enables the Duke to recruit Hippolito as Leantio's assassin. Finally, it is the foreshortened life of Livia's love affair that causes the conclusion of the others. Livia's grief at Leantio's murder turns her into the unrelenting destroyer who brings not only the incestuous relations of her brother and her niece but also the play to its catastrophic end.

But the love interests which pattern **Women Beware Women** are themselves formed by an internal pattern. All three love affairs share two distinct traits. The first is that the ages of the partners in each liaison differ substantially: Bianca is sixteen and the Duke is fifty-five; Isabella is probably Bianca's age, and her uncle Hippolito is presumably old enough to be her father; Leantio cannot be much older than Bianca, and Livia is thirty-nine. The second characteristic seems almost a corollary of the first; the older partners in the relationships seem to possess parental stature while the younger partners seem to share the status of children. One might naturally expect such overtones in the case of the explicitly incestuous Isabella and Hippolito, but their presence in the other two affairs suggests that the pattern of love in **Women Beware Women** is ultimately something very close to incest.

The theory that sexual relations in **Women Beware Women** resemble parent-child relations affords insight into the love affair of the Duke and Bianca, and particularly into the character of the latter, whose change of heart continues to be one of the play's chief critical problems. As J. R. Mulryne summarizes it [in the Introduction to his edition of *Women Beware Women*, 1975], the problem is that at the beginning of **Women Beware Women,** Bianca "seems a self-effacing, virtuous girl," but that with her seduction by the Duke, she changes to "a strong minded even aggressive woman wholly adapted to the hypocrisy and compromise of Florentine society." The audience's first impression of Bianca, however, is not only that of a virtuous young woman but also that of an isolated and frightened girl. Throughout most of the play's first scene, Bianca is silent. This emphasizes the fact that Bianca is a stranger except for the brittle matrimonial bond which ties her to Leantio. Moreover, the very nature of the dialogue draws attention to Bianca's alienation. The play opens with a long and familiar exchange between Leantio and his mother. Their intimacy—something quickly strengthened by Leantio's humorous knowledge of his mother's foibles and by the asides the two of them share out of Bianca's hearing—emphasizes Bianca's apartness. The dialogue itself refers frequently to Bianca's position as an emotional novice to the state of marriage, as well as a newcomer to a strange household and city. Finally, when Bianca is invited to join the conversation, she shows that she understands her position:

> I have forsook friends, fortunes, and my country;
> And hourly I rejoice in it.
>
> (131-132)

She wants to be accepted by her new social group, and to create intimate familial ties to Leantio and her mother-in-law:

> Here's my friends,
> And few is the good number. Thy successes
> Howe'er they look, I will still name my fortunes;
> Hopeful or spiteful, they shall all be welcome:
> Who invites many guests, has of all sorts
> As he that traffics much, drinks of all fortunes:
> Yet they must all be welcome, and used well.
> I'll call this place the place of my birth now—
> And rightly too, for here my love was born,
> And that's the birthday of a woman's joys.
> You have not bid me welcome since I came.
>
> (132-142)

Yet these lines give one the sense that Bianca is nervous. Her protestation to a strange mother-in-law that "Here's my friends" makes Bianca seem emotionally needy, and it is impossible not to feel that in her repeated reference to good and bad fortune, Bianca is expressing her own insecurity. Finally, the close of her speech with the appeal for a kiss is not merely light coquetry, but primarily a sign of Bianca's need for reassurance and protective love.

In the next scene in which we see her, Middleton continues to reenforce our sense of Bianca's haplessness. When Bianca appears at the window to watch Leantio depart, the latter's attitude toward his bride is disconcertingly physical. When Bianca pleads—quite touchingly—with Leantio to remain home for "this one night," he vulgarly replies:

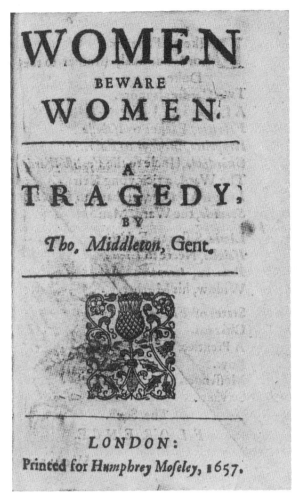

Title page of a 1657 octavo edition.

Alas, I'm in for twenty, if I stay,
And then for forty more, I have such luck to flesh:
I never bought a horse, but he bore double.
If I stay any longer, I shall turn
An everlasting spendthrift; as you love
To be maintained well, do not call me again,
For then I shall not care which end goes forward.
                                        (I.iii.50-56)

The audience cannot help but sympathize with Bianca as she is left alone for the first time with a strange mother-in-law who coldly reproves her for her tears. It is at this point, when Bianca feels most deserted and most in need of attention, that Middleton chooses to introduce her to the sight of the Duke. Before the latter's entrance, Leantio's mother refers to him as "a goodly gentleman of his years" (91) and Bianca asks "Is he old then?" When the mother replies "About some fifty-five," Bianca significantly remarks "That's no great age in man, he's then at best / For wisdom and judgement" (93-94). The reason that this is significant is that she has just been abandoned by a young husband. The Duke is a man who is old enough to be her father, and Bianca is immediately attracted to such a *mature* man's "wisdom and judge-

ment." After the Duke's entrance and exit, Bianca comments:

Methinks my soul could dwell upon the reverence
Of such a solemn and most worthy custom.
                                        (104-105)

But she asks the mother, "Did not the Duke look up? methought he saw us." Middleton has introduced us to Bianca almost as if she were an orphan deprived of attention and love. It is hard not to feel that in responding to the Duke's acknowledgment of her presence, Bianca is responding warmly to a situation from her past and one that is familial in nature.

In the scene that presents Bianca's seduction (II.ii.), Middleton re-creates some of the conditions that prevailed in the scene that introduced us to Bianca. She is once more in an exposed social position. Middleton invokes a whole social situation, with Livia and the mother confortably within it and Bianca outside. As Mulryne notes, the two older women refer to matters of neighborliness and social duty. The audience is continually aware of their social skills and repeatedly reminded of the long years of experience that enabled them to build these skills. Moreover, the theatrical brilliance of the chess game emphasizes Bianca's defenselessness as the pawn taken by the more powerful chess piece. In this setting, it is very clear that Bianca is a frightened and inexperienced girl.

The moment at which she turns and sees the Duke, Bianca reacts with terror. The Duke, on the other hand, is superbly self-assured, and he skillfully gives Bianca what she needs most—reassurance:

Prithee tremble not.
I feel thy heart shake like a turtle panting
Under a loving hand that makes much on't.
Why art so fearful? as I'm a friend to brightness,
There's nothing but respect and honour near thee.
                                        (321-325)

It is apparent from these lines that the Duke treats Bianca like a frightened child—there is an implied paternal embrace—and this is why he succeeds in seducing her so readily. He offers her the security that she so desperately needs. Along with his threats of force and his praise of her beauty, the Duke expresses a kind of cherishing tenderness such as Bianca might have experienced at her father's house in Venice:

thou seem'st to me
A creature so composed of gentleness
And delicate meekness, such as bless the faces
Of figures that are drawn for goddesses
And make art proud to look upon her work. . . .
                                        (340-344)

Finally, in persuading Bianca to "make more haste to please me" (368), the Duke resorts to a quasi-parental argument; Bianca should, he argues, behave like an obedient child:

She that is fortunate in a duke's favour
Lights on a tree that bears all women's wishes:
If your own mother saw you pluck fruit there,
She would commend your wit, and praise the time
Of your nativity.

(371-375)

Although the changed Bianca who appears after her seduction is almost always described as sophisticated and corrupt, I think it is even more accurate to say that she has become *more* rather than less childlike. After her seduction by the Duke, Bianca behaves like a spoiled, willful child, who is accustomed to getting her own way. In the scene following, the Mother complains that Bianca

. . . was but one day abroad, but ever since
She's grown so cutted, there's no speaking to her.
Whether the sight of great cheer at my lady's,
And such mean fare at home, work discontent in her,
I know not; but I'm sure she's strangely altered.

(III.i.3-7)

Bianca now enters; nothing satisfies her:

This is the strangest house
For all defects, as ever gentlewoman
Made shift withal, to pass away her love in!
Why is there not a cushion-cloth of drawn work,
Or some fair-cut-work pinned up in my bed-chamber,
A silver-and-gilt casting-bottle hung by't?
Nay, since I am content to be so kind to you,
To spare you for a silver basin and ewer,
Which one of my fashion looks for of duty. . . .

(16-24)

The "new" Bianca is really a reversion to an earlier Bianca. She is like a child under the influence of the fantasy that her present parents are not her actual parents. (Her real parents are a king and queen.) Bianca now also resembles the fairy-tale princess who felt the presence of a pea beneath fourteen feather mattresses. What complicates things is that Bianca *really* is from a wealthy household, and her experience with the Duke, and her father, has wakened her memories of her actual father:

I ask less now
Than what I had at home when I was a maid
And at my father's house; kept short of that
Which a wife knows she must have—nay, and will—
Will, mother, if she be not a fool born—
And report went of me that I could wrangle
For what I wanted when I was two hours old;
And by that copy, this land still I hold.

(52-59)

It is impossible not to notice that Bianca now speaks of herself as she was, as a child "at [her] father's house," having her will, getting "what [she] wanted." And after Bianca's departure, the Mother's soliloquy remarks again upon Bianca's "alteration," suggesting a comparison of her to "a very young thing":

'Tis the most sudden'st, strangest, alteration,
And the most subtlest that ev'r wit at threescore
Was puzzled to find out. I know no cause for't; but
She's no more like the gentlewoman at first
Than I am like her that nev'r lay with man yet,
And she's a very young thing where'er she be.

(63-68)

When we see Bianca again, during the banquet of Act III, scene ii, our impression is once more of a woman who is almost a child. The reasons for this effect are the circumstances. On this occasion, we see Bianca once again with the Duke; and although she is not the occasion of the banquet, the Duke persists in turning his own and therefore everyone's attention to her at every possible opportunity. It is almost as if he were a proud father showing off his daughter. The effect of such spoiling on the Duke's part is seen clearly at the end of Act IV. Bianca and two ladies make seemingly inconsequential chatter that serves to define sexual relations by reference to good and bad time-keeping. But the conversation also serves to define the new Bianca. She is the most boastful, petulant, and immature of the three. After their departure, Bianca meditates upon her fate, and it is significant that she thinks about her own girlhood and about the destinies of the daughters she may have. One easily infers that Bianca—despite her anticipation of motherhood—is redefining herself as a child rather than as the young wife of the first act.

At this point Leantio enters, and these two supposedly now worldly young people have an infantile argument that concludes with Leantio's threat to murder Bianca. Bianca is upset but not overly anxious. The reason for her confidence is her secure filial trust in the Duke's care and power. When the latter enters, it is clear that Bianca expects what all children presume—to be taken care of. And the Duke, of course, complies, sending Bianca to bed as if she were his troubled daughter:

DUKE: Do not you vex your mind; prithee to bed, go.
All shall be well and quiet.
BIANCA: I love peace, sir.
DUKE: And so do all that love; take you no care for't.
It shall be still provided to your hand.

(IV.i.123-126)

From Bianca's adultery with the Duke, we turn now to Isabella's incestuous relation with Hippolito. Although the former is not really incest, we have recognized that the two lovers behave in a manner that resembles parent and child, and that Bianca becomes increasingly child-like as the affair progresses. Moreover, we have seen that the two lovers seem particularly attracted to the roles determined by the quasi-incestuous dynamics of their relationship. Isabella and Hippolito seem, on the other hand, horrified by incest. Although Hippolito is less disturbed than his niece—she is disturbed enough to abstain, he is not—his references to incest are never less than fearful:

I would 'twere fit to speak to her what I would, but
'Twas not a thing ordained; Heaven has forbid it,
And 'tis most meet that I should rather perish

Than the decree divine receive least blemish.
Feed inward, you my sorrows, make no noise;
Consume me silent, let me be stark dead
Ere the world know I'm sick.

(I.ii.154-160)

When Isabella tries to wrest the secret of her uncle's distress from him, his evasiveness is tortured:

You of all creatures, niece, must never hear on't;
'Tis not a thing ordained for you to know.

(207-208)

After the affair is consummated, Hippolito continues to show the distress of shame and guilt. He tells himself that he and Isabella must "keep our acts hid from sin-piercing eyes" (II.i.238), and later meditates that "I know myself / Monstrously guilty . . . " (IV.ii.4-5). Finally, at the time of his death, Hippolito speaks of "a fearful lust in our near bloods, / For which I am punished dreadfully . . . " (V.ii.153-154).

But it is to Isabella, particularly, that the prospect of incest is too distasteful even for words. When she learns what her uncle's feelings really are, Isabella exclaims

What's that?
Methought I heard ill news come toward me,
Which commonly we understand too soon,
Than over-quick at hearing. I'll prevent it,
Though my joys fare the harder; welcome it—
It shall nev'r come so near mine ear again.
Farewell all friendly solaces and discourses;
I'll learn to live without ye, for your dangers,
Are greater than your comforts. What's become
Of truth in love, if such we cannot trust.
When blood that should be love is mixed with lust.

(I.ii.219-229)

And at the end of the fourth act, when Isabella learns that Hippolito actually is her uncle and that her adultery with him has been indeed incestuous, she reacts with genuine horror:

Was ever maid so cruelly beguiled
To the confusion of life, soul and honour, . . .
Oh shame and horror!
In that small distance from yon man to me
Lies sin enough to make a whole world perish.

(IV.ii.126-127, 130-132)

But Isabella's horror of incest seems overdetermined; her conscious repugnance for incest with her uncle seems to conceal an unconscious attraction to it. Before Hippolito discovers his feelings to Isabella, for example, Fabritio tells us:

Those two are nev'r assunder; they've been heard
In argument at midnight, moonshine nights
Are noondays with them; they walk out their sleeps
  [together]
. . . they're like a chain,

Draw but one link, all follows.

(I.ii.63-65, 68-69)

And when they enter, Guardiano, with unconscious irony, remarks:

Oh affinity,
What piece of excellent workmanship art thou?
'Tis work clean unsought, for there's no lust, but
  love in't,
And that abundantly—when in stranger things,
There is no love at all, but what lust brings.

(69-73)

In the same scene, Isabella repeatedly calls our attention to the depths of her feeling for her uncle:

What, are you sad too, uncle?
Faith, then there's whole household down together:
Where shall I go to seek my comforts now
When my best friend's distressed? What is 't afflicts
  you, sir?
. . .
You made profession once you love me best—
'Twas but profession!
HIPPOLITO: Yes, I do't too truly,
And fear I shall be chid for't. Know the worst then:
I love thee dearlier than an uncle can.
ISABELLA: Why, so you ever said, and I believed it.

(185-188, 210-214)

Even clearer evidence, however, of Isabella's sexual attraction to her uncle is the ease with which Livia is able to convince her niece that her uncle is not really her uncle. Obviously, Isabella wants very much to believe Livia:

Would I had known [this]
But one day sooner! he had then received
In favours what, poor gentleman, he took
In bitter words—a slight and harsh reward
For one of his deserts.

(II.i.184-188)

Moreover, once Isabella's conscience has been mollified, she aggressively pursues her uncle with a celerity that is startling:

Are you returned [?] . . .
. . . I will keep you fast now,
And sooner part eternally from the world
Than my good joys in you. Prithee, forgive me.
I did but chide in jest; the best lovers use it
Sometimes; it sets an edge affection.
When we invite our best friends to a feast
'Tis not all sweet meats that we set before them.
There's somewhat sharp and salt, both to whet appetite
And make 'em taste their wine well; so, methinks
After a friendly, sharp, and savoury chiding,
A kiss tastes wondrous well and full o' th' grape—
[*kisses him*]
—How think'st thou, does't not?

(192-203)

It seems to me that the factors that determine Isabella's incestuous behavior are rather like Bianca's. Isabella's choice of her uncle expresses a neurotic need to be protected and loved as an infant daughter would be by her father.

The situation in which Isabella finds herself at the beginning of the play is a frightening one for a young woman we can presume to be not above, and probably less than, sixteen. Isabella's heartless father is about to give her away to the idiotic Ward in what promises to be a loveless and joyless marriage. Isabella is at the stage in life when—to paraphrase Genesis 2:24—"a [woman] leaves [her] Father and [her] mother and cleaves to [her] husband." Isabella is, therefore, relinquishing parental bonds for genital bonds. And one aspect of the Ward that is quite as remarkable as his idiocy, is his exaggerated and violent genitality.

Whenever the Ward and his man Sordido are on stage, they make lewd and lascivious jests and jokes. Moreover, the Ward is never without his phallic trap-stick, and whenever he enters, he is talking about the violence he has just committed with it: "Beat him? I beat him out o' th' field with his own cat-stick" (I.ii.87-88). He brags that he also "beat [my lady's tailor] too" and Sordido adds "Now you talk on 'em, there was a poulterer's wife made a great complaint of you last night to your guardiner, that you struck a bump in her child's head, as big as an egg" (94-97). The Ward's violence is apparently boundless; it disregards familial ties. He proudly boasts "When I am in game, I am furious; came my mother's eyes in my way, I would not lose a fair end—nor were she alive, but with one tooth in her head, I should venture the striking out of that. I think of nobody, when I am in play, I am so earnest" (98-103). The point is that Middleton directly associates this violence with the Ward's bestial sexuality:

> "I can stoop gallantly, and pitch out when I list; I'm dog at a hole. I mar'l my guardiner does not seek a wife for me; I protest I'll have a bout with the maids else, or contract myself at midnight to the larder woman in presence of a fool or a sock-posset . . . I feel myself after any exercise horribly prone: let me but ride, I'm lusty—a cockhorse straight, i' 'faith . . . I'll forswear eating eggs in moonshine nights; there's never a one that I eat, but turns into a cock in four-and-twenty hours; if my hot blood be not took down in time, sure 'twill crow shortly."
>
> (113-125)

As the Ward says these things, Isabella watches in silence; the audience can imagine her response.

This contrast of their marriage-to-be with the relations of Hippolito to Isabella emphasizes the tenderness of the latter. We cannot help but remember and compare what the Ward threateningly boasts of doing "in moonshine nights" to what we know of the activities of Isabella and Hippolito at such times:

> Those two are never asunder; they've been heard
> In argument at midnight, moonshine nights
> Are noondays with them.
>
> (I.ii.63-65)

In Hippolito and Isabella's relationship, there *is* suppressed lust that eventually becomes incest. But for now, the important thing to notice is that Middleton characterizes Hippolito's relation to Isabella as comfortingly oral rather than disturbingly genital, as in the case of the Ward.

One of the chief reasons that I believe the Hippolito-Isabella liaison suggests father-daughter, rather than uncle-niece, incest is that it is easier to identify Hippolito as the girl's father than Fabritio. It is difficult to imagine the foolish Fabritio as the father of anyone except the idiotic Ward. Middleton not only creates the two characters in the same image, but also explicitly allies them by such remarks as Livia's, after Fabritio's exit and before the Ward's entrance:

> And here comes his sweet son-in-law that shall be.
> They're both allied in wit before the marriage;
> What will they be hereafter, when they are nearer?
> Yet they can go no further than the fool:
> There's the world's end in both of 'em.
>
> (II.i.76-80)

Since Fabritio's character is so unlike that of any other member of his family, and since he shows no discernible affection for his daughter, it seems natural that the audience perceives Hippolito as a paternal surrogate. Encouraging this perception are Livia's role as a surrogate mother and the fact that Hippolito's relationship with his sister seems somewhat more than fraternal. Isabella's choice of Hippolito suggests that it is a return to a female child's first love object—her father.

Just as the relationships of the Duke and Hippolito, with Bianca and Isabella, tend to the paternal and protective, Livia's relationships with Leantio and Hippolito are essentially maternal and nurturing. Since Leantio is perhaps the play's central figure, and because Livia's connection with him is so significant, we must first try to understand his filial nature rather carefully.

The first thing the audience notices about Leantio is that he is excessively possessive. When his mother asks him to identify Bianca, at the beginning of the play, Leantio replies:

> Oh you have named the most unvalued'st purchase,
> That youth of man had ever knowledge of.
> As often as I look upon that treasure,
> And know it to be mine—there lies the blessing—
> It joys me that I ever was ordained
> To have a being, and to live 'mongst men.
>
> (I.i.12-17)

Possessiveness is the tonic that characterizes Leantio. In regard to the latter's feeling for Bianca, Middleton repeats this chord again and again. But the corollary of such excessive possessiveness is the neurotic sexual jealousy which also characterizes Leantio. Although the audience has no hint that Leantio has any need to be so concerned, imagined threats to his conjugal pleasure seem to consume most of his energies; he worriedly warns his mother to watch what she says before his wife, because Bianca is a woman and

A woman's belly is got up in a trice:
A simple charge ere it be laid down again.

(82-83)

Leantio's erotic possessiveness and jealousy suggest that he wants to own the affections of Bianca utterly. Only one man, however, ever seems to succeed in approaching such complete possession of a woman—an only son in relation to his first love object, his mother. In actuality, however, a son does have a potent rival in his father. In comparison to his sexually mature father, the male child feels himself to be sexually inadequate. Such inadequacy offers insight into one of the characteristics of Leantio that has often been remarked upon, but rarely satisfactorily explained—his vulgarity. In the first scene, for example, Leantio assures the Mother that

I'll prove an excellent husband—here's my hand—
Lay in provision, follow my business roundly,
And make you a grandmother in forty weeks!

One also notices that Leantio's closing soliloquy is filled with sexually charged words like "pride," "bloods," "choice treasures," "jewel," "gem," and "keys." And in the third scene, after the pleasure of sharing Bianca's bed, Leantio crudely remarks:

Methinks I'm even as dull now at departure
As men observe great gallants the next day
After a revels; you shall see 'em look
Much of my fashion, if you mark 'em well.
'Tis ev'n a second hell to part from pleasure
When man has got a smack on 't. As many holidays
Coming together makes your poor heads idle
A great while after, and are said to stick
Fast in their fingers' ends' ev'n so does game
In a new-married couple for the time;
It spoils all thrift, and indeed lies a-bed.

(I.iii.1-12)

He subsequently boasts of his sexual prowess: "I have such luck to flesh: / I never bought a horse, but he bore double" (51-52). Leantio's lewd language seems to me to be a species of self-exposure that is motivated by sexual anxiety or defensiveness. Like the child who exposes himself to show that he still possesses the genital whose loss he fears, Leantio tries to belie his worried virility through boastful vulgarity that borders on the obscene.

In comparison to the Duke—who is, as we have seen, a father figure—Leantio does indeed prove sexually inadequate. In the banquet scene, Middleton creates two centers of dramatic interest. The first, of course, is the Duke's attention to Bianca as he flatters her, praises her, kisses and fondles her, and finally takes her off in his coach to his palace. But because Leantio so frequently punctuates the action with asides, the audience also focuses upon his discomfort as he watches the Duke and Bianca and wrestles unsuccessfully with his jealousy:

A kissing too?
I see 'tis plain lust now, adultery boldened.
What will it prove anon, when 'tis stuffed full
Of wine and sweet meats, being so impudent fasting?

(III.ii.36-39)

Increasing Leantio's torment are Bianca's repeated, if implicit, scoffs in his direction. Leantio reacts to his loss of Bianca as to a loss of manhood, as if indeed he were losing a part of his body. After her departure with the Duke, he cries:

Oh, hast thou left me then, Bianca, utterly!
Bianca! now I miss thee—Oh return,
And save the faith of woman. I nev'r felt
The loss of thee till now; 'tis an affliction
Of greater weight than youth was made to bear—
As if a punishment of after-life
Were fallen upon man here, so new it is
To flesh and blood; so strange, so insupportable
A torment—ev'n mistook, as if a body
Whose death were drowning, must needs therefore suffer it
In scalding oil.

(III.ii.243-253)

Before turning our attention to the relations of Leantio and Livia, it is necessary to recall that from her first appearance in the play, Livia is a figure we associate with the maternal and protective. With the exception of Hippolito, for example, she is the only character who offers the hapless Isabella what seems like protection and warmth. But it is her relation to her younger brother Hippolito that first serves to define her. Put simply, she has incestuous feelings for him. This is obvious when Livia greets him and kisses him, and when Hippolito blushes response:

My best and dearest brother, I could dwell here;
There is not such another seat on earth
Where all good parts better express themselves.
HIPPOLITO: You'll make me blush anon.
LIVIA: 'Tis but like saying grace before a feast, then,
And that's most comely; thou art all a feast,
And she that has thee, a most happy guest.

(I.ii.146-152)

Roma Gill [in her edition of *Women Beware Women*, 1969] remarks that "[Livia's] tenderness towards [Hippolito] and her readiness to serve his will at whatever cost to herself and her own 'honesty' speak a more than natural affection and hint a one-sided incestuous attraction. If this is admitted, then the procuring of Isabella seems less like an evil game and more an attempt to provide some acceptable substitute for herself. Through Isabella, Livia can indulge, vicariously, her own desires." This is a perceptive remark, but I suspect that Livia's feelings for Hippolito express something that is closer to mother-son, than sister-brother, incest. In the next scene in which we see them together, Livia's sexual feelings seem complicated by maternal tendencies to protect, comfort, and nurture:

I love you so,
That I shall venture much to keep a change from you
So fearful as this grief will bring upon you—
'Faith, it even kills me, when I see you faint
Under a reprehension . . .
Thou keep'st the treasure of that life I love
As dearly as mine own.

(II.i.18-22, 26-27)

And when Hippolito leaves her, Livia meditates:

Beshrew you, would I loved you not so well!
I'll go to bed, and leave this deed undone;
I am the fondest where I once affect,
The carefull'st of their healths and of their ease,
    forsooth,
That I look still but slenderly to mine own.

(63-67)

One might emend Gill's remark with the suggestion that Livia also betrays Isabella to Hippolito because a mother is usually less ambivalent about a son than about a daughter.

It is dramatically appropriate that Livia's love affair with Leantio begins only after Hippolito and Isabella consummate their passion. Leantio is in a sense Hippolito's replacement. In an equally vivid sense, Livia replaces Leantio's mother. Indeed the last moment in the play when we observe the Mother, she is conversing with Livia and the topic of their conversation is Leantio:

LIVIA: Is that your son, widow?
MOTHER: Yes, did your ladyship
Never know that till now?
LIVIA: No, trust me, did I.
Nor ever truly felt the power of love
And pity to a man till now I knew him.

(III.ii.62-65)

It is significant that Livia describes the motivation of her passion for Leantio as a maternal characteristic, "pity." She enters his life at the moment when he is most wounded, and her first attempts to communicate with him are attempts to succor him. At first Livia is not able to attract Leantio's attention; he is too unhappy to notice her. But the young man's misery only enflames her love. He finally acknowledges her and asks "what would you say to me"? (270) Significantly, her first words are

Nothing, but ev'n in pity to that passion,
Would give your grief good counsel.

(III.ii.273-274)

And the lines that follow are not only filled with similar sentiments but also show that Livia's love for Leantio is a desire to care for and take care of him.

The circumstances of Leantio's murder and Livia's subsequent revenge are related to the incest motif. As I suggested before, Leantio is Hippolito's replacement. Given the kind of relation which Hippolito had to Livia, it is easy to see in his determination to murder Leantio not only his ambition

for his sister's marriage to Lord Vincentio—which would be frustrated by her affair with the factor—but also sibling rivalry with the man who had taken his place. Moreover, Livia's reaction to her brother's murder of her lover is surely one of the most searing episodes in the drama of the times. In the Middleton canon, the scene that most nearly approaches this kind of intensity is the moment in *A Fair Quarrel* when Lady Ager reacts to the supposed death of her son, Captain Ager, in a duel. What I mean to suggest is that Livia's grief at Leantio's loss is more like that of a mother than that of a lover. Her terrible revenge—instinctive and unhesitating—upon her brother and her niece is like that of a she-bear who has lost a cub.

In light of my remarks about *Women Beware Women*'s involvement with the incest motif, one might well ask how the latter is related to the play's final catastrophe. One obvious relation is that the concluding masque recapitulates much of the previous action. The most important recapitulation, of course, is Livia's role as Juno Pronuba, the mother Goddess who arranges marriages. This has been Livia's place in the play from the beginning: she has arranged the relationships of the Duke and Bianca and of Hippolito and Isabella; and she advised the latter to proceed with her marriage to the Ward. As we have also seen, she has played the role of mother not only to her younger brother and her niece but also to her lover. Moreover, in the masque, just as in the rest of the play, this double role had disastrous consequences for Livia as well as for the others.

The chief problem the masque presents is the fact that its atmosphere differs so markedly from the first four acts. The opening acts present the characters realistically—the dramatic method is mimetic—but the final act subjects them to caricature as Middleton's dramaturgy takes a sudden turn into allegory and farce. I suspect that the reason for this has to do with the psychologies of audience response and of Middleton himself. In the opening acts of *Women Beware Women*, Middleton succeeds, perhaps not entirely consciously, in making the morally reprehensible, incestuous tangle of relationships uncomfortably sympathetic. The relationship of the Duke and Bianca is more attractive than that of the latter and Leantio, and Isabella and Hippolito are surely far preferable to Isabella and the Ward. And while the chorus of "enough" that concludes Livia's bargain with Leantio is distasteful, it seems impossible for the audience to be unaffected by compassion at Livia's heartbreak upon her loss of her lover. Middleton's purpose in the final scene may be, therefore, to disengage his audience from a sympathetic response to the masquers. Although the final masque is brilliant, and theatrically effective, it is too little, too late, for such a purpose. Classroom experience suggests that many readers do not become sufficiently detached in order to regard Middleton's characters as simply moral defectives.

Women Beware Women seems unquestionably ambivalent about the involvement of sexual partners of widely varying ages. On the one hand, it seems to ask its audience to deplore it; but, on the other, it also depicts such involvements in a manner that is undeniably seductive. I suspect that the sources of this ambivalence are Middleton's own experiences in early life. The dramatist's parents were in their forties when he was born, and Middleton lost his father when he was only five years old. Within a few months, Mrs. Middleton rashly remarried a man twenty years her junior. Her second husband—like Leantio, a factor—was a dissolute adventurer. Although he did not live with the family for long, he brought upon the Middletons endless quarrels and litigation. For approximately fifteen years, in spite of the limited legal rights possessed by Elizabethan women, Mrs. Middleton fought tenaciously to protect herself and her small family. For the most part, she succeeded. It is difficult to judge how Middleton felt about his mother. Since he was an eldest child, they may have been very close; and he certainly must have appreciated the tenacity with which she protected both him and his sister from disaster. But it is also easy to believe that as a young boy he resented her for re-marrying so precipitously after his father's death. And as he matured he must also have resented the fact that his mother's mistaken marriage continued to threaten his well-being. Since the young Middleton seems to have been morally precocious, one can probably assume that he was contemptuous of the urgings that led a woman in late middle age to choose a man young enough to be her son as her sexual partner. Middleton must have displaced some of his hatred of his stepfather onto the factor Leantio. The latter does not love the older Livia but merely uses her for his own purposes. Because of Livia's almost maternally protective care of Leantio, however, one images that Middleton could easily have identified with Leantio when he remembered how his mother protected him from financial and emotional ruin. Reading Middleton's biography into the life of his drama is, of course, unsafe, but when one looks at **Women Beware Women** one is struck by an unmistakable sexual pattern which mixes age with youth, even if one must finally acknowledge that Middleton's attitude to this pattern is irresolvably ambivalent.

Laura Bromley (essay date 1987)

SOURCE: "Men and Women Beware: Social, Political, and Sexual Anarchy in *Women Beware Women*," in *Iowa State Journal of Research,* Vol. 61, No. 3, February, 1987, pp. 311-21.

[*Bromley maintains that the corruption and immorality in* Women Beware Women *are caused by the collapse of the social structures of family, class, and church.*]

In the last scene of **Women Beware Women,** the characters moralize about the cause of their downfall: "Lust and forgetfulness has been amongst us, / And we are brought to nothing" (V.ii.146-47), declares Hippolito; Livia admits, "My own ambition pulls me down to ruin" (V.i.133); and Bianca laments, "Like our own sex, we have no enemy, no enemy" (V.i.215) (Thomas Middleton, **Women Beware Women,** ed. Mulryne. All quotations are taken from this edition). If we accept these aphorisms as summarizing the text of the play, we conclude that Middleton wants to show that men and women are sinful and corrupt, and the forms of evil most prevalent and most destructive are lust and greed for money and power. Most critics following this

line, stress the immorality of the characters and their society. (See, for example, Bradbrook, Mulryne, Parker, Ribner, and Schoenbaum.) But an examination of the subtext of the play reveals more topical and specific causes of human tragedy than original sin and social corruption. Middleton is concerned with the breakdown of established structures and standards during a period of social change. He connects the solipsism of his characters with the weakening of the institutions and relationships that traditionally provide the values that guide individuals, offering alternatives to the blind pursuit of pleasure and profit. In **Women Beware Women,** the consequences of freedom from the old rules without new directions are anarchy, anxiety, and alienation.

Many of the conflicts in the play are generated by the women's desire for autonomy, but a study of power relations in the play cannot be limited to those between men and women, as in some recent feminist criticism (Foster and Juneja, for example), for the battle between the sexes is part of a broader and more complex struggle for ascendancy between generations and classes. (Some attention is paid to conflicts between classes, sexes, and generations by Batchelor, Gill, Rowe, and Wigler.) Middleton is certainly interested in exposing and satirizing outmoded social standards. As his ironic treatment of character and situation makes clear, husbands should not lock up their wives, fathers should not force their daughters to marry rich fools, brothers should not kill their sisters' lovers in the name of family honor. But when they are released from the dominance of foolish or tyrannical men, Bianca, Isabella, and Livia choose new forms of bondage. They break with their male relatives only to bind themselves to equally self-serving lovers. Each female character seeks, and attains, liberation from the obligations imposed on her not only as a member of a sex, but as a member of a family and a class, only to suffer a crippling displacement; to break bonds is to be cast adrift. Having fought free of the requirements of rank, Bianca fulfills them in marriage to the Duke. Isabella is made a "stranger" like Bianca by her Aunt Livia's lie that she is her mother's illegitimate child. But when freed to choose without regard to her family, she ties herself to Hippolito, her father's brother. The only use to which Livia can put her wealth and independence is the indulgence of her own sexual appetites and those of her brother, Hippolito, and the Duke. Sexual freedom, for the women as well as the men, means license.

Freedom is illusory, for both men and women are disoriented, displaced "strangers" in the world of **Women Beware Women.** (The frequency with which Middleton uses the word "stranger" has been noted by Brian Parker [194].) It is not free choice but insecurity—economic, social, and psychological insecurity—that finally attaches Bianca to the Duke, Isabella to Hippolito, and Livia to Leantio. Middleton locates the sources of this insecurity in the breakdown of traditional social hierarchies and in the loss of authority in the family, state, and church. From this perspective, the most important distinction is not between men and women, but between young and old, or between those who are established in society and those who are trying to make a place for themselves.

Leantio is a pivotal character in this regard because he is young, bourgeois, without a father or inherited wealth or rank. He is usually said to be priggish, ineffectual, and self-satisfied. But his failures may more clearly reflect problems rooted in the social system than do those of more diabolical characters, like the Duke, or of caricatures like Fabritio or the Ward. What sets Leantio apart, making him pathetic or ridiculous to the other characters—and vulnerable to them—is that he believes in authority. He feels guilty for having stolen Bianca from her parents and home, and he fears and expects punishment from the authorities in Florence. We see Leantio as crude and smug at the beginning of the play, gloating over his possession of Bianca, a treasure beyond his means. Yet he has a clear sense of his own duties, and tries to balance his passion for his wife with his need to make a living for her and for his mother. His desire for domestic contentment is sincere, if unrealistic. He sees in black and white terms—one marries or burns—yet he is clearly devoted to Bianca and to his conception of "a good husband." He vows to his mother, "I'll prove an excellent husband, here's my hand" (I.i.107). It is important to remember that he hides Bianca not primarily out of fear of her wandering eye—for, unlike his mother, he cannot imagine that her satisfaction could be less than his own—but as a precaution against her discovery, which would result in her being returned to Venice and her family.

In short, Leantio means well, tries to do good, but, because of his simple code, is without the means to cope with the defection of his wife and mother. Because he believes in the moral authority of the Duke and believes that his loss of Bianca is just, he falls victim to those around him, who have no scruples. Unlike the character Pietro in Celio Malespini's *Ducento Novelle,* who is based on an historical person and who is the likely source of Middleton's characterization (Mulryne xxxviii-xl), Leantio never acquiesces to Bianca's affair for his own protection. He cannot, however, hold out against the power of the Duke and of Livia, and he allows himself to be gradually seduced by the glamour of wealth. The qualities that, in a society with a more fully articulated middle-class ethos, would sustain him in fruitful relations with others—his doggedness, earnestness, and loyalty—here betray him. Bewildered and grieved that Bianca is "my wife till death, yet no more mine" (III.iii.320), Leantio is prompted by his bourgeois practicality and instinct for self-preservation to rationalize that, since he has lost Bianca,

> . . . my safest course
> For health of mind and body is to turn
> My heart and hate her, most extremely hate her.
> (III.iii.337-39)

Virtue is defined by society and depends on relations with others, and Leantio is alone because no one else plays by the old rules. With the breakdown of authority in the family and, as will be seen later, in the state and church, there is no higher good to which one defers, in the name of which one refrains from purely self-interested behavior.

There are no stable, nurturing families to guide Leantio, Bianca, Isabella, or the Ward in *Women Beware Women.*

Instead, the older generation, which should guide these young people, has forfeited legitimate authority through its moral bankruptcy. Parents and surrogate parents exploit their dependents. Having left her wealthy family, Bianca stresses her affiliation with and dependence on Leantio and his mother:

> I have forsook friends, fortunes, and my country
> And hourly I rejoice in't . . .
> . . . Thy successes
> Howe'er they look, I will still name my fortunes.
> (I.i.131-34)

Yet her husband cannot protect her, and her mother-in-law exposes her to harm through her stupidity and self-indulgence as she succumbs to Livia's pressures and temptations. In the first scene of the play, Leantio's mother is shown to be a woman who knows the ways of the world and accepts them. She has no hope that Bianca will be satisfied with her son, whose old-fashioned notions of marriage she mocks. Indeed, her view of Leantio is so pragmatic and disinterested that it is soon apparent that Leantio's insistence in his asides on her as a loving "good mother" are as naive and self-deluded as his view of Bianca's potential to be a traditional "good wife."

Far from being a "good father," Fabritio is a parody of the protective father arranging a marriage to secure the economic and social well-being of his daughter. His failure as a father is not less disturbing because he is overruled by Livia, who sees him as the dangerous fool he is. Indeed, Livia's abuse of her own authority has the most terrible and far-reaching effects. Isabella is a marriageable young woman with no mother and no female friends. Into this gap steps the selfish, calculating surrogate mother, her Aunt Livia, who plays on what is not only Isabella's desire for the intimacy she has experienced with Hippolito, but surely also her need for a father. Hippolito is the "good father" Isabella has missed, an uncle with power, authority, and, from Isabella's point of view, the wisdom and love to use it properly.

It is particularly ironic that Livia should advance her scheme to pander to Hippolito's desire for his niece by creating a fiction that makes Isabella what she is in essence, a "stranger" in this unnatural family. She tells Isabella that she is the illegitimate child of her mother and her mother's lover, insisting that "you are no more allied to any of us, / . . . / Than the merest stranger is" (II.i.135, 138). Thus Livia "frees" Isabella to marry whomever she pleases, knowing that this will bind her in an incestuous affair with Hippolito, by displacing her from her family: her father, aunt, and uncle. Moreover, her lie depends on Isabella transferring her trust from her natural mother, whose adultery she believes in immediately, to Livia. Livia also mercilessly entraps the real stranger, Bianca, to whom she owes courtesy and charity, in order to feel her power and to strengthen it by serving the Duke.

Of Hippolito's seduction of his niece, little need be said. Like Livia, he preys upon Isabella's need, masking his sexual interest in her as disinterested friendship. While the incestuous nature of their affair is hidden from Isabella by Livia, Hippolito knowingly corrupts her. Here Middleton departs from his source (Mulryne xlv), in which the character on which Hippolito is based is also deceived by Livia's lie, in order to emphasize the cold-bloodedness of his sin. Hippolito restrains himself only long enough to utter the few lines that deepen his guilt by revealing his consciousness of it:

> I would 'twere fit to speak to her what I would; but
> 'Twas not a thing ordained, Heaven has forbid it;
> And 'tis most meet that I should rather perish
> Than the decree divine receive least blemish.
>   (I.ii.152-55)

Fifty-five lines later, he declares his love to his niece. Finally, as if to underline the failure of guardianship in mothers and fathers, aunts and uncles, Middleton gives us Guardiano, the shrewd and cynical guardian of the Ward, the man who helps Livia ensnare Bianca for the Duke and brags about his past accomplishments as court pander.

To turn from the breakdown of family structure to that of class structure, it is useful to return to Leantio, with his middle class virtues of persistence and diligence. Not only is Leantio without orienting family relationships; he is also without a network of peers in a bourgeois milieu. He and his mother are the only characters in the play who are concerned about making a living. There are no signs of the social system in which he has his place, and he is seen in connection with no other men, although he mentions the "rich master" whom he serves as a factor. A businessman, he is far from the underemployed, rebellious De Flores or Bosola, Flamineo or Iago, nursing their social and economic grievances, unable to rise in civil society, men who feel justified in selling their services to the highest bidder. But he is equally far from the independent, prosperous merchants and entrepreneurs of Middleton's city comedies, like Yellowhammer and Quomodo. Middleton goes to great lengths in the first scene to establish that Leantio's work is both honest and risky. Diligence and merit may possibly pay off, but Leantio works for wages and clearly has little chance of establishing himself and achieving economic security.

Class lines are loosely drawn in *Women Beware Women.* This society is not really concerned with Bianca's marriage to a man of lower station or with Livia's liaison with Leantio. Hippolito's protests about family honor are as absurd and anachronistic as Fabritio's attempts to enforce the marriage of Isabella and the Ward. But power is still rooted in money and rank—in the aristocracy. The Duke, who wields power by virtue of his social, economic, and political standing, is an authority in the public world as well as in Leantio's private world. The Duke takes what he wants, and Leantio finds himself cuckolded by his surrogate father, who engages in a kind of symbolic incest that is obviously related to the actual incest of Hippolito and Isabella. (Patterns of incestuous love are explored by Wigler [183-201].)

Leantio's defiance of the social rules in "stealing" Bianca dooms him, then, not because the Duke asserts his rightful authority to punish him, but because the rules exist only in Leantio's imagination. As in the case of De Flores, Bosola, and Iago, selling himself turns out to be a more reliable means of support for Leantio than selling his labor, so he resigns himself to accepting first the captainship from the Duke, and then the position of Livia's kept man. Leantio is impotent because he knows that he has morally compromised himself, but also, and more importantly, as Middleton takes care to show, because no economic or political challenge to established power is possible. In spite of Schoenbaum's insistence on the similarity of *Women Beware Women* to Middleton's comedies, particularly in its bourgeois milieu (127-29), there are only the feeblest signs of life in this play of a vital middle class society like the one realized in the comedies, where young people can successfully oppose the tyranny of parents who control their money and marriages. As George Rowe argues, "The world of *Women Beware Women* . . . is . . . hostile to comic values" (197). The power and privilege of the Duke and, to a lesser extent, of aristocrats like Livia and Hippolito, keep them safe from attacks from without. Inbreeding seems an almost inevitable consequence of the boredom and sterility of the courtier's world.

Along with the social mobility made possible by the blurring of class lines comes social anxiety. Bianca comes to Leantio with no dowry or other wealth but with a taste for luxury that only lies dormant, ready to be stirred back to life by the Duke. Much like Leantio's mother, who professes to abundant natural maternal affection but expresses only pragmatic considerations, Bianca gives signs of her appreciation of wealth and power while professing that with her husband's love she is "as rich as virtue can be poor" (I.i.128). Expectations about position, money, and responsibility are all vague for Leantio and Bianca in the first scene of the play, but only Leantio is surprised when Bianca, seeing herself through the Duke's eyes, suddenly sets a higher price on herself.

Leantio cannot offer Bianca the kind of noble household in which she could find occupation as well as ample provision for her material and social needs, yet he expects that she will be a traditional wife, leading a sheltered existence and fulfilling herself through him. Leantio needs a wife like Quomodo has found at the beginning of *Michaelmas Term* or like Yellowhammer has in *A Chaste Maid in Cheapside*: an equal, a helpmate, a business partner. In choosing a woman of wealth and breeding, he manifests the same yearning for what is beyond his scope that brings Bianca to look at the Duke. Like Bianca herself, he is a "stranger" in Florentine society with no stronghold and no defense against the power of wealth and rank wielded by the Duke and Livia.

Bianca finds no place for herself and no security with Leantio. When she first sees the Duke in procession from the window of their house, she remarks not upon his person, but upon his position, including the stable tradition behind it and the ceremony that expresses it:

> . . . 'Tis a noble State.
> Methinks my soul could dwell upon the reverence

Of such a solemn and most worthy custom.
(I.iii.102-04)

It is not only economic and social insecurity, but the need for a personal relationship with a stable authority figure that finally ties Bianca to the Duke, as it ties Isabella to Hippolito and Leantio to Livia. It is not a sign of Leantio's fatuousness that, in the course of one scene, he goes from blessing to cursing the married state. Rather, it is a sign of his understandable confusion about his place, including his duties as a husband and those of his wife.

Leantio's bewilderment and pain at the loss of his wife are not amusing, but pitiful. In spite of his faults, Leantio provides a striking contrast with the other characters, who behave more consistently because they are always guided solely bt the principle of self-interest. At the beginning of the play, he expresses his belief in romantic love and in marriage as a sacrament. His pardon for eloping with Bianca is "sealed from heaven by marriage," which is a shelter for their "quiet innocent loves" (I.i.45, 52). His confused conception of marriage as a safeguard against whoredom and as a peaceful haven are soon refuted by his experience, but for the other characters marriage, like family, class, and other networks of relationships, no longer helps to define one's place and duties. They suffer from none of Leantio's delusions.

Isabella speaks abstractly about the ideal of marriage as "the most blest estate" (I.ii.178), but complains bitterly of her own common experience: enforced marriage, marriage as "thralldom" (I.ii.170), marriage as a transaction in which women are "bought and sold" (III.iv.36). She and Hippolito agree that her marriage to the Ward will be no impediment to their pursuit of pleasure. On the contrary, in Hippolito's words,

This marriage now must of necessity forward,
It is the only veil wit can devise
To keep our acts hid from sin-piercing eyes.
(II.ii.236-38)

The Duke and Bianca are amused, rather than horrified, at Isabella's marriage to the repulsive, idiotic Ward, assuming that she will soon take a lover. And the Duke, like Leantio, believes that the act of marriage in itself can expiate past sins.

All of these vague, self-serving conceptions of marriage appear to be on the verge of being dispelled by the righteous wrath of the Cardinal, who is God's representative on earth, but also the Duke's brother. He enters in Act IV directly after the Duke has incited Hippolito to kill Leantio, his sister's lover. In an impassioned speech, the Cardinal delivers the Church's position on adultery, denouncing the Duke for his sin and reminding him of his responsibilities as a ruler and example to his people. The Duke declares his repentance and promises himself that as soon as Bianca's husband, Leantio, is murdered, he will "make her lawfully mine own, / Without this sin and horror" (IV.i.273-74).

The Cardinal's moral outrage, like all other right feeling in the play, is gradually eroded by expediency. He interrupts the marriage of the Duke and Bianca:

Cease, cease; religious honours done to sin
Disparage virtue's reverence, and will pull
Heaven's thunder upon Florence—holy ceremonies
Were made for sacred uses, not for sinful.
(IV.iii.1-4)

There is little to sustain the Cardinal's view of himself as a man of God, however, and it eventually gives way to his view of himself as a courtier and statesman and to his desire to ingratiate himself with the real power in Florence, the Duke. Most critics, with the notable exception of David Holmes (163-64), see the Cardinal as the voice of morality, and certainly his doctrine is sound and his language is convincing. But he only gives lip service to orthodox Christian values. The spiritual world of which the Cardinal is a part, like the bourgeois, mercantile world of Leantio, is absent from the play, as are its rules and rewards. After a few words of casuistry from the beautiful Bianca, the Cardinal backs down and the marriage proceeds. Soon he is prevailed upon by the Duke to kiss Bianca, and he declares, "I profess peace and am content. . . . You shall have all you wish" (V.ii.14, 16).

No other codes of belief and behavior are present in the play. There is no higher authority imaginatively or actually present in the name of which, or empowered by which, one can refrain from opportunism. The license of the Duke, and the license he gives others, exemplify the lawlessness of this society. Far from judging the lawless marriage of Leantio and Bianca, the Duke compounds the crime by taking Bianca for himself, forcing himself on the vulnerable young stranger in his state. Guardiano, who has pandered for the Duke before, tells us that the Duke's lust is dominant and willingly served by Hippolito, Livia, and himself. The Duke mingles freely with the citizens, maintaining no higher standards, eliciting no love or respect, surrounded by no loyal servants. Behind the form of the procession which so attracts Bianca is disorder; there is no hierarchy, but anarchy, or the tyranny of greed and lust.

In the world of *Women Beware Women,* individuals fight to liberate themselves from the dominance of corrupt and corrupting authority only to find themselves without ordering principles and without freedom. Unable to define themselves by reference to stable structures of family, class, or church, they impulsively seek security in alliances, particularly those which appear to ensure their profit and pleasure. Certainly, as is often noted, they are lacking in moral strength, but Middleton emphasizes the dissolution of the usual sources of this strength. At the end of the play, the characters simply do each other in, dying in the same confusion in which they lived. They are less the victims of each other than of themselves, and less their own victims than those of a society of displaced persons.

LITERATURE CITED

Batchelor, J.B. "The Pattern of *Women Beware Women."*
Yearbook of English Studies 2 (1972): 78-88.

Bradbrook, M.C. *Themes and Conventions of Elizabethan Tragedy.* 2nd ed. Cambridge: Cambridge UP, 1980. 102-32.

Foster, Verna Ann. "The Deed's Creature: The Tragedy of Bianca in *Women Beware Women.*" *Journal of English and Germanic Philology* 78 (1979): 508-21.

Gill, Roma. "The World of Thomas Middleton." *'Accompaninge the players': Essays Celebrating Thomas Middleton, 1580-1980.* Ed. Kenneth Friedenreich. New York: AMS P, 1983. 15-38.

Holmes, David. *The Art of Thomas Middleton.* London: Oxford UP, 1970. 158-67.

Juneja, Renu. "The Widow as Paradox and Paradigm in Middleton's Plays." *The Journal of General Education* 34.1 (1982): 3-19.

Mulryne, J.R. Introduction. *Women Beware Women.* By Thomas Middleton. London: Methuen, 1975. xix-lxxix.

Parker, R.B. "Middleton's Experiments with Comedy and Judgment." *Jacobean Theatre.* Stratford-upon-Avon Studies 1. Ed. John Russell Brown and Bernard Harris. 1960. New York: Capricorn Books, 1967. 192-99.

Ribner, Irving. *Jacobean Tragedy.* London: Methuen, 1962. 137-52.

Rowe, George E., Jr. *Thomas Middleton and the New Comedy Tradition.* Lincoln: U. of Nebraska P, 1979. 194-200.

Schoenbaum, Samuel. *Middleton's Tragedies.* New York: Columbia UP, 1955. 102-32.

Wigler, Stephen. "Parent and Child: The Pattern of Love in *Women Beware Women.* " *'Accompaninge the players': Essays Celebrating Thomas Middleton, 1580-1980.* Ed. Kenneth Friedenreich. New York: AMS P, 1983. 183-201.

THE CHANGELING

William Empson (essay date 1935)

SOURCE: "Double Plots," in *Some Versions of Pastoral*, 1935. Reprint by New Directions, 1968, pp. 27-86.

[*Empson was an English critic, poet, and editor who is best known for* Seven Types of Ambiguity *(1930), his seminal contribution to the formalist school of New Criticism. Empson's critical theory is based on the assumption that all great poetic works are ambiguous and that this ambiguity can often be traced to the multiple meanings of words. Empson analyzes a text by enumerating and discussing* these various meanings and examining how they fit together to communicate the poem's ideas and emotions. In the following excerpt from a study that was first published in 1935, Empson addresses how the comic subplot of The Changeling *relates to and amplifies the main plot, thereby presenting the first modern critical argument that the play is thematically unified.*]

Swinburne said of ***The Changeling*** that 'the underplot from which it most absurdly and unluckily derives its title is very stupid, rather coarse, and almost vulgar,' after which it is no use saying, as he does, that it is Middleton and Rowley's greatest play, 'a work which should suffice to make either name immortal'; the thing might have good passages but would be a bad play. And however disagreeable the comic part may be it is of no use to ignore it; it is woven into the tragic part very thoroughly [A. C. Swinburne, Introduction to *Thomas Middleton,* ed. Havelock Ellis, 1887]. Not that this interferes with the accepted view that the comic part is by Rowley and most of the tragic part by Middleton; the sort of unity required depends on the order of the scenes, which they would presumably draw up together, and on ironies which they could work out separately.

The chief reason why modern critics have passed over the comic part is that it forces one to take the unembarrassed Elizabethan view of lunatics, and though still alive in the villages this seems mere brutality to the cultivated. They were hearty jokes, to be treated like animals, and yet were possessed by, or actually were, fairies or evil spirits; they had some positive extra-human quality; they might say things profoundly true. No doubt it was crude to keep a lunatic as a pet, but we may call Shakespeare and Velasquez in evidence that the interest was not as trivial as it was brutal; and though no other Elizabethan could write the part of the madman-critic as Shakespeare could, so that their lunatics are less pleasant than his, this was chiefly for lack of his surrealist literary technique; they could assume the same attitude to lunatics in the audience as he could. People nowadays can swallow the idea in terms of painting or metaphor but to feel it at first hand about a realistic stage lunatic is too much. Certainly if the chorus of imbeciles here was merely convenient or merely funny the effect would be disgusting; but the madhouse dominates every scene; every irony refers back to it; that is why the play is so much nearer Webster than either of its parts.

Though their tones are different the two plots are very alike; in both the heroine has been married for social convenience to a man she does not love, so that there is a case for her if she cuckolds him. In the comic story she gets enough fun out of her lovers to keep up her spirits without being unfaithful to him even in detail; no doubt this is coarse and flat enough, but the contrast is not pointless. Beside the tragic characters she is sane; living among madmen she sees the need to be. This in itself compares the madmen to the tragic sinners, and a close parallel is used to drive it home. The idea of the changeling, a child stolen into the fairies' world, a fairy child replaced for it, makes you feel that the shock of seeing into a mad mind is dangerous; it may snatch you to itself. This shock is in all the discoveries of the play. When Antonio, disguised as a lunatic, makes love to Isabella, she breaks after three lines of his rhetoric into hearty laughter: 'you're a fine fool indeed . . . a parlous fool'; he is a changeling the other way round, she finds, but that is the same thing; he may snatch her into his world. It is in the next scene, so that we are forced to compare them, that we have the discovery the critics have praised so justly in isolation:

> Why tis impossible thou canst be so wicked
> Or shelter such a cunning cruelty
> To make his death the murderer of my honour.

The real changeling from which the play 'derives its title' is De Flores.

One need not look at all the jokes about the jealous mad-house keeper; they simply repeat that love is a madness. There is a more striking parallel between De Flores and the subordinate keeper Lollio, who has some claim to be count-ed among the fools. He demands 'his share' from Isabella as a price for keeping his mouth shut about Antonio, just as De Flores does from Beatrice. This is not irony but prepa-ration ('device prior to irony'); coming in the scene after De Flores commits the murder and before he demands his reward it acts as a proof of Isabella's wisdom and a hint of the future of Beatrice. Isabella threatens to make Antonio cut Lollio's throat, which does not impress him; when the tragic scene they foreshadow is over we find them smack-ing the threats at each other as casually as ever. I don't say that this is delicate, but it is a relief; Isabella is a very impressive creature; and the assumption in the tragic part that Alsemero will take his maid's virginity without discov-ering she is not his wife is more really brutal than anything in the asylum scenes.

The two stories get their connection of plot from the two lovers of Isabella, who leave Beatrice's court to be dis-guised as madmen and are brought back with other mad-men to amuse it in the masque at her wedding. This was not merely a fine show on the stage but the chief source of the ideas of the play. The antimasque at a great wedding, con-sidered as subhuman, stood for the insanity of disorder to show marriage as necessary, considered as the mob, ritually mocked the couple (for being or for not being faithful, in-nocent, etc.), both to appease those who might otherwise mock and to show that the marriage was too strong to be hurt by mockery. We have been shown the chief thing the madmen of the play stand for, when Isabella seemed likely to take Antonio seriously.

> (Cries of madmen are heard without, like those of birds and beasts.)
> LOLLIO. Cuckoo, cuckoo.
> ANTONIO. What are these?
> ISABELLA. Of fear enough to part us.

Fear parted Beatrice from Alsemero, the husband won falsely; the madmen brought in to be mocked form, for her as for Isabella, an appalling chorus of mockers, and assim-ilate her to themselves. The richness of the thought here does not come from isolated thinking but from a still hearty custom; to an audience which took the feelings about a

marriage masque and a changeling for granted the ideas would arise directly from the two plots.

So the effect of the vulgar asylum scenes is to surround the characters with a herd of lunatics, howling outside in the night, one step into whose company is irretrievable; looking back to the stock form, this herd is the 'people' of which the tragic characters are 'heroes.' Beatrice too becomes a changeling;

> I that am of your blood was taken from you

she tells her father. Morally a child such as the fairies can steal, and fearing De Flores as a goblin, she puts him to a practical use to escape him; he could then steal her; she must realise his way of feeling and be dragged into his world. It is the untruth of the appeal that makes it so terri-ble, and the hint of the changeling idea given by the other plot that makes us accept it. As a finale this connection is at last made obvious; the venomous courage of De Flores is united to the howling of the madmen.

> BEA. Alsemero, I'm a stranger to your bed.
>   Your bed was cozened on the nuptial night,
>   For which your false bride died.
> ALS. Diaphanta?
> DE F. Yes, and the while I coupled with your mate
>   At barley-break; now we are left in hell.
> ALS. We are all there, it circumscribes us here.

We have heard about barley-break before. 'Catch there, catch the last couple in hell' scream the lunatics in the darkness at the back of the stage, when Antonio discloses his plot to Isabella; the two parts are united, and they are all there together.

M. C. Bradbrook (essay date 1935)

SOURCE: "Thomas Middleton," in *Themes and Conven-tions of Elizabethan Tragedy,* Cambridge at the University Press, 1935, pp. 213-39.

[*Bradbrook is an English scholar noted especially for her commentary on the development of Elizabethan drama and poetry. In her criticism, she combines both biographical and historical research, paying particular attention to the stage conventions of Elizabethan and earlier periods. In the following excerpt from her influential essay on Middleton, she evaluates the naturalistic treatment of character in* The Changeling *and provides an elaboration of William Emp-son's contention that the tragedy is well unified.*]

Middleton's tragedies are as similar in their methods of construction as they are different from the plays [of other Elizabethan dramatists]. Rowley's name appears on the title page of *The Changeling,* but it is difficult to see the pos-sibility of his sharing in the main plot, for its unity is of a kind which not even the most sympathetic collaboration could achieve.

The connection between the two plots of this play is, however, very carefully worked out. It is indicated even in the title, "The *Changeling*", which describes both Antonio, the innocent, and Beatrice-Joanna, the inconstant woman (a usual meaning—*vide* **Anything for a Quiet Life,** 2. 1. 71, and *N.E.D.* [*New English Dictionary*] *sub verb*).

The construction of the play is masked by the greater naturalism of the treatment. Compared with the characters of earlier plays, Middleton's are fuller, more natural and human. Their motives and actions may be conventionally "Italianate" (they have vestigial remains of the Revenge code in the melancholy of Tomazo the revenger and the appearance of the ghost), but their feelings and responses are normal. Beatrice-Joanna's famous outburst, when the murderer demands possession of her as a reward:

> Why 'tis impossible thou canst be so wicked
> Or shelter such a cunning cruelty
> To make his death the murderer of my honour—
>
> (3. 4. 121 ff.)

is only the most obvious illustration of Middleton's interest in the way the mind works. Deflores' brief plea to the man he has cuckolded, when he hears Beatrice-Joanna crying out in futile anger:

> Let me go to her, sir—
>
> (5. 3. 112)

is so assured of his right to calm her that the husband can but send him in.

The construction of the play is, however, partly dependent on themes: briefly it may be described as a study in the conflict of passion and judgment, and of the transforming power of love. All the characters (save Alsemero) are entirely at the mercy of their feelings, which are instinctive and uncontrollable. Judgment is blinded, so that the characters practise all kinds of deception and self-deception to gain their ends. Love is "a tame madness", a kind of possession which seizes upon a man and "changes" him so that he is no longer recognisable. In the main plot the themes are worked out naturalistically; in the subplot the use of the madmen, and of more literal transformations, as well as more farcical action, makes a kind of phantasmagoria. The key words are "change", "judgment" and "will" (in the sense of instinctive desire, often of sensual desire, as in Shakespeare). The connection between plot and subplot is summed up in the final scene where the structure of themes is explained.

> *Alsemero.* What an opacous body had that moon
> That last changed on us! here is beauty changed
> To ugly whoredom; here servant-obedience
> To a master-sin, imperious murder;
> I, a supposed husband, changed embraces
> With wantonness—but that was paid before—
> Your change is come too from an ignorant wrath
> To knowing friendship. Are there any more on's?
> *Antonio.* Yes sir I was changed too from a little ass
> as I was to a great fool as I am: and had like to ha' been
> changed to the gallows, but that you know my innocence

> always excuses me.
> *Franciscus.* I was changed from a little wit to be
>   stark mad
> Almost for the same purpose.
> *Isabella* (to her husband). Your change is still behind,
> But deserve best your transformation.
>
> (5. 3. 199ff.)

"Transformation" is a useful word to describe the character changes in the play: people are changed in the eyes of others, and they are also changed radically in themselves by the power of love.

The play opens with Alsemero falling in love. It was "in the Temple" which he instinctively feels to be an omen (the use of omens as what would now be called promptings of the unconscious mind plays a large part in the play). In any case he is already transformed; from an ardent traveller he becomes a loiterer, from a woman hater a courtier so that his friend cries:

> How now: the laws of the Medes are changed sure:
> salute a woman: he kisses too: wonderful!
>
> (1. 1. 60)

This sense of shock and discovery is the same in kind (though not in intensity of course) as the "discoveries" of Beatric-Joanna, of Isabella and of Alsemero.

The dialogue which follows states the main theme. Alsemero roundly declares his love, to which Beatrice-Joanna replies:

> Be better advised, sir:
> Our eyes are sentinels unto our *judgments*
> And should give certain *judgment* what they see;
> But they are rash sometimes and tell us wonders
> Of common things, which when our *judgments* find
> They can then check the eyes and call them blind.
>
> (1. 1. 73ff.)

Alsemero has seen her twice, however, and this he considers amply sufficient for the co-operation of eyes and judgment.

Deflores is then introduced, and Beatric-Joanna's instinctive hatred of him. "She knows no cause for't but a peevish *will.*" Beatrice-Joanna and Alsemero have a long discussion on the idiosyncratic character of the will (compare *The Merchant of Venice*, 4. 1. 44-62) and its instinctive precritical judgments. Beatrice-Joanna's father then appears and a conversation, in which asides and equivocations are frequent, shows to what extent Beatrice-Joanna's "will" is already transforming her. She says:

> I shall *change* my saint, I fear me: I find
> A giddy turning in me—
>
> (1. 1. 158-9)

an echo of Alsemero's "I keep the same church, same devotion" which points the contrast between them. Her father explains to Alsemero that she is betrothed to Alonzo de

Piracquo: immediately his plans change, he must go away. The father will have her married at once, "I'll want my *will* else". Beatrice-Joanna adds aside, "I shall want mine if you do it". Finally Deflores, remaining to soliloquise, reveals his plight as the same one:

> I know she hates me
> Yet cannot choose but love her: no matter,
> If but to vex her, I will haunt her still:
> Though I get nothing else, I'll have my will.
>
> (1. 1. 237-40)

The second act opens with Beatrice-Joanna busily deluding her own judgment. Alsemero's friend has just arranged an assignation, and she catches at his discretion as a justification for herself.

> How wise is Alsemero in his friend,
> It is a sign he makes his choice with *judgment:*
> Then I appear in nothing more approved
> Than making choice of him. . . .
>
> (2. 1. 6ff.)

She loves "with intellectual eyesight" as Alsemero thought he did.

Instead of Alsemero, Deflores arrives. He describes his own infatuation coolly (he is well aware of his ugliness, so that only "intellectual eyesight" could ever endure him) yet he does not despair, and when Beatrice-Joanna turns on "this ominous ill-faced fellow" he endures her patiently. He has a certain self-knowledge which sets him above the others, if it does not give him self-mastery.

> Why am I not an ass to devise ways
> Thus to be railed at? I must see her still,
> I shall have a mad qualm within this hour again
> I know't.
>
> (2. 1. 77ff.)

When he is gone Beatrice-Joanna enlarges on the feeling of danger he inspires in her. The scene concludes with an interview with her unwelcome lover, Piracquo. He refuses to recognise her very plain dislike of him, since love has overpowered his judgment too. His brother comments on his incredulity:

> Why, this is love's tame *madness,*

a significant link with the subplot.

All this interweaving of self-deception and self-awareness is supported by dialogue of the greatest ease and naturalness. There is no sustained heroic pitch as in Tourneur or Webster; the climaxes of feeling are simply expressed, not in obviously rich and poetic language.

> I have within my eyes all my desires. . . .
>
> (2. 2. 8)

> Here was a course
> Found to bring sorrow on her way to death

> The tears would ne'er have dried till blood had choked 'em.
>
> (2. 2. 37-9)

The scene in which Deflores is given the commission to kill Piracquo is one of ironic comedy. Having seen her secret interview with Alsemero he has hopes for himself and when Beatrice-Joanna seems more friendly he is really deceived into thinking her judgment is changed.

> *Beatrice-Joanna.* You've pruned yourself, methinks: you were not wont
> To look so amorously.
> *Deflores.* Not I—
> 'Tis the same phisnomy to a hair and pimple
> Which she called scurvy scarce an hour ago.
> How is this?
> *Beatrice-Joanna.* Come hither; nearer, man.
> *Deflores.* I'm up to the chin in heaven!
>
> (2. 2. 74ff.)

At first he coaxes her into speaking because he half believes she is in love with him. She is trying to get her request out naturally and he makes things easy by importuning her.

> *Beatrice-Joanna.* Oh my Deflores!
> *Deflores.* How this? she calls me hers?
> Already, my Deflores—You were about
> To sigh out somewhat, madam? . . .
> *Beatrice-Joanna.* Would creation—
> *Deflores. Ay well said, that's it.*
> *Beatrice-Joanna.* Had made me man.
> *Deflores.* Nay that's not it.
>
> (2. 2. 97ff.)

He may be ironical, but it is hardly likely. They part mutually deceived, Beatrice-Joanna rejoicing at being rid of him and he in having won her.

The murder is quickly done and the great discovery scene follows. Beatrice-Joanna is congratulating herself on her judgment.

> So wisdom by degrees works out her freedom.
>
> (3. 4 .13)

Deflores is something more than complacent as he enters and shows her the severed finger of Piracquo. She is horrified, for she had not visualised the murder; Deflores the hired assassin was to stand between her and the dirty business of the stabbing. He is quite calloused physically, and cannot understand her qualms at sight of the ring—"the first token my father made me send him". When she tells him to keep the jewel, however, her coarseness is exposed in turn by his retort:

> 'Twill hardly buy a capcase for one's conscience though
> To keep it from the worm, as fine as 'tis.
>
> (3. 4. 45-6)

His anger rises as he realises her attitude towards himself. The barriers of her modesty, dignity and stupidity are not easily broken; she only thinks of him as a servant and at first actually appeals to him on those grounds.

> Think but upon the distance that creation
> Set 'twixt thy blood and mine and keep thee there.
>
>   (3. 4. 131-2)

Deflores' reply suggests that she has become "transformed": she is no longer the woman she was, since her love has altered.

> 'Twas chang'd from thy first love, and that's a kind
> Of whoredom in the heart, and he's chang'd now
> To bring thy second on, thy Alsemero.
>
>   (3. 4. 144-6)

She is "the deed's creature", and one with him. It will be seen that later both Beatrice-Joanna and Alsemero acknowledge her transformation.

Deflores' speeches have also a naturalistic interpretation. The pain of his disillusion can be felt behind his violence; it breaks out finally in an appeal to her pity, as direct as hers to him:

> I live in pain now: that shooting eye
> Will burn my heart to cinders.
>
>   (3. 4. 152-3)

When she submits he drops to a tenderness heard again in the final scene. It is one of Middleton's most daring and most perfectly managed modulations of feeling:

> Come rise and shroud your blushes in my bosom:
> Silence is one of pleasure's best receipts:
> Thy peace is wrought for ever in this yielding.
>
>   (3. 4. 167-9)

The last two acts are worked out in the same manner as the first three. Beatrice-Joanna makes the same mistake with Diaphanta as she did with Deflores. "'Tis a nice piece gold cannot purchase", and so she bribes her maid to take her place on the marriage night.

Diaphanta's lust nearly wrecks the plan, as Deflores' had done. He arrives and suggests an alarm of fire, but Beatrice-Joanna is as slow now as heretofore to see the point of his proposals.

> *Beatrice-Joanna.* How, fire, sir? that may endanger
>   the whole house.
> *Deflores.* You talk of danger when your fame's on
>   fire?
>
>   (5. 1. 33-4)

The trick of the "magic" glass of water by which Alsemero tests her virginity is not out of place, for it belongs with the "omens" and other irrational elements rather than with the naturalism of character and speech; it is also reinforced by the stronger suggestion of "magic" in the subplot.

Alsemero is the only character whose "will" does not overpower his judgment. Beatrice-Joanna fears his clear sight (4. 1. 1-17). He is contrasted with Piracquo who would not hear a word against his betrothed:

> Were she the sole glory of the earth,
> Had eyes that could shoot fire into King's breasts
> And touched, she sleeps not here.
>
>   (4. 2. 106-8)

The quarrel with Tomazo de Piracquo seems "ominous" to him; but his innocence relieves him. At the moment of discovery he remembers his early scruples:

> O the place itself e'er since
> Has crying been for vengeance! the Temple. . . .
>
>   (5. 3. 73-4)

Beatrice-Joanna now appears hideous to him, even physically hideous, and in that is akin to Deflores. Her transformation is complete, through the discovery of her deceit.

> The black mask
> That so continually was worn upon't
> Condemns the face for ugly ere't be seen.
>
>   (5. 3. 3.5)

> O thou art all deformed.
>
>   (5. 3. 78)

Beatrice-Joanna miscalculates a third time: she confesses murder but denies adultery, thinking Alsemero will pardon the greater crime, since it was done for his sake. She knows him no better than Deflores or Diaphanta; he rejects her with horror and it is left for Deflores' resolution to cut the thread, by murder and suicide. Beatrice-Joanna recognises her transformation, at first indirectly: of the word "whore" she says:

> It blasts a beauty to *deformity*
> Upon whatsoever face that breath falls
> It strikes it ugly.
>
>   (5. 3. 33-5)

Finally she recognises her union with Deflores, and the significance of her first "will" to dislike him (5. 3. 157-60).

The revenge of Tomazo de Piracquo is also a matter of will. At first he likes Deflores, but later he feels an in-explicable recoil from him.

The subplot is connected with the main plot chiefly by implication. It acts as a kind of parallel or reflection in a different mode: their relationship is precisely that of masque and antimasque, say the two halves of Johnson's *Masque of Queens*. The direct links at the end have already been mentioned: there is also a scene of parallel action, first noted by Mr Empson, in which Isabella, the wife of the madhouse keeper, is detected with her lover by a servant Lollio. He proceeds to exact the same price from Isabella that Deflores did from Beatrice-Joanna:

Come, sweet rogue: kiss me, my little Lacedemonian:
let me feel how thy pulses beat: thou hast a thing about
thee would do a man pleasure, I'll lay my hand on it.

(3. 3. 247-50)

Her reply is an inversion of Beatrice-Joanna's. She threatens in turn:

Be silent, mute,
Mute as a statue, or his injunctions
For me enjoying, shall be to cut thy throat,
I'll do't, though for no other purpose.

(3. 3. 253-6)

Deflores enjoyed Beatrice-Joanna in return for cutting a throat.

Isabella has two lovers, who are disguised as a fool and a madman in order to gain access to her. Antonio, the fool, throws off his hideous disguise, which he calls a *deformity* (3. 3. 195) and appears as her lover suddenly:

This shape of folly shrouds your dearest love,
The truest servant to your powerful beauties,
Whose *magic* had the force thus to *transform* me.

(3. 3. 127-9)

It is parallel to Deflores' appearance as the lover of Beatrice-Joanna. The quality of the surprise is similar (not, of course, the intensity). The other lover never actually encounters her, but sends a letter in which he says:

Sweet Lady, having now cast off this counterfeit cover
of a madman, I appear to your best *Judgment* a true and
faithful lover of your beauty . . . (Love) shapes and
transhapes, destroys and builds again. . . .

In the same scene Isabella puts on the disguise of a madwoman to meet the fool; but she is only temporarily transformed. Her speeches are full of references to Dedalus and Icarus, which suggest the dangerous nature of their secret and the preciousness of the reward. But the fool does not recognise her, and so she returns to her former state, and is never actually unfaithful to her ridiculous husband.

The chorus of madmen depict the bestial element in man, rather as Caliban does [in Shakespeare's *The Tempest*], or the rout in [Milton's] *Comus*. At the climax of the subplot, when Isabella is hard pressed by Antonio, Lollio cries "Cuckoo! cuckoo!" and there is the direction:

Madmen above, some as birds, others as beasts.

Bullen and other editors rearrange this, but it clearly means that the madmen appear on the upper stage in the masquing habits which they are to wear at their entertainment at Beatrice-Joanna's wedding. They are a symbolic presentation of evil. Isabella explains:

They act their fantasies in any shapes [i.e. costumes]
Suiting their present thoughts.

Already they have been heard within crying at the game of barley-break:

Catch there: catch the last couple in hell!

(3. 3. 173)

The old worn pun gains in horror when Deflores echoes it to Alsemero in the final scene:

I coupled with your mate
At barley-break: now we are left in hell.

(5. 3. 165-6)

Vermandero adds, "It circumscribes us here", thinking of the actual chalk ring.

The supernatural element in the main plot is veiled: it depends on the omens and the "magic" effects of Alsemero's chemistry. The subplot is fantastic and pictorial. The masque of madmen, ostensibly prepared for the wedding, is actually given in rehearsal before Isabella at the end of Act 4. She is summoned to it:

Away then, and guide them in, Lollio:
Entreat your mistress to see this sight.

The importance of this masque can be gauged by the comparison with that in Ford's *The Lover's Melancholy* (3. 3). Here the doctor Corax has a masque of melancholy men to cure the melancholy of the Prince. The different types of the disease are taken from Burton, and each is symbolically dressed. For instance, Lycanthropia has "his face whited, with black shag hair, and long nails and with a piece of raw meat". The wanton melancholy is "a Sea-Nymph big-bellied, singing and dancing", the point of this being of course that *mermaid* was slang for prostitute.

The Prince remaining unmoved, Corax adds:

One only kind of Melancholy
Is left untouched: 'twas not in art
To personate the shadow of that fancy:
'Tis named love-melancholy . . .
Love is the tyrant of the heart: it darkens
Reason, confounds discretion: deaf to counsel
It runs a headlong course to desperate madness.

The Prince, like Claudius in *Hamlet,* breaks off the revels abruptly. The significance of this passage with its symbolic treatment of madmen and the connection between love and madness involved in the symbolism is perhaps all the stronger for there being no trace of any direct influence of Middleton.

Throughout the scenes of the subplot of **The Changeling,** riddling games and tableaux keep up the bizarre horror.

Here's a fool behind a knave, that's I: and between us
two fools there is a knave, that's my master: 'tis but we
three, that's all.

We three, we three, cousin.

(1. 2. 202ff.)

This is the husband posed between Lollio, his servant, and Antonio, his "patient", both of whom are deceiving him at the moment when they so firmly assert that he is the knave and they the fools. So Isabella is posed between her husband and her two lovers throughout the play. So Beatrice-Joanna is posed between her husband and her two lovers, Piracquo and Deflores, in the one scene where the supernatural is allowed to intrude overtly into the main plot, and the silent ghost of Alonzo appears to Deflores and Beatrice-Joanna as they plot the second murder, that of the waiting woman Diaphanta. Yet even here the tone is kept quiet: to Deflores the ghost is only a "mist of conscience", while Beatrice-Joanna does not even see it clearly enough to recognise it: it felt an "ill thing" that left a shivering sweat upon her. So firmly does each half of the play retain its own proper atmosphere, and yet so closely are they interwoven with each other.

Peter Morrison (essay date 1983)

SOURCE: "A Cangoun in Zombieland: Middleton's Teratological *Changeling*," in *"Accompaninge the players": Essays Celebrating Thomas Middleton, 1580-1980,* edited by Kenneth Friedenreich, AMS Press, 1983, pp. 219-41.

[*Morrison disputes those critical interpretations that regard* The Changeling *as unified around the concept of change or mutability, countering that "if* The Changeling *is unified at all . . . it is certainly not so by virtue of abstract concept or formal structure but by such things as symbol, image, mood."*]

> Men very hot and dry, are never faire, save by miracle, but rather hard-favored, and ill shaped: for the heat and dryness (as Aristotle affirmeth of the Ethiopians) wrieth the proportion of the face, and so they become disfigured. . . . Whence it is manifest, that much beautie in a man, is no token of much heat.
>
>   Huarte-Navarro, *The Examination of Men's Wits*

> The true meanings of words are bodily meanings, carnal knowledge; and the bodily meanings are the unspoken meanings. What is always speaking silently is the body. The unspoken meaning is always sexual. Of sexuality we can have only symbolical knowledge, because sexual is carnal. Death and love are altogether carnal; hence their magic and their great terror.
>
>   Norman O. Brown, *Love's Body*

[There] is no shortage of twentieth-century criticism on *The Changeling*—major studies of the play number in the neighborhood of forty, and a comprehensive critical bibliography would probably list over one hundred entries. The reasons for this (at least the primary ones) are apparent: *The Changeling* has always been a highly-regarded play, and, since Eliot at least, it has been a commonplace to rank it as a tragedy that is among the finest, if not *the* finest, produced by one of Shakespeare's contemporaries. Moreover, *The Changeling* invites critical discussion, for though its power is widely recognized and admired, just how the play works and what it might mean have proven thorny and challenging issues.

Until 1950 it was commonly argued that the play did not work, at least as a whole, and that its meaning was to be found in the handful of compelling scenes that concentrate on the progressive moral degeneration of Beatrice—on, in Eliot's fine phrase, Beatrice's gradual "habituation" to sin. Empson was the first to question this line of reasoning, noting in brief but cogent observations that *The Changeling* necessarily lacked meaning if it lacked unity and that the number of seemingly incidental or minor scenes in the play—especially those involving the comic subplot—comment ironically and substantially on the central action involving Beatrice and De Flores.

It is to Empson's position that the vast bulk of criticism on the play can be traced, a criticism given over almost entirely to working out in full the elaborate and complex interconnections of plot, character, imagery, and theme that are then offered up as the structural core of the play. With the exception of a very few contemporary essays, this body of criticism—for all its elaborations—can be characterized in a reasonably uncomplicated way. Two generalizations will suffice. The first is that *The Changeling* raises three knotty, and so often contentious, problems:

1. What(who) is(are) a(the) changeling(s)?
2. How are the two plots related?
3. What is the "moral vision" of the play?

The second is that to offer an opinion on any of the three questions is necessarily to offer an opinion on the other two, for the three problems are the same problems.

Of the three-questions-that-are-one-question, it is probably the first—which stems from the rich ambiguity inherent in the title of the play—that has been most assiduously pursued as the best way to get at the rest, this particular tradition being more or less inaugurated in 1954 by Holzknecht's influential essay. In observing via the *OED* that a "changeling" was known in the seventeenth century as an "inconstant person," not merely as a "fool," or as a "fairy child left in exchange for one stolen," Holzknecht made room for an energetic formalism latent in Empson's earlier discussion of the play. This approach to *The Changeling* feeds from the title in order to argue that the play can only be understood in light of the complex dialectics of metamorphosis and the deeply ironic (and in this case tragic) juxtaposition of constancy and inconstancy. The play proves full of changelings; so the title is fully appropriate and the subplot richly connected to the main plot by intricate inversion and by the fact that the changelings (fools) in Alibius' asylum are grotesque parodies of the changelings (inconstants) in Vermandero's castle. Williams' summary acceptance of this argument is representative of the tradition:

> The thematic interrelation of the two plots is evident in the ramifications of meaning afforded by the title of the play. The denotation of the word "changeling" familiar to the modern audience is "an infant exchanged by fairies for another infant"; it is the only meaning not relevant to the play. A changeling for this play is a waverer or a fickle person, a person surreptitiously put in exchange

for another, or an idiot (*OED*). All of these meanings are relevant to one or more of the characters in the play, and all involve the concept of transformation.

The appeal of this position is manifest. Because it allows—encourages, in fact—myriad internal connections and disconnections, it makes the play ripe for formalist inquiry. Moreover, it affirms the particular power of the Beatrice/De Flores scenes by locating them within the context of the whole play. Moreover, it has been this argument that has been wholly responsible for justly discarding the earlier opinion that *The Changeling,* however powerful and compelling, was nevertheless a play of two or three great scenes and a half-dozen lamentable ones. No one can any longer doubt that the two plots of the play are closely related in numerous ways and that their interrelation expands the moral vision of the play and so heightens its power.

Nevertheless, successful and substantial as this method of inquiry has proven, it seems apparent—thirty years after the publication of Empson's essay—that criticism has by-and-large failed to answer the challenge of *The Changeling,* which for all its dismantling remains today a play as troublesome and as baffling and as disturbing as it appeared to its critics in the earlier half of this century. This is largely due to the fact that modern criticism of the play . . . has tended to rely on a hermenuetics predicated on two key assumptions, neither of which are questioned (though both are questionable) and the elaboration of which has shifted attention away from the most compelling quality of *The Changeling* and so has whitewashed the most unsettling and determinant quality of the play: our intense fascination with and absorption in the extraordinary pathological intensity of Beatrice and De Flores' violent sexual union.

The first of these assumptions is that the play is powerful *because* it is unified—that is, because *The Changeling* is recognized as powerful, because it is apparently "meaningfull," it is therefore assumed to be integrally unified. The task of criticism then becomes to validate this equation by demonstrating the various ways (presumably leading eventually to a complete schematic) in which the play is in fact unified. The central problem with this argument lies in the fact that *The Changeling* in many ways obviously lacks rather than exhibits the formal unity for which it has been so richly praised.

No amount of ingenuity, for example, can make sense out of the play's time scheme, even though a precise understanding of the order of events is essential to render whole sections of the action credible. Piracquo, who apparently has been in Alicante ("five days past") where Beatrice has seen and accepted him, manages to rearrive on two separate occasions, once in I.i. where Vermandero brings Beatrice "news" that he saw her husband-to-be "lately," and then again in II.i. (a day or so later, one gathers) where he appears with his brother "new alighted." The wedding, expected "within this sevennight" in I.i. and extended "three days longer" in II.i., seems to take place as scheduled (Alibius proceeds with his entertainment plans as if there were no delay), though this hopelessly confuses the specifics of Piracquo's murder, which at one point apparently occurs immediately following his second arrival, at a second point apparently just prior to the wedding, and at a third point—the actual day of the wedding—"ten days since," which leads Vermandero to suspect Franciscus and Antonio even though it is perfectly clear from I.i. that both of them left the castle prior not only to Piracquo's disappearance, but even to his *arrival.* Yet Vermandero in V.iii. proudly displays the suspected murderers as having been "disguis'd / E'er since the deed was done," an obvious impossibility no one—including the accused—even think to question. Moreover, nobody seems to miss Piracquo until he fails to show up the morning of the wedding, though the impresson left in III.ii. is that he and his brother are live-in guests at Vermandero's castle and that his disapperance would be promptly noticed.

Additional examples of confusion abound. Beatrice, who in III.iv. is apparently genuinely surprised to discover that lust, not greed, has motivated De Flores, nevertheless seems to know in II.ii. exactly why De Flores will be eager to do her bidding. In IV.i. Beatrice fortuitously discovers Alsemero's "physician's closet," though she has no reason at all to search through her husband's possessions—the real motive for the discovery (one Middleton makes no effort to disguise) being only that the plot requires that it be made. Tomazo, who in IV.ii. calls De Flores "kind and true one" and praises his "wondrous honest heart," reappears a day later (V.ii.) claiming he has never trusted De Flores, whose sight is "poisonous" to him. Finally, the entire subplot is never resolved, a lapse so glaring that it leads Levin to speculate that the play is missing (by authorial or editorial oversight or omission) an entire scene.

Though the anti-masque of fools and madmen is elaborately prepared for (the discovery of Antonio and Franciscus obviously to be tied to the performance), it is completely forgotten in the wholesale, bandwagon unmasking with which the play closes. Moreover, Lollio simply disappears, though the last time we see him (IV.iii.) he has just cooked up an imminent (but not forthcoming) confrontation between Antonio and Franciscus by falsely promising each of them Isabella (without her knowledge) if one eliminates the other. Alibius, too, has his own plans to generate additional profit from his fools and madmen via their performance at the wedding; but the carefully initiated scheme simply drops out without any development or resolution. To this list we might also add the distinction several times drawn between madmen and fools, an apparently significantly matter that proves to be nothing more than a red herring.

Moreover, the disunity and disorganization apparent in the "workings" of the play are equally—and more significantly—characteristic of its larger formal patterns and consequently must be a serious concern in any discussion of the play's meanings or attitudes. *The Changeling* is not merely a play of dubious genre (it was first entered in the *Stationers' Register* as a comedy), it is a play of *indeterminant* genre, which is a wholly different matter, and one almost invariably avoided by Middleton's critics. Only Pentzell has seen fit to raise this issue, yet his observations are certainly correct, and their significance—I take it—nothing short of essential. One need not agree with Pentzell's as-

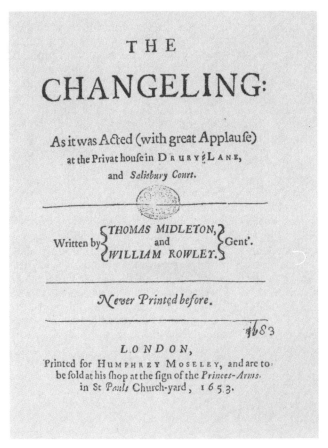

THE

CHANGELING:

As it was Acted (with great Applause)
at the Privat house in DRURY LANE,
and *Salisbury Court.*

Written by {THOMAS MIDLETON,
and   Gent'.
WILLIAM ROWLEY.}

Never Printed before.

1653

LONDON,
Printed for HUMPHREY MOSELEY, and are to
be sold at his shop at the sign of the *Princes-Arms.*
in St *Pauls* Church-yard, 1 6 5 3.

Title page to a 1653 edition.

sessment that *The Changeling* is best defined as "manner-ist," but certainly its lack of closure, its *ad hoc* commingling of conventions, situations, and characters often opposite in kind, its unassimilated congestion of intense psychological realism and flat formalism, its obvious stitchery and loose ends, argue that the play is anything but the brilliant multi-faceted jewel it has so often been made out to be. And yet the compelling power of *The Changeling* is undeniable—this is not a flawed play that has moments of greatness; it is a great play that openly flaunts its flaws.

Closely related to this matter is a second premise, equally problematic and equally common, which is that the concept of "change" lies at the very center of the play and that it is this abstraction to which all the actions and reactions of the play inexorably lead. *The Changeling,* that is, is said to be "about" change because it is "about" changing and changeable people. Other than the fact that this argument is meaningless, several difficulties stem from its assertion. The first is that it is far too general to be of any help, however it may be that *The Changeling* is in some sense concerned with change. To say that the characters of the play change, or are changed, is to make a comment applicable to virtually any play, or to anything that has characters in it at all, for that matter. And although it is true that the characters in *The Changeling* themselves call attention to the issue (especially in the concluding scene), what they have to say is so

patently vapid and formulaic as to render the whole matter utterly absurd, at least insofar as any useful generalizations about "change" are concerned.

Secondly, the thematics of mutability belong to one side of a structural dialectic (the other pole being that of stability) invariably bewildered in the reversals and paradoxes of metaphysical relativism. Because it is all too easy to see every character in *The Changeling* as a "changeling" with respect to something or someone else, the play can be seen as a kind of shell game in which we are expected to uncover the "real" changelings—the assumption here being that to find the "real" changelings is to find the key to the only valid interpretation of the play. The inevitable result of this line of thought—a culmination inherent in Holzknecht's essay twenty years earlier—is Jacob's argument that change is the only constant in *The Changeling,* that "every major character is both changing and unchanging," that the only true changelings are thus those who do not change, and that since the only unchanging state is death, the real changelings of the play must be those who die.

Here we have arrived at a textual criticism which is perfectly bemused by itself and entirely disassociated from the emotional center of the text which is its concern. It is particularly interesting in this light, I think, that the full elaboration of Empson's argument for structural unity should generate a criticism that has almost entirely avoided the central point of Empson's own analysis: that the madhouse dominates *The Changeling* in every scene, that De Flores is the fairy-child changeling and as such shares a heritage with the fools and madmen, and that the whole of the bestial horde (and Beatrice's eventual conversion to their ranks) evidences throughout the play how foolish, fragile, and tenuous are the comfortable assumptions for rational order made by civilized man.

In fact, the thematics of transformation in *The Changeling* derive from—and point toward—an understanding of mutability more primal, more unsettling, more incapable of rational analysis and reduction than that which is generally assumed or argued for. The essential power of the play does not lie in the complex, brainy ethics and metaphysics of mutability, but in the hollow, brooding tension between its own frightening dispassion and the blunt release of primordial violence, madness, and sexuality within an impotent, repressive, wedding-cake civilization manned by straw moralists and sanctimonious fools dressed as gentility. *The Changeling* is a monster story: the monster loses, but the winners are frauds. Because of this, the play ends with a question and so generates, at the very least, ambiguous and unsettling responses to its characters and to its story. Much of the strength of the play lies in its obsessive irresolution, in its lack of effective catharsis or anagnorisis; if *The Changeling* is unified at all, then, it is certainly not so by virtue of abstract concept or formal structure but by such things as symbol, image, and mood.

If we begin from these premises, it is clear that *The Changeling* provides us no grounds for explaining away, let alone moralizing, the liaison between Beatrice and De Flores, even though coming to some resolution of the events in the play requires it. However bewildered and misguided she is or savage and pathetic she becomes, Beatrice is neither naïf nor lamia; neither is De Flores, for all his cunning and violence, an amoral destroyer in the mold of Iago. Both inherit a destiny that amazes them more than it does the members of Vermandero's household who gather at the final unmasking. For his part, De Flores is motivated by a love for Beatrice that he fully recognizes as irrational and even perverse. He is "enjoined" to pursue her despite her scorn and revulsion; for this, he is an "ass" who must constantly devise circumstances to trigger her contempt, a "common Garden bull" who backs off only as preparation for a new barrage of harassment and disgust. It is an affliction, moreover, that is getting worse rather than better:

> Whatever ails me? Now a-late especially
> I can as well be hang'd as refrain seeing her;
> Some twenty times a day, nay, not so little,
> Do I force errands, frame ways and excuses
> To come into her sight, and I have small reason for't
> And less encouragement; for she baits me still
> Every time worse than other, does profess herself
> The cruelest enemy to my face in town,
> At no hand can abide the sight of me,
> As if danger, or ill-luck, hung in my looks.
>
> (II.i.27-36)

Unable to explain his compulsion even to himself, De Flores rationalizes his odd behavior by appealing to pragmatic expedients which at least give him a measure of distance and a working excuse: Beatrice's contempt for him is as extreme and as irrational as his desire for her; moreover, experience offers some hope in that others worse favored than he have had remarkable success. "I ha' seen," he concludes, "Women have chid themselves abed to men."

The simple fact, however, is that ugly and despicable De Flores, who knows his case to be triply hopeless (he is loathsome; he is a servant; she is already betrothed), is hopelessly and stupidly in love with Beatrice-Joanna. What he stumbles on, unbelievably, deliriously stumbles on, is a sudden and unexpected opportunity not only to win in one moment Beatrice's devotion and gratitude but to become her sexual partner as well—indeed, her sexual author and sexual proprietor. There is no question that De Flores will pay her asking price, not because he is without conscience but because he is driven by a far higher imperative against which the conventions of social morality are a trifle. It is only after the fact that De Flores comes to apprehend how the fortuitous circumstances that brought him Beatrice-Joanna were the workings of a social and psychological destiny necessitating their union and completely validating his actions and his existence. Victim as well as villain, De Flores elects to embrace the opportunity that will simultaneously save him and damn him. In the end, De Flores knows that Beatrice is wholly his; more importantly, he has also come to know that this is the only thing he wanted, and that he can richly "thank life for nothing / But that pleasure."

Beatrice's anxiety is much more acute because she does not

bear the external deformities that encourage De Flores to accept his alienation when the opportunity for fulfillment arises. Beatrice must struggle with her beauty, her status, her sex, each of which is a powerful enemy that strongly interferes with any desire or opportunity she may have for genuine growth or self-realization. Because she is young, rich, beautiful, and the daughter of a lord, Beatrice is vain, chaste, coy, arrogant, inconstant, and wholly insecure and unhappy. Emotionally powerful, Beatrice is effectively powerless; and it is her lack of power that eventually consigns her to her unhappy destiny. She is a member of a society whose elaborate and empty fictions can account neither for her feelings nor her being. A sad inheritress of a social structure predicated on a smug, masculine, thorough-going but thoroughly impotent dualism, she is understandably incapable of working out an effective formula in which she can order her various desires: security, admiration, passion, purity. She "falls in love" with beautiful men because, being a beautiful woman, she has no other alternative; betrothed to one Spanish nobleman but terrified of her sexual identity, or lack of identity, she must of necessity "change her saint" as the opportunity arises, which it constantly must. Piracquo must be followed be Alsemero who must in turn be followed by another lord, yet more beautiful, yet more noble, yet more desirable. Paying dutiful lip service (because there is no other kind of service paid) to an ethic that inexorably divides sanctity and lust, "true" and "false" devotion, Beatrice has no way to reconcile her sexual desires with her sense of self: she must both love and loathe her sexual arousal.

To Beatrice lust is "ugly" and "poisonous" because the only language she has ever been taught defines her emotions precisely in those terms; she must see her passion and her beauty as contradictory—the first a devotion based on blood and guilt, the second a devotion based on spirit and virtue. De Flores' ugly and loathsome face, so perfectly and so visibly contrary to her own beautiful one, is thus for her an inescapable and certain goad. She must be at once repelled and drawn to him, as she must recognize that her "giddy turning" is the signature of a destiny that will destroy her if she cannot discover some way, powerless as she is, to avoid it. Beatrice does, in fact, seek to avoid it in the only way she knows how: she appeals to Alsemero, her new love, hoping that he will guide her from the labyrinth by offering a sexual love that is itself beautiful.

But Alsemero can offer Beatrice nothing of the kind. He too is a beauty, and all his modes of knowing are confined to a structure wholly inappropriate to the circumstances of existence. Well-meaning but stupid, dutifully caring but completely insensitive, Alsemero simply cannot speak the mad language Beatrice needs to hear (she, of course, can hardly speak it herself), so he can never understand her and never love her. By turns condescending, supercilious, self-assured, honorable, upright, reassuring, paternal, smug, virtuous, Alsemero has no way of hearing, let alone responding meaningfully to, Beatrice's confusion and despair. Moreover, he is as confused by his sexual identity as is Beatrice, incapable of seeing women as anything other than virgins or whores and so consequently deeply troubled by his own sexual motivations. At the end of the entire debacle, nothing relieves Alsemero more than to hear Beatrice confess that it was not her but Diaphanta who shared his wedding-night bed; it is this admission that allows Alsemero to proclaim himself free of infection and so confidently and condescendingly to reassure his father-in-law that he has nothing to lament, since "Justice hath so right / The guilty hit, that innocence is quit / By proclamation and may joy again." And it is precisely this universal capacity for moral handwashing that allows Alsemero to divert attention from the "broken rib of mankind" at his feet by engaging the whole company in a catholic and utterly bloodless rumination on the curiosities of change and the strange transformations brought about by the recently opacous moon. Alsemero is a zombie.

Beatrice, of course, neither knows this nor would know what to do if she *did* know it. What she does know is that her eyes clearly tell her that Alsemero, not Piracquo, is the man meant for her, which means that Piracquo stands between her and the true devotion that is her rightful destiny. To powerless, passionate, fearful Beatrice, beautiful and noble Alsemero is home:

> I have within mine eye all my desires;
> Requests that holy prayers ascend heaven for
> And brings 'em down to furnish our defects
> Come not more sweet to our necessities
> Than thou unto my wishes.
>
> (II.ii.8-12)

It is Alsemero, Beatrice mistakenly believes, who can heal the monstrous and alien defects within her by dissolving the grip of necessity they exercise over her: Alsemero will make her whole. "W'are so like / In our expressions, lady, that unless I borrow / The same words, I shall never find their equals," Alsemero graciously responds, all the while entirely misapprehending the nature and substance of Beatrice's appeal to him.

To the genuine dilemma both lovers face (presumably they both face it) occasioned by Beatrice's promise to Piracquo and Vermandero's correlative command, Alsemero the zombie can think of nothing other than the obvious, and obviously stupid, solution: he will challenge Piracquo to a duel of honor and so valorously and nobly solve both problems in a single action. With no answer of her own, this is nevertheless precisely what Beatrice does not want to hear from her professed equal-thinking lover:

> How? Call you that extinguishing of fear
> When 'tis the only way to keep it flaming?
> Are not you ventured in the action
> That's all my joys and comforts? Pray, no more, sir.
> Say you prevail'd; you're danger's and not mine
>   then.
> The law would claim you from me, or obscurity
> Be made the grave to bury you alive.
> I'm glad these thoughts come forth; oh, keep not one
> Of this condition, sir. Here was a course
> Found to bring sorrow on her way to death;
> The tears would ne'er ha' dried till dust had chok'd 'em.
>
> (II.ii.29-39)

It is at this moment that Beatrice decides that she must take things into her own hands, wholly unprepared and misled though she is. Actually, being incapable of decision-making, Beatrice decides nothing. What "occurs" to her, with the force and conviction of inspiration, is that ugliness must fight ugliness if beauty is to be kept free of stain. Hence the obvious, inescapable answer to the newly-monstrous Piracquo is the eternally-monstrous De Flores, whose explicit deformity clearly names him as "blood-guilty." Beatrice does not share her plan with Alsemero because she knows she *cannot* share it with him—committed as he is to being noble, Alsemero must reject murder-by-contract while offering in its place only the equally absurd alternatives of a love-duel (which, regardless of the results, must prevent their love) or stoic and sad acceptance of their destiny (which must also prevent their love).

Though Beatrice makes the wrong choice, then, she makes the only choice she can: she must kiss poison, stroke the serpent, if she wishes to inherit the earthly paradise she feels is rightfully hers. Consequently, it is an especially hypocritical Alsemero, horrified by uncovering blackest sin and infection in the creature he has lusted after and even (as he thinks) mated with, who condemns Beatrice for the very crime he himself offered to commit in the name of honor, nobility, and, of course, sanctity. As for the very human and urgent matter of sexual love and carnal intercourse, Alsemero has nothing but a pathological preoccupation with purity, a distrust of eros, a few wedding-night jokes, and a chemical virginity test taught him by a Chaldean. "Oh, were she the sole glory of the earth, / Had eyes that could shoot fire into kings' breasts, / And touch'd, she sleeps not here," Alsemero self-righteously proclaims, never imagining for a moment that his utter failure as a lover, as a husband, indeed as a human being, has put a firm stamp of approval on the pathetic script Beatrice must act out.

The blackest moment of *The Changeling* is not the spectacle of a thoroughly-broken and harried Beatrice being ceremoniously hauled before her domestic tribunal; it is witnessing Beatrice in her last act beg forgiveness of those—zombies all—who are wholly incapable of forgiveness and whose incapacity and inertia have, to such a great extent, driven her to a miserable end. Deprived of any strength, any self-knowledge, any capacity for imaginative response, Beatrice is a victim, as she is also a sad artificer, of the social order in which she is constrained to exist. It is only De Flores who genuinely understands her, only De Flores who genuinely responds to her and genuinely loves her, and so it must be De Flores who destroys her—the alternative of their free, mutual, carnal, ecstatic human love completely unavailable in Alicante, or, more accurately, available only to the insane, the maimed, the alien, all of which the social order quickly destroys, or else cages for general amusement and entertainment.

In Middleton's Alicante, only the weak survive, which they do with a vengeance. They do so by denying their humanity—that is, denying their mortality, mutability, carnality. One, of course, can deny none of these, which means they must be enervated and eviscerated by redefinition and transformation. In short, to achieve the *stasis* that is the aim of socialization, social man must commit to the elaborate construction of a doublespeak that both names and transfigures (to misapply Yeats) "all that dread." Any eruption of the *grundsprache*—the atavistic language in which eroticism, death, mutation, the *ec-static* are primal roots of meaning—must therefore be suppressed, or radically sublimated in the form of social rituals (such as courtship), innuendoes, puns, rationalizations, obscenities, gibberish, banter. As a suitor, nothing preoccupies Alsemero more than speaking a language which achieves his end (sexual fruition) while concealing his motives, especially from himself, in a cloud of reassurance and rational moralizing. He loves Beatrice's beauties "to the holy purpose," he tells himself, thereby countering Jasperino's suggestion that his unusual behavior indicates a change of heart: "I keep the same church, same devotion." Disturbed by his appetite but determined not to give it its proper name, Alsemero is perfectly unprepared to respond to Beatrice while perfectly prepared to play the polished suitor he has never yet been. In the deep science of zombie love, Alsemero is skillful; he can "sing at first sight."

To Beatrice, who sings this language herself, Alsemero holds forth the promise of transforming her sexual dread to bliss by sublimating the beast that haunts her. What Alsemero does instead is to dismiss the beast, as he must, by a rhetorically appropriate but utterly jejune rationalization that avoids the issue Beatrice cannot allow herself to articulate. De Flores, she confesses, is her "infirmity," for which she cannot account other than "his or hers, of some particular thing / They must abandon as a deadly poison, / Which to a thousand other tastes were wholesome. / Such to mine eyes is that same fellow there, / The same that report speaks of the basilisk." Alsemero responds by assuring her that he too has the same infirmity ("we are so like in our expression, lady," etc.) and glibly converting the whole matter into another instance—exactly as he does at the end of the play with his ruminations on change—of an ancient truth that calls for elucidation: in this instance, *de gustibus non est disputandem.* "Some people hate oil, some wine, some the scent of roses," Alsemero concludes, "and you just happen to hate De Flores." Necessarily dissatisfied with this answer as she is later alarmed by his suggestion that he solve the whole problem by challenging Piracquo to a duel, Beatrice presses Alsemero to share his infirmity with her. His inane answer ("what might be your desire perhaps, a cherry") underscores how completely removed Alsemero and his social habits are from the world of experience Beatrice is struggling to cope with.

To these examples we can add the remainder of Alsemero's impoverished lexicon, including the juvenile virginity test (where he once again conceals his true motives) and his final castigation of Beatrice as a "whore," which, in the social niceties of Alicante, is the ultimate obscenity one zombie can hurl at another (and so Beatrice, never set free, is properly horrified at hearing herself so named). "Oh, thou art all deformed," Alsemero says, staring at Beatrice's face with the same horror and revulsion Beatrice has felt for De Flores—a revulsion Alsemero has dismissed as but a "frequent frailty in our nature." Compared to this, Beatrice's admiration of ugly De Flores as a "man worth lov-

ing," too little, too desperate, too late though it is, has an authority nowhere found in the language of her lover, her friends, her father.

Nowhere, that is, except in the language of De Flores, whose lexical alternative to Alsemero's "glass with the letter M" ("And question not my purpose") is Piracquo's severed finger, ring still attached, waved in Beatrice's face as frankly symbolic of the unambiguous bargain they have struck. Deformed as he is, De Flores is no scholar nor one of love's artful singers. His courtship, hopeless as he knows it to be, is articulated in the bald, biological ritual of thrusting his ugly face into Beatrice's beautiful one at every available opportunity, even if he has to "frame ways and excuses," even if he has to be an "ass" to do it. Nothing unsettles Beatrice more than this blunt grammar, which addresses her own desires and so her own self contempt—addresses both the terrifying loving and loathing Alsemero will not recognize—so clearly that she cannot allow herself to understand. She "dares" not. A spectator, as she thinks, not an inmate of the asylum whose members are to dance at her wedding, Beatrice hears in the howling gibberish of the bestial mob an all-too-sensible, all-too-disturbing appeal. De Flores is neither madman or fool, but he is of their kind and in their image by the simple fact of his deformity and alienation. He is the repressed, alien self whose name must never be mentioned, a name that "blasts a beauty to deformity."

"All Freaks," Leslie Fiedler comments [in his *Freaks: Myths & Images of the Secret Self,* 1978], "are perceived to one degree or another as erotic. Indeed, abnormality arouses in some 'normal' beholders a temptation to go beyond looking to *knowing* in the full carnal sense the ultimate other." For sexually-charged Beatrice, De Flores is truly the "ultimate other," an unambiguous, monstrous manifestation of her secret self her social world has at once engendered and then forbidden her to explore. The terrible seduction scene Beatrice must endure, replete with her pathetic dodges, disclaimers, protestations, denials, and humiliations, is a sad measure of the madness the normal world requires of her. For his part, De Flores is tortured by none of the psychological anguish Beatrice must undergo in search of her sexual identity. Once he discovers, rapturously discovers, that what he has only surmised is in fact true—that by becoming monstrous he has become indispensable to Beatrice—De Flores gladly embraces his monstrosity and challenges Beatrice to accept hers. "Though thou writ'st maid," De Flores tells a terrified, trembling, wholly aroused Beatrice:

> . . . thou whore in thy affection,
> 'Twas chang'd from thy first love, and that's a kind
> Of whoredom in thy heart; and he's chang'd now
> To bring thy second on, thy Alsemero,
> Whom (by all sweets that ever darkness tasted),
> If I enjoy thee not, thou ne'er enjoy'st.
>
> (III.iv.143-148)

Treated as a monster, De Flores responds in kind. Changeling Beatrice, playing at love, gets what she desires and despises—changeling De Flores.

This returns us to Middleton's much-worried title and to the obscure "cangoun" of my own; it also brings us back to the general issue of change in the play. As noted earlier, the title of the play has been lugged in on behalf of every conceivable claim for the endless nuances of "changeability" and "changeableness" singular to the play. That this is by-and-large a misguided endeavor, fed though it is by the characters of the play and supported by the editors of the *OED,* is indicated by a number of things that point in a very different direction. The first is that, for all the declamations to the contrary, no one changes in Middleton's zombieland—no one *really* changes, that is. It is the terrible absence not the preponderance of transformation that rules the world of the play, for genuine mutability is the one thing the walking dead of Alicante must deny and resist at all costs. As change is the single great enemy of sexual and social ordering, change must consequently be denatured and absorbed if the *status quo* is to survive. This is why Alsemero encourages the cataloguing of changes at the end of the play and why everyone joins right in. Readily describing an endless variety of "changes" that are somewhere on the order of a change from Gleem to Crest, the robots of Alicante quickly regroup, suffering no more than a momentary, horrifying glimpse into the consequences of their own alienation, of their own beauty. In Alicante, in fact, there is no alternative for real, meaningful, purposive, substantive change: since it is only in this activity that human beings can hope to discover themselves or hope to live full and valuable lives, Beatrice's failure in love—indeed, everyone's failure in life—is foredoomed.

In addition, there is good reason to doubt the editors of the *OED* and to recognize, as Empson did, De Flores as Middleton's changeling. According to the etymology provided in the *OED,* the English word "changeling" is a diminutive of the French root *"change,"* its earliest usages (a "changeling" as a "changeable person") understandably directly pointing toward that root. But it is highly unlikely that a root which is an abstract verb should be converted into a highly particular substantive and then applied to a most specific group of creatures (fools, idiots, deformed "fairy" children) long known to Western folklore and long antedating the first citation of the term given by the *OED.* Kiessling [in his *The Incubus in English Literature: Provenance and Progeny,* 1977] traces changeling stories at least back to the ninth century, arguing that monstrous offspring have been long understood in Western literature as progeny of the child-stealing night creatures—those children clearly not "in the image" just as clearly being "in the other image." These creatures are "changed" not merely because of the machinery of myth defines them as *ex*-changed but because they are mutants, monsters, aliens, freaks—"changed" beings in the primal sense of otherness. A group of Old French and Middle English words etymologically similar to "change" but closely associated with the image of the imbecile and the monster indicates this root—these words apparently derive from the Old French *"cangoun"* (the deformed, exchanged child) and include substantive variants such as "cangun" and "congoun" as well as the derivative adjectives "chang," "cang," "cange" and others.

In Middle English texts the word is most commonly used to indicate a fool or idiot, commonly in connection with the corresponding characteristic of "lewd" or "lustful," such as occurs in the compound *"cangeien"* or the phrase *"cang ehen"* (lustful eyes) in the following sentence from the *Ancren Riwle:*

> *. . . tu a sunful mon art . . . to keasten cang ehen up o yung wummon.*

> (. . . you are a sinful man . . . to cast lewd eyes upon a young woman.)
>
> *Ancren Riwle,* 14b.

Another citation from the same text indicates the most common adjectival form of the root; in this case the phrase *"cang men"* means "fools":

> *Worldes weole . . . bidweolieð cang men to luuien a schadewe.*

> (Worldly happiness . . . beguiles fools to love a shadow.)
>
> *Ancren Riwle,* 52a.

More specific application of the term, particularly with regard to the legend that attributed deformity, mutation, and forms of imbecility to the work of malign spirits (and a related legend that attributed special concupisence to those changeling creatures), is evident in this warning against marriage from *Hali Maedenhede:*

> *Bisih þe, seli meiden, beo þe cnot icnut aenef of wedlac, beo he cangun oð er crupel, beo he hwuch-se eauer be, þu most to him halden.*

> (Beware, silly maiden, once the marriage knot is tied, no matter if he is an idiot or a cripple or whatever else he may be, you must nevertheless keep to him.)
>
> *Hali Maedenhede,* 479-481.

Here the term *"cangun"* is treated as syntactically parallel to *"crupel"* and might be translated either as "an idiot" or as "a changeling." That the word includes as one of its fundamental meanings the deformed changeling child (that it is not, in other words, merely a general term to denote a fool) is apparent in a final example from the *Ancren Riwle* in which both the general adjectival and particular substantive forms of the root appear:

> *Cang dohter inwurð as mone i wonunge, priueð as þe cangoun, se lengre se wurse.*

> (A foolish daughter is worth a waning moon; like the changeling, the longer she lasts, the worse she becomes.)
>
> *Ancren Riwle,* f.29r.

The *"cang dohter"* in this citation is a translation of the *fatua filia* of *Ecclesiasticus* 22.3, so here *"cang"* means "foolish." *"Cangoun,"* however, means "changeling," and in particular the monstrous fairy child exchanged for the beautiful human one, a child that only gets progressively worse the longer it survives.

This suggests that we understand the changeling—in its most fundamental sense—as a member of a class of creatures who are aliens by virtue of their mutation, or mutants by virtue of their alienation; this class includes among its members beings such as freaks, idiots, retards, monsters, feral children, dwarfs, hunchbacks, Moors, wild men, cripples, giants and the like. It also suggests that there is a primal association, built into language and intrinsic somehow to the act of socialization, that unites the concept of change with the image of the mutant—an etymological heritage misrepresented in the definition of "changeling" in the *OED* but powerfully, numbly articulated within Middleton's play. It is particularly interesting in this light that another common root for change, the Indo-European *"al"* (Greek *allos*) means "other" as well. From this root we get the words "alter," "alien," and even "adulter." This points to the existence of the mutant within the *status quo* as a profoundly disturbing reminder of the obdurate mutability and mortality, the essential and irreducible reality, of human kind—a fact those of the tribe created in *imago deus* are perpetually and necessarily preoccupied with denying, avoiding, rationalizing, repressing.

It is this notion of the changeling—this *image,* really—that is so fundamental to Middleton's play. What remains hovering over the wreckage, what remains as the iconographic center of *The Changeling,* is De Flores' silent, scrofulous, pock-marked face, visible most clearly in the circle of beauties posturing over the corpses that lie at their feet. Two earlier and parallel images which have been hinted at but hidden from us throughout, both of them equally mute and grotesque, finally appear in the terrible celebration of the closing scene. The first is that of the bored gentry of Alicante who seek amusement by visiting the freaks, fools, and madmen on display at Alibius' asylum; the second is that of the bestial anti-masque, the madman's morris, planned as the special entertainment for Beatrice's wedding. In the frozen antics of those left posed over Beatrice and her monster-lover, we see a savage mimicry of those earlier spectators, seeking reassurance and fleeing life by collectively mocking and scorning the true self, the terribly beautiful and horrible self, they secretly know is also theirs.

To this degree, *The Changeling,* with its incessant savagery, its utter rejection of sentimentality, its vision of society bleak to the point of nihilism, poses a naked challenge to its readers and to its audience—the same challenge faced and failed by the gentry of Alicante. That challenge can be voiced in a single word: change. Dispassioned ruminations on the intricate variations of transformation in *The Changeling* miss the point of the play as surely as the zombies of Alicante misapprehend the beasts they compliment themselves on having destroyed. Eventually, the criticism demanded by *The Changeling* is not that of rational discourse, but that of personal action and commitment to the reformation of man and the construction of a social order responsive to, rather than repressive of, the suffering, beauty, love, lust, hatred, and death that are the radicals of the human condition. To this end, *The Changeling* is itself no beauty: it is a mutant made of farce and fury, a monster made of passionate shrieks and blank stares, a freak half-finished with an arm too many or a leg too few. Art,

changeling art, Middleton seems to suggest, may be capable of effecting the transformation man and society must have; if there is any hope in Middleton's vision, this is it. *The Changeling,* however, leaves little doubt as to what its author thinks the real chances are.

BIBLIOGRAPHY

Brodwin, Leonara Leet. *Elizabethan Love Tragedy, 1587-1625.* New York: New York University Press, 1971: 151-179.

Eliot, T. S. "Thomas Middleton." *Elizabethan Essays.* London: Faber & Faber, 1934: 87-100.

Empson, William. *Some Versions of Pastoral.* Norfolk: New Directions, 1950: 48-52.

Holzknecht, Karl. "The Dramatic Structure of *The Changeling." Renaissance Papers: A Selection of Papers Presented at the Renaissance Meeting in the Southeastern States,* ed. Allan H. Gilbert. Orangeburg: University of South Carolina Press, 1954: 77-87. The essay is reprinted in *Shakespeare's Contemporaries,* ed. Max Bluestone & Norman Rabkin. Englewood Cliffs: Prentice Hall, 1961: 263-272.

Jacobs, Henry E. "The Constancy of Change: Character and Perspective in *The Changeling." Texas Studies in Language and Literature,* 16 (1975): 651-674.

Johnson, Paula. "Dissimulation Anatomized: *The Changeling." Philological Quarterly,* 56 (1977): 329-338.

Jordan, Robert. "Myth and Psychology in *The Changeling." Renaissance Drama* (New Series), ed. S. Schoenbaum, 3 (1970): 157-165.

Levin, Richard. *The Multiple Plot in English Renaissance Drama.* Chicago: University of Chicago Press, 1971: 34-48.

Pentzell, Raymond J. *"The Changeling:* Notes on Mannerism in Dramatic Form." *Comparative Drama,* 9 (1975): 3-28.

Roy, E. "Sexual Paradox in *The Changeling." Literature and Psychology,* 25 (1975): 124-132.

Williams, George W., ed. *The Changeling.* (Regents Renaissance Drama.) Lincoln: University of Nebraska Press, 1966. Introduction.

FURTHER READING

BIBLIOGRAPHIES

Steen, Sara Jayne. *Thomas Middleton: A Reference Guide.* Boston: G. K. Hall, 1984, 297 p.

Annotated list of materials relating to Middleton published from 1800 to 1978.

Tannenbaum, Samuel A. *Thomas Middleton: A Concise Bibliography*. Elizabethan Bibliographies Number 13. New York: Samuel A. Tannenbaum, 1940, 35 p.

Primary and secondary bibliography including sections on Middleton's plays, masques, prose works and poems, collections, and biographies of the author.

Wolff, Dorothy. *Thomas Middleton: An Annotated Bibliography*. New York: Garland Publishing, 1985, 138 p.

Divides its entries into book-length works on Middleton and journal articles. Features a section on foreign-language studies.

OVERVIEWS AND GENERAL STUDIES

Asp, Carolyn. *A Study of Thomas Middleton's Tragicomedies*. Jacobean Drama Studies, No. 28. Salzburg: Institut für Englishe Sprache und Literatur, 1974, 282 p.

Provides a general introduction to Middleton's efforts in the genre and gives special consideration to *A Fair Quarrel*, *The Old Law*, and *The Witch*.

Barker, Richard Hindry. *Thomas Middleton*. New York: Columbia University Press, 1958, 216 p.

Important biographical and critical overview of the playwright and his work.

Brittin, Norman A. *Thomas Middleton*. Twayne's English Author Series. New York: Twayne Publishers, 1972, 176 p.

Overview of Middleton's life and career that attempts to "provide a guide to the whole body of Middleton's work in the light of contemporary scholarship."

Covatta, Anthony. *Thomas Middleton's City Comedies*. Cranbury, N.J.: Associated University Presses, 1973, 187 p.

Argues that Middleton's comedies "should be studied not as social documents but as fictions," best seen as "dramatic constructs, put together by a man of considerable intelligence, wit, and dramatic skill."

Dominik, Mark. *Shakespeare-Middleton Collaborations*. Beaverton, Ore.: Alioth Press, 1988, 173 p.

Contends that *Timon of Athens*, *A Yorkshire Tragedy*, and *The Puritan* are all works that "show mixed Shakespearean and Middletonian characteristics."

Ellis-Fermor, Una. "Middleton." In her *Jacobean Drama: An Interpretation*, pp. 128-52. London: Methuen & Co., 1958.

Seeks to identify the essential characteristics of Middletonian drama, finding that the playwright's keen powers of observation were a source of both his strength and his shortcomings. "Faithful to his observation and to the record of underlying psychological laws which it revealed to him," Middleton was, she states, "untouched by the heroic, the romantic and the pathetic mood, to the very belittling of [his] human figures."

Ewbank, Inga-Stina. "The Middle of Middleton." In *The Arts of Performance in Elizabethan and Early Stuart Drama: Essays for G.K. Hunter*, edited by Murray Biggs and others, pp. 156-72. Edinburgh: Edinburgh University Press, 1991.

Examines Middleton's tragicomedies, particularly *The Witch*, *A Fair Quarrel*, and *More Dissemblers besides Women*. Ewbank finds that Middleton's skepticism toward human nature is the source of the "theatrical energy" of these plays.

Farr, Dorothy M. *Thomas Middleton and the Drama of Realism*. Edinburgh: Oliver & Boyd, 1973, 139 p.

Considers seven of Middleton's plays, including *A Chaste Maid in Cheapside*, *The Changeling*, *Women Beware Women*, and *A Game at Chess*.

Hallett, Charles A. "Middleton's Overreachers and the Ironic Ending." *Tennessee Studies in Literature* XVI (1971): 1-13.

Scrutinizes what he feels are the failings in Middleton's dramatic technique in his early comedies, citing the playwright's "inability to merge theme, plot, and character into a unified whole."

Heinemann, Margot. *Puritanism and Theatre: Thomas Middleton and Opposition Drama under the Early Stuarts*. Cambridge: Cambridge University Press, 1980, 300 p.

Sets out to examine Middleton's work "in relation to the society and social movements of his time, and, in particular, to trace what connections it may have had with radical, Parliamentarian or Puritan movements and groupings."

Hibbard, G. R. "The Tragedies of Thomas Middleton and the Decadence of Drama." *Renaissance and Modern Studies* I (1957): 35-64.

Examines *Women Beware Women* and *The Changeling* for evidence that Middleton was "a man with fresh intuitions about the nature of tragic experience, seeking to embody those intuitions in dramatic form, trying hard to escape from the shackles of the past and never quite managing to do so."

Holmes, David M. *The Art of Thomas Middleton: A Critical Study*. Oxford: Clarendon Press, 1970, 235 p.

Proposes to "provide an appreciation of [Middleton's] art and of the point of view and feeling that underlie it."

Holtz-Davies, Ingrid. "*A Chaste Maid in Cheapside* and *Women Beware Women*: Feminism, Anti-feminism and the Limitations of Satire." *Cahiers Élisabéthains* 39 (April 1991): 29-39.

Detects "misogynist tendencies" in the two plays that "cannot be attributed to the depiction of individual characters but only to the sensibility which created these plays."

Jackson, MacD. P. *Studies in Attribution: Middleton and Shakespeare*. Salzburg: Institut für Englische Sprach und Literatur, 1979, 228 p.

Applies a number of linguistic, bibliographic, and other tests to a variety of plays known to be by Middleton or attributed to him in an effort to more clearly define the author's canon.

Kirsh, Arthur C. "Middleton." In his *Jacobean Dramatic Perspectives*, pp. 75-96. Charlottesville: The University Press of Virginia, 1972.

Maintains that, despite the heterogeneity of Middleton's output, all the plays in which he had a hand "reveal an identical and powerful dramatic 'point of view'."

Leggatt, Alexander. *Citizen Comedy in the Age of Shakespeare.* Toronto: University of Toronto Press, 1973, 167 p.

Considers numerous plays by Middleton, including *A Mad World My Masters*, *A Chaste Maid in Cheapside*, and *Michaelmas Term* in an investigation of the general characteristics of the genre of comedy set in London's urban milieu.

Schoenbaum, Samuel. *Middleton's Tragedies: A Critical Study.* New York: Gordian Press, 1970, 275 p.

Influential investigation of Middleton's principal efforts in the genre, divided into two sections: the first offers critical assessments of the plays; the second considers problems of attribution and the canon of Middletonian tragedy. Schoenbaum's criticisms of *The Revenger's Tragedy* are reprinted in the entry above.

Steen, Sara Jayne. *Ambrosia in an Earthen Vessel: Three Centuries of Audience and Reader Response to the Works of Thomas Middleton.* New York: AMS Press, 1993, 240 p.

Reprints extracts of commentary on Middleton's plays, from the earliest appreciations by his contemporaries to late nineteenth-century criticism and reviews.

A MAD WORLD MY MASTERS

Farley-Hills, David. "A Satire against Mankind: Middleton's *A Mad World, My Masters*." In his *The Comic in Renaissance Comedy*, pp. 81-107. Totowa, N.J.: Barnes & Noble Books, 1981.

Analyzes the play as both a realistic commentary on contemporary life and a morality play.

Marotti, Arthur F. "The Method in the Madness of *A Mad World, My Masters*." *Tennessee Studies in Literature* XV (1970): 99-108.

Argues that "because, in this comedy, Middleton expresses the problem of perception through various theatrical means, the relation of illusion to reality comments on the nature of the dramatic art itself."

Slights, William W. E. "The Trickster-Hero and Middleton's *A Mad World, My Masters*." *Comparative Drama* III, No. 2 (Summer 1969): 87-98.

Describes Follywit as a combination of two character types derived from ancient Roman comedy: the adolescent and the witty slave.

Takase, Fumiko. "Thomas Middleton's Antifeminist Sentiment in *A Mad World, My Masters*." In *Playing with Gender: A Renaissance Pursuit*, edited by Jean R. Brink, Maryanne C. Horowitz, and Allison P. Coudert, pp. 19-31. Urbana: University of Illinois Press, 1991.

Evaluates the "persistent association of woman with lust and the devil" that Middleton exploits in the comedy. Takase concludes: "By reducing the actions of everyone, men and women, to the single instinct of lust. . . , the

dramatist strips humankind of all disguise and portrays the human race as devoid of any passion except lust. . . . If women are the pit of hell, men 'willingly' fall into it."

THE REVENGER'S TRAGEDY

Ayres, Philip J. *Tourneur: "The Revenger's Tragedy."* London: Edward Arnold, 1977, 62 p.

Examines several "dimensions" of the play, including the ironic, the comic, the tragic, and the social. Ayres also provides information on background and sources and recent stage productions of the tragedy.

Eliot, T. S. "Cyril Tourneur." *The Times Literary Supplement* (13 November 1930): 925-26.

Asserts that "for closeness of texture . . . there are no plays beyond Shakespeare's, and the best of Marlowe and Jonson, that can surpass *The Revenger's Tragedy*." Eliot ascribes the play to Tourneur.

Foakes, R.A. Introduction to *The Revenger's Tragedy* by Cyril Tourneur, pp. xix-lxix. Cambridge, Mass.: Harvard University Press, 1966.

Wide-ranging overview of the play that considers such issues as date, text, sources, and authorship, as well as an aesthetic appreciation.

Gibbons, Brian. Introduction to *The Revenger's Tragedy* by Cyril Tourneur, pp. xi-xxx. New York: Hill and Wang, 1967.

General survey of the play that includes a discussion of the authorship controversy. Gibbons concludes that "it seems reasonable to ascribe the play to Cyril Tourneur, allowing that it reveals the influence of Thomas Middleton," among others.

Murray, Peter B. "The Anonymous *Revenger's Tragedy*." In his *A Study of Cyril Tourneur*, pp. 144-257. Philadelphia: University of Pennsylvania Press, 1964.

Exhaustive stylistic, structural, and linguistic analysis of the play. Murray maintains that "the great weight of the internal evidence" indicates that Middleton wrote the tragedy.

THE ROARING GIRL

Comensoli, Viviana. "Play-making, Domestic Conduct, and the Multiple Plot in *The Roaring Girl*." *Studies in English Literature 1500-1900* 27, No. 2 (Spring 1987): 249-66.

Argues that, taken together, the comedy's three plots "convey the concern at the heart of the play with the degeneration of marriage and the family, a tension sustained in the antithesis between the household . . . and the city."

Miller, Jo E. "Women and the Market in *The Roaring Girl*." *Renaissance and Reformation* XIV, No. 1 (Winter 1990): 11-23.

Asserts that "Moll Cutpurse invites us to reevaluate our responses to her and to understand better the freedom and nobility of the tomboy figure on the Renaissance stage who ignores and disrupts her society's rigid constraint of women's subjectivity."

Mulholland, P. "Let her roar again: *The Roaring Girl* Revived."

Research Opportunities in Renaissance Drama XXVIII (1985): 15-27.

> Detailed discussion of a modern production of the play.

Rose, Mary Beth. "Women in Men's Clothing: Apparel and Social Stability in *The Roaring Girl*." *English Literary Renaissance* 14, No. 3 (Autumn 1989): 367-91.

> Examination of Moll Cutpurse that demonstrates how "society's effort to assess the identity of this female figure in male attire becomes the central dramatic and symbolic issue of the play."

A CHASTE MAID IN CHEAPSIDE

Altieri, Joanne. "Against Moralizing Jacobean Comedy: Middleton's *Chaste Maid*." *Criticism* XXX, No. 2 (Spring 1988): 171-87.

> Denies that *A Chaste Maid* is a critique and parody of the conventions of New Comedy, with their stress on romance and marriage; rather, Altieri claims, the play is "based on the trickster comedy which creates its plot-grounding errors from deceptions as opposed to the recognitions of romance."

Van den Broek, A .G. "Take the Number Seven in Cheapside." *Studies in English Literature 1500-1900* 28, No. 2 (Spring 1988): 319-30.

> Proposes that the plot of *A Chaste Maid* enacts the ending of one seven-year "social contract" and the beginning of another. Middleton, Van den Broek states, "depicts Cheapside society at a critical point, following a . . . period of decadence and depravity. A change is inevitable."

WOMEN BEWARE WOMEN

Bromham, A. A. "The Tragedy of Peace: Political Meaning in *Women Beware Women*." *Studies in English Literature 1500-1900* 26, No. 2 (Spring 1986): 309-29.

> Seeks to show "through an examination of verbal and image series and of the use of setting and spatial perspectives, how motif and dramatic effect are integrally

related to political viewpoint" in the play.

Dawson, Anthony B. "*Women Beware Women* and the Economy of Rape." *Studies in English Literature 1500-1900* 27, No. 2 (Spring 1987): 303-20.

> Examines "what rape means in the social and political economy" depicted in the play, specifically its "relationship to sexual blackmail, social institutions, and political power."

Thomson, Leslie. "'Enter Above': The Staging of *Women Beware Women*." *Studies in English Literature 1500-1900* 26, No. 2 (Spring 1986): 331-43.

> Attempts to resolve several complex problems the play presents in terms of staging.

Tricomi, Albert H. "Middleton's *Women Beware Women* as Anticourt Drama." *Modern Language Studies* XIX, No. 2 (Spring 1989): 65-77.

> Contends that the play is a "major political tragedy" and explores the ways in which Middleton "sought to deconstruct the symbolism of power and privilege" with this work.

THE CHANGELING

Simmons, J. L. "Diabolical Realism in Middleton and Rowley's *The Changeling*." *Renaissance Drama* n.s. XI (1980): 135-70.

> Investigates the play's relation to Renaissance views of human psychology and the belief that alien personalities could invade a person's mind. Conjointly, he explores "the artifice whereby the two collaborators were able to exhibit and, simultaneously, to incorporate the alien within the violated personality."

Taylor, J. Chesley. "Metaphors of the Moral World: Structure in *The Changeling*." *Tulane Studies in English* 20 (1972): 41-56.

> Contends that the play is unified by "the Renaissance concept of moral perfection, a concept which offers an implicit alternative to the moral failures of the characters and to the inconstancy which makes them changelings."

Additional coverage of Middleton's life and career is contained in the following source published by Gale Research: *Dictionary of Literary Biography,* **Vol. 58.**

Luigi Pirandello
1867-1936

INTRODUCTION

One of the most important dramatists of the twentieth century, Pirandello prompted a reevaluation of traditional stagecraft through his innovative use of philosophical themes and experimentation with dramatic structure. Preoccupied with the relationships of reality to appearances and of sanity to madness, he often portrayed characters who adopt multiple identities, or "masks," in an effort to reconcile social demands with personal needs. He was closely associated with the Theater of the Grotesque, a dramatic school that stressed the paradoxes and contradictions of life, and was also deeply concerned with making literature a more truthful and effective means for conveying human experience. Toward this end he developed the aesthetic theory of "humorism," which he defined as a mingling of comedy and tragedy to produce simultaneous emotional awareness of both of these aspects of the human condition.

BIOGRAPHICAL INFORMATION

Pirandello was born in Sicily to a prosperous sulphur merchant. Although his father initially sent him to study commerce at the local technical institute, Pirandello found the subject uninteresting and transferred to an academic secondary school, where he excelled in oratory and literature. After graduation, Pirandello attended universities in Palermo, Rome, and finally Bonn, where he earned a doctorate in Romance philology. After his father arranged Pirandello's marriage to Antonietta Portulano, the daughter of a business partner, the couple settled together in Rome and had three children. To support his family, Pirandello was forced to take a position as professor at a women's normal school. In 1904 he realized his first critical success with the novel *Il fu Mattia Pascal* (*The Late Mattia Pascal*), but this was overshadowed when his father's sulphur mines, in which Pirandello was heavily invested, were destroyed in a flood. All of Pirandello's wealth, including his wife's dowry, was wiped out. Upon hearing the news, Antonietta suffered an emotional collapse; she subsequently became delusional and hostile, and was eventually institutionalized. The pressure of Pirandello's personal situation spurred a period of intense creativity from 1916 to 1922, which culminated in the production of his two greatest dramas, *Sei personaggi in cerca d'autore* (*Six Characters in Search of an Author*) and *Enrico IV* (*Henry IV*). Pirandello quickly went from being an author with a respectable but modest reputation to being one of the major literary figures in Italy. In 1934 he was awarded the Nobel Prize in literature. He died in 1936.

MAJOR WORKS

Although Pirandello's first dramas were not staged until he was forty-three years of age, by the time of his death he had written over forty plays. In his most famous work, *Six Characters in Search of an Author*, Pirandello described the plight of six characters who interrupt the rehearsal of another Pirandello play to demand that their stories be acted out. His acknowledgment of the stage as the location of a theatrical performance—a place where life is only simulated—startled audiences and critics alike and heralded the self-conscious use of the theater that is a hallmark of modernist drama. Pirandello followed the success of *Six Characters* with *Henry IV*, which many critics consider his greatest work. Written four years after he had his wife committed, *Henry IV* is an expression of the concern with madness that had been prevalent in Pirandello's personal life and in his art. The play depicts a man who, as the result of an injury suffered at the hands of a rival, believes he is Henry IV. Eventually, he regains his sanity but in a fit of rage kills his rival, so that he must feign continued madness to avoid the consequences of his deed.

CRITICAL RECEPTION

Pirandello described his dramatic works as a "theater of mirrors" in which the audience sees events on stage as a reflection of their own lives: when his characters' doubt their own perceptions of themselves, the audience experiences a simultaneous crisis of self-perception. In questioning the distinction between sanity and madness, he attacked abstract models of objective reality and theories of a static human personality. For these reasons, many critics have labelled him a pessimist and a relativist; others, noting the strong sense of compassion for his characters that Pirandello conveys, contend that Pirandello is not preaching a definable ideology, but is simply expressing his acute consciousness of the absurdities and paradoxes of human life.

PRINCIPAL WORKS

PLAYS

Liolà 1916
Cosí è (se vi pare) [*Right You Are! (If You Think So)*] 1917
Il piacere dell'onestà [*The Pleasure of Honesty*] 1917
L'uomo, la bestia e la virtù [*Man, Beast, and Virtue*] 1919
Sei personaggi in cerca d'autore [*Six Characters in Search of an Author*] 1921
Enrico IV [*Henry IV*] 1922
Vestire gli ignudi [*Naked*] 1922
Ciascuno a suo modo [*Each in His Own Way*] 1924
Come tu mi vuoi [*As You Desire Me*] 1930
Maschere nude [*Naked Masks*] 10 vols. 1930-38
Questa sera si recita a soggetto [*Tonight We Improvise*] 1930
I giganti della montagna [*The Mountain Giants*] 1937

OTHER MAJOR WORKS

Mal giocondo (poetry) 1889
Amori senza amore (short stories) 1894
Beffe della morte e della vita (short stories) 1902
Il fu Mattia Pascal [*The Late Mattia Pascal*] (novel) 1904
Erma bifronte [*Two-faced Herma*] (short stories) 1906
L'esclusa [*The Outcast*] (novel) 1908
L'umorismo [*On Humor*] (essay) 1908
I vecchi e i giovani [*The Old and the Young*] (novel) 1913
Il carnevale dei morti (short stories) 1919
Novelle per un anno. 15 vols. (short stories) 1922-37
Uno, nessuno e centomila [*One, None, and a Hundred Thousand*] (novel) 1926

AUTHOR COMMENTARY

Pirandello Confesses . . . Why and How He Wrote *Six Characters in Search of an Author* (1925)

SOURCE: *The Virginia Quarterly Review,* Vol. 1, No. 1, April, 1925, pp. 36-52.

[*The following is a translation of Pirandello's preface to* Six Characters.]

I had to, to escape from . . . well, that is what I am going to explain.

As I have written elsewhere, the lively little maid-servant who for years and years now (though it seems as though it were only since yesterday) has been waiting on my writing, is for all that not so new at her work. She is often of a somewhat scornful and jesting humor, this *Fantasia* of mine. If, now and then, she is of a humor to dress in black, there is no denying that her solemn apparel is often extremely odd. But if you think that this is her usual style of dress, you are very much mistaken. Time and time again I've seen her put her hand in her pocket and pull out a fool's cap, red as a cox-comb, and all a-jingle with its tiny bells. This she claps on her head, and off she goes! Here today, and somewhere else tomorrow!—And she persists in bringing back with her the most disgruntled beings imaginable and filling up my house with them—men, women and children, all involved in the most extraordinary and complicated situations—their plans frustrated, their hopes deluded—in short, people it is often very uncomfortable to deal with.

Well, a few years ago *Fantasia* was unfortunately inspired—or it may have been just an unlucky whim on her part—to unload a whole family on me. I don't know where in the world she had fished these people up from, but she insisted that they were material for a perfectly gorgeous novel.

A man of about fifty, in black coat, light trousers, his eyebrows drawn into a painful frown, and in his eyes an expression mortified yet obstinate; a poor woman in widow's weeds, leading a little girl of about four by one hand and a boy of ten or so by the other; a pert, bold young miss, also in black, but an equivocal and brazen black it seemed, as she moved about in a constant flutter of disdainful biting merriment at the expense of the older man; and a young fellow of twenty-odd who stood apart from the others, seemingly locked within himself, as though holding the rest in utter scorn . . . in short, the Six Characters just as they appear on the stage at the beginning of my play. At once they began telling me their misfortunes, first one, then another, each in turn silencing all the rest, as each in turn shouted out his story; and there they were flourishing their scattered passions in my face, just as in the play they flourish them in the face of the thoroughly misunderstanding Manager.

Can an author ever tell how and why his imagination gives birth to a certain character? The mystery of artistic creation is the mystery of birth itself.

A woman may desire a child, but the desire, however intense it may be, does not suffice to create; and then one fine day she discovers that her desire is to be realized, but she cannot tell at what precise moment the life within her came into being. And in just the same way the artist, who gathers within himself innumerable germs of life, can never say how, or why, or at what precise moment one of these particles of life has lodged in his imagination, there to become a living creature inhabiting a plane of life superior to our voluble and vain daily existence.

Well, all I can say is that, without my having sought them at all, there they were, those six characters you now can see on the stage, so alive you could touch them, so alive you could fairly hear them breathe. And there they stood, each with his secret torment, but bound to all the others by birth and by the tie of events experienced together, waiting for me to let them into the world of art by making of their persons, their passions, and their vicissitudes, a novel, a play, at the very least a short story.

They had come into the world alive and they wanted to live. Now no matter how strikingly individualized a character may be, I have never represented man, woman, or child, for the mere pleasure of representation. I have never related a single experience for the mere pleasure of relating it; I have never described a landscape for the mere pleasure of describing it.

There are authors—and they are not so few—who *do* write for the pleasure they take in the writing alone, and who look for no other satisfaction. Such writers one might describe as historical.

Can an author ever tell how and why his imagination gives birth to a certain character? The mystery of artistic creation is the mystery of birth itself.

—Luigi Pirandello

But there are others who, in addition to deriving the pleasure I have described, feel a spiritual need that will not permit them to use characters, events, or scenes which are not impregnated, so to speak, with a special sense of life that gives them a universal significance and value. Such writers are, properly speaking, philosophical. And to this latter group I have the misfortune to belong.

I hate symbolic art, for it makes a mechanical structure, an allegory, out of all representation, destroying its spontaneity, reducing the creative impulse to an empty and shortsighted effort; for the mere fact of giving an allegorical meaning to what is being represented indicates that the representation proper is held in low esteem, as having in itself no truth, whether real or imaginary. Such a representation has been prepared simply for the purpose of demonstrating some moral truth. But the spiritual need I referred to a moment ago cannot be satisfied by allegorical symbolism, except in the rare instances where, as in Ariosto, the motive

is lofty irony. For the latter derives from a concept, or rather *is* a concept that is trying to become an image; but the former, on the contrary, tries to find in the image itself, which should be alive and spontaneous in every aspect of its expression, a meaning that will give it significance.

Now, for all my prying and searching, I could not succeed in finding any such meaning in these "characters." And I concluded therefore that there was no particular obligation on my part to give them the life for which they were clamoring.

"I have already tormented my readers with hundreds and hundreds of stories," I thought to myself. "Why should I bother them with an account of these six unfortunates, and their wretched plight?"

And acting on this feeling, I pushed them out of the way. Or rather, I did everything I could to get them out of the way.

But one doesn't give life to a character for nothing!

These creatures of my brain were not living *my* life any longer: they were already living a life of their own, and it was now beyond my power to deny them a life which was no longer in my control.

Persisting in my intention of driving them out of my mind, I found to my consternation that almost completely detached as they were now from any supporting narrative, emerging miraculously from the pages of the book containing them, they went right on living their own lives; from which at certain moments during the day they would turn aside to confront me in the solitude of my study. Now one, now another, now two of them together, would come to tempt me and propose scenes that I was to set down in dramatic form or simply describe; and they were always at great pains to point out the effects to be derived from their suggestions, and the singular and novel turn that some unique situation might take and the interest it would arouse, and so on, and so on.

For a moment I would give in; and this momentary weakening, this brief surrender, was enough for them to draw out of me additional life, and naturally with every particle of life that they thus acquired they grew all the better able to convince me, their powers of persuasion growing with their life, increasing as the life in them increased. And so it became more and more difficult for me to get rid of them in proportion as it became easier for them to appear before me and tempt me. Finally, as I have already suggested, they became an obsession—until suddenly I thought of a means of getting out of my predicament.

"Why not," thought I, "represent this unique situation—an author refusing to accept certain characters born of his imagination, while the characters themselves obstinately refuse to be shut out from the world of art, once they have received this gift of life? These characters are already completely detached from me, and living their own lives; they speak and move; and so, in the struggle to live that they have persistently maintained against me they have become dramatic characters, characters who can move and speak of their own initiative. They already see themselves in that light; they have learnt to defend themselves against me; they will learn how to defend themselves against others. So why not let them go where the characters of a play usually go to attain full and complete life—on a stage? Let's see what will happen then!"

Well, that's what I did. And of course things turned out just as they had to turn out: there was a mixture of the tragic and the comic, of the fantastic and the real, in a situation as humorous as it was novel and complicated. The play all of itself, by means of the breathing, speaking, moving characters in it, who carry the action and suffer its conflicts and clashes in their own persons, demands to be acted at any cost. It is the vain attempt to improvise on the stage the carrying out of this demand that constitutes the comedy.

First, the surprise of the company of actors who are rehearsing on a stage littered with sets and properties, a surprise mixed with incredulity at seeing those six characters appear on the stage and announce that they are looking for an author; then the mother's sudden faint and the instinctive interest of the actors in the tragedies they sense in her and in the other members of that strange family; then the confused, ambiguous conflict that unexpectedly takes possession of that empty stage so little prepared to receive it; and, finally, little by little, the rising tide of that interest as the conflicting passions of father, step-daughter, son, and mother, break out and try to dominate each the other with tragic and lacerating fury.

And, lo, those six characters who had of their own initiative stepped up on the stage, suddenly find in themselves that sense of universal significance which I had at first sought in vain; they find it in the excitement of the desperate struggle each character carries on with the others and in the struggle that all of them together carry on with the Manager and the Actors who fail to understand them.

Unintentionally, without knowing it, each one of them, in defending himself against the accusations of the others, under the pressure of his agitation gives out as his own vivid passion and torment, passions and torments that for years have been those of my own being; the impossibility (we take it as a heart-rending deception) of establishing a mutual understanding on the empty abstractions of words; the multiple personality of every one of us, a composite with as many faces as there are possibilities of being in each of us; and finally the tragic conflict between Life, which is forever fluid, forever in flux, and Form, which hardens Life into immutable shapes from which Life itself withdraws.

Two of those characters in particular, the Father and the Daughter, recur again and again to the frightful and unchangeable fixity of their form in which both see the essence of their being perpetually imprisoned; for the one that unalterable shape is punishment, for the other vengeance; and this form, which is themselves, they defend against the vapid jests and the meaningless chatter of the actors, trying to make the commonplace Manager accept it, while he of course is intent on changing it and adapting it to the so-called requirements of the theatre.

The six characters are not seemingly all in the same stage of formation. This is not because some of them are of first, and some of secondary, importance, finished pictures and studies in the rough. That would be nothing more than the most elementary sort of perspective, necessary to any architectural composition of scene or narrative. Neither is it because they are not all completely formed for the purposes they serve. All six are at the same stage of artistic realization and all six are on the same plane of reality—and this is the strange part of the play. Yet the Father and the Step-Daughter, and also the Son, are realized as *mind,* while the Mother is *nature;* and the Boy who looks on and makes gestures, and the Child, both absolutely inert, are no more than onlookers taking part by their presence merely. This creates a perspective of another sort. Unconsciously I had felt that I must realize some of the characters (artistically speaking) more completely, others less so, barely suggesting others still as elements of a story to be narrated or represented; those who are most intensely alive, the Father and Step-Daughter, naturally come forward and direct and drag along the almost dead weight of the others; of whom one, the Son, is reluctant, while the Mother, like a resigned victim, stands between those two small creatures, the children, who have scarcely any being except that of appearance, and who need to be led by the hand.

And that is just how they ought to appear—in the stage of creation arrived at in the author's imagination at the moment he attempts to drive them away from him.

When I stop to think of it, to understand this artistic necessity, and then unconsciously to comply with it and resolve it by means of this perspective seem to me nothing short of a miracle. The truth of the matter is that the play was conceived in one of those moments of illumination when the imagination acts with untrammelled spontaneity, and when, for a wonder, all the faculties of the mind are working together in a superb harmony. No human brain, coldly attacking this problem, could ever have succeeded, no matter how hard it tried, in grasping and satisfying all the necessities of this form. Therefore whatever I may say in order to throw light on its significance and importance should not be interpreted as something I thought out before I set to work—as a defence of that work in short; but as a progressive discovery which little by little I have been able to make and which I shall certainly never complete in the brief span of my mortal life.

I have tried to represent six characters in search of an author. Their play does not take shape precisely because the author they are looking for fails them; and the play actually presented consists of their vain attempt to induce him to satisfy their wishes—by giving them a play, a comedy, to act; but the play is a tragedy also, because these six characters fail of attaining their purpose. The author turns them down!

But can an author represent a character even while he is refusing to deal with him? It seems clear enough that, in order to represent a character, an author must first welcome him into his imagination before he can "express" him. And that is what I did. I took those six characters in and realized them; but I took them in and realized them *as having been turned down.*

But let us understand precisely what it was that was turned down; not the characters evidently, but their play—the very thing that interested them above all else, of course. But it didn't interest me at all, for the reasons I have pointed out.

And what, for a character in a play, constitutes his comedy or tragedy as the case may be?

Every creature born of the imagination, every being art creates, must have his own play, that is to say, a play of which he is the hero and for which he is the dominating character. That play is the *raison d'être* of that particular character; it is his life process; it is necessary for his existence.

So far as the six were concerned, I accepted their existence: but I refused the reason for their existence; I accepted the organism as it had developed but in place of its own function I assigned to it another more complex function in which its own original function scarcely figured at all. A terrible and desperate situation for both of them, Father and Step-Daughter, for of all the six it was they who were most eager to live, who were most fully conscious of being characters, that is to say, absolutely dependent on a play, on their own play, since that is the only one they are capable of imagining. Yet that is the play that is turned down! An impossible situation in short, a situation they must get out of at any cost for it is a matter of life and death. True, I did give them another *raison d'être* than their own, another function—nothing less than the "impossible" situation, the dramatic situation, which consists of being turned down and in search of an author; but they cannot even suspect—since they already have a life of their own—that this has now become their real reason for being, and a sufficient cause for their existence. If anyone should tell them so they wouldn't believe it;—how is it possible to believe that the only reason for one's existence resides wholly in a ceaseless torment that seems as unjust as it is unexplainable?

I cannot imagine therefore why I was found fault with because the character of the Father, instead of remaining what he should have been, went beyond his own characteristics and rôle as a character, at times trespassing on the author's own activities and adopting them as his own. I, who can understand those who do not understand me, see plainly enough that the blame comes from the fact that this character gives out as his own a work of the spirit that is recognized as being mine. That he does so is perfectly natural and of no significance whatever. This travail of spirit in the character of the Father derives from causes and reasons which have nothing to do with the drama of my personal experience—a consideration which of itself would rob the criticism in question of all semblance of consistency. However, I wish further to make it plain that the inherent activity of my mind—an activity that I have every right to let one of the characters reflect provided I make it organ-

ic—is one thing; while the activity my mind carries on for the purpose of realizing this work, the activity which succeeds finally in giving shape to the play of those six characters in search of an author, is quite another. If the Father participated in this activity, if he helped to form the play the essence of which is the authorlessness of those six characters, why then—then only!—would one be justified in saying that the Father is at times the author himself, and is therefore not what he should be! But the Father exists as a character in search of an author: he suffers that destiny, he does not create it; he endures it as an inexplicable fatality, and the situation in which he finds himself is one against which he rebels with all his strength, trying to remedy it; he is therefore really a character in search of an author and nothing more, even though he does express as though it were his own the activity of my mind. If he really did share in the author's activity that fatality would be easily explained; that is to say he would be admitted—as an *unadmitted* character—into the very centre and core of the poet's creative imagination, and would no longer have any cause to feel despair because he could not find anyone to affirm and compose his life as a character; I mean that he would accept willingly enough the *raison d'être* given him by the author and would without a moment's hesitation throw his own overboard, promptly consigning the Manager and the Actors, to whom he had appealed as his only recourse, to the devil.

There is one character, the Mother, on the other hand, to whom the mere fact of having life, considered as an end in itself, is not of the slightest importance. For she never doubts for a moment that she is already alive, nor does it ever occur to her to inquire in what respect and why she is alive. In other words she is not aware of being a character, for she is never, not even for a single moment, detached from her "part." She doesn't even know she has a "part."

This makes her perfectly organic. In fact, her rôle as mother does not permit her to be mentally active. And she has no "mind;" she lives in a stream of feeling that never ceases, so that she cannot become conscious of her own life, that is to say, of her being a character. But for all that, even she, in her own way and for her own ends, is searching for an author. At a certain moment she seems pleased at being brought before the Manager. Because she hopes to gain more life through him? No; but because she hopes the Manager will give her a scene to act with her son, a scene into which she would put a large part of her own life. But the scene does not exist: it has never nor could it ever have taken place. That shows to what a degree she is unaware of being a character, unaware that is, of the life she may possess, fixed and determined moment by moment in every gesture and in every word she speaks.

She comes on the stage with the others, but she does not know what she is being made to do. Apparently she imagines that the mania for life which is constantly assailing her husband and daughter, and on account of which she too is dragged on to a stage is nothing more than another of the usual incomprehensible eccentricities of that cruelly tormenting and cruelly tormented husband of hers, or—and this is what for her makes it so frightful—another questionable move on the part of her poor erring daughter. She is entirely passive. The circumstances of her life and what they have come to mean in her eyes, her own nature, are all given by the other characters, never by herself, and only once as her natural instinct rises up rebelliously in her does she contradict them to make it clear that she had no intention of abandoning either her husband or her son; but that the child was taken away from her and that her husband forced her to abandon him. She is able to set you right on questions of fact, but she does not know and she cannot explain anything else.

Briefly, she is *nature,* nature fixed in the form of a mother.

As to the new kind of satisfaction I found in this character, I must say a word. Nearly all my critics, instead of defining the Mother as un-human—this seems to be the peculiar and incorrigible nature of all my characters without exception—have been good enough to note "with unaffected pleasure" that at last my imagination had given birth to an extraordinarily *human* character. This unlooked for praise I explain in this fashion: my poor Mother is tightly bound to her natural function as mother, and cannot possibly function mentally or spiritually; that is to say, being hardly more than a piece of flesh living completely in the functions of bearing, suckling, nursing and loving her progeny without ever needing to use her brain, she realizes in herself the perfectly typical "human being!" Of course! For nothing is more superfluous in the human organism than the mind!

My critics expected with this praise to dismiss the Mother and made no attempt to penetrate to the kernel of poetic values this character possesses in the play. A "most human" figure, yes, since the character entirely lacks mental activity, that is to say, is unaware of being what she is and takes no interest in explaining to herself how it happens that she is as she is. But the fact that she does not know she is a character in a play does not prevent her from being one. That is her dramatic situation in my *Six Characters.* And the most vivid expression of this situation flashes out in her cry to the Manager when he tells her to pause and consider that as all these things she is relating have already occurred they should not cause her to weep afresh. "No, it is happening now, it is always happening! My torture is not feigned! I am alive, I feel every moment of my torment. My torment too is alive and in every breath I draw!"—She feels all this, without understanding it, as something inexplicable therefor: but she feels it with such terrible force that it does not even occur to her that it could be explained to her or to the others. She feels it—that suffices. She feels it as grief, and this grief at once cries out. And that is how she reflects the hardening of her life in a form—the same thing that in quite another fashion torments the Father and the Daughter. With them it is mind; with her, nature. The mind rebels and tries to draw whatever advantage it can from its torment; but nature, unless stimulated by the senses, can only weep.

The conflict between Life and Form is inexorably a condition of the spiritual order; it is also inherent in the natural order. Life, which abandons its fluidity in order to become fixed in our bodily form, little by little kills its form. In the irreparable and continuous aging of our bodies the nature fixed in those particular forms has an eternal cause for complaint. The Mother's plaint is both passive and perpetual. Revealed through three different faces, made significant in three distinct and simultaneous conflicts, it is in this play that the dramatic struggle between Life and Form finds its most complete expression. Moreover, in that poignant outburst of hers to the Manager, the Mother also brings out the particular significance of the form of life created by the human spirit: that is to say, the artistic form—a form which does not congeal, which does not kill, its own life and which life does not devour. If the Father and the Daughter were to begin their scene a hundred thousand times, invariably, at the appointed moment, in the second when the life of the work of art is to be expressed by the Mother's cry, that cry would resound—unchangeable and unchanging in form, not as a mechanical repetition is unchanging, a repetition required by external forces, but alive and as though new each time, and each time suddenly born to live forever—embalmed alive in imperishable fixity! Always, when we open the *comedy,* we find the living Francesca confessing her sweet sin to Dante; and though we should read that passage a hundred thousand times in succession, Francesca will still a hundred thousand times repeat her words, not mechanically, but as though each time were the first, and with such vivid and sudden passion that the poet each time will turn faint with his emotion!

All that lives, by the sheer fact of living, has a form and so must die; all except the work of art which, on the contrary, lives forever insofar as it is form.

The birth of a creation of the human imagination, that step across the threshold from nothingness to eternity, can occur suddenly, when some necessity has served as its matrix. In a play that is imagined a character does and says whatever is necessary, he is born just the character he ought to be. That is how Madame Pace comes to life among the six characters, with all the effect of a miracle or a surpassingly clever trick realistically portrayed. But it isn't a trick. That is a real birth, and the new character is alive, not because the character was alive before, but because successfully ushered into life, as required by the very fact of her being a character—she is obliged to be as she is. As she steps on the scene there is a break therefore, a sudden change in the planes of reality on the stage, because a character can come to life that way only in the imagination of the poet and not on the boards of the stage itself. Without anyone's noticing it, I suddenly changed the nature of the scene; at that precise moment I took it back into my imagination but without removing it from the sight of the audience; that is to say, instead of the stage, I showed them my imagination in the act of creating, as though it were a kind of stage. The sudden and uncontrollable transformation of some form of appearance from one plane of reality to another is a miracle of the same kind as that accomplished by the Saint who animates his statue, which for that moment is certainly neither of wood nor of stone. But it is not an arbitrary kind of miracle. That stage, since it receives the imagined reality of the six characters, does not exist of itself as a fixed and immutable fact, just as nothing in the play exists in advance—everything is actually in the making, everything about it moves and changes, always impromptu, always tentative. Even the plane of reality in which all this form-less life moves and flows in its eager search for form is thus organically displaced. When I conceived of having Madame Pace come to life then and there on that stage, I felt sure I could carry out my conception, and I did so; if I had noticed that this sudden birth suddenly and in a twinkling broke in upon and gave another shape to the plane of reality of the scene, I would certainly never have attempted it, for I would have been appalled by its apparent lack of logic, which would thus have inflicted an unfortunate injury on the beauty of my play. But the fervor of my imagination saved me; because, in the face of a deceptive logic, that fantastic coming to life is demanded by an artistic necessity that is mysteriously and organically correlated with the life of the whole work.

When anyone tells me that my play is not as good as it might be because, instead of being smooth and stately, it is chaotic in expression, and sins by its romanticism, I am forced to smile.

I can understand of course why this criticism is made. As I have written this play, the dramatic presentation of the six characters appears tumultuous and unruly. It never proceeds in an orderly fashion: it lacks logical development—there is no stringing together of events. True enough! Had I gone out to look for it with a lantern I could not have found a more disorderly, eccentric, capricious and complicated manner, a more *romantic* manner, in short, of presenting the drama in which the six characters are involved. True again! But as it happens, that is not the play I have present-ed. The play I am dealing with is quite another play—I need not repeat what that play is! But aside from the var-ious excellences to be found in it according to one's taste, it contains a sustained satire of romantic methods; for while my characters are in such a fever to outdo themselves in the parts each of them has in one play—their play, I am pre-senting them as characters in another play—my play! This they neither know nor suspect. As a result the extreme agitation their passions cause in them—a trait of romantic treatment—is humorously superimposed on sheer void. And the play of the six characters, represented not as it would have been composed by my imagination if my imagination had accepted it, could not have a place in my work except as a "situation" to be developed somehow or other, and could not come out except in eruptive, incoherent commands, in violent short-cuts, chaotically, in short, perpetually inter-rupted, led off the track, contradicted, actually *denied* by one of its characters, and not even seen by two of them!

One of the characters—the Son, who denies the conflict which makes him a "character"—derives his importance, his "substantiality," from the fact, not that he is a character in the play-in-the-making,—for he scarcely appears at all in that capacity—but that he is a character in my representa-tion of the play-in-the-making. He is in short the only one who lives as a "character in search of an author" and noth-ing else; to such a degree that the author he is looking for is not a dramatic author. This too could not very well be otherwise. Moreover, not only is the attitude of this charac-ter completely organic in my conception, but he heightens the general confusion and disorder, besides being another element of romantic contrast.

It was precisely this organic and natural chaos that I had to represent. But to depict chaos does not mean that one must proceed chaotically, romantically! The method I have used is the very opposite of chaotic. It is clear, simple, and or-derly, as is evident from the way the plot, the characters, the several planes of reality, imaginary and real, the dramatic and comic values, have all been accepted by the playgoing publics of the world; and for those who have eyes to see further the play contains still other values, by no means the usual values, and of no mean scope. Great is the confusion of tongues among men if there are words in which criti-cisms of this nature can find expression. The confusion is the confusion of the law of order itself which this play of mine observes in every particular, and which makes it a classical and typical play, while at the same time forbidding its ultimate catastrophe to find expression in a single word. It is made clear to everyone witnessing the play that Life cannot be created by artifice, that the play of the six char-acters, lacking as it does an author to nourish it in the womb of his spirit, cannot be represented for the vulgar satisfac-tion of someone who wishes merely to know how an event developed. This event is recorded by the Son in the material succession of its moments, but it is entirely devoid of mean-ing and therefore does not need even a human voice to express it; but, with its own material voice, and for the simple reason that the event had happened before, it hap-pens again. Ugly and useless, catastrophe swoops down with the detonation of a weapon—a piece of mechanism—on the stage, shattering and throwing to the four winds the sterile attempt of characters and actors to make their play without the help of the poet.

If I dare not heed the statement which G. B. Shaw has seen fit to make—that *Six Characters in Search of an Author* is the most original and dynamic play ever written in any nation, or at any time, whether ancient or modern—I can at least feel in all conscience that the appearance of the *Six Characters* marks a date in the history of the Italian theatre which it will not be possible for the supporters of the "old" drama to ignore.

OVERVIEWS AND GENERAL STUDIES

Eric Bentley (essay date 1946)

SOURCE: "Varieties of Comic Experience," in *The Play-wright as Thinker: A Study of Drama in Modern Times,* Reynal & Hitchcock, 1946, pp. 127-57.

[*In the following excerpt, Bentley characterizes Pirandello as a pessimist who speaks for the people "who have lived through the extraordinary vicissitudes of the twentieth cen-tury, uncomprehending, passively suffering."*]

Since Shaw and Wilde no dramatist has written first-rate drawing-room comedies. The best have been by our Maughams and Behrmans and Bernsteins. Writers have been turning from the formality of the drawing room to-ward a grotesqueness which, in its nearness to *commedia dell' arte* or to Aristophanes, may seem more primitive, yet which, in its psychological depth and intricacy, may well be more sophisticated. Strindberg . . . sometimes achieved comedy by giving a quick twist to one of his own tragic themes. Wedekind aimed at tragedy, but by the novel method of using almost exclusively comic materials, thus reversing the technique of Strindberg's comedies. In Italy *it teatro del grottesco* arose. Its spokesman Luigi Chiarelli said: "It was impossible [in the years immediately preceding 1914] to go to the theater without meeting languid, loquacious granddaughters of Marguerite Gautier or Rosa Bernd, or some tardy follower of Oswald or Cyrano. The public dropped sentimental tears and left the playhouse weighed down in spirit. The next evening, however, it rushed in numbers to acclaim a naughty skit like *The Pills of Hercules,* in order to re-establish its moral and social equilibrium." From Chiarelli's scorn for the New Drama, already old, of Dumas and Hauptmann, Ibsen and Rostand, came his own play, *The Mask and the Face.* The year of its première—1916—was the year Luigi Pirandello embarked on his second career: that of playwriting.

Right You Are (if you care to think so!) (1917) has often been regarded as the quintessential Pirandello. The basis of the play is some sort of "bourgeois tragedy," something that would have stirred the audiences of the old-new drama which Chiarelli had laughed at. The domestic unhappiness of a husband, a wife, and a mother makes up the tragic triangle. A commentator named Laudisi is the *raisonneur à la* Dumas.

The peculiar thing about the situation in this domestic tragedy is that we do not know what it is: a fact that is as much second nature to Pirandellians as it is disconcerting to others. The peculiar thing about the *raisonneur* is that instead of giving us the correct view of the tragedy he tells us that all views are equally correct. But then, according to Pirandello, *this* is the correct view.

The man lives with his wife on the top floor of a tenement while the mother lives at his expense in a lavish apartment. The wife never leaves the tenement, and the mother never goes nearer the daughter than the yard below from which she shouts up to the daughter. This state of affairs not unnaturally sets tongues wagging. Asked for an explanation, the husband says the mother is deluded. She thinks the wife is her daughter, though actually she is the husband's second wife. Her daughter, his first wife, died, though the mother dare not believe it. . . . We are settling down to believe this version of the story when we hear from the mother as equally convincing version. The son is deluded. He has never recovered from the delusion that his wife died, and they have had to let him marry her again under the impression that she was another person.

Neither mother nor husband seems to have an axe to grind. Each is solicitous for the other's good. Each has a good reason for strange conduct. The mother needs to see her daughter often and must pay her visits. The husband must keep her in the street so that she shall not discover her error. Pirandello is at great pains to balance the two interpretations exactly, to tug our feelings now this way, now that,

now up, now down, on the alarming switchback of his thinking. We may think ourselves on the right track, for example, when the husband, untrue to his story, is furiously angry with the old lady and tries to convince her that his wife is not her daughter. But, as soon as she leaves, his rage subsides. He was just play-acting, he tells us, to confirm her impression—so necessary to her peace of mind—that he is mad.

In the end the wife herself is summoned to unravel the mystery. She says: "I am the daughter of Signora Frola [the mother], and I am the second wife of Signor Ponza [the husband]." The *raisonneur* of the play, who already has told as that there is no one true version of the story but that all versions are equally true, steps forward, and his peals of laughter end the play. Whereupon one school of critics praises Pirandello for his profound "philosophy of relativity," and another condemns him as "too cerebral"—only "mentally dramatic," as George Jean Nathan has it, **Right You Are** being "written for intelligent blind men." The critical boxing ring would seem to be set for a bout concerning the drama of ideas.

Like Shaw, Pirandello has not been averse to the report that his drama is all intellect—no man minds being thought a mighty brain—and here are some of his words: "People say that my drama is obscure and they call it cerebral drama. The new drama possesses a distinct character from the old: whereas the latter had as its basis passion, the former is the expression of the intellect. . . . The public formerly were carried away only by plays of passion, whereas now they rush to see intellectual works."

Such is the Pirandello legend. Around every great man there grows a legend which, whether fostered by himself or not, is always a distortion, sometimes a gross distortion of his real nature—if we may assume the existence of so un-Pirandellian an entity. The omission which I disingenuously made in the above quotation from Pirandello is a casual remark that happens to be more revealing than the pontificality of the rest. It is this sentence: "One of the novelties that I have given to the modern drama consists in converting the intellect into passion." Let us discount here the claim to originality. Strindberg had already perfected the art referred to. A succession of dramatists from Vigny on had announced a new drama of thought and intellect. The essence of Pirandello is not his intellectuality. It is his conversion of the intellect into passion. Perhaps Strindberg had done that too; it is the theory behind his naturalistic tragedies; yet in Strindberg passion summons intellect to work its will, while in Pirandello passion and intellect torture each other and join in a mutual failure. The quintessence of Pirandellism is this peculiar relation of intellect to feeling.

Ostensibly Pirandello's plays and novels are about the relativity of truth, multiple personality, and the different level of reality. But it is neither these subjects nor—precisely—his treatment of them that constitutes Pirandello's individuality. The themes grow tiresome after a time, and those who find nothing else in Pirandello give him up as a bad job. The novelist Franz Kafka was long neglected because his world also gave the impression of philosophic obsession and willful eccentricity. Then another and deeper Kafka was discovered. Another and deeper Pirandello awaits discovery.

Before he can be discovered the perpetual "cerebration" concerning truth, reality, and relativity will have to be set on one side. At face value the argument of **Right You Are** is that, since both mother and husband give a contradictory but equally plausible account of the same events, and since the daughter jumbles the two incomprehensibly, therefore, there is no objectively true version of the story. This is a complete *non sequitur*. All events can be reported in different ways. This might only mean that some reports must be wrong, not that there is no right view. There is actually nothing in the plot of **Right You Are** to indicate that there can be no correct version of the story. The unusual thing is that we do not know what it is. This is very Pirandellian—not only, however, in that it is used to bolster a rather confusing, if not confused, discussion of truth, but also because it leads us to what we might venture to think is the real Pirandello.

The wife's longest speech—of three sentences—is as follows: "And what can you want of me now, after all this, ladies and gentlemen? In our lives as you see there is something which must remain concealed. Otherwise the remedy which our love for each other has found cannot avail." The concealment which leads on the superficial, pseudometaphysical level to a discussion of truth is here very differently associated. There *is* a true version of the story but it must not be known lest the lives of three people concerned be shattered. But, someone will protest, could not Pirandello use the prerogative of the omniscient author and tell *us* without telling the characters what the remedy is which their love has found? He could. But his refusal to do so is more to his purpose. The truth, Pirandello wants to tell us again and again, is concealed, *concealed*, CONCEALED! It is not his business to uncover the problem and solve it for us as in a French *pièce à thèse*. The solution of the problem, the cure for these sick human beings, is to leave their problem unsolved and unrevealed. The unmasker of illusions is at best a Gregers Werle [in Ibsen's *The Wild Duck*], at worst one of the gossips of **Right You Are.** On the superficial level Pirandello is protesting against the spurious helpfulness of the scandalmonger, the prying reporter, and the amateur psychoanalyst; at a deeper level he is asking that the human soul be left a little territory of its own—which also was one of the themes of Kafka.

As for dramaturgy, if the "remedy" were explained, the play would inevitably be built around this keystone of the whole problem. Pirandello could not afford—whatever the inducements—to have the emphasis so distributed. He wants to accent the refusal to search for a keystone. So he has his *raisonneur* argue that there is no keystone—an argument which sticks in people's minds as if it were the substance of the play. Actually the play is not about thinking but about suffering, a suffering that is only increased by those who give understanding and enquiry precedence over sympathy and help. Pirandello took from the *teatro del grottesco* or from his own fiction the antithesis of mask and face, the mask being the outward form, the face being the suffering creature. At its crudest this is the theme of the clown with a tender heart. Already in Chiarelli the mask

and the face had, however, the broader meaning of the social form, identified with tyranny, and the individual soul which it sought to crush. In his best-known plays Pirandello elaborates on this antithesis. We see a central group of people who are "real." They suffer, and need help, not analysis. Around these are grouped unreal busybodies who can only look on, criticize, and hinder. In **Naked,** which is the first Pirandello play to read since it does not lead one off on the false trail of relativity and truth, the mystery is dissolved, as in **Right You Are** it is not, and the result is the destruction of the protagonist. Note that this mystery, constituted by the illusions without which the heroine could not live, is not the Mask. The Mask is the social and antihuman tyranny of, for example, a novelist for whom the heroine's unhappy lot is grist to the mill. The Mask is the interference of the mechanical, the external, the static, the philosophical, with our lives. Thus not only the smug novelist of **Naked** and not only the disingenuous truth seekers of **Right You Are** are the Mask. Pirandello himself—and every novelist and playwright—is the Mask. His material is the flux of suffering: his art stops the flow; its stasis is at once its glory—in immortalizing the moment—and its limitation, since life, being essentially fluid, is inevitably misrepresented by art. In drama, life wears a double mask: the mask imposed by the dramatist and that imposed by stage production. Three plays are devoted to this fact. In the best of them—**Six Characters in Search of an Author**—the three levels of reality are played off against one another throughout, and a fourth level is implied when we find one character judging another by what he happened to be doing on one shameful occasion, in other words by one isolated fact, which, wrongly taken as typical, becomes a Mask on the face of the real man. What if all our characterizations are like this? Just as we found, Pirandello argues, that there is no objective truth, so we find also that there are no individuals. In the one case we have only a number of versions or opinions. In the other we have only a succession of states of mind and being.

Exactly as in the matter of truth, so in the analysis of character the extreme conclusion is a *reductio ad absurdum* too barren to be the real motive force of such powerful works as Pirandello's. His characters in fact are effective not in direct relation to these conceptions, but because these conceptions enable him to suggest beneath the Mask of the physical presence the steady ache of suffering humanity. What a pessimist Pirandello is! says someone. Certainly. But again the point of Pirandello is not his philosophy—of relativity, personality, or pessimism—it is his power to conceal behind the intellectual artillery barrage the great armies of fighters and the yet greater hordes of noncombatants and refugees. Pirandello is a pessimist. So also must many of the people of Europe be, people who have lived through the extraordinary vicissitudes of the twentieth century, uncomprehending, passively suffering. Modern people may be no more passive and uncomprehending than their ancestors; but surely they are more aware of their helplessness. Even as Proust speaks for the passive semiaristocrats whom our new order has swept out of existence, so Pirandello, like Kafka, like Chaplin, speaks not for the aware and class-conscious proletarian but for the unaware, in-between, black-white-cotton-coated, scapegoat.

All this is in ***Right You Are.*** In a note to the director of the play one might write as follows:

"Make a marked distinction between the enquirers into the story, who are a sort of chorus representing what Pirandello regards as the Mask and the three 'real people' involved in the domestic tragedy. The Three are typical people of a middle-class tragedy in that they express grief and arouse pity without terror. Note how Pirandello's initial descriptions of the characters and his subsequent stage directions stress alike the genuineness and acuteness of their sufferings.

"Now the odd thing is that the wholly sad theme is placed in a satiric frame. Since this contrast, already familiar to you in the *teatro del grottesco,* is the play, you had best be careful to secure the exact balance that is needed. The Three must act with unmitigated and uninterrupted pathetic force. But the Chorus—as we may call the other characters—must never enter into their sufferings. They must be as detached as a callous doctor at a deathbed. They must not, out of consideration of their Three colleagues, play down their own frivolity any more than the Three must soften their agony in order to come closer—as there is a natural tendency to do—to the mood of the Chorus. Only if the contrast between the two groups is kept sharp will the effect of the grotesque be attained. Otherwise the effect will be of blurred incongruity.

"You already understand how and why this bourgeois tragedy differs from tradition in not revealing its true nature. That is a primary irony which your production can point up by making the alternation of explanations go snip-snap so that the brilliance is its own justification. Otherwise your audience will regard all this as the lumbering preparation for a denouement which, after all, never takes place. An almost equally important irony is that between the celebrated 'cerebral' dialogue of Pirandello and the deep agony which—as your Three must make clear—is the core of the action. This irony is more than the contrast between the Three and the others. The Three actually join in the intricate analysis of cause and effect, motive and act, which is the constant subject of discussion. The point is that these analyses are not 'coldly intellectual.' They are positively maniacal. (You might look up Pirandello's essay on humor where he maintains that the humorist takes a wild pleasure in tearing things to pieces by analysis.) By its maniacal quality the 'cerebration' enters into relationship with the agony, a relationship at once logical and psychological.

"You recall how in *Cyrano de Bergerac* Rostand rendered Hugoesque tragedy palatable by making it over into a tough-jointed tragi-comedy. The grotesque contrasts of ***Right You Are*** might be regarded as Pirandello's way of making 'bourgeois tragedy' work—by making it over into a tough-textured comedy. Perhaps comedy is not the best word for such a play, but then you as a practical man are less interested in that question than in the correct interpretation of the play whatever its generic name. For you the significance of Pirandello's version of bourgeois tragedy is that it sets the audience at a distance, preserving them both from tears and from boredom. Do not be shocked when they laugh *with* your Chorus *against* the Three or when they are amused with Laudisi the *raisonneur* when perhaps weeping would seem more in order. Their laughter is significant. For one thing it is what enables them to stomach the unmixed horror of Pirandellian diet. It is not stupid laughter exactly. Pirandello has 'comedified' his tale. If the laughter he arouses prompts an unflattering interpretation of human nature, that is intended. The old theatrical business, at which you are adept, of mingling laughter and tears was never more calculated, more intricate, more meaningful, or more depressing than here.

"Accentuate then—do not soften—the clashes of sound and color of which the play is composed. If you let it work, you will find the whole thing ultra-theatrical. I should say: if you let *them* work, for a Pirandello play is made up of actors, not of props and scenery. That must be why our friend Mr. Nathan thought it was written for blind men. But remember that actors—especially the actors of the *commedia dell' arte* whose skill Pirandello wished to revive—once were, and can be again, the main part of the show. Tell your actors to let go. Have them shout, swagger, gesticulate—at least in the earlier rehearsals. For you have to get them to act and talk instead of strolling and muttering like mannequins with a pin loose. And if they perform their role from outside instead of pretending to *be* the people who are not people, Pirandello would be better served. As you know, he called all his plays Naked Masks—not naked faces. Let your actors remember that. Naked Masks—a violent oxymoron indeed! Is not such a figure of speech a pointer, for you and the rest of us, to the strange genius of its author!"

Martin Esslin   (essay date 1969)

SOURCE: "Pirandello: Master of the Naked Masks," in *Reflections: Essays on Modern Theater,* Doubleday & Co., Inc., 1969, pp. 49-57.

[*Esslin, a prominent and sometimes controversial critic of contemporary theater, is perhaps best known for coining the term "theater of the absurd." His* The Theater of the Absurd *(1961) is a major study of the avant-garde drama of the 1950s and early 1960s, including the works of Samuel Beckett, Eugene Ionesco, and Jean Genet. In the following essay, he provides an overview of Pirandello's work, stressing his influence on modern theater.*]

Among the creators of the contemporary theatre Luigi Pirandello stands in the very first rank, next to Ibsen, Strindberg, and Shaw. And even though his plays may be less frequently performed in the English-speaking world than those of either Shaw or Ibsen today (Strindberg is equally unjustly neglected), his living influence in the work of the dramatists of our own age is far stronger, far more active than that of those two giants. For Pirandello more than any other playwright has been responsible for a revolution in man's attitude to the world that is comparable to the revolution caused by Einstein's discovery of the concept of relativity in physics: Pirandello has transformed our attitude to human personality and the whole concept of *reality* in human relations by showing that the personality—character in stage terms—is not a fixed and static entity but an infinitely fluid, blurred, and *relative* concept. People appear different to different fellow human beings, they act differently in different contexts, they react differently to differing situations. And where is the Archimedean point outside that fluid reality from which we might judge which of these different manifestations of a human personality is the true, the *real* one? There is no such point, just as there is no fixed point in the physical universe from which all velocities could be measured.

A man keeps his wife confined to his house, and that makes the neighbors talk. He does not even allow his mother-in-law to come and see her. All she may do is to look at her from the street as she appears at the window. The man has his explanation: He has lost his first wife in an earthquake in another town and has now remarried. The dead woman's mother will not believe that she is dead and he cannot bring himself to hurt her, so he pretends that the old lady still *is* his mother-in-law but keeps her from his wife in order to spare her the shock of finding someone else in her daughter's place. But the mother-in-law also gets a chance to tell *her* story. She knows that her son-in-law thinks he has remarried, but in fact the earthquake so unhinged his mind that he thought his wife was killed and in order to make him go on living with her the family had to pretend that he has remarried. Each of the two explanations is put forward with perfect logic and apparent sanity, each would perfectly fit the situation. But only one of them can be true. Finally the young woman at the center of the dispute appears, heavily veiled. She is asked: Which of the two are you? And replies: "I am the old lady's daughter and I am this man's second wife. And for myself, I am nobody! Nobody at all!" But the bystanders object, she must be either one or the other. "No! As far as I am concerned, I am just whoever you think I am. . . . "

And indeed the alternative between only *two* possible solutions is far too simple. There is an infinity of other solutions. The young woman may be neither the daughter of the lady nor the second wife of the husband. She may be trying to keep two equally disturbed minds from cracking up. Or she herself may suffer from a form of insanity which makes it necessary for her to think that both characters she embodies must co-exist. In other words we are faced with a multiple system of delusions which is kept in a precarious balance, and each of these delusions undermines the foundations of the other two. It is a closed system without an exit: each person's illusions are *his* reality.

Again and again this basic problem of illusion and reality, so neatly and logically worked out in the plot of the play ***Right You Are If You Think You Are,*** occurs in different variations in Pirandello's vast *oeuvre* of more than forty plays, seven novels, and some two hundred stories.

He himself lived his life caught up in such an inextricable net. He was the son of wealthy owners of sulphur mines near his native Sicilian city of Girgenti (today renamed Agrigento). At the age of twenty-six he married the daughter of one of his father's partners. Nine years later a mining disaster caused the ruin of the family fortunes of Pirandello's own and his wife's parents. Signora Pirandello was

paralyzed as a result of the shock; she could not move her legs for six months and after that developed the symptoms of extreme paranoia. She was so jealous of her husband that no woman was allowed to enter their home, maidservants had to be more than fifty years of age and were not permitted to live in the house. Pirandello had to hide his manuscripts as his wife suspected secret love letters in any piece of paper with writing on it. He never went out without taking one of his children with him, so as to have a witness for every minute of the day. Yet Pirandello loyally suffered all these tribulations rather than have his wife removed to an asylum. It was only after sixteen years, in 1919, that her condition made it necessary for her to go to a sanatorium, where she survived for another forty years.

So he himself was confronted with the problem: in his wife's disturbed mind he appeared as a totally different character from the image he had of himself. And yet, who was to decide which image was the true one, which was illusion, which reality? Who is sane? Who is mad? The mad are convinced *they* are sane. So every one of us who swears that he is sane may in fact be mad without knowing it.

The hero of Pirandello's greatest play, ***Henry IV,*** is a case in point. As a young man, while impersonating the German Emperor Henry IV in a historical pageant, he fell from his horse as a result of a practical joke engineered by his rival in love. For many years, in consequence of the blow he suffered, he has been mad, thinking that he actually *is* the medieval Emperor. So as not to expose him to an unbearable nervous shock he has been surrounded by costumed servants in a reconstructed medieval court. Then one day the patient realizes the masquerade, he becomes sane, but because he rather likes the comfort of living outside his time, he keeps up the deception, he continues to pretend that he believes himself a medieval Emperor. His friends, unaware of his state of mind, prepare an elaborate shock therapy to cure him: they will confront him with the daughter of his former love, who resembles her exactly, so as to take him back to the exact point where his madness started. As he has long seen through his masquerade the shock treatment does not have the desired effect. He merely gets so furious with his erstwhile rival that he kills him, knowing he will have to go on pretending to be insane to escape the consequences of the murder. This is a complex enough pattern, but as Eric Bentley has pointed out in a brilliant essay on ***Henry IV*** it is in fact still more complex: is the hero's withdrawal from reality, after he has realized that he is living in the twentieth century and not in the eleventh, the act of a sane man? Hardly. It might be seen as a different type of insanity. And is the murder of his old rival in a fit of rage the action of a sane man? Surely not. So in fact our hero may believe himself to have returned to normality, but this itself is merely a further illusion. . . .

The man who thinks he is the Emperor Henry IV wears elaborate medieval costume, he is *masked* in the sense in which the costumed participants of a masked ball are referred to as *masks*. Pirandello gave the edition of his collected plays the over-all title ***Maschere nude (Naked Masks).*** We all in our daily lives, he suggests, are like the masks in a masked ball, the masks of the old Italian

Commedia dell'Arte, stereotyped characters with roles prescribed by long tradition. He, the dramatist, sets out to strip these masks off his characters, to tear off their disguise, their conventional costume, to get at the naked truth. But he finds that it is impossible ever to establish the absolute truth about any living human being, simply because, life being change, change in the observer as well as in the observed, there can never be an absolute—that is, *fixed*—truth about anyone.

If we are all costumed masks enacting stereotyped roles, then the dividing line between the actor on the stage and the spectator in the stalls becomes blurred. Many of Pirandello's plays deal with the problem of stage illusion vs. illusion in life, stage truth vs. truth in life. His most famous play, *Six Characters in Search of an Author* (first performed in 1921), poses the problem in the most ingenious manner. A theatre is invaded during a rehearsal by a group of six characters who have been conceived in the mind of an author but discarded by him as being too melodramatic. Once brought to life, however, they demand their existence on the stage. They enact their predicament. The actors become interested and try to make them the basis of a play. So now the roles are taken by the actors. But, the characters protest, the actors only translate the truth of the imagination of an author back into stage stereotypes. The fiction is more real than its enactment by flesh-and-blood professionals.

This is the core of Pirandello's concern, the nature of human consciousness of itself, of reality as reflected in our minds. If it is impossible to find an objective yardstick of reality we are thrown back into a universe of interlocking subjective viewpoints between which it is impossible to determine a greater or lesser degree of objective truth. As Pirandello told Domenico Vittorini in 1935 (a year before his death): "The last generation looked upon nature and man as something existing in unchanging, clear-cut and solid form outside of us. To me reality is something that we mold through the power of our imagination. . . . We say 'I am one' and we look upon ourselves as well as upon fellow men as solid and clear-cut personalities, while in reality we are the juxtaposition of infinite, blurred selves. . . . "

Pirandello, who had spent some time as a student at Bonn University in Germany and had been greatly influenced by German philosophy, embodied some of the principal trends in modern thinking—Bergson's dynamic vitalism with its insistence on the fluidity of human personality, phenomenology, existentialism—in a vigorous and original type of philosophical drama. He was aware of this. In the preface to *Six Characters in Search of an Author* he distinguished between two types of writers: those who merely want to tell a story "are . . . historical writers. But there are others who, beyond such pleasure, feel a more profound spiritual need on whose account they admit only figures, affairs, landscapes which have been soaked, so to speak, in a particular sense of life and acquire from it a universal value. These are, more precisely, philosophical writers. I have the misfortune to belong to these last."

Yet, while he used the stage as a laboratory for the demonstration of a philosophical view of the world, Pirandello was anything but a cerebral dramatist. He was, above all, a man haunted by images. The subject matter of *Six Characters in Search of an Author* is, after all, basically a dramatization of the playwright's mind haunted, invaded, by characters who simply will not let him alone. The scene at the core of the play, that of the father, who furtively frequents houses of assignation, being confronted by his own stepdaughter, who is forced to eke out her existence by selling herself, is one the author does not want to deal with, that he discards, and yet one to which the figments of his subconscious mind force him to return. In that sense the stage itself that the characters invade is simply the author's own consciousness. He wants to repress the Oedipal, incestuous situation that haunts him, but he cannot do it, the play insists on being written: "Creatures of my spirit, these six were already living a life which was their own and not mine any more, a life which it was not in my power any more to deny them."

Pirandello was fully aware of the uncontrollable forces at the basis of human personality. As he told Vittorini: "There are emotions and acts that are uncontrollable because of the blurred character of our personality." One might put it the other way round: Because our personality is composed of forces that are beyond our conscious control, it is bound to be fluid and blurred; because we are not wholly conscious of our own motivations we cannot distinguish between illusion and reality. Pirandello's plays can therefore be studied, not merely as the product of a brilliant philosophical mind, but also as the expression of a personality haunted by images welling up from the depths of a deeply troubled soul.

Pirandello's influence pervades all contemporary drama. His contribution is so rich that the most diverse tendencies have been able to find nourishment in aspects of Pirandello's thought or practice. His insistence, for example, that the stage is an illusion shot through by the reality of the actors themselves, who become real precisely when they fall out of their roles and address the audience as themselves, undoubtedly had its influence on the anti-illusionist theatre of Brecht. Brecht's alienation effect, after all, is based on the recognition that the audience should be made aware of the illusionistic character of the stage, so that the actors could be in a position to comment themselves, as themselves, on the action they are demonstrating to the audience.

The same Pirandellian idea, in a completely different guise, appears in Genet's mirror technique in plays like *The Maids, The Balcony,* and *The Blacks.* The opening scene of *The Balcony* where we are shown a bishop confessing a sinner, only to discover that the bishop isn't a bishop at all but a little man who comes to a brothel where he indulges himself in dressing up as a bishop, derives directly from Pirandello's *Henry IV.* Similarly in *The Blacks* we are gradually made to realize that the action we have been watching was merely put on for our benefit in order to distract attention from a real murder which has been happening off stage; in other words, Genet is using the Pirandellian concept of various levels of illusion between stage and reality.

Anouilh uses a similar device in a number of his plays. In

Le Rendezvous de Senlis, for example, the hero engages two actors to impersonate his parents so as to give his beloved the illusion that he has a solid family background. And in one of his latest plays, *La Grotte,* Anouilh confronts us with an author who is trying to write a play by producing the characters for us on the stage and trying them out in various situations, with the characters finally becoming autonomous enough to refuse to go along with their author. Thornton Wilder has used many Pirandellian ideas and techniques in plays like *Our Town* and *The Skin of Our Teeth.*

The dramatists of the Theatre of the Absurd who put the images of their dreams and obsessions on the stage without even the pretense of a realistic framework continue Pirandello's subjectivist approach to reality. In **Six Characters** we still have a background of a real theatre with real actors against which the creatures of the author's imagination are contrasted. In the plays of Ionesco or Beckett the characters are clearly enough merely the emanations of the playwright's subconscious. Yet at the same time both Ionesco and Beckett retain the Pirandellian effect of letting the audience become aware of the fact that these fantasies are being embodied by actors who are real people and do not always pretend to be the characters they portray. The two tramps in *Waiting for Godot,* the master and the servant in *Endgame* frequently refer to their position as actors on a stage.

In a play like Peter Weiss's *Marat/Sade,* Brechtian alienation effects and absurdist projections of the consciousness of madmen onto a stage are cunningly mingled, but ultimately the whole elaborate structure of interlocking levels of subjectivity, of madness encompassed in madness, derives from Pirandello: these are Sade's characters who are trying to liberate themselves from their author, while we the audience of today are confronted by an audience of 1809 watching a play portraying events of 1792, illusions within illusions on the pattern of Pirandello's **Henry IV.**

Moreover, by confronting stage reality and the reality of life and showing both up as illusions, Pirandello can also be said to be a forerunner of the Happening. A play like **Each in His Own Way,** which Pirandello visualized as being staged in the foyer of the theatre as well as in the auditorium and on the stage, is a case in point. The play opens with the direction: "The performance of this play should start on the street outside the theatre. . . . " Newsboys are to distribute a newspaper containing an item referring to an event that is said to have been made the subject of the play. As the audience enters the foyer it is to witness the attempts of three elegant gentlemen to dissuade a lady, the supposed subject of the play, from going to see the performance. And the performance itself is to be constantly interrupted by the supposedly real characters, who are the models of the fictitious characters on the stage, protesting against the way they are being dealt with, the whole thing finally ending in such an uproar that the manager has to announce the abandonment of the performance.

This surely must be one of the first scenarios for a Happening. Much of it is embodied in a detailed script, but a good

many incidents are left to be improvised by the actors, and of course, once the scandal has broken out, it might well acquire a degree of spontaneity that even Pirandello did not bargain for.

Indeed, the objectives of the Happening are largely identical with Pirandello's. The participants in the Happening are to be made aware of the shifting ground on which they stand—that reality may be illusion, illusion reality, and that the world itself is a vast stage on which illusion merges into reality, which in turn may reveal itself as just another layer of illusion.

Pirandello received the Nobel Prize for Literature in 1934. He died in 1936. Today, more than a hundred years after he was born, the time seems ripe for an intensive revival of interest in Pirandello's work for the theatre. There are still many of his plays that have not yet been performed in English, that have not even been translated. For sheer inventiveness there are few dramatists' *oeuvres* that can rival the as yet untapped wealth of Pirandello's massive achievement.

The theatre as Pirandello represents it in
***Six Characters in Search of an Author* is**
very much like life itself, always at odds
with itself, always getting in its own way,
yet always pursuing and, in the end,
having its way.

—*Lionel Trilling, in his* The Experience
of Literature, *1967.*

Anne Paolucci (essay date 1974)

SOURCE: "Art for Life's Sake," in *Pirandello's Theater: The Recovery of the Modern Stage for Dramatic Art,* Southern Illinois University Press, 1974, pp. 7-21.

[*Below, Paolucci discusses the defining characteristics of Pirandello's drama, emphasizing the dramatist's concern with depicting the nature of personality and consciousness.*]

Pirandello came to the theater late in life, when he was close to fifty, and long established as a poet, short-story writer, and novelist of considerable fame. He was born on June 28, 1867 in Girgenti, Sicily (since renamed Agrigento to recall its original Greek name). The chronology of his pre-dramatic writings begins with a collection of poems, **Mal giocondo (*Joyful Pain*),** which appeared when he was twenty-two. A second collection, **Pasqua di Gea (*The Easter of Gea Tellus*),** followed in 1891. Then came his first volume of short stories, **Amori senza amore (*Loves without Love*),** in 1894; his **Rhine Elegies** (1895) and verse translations of Goethe's *Roman Elegies* (1896); his earliest novels, **L'esclusa (*The Outcast*),** 1901, and **Il turno (*The Turn*),** 1902; new volumes of short stories spread out over a dozen years; the novel that gave him an international reputation, **Il fu Mattia Pascal (*The Late Mattia Pascal*),** 1904; and his much-discussed literary essay, **L'umorismo (*On Humor*),** 1908. These works in their very titles suggest the themes of the major plays to come: the confounding of opposites, complexities of family relationships, adultery, unrequited love, death, the multiplicity of personality, the irony of self-consciousness—to name only a few.

Pirandello's first efforts at playwriting were, in fact, not so much plays in the strict sense, as short stories and novels adapted for stage representation. He used to insist, right down to the completion of *Six Characters in Search of an Author* in 1921, that he really had no interest in playwriting as such, that he looked down upon stage representation as a mere technique for communicating the substance of stories that are much better told, for intelligent readers, in narrative form. Later, he most emphatically acknowledged that his first notion of dramatic art was all wrong. While that notion lasted, however, he used to shudder at the thought of submitting his imaginative creations to the "whims" of directors and actors. He much preferred, he said, the direct communication of lyric poetry and the fully controlled narrative techniques of the novel and short story.

But then, apparently, he experienced the kind of reversal that T. S. Eliot tells us about in "The Three Voices of Poetry," where he acknowledges that he did not learn what drama was really all about until *after* he had written *Murder in the Cathedral*. Like Pirandello, Eliot had written lyric poems and had narrated (in verse) a variety of tales. When he first tried to write plays, with his pageant-play *The Rock* and then *Murder in the Cathedral,* he thought his task was merely to *stage* his poems and narratives. "The third, or dramatic voice, did not make itself audible to me," he confesses, "until I first attacked the problem of presenting two (or more) characters in some sort of conflict, misunderstanding, or attempt to understand each other, characters with each of whom I had to try to identify myself while writing words for him or her to speak." Eliot then introduces an illustration as genial as Pirandello's account of the hole torn in a puppet theater which transforms Orestes into Hamlet.

> You may remember that Mrs. Cluppins, in the trial of the case of Bardell *v.* Pickwick, testified that "the voices was very loud, sir, and forced themselves upon my ear." "Well, Mrs. Cluppins," said Sergeant Buzfuz, "you were not listening, but you heard the voices." It was in 1938, then, that the third voice began to force itself upon my ear.

It was in 1916, when he was forty-nine, that the "third voice" began to force itself on Pirandello's ear. By 1921, it had possessed him completely. In Pitoëff's words, from that moment "theater is in Pirandello; Pirandello is theater." And Ionesco confirms the judgment, saying: "[Luigi Pirandello] is the manifestation of the inalterable archetype of the idea of the theater which we have in us."

What poetry's third voice (and it was always *poetry* that talked to Pirandello) forces on the imagination is recognition that all the world's a stage and that all the men and women who appear on it generation after generation are caught up in its perpetually renewed drama of genuinely free personality. That vision of the world gave birth to trag-

edy and comedy among the ancient Greeks. Without seeking it, Pirandello relived the experience of that birth in himself.

In our everyday existence, we sense personality—human willful self-centeredness—all around us and in ourselves. But it is so mixed, so confused, that we cannot focus our attention on it easily. Our naïve self-concern in the pursuit of immediate goals and needs easily distracts our attention. Art no less than religion is a response to that all-pervading sense of personality in and around us: that mighty presence, as Wordsworth called it, in its first manifestation to him, when it haunted him like a passion—long before he learned to hear in it

> The still, sad music of humanity,
> Nor harsh, nor grating, though of ample power
> To chasten and subdue.
> ["Lines Composed a Few Miles
> above Tintern Alley"]

From the lyric voice of poetry, Wordsworth had passed to that of lyrical narration; but he never heard the third—the dramatic voice of multiple personality, which is sad music still, but with power to purge us of our self-assertive and exclusive concern for ourselves.

Pirandello had his lyrical and narrative times. Viewing the confusion of wills around us, his first response was an anguished lyrical cry of sympathy, like Shelley's

> Me, who am as a nerve o'er which do creep
> The else-unfelt oppressions of this earth.
> ["Sympathy"]

Later, coming out of himself in his short stories and novels, Pirandello tried to represent sympathetically the confusion of wills in others (a confusion that impinges on our consciousness daily), seeking to give it a meaningful and communicable form. His narratives succeed; but as he develops his narrative skills, it soon becomes clear that it is the depths of willful personality that most interest him—which is to say that, though not quite consciously yet, he is all the while in search of theater.

When Pirandello finally hears that third voice—characters speaking for themselves to one another—his poet's eye leaps at once to the frenzied heart of the matter, and he bodies forth his dramatis personae as *maschere nude* (naked masks), which is the perfect Italian equivalent for the personae of drama in the ancient sense of the term. Personality in its nakedness is a phrase and a thought that takes us to the vital center of dramatic art. Pirandello places himself at that center; and from there, everything he sees, everything he remembers, everything that his friends—especially old Sicilian friends—tell him about life becomes dramatically provocative.

It has been observed that in any old Italian villa, or *palazzo,* or humble cottage, or city apartment, or rooming house, one can meet the very people Pirandello gives us in his plays—people as odd, as complex, as involuted. If we don't

Pirandello in his study, 1913.

see them there, if we don't see them in our own homes, in ourselves wherever we are, it is because we just don't want to see them, because we resist the experience. Pirandello, as he makes clear in his short stories, saw with a lyric poet's eye the alienated types who feel themselves rejected in their families, in their village society, at work and at play. He saw also the opposite types who impose their will on everybody around them, forcing acceptance of what they insist is the truth of a situation when to most others—and to the alienated most of all—the situation is nothing of the sort. In Sicily such willfulness is, of course, at the heart of the lifestyle of the *mafiosi,* in whom a notorious sense of honor drives out every ordinary sense of truth when truth is likely to offend honor.

Alienation and aggressive self-assertion for honor's sake were most intense in the Sicily of Pirandello's youth. Yet, the tension between them was drawn to such extremes as to embrace within its range the infinite variety of personal conflicts that make up the social experience of men, women, and children everywhere.

Pirandello held up his dramatic mirror for all the world to see itself in it. He fashioned that mirror, first of all, with the materials of his native Sicily. His first significant play—the one which, in Eric Bentley's judgment, Americans ought to start with—has all the power and charm of the Sicilian world that fascinated Goethe when he wrote "Kennst du das Land?" It celebrates the ordinary, everyday life of rural, Arabic Sicily, whose exultant moods are splendidly voiced

in the natural poetic genius of Liolà. Written originally in Girgenti dialect and first performed in 1916, *Liolà* springs full-blown into dramatic being, without laborious preparation, out of Pirandello's storehouse of narrated tales. It is deceptively light and comically realistic; but . . . the surface realism is under great tension, and the comic spirit cuts through the fibers of that surface until we sense the pressure of a world of tortured self-consciousness about to burst through from below.

After *Liolà,* Pirandello plunges headlong into that tortured underlying world. He starts, as a rule, with a seemingly solid, everyday situation which he then proceeds to tear apart. He does this in a parallel series of plays, one of which explores dramatically why theater came into being in the first place and why so many people still feel that its representations of human conflict can give meaning to man's earthly existence more adequately than most other forms of experience; while the other, plunging deeper, explores the lowest depths of human motivation, where we experience most directly the need for a theatrical catharsis to shape a personal self for ourselves out of the fragmented chaos of passions and emotions which is our everyday existence.

The first series consists of Pirandello's so-called theater plays [*Six Characters in Search of an Author, Each in His Own Way, Tonight We Improvise*], with which he invaded the modern stage to recover it for dramatic art. In them he attempts to do for a thoroughly self-conscious age what Aeschylus, Sophocles, Euripides, and Aristophanes did for a Greek society which was anything but self-conscious. It was not until Greece had had its great tragedies that Socrates, a contemporary of Aristophanes, first took to heart the oracular utterance: Know Thyself. Even in Shakespeare's time, when Hamlet takes the place of Orestes, self-consciousness is not all-pervading, as it has become in our post-Kantian age.

What can the theater be for a self-critical, thoroughly self-conscious age like our own? Surely not the setting for a communal, religious, political ceremony such as it had been for the Greeks. What then? To answer that question, Pirandello takes our modern theater apart for us. He shows us its inner operation, how it works to shape personality *for* us on the stage, and *in* us through the dramatic catharsis we experience. . . .

But what are we before dramatic art—which is our universal legacy in the Western world—succeeds in purging us, vicariously, to give us inner form? Pirandello shows us that too. In a series of plays, starting with *The Life I Gave You* and *It Is So (If You Think So),* and running through *As Well As Before, Better than Before,* and *At the Exit,* to *Henry IV,* Pirandello forces us to experience for ourselves what happened to poor Orestes when a hole was torn through the marionette sky of his "classical" tragedy.

In this second series of plays on the complex depths of character, not less than in his theater plays, Pirandello anticipates the experimental efforts of our contemporary existential drama, our theaters of the absurd, of revolt, of protest, our "happenings." In one fell swoop, he—more than any other single playwright of this century—has shown the dramatic potential of certain philosophical questions *as theater,* translating difficult ideas into ingenious and immediate realities for the stage, redefining traditional "character" and "action" for the purpose, and transforming conventional language into a series of exchanges which defy standard "communication." He paved the way for the fragmentation of language which we find in Ionesco; he turned dramatic statement into a provocative reassessment of perception and experience, of the kind we find in Giraudoux and Genet; he explored the age-old questions of death and life in modern myths which invite comparison with Camus, Sartre, and Beckett. One must stress, however, that in all his ingenious reversals of traditional values and dramatic concepts, he never sacrificed the notion of "organic" theater.

It is worth noting here that the personae, or masks, of the ancient Greek theater were meant to *conceal* the confused complexity that makes us, before character is defined, some twenty several men at least each several hour. Those Greek masks were worn by actors who did not have to make their own faces and bodies into masks. They simply "put on" their dramatic personalities, and the playwright's words were intelligible to the audience on their own merit, regardless of whether the actors took emotional possession of them. The lines were recited; acting counted for next to nothing. In the modern theater, starting with the age of Shakespeare, *wearing* personality and *reciting* the playwright's words in an external fashion no longer sufficed—for the same reason that it was no longer acceptable dramatical-

ly to hold characters responsible for deeds they have not intentionally committed, as in the Oedipus cycle of Sophocles.

Pirandello grasped fully the difference between the ancient and the modern sense of personality. The modern consciousness of right and wrong, the Judaic-Christian "conscience" and notion of guilt, the subjective attitude of self-conscious individuality as distinguished from the objective fact of accomplished deeds, have dictated a new mold for modern drama. The heroes of modern drama since Shakespeare's time have made their tragic decisions in the complex depths of personality, where the sanctions of moral law or social responsibility have no compelling force. Whether morally justified or wrong and criminal in their deeds, they invariably act as they do, not out of interest in the "ethical vindication" of the external absolutes they subscribe to but for the simple reason that they are the kind of men they are.

This new dramatic imperative of the modern world was given its first memorable expression in Shakespeare; but Pirandello is the first dramatist to express dramatically a *total* absorption in it. Shakespeare had already revealed that, when we look deeply into the motives of our actions, even when caught on the horns of a tragic dilemma, we are always faced with an absurdity that borders on the comic. Greek society, with its objectively confirmed absolutes of family and political values, concealed from itself the sense of "comic relief" that inevitably gnaws its way into our consciousness in moments of high, even tragic, drama.

That sense of comic relief, in tragedy, already strong in Shakespeare, becomes all-pervasive in Pirandello. His one major literary essay, *On Humor,* was devoted to an analysis of its significance for the full development of personality. It is ultimately a humorous experience to know oneself self-consciously. Each of us is an individual claiming "personal" rights objectively before the law; but each of us is also a moral subject claiming rights (and wrongs) of conscience, a family member claiming the love of parents, brothers and sisters, children, a "burgher" in the rat race of civil society, manifesting needs and struggling to secure the cooperation of others for the satisfaction of those needs, and, finally, a "citizen" with the rights and responsibilities of integration in a political fraternity. In those several roles, we manage to maintain a sense of personal unity on the strength of habit. But that unity is threatened again and again by the strain we feel internally as we pass out of one role into another, even in the course of a single ordinary day. In such moments, we are apt to see ourselves suddenly as we imagine "others" see us. We hold up a mirror to ourselves and, whether consciously or not, share at least for a moment in the essential process of creative art.

That is Pirandello's tour de force. We see ourselves mirrored, but we're aware that we are somehow not what we seemed, and the mirrored image embarrasses us, often to the point of laughter. We may instinctively reject the image. But not for long. Sooner or later, we admit to ourselves that we are what we were embarrassed to see mirrored back to us. And then our "humor" becomes a painful awareness of the grotesque posturing our lives must seem to be to others.

Humor, says Pirandello, is the uneasy acknowledgment of the trial of personality as it is forced to recognize its many masks. This is what links humor, or comedy, with tragedy in the historic origin of drama among the Greeks. In an essay on the history of the Italian theater—completed late in his life—Pirandello tells us that the Greeks conceived their plays as trials, offering the public what is, in fact, the very essence of theater:

> a public trial of human actions as they truly are, in that pure and everlasting reality which the imagination of poets creates as an example and warning for our commonplace and confused natural life—a trial both free and human, which spurs the consciences of the judges themselves to an ever loftier and more rigorous moral life. This, in my judgment, is the value of the Theater.

A public trial, both free and human—to catch our consciences. Again and again, in the Greek theater, the question is raised: What does it mean to be free? And in the answers provided by Aeschylus, Sophocles, and Euripides, the Greek audience—through emotional vicarious involvement in the dramatized action—experienced the arrogance of freedom, which makes us claim responsibility for all that we do or suffer to be done to us, despite the fact that, by objective analysis, by scrutinizing ourselves and our situations in detail, it is easy to "see" that a hundred, a thousand, a hundred thousand "forces"—internal as well as external—act on us to make us do what we do.

Pirandello displays the full complexity of that kind of "trial." We are one, externally, in our many social and legal masks; but under analysis, our oneness disintegrates, breaks up into fragments. We are one—or, rather, we are a hundred thousand different "ones," as many as there are others around us mirroring our reflection differently each moment.

The dialectical struggle of the will to hold that complexity together is what Pirandello puts on display as a public trial. It is the common denominator of all his plays, and that is why we must dwell on it here. The Greeks, whose sense of family memberships and social commitment was much stronger, depicted that public trial or struggle in relatively simple terms. Shakespeare's trial of personality coming to know itself is much more complex. But Pirandello's burden—which is the moral burden of our age—is to deal with a world in which, the minute we stop seeing ourselves as one, we immediately see ourselves as no one, or as a hundred thousand ones. It is the same dramatic purpose at work, however: to put on public trial the complexities of human nature and conduct. When we look around us in everyday life, all we get is an image of ourselves in a shattered mirror. The playwright's burden is to give us something else: the reality of our fragmented wills, indeed, but so nakedly exposed, so focused, that it makes us whole at least in the shock of self-knowledge that makes us free.

Pirandello's is "difficult" theater, to say the least. But not more difficult than the reality which is the subject matter. The encrustations of habit are not easily cracked. How exactly do we go about "seeing ourselves" in the depths of our consciousness? Pirandello pictures it for us, usually, by having one of his characters look at his reflection in a mirror. That way we can get to see ourselves as others see us. And, as we usually try to get into the real consciousness of other people by looking steadfastly into their eyes, so we imagine we can do the same with our mirrored image; and with better results, since we are, after all, looking out of the same eyes we are looking into. That's our instinctive expectation. Yet, when we try it, what we actually see is an utterly distracting look with which we are not in the least able to identify ourselves. We realize at once that we can do better by closing our eyes, by not looking out at all, so that the mind's eyes may turn inward upon themselves.

Consciousness turned inward is self-consciousness. Even before a mirror, consciousness is very different from self-consciousness. Consciousness, at best, must have a naïve confidence in its sensory experience. Facing the world of things it can see, hear, smell, taste, and touch, things that are *here* and *now,* consciousness says simply: *così è—it is so.* But that initial sense of certainty is easily destroyed. The *here* and *now* which is the basis of our certainty of things disappears the moment we turn our attention away. *It is so* only if that's how you see it: *se vi pare.*

So we turn away from things that only appear to be and focus our consciousness inward upon itself (as Socrates advised). There, needless to say, we get a totally different impression of things. Our first impulse, then, is to empty our consciousness of all its sensory impressions, so as to see it in its nakedness. The immediate effect is like an empty mirror reflected into an empty mirror ad infinitum. There is great depth, but no content. We have, indeed, our *self* mirroring itself; but, without specific content, it could be *any* self, in any body; and that, we quickly recognize, is the antithesis of what is ordinarily meant by personality.

We were *somebody,* however confused, in simple consciousness. Now, in our first attempt at self-consciousness, we are suddenly *nobody.* Pirandello forces the sensation of this experience on us repeatedly in his plays. It is by no means a theatrical stunt. But neither is it a psychological or phenomenological tour de force that were better left to philosophers. The ancient Greek drama, in fact, discovered its tragic and comic masks—its dramatis personae—in the very depths of this dialectic of self-consciousness. The nothingness, the nobody or anybody we initially find there is the naked will whose task it is to shape us a proper persona, or mask, which will hold together, according to its strength, the confusion of our everyday conscious experience which makes us twenty several men at least each several hour.

But there is a dilemma in the experience of the naked will mirroring itself in empty self-consciousness. Which is the original, real will and which the mirrored image? Which was the original consciousness that emptied itself of its empirical experience of the world to study itself and which—in the act of self-reflection—is the reflected consciousness?

The question is worth exploring even apart from its strictly theatrical importance (which is critical for any serious study of the idea of drama) if for no other reason than that it has literally revolutionized our contemporary society, on and offstage. Students of Karl Marx know how fascinated he was by Hegel's discussion of the dilemma of self-consciousness in the *Phenomenology*. Whether he actually read Hegel or not, Pirandello certainly knew the experience and has dramatized it with great daring, and convincingly, in many plays. It is a dilemma each of us can experience for himself. In what is perhaps his most brilliantly conceived novel, ***Uno, nessuno, e centomila*** (***One, No One, and a Hundred Thousand***), Pirandello explores the progression from full consciousness, as somebody, to empty self-consciousness, as nobody in particular, to the third level of awareness that combines the fullness of the first with the infinite self-reflection of the second, in a dizzying experience of mirrored fullness where the confusion is a thousand times, a hundred thousand times what it originally was, and we are no closer than before to discovering which is the original self-conscious will and which the reflected image.

In his *Phenomenology,* Hegel reminds us that entire ages, entire civilizations—as, for instance, the ancient Hindu— have been wrapped up in it, to the point of abandoning any commonsense awareness of our so-called objective world. Each of us, even here in the West, where empirical science reigns, must plunge into it at least momentarily if we are ever to know what "knowing" really is. Hegel characterizes the experience as that of the "unhappy consciousness." It is difficult to come out of it without an act of "hybris," as the ancient critics of drama defined the term—without an arrogant assertion of willful self-mastery, such as the protagonists of the Greek tragedies displayed onstage for the moral edification of the Greek citizenry.

It takes a creative, dramatic arrogance to make "one" out of the division of mirrored consciousness mirroring its mirrored consciousness. In that experience, our original naïve consciousness is literally beside itself, as if it were another self; and when it seeks to overcome that division, it literally *crowds* itself in infinite self-reflection, like that fiend in William Blake's cloud who *crowds,* in his fierce madness, after night.

In the end, one side of mirrored self-consciousness must overwhelm the other—or surrender itself to the other (which is really the same thing)—if we are to be made whole. Hegel calls it a conflict between lord and bondsman, or master and servant, in which the roles end up being reversed before they are confounded. Karl Marx, as we know, saw his Communist revolution of the proletariat as accomplishing in civil society precisely the reversal of roles which Hegel indicates as the inevitable outcome of the master-servant struggle in the divided self-consciousness. Following Hegel's specific indications, the author of the *Communist Manifesto* argued that, by arming its servants with industrial skills and the weapons of war, the bourgeois ruling class of modern industrial society was giving its very being, with all its strength, to its enemy and thus virtually committing suicide. Marx's "final solution" to the bour-geoisie-proletariat struggle (in which the proletariat triumphs absolutely with its dictatorship) is the antithesis of Hegel's view of the ultimate outcome. Hegel emphasizes that the I-Thou opposition in self-consciousness is truly resolved not when one side insists that the other side is nothing, a *not*-I, but when the opposed sides of consciousness recognize their higher unity as "we" in creative reason.

Pirandello's dramatization of the experience follows the course of the Hegelian analysis. Out of the dramatized conflict in play after play written late in his career, he brings us to a new sense of "we," of a unity of personality in self-consciousness; and in that unity or synthesis, the Greek tragic catharsis finds its modern equivalent.

Just as he explored in one series of plays what the stage is and has been for civilized society, and in another the depths of personality that provide the substance of dramatic art, so Pirandello gives us a third series of plays that dramatize, onstage, the experience of dramatic catharsis itself. His last great plays—the so-called myths of ***The New Colony, Lazarus,*** and ***The Mountain Giants,*** taken together with ***Diana and Tuda*** and ***When Someone Is Somebody,*** are an integral and culminating part of Pirandello's dramatic world. They can stand alone, of course, on their own merits as distinct works of art; but, like Shakespeare's *Tempest* and, even more, like his *Henry VIII,* they reveal their full dramatic significance only to those who are thoroughly at home in the dramatic world of which they are the culminating achievement.

In ancient Greek drama, the tragic catharsis was by no means complete in the first or second work of a grand trilogy. Aeschylus's *Prometheus Bound* needs not only a Prometheus unbound to complete its dramatic effect, but also a play establishing Prometheus in Attica as a benignant deity. In the *Agamemnon-Cheophori-Eumenides* trilogy, the cycle is not complete until Orestes is tried in a rational court and acquitted by a vote of Athene which puts the family curse to rest. Sophocles's trilogy of *Oedipus Tyrannos, Antigone,* and *Oedipus at Colonus* gives us, in fact, three distinctly different masterpieces, in which the third takes on a transcendent importance it could not otherwise have had as a work of art, when it is read as the culmination of that particular trilogy.

In his last plays, Pirandello is in effect drawing the chief meridians of his theatrical world upward to converge at a single pole. This whole business of life can be for us all no more than a tale told by an idiot unless we get deep enough below the surface of conventional values to the substantive core. What blind Oedipus "saw" at Colonus, what Orestes experienced in Athene's court of ultimate appeal, what Shakespeare reveals to us in the magic art of Prospero and in Cranmer's prophecy at the christening of the child destined to become Queen Elizabeth—such is the substance of Pirandello's myth plays. In them he gathers up all that he had already dramatized, into a new synthesis, to show us its social, religious, and artistic reality, in its rightness, its holiness, and its beauty.

Pirandello's theatrical world is planted deep in the common soil of human experience, with a sturdy weathered and twisted trunk of theatrical expertise that enables him to review for us dramatically the meaning of theater, and with marvelous branches of evergreen leaves that come and go imperceptibly, laden with seasonal fruit. Just before he died, Pirandello had a vision of such a tree—the great Saracen olive of Sicily. He explained to his son, on the morning of the day before his death, that with that tree planted in the center of the stage, for the curtain to come down in the unwritten final act of *The Mountain Giants,* he would solve everything he meant to show. That great tree, whose roots he had revealed in his masterful *Liolà,* was meant to symbolize the completion of his theater.

Pirandello has gone deeply into the secret chamber of man's heart and has discovered tragic wants. He has seen that there are things that we dare not confess even to ourselves, moral deeds that lie like heavy stones in the depth of our conscience.

—*Domenico Vittorini, in his* The Drama of Luigi Pirandello, *1935.*

Umberto Mariani (essay date 1989)

SOURCE: "The 'Pirandellian' Character," in *Canadian Journal of Italian Studies,* Vol. 12, Nos. 38-9, 1989, pp. 1-9.

[*In the essay below, Mariani examines how figures in Pirandello's plays create their own "subjective realities."*]

> "Ogni fantasma . . . deve avere il suo drama."
> (Preface to *Sei personaggi in cerca d'autore*)

In the structure of the most representative works of Pirandello, the major works of his maturity, a fundamental opposition recurs with increasing clarity between those characters who endure, question, or reject the values and conditions to which their society is determined to bind them—with its customs, its prejudices, its philistinism, its definite claim to wisdom, knowledge, self confidence—and the representatives and supporters of that society. This is the opposition through which the Pirandellian character reveals itself. The "Pirandellian" character, therefore, is not any charater in any work by Pirandello, but that character who rebels against the pretensions of social forms and thereby sets himself in opposition to the "bourgeois" characters who are his antagonists and are the functional embodiments of that fundamental opposition. The fact that the "Pirandellian" character too for the most part comes from a bourgeois background does not at all diminish the fundamental opposition, but rather defines with necessary precision its essentially formal, spiritual, ethical, nature.

The Pirandellian character is one who suffers then, enduring thereby a time-less essential condition, but he also endures the particular condition of twentieth-century man—

perhaps one of the reasons for the vitality and modernity of Pirandello's work and particularly of his theater. His character has lost the feeling of comforting stability, of self confidence of the bourgeois world of the end of the century; he is assailed by doubts about his identity and the possibility of ever realizing or communicating it, establishing a normal, functioning relationship with the society he happens to live in; he has lost the feeling of unity, of a community of thought and belief, and of faith in the means to communicate basic values that the late nineteenth-century bourgeois world enjoyed; he suffers from his loss and denounces it more dramatically than do the characters of Svevo.

As the old century came to its end and the new approached the catastrophe of the First World War, the bourgeoisie in Europe and particularly in Italy was progressively losing the dominant position it had enjoyed during the struggle for Italy's reunification and the period that followed. With the political tradeunionist mass movements of the proletariat on one side and the rise of the new industrial baronies on the other, the bourgeois intellectual saw his own role becoming increasingly irrelevant. Yet that bourgeois world had once seemed so solid, secure, indeed so complacent in the principles and the institutions which ruled social behavior; it had seemed especially confident in its positive faith in the omnipotence of scientific knowledge. Now instead the bourgeois intellectual felt betrayed. The promises of that security had not been kept: scientific knowledge had been unable to guarantee anything positive; the moral convictions had often revealed themselves as hypocritical masks concealing under an apparent harmony a mediocre reality, indeed a reality that was disintegrating, no longer sustained by the now empty forms of its false ideals, so different, on their utilitarian underside, from the heroic values of the first half of the century. The Pirandellian character has discovered the meanness, the hypocrisy, the pretentiousness, the shabby values of petit bourgeois ideals.

Once the old values, the empty ideals have been degraded and rejected, it becomes impossible to hold onto the unified vision of reality that society fostered; reality breaks down into a meaningless succession of events which some segments of the middle class may still think it controls, while the Pirandellian character has clearly perceived the fragmentation and decay of a reality which has lost all credibility in spite of his antagonist's continuing claims to certainty and self-assurance.

And if historical reality in its intellectual, ethical, and social aspects breaks down, can the certainties and assumptions regarding the individual himself, the integrity of the person, his very identity, avoid collapse? The Pirandellian character must bear not only the disintegration of the social reality amidst whose assurances he was raised, but also the disintegration of his own personality, of the comforting certainties regarding his identity, his personal worth; he must live what Pirandello in the famous preface to the *Sei personaggi* will call the drama of "life devoid of form". The crisis of the structures of social life and of behavior is reflected in the individual soul, which is unable to stay afloat following the shipwreck of the forms of objective, external, social reality. The Pirandellian character proclaims the loss of his own form, of his unity, of the certainty of his knowledge, and understanding of his own truth, and of its communicability; this is the condition at the root of the drama he brings with him onto the stage.

The Pirandellian character, however, does not accept but suffers from and denounces the loss of his form as an unjust privation. He feels the need of that form, that consistency, that unity and self-assurance, for an existence supported by a system of values and ideals. He asserts that need as a fundamentally human and insuppressible one: the need to know one's identity and to communicate what one is, the need to identify with, to integrate oneself into a stable society, to enjoy its recognition, to find a sense of security in it. And he aspires to this tenaciously as to a conquest by right.

From the exile of this "life devoid of form" the Pirandellian character yearns, then, for a form, declares his need for an enduring structure, which, however, cannot be the reality that shamefully disintegrated shortly before, the hypocritical forms of bourgeois behavior with their devalued content. He is not a nostalgic reactionary. To be different from the old one, the new form must possess an absolute, unassailable unity and solidity—that is, an impossible, unattainable unity and solidity. For the worst aspect of the wornout values of the late 19th century had been their very claim to be absolutes. The bourgeois world against which the Pirandellian spirits rebel were too guilty of presumption, of an unjustified, complacent, even arrogant confidence in its social institutions, its customs and codes of behavior, its scientific faith for them to be inclined to trust any belief bearing even the slightest implication of certainty.

The new form then, toward which the Pirandellian character so passionately aspires, if it must differ from the one that has failed, if it must be, and not only seem, unassailable, absolute, cannot exist, is impossible in the real world. Therefore, he does not like to explain or define it; he knows his is an unappeasable need, an unattainable goal. He knows that his loss is final; yet he resents it, he cannot resign himself to the chaos of formlessness and of insignificance. This is his conflict, his drama. Exiled as he is in the limbo of formlessness, the Pirandellian character lives a drama not dissimilar from that of the souls in Dante's limbo, who "without hope live in desire". The Pirandellian character mounts the stage to bear witness to this existential condition, this conflict which is his drama. He declares his loss and his irrepressible need for what he has lost as well as his tragic knowledge that he cannot achieve what he seeks and needs; a universe of certainties, an absolute that would allow him to affirm himself, values that would create and define a reality for him. He defines his ultimate tragedy as that of being destined to pursue forever his lost unity in the chaos of endless disintegration, the drama of "a life devoid of form yet longing for a form".

The characters of many dramatists who came after Pirandello, more or less conscious of this destiny of the impossibility of attaining that unassailable absolute reality, are resigned to the fall into formlessness, have made peace with chaos; they represent the definitive loss of an essential human dimension, and their theater moves towards silence. But the Pirandellian character, although he knows that he will never arrive at an acceptable solution, does not cease to search for it, to declare his need for it, even to pursue utterly unsatisfactory solutions, so strong is his longing for form, for a reality which can be shared. He will assert in *Cosí è, se vi pare* his awareness of the relativity of reality and maintain an uneasy family *menage*. He will choose in *Enrico IV* a reality fixed by the history of eight hundred years earlier. In *Sei personaggi* he will seek a definitive artistic form or, failing to obtain it from his creator, at least a momentary expressive form in the acting of a theatrical company. The six characters are clearly driven by the need for a profound form of communication, impossible to attain even through the eloquence of the highest artistic creation, let alone through a play whose plot exists only orally, in fragments, in a form that is still in flux, continually contested, wide open to betrayals of interpretation. They are conscious of pursuing only compromises, utterly unsatisfactory goals because the satisfactory ones are unattainable or unknowable or non-existent; they even complain about the definitive artistic form which they seek with such persistence and intelligence as the best possible means of communication (and even as a guarantee of immortality) because artistic form, despite its eloquence, cannot avoid fixing and simplifying the reality it tries to represent while real life is complex, rich, in endless flux.

This traumatic discovery of an irreparable loss is, then, the existential condition of Pirandello's characters and the cause of their insoluble conflict with life in our time; it is at the source of his inspiration; an inspiration of an eminently moral nature. Hence Pirandello's compassion for the fate of contemporary man, victim of that trauma and loss, and his denunciation of false values, of the social myths of honor, respectability, manners, behind which the bourgeois world hid its moral void.

Just as the Pirandellian character tries to unmask those myths, so he argues with the artistic forms that represented and celebrated them, especially bourgeois comedy, the forms of which are assumed by some Pirandellian characters in order to denounce their contradictions and their hollowness. Instead of opposing them uncompromisingly, these characters prefer to embody recognizable situations and characters of a bourgeois reality in order to protest its alienating and alienated qualities, they present themselves to a public and even to professional actors familiar with the forms and content of bourgeois drama, wearing its clothing and using its language, in order to unmask its mechanical nature, its conventionality, its equivocal familiarity. They make extensive use of dialectics, as the bourgeois characters used it to defend bourgeois conventions, but they do so in order to tear them apart, and to condemn reasoning itself as an abuse, a means of repressing free and genuine feelings, or at least to underline its function as a means of reaching a more acute awareness of the absurdity of one's suffering; they use words to complain about their inadequacy as a means of communication. They make use of all these means of communication to attest to both their condemnation to incommunicability and their need to communicate.

And while using the accepted, traditional theatrical forms to discredit them, the Pirandellian character also uses them to demonstrate the validity of new, experimental, open forms, bringing the theater into the theater. The tragedy of the character is irresoluble, and the new theater must remain open, with no solutions. It must invade the outworn forms of bourgeois drama, break up its structures, invalidate its dénouements, laugh at its conclusions, propose non-conclusions; it must tell the respectable audiences that the third act they are expecting is a fraud that should be suppressed, or ignored or dismissed with sardonic laughter, that even the physical space of the stage is a convention and can be profitably enlarged to include the orchestra, the lobby, the nearby streets, any imaginable place.

Pirandello reflects an important moment of the "crisis of passage" from nineteenth-century positivist bourgeois culture to the irrationalistic avantgarde culture of the twentieth century. But while various revolutionary and experimental currents of his time and thereafter embraced and cultivated a post-positivistic irrationalism and nihilism, Pirandello deplores and longs to escape them, without, however, yielding to nostalgia for a past that perpetrated so cruel a hoax on his characters. Although it was a rich source of symbolism for him, the discovery of the irrational, of the unconscious, of multiplicity, which took the place of that lost unified view of bourgeois culture, could not compensate for that definitive tragic loss; rather, Pirandello's lucid sensibility generated bewilderment, compassion, and moral indignation.

The most important element of the positivist vision of reality had been the certainty, fostered by centuries of Aristotelianism and later of modern science, of the existence and knowability of an objective reality that included man but was not of his making. Not a product of his ability to conceive, interpret, and incorporate inner concepts into his vision of exterior reality, as man had done through the centuries, from the earliest mythological interpretations of reality through numberless philosophical systems from the presocratics to Kant and Hegel; but an objective reality, which the human mind, especially after the introduction of the scientific method of inquiry some centuries earlier, had been exploring with increasing depth. The discoveries in the fields of the exact sciences were at the root of that certainty, but the overwhelming influence of Aristotelian thought through the centuries on the mental attitudes of people of average education accounted for the tendency to stretch that certainty beyond the limits of scientific knowledge to the social sciences and even to individual and collective perceptions of inner and exterior realities. These are areas in which objective knowledge is impossible, and in which, therefore, no certainty, no dogmatism was justifiable: areas in which consciousness can at most be subjective, a stream of opinions derived from a stream of totally subjective impressions and perceptions of a reality created by the individual to satisfy inner existential needs or by a dominant group able to impose its own vision of things on others.

The relentless pressure of the group on the individual to conform usually succeeds. The individual accepts, however reluctantly, the ideas, ideals, values, forms, and behaviors defined and proposed by society. Otherwise the conflict would be unendurable. But he wears a mask, imposed and accepted. Or the individual may refuse it, but only to create one of his own, in order to survive, to fight society with its own weapon, to function in it, or in spite of it, to communicate to others one's perception of oneself, "to communicate oneself", to seek in others a confirmation of one's perception of oneself, of one's identity.

Thus Mattia Pascal, who though he could rid himself of a suffocating reality, must soon create for himself a new reality to face a society geographically different but equally exacting of the individual, and finally, oppressed by the alter reality too, he escapes to return to the previous one—by which, however, since he is officially dead, he is relegated to a limbo that allows him no satisfactory social integration, though unwittingly allowing him a bit of the longed-for freedom. Thus the Ponza family, having created the unusual family *menage* that allows the two survivors of the real or fictitious loss of wife or daughter to go on living and maintaining their individual vision of reality, must fight, tooth and nail, a society that does not deem the creation of a private reality acceptable, let alone its externalization in social relationships. Thus Henry IV, an object of derision for society even before the accident that caused his madness—a derision of which the joke that precipitated the accident was only one episode—creates for himself a new reality when he awakens from twelve years of madness in order to survive the new situation and repay society to some degree for his loss; and after rejecting that new reality for a few hours, he must revive it at the end of the play, having killed the person most directly responsible for his loss.

But we are dealing always with imposed, subjective realities, all relative, not absolute, all different in content, fashioned by different individuals, even when some of them think they have a very similar view of things and therefore group together to try to impose it on the whole society. An objective reality, outside the field of the exact sciences, if it exists at all is beyond our possibility of knowing it; and if we cannot know it, we cannot speak of it or even simply affirm its existence.

And if objective reality cannot be known, created reality becomes an inevitable necessity for everyone. Pirandello wrote: "Io penso che la vita è una molto triste buffoneria, poiché abbiamo in noi senza poter sapere né come, né perché, né da chi, la necessità di ingannare di continuo noi stessi con la spontanea creazione di una realtà (Una per ciascuno e non mai la stessa per tutti) la quale di tratto in tratto si scopre vana e illusoria." Even the madness Henry IV invents in order to face the reality he wakes up to and take whatever little revenge he can on his persecutors, is accepted by the latter to confirm their opinion of their own sanity; in order not to be too deeply shocked by his terrible words, since they are those of a madman; hence even after the revelation of his recovery it will not be too difficult for them to become convinced once more of his madness and to consider Belcredi's murder the act of one mentally deranged, and not what it really is: a vindictive gesture made in blind rage by a man who has persuaded himself to reenter the unforeseeable and uncontrollable present from an orderly and controlled reality fashioned after a known and totally predictable historical model.

This reality created by each individual with or against the pervasive or compelling pressure of other individuals or an entire group, being relative, illusory, personal, is not so different in its fundamental subjectivity from the created reality of a work of art, which, however, conceived at a deeper level of consciousness, wrought upon by longer reflection, more acute intelligence, and more intense concentration, probably comes closer to achieving some semblance of truth ("less real, perhaps, but truer"). The reality created by the artist must perforce possess qualities which the reality created by each individual in his everyday living does not possess, and will lack some qualities that are present in daily life: artistic reality is fixed forever in a definitive text, which, if genius has concurred in shaping it, may confer to the artistic creation and its characters an immortal vitality, while the reality created by everyday living is in flux, constantly changing, not capturable in memory, perishable. Artistic reality captures a particular moment, creates an ideal moment, frozen, abstracted from the context of the flux of everyday reality. In that respect it impoverishes the vitality that derives from movement, from multidimensionality, from contradiction, in favor of a vitality that comes from its ideal sublimation, its distillation into the most effective form of communication, artistic form.

The two realities, however, do have in common the basic quality of their subjectivity. And they maintain a strong interdependence: everyday reality to the eyes of the "humorist" (as Pirandello often called himself in his lengthy elaboration of the concept of literary humor) reveals the presence of a tragic contradiction which he tries to represent. His art then expresses the feeling of the author as he confronts that tragic condition, "the feeling for the reverse". His work, that is, in which the tragedy of his characters may be *less real, perhaps, but truer,* gives form to the artist's sense of the tragedy, *less true, perhaps, but more real,* of everyday reality. Art is not the mirror of life but a mirror for life. Life looking at itself would never be able to see the fundamental contradiction that is revealed to it when it looks at itself as it is mirrored in the work of art. Art is not a mirror of life, but it holds up a mirror to life which sees itself in it the way the artist's eye sees it, in its essence, its most secret reality—which is no less real. The "humoristic"—that is, tragically contradictory—condition that art reveals, is equally present, if unrevealed, in everyday reality. The "humorist" laments that tragic reality in all sincerity, deeply, because it is real, is inherent in everyday life, and cannot merely be treated ironically as an exclusively "fictitious" reality, belonging to the work of art alone.

This is one of the reasons why Pirandello considered the term "irony" inadequate to designate the feeling that he chose to call *"umorismo".* He rejected both irony as a term of traditional rhetoric, that is saying something with any degree of invective or sarcasm while meaning its opposite, a contradiction that is obvious, "fictitious", one of words not of substance; and irony in the sense meant by Schlegel: "per il poeta l'ironia consiste nel non fondersi mai del tutto con l'opera propria, nel non perdere, neppure nel momento del patetico, la coscienza della irrealtà delle sue creazioni, nel non essere lo zimbello dei fantasmi da lui stesso evocati, nel sorridere al lettore che si lascerà prendere dal giuoco, e anche di se stesso che la propria vita consacra a giocare." The awareness of the "humorist" goes beyond (it does not stop before taking that step, as some would have it) the awareness of the unreality of the work of art, of the merely fantastic, fictitious elements that Schlegel reminds us of. The feeling of the "humorist" springs from the awareness of the contradiction that tragically dominates everyday reality, the life of man, before becoming the theme of the work of art. If the smile of the romantic poet, according to Schlegel, is born of the awareness that pathos is after all the soul of a fictitious work, the lament of the "humorist" is born of the *feeling* for what in life and not just in the work of art is tragically reversed.

Pirandello's distinction between the comic and the humoristic lies in this tragic quality: "the comic is the perception of the opposite"; it causes laughter because something is *amusingly* reversed; but if "the perception of the opposite" is followed by reflection revealing the tragic underside of the comic and producing the *"feeling for* the opposite", compassion for the victims of the contradiction, "then I cannot laugh as before", one is no longer confronting something amusingly overturned by something *tragically* overturned. The humoristic is what at first prompts laughter but upon reflection must lead us to tears, to deep anguish.

The deep current of sympathy that ties the author to the "Pirandellian" characters, the seriousness of the writer before their drama, is due not to the fact that he "is not aware of the 'unreality of what he creates'," but to the fact that his characters are the expression of a moral torment, "the *feeling for* the opposite", and embody in a *less real, perhaps, but truer* form the *less true, perhaps, but more real* tragedy of humanity in our time. It is a sympathy which is felt especially deeply when the "Pirandellian" character reacts with fierce indignation to any insult to his suffering, his sincerity, his authenticity—in a word to his human dignity.

Pirandello's whole theory of "humorism" affirms, in fact, that his art springs from a matrix that is deeply ethical, not merely preoccupied with questions of form. And when he says that the characters in his work may be "less real, perhaps; but truer", he is talking about a truth not exclusively epistemological, but ethical as well, a truth concerned with good and evil, with injustice and understanding and compassion.

Mary Ann Frese Witt (essay date 1991)

SOURCE: "Woman or Mother? Feminine Conditions in Pirandello's Theater," in *A Companion to Pirandello Studies,* edited by John Louis DiGaetani, Greenwood Press, 1991, pp. 57-72.

Women as objects of desire, scorn, fear, as victims or as traps; conflicts arising over pregnancy and female identity—these lie at the very heart of Pirandello's dramatic plots. The triangular basis of a number of plays (old man-young woman-young man; husband-wife-lover) might place Pirandello squarely in the tradition of both classical and *boulevard* comedy were it not for the absence of, or at least the lack of emphasis on, romantic love. For Pirandello there can be no comic resolution, no affirmation of eros, fertility, or even delight in seeing the duper duped, because these have become the very sources of the problems that he explores in their agonizing and endless labyrinths. Even *Liolà,* long hailed as a life-affirming, sun-drenched masterpiece, poses, as we will see, social and psychological questions that undermine its comic surface. Pirandello's humorism often subverts a classically comic situation, engaging the reader or spectator in a *sentimento del contrario.* In *Think It Over, Giacomino,* for example, we have what could be, in Harry Levin's terms, a classical conflict between "killjoy" and "playboy," centered, naturally, on the possession of a woman. In this play, however, it is the old man (normally the killjoy) who must persuade the young man (normally the playboy) to fulfill his role as lover. In addition, the woman in question is valued not as an object or a subject of erotic desire but primarily in her role as mother of a child, a condition not infrequent in Pirandello's works.

"Non è una donna, è una madre," (She's not a woman, she's a mother) says the Father of his wife in *Six Characters in Search of an Author.* The statement is revealing in that not only this character but also the playwright himself appears to view the other gender as a series of categories, or dramatic roles, roles defined not by the character herself but by others' views of her. We are privileged to witness the Father's sense of himself as both *man* and *father,* and indeed his agonizing consciousness (like that of other male characters such as "Enrico IV" and Leone Gala) of the fact that a man in his life plays many parts. Pirandello's female characters often play one or more roles assigned to them by the absent but controlling author and by the male characters in their lives. These roles can be defined broadly as those of *madre/moglie/figlia/donna* (mother/wife/daughter/woman.) The *figliastra,* the stepdaughter, struggles against this categorization. Here I would like to examine some major examples of what I take to be the two primary categories, those of *mother* and *woman,* and to attempt to redefine the nature of the female in Pirandello's theater.

Pirandello's veneration of motherhood, along with his fascination-repulsion toward pregnancy, surely stem in part from his upbringing in what his biographer Giudice terms "atavistic Muslim-Catholic Sicily" with its taxonomy of women and girls as Virgin, Mother, or Dishonored, as well as his deep attachment to his own mother and his distrust of his father. The formative episode between Luigi's father Stefano and his niece—Stefano made the girl pregnant and arranged for her to marry a man who would legitimize her unborn child—no doubt served as a model for many of the dramatist's situations. Pirandello's conflicts with his father, leading to a final acceptance of authority, may, as Giudice suggests [in *Pirandello: A Biography* (1975)], have prepared him for his later commitment to fascism. Certainly his attitudes toward motherhood agree with fascist ideology on the subject, in part no doubt because both have their origins in the same "atavistic" values. In the development of Pirandello's aesthetics and thought, as in early fascist

ideology, we witness a curious combination of a revolutionary, modernist critique of bourgeois institutions such as marriage and the family with an attachment to the most traditional archetypes.

"La madre è una costruzione irreducible" (the mother is an irreducible construction), says Baldovino in *The Pleasure of Honesty.* The fascist critic Ascanio Zapponi interprets this phrase to mean that on this "instinctive" as opposed to "intellectual" basis, in conformity with fascist ideology, one can begin to construct. Baldovino makes this remark just after delivering a most Pirandellian speech on the "construction" of one's personality in various situations. About to step into his new role as husband of his friend Fabbio's pregnant mistress Agata in order to keep her "honest," Baldovino curiously asks if there is a mother involved and upon hearing that there is makes the remark quoted above. The stage directions for Agata's mother, Signora Maddalena, describe her as: "fifty two years old . . . full of passion for her daughter, she only sees through her eyes." If our "constructions," as Baldovino maintains, are masks that hide our most intimate feelings—what we are for ourselves as opposed to what we are for others—then it appears that maternity is the one construction in which social role and intimate feelings coincide, a role so all-consuming that it eclipses all others. Paternity, as Baldovino himself will show, can be intellectually constructed, whereas maternity need only be instinctively accepted. *The Pleasure of Honesty* has been seen as Pirandello's optimistic comedy in which love triumphs over reason, but in fact the real triumph is not that of love but of maternity. At the beginning of the third act, Maddalena says of her daughter that she is now nothing but a mother and at the end of the play, when Agata has chosen to follow him and leave her lover, Baldovino says to his wife: "con la maternità, l'amante doveva morire. Ecco, voi non siete piu altro che madre" (with maternity, the lover [in you] had to die. Now you are nothing but a mother.) The plays's happy ending thus allows Agata to assume her "irreducible" maternal state and Baldovino to "construct" his paternal one. The biological father, as often in Pirandello, can be dispensed with.

Several Pirandellian situations postulate a variation on the cuckold theme, with a man donning the mask of paternity for another man's child or children. *Think it over Giacomino* is perhaps the prototype; others include *All for the Good*; *Man, Beast, and Virtue*; *The Life I Gave You* (although offstage); and *Liolà.*

Critics from Gramsci to Bentley and beyond appear to have accepted at face value Pirandello's claims in his letter to his son Stefano that *Liolà,* written as a summer vacation diversion, is "full of songs and sunshine and is so light-hearted that it doesn't seem like one of my works at all." Yet [as Susan Bassnett-McGuire points out] the plot of *Liolà* is basically that of Machiavelli's *La Mandragola* (a comedy to be sure, but scarcely "light-hearted"). She maintains that, while Liolà may be pro-life, he is profoundly antifeminist, a stance that sours his proclamations of sun and song. I would argue that the question of feminism or antifeminism doesn't even enter the picture. Rather, what makes it impossible (at least now) to read *Liolà* as a primarily light-hearted comedy is the fact that the play makes sense only within the Sicilian codes that Pirandello establishes as parameters and that even within these codes Liolà's primary project is to rob women of all dignity and autonomy. For example, Liolà prides himself on his "generous offer" to marry Tuzza, and he justifies his own promiscuity, which results in several pregnancies, with a folksy formulation of the most traditional double standard: "Everyone knows how my children were born!—Girls who went astray [*Ragazzotte di fuorivia*]. It's bad to force a well-guarded gate, but he who travels on an open and beaten road . . . ." Liolà also justifies his activities by generously offering to raise the children he has fathered, but of course what he does is to let his mother handle the work while he plays with them. Thus, his women are denied the only status that in the Sicilian code could give them dignity, that is, maternity. And Liolà has the best of both worlds! In a sense he is indeed the product of his author's summer fantasies—a male mother. Creative and fecund both as poet and progenitor, he enjoys the "irreducible" state of motherhood without what Pirandello sees as its bestial, instinctive, limiting aspects—functions divided between the natural mothers and the grandmother.

The treatment of maternity and woman in this play is also developed in the comparison of the "good" woman Mita with the "bad" woman Tuzza, both of whom attempt to deceive Uncle Simone into believing that their children, fathered by Liolà, are his. Acting on her own behalf, with her mother, Tuzza attempts to defend her interests and fails. Mita, on the other hand, submissive and docile, does exactly what Liolà tells her to do and succeeds. As in classical comedy, Liolà the playboy outsmarts Uncle Simone the killjoy (fathering a child on his wife), and yet the happy ending is deeply troubled. Tuzza's desperate attempt to kill Liolà out of jealousy and revenge anticipates Enrico IV's successful stabbing. If Liolà seemed to challenge the stifling moral and social order of the Sicilian village in his defiance of the institutions of marriage and property, that order is firmly reestablished in the end. The unwed Tuzza is the dishonored woman, unhappily married Mita the honored mother, and Liolà the happy father-mother, having expropriated the maternal rights of the dishonored girls. The purported champion of "nature" against "society," Liolà has in the end affirmed the necessity of hypocrisy and trickery for the maintenance of the social order.

Motherhood triumphant and legitimized rather than love triumphant thus constitutes the outcome of both of these early Pirandellian "comedies." Maternity is perhaps more properly the stuff of comedy in **Man, Beast, and Virtue** (1922), whose situation constitutes a farcical variation of those in **Liolà** and **The Pleasure of Honesty**. Here a lover must desire that his mistress's husband perform his conjugal duties so that the child she is carrying will appear to be his and her "honor" thus preserved. Whereas Agata actually chooses her husband over her lover (evolving, as we have seen, from *amante* to *madre*), Signora Perella, like Mita, submissively follows her lover's plan to deceive her husband. She thus assumes several roles, dependent on the two men's perceptions of her. In his attempt to seduce Captain Perella to make love to his wife, Paolino at one point brings out a makeup kit to paint a "horrible mask" on his beloved.

He explains his reasons for doing so in terms of his perception of the role that the captain will assign to his wife. "Non ti vuole madre! E tu la darai a lui, codesta maschera, alla sua bestialità!" (He doesn't want you as a mother. You must wear this mask to appeal to his bestiality!). Paolino soon finds, however, that he has misjudged his audience. Upon seeing his wife, the captain roars with laughter, because she is playing the wrong role. He explains to Paolino: "Benissimo, si . . . Se fosse una . . . lei m'intende! Come moglie, no . . . e buffa!" (Yes, she looks great . . . If she were a . . . you know what I mean. But as my wife, no . . . she looks ridiculous). In a later conversation the captain makes clear that the distinction between the categories of wife and woman is in his mind a clear one. "Come c'entrano adesso le mogli, scusi? Noi stiamo parlando delle donne . . . " (What do wives have to do with the subject? We're talking about women), he says to Paolino, who argues in defense of his own interests that there *are* times when a husband should treat his wife like a woman.

Signora Perella is thus *moglie* to the captain, *donna* to Paolino, *madre* to her son, and, finally, thanks to an extraordinary love potion administered to her husband, a dignified *madre* in the social order. Her modest and "virtuous" nature, praised by Paolino, along with her expectant state, gives her yet another role in her lover's eyes. As Pirandello tells us in the stage directions, she sits in the moonlight in the pose of "Ecce Ancilla Domini" while Paolino holds out a lily in the position of the angel making the annunciation, the latter proclaiming "Oh santa mia!" Elevated from *donna* to *Madonna*, finally secure as *madre*, Signora Perella appears to exist only as she is painted, perceived, or taken by lover or husband. A comic model of one of Pirandello's basic female types, she is as she is desired and, for herself, no one.

More than in any other play, motherhood is presented in **La vita che ti diedi (The Life I Gave You)** with its almost entirely female cast and its ostensibly female concerns. The action of this play that has been called a tragedy is, however, dominated by an absent male—the dead son of the main character Donn'Anna. The central problem is that of *allontanamento*—the changing and distancing of the fundamental mother-child tie. The primary situation, Donn'Anna's reaction to the death of her son, appears as the extreme form of the secondary, "normal" situation of her sister Donna Fiorina who finds her young adult children, returned after a year at school, transformed into "other people" and no longer really hers. In fact, as Donn'Anna remarks, her son was already "dead" to her when he defied her by leaving home. The life she desperately attempts to preserve is his life as he was before he left home, a life she seeks to preserve in his room. "Io voglio quella sua stanza la com'ere; che stia la viva, viva della vita che io le do, ad attendere il suo ritorno" (I want his room to be as it was, alive with the life I give it, waiting for his return).

With no realistic cause attributed to it, the son's actual death seems to be somehow a logical outgrowth of his "death" to his mother. Her desperate attempt to keep her son "alive" includes enticing Lucia, the married woman who carries his child, to come to her villa and stay in her son's room. By keeping Lucia with her while she gives birth to her son's child, Donn'Anna will gain a daughter, while the "life she gave" will be given back to her. This scheme is complicated when Lucia's own mother Francesca, referred to as "l'altra madre," comes to reclaim her daughter and to convince her to go back to her other children. Donn'Anna at last realizes the folly of her scheme—her role as mother is finished; Lucia, not she, will be the mother. "Sarai tu la madre allora; non piu io! . . . Lo riavrai tu, la, mio figlio—piccolo com'era—mio— . . . e io ora, muojo, muojo veramente qua". . . *E piangera, piangera come non avra mai pianto.* . . (You will be the mother, not I! You'll have my son as he was when he was little— . . . and I am now really dying, dying here . . . *And she cries as she has never cried before*). Like Signora Morli, Lucia cannot remain "una e due" and will reassume the maternal role. The resolution of this "tragedy" is not unlike that of Pirandello's comedies in that the young woman ends by reaccepting her assigned roles of *figlia* and *madre,* obeying her mother by returning to her husband while carrying the lover's child. Here, however, the protagonist Donn'Anna also assumes a new role, transforming herself from *madre* to *mater dolorosa,* which means for her a kind of death in life. Having lived entirely in the irreducible construction of motherhood, she "dies" when she no longer exists in that capacity. She foresees a similar destiny for Lucia: "Vai, vai, figlia,—vai nella tua vita— . . . povera carne macerata anche tu.—La morte a ben questa" (Go daughter, go into your life . . . poor broken flesh like mine.—This is what death is). The mother's lot is to "break her body" (as Pirandello says elsewhere), giving life only to move toward a status of death in life when her children—whether by death or *allontanamento*—are no longer hers.

The figure of *mater dolorosa,* sometimes a "widow" of both husband and son, was a familiar one on the European scene following World War I. In the interest of glorifying sacrifice to the *patria* as well as in what seemed to be a fanatic fervor to increase the Italian birth rate, Mussolini, in the early years of his fascist government as well as throughout the regime, attempted to raise to a level of almost mystical veneration the images of both the young mother and the sacrificing mother. In 1923, the year in which **La Vita che ti diedi** was written, the first congress of fascist women was held. As recounted by Maria Antonietta Macciocchi [in her *La Donna 'Nera': Consenso femminile e fascismo* (1977)], both Mussolini's discourse and that of the fascist women themselves portray the Duce as not only the Super Male, Husband, and Lover of all women, but also in some mystical sense both father and mother of their children. In the words of the Marchesa di Casagrande's address to the Duce: "Esse (le madri) li hanno allevati (i figli) ma voi li avete ispirati; avete posto con la vostra anima nei loro cuori non una fiaccola ma un rogo vivo . . . Sono vostri soldati, fiori purissimi della primavera italica . . . Per il nostro amore . . . auspice il Duce, siamo convenute da tutte le terre che piu hanno udito il ruggito del leone di San Marco, per gettare la semenza che dovra germinare i fiori della nuova Primavera" (The mothers raised the children, but you inspired their birth; you placed in their soul not a torch but a living fire . . . They are your soldiers, the purest flowers of the Italian spring . . . Out of our love . . . under the auspices of the Duce, we have convened here from all the lands that have heard the roar of the lion of Saint Mark, to sow the seed from which will sprout the flowers of the new spring). Sacrifice and reproduction, the roles assigned to women in **The Life I Gave You,** are here glorified through bombastic rhetoric and erotico-mystical devotion to the Duce. Macciocchi theorizes that what fascist discourse really implies is the castration of all Italian males except for the Duce—he alone will be the *Maschio-Marito,* the real father, as the Marchesa states, of the sons of the new Italy. Certainly the "giorno della fede," December 22, 1935, when Mussolini asked Italian women to give him their wedding bands to help support his Abyssinian campaign, must have had something of the aura of a mystical mass marriage. (Pirandello contributed his Nobel Prize medal to the campaign.) The man for all women—Pirandello appears to have written around that time a story with that title ("L'Uomo di tutte le donne") concerning a man whom all women find irresistible, a man who has fathered most of his friends' children.

It would be impossible here to discuss at any length the thorny question of the extent of Pirandello's commitment and artistic relationship to fascism, but his preoccupation with the reproductive and sacrificial functions of women, their "irreducible" roles as mother, at least, seems to coincide with images upheld by the regime. **The Life I Gave You** is also remarkable for its absence of fathers. Not a word is said about Donn'Anna's husband, who presumably fathered the son she has lost; neither the children of her sister Donna Fiorina nor Lucia appear to have a father. The only father discussed, but more as son and lover than as father, is the great absent one, the sacrificed son whom his mother hopes to see reborn in Lucia. Perhaps the women praying to the Virgin at the opening of the play ("Mater Christi, Mater Divinae Gratiae, Mater purissima") indicate that the primary relationship is that between mother and child and that the mother-son relationship in particular in some sense recapitulates the model of the Virgin Mother and Christ. The official father (the presumed case of Lucia's husband here and a major theme in the comedies discussed above as in **Think it Over Giacomino**) often plays the role of St. Joseph in Pirandello. Presumably a nonbeliever in the Christian God, but profoundly influenced by Catholic culture, did Pirandello transfer his ambivalent feelings about his own father to a veneration of the Father of the new sons of Italy, the one who could transform Italian mothers into Madonnas, in a new secular trinity?

The state of maternity becomes even more idealized in Pirandello's late "myth plays." **The New Colony,** in particular, recounts the transformation of prostitute to Madonna. With her new ideal of loving one man, the father of her child, but looking after and caring for all in the utopian community, the prostitute La Spera discovers the "miracle" of milk returning to her breasts while becoming a "queen and saint," "transfigured." She is also an object of value in the community: until a shipment of women arrives, her lover Currao's power over the others comes from the fact that he "owns" her. When Currao eventually wants to leave her to marry a young virgin, and to take his son, La Spera resists mightily. If Currao really cared for him, she reasons, he would give him to his mother, because only a mother can give him real love. In the end, it would seem that La Spera has become not only Madonna but Mother Earth. When Currao attempts to take the child by force, La Spera grasps him in a "mother's desperate embrace," the earth trembles, the island and its inhabitants sink into the sea, and La Spera remains alone on a rock, nursing her child upon the waters! The "irreducible construction" alone survives the attempts to construct new men in a new society. It is on this rock, Pirandello seems to imply, that such attempts can begin anew.

More could be said about mothers and maternity in Pirandello's drama: the metaphorical value of the maternal villa or palace in *Each in His Own Way, Henry IV,* and *The Life I Gave You*; the mother-son relation in *Each in His Own Way*; the mother-daughter relation in *Tonight We Improvise*; the suffering mother in *The Other Son*; and of course the mother figure in *Six Characters,* to mention a few. Roberto Alonge (1978) has discussed at some length mother figures and what he calls "the problematic of Mother Earth" in the late plays, arguing that Pirandello's vision coincides with the fascist dream of a return to a precapitalist, agrarian society. My analysis intends to show that the preoccupation with maternity, while it takes different forms, is central to Pirandello's theater from beginning to end. I would, however, like to explore here a different facet of Pirandello's fascination with maternity, not so much in his dramatic works as in his dramatic theory: his particular use of the traditional metaphor of maternity as artistic creation.

"Si pensi che il mistero d'ogni nascita artistica e il mistero stesso d'ogni nascita naturale; non cosa che si possa apposta fabbricare ma che deve naturalmente nascere" writes Pirandello in 1934. (The mystery of every artistic birth is the same mystery as that of natural birth; it is not something that you can make on purpose but something that must be born naturally.) Arguing against art as a form of conscious propaganda, he does *not,* as some of his commentators believe, take a stance in favor of "pure" art. Theater, for example, is for him the form that most intimately mirrors contemporary moral values. The birth metaphor as used here implies a primitive concept of the reproductive process. There seems to be no possibility of intentionality, and there is no mention of a father. Artistic birth, it would seem, simply flowers as the mysterious result of the influences ("germs") that enter the artist's mind, influences that are inevitably tied to the social fabric but that will not result in *conscious* propagation.

Pirandello had already developed the birth metaphor more extensively in the preface to *Six Characters* where he used the same words: "Il mistero della creazione artistica e il mistero stesso della nascita naturale." Just as a woman, in his view, cannot decide to become a mother, but one day finds herself a mother, "Cosi un artista, vivendo, accoglie in se tanti germi della vita, e non puo mai dire come e perche, a un certo momento, uno di questi germi vitali gli si inserisca nella fantasia per divenire anch'esso una creatura viva in un piano di vita superiore alla volubile esistenza quotidiana." (Thus an artist, by living, lets into himself so many germs of life, and he can never say how or why, at a certain moment, one of these vital germs inserts itself in his fantasy to become a living creature, living on a plane superior to that of inconstant daily existence.) The allegorical figure "Fantasia," introduced previously as Pirandello's servant, here joins the birth metaphor to appear as an egg, or perhaps a womb. If the "germs" come from outside, they come from no particular source and are appropriated by the artist, so that the process of artistic birth now appears as a kind of parthenogenesis.

The problem of the Six Characters as posed in this preface and in the novella entitled *La Tragedia di un personaggio* appears to be, in the terms of this metaphor, that they are searching for a maternal space—a womb—in order to be artistically born, and thus come to eternal life. Dr. Fileno, the character-protagonist in *La Tragedia*, explains with an example. "Mi dica lei chi era Sancho Panza! Mi dica lei chi era Don Abbondio! Eppure vivono eterni perche—vivi germi—ebbero la ventura di trovare una matrice feconda, una fantasia che li seppe allevare e nutrire per l'eternita" (Tell me, who was Sancho Panza! Who was Don Abbondio! And yet they have eternal life because as living germs they had the good fortune to find a fertile womb, a fantasy that was able to raise and nurture them for eternity), words that are repeated by the Father to the director in the play. The metaphor now makes the character seem either an Aristotelian *homunculus* or an embryo somehow formed elsewhere and the author a kind of male surrogate mother. Dr. Fileno asks Pirandello-as-author to "riprendermi e darmi la vita che quell'imbecile non ha saputo darmi" (take me back and give me the life that that imbecile [his previous author] was unable to give me). Is the search for an author thus prompted by the fear of *allontanamento* (the problem of *The Life I Gave You*) and the desire for a return to a blissful pre-birth or pre-Oedipal state? A character's eternal life, it would seem, must be sought through a kind of regression/rebirth through a male mother.

It is clear that if the process of artistic creation is described in metaphorical terms taken from female processes, an author for Pirandello can only be male. Careful to distinguish between lofty, immortal artistic birth and lowly, mortal carnal birth, Pirandello reinforces this distinction in the preface with his description of the character of the Mother. Unlike the other characters, the Mother is not in search of an author because she has no spirituality and thus no consciousness of being a character. Living entirely by instinct, she is entirely passive and carnal: "quasi un ciocco di carne compiutamente viva in tutte le sue funziomni di procreare, allatare, curare e amare la sua prole, senza punto bisongo percio di far agire il cervello" (almost a block of flesh complete in its functions of giving birth, nursing, caring for and living its offspring without having to use the brain at all). The author thus succeeds in expropriating the birth process from its lowly female context to endow it with the mental and spiritual capacities proper to the male. It is no wonder that Liolà, the male mother, was also a poet. Seen in this light, Pirandello's obsession with maternity may signify not so much an interest in women and mothers per se as a kind of womb envy, or a preoccupation with the metaphorical value of the low form of birth for the high. In any case, as we have seen, motherhood provides Pirandello's female characters with a fundamental role in society, as in the dramatic text.

In contrast to the irreducible mothers, women who appear as *donna* in Pirandello's drama seem shifting, illusory, unstable, and theatrical. As traditional Pirandellian criticism points out, the plays written with roles for Marta Abba, from about 1924 on, present beautiful, mysterious, solitary, often lost and victimized, but fascinating creatures. These may appear to be "strong" female roles—as indeed from the point of view of an actress they undoubtedly are—but what has not been sufficiently pointed out is the fact that Pirandello's concerns with role and identity or with the theater as metaphor for life are quite gender specific. The veiled woman who appears at the end of *Così è (se vi pare)* (*Right You Are, If You Think You Are*) is not, as has been often supposed, an allegory for the illusiveness of truth but rather a figure of the mobility of female identity, subject as it is to the perceptions of those whose roles give them a more solid grounding: in this case the mother and the husband. In this reading, it is clear that Lina/Giulia Ponza can be both Signora Frola's daughter and Signor Ponza's second wife, for like an actress she can play her assigned parts of both *figlia* and *moglie* while being, for herself, no one. The figure of the woman without a proper identity who plays the parts assigned by what we might call her "authors" will become even more prominent in the Marta Abba plays, but the antecedents are to be found throughout the early Pirandello.

The Sicilian comedy *Il Berretto a Sonagli* (*Cap and Bells*), written in 1918, is a case in point. The first part of this play takes place in an entirely female world in which women, organized by the jealous wife Beatrice, actually seem to be controlling the plot. It soon becomes clear, however, that the action is really dominated by the great absent one, Beatrice's husband, the bank president. When Beatrice tries to engage Ciampa, the humble employee whom Beatrice's husband has cuckolded, on her side, Ciampa opts to maintain appearance, "honor," and the patriarchal order. To do otherwise would be to acquiesce to female plotting and thus to anarchy. Ciampa gets his way by invoking the old Sicilian code—he could kill both his wife and Beatrice's husband and get away with it. Beatrice, in order to save her husband's life, consents to play the role that Ciampa assigns her: she will feign madness to the point of allowing herself to be sent to an asylum in order to discredit the accusations she has made. Ciampa, one of Pirandello's great roles for the *attore brilliante* Musco, understands at a level beyond the grasp of the other (primarily female) characters the nature of social hypocrisy and the inevitability of theatrical "masking" in life. In a manner consistent with Pirandello's later male protagonists, however, Ciampa *chooses* not only the role he himself will play, but also the "mad" mask that Beatrice will don. While it is true that Beatrice acquiesces in the choice that Ciampa has made for her, she does so under the control of the absent one—out of duty to her husband, whose life Ciampa now controls. We thus have a paradoxical, humoristic situation in which a husband/lover and cuckolded husband act in collusion against the wronged wife. (Ciampa's wife, it should be noted, appears

on stage only briefly and seems entirely under the control of her husband and her lover.) The hypocrisy of the patriarchal social order is exposed, yet it must be maintained, not torn apart by female plotting. Ciampa will be satisfied with the appearance of keeping his wife under lock and key and by manipulating the Sicilian code to his own advantage.

The much later "theatrical" play *Questa Sera si recita a soggetto* (*Tonight We Improvise*) (1930) plays, with some variations, on the theme of female roles. In the play within the play, or the subject of the proposed improvising, we have as in *Cap and Bells* an intially all-female world presented: in this case a mother and four daughters attempt to control their own style of life in opposition to prevailing Sicilian codes. Here it is an absent father, in conjuction with the codes, who dominates. One of the daughters, Mommina, because of her father's death and a scandalous affair with a singer, feels obliged to marry a jealous Sicilian in order to protect the family honor. Mommina, who would have become an opera singer, is virtually imprisoned by her husband. Determined to confine her entirely to the role of mother, the husband attempts to control her very thoughts. Mommina's attempt to leave her prison in imagination by performing an imaginary *Trovatore* for her daughters results in her death. In Pirandello's theatrical labyrinth, the actress who plays the role of Mommina is also supposed to have a heart attack and die. Here the woman appears as victimized by roles in both life and art.

As if extending the truncated role of Signora Ponza, the actress Delia Morello in *Each in His Own Way* first appears to the audience wearing a thick veil. Delia, it soon becomes apparent, is ready to accept her role as "written" either by Diego or Francesco or, in the end, by Michele Rocca. In Delia Pirandello creates not a new type of woman but a new incarnation of his vision of woman: woman as actress, or the condition of actress as metonymical with the nature of woman. Several of Pirandello's female characters recall in one form or another Signora Ponza's final words. Ersilia in *Vestire gli ignudi* (*To Clothe the Naked*), who is in a sense searching for both a veil and an author, confesses that she has never had the strength to be anything. Tuda's last words in *Diana e la Tuda* are "Io che ora sono cosi: niente . . . piu niente . . . " (Now I am nothing . . . nothing at all). The unknown woman in *Come tu mi vuoi* (*As You Desire Me*) puts herself into the hands of Boffi saying, "—non conosco piu nulla e non mi conosco . . . un corpo senza nome in attesa che qualcuno se lo prenda!" (I don't know anything; I don't know myself. I'm a nameless body waiting for someone to take it!). The lack of existential identity expressed by these characters posits woman as enigma for herself as for others, driving men to speculate about this enigma and to try to capture it in a comprehensible and controlled way. Ersilia is offered a role by each of her former lovers as well as by her writer. The unknown woman, using the picture of Cia as model, dresses herself to play the part. Again like a more developed Signora Ponza, she is revealed in the end to exist only in the roles created for her by others. By virtue of the fact that her only choices appear to be Bruno's wife or Salter's mistress, she remains *l'ignota*, her only identity that of a relative being.

What we might call the Signora Ponza syndrome, or the relativity of female identity, is evident even and perhaps especially in what at least one critic has seen as Pirandello's feminist play, *Trovarsi (To Find Oneself)*, 1932. On one level the plot does indeed concern a gifted, intelligent, beautiful woman (the play is dedicated to Marta Abba) who renounces marriage to the man she loves in order to continue her acting career. On closer look, however, we are dealing not with a liberation from bourgeois marriage (the capricious young Swedish artist Elj is anything but a Sicilian husband), but the failure of a woman to realize herself sexually on the one hand and the profession of actress as a metonymical with the non-identity of woman as individual on the other.

The first act of *To Find Oneself,* like that of *Each in His Own Way,* presents the secondary characters' discussion of the actress. What is Donata Genzi's true nature, what is she like as a woman, and indeed can an actress have a life as a woman? The dialogue again picks up the words of Signora Ponza's self-definition: "LA MARCHESA BOVENO: Be' sara pure in qualche modo, nella vita; e si potra dir come! Tranne che per voi una 'vera' attrice non sia piu una donna! (Well, she must be some way in life, and we'll be able to say how! Unless, as you think, a 'true' actress is no longer a woman!). SALÒ: Una no; ecco: tante donne! E per se, forse, nessuna (A woman no; *many* women! And for herself, perhaps, no one"). Salò maintains that a life as *donna,* which seems to imply for all the characters a love life, is excluded by the "abnegation" which the condition of actress implies: "negare se stessa, la propria vita, la propria persona, per *dar*si tutta e *dar*la tutta ai personaggi che rappresenta" (to deny one's self, one's own life and person to *give* oneself entirely and *give* it entirely to the characters one plays). Donata's very name contains the duality which discussion about her person has prompted: *donna/data,* the woman/the given one.

Once Donata the actress has made her entrance, the discussion continues, now with the added dimension of Donata's own narcissistic speculations. "How can you know what I really am," she asks the other characters, "if I don't know myself?" To play different roles on the stage, return to one's dressing room, take off the makeup, and be unable to "find oneself"—Donata postulates the problem to be solved, but in a way that is neither philosophical nor strictly dramatic. Pirandello seems to have invented a particular style for her alone.

As Donata says: "Cose a cui si pensa senza volerlo, quasi di nascosto da noi stessi . . . sogni . . . pena di non essere . . . come dei fiori che non han potuto sbocciare . . . —ecco, finche si resta cosi, certo non si ha nulla; ma si ha almeno questa pienezza di liberta . . . " (things we think about without wanting to, as if hidden from ourselves . . . dreams . . . pain of nonbeing . . . like flowers that were unable to bud . . . —as long as things stay like that we have nothing, but at least we have this fullness of freedom . . .). These sentence fragments, held together by ellipses and sometimes accompanied by protests of inability to express herself, typify Donata's long "speeches" throughout the play. Here Pirandello almost seems to be attempting his own

version of *l'écriture feminine,* a writing that seems to emanate from the subconscious without consciously imposed grammatical and syntactical structures. Donata, one might say, does not "think like a man."

Donata's attempt to "find herself" is performed almost as an experiment but an experiment incited by a capricious, unmeditated act. To the fullness of freedom as mere potential, Donata opposes the notion of "throwing oneself" into life and accordingly throws herself on the next man she finds, the young Swedish-Italian aristocrat-sailor-painter Elj. The end of the first act, then, finds both Elj and Donata ready to leave the villa of Donata's friends, a closed space that has been dominated by social interaction and narcissistic speculation, to "throw themselves" into a boat on a stormy, dangerous sea.

As the second act opens, Elj has saved Donata from drowning, brought her to his house, and the two have become lovers. Renée Moliterno points out the "surprising" (for its time and for Pirandello) nature of the dialogue between Elj and Donata in its reference to sexual intimacy. "You thought too much of yourself," Donata tells her lover the morning after, adding that that is perhaps simply in the nature of men. Donata's attempt to be a woman rather than an actress has then failed on one important count. When Elj tells her how he loves the gestures she uses with him, Donata realizes that these are the same gestures she is famous for on the stage. Her awareness that the woman/actress dichotomy is more complex than she had thought prompts another meditation in what we now recognize as the Donata style:

> Sai, è . . . è per forza cosi . . . perche io sono stata sempre vera . . . sempre vera . . . ma non per me . . . ho vissuto sempre come di la da me stessa; e ora voglio essere 'qua'—'io'—'io'—avere una vita mia, per me . . . devo trovarmi!
>
> (You know, it's . . . of course it's this way . . . because I have always been true . . . always true . . . but not for me . . . I've always lived as if above myself; and now I want to be 'here'—'I'—'I'—to have my own life, for me . . . I have to find myself!)

Elj asks Donata to be his wife, but the capricious young man who lost his mother at an early age, whose primary desire is to return to the sea that he envisages as a woman, and whose uncle, when he comes to speak with Donata, treats him like a spoiled child, seems to be seeking a mother as well as a lover and in any case a woman who will tolerate his capriciousness. Unable to decide on the marriage, at the end of the second act, Donata, with the advice and help of Elj's uncle, sets up another experiment. She will return to the theater to allow Elj to see her on the stage.

The play thus has a dialectical structure: the first act concerns the actress who desires to be a woman; the second act the woman who still desires to be the actress; the third act sets up and accomplishes the synthesis of actress/woman. The synthesis, however, does not resolve the tensions between the two modes of being and on one level appears to separate them even further. Elj cannot tolerate seeing Donata on the stage using the gestures of intimacy that he desires for himself alone (making a spectacle of herself, giving herself to the public). He walks out of her life, vowing to return to the sea. Donata must choose, it would seem, between being an actress and being a woman. On another level, however, what Donata discovers upon returning to the stage is that being a woman and being an actress are one and the same, or that acting is the quintessential mode of being a woman. When Giviero congratulates her for her triumphant performance as actress, she corrects him: "Ancora dite dell'attrice? No! no! Io me son sentita felice come donna! come donna! Felice di potere ancora amare! Questa era la mia vittoria! . . . mi sono liberata!" (Do you still speak of the actress? No! no! I felt happy as a woman! As a woman! Happy to still be able to love! That was my victory! . . . I have freed myself!).

In her attempt to love as a woman, it would seem that Donata discovered that loving is also a form of acting, and back on stage she rediscovers that acting is a form of loving. Donata says in a visionary trance: "Io posso avere tutto l'amore che voglio—e darlo!—io, tutto l'amore! e a me l'amore di tutti!" (I can have all the love I want—and give it—I, all the love! And for me the love of all!). Donata's fundamental narcissism affirms itself in the process of "finding" herself, as does her Pirandellian awareness that the self cannot be found because it is after all nothing but a series of creations or constructions. The play ends with her words: "Vero e soltanto che bisogna crearsi, creare! E allora soltanto, ci si trova" (The only truth is that one must create oneself, create! Only then does one find oneself). The original dichotomy is bridged as the figure of Donata no longer seeks to be *donna* or *data* but resolves itself as *donna data,* the given woman, the woman offered to the public as *tante donne,* many women. While it is true that the actress, unlike other women, can in a sense liberate herself from the anguish of being "for herself, no one," it is also true that as a player of roles or a wearer of masks created by men, existing only in the myriad forms perceived in the mirror of the audience, the condition of actress is a heightened, condensed, artistic representation of what it means, in the Pirandellian world, to be a woman.

It might be objected that what I have postulated as the feminine condition, or more properly the condition of *donna,* woman, in Pirandello's theater is quite simply the human condition which for Pirandello is by definition theatrical. This is in a sense true, but I would argue that the feminine condition represents (paradoxically, since the female for Pirandello as for many other male writers is not Man but Other) at once the most radical and the purest form of Pirandellian theatricality, This would explain why so many of Pirandello's characters are women. The helplessness experienced before the awareness that the self does not exist; the acceptance of the fact that facets of self can be found only by playing the roles created by others—such intuitions are endemic to Pirandello's women. Men, in Pirandello's theater, are not infected by the Signora Ponza syndrome. "Henry IV" loses his name, but not, entirely, his sense of self, for he chooses his roles and manipulates the other characters in his fake medieval world. The difference

between a title such as *As You Desire Me* and *Henry IV* is symptomatic. Both imply a loss of "real" identity and the adoption of a theatrical one, but whereas the man assumes his persona, the woman exists only "as wanted."

The one way for a woman in this Pirandellian world to escape the condition of relativity is to assume her instinctive destiny, the irreducible construction of motherhood. This condition, however, is also part of a social code, and its security depends on the willingness of a man to play the part of (not necessarily to be) the father. The fundamental relation between a mother and her "creatures" appears to be one that men both admire and envy. Pirandello, as we have seen, appropriates the state of motherhood by incorporating it into his metaphor for artistic creation. By relegating the domain of the instinctual and the carnal to women, the male mother gives birth to and nourishes spiritual children, combining the best of both worlds. Pirandello's veneration of *Madre/Madonna,* as well as his portrayal of women as relative being, coincide with the fascist discourse of the period, while bearing the unique stamp of the conservative Sicilian who became a radical modernist.

SIX CHARACTERS IN SEARCH OF AN AUTHOR

PRODUCTION REVIEWS

Stark Young (review date 22 November 1922)

SOURCE: "Brains," in *The New Republic,* Vol. XXXII, No. 416, 22 November 1922, pp. 335-36.

[*An American playwright, poet, and novelist, Young was a prominent member of the Agrarian group of Southern poets with Allen Tate, John Crowe Ransom, Robert Penn Warren, and several others, from 1928 until the mid-1930s. He served for twenty years as drama critic for such journals as the* New York Times, *and the best of this criticism is collected in* Immortal Shadows: A Book of Dramatic Criticism *(1948). He is especially acclaimed for his translations of Anton Chekhov's dramas. In the following review of the 1922 stage production of* Six Characters in Search of an Author *in New York City, he maintains that Pirandello's drama shows a "brilliant originality" and is a "fine theatrical piece."*]

We can judge the excellence of a man's legs by how well he can run or jump or dance, and can see easily enough how much eye for color he has. And we can judge his ear for music. We know how strong his muscles are by what he can lift, move or endure. Happily by some kind fortune this does not hold of the mind. We have no reason to believe that there is any higher average of mental endowment of its kind than there is of the eyes for color or of muscles or musical ears. But there is no straight-off way of judging these hidden gifts; and any man is free to think his invisible powers as good as the best. No matter what outward signs and fruits there be, he can go on consoling himself with his unseen depths. For Pirandello's play at the Princess this is a fine thing; otherwise many of our theatre audiences when they run into such subtlety of analysis, originality of invention and brilliant and poignant stress of mentality, would be overwhelmingly put in their places. And without this secure and unseen certainty of their own powers many of our citizens might be upset to hear that these metaphysical, tragic, accurately fantastic and laughable plays by Pirandello are to no small extent mouthpieces of much of young Italy; that on the streets of Rome a year or two ago there was a mob with six hundred persons in it over one of these dramas; and that when one of these works is performed, in the intervals between the acts the aisles and the foyers of an Italian theatre are crowded with discussion like a hot debating academy. However—

The rehearsal of a Pirandello play, ill thought of by the director, is about to begin when six characters from the author's brain appear. They wish to be allowed to react themselves and to set forth the event that is a part of what they are. There are the father and his son, the son's mother and three other children by a man with whom the husband, driven by a demon of experiment, has let the wife elope. One of these children is the daughter who has run away and gone to the dogs; the other two are dead but are present on the scene because they have been given a reality and are therefore unchanging. The director at last consents to see their story. They recreate parts of scenes, the actors are assigned roles and try them, to the great amusement of the realities of whom they are to create the illusion. The father argues metaphysics with the director. The play is halted. It goes on again. The father, repulsed by the son, is more and more attracted to the young woman, who gives way to him. The mother intervenes. The life of these six characters emerges somehow, real and unreal at once. The theatre is mocked for the absurdity of its medium and its inadequacy for any revelation of truth. In the end the little girl is drowned in the fountain and the boy shoots himself. The agony of the mother is terrible and overpowering. Nobody on the stage knows any longer which is reality and which is illusion. The mother goes out with the dead boy in her arms. Is he wounded? the director asks, Is he really wounded? He is dead, some of the actors cry. No, other actors say, it is fiction, don't believe it. The father cries that it is not fiction, it is reality, and runs out. Fiction, reality, the director says. He has never seen anything like it. And they have made him lose a morning.

The play is transplanted from Italy without any great sense of loss and with a very wise omission of any attempt at Italian production or method of acting. Italian dramatists instinctively write for the actors, and this play of Pirandello's is easily accessible to acting and full of possibilities. And this, together with Mr. Pemberton's plausible casting of the characters and his excellent directing, partly accounts for the high level that we get throughout the performance.

As the father Mr. Moffat Johnston was admirable. He got remarkably well into the reading of his many long speeches their essential quality, which was a strange mixture of an-

alytical and physical passion and of boldness and fear, candor and shame. Mr. Dwight Frye brought a convincing imaginative insight to the part of the son, whose life had been outraged by the contrast between his idea of parents and his actual instance of them, and whose place in the whole situation was violently against his will and at the same time an inner necessity. Mr. Frye is a beginner with something very much beyond what the New York stage expects of its young men; he has talent and intelligence; though he should get his r's rightly placed—his "father" and "mirror" and "horror" come off with great travail so far—he should work on his English as Miss Woodruff must have done, whose whole tone and accent is better than last year. And Miss Florence Eldridge needs to cherish her speech now and then; she has a way of speaking too fast and of slurring her consonants till they are lost. But as the daughter her work was astonishingly good; it was impetuous, flickering, sometimes crude, sometimes leaping up, sometimes darkened from within. She achieved the ebullience and tragedy of the character, the necessity for living and for speaking out, the tears and animation and mind. Against the more stolid and upright bodies of the director's own company of actors, Miss Eldridge created something strangely real and unreal and irrepressible. There were moments when she seemed to be a flame; behind her eyes and brow there seemed to shine the light of some youthful and urgent and eternally fixed reality, and about her movement the force of some haunting fatality and enthusiasm. The part of the mother it would be hard to imagine done with more rightness than Miss Wycherly gave to it. As the woman who had loved this man but who had been blind to him and misjudged him, and who had borne four children only to have them dashed from her by death and shame and pride, her suffering was the deepest of all the six; the deep degree of it pushed her grief beyond the actual and gave to it a kind of eternity. Miss Wycherly got this effect. Her eyelids, her brow, her hands, the line of her figure, her cries, had about them that last and final tragic reality of the eternal type.

The translation used of Pirandello's play is not a bad one. The philosophic speeches fare best; as a matter of fact they come over very straight into the English. There are vulgarities now and then that fall below the original—"sopporto la sua vista," for example, is hardly "stand for his face." And to tag on at the very last the bit where the director turns to the actors and says to get on with The Bride's Revenge seems uselessly silly. It is the wrong sort of humor. And what's worse, it is quite out of the key of Pirandello, who ends on reality and unreality and a hint of satire in the director's notion of losing a morning's time. This addition at the very last is a perfect example—more obvious than any Pirandello allows himself to use in the play—of exactly what he satirizes in the theatre, the catering, and fear of not making a go of it, and thick intrusiveness. I hope Mr. Pemberton will risk lopping it off.

In *Six Characters in Search of an Author* Pirandello first of all manages to contrive a fine theatrical piece. It exhibits everywhere one of his most noticeable gifts—something that may be seen already even in so early a work as his *Sicilian Limes,* translated in the last number of the Theatre

Initial crowd reaction to *Six Characters in Search of an Author*:

Things started to go badly from the first, when the spectators came into the theatre and realized that the curtain was raised and that there was no scenery. The first protests were heard from people who were irritated by what they considered to be gratuitous exhibitionism—and though Pirandello had not yet caused any major outrage, he did not have a good reputation. The play began and the first oddities were noticed: a stage-hand in a green overall started nailing planks on to the stage; the producer looked out from the wings and sent him about his business; some actors dressed in their everyday clothes strolled in chatting to each other; the manager of the troupe started talking about this and that with his secretary. Then, once the action had begun, there was an additional provocation when the manager said: 'What can I do if . . . we have to perform plays by Pirandello which nobody understands and which never satisfy anybody, not the actors, the critics, or the audience?' And finally there was the extraordinary arrival from the back of the auditorium, announced by one of the doormen, of the curious six characters. All this was enough to enfuriate anyone who had gone to the theatre to spend a pleasant evening. The first catcalls were followed by shouts of disapproval, and, when the opponents of the play realized that they were in the majority, they started to shout in chorus, *'ma-ni-co-mio'* ('madhouse') or *'bu-ffo-ne'* ('buffoon').

Of course the play did not lack its supporters who endeavoured to defend it, thereby creating an even greater confusion. As the commotion increased the play was strenuously performed by the actors, but only very little of it could be heard, especially since, at one point, members of the audience started to exchange blows and there was a general riot.

Gaspare Giudice, in his Pirandello: A Biography, *1975.*

Arts Magazine—the ability to set forth quite well enough what needs to be known and at the same time to clear it out shortly and make ready for what he really wishes to stay on and emphasize. *Six Characters in Search of an Author* shows a brilliant originality and invention in the situation. The machinery is highly expert with which the double line of incident is established. The transitions, which are so frequent and so varied in event and idea, are facile and profound. Pirandello's play is thought become theatric. And his thought is subtle, and subtle not through the sense of any vagueness but through luminous combinations of precise ideas and suggestions. This drama of his is satirical about the theatre but also in the same way about life. The blind and unending and unconcluded shifting of life is portrayed as it struggles against the accidents and illusion of society. No philosophy is pure, no theory gets a chance to exist in its clear reality, exactly as nothing that one of these characters thinks or feels or intends ever means to another character what it means to him.

Six Characters in Search of an Author has a plot suspense and a thought suspense. You are keen to see what happening will come next; your mind is excited by the play of

thought till your head seems to hold a kind of cerebral melodrama. But the greatest achievement in Pirandello's play is that the sum of it is moving. It gives the sense of spiritual solitude. Under this fantasy and comedy and brilliant mockery and pity, it releases a poignant vitality, a pressure of life. It moves you with the tragic sense of a passionate hunger for reality and pause amid the flux of things.

Desmond MacCarthy (review date 20 June 1925)

SOURCE: "Pirandello," in *New Statesman,* Vol. XXV, No. 634, 20 June 1925, pp. 282-83.

[*MacCarthy was one of the foremost English literary and drama critics of the twentieth century. He served for many years on the staff of the* New Statesman *and edited the periodical* Life and Letters. *In the following favorable review of the Roman Art Theatre Company's stage production of* Six Characters in Search of an Author, *he examines the work's major themes and terms it "a remarkable play."*]

It was thanks to Mr. Cochran we saw [Elenora] Duse act when she visited England for the last time. It is due to his enterprise that we now have a chance of seeing the Roman Art Theatre Company perform Signor Pirandello's plays at the New Oxford Theatre. They opened with *Six Characters in Search of an Author,* which the Stage Society performed in the spring of 1922. I remember thinking that performance a good one, and Mr. Franklin Dyall in the part of the Father made an impression on me so vivid at the time that between the acts at the New Oxford last Monday I was able to call up his shade. This is a considerable compliment, for the vehemence and brilliance of Signor Lamberto Picasso in the part was so overwhelming that one might have expected no other interpretation to be conceivable beside it. Yet I could still just see the black, often motionless, macabre figure of Mr. Franklin Dyall beside Signor Picasso's dead-white, red-haired, distracted, gesticulating "Father." There could be, of course, no doubt which of the two was nearer the character created by the author, but I can assure Signor Pirandello that Mr. Dyall's interpretation was far from being a travesty of the character such as "The Father" on the stage would have protested against. When, however, one compared the two performances as wholes, and considered the passionate and splendid acting of "The Stepdaughter" (Signorina Marta Abba), one saw how faint a reflection of the original the Stage Society's performance had really been, though at the time it deserved all the praise it got. Nor is this to be wondered at. After all, it is an Italian play, and Italians must be its best interpreters, let alone the fact that the Roman Art Theatre has the author himself to guide them. Moreover, when we act Signor Pirandello's plays we suffer under a serious disability. The authorised translation of his works which we have to use is limp, confused and written in shocking bad English. All beauty and subtlety disappear. There is an Italian proverb "Traduttori, traditori." It certainly applies to Signor Pirandello's American translator. A few weeks ago a review of the latest volume of the translation of his collected plays appeared in this paper, showing, as far as space allowed, how carelessly and badly the work had been done. When Signor Pirandello appeared himself on the stage at the New Oxford between Acts I. and II. and challenged questions, he was accompanied by an interpreter who seemed to have difficulty in seizing Signor Pirandello's own points and was ludicrously incapable of communicating replies in intelligible English. This did not really matter; it was even amusing. Under the spell of the play, in which the distinction between reality and imaginative creation is so cunningly blurred, the audience could hardly believe in the reality of Signor Pirandello himself. The interpreter at his side stood so clearly in the same relation to himself as "The Leading Man" to "The Father" in the play, that the interlude became comically indistinguishable from the performance. It illustrated the same theme. If I had the nerve to bellow in public, I should have shouted: "Do you know your translator is as bad as your interpreter?" . . .

Six Characters in Search of an Author is a play which has attained to European fame. When the Stage Society produced it A. W. wrote a note upon it for the programme. I will quote a passage from it:

> It is neither a play within a play, nor yet a play in the making. Rather it is a trial—possibly an indictment—of the modern theatre. The author has created Six Characters and imagined for them a situation of poignant intensity. And then, doubtful of the theatre's adequacy to his intentions, he abandons his play—it is not to be written. But the characters remain; he has endowed them with life and they refuse to relinquish his gift. A theatrical stock company meets to put another Pirandello play into rehearsal, and as they begin their work, the six characters arrive, and demand that their story shall be given the dramatic representation for which it was destined.

This is indeed something new in the way of a plot, one requiring an enormous amount of ingenuity from the dramatist. The curtain goes up on an empty stage. The actors drop in for rehearsal; the dictatorial, matter-of-fact manager is bustling about giving orders. Quarrelsome, snappy chatter follows, and at last after one disgusted individual has gone off in a huff, the rehearsal begins to get under way. At this point enter from the body of the theatre a grotesque and gloomy procession, a pale distraught man in a black cloak, a widow in streaming weeds, a girl, about eighteen, also in black, a grim youth about twenty-two, a small girl of eight and a boy about twelve. These people are "characters" in a play Signor Pirandello intended to write. The actors turn and stare; the manager naturally asks these strange apparitions what the devil they want. They want to be given the chance of living through the story which their creator has written for them. That story and their relations to each other gradually emerge as the acting proceeds. These are agonising and complicated. Politely, gravely, but with a mesmeric intensity "The Father" explains to the dumbfounded manager that a nebulous unattached existence has become intolerable to them. They must fulfil their destiny. Will the company kindly impersonate them and bring rest to their perturbed spirits? The impression produced at first on the manager and the actors is best expressed in the simple words, "Well, I'm blowed!" Interrupted by the titters of the

actors and the passionate ejaculations of the other "characters," each of whom are desperately anxious that his or her version of their terrible predicament shall be properly expressed, "The Father" actually succeeds in persuading the manager that their story may make a better play than the philosophic, incomprehensible stuff Signor Pirandello has actually provided.

Now it is of the utmost importance dramatically—this is an effect which the Roman Art Theatre Company brought off to perfection—that "the characters" by their intensity should impinge on the audience so violently that the living people on the stage seem mere shadows beside them. Here lay the enormous superiority of this performance as compared with the English one.

"The characters" in the play are not "real people," but, like masterpieces of fiction, in a sense they have more "life" in them. (Signor Pirandello himself seems to take this phenomenon with a philosophic seriousness which strikes me as regrettable, but this is a point I shall leave to a future discussion of his drama when I have seen more of it.)

The story "The Father" unfolds, with illuminating passionate interruptions from the other "characters," is briefly this: "The Widow" is his wife. After bearing him a son (the grim youth) she ran off with his secretary, taking her baby with her. By this man she had the other children. He saw nothing of them. He had no idea that after the death of his wife's lover they had fallen into abject poverty. He was left in a very humiliating position. He was not old enough to be indifferent to women and yet too old to be loved by them . . . in short, he was in the habit of occasionally buying what he could not otherwise get. Now, it is unfair to think the whole of a man is in all his actions, yet others are apt to judge him as though that were the case. Then a most terrible thing happened. He went to a certain house which, under the pretence of being a dressmaker's, was the kind of house where such bargains are struck. There, without recognising her, he met his wife's daughter, "the girl you see over there." They were interrupted in time by the mother who had come to see her daughter. But imagine how fearful is his predicament now! He has taken the whole family back to live with him. The girl only sees him now in the light of that interview. He is to her merely *that* elderly salacious man. He has no control over her; the sinister surliness of his own son has driven her from home on to the streets. Subsequently the silent little maniac of a boy drowned his small sister and shot himself. The scene at the dressmaker's in particular takes the manager's fancy. He agrees that "the characters" should go through their lives before the company and that after shorthand notes have been taken, the actors and actresses should impersonate them. This is just what "The Father" and "The Stepdaughter" want. But when after going through (with pain which communicates itself to us) their crucial scene, which is interrupted by "The Mother's" cry of horror, they see a real actor and actress act it, they are frantically disgusted. It is a complete travesty of themselves and "reality." Here the element of comedy enters. The actors' travesty is most amusing. Signor Pirandello has illustrated what every imaginative dramatist or creator is apt to feel when his characters are impersonated on the stage. In part *Six Characters in Search of an Author* has been inspired by the humorous sufferings of a dramatist at the inevitable distortions due to the substitution of the personality of the actor for that of the character as he imagined it. But the play also carries a deeper suggestion, a suggestion of the limitations of all art in expressing reality, especially the art of the stage. But there is also a third suggestion in the play. There is no doubt, I think, that Signor Pirandello intends us to take rather seriously the metaphysics which "The Father" propounds to "The Manager" when the latter denies "reality" to "the characters." This dialogue does, however, serve also a better purpose. It intensifies the confusion in our minds. Consequently the relation between "The characters" who usually move in a light tinged with red while the actors remain in white daylight, gains plausibility.

In conclusion, there is a question I should like to see answered. Has the Censor removed the ban upon *Six Characters in Search of an Author* in the English language? No incest takes place. Apart from the fact that it is a remarkable play, and one thousands would enjoy and not forget, it is rather important that we should not figure as a nation of idiots in the eyes of Europe. The Censor has been active lately. I hear on good authority that he struck the word "bird-droppings" out of a play the other day.

CRITICAL COMMENTARY

Olga Ragusa (essay date 1980)

SOURCE: "Sei personaggi in cerca d'autore," in *Luigi Pirandello: An Approach to His Theatre,* Edinburgh University Press, 1980, pp. 137-69.

[*Ragusa is an Italian-born American critic and educator with a special interest in Italian literature. In the following excerpt, she offers a thematic and structural analysis of* Six Characters in Search of an Author.]

Multifacetedness (*poliedricità*), wrote Lampedusa, is the distinguishing characteristic of works of absolute first rank. Because *Sei personaggi* possesses this quality and presents different aspects of itself to different viewers, I judge it a work difficult enough to require exegesis and rich enough to withstand it. Of the three bodies of material that for purposes of analysis can be seen as constituting distinct structural elements in the play—(1) the story of the Characters' lives, (2) the attempt on the part of Manager and Actors to turn this story into a play, and (3) Pirandello's own telling of the story within his representation of the Company's attempt to give it shape—it is the first that in early productions attracted the greatest share of attention and that continues to awaken a good deal of perplexity even today. An inveterate habit of mind demands an answer to the question. 'What exactly did happen?' and conceives of the question as referring to Father, Mother, and their offspring, rather than to that odd group of beings who one day appeared on a stage set for a rehearsal. Only after a satisfactory answer has been given can the reader or viewer go on to consider and appreciate other aspects of the work before him.

The story of the Characters as it unfolds on stage begins in good epic fashion *in medias res* or, if more properly dramatic terminology is preferred, close to its *dénouement.* The Father is in his fifties; the Son is twenty-two. This is the first chronological fact given: it is spelled out in the stage directions and made visually apparent in performance through make-up and the assignment of parts. Chronology appears again when twice in rapid succession the Stepdaughter says that she has been an orphan for two months and that for that length of time she, the Mother, and her siblings have been wearing mourning for her father. The Stepdaughter's father is not *the* Father, whose only child is the Son. The blood relationship of the Six, by normal standards confusing, could not be more explicitly stated than it is in the very first few minutes of the play. But Manager and Actors, already disconcerted by the Father's initial presentation of himself as a character (while they see him as a person), are further bewildered by this intricate family relationship. Their questions, quips, and remarks, however, serve to elicit a full clarification of the facts.

These facts must be fully established to satisfy the natural curiosity of the audience in the hall and of the other audience, Manager and Actors, on stage. They are moreover the facts that explain the particular intensity of the feelings of Father, Stepdaughter, and Mother (the only three of the Six who speak at first), an intensity which keeps the Characters more tightly enclosed within their relationship than the Members of the company are united by their community of shared work and professional pride.

The emotions displayed by the Characters have been building up over a long period of time. They are emotions typical of the long, intimate, and ambivalent association that characterizes family life. Their intensity can also be measured by the fact that Stepdaughter and Father, in different degrees and for different reasons, have lost their sense of shame and reserve. Secrets normally shielded by the bourgeois family are here pulled into full public view. The Stepdaughter especially is driven by a ferocious fury to unmask the Father's motives in taking the family back home with him; and in her vindictive grudge against him, however justified, she does not hesitate to reveal her own degradation at the hands of Madama Pace, the brothel keeper. It is significant that the scene she cannot wait to act is judged damaging to her reputation by both the Mother and the Manager, the two guardians of propriety in the play. As for the Father, the life-time of isolation he has behind him has obliterated his sense of self-awareness to the point that he permits himself to be dragged into performing the very scene (his meeting with the Stepdaughter at Madama Pace's) he should have every reason to want to keep hidden. His need to justify his actions, especially his original decision about the Mother, has been pent up so long that it now sweeps all restraints before it. The Son's contempt both for the Father's empty phrases and the Stepdaughter's vilification, his refusal to have anything to do with the others (so that he even rejects his Mother), his complete withdrawal—a reaction to hurt just like the Stepdaughter's aggressive pushing forward—all these are the results of long pent-up resentments.

To know what the Characters' relationship is and for how long their association has lasted is not however sufficient to form a judgment. That a judgment is being asked for is obvious: the Father, not the Stepdaughter, finds himself in a symbolic court of law and it is he who presents the evidence for his defence. The evidence forms the retrospective exposition of the story. The Manager sits down to listen to it and the Father begins it in the imperfect, the *de rigueur* tense for background information in historical narrative: 'C'era con me un pover'uomo . . . ' [There was a poor devil of a man working for me . . .].

The Father, who was married to a woman of humble background, mother of a child that for its health had been sent to a wet nurse in the country, noticed the mutual sympathy that developed between his employee (the *pover'uomo*) and his wife, the support they sought in one another for putting up with his irascibility. Finding the situation intolerable—not because of jealousy, he says, but because the drawing together of the two implied a tacit criticism of his very being—the Father fired the man. The Mother remained at home, a lost soul, 'come una di quelle bestie senza padrone, che si raccolgono per carità' [like an animal without a master that one takes pity on and carries home]. Not out of cruelty, the Father says, (just as it had not been out of cruelty that he sent the Son away) 'quanto per la pena—una pena angosciosa—che provavo per lei' [as because of the pain—a veritable anguish—that I felt on her account] he sent the Mother to join the other man, better suited than he was to live in harmonious unity with her. But, as such stories go, what had been intended to correct circumstances actually complicated them. Upon his return home, the Son felt estranged and no bond developed between him and his father. As for the Father, he describes himself too as wandering through the empty rooms 'come una mosca senza capo' [like a fly without a head].

It is thus that the Father in his loneliness began to take an interest in the Mother's new family, particularly the Stepdaughter, who had reached school age and whom he could watch on her way to and from school. Of the other children the Boy was still too young to go to school and the Little Girl (who is four to the Stepdaughter's eighteen when they appear on stage) had not yet been born. Some time after the Father had become interested in the Mother's new family, they moved away and remained away for a number of years. Then, upon the other man's death, they came back to the city and it was at that time that the encounter at Madama Pace's took place. Horrified to see what poverty had done to his wife and her children, the Father took them back into his home. The Son resented the intrusion of the strangers, his mother's bastard children, and though he had no affection for his father, was antagonized by the Stepdaughter's insulting behaviour towards him. The Mother, rejected by her Son, could think of nothing but of winning back his love. The Boy, like his own father 'umile' [humble] (as the Father repeats), was completely lost in the new environment, and indeed ended up by committing suicide. Before that happened, however, the Little Girl, neglected by the Mother in the same way as the Boy was, drowned in the garden fountain. As a result of this accumulation of tragedies the Stepdaughter left home.

These facts, which constitute the entire story (as distinct from specific episodes) of the six Characters' lives, all emerge in the course of Act 1 though not in this order and not as schematically summarized. They are surrounded and engulfed by the emotional reactions of all concerned and their motivations are variously played out, interpreted by those who were affected. But the *dénouement,* the finale of the drama to be made, is already clearly hinted at by the Stepdaughter in her initial appeal to Manager and Actors. 'Senta, per favore', she pleads with the Manager, 'ce lo faccia rappresentar subito, questo dramma, perchè vedrà che a un certo punto, io—quando quest'amorino qua [the Little Girl]—vede com'è bellina? cara! cara! ebbene, quando quest'amorino qua, Dio la toglierà d'improvviso a quella povera madre: e quest'imbecillino qua [the Boy] farà la più grossa delle corbellerie, proprio da quello stupido che è—allora vedrà che io prenderò il volo! Sissignore! prenderò il volo! il volo!' [Just listen: let us play it for you right now, this drama, for at a certain point you'll see that I—when this little darling—look how sweet she is! Sweetie! Sweetie!—well, when God will suddenly take this darling away from that poor mother of hers, and that little idiot there will do the stupidest of things, like the nitwit he is—then you will see me getting out! Yes sir! Getting out! Out!].

Reproduced without the accompanying stage directions and read without being able to see the gestures and actions, the Stepdaughter's words with their broken syntax, the interruptions and resumptions, reflect in miniature the process by which the facts of the story are revealed. These facts are repeated, with the exception of the Stepdaughter's flight, at the end of the act when in answer to the Manager's comment that children are a nuisance on stage the Father reassures him: 'Oh, ma lui [the Boy] glielo leva subito, l'impac-cio, sa! E anche quella bambina, che è anzi la prima ad andarsene . . .' [But he won't be a nuisance for long. Nor will the little girl, no, for she's the first to go . . .].

Obviously Pirandello was convinced that the facts of the story as recounted in Act I of the definitive version of the play (the text we have been following in our own reconstruction) were sufficiently explicit for the spectator to grasp. This explains why he felt that he could excise from the original version the part of the Father's long speech that followed the sentence just quoted. In those lines the Father had given an interpretation of the *dénouement:* the very interpretation which forms the basis of Eric Bentley's 'Father's Day' (from a Freudian point of view one of the best pieces written *not* on Pirandello's play but on the inner story which it tells). Through the ending, says the Father, the original family is reconstituted, Father, Mother, and Son 'resi, dalla scomparsa di quella famiglia estranea, estranei anche noi l'uno all'altro, in una desolazione mortale, che è la vendetta . . . del Demone dell'Esperimento che è in me . . .' [ourselves alienated from each other by the disappearance of that alien family, alienated and utterly desolated—the revenge of the Demon of Experiment that I carry inside me].

The second recurrent structural element in *Sei personaggi* consists of the repeated efforts of Manager and Actors to create the illusion of reality on stage with the 'real' reality which the Characters bring them. In contrast to the Six, who are tragic if for no other reason than because they feel their predicament, Manager and Actors are comic. Like characters of comedy in general they may be described as believing in what they can touch, see, and understand and eager to preserve their sense of dignity. They may be seen as working out their problems on the level of action rather than abstract thought, as being strictly empirical. Whenever attention shifts to them there is a resultant change in tone. The audience identifies with them in their patronizing humouring and more often intolerant rebuffing of the Characters, in what Hobbes calls the 'sudden glory' of abruptly perceiving one's superiority to others. But because of the play's dynamic movement the identification does not hold. The language of the Characters, especially that of the Father, the furthest removed in its specious (the word is Pirandello's) ratiocination, is again and again the more powerful one and repeatedly engulfs and drowns out the more trivial language of the Actors.

This situation is similar to that in *Cosí è (se vi pare),* Manager and Actors taking the place of the small town gossips who in that play are the uncomprehending spectators of the anguished, harrowed family in their midst. The parallel, however, does not of course imply identity. Signora Frola and the Ponzas are persons not characters; the Agazzis, Sirellis, and the others are ordinary citizens not actors. The setting is a middle-class apartment not a stage. Laudisi, though like the Father the spokesman for typically Pirandellian ideas that recur in all the writer's works, is not the Father. Yet the pattern of the one play fits into that of the other, and the audience that identifies at first with the outer group ends up, if the lesson of the parable has been successfully imparted, discovering its oneness with the inner. The epithet *pazzo* [mad] used by the Manager to brand the Father and his family when they appear on stage is also the pivot for the action of *Cosí è (se vi pare).* 'Comedy justifies, defends, or elevates us in relation to the oddity, the alien, the scapegoat. It enables us to surmount our doubts about those that are different by laughing them out of existence' (R. J. Dorius). This is the mechanism that tries to function in *Cosí è (se vi pare)* but which Laudisi interferes with and the inner group itself succeeds in deactivating. It is also the mechanism that Manager and Actors instinctively have recourse to every time the Father soars too high in asserting his uniqueness.

We shall see when we turn to the third recurrent structural element in *Sei personaggi* that as potential characters Father and Stepdaughter are thoroughly acquainted with the experience of literary creation. As non-authors, Manager and Actors have no first-hand knowledge of that experience and as non-characters, they are ignorant of the particular anguish of a transitional state of existence between non-being and being that Father and Stepdaughter experience and express. But as members of a theatrical company they are well versed in the techniques of stage-craft, and their long association with the life of the theatre has acquainted them at least superficially with most of the theoretical notions that have had currency in the history of drama. (Pirandello's own equally empirically derived knowledge

in this area constitutes the core of his Introduction to Silvio D'Amico's 1936 edition of *Storia del teatro italiano,* an expanded version of an article that had appeared the previous year in the review *Scenario*). The stage business constantly interrupts the Characters' efforts at telling, or rather, portraying their story, thus providing a commentary perceived immediately as comic by the audience. In their totality the incidental observations that accompany it lay down the 'rules' that the inner episodic, unfinished play, which remains a fragment, should have followed.

The play begins with an unset stage: the directions, calling for a raised curtain, no wings or scenery, and a stage almost completely dark and empty, have remained unchanged in successive editions of the play. The Company's very first action shows the audience the expertise of its technical staff, from stage manager (a character added in the 1925 edition) to stage crew. Immediately following but still prior to the entrance of the Characters, Manager and Actors prepare themselves for the rehearsal of a play. It happens to be a play by Pirandello, the same author who is responsible for having gathered together the audience in the theatre, and this fact provides a particularly lively and pointed context within which some stage conventions can be quickly sketched. The introductory scene can thus be seen as a frame for the whole play, underlining its specific genre of play-within-a-play.

Reflecting Pirandello's characteristic use of repetition and complication by way of repetition, the first part of Act II, up to the appearance of Madama Pace, reproduces with a greater abundance of details the business of setting up a play already gone through in Act I. But whereas in that instance there already was a text of the play and the Manager's task was therefore limited (he explained the author's intentions and because of the particular play being rehearsed tried to overcome his Company's resistance to the 'incomprehensible' Pirandello), in Act II more is at stake. Here there is no written play and consequently everything, including the assignment of parts, the selection of props, the application of make-up, as well as the meaning of the author, remains to be settled and thus becomes the subject of prolonged and heated argument between the Characters, and the Manager and Actors. By Act III some of the friction has gone, some of the stage conventions have been accepted. As a result, the curtain rises on at least part of the shadow setting (*simulacro di scena* are Pirandello's words) already in place: a small garden fountain is seen where previously Madama Pace's famous parlour had been erected piece by piece before the eyes of the audience. Other props are added in the course of the first part of the act, in another repetition, this time on a reduced scale, of what had occurred in Acts I and II.

We can now ask what kind of play Manager and Actors have in mind as the vehicle for the raw material of the Characters' lives. It comes as no surprise that in terms of both dramaturgy and stage practice, Manager and Actors are traditionalists. Like the audience in the theatre they feel that art must give a recognizable structure to reality, that it must reduce chaos to order.

A first distinction is made by the Manager when he enunciates the basic characteristic of drama: on stage there is action, event, not narration. 'Ma tutto questo è racconto, signori miei!' [But all this is story telling, my friends!], he exclaims interrupting the Stepdaughter's recollection of the Father waiting for her at school when she was a child. A little earlier the Stepdaughter, shouting down the Father, had raised the same objection: 'Qui non si narra! Qui non si narra!' [This is no place for story telling!]. (For Pirandello speaking in his own voice on this point, see *L'azione parlata*: 'Ogni sostegno descrittivo o narrativo dovrebbe essere abolito su la scena' [All descriptive and narrative props should be banished from the stage].) At the end of Act I the Actors, who up to that point have been little else than spectators vis-à-vis the entanglements of Characters and Manager, in a brief excited choral scene give its technical name to the kind of play that seems to be in the making: *commedia dell' arte,* the improvised drama gone out of fashion two centuries before and to which *they* would not deign to stoop. Thus the act that had begun with the reading of stage directions from a script ends symmetrically with the reiteration that, on the stage of *Sei personaggi,* written—that is, fully structured—plays are performed, not plays for which only a rudimentary sketch exists.

As far as dramaturgy is concerned, the most important point made regarding the kind of play the Company is accustomed to performing and the audience to viewing is the Manager's enunciation of the rule of unity of action or coherence. 'Ma io voglio rappresentare il mio dramma! il mio!' [But I want to play *my* drama. Mine!], the Stepdaughter cries passionately in Act II in the course of her tug-of-war with the Father. The Manager's answer runs the whole gamut from annoyance to persuasion to conciliation. There is not only the Stepdaughter's drama, he says, but the drama of the others as well. One character cannot simply take over the stage for himself and crowd out the others: 'Bisogna contener tutti in un quadro armonico e rappresentar quel che è rappresentabile!' [Everyone must be placed within the frame of one harmonious whole. Only what is performable can be performed]. And after all, he concludes, it will be in the Stepdaughter's own interest to play down her drama at this particular juncture in the story if she wishes to win greater audience sympathy.

Beyond these theoretical desiderata—a play is action not narrative; it must be written down not improvised; it must have unity—there is the whole area of dramatic practice. Unity, for instance, may be achieved through unity of place but it can equally well be achieved by starting the action with an event already far along in the development of the situation. The problem of unity of place appears in Act III apropos the Stepdaughter's observation that not all of the second act of the proposed drama can be set in the garden because the events that concern the Son and the Boy actually took place in the house. The problem of the relationship between preceding action (*antefatto*) and dramatic action appears in Act I when the Father agrees that the narrative part of the Characters' lives will not be represented but only referred to. And in fact the three acts of the drama to be composed focus on three scenes that took place at the end of the story to be told: the Father meets the Stepdaugh-

ter when she is a fully grown young lady and not when she is a child; the children will play the scene of their death and not moments of their life with their own father; Mother and Son will come together at the moment of their reunion and not at their separation ten years earlier. As we have already pointed out in connection with the story of the six Characters, the action on stage is the epilogue of a situation created much earlier. In this respect *Sei personaggi* repeats the pattern of Pirandello's earliest extent play, *La morsa* (1892), whose original title was *L'epilogo.*

Problems of acting or interpretation are furthest removed from the area of theory and are most central to practice. In *Sei personaggi* they are dealt with directly in Act II and their presence there contributes to making that act the busiest, most animated, varied and colourful of the play. Friction between the Characters and the Actors starts early in the act when the Manager assigns their roles to the Members of the Company. It is significant that he should find no difficulty in doing so, while the Father and the Stepdaughter find it impossible to recognize themselves in the Actors that will play them. Even with the best make-up, the Father observes, the Leading Man will hardly resemble him, and as for playing him as he really 'is' that is obviously an impossibility. The Stepdaughter, for her part, simply laughs in the Leading Lady's face. Yet a little later, immediately after the scene with Madama Pace and the meeting between Father and Stepdaughter, Leading Lady and Leading Man take the initiative and propose to rehearse the scene just 'played' by the two Characters. Within the world of *Sei personaggi* this becomes a rehersal of a rehearsal, in its turn even further distanced from the audience when the Manager gets up on stage to show his actors how it should be played.

Pirandello's stage directions at this point (they are already in the original edition) call for a scene that is not a parody of the one just performed but one that might be described as a clean, corrected copy of it, the artful imitation of reality. The Manager demands ease, *souplesse,* in the acting. But the performances delivered are wooden, exaggerated, conventional. For the Characters they are a torture to watch (though the Stepdaughter's sense of alienation is expressed paradoxically in frenzied peals of laughter). For the audience in the hall they are irresistibly funny, caricatures. But for the Manager and Actors they are exactly what they expect them to be, not yet perfectly timed, still capable of being improved, but essentially correct. The Leading Man is playing 'un vecchio, che viene in una casa equivoca . . . con l'aria spigliata, sbarazzina d'un vecchio galante' [an old man who enters a house of ill repute . . . with the self-possessed roguish air of an elder Don Juan]. The Leading Lady plays a world-weary prostitute 'socchiudendo penosamente, come per disgusto, gli occhi' [closing her eyes painfully as though in disgust]. What in the original 'performance' of Father and Stepdaughter were words and gestures indissolubly united in genuine psychological reactions, in the Actors' interpretation become so many discrete and separate samples of emotions, for each one of which there is a set and predetermined tone, a studied and practised posture. Obviously, in the eyes of Manager and Actors, the Characters are types not persons, interchangeable with the cast of stock characters the Company excels at

Six Characters in Search of an Author, *1923.*

playing. This fact provides an ironic retrospective comment on the Manager's boast in Act I that his Company has given life to immortal works 'qua, su queste tavole' [here, on these boards], and earlier in Act II that his actors have given 'corpo e figura, voce e gesto' [body and face, voice and gesture], that is expression, to much loftier subject-matter than the paltry story that the Characters have brought him. The scene almost seems to have been written to illustrate the reasons for Pirandello's well-known reservations about the theatre as an art form (an excellent comprehensive statement, particularly relevant to this aspect of *Sei personaggi,* is the 1908 essay *Illustratori, attori, e traduttori*), or to support the Stepdaughter's conjecture in Act III that their author had rejected the Characters because of his discouragement with the theatre as it was usually made available to the public at that time.

We could perhaps step back for a moment and try to cast the action of the inner story of *Sei personaggi,* the story that tells the content of the Characters' lives' into the mould of the traditional three-act play. The differences between the first and definitive versions of the play indicate that Pirandello must have done something like that at some point, must have passed, that is, from what the ancient theories of rhetoric called *inventio* to *dispositio,* or from what Alfieri called *ideare* to *stendere,* from the 'thinking up' of the subject to its arrangement into scenes. We have already noted that there are three scenes into which what would otherwise be the narration of the Characters' story is to be absorbed: the meeting between Stepdaughter and Father,

the death of the children, and the Mother's pleading of her case with the Son. Of these only the first one, the encounter at Madama Pace's, is set off in the text, explicitly labelled 'The Scene', and played through in its entirety. The second one is set up by the Manager, but though its *dénouement* (the revolver shot with which the Boy kills himself) takes place, it is not actually played. The reason for this is that it intersects what should have become the third scene, which to suit modern stage conventions is first transferred from inside the house (where it reputedly took place) to the garden and is then violently rejected by the Son who claims that it never took place because he walked out on his Mother—in a play on words—'Proprio per non fare una scena!' [precisely in order not to make a scene]. Under normal circumstances these three scenes could have turned into the necessary three acts. As it is, they are out of phase from the beginning, 'The Scene' being played in Act II, the second act of the play-to-be-made being announced at the beginning of Act III (why the whole adventure in the theatre which *Sei personaggi* describes should have begun with the rehearsal of Act II of another play now becomes apparent in retrospect), and the third act never being even begun. That something like this outline must at some time have occurred to Pirandello can be deduced from the displacement of the second scene from the beginning of Act II (where it was in the original version) to Act III. The only scholar who has so far compared the different editions of the play, Jørn Moestrup, attributes the displacement to Pirandello's desire to maintain suspense by avoiding foreknowledge. This explanation, if not perhaps actually incorrect, is certainly insufficient. We have already shown how the story of the six Characters is revealed in its entirety in Act I. It would seem more likely therefore that the second scene was moved to Act III not only because it is the conventional tragic climax but also because there was no place for it in Act II, the act reserved for 'The Scene'.

We come now to the third body of material that can be isolated as a distinct structural element in the play: the discussions of the peculiar state of being of a character and, subsidiary to that, the consequences for the author that result from it. In those parts of *Sei personaggi* that dramatize the problematic interplay of characters and actors, it is the character's strong personal traits, his unique individuality, the fact that he is *someone* ('Perchè un personaggio ha veramente una vita sua, segnata di caratteri suoi, per cui è sempre "qualcuno". Mentre un uomo . . . un uomo così in genere, può non esser "nessuno"' [Because a character really has a life of his own, marked with his special characteristics; for which reason he is always 'somebody'. But a man . . . a man in general, may very well be 'nobody'], says the Father in Act III), that may stand in the way of his being adequately represented by an actor professionally trained but incapable of 'that supreme renunciation of self', that 'spiritual creative activity of the rarest kind', which Pirandello speaks of as the mark of the great actor in his essay on Eleonora Duse (*The Century Magazine,* June 1924). In the other parts, those that deal with the relationship of characters and author, it is the character's need for untrammelled development that may find itself in conflict with the shaping imagination of the author. And indeed in speaking of the creative moment elsewhere in his work Pirandello returns over and over again to his basic claim that no worthwhile work of art can be produced, no living and breathing character be given life unless the author 'si sia veramente immedesimato con la sua creatura fino a sentirla com'essa si sente, a volerla com'essa si vuole' [has really become identified with his creature to the point of feeling it as it feels itself, of wanting it to be as it wants itself to be] (*L'azione parlata*).

It was pointed out earlier that the paradoxical situation of characters coming to importune an author was fixed from the beginning of Pirandello's conception of the work. This paradox gives the play its title and is its most striking invention as well as its structural keystone. It calls for attention. Obviously, characters are not persons. It is true that in familiar discourse the word 'character' may be used as a synonym for 'person', specifically, 'a person who is peculiar and eccentric'. But when the word occurs in conjunction with the concept of authorship, it is removed from the every-day world to the world of fiction. In that context characters are distinguished from persons, the former being creations of authors, the latter products of procreation and environment. A character should not normally be thought of as having a life outside the work of which he is a part, nor of existing prior to the creative act of his author.

Yet Pirandello felt . . . that he was 'visited' by his characters—by some more insistently than others—*before* they had a place in the man-made world of art. Being 'visited' by a character, a figment of the imagination, means that a particularly close relationship exists between the author and the character, not necessarily in the sense of an autobiographical identification but in the sense of the 'archaic image' as described by Jung: 'the image . . . presents itself more or less suddenly to the consciousness as the latter's product, similarly to a vision or a hallucination, but without the pathological character of these'. Other writers besides Pirandello have described the phenomenon, but none, as far as I know, has made as much of it as he. Chekhov, for instance, is reported to have remarked: 'There is a regular army of people in my brain begging to be summoned forth, and only waiting for the word to be given'. Ibsen wrote: 'Often my characters astonish me by doing or saying things I had not expected—yes, they can sometimes turn my original scheme upside down, the devils!' Dickens confessed: 'My notion is always that, when I have made the people to play out the play, it is, as it were, their business to do it and not mine'. That many writers felt the characters in their works to be more alive than the persons of flesh and blood that surrounded them in their daily lives is borne out by Balzac's feeling that through his novels he was contributing to the citizenry of France. But if we examine these instances in the light of Pirandello's more complex statements, we note that it is not so much the autonomy of the character that astonishes Pirandello as the demand the character makes on him and that he must answer with an act of love. The rejected character, the character without an author, is the one that has been denied this kind of love. Pirandello's *immedesimarsi,* the author's identification with his creature 'to the point of feeling it as it feels itself, of wanting it to be as it wants itself to be', is quite different from the identity of sensations felt by Mme Bovary and Flaubert when, as is reported, he had the taste of arsenic in *his* mouth as he was describing *her* death. As for Flaubert's frequently quoted remark, 'Mme Bovary c'est moi', I would interpret it as meaning that he understood Emma through himself, that he lent her something of himself, in contrast to Pirandello's understanding his characters by listening to their 'reasons', by foregoing some of his own ego for their sakes.

The basic situation of *Sei personaggi,* then, is a variation on a theme familiar to Pirandello and not unknown to other writers. The variation means that contrary to what is the case for Dr Fileno [in *La tragedia di un personaggio*] for instance, the Six in the play encounter not an author but the Manager and his Company of actors. If the invention of having characters act as though they were persons, with the spontaneity of the undetermined, is paradoxical, then when these characters-turned-persons are forced to become actors (even if only in a rehearsal), something fundamental happens in the history of the theatre. Actors and characters as different entities cannot simultaneously occupy the same stage. Characters are essences; actors are roles. The creation of illusion on stage demands that the actors become the characters for the duration of the performance. In Pirandello's play the Characters are in the end forced off the stage. There is no room for them in that particular space which is the space reserved for actors, that is, for persons who have studied and learned the parts they are to play. The Characters have 'lived' their parts, each one his own part, each one in his own incommunicable experience of it. The parts have not been orchestrated; they make little sense as a whole.

Instead of a story there will be fragments of a story. Instead of a resolution there will be the empty stage at the end. The audience that in accordance with a well-established custom has come to abandon itself to the conventional creation of illusion will go home unsatisfied, its expectations frustrated. Catharsis has not taken place, and the experience of the play is replaced by heated discussions, not as in normal after-theatre conversations of its performance, but of its very meaning. (For Pirandello's own dramatically detailed reconstruction of audience reaction to his works, see the First Choral Interlude of *Ciascuno a suo modo* and especially the lines spoken by One of the Author's Champions.)

In the Preface to *Sei personaggi* Pirandello wrote what is surely one of the most lucid and comprehensive analyses of the play. One passage summarizes what happened once he, in the *persona* of the author, decided to let loose on stage the Characters, who had so to speak served their acting apprenticeship in trying to get him to write their story: 'è avvenuto naturalmente quel che doveva avvenire: un misto di tragico e di comico, di fantastico e di realistico, in una situazione umoristica affatto nuova e quanto mai complessa; un dramma che da sé per mezzo dei suoi personaggi, spiranti parlanti semoventi, che lo portano e lo soffrono in loro stessi, vuole a ogni costo trovare il modo d'esser rappresentato; e la commedia del vano tentativo di questa realizzazione scenica improvvisa' [what had to happen happened, and the result was a mixture of tragic and comic, of fantastic and realistic, in a completely new and extremely complex humoristic situation: a drama that seeks at all costs to represent itself by means of its characters, breathing, speaking, self-propelling, who carry it within them and suffer it; and the comedy of the vain attempt, at this sudden theatrical realization]. It should come as no surprise that Pirandello's answer to 'what happened' once he set the play-within-the-play, or better the drama-within-a-comedy, in motion refers not to the first of the linked terms but to the second, not to the substance or plot of the inner story but to the shaping of the work, the artifact created by the outer story. In choosing as the genre designation for his play the expression *commedia da fare* [comedy to be composed], which we read on the title page of the 1921 edition and which fits perfectly into the mould *romanzo da fare* used to refer to the work initially, Pirandello underlined his awareness of the comparative importance of its two indissolubly joined halves. . . .

[*La tragedia di un personaggio* is] in many ways indispensable for a proper and satisfying understanding of *Sei personaggi.* But the strong analogies between the two works do not, of course, obliterate the differences. Thus, while Dr Fileno and the Father are both in search of an author, Dr Fileno is already a character while the Father is seeking to become one. If as a character in *La tragedia di un personaggio* Dr Fileno is at least twice removed from being a person, the Father's status is as yet problematic. He finds himself in a no man's land, in transition to a place for which he longs—a kind of Paradise of Essence—and which he may never reach. Indeed, *is* he a character or is he only one of *the* Characters? The difference in the meaning of the word brought about by its capitalization deserves attention.

For the Father (as are the other five, but not Madama Pace) is nameless, just as the protagonist of *Enrico IV* is nameless, his identity in the void of the ellipsis points which appear in that play's *dramatis personae: . . .* (Enrico IV).

In order to acquire a name the Father would have to convince an author that he should be given one. But the only author the Father has met so far is the one who, as we have seen, left some fragments of a projected novel, in which the gentleman on his way to signora Pace's cannot actually yet be said to be the Father. As for the author of the Preface, *he* did not encourage the fictional realization of the Six; he blocked it. 'Siamo qua in cerca d'autore' [We are here looking for an author], the Father says as he leads his little band up to the stage. But on the stage of *Sei personaggi* there are no authors, and the Father will have to plead his case before what are at best humble craftsmen. In *La tragedia di un personaggio* Dr Fileno, already in the privileged state of being really a character, had been luckier.

The fact that it is craftsmen and not an author that the Father will be addressing makes all the difference. The variation on the theme—the lucky find made by the author of the Preface to rid himself of the characters he didn't want to coddle, didn't want to give fictional life to—has far-reaching formal results. The encounter becomes a sequence of misunderstandings. Between Dr Fileno and his author there were no misunderstandings. The author knew what was wanted of him; he knew how much of himself he would have had to give to satisfy the character; by an act of judgment he refused to become involved. Not so the Manager and his Company of actors. They are seduced, willing to help. They listen and watch. They comment and analyze. They imitate. They question. But they are unable to help. Potential creators with the unfashioned raw material which the Characters bring them of what the magician (i.e., a kind of author) in *I giganti della montagna* calls 'fictious reality', they cannot rise to the challenge, imprisoned as they are in material reality.

Three times, once in each act, the Father comes forward to try to explain what the nature of the Characters is. Each time the explanation is interrupted. The Characters and the Actors do not speak the same language. The Actors cannot understand the Father. When in Act I he asks, 'Non è loro ufficio dar vita sulla scena a personaggi fantasticati?' [Isn't it your job to give life to creatures of fantasy on stage?], the Manager interprets the question as a slur on the actor's profession. 'Ma io la prego di credere che la professione del comico, caro signore, è una nobilissima professione!' [But I beg of you! The actor's profession is a very noble one], he counters indignantly.

When in Act II Madama Pace miraculously appears at the very moment she is needed, the Father is radiant but the Manager is again indignant, 'Ma che trucchi son questi?' [What kind of tricks are these?], and the Actors echo him: 'Ma dove siamo insomma?' [What goes on around here?], 'Di dove è comparsa quella lì?' [Where on earth did *she* come from?], 'Questo è il giuoco dei bussolotti!' [Hocus pocus!]. The Father's exhortation ('Ma scusino! Perchè vogliono guastare, in nome d'una verità volgare, di fatto, questo prodigio di una realtà che nasce, evocata, attratta, formata dalla stessa scena, e che ha più diritto di viver qui, che loro; perchè assai più vera di loro?' [But pardon me! Why would you want to destroy in the name of a vulgar, factual truth, this miracle of a reality which is born, called forth, attracted and formed by the stage itself and which indeed has more right to live here than you because it is much truer than you?]), would fall on completely deaf ears if the scene between the Stepdaughter and Madama Pace which has immediately come to life were not so compelling—so 'natural'—that Manager and Actors are momentarily rapt in it (incidentally, an illustration of the aptness of Simoni's distinction between the success of the artist and the failure of the philosopher . . . But the truce, in spite of this magnificent demonstration of both what a character is and what literary creation is, is short-lived. From the realm of art, Manager and Actors quickly fall back into the shoptalk of their trade.

Act III contains the Father's longest and most complex gloss on the condition of being a character. It begins with the Manager's taunt, 'E dica per giunta che lei, con codesta commedia che viene a rappresentarmi qua, è più vero e reale di me!' [And you'll be saying next that you, with this comedy of yours that you brought here to act, are more true and more real than I am!]. And it continues as the Father, following the lead shown by Dr Fileno and repeating parts of his defence *verbatim,* calls upon the experience of literary creation to explain his point. In underlining the close link between author and character—a link made even closer by his addressing an author already singled out as potentially receptive to his plea—Dr Fileno had begun his defence with the words: 'Nessuno può sapere meglio di lei, che noi siamo esseri . . .' [No one can know better than you that we are beings . . .]. Between Father and Company of actors, on the other hand, there is no common ground of experience and so the Father's speech begins: 'Non l'ha mai visto, signore [i.e., he has never seen a character getting out of his part and philosophizing about himself], perchè gli autori nascondono di solito il travaglio della loro creazione' [You have never seen such a case, sir, because authors, as a rule, hide the labour of their creation]. There follows a recapitulation of the genetic moment in a character's life, until the Father's abstract, verbal presentation is replaced by the scene which the Stepdaughter, stepping forward in a dream-like trance, plays out. She enacts, in other words, the temptation scene barely hinted at in the second fragment of the novel mentioned earlier ('Soprat-tutto lei, la ragazza. La vedo entrare . . . ' [She especially, the girl. I see her coming in . . .]), described with greater pathos and wonder in '**Colloqui coi personaggi**' ('Nell'ombra che veniva lenta e stanca . . . ' [In the darkness that gathered slow and tired . . .]), and related specifically, in the Preface, to Pirandello's decision to turn novel into play.

The Father's three passages stand out within the overall structure of the play and form one thematic unit within its strategy. When the theme re-emerges in the last act, the Manager's mocking lines contain the same two adjectives, *vero* and *reale,* that the Father had used in Act I. Actors, he had said, give life to 'esseri vivi, più vivi di quelli che respirano e vestono panni! Meno reali, forse; ma più veri!'

[living beings more alive than those who breathe and wear clothes: beings less real perhaps, but more true!]. In the linking and at the same time separation of *vero* and *reale* there lie, quite incidentally and curiously embedded, echoes of the history of the development of a literary concept—realism, naturalism, or what in Italy was known as *verismo*—by the 1920s completely surpassed in the work of Pirandello. The importance of *Sei personaggi* in the literature of the twentieth century derives also from the statement of the non-mimetic function of art so insistently repeated in its exploration of the relationship between character and author.

In analyzing the dramatization of the inner story of the Characters' lives and the interplay of characters and actors on stage, [we can see that some changes took] place in the text between the original and definitive versions. These changes consist of excisions, additions, and transpositions, and concern all three aspects of the play. In addition to the Father's speech toward the end of Act I, Pirandello dropped the important lines of the Son in Act II in which the latter rebelled against the Father's forcing upon his children a recognition of their parents' needs as man and woman; an exchange between Father and Manager at the beginning of Act III in which the Father reiterates Pirandello's conviction that men reason because they suffer; and by transposing the beginning of Act II to Act III, the attempt at a scene between Mother and Son. But of considerably greater significance are the additions which radically change the beginning and the ending of the play. Instead of the Manager's lines with which the play originally ended: 'Finzione! Realtà Andate al diavolo tutti quanti! Non mi à mai capitato una cosa simile! E mi hanno fatto perdere una giornata!' [Pretence? Reality? To hell with it all! Never in my life has such a thing happened to me. I've lost a whole day over these people, a whole day!], there is now a pantomime which changes the resolution of the story—the reconstitution of the original family and the departure of the Stepdaughter—into visual terms and emphasizes for the last time the radical, essential, metaphysical distinction between the Characters and the Actors. The beginning of the play is correspondingly more elaborate: the 'frame' has been expanded. The addition of the Stage Manager with his liaison function serves to break up into its components the realistic rendition of theatrical life on stage and thus to spell it out in its particulars. No doubt reflecting Pirandello's increased familiarity with the practices in the theatre, the stage directions in the later version also pay greater attention to lighting effects.

But the most important innovations are the two stairways, left and right respectively, that connect the stage with the auditorium. The stairways did not exist in the original version, which was written for a typical proscenium stage, like the one of the Teatro Valle at the time with a framed playing area strictly separated from the audience. Thus while the Actors continue to enter from the back of the stage, the Manager now uses one of the two stairways. He is dressed in street clothes, and his progress from the auditorium door down the aisle and up the stairway is watched by the Actors. As a matter of fact, in order to attract attention to the unusualness of the proceedings, the Actors are made to interrupt the dance they had just begun.

The entrance of the Characters who in the original version had used the door on stage now repeats and amplifies that of the Manager. Like him they come up from the auditorium, preceded by the Stage-Door Man, but Manager and Actors will become aware of their presence only at the end of their walk down the aisle. When the Father says the words, 'Siamo qua in cerca d'un autore', with which the action proper begins, he is standing at the foot of one of the stairways. He will be preceded by the Stepdaughter who in her first demonstration of aggressiveness and insubordination pushes him aside as he has just barely begun to speak. The Father then follows the Stepdaughter up the steps; the Mother, the Little Girl and the Boy remaining on the lowest level, the Son hanging back, still on the auditorium floor. This tableau is held as the dialogue between Father and Manager engages the emotional reactions of the Actors in an initial skirmish. With the Father's lines: 'Mi dispiace che ridano cosí, perchè portiamo in noi, ripeto un dramma doloroso, come lor signori possono argomentare da questa donna vestita di nero' [I'm sorry to hear you laugh, because, I repeat, we carry a painful drama within us, as you all might deduce from the sight of that lady there, veiled in black], identical words in the two editions, with the exception of the addition of *doloroso* in the later one), attention shifts to the Characters again. The Father helps the Mother up the remaining steps, and a new tableau—the Mother, the Little Girl and the Boy close together, the Son standing to one side at the back, the Stepdaughter also standing apart from the others, downstage, leaning against the proscenium arch—is formed on one side of the stage. This action, in which there is no dialogue, is accompanied by a play of lights which serves to divide the stage in two, creating the same kind of distance between Characters and Actors that already exists by virtue of the stage itself between spectators and performance. At the end of the action the Actors applaud, thus underlining the theatrical nature of what has just occurred: among other things the Father is an accomplished director whose gifts are recognized by the professionals before whom they have been displayed.

The stairway will not be used by the Characters again until the very end of the play when the Stepdaughter runs down it for her spectacular exit. In Act II its role is that of simple passageway from stage to auditorium floor, used by the Manager (as he had already used it in Act I) in his frequent moves from and to the stage as he observes the effectiveness of 'The Scene' being enacted. The difference in essence between Madama Pace and the Characters is stressed by the fact that she does not use the stairway but enters from the back of the stage as she had done in the original version. Her sudden appearance, however, greeted in the original version by no more than deep amazement and indignation on the part of Manager and Actors, sets off a lively by-play in the definitive version as they rush off the stage with a yell of terror, running down the stairs and starting up the aisle as though fleeing. In Act III the stairs are twice on the verge of being used by the Characters. The first time is when the Son tries to walk out on the scene with the Mother but is held back within the acting space on stage: his trance-like walk from stairway to stairway is watched with fascinated awe by the Actors. The second time is during the violent flare-up between father and son as the Father grabs the Son and shakes him only to be grabbed in turn. Then in an escalation of hatred and rebellion—in the definitive version as against the earlier one—the Son throws the Father to the ground next to the stairway. Again attention is directed to this architectural feature which in the strategy of communication of *Sei personaggi* acts at once as link and barrier.

Of the changes we have been reviewing, the excisions (whose main function is to add to the *antefatto* which it is up to spectator or reader to reconstruct) and the transposition of material from Act II to III (which results in a better articulation of the compositional elements of the plot) stem from 'literary' rather than 'theatrical' considerations. They could conceivably have occurred even if *Sei personaggi* had never been performed and if in the years between 1921 and 1925 Pirandello had not increased his personal involvement in the production of his plays to the point of desiring and planning his own company and theatre, the Teatro d'Arte, which opened its doors in Rome at the beginning of April 1925.

The new conception of acting space, however, and the suggested use of masks—the other major innovation in the definitive version—are no doubt to be attributed to Pirandello's contacts with milieus in which discussions of theatre architecture were the order of the day and with production of *Sei personaggi* whose actors and director had not been briefed and rehearsed directly by him. One of the most famous new theatres of the time was the Berlin *Komödie*, built by Oskar Kaufmann for Max Reinhardt in 1924, with loges opening directly on to the stage to facilitate that union of audience and performers already called for in the 1915 *Manifesto del teatro futurista sintetico*. Virgilio Marchi, the architect who rebuilt the theatre of the Palazzo Odescalchi for Pirandello's company, was himself a Futurist and he, too (as demonstrated by the setting and staging of *Sagra del Signore della nave,* the one-act play with which the theatre was inaugurated), was concerned with breaking down the traditional separation of auditorium and stage. As far as Pirandello's experience of *Sei personaggi* in the interpretation of other directors is concerned, the most important was that afforded by his first trip to Paris in April 1923. At the *Comédie des Champs Elysées* he witnessed the entrance of the Six Characters not from the door on stage as his directions called for but, as 'invented' by Georges Pitoëff, lowered from above by means of an old freight elevator with which that stage happened to be equipped. Alarmed by this departure from his conception when he had first heard of it in correspondence with Pitoëff, Pirandello was so taken by it when he saw it enacted that he adopted it, according to one report, for a later performance under his own direction (see, Jean Hort, *La Vie héroïque des Pitoëff,* Geneva 1966). Of similar significance, though Pirandello was not present at any of its performances, was the Max Reinhardt production of *Sei personaggi* which ran at the *Komödie* from 30 December 1924 till 8 March 1925. Max Reinhardt's Characters made their entrance neither from the stage door, nor from the auditorium door, nor from above, but were on stage from the beginning, hidden from the audience until a violet light made them appear out of the darkness like 'apparitions' or ghosts.

It is probably impossible fifty years after the event to go back and pinpoint the exact cue from which Pirandello derived the double means (stair and masks) by which to underline in truly spectacular and theatrical fashion the play's fundamental *donnée:* the difference in essence between characters and persons, and the accompanying superiority of art (not artifice) to life. This aspect of the play, which constitutes its uniqueness in Pirandello's dramatic corpus, was obscured when in 1933 he joined *Sei personaggi* to *Ciascuno a suo modo* and *Questa sera si recita a soggetto* to form the first volume of his collected plays. Seen as one of the trilogy of the theatre-within-the-theatre, *Sei personaggi* does indeed illustrate one fact of the interaction of characters, actors, author, manager or director, drama critics, and spectators which should result in the creation of the illusion of life on the stage. In the Preface, however, which 'completes' the play, and was indeed written well before *Questa sera si recita a soggetto* (though not before *Ciascuno a suo modo*), the emphasis was elsewhere.

As portrayed in the Preface, *Sei personaggi* is not primarily (as it appears in the Premise to the trilogy) the representation of the conflict between characters and actors and manager taking place in the theatre but the representation of the author's creative act which takes place in the mind and is externalized (or concretized and 'personified') through the medium of the stage. Such is the meaning, Pirandello says explicitly, of the sudden appearance of a seventh Character, Madama Pace, who does not arrive in the theatre with the others but 'materializes' when the action calls for her presence: 'È avvenuta una spezzatura, un improvviso mutamento del piano di realtà della scena, perché un personaggio può nascere a quel modo soltanto nella fantasia del poeta, non certo sulle tavole d'un palcoscenico. Senza che nessuno se ne sia accorto, ho cambiato di colpo la scena: la ho riaccolta in quel momento nella mia fantasia pur non togliendola di sotto gli occhi agli spettatori; ho cioè mostrato ad essi, in luogo del palcoscenico, la mia fantasia in atto di creare, sotto specie di quel palcoscenico stesso' [A break occurred, a sudden change in the level of reality of the scene, for a character can be born in this way only in the poet's imagination, not on a stage. Without anyone having noticed it, I all of a sudden changed the scene: I gathered it up again into my own imagination without, however, removing it from before the eyes of the spectators. That is, I showed them, instead of the stage, my imagination in the act of creating—my imagination in the form of this same stage].

The full implications of this important passage so necessary to a total understanding of the play are easily overlooked in the thematic richness of the Preface which recapitulates the history of the genesis of the play and offers a probing analysis of its constituent elements. But the dominant chord is actually sounded at once with the introduction at the beginning of the Preface of yet another 'character', Pirandello's unconventional little servant maid, Fantasia, the fleshed-out image of the writer's creative faculty. In his fictionalized retelling of the historical facts which we have used in this chapter to throw light on the making of the 'comedy to be composed', Pirandello is concerned with what in *I giganti*

della montagna Cotrone refers to as 'the real miracle': 'E il miracolo vero non sarà mai la rappre-sentazione, creda, sarà sempre la fantasia del poeta in cui quei personaggi son nati, vivi . . . ' [And the real miracle will never be the representation itself, but always the fantasy of the poet in which those characters were born living . . .]. In Pirandello's conception fantasy, or better, imagination, is a life-giving force similar to nature in its overwhelming drive to creation. Metaphors of birth, gestation, survival, and death recur time and again in his remarks on the psychology of literary invention. Indeed, nowhere has the organic metaphor, so deeply embedded in the aesthetics of Romanticism, been developed as fully as in the work of Pirandello. In the midst of a totally pessimistic view of life which cannot remove its gaze from the inevitability of death, Pirandello has triumphantly affirmed the immortality of the work of art: 'Tutto ciò che vive, per il fatto che vive, ha forma, e per ciò stesso deve morire: tranne l'opera d'arte, che appunto vive sempre, in quanto è forma' [All that lives, by the fact itself that it lives, has form, and for that very reason must die; except the work of art, which lives forever precisely because it is form].

Because of the importance of this aspect of Pirandello's thought and because the text of *Sei personaggi* and its becoming are a full illustration of it, my discussion of the play has assumed its present form.

Pirandello has made it clear that the story of the characters is not his primary interest, nor is the philosophical question of reality versus illusion. His play is thought become theatric.

—*Lander MacClintock, in* **The Age of Pirandello**, *1951.*

Anna Balakian (essay date 1991)

SOURCE: "Pirandello's *Six Characters* and Surrealism," in *A Companion to Pirandello Studies,* edited by John Louis DiGaetani, Greenwood Press, 1991, pp. 185-92.

An affinity has often been seen between the theater of Pirandello and the surrealist mode because both adhere to such notions as the "absurd," the unconventional, the iconoclastic, and the shocking to stir the receivers of the created work. Let us examine these elements from the angle of Pirandello's *Six Characters in Search of an Author* as well as of the surrealists' position, to determine the nature of affiliations and of differences.

Undeniably, his reception in Paris had much to do with Pirandello's subsequent fame. He wrote *Six Characters* in 1921, but it was not until the play was presented in Paris in 1923 that notoriety was accompanied by sincere curiosity and serious appraisal. Apparently, the influence of innovations is more dramatic when it crosses national frontiers than within a national literature. This phenomenon is manifest in the way Europeans embraced Edgar Allen Poe, for instance, in the nineteenth century, and in the twentieth century in the way Albert Camus was received in the United States or Faulkner in the Soviet Union.

Curiously, France, the country historically noted for generating avant-gardism in poetry and painting, was rather slow in its renovation of theater. In the first two decades of this century, we see artists and poets adapt to a new world of relativism brought about by advances in physics and mathematics which distributed the three-dimensional perception of the cosmos, and by experimentations in psychiatry that let down the barriers between the conscious and the unconscious. In response, the avant-garde brought about radical changes in aesthetics such as cubism, which took place in Paris whether its perpetrators were French or whether they came from other countries to practice their art in Paris. But theatrically the only innovators identified with the avant-garde were those who were attracted to the applications of Grand Guignol Theater by Alfred Jarry and to Apollinaire's feeble attempt at experimental theater in 1918 in his play *Les Mamelles de Tirésias.* Apollinaire had been truly avant-garde as a poet, breaking the rules of prosody, playing havoc with time perceptions, and simulating simultaneity. In contrast, in his play he was serving an ideology rather than theater as a genre. In the wake of World War I, he had a message to offer rather than a new form: he deemed his plea to repopulate France to be a universal concern, relating his protagonist not to a particular society but to the universe as a whole in terms of the human power to produce 40,049 children in one day. Therefore, his theatrical presentation took on the semblance of a universal stage setting transportable from one continent to another. When he qualified his vista as "surrealist" in the introduction of his play, thus using that label for the first time to distinguish a form of art, the word would have a great reception. But his caricature of the burgeoning feminist woman of his time and his benign ridicule of humanity as a whole were still expressed within the normal stage we are accustomed to. He maintained a clear division between audience and stage, between actors and viewers, with the clear understanding that everyone involved in bringing the text to performance was subservient to the author of the text. The truth is that his play neither supports nor demonstrates his long introduction about the needs of the new theater; his second play, *Couleur du Temps,* is even more conventional.

While profound changes were taking place in poetic discourse in terms of renovation of the image and the representation of reality in painting and poetry, theater remained the same. The most popular, prolific, and durable theater was still that of the boulevards' romantic boudoir triangles, the psychological plays of Ibsen and of his followers, or the social theater of François de Curel or Henri Brieux, or even the surviving naturalist theater of Henri Becque. All of these works may have developed fresh insights on humanity and society, but they did not offer fresh, unpredictable forms of representation in the script or new presentations on the stage.

When, therefore, Pirandello burst on the scene, only Louis Aragon in France, a very young pre-surrealist, had questioned the general idea of the changing concept of beauty in the arts in a little satirical novel, *Anicet.* He had derided all the experimentations of the moment called "modern" as pretentious and shallow; he had challenged all the so-called innovators including Picasso, Charlie Chaplin, Cocteau, the Dadas, and even his dear friend André Breton under very thin disguises.

None of these early avant-gardes had raised the disturbing issues that were to be central both to Pirandello and the surrealists, namely, how the notion of beauty had changed in the modern world, what relativism had done to the definition of reality, what artists could expect of their art in terms of their own survival, in terms of its survival as intended by its author, and in terms of the fading barriers between reality and illusion. Finally, although in the past so much theory of the arts had concentrated on the effect of the work of art on the reader or viewer, was it not time to observe the effect of the viewer or reader on the work itself?: How can we understand each other if into the words which I speak I put the sense and the value of things as I understand them within myself while at the same time whoever is listening to them inevitably assumes them to have the sense and value that they have for him? (Father, *Six Characters,* Act I) [translation mine].

The question is particularly pertinent to both Pirandello and the surrealists and, as we will see, in quite different ways. When *Six Characters* hit Paris, surrealism was not yet officially declared, although André Breton and his colleagues were pondering what artistic forms their revolution was to promote. Dada had made its official arrival in Paris in 1920 but had identified with no special art form; collage and theatrical improvisations were fragmentary and meant to be executed or performed before randomly selected audiences. Neither the authors nor the viewers took these shows as dramatic structures. What interested the Dadas and the rising coterie of surrealism in the dramatic form was dialogue, which was viewed as a form of linguistic ping-pong with no special consequence for dramatic action: two streams of thought, two soliloquies interrupting each other rather than responding logically to each other, their incongruities often revealing underlying hostilities in the interlocutors.

Even after Breton's official Manifesto established certain basic principles for surrealism, the series of playlets written by Breton, Soupault, Aragon, Desnos, Tzara, and even the more extensively structured plays of Roger Vitrac were deemed extensions of poetry to illustrate perceptions such as the power of love at first sight, the impact of chance meetings, the melding of dream and the wakeful states, the capacity of language to trigger the imagination of the spectator, the need for the individual to break through the constriction of social institutions and to demonstrate that in the modern world beauty had to be convulsive, explosive, unpredictable, or not at all. In that particular context the "absurd" is something sublime and devoutly to be wished; it is a resource of the imagination. But the dramatic works of the first generations of surrealists were only blueprints for a new form of poetic discourse rather than finished dramatic works. These fragmentary efforts made it obvious that the dynamism of theater would be difficult to convey through the medium of the existing theater unless there first occurred a massive transfiguration of the structure and function of stagecraft, willed or encouraged by the author. The surrealists did not probe or even evoke the questions that touch theater art integrally. In fact, these issues were totally ignored as they would be by people who are unversed; these people, however, were supremely versed and thereby knew what they were destroying, as was the case with Pirandello. In relation to the spectators, what the surrealists hoped to do was to raise the level of imaginative power, but they did not have in mind any specific creation regarding the interplay between author and producer, or actor and audience, at least not until Antonin Artaud's *The Theater and Its Double,* which proposed theatrical devices affecting audience behavior. But Artaud's treatise, which he really did not implement, is posterior to *Six Characters,* which contains both thesis and praxis within a single work.

When we look at *Six Characters* from the point of view of this cursory description of the salient characteristics of fragmental surrealist plays, the differences are jarring. First, Pirandello came to his rebellion as a theatrical craftsman who had mastered conventional theater. He was a professional who wanted to break the rules and not an amateur who knew no better. The impact of the aberration of form becomes much more notable when it is willed and when the rejection or negation carries the weight of new values. Pirandello's flaunting of the rules had affirmative intentions. When in the beginning of the play he has the Director telling his crew that they have to use Pirandello's plays because there is a sudden dearth of plays coming from Paris, he is expressing Pirandello's exasperation with the state of the theater. A few minutes later the characters are telling the Director the reason for their orphaned state: "He [the author] abandoned us in a fit of depression, of disgust for the ordinary theater as the public knows it and likes it," . . . is the way the Stepdaughter explains why the characters were abandoned.

Pirandello dissects the theater to find out what ails it. He wants to break down the barriers between generator, director, performer, and receiver (audience). In contrast, the surrealists wanted to break down the divisions between the genres; for them theater was nothing more than an oral poem. In poetry the surrealist effects are essentially dependent on rapid, unexpected sparks of recognition and revelation, but the all-in-one-piece impact of a poem or a painting has so far proved inaccessible to the longer time span and larger space of the dramatic piece. The *sine qua non* of a poem, whether written or oral, is its ability to manipulate words. The cult of language, no matter in what genre, is the mark of surrealist writing: automatically eruptible, analogically contrived and hallucinatory in its repercussions. Pirandello sometimes found language to be a veritable barrier to the search for truth, and he denigrates the artist's dependence on it as a crutch in his inability to get to the core of human problems: "Words, words . . . the consolation of finding a word" is said in derision.

For the surrealist there is no discrete separation between the poetic and the dramatic forms. Poetry includes all the others, which the surrealists are ready to mutate or even mutilate if they can thereby enhance the power of poetry and extend its domain. Pirandello wants to break down the rules the better to preserve the theater. What does he do in *Six Characters* in his effort to strengthen what he considers to be a debilitated form? He is questioning the problem of survival and reality. The first premise is that the work has more chance of survival than its author. "Man, the writer . . . the instrument of creation will die. But what is created by him will never die" (Father, Act I). This thought had already been the matrix of the symbolist aesthetics. But once the work attains its independence from the author, it is in turn prone to mutability because it will have to combat and resist other factors endangering its integrity as it gets to mean different things to successive audiences. But unlike the late twentieth-century Derridian "différance" which relates to the privileged reader's inclinations to change the meaning of a text, that of the theater performance is more vulnerable. It is subjected to a triple tier of interpretation because it has to go through the process of its theatricalization in the hands first of the director, second of the actors, and only finally of the audience.

So, in truth the fate of this created reality (which is presumably "fixed") is as precarious as that of the human one. If human reality is ephemeral because of the impact of time, which turns today's reality into a yesterday no more substantial than an illusion, the theatrical reality that we call illusion and that at first glance seems impermeable to the ravages of human time, is just as vulnerable because of the future impact of rethinking on the part of producers, performers, and the changing responses of succeeding audiences. On the contrary, the variability of interpretation in the case of the surrealist author or painter is a cause not of fear but of exhilaration, an indication of the richness of the work. What Dali called "the delirium of interpretation" was an inherent goal of surrealist poetics. In fact, the palimpsestic character of surrealist discourse is part of the scheme. "Donner à voir" in Eluard's words and "faire voir" in Breton's are sheer invitations to receive not the perception of the creator of the work but the energy generated by the vision for uses other than the creator's. The astonishment of the Six Characters at being represented in ways they do not recognize would be deemed puerile by the surrealists.

In the case of *Six Characters,* the question of viability becomes even more complicated because at a certain junction reality intervenes to destroy illusion. Or in other words a real-life event—the actual drowning of a little girl and the suicide of the boy—brings art and reality into collision, violating the created reality of the fixed characters. They cannot be represented if they no longer exist. The play is pulverized before the very eyes of those who want to perform it. However relative truth may be and however dependent reality may be on point of view, these become totally academic problems as soon as the created reality disintegrates. The conclusion of the problematics of the creative process, which is the center of Pirandello's preoccupation, is a state of nihilism. It takes on a more concrete form in the idiotic laughter with which the play ends in the definitive version of the script. This is not the laughter of effervescence we sometimes meet in surrealist expression.

Surrealism forestalls the frustrations of art by its preliminary pronouncement that life is more important than art. Art is only a means of making life richer, more enjoyable. This philosophy is a safety valve against nihilism. The surrealists, who considered the sheer power of living in high gear a more satisfactory occupation than writing or painting, could not worry too much about the state of art. On the contrary, Pirandello starts in *Six Characters* by expressing his dissatisfaction with the theater of his time, picks some of the trite dramatic themes of the day (the infidelity of the Mother, the incestuous leanings of the Father, the disengagement of the Son from daily life, the prostitution of the Stepdaughter because of economic necessity), and he uses a banal plot as a vehicle for his meditation on the metaphor which theater becomes for life's problems. They emerge from these situations that have become graver in a world trying to adapt to a relativist point of view. Where the short view of the march of time might suggest that psychology was beginning to make us understand each other better than in the past, the long view that Pirandello perceived was that when truth became a relative concept, interrelationships between humans became even more impossible than under the absolute code of yore. "We think we understand one another. But we never really understand." Understanding of each other's character was never a high priority for the surrealists; instead, they reversed the mystery of human personality. What held the group together were their tropism toward certain objects, landscapes, and people, the visions they shared, the paintings to which they were drawn, and the artists they admired in mutual and sometimes illogical unison.

The primordial process of theater was and always has been the representation of life, and the creation of illusion has been only a means of reinforcing that reality. The indeterminacy of reality in the modern world made the normal process of creating that no longer reliable. Pirandello leaves us with the picture of the artist finding his art inadequate and revealing the quagmire through the deterioration of the medium. To his viewers the image of the disintegration of theater became a source of new freedom for the art. By letting the audience share his secret, Pirandello revealed to himself as well as to the adept viewer an infinite number of new channels open to theater.

Pirandello's efforts at philosophizing were expressed in the discourse of his play, but the form in which this discourse was couched proved to have more substantive value and more impact on the future of theater than the content of that discourse. He had unwittingly liberated the structure of theater for the rest of the century. A seeming informality in stage-craft opened the possibilities of audience involvement; plot irresolution became acceptable, and the curtain separating illusion from reality vanished. If the freedom of the characters from their author's intentions was already an impudent step, an even more far-reaching break in the definitive version of the play occurred when Pirandello's stage directions bid the characters to burst into the arena of the audience.

Among the surrealists who had no more faith in the theater than in the novel, the only erstwhile surrealist with sustained interest in the theater was Artaud, whose existence as an actor and sometime playwright prevailed longer than his adherence to surrealism. When in his theoretical work in drama Artaud used the metaphor of the plague, he was only reinforcing Pirandello's earlier notion of the importance of audience participation. But in Artaud's case it became a greater social than philosophical phenomenon, and neither the course of his tragic life nor his unsustained qualifications as a playwright made it possible for him to achieve an *oeuvre.*

Pirandello's philosophy and aesthetics are very closely linked together. He mingles his sense of the precariousness of life with the perilous state of art. Actually, in the last analysis the Six Characters are not so much in search of an author as of a performance, which Pirandello determines to be the essential character of theater itself. It has often been pointed out that the Characters lack the cohesion to become performable because the author has abandoned them. But in reality there is an element of rebellion on the part of the Characters against their author:

> When a character is born he immediately acquires an independence. . . . Even of his own author. That everyone can imagine him in a whole host of situations which his author never thought of placing him. He can even imagine acquiring sometimes a significance that the author never dreamed of giving him.

But performance is the essential character of theater. The play ceases to exist if not performed at all; therefore, it is more precarious than poetry or the novel. If indeed the author had scrapped the trivial material, then the Characters' second and more theater-related problem was caused by the fact that they would cease to exist no matter how good or bad their script might be unless a director and performers were to be found—and only then could they seek the judgment of the audience. Otherwise, their independence would serve no purpose, and they would be the embodiments of imperfect drafts of a work of art drifting weightlessly and reaching no one. If then a play is not a play unless it is performed, neither is it performable if its author has aborted it.

By deconstructing the mechanism of theater, Pirandello was able to demonstrate which of the elements were trappings and which were the essentials. By having the author challenged by the producer (or in the more appropriate French word the "réalisateur"), Pirandello launched in Europe the era of the great impresarios who gave their own imprints to a play and even in some cases managed to give cohesion to some loosely constructed ones. In a subsequent age, which did not produce great drama, the permissibility practiced by this new breed of directors made it possible for playwrights such as Thornton Wilder to endow drama with a certain contrived informality, giving the director more opportunity to exercise his own creativity.

The surrealists did not care specifically for the destiny of the theater. Their basic hypothesis was that a liberated mind could energize any form of writing as well as any of the other media of the arts, which were like instruments whereby man could demonstrate his psychic liberation and heightened imagination, or derive through his work a better understanding of his own mettle.

The questions Pirandello asked about the creative process were not as novel as the renovations of the craft that he put thereby into motion. Those who observed his feat were impelled toward a freer concept of theater, which in turn opened up a larger vista for dramatic representation.

In an age deeply stricken with the sense of mortality, the most fragile of the arts became the most representative of the "brave new world," whose bravura masked some muffled sobs and whose laughter suggested a feeble effort to distance from itself the impending void. Beyond the tower of despair, Pirandello had superposed the reverberations of the Stepdaughter's hysterical laughter to the earlier and more conventional sobbing with which he had originally ended his play. But neither the sobbing nor the ironic laughter is compatible with the philosophy of surrealism, which emphasizes the immediacy of life as a multi-dimensional and ever renewable reality to be espoused.

It it true that many midcentury unconventional dramatists such as Arrabal, Ionesco, Henri Pichette, and Yacine Katab were labeled neo-surrealist. Generally, however, that was a journalistic perception based on the assumption that any extravaganza in the arts is tinged with the "surrealistic." A very small number of playwrights in the era following that of the peak both of surrealism and of Pirandello would truly qualify as surrealists, although few are totally untouched by the spirit of surrealism. Those who in effect followed faithfully the surrealist line have not attained universal recognition and have emerged in countries whose literature still remains largely unfamiliar to the world at large. (But that is another issue deserving, and not getting, sufficient critical attention!) The real filiation of the noted men of the theater of the late twentieth century is with Pirandello.

A truer perspective would suggest, then, that Pirandello and the surrealists shared a moment in the history of the arts but followed parallel rather than converging paths in their spectacular irreverence for the traditional.

HENRY IV

PRODUCTION REVIEWS

Stark Young (review date 6 February 1924)

SOURCE: "The Pirandello Play," in *The New Republic*, Vol. XXXVII, No. 479, 6 February 1924, p. 287.

[*In the following review of the New York City stage production of* Henry IV, *Young criticizes the acting as weak but lauds the drama's "intellectual beauty."*]

The Pirandello play at the Forty-Fourth Street Theatre is important not by reason of any display or novelty or foreign importation but through the mere occurrence on our stage of a real intellectual impact, a high and violent world of concepts and living. So far as the practical end of it goes Pirandello's *Henry IV* is difficult for our theatre. Its range and complexity of ideas are made more difficult by the presentation that it gets now and that it would be almost sure to get one way or another in any of our theatres.

The play is fortunate in its translation, certainly; Mr. Livingston's rendering is both alive and exact, and especially in the second act, where the thought is more involved, Mr. Livingston achieves an unusual quality of distinction. Mr. Robert Edmond Jones's two settings—save for the two portraits in the first scene, which obviously should be modern realistic in the midst of the antique apartment—are ahead of anything Pirandello would be apt to get in Italy, more precisely in the mood and more beautifully and austerely designed. Otherwise the trouble begins with the acting. Even bad Italian actors would, congenitally even if in no other way, be closer to this Italian play and its necessities than bad actors of our own might be. The actors in the opening moments at the Forty-Fourth Street Theatre could not even cope with the necessary delivery of the words. They not only could not whack out the stresses needed for the mere sense of the lines, but had no instinct for taking the cues in such a manner as would keep the scene intact. All that first part of the scene Pirandello means to keep flowing as if it were taking place in one mind; and the actors should establish that unity, speed and continuity by taking fluidly their lines as if from one mouth. Miss Lascelles's portrayal of Donna Mathilde is not definite or elegant enough; it is muffled and it is not full enough of a kind of voluptuous incisiveness. Mr. Louden's Doctor is wrong, too flat and narrow; the part is rough and tumble—out of the old Commedia very nearly—and a satire on specious scientific optimism and incessant explanation. And Mr. Korff's troubles with the language make his lines, which are hard enough already to grasp, confused and elusive.

Much of the meaning of Pirandello's *Henry IV* will depend of course on the actor who does the central character. Mr. Korff is a very good actor indeed in a certain style. He has a fine voice and a good mask in the manner of the Flemish or German schools of painting. But his portrayal of Henry IV lacks most of all distinction and bite. It is too full of sentiment and too short of mental agitation; it has too much nerves and heart and too little brains. The average audience must get the impression from Mr. Korff that we see a man whose life has been fantastically spoiled by the treachery of an enemy, that the fall from his horse began his disaster, which was completed by the infidelity and loose living of the woman he loved. But this weakens the whole drama; the root of the tragic idea was in the man's mind long before the accident; Pirandello makes that clear enough. The playing of this character, which is one of the great rôles in modern drama, needs first of all a dark cerebral distinction and gravity; the tragedy, the irony, the dramatic and philosophical theme, depend on that. Mr. Korff has theatrical power and intensity, but too much waggling of his head; he is too grotesque and undignified vocally; he has too little precision and style for the part; and not enough intellectual excitement and ideal poignancy. And the very last moment of the play he loses entirely by the rise that he uses in his voice and by the kind of crying tumult that he creates. Pirandello's idea cannot appear in such terms as Mr. Korff's. Pirandello is concerned first and last with a condition of life, an idea, embodied in a magnificent personage, not with personal ills and Gothic pities.

A man dressed as Henry IV of Canossa fame rides beside the woman he loves, who goes as Mathilde of Tuscany. His horse is pricked from the rear and lunges; the man when he comes out of his stupor believes himself to be the real Henry IV. For years the river of time flows past him; his beloved marries and has a daughter, she becomes the amante of his rival. He chooses, when his reason returns, to remain in the masquerade of the character that for an evening's pleasure he has put on. Life has cheated him, made a jest of him, he gets even with life by remaining permanent in the midst of everlasting change. All men play a part in life; he plays his knowingly. And the people who come out of life to him must mask themselves before they are admitted; he makes fools of them. The woman he has loved comes with his nephew and the doctor to see him, bringing also her amante—well played by Mr. Gamble— with her and her daughter, who is the image of what she herself was in her youth. They are the changing Life brought now against the fixed Form in which the supposed madman lives. Driven by the sense that years have passed and are recorded on these visitors from his past and that he has not lived, he tells his attendants of his sanity and his masquerade. They betray his secret. In the end he sees that in the young daughter alone can he recognize his renewal and return to life. There is a struggle when he tries to take her, and he kills the amante. Necessarily now, after this crime, he remains shut up in the mask under which he has masqueraded.

With this the Pirandello theme appears; the dualism between Life on one hand and Form on the other; on the one hand Life pouring in a stream, unknowable, obscure, unceasing; on the other hand forms, ideas, crystallizations, in which we try to embody and express this ceaseless stream of Life. Upon everything lies the burden of its form, which alone separates it from dust but which also interferes with the unceasing flood of Life in it. In *Henry IV* this man who has taken on a Form, a fixed mask in the midst of flooding, changing Life, remains in it until the moment when his passion and despair and violent impulse send him back into Life. But only for a moment: the impetuous violence of the Life in him expels him into his masquerade again: in the struggle between Life and Form, Life is defeated, Form remains.

Nothing in town is to compare to Pirandello's *Henry IV*— well or badly done—as worth seeing. If there is a tendency in many of his plays to think, talk, analyze, without embodying these processes in dramatic molds that carry and give them living substance—and I think that is one of Pirandello's dangers, his plays too often when all is said and done boil down too much to single ideas—this fault cannot be

laid on his *Henry IV.* In this play Pirandello has discovered a story, a visual image, and a character that completely embody and reveal the underlying idea. This drama has a fantastic and high-spirited range in the spirit of the Italian comedy tradition; it has also a kind of Shakespearean complexity and variety; and in the second act, at least, something like a great poetry of intellectual beauty.

Frances Birrell (review date 21 June 1924)
SOURCE: "Pirandello at Cambridge," in *The Nation and the Athenaeum,* Vol. XXXV, No. 12, 21 June 1924, pp. 379-80.

[*Below, Birrell provides a favorable review of the Cambridge stage production of* Henry IV, *describing the play as "cerebral" and the representation as "exciting and consistent."*]

Pirandello is, to my mind, easily the most important playwright who has appeared in Europe since Chekhov, and it is lamentable that a combination of circumstances have hidden him from English playgoers. The Censor, in a moment of egregious folly, stopped *Six Characters in Search of an Author* (magnificently produced for the Stage Society by Komisarjevski), and a recent translation of *Three Plays* by Pirandello, unsatisfactory as it is, got less attention than it deserved.

Our thanks are therefore once more due to Cambridge for its courage in performing the author's masterpiece *Henry IV.,* and producer and actors are to be congratulated on the great measure of success achieved in a very difficult task. All through, the production was exciting and consistent; it went with admirable smoothness, while the acting of the title *rôle* was splendid. It is a difficult because a novel play, and sometimes none too easy to follow. Hence, though I was carried away at the moment, I am, on reflection, not quite so satisfied with the interpretation. Still, I may be wrong myself, and hope any criticism will be regarded as friendly discussion, not as fault-finding.

The dry bones of the play are these. A young Italian student appears in a pageant as the Emperor Henry IV, with the lady he secretly loves and with his rival in her affections. All his circumstances bear a superficial resemblance to those of the real Emperor. In the course of the pageant he falls from his horse and gets a "fixation" that he really is the Emperor, and bases all his life and surroundings on his prototype. The delusion lasts twelve years, but he prefers to live in it for eight years more, at which point the play opens. His relations, accompanied by a brain specialist, arrive to effect a cure, but their grotesquely impercipient conduct brings him to see what horrible experience his "real" life would let him in for, and confirms him in his desire to remain Henry IV.

The play is as "cerebral" as anything could be, the desire of the author being, I think, to suggest that his "delusion" life is as reasonable as his "real" life, while the general impression should remain that he is fundamentally the only sane and sensible person in the play. Similarly in *Six Characters,* only the "characters," not the actors, are really real.

This is where the A.D.C. performance divagates from my idea of the play. Henry IV. becomes a problem: Was he mad or was he not? Was he mad all the time, some time, or never? Was he a "borderline" case? The same controversy has raged unprofitably round Hamlet. The part of the doctor reinforces this interpretation. He was incapable and even disastrous, but not because he was a drivelling idiot—on the contrary, within his limits, he was a serious and intelligent man—but because his intelligence was concentrated on an unreal state of affairs. If madness, ordinarily so-called, does not exist, a mad doctor is an absurdity. The producer faced the difficulty and "guyed" the part. It is the stupidity of the medical profession which precipitates the catastrophe. But I do not believe that this was the intention of the author. He did not perhaps intend so much contrast between Henry IV. and everyone else. No doubt, on this particular day of the play, he was worked up by the imbecile persecution to which he was being subjected. Otherwise he would behave as naturally as his difficult position would admit. His decision to remain Henry IV. is the result of an intellectual process. By this means the basic idea behind much of Pirandello's art is indicated. Are not these terms "reality" and "fiction" merely convention? Would it not be truer to say that nothing is but thinking makes it so? Pirandello is preoccupied with mental states even more than personal relations, and his drama is of the brain. His idea may be philosophically unimportant, but aesthetically it is satisfactory, and he is a great artist.

Such are only my personal views, and no doubt the producer can justify his own conception. In any case, the performance was most interesting, and my remarks are meant to do no more than stimulate intelligent interest in a remarkable writer.

CRITICAL COMMENTARY

June Schlueter (essay date 1979)

SOURCE: "Pirandello's *Henry IV*," in *Metafictional Characters in Modern Drama,* Columbia University Press, 1979, pp. 19-34.

[*In the following essay, Schlueter examines the dual nature of Pirandello's characters in* Henry IV, *maintaining that the protagonist is the prototype for metaphysical characters in modern drama.*]

To say that self-conscious modern drama began with Pirandello would be like saying that realism began with Balzac, naturalism with Zola, or surrealism with Breton: all of these are oversimplifications that wrongly imply a literary concept is the pure product of one man's genius rather than the outgrowth of a complex combination of prevailing values and attitudes—and the need to find expression for those values and attitudes—which are the temper and ripeness of a particular era. Pirandello was not alone in his dramatic achievement, nor was he even the first. Indeed, it is ulti-

mately impossible to fix with exactness the first modern dramatic rendering of the "other tradition." Depending on one's specific criteria, any one of a number of playwrights—Ibsen, Chekhov, Shaw, Zola, Maeterlinck, Strindberg, Jarry, Apollinaire, Chiarelli, Schnitzler, and several others—might qualify as being the playwright of seminal importance. Yet it is not difficult to understand why the phrase "after Pirandello" has become a critical commonplace, for, as Francis Fergusson notes in *The Idea of a Theater,* Pirandello is symbolically, if not chronologically, the point at which a new form of drama emerged.

In the early 1920s, the plays of Pirandello were performed in New York, London, Paris, Berlin, and Vienna, as well as in Pirandello's native Italy. Possibly the strongest and most immediate impact of the playwright was felt in France, where the 1923 production of *Six Characters in Search of an Author* at the Comédie des Champs-Elysées in Paris greatly excited the critics. [In *Retours à pied* (1925)] Henri Beraud, for example, acclaimed the play as having "overwhelmed my soul," and Pierre Brisson called it "a new achievement in the contemporary history of the theater "[*Au Hasard des Soirées* (1935)]. It was this play about which Georges Neveux would later remark: "The entire theatre of an era came out of the womb of the play, *Six Characters* " ["Pirandello vous a-t-il influenceé?" *Arts,* No. 602 (16 January 1957)]. Within two years, the Sicilian's reputation secure, Pirandello's plays were "everywhere":

> at the Atelier, at the Renaissance, at the Théâtre des Arts; he is being played in three theaters at the same time—a fact without precedent for a foreign author; it's a rage, an infatuation, a fancy, a craze.

In 1926, Gaston Rageot christened Pirandello "the great dramatist of the western world "[*Revue politigue et littéraire,* 19 June 1926]. Nor was the playwright's significance to diminish. In his 1947 study of the French theater [*Le Théâtre français contemporain*], Marcel Doisy testifies to Pirandello's continuing impact:

> Surely no man of the theater since Ibsen had given Europe so totally renewed conceptions of the theater, a more violently original artistry together with so personal a technique. . . . And it certainly seems as if his revelations are still far from being exhausted. . . . Pirandello might easily remain one of the guiding lights of the period which is opening.

The canon of Pirandellian drama is like a symphony, stating and restating, embellishing, varying a single theme. Virtually all of Pirandello's plays reflect the artist's nearly obsessive preoccupation with the relationship between reality and illusion, be it with respect to the philosophical conception of the relativity of truth, the fluid and multiple nature of the personality, or the persistent division between life and art. In his rendering of the multiplicity of identity, the playwright, undoubtedly influenced by the *teatro del grotesco,* repeatedly distinguishes between the "mask," which all of us assume, and the "face," which constantly remains veiled. In his inquiry into the relativity of truth, he constructs and demolishes layers of illusion, probing into the multiple perceptions and identities of his characters to reveal yet conceal the "naked mask." In his fascination with his own power as artist-creator, he dramatizes the dialectic between the fluid, spontaneous, sprawling nature of life and the fixed, predictable and contained nature of art. But as Robert Brustein points out in *The Theatre of Revolt,* the areas of Pirandello's dramatic inquiry are all facets of the same subject:

> The typical Pirandellian drama is a drama of frustration which has at its core an irreconcilable conflict between time and timelessness or life and form; and whether the author is reflecting on human identity or (his other major subject) the identity of art, the terms of the conflict remain essentially the same.

For Pirandello, the metafictional character is the dramatic embodiment of this multiple single theme.

Because Pirandello is so concerned with the nature of identity, nearly every one of his major characters (Signora Ponza in *Right You Are* or Leone in *Rules of the Game,* for example) possesses a "mask" as well as a "face." And because he is so concerned with the nature of theater, many (such as the characters in *Each in His Own Way* or *Tonight We Improvise*) also possess an expressed awareness of their identities as actors. In fact, most of Pirandello's characters may be called metafictional characters, for whether their acting role is psychological or social on the one hand, or theatrical on the other—or both—they serve as symbols of the playwright's concern with the multiple facets of the relationship between reality and illusion.

One Pirandellian character in particular may well be called the prototype of the metafictional character in modern self-conscious drama, and that is the protagonist of *Henry IV.* As Brustein perceives:

> In Henry's character, Pirandello's reflections on the conflict between life and form, on the elusiveness of identity, and on man's revolt against time, achieve their consummation. . . . Henry is the culmination of Pirandello's notions (developed more elaborately in his theatre plays) about the timeless world of art.

In terms of its presentation of the complexity of identity, *Henry IV* (1922) is perhaps the richest of the Pirandello canon. No character in that play exists singularly as a fictive creation, but each moves from one self to another as the action shifts from the distant past to the recent past to the present. Donna Matilda, the protagonist's former love, possesses no fewer than five identities: she is at once the middle-aged Donna Matilda of the present; the masked Donna Matilda of twenty years earlier; the Marchioness Matilda of Tuscany of eight hundred years earlier; the Duchess Adelaide, mother of Empress Bertha of Susa, who was the historical eleventh-century king's wife; and, through her daughter, the youthful Donna Matilda chronologically misplaced. Which of these several selves she is at a given moment is dependent upon the role she voluntarily assumes (as when she pretends, upon first seeing the "madman," to be Adelaide), or, more commonly, the identity

imposed upon her by the protagonist. That character's perceptions, depending on whether they emanate from the eleventh-century king, the love-struck young man of twenty years earlier, or the middle-aged man of the present, permit Donna Matilda to move through a twenty-year time span of reality and an eight-hundred-year time span of fantasy, and to be several selves simultaneously. The central symbol of this fluidity and multiplicity of identity is the masquerade: the protagonist's delusions began at a masquerade pageant; Donna Matilda is masquerading as a character from both the protagonist's past and Henry IV's past; those in the group of characters who visit the castle are donning masks which conceal the face in the ultimate hope of revealing the face of the protagonist, who is the master masquerader.

Even with this multiplicity of selves, however, there exists a basic duality which creates the metafictional character. Every character in *Henry IV* possesses a double identity within the fictive world; every character, already fictive, plays the part of a fictive character in the fiction within the fictive world of the play. In the face of such role playing within role playing, we are forced to differentiate between the two fictive roles, one of which we accept as the "real" fictive character. Thus we have the young men who cater to Henry's whims possessing one identity when they talk among themselves, use electric lights, and smoke cigarettes, and another identity when they are in the presence of the eleventh-century monarch. Similarly, the throne room guests who hope to cure the would-be king are "real" in their capacities as former love, her lover and her daughter, the nephew, and the doctor; they are fictive when they wear the masks of personages from the past of the historical Henry. The double identities of all the characters in the play, however, are dependent upon the double identity of the central character, the man who believes—and does not believe—himself to be Henry IV, king of the Holy Roman Empire.

Before looking at the duality of the protagonist of *Henry IV,* however, it might be appropriate to examine the dialectic which is responsible for creating the character which belongs to both the world of fiction and the world of reality, and to that end turn to another Pirandellian play, which was written one year earlier than *Henry IV,* and is somewhat less developed in terms of this concept. For in *Six Characters* (1921), two groups—the Characters and the Actors—rather than a single character, embody the two fictive identities. Our response therefore (or at least our initial response) is comfortably divided; since it is a *donnée* of the play that we do not accept the fictive creations (i.e., Characters and Actors) equally, we must imaginatively endow one group with the status of "real." We readily choose the Actors—a group of men and women realistically rehearsing a play when we happened upon them—and remind ourselves of the premise of drama involving the creation of any dramatic character: the actor, of course, is real; the character, fictive. Even though the premise is not so simply applied here, since in this case the Actors are no more real than the Characters (they, too, are fictive creations being played by real people), their juxtaposition with the Characters, who are, by self-admission, fictive, authenticates their reality.

Initially, then, there is no problem in isolating reality from illusion. Six Characters appear on stage during a rehearsal of a Pirandello play and declare themselves to be the products of an author's imagination, an author who has created but abandoned them. Their intrusion upon the world of the Actors readily allows us to establish the dichotomy of fictive (the Characters) and "real" (the Actors). Gradually, however, Pirandello (predictably) upsets this distinction.

The Characters, who wish only to be immortalized though the written text, insist upon their autonomy, claiming an existence independent of the play which attempts to portray them. They find that the Actors cannot portray them with fidelity, for the Actors themselves interpret and create, making of the Characters something quite different from what the Characters claim is their true identity. The Characters want only fidelity to what they know as their own experience, but cannot find it in the reflection of art. They enact (or re-experience) their tragic story and then watch the Actors imperfectly perform the same scene. We soon find that the failure of the Actors to record accurately the experience of the Characters lends a validity to the Characters, upsetting our earlier delegation of them to the world of illusion and of the Actors to the world of reality.

Yet the characters do not claim reality; they reaffirm the fact that they are illusion:

> THE FATHER: Now . . . , if you consider the fact that we . . . as we are, have no other reality outside of this illusion . . .
>
> THE MANAGER: . . . And what does that mean?
>
> THE FATHER: . . . As I say, sir, that which is a game of art for you is our sole reality.

The audience must now adjust its thinking to include the possibility that illusion is more real than reality, particularly since the Characters retain their identities irrespective of time. As the father questions the manager's identity, asking him who he is and pointing to his changing reality, the present being "fated to seem a mere illusion" tomorrow, we add to our thinking the further possibility that perhaps reality is illusion. The Characters, who have no reality beyond the illusion, are thus as real as the "real" individual whose identity is an illusive one. Through the exploitation of the dichotomy between the real and the fictive, Pirandello has dramatized several concerns: the fluidity of identity, the philosophic relationship of reality and illusion, and the relationship of life and art.

Yet one character does not embody the dichotomy of the real and the fictive. In *Six Characters* it is simply a case of our being manipulated into viewing a given set of characters as "real" and then as fictive, and vice versa, to dramatize that dichotomy. The principle with which we are concerned here is intact, but we must look ahead to *Henry IV* for the single metafictional character which is "real and false at the same time."

When *Henry IV* opens, Berthold, a newcomer to the castle, is being initiated into the routine of an attendant of Henry IV. Having believed the madman to be the "other" Henry IV, the sixteenth-century king of France, Berthold is in frantic need of background details, which the other attendants gladly supply (and which Pirandello obliges us with as well). The man who believes himself to be Henry IV has been acting the role for some twenty years. Two decades earlier, dressed as the eleventh-century king at a masquerade pageant, and youthfully in love with Donna Matilda, herself dressed as Matilda of Tuscany, Henry's historical enemy, the protagonist was thrown from his horse and became fixated in the identity of the mask he wore. Donna Matilda describes the tragic event:

> I shall never forget that scene—all our masked faces hideous and terrified gazing at him, at that terrible mask of his face, which was no longer a mask, but madness, madness personified.

We and the attendants soon learn, however, that the madman recovered from the fixation eight years earlier, but, choosing not to return to the real world from which he had been absent for twelve years, hid his lucidity and continued the illusion of his delusion.

The double existence of the protagonist in *Henry IV,* then, is manifested, on the one hand, in the "real" self, the man (whose name we never learn) who twenty years earlier was enamoured of Donna Matilda, dressed the part of Henry IV, and, twelve years after that, consciously regained his identity but did not reveal this fact to others. On the other hand, it is manifested in the fictive self, that of the eleventh-century king of the Holy Roman Empire, which for twelve years was the result of the madness of the protagonist and for eight years the result of his "lucid madness." For eight years, then, there has been an overlapping of the "real" and the fictive selves, for while Henry was unaware of his masquerade at first, he is now, and has been for eight years, supremely aware of it, yet persists in maintaining it.

Translated into social terms, Henry is an extreme example of the individual who as social animal adopts roles in order to fulfill the image others have of him. Yet there is a strange superiority in the kind of role playing to which the protagonist is committed as compared with the kind of role playing in which the social individual—and the castle guests and valets—indulge. When he is actually mad, the protagonist is playing a role in earnest; he is so totally committed to his identity as Henry that any distinction existing between fiction and reality dissolves, inextricably merging, at least for Henry, the mask and the face. When he is lucidly mad, though, he is playing the role in full consciousness that it is an illusion, but his madness is being sustained not in deference to any demands of society, but for his own purposes: first, because he is psychologically unable to rejoin a world from which he has been absent for twelve years, and secondly, for his own amusement. For eight years the protagonist has been in complete command of his role and in partial command of those of others, which he creates and manipulates in relation to his own. By contrast, the make-believe of the castle guests and the valets is one which is created exclusively for the benefit of Henry.

Recognizing them as fools, Henry can chide the valets for not having "known how to create a fantasy for yourselves, not to act it for me."

On a psychological level, Henry is also superior, for he is the only one who can believe "the moon in the pond is real." The others, rigidly fixed in a concept of themselves, are incapable of simultaneously believing and not believing the lie. Where Henry dyes his hair for a joke, the Marchioness does it seriously in an effort to fulfill her own static image of herself. But Henry tells his former love:

> I assure you that you too, Madam, are in masquerade, though it be in all seriousness; and I am not speaking of the venerable crown on your brows or the ducal mantle. I am speaking only of the memory you wish to fix in yourself of your fair complexion one day when it pleased you. . . .

Henry alone possesses what Doctor Dionysius Genoni characterizes as "the peculiar psychology of madmen; . . . [he can] detect people who are disguised; . . . recognize the disguise and yet believe in it; . . . [and he can understand that] disguise is both play and reality." Only the protagonist can "act the madman to perfection":

> and I do it very quietly, I'm only sorry for you that you have to live your madness so agitatedly, without knowing it or seeing it.

The protagonist's duality may exist in terms of identity, in both social and psychological terms, and indeed it may offer a perspective on social roles and the psychological concept of self, but it is surely not limited to that concern in this play (or, for that matter, in any of the other plays in this study).

Pirandello's other great subject is the relationship between life and art, and the protagonist's duality is well worth considering in aesthetic terms. If the middle-aged protagonist is the "real" self and the eleventh-century king the fictive self, then we may also equate the division of sanity and madness ("madness," "fantasy," "unreality," "illusion" all suggesting creative genius and the product of that genius) and the division of life and art. From the psychological crisis of the protagonist, then, emerges a metaphor not only for the self in its social and psychological manifestations, but for the play itself, through which the playwright may examine the validity of art in the face of an uncertain reality.

The distinction that exists between life and art has long been a concern of literary creators, especially so among modern writers. In his 1889 essay, "The Decay of Lying," Oscar Wilde, through the voice of his fictive Vivian, proclaims the superiority of art:

> My own experience is that the more we study Art, the less we care for Nature. What Art really reveals to us is Nature's lack of design, her curious crudities, her extraordinary monotony, her absolutely unfinished condition. Nature has good intentions, of course, but, as Aristotle once said, she cannot carry them out. When I

look at a landscape I cannot help seeing all its defects. It is fortunate for us, however, that Nature is so imperfect, as otherwise we should have no art at all. Art is our spirited protest, our gallant attempt to teach Nature her proper place.

In his inquiry into the relationship of reality and illusion in *Henry IV,* Pirandello focuses particularly on an aspect of art existing as part of the orderliness suggested by Vivian and clearly distinguishing it from reality, and that is time-lessness.

Like the characters in *Six Characters,* man, a temporal creature, is constantly seeking relief from the flux of existence, a means of freezing what Pirandello, in his 1920 essay, *On Humor,* calls "the continuous flow":

> Life is a continuous flow which we continually try to stop, to fix in established and determinate forms outside and inside of ourselves because we are already fixed forms, forms that move among other immovable ones, which follow the flow of life until the point when they become rigid and their movement, slowed, stops.

The means by which we attempt to achieve permanence is illusion:

> The forms in which we try to stop and fix this continuous flow are the concepts, the ideals, within which we want to keep coherent all the fictions we create, the condition and the status in which we try to establish ourselves.

For twelve years Henry was the realization of this striving; he had succeeded in suspending his susceptibility to the "poisonous ingenuity of time" which Beckett describes in *Proust:* "There is no escape from the hours and the days. Neither from to-morrow nor from yesterday." While *chronos* continued on its course, Henry remained the young king of Germany, reliving the events of a concentrated period of time from 1076, when the historical king penitently knelt before Pope Gregory VII, to 1080, when he was supreme ruler over the entire empire, including the pope. For Henry, immovably fixed in history, the past, present, and future were a concentrated and constant reality.

For eight years, however, the protagonist has been only pretending to be Henry IV. Within his self-created fiction, he—or at least his mask—is still immune from time, a delusion which the others, by responding to him as though he were Henry, support. For the protagonist himself, however, his susceptibility to time is the one certainty of his sanity. He may yet dress as Henry IV and "relive" the events of the eleventh century, but for eight years he has been aware of his own greying hair and of the absence of much of a resemblance between the portrait of the youthful man dressed as Henry IV and the middle-aged man his mirror reflects. The fact is that while the fictive side of the protagonist's double existence has remained fixed, the "real" side has moved irretrievably forward in time.

It is not difficult to see the emerging metaphor of life and art in the protagonist's dual nature. Life, which is subject to time, is a progression of haphazard events, none of which can be relieved. Art, which transcends time, freezes events into a permanent, repeatable pattern. The unnamed protagonist, then, who frets over his greying reflection, is the embodiment of life. Henry, the other part of the double character, in his immunity from time, his capacity to relive events in the past as a present reality, his ability to give permanence to illusion, is the embodiment of the spirit and function of art.

The relationship between art and reality which is embodied in Pirandello's central character is externally symbolized by the portraits of Donna Matilda and the youthful protagonist which hang on the wall of the throne room. Originally, these portraits, which reflected the young couple in their masquerade pageant costumes, were thought by the protagonist to be images; when he regained his sanity and became aware of his own temporality, he preserved the portraits as a means of fostering the youthful image he knew no longer was fact. The portraits, after all, as art, possessed the very quality of permanence of Henry's madness:

> A portrait is always there fixed in the twinkling of an eye: it can bring back everything: movement, gestures, looks, smiles, a whole heap of things.

But the portraits, once reflectors of reality and now betrayers of it, soon become reality. Like the portrait in Oscar Wilde's novel, they become "animated inanimate duplicates" [C. F. Keppler, *The Literature of the Second Self* (1972)], but to an even greater degree than in the portrait of Dorian Gray, which ages within its frame. Here the portraits, replaced by Donna Matilda's daughter and the protagonist's nephew, emerge from the frames which enclose them and assume living from. Just as the young protagonist had twenty years earlier become the realization of an illusion, so the portraits are no longer art, but reality.

The doctor's plan was to present the protagonist with a double image—the youthful couple and the aged couple—in hopes of telescoping time and shocking the madman into sanity. But because the protagonist is already cured *before* the shock treatment, the performance is a perilous one: the portraits are acquiring life before a man who finds security in the fact that his real self is indeed subject to time. For the madman, perceiving the live forms of Donna Matilda (actually her daughter) and himself (actually his nephew) as they were twenty years earlier and, immediately after, the live forms of the present Donna Matilda and himself, might have resulted in the restoration of his personality. But for the man whose sanity rests so seriously on his awareness of time as a continuum, a perception now seriously disturbed, the reincarnation could just as readily result in convincing the protagonist that he is the eleventh-century king. In fact, the treatment is abruptly discontinued when the others enter the throne room to announce their discovery that Henry is already cured. The face before them now is no longer that of Henry IV; it is the "naked mask."

And it is as the naked mask that the protagonist responds, embracing Frida as his youthful love Matilda, joyfully pouring forth twenty years of suppressed emotion. But he is embracing Frida for an even more important reason: the young woman, once frozen in form, is now pure life. It is this spontaneity and freedom which he so enthusiastically, almost frenetically, embraces, only to be thought a madman for doing so.

Seeing the impossibility of life without illusion, and without love, the protagonist must return to the mask of his madness, where illusion is tolerated and love is an eternal force. He cries his torment, which "is really this: that whether here or there [Pointing to his portrait . . .] I can't free myself from this magic." By slaying Belcredi, he permanently seals himself in the "eternal masquerade." As the dying man is carried offstage crying, "No, no, you're not mad! You're not mad. He's not mad!"—a sentiment not shared by the others—the protagonist, "with the most lucid consciousness," slips permanently into the role of Henry IV.

Admirers and detractors of Pirandello alike have long commented on the playwright's incessant hammering away at the theme of reality and illusion. The playwright himself in fact playfully comments on his own endless preoccupation in *Each In His Own Way* (1924), where, in an interlude in which the first act is criticized by defenders and opponents of Pirandello, a spectator complains: "But why is he always harping on this illusion and reality string?" The aspect of the relationship of reality and illusion which presents itself most readily to readers of Pirandello's plays is that of relativity. But the playwright's preoccupation extends considerably beyond the dramatization of the way in which we "simulate and dissimulate with ourselves, splitting or even multiplying ourselves," to the central philosophical question underlying all his drama: exactly what the relationship between reality and illusion consists of.

In a 1923 essay which shows considerable sensitivity to Pirandello's philosophy ["Life Versus Form," in *Studi sul teatro contemporaneo*], Adriano Tilgher discusses the dialectic of life and form which is at the core of virtually every essay, short story, and play the Sicilian wrote. Tilgher observes that man is unique among living things in possessing consciousness of life. Unlike a tree, which is "completely immersed in its own vital sense," not distinguishing itself from its environment, man possesses both life and the feeling of life. This unique consciousness, detaching itself from life, creates a new life of forms—"the concepts and ideals of our spirit, the conventions, mores, traditions and laws of society." These forms, however, conflict with the free flow of life, imprisoning man within their molds, and, finally, replacing life as the only seeming reality.

Robert Brustein, discussing the affinities of Pirandello and Bergson [in *The Theatre of Revolt*] similarly summarizes this relationship, characterizing the playwright's concept of life:

> Life (or reality or time) is fluid, mobile, evanescent, and indeterminate. It lies beyond the reach of reason, and is reflected only through spontaneous action, or instinct. Yet man, endowed with reason, cannot live instinctually like the beasts, nor can he accept an existence which constantly changes. In consequence, he uses reason to

fix life through ordering definitions. Since life is indefinable, such concepts are illusions. Man is occasionally aware of the illusory nature of his concepts; but to be human is to desire form; anything formless fills man with dread and uncertainty.

And Pirandello himself describes the conflict in *On Humor*:

All phenomena either are illusory or their reason escapes us inexplicably. Our knowledge of the world and of ourselves refuses to be given the objective value which we usually attempt to attribute to it. Reality is a continuously illusory construction. The obstacles and the limitations we place upon our consciousness are also illusions. They are the conditions of the appearance of our relative individuality. In reality, these limitations do not exist.

Art, then, and all of man's illusions, are created in response to this dialectic. And their absolute necessity is understood perhaps most immediately in the novel, *The Late Mattia Pascal,* which Tilgher describes:

To enjoy life in its infinite nakedness and freedom, outside all constructed forms into which society, history, and the events of each individual existence have channeled its course, is impossible. Mattia Pascal tried that, who, palming himself off as dead and changing name and aspect, believed he could start a new life, in the enthusiasm of a boundless liberty. He learned at his own expense that, having cut himself off from all social forms and conventions, he was only allowed to witness other people's life as a foreign spectator, without any further possibility to mingle with it and enjoy its fullness. Since he had estranged himself from the forms of life, it now no longer conceded itself to him except superficially, externally.

The experience of Henry IV is a similar one of alienation. But in his case, the would-be king has cut himself off from both life and the forms others lived by, creating a unique form of his own which enabled him totally to live his illusion. And when, like Pascal, he attempted, if only for a moment, an affirmation of pure life without form, he was branded as a madman. Neither achieved the balance of life and form which Pirandello believes is the wisdom of life and which Tilgher so appropriately describes:

To accept the Forms or constructions into which Life has been forced; to participate in them with heartful belief and yet avoid crystallizing oneself in one of them or in one of their systems, but to retain so much spiritual fusion or fluidity that one's soul may go on from form to form without finally coagulating in any, without fearing the impurities it inevitably carries along in its ceaseless flow, since that very flowing will purify it: here is the practical wisdom of life.

The protagonist's retreat into illusion, then, is not a denial of an absolute reality in deference to twentieth-century relativism, but rather an affirmation of the unceasing interdependence of reality and illusion, of life and form, which must characterize life if man is to make any sense of a reality of which he sees only the shadow.

Illusion, then, is not only a competing force simultaneously reflecting and contradicting reality; it is a necessity, for it constitutes the only reality mankind is capable of perceiving and affirms man's constant need for form. And art offers us a packaged epitome of the "magic" from which Henry and we cannot escape, within the fictionalized reality that is its world. In 1920 Pirandello spoke of his feelings about his art:

I think that life is a very sad piece of buffoonery; because we have in ourselves, without being able to know why, wherefore or whence, the need to deceive ourselves constantly by creating a reality (one for each and never the same for all), which from time to time is discovered to be vain and illusory. . . . My art is full of bitter compassion for all those who deceive themselves; but this compassion cannot fail to be followed by the ferocious derision of destiny which condemns man to deception.

For Pirandello, art is a redeeming force through which man preserves the illusion which must eternally coexist with reality, and a purgative for the constant frustration of man's final inability to know. And the double character is the distillation of the dialectic between life and form, reality and illusion, that is the playwright's single theme.

After the dissections, demolitions, and restructurings of reality which have taken place over the past two decades at the hands of such playwrights as Beckett, Ionesco, Stoppard, and Handke, the blatantly manipulative plays of Pirandello may no longer seem the fascinating inquiries into the nature of illusion and reality they once were, but may now appear to be naive and rather tiresome be-laborings of a theme treated by others in more sophisticated ways. Yet Pirandello's creation of the metafictional character in *Henry IV* must remain the prototype for modern drama, for through it he has perfectly distilled the dialectic between life and form, reality and illusion, that is his own and the modern playwright's recurring theme.

He appealed not because he flouted tradition but because his art mirrored, and put to discussion, the problems of his age. It is here that we have to see his importance; all other aspects of his work are secondary.

—Oscar Budel, in his **Pirandello, 1969.**

Susan Bassnett (essay date 1991)

SOURCE: "Henry IV—The Tragic Humorist," in *A Companion to Pirandello Studies,* edited by John Louis DiGaetani, Greenwood Press, 1991, pp. 231-43.

Luigi Pirandello is generally considered one of the great seminal dramatists of the twentieth century, ranked alongside Ibsen, Strindberg, Chekhov, and Brecht. Plays like *Six*

Rex Harrison in the title role of Henry IV, *Her Majesty's Theatre, London, 1974.*

Characters in Search of an Author and **Henry IV** have been widely translated and produced frequently by both professionals and amateurs. Outside Italy, it is perhaps less widely known that Pirandello was also a gifted prose writer, producing no less than 7 novels and 14 collections of short stories, together with a substantial body of critical essays and theoretical writings. If we add to these his 6 collections of poetry, and the total of 16 one-act plays and 27 full-length plays, the true size of his literary output begins to appear.

In spite of the popularity of some of his plays, not very much of the great body of Pirandellian texts has been translated into English. As a result, a curious distinction has arisen between the Pirandello familiar to Italian readers and the Pirandello known to English-speaking readers. The Italian Pirandello comes across as a witty, cynical writer, deeply concerned with the problem of fragmented personality and the ironies of multiple identity, whereas the English Pirandello emerges as altogether more serious, more intellectual or "cerebral" as he has often been described. And, of course, in English Pirandello is regarded primarily as a dramatist, which is a somewhat restrictive view since the links between his prose works and his theater works are an essential clue in our understanding of his work as a whole.

Pirandello began writing for the theater as early as 1898, when he wrote the one act play *L'epilogo* (*The Epilogue*) that was published but not produced. It was not until 1910

that a Pirandello play was staged, when Nino Martoglio directed two one-act plays and Pirandello began to write full-length pieces. Throughout his life he was to write short stories and novels alongside plays, however, and a considerable number of his plays are based on earlier prose works. In his essay "**Spoken Action**" ("**L'azione parlata**") written in 1899, Pirandello emphasized the close relationship between prose narrative and theater, and argued that for what he called the "miracle" of theater to occur, a new language had to be developed:

> a language that is itself spoken action, a living language that moves, the expression of immediacy, at one with action, the single phrase that must belong uniquely to a given character in a given situation: words, expressions, phrases that are not invented but are born when the author is fully at one with his creation so as to feel what it feels and want what it wants.

Critics and biographers have made much of the fact that the bulk of Pirandello's theater output stems from the period after his wife Antonietta had been put into a nursing home because of her mental illness. This illness took the form of manifestations of pathological jealousy, and in 1918, when Pirandello's eldest son Stefano came back from the First World War, the family decided to have Antonietta committed. Whatever the connection between this occurrence and Pirandello's writing for the theater, the fact remains that the theme of jealousy runs as a leitmotif throughout Pirandello's work and was obviously a human predicament that he found compellingly significant.

Approaching the theater of Pirandello, it becomes immediately obvious that there are no easy labels to attach to this work. Some of his plays, notably the theater-in-the-theater trilogy, show his ability to experiment with theater form, while others conform to the well-made three-act play of the naturalist theater tradition but deal with the theme of multiplicity in human relationships and the tragedy of man's search for a universally recognized identity. Time and again Pirandello explores themes that were to recur later in the century in the theater of the absurd and the theater of cruelty. The fact that it is impossible to label Pirandello clearly is a nicely ironic touch that he would himself have liked, for in all his work he was concerned primarily with the idea of the impossibility of truth. Again and again his writings illustrate the idea of relativity, of a many-sidedness that denies the existence of a single absolute. Even language, the instrument of man's daily communication, is inadequate. As the Father says in *Six Characters in Search of an Author*:

> Don't you see that the whole trouble lies here? In words. Each of us has within him a whole world of things, each one has his own special world. And how can we ever come to an understanding if I put into the words I utter the sense and value of things as I see them.

Nor is identity a unique fact. In *Right You Are (If You Think So)* Signora Ponza, the mystery lady that the Neighbors in the play seek to explain, refuses any single definition of her relationship to the man claiming to be her husband and the woman claiming to be her mother and says simply, "I am whoever you believe me to be." Pirandello acknowledges the impossibility of single definitions or simple solutions and offers us a vision of the world in which nothing is ever certain.

The titles of many of his plays further illustrate Pirandello's tendency to make us think twice about our notions of security. *Cosí è (se vi pare)*, [*Right You Are (If You Think So)*], *Ciascuno a suo modo (Each in His Own Way)*, *Come prima, meglio di prima (As Before, Better Than Before)*, *O di uno o di nessuno (Either Someone's or No-one's)*, *Non si sa come (You Don't Know How)*, *Sogno, ma forse no (A Dream, But Perhaps It Isn't)*—all these play titles are enigmas, deliberately ambiguous in their construction. And the titles reveal another significant Pirandellian element—humor, a feature that, unfortunately, does not always come across so clearly in English translation but that is a lynch pin in all his works.

If we consider for a moment what Pirandello means by *humor,* various difficulties arise. Clearly, he does not mean "comedy" as such, for his themes are all too often suffering, death, and human misery. Pirandello belonged to an age of de-structuring, to the world of cubism and Dada, the world in which ideal order had ceased to be the concern of art. In place of an image of ideal order, art in the early twentieth century substituted an image of fragmentation, of a whole broken into myriad particles, an image that mirrors the

splitting of the atom and the theory of relativity in the scientific world. In Italy, the Futurist Manifesto of 1910 had proclaimed the destruction of the past: "Sweeping the whole field of art clean of all themes and subjects, which have been used in the past. Alleviate all attempts at originality however daring, however violent."

In such a world, humor derives from the clash between the desire for fixity and stability and the impossibility of achieving that goal. Life, as Pirandello says in his essay *On Humor* published in 1908, is like a vast river that continually overflows its banks and cannot be controlled. All man can do is to create illusory safeguards in art and life as a way of dealing with the inexorability of that great tide: "Concepts and ideals by means of which we hope to give coherent enduring shape to all the fictions we create for ourselves, to the conditions and the state in which we tend to settle down and establish ourselves." In *Tonight We Improvise,* Hinkfuss, the director whose speeches show close links to *On Humor*, explains the paradox that is life: "Life must obey two necessities, both opposites, which prevent it from either lasting consistency or constant motion. If life were always in motion, it would never be consistent: if it were always consistent, it would not long move. And life must be consistent in motion."

The irony of this problem takes on another dimension when we come to the question of the relations between life as both consistency *and* motion and art. For the world of art is a means of freezing and fixing within the frame of form. Every time we pick up a novel, the characters do the same thing, though our perceptions may alter. But the problem here, the "humor," is that the work of art has immortality and "lives" forever precisely because it is not life.

It is easy to see why Pirandello increasingly came to write for the theater, since theater is the ultimate paradox: the play is a fixed work of art brought to life by human beings who assume roles, and, although the text is *fixed,* the *process* of performing that text ensures that it will never be the same twice. It moves and is fixed; theater, in other words, is a mirror-life.

The other great irony about the life/theater dichotomy is that theater, no matter how moving or realistic or surreal or unintelligible, is made up of signs. When an actor wears a crown, he is a king in the world of the play since the crown carries the sign-value of kingliness, and we accept that sign without questioning whether or not the crown is really made of gold. Similarly, when an actor dies, we accept the sign of death in the playing, but if an actor *did* die on stage, this would cease immediately to be theater and become life. Fascinated by this multilayered nature of theater, Pirandello played with the possibilities the medium had to offer. Erving Goffman, a sociologist rather than a theater specialist, has prepared a neat resume of Pirandello's various experiments in his book *Frame Analysis.* Goffman suggests that Pirandello used three main formats to explore the issues of motion versus fixity, appearance versus reality. In the first type of theater, "the traditional respect for the projected characters is sustained." Into this category belong the plays that follow the traditional naturalistic format. In the second category are those plays like *Six Characters,* where "the conventional performer-character line is attacked but the attacks stop at the stage-line." So *Six Characters* is still a three-act play, in spite of the various devices used to give the impression of breaking the form, and it is in the third category that Pirandello breaches the line between onstage and auditorium, in plays such as *Tonight We Improvise* and *The Mountain Giants.*

Considerable attention has been given to Pirandello's experiments with theater form. Indeed, his reputation is largely that of an innovative dramatist, but of all his plays the one that stands out in terms of emphasis on a single character is *Henry IV.* This is the most frequently performed play by Pirandello in English, and has frequently been compared to *Hamlet.* Discussing Henry IV [in "On *Henry IV,*" *ITI World Theatre* 16, No. 4 (1967)], the Czech director Vaclav Hudecek describes Henry as the epitome of twentieth-century man: "The desire to take one's bearings in this absurd world, ceaseless efforts to draw up the map of oneself and the mental dispersion resulting from the conglomerate of these confused sentiments characterize the man of the second half of the XXth century. All this can be found in Henry."

The first production of *Henry IV* (*Enrico IV*) took place on February 24, 1922, at the Teatro Manzoni in Milan. Ruggero Ruggeri played Henry, and this was to remain one of his most successful roles for years to come. The only other contemporary actors who achieved a similar success with the role were Lamberto Picasso and Leonardo Bragaglia. Each played Henry with different emphasis: Ruggeri focused on what he saw as an essential lyricism in the role, whereas Picasso stressed the bitterness and terse irony of the character. Writing to the director Virgilio Talli, Silvio d'Amico described the play as: "quite fantastic. Absolutely unlike anything that has been seen in the theatre before, and there is no doubt that it is a work of major importance."

The success of the play in Italy, combined with the international reputation that Pirandello had so suddenly acquired following the scandalous *Six Characters* in 1921, meant that *Henry IV* was translated into English shortly after its Italian premiere. Edward Storer's version was published in 1923, and the first U.S. production, retitled *The Living Mask,* was presented at the 44th Street Theater in New York on January 24, 1924. Stark Young's review of the first night [in *The New Republic,* 6 February 1924] criticized the actors for their excessive sentimentality but stressed the importance of the play as a milestone not only in the Pirandello's development as a dramatist, but also in world theater.

Nothing in town is to compare to Pirandello's *Henry IV*—well or badly done—as worth seeing. If there is a tendency in many of his plays to think, talk, analyze, without embodying these processes in dramatic moulds that carry and give them living substance—and I think that is one of Pirandello's dangers, his plays too often when all is said and done boil down too much to single ideas—this fault cannot be laid on *Henry IV.* In this play Pirandello has discovered a story, a visual image, and a character that completely embody and reveal the

underlying idea. This drama has a fantastic and high-spirited range in the spirit of the Italian comedy tradition; it also has a kind of Shakespearean complexity and variety; and in the second act, at least, something like a poetry of intellectual beauty.

London had to wait a year longer for the play to arrive, but in compensation it was first performed in Britain by Pirandello's own company with Ruggero Ruggeri in the title role. The company toured with four plays (*Six Characters, Henry IV, Right You Are,* and *Naked*). *Henry IV* was by far the most popular, judging by the enthusiastic response of reviewers. *The Times* on June 19, 1925, also raised the comparison with Shakespeare, and *The Manchester Guardian* reviewer, one day later, pointed out that, despite his own inadequate Italian, the play was obviously a great work: "no one of ordinary sensitiveness could miss the fact that Pirandello has put on the stage a great tragic figure and found a great actor to make it live for us."

The plot of *Henry IV* is, as reviewers noted, straightforward. Some twenty years before the action begins, a group of young Italian aristocrats had staged a masquerade—each guest had elected to come as a famous historical character. One of these young men had chosen to come as the Emperor Henry IV, carefully studying the background to his role to ensure greater authenticity. During the masquerade he had fallen from his horse, hit his head, and, as a result of the cerebral damage caused by the fall, had awakened suffering from the delusion that he was indeed Henry IV. Being of a sufficiently wealthy background for private nursing to be arranged, the young man was shut away in a country villa instead of an asylum. In order to humor his delusion, the villa was decorated to look like a medieval castle, with successive servants and nurses dressed in costumes of the time of Henry IV.

The play starts with a joke. The latest in a series of servants, Bertoldo has just arrived at the villa in the wrong costume, having confused his Henries and believing he has come to the court of Henry IV of France. His arrival provides a means of filling in the details of Henry's madness for the audience, and shortly after this introduction, visitors are announced. The young Marquis di Nolli, Henry's nephew, his fiancee Frida, her mother Matilda, and her mother's lover, Belcredi, have come to visit Henry, bringing with them a psychiatrist. The servants insist that they dress up before meeting Henry, and as they prepare to be received into his presence, further details come to light. We learn that there was once something between Matilda and Henry at the time of the masquerade, in which both she and Belcredi were involved, and we learn also that Belcredi views Henry's madness with a certain cynicism. Their uneasiness as they wait for Henry creates a sense of tension, and when he does finally appear, toward the end of Act I, his entrance comes as a shock. For Henry is now nearly fifty years old, pallid and with greying hair, but he has dyed parts of his hair yellow and is heavily made up in an attempt to hide the ravages of time. He looks, in short, the perfect picture of a madman. In the scene that follows, however, his madness is more difficult to pin down, and he seems at times to be playing with his distinguished visitors, making them more ill at ease than ever.

Act II begins with the Visitors discussing their impression of Henry. The Doctor talks in learned terms about madness, but neither Matilda nor Belcredi, for different reasons, is convinced that he is mad at all. The Doctor devises a plan which, he hopes, will cure Henry by jolting him into the twentieth century. Matilda's daughter, Frida, who looks now as her Mother did twenty years before, is to dress up in her costume. There are two life-size portraits in the room, one of Henry and one of Matilda at the time of the masquerade. Frida and Di Nolli will stand in front of the portraits, and when Henry appears Frida will step down out of the frame, as it were. This plan, according to the Doctor, will shock Henry into an awareness of normal time.

While the visitors are offstage preparing for this moment of truth, Henry reveals to his group retainers that he is not mad at all. Some years previously he had found his madness "cured," but he has gone on living as Henry IV because he has chosen to do so. The sane Henry reflects bitterly on the irony of madness—madmen "construct with logic," they live apart from the terror that sane people face, the terror of knowing that nothing in life can ever be fixed and that time destroys everything. Henry achieves tragic stature in this second act, in contrast to the shallowness of the retainers who do not understand the profundity of what he says to them.

The crisis comes in Act III, a brief act that moves at a rapid pace. Frida plays her part and steps out of the picture frame, and Henry is goaded into telling the visitors about his years of madness and sanity, how he has lived twenty years shut away in a masquerade that has become his reality. This is my life, he tells them, but even as he does so he is forced to recognize the inevitability of the passing of time. No longer able to recognize the aging Matilda, he seizes Frida in a sudden vain attempt to hold on to the love of his imagination. Belcredi intervenes, shouting that Henry is not mad and cannot hide behind a mask of madness. In a wild gesture of retaliation, Henry stabs him. This gesture confirms everyone's belief that he is mad, and the play ends with Henry condemned to live out the rest of his life as Henry IV, trapped forever in the guise of a madman. "Here together . . . forever" are the last words of the play. Henry has stepped out of his role for an instant, but his action in that split second of time has forced him back into it, permanently.

When Henry first appears, he talks about life in terms that recall *L'umorismo,* where Pirandello discusses the flux that moves forever beneath the bounds man imposes in an attempt to order his consciousness and construct a personality for himself. Henry warns of the dangers of not resigning oneself to what is, and of the need to cling to something in a moving universe:

> There's not much you can say: we're all fixed in all good faith in a splendid concept of what we are. However, Monsignor, while you're standing there so firmly, holding on tight with both hands to your sacred robes, something is slipping away out of the sleeves, slipping slithering like a serpent . . . something you don't even notice. *Life,* Monsignor!

Since Henry is talking to the Doctor in disguise, this speech is especially ironic and meaningful on various levels: life slips away, consumed by time, while man clings to his own illusion, his own mask of false security, his "borrowed robes" of faith. Here, the Doctor is disguised visibly as Monsignor Ugo de Cluny, from the eleventh century. It is even more ironical that at this point both characters and audience believe Henry to be mad, and imagine that he is unaware of the Doctor's "real" identity. The notion of Henry acting a part has still not become relevant, although Di Nolli and Belcredi did comment earlier on how madness has turned Henry into a great actor—he has become, with madness, a magnificent, terrifying actor.

The levels of disguise operating in this speech are numerous. The play is being performed by actors, therefore persons in assumed roles; the retainers and visitors are disguised in eleventh-century costume; Henry is in costume and is playing the role of a madman; and finally, the disguise to which Henry refers is the existential disguise man assumes for security, a notice to which he returns again and again. He is repeating the same facts as expressed by R. D. Laing [in *The Divided Self,* (1965)] when he states that "a man without a mask is indeed very rare. One even doubts the possibility of such a man. Everyone in some measure wears a mask."

The madman as prophet, the fool speaking truths, is by no means an original idea. Like the Fool in *King Lear,* or like Lear in his real madness and Edgar in his feigned madness, Henry is beyond social conventions and can say what he likes. When he is on stage, he dominates the scene and the others seem cowed before him. His madness, real or not, gives him a power over the "normal" world because, since he is not subject to its laws, he is the personification of what man most fears—unpredictable and inexplicable action. On the other hand, as Laing says, unpredictable actions are not grounds for declaring someone to be insane, and he admits that many people regarded as normal are deeply psychotic. He also mentions the relativity within madness:

> I am aware that the man who is said to be deluded may be in his delusion telling me the truth, and this in no equivocal or metaphorical sense, but quite literally, and that the cracked mind of the schizophrenic may *let in* light which does not enter the intact minds of many sane people whose minds are closed.

Again, like the Fool in *King Lear,* Henry is called Henry IV throughout, and we never learn whether this was in fact his name before the accident. Pirandello does not alter his name according to whether or not he is playing a role, as in the case of the actors in *Questa sera si recita* . . . where the stage directions alternate between referring to them as members of the company or as characters in the play. Henry begins and ends the play as Henry. He is cut off from life in the twentieth century, and therefore his name in that period is as meaningless as all the other details of the century that he rejects, such as clothes, cigarettes, or electric light.

The relativity of madness is the pivotal point of the whole play and from this various other aspects of relativity are touched on. In this respect, *Henry IV* provides almost a resume of the principal themes of Pirandello's theater—the relativity of perception and of language, the relativity of freedom, existence seen as imprisonment in itself, the notion of life as a game wherein each person plays an assigned role. The first scene of the play, which serves as a comic vehicle to provide the audience with details of Henry's situation, immediately introduces some of these themes. When Bertoldo discovers that he has read up on the wrong time period, like an actor learning the wrong part, he asks the others who he is supposed to be in the eleventh-century court where they play their roles. Landolfo replies: "And you can comfort yourself with the fact that we don't know who we are either. He's Arialdo; he's Ordulfo; I'm Landolfo . . . That's what he calls us. We're used to it now. But who are we? Names of that time period." The retainers exist only as names and have no place in history, no part other than what Henry determines they will play. They exist because of Henry and for him; he alone has a notion of who they are, because, as Landolfo says, he has at least labeled them with names. In assuming these roles, they have sacrificed not only any identity they may have had in the twentieth century, but because they do not believe in what they are doing, they also treat the whole thing as a joke and do not even live as people in the eleventh century. Just as the Spectators in *Each in His Own Way* were characterized and named by their opinions, so these retainers have lost everything except the names given to them by a man they believe is mad.

Landolfo explains further that they are puppets, to be manipulated by Henry:

> We're like this, without anyone to give us a clue or give us a scene to play. How shall I put it? The form is there, but without any content. We're worse off than the real privy counsellors of Henry IV because, true, no one gave them a part to play either, but at least they didn't know they were supposed to be playing one. They played a part because they played it. Only it wasn't a part, it was their life.

This speech takes us back to *Questa sera si recita,* where the actors claim that they must live their roles or be nothing. The four retainers, superficially comic though they appear to be, are trapped in an even more tragic situation than Henry or Giovanni who play their roles with a kind of conviction. The retainers' role-playing is without direction or purpose, and they are entirely at the whim of a madman. If we extend this situation onto a more universal level, the retainers can be seen as a man and the madman in control is chance, or god. Gloucester's words in *King Lear* (IV,i) apply to this play with the same existential force of all time:

> 'Tis the time's plague, when madmen lead the blind.

While the retainers exist only as names chosen by Henry, he possesses an awareness of the relativity of identity beyond that of any other character in the play. In Act II, when the Visitors leave, Henry cries out bitterly against the relativity of language itself, the meaninglessness of names and labels:

What do they succeed in imposing? Words! Words that everyone understands and repeats in his own way. But then, that's how so-called public opinion is formed. But woe betide the man who finds himself branded with one of these words some day, that everyone repeats, like "madman" for example.

In Act I, Henry reminds the Visitors of the importance of knowing who they are, over and above the labels they bear:

> "I feel the spirit of the times and the majesty of whoever knows how to be what he ought to be: a Pope!"

Henry then continues, reminding them that chance can destroy even the apparent security of Popes:

> I tell you that tomorrow the roles could be reversed. And what would you do then? Would you by any chance laugh at a Pope dressed as a prisoner?—No.—We'd be even. Today I'm wearing the mask of a penitent; tomorrow he'd be wearing that of a prisoner. But woe betide the person who doesn't know how to wear his mask, be it that of a king or of a Pope.

The roles can be changed without warning, and only those who manage to keep on playing their parts can have some relief from the processes of change and subsequent pain. But even this relief is illusory, as demonstrated by Henry himself, who continues to play his role and remains trapped in that role forever. His escape into his own world of "madness" is seen to be another form of imprisonment. Henry may be free from many of the restraints that confine people in the "sane" world, such as social convention, consecutive time, and coexistence with others, but he is just as subject to the passing of time and is confined in the world of his own creating. Belcredi sums up the position of all humankind, mad or sane:

> This is the illusion: that we'll go out of life through a door in front of us. It isn't true. If you begin to die as soon as you're born, then whoever started first is ahead of us all. And old father Adam is the youngest of the lot.

In this dark vision, the madman has a special place, for the madman is free to follow any pattern or nonpattern he chooses. And in this freedom to separate themselves from the need to have fixed beliefs and forms, madmen come closer to the essence of life itself.

If life is inconstancy and motion, as Pirandello reiterates in play after play, and man is constantly striving to create a niche for himself beyond that movement, then the madman, unaware of his "privilege," is the one with the insight into what being alive means. In a universe of motion, the madness is to strive for fixity, not to live out a life of formless movement. In *On Humor* Pirandello tells us that:

> The collective consciousness, the soul of the race of which we are a part lives within each of us; and the ways in which others judge and feel and act pressure us subconsciously. In society, masks, disguises and pretence control operations—the more habitual they become, the less we are aware of them; and in the same way, we

mask our real self, pretending to be other than we are, adopting a dual, even a manifold "persona".

In such a context, the "sane" man is the more mad since he lives out a daily delusion that constancy is possible. The irony of the play is in the realizations: those declared by some to be "mad" because they do not conform to the social norms are less "mad" than those who believe in the existence of absolutes, but whatever their state of madness or sanity, all men are condemned to exist in a world of motion and time, from which even illusion is no valid escape. Moreover, since illusion is itself formless, man seeks stability through an indefinable abstract, the ultimate absurdity.

Walter Starkie [in his *Luigi Priandello 1867-1936* (1967)] uses a musical image to describe the structure of this play: "Like a theme ever recurring through the mazes of orchestration of a symphony, the idea of distance and time is repeated again and again in this play." This seems to be an excellent image, but I would also add the themes of art as fixity and life as motion, the relative freedom of the madman and the artist, and the notion of what the individual sees and how he translates that visual experience into a highly personal understanding. Time and history are crucial, but so also is the problem of perception, the idea of life itself as madness, the impossibility of ever judging sanity by other than purely relative means. Henry is supposedly mad in Act I, declares himself sane in Act II, commits a "mad" gesture in Act III, where, it must be noted, the stage directions are deliberately ambiguous, and Henry is described as laughing like a madman. But Henry is consistent in his real or feigned madness. The truths he speaks in Act I when we all believe he is mad are reiterated in Act II when he "proves" his sanity by admitting that he knows he is playing a role and living in another time period. He changes moods abruptly, moves about in time, and physically he moves rapidly round the stage, going from person to person in Act I. In Acts II and III he moves in and out of apparent sanity; his moods seem more controlled, his movements are less pronounced, but his cynicism and sufferings are constantly present.

As the play progresses, it becomes increasingly clear that we are being shown that language, perception, and finally reality are all relative, and that the great problem facing man is how to communicate with his fellows. Henry, the madman, must follow up his words with actions to prove their "truth" to the others, so he has to show the four retainers how he can act and construct scenes before they believe he is "cured," and in the final act he communicates by committing a violent action, murder, which ironically "proves" to the others only that their beliefs are confirmed and he is mad after all. His final gesture, the murder of Belcredi, is inevitable because on one level it is his last desperate attempt to show that his role is real and not a game and cannot be dismissed as easily as the others presume, and on another level it is the action of a man trapped into a corner and forced to react. The world he has been keeping himself from has finally caught up with him, and like Leone Gala in the *Rules of the Game* he is forced to recognize that he cannot exist in isolation, in his own private dream world.

The Visitors are real, their attempts to "cure" him do happen, and he can no longer insist on closing himself in the eleventh century to escape. At the conclusion of the play, the realization of how this reality has trapped him forever forcibly in a role he previously played of his own free will is emphasized by the stage directions, and by Henry's words:

> Yes, now . . . inevitably . . . (gathers his retainers round him, as if to shield himself,) here together, here together . . . forever!

Others have broken his safe world of illusion and destroyed it, and he is caught in his own game, condemned to play it forever. The parallels with Leone Gala are quite clear: the one sought a world without emotion, a rational world, the other sought a world of unconfined movement, and both tried to keep complete control. Both ultimately share the same fate: immobility. The warning is plain; society may be represented by the petty, unpleasant characters who come to visit Henry, but they have not tried to define the world they live in. Matilda is condemned to being a jealous, unhappy, middle-aged woman, and the Doctor is condemned to being a phony who puts his trust in inadequate laws of science. They have no choice, no matter how they may try to forget. But Henry is finally condemned to being the mad Emperor because he tried consciously to play a role and create an illusion to save himself pain. No one can escape in the end, and the fake world of recreated history is as inadequate as the makeup Matilda wears to disguise her age.

The disguise motif, so crucial to the play, moves from being comic in the first scene to the tragic moments at the end of the play, when Henry realizes that he will never be able to take off his costume. When the three retainers meet Bertoldo, who is erroneously wearing sixteenth-century costume, and one of the lackeys lights up a cigarette, the whole notion of costume becomes farcical. Later, when Matilda, the Doctor, and Belcredi are forced to dress up in order to meet Henry, they do so with a mixture of amusement and uneasiness and when Frida, the living portrait, appears wearing her mother's costume, she can only comment on its size and how uncomfortably it fits her. For Henry alone the costume he wears is real because he has chosen to wear it and made it his. By the end of the play, he has been reduced to the same fate as all other men, forced to wear his costume, his disguise, regardless of his will. The one moment of instinct, when he broke the ordered world of recreated life, when he cheated (in a sense) and performed an unscripted act, leads to his downfall. His own personality erupted through the character of Henry IV to make him commit an act that the Emperor never conceived. As he gathers his retainers about him, the fear of this improvised action, the knowledge that he has broken out of his role, that he is doomed to remain Henry IV forever suddenly touches him and appalls him. Yet even in this final tragic moment, the bitter irony that characterizes the play is apparent. Henry has "proved" his madness, and Belcredi (the only one who knew that, as the stage directions indicate, the action was provoked by the life of his own pretense) is dead. Henceforth, the Visitors will have no doubts about Henry's madness, and the last vestiges of communication, the game he was able to play with them for so long, will no longer exist.

Henry IV is therefore a play that takes us into the heart of Pirandello's vision of the world. It is a play about the relativity of madness, and the question of what constitutes the boundaries of madness is a recurrent theme in twentieth-century art, especially in the theater.

In *Madness and Civilization,* Michel Foucault comments that "The ultimate language of madness is that of reason, but the language of reason enveloped in the prestige of the image, limited to the locus of appearance which the image defines." Madness is therefore the point of overflow, the moment when all supposed boundaries of reason are swept away. By choosing to write a play about madness, Pirandello found a way of exploring the ideas set out in *On Humor.* A close analysis of the play reveals with what bitter irony he deals with the plight of one man as a metaphor for the plight of all humankind. Henry's predicament is a sign of man's predicament, caught between structures and definitions in a world over which he has no control. It is a vision of the world that is at the same time humorous and tragic. If we laugh at Henry's absurdities, it is because the pain is too great for tears.

FURTHER READING

BIOGRAPHY

Guidice, Gaspare. *Pirandello: A Biography,* translated by Alastair Hamilton. Oxford: Oxford University Press, 1975, 221 p.
> Abridged translation of the standard critical biography.

OVERVIEWS AND GENERAL STUDIES

Bassnett-McGuire, Susan. *Luigi Pirandello.* New York: Grove Press, 1983, 190 p.
> Thematic survey of Pirandello's dramas.

Bazzoni, Jana O'Keefe. "The Carnival Motif in Pirandello." *Modern Drama* XXX, No. 3 (September 1987): 414-25.
> Emphasizes the importance of the carnival motif, concluding that "Pirandello's drama is carnevalesque because it celebrates the struggle of the human spirit for freedom, for self-knowledge, and for communion."

Bentley, Eric. "*Enrico IV*" and "*Six Characters in Search of an Author.*" In his *Theatre of War,* pp. 32-44, pp. 45-63. New York: Viking Press, 1972.
> Examines the defining characteristics of both dramas.

————. *The Pirandello Commentaries.* Evanston: Northwestern University Press, 1986, 119 p.
> Includes ten essays written between 1946 and 1986.

Bishop, Thomas. *Pirandello and the French Theater.* New York: New York University Press, 1960, 170 p.
> Traces Pirandello's influence on the major French playwrights of the twentieth century.

Cambon, Glauco, ed. *Pirandello: A Collection of Critical Essays.* Englewood Cliffs, N.J.: Prentice-Hall, 1967, 182 p.
> Contains thirteen essays by prominent critics.

Chomel, Luisetta. "Pirandello's Notion of Time." *Canadian Journal of Italian Studies* 12, Nos. 38-9 (1989): 26-39.
> Concludes that the time motif punctuates Pirandello's writings from "the poetic beginning to the last plays, in different forms and various degrees of intensity."

Della Fazia, Alla. "Pirandello's Mirror Theater." *Renascence* XV, No. 2 (Fall 1962): 37-40.
> Examines the function of mirror imagery in Pirandello's dramas.

Della Terza, Dante. "On Pirandello's Humorism." In *Veins of Humor,* edited by Harry Levin, pp. 17-33. Cambridge: Harvard University Press, 1972.
> Discusses Pirandello's theory of humor as put forth in *L'umorismo* and examines its application to his work.

DiGaetani, John Louis. *A Companion to Pirandello Studies.* New York: Greenwood Press, 1991, 443 p.
> Collection of critical essays. Includes a primary bibliography and production histories of *Six Characters in Search of an Author* and *Henry IV.*

Fabbri, Diego. "A Rip in a Paper Sky." *World Theatre* XVI, No. 3 (May-June 1967): 218-23.
> Examines Pirandello's original dramatic techniques and notes that his greatness lies in the tragic vision by which he produces catharsis in his audiences and readers.

Heffner, Hubert C. "Pirandello and the Nature of Man." In *Modern Drama: Essays in Criticism,* edited by Travis Bogard and William I. Oliver, pp. 255-75. London: Oxford University Press, 1965.
> Disputes the view that "dissolution of the ego" is Pirandello's most important contribution to modern drama. Heffner analyzes elements of dramatic characterization and human personality in order to demonstrate that "the ego does not disappear in Pirandello's character; it grows more complex, taking on some of the aspects of change which we find in human personality."

Lavrin, Janko. "Luigi Pirandello." In his *Aspects of Modernism: From Wilde to Pirandello,* pp. 231-47. London: Stanley Nott, 1935.
> Discusses the major themes in Pirandello's dramas.

Lucas, F. L. "Part IV—Luigi Pirandello." In his *The Drama of Chekhov, Synge, Yeats, and Pirandello,* pp. 358-438. London: Cassell, 1963.
> Brief essays on each of Pirandello's plays.

MacClintock, Lander. "Pirandello, the Perfect Pessimist." In his *The Age of Pirandello,* pp. 175-229. Bloomington: Indiana

University Press, 1951.

Chronicles Pirandello's career and assesses his impact on Italian theater.

May, Frederick. "Three Major Symbols in Four Plays by Pirandello." *Modern Drama* VI, No. 4 (February 1964): 378-96.

A study of the role of images of mirrors, water, and the color green in *Six Characters in Search of an Author*, *Henry IV, A Dream (But Perhaps It Isn't)*, and *Man, Beast, and Virtue*.

Mazzaro, Jerome. "Morality in Pirandello's *Come tu mi vuoi*." *Modern Drama* XXXVI, No. 4 (December 1993): 556-68.

Thematic and structural analysis. Mazzaro maintains: "The play illustrates not so much what people should do under ideal circumstances as what kinds of action may be taken when individuals can no longer live under existing conditions."

Palmer, John. "The Plays of Luigi Pirandello." *The Nineteenth Century and After* 97, No. DLXXX (June 1925): 897-909.

Provides an overview of Pirandello's work.

Phelps, Ruth Shepard. "Pirandello's Plays." In her *Italian Silhouettes*, pp. 116-41. New York: Alfred A. Knopf, 1924.

Study of Pirandello's plays.

Ragusa, Olga. *Luigi Pirandello*. New York: Columbia University Press, 1968, 48 p.

Introductory survey of Pirandello's work.

————. "Luigi Pirandello." In *European Writers in the Twentieth Century*, edited by George Stade, pp. 389-416. New York: Charles Scribner's Sons, 1989.

Comprehensive survey of Pirandello's work.

Review of National Literatures 14 (1987): 190 p.

Special issue devoted to Pirandello. Contains nine articles, including "Pirandello's Introduction to the Italian Theater," by Anne Paolucci; "Pirandello's Scandalous Docile Bodies," by Jennifer Stone; and "*Six Characters*: An American Opera," by Antonio Illiano.

Rey, John B. "Pirandello's 'Last' Play: Some Notes on *The Mountain Giants*." *Modern Drama* XX, No. 4 (December 1977): 413-20.

Offers an explanation for the unfinished state of Pirandello's *The Mountain Giants*.

Roland, Alan, and Rizzo, Gino. "Psychoanalysis in Search of Pirandello: *Six Characters* and *Henry IV*." In *Psychoanalysis, Creativity and Literature: A French-American Inquiry*, edited by Alan Roland, pp. 323-51. New York: Columbia University Press, 1978.

Discusses Pirandello's two major dramas in psychoanalytical terms, maintaining that "over the years, critics and audiences have endeavored to understand these enigmatic and profoundly psychological works only to discover still deeper and more complex layers of meaning."

Sogliuzzo, A. Richard. *Luigi Pirandello, Director: The*

Playwright in the Theatre. Metuchen, N.J.: Scarecrow Press, 1982, 274 p.

Determines that Pirandello's consciousness of the demands of theatrical production influenced the creation of his plays.

Starkie, Walter. *Luigi Pirandello: 1867-1936*. Berkeley: University of California Press, 1967, 304 p.

Book-length critical study of Pirandello's work.

Tener, Robert L. "The Geography of Human Limits: A Study of Pirandello's Plays." *Canadian Journal of Italian Studies* 13, Nos. 40-1 (1990): 38-51.

Claims that "Pirandello's use of spatial images and intimate relationships to home and land constitutes one of the more complex aspects of his dramas."

Vittorini, Domenico. *The Drama of Luigi Pirandello*. Philadelphia: University of Pennsylvania Press, 1935, 351 p.

Critical analysis of Pirandello's drama.

Williams, Raymond. "Luigi Pirandello." In his *Drama from Ibsen to Eliot*, pp. 185-95. London: Chatto & Windus, 1965.

Asserts that Pirandello's drama destroyed the "illusion of reality" that had been the foundation of naturalist drama.

RIGHT YOU ARE! (IF YOU THINK SO)

Ascoli, Albert Russell. "Mirror and Veil: *Così è (se vi pare)* and the Drama of Interpretation." *Stanford Italian Review* VII, Nos. 1-2 (1987): 29-46.

Asserts that the message of Pirandello's play is "the paradoxical, self-cancelling news that no single and definitive interpretation is ever possible."

Holman, Richard. "Farce after Existentialism: Pirandello's *It Is So! (If You Think So)*." In *Themes in Drama*, edited by James Redmond, pp. 201-06. Cambridge: Cambridge University Press, 1988.

Analyzes the unique farcical aspects of Pirandello's comedy and also asserts that the playwright "takes on a social aspect of morality which is necessary if the world is to be a well-ordered place: that is, the notion that we can understand and hence judge the actions of others."

SIX CHARACTERS IN SEARCH OF AN AUTHOR

Charney, Maurice. "Shakespearean and Pirandellian: *Hamlet* and *Six Characters in Search of an Author*." *Modern Drama* XXIV, No. 3 (September 1981): 323-29.

Compares the two plays, concluding that "there is a remarkable similarity in the central experience."

Clark, Hoover W. "Existentialism and Pirandello's *Sei Personaggi*." *Italica* XLIII (1966): 276-84.

Compares existentialist elements in *Six Characters in Search of an Author* with the tenets of modern existentialist thought.

Fergusson, Francis. "The Theatricality of Shaw and Pirandello."

In his *The Idea of a Theatre*, pp. 178-93. Princeton, N.J.: Princeton University Press, 1975, 221 p.

> Praises *Six Characters in Search of an Author* for its sophisticated subversion of the limiting conventions imposed on theater by modern realism.

Trilling, Lionel. "Commentary." In his *The Experience of Literature: A Reader with Commentaries*, pp. 359-62. Garden City, N.Y.: Doubleday & Company, 1967.

> Trilling maintains: "Of all the theatre's many celebrations of its own mysterious power, of all the challenging comparisons it makes between its own reality and that of life, Pirandello's *Six Characters in Search of an Author* is the most elaborate and brilliant."

HENRY IV

DeVivo, Albert. "*Henry IV* and Time." *Canadian Journal of Italian Studies* 12, Nos. 38-9 (1989): 40-50.

> Uncovers Pirandello's view of time through a close reading of *Henry IV*'s dialogues, concluding that the structure of the play "validates Henry's philosophy of real time as flux."

Maceri, Domenico. "History and the Dialectic in Pirandello's *Henry IV*." *Selecta* 3 (1982): 26-30.

> Asserts that in his drama Pirandello disturbs "the sense of universal and timeless qualities in man which permit us to identify with characters separated from us by centuries."

Additional coverage of Pirandello's life and career is contained in the following sources published by Gale Research: *Contemporary Authors,* Vol. 104; *DISCovering Authors; Twentieth-Century Literary Criticism,* Vols. 4, 29; and *World Literature Criticism.*

Eugène Scribe
1791–1861

Full name Augustin Eugène Scribe.

INTRODUCTION

Scribe was one of the most prolific and successful French dramatists of the nineteenth century. His output—variously estimated at between three and four hundred works, written either alone or with collaborators—consists of opera libretti and *comédies-vaudevilles* (brief topical farces), as well as full-length plays. Scribe's great popularity with contemporary audiences derived in large part from his unrivalled skills as a craftsman; indeed, Scribe is considered the originator of the *piéce bien faite*, or well-made play, a genre characterized by intricate, carefully constructed plots. Although his works are seldom produced today, Scribe's masterful stage technique profoundly influenced the works of his contemporaries and successors throughout Europe and America.

BIOGRAPHICAL INFORMATION

The son of a silk merchant and his wife, Scribe was born and raised in Paris. His family suffered financial hardships following his father's death in 1798, but Scribe received a scholarship that enabled him to attend the Collège de Sainte-Barbe, a well-regarded secondary school. After graduating, he studied law at his mother's urging; when she died in 1811, however, Scribe abandoned his studies and decided to pursue a career as a dramatist. His earliest works were failures, and it was not until 1815 with the staging of *Encore une nuit de la Garde Nationale* (*Another Night in the National Guard*), a one-act *comédie-vaudeville*, that Scribe achieved his first success. This production is also notable because it marked the establishment of a royalty system for playwrights in France: rather than accepting a single payment for the play, Scribe insisted on receiving a percentage of its profits. Following the production of *Another Night*, Scribe went on to write several enormously popular plays every year until shortly before his death; in addition, he composed libretti for over one hundred comic and grand operas. Throughout his career, in order to meet theater managers' demands for new plays, Scribe often enlisted the aid of collaborators, including Germain Delavigne, Charles-Gaspard Delestre-Poirson, Henri Dupin, and Ernest Legouvé. This practice earned Scribe a reputation for running a "play factory," and some of his contemporaries claimed that his contributions to the dramas were negligible. Such charges notwithstanding, Scribe was elected to the prestigious Académie Française in 1836. By the end of his life, he had amassed a fortune from his works, and he lived lavishly, frequently entertaining guests at his country estate at Séricourt and becoming well known for his generosity toward his collaborators. When he died in 1861, thousands attended his funeral in Paris, causing business in the city to come to a standstill.

MAJOR WORKS

Scribe spent the early part of his career writing primarily *comédies-vaudevilles*, and he is credited with revolutionizing the genre through his innovations in form and subject matter. He broadened the scope of the *comédie-vaudeville* by transforming it from a one-act farce depicting an incident from everyday life into a two- or three-act play that had a complex plot with well-planned surprises and a logical denouement. Scribe emphasized topical satire in these works, offering audiences studies of the vices and follies of contemporary life. Thus, in such pieces as *Le Mariage de raison* (*The Marriage of Convenience*) he condemned impulsive marriages; in *Le Solliciteur* (*The Applicant*), he denounced corrupt politicians; and in *Le Charlatanisme* (*Quackery*) he censured unethical journalism.

Though often noted for their accurate depiction of nineteenth-century French society, Scribe's full-length plays are primarily praised for their superb construction. Expanding upon the technical innovations of his *comédies-vaudevilles*, Scribe composed these works according to a precise structural formula which has become known as the well-made play. Distinguished by tightly constructed, fast-moving plots in which action takes precedence over character development, Scribe's well-made plays display several common structural features, including a clear exposition of the subject in the first act, a series of reversals in the protagonist's fortunes, a pattern of mounting suspense leading up to a striking climax, and a credible denouement. Scribe considered a carefully designed plot so essential to the success of his plays that he once remarked, "When I have finished my plan, I have nothing more to do." Critics agree that Scribe's most popular well-made plays—including the comedies *Bertrand et Raton* and *Bataille des dames* (*The Ladies' Battle*); the historical drama *La Verre d'eau* (*The Glass of Water*); and his only tragedy, *Adrienne Lecouvreur*—reveal him to be a master of theatrical effect who knew what would please playgoers.

Commentators have observed that Scribe also applied the principles of the well-made play to his libretti, which he constructed within a dramatic framework that combined an emphasis on spectacle with logically ordered, increasingly suspenseful scenes. He is also recognized for introducing a number of changes into French opera, notably the expansion of the role of the chorus by using it as an essential part of the action rather than merely as an element of the background. As a librettist, Scribe is best known for his work with composers Giacomo Meyerbeer and Daniel Auber; however, he also provided libretti for the operas of other famous composers, including Gaetano Donizetti, Jacques Offenbach, and Giuseppi Verdi.

CRITICAL RECEPTION

Scribe's works were extremely popular in his day, although critics often condemned them as possessing flat characters, lifeless dialogue, and shallow subjects. Most conceded, however, that Scribe was an excellent craftsman with a talent for adapting his plays to suit the fluctuating tastes of his audiences. Recent commentators, while acknowledging the artistic flaws of Scribe's works, recognize the extent of his technical achievement and the lasting impact of his stagecraft. Several studies have been devoted to assessing the contribution the well-made play has made to modern drama, and Scribe is often admired for furnishing dramatists with a formula that is both adaptable to many subjects and guaranteed to please the public. Numerous scholars have pointed out that such playwrights as Alexandre Dumas *fils*, Georges Feydeau, Henrik Ibsen, Bernard Shaw, as well as countless others are indebted to the techniques that Scribe pioneered.

PRINCIPAL WORKS

PLAYS

Les Dervis (with Germain Delavigne) 1811
[*The Dervishes*]
Encore une nuit de la Garde Nationale; ou, Le Poste de la barrière (with Charles-Gaspard Delestre-Poirson) 1815

[*Another Night in the National Guard; or, The Guard Post at the City Gate*]
Le Valet de son rival (with Delavigne) 1816
[*His Rival's Valet*]
Le Solliciteur; ou, L'Art d'obtenir des places (with Jean-Gilbert Ymbert and Antoine-François Varner) 1817
[*The Applicant; or, The Art of Obtaining Employment*]
Les Frères invisibles (with Honoré Mélesville and Delestre-Poirson) 1819
[*The Invisible Brothers*]
Valérie (with Mélesville) 1822
Rodolphe; ou, Frère et soeur (with Mélesville) 1823
[*Rodolphe; or, Brother and Sister*]
Le Charlatanisme (with Edouard-Joseph Mazères) 1825
[*Quackery*]
Le Mauvais Sujet (with Camille) 1825
[*The Worthless Fellow*]
Le Mariage de raison (with Varner) 1826
[*The Marriage of Convenience*]
La Chatte métamorphosée en femme (with Mélesville) 1827
[*The Cat Changed into a Woman*]
Dix ans de la vie d'une femme; ou, Les Mauvais Conseils (with Thomas Terrier) 1832
[*Ten Years from the Life of a Woman; or, Bad Advice*]
Betrand et Raton; ou, L'Art de conspirer 1833
[*Betrand and Raton; or, The Art of Conspiracy*]
La Passion sécret 1834
[*The Secret Passion*]
L'Ambiteux 1834
[*The Ambitious Ones*]
La Camaraderie; ou, La Courte Échelle 1837
[*The Clique; or, The Helping Hand*]
Les Indépendants 1837
[*The Independent Ones*]
La Calomnie 1840
[*Slander*]
La Grand'mere; ou, Les Trois Amours 1840
[*The Grandmother; or, Three Loves*]
Japhet; ou, La Recherche d'un père (with Louis-Émile Vanderburch) 1840
[*Japhet; or, The Search for a Father*]
Le Verre d'eau; ou, Les Effets et les causes 1840
[*The Glass of Water; or, Causes and Effects*]
Une Chaîne 1841
[*A Chain*]
Oscar; ou, Le Mari qui trompe sa femme (with Mélesville) 1842
[*Oscar; or, The Husband Who Deceives His Wife*]
Le Fils de Cromwell; ou, Une Resauration 1842
[*The Son of Cromwell; or, A Restoration*]
La Tutrice; ou, L'Emploi des richesses (with Paul Duport) 1843
[*The Guardian; or, The Use of Riches*]
Le Puff; ou, Mensorge et vérité 1848
[*Puffery; or, Lie and Truth*]
Adrienne Lecouvreur (with Ernest Legouvé) 1849
Les Contes de la reine de Navarre; ou, La Revanche de Pavie (with Legouvé) 1850
[*Tales of the Queen of Navarre; or, Pavia's Revenge*]
Bataille des dames; ou, Un Duel en amour (with Legouvé) 1851
[*The Ladies' Battle; or, A Duel of Love*]

Mon Étoile 1854
  [*My Star*]
La Czarine 1855
  [*The Czarina*]
Feu Lionel; ou, Qui vivra verra (with Charles Potron) 1858
  [*The Late Lionel, or, Live and Learn*]
Les Trois Maupins; ou, La Veille de la Régence (with Henry Boisseaux) 1858
  [*The Three Maupins; or, The Eve of the Regency*]
Rêves d'amour (with Charles-Henry Desnoyers de Biéville) 1859
  [*Dreams of Love*]
La Fille de trente ans (with Émile de Najac) 1859
  [*The Thirty-year-old Woman*]
La Frileuse 1861
  [*The Chilly One*]

LIBRETTI

Leicester; ou, Le Château de Kenilworth (with Mélesville; music by Daniel Auber) 1823
  [*Leicester; or, The Castle of Kenilworth*]
Le Valet de chambre (with Mélesville; music by Michel Enrico Carafa) 1823
  [*The Valet*]
La Neige; ou, Le Nouvel Eginhard (with Delavigne; music by Auber) 1823
  [*Snow; or, The New Eginhard*]
La Maçon (with Delavigne; music by Auber) 1825
  [*The Mason*]
La Dame blanche (music by François Boieldieu) 1825
  [*The White Lady*]
La Somnambule; ou, L'Arrivée d'un nouveau seigneur (with Pierre Aumer; music by Ferdinand Hérold) 1827
  [*The Sleepwalker; or, The Arrival of a New Master*]
La Muette de Portici (with Delavigne; music by Auber) 1828
  [*The Mute Woman of Portici*]
Le Comte Ory (with Delestre-Poirson; music by Gioacchino Rossini) 1828
  [*Count Ory*]
Fra Diavolo; ou, L'Hôtellerie de Terracine (music by Auber) 1830
  [*Fra Diavolo; or, The Guest-House of Terracine*]
Manon Lescaut (with Aumer; music by Jacques Halévy) 1830
Le Philtre (music by Auber) 1831
  [*The Philter*]
Robert le Diable (with Delavigne; music by Giacomo Meyerbeer) 1831
  [*Robert the Devil*]
Gustave III; ou, Le Bal masqué (music by Auber) 1833
  [*Gustavus III; or, The Masked Ball*]
Ali-Baba; ou, Les Quarante Voleurs (with Mélesville; music by Luigi Cherubini) 1833
  [*Ali Baba; or, The Forty Thieves*]
La Juive (music by Halévy) 1835
  [*The Jewess*]
Les Huguenots (music by Meyerbeer) 1836
  [*The Huguenots*]
Le Domino noir (music by Auber) 1837
  [*The Black Domino*]

Les Martyres (music by Gaetano Donizetti) 1840
  [*The Martyrs*]
Dom Sébastien, roi de Portugal (music by Donizetti) 1843
  [*Don Sebastian, King of Portugal*]
Le Prophète (music by Meyerbeer) 1849
  [*The Prophet*]
La Nonne saglante (with Delavigne; music by Charles Gounod) 1854
  [*The Blood-Stained Nun*]
Les Vêpres siciliennes (with Mélesville; music by Giuseppe Verdi) 1855
  [*The Sicilian Vespers*]
La Chatte métamorphosée en femme (with Mélesville; music by Jacques Offenbach) 1858
  [*The Cat Changed into a Woman*]
L'Africaine (music by Meyerbeer) 1865
  [*The African Woman*]

OVERVIEWS AND GENERAL STUDIES

A. B. Walkley (essay date 1925)

SOURCE: "Scribe," in *Still More Prejudice*, Alfred A. Knopf, 1925, pp. 44-8.

[*Walkley attacks Scribe's plays as the productions of a hack pandering to the tastes of a bourgeois audience.*]

Scribe, the greatest of all theatrical purveyors, died so long ago (1861), and is so completely forgotten, that it is high time to have a book about him. A Professor in the University of California, Dr. Neil Cole Arvin, obliges with one— *Eugène Scribe and the French Theatre,* written from that distance which lends enchantment to the view as well as some errors in perspective. Was Scribe really so important in the history of the theatre? Did he so markedly influence his successors? "Practically every innovation, every reform, every novelty found in the drama of the nineteenth century," says Dr. Arvin, "originated with Scribe, and the highest point in the development of the main *genres* of dramatic literature was reached in his plays." This, if true at all, is only true of the technicalities, the machinery of the theatre, the mere stage-carpentry—things that matter very little and may almost be said to invent themselves. Everything of value in the modern theatre, its intellectual dialectic, its emotional sincerity, its fundamental verisimilitude, has been a revolt against that shallow theatricality which we call Scribism.

Of Scribe's own 300 and odd plays, which were once to be seen not only in Paris but in every theatre in Europe, the sole survivor to-day is **Adrienne Lecouvreur**—and that from the mere accident that its heroine caught the fancy of Sarah Bernhardt. Now that Sarah is gone, I doubt if we shall ever see **Adrienne** again. Scribe's great success— commercial success—in his day was, like other commercial successes, the result of three things: a natural instinct for the business, industry and skill in meeting a popular demand, and a certain mediocrity of mind. Scribe was born for the theatre and scribbled plays almost from infancy. He consistently catered for the tastes of his public—that curious, mixed *bourgeoisie* of his time, the Royalists of the Faubourg St. Germain, the ex-Imperialists of the Faubourg St. Honoré, and the new rich of the Chaussée d'Antin. These various interests he was careful to conciliate, generally by a system of mixed marriages. The Royalist heroine married the Imperial colonel's nephew, or the young marquis, ruined at cards, but an accomplished horseman, married the banker's daughter. The proper thing was to marry for money, an eminently *bourgeois* ideal; the passion of love Scribe left to the romantic playwrights. Indeed, money plays as conspicuous a part in Scribe's theatre as in the novels of his contemporary Balzac. But Balzac gives you, what Scribe could not, the passion as well. Scribe's essential mediocrity and shallowness of mind was, no doubt, the chief factor in his success: it kept so steadily on the mental level of his materialistic public. Like theirs, his moral code was strictly prudential and regulated by the social proprieties. Husbands always triumphed over lovers, and the cause of passion is always sacrificed to that of "la famille." "Respectability" was the chief ideal. As for history, that was a collection of trivial anecdotes, all illustrating the dictum "What great events from little causes spring." Thus Scribe wrote a play about Walpole (*L'Ambitieux*), in which that Minister's fortune hangs in the balance through George II.'s discovery of a love-letter tied up in the Royal mistress's handkerchief; and a play about Queen Anne (*Le Verre d'Eau*), in which the political history of England is vitally affected because the Duchess of Marlborough drops a glass of water in the Queen's lap. Indeed, Scribe's history is as childish as any in Hugo or Dumas *père,* without their excuse of making the absurdity a pretext for passionate or romantic adventure.

If there is hardly any passion in Scribe (because it is not "respectable," because it is a nuisance to "the family," because it is not correct form in the Chaussée d'Antin), still less are there any characters (because puppets will do just as well, or even better, to carry out a plot which is merely an ingenious combination of incidents). Dr. Arvin prefers to say that "this conception of dramatic art by its very nature relieves the author of the responsibility of taking account of characters, sentiment, or passion." He might as well say that it relieves the author of the responsibility of authorship. Can you think of Balzac without thinking of his characters? We say a Hulot, a Mme. Marneffe, a Père Goriot, a Rubempré, a Coralie, a Rastignac, and know them better than our own blood-relations. A list of Scribe's characters would be a list of meaningless, unidentifiable names. Is it to be wondered at that he is clean forgotten?

He might, even so, have escaped oblivion, had he had the advantage of a style. But that invaluable preservative was wholly lacking; it was Théophile Gautier's perpetual grievance against him that he had no style. It is easy to overstress the point, no doubt. Balzac had no style, or a very bad one, and yet has more enthusiasts to-day than he ever had in his lifetime. Labiche had no style, but his eleven volumes of collected plays are still, despite the drawback, a perpetual feast of delight. On the other hand, I think some of the plays of Dumas *fils* live as much by their style as by their dramatic quality, or so at least I thought when I saw *Le Demi-Monde* in London the other day. The importance of style, the most personal or elements, in dramatic work will always be a disputable question, for it is the peculiarity of the dramatist that he never

---

> **Scribe and public taste:**
>
> [Scribe] threw himself heart and soul into the present, and took the public taste as he found it. Eager for novelty—unscrupulous as to taste—impatient of analysis and laborious exposition of character—intolerant of mere polish or beauty of dialogue—more pleased with a bold and rough outline than a finished cabinet picture—above all things demanding variety of movement, of scene, of incident, of the subjects of ridicule—and thus following all the changes of the inconstant character of a Parisian public—he presented his pictures to the world, scarcely dry, on his gay though somewhat clumsy canvas, and every one was delighted with the resemblance; for in the playful *malice* of his portraits every one thought he recognized, not his own portrait, but those of his friends. . . .
>
> *George Moir, in* The Foreign Quarterly
> *IX, No. xxii, May 1832.*

speaks in his own person. Yet every dramatist of mark has his own, unmistakable fashion of speech; Congreve's is distinct from Farquhar's, Goldsmith's from Sheridan's, Maugham's from Shaw's.

Scribe's, however, was the pedestrian slipshod which we call "no" style. It was the common language of the classes with no ear for language, the busy philistine *bourgeoisie* for whom Scribe wrote. No wonder the poets and critics and the whole æsthetic and literary world were banded against him!

Martin Lamm   (essay date 1948)

SOURCE: "Scribe and Hebbel," in *Modern Drama,* translated by Karin Elliott, Basil Blackwell, 1952, pp. 1-15.

[*The following excerpt is taken from a work that first appeared in Swedish in 1948. Using the historical drama* The Glass of Water *as his model, Lamm investigates Scribe's dramatic technique and assesses his influence on subsequent playwrights throughout Europe, most notably Henrik Ibsen.*]

[The German poet and playwright Friedrich Hebbel] writes in his diary; "A real drama can be compared with a big building, which has as many rooms and passages under the ground as above it. Ordinary people only see the latter, but the builder knows both".

Scribe never wrote a "real drama" in this sense. There are no underground passages and rooms in his works; everything is above the ground. He took to heart La Bruyère's maxim, that writing a book is as much a craft as making a clock. In his chosen craft, moreover, Scribe achieved a mastery which was to stand his successors during the next fifty years in good stead. In particular, his skill in the construction of plots provided a firm framework which the shapeless bourgeois dramas had previously lacked. He succeded in writing plays which gave a real impression of contemporary life; he dealt with live issues in a way which made the stage seem their natural setting. It remained for the next generation of playwrights to give the stage drama greater depth. Scribe was not the man to compose literary drama; he wrote for a wider public. To some extent he resembles those playwrights who created the folk drama of the late renaissance in Spain and England. Like them he was an educated man and had originally intended to become a lawyer. Economic reasons had compelled him to turn to playwriting. He wrote his plays to be acted, not to be read, but he knew how to use his education to the best advantage. He was the first of the 19th century playwrights to succeed in living by his pen alone. Hitherto authors had received only a single and very meagre payment for their plays. Scribe however introduced a system of royalties which made him a millionaire and the owner of a great chateau in France. He also formed an association of playwrights to defend their interests against the theatre directors, thanks to which dramatic authors were enabled for the rest of the century to devote themselves wholly to their craft.

It was this system of royalties which Scribe introduced that enabled the younger Dumas, Augier and Ibsen to live a life free from financial worries.

The changes which Scribe introduced into the drama were the most valuable of all reforms during this period. There had been no lack of good poets, shrewd psychologists and profound thinkers ready to try their hand at drama in the early 19th century. The majority, however, had little stage sense, or if they had, stifled it with their theories. Scribe had no great gift for characterization, no high moral or philosophical ideas; he had no style, and was indifferent to all aesthetic theories; but he understood stagecraft better than anyone. His skill at weaving plots was such that he gave to the 19th century drama just what it had hitherto lacked—a firm internal structure. It is surprising to note how rapidly modern drama developed after Scribe, though his disciples soon revolted against the excessive artificiality of their master's plots.

Scribe's dramatic works, including those which he wrote in collaboration with other authors, are estimated at three or four hundred. Not all of these are plays. Scribe also completely transformed the libretti of opera and opéra comique. Opera had not yet shaken itself free from the classical subjects, and the same situations and themes were repeated again and again. Scribe was the creator (as far as the text is concerned) of Grand Opera, his first work being *La Muette de Portici* (*The Mute from Portici*). Later he wrote some of the best-known operas of his day, *Les Huguenots* (*The Huguenots*), *Le Prophète* (*The Prophet*), *L'Africaine* (*The African Woman*), and many more. As an opera librettist, his taste was for romantic and colourful subjects, though otherwise he was no romantic. Many of his libretti were not original, but adaptations of others' work; he even had the courage to rewrite Shakespeare's *The Tempest* as an opera. Of all Scribe's works, his elegant comic operas have perhaps held their place on the stage longest—*La dame blanche* (*The White Lady*), *Le domino noir* (*The Black Domino*), *Fra Diavolo*, and many others.

It was for the half-musical Vaudeville theatre that Scribe wrote his first and most of his later plays, and it was here that he first won his reputation. Vaudeville was a light form of drama, dating back to the 17th century. The name really referred to the couplets which occurred in it. For instance in Beaumarchais' *Le mariage de Figaro* (*The Marriage of Figaro*), which is a comedy, there is a vaudeville, that is a series of couplets, at the end of the play. During the 18th century the name came to signify a short musical play with a delicate and sometimes improvised plot, with interspersed couplets, which often have a topical or political significance. During the 18th century this peculiarly French form spread all over Europe.

The reason why Scribe came to write so many vaudevilles or vaudeville-comedies was that the Théâtre Français had special priveleges for the production of both comedies and tragedies. But Scribe was too prolific a writer for the Théâtre Français to take all his works. He had therefore come to an agreement with the Director of the Gymnase Theatre, whereby the latter undertook to stage all Scribe's vaudeville plays—an arrangement, incidentally, which made this director a multi-millionaire.

Scribe was least happy as a writer of lyrics, and he gradually whittled away the couplets until he had removed from vaudeville the last traces of the pastoral drama and the rural idyll. Instead he invested it with a lively Parisian atmosphere. He devoted his attention to devising more elegant and ingenious plots, based on stories both old and new, real and imaginary. Even at this stage he was giving expression to a sober bourgeois attitude that was later to be reflected in modern French drama.

It was above all as a writer of vaudeville that Scribe made his name. In this capacity he became a master from whom Heiberg, Hertz and Hostrup learned much, as did also the distinguished Swedish vaudeville playwrights of whom Blanche was the best. Even when, in his more serious plays, he deals with social problems, there always lingers a faint echo of the gaiety of vaudeville.

Scribe's straight plays are either historical comedies or domestic dramas. In both types his technique is the same, but as his historical plays have retained their popularity longer it is proposed to deal first with them, and in particular with his play *Le Verre d'Eau* (*The Glass of Water*). This drama was first produced in 1840 and is still being played to-day. This play gives in essence Scribe's whole philosophy of dramatic art, in so far as he can be said to have had one.

The Glass of Water has the high-sounding sub-title, *Les effects et les causes*. A glass of water spilt on Queen Anne's dress by the Duchess of Marlborough is the cause of her own disgrace, the collapse of the Whigs, the rise of Bolingbroke and ultimately a revolution in English foreign policy. Scribe wishes to show that from the most trivial incident can result the most catastrophic reversals of fortune. This point of view is put by Bolingbroke himself in his famous tirade in the first act; he concludes it by telling how he became a statesman and a Minister of the Crown because he could dance a saraband, and was dismissed because he caught a cold.

This discovery made by Scribe and Bolingbroke is as old as the hills, and many authors at many times have expressed it in more or less the same terms. Scribe found it first in Voltaire who had previously quoted this very same historical incident, the spilling of a glass of water. In direct contrast to Schiller, Scribe conceived a historical event as the result of cunning intrigue, and as set in motion by trivial causes such as personal ambition or vanity. This conception naturally deprived his plays of all semblance of historical reality, but enhanced their dramatic quality. About the actual clash of ideas behind the conflict between Bolingbroke and his enemy we learn nothing.

Significantly enough, it is only against the Duchess of Marlborough that Bolingbroke is fighting; as plotters and counter-plotters they are well matched in cunning. The remaining characters—the Queen who is always vacillating, and the young lovers, Masham and Abigail Churchill—are mere puppets in their hands. The whole play hinges on the rather improbable supposition that Masham is the unconscious object of admiration of two rivals, the Queen and the Duchess. Bolingbroke contrives to make good use of their jealousy, and by the fourth act causes a quarrel to break out between them, at the very moment when the Queen bids Masham hand her the fateful glass of water. The jealous Duchess seizes it and spills the water over the Queen's dress.

Scribe often builds his plays round two young people who fall in love, and are happily united at the end of the fifth act. But their fates are playfully interwoven with serious political struggles and they are used as catspaws by both sides for their own ends. The general idea is to allow the characters to fall victims to all kinds of misunderstandings, which the audience knows all about already and therefore finds all the more entertaining to watch as they see the characters becoming innocently and unconsciously embroiled. If Masham is anxious to confide in one or other of the noble ladies, or they are about to confess their affection for him, the author is sure to interrupt their conversation by some device which leaves them with false impressions of each other's feelings. Letters are intercepted, secret whisperings overheard and misunderstood, assignations are made, but the person who turns up is always the one whose presence is least desired; this is all according to the convention.

Plots of this kind go far back into dramatic history, and are to be found fully developed in the French playwrights of the 18th century, Marivaux and Beaumarchais. One can even find 18th century examples of comedy based on some historical incident—a type of which Scribe was so fond. What was new in Scribe was the importance which he gave to the plot. In *The Glass of Water* the love of the Queen and the Duchess of Marlborough for Masham is regarded solely as a factor in the development of the plot, and the author makes no effort whatever to explain their motives in psychological terms.

The Exposition, which was such an important element in most 19th century drama, is almost entirely missing in Scribe's works. He plunges straight into the action, and from the first moment dramatic tension is high. Scribe then gives himself plenty of time; the real climax is not reached until the fourth act, the fifth being reserved for setting all to rights. Meanwhile the audience is held in suspense. Every new character who appears on the stage adds a new twist to the plot, and leads the audience to look for a solution in a different quarter. To ensure that they fully appreciate the dangers of the situation, the author allows the principal characters to exchange asides which show how the game is going. At the end of the third act Bolingbroke whispers to Abigail, "The match goes well". "It is lost", says Abigail. "It is won", answers Bolingbroke.

At the end of the fourth act comes the big scene which everyone has been waiting for, the same which later on, in the plays of Dumas the younger and Augier was to be known as the *scène à faire*. In *The Glass of Water* we have in this scene the fateful glass of water which brings disgrace to the Duchess of Marlborough. The purpose of this technique is of course to ensure that right up to the moment when the curtain rises for the last act the spectator's heart shall be in his mouth. Plays were constructed on this principle not only by the younger Dumas and Augier, but also by Ibsen in his earliest plays.

The last act, however, always brings a happy solution to every problem. The plot is by now so complicated that the audience is quite incapable of guessing the solution, though at the same time entirely confident that all will be well in the end. The dramatic critic Sarcey, who, unlike his contemporaries, cherished an abiding affection for Scribe, was very irritated when the great tragic actress, Madame Bartet, overacted her part in one of Scribe's plays and gave her despair too realistic an expression. The incident occurred in a scene in *La bataille de dames* (*The Ladies' Battle*), when her lover was being dragged away to execution by the police. So movingly did the actress depict the agony of young Léonie that Sarcey felt himself compelled in the name of the public to reprove her. "Dear Lady", he said, "Pray do not be so anxious. You are in M. Scribe's hands; he is a fine fellow and he won't let you down. In the last act he will restore your handsome lover and see that you are married. Your young man pretends to put his head on the block, and we pretend to believe that he may lose it. You must pretend to be anxious, because courtesy demands it, but if you are more than reasonably anxious you embarrass both the author and all of us. The emotion that you show must bear some relation to the truth of the situation—and the truth is that none of this is really true: it has never happened".

This passage shows the atmosphere of unreality which pervades Scribe's plays. They are good theatre, and good theatre they are meant to be: they have no pretensions to reality.

The last line of a Scribe play often contains some allusion to the title. In *The Glass of Water*, Bolingbroke hands Masham his seals of office, and receives the answer, "And all this thanks to a glass of water". *The Ladies' Battle* ends in the same way; "It's not enough to play well in order to win", says the triumphant Countess. "True", replies her opponent, "you need to hold the aces and kings". At which the Countess, with a glance at the happy lover, exclaims, "Especially the King, when ladies wage war". Allusions to card games or chess are characteristic of Scribe, and may be noted in as late a play as Strindberg's *Gustav III.*

Plots such as those of Scribe would seem quite incredible if he had not also created characters expressly for them. These characters fall into two categories, the intriguers and their victims.

At the centre of his plays there is always a brilliant conspirator, who carries on his intrigues for the sheer joy of intriguing. To enable him to display his art in all its glory, it is necessary that the other characters shall be, if not fools, at least easily led and unsuspecting. The audience are in the chief conspirator's confidence from the very first moment, and by means of his asides they are kept informed of the progress of his plots. Thus they can derive great amusement from the spectacle of those poor credulous wretches who think they are behaving as heroes, when in fact they are being used as pawns by others, or else are chivvied along in ignorance of the fearful dangers around them, until at last they are safe in their lovers' arms, as happens to Masham in *The Glass of Water*. If ever Scribe tries to create a real character he fails miserably, and his dramas are almost always at their best when they are so full of incident that no one has any time to gain a real impression of the characters.

The dialogue is also determined by the plot. In no way does it resemble ordinary conversation—indeed, it hardly pretends to do so. A typical dramatic dialogue of Scribe's is one where the brilliant characters sparkle like fireworks, while the stupid, the pompous and the gullible betray themselves in every sentence they utter. Scribe's style is considered to be dull, but it is at any rate economical: it carries the reader straight into the action and anchors his attention there.

It is above all in these historical plays that Scribe's virtuosity as a constructor of plots is made plain. For the development of modern drama, however, his contemporary plays have been of at least equal significance. On the whole they are written after the same pattern; but however slight their connexion with real life, these plays, because of the subject with which they deal and the technique employed, have had a considerable effect on modern drama as developed by Augier and Dumas the younger.

The construction of *La Camaraderie (Comradeship)* is similar to that of the historical plays. Conspiracy and intrigue are represented in a contemporary setting of cliques and coteries. The play introduces us first to a group of people who have made a compact to secure each other's advancement to posts of honour and profit by every available means. To this end they influence opinion in journals and salons, and whisper confidences in the ears of ministers—with such success that all members of the group achieve fame and distinction, while outsiders are discredited and disgraced. As the leader of the conspiracy we find Madame de Mirémont, a former schoolmistress, who has succeeded in marrying a peer of France. There is also a hero, an honest young lawyer who is pushed forward to advancement without his being aware of it. Exactly like Masham in *The Glass of Water,* he falls in love with a girl, and to win her hand must secure election to Parliament. To achieve this his friends succeed in persuading the influential Mme. de Mirémont that he is in love with her. The ruse is not discovered until too late, when she can no longer take counter-measures, and in the final scene the hero makes this naive recantation: "How wrong I was to lament my fate and the wickedness of mankind. Why, even this morning, I was cursing the age for its plots and intrigues. Now I perceive that friendships can indeed be disinterested, and that one may succeed without recourse to cliques and shameful manœuvres". The play was immensely popular because it openly satirized the cliques which have always flourished in French politics. It is superficial, but it is also witty and entertaining, and it is certainly a forerunner of the "Comedy of Manners", in which Augier was later to display the sores on the body of French society.

Une Chaîne (A Chain) is probably the play of Scribe's which most foreshadows the dramas of the younger Dumas, a playwright on whom Scribe's technique was to have great influence. It tells of a young man who falls in love with a girl, but feels himself still bound to a former mistress, as if by a heavy chain, and it introduces several characters who are later to become stock figures in modern French drama; the *grande dame* who falls in love with a young genius, the deceived husband whose duelling pistols are always cocked, the innocent girl led to the altar without knowing anything about her husband or the extent of his affections, and finally the honest and prosperous father-in-law from the country. The issue is really a profoundly serious one, but Scribe cannot resist the temptation to contrive intrigues and really succeeds (without unduly straining our credulity) in presenting a series of highly dramatic situations.

The play shows both Scribe's strength and his weakness. It was written in 1841, and portrayed both characters and situations with a realism that modern drama was not to develop to the full until ten years later. As soon as the complexities of the plot begin to appear, the atmosphere changes, the characters become mere puppets in the author's hands, and the whole thing becomes just an ingenious piece of stagecraft. The novel at this period had already achieved a much higher degree of realism. Ten years before *A Chain* appeared, Stendhal had written in France *Le Rouge et le Noir,* a study of a similar situation, but executed with supreme realism and with very shrewd psychological insight.

The attention which Scribe gave to his plots was a very necessary element in the reform and growth of drama, which needed to recover some of the logic it had lost since the great days of the French classical period. The trouble is, however, that the mechanism of Scribe's plots is too obvious, and dramatic tension becomes the dominating factor in his plays. The play becomes a sort of chess problem where the spectator is presented with a situation for which there seems no solution until the author's skill suddenly reveals the move which resolves it. Scribe was once watching a performance of one of his own early plays whose plot he had forgotten; turning to his neighbour he said, "I am curious to see how I got myself out of this one". Perhaps it is the weakness of Scribe's plays that the spectator is more interested in the author's solution to the problem than in the psychological consistency of his characters' behaviour.

Scribe was very fond of placing one character at the mercy of two powerful personalities, each pulling him in a different direction. The typical example of this is *The Glass of Water,* where young Masham is tossed like a shuttle between the Duchess of Marlborough and Bolingbroke. Again in *Comradeship* the hero is placed between two intriguing ladies, and with various modifications the same situation is found in most of his main plays. The solution is usually so contrived that the main conspirator achieves his object, and removes the last obstacle to the union of the young lovers in the final scene.

By his skill in the construction of plots Scribe became the obvious teacher, to whom young dramatists of succeeding generations looked. It is said of Sardou, his most faithful disciple and the heir of his crown, that he began his career by reading the first act of a Scribe drama with which he was not familiar, then composing the rest of the play, and finally comparing the result with Scribe's original.

The more ambitious playwrights of the realistic modern drama school which followed Scribe also made use of his technique. This holds true even of the younger Dumas, who rather ungratefully described Scribe as the Shakespeare of the shadow theatre, the master who could construct plays with characters who never came alive. Naturally Björnson and Ibsen were not such close intimates of Scribe, but in their young days, when they were theatre directors, they came much under his influence, because the Norwegian repertory gave pride of place to his plays. Björnson, indeed, in his early theatre reviews expressly warned his contemporaries not to omit that stage in development which could be described by the name of "the man with the new theatre machine". The influence of Scribe on Björnson's plays is apparent, not only in the early Norse dramas, but also in later contemporary plays. In his great feminist play, *Leonarda,* a forerunner of Ibsen's *A Doll's House,* the resemblance to *The Ladies' Battle* was so plain that he found it advisable to make one of his heroines say that she had just read the play.

The influence of Scribe also dominated Ibsen when he wrote his early historical plays, especially *Fru Inger til Östråt (Lady Inger of Östråt),* while his first contemporary play, *De unges forbund (The League of Youth),* has as its hero, Stensgård, a mere puppet of the Scribe type who is tossed to and fro between two experienced plotters, Daniel Hejre and Lundestad. Gradually Ibsen cut the threads that

bound him to Scribe's involved plots, but he never quite succeeded in freeing himself entirely from the tendency to over-elaborate his plots. Without those years of apprenticeship to Scribe, however, he might never have become the greatest master of technique in modern drama.

The improbability of Scribe's plots:

His skill in the conduct of his plots is perhaps the best known and the most popular feature of his character. The incidents are seldom complex: they succeed each other naturally: nothing lingers, nothing requires explanation. Indeed his extraordinary skill in this respect, and his confidence in his own powers of managing any theme however perilous, sometimes lead him into the selection of plots, the basis of which involves some absurdity or improbability which all the dexterous tact of his development can hardly redeem. . . . It is perhaps the best proof of his felicitous management in this respect, that with every scene the improbability appears to decrease, till at last, when the curtain falls, we have altogether resigned ourselves into the hands of the dramatist. There are but few of his works in which some scene is not to be found, where the situations are of the most trying kind, hovering on the brink of improbability, or treading the verge of melodramatic exaggeration, and yet by the aid of an admirable discretion, and an unfailing command of natural and at the same time effective and witty dialogue, he winds himself out of all his entanglements just as we had begun to think his case hopeless.

George Moir, in The Foreign Quarterly
IX, No. xxii, May 1832.

Patti Gillespie   (essay date 1975)

SOURCE: "Plays: Well-Complicated," in *Speech Monographs* Vol. 42, No. 1, March, 1975, pp. 20-8.

[*Gillespie closely examines the structure of Scribe's dramas in an attempt to formulate a precise definition of the term "well-made play."*]

Considerable confusion surrounds the meaning of the phrase *well-made play.* This confusion can be lessened by agreeing to restrict its use to those plays written in or after the nineteenth century, by or in the manner of Eugene Scribe. But even then the phrase lacks precision since little agreement exists about which features of Scribe's plays combine to call forth the designation *well-made.* The consistency with which various critics speak of the well-made play *form* or *formula* seems to imply an awareness of some pattern in the over-all structure, but the infrequent attempts to discover the pattern have not been successful.

Perhaps a key to this presumed form, or formula, or over-all structure, is an understanding of how Scribe built and resolved complication. Aristotle identified complication and denouement as the formal parts of plot, and critics are fond of remarking that Scribe relied on "lots of plot" as he wrote his plays. Although random remarks concerning complications in Scribean drama appear throughout the critical literature, no systematic study of Scribe's construction of complications has been undertaken and reported. A methodical inquiry into these techniques seems warranted, for it should provide valuable information about recurring features of construction throughout the body of Scribe's plays. And these recurring features, once identified, should constitute a very important part of any eventual definition of the phrase *well-made play*.

Before turning to the analysis of the plays themselves, however, the meanings of certain terms should be clarified. A play has two formal parts: complication and denouement. The play is divided into these parts by the crisis. A *complication* is anything which alters or threatens to alter the course of an action. A *crisis*, or turning point, is reached whenever no further entanglement or involvement of a complication is possible. For the untangling or resolving of complication, the French adopted the term *denouement*. *Line of action* will be used to designate a related series of complications. The number of complications within any given play may be vast, for a single line of action may encompass numerous complications, and many plays develop more than one line of action.

But dealing with complications can be simplified by agreeing that a play has a major complication, the resolution of which precipitates, or allows, an end to the play. Similarly, a single complication may have its own crisis and resolution; therefore, a play will have several crises. But the major crisis of the play occurs when the play's major complication reaches the point at which its further entanglement is impossible. An example will clarify. The major complication of *Hamlet* is initiated when the young prince accepts the three-fold charge from the ghost of his father; the major crisis is the famous mousetrap scene; the complication ends with the death of Hamlet.

Clearly, the relative position of the play's major crisis determines in large measure the form of the play's complication and denouement. Three basic patterns are possible. If the crisis is early, the play will build complications fairly rapidly to the point where further involvement is impossible; the play will then rather slowly resolve its complications. If the crisis is very late, the complications will build for an extended period and then resolve abruptly: the denouement will be short. When the crisis occupies an intermediate position, the knotting of the complications and the untying (the denouement) will adjust accordingly. To clarify and to provide a convenient point of reference, two examples will serve. Shakespeare frequently employed an early crisis, a crisis located in what is now the third act of his five-act play. Moliere, on the other hand, placed the crisis of *Tartuffe* in the fourth act and used the whole fifth act for the denouement. Such a crisis, I will call intermediate. The term *late crisis* will designate a crisis in the fifth act of a five-act play or in a proportionately similar position in the case of one-, two-, three- or four-act plays.

Scribe employs all three structural patterns, but he shows a decided preference for crises in the intermediate and late

positions. Of the thirty-five plays [which contain no music], only *Dix Ans de la vie d'une femme* and *Le Mauvais Sujet* display an early crisis and extensive denouement. Significantly, these two plays are early works and are atypical in another respect: both posit a change in the ethical disposition of the leading character.

In *Le Mauvais Sujet,* Estelle and Raymond are happily contemplating marriage, but the arrival and subsequent intervention of the mysterious and malevolent Robert complicates the action. About midway through the play's single act, Robert undergoes a spiritual conversion because he discovers that his father has forgiven him. He becomes the benefactor of the play's sympathetic characters and hastily eliminates those very obstacles he had earlier contrived. Robert then leaves the village as secretly as he had come, sacrificing his own happiness for that of his friends and family. Only after his ship sails do the characters guess his true identity. The crisis, Robert's reformation, occurs about midway in the action; the denouement explores the changed attitudes of Robert and shows his attempts to undo the wrongs which he committed in his past.

In *Dix Ans de la vie d'une femme,* Adele's foolish decision to obey her friends rather than her husband, Darcey, leads directly to a life of adultery. The crisis is reached in Act III when Darcey exposes Adele's sin to the entire family. The denouement begins with the decision that Adele's punishment will be estrangement from Darcey; the rest of the play portrays her consequent moral decline and progressively worsening economic plight. As in *Le Mauvais Sujet,* the play's final resolution depends upon the removal of the protagonist from the dramatic action; whereas Robert sails away, Adele dies (repentant but not forgiven). In both plays, the ending is less a resolution of the play's major complication than a contrivance for stopping the action.

With respect to the position of the crisis, the remaining thirty-three plays are about equally divided, the late crisis being slightly more prevalent. Five of the six one-act plays and nine of the eleven three-act plays have this construction; among the five-act works, the late crisis is rare but not absent. Usually the late crisis takes the form of a major plot discovery (e.g., *Rêves d'amour*); less often it is a threat to a sympathetic character (e.g., *La Passion secrète*), a decision by a principal character (e.g. *Valérie*), or a confrontation (e.g., *Le Puff*). Whatever its form, the late crisis leads almost immediately to the play's resolution, the rapidity of which is most often made possible by the direct and successful intervention of an agent aligned with the sympathetic characters. Although the interfering agent may be new to the action (e.g., *Le Valet de son rival*), typically he has been a participant throughout but assumes a new position of strength by means of information only recently acquired (e.g., *Les Indépendants*). Less often the speedy resolution is made possible by an agent's conversion (e.g., *La Czarine* and *La Frileuse*), or by another discovery (e.g., *Rodolphe*). In plays dependent on deception, the resolution may merely be the successful completion of the trickery and abysmal (and acknowledged) defeat of one agent (e.g., *La Grand'mère* and *Le Valet de son rival*). Whatever the instrument of resolution, in Scribe's plays which have a late crisis, the denouement is less an untangling than a cutting-through the mass of complications.

Japhet, Feu Lionel, La Tutrice, and most of Scribe's five-act plays have an intermediately-placed crisis. This crisis is also usually a major plot discovery, but on some occasions a deed (e.g., *La Tutrice*) or a confrontation (e.g., *Le Fils de Cromwell*) may substitute for, or strongly supplement, the discovery.

Obviously, plays with an intermediately-placed crisis have more extensive denouements than those with a late crisis. The way in which Scribe uses the lengthy denouements is varied. The denouement most often develops (often to a crisis) numerous minor lines of action preparatory to resolving both them and the principal line of the play. In *Bertrand et Raton,* for example, the crisis is at the end of Act IV. The early part of the fifth act portrays the plight of the young lovers, dramatizing their helplessness and inability to extricate themselves from their dilemma; the rest of the act reinforces the didactic purposes of the play: suggesting that governing is best left to the aristocrats and politicians and showing the ineptitude of the people and the fickleness of the mob.

An intermediate crisis not infrequently gives rise to another complication; the denouement then is itself the initiation, development, and resolution of this complication. In *La Calomnie,* for example, the discovery of the identity of the count's real lover will presumably end the threat to Cecile's reputation and restore her happiness. Instead, the discovery (the major crisis) initiates another complication. Before the crisis, Raymond has only to put an end to the rumors about Cecile; his strategy is simple—he will learn and then reveal the identity of the real lover. After the crisis, Raymond must dispel the rumors still, but he must do so without revealing that Herminie (his sister) is the true culprit. Act five is devoted to exploring alternative solutions to the dilemma and to selecting and effecting one of these.

In most plays of trickery depending on a conflict between wits, the action after the crisis is devoted primarily to the unsuccessful efforts of the antipathetic wit to regain the advantage lost at the play's crisis. In *La Camaraderie,* for example, Cesarine employs all of her wiles to recoup her losses and to reverse the trend toward Edmond's nomination which she herself had mistakenly engineered. The play ends when the absolute defeat of Cesarine by Zoe is irrevocable and painfully clear even to Cesarine.

In *Les Trois Maupins* and *La Tutrice* there is a significant lapse of time between the act containing the crisis and the one setting forth the denouement; therefore, both plays devote a large proportion of the action after the crisis to an exposition of interim events and developments. Only following these explanations does the active process of disentanglement begin and the play's final resolution emerge. Clearly when Scribe uses the intermediate crisis and the fairly extensive denouement, his purpose and forms vary considerably.

Certain practices of Scribe with respect to major complication, crisis, and denouement are now clear. Scribe generally avoided an early crisis, but he used the intermediate and late crisis almost equally, seeming to prefer the former for his five-act plays and the latter for his one- and three-act works. The major crises are usually discoveries, but other devices are not rare. Rapid denouements most often depend upon the direct intervention of an agent late in the action; conversions, decisions, or discoveries may suffice for the resolution, however. Denouements following intermediately-placed crises usually develop secondary lines of action to a crisis or begin and develop new complications; secondarily, they may reinforce the play's didactic statement or explain interim events.

Having considered Scribe's practices with respect to the formal parts of plays, a closer examination of the complications themselves is possible. In some plays, action is relatively simple. Although a few minor and seemingly unrelated complications may be introduced prior to the initiation of the play's principal action, once the major complication is underway, other complications become subsidiaries to it. The minor complications are then either quickly resolved or become a means for adding to the suspense and entanglement of the major complication. The resolution of the major complication effects or is effected by the resolution of the minor, subsidiary complications.

Rodolphe, an early one-act play, provides one excellent example of how Scribe handles complications in plays with rather simple constructions. Rodolphe is the legal guardian of Therese, but he has been posing for years as her brother to avoid any appearance of impropriety. He now loves her, but he fears to reveal the truth lest she reject his suit, or worse still, marry him from a sense of obligation only. Therese loves Rodolphe but consents to wed another in order to suppress her own evil, "incestuous" emotions. The dilemma is solved by a double discovery: Rodolphe learns of Therese's love and Therese learns that Rodolphe is not her brother.

The play's development from complication to crisis and denouement is direct. The major complication is introduced in the play's opening scene when Rodolphe reads aloud a letter recently composed for a suitor of Therese. In the letter he describes their real relationship; in his musings he tells of his love. A series of supportive complications then follow quickly: Antoine declares his love for Therese; whereupon Rodolphe, frenzied by jealousy, insults his former partner and friend; Therese discovers that her love for Rodolphe exceeds the fraternal and falsely concludes that her emotion is vile. Therese promotes a reconciliation between the men and then asks Antoine to marry her; Rodolphe mistakenly concludes that Therese does not love him, and so announces his intention to depart forever. The mutual discoveries and confessions then follow and begin the play's denouement. The final resolution occurs when Antoine returns to the stage having read Rodolphe's letter to the suitor. Knowing the real relationship and realizing their mutual love, Antoine insists on giving up Therese so that she and Rodolphe will be free to marry.

In **Rodolphe,** the several complications occur sequentially. Some interlock, that is, the initiation of a second precedes the resolution of the first; some do not. Although several episodic and minor complications exist, the series as a whole serves to supplement the major complications directly and in some important way. The action of this play, therefore, might be conveniently schematized as simple and linear.

La Passion secrète is another relatively simple construction, but it differs significantly enough to warrant its brief consideration. The initiation of the major complication in this play is much later than that in **Rodolphe.** Prior to its commencement, several questions are raised and answered; the answer to each question raises yet another question. Following the interrogative series and the introduction (but not the development) of two monetary complications, the last question is answered, and the play's principal complication is introduced: the woman, Albertine, is a compulsive gambler in need of money. Albertine steals, and immediately a number of threatening complications develop: Albertine is asked to return some money and to provide other money for a dowry; as a villain barters for her body, Albertine's final attempt to secure a loan fails. The timely intervention of Leopold resolves all complications.

While the questions and complications of Act I are sequential and interlocking like those in **Rodolphe,** the complications in Act III develop differently. Several supportive complications in Act III are introduced early and then abandoned for a time. They are later developed quickly and sequentially to a crisis. Each is suspended at this stage of its development and held at the crisis while all are connected to the play's major complication. Since none of the minor complications can be resolved prior to the resolution of the major complication, the major crisis and resolution gain great force. The result is of the threat increasing geometrically rather than arithmetically. The suspense of impending doom is cumulative and might be compared with an assault or bombardment. **La Passion secrète,** then, differs from **Rodolphe** both in the point at which the play's major complication is initiated and in the way by which the supportive complications are related to the principal line. But like **Rodolphe, La Passion secrète** is essentially a linear development in which all the secondary lines of action contribute more or less directly to the construction of the play's principal complication.

Few of Scribe's plays are so simple, and few can be profitably schematized as linear progressions. Most display many lines of action developing simultaneously on several levels. These plays might be better conceptualized as planar instead of linear arrangements. An example can illustrate.

The story line for **Feu Lionel** is rather complicated and its structure sufficiently representative to serve the purpose. Lionel, under the name of Rigaud, has been living at the home of Bremontier and has fallen in love with his daughter, Alice. Lionel has been a perpetual failure in love and finances and is disguised as M. Rigaud because he tried

Sarah Bernhardt as Adrienne Lecouvreur.

(and failed) to commit suicide. He is ashamed to face his friends, and he fears that Alice would find him ridiculous and cease to love him should she learn the truth. Montgiron, his former friend and lawyer, promises to help him keep the secret; but the arrival of an officious Baronne and then of the foolish Robertin threatens to expose Lionel's real identity. Developing concurrently with this story are two secondary lines: (1) the Baronne is negotiating with Bremontier to close a business deal involving the transfer of a piece of land, and (2) Robertin is trying to establish with certainty the death of Lionel so that he may be declared the only surviving relative of a wealthy person and thus inherit a vast sum of money. Alice eventually discovers the truth, but she loves Lionel in spite of his foolishness. She will marry him if only he will confront his friends. The sting of the confrontation is reduced for Lionel when Montgiron invents a bet which allegedly caused Lionel to undertake the impersonation: he wagered that if Lionel were to disappear, the capriciousness of the Baronne would be proved. Ridicule shifts from Lionel to the Baronne and Robertin, whose incipient courtship crashes forthwith.

The development of the complications is clear if intricate. Before the initiation of the play's principal action, two questions are raised successively and then answered almost simultaneously. "Who is Rigaud?" and "What is the connection between Rigaud and Montgiron?" are both answered in Act I when the old friends engage in a long expository dialogue: Rigaud is Lionel.

The major complication begins to develop immediately: Rigaud must not be exposed because he would become an object of ridicule. Threatening complications follow quickly. The Baronne, a former lover of Lionel, arrives unexpectedly: Robertin, a prospective heir, appears and is determined to investigate the circumstances surrounding Lionel's death. The major complication becomes intricately and irrevocably tied to the developing love between Alice and Lionel: Alice is told of a hypothetical case in which a man tried to commit suicide, failed, and chose to assume another identity rather than face the ridicule of his friends. Alice giggles uncontrollably during the recital of the story. At its completion she launches an indignant and self-righteous condemnation of such a man and declares that she herself could never be sympathetic with such a foolish person. By this device Scribe makes the play's major complication (the identity) into a threat to the secondary complication (the love). Another threat to the love interest is immediately posed: Montgiron becomes a serious suitor for Alice's hand. All of these complications are temporarily suspended while the intricacies of a financial relationship between the Baronne and Robertin are discovered, explored, and related to the business of Bremontier and the identity of Lionel.

The play's final resolution depends upon the interference of Montgiron who promotes Robertin's courtship of the Baronne and who informs Alice of the true identity of Rigaud. Alice's demand for a public confession resolves the two major complications; the confession also exposes the falsity of Robertin's claims to fortune. Montgiron's happy notion to introduce the bet serves to mitigate the ridicule destined for Lionel, redirecting it to Robertin and the Baronne; moreover, the bet serves to expose the perfidy of the Baronne as a business woman and to tie off the Robertin-Baronne affair. The appropriate dispensation of the lands and monies completes the play's resolution and brings the action to a conclusion, each complication having been resolved and some connection having been made.

Five features appearing in *Feu Lionel* recur often in the thirty-five plays. For convenience these techniques are listed and briefly explained. Their use in *Feu Lionel* is indicated and the titles of one or two other plays in which the technique is particularly clear are offered for those who wish to explore them more fully.

1. Questions of identity or intent are raised and answered prior to the initiation of major lines of action. In *Feu Lionel,* "Who is Rigaud?"; "Rigaud is Lionel." See also *Bataille de dames* and *Les Frères invisibles.*

2. Two or more important lines of action are interwoven intricately so that a threat to one ramifies at once in the other. A love interest is usually the basis of at least one

of the interdependent lines of action. The Baronne's deal with Bremontier and Robertin's desire for inheritance threaten to expose Lionel's identity. See also *Japhet* and *Une Chaîne.*

3. Important complications are frequently abandoned for stretches of dramatic time in order to permit the exploitation of decidedly minor complications which may or may not relate integrally to the development of the play's principal action. Although the minor complications generally connect with the major lines, they often are developed internally far beyond what is required in terms of their ultimate contribution to the overall construction. In *Feu Lionel* the several threats to the love story are suspended while the finances of Baronne and Robertin are explored. (See also the Melanie line in *La Fille de trente ans* and the loves of Josseline in *Mon Étoile*).

4. The internal development of a complication or line of action usually proceeds in a fairly regular sequence, either interlocking or freed, that is, a sequence of the sort described in *Rodolphe.* Scribe varies this pattern from time to time. He may develop complication within complication, that is, he may build and resolve successively smaller complications within the frame of the next larger complication. This technique is observable in *Feu Lionel.* Less frequently he turns to an "assault" technique described for Act III of *La Passion secrète.* Although each of the three developmental patterns can be seen in many, perhaps even most, of Scribe's plays, *La Fille de trente ans* is a particularly good play in which to observe Scribe's use of the three forms. . . .

5. By interweaving the important complications early in the play and by deftly and unobtrusively connecting certain of the minor complications to these and to each other from time to time during the course of the play, Scribe manages to cement all but a few lines prior to the play's crisis. At the crisis, these few remaining strands are made to converge. In *Feu Lionel* the secret identity is threatened by Robertin and the Baronne. The revelation of the secret threatens the love affair. The rival suitor reveals the secret of Lionel's identity, ending the first complication. Alice remains in love and requires a confession, ending the second. The one-time suitor superintends the rewards and punishments and ties-off all lines of action.

But plays like *Feu Lionel* are not Scribe's most complex constructions. Some of the political plays and comedies of social comment posit large frames which surround the plays' story. For example, in *Le Verre d'eau,* the complication of the war between France and England is introduced in the first scene of Act I and then abandoned while first the love interest and then the wits' battle get underway and develop. Although mentioned from time to time, the political action receives scant attention until the play's crisis and denouement. In such extra levels, Scribe may have striven for an effort like Shakespeare achieved in *Hamlet.* That Shakespeare successfully exploited the Fortinbras complication to present ramifications in a political sphere while Scribe fails to achieve a similar resonance seems due to a limited genius rather than a faulty conception.

In summary, Scribe generally avoids an early crisis; he shows a slight preference for a late crisis in the short plays and an intermediately-placed crisis in the five-act plays. The crises most often take the form of discoveries. Lengthy denouements usually develop secondary complications to a point of crisis or introduce and develop a new complication (one initiated at the crisis). Rapid denouements are most often attributable to the direct intervention of agents in a position of power.

All of Scribe's plays develop several lines of action, each with many internal complications. Scribe generally ties two of the important lines together early in the play and connects various minor lines to one another and to the major lines throughout the play. By this means, he prepares the way for the rapid converging of all lines during the play's denouement. Some plays use a framing complication which seems intended to add another dimension to the play's meaning.

The implications of these practices are several and significant. Although Scribe employed an abundance of complications, he usually chose a late point-of-attack and a loose antecedent-consequence scheme of probability and unity. It is the combination of these three techniques that becomes an important component of the well-made play, and it is this combination which created many of the problems in Scribe's plays to which critics allude.

To appreciate the nature of the problem, one might imagine placing a Shakespearean network of complications and "subplots" inside of a Racinean (Neo-Classical) construct with its late point of attack and "causal" scheme of probability. Obviously, the richness, diffusion, and complexity of the Elizabethan drama is ill-accommodated by the sparse, compressed, and restricted constructions of the French Neo-Classical writers. Thus, Scribe's multitudinous complications and lines of action strain under the late point of attack and antecedent-consequence scheme of probability and unity.

The strain of this combination is intense, often approaching a kind of breaking point. Only the greatest ingenuity and technical skill will permit the convergence of the several lines of action *and* the final resolution of all important complications within the narrow constructive principles which Scribe adopted for his plays. The manipulations necessary to achieve the play's ending become apparent to someone familiar with a body of the plays and therefore the plots are dubbed "mechanical." The profusion of complications becomes silhouetted against the stark pseudo-Aristotelian structure and leads to critical comments that well-made plays have "lots of plot."

It is the combination of these three techniques which is central to Scribe's dramaturgy. It is this combination and its significance which past critics have failed to recognize and specify. It is this combination which must be cited as an important component of Scribe's plays and which must occupy a prominent place in the definition of well-made play.

Scribe's skill as manipulator of characters:

It is a mistake . . . to regard M. Scribe as a comedy-writer at all, though he has doubtless produced many cleverly constructed comedies, as he has also produced cleverly constructed novels, and narrative and dramatic scenes of all kinds. Neither should we take M. Scribe at his own word, and regard him as a song-writer; for, in spite of the number of ingenious opera-books that he has given to the world, and the great success they have attained, no one knows him by his songs. He was, above all, a maker of plots; and it was surprising what combinations he could bring about with only a few well-known characters, who from unreal, which they seemed at first, became at last conventionally true, by the mere force of a convention established between the dramatist and his public. His young widows and his colonels might not vary very much (though the colonel, of course, turns up in many pieces as an admiral, or a member of the diplomatic service), but they were always being placed in new positions; and M. Scribe knew more of the permutations and combinations to be effected with half a dozen characters than any dramatist who has lived since Lope da Vega. Say that his personages were like chessmen—varying about as much as the knight and the castle of one pattern will vary from the knight and the castle of another—he was still a most ingenious chess-player, sure of every move he made, and capable of winning the game in five hundred different ways.

Sutherland Edwards, in The Temple Bar *II, April 1861.*

Hans Heinsheimer (essay date 1977)

SOURCE: "The Scribe Factory," in *Opera News,* Vol. 41, No. 12, January 29, 1977, pp. 17-19.

[*In the essay below, Heinsheimer surveys Scribe's work as a librettist, commenting on his prodigious output and his unparalleled success.*]

A Dutch inn, villagers dancing, soldiers drinking, wandering Anabaptists preaching revolt, an army camp in Westphalia, skating on a frozen lake, a maiden jumping into a river to save her honor, a coronation in a German cathedral, a dungeon, a bacchanale, finally a fire and an all-consuming explosion—operatically most effective, historically most incorrect. (The real prophet, unromantically named Jan Beuckelszoon, was captured and executed.) All this was the stuff that made Augustin Eugène Scribe the most successful, most influential, most significant, most powerful and probably the richest fashioner of opera librettos of his time.

He was also the most prolific. *Le Prophète* was the fifty-first work with a Scribe (or at least partially Scribe) libretto to be performed at the Opéra or the Opéra Comique since 1823, when at age twenty-four he had switched from writing vaudevilles to trying his hand at opera. In his first year of association with the musical theater, his name appeared on the playbill of three operas at the Comique—Auber's *Leicester, ou le Chateau de Kenilworth,* based on the novel by Sir Walter Scott, his *La Neige, ou Le Nouvel Eginard,* originally written for Boieldieu, and a one-act opera, *Le Valet de Chambre* by Michele Carafa, an Italian who had been an officer in Napoleon's army, became a full-time composer after Waterloo and wrote—*Sic transit gloria mundi*—two dozen operas.

Among the works Scribe helped to create between 1823 and 1849, the year of *Le Prophète,* were twenty-seven operas with music by Auber, including *La Muette de Portici* (1828), one of the great opera successes of all time; a second superhit, *La Dame Blanche* (1825), with Boieldieu; three operas for Meyerbeer, beginning with *Robert le Diable* (1831) and including *Les Huguenots* (1836) and *L'Africaine,* composed much later and produced only in 1861, after both composer and author were dead. The list further includes Rossini's *Comte Ory* (1828), one of the last works of the semi-retired composer, and *La Juive* plus several other works by Halévy, among them a full-length ballet based on the story of Manon Lescaut—the first time (1830) that Manon appeared on the opera stage. Scribe used the subject again twenty-five years later for an opera for Auber, long before Massenet. There were two works by Donizetti, one by Cherubini and a large number of operas whose composers have disappeared behind the spiderweb of time. In one single year (1839) there were seven Scribe premieres in Paris.

Scribe died in 1861 at the age of seventy in a cab on the way to visit a friend, to the stunned consternation of the cabbie, who "drove home in all haste" to deliver what was left of his famous customer to an equally stunned household at Scribe's sumptuous town house at 12 Rue Pigalle. In the twelve years left to him after *Le Prophète,* the pace and density of success had slackened. He had written a farce dealing with a dog by the name of Barkouf for Jacques Offenbach, which helped to fulfill Offenbach's lifelong desire to have one of his works performed at the Opéra Comique but accomplished little else (1860). He also added Charles Gounod to the catalog of famous composers competing to work with him.

The story of *La Nonne Sanglante (The Bleeding Nun)* sheds light on the mores of the libretto business in Scribe's time. The work was originally written for Halévy, who refused to set it. Then Meyerbeer got hold of it, but Scribe, knowing how long the composer took to finish a score, is reported to have remarked, "I am growing old, and I should like to see a performance of my work." Berlioz, who was next in line, even wrote some music and hoped for a production in 1849, but he made little progress, and Scribe asked him to relinquish the work. The script was then offered to Félicien David, who declined, finding the time fixed by the management of the Opéra too short. Albert Grisar, a prolific opera composer, was approached, even Verdi. They all found the tale, based on *The Monk* by M. S. Lewis, repellent. After it had been peddled for four years, Gounod agreed to write the music, and the work was brought out at the Opéra on October 18, 1854, with a result that fully justified the judgment of the earlier candidates.

Berlioz in his *Memoirs* recalls the incident: "When on my return to Paris I met Scribe, he seemed a trifle abashed at having accepted my proposition and taken back my poem on *La Nonne.* 'But,' he said to me, 'you know how it is, the priest has to make a living from the altar.' Poor man! He really could not wait; he has only two or three hundred thousand francs income, a town house, three houses in the country, etc." On the door of one of these country houses, incidentally, his palatial domain of Sericourt (Seine-et-Marne), the multi-millionaire Scribe had mockingly and revealingly affixed this distich:

> Le théâtre a payé cet asile champêtre,
> Vous qui passez, merci, je vous le dois peut-être.
>
> (For this retreat far from the town the stage has paid.
> Thanks, passerby! Perhaps I owe it to your aid.)

In the dozen years after *Le Prophète,* his last big, undisputed triumph, Scribe's superficial treatment of people and events, the bending of history to achieve theatrical effects, the papier-mâché people he created—all this became more and more noticeable as Violetta, Rigoletto, Berlioz' Dido, Gounod's Marguerite and the Wagnerian mythic figures began to appear. "A brisk, animated style, neither forceful nor correct, no development of the characters, but also a savoir-faire till then unexampled in the building up of a plot and bringing about the dénouement," such were the defects and merits recognized by his own contemporaries.

"His style," said one of them, "is simply the jargon of his period, that of the *Restauration.* He became a tragic and lyric poet without becoming a great versifier and without ceasing to be a vaudevillist, a *chansonnier,* even when he took up lofty subjects manifestly beyond the powers of his Muse." When he was made a member of the Académie Française in 1836, an honor to which a genius like Balzac aspired in vain all his life, the man who delivered the eulogy, with whatever is the French equivalent for tongue-in-cheek, said, "The secret of your prosperity is opportunely to have seized the spirit of the age and to have written the kind of play that suits it best and bears the greatest resemblance to it."

His qualities, both pro and con, came strikingly to the forefront during his one and only collaboration with Verdi, *Les Vêpres Siciliennes* for the Paris Exhibition of 1855. Years later, there was a typical Scribian postlude to the brief encounter. Verdi learned that the *Vêpres* libretto was not even an original effort: it was a rehash, with change of scenery, of Donizetti's *Duc d'Albe,* written fifteen years earlier.

After the July revolution of 1830 had toppled the last Bourbon and put the bourgeois king "Louis Philippe Egalité" on a deglamorized throne, Louis Véron, a physician and successful newspaper publisher, was appointed to head the Paris Opera. "I hesitated for nearly a fortnight," Véron wrote in his memoirs, "but after reflecting I said to myself: the bourgeoisie will want to enjoy its newly won dominating status. It will want to amuse itself. And the Opéra will become the focal point for its amusement. It will become what Versailles had been for the old regime."

Véron did not carry out the six years of his contract but retired from the Opéra after five years a lifelong millionaire—a fact difficult to believe in our days of subsidies and donations never quite catching up with opera deficits. The doctor who had so perceptively taken the pulse of the time owed much of his good fortune to Scribe's instinct for the public taste. In 1825 Scribe had sensed the romantic appeal of fog-shrouded castles and armored nobility, making a libretto from two novels by Sir Walter Scott. The result was **La Dame Blanche,** score by Boieldieu, which at once began a victory procession around the world and within less than thirty-five years had its thousandth performance in Paris.

Three years later, with the stirring of unrest that soon was to lead to the revolution of 1830, *La Muette de Portici* (music by Auber) again fitted the moment. The opera was based on a historical event, the revolution in Naples against the Spanish occupation in 1647. Again Scribe adjusted history: at the end of the opera the mute heroine (a dancing role) casts herself into the sea during an eruption of Mt. Vesuvius, an event that in reality had taken place sixteen years earlier. First performed in 1828, *La Muette* was appropriately on the program of the Opéra on Friday, July 23, 1830, the day before the fighting broke out. The opera reopened the house three weeks later after the revolution. A performance in Brussels the same month touched off a public uprising that resulted in Belgium's breaking away from Dutch rule. So Scribe not only rewrote history, he made it.

As for Véron, no sooner had been taken over the management (and the box office) of the Opéra than Scribe, in 1831, was ready with **Robert le Diable,** the first French opera written by Meyerbeer and a spectacular, long-lasting success. It was followed by Auber's **Philtre,** likewise successful but—again the strange mores of the libretto community—pushed off the boards when, only one year later (1832), Donizetti's *Elisir d'Amore* was produced in Milan, its text by Felice Romani based on the same Scribe libretto. Véron produced four additional operas by Auber and Scribe, among them **Gustave III, ou le Bal Masqué,** which twenty-six years later in a humanized dramatization by Antonio Somma became Verdi's *Ballo in Maschera.*

There was also **Ali Baba et les Quarante Voleurs,** the only collaboration of Scribe with Cherubini and the seventy-three-year-old composer's last opera. Then in 1835 came another huge success, with music by Halévy—*La Juive.* Véron produced these lavishly, without consideration for expense, but—oh, happy times of a vanished past!—got all his money back many times over. No small wonder he reflected on Scribe in his memoirs in a vein very different from that of other contemporaries:

> It is supposed that nothing is easier to write than an opera libretto—a grave error. A five-act opera cannot survive without a highly dramatic plot, one that engages the passions of the human heart, and has a strong historical interest. This plot must also be comprehensible to the eye alone, like a ballet, and the chorus must play an important part in the action. Each act must offer contrasts of décor, of costume and especially of dramatic situation. I do not hesitate to state that of all dramatic writers M. Scribe is the one who best understands opera. He excels in the choice of

subjects, in creating interesting situations for musical treatment according to the genius of the composer.

The **Oeuvres Complètes d'Eugène Scribe de l'Academie Française** consist of seventy-six volumes, of which twenty-six were needed to accommodate the librettos. Of these only a few are based on existing plays or novels; in addition to Scott and the Abbé Prevost, whom he discovered as a candidate for operatic glory, Scribe used Shakespeare, Racine and a few others, but the bulk of his work is original. How was such an enormous output possible? Through extraordinary working methods. While many of Scribe's librettos carry only his own name, particularly the big works for Meyerbeer, Halévy and Auber, many show an additional acknowledgment in small, elegant print, "en société avec. . . . "

Wagner had been an eager beseecher of the man who had the keys to all the Parisian opera houses in his pocket. He had ardently hoped Scribe would write a libretto from his own elaborate scenario to *The Flying Dutchman,* one that would open at least one door. After Scribe refused, Wagner referred to "the Scribe factory." The *Dictionnaire des Contemporains* describes it:

> M. Scribe was obliged to establish a veritable atelier, where a host of ordinary and extraordinary collaborators contributed several items—one perhaps the idea, a second the plot, a third the dialogue, a fourth couplets. Scribe himself, endowed for his task with an incredible aptitude and perseverance, supervised and directed everything. Sometimes he would furnish the sketch, or he would revise and polish the work or remodel it in part. Finally he signed it with his name, but always placed on the playbill and in the published libretto the name of his chief collaborator beside his own.

The eulogist at the Académie summed it all up rather nicely: "Without your collaborators you perhaps would not have written all your plays, but without you they would not have succeeded."

There were many workers in the factory—men like Dupin, Brazier, Varner, Carmouche, Bayard, Xavier and Vernon de Saint-Georges, who, sans Scribe, wrote the libretto for Donizetti's *Fille du Régiment,* and others. Their leader was Scribe's old companion Germain Delavigne, with whom he had already shared his first flop, a play they collaborated on in 1810 when Scribe was nineteen years old, and whose name appears on the texts of many operas, beginning with **Le Maçon** in 1825 (music by Auber) and ending with the ill-fated **Nonne Sanglante** of 1854.

The second prominent member of the club was Honoré Mélesville, coauthor of Scribe's first operatic attempts of 1823—Auber's **Leicester** and the Carafa one-acter—and continuing through 1839. Most of the members of the *société* were also active independently. Mélesville wrote the libretto for Hérold's *Zampa,* which had its first performance at the Comique in 1831. That year also saw the first arrival of Bellini's **Somnambula** in March, **Le Philtre** in June, **Robert le Diable** in November and **Norma** in December. What fabulous times!

Today, like so many libretto writers, Scribe resides sadly in the twilight zone of opera history, in whose arid soil posthumous laurel grows sparsely. The public knows a little about Schikaneder, Da Ponte, Hofmannsthal—but who wrote *Tosca, Fidelio, Carmen, La Traviata, Die Fled-er-maus*? The author of *Le Prophète* is known best, if not only, by the street alongside the Paris opera house, called Rue Scribe since 1864, three years after his death. And even this recognition is caused less by opera associations (shared by neighboring streets named for Gluck, Meyerbeer, Auber and Halévy) than by the fact that No. 12 houses the American Express office. Scribe probably did not expect more. For his tomb he prepared an epitaph that spells out the fulfilments as well as the self-imposed limitations of his aspirations:

Vivant, j'eus des amis, quelque gloire, un peu d'or.
Ci-gît qui fut heureux, et qui l'est plus encore.

(While living I had friends, gold, glory, if you will. Here lies one who was happy, and now is happier still.)

Scribe's effect on his audience:

Once involved in the inextricable network of plot, counterplot, and intrigue which Scribe weaves about you, you are no longer master of yourself. You must submit forthwith to his guidance. Even against your will, you must, for the time being, suspend the exercise of your taste and judgment, and admire blindly whatever he sees fit to present to you. Your eyes are riveted upon the stage, and you feel no inclination to withdraw them. The most common expression amuses you; a dialogue which you would never have consented to read, commands your fixed attention. You follow eagerly all the intricacies of the plot, from the commencement to the conclusion of the piece. When it is finished, perhaps you ask, "After all, what does it amount to?" Your question comes too late. The five acts have been played. You have followed them to the end with unflagging interest. The effect which the author had in view has been produced.

Eugène de Mirecourt, quoted in The North American Review *XCVII, No. 201, October 1863.*

Douglas Cardwell (essay date 1983)

SOURCE: "The Well-Made Play of Eugène Scribe," in *The French Review,* Vol. LVI, No. 6, May, 1983, pp. 876-84.

[In this essay Cardwell provides a detailed overview of the characteristics of Scribe's dramas.]

Eugène Scribe has long been acknowledged as the developer, or inventor, of what is commonly called the well-made play, and there is an abundance of literature on translations, adaptations, and imitations of his works as well as general agreement on the importance of his influence on both

French and foreign playwrights well into this century. The reaction against his plays—which began during his lifetime and continues today in the revolt against the "bourgeois" theater that he typifies for many, and of which he is indeed a primary source—serves as additional proof of his importance in the history of theater and of the power of the forces he organized and directed, as does also the viewing of many current films and television programs, which bear his stamp as clearly as do the plays of Augier, Feydeau, Ibsen, or Shaw.

The essence of that power, the nature of that stamp, however, have generally defied definition; his admirers have had as little success as his detractors. Both groups have tended to emphasize his technical skill, usually without explaining it and without considering other factors that might have contributed to his success. Alexandre Dumas *fils* dismissed him as a "prestidigitateur de première force," while others commented on the absence of style and character development, but these typical generalities fail to answer satisfactorily the question raised so often and so despairingly by Théophile Gautier:

Comment se fait-il qu'un auteur dénué de poésie, de lyrisme, de style, de philosophie, de vérité, de naturel, puisse être devenu l'écrivain dramatique le plus en vogue d'une époque, en dépit de l'opposition des lettrés et des critiques?

Gautier correctly perceives that Scribe's undeniable technical skills do not adequately explain his success but cannot do better than to blame the philistine audiences of the time who made Scribe the first Frenchman to get rich by writing plays while neglecting the playwrights favored by the crimson-vested defender of *Hernani.* Most critics have been kinder to the audiences, but not to Scribe, and they have continued to refer to technical skill, theatrical tricks, a basic structure, a formula, which would define the well-made play and explain its success.

The most recent and most elaborate attempt to reduce the well-made play to a formula comes from Stephen S. Stanton, who claims that "True examples of such drama display seven structural features," which he lists [in his introduction to *Camille and Other Plays,* 1957]. The list is apparently based on a small number of Scribe's plays, especially *Le Verre d'eau,* which is included in his anthology. While one might use the phrase "true examples" to imply that any Scribe play that fails to exhibit the listed features is not "well-made," it is not logical to suppose that, having found a formula for success, Scribe used it only a few times and ignored or abandoned it in the remainder of his plays. Surely any attempt to define the well-made play as exemplified by Scribe must take into account the thirty-five plays included in the series *Comédies-Drames* by the editors of the only complete edition of his works [*Œuvres complètes d'Eugène Scribe,* 76 volumes, 1874-85]. Stanton's list is at the same time too specific and too general: too specific, because it excludes many of those plays; too general, because one could follow it to the letter and still not produce a well-made play. A few adjustments will not solve the problem, for the difficulty lies not simply in finding a more accurate formula, but in the fact that accuracy is incompatible with the brevity of a formula. The most remarkable feature of these plays, when viewed collectively, is their variety. The lowest common denominator is just not low enough to be of much use. Thus the search for a formula that will explain the structure of the well-made play is doomed to failure. There is no general structure that is common to all such plays. One can, however, describe common practices and tendencies in order to understand better the meaning of that term as it applies to Scribe. The emphasis will be on the typical rather than on the exceptional, but the fundamental fact remains that the range of possibilities is too broad for the description to serve as a prescription. It takes more than the application of rules to construct a well-made play.

Scribe's works include several types of play. Not only are there the expected comedies with various themes and settings—social, historical, political—but also a play that anticipates the *pièce à thèse* (*La Calomnie*) and a serious drama (*Adrienne Lecouvreur*). *Dix ans de la vie d'une femme* is a pre-naturalist play that traces in dismal detail the decline and death of a woman who falls under the influence of the wrong friends, and there is even a melodrama (*Les Frères invisibles*). It is certainly not possible to deny the flexibility and variety of the well-made play.

For the exposition there are some clearly defined principles. It must be complete, not in the sense that every detail about previous events that is to be included in the play must be in the exposition, but rather that there must be at least an allusion to every event, though the details may be filled in later if it suits the purposes of the playwright. The exposition must not precede all the action, but be mixed in with the first part of it. The play begins with an event that precipitates a crisis in an already unstable situation, which arouses the interest and curiosity of the audience and gives more life and energy to the exposition. Often an action illustrates the exposition: when an unexpected visitor shows up for breakfast in the first act of *Les Trois Maupin,* the tip he gives the "servant" is used to buy the groceries needed to feed him, thus graphically demonstrating the previously mentioned poverty of the family. Scribe avoided monologues and dialogues in which the characters exchange information already known to both of them in favor of scenes that seem more natural and that often help to advance the action. The "dilution" of the exposition with action obviously prolongs it, and in the longer plays, which require a great deal of exposition, it is not unusual for it to extend into the beginning of the second act. Generally it is spread over the first quarter of the play.

The action of the well-made play is made up of attempts to overcome a series of obstacles, culminating in the major obstacle that will hold up until the dénouement. Obstacles can be of any type, though they very often have to do with communication—either achieving it or preventing it. There must be several obstacles in each play, and they must be arranged in ascending order of difficulty, except that a major obstacle may have satellite lesser obstacles that serve to make it more imposing, in which case it is the total weight of the problems a protagonist faces that increases as the play progresses as much as the weight of the individual problems. The reversals associated with each obstacle usually come in pairs, the first favorable and the second unfavorable, so that the hero's difficulties afford only brief respites before the final victory. Often the action includes a near-solution (in some cases one that would result in an unsatisfactory dénouement) to add excitement and suspense as well as to prepare the real solution. The action also includes situations, known as *scènes à faire,* that the audience longs for but regards as uncertain, or dreads but believes to be unavoidable. They usually involve a direct confrontation between protagonist and antagonist, or their representatives, from which one will emerge the victor (at least provisionally). The *scène à faire* generally comes fairly late in the action and points the way to the dénouement. There are usually secondary *scènes à faire* as well; sometimes one becomes part of the dénouement, as does the threatened *scène à faire* that is avoided at the last minute to save the happy ending. Though the antagonist may get his just deserts in some other fashion, the scene usually depends upon the decisive communication of a key piece of information, or upon its prevention. The scene is carefully prepared, highly dramatic, and, despite its structural importance, designed primarily for the emotional satisfaction of the audience.

In its broadest formulation, the structure of a Scribe play usually centers around a single character whose decisions and actions vitally affect the fates of the other characters. In many of the plays a decision is made and then changed several times, with appropriate reactions by the other characters, before the final curtain. The action swings back and forth without making any real progress until the end. In another group of plays, the action is linear, with steady progression from beginning to end. In *Rêves d'amour,* for example, Jeanne flees from Henri throughout the play, while Henri overcomes obstacle after obstacle before finally catching her in the last scene. And in *Dix ans de la vie d'une femme,* the morals and situation of the title character go down steadily from beginning to end, with only the most illusory upswings.

Scribe's basic dramatic device is the *quiproquo.* There are usually several in one play; one may be the basis for the main action, but this is not always the case (in *Les Contes de la reine de Navarre,* for example, there is a succession of *quiproquos,* as Marguerite tries one scheme after another to try to free her brother). Usually the misunderstanding is an accident, often without the knowledge of any of the parties to it, but sometimes it is induced with intent to deceive, and often exploited. The use of the *quiproquo* is part of a broader pattern in which the revelation or continued concealment of a secret, the receipt of certain information by the correct person, or the prevention of its discovery by the wrong person is essential to the proper outcome of the action. Various bits of information may, in the course of the play, be communicated, withheld, distorted, falsified, or invented, causing the many ups and downs in the action. One visible indication of the importance of communication in Scribe's plays is the constant use of letters and various documents and papers. (Over one-fourth of all scenes involve some form of paper stage property, and only eleven of the one hundred thirty-three acts have no such scene.) The secret or *quiproquo* is usually made obvious to the spectator from the beginning, or at least early, but not always (in **Oscar** the audience must wait until the end of the play to learn the true identity of the woman with whom Oscar had a rendezvous, after two other candidates are implicated, then cleared). In this Scribe follows the policy that he reportedly claimed to be the secret of his art. Octave Feuillet, in the speech he gave when taking Scribe's seat at the Académie Française, quotes him as saying:

> Le publique m'aime parce que j'ai soin de le mettre toujours dans ma confiance; il est dans le secret de la comédie; il a dans les mains les fils qui font jouer mes personnages; il connaît les surprises que je leur ménage, et il croit les leur ménager lui-même; bref, je le prends pour collaborateur; il s'imagine qu'il a fait la pièce avec moi, et naturellement il l'applaudit.

He may indeed have done this for the reason he states, but there is also more potential for drama and suspense when the audience knows the secret than when it does not, for then it is constantly aware of what is at stake. Nevertheless, this does not prevent Scribe from springing a few surprises on the audience.

Each scene must make a definite contribution to the development of the action. As could be expected in plays where communication is so important, the combination of characters to be found onstage at a given moment is determined mainly by the potential for the transfer of information. Some bit of information received or imparted, some act or failure to act, some decision or indecision marks every scene. A very important part of the structure of the well-made play is thus determined by the arrangement of the entrances and exits of the characters and the onstage combinations that result. The scenes are usually tightly linked together, as each prepares the next; the author must thus ensure that each succeeding scene has a combination of characters that will permit the action to move forward according to plan. He avoids, however, certain necessary combinations as long as possible or, even more tantalizingly, permits and then interrupts them, before finally satisfying the carefully cultivated desire of the audience to witness the expected outcome. He must also avoid excessive and increasingly hard-to-justify entrances and exists by any of the characters. In Scribe's plays, major characters average at least three scenes per appearance, sometimes more than four—scarcely a frenzied pace. Though there should be two or three characters onstage most of the time in order to control the spread of information properly, more are needed here and there for the sake of variety. Often most or all of the main characters are on stage for the last scene, for the long-awaited revelation of the facts that will make possible the happy ending, or that will give certain characters (and the audience) some anxious moments before the danger of a fatal revelation is dissipated, often by means of the artful lie. At the end of *Le Verre d'eau,* for example, disastrous scandal is averted when Bolingbroke asserts that he has sent Masham to see his wife Abigail in the queen's apartments. In fact Masham is not married and has come to see the queen.

Typically, one character will dominate each act, but the same person does not dominate all the acts in a play. In **Adrienne Lecouvreur,** the dominant characters are, in turn, the princess, Michonnet, Adrienne, the princess, and Adrienne. This domination is indicated by the fact that the character is onstage through most or even all of the scenes of the act, but it is not usually limited to that constant presence. The character may be actively seeking to affect the outcome of the action, or undergoing successive shocks as others act for or against him, or merely looking on as others struggle (as a prelude, of course, to more direct action later on). The act usually ends on a definite shift in the fortunes of a main character and often has as its purpose the preparation of that shift.

One of the most obvious areas of structural variation is in the number, length, importance, and relationship to the main plot of the sub-plots. Most plays have at least one sub-plot, and there may be as many as seven, usually quite solidly linked to the main plot. In **Le Verre d'eau,** for example, the love-plot of Masham and Abigail and the plot of Bolingbroke to return to power become interdependent as the three characters work together to obtain their several ends. In other plays, the sub-plot is more parallel than dependent (in **Les Trois Maupin** the rise of Henri in society and in the military, due to the protection of amorous ladies at court, is independent of his sister's rise to fortune while masquerading as a famous singer, also at Versailles, though their contemporaneous presence there does lead to some exciting complications in the action). The importance of the sub-plot varies from negligible to virtual equality with the main plot. Even though the plots generally stretch from the first act to the last, they can start anywhere and end anywhere. They do have to end, for a stable situation must be established before the final curtain; a "lady or the tiger?" ending is not permitted in a well-made play.

The dénouement must first of all be swift, often taking place in the last scene. There are several ways of bringing about the final reversal; by whatever means, it usually comes at the moment when all hope seems lost, when a solution seems either impossible or too late to prevent the catastrophe. The reversal must be unpredictable, and much of the art of the well-made play lies in the preparation of its elements in such a way that the audience will not be able to put them together before the right moment, but will quickly recognize the logic of the solution once it is presented to them.

While this summary of general tendencies, common practices, and even a few rules offers a kind of *portrait robot* of Scribe's plays, the many exceptions and variations emphasize their irreducibility, and the aesthetic choices implied by the characteristics cited indicate that the well-made play as developed by Scribe is as much a philosophy as it is a form. As Ferdinand Brunetière pointed out, Scribe practices the theatrical equivalent of "l'art pour l'art," treating the theater as the Parnassians treated poetry. Unlike them, however, a primary principle of his philosophy is a concern for pleasing his audience, which he saw as the general public, not an elite.

In the speech he delivered at his reception into the Académie Française, Scribe expressed a part of that philosophy:

> Vous courez au théâtre, non pour vous instruire ou vous corriger, mais pour vous distraire et vous divertir. Or, ce qui vous divertit le mieux, ce n'est pas la vérité, c'est la fiction. Vous retracer ce que vous avez chaque jour sous les yeux n'est pas le moyen de vous plaire: mais ce qui ne se présente point à vous dans la vie habituelle, l'extraordinaire, le romanesque, voilà ce qui vous charme, c'est là ce qu'on s'empresse de vous offrir.

Scribe's own plays show that this statement cannot be accepted literally, but with minor emendations it can be made to fit them with reasonable accuracy. It is apparent that he sought above all to entertain rather than to instruct or to correct his audience, which explains in large part the reaction against him by Dumas *fils* and the other writers of the *pièce à thèse*. Though there is a lesson in most of his plays, it is treated lightly and with good humor (*La Calomnie* is the exception among plays labeled "comédie"), so that the spectator has no sense of being preached to. There are also no lessons that his audience would not agree with, at least when applied to someone else. The primacy of entertainment is the root of Scribe's philosophy of the theater, from which grow the principles that he observed almost without exception. He himself indicated some of these principles in his preface to the *Théâtre de J.-F. Bayard:*

> C'était la gaieté, la verve, la rapidité, l'entrain dramatique! L'action une fois engagée ne languissait pas! Le spectateur, entraîné et pour ainsi dire emporté par ce mouvement de la scène, arrivait joyeusement et comme en chemin de fer, au but indiqué par l'auteur, sans qu'il lui fût permis de s'arrêter pour réfléchir ou pour critiquer. . . .

> Le faux et le larmoyant sont faciles; c'est avec cela que l'on fabrique du drame! voilà pourquoi nous en voyons tant! La vérité et la gaieté sont choses rares! La comédie en est faite! voilà pourquoi nous en voyons si peu!

> Peu d'auteurs ont possédé à un degré aussi élevé que lui, l'entente du théâtre, la connaissance de la scène et toutes les ressources de l'art dramatique! Sujet présenté et développé avec adresse, action serrée et rapide, péripéties soudaines, obstacles créés et franchis avec bonheur, dénoûment inattendu, quoique savam-ment préparé, tout ce que l'expérience et l'étude peuvent donner venait en aide chez lui à ce qui vient de Dieu seul et de la nature, l'inspiration, l'esprit, la verve et cette qualité la plus rare de toutes au théâtre: l'imagination, qui invente sans cesse du nouveau ou qui crée encore, même en imitant.

Scribe was talking about Bayard, but the qualities he picks out and the values he reveals in expressing them represent as much a portrait of himself as a description of his colleague and collaborator. The first paragraph expresses the

goal; the last indicates the means. Both are exemplified by Scribe's plays.

The reference to truth apparently contradicts the insistence on fiction in the passage cited earlier, but a careful reading of his plays clearly reveals that it is a certain combination of truth and fiction that is intended. Scribe's concept of truth is related to audience acceptance, or plausibility, a concern of most playwrights, but a special problem for Scribe, with his emphasis on the fictional, the extraordinary, and thus upon plot and the maintenance of suspense. This required characters that the audience can identify with and care about and, even more important, a basic situation and events that develop it and that are interesting. This means that they must be uncommon, for as Scribe pointed out in the passage quoted above, what one sees every day is not entertaining; but at the same time they must not be impossible, for then the spectator ceases to believe and loses interest. The same result follows a too-great consciousness of the fact that the playwright is in complete control, which can be caused by events that are too predictable or too capricious. The response to the danger of predictability leads Pierre Voltz to begin his definition of the "pièce bien faite" by calling it "une pièce où la part du hasard reste grande, puisque les événements passent au premier plan et doivent faire naître l'intérêt par leur imprévu" [*La Comédie* (1964)]. The other extreme is avoided by the careful preparation that precedes the coincidences and other apparent interventions of chance, so that the audience accepts them as perfectly justified or even natural. Indeed it could be argued that the primary and most consistent characteristic of the well-made play is the thoroughness with which every action, every event, even every entrance and exit is prepared, explained, justified.

Another part of the solution is to imbue the fictions with an aura of reality, a process that leads Scribe to introduce a new degree of realism in the theater, and some critics, at least, have seen a definite resemblance between the world he portrays and contemporary France. Stendhal praises him for being "le seul homme à le ce siècle qui ait eu l'audace de peindre, en esquisse il est vrai, les mœurs qu'il rencontre dans le monde" [*Mémoires d'un touriste*]. The characters, the setting, the problems are all taken (except in his historical plays, and some would say even in them) from the society of his time. It is only the plot and certain situations that are manifestly fictional, and it is only there that one finds any substantial amount of "l'extraordinaire, le romanesque" of which Scribe spoke. Real life is not quite so full of happy endings, of coincidences, of elections—as Stendhal noted in the sequence of the passage quoted above—that are made in twenty-four hours, and not quite so many millions belong to unattached heiresses or handsome young men. The structure of Scribe's plays is thus totally artificial—while it may be flexible to fit the individual situation, it is still a kind of abstraction, imposed from the outset and designed to meet dramatic needs rather than to duplicate "real life." To hide this artificial skeleton, in addition to the measures described above and generally the suspense-building devices of which he makes such skillful use, he fleshes out his plays with many details chosen from reality; hence, the use of contemporary manners, life-style, and surroundings and the presence and especially the manipulation of an abundance of stage properties, which are, to all appearances, real, and whose significance in the action and variety of uses represent an important innovation in stagecraft. Even his much-criticized style, by corresponding closely to the actual spoken language of the day, is part of the reality he transfers to the stage to help maintain the plausibility of his plots and thus to permit him to hold the interest of the spectator.

To hold the interest of the spectator requires, of course, more than plausibility, and the study of Scribe's statements and plays shows us how he chose to go about it. He offered his audience involvement and excitement while they were in the theater and a sense of satisfaction to savor on the way home. Since audiences always love romance, every play has a love interest. Sometimes it is primary, but often it supports, by eliciting greater audience sympathy and involvement, a main plot that carries a social or moral message, or even, in a few plays, political commentary (*Bertrand et Raton, L'Ambitieux*). He avoided ideas, events, or characters that would shock or displease and sought those with which the audience could most easily identify. In part because of that identification and also perhaps due to an innate gentleness and "gaieté," the comic elements in his plays arise from situation or language rather than from serious character flaws or farcical action. He enlivened his plays with a wide variety of characters, with amusing as well as admirable traits, but seldom is a character subject to ridicule. There are few real villains, and punishments for misdeeds are seldom cruel. The problems are real, or at least realistic, but the solutions are simpler than in real life, less painful, for the purpose is to distract the spectator from his problems, not to force him to confront them. The plot takes precedence over the message, and also over character development, a choice deplored by critics but apparently not regretted by audiences. Scribe kept them concentrating on the action, wondering how the play would end and how it would get there. He appreciated the visual as well as the verbal nature of drama, as can be seen in his emphasis on sets, on movements and stage business, and especially on the multiplicity of stage properties. His expositions are thorough, so that the action will be easy to follow and the motivations of the characters clear. He made the audience privy to most of the secrets, so that they would have a feeling of complicity with the author, but reserved some ingenious surprises, to avoid the boredom that would result from excessive predictability. The final surprise, of course, is the manner of producing the reversal that precipitates the dénouement that, in addition to being logical and credible, is complete, with no loose ends left dangling. It is also the ending the audience has come to desire, including the achievements of justice and the marriage of the two—or four—most sympathetic young people (exceptions: *Adrienne Lecouvreur* and the atypical melodrama *Les Frères invisibles,* which end in murder and suicide, respectively). Coincidences are frequent—often to simplify and expedite the development of the plot—but plausibly justified. Scribe scrupulously, even ruthlessly, eliminated non-essentials so that nothing slows down the action or diverts attention from it and exploited fully the dramatic potential of each situation and action. This extreme dramatic efficiency results in

the use of the fewest possible characters: in a complex plot, they will often play multiple roles. Masham, for example, is the lover of Abigail, the object of the rivalry between the queen and the duchess, and the killer (in a duel) of Bolingbroke's cousin (*Le Verre d'eau*).

If these principles seem familiar—and they should—that is a measure of Scribe's success through the years, for they do not permit us to distinguish him from many of his successors, but they do differentiate him from his predecessors; though some followed a few of these principles, none adopted them all, and the new combination reveals his originality, as does his ability to use appropriately and imaginatively all the techniques, all the tricks and devices available to the playwright, impressive in their variety and their complexity. Attempts to reduce them to common factors only serve to emphasize this, as can be seen in the case of Michael Kaufmann, whose long list of devices, situations, and actions that are repeated in Scribe's plays includes scarcely any items repeated more than a few times [*Zur Technik der Komödien von Eugène Scribe* (1911)]; and when one looks at the examples listed and at their contexts, it becomes apparent that the general circumstances, the significance, the importance, the types of characters involved, and often even the effect are so different that the various instances can be said to be repetitions only in the most superficial sense. Thus in the end Kaufmann brings new evidence of Scribe's ability to renew constantly the means at his disposal. He did not invent new ones, but as Gustave Larroumet said, "dès ses premières pièces, la façon dont le sujet est conçu, développé, conduit au dénouement, dénote un inventeur, et à un tel degré, que cette invention est du génie" ["Le Centenaire de Scribe," Preface to *Les Annales du Théâtre et de la musique, 17e année,* edited by Edouard Noël and Edmond Stoulling (1891)]. His philosophy of the theater led him to choose a form that was "dénué de poésie, de lyrisme, . . . de naturel," precisely because it resulted in a greater degree "de vérité, de naturel," according to his own definition and, apparently, that of his audience. It is not the mechanical application of a formula, but the deliberate choice of the elemental aspects of drama, developed with unusual imagination and skill, and a finely-honed sense of how to involve and satisfy an audience that constitute the well-made play of Eugène Scribe.

FURTHER READING

Arvin, Neil C. "The Technique of Scribe's *Comédies-Vaudevilles.*" *Modern Philology* XVI, No. 3 (July 1918): 47-53.

> Asserts that "Scribe was the greatest technician in the history of the French drama and . . . all the dramatists of the nineteenth century who aimed at constructive excellence profit, consciously or unconsciously, from the new models which he gave to dramatic art."

———. "The *Comédie-Vaudeville of Scribe.*" *Sewanee Review* XXVI, No. 4 (October 1918): 474-84.

> While admitting that Scribe's short plays are "devoid of

literary value and written in a mediocre, prosy style," Arvin insists they are historically valuable for the picture they paint of nineteenth-century Parisian society.

———. *Eugène Scribe and the French Theatre, 1815-1869.* Cambridge, Mass.: Harvard University Press, 1924, 268 p.
Seminal study of Scribe's life, career, and milieu.

Koon, Helene and Switzer, Richard. *Eugène Scribe.* Boston: Twayne Publishers, 1980, 174 p.
Biographical and critical survey of the playwright.

Legouvé, Ernest. "Eugène Scribe." In *Papers on Playmaking,* edited by Brander Matthews, pp. 254-74. New York: Hill and Wang, 1957.
Reminiscence and appreciation of Scribe by his collaborator on such plays as *Adrienne Lecouvreur* and *The Ladies' Battle.*

Matthews, Brander. "The Pleasant Land of Scribia." In his *Principles of Playmaking: And Other Discussions of the Drama,* pp. 133-146. New York: Charles Scribner's Sons, 1919.
Characterizes Scribe's accomplishment as a limited one: "He is successful in achieving all that he is ambitious of attaining—the entertainment of the spectators."

———. "Eugène Scribe." In his *French Dramatists of the 19th Century,* pp. 78-104. New York: Charles Scribner's Sons, 1924.
Concedes that Scribe's characters are lifeless but praises the playwright as "the inventor of the comédie-vaudeville, as the improver of grand opera," and as "a play-maker of consummate skill."

Nicoll, Allardyce. "The Coming of Realism." In his *World Drama: From Aeschylus to Anouilh,* pp. 485-518. 1949. Reprint. New York: Harcourt, Brace & World, 1965.
Examination of Scribe's career in the context of French theatrical history.

Pendle, Karin. *Eugène Scribe and French Opera of the Nineteenth Century.* Studies in Musicology, No. 6. 1970. Reprint. Ann Arbor, Mich.: UMI Research Press, 1979, 627 p.
Critical discussion of Scribe's libretti, his collaborators, the theaters for which he wrote, and his influence on the development of both comic and grand opera.

Smith, Hugh Allison. "Scribe and the Well-Made Play." In his *Main Currents of Modern French Drama,* pp. 108-21. New York: Henry Holt and Company, 1925.
General assessment of the merits and faults of Scribe's dramatic technique.

Stanton, Stephen S. "Scribe's *Betrand et Raton*: A Well-Made Play." *Tulane Drama Review* II, No. 1 (November 1957): 58-70.
Detailed examination of the play that seeks to demonstrate that Scribe "did more than any other dramatist to restore to modern theater the classical practice of Molière—to enlighten mankind through the ridicule of human folly."

———, ed. *"Camille" and Other Plays.* New York: Hill and Wang, 1957, 306 p.
Includes translations of *A Peculiar Position* and *The Glass of Water,* as well as an introduction in which Stanton discusses Scribe's development of the well-made play.

———. "Ibsen, Gilbert, and Scribe's *Bataille des Dames.*" *Educational Theatre Journal* XVII, No. 1 (March 1965): 24-30.
Analyzes the influence of Scribe's play on Henrik Ibsen's *Feast at Solhaug* and William Schwenk Gilbert's *Engaged.*

Walkley, A.B. *"Adrienne Lecouvreur."* In his *Drama and Life,* pp. 279-82. London: Methuen & Co., 1907.
Review of a 1905 staging of Scribe and Ernest Legouvé's play, with Sarah Bernhardt in the title role.

Additional coverage of scribe's life and career is contained in the following source published by Gale Research: *Nineteenth-Century Literature Criticism, Vol. 16.*

Lucius Annaeus Seneca
c. 4 B.C.–65 A.D.

INTRODUCTION

An influential and prolific philosopher and playwright, Seneca was a respected man of letters who actively participated in the politics of his time. As a tutor and advisor to the young emperor Nero, Seneca helped to direct Roman political policy between the years 54 and 62, ensuring a greater measure of tolerance and justice in the empire. Critics have praised the prose in Seneca's essays, letters, and treatises as one of the foremost examples of the "pointed," or epigrammatic style of the Silver Age. They have also admired its instructional tone and skillful use of colorful and unusual figures of speech. Seneca's tragedies, alternately extolled for their powerful depictions of extreme circumstances and mental states and censured for their presentation of lurid onstage violence, have had a strong impact on European drama, particularly that of Elizabethan England. Playwrights to the present day have drawn on Seneca's works for elements of characterization, plot, and mood, attesting to his lasting influence.

BIOGRAPHICAL INFORMATION

Seneca was born in what is present-day Cordoba, Spain, the second son of Seneca the Elder, a famous rhetorician and teacher. As a child he was brought to Rome, where he embarked on the study of grammar and rhetoric, eventually turning to the study of philosophy. Following a stay in Egypt with his aunt and uncle—who was the provincial governor—Seneca returned to Rome in 31 to take the post of quaestor (a Roman official chiefly concerned with financial administration). He was eventually admitted to the Roman Senate. Around this time Seneca began to establish what was to become a successful career as an orator and author. It may have been his popularity and professional stature, biographers speculate, that led to his fall into disfavor with the emperor Gaius (Caligula). Subsequently, Caligula's successor Claudius accused Seneca of adultery with Claudius's niece Julia and exiled him to Corsica. When the emperor's wife Agrippina interceded on Seneca's behalf, he was allowed to return to Rome in 49. It was then that he became Nero's tutor and assumed the office of praetor (a judicial post). When Nero rose to power five years later, the inexperienced emperor relied on the guidance of Seneca and the praetorian prefect Burrus. Historians note that although Seneca's influence on Nero was beneficial, he must have followed the emperor's wishes in order to preserve his position at court. Seneca therefore may have been an accomplice to—or at least a party to the coverup of—Nero's murder of Agrippina in 59. With Nero's behavior growing increasingly erratic and dictatorial, and with the death of Burrus, Seneca retired from public life to devote himself to writing. In 65 he was implicated in an unsuccess-

The only known likeness of Seneca, dated c. 240.

ful conspiracy against Nero and was ordered to take his own life. He complied. His final act, judged a heroic one, was recorded by Tacitus in his *Annals*.

MAJOR WORKS

Although a number of Seneca's works have been lost, a good portion of his output has survived, including writings on science, geography, and philosophy, as well as ethical treatises, essays, and epigrams. In his prose works Seneca stresses the importance of life experience, knowledge of natural phenomena, common sense, and tolerance, guiding his reader toward the ideal of a life well lived. His chief poetic works are the nine tragedies written around the period 45 to 55. Eight are based on existing Greek models: *Hercules Furens* (*Mad Hercules*), *Troades* (*The Trojan Women*), *Medea*, and *Phaedra* take after similarly titled plays by Euripides; *Oedipus*, *Phoenissae* (*The Phoenician Women*), and *Hercules Oetaeus* (*Hercules on Oeta*) follow plays by Sophocles; and *Agamemnon* derives from Aeschylus's like-named play. *Thyestes* seems to have no Greek precedent. *The Phoenician Women* survives only in fragments and Seneca's authorship of *Hercules on Oeta* has at times been disputed. A tenth play, *Octavia*, which was formerly attributed to Seneca, is now generally considered the work of some other writer.

Critics have noted that, despite structural similarities, Seneca's dramas differ significantly from their Greek models. The elaborate rhetoric, argumentation, and complex verbal exchanges in Seneca's plays are quite unlike the spare dialogue of Greek tragedy. Moreover, the atmosphere of gloom, disease, insanity, and physical horror that pervades his plays is antithetical to the spirit of Greek drama. Repeatedly in Seneca's plays passion leads to madness, which in turn causes chaos and abnormal occurrences in the natural universe. The verbal, visual, and thematic exaggeration of his tragedies contrasts markedly with Seneca's fundamental Stoic philosophy, and thus serves to warn against the dangers of excessive emotion and to emphasize the theme of fate that is central to tragedy. The extreme verbosity and graphic violence of the plays have led some to question whether they were meant to be performed on stage at all or intended merely for presentation in dramatic readings.

CRITICAL RECEPTION

Reaction to Seneca's work has consistently been mixed. In his own time, the plays were popular among young people who strove to imitate their sophisticated and witty rhetorical style. They were criticized by Caligula, however, and later they were censured by Quintilian, who charged that Seneca had corrupted the writing style of generations of students. Early Christian writers admired his philosophical writings, finding in them similarities to their own beliefs; but St. Augustine perceived a certain hypocrisy inherent in Seneca's role at Nero's court. In the Middle Ages, Seneca's works, along with Cicero's, were essential educational texts. He was studied and quoted by Petrarch, Chaucer, and Dante.

The introduction of Seneca's plays to England—through Thomas Newton's 1581 edition of *Seneca His Tenne Tragedies*—marked an important event in the history of English drama because so many playwrights were to imitate Seneca's style and themes. Thomas Kyd, Christopher Marlowe, Ben Jonson, John Webster, and William Shakespeare all admired Seneca's tragedies and modeled their works on them. Scholars list the plays of Seneca among the most significant influences on Elizabethan tragedy, noting that many stock characters and situations derive from these works. On the European continent, Seneca served as a model for seventeenth-century playwrights Pierre Corneille and Jean Baptiste Racine. Championed in the eighteenth century by Jean Jacques Rousseau and Denis Diderot, Seneca was attacked or ignored in the nineteenth. The noted German critic August Wilhelm Schlegel, for example, faulted Seneca's tragedies for their "display of bombast, which distorts everything great into nonsense."

Twentieth-century commentators have continued these earlier debates. While some have argued that Seneca's works set the standard for Latin Silver Age literature, others have disparaged their rhetorical contrivances and florid style. Increasingly, however, scholars have shown interest in Seneca's handling of characterization, stressing the play-

wright's often subtle psychological insight. Even as his specific contribution to drama has undergone continual re-evaluation, Seneca has throughout the centuries remained an important and powerful influence on playwrights.

PRINCIPAL WORKS

PLAYS*

Hercules Furens (*Mad Hercules*)
Troades (*The Trojan Women*)
Phoenissae (*The Phoenician Women*)
Medea
Phaedra
Oedipus
Agamemnon
Thyestes
Hercules Oetaeus (*Hercules on Oeta*)

OTHER MAJOR WORKS

Apocolocyntosis Divi Claudii (*Pumpkinification of the Divine Claudius*) (satire)
Consolationes (*Consolations*) (essays)
†*Dialogi* (*Dialogues*) (essays)
De Beneficiis (*On Giving and Receiving Favors*) (essays)
Ad Lucillum Epistulae Morales (*Moral Letters*) (essays)
Quaestiones Naturales (*Natural Questions*) (treatise)

*No dates for Seneca's plays are known; all were written between c. 45 and 55 A.D. The ordering here reflects that of the so-called E group, based on the *Codex Etruscus*, the most trustworthy of the surviving ancient manuscripts of Seneca's dramas. Another important grouping, called A, lists the plays as follows: *Hercules Furens, Thyestes, Thebais* [*Phoenissae*], *Hippolytus* [*Phaedra*], *Oedipus, Troas* [*Troades*], *Medea, Agamemnon, Octavia*, and *Hercules Oetaeus*. *Octavia* appears only in A, and, although scholars once considered it a Senecan play, it is now judged to be the work of some other dramatist.

†Contains such pieces as *De Clementia* (*On Mercy*), *De Ira* (*On Anger*), *De Providentia* (*On Providence*), and others.

OVERVIEWS AND GENERAL STUDIES

Clarence Valentine Boyer (essay date 1914)

SOURCE: "Seneca," in *The Villain as Hero in Elizabethan Tragedy*, 1914. Reprint by Russell & Russell, 1964, pp. 13-20.

[*Boyer looks at* Medea *and* Thyestes, *Senecan plays in which the principals are cast as "villain-heroes," and he examines the possible influence of such characterization on Elizabethan drama.*]

The influence of Seneca on Elizabethan drama has been carefully though not exhaustively studied, so that there is general agreement as to the fact, if not the extent of his influence. To Seneca is usually attributed the introduction of the ghost and the chorus, the division of the play into five acts, as well as the introduction of various themes, such as revenge. It is the question of themes and the manner of treating them that concerns us here. All of Seneca's themes are violent and sensational. It is true that with the exception of *Octavia* they are taken from Greek sources, but owing to the manner of treatment they radiate anything but a Greek atmosphere. In the selection of characters, Seneca is faultless. Even Aristotle might be said to approve his choice, for the Greek critic remarks: "The best tragedies are founded on the story of a few houses—on the fortunes of Alcmaeon, Œdipus, Orestes, Meleager, Thyestes, Telephus, and those others who have done or suffered something terrible." But in the general management of his subjects, Seneca makes many of these tragedies not terrible, but shocking, horrible, revolting; hence they do not produce tragic pleasure. Revenge is, indeed, the impelling force which drives many of Seneca's characters to their monstrous deeds; but revenge is not, as some critics maintain, always represented by him as a sacred duty, as it came to be later on in Elizabethan drama, in the *Hamlet* type of play, for instance. It may be the death of a relative for which vengeance is sought, and the revenge may be associated with some supernatural force, as e.g. the ghost. But the ghost, in ***Thyestes*** at any rate, does not appear to urge Atreus to revenge as a sacred duty; on the contrary, it urges him to revenge that both he and Thyestes may suffer for their wickedness and that of their ancestors. The revenge itself is represented as sinful; it is undertaken for personal injuries, and is born of malice rather than of duty.

In thus representing faithlessness, cruelty, murder, revenge, and lust as governing the hearts and minds of men in high places—even in his appeal to magic and the supernatural—Seneca offered themes both familiar and pleasing to the audiences of the Elizabethan theatre. At the same time Seneca stood for antiquity, and his name, technic, and moralizing passages exerted a paramount influence with the classicists. Now among the plays of this authoritative and highly appreciated dramatist we find two that clearly suggest the villain-hero type, viz. *Medea* and *Thyestes*. Considering the remarkable influence of Seneca upon the Elizabethan drama in general, it would not be at all surprising if his influence extended to the shaping of the villain-hero type in particular.

Seneca follows Euripides in making Medea a villain as well as the heroine, but in the process he transforms her into a monster. In the first part of the Greek play, all our sympathy is awakened for Medea. We despise Jason. It is not until the heroine contemplates revenge that our sympathy is in the least abated. We could almost forgive her for an open murder of her enemies. When she contemplates the murder of her children, however, she begins to appear monstrous; but this feeling again merges into pity when we see how she suffers at the thought of losing them. Moreover, Euripides seeks to lessen the horror of the deed by laying stress upon the fact that Medea is killing her children to keep them from being killed by her enemies. But when she actually murders them, and triumphs in the car above Jason's head,

rejoicing in her victory over him, and showing no signs of mother-pity, our aversion once more masters us. Nevertheless, the feeling that we carry away from a perusal of the play is one of mingled pity and aversion in which the former is fully as powerful as the latter.

In Seneca's tragedy the effect is quite different. Medea herself opens the play with a blood-curdling soliloquy, calling upon the powers above and below to damn for ever Jason, Creon, and Creüsa:

> . . . and ye
> Whose aid Medea may more boldly claim, thou
>   world
> Of endless night, th' antipodes of heavenly realms,
> Ye damned ghosts, thou lord of hades' dark domain,
> Whose mistress was with trustier pledge won to thy
>   side—
> Before ye all this baleful prayer I bring: Be near!
> Be near! Ye crime-avenging furies, come and loose
> Your horrid locks with serpent coils entwined, and
>   grasp
> With bloody hands the smoking torch; be near as
>   once
> Ye stood in dread array beside my wedding couch.
> Upon this new-made bride destruction send, and
>   death
> Upon the king and all the royal line! But he,
> My husband, may he live to meet some heavier
>   doom;
> This curse I imprecate upon his head; . . .

This dire curse at once alienates sympathy. We get the impression that Medea is an evil woman, and this impression becomes fixed, for the act is closed by the chorus immediately following this soliloquy. Medea does not tell of her own wrongs until Act II; and when she there enumerates the crimes she has been guilty of for Jason's sake, the cruelty of the deeds swallows up the reason for them. In Act III, in a conference with Jason, she learns that he loves his children, but she only makes use of this discovery to inflict brutal punishment. In Euripides, her children are to be banished, and she seeks to have them protected. In Seneca, the children are safe in the father's hands, which makes her slaughter of them the more revolting. In the fourth act she appears chanting horrible incantations, and herself steeps the bridal gifts in the brew that is to make them fatal. Finally, in the fifth act, she slays her children before the audience, and exults in the suffering of Jason. Her own hesitation over killing the children is scarcely touched as a motive. The result is that she becomes an extremely unsympathetic protagonist. The effect of the combination of villain and protagonist is disappointing; the emotions called forth are as untragic as Aristotle predicted.

In the tragedy of ***Thyestes*** the murderer Atreus appears as the villain. The mere fact that he is a murderer, however, does not make him a villain. We must remember that the wilfulness of the act is as important as the act itself. With the exception of Medea, none of the classical criminals seems to be acting altogether voluntarily. Thyestes suffers because he is the son of a doomed house; and even Atreus is inspired by the Ghost of Tantalus, who in turn is driven on by the Fury to do his allotted part. But in the case of Atreus this motive is lost sight of in his horrible cruelty and exultation in torture. He is one of the most monstrous creations in dramatic literature. As he prepares his brother's children as a feast for the parent, and glories in his wickedness, he is actually loathsome. With him we may fairly say it is crime for crime's sake.

> ATREUS. . . . 'Tis sweet to note
> The father's frantic grief when first he sees
> His children's gory heads; to catch his words,
> To watch his colour change; to see him sit,
> All breathless with the shock, in dumb amaze,
> In frozen horror at the gruesome sight.
> This is the sweet reward of all my toil—
> To see his misery, e'en as it grows
> Upon his soul.

Atreus is, in fact, the paragon of villains; the question is whether he is also the hero. The play is named after Thyestes, and, according to the Greek conception of the gods punishing evil from generation to generation until the original sin had been balanced by the punishment, the fate Thyestes meets with in this tragedy for the sins of his ancestors would doubtless have made him the protagonist in the estimation of a Greek audience. For Thyestes and Atreus were the sons of Pelops who was served as a dish to the gods by his father Tantalus; and from Atreus sprang Agamemnon who was killed by his wife. This whole family was so submerged in crime, and was so well known to the Greeks, that the tragic end of any one of them would have made that one the protagonist in their eyes. It is to be said also for Seneca's tragedy that the audience is informed by narration of the evil deeds committed in the past by Thyestes against his brother. But Thyestes is repentant, and has already suffered for his past sins by poverty and banishment when he is introduced to us. Consequently we are inclined to sympathize with him. When Tantalus and the Fury have retired after a prologue called Act I, Atreus appears in soliloquy and at once becomes the centre of interest. We hope that his scheme to entice his brother back will not be successful; we are most interested in him from beginning to end, because we wish him to fail in everything which he attempts; we are so filled with loathing and hatred for him that we have little or no feeling, not even of pity, left for anyone else. It is not the effect of his machinations upon Thyestes as a hero with whom we are in sympathy that is the centre of interest, but his own frightful crimes, his colossal wickedness, his conflict with moral law. Moreover, he has the chief acting part and speaks the greatest number of lines, so that he may reasonably be classed as the hero according to our definition.

Unless the Elizabethans were thoroughly familiar with Greek legendary history and the Greek idea of retribution, as well as with the classic method of presenting merely the culmination of an action, they must have been much impressed by the preponderating part played by the criminals. Consider for a moment the startling nature of the Senecan themes:

Œdipus is guilty of incest, and gouges out his own eyes; Clytemnestra commits adultery, and murders her husband; Medea slaughters her own children, and hurls them down to her husband from the housetop; Atreus makes his brother drunk at a banquet, and serves him the flesh of his own children!

Considered in the bald outline, could any facts be more gruesome? And yet these plays were constantly read by the Elizabethan poets, and were regarded as the best examples of dramatic art. Violence and murder were before them as model themes for imitation, and in at least two of Seneca's plays the protagonists were themselves villains. Having the sanction of classicism, and appealing to the imagination of that era, these tragedies undoubtedly exercised some influence in directing the Elizabethan playwright's choice and handling of theme, so that Seneca, if he did not furnish the actual models, may be said at least to have suggested the plot with the villain as hero.

The Elizabethans, however, must be credited with one distinct advance. The tragedy of *Thyestes* does not end unhappily for Atreus: he is successful in his designs and suffers no punishment. The same is true of Medea. Of course, the fact that the plays open only with the last phase of an action, and that those who do meet with misfortune are suffering because of their own past or the deeds of their ancestors, and likewise the fact that he who triumphs now will suffer in the play to follow, makes it excusable for the villain to succeed; but the effect, nevertheless, upon the reader at the close of one of these tragedies is anything but pleasing; it is distressing. Successful villainy adds shock to the horror of the crimes. If these plays served in any way as models for the Elizabethans, the reversal of fortune at the end for the villain-hero was their own addition. In presenting the whole of an action, though they were not squeamish in the actions they imitated, they recognized that a spectator demands at least some satisfaction for his moral sense if he cannot be elevated, and they consequently saw to it that the villain perished for his crimes before the curtain fell, though they had to strain a point to kill him.

T. S. Eliot (essay date 1927)

SOURCE: "Seneca in Elizabethan Translation," in *Selected Essays,* Harcourt, Brace Jovanovich, Inc., 1950, pp. 51-88.

[*Perhaps the most influential poet and critic to write in the English language during the first half of the twentieth century, Eliot is closely identified with many of the qualities denoted by the term Modernism: experimentation, formal complexity, artistic and intellectual eclecticism, and a classicist's view of the artist working at an emotional distance from his or her creation. The following essay was originally published in 1927 as an introduction to the Tudor Translation Series edition of Thomas Newton's 1581 rendering of Seneca's plays, entitled* Tenne Tragedies. *Eliot focuses on Seneca's effect on the development of the Elizabethan Tragedy of Blood, his impact on the dramatic language of the period, and his influence on the intellectual ideas contained in the plays of William Shakespeare, Ben Jonson, Thomas Kyd, and others.*]

The influence of Seneca upon Elizabethan drama has received much more attention from scholars than from literary critics. The historical treatment has been very thorough. The admirable edition of the works of Sir William Alexander, Earl of Stirling, by Kastner and Charlton (1921), has a full account of this influence both direct and through Italy and France; in this introduction also will be found the best bibliography of the subject. Dr. F. S. Boas, especially in his edition of Kyd's Plays, has treated the matter at length. Professor J. W. Cunliffe's *Influence of Seneca on Elizabethan Tragedy* (1893) remains, within its limits, the most useful of all books, and Mr. Cunliffe has handled the question in a more general way in his *Early English Classical Tragedies*. Indirect Senecan influences have also been studied in detail, as in Professor A. M. Witherspoon's *Influence of Robert Garnier on Elizabethan Drama*. And work which is now being done on the earlier drama (see Dr. A. W. Reed's recent *Early Tudor Drama*, 1926) will enable us to understand better the junction of the Senecan influence with the native tradition. It is not fitting that a literary critic should retrace all this labour of scholarship, where either his dissent or his approval would be an impertinence; but we may benefit by this scholarship to draw certain general conclusions.

The plays of Seneca exerted their influence in several ways and to several results. The results are of three main types: (1) the popular Elizabethan tragedy; (2) the "Senecal" drama, pseudo-classical, composed by and for a small and select body of persons not closely in touch or in sympathy with the popular drama of the day, and composed largely in protest against the defects and monstrosities of that drama; (3) the two Roman tragedies of Ben Jonson, which appear to belong between the two opposed classes, to constitute an attempt, by an active practising playwright, to improve the form of popular drama by the example of Seneca; not by slavish imitation but by adaptation, to make of popular drama a finished work of art. As for the ways in which Seneca influenced the Elizabethans, it must be remembered that these were never simple, and became more complicated. The Italian and the French drama of the day was already penetrated by Seneca. Seneca was a regular part of the school curriculum, while Greek drama was unknown to all but a few great scholars. Every schoolboy with a smattering of Latin had a verse or two of Seneca in his memory; probably a good part of the audiences could recognise the origin of the occasional bits of Seneca which are quoted in Latin in some of the popular plays (*e.g.* several times by Marston). And by the time that *The Spanish Tragedy* and the old *Hamlet* had made their success, the English playwright was under the influence of Seneca by being under the influence of his own predecessors. Here the influence of Kyd is of the greatest importance: if Senecan Kyd had such a vogue, that was surely the path to facile success for any hard-working and underpaid writer.

All that I wish to do is to consider certain misconceptions of the Senecan influence, which I believe are still current in our opinions of Elizabethan drama, although they do not appear in works of scholarship. For such a purpose the contemporary translations possess a particular value: whether they greatly affected the conception of Seneca, or greatly extended his influence, they give a reflection of the appearance of Seneca to the Englishman of the time. I do not suggest that the influence of Seneca has been exaggerated or diminished in modern criticism; but I believe that too much importance has been attached to his influence in some directions, and too little to his influence in others. There is one point on which every one is agreed, and hardly more than one: the five-act division of the modern European play is due to Seneca. What I chiefly wish to consider are, first, his responsibility for what has been called since Symonds' day the Tragedy of Blood—how far Seneca is the author of the horrors which disfigure Elizabethan drama; second, his responsibility for *bombast* in Elizabethan diction; and third, his influence upon the *thought,* or what passes for thought, in the drama of Shakespeare and his contemporaries. It is the first which I think has been overestimated, the second misconstrued, the third undervalued.

Certainly, among all national dramas, the Elizabethan tragedies are remarkable for the extent to which they employ the horrible and revolting. It is true that but for this taste and practice we should never have had *King Lear* or *The Duchess of Malfy;* so impossible is it to isolate the vices from the virtues, the failures from the masterpieces of Elizabethan tragedy. We cannot reprehend a custom but for which one great experiment of the human spirit must have been left unmade, even if we cannot like it; nor can we wholly deplore anything which brings with it some information about the soul. And even leaving Shakespeare apart, the genius of no other race could have manipulated the tragedy of horror into the magnificent farce of Marlowe, or the magnificent nightmare of Webster. We must therefore reserve two measures of comparison: one, that between the baser tragedy of the time and the best tragedy of the time, the other (which is perhaps a moral measure, the application of which would lead us too far for the present discussion) between the tragedy of the time as a whole and another tragedy of horror—we think of Dante's Ugolino and the Oedipus of Sophocles—in which, in the end, the mind seems to triumph. Here, the question of Seneca's influence is capital. If the taste for horror was a result of being trained on Seneca, then it has neither justification nor interest; if it was something inherent in the people and in the age, and Seneca merely the excuse and precedent, then it is a phenomenon of interest. Even to speak of Seneca as offering a precedent and excuse is probably to falsify; for it implies that the Elizabethans would otherwise have been a little uneasy in conscience at indulging such tastes—which is ridiculous to suppose. They merely assumed that Seneca's taste was like their own—which is not *wholly* untrue; and that Seneca represented the whole of classical antiquity—which is quite false. Where Seneca took part is in affecting the type of plot; he supported one tendency against another. But for Seneca, we might have had more plays in *The Yorkshire Tragedy* mould; that is to say, the equivalent of the *News of the World* murder report; Seneca, and particularly the Italianised Seneca, encouraged the taste for the foreign, remote, or exotic. No doubt *The Jew of Malta* or *Titus Andronicus* would have made the living Seneca shudder with genuine aesthetic horror; but his influence helped to recommend work with which he had little in common.

When we examine the plays of Seneca, the actual horrors are not so heinous or so many as are supposed. The most unpleasantly sanguinary is the *Thyestes,* a subject which, so far as I know, was not attempted by a Greek dramatist. Even here, if the view that the tragedies were intended only for recitation is true, the cultivated Roman audience were listening to a story which was part of their Hellenic culture, and which is in fact a common property of folklore. The story was sanctified by time. The plots of Elizabethan tragedy were, so far as the audience were concerned, novelties. This plot of *Thyestes* is not employed by any Elizabethan, but the play has undoubtedly more in common with the Tragedy of Blood, especially in its early form, than any other of Seneca's. It has a particularly tedious Ghost. It has, more emphatically than any other, the motive of Revenge, unregulated by any divine control or justice. Yet even in the *Thyestes* the performance of the horrors is managed with conventional tact; the only visible horror is the perhaps unavoidable presentation of the evidence—the children's heads in a dish.

The most significant popular play under Senecan influence is of course *The Spanish Tragedy,* and the further responsibility of Kyd for the translation of the pseudo-Senecan *Cornelia* of Garnier has marked him as the disciple of Seneca. But in *The Spanish Tragedy* there is another element, not always sufficiently distinguished from the Senecan, which (though it may have relations among the Italian Renaissance progeny of Seneca) allies it to something more indigenous. The Senecan apparatus, it is true, is impressive. The Ghost, and Revenge, who replace the Tantalus and the Fury of the *Thyestes,* use all the infernal allusions—Acheron, Charon, and the rest—so dear to Seneca. Temporary insanity is an expedient well known to Seneca. But in the type of plot there is nothing classical or pseudo-classical at all. "Plot" in the sense in which we find plot in *The Spanish Tragedy* does not exist for Seneca. He took a story perfectly well known to everybody, and interested his auditors entirely by his embellishments of description and narrative and by smartness and pungency of dialogue; suspense and surprise attached solely to verbal effects. *The Spanish Tragedy,* like the series of Hamlet plays, including Shakespeare's, has an affinity to our contemporary detective drama. The plot of Hieronymo to compass his revenge by the play allies it with a small but interesting class of drama which certainly owes nothing essential to Seneca: that which includes *Arden of Feversham* and *The Yorkshire Tragedy.* These two remarkable plays are both based on contemporary or recent crimes committed in England. Unless it be the hint of divine retribution in the epilogue to *Arden,* there is no token of foreign or classical influence in these two plays. Yet they are bloody enough. The husband in *The Yorkshire Tragedy* kills his two young sons, throws the servant downstairs and breaks her neck, and nearly succeeds in killing his wife. In *Arden of Feversham* the wife and her conspirators stab the husband to death upon the stage—the rest of the play being occupied by a primitive but effective police inquiry. It is only surprising that there are not more examples of this type of play, since there is evidence of as lively a public

interest in police court horrors as there is today. One of the pieces of evidence is associated with Kyd; it is a curious little account of a poisoning case, *The Murder of John Brewen.* (A little later, Dekker was to supply the deficiency of penny journalism with his Plague Pamphlets.) In Kyd, whether *Arden* be by him or by an imitator, we find the union of Senecan with native elements, to the advantage of both. For the Senecan influence is felt in the structure of the play—the structure of *The Spanish Tragedy* is more dramatic than that of *Arden* or *The Yorkshire Tragedy;* whilst the material of *The Spanish Tragedy,* like that of the other two plays, is quite different from the Senecan material, and much more satisfying to an unlettered audience.

The worst that can be urged against Seneca, in the matter of responsibility for what is disgusting in Elizabethan drama, is that he may have provided the dramatist with a pretext or justification for horrors which were not Senecan at all, for which there was certainly a taste, and the taste for which would certainly have been gratified at that time whether Seneca had ever written or not. Against my use of *The Yorkshire Tragedy,* it may be said that this play (the crime in question was committed only in 1603) and *Arden* also were written after the success of *The Spanish Tragedy,* and that the taste for horrors developed only after it had received Senecan licence. I cannot *prove* the contrary. But it must be admitted that the greater number of the horrors are such as Seneca himself would not have tolerated. In one of the worst offenders—indeed one of the stupidest and most uninspired plays ever written, a play in which it is incredible that Shakespeare had any hand at all, a play in which the best passages would be too highly honoured by the signature of Peele—in *Titus Andronicus*—there is nothing really Senecan at all. There is a wantonness, an irrelevance, about the crimes of which Seneca would never have been guilty. Seneca's Oedipus has the traditional justification for blinding himself; and the blinding itself is far less offensive than that in *Lear.* In *Titus,* the hero cuts off his own hand in view of the audience, who can also testify to the mutilation of the hands and the tongue of Lavinia. In *The Spanish Tragedy,* Hieronymo bites off his own tongue. There is nothing like this in Seneca.

But if this is very unlike Seneca, it is very like the contemporary drama of Italy. Nothing could better illustrate the accidental character of literary "influence"—accidental, that is, with reference to the work exercising the influence—than the difference between Senecan drama in Italy and in France. The French drama is from the beginning restrained and decorous; to the French drama, especially to Garnier, the Senecan drama of Greville, Daniel and Alexander is allied. The Italian is bloodthirsty in the extreme. Kyd knew both; but it was to the Italian that he and Peele yielded themselves with sympathetic delight. We must remember, too, that Italy had developed stagecraft and stage machinery to the highest point—for the most sumptuous masques in England, Italian managers, engineers and artists were brought over; that the plastic arts were much more important in Italy than elsewhere, and that consequently the spectacular and sensational elements of drama were insisted upon; that Italian civilisation had, in short, everything to dazzle the imagination of unsophisticated northerners emerging into a period of prosperity and luxury. I have no first-hand acquaintance with Italian plays of this epoch; it is a library which few readers would penetrate in pursuit of pleasure; but its character and influence in England are well attested. It is possible to say that Seneca hardly influenced this Italian drama at all; he was made use of by it and adopted into it; and for Kyd and Peele he was thoroughly Italianised.

The Tragedy of Blood is very little Senecan, in short, though it made much use of Senecan machinery; it is very largely Italian; and it added an ingenuity of plot which is native.

If we wished to find the reason for the sanguinary character of much Elizabethan drama—which persists to its end—we should have to allow ourselves some daring generalisations concerning the temper of the epoch. When we consider it, and reflect how much more refined, how much more *classical* in the profounder sense, is that earlier popular drama which reached its highest point in *Everyman,* I cannot but think that the change is due to some fundamental release of restraint. The tastes gratified are always latent: they were then gratified by the drama, as they are now gratified by crime reports in the daily press. It is no more reasonable to make Seneca responsible for this aspect of Elizabethan drama than it is to connect Aeschylus or Sophocles with *Jude the Obscure.* I am not sure that the latter association has not been made, though no one supposes that Hardy prepared himself by close application to the study of Greek drama.

It is pertinent to inquire, in this context, what was the influence of Seneca, in the way of horrors, upon the small body of "Senecal" dramatists who professedly imitated him. But this collation is relevant also to the question of Seneca's influence upon language; so that before making the comparison we may consider this latter question next. Here, the great influence of Seneca is unquestionable. Quotation after quotation, parallel after parallel, may be adduced; the most conspicuous are given in Cunliffe's *Influence of Seneca,* others in Lucas's *Seneca and Elizabethan Tragedy.* So great is this influence that we can say neither that it was good nor that it was bad; for we cannot imagine what Elizabethan dramatic verse would have been without it. The direct influence is restricted to the group of Marlowe and to Marston; Jonson and Chapman are, each in his own way, more sophisticated and independent; the later or Jacobean dramatists, Middleton, Webster, Tourneur, Ford, Beaumont and Fletcher, found their language upon their own predecessors, and chiefly upon Shakespeare. But none of these authors hesitated to draw upon Seneca when occasion served, and Chapman owes much, both good and bad, of his dramatic style to his admiration for Seneca. No better examples can be found, however, of plays which, while not Senecan in form, are yet deeply influenced by Seneca in language, than the *True Tragedy of Richard Duke of York,* and the Shakespearean *Richard II* and *Richard III.* These, with the work of Kyd and that of Marlowe and of Peele, and several of the plays included in the Shakespeare Apocrypha, have a great deal in common.

The precise pilferings and paraphrases have been thorough-ly catalogued by the scholars I have mentioned, and others; hardly a dramatist, between Kyd and Massinger, is not many times indebted to Seneca. Instead of repeating this labour, I prefer to call attention to his universal influence. Not only the evolution of the dramatic structure, but the evolution of the blank verse cadence, took place under the shadow of Seneca; it is hardly too much to say that Shakespeare could not have formed the verse instrument which he left to his successors, Webster, Massinger, Tourneur, Ford, and Fletcher, unless he had received an instrument already highly developed by the genius of Marlowe and the influence of Seneca. Blank verse before 1600, or thereabouts, is a crude form of music compared to blank verse after that date; but its progress in fifteen years had been astonishing. In the first place, I believe that the establishment of blank verse as the vehicle of drama, instead of the old fourteener, or the heroic couplet, or (what might have happened) a particular form of prose rhythm, received considerable support from its being obviously the nearest equivalent to the solemnity and weight of the Senecan iambic. A comparison of the trotting metre of our translations with Surrey's translation of Virgil will show, I think, that while the former has undeniable poetic charms of its own, the latter would reveal more resources to the ear of the dramatist. The pre-Marlowe versification is competent, but extremely monotonous; it is literally a *monotone,* containing none of the musical counter-rhythms which Marlowe introduced, nor the rhythms of individual speech which were later added.

> When this eternal substance of my soul
> Did live imprison'd in my wanton flesh,
> Each in their function serving other's need,
> I was a courtier in the Spanish court:
>   (Prologue, *Spanish Tragedy*)

But to illustrate the early use of this metre under Senecan influence, a worse play serves our purpose better; the Senecan content justifies our quoting at some length from *Locrine,* an early play of no merit whatever. Here is the Revival of Learning in the brain of a fourth-rate playwright:

> HUMBER. Where may I find some desert wilderness,
> Where I may breathe out curses as I would,
> And scare the earth with my condemning voice;
> Where every echo's repercussion
> May help me to bewail mine overthrow,
> And aid me in my sorrowful laments?
> Where may I find some hollow uncouth rock,
> Where I may damn, condemn, and ban my fill
> The heavens, the hell, the earth, the air, the fire,
> And utter curses to the concave sky,
> Which may infect the airy regions,
> And light upon the Brittain Locrine's head?
> You ugly sprites that in Cocytus mourn,
> And gnash your teeth with dolorous laments:
> You fearful dogs that in black Lethe howl,
> And scare the ghosts with your wide open throats:
> You ugly ghosts that, flying from these dogs,
> Do plunge yourselves in Puryflegiton:
> Come, all of you, and with your shriking notes
> Accompany the Brittain's conquering host.
> Come, fierce Erynnys, horrible with snakes;

Come, ugly Furies, armed with your whips;
You threefold judges of black Tartarus,
And all the army of you hellish fiends,
With new-found torments rack proud Locrine's
    bones!
O gods, and stars! damned be the gods and stars
That did not drown me in fair Thetis' plains!
Curst be the sea, that with outrageous waves,
With surging billows did not rive my ships
Against the rocks of high Cerannia,
Or swallow me into her wat'ry gulf!
Would God we had arriv'd upon the shore
Where Polyphemus and the Cyclops dwell,
Or where the bloody Anthropophagi
With greedy jawes devours the wand'ring wights!

Enter the ghost of ALBANACT

But why comes Albanact's bloody ghost,
To bring a corsive to our miseries?
Is't not enough to suffer shameful flight,
But we must be tormented now with ghosts,
With apparitions fearful to behold?

GHOST. Revenge! revenge for blood!

HUMBER. So nought will satisfy your wand'ring ghost
But dire revenge, nothing but Humber's fall,
Because he conquered you in Albany.
Now, by my soul, Humber would be condemned
To Tantal's hunger or Ixion's wheel,
Or to the vulture of Prometheus,
Rather than that this murther were undone.
When as I die I'll drag thy cursed ghost
Through all the rivers of foul Erebus,
Through burning sulphur of the Limbo-lake,
To allay the burning fury of that heat
That rageth in mine everlasting soul.

GHOST. *Vindicta, vindicta.*

                  [*Exeunt.*]

This is the proper Ercles bombast, ridiculed by Shakespeare, Jonson, and Nashe. From this, even to *Tamburlaine,* is a long way; it is too absurdly distorted to serve even as a burlesque of Seneca; but the metre has something Senecan about it. From such verse there is a long distance to the melodies of

Now comes my lover tripping like a roe,
And brings my longings tangled in her hair.

or

Welcome, my son: who are the violets now
That strew the green lap of the new-come spring?

or

But look, the morn, in russet mantle clad,
Walks o'er the dew of yon high eastern hill:

that is to say, to the *lyrical* phase of blank verse, before Shakespeare had analysed it into true dramatic differentiation; it belongs to the first or *declamatory* phase. But this declamation is in its impulse, if not in its achievement, Senecan; and progress was made, not by rejection, but by dissociating this type of verse into products with special properties.

The next stage also was reached with the help of a hint from Seneca. Several scholars, Butler in particular, have called attention to a trick of Seneca of repeating one word of a phrase in the next phrase, especially in stichomythia, where the sentence of one speaker is caught up and twisted by the next. This was an effective stage trick, but it is something more; it is the crossing of one rhythm pattern with another.

    —Sceptrone nostro *famulus* est potior tibi?
    —Quot iste *famulus* tradidit *reges* neci.
    —Cur ergo *regi* servit et patitur iugum?

                              (***Hercules***)

Seneca also gets a kind of double pattern by breaking up lines into minimum antiphonal units:

Rex est timendus.
                    Rex meus fuerat pater.
Non metuis arma?
                  Sint licet terra edita.
Moriere.
       Cupio.
            Profuge.
                Paenituit fugae.
Medea,
     Fiam.
          Mater es.
             Cui sim vides.

                              (***Medea***)

A man like Marlowe, or even men with less scholarship and less genius for the use of words than he, could hardly have failed to learn something from this. At any rate, I believe that the study of Seneca had its part in the formation of verse like the following:

    —Wrong not her birth, she is of royal blood.
    —To save her life, I'll say she is not so.
    —Her life is safest only in her birth.
    —And only in that safety died her brothers.

It is only a step (and a few lines further) to the pun:

Cousins, indeed; and by their uncle cozen'd.

Some of the effects in such plays as *Richard II* and *Richard III* are indeed of pre-Marlowe origin, as:

I had an Edward, till a Richard kill'd him;
I had a Henry, till a Richard kill'd him;
Thou hadst an Edward, till a Richard kill'd him;
Thou hadst a Richard, till a Richard kill'd him.

which is already in even *Locrine,* as:

> The boisterous Boreas thundreth forth Revenge,
> The stony rocks cry out on sharp revenge,
> The thorny bush pronounceth dire revenge,

but in the following lines from Clarence's Dream we see an immense advance over *Locrine* in the use of infernal machinery:

> I pass'd, methought, the melancholy flood,
> With that grim ferryman which poets write of,
> Unto the kingdom of perpetual night.
> The first that there did greet my stranger soul,
> Was my great father-in-law, renowned Warwick;
> Who cried aloud, "What scourge for perjury
> Can this dark monarchy afford false Clarence?"

The "kingdom of perpetual night" and the last two lines are a real approximation in English to the magnificence of Senecan Latin at its best; they are far from being a mere burlesque. The best of Seneca has here been absorbed into English.

In *Richard II,* which is usually dated a little earlier than *Richard III,* I find such interesting variations of versification that I am convinced that it is a slightly later play, or else that there is more of Shakespeare in it. There is the same play of words:

> Give Richard leave to live till Richard die.

> A brittle glory shineth in his face;
> As brittle as the glory is the face.

but there is less stichomythia, less mere repetition, and a dexterity in retaining and developing the same rhythm with greater freedom and less obvious calculation. (See the long speeches of Richard in Act III, sc. ii. and sc. iii, and compare with the more carefully balanced verses of Queen Margaret's tirade in *Richard III,* Act IV, sc. iv.)

When blank verse has reached this point, and passed into the hands of its greatest master, there is no need to look for fresh infusions of Seneca. He has done his work, and the one influence on later dramatic blank verse is the influence of Shakespeare. Not that later dramatists do not make great use of Seneca's plays. Chapman uses him, and employs the old machinery; but Seneca's influence on Chapman was chiefly on Chapman's "thought." Jonson uses Seneca deliberately; the superb prologues of *Envy* and *Sylla's Ghost* are adaptations of the Senecan ghost-prologue form, not an inheritance from Kyd. Massinger, a most accomplished dramatist and versifier, sometimes falls back most lamentably upon ghosts and spectacles. But the verse is formed, and Seneca no further responsible for its vices or virtues.

Certainly, Elizabethan bombast can be traced to Seneca; Elizabethans themselves ridiculed the Senecan imitation. But if we reflect, not on the more grotesque exaggerations, but on the dramatic poetry of the first half of the period, as a whole, we see that Seneca had as much to do with its

merits and its progress as with its faults and its delays. Certainly it is all "rhetorical," but if it had not been rhetorical, would it have been anything? Certainly it is a relief to turn back to the austere, close language of *Everyman,* the simplicity of the mysteries; but if new influences had not entered, old orders decayed, would the language not have left some of its greatest resources unexplored? Without bombast, we should not have had *King Lear.* The art of dramatic language, we must remember, is as near to oratory as to ordinary speech or to other poetry. If the Elizabethans distorted and travestied Seneca in some ways, if they learned from him tricks and devices which they applied with inexpert hands, they also learned from him the essentials of declaimed verse. Their subsequent progress is a process of splitting up the primitive rhetoric, developing out of it subtler poetry and subtler tones of conversation, eventually mingling, as no other school of dramatists has done, the oratorical, the conversational, the elaborate and the simple, the direct and the indirect; so that they were able to write plays which can still be viewed as plays, with any plays, and which can still be read as poetry, with any poetry.

It is improper to pass from the questions of Seneca's influence upon the Tragedy of Blood and upon the language of the Elizabethans without mentioning the group of "Senecal" plays, largely produced under the aegis of the Countess of Pembroke. The history of this type of play belongs rather to the history of scholarship and culture than to the history of the Drama: it begins in a sense with the household of Sir Thomas More, and therefore is doubly allied to the present subject by Jasper Heywood; it is continued in the conversations at Cambridge of Mr. Ascham, Mr. Watson, and Mr. (later Sir John) Cheke. The first to attack openly the common stage was Sir Philip Sidney, whose words are well known:

> Our Tragedies and Comedies (not without cause cried out against), observing rules neither of honest civility nor of skilful Poetry, excepting *Gorboduc* (againe, I say, of those that I have seen), which notwithstanding, as it is full of stately speeches and well sounding Phrases, climbing to the height of Seneca his style, and as full of notable morality, which it doth most delightfully teach, and so obtain the very end of Poesie, yet in troth it is very defectious in the circumstances, which grieveth me, because it might not remain as an exact model of all Tragedies. For it is faulty both in place and time, the two necessary companions of all corporal actions. . . . But if it be so in *Gorboduc,* how much more in all the rest, where you shall have Asia of the one side, and Afric of the other, and so many other under-kingdoms, that the Player, when he cometh in, must ever begin with telling where he is: or else the tale will not be conceived? Now ye shall have three Ladies walk to gather flowers, and then we must believe the stage to be a Garden. By and by, we hear news of shipwrack in the same place, and then we are to blame if we accept it not for a Rock.

It was after Sidney's death that his sister, the Countess of Pembroke, tried to assemble a body of wits to compose drama in the proper Senecan style, to make head against the popular melodrama of the time. Great poetry should be both an art and a diversion; in a large and cultivated public like the Athenian it can be both; the shy recluses of Lady Pembroke's circle were bound to fail. But we must not draw too sharp a line of separation between the careful workman who laboured to create a classical drama in England and the hurried purveyors of playhouse successes: the two worlds were not without communication, and the work of the earlier Senecals was not without fruit. . . .

I wish only to call attention to certain characteristics of Senecal Tragedy in its final form, in the work of Greville, Daniel and Alexander. I would only remind the reader that these final Senecal plays were written after any real hope of altering or reforming the English stage had disappeared. In the early Elizabethan years appeared a succession of tragedies, mostly performed by the Inns of Court, and therefore not popular productions, which might in favourable circumstances have led to a living Senecan drama. Notably, *Gorboduc* (mentioned by Sidney above), *Jocasta,* and *Gismond of Salerne* (three of the four plays contained in Cunliffe's *Early English Classical Tragedies*). When *The Spanish Tragedy* appeared (with, as I have suggested, its particularly non-classical element) these feeble lights were snuffed out. I pass on to the finished Senecal product, because I am only concerned to elicit the effect of Seneca upon his sedulous admirers and imitators who professed to be, and were, men of taste and culture.

The Monarchic Tragedies of Alexander, Earl of Stirling, are the last on our list, composed under the auspices of the scholarly King James I. They are poor stuff: I imagine that they are more important in the history of the Union than in the history of the Drama, since they represent the choice, by a Scotsman of accidental eminence, to write verse in English instead of in Scots. Their faults are the faults of the other plays of the group; but they have not the virtues of the others. The two plays of Fulke Greville, Lord Brooke, the friend and biographer of Sidney, have some magnificent passages, especially in the choruses; Greville had a true gift for sententious declamation. But they have much dullness also; and they do not imitate Seneca nearly so faithfully as either those of Alexander or those of Daniel. Greville not only cannot stick to one chorus, but will introduce, on one occasion, a chorus of "Bashas or Caddies," and after the next act, a chorus of "Mahometan Priests"; he introduces the still more doubtful practice of supernatural figures, a "dialogue of Good and Evil Spirits," or even a chorus of two allegorical figures, "Time and Eternity" (ending indeed with the fine line spoken by Eternity: *I am the measure of felicity*). The best, the best sustained, the most poetic and the most lyrical, are two tragedies of Samuel Daniel: *Cleopatra* and *Philotas*. They contain many lovely passages, they are readable all through, and they are well built.

Now, in comparison with the supposed influence of Seneca on the barbarity of Elizabethan tragedy, and his supposed bad influence upon the language, what do we find in the plays of those who took him as their model in their attack upon the popular stage, in that attack in which Daniel, in his dedication of *Cleopatra* to the Countess of Pembroke, declared himself the foe of "Gross Barbarism"? Deaths there are, of course, but there is none of these tragedies that is not far more restrained, far more discreet and sober, not only than the Tragedy of Blood, but than Seneca himself. Characters die so decently, so remote from the stage, and the report of their deaths is wrapped up in such long speeches by messengers stuffed with so many moral maxims, that we may read on unaware that any one concerned in the play has died at all. Where the popular playwrights travestied Seneca's melodrama and his fury, the Senecals travesty his reserve and his decorum. And as for the language, that, too, is a different interpretation of Seneca. How vague are our notions of bombast and rhetoric when they must include styles and vocabularies so different as those of Kyd and Daniel! It is by opposite excesses that Senecals and popular dramatists attract the same reproach. The language of Daniel is pure and restrained; the vocabulary choice, the expression clear; there is nothing far-fetched, conceited, or perverse.

> CLEOPATRA. What, hath my face yet power to win a Lover?
>   Can this torne remnant serve to grace me so,
> That it can Caesar's secret plots discover,
>   What he intends with me and mine to do?
> Why then, poor beauty, thou hast done thy last,
>   And best good service thou could'st do unto me;
> For now the time of death reveal'd thou hast,
>   Which in my life did'st serve but to undo me.

The first two lines are admirable; the rest are good serviceable lines; almost any passage from *Cleopatra* is as good, and some are far better. The whole thing is in excellent taste. Yet we may ponder the fact that it would not have made the slightest difference, to the formation of our Augustan poetry, if Daniel and his friends had never written a line; that Dryden and Pope are nearer allied to—Cowley; and that they owe more to Marlowe than to the purest taste of the sixteenth century. Daniel and Greville are good poets, and there is something to be learned from them; but they, and Sir John Davies who somewhat resembles them, had no influence. The only one of Lady Pembroke's heroes who had influence is Edmund Spenser.

Within the limits of an essay it is impossible to do more than touch on the influence of Seneca upon the "thought" of the Elizabethans, or more exactly, upon their attitude toward life so far as it can be formulated in words. I would only say enough, at this point, to remind the reader that Seneca's influence upon dramatic form, upon versification and language, upon sensibility, and upon thought, must in the end be all estimated together; they cannot be divided. How the influence of Seneca is related, in the Elizabethan mind, with other influences, perhaps those of Montaigne and Machiavelli, I do not know; and I think it is a subject still to be investigated. But the frequency with which a quotation from Seneca, or a thought or figure ultimately derived from Seneca, is employed in Elizabethan plays whenever a moral reflection is required, is too remarkable to be ignored; and when an Elizabethan hero or villain dies, he usually dies in the odour of Seneca. These facts are known to scholars; but if known, they are usually ignored by literary critics. In a comparison of Shakespeare with Dante, for instance, it is assumed that Dante leant upon a system of philosophy which he accepted whole, whereas Shakespeare created his own: or that Shakespeare had acquired some extra- or ultra-intellectual knowledge superior to a philosophy. This occult kind of information is sometimes called "spiritual knowledge" or "insight." Shakespeare and Dante were both merely poets (and Shakespeare a dramatist as well); our estimate of the intellectual material they absorbed does not affect our estimate of their poetry, either absolutely or relatively to each other. But it must affect our vision of them and the use we make of them, the fact that Dante, for instance, had behind him an Aquinas, and Shakespeare behind him a Seneca. Perhaps it was Shakespeare's special rôle in history to have effected this peculiar union—perhaps it is a part of his special eminence to have expressed an inferior philosophy in the greatest poetry. It is certainly one cause of the terror and awe with which he inspires us.

Philip Whaley Harsh (essay date 1944)

SOURCE: "Seneca," in *A Handbook of Classical Drama,* 1944. Reprint by Stanford University Press, 1963, pp. 401-36.

[*In the following excerpt, Harsh examines Seneca's works against the backdrop of his life and times.*]

Seneca . . . was a man of the highest social, political, and economic status. He early distinguished himself in literature, as his father had done in rhetoric, and he left an impressively large body of writings. Much of this has survived to make him the most influential Latin prose writer after Cicero. His primary interest was clearly moral philosophy; but his activity in letters, as in business, extended far and wide. Among his lost works was one on the geography of India, one on the form and one on the movement of the earth. These, like his extant work entitled *Natural Questions,* are noteworthy here because the scientific interests which they reveal are observable in his tragedies.

Nine tragedies of Seneca have been preserved. These are all written on the conventional Greek tragic subjects. Influence of intermediate adaptations, sometimes demonstrable, may be assumed in most cases, and always Seneca has himself made important changes that are apparently original. In general, however, five of his tragedies are modeled primarily after Euripides (the *Mad Hercules,* the *Trojan Women,* the *Phoenician Women,* the *Medea,* and the *Phaedra*), two after Sophocles (the *Oedipus* and the *Hercules on Oeta* [*Trachiniae*]), and one after Aeschylus (the *Agamemnon*). Seneca's *Thyestes* is the only tragedy for which no corresponding Greek original has survived.

A tenth play, the *Octavia,* is preserved. This tragedy concerns a contemporary historical situation and presents Seneca himself as an important character. For various reasons it is often assumed that this play was written after the death of both Seneca and Nero.

Tragedy Under Seneca

The leap from Greek tragedy to Seneca is one of almost five hundred eventful years. Of the extensive corpus of tragedies produced in both Greece and Italy during this period, however, only a series of names and titles and a few hundred short fragments have survived. Probably one Greek play, the *Rhesus,* also belongs to this period. In the field of tragedy changes were certainly enormous, but no approach to an adequate picture can be obtained. One point of interest in connection with Seneca may be mentioned: "philosophical" tragedy not designed for production in the theater seems occasionally to have been written.

Turning to Seneca's tragedies from the extant Greek plays, we appear to be on familiar ground. The same old subject material is being mulled over once more: Oedipus and Agamemnon are still stamping across the scene. If we are satisfied with this first appearance, or if we insist upon absolute literary criteria, we shall find the plays of Seneca so far inferior to the Greek tragedies that we may be tempted to view the Roman plays as the worthless product of an incompetent writer. Judged by the criteria of Aristotle, however, some of the plays of Shakespeare himself would come off poorly. The comparison of Seneca's plays with the very best Greek masterpieces is likely to obscure more than it reveals unless designed primarily to discover the intent of Seneca in making his changes. Such comparison is so obvious, furthermore, that one never thinks of comparing Seneca's best with the only other plays that have survived from this half-millennium, the *Rhesus* and the *Octavia,* to which either Seneca's *Trojan Women* or his *Phaedra* is much superior. Critics forget, also, that many Senecan faults are found in plays such as the *Rhesus* or Euripides' *Orestes.*

It is unnecessary here to point out all the respects in which the Greeks wrote better Greek tragedies. Certainly if Seneca's purpose had been to imitate the Greeks of the fifth century, a man with far less talent could have done a much more competent job. Nor is it likely that one who was such a competent writer in other fields should continue writing tragedy unless he felt that he was achieving his purpose, or that he would be so conceitedly prejudiced that he could not perceive something of the true qualities of his work. The inevitable conclusion is that most critics condemn Seneca for not doing what he never had the slightest intention of doing. Actually his plays are vastly different from the Greek tragedies of the fifth century, though they are doubtless not masterpieces judged by any standard. His strong personality has left its impress on every phase of them, and they are thoroughly Roman productions.

The primary purpose of Seneca in writing his tragedies is one of the most disputed problems in classical drama. Any attempt at a satisfactory solution, therefore, must be conjectural. The various interests of Seneca can be determined from his tragedies, from his other writings, and perhaps from a knowledge of his life. Obviously the plays must be interpreted in the light of these interests, more so with Seneca than with the previous classical dramatists. These were all practical men of the theater or at least had intimate contact with actual production. They were all professional dramatists in the best sense of that term. But Seneca was not. Most critics would call him a dilettante. His tragedies are marked not so much by the superficiality of the dilettante, however, as by the disproportion of the amateur. The perfection of the artistic whole is sacrificed to the author's special interests. This characteristic is a vice which he shared with many in a nervous and intellectually chaotic age. These special interests of Seneca, furthermore, were sometimes incompatible with dramatic effectiveness.

Several of Seneca's interests have a tinge of pedantry. He is inordinately fond of detailed geographical descriptions. The Romans of his day had achieved a far larger world than any previous people, and they were conscious and justifiably proud of this. Even now it is thrilling to read Seneca's references to the antipodes or his prediction of the discovery of America in the *Medea* (375-79). Such a bold stretch of the human imagination, though anticipated by others, is undeniably admirable. His detailed catalogue of the districts of Attica at the opening of the *Phaedra,* however, must have been almost as boring to the Roman as it is to the modern reader. Many another catalogue is equally so, as are his lists of hunting dogs and his series of rare wild animals. He could well have been more sparing also with his vast mythological lore—his plays require a far more detailed knowledge of Greek legends than the Greek tragedies do.

All critics recognize one interest and one effect consistently achieved in Seneca's tragedies: rhetorical display. Brilliant sophistic argument, arresting epigrammatic point, vivid description of sensational events—these qualities were highly prized in Seneca's day, and these he achieved undeniably well. It is often concluded, therefore, that the tragedies were designed merely as a vehicle for this rhetorical display and that they were written not for actual production but for reading. Still we should not be too ready to assume that a man of Seneca's stature—history and his other writings prove that this was not small—should indulge in mere display and should write tragedies as a schoolboy's exercise.

The question of production is an old and still hotly disputed one. There is no external proof that any of his plays were ever produced. Most critics who analyze from the point of view of Greek tragedy and Roman rhetoric are convinced that the plays were written for reading or recitation. The extreme violence of many scenes is cited. Certainly the slaughter which the mad Hercules wreaks would tax modern stagecraft to the utmost—we need not assume that Roman stagecraft of this period was much less skillful. But this slaughter may be enacted behind the scenes. Certainly the assembling of the body of Hippolytus is done on stage, and some critics cite this as a scene impossible of presentation. But the scene at the end of Euripides' *Bacchae,* now lost, may have been almost as gory. In short, there is no proof here.

The strongest indication that the plays were not intended for the theater, in the opinion of the present writer, lies in the minuteness with which the actions of characters on stage are described. When Phaedra rushes up to Hippolytus and

faints, for instance, the Nurse does not cry out in a natural fashion and come to her aid; but in the fashion of a medical casebook she describes how Phaedra's body falls lifeless to the ground and how a deathlike pallor spreads over her face. Even plainer are the words of Hippolytus when he is on the point of slaying Phaedra: "See, I have grasped your hair and forced your shameless head back with my left hand. . . ." Though a certain amount of such description is natural in ancient drama where stage directions were not explicitly added, this description is so much commoner in Seneca than in other extant plays that it seems designed to replace the action of the real theater. The assumption that the plays were not written for production appears attractive, therefore; but it is by no means proved, and the plays should be read without prejudice on the point.

Certain dramatic qualities are sadly lacking in the plays of Seneca, especially dramatic action. This is most clearly brought out by a comparison of the number of scenes in the extant tragedies. The seven plays of Aeschylus have an average of approximately eight and one-half scenes each, the plays of Sophocles and Euripides fifteen scenes, and those of Seneca approximately nine scenes. Seneca is careless of motivation of entrances and exits, realistic dialogue, preparation for subsequent events, and the various other details of technique which the Greek masters had developed to such perfection. The plays tend to seem collections of scenes, therefore, rather than dramatically articulated units. Often action is managed awkwardly. Medea calls for her children who are within the house, and one line later they seem to be standing before her awaiting her orders. Such unnatural, schematic action is characteristic of the informality of Old Comedy. Still more important, the characters often are implausibly or desultorily presented, unity of subject seems to be violated by apparently extraneous material, and the plays usually open on such a shrill note of horror that no opportunity remains for an effective reversal of fortune.

In contrast to these various undramatic features, extremely theatrical and spectacular scenes are not infrequent. The opening scene of the *Phaedra* seems to be designed as colorful pageantry—thoroughly according to the Roman tradition of overelaborate stage effects. The scene between Andromache and Ulysses in the *Trojan Women* is splendid theater. So is the scene between Phaedra and Hippolytus. Many of the final scenes, however horrible, are eminently spectacular.

That rhetorical display is one of Seneca's most striking characteristics is obvious; but sometimes it may serve as a means to a less obvious end. The first choral song of the *Phaedra,* for instance, is pertinent to the situation and its poetry would be very acceptable if the whole passage did not end with the point that love overcomes even a stepmother. Again Hippolytus, delivering a fine Stoic speech excoriating civilized man and his crimes, cites all sorts of crime within the family except the crimes of the stepmother. It would be unfair, he intimates, to argue from such an extreme and indisputable example. But this seems a jarring note in his characterization; for hitherto Hippolytus has revealed no prejudice or cause for such at least against his own stepmother, and in the ensuing scene with her he seems to have no prejudice. Consistency of character appears here to have been sacrificed to rhetorical point. But many sententious pronouncements on stepmothers are found in this tragedy of Seneca as in several others, and although the stepmother theme was a rhetorical commonplace we must consider the possibility that Seneca was interested not primarily in rhetorical display but in stepmothers. Nor is this alternative as ridiculous as it at first seems; for the mother of the Emperor Nero as a stepmother had run the gamut of crimes, and this theme is very properly an important one in the historical tragedy *Octavia*.

The theme of the tyrant is even more frequent in Seneca. Those speeches in which the Nurse tries to dissuade Phaedra from pursuing Hippolytus, for instance, read like a lecture of Seneca to his pupil Nero urging him not to embark upon a career of crime. "I am not unaware," she says (136-39), "how unwilling to be guided to an honorable course is royal pride, callous and unaccustomed to the truth. But I shall bear whatever fate may chance to be mine; courage is given to one who is old by the thought that death soon will bring freedom." Unfortunately, however, this play like all the others cannot be dated. The assumption of any reference to the ruling family, therefore, is purely conjectural.

The use of drama as more or less subtle political criticism had a long tradition in Rome. Extended allegory was not necessary; a single line even of an old play was often interpreted in the light of contemporary events and greeted with applause or hissing. During the time of Seneca, when the tyrannies of the emperors made open criticism of political policies extremely dangerous, all genres of literature were used for covert criticism. A certain Cremutius Cordus wrote a history in order, perhaps, to praise Brutus and to call Cassius "the last of the Romans." Cordus was forced to commit suicide. Another contemporary of Seneca, Curiatius Maternus, wrote tragedies with a political purpose and sometimes on Roman historical figures. These were publicly read by the author and were apparently not intended for production in the theater. One of the men under whom Seneca in his youth mastered rhetoric, Mamercus Aemilius Scaurus, is said to have incurred the wrath of the Emperor Tiberius by writing a tragedy, *Atreus,* in which a commonplace from Euripides' *Phoenissae* (393) was included— "One must bear the follies of his rulers."

Every play of Seneca has somewhat similar lines. It is not inconceivable that Seneca, though no extremist, should write a whole play for one well-placed line of this type. The subject material of Greek tragedy was ideal for such application. The more commonplace a theme might be there or in contemporary rhetoric, such as the theme of the tyrant or that of the stepmother, the safer the author would feel in dwelling upon it; and the audience would doubtless be no less keen in applying it where it seemed most apposite in the contemporary situation. That Seneca had a political purpose in writing his tragedies, therefore, is an easily conceivable, though at present not widely accepted, hypothesis.

Inextricably bound up with a possible political end are Seneca's very certain moral and philosophical interests.

The inevitability that one dreadful crime will lead to another, for instance, is an obvious theme in the *Thyestes* and the *Agamemnon,* and indeed this is the theme of Aeschylus himself in his trilogy on Orestes. Not only interpretation of the legends is affected by philosophical concepts but portrayal of characters also, the choral lyrics, the action, and perhaps even the form of the play. If crime must lead to crime, then the individual characteristics of those who come late in the vicious cycle do not determine the course of events and so need not be dwelt upon. Indeed, if determinism is accepted, then tragedy of character becomes meaningless. Perhaps this in part is the explanation of the very desultory treatment which is given the character of Oedipus or that of Clytemnestra.

Many of Seneca's figures are almost ideal Stoics. Even his women and children face disaster and die with a fortitude which may well stifle pathos and preclude dramatic effectiveness. The choral lyrics, where intensity of feeling is most desirable, are emotionally reserved. Such stringent inhibition of the softer emotions results in a lack of genuine pathos in Seneca's plays—perhaps their one greatest shortcoming.

Violent emotions and their outrageous crimes, however, are most frequent and constitute another obvious special interest of Seneca. His portrait of Medea is not, like that of Euripides, a detailed psychological study of a more or less normal woman driven by a series of events to abnormal crime. It is rather a livid exaggeration of the conventional barbaric sorceress. His motive is apparently not to explain an abnormal action but to display a sensational figure who is more than abnormal from the first line of the play. He deliberately strives to create a climax that is fantastically horrible; and no one will deny that he succeeds.

Closely allied with Seneca's interest in the horrible is his enthusiasm for the mystic. This appears superficially in rites of magic, ghosts, and concern with the underworld. The pathetic fallacy, also, is carried to mystical lengths. The whole cosmos reacts to the crime of Atreus. But these external manifestations are merely the dark background for the mysticism of man's own soul. Thyestes is overwhelmed with the consciousness of his guilt (*Thyestes* 513), and an inexplicable premonition of ill chokes his enjoyment of the banquet. Even more significant is the obsession of death which many Senecan characters display. This obsession was the author's own, as may be observed also in his prose works—and justifiably so, for his health was extremely delicate and, in an age precarious for all of his class, he lived in unusually close and dangerous relation to the tyranical emperors. In his tragedies death is at once the ultimate of the horrible and the supreme release from toil and suffering. This avid mysticism and obsession of death is the intellectual ground that later proved so fertile a seed plot for Christianity.

Seneca has chosen his material with a keen regard for his special interests. There must be no romantic recognitions and no sweetness—no *Alcestis* or *Iphigenia in Tauris*. All his plays with the possible exception of the mystic *Hercules on Oeta* are tragedies in the modern sense of that word. All are filled with the qualities for which he was famous in the Renaissance—*atrocitas, gravitas, maiestas.* The Greeks of the fifth century were the youths—eternal youths—of the ancient world; Seneca was its disillusioned old age.

Interpreted as expressions of his intellectual interests, we conclude, the tragedies of Seneca are successful productions. The author was a serious thinker and an eloquent writer despite his many faults. He was not a great dramatist and made no attempt to be; but his plays have certain dramatic virtues, and their historical importance as drama has been tremendous. Largely neglected in ancient and in medieval times, they emerged in the fourteenth century as the only well-known classical tragedy, and their rule over Italian and French drama continued for many centuries. In the England of Shakespeare's day, too, they were immensely popular. Nor should we be too ready to deplore history's preference for Seneca, because of his language, above the Greeks. His intellectual outlook, like his language, was a part of the immediate tradition of Italy and France: the Greeks were essentially foreign. Even as drama, Greek tragedy with its chorus and with its Greek divinities, though vastly superior, could never have been so readily and so thoroughly assimilated.

STRUCTURE.—By the time of Seneca, dramatists as well as critics seem to have approved the rule of five acts, for all his plays except possibly the *Oedipus* have four divisional choral songs. The rule of three speaking characters, too, is observed, though some scenes, as that at the end of the *Agamemnon,* would require four actors. The unities of time and place are normally respected. A change of scene, however, seems to occur in the *Hercules on Oeta* and possibly elsewhere. The background of the *Medea,* furthermore, seems vague and uncertain. Strict unity of subject is often sacrificed to the author's peculiar interests.

In metrical usage Seneca is conservative. His characters almost invariably speak in simple iambic verse. Three short passages in trochaic verse of seven and one-half feet occur. Occasionally a character, such as Hecuba at the opening of the *Trojan Women,* is given anapestic or other lyric measure. The choral meters are monotonously simple.

The tragedy often begins with a monologue-prologue delivered by the main character. This form is doubtless descended from the Euripidean prologue; but Seneca does not use it primarily for purposes of exposition. Indeed, lack of adequate exposition is a typical feature of a Senecan play. One can hardly avoid the impression that the audience and even the characters themselves are thoroughly acquainted with their past, present, and future before the action begins. Any exposition given often appears inevitable or fortuitous. The Senecan prologue is normally used to create the mood of the play, and this mood is frequently that of horror. A dire note is struck at the very first and is maintained throughout. The prologue may develop into a semblance of a dialogue, but usually it constitutes the whole first act. Ghosts and spirits are used twice in prologues and a major ivinity is used once.

The chorus in Seneca is primarily an interlude. It is sometimes withdrawn after a lyric, as apparently in earlier Roman tragedy, but again it may remain on stage and even engage in conversation with a messenger or some character. This is rare, however, and occurs only when no other speaking character is on stage. Sometimes two different choruses are used. In the *Agamemnon,* for instance, a group of Trojan captives constitutes the second chorus. The lyrics themselves occasionally rise to poetic heights of real beauty, but too often they are pedestrian. A distinct effort is still made to give them at least a superficial connection with the action. In general, however, little of the Greek subtlety in adapting the chorus to the needs of the play can be observed, and it is regrettable that the chorus was not wholly eliminated.

The absence of an organic chorus creates certain difficulties of staging to which Seneca is not wholly impervious. On the huge Roman stage, as in Roman comedy, the entrance of a character in mid-scene becomes a distinct problem. Such entrances are accompanied by a soliloquy, which is often an aside. Asides are not unnatural under these conditions, and they are accordingly much more common than in Greek tragedy. Such soliloquies are employed to reveal information which it might be difficult to convey in the ensuing dialogue. Indeed, Seneca is inordinately fond of soliloquies of every type.

Usually at the beginning of the second act the dramatic action is initiated. Frequently this takes the form of a subaltern's attempting to deter the main character from crime. Such a scene is designed, of course, to bring out the criminal determination of the main character. The entrance of a new character may develop a complication. The act usually ends with the formation of a definite criminal plan.

The third act, as in the *Thyestes,* may be given over to the presentation of the victim and may end with his entrapment. The fourth act may give a description of the catastrophe and the fifth a vivid illustration of it. Normally there is no sharply marked peripety or any strong emotional contrast between the opening and the close of the action. The situation is very bad at the beginning, and it rapidly becomes much worse.

Seneca uses no *deus ex machina,* unless the appearance of Hercules at the end of the *Hercules on Oeta* can be called such. Far from having any prejudice against violent deeds on stage, he delights in making his finale fantastically horrible and bloody. So we see Jocasta stab herself in her "capacious womb," and so we hear the thud of the bodies of Medea's children as she flings them from the housetop.

1. Mad Hercules (Hercules Furens)

The *Mad Hercules* shows many dramatic faults and much overdone rhetoric, but individual scenes in it are very impressive. The subject doubtless made a strong appeal to Seneca for several reasons. It is perfectly adapted to the themes of the stepmother and the tyrant. Both these were dear to his heart, and they furnish some of his finest rhetorical effects. "No greater victim can be sacrificed to Jupiter and no richer one than a king who is unjust," says Hercules as he is about to sacrifice while his hands still drip the blood of Lycus. Effective also is Hercules' apostrophe to his own hands as the tools of his stepmother (1236). The fantastic exaggeration of his labors also must have teased the imagination of Seneca, and the long description of the underworld is well fitted to serve both moralist and rhetorician. Seneca obviously took delight also in depicting the growing frenzy of Juno and especially the seizure of Hercules—a magnificent scene. Still more attractive perhaps was the contemplation of the sufferings of this Stoic saint which so clearly emphasize Fortune's envy of virtue and her ironic fickleness in bestowing her favors (esp. 524-32).

SOURCES.—Euripides introduced this subject into tragedy in his still extant *Heracles;* and, though there were later Greek versions and perhaps one Roman adaptation, Seneca seems to have followed the original play. The incidents, at least, are the same, but fundamental changes in treatment and interpretation have been made. Since these affected every part of the play they may best be noted in the general consideration.

DISCUSSION.—Seneca has added a conventional prologue spoken by Juno. Her catalogue of the various loves of Jupiter and their mementos in the sky seems a little ridiculous but is a part of the stepmother theme. More important is her recitation of the great accomplishments of Hercules and her great anger at his success. Finally, raising her voice to the screech of hysteria, she foretells his madness and adumbrates its results. Thus the loud note of horror which usually characterizes the opening of a Senecan tragedy is here clearly sounded.

Another effect of the prologue is even more important. The foreknowledge here imparted casts a shade of irony upon the glory of Hercules' return, and thus Euripides' magnificent contrast between the returning hero and the murderer of wife and children is largely lost. No such contrast really exists in the life of Hercules as Seneca presents it. All has been and still remains a titanic struggle against a superior power. The climax of this struggle and Hercules' inevitable ruin is the subject of Seneca's tragedy. In the prologue and throughout the play the fantastic exaggeration of Hercules' accomplishments raises the hero so far above human accomplishment that he loses much of his human appeal. But he gains the superhuman stature requisite for contest with divinity. Juno's prologue, therefore, serves the Senecan interpretation of Hercules well, however far this may be from the Aristotelian concept of the most effective tragic character. The prologue also concentrates attention upon Hercules alone, whereas the opening of Euripides' play emphasizes the plight of his family.

As an explanation of Hercules' madness, Juno's conventional prologue replaces the very unconventional scene of Iris and Lyssa in the center of Euripides' play. The elimination of that scene allows the gradual seizure of Hercules to be depicted on stage without supernatural interference in its presentation. But while Iris and Lyssa poetically symbolize the madness which at that moment is at work within the

palace, Juno's prologue, though ending on the pitch of frenzy, comes long before the actual madness and is immediately followed by the chorus' idyllic description of dawn and Stoic praise of the simple life!

The second act begins in no less declamatory fashion than the prologue. Amphitryon now prays for relief from misfortune and holds forth on the eleven previous labors—the securing of Cerberus is still in progress—for some seventy-five verses, and Megara closes the series with a mere thirty on much the same subject. Both invoke Hercules as if he were a god. Thus the first three hundred and eight verses pass in only four units. This disturbingly awkward opening is caused by Seneca's failure to recast the first of his play—or rather the first of Euripides' play—after he has added the prologue by Juno. The endless repetition of the labors has its justification—emphasis on the endless struggle which Hercules' life has been. The effect is well designed, therefore, but it is not well executed. The repetition is too monotonous and boring.

The scene with Lycus, except for the further intrusion of the labors, is far better. Seneca gives the tyrant the very plausible motivation of wishing to marry Megara in order to make his reign a more legitimate one. This is an improvement over Euripides, designed no doubt to facilitate Seneca's theme of the tyrant. If the play was written during the reign of Nero, however, it was an obvious motivation; for Nero himself had a somewhat similar reason for marrying Octavia, the daughter of Claudius. Nero's relation to Octavia also was somewhat similar, for Claudius and his son were to be or had been murdered for the benefit of Nero, and according to Seneca he who derives the benefit from a crime is the guilty party. After Lycus has withdrawn, Amphitryon at the end of the scene foresees the return of Hercules.

The labors are now once more attempted, this time by the chorus, and special emphasis is given the return from the underworld. Following their fanfare, Hercules appears. After an entrance monologue in which he boasts of his triumph over death, he hears of Lycus' outrages and immediately goes off to slay him. He has shown no tenderness in greeting wife and children; and, since Theseus has entered with him as a speaking character, Megara can say nothing if the rule of three speaking actors is to be maintained. Thus one of the most pathetic episodes of Euripides' play is eliminated. But this is consistent with Seneca's procedure; for he makes no effort to humanize Hercules, at least before the climax, and Megara and the children are carefully kept in the background throughout.

Theseus has been brought on with Hercules in order, no doubt, that he may declaim on the underworld and Hercules' accomplishments there. This description enables the author to bring out the Stoic conception of retribution after death and to apply it especially to the tyrant. Such a conception is a natural counterpart or consolation for a view of life as a laborious and finally unsuccessful struggle, but no effort is made to bring out this connection with the theme of the play and so to justify the inclusion of the scene. Theseus' description itself, of course, is sensational and colorful.

Dramatically Theseus' entrance with Hercules is very plausible and avoids the abruptness of his appearance later, as in Euripides. But this advantage is small gain and apparently involves the extreme inconvenience of removing him at the climax when Hercules is about to slaughter wife and children.

After a choral song contemplating the underworld and death but ending on an ironically joyful note concerning the success of Hercules, the hero returns with the blood of Lycus upon his hands. As he prepares to sacrifice in spite of this defilement, the madness gradually comes over him. The actual presentation of this scene has been made possible by having Lycus slain somewhere off stage and not trapped within the palace as in Euripides. This, too, is a distinct gain for Seneca, but precisely how the following carnage could have been portrayed in the theater is quite uncertain. Some assume that it was not designed ever to be portrayed, others that the carnage takes place behind the scenes while Amphitryon views and reports it. Amphitryon's detailed description does not necessarily decide the matter, for contemporary action on stage is often so described in Seneca. The seizure itself is plausibly managed and does not include those manifestations which the comic poets considered a little puerile and ridiculous in Euripides.

After a choral lyric of grief that is too rhetorical to be very effective, Hercules awakens, and through his own deductions he is made to realize what he has done. His gradual enlightenment and his desire to die are depicted with genuine pathos. He is finally persuaded to live, not so much by Theseus' exhortation to withstand adversity, the prime consideration in Euripides, as by Amphitryon's appeal to filial piety. This, too, is as we should expect in Seneca, where suicide is often praised as the one escape from misfortune.

2. Trojan Women (Troades)

The **Trojan Women** has often been considered the best of Seneca's plays. It is certainly an impressive spectacle of the mutability of fortune, the woes of the vanquished, and the insolence of the victorious. The whole is overcast by the irony of the victors' own coming destruction. The outlook of the play, then, is similar to that of the Trojan Women of Euripides; so is the structure, which achieves a certain unity of tone and theme even though the two main incidents of the play are only superficially connected. The scene between Andromache and Ulysses, an important source for Racine, is brilliantly written and would doubtless be very effective in any theater. On the whole, however, the play lacks that consummate finish of dramatic technique which usually characterizes Greek tragedies.

SOURCES.—The murder of Astyanax and the grief of Andromache form one of the main episodes in Euripides' Trojan Women. The death of Polyxena is an important part of his Hecuba. Seneca follows the main outlines of Euripides in relating these events, and distinct echoes of both plays are found; but major changes have been made. The question of sacrificing Polyxena is here made the subject of a spirited and dramatic debate; Andromache has a premonition of the danger and hides Astyanax in Hector's tomb,

but eventually she is forced by the crafty Ulysses to reveal his whereabouts. This hiding of Astyanax occurred also in a Latin tragedy of Accius entitled *Astyanax,* in which also Calchas seems to have motivated the murder. But the use of the tomb of Hector for this, considered fantastic by some critics, may be original with Seneca.

Variouis other important changes have been made: Hecuba is not the center of Seneca's play; more speaking characters are brought on stage; the choral songs though effective do not have the beauty or depth of pathos of those in Euripides. Seneca's play may well be the product of contamination, since this combination of Astyanax and Polyxena is not known to have occurred in any previous play.

Various other plays may have been drawn upon for details. Sophocles wrote a *Polyxena* and also a *Captive Women* (*Aichmalotides*), which may possibly have covered some of the same material as Euripides' *Trojan Women.* Accius wrote a *Hecuba* and apparently a *Trojan Women* besides the *Astyanax* just mentioned. Still other plays had been written on these subjects in both Greek and Latin.

DISCUSSION.—Hecuba, at once the most venerable and the most pathetic survivor of the destruction of Troy, opens and closes the play. Her prologue emphasizes the mutability of fortune, the sacrilegious violence of the conquerors, and the enslavement awaiting the women. These thoughts very naturally develop into an antiphony between her and the chorus, which contains genuine tears for the dead and for the even more unfortunate living. Emotionally, this is an effective opening of the play. From the dramatic point of view, however, we should have expected some significant reference to Polyxena, Andromache, and Astyanax, the characters about whom the main incidents of the play devolve. Actually Hecuba twice refers to Cassandra, who does not appear as a character in the play. At the end of this lyric exchange, furthermore, Hecuba very ineffectively withdraws (or becomes silent).

The Herald now comes on for a more typical Senecan prologue of horror reporting the appearance of the ghost of Achilles. Since the Herald immediately departs when his report is given, his speech also has that detachment which usually characterizes a Senecan prologue. The creation of Senecan atmosphere is doubtless the main purpose of this sensational speech, for the information which it gives could easily have been worked into the conversation between Pyrrhus and Agamemnon.

Agamemnon here, reminiscent of the Agamemnon of Euripides' *Hecuba,* is a very cautious and restrained conqueror. He is keenly aware that the Greeks have gone to excesses and that the momentary whim of fortune is just as formidable as an armada of a thousand ships or a struggle of ten long years. Indeed he forebodes the disasters which actually overtake the Greeks and himself. Thus the ominous theme of Hecuba's prologue is elaborated to cast a grim irony over the present insolence of the victors. With such farsighted Stoic characters, Seneca's play has no need of a divine prelude like that of Euripides' *Trojan Women.* This substitution of vague human foreboding for supernatural explicitness might be considered a distinct improvement.

The quarrel between Pyrrhus and Agamemnon over the sacrifice of Polyxena begins with long and comparatively restrained speeches. But it soon develops into a rapid and excited contest of abuse which is one of the most dramatic dialogues in Seneca. Finally Calchas is called in to settle the matter like a *deus ex machina*. All critics have laid the severest strictures upon the abruptness here, and perhaps this, like the appearance of the children in the ***Medea*** (845), is another example of that dramatic awkwardness which is not infrequent in Seneca. Still this scene could be staged very effectively by having Calchas and various other figures enter along with Pyrrhus and Agamemnon at the beginning of the scene. The sacred insignia would clearly mark out the priest who sacrificed Iphigenia. He would stand by ominously silent and contemptuously superior to this futile logomachy over reason and justice—the priest waiting for the kings to appeal to him as he knows they eventually must. The end of this act is admittedly abrupt, but Agamemnon can say nothing after Calchas' pronouncement ex cathedra.

The pronouncement of Calchas not only settles the dispute over Polyxena; the fate of Astyanax, also, is brusquely determined in three short lines. Thus the action of the remainder of the play is foretold. The following chorus on death as the end of all is not inapposite, and this pagan conviction is here expressed with depressing certainty.

The third act is masterly. The appearance of the ghost of Hector to Andromache, corresponding to that of the ghost of Achilles to the Greeks, is well conceived. Andromache's finding the features of her dead husband in the face of her son is both moving and significant for the dilemma which she is soon to have thrust upon her. The genuine pathos here and the obviously inevitable tragic outcome prevent any semblance of melodrama in the spectacular scene with Ulysses. Andromache's turmoil of spirit is depicted with keen psychological insight, though the incoherency of her lines is sometimes destroyed by benighted modern editors. In these scenes, furthermore, Seneca has placed at least some restraint upon his inveterate fondness for rhetorical effect.

In the ensuing lyric the chorus contemplate to what homes they may be taken in Greece. This adaptation of a Euripidean choral theme is not well done, but the suggestion of imminent departure is effective.

The fourth act moves rapidly but lacks the brilliance of the third. Andromache's wrangling with Helen immediately after Astyanax has been taken off to die detracts from the pathos of her suffering. Euripides chose the wiser course when he allowed her to make her final exit along with Astyanax, for anything that she can say after this must appear anticlimactic. Nor is the defense of Helen really pertinent to this scene, although the pity of an enemy adds to the pathetic tragedy of Polyxena. Significant for the play as a whole, however, is the resumption of the theme of the destruction to be visited upon the Greeks. Hecuba prophesies woes for Ulysses (994), and prays that the seas may be

as savage to the Greeks as the Greeks are to their suppliants (1006).

The fifth act combines the stories of Astyanax and Polyxena, but only in an external fashion. The speech of the Messenger must be divided between these two unrelated events—a division not characteristic of messenger speeches in Greek tragedy—and the resultant awkwardness is aggravated by the Messenger's offering a choice as to whose misfortune he should relate first. Incidentally both Astyanax and Polyxena die like Stoics. The play ends effectively with Hecuba's ironic *propempticon* to the Greeks amounting to a curse and a prophecy that the sea will give them the welcome which they deserve.

3. Phoenician Women (Phoenissae)

Scholars have not agreed on an explanation of the scenes preserved under this title. Perhaps they are mere independent studies; perhaps they are parts of a complete or projected tragedy.

Doubtless Euripides' *Phoenissae* was Seneca's chief model. That play was one of the most famous of all Greek tragedies and contained perhaps the most widely known discussion of tyranny in classical literature. It was a dangerous play during Seneca's day, as Mamercus Scaurus, his contemporary and one of his rhetorical models, had discovered under Tiberius. The general subject had been treated in various other Greek and Roman tragedies, including Sophocles' *Oedipus at Colonus,* and in epic verse. The Roman historical legend of Coriolanus as related in Livy (2. 39-40) may well have contributed to the scene with Jocasta.

The first scene is one between Oedipus and Antigone. Oedipus asks that he be allowed to go the way which, even in his blindness, he will find more easily alone—the way of death. But Antigone replies that she will never leave him. Incidentally she reveals that Polynices is leading his army against Thebes, and that Jocasta is still alive. This conversation develops into a Senecan discussion of suicide somewhat like that in the ***Mad Hercules.***

The scenes with Jocasta either include a change of locale from Thebes to the battleground or else Jocasta leads the brothers on stage in a unique manner. Here Jocasta does most of the talking, making a passionate appeal especially to Polynices and ending on the Senecan theme of the folly of kinghood. The attitudes of the two brothers are much the same as in Euripides.

4. Medea

This is a tragedy of revenge written with special emphasis upon the inhuman fury and weird sorcery of a barbaric Medea. Indeed this play is an important source of knowledge of ancient magic, and a comparison with the witches' scenes in *Macbeth* is sufficient to prove that in literature, at least, ancient magic was not so very different from modern.

SOURCES.—The story of Medea was one of the most popular among both Greek and Latin dramatists, and it was treated in various other genres as well. Especially famous in Latin literature was the tragedy which the brilliant young Ovid wrote. Seneca, an admirer of Ovid, seems to have been influenced considerably by that play as he doubtless was by still other treatments.

The plot of Seneca's play, however, is essentially that of the *Medea* of Euripides; and doubtless this famous masterpiece was his chief source and model. But fundamental changes, as usually in Seneca, have been made in the characters and tone of the play, and much of its dramatic action has been deleted. Aegeus and the Paedagogus are eliminated. Jason appears only twice; and he is very different from the Jason of Euripides. Here he is weaker, more ingenuous, and more appealing. He has been forced into the marriage; and his entreaties alone, as Creon himself reveals, have saved Medea from being put to death. Jason here is also extremely fond of his children. Indeed, he insists that he chose submission to Creon rather than death only in order to save his sons. In part this more human portrayal of Jason is designed to bring out the inhumanity of Seneca's Medea; for whereas Euripides' great achievement had been to make Medea entirely human and understandable, Seneca deliberately presents her as a fantastic exaggeration of that barbaric sorceress which she is normally represented as being in ancient literature.

DISCUSSION.—Medea herself opens the play with a hysterical monologue. She screeches for vengeance. She prays that death may come upon Creon and his daughter and that life may be made a miserable burden for Jason. She flagellates herself and casts about for a crime worthy of her maturity. Thus is sounded the usual Senecan note of horror. Entirely gone is the careful emotional preparation for the appearance of Medea which the prologue of Euripides' play contains, as well as its vague and uncertain forebodings. Gone too is the effective scene with the children, who do not appear in Seneca's play until they are sent with the poisoned gifts, when they are present for only four lines. All this, of course, is in strict accord with Seneca's desire to present Medea in a very unfavorable but very intense light.

Seneca's chorus, as might be expected, is bitterly opposed to Medea and sympathetic with Jason and their king. So the first choral lyric is a gay song in honor of the marriage which is now to be consummated.

Naturally the strains of this festive song gall Medea and stimulate her to greater fury. She recalls in detail the crimes which she has committed for Jason's sake. Still she is obviously in love with him, as she reveals by her conviction that Creon alone is responsible and by her momentary resolve to take vengeance only upon him. The Nurse makes a desperate attempt to curb Medea's wrath, but this serves merely to reveal her determination more sharply. The next scene with the imperious Creon allows Medea a spirited defense. It also adds direct description of her character and her witchcraft. She is one, says Creon, who combines the natural deceit of a woman with the aggressiveness of a man (267-68). After finally granting her one more day within the realm, Creon hastens off to the marriage—an effective detail.

The chorus deprecates the impious boldness of man in inventing ships and overcoming those barriers which the gods placed between the lands. Medea was worthy freight for the first vessel! Then, by a shocking anachronism, Seneca marvels at the vast extent to which man's ingenuity has expanded the world of his own day, and predicts that in a day to come new continents will be revealed—his famous prediction of the discovery of America.

After her Nurse has described her utter madness, Medea comes on again for more self-flagellation. This soliloquy reveals a hardening of her attitude toward Jason and prepares for his entrance just as her former soliloquy has prepared for the entrance of Creon. The scene with Jason gives Medea another opportunity for a brilliant speech justifying her position and incriminating Jason. But Jason stands up well against all her charges, and the sincerity of his defense has been carefully guaranteed by his entrance monologue as well as by the previous statements of Creon and by the free admissions of Medea. Jason resolutely refuses Medea's plea to return to her and seek life elsewhere. Only at this point does Medea, who has never shown much regard for her children, give up hope of recovering him and begin definitely to plot for a vengeance upon him far worse than that upon Creon. In the course of this scene, when Medea asks that the children be allowed to go with her Jason very naturally reveals his great love for them. Medea immediately realizes where her vengeance upon him can strike deepest. Thus Seneca skillfully works into this scene the main function of Euripides' scene of Medea and Aegeus. Seneca has no other use for that scene, for he is wholly unconcerned with any semblance of a realistic escape at the end of the play. As soon as Jason departs, Medea plunges into a tantrum and announces her plan to send the poisoned gifts.

Remarking the limitless fury of a woman spurned, the chorus ponder the ill fate of those who sailed on the first ship and pray that Jason, their leader, may be spared. So this lyric harks back to the previous choral song and sounds an effectively ominous note.

The scenes of witchery, like the sacrifice and the raising of the ghost in Seneca's *Oedipus,* are essentially a digression. Still they are not so very much out of place here, since Medea's sorcery has been emphasized from the first and an atmosphere of horror and diabolical crime has been consistently maintained. The metrical variation in this scene is noteworthy. She enters with excited trochaics, lists her magical accomplishments in staid iambics (well suited to the realm of facts!), shifts to lyric iambics in making her offerings, and then to anapests for her "prayers." At the end of the scene, which reaches its climax with Medea's barbaric gashing of her own arms, the children are abruptly dispatched with the gifts.

After a short choral lyric describing Medea's fury, a messenger reports the catastrophe. For once Seneca rejects the opportunity of making a long glowing description of horror. Indeed, so short a report is unique in ancient tragedy; but the innovation is as welcome as it has been long awaited. A conventional messenger's speech here, furthermore, would be quite useless, for Medea in her incantation has directed with revolting detail the effects which the gifts are to have upon the bride.

Medea's last soliloquy, in which she finally determines upon the slaughter of her children, is an amazing confusion of natural human emotions, including even remorse, of the mysticism of madness, and of sophistry strained almost to the ridiculous. She wishes that she, like Niobe, had borne fourteen children instead of two in order that her vengeance might be greater! There is here no thought of saving the children from destruction at the hands of her enemies, as in Euripides. Here all is vengeance.

Jason enters with soldiers, coming not to save his children primarily, as in Euripides, but to punish Medea. As Medea has just slain one of her children before the eyes of the audience in order to satisfy the Avenging Furies of her brother, so now, having mounted to the roof of her dwelling, she slays the other before Jason and despite his most abject entreaties. Then she apparently flings the bodies down to him. This ghastly scene is most dramatic and is a fitting climax to a play that from the very first has sounded the note of horror. It is less effective than the final scene in Euripides, because Medea is less human and the children here have never been effectively presented. It is less tragic, too, because the heavy grief that falls upon life, which must go on even after such a catastrophe, is really more tragic than the catastrophe itself. But Seneca has undeniably achieved a harrowing and spectacular finale.

5. *Phaedra* (*Hippolytus*)

The ***Phaedra*** is one of Seneca's best plays. His interpretation is very different from that of Euripides in his extant *Hippolytus.* No effort is made to soften the character of Phaedra. This villainess plays the main role of the tragedy, and perhaps Seneca's primary interest lay in the study of her character. There is nothing mystical about Seneca's Hippolytus, who worships Diana as any other huntsman would and who is a more normal human being than the Hippolytus of Euripides, though he does hate women and civilization for various philosophical reasons. The theme of the stepmother is prominent in the play, and it is conceivable that certain passages are directed toward the imperial family.

SOURCE.—Euripides wrote two plays on the story of Phaedra and Hippolytus, of which only the later *Hippolytus Crowned* has been preserved. Seneca's ***Phaedra*** shows certain similarities to this play but in the main appears to be an adaptation of Euripides' earlier *Hippolytus Veiled.* Several other dramatists, however, are known to have treated the subject. Various lines in Seneca's play, especially in the first scene between Phaedra and her Nurse, loosely correspond to certain fragments of Euripides' earlier play, although it is sometimes assumed that there was no Nurse in that play. Seneca's treatment has many points in common with an imaginary love letter of Phaedra written by Ovid. We know that on some points Ovid is following Euripides' earlier play, and it may be that both Seneca and Ovid are

independently following Euripides rather than that Seneca is following Ovid.

INFLUENCE.—In his *Phèdre* (1677) Racine used to the best advantage not only Seneca's ***Phaedra*** but Euripides' extant *Hippolytus* as well. A complete analysis of Racine's indebtedness is beyond the limits of the present consideration, but the following motives may be mentioned as due to Seneca: Phèdre dominates the action throughout the play; the infidelity of Theseus is stressed; Phèdre confesses her love to Hippolytus in person, and her words are at times very close to those of Seneca; Phèdre beseeches the contemptuous Hippolytus to slay her and retains his sword; Phèdre dies on stage after confessing the truth.

The subject has been dramatized also by Gabriele d'Annunzio (*Fedra,* 1909).

STRUCTURE.—The play opens with a long passage in anapestic recitative by Hippolytus. Although his catalogues of places, dogs, and animals are elaborated with brilliant pedantry—witness the inclusion of the bison—still this scene could be staged as a colorful and spectacular extravaganza. It is more proper to the pageantry of modern opera, however, than it is to an exposition scene in serious drama. It is wholly a prelude. The lines of Hippolytus do end with a prayer to Diana; but this prayer is no more than that of an ordinary huntsman, and there is not, as in Euripides, any suggestion that Hippolytus is guilty of sacrilege toward Venus. After this prelude, Phaedra comes on with her Nurse. Her languishing complaints strongly contrast with the animal exuberance of Hippolytus and emphasize the gulf between these two. The conversation between Phaedra and the Nurse furnishes the real exposition of the play. Here the Nurse is already acquainted with Phaedra's passion, and the scene consists not of the Nurse's seducing Phaedra, as in Euripides, but of Phaedra's seducing the Nurse. Like a Stoic philosopher the Nurse preaches restraint and continency. She inveighs against royal license. She systematically eliminates every possibility of committing such a crime successfully. But Phaedra will not hear her, and by artfully threatening suicide, mistress bends servant to her will. The Nurse agrees to approach Hippolytus—the first step in the complication—and here the act ends (first act, 273 lines).

The subsequent choral song (84 lines) is strictly pertinent to the situation: love is supreme master of all the world. The poetry of the song is spoiled by the epigram at the end— love overcomes even the savage stepmother.

The second act (378 lines) opens with a realistic description of the manifestations of Phaedra's passion by the Nurse. Phaedra herself comes on, and her words and actions corroborate the description. This scene is reminiscent of the scene between Phaedra and the Nurse in Euripides' extant play; but its function here is somewhat different, for it is preparing for Phaedra's madly throwing herself at Hippolytus and perhaps for her madly taking revenge upon him. The action moves into new ground with the entrance of Hippolytus, who comes on at precisely the most convenient moment. The gross efforts of the Nurse to seduce him to a life of luxurious wantonness only offend him. After the

A Spanish production of Seneca's Medea *at Teatro Español in Madrid.*

Nurse has failed, Phaedra rushes up to faint in Hippolytus' arms. As she is revived, or pretends to be so, she steels her determination and makes her confession in a brilliantly written scene. She begs Hippolytus not to call her by the name of mother but rather by that of slave. She urges him to take her royal power—and herself. She tries to convince him that his father is dead. In Hippolytus she sees the more ideal Theseus. Finally she throws herself at his feet; but he is frightened and revolted by her crude advances. He abandons his sword and flees as Phaedra pretends to swoon and the Nurse comes to her rescue and calls for help in an effort to save her mistress by indicting Hippolytus.

The second choral song (88 lines) describes the flight of Hippolytus, dwells upon his beauty, and forebodingly suggests that flight will not bring him safety.

The leader of the chorus denounces Phaedra for her false charge and her base artifice. He then introduces Theseus. Theseus enters expressing his great relief at having escaped from Tartarus. He is startled by the sounds of grief. The Nurse appears and abruptly warns him that Phaedra is on the point of suicide. At the command of Theseus the doors of the palace are opened and Phaedra is revealed. But she artfully refuses to confess her secret until Theseus threatens to put the Nurse to torture. Refusing to name Hippolytus, Phaedra indicts him by means of his sword—an effective dramatic gesture. In a long monologue Theseus then calls

upon his father Neptune to destroy Hippolytus. This short third act (135 lines) constitutes the climax of the play and practically the reversal of fortune for Hippolytus.

The choral song which follows (30 lines) loftily ponders why the universe is so marvelously controlled but mankind is left to the mere whims of chance. This is a not unnatural reaction to the apparent triumph of the wicked Phaedra and to the ruin of the innocent Hippolytus.

The fourth act (134 lines) consists of the Messenger's report of the destruction of Hippolytus. This strikes the modern reader as too long and too much concerned with the miraculous. Significant description of Hippolytus himself and of the reaction of friends and servants is not as effectively emphasized as in Euripides; but occasional phrases (1005, 1067) do reveal Hippolytus' pathetic admiration for his father.

The last choral song (31 lines) opines that Fortune is most likely to strike down the great, as it has struck down Theseus. He has returned from the underworld only to meet even worse calamity in his own house.

The fifth act (127 lines) begins with the appearance of Phaedra. She calls down imprecations upon herself; but her dominant emotion is grief at the death of her beloved Hippolytus. She confesses her guilt and commits suicide. In excited trochaic meter Theseus, overwhelmed with remorse, curses himself in the most extravagant manner. He finally attempts to compose the mangled body of his son and with his last words curses Phaedra.

DISCUSSION.—Structurally Seneca's play is not very different from Euripides' extant *Hippolytus.* Some scenes in the Greek play, however, have no equivalent in the Latin. The divinities of prologue and epilogue have been entirely eliminated. Seneca's play develops wholly on the human level, and he manages to reveal the truth to Theseus without divine revelation—a weak and often criticized device in Euripides' play. In Seneca, furthermore, there is no choral song between the opening scene with Hippolytus and the first appearance of Phaedra. This is awkward. Indeed the whole beginning of this play with its interminable speeches is very poorly managed.

Seneca has added some excellent scenes. That between Phaedra and Hippolytus is the best of these. Its psychology is keen and subtle. Its theatrical effectiveness is equal to almost anything in ancient drama. The scene wherein Phaedra indicts Hippolytus, furthermore, is a brilliant one. Lastly, the scene of Phaedra's confession and suicide is spectacular, though the lack of any effective exchange between Phaedra and Theseus perhaps robs this scene of the dramatic effectiveness which it might be made to possess.

But Seneca has suffered the very serious loss of the scenes between Hippolytus and Theseus which play so important a part in Euripides.

A comparison of one other item of structure in each play is very significant—the "curtain" of the second act. In Euripides' extant play, when Hippolytus denounces Phaedra and flees the scene, Phaedra bursts into a short lyric lament, and this is immediately followed by the scene in which Phaedra dismisses the Nurse as her bane and determines to die in a last resort to save her good name and the honor of her children, and also to punish Hippolytus for his haughty disdain. Thus Euripides at the exit of Hippolytus refuses a spectacular curtain and its consequent suspense. He prefers to end the episode with ominous foreshadowing of the tragedy, but not before he has thoroughly motivated the most dreadful of Phaedra's actions—her denunciation of Hippolytus. Seneca omits this motivation. Here the Nurse hastily forms the plan for denouncing Hippolytus. His act ends so quickly after the departure of Hippolytus that his curtain is a spectacular one, though the suspense has been spoiled by the Nurse's announcement of her plan. Racine, as we might expect, has this spectacular curtain; but he also maintains the greatest suspense by ending his second act before Phaedra has had time to consider her future course.

Phaedra is drawn with great skill. Forced into marriage with a man notorious for mistreatment of his wives, and now deserted and betrayed, she is intensely miserable in her solitude. Small wonder is it, then, that this Phaedra, the undisciplined child of a royal house whose women were distinguished for their worse than licentious conduct, should fall in love with her beautiful stepson. Almost incredibly selfish, this Phaedra shows no hesitation in making known her passion to the Nurse, and she complains only that she does not, like her mother, have the inventive genius of a Daedalus to pander to her desires. She freely admits the criminal nature of such a union, but her moral consciousness is so obtuse that she feels no obligation to struggle against her passion or even to rationalize away its criminal aspect. Madness rules over her, as she herself expresses it (184). She cannot bring herself rationally to consider the possibility of her husband's return or the impossibility of seducing Hippolytus. She is driven by a passion that is reckless of everything but its own desire.

Still, Phaedra maintains enough equilibrium to practice deceit most artfully. She wins over the Nurse to her aid by an apparently insincere resolve to commit suicide. She faints most opportunely in the arms of Hippolytus (cf. 426). She begs Hippolytus to slay her, but this device—if it is device—is unfortunately without result. Seneca has not given Phaedra any expressed motivation for denouncing Hippolytus to Theseus. The Nurse in first suggesting such a course is motivated by the desire to cover their guilt. Perhaps Seneca felt that Phaedra's selfishness and her passionate weakness make further motivation unnecessary, or perhaps this is another instance of Seneca's tendency to write a collection of scenes and not a dramatically articulated play. But Phaedra goes to such extremes of artfulness in her deception of Theseus (cf. 826-28) that she must be considered morally responsible for this course of action even though the Nurse has been the first to suggest it.

In her final scene Phaedra is still the same. She taunts Theseus with his guilt, though this guilt is very slight compared to her own. She commits suicide not so much because of remorse as in a last desperate effort to be with Hippolytus and satisfy her insatiable passion.

The final scene has been severely condemned as an atrocious violation of propriety. This gory handling of the limbs of Hippolytus, however, seems to be not so very different externally from the original final scene of Euripides' *Bacchae.* Such matters are largely governed by superficial convention, though it must be admitted that for the modern reader Seneca's scene, far from achieving any great pathos, is revolting.

6. Oedipus

In his **Oedipus** Seneca appears most interested in presenting the portrait of a tyrant who from first to last was a curse upon his people and who himself was strangely obsessed with a premonition of his dreadful guilt. As a background for this mystic consciousness of sin, all the horror of the play is apposite, and even the callous sensibilities of one who has seen the slaughter of war or gladiatorial combats must be stimulated by this remarkable display. Those of more delicate sensibilities are likely to be repelled by it.

SOURCE.—Seneca follows the main lines of Sophocles' famous tragedy, but his purpose is so very different that the two plays are hardly comparable. His minor details may come from other sources. A host of Greek dramatists had treated the subject, and the young Julius Caesar, also, had taken a fling at it.

DISCUSSION.—Seneca has not only exhausted the natural possibilities of the subject for sensational and dreadful effects. He has introduced extraneous scenes, also, and germane and extraneous alike are strung together by the flimsiest dialogue in order to retain the semblance of a drama. Seneca makes no attempt to construct a logical and inevitable progression of events or to individualize the characters into something more than puppets of fate. Since the career of Oedipus is to be interpreted as an illustration of determinism (980-94), portrayal of character is superfluous for Seneca except that he wishes to present Oedipus as a tyrant obsessed with a consciousness of his guilt. Only the curtest respects, furthermore, are paid to details of dramatic technique. The most difficult problem in dramatizing the material is to avoid the embarrassment of two discoveries. Sophocles accomplished this only by the implausible expedient of identifying the shepherd who exposed Oedipus with the one survivor of Laius' struggle with the "robbers." Seneca has eliminated this implausibility, but he has two discoveries. Jocasta's revelation of the nature of Laius' death convinces Oedipus that he is the murderer. Mechanical haste in bringing on the Corinthian, however, prevents this untimely climax from becoming disturbingly obvious. But smooth articulation of the dramatic action also appears to be of little concern for Seneca; it is hardly pertinent to his chief interests.

"Seneca . . . ," we read in the preface of the *Oedipus* of Dryden and Lee, "as if there were no such thing as nature to be minded in a play, is always running after pompous expression, pointed sentences, and philosophical notions, more proper for the study than the stage: the Frenchman followed a wrong scent; and the Roman was absolutely at cold hunting." Certainly the material furnishes Seneca an excellent excuse for delivering Stoic sermons on several of his favorite subjects, especially the principle that a king who inspires fear must himself be subject to it—a good theme for Seneca's pupil Nero. The quarrel of Oedipus and Creon, so nicely prepared for and worked into the progression of events in Sophocles, is here used for this sermon and has no important effect upon the action.

The play opens with a long soliloquy—though Jocasta may be present—in which Oedipus reveals the horror of his own conscience and his dark past. The consumption of the plague, also, is dwelt upon. Finally, another harrowing picture out of Oedipus' past, his clash with the Sphinx, is presented.

The chorus now continue with a depressingly vivid description of the plague.

Creon's chilling account of receiving the oracle brings more horror, and the oracle itself is all too plain. Like several other references, the oracle foretells the misfortunes of Oedipus' sons as well as those of the king himself. These references contribute to the general gloom of the play, but being extraneous they tend to disrupt its logical unity. The fearful curse which Oedipus pronounces upon the murderer is no less obvious than the oracle, thus losing the simple and effective irony of the curse in Sophocles. But the revolting details of an unnatural marriage have been added.

At this point the Sophoclean tradition of events is abandoned in order to insert the account of the sacrifice. This is gory in the extreme and doubtless original with Seneca. The bull's fleeing the light of day, of course, suggests Oedipus' blinding himself, as the manner of the heifer's death suggests the suicide of Jocasta. The splanchnology, too, is painfully clear in its application to the house of Oedipus.

Here, perhaps as temporary relief, Seneca has kindly introduced a choral dithyramb to Bacchus, which constitutes a fine display of geographical erudition.

The dreadful sacrifice leads only to a still more harrowing episode, the exorcism of the ghost of Laius. Returning from this ordeal, Creon is very loath to reveal its results to Oedipus. His reluctance is nicely brought out in the assignment of lines. Oedipus is given precisely two lines and Creon precisely one during several exchanges—a dramatic subtlety used in the opening scene of Aeschylus' *Prometheus.* But of course Creon is eventually brought to his gruesome description. It begins in the best classic manner with an account of the place where the rite was performed. But the best classic manner quickly gives way to more of the magic, the supernatural, and the horrible.

At first glance Seneca would appear to have lost an opportunity for exploiting the horrible by not having Jocasta on stage when the discovery of Oedipus' identity is made, or at least by not portraying her reactions when this point is being approached. In Seneca's version, it is the Corinthian who tries to deter Oedipus from pursuing this knowledge. In Sophocles the Corinthian is characterized by optimistic eagerness, which effectively contrasts with Jocasta's efforts to deter Oedipus and with the reluctance of the shepherd of Laius. In Seneca the loss of Jocasta's reactions is a serious one; but it is apparently necessary, for they must be reserved intact for the final scene.

The Messenger's description of Oedipus' blinding himself is another masterpiece in depicting the horrible. It is almost forgotten, however, after we have seen what Seneca has in store for us and what he can accomplish when he extends himself; for the final scene is horrible beyond all words. Jocasta commits suicide by plunging Oedipus' sword into her "capacious womb," and the blinded Oedipus seems to stumble over her corpse as he shuffles off into miserable exile.

7. Thyestes

The *Thyestes* in its own crude way is a powerful tragedy of revenge. A secondary theme, crime's perpetuation of crime, is given strong emphasis especially in the opening scenes and at the very close of the play. This theme is carried on in the *Agamemnon,* where vengeance for vengeance is foreshadowed. Such a theme was a timely one for the court of Nero. That Emperor had murdered or was soon to murder his stepbrother Britannicus and his own mother, who incidentally had murdered her husband, the Emperor Claudius. Uncertainty as to the dates of these plays, however, precludes any assumption of a definite reference to these contemporary events.

The *Thyestes* surpasses many of Seneca's plays in its technical execution and theatrical qualities. Dramatic dialogue is maintained throughout. Only one iambic speech extends to fifty lines. The dramatic action is straightforward, though it could hardly be otherwise in a plot of such simplicity. The tone, as usually in Seneca, is dire and unrelieved. Great care has been taken to integrate the choral lyrics with the dramatic action, but these are somewhat too long and at times too boring.

SOURCE AND INFLUENCE.—The story of Atreus and Thyestes was one of the most frequently dramatized Greek legends. Sophocles wrote an *Atreus*. We know of some nine Greek plays entitled *Thyestes,* including one tragedy by Euripides and perhaps two by Sophocles. Still other titles were used, such as Euripides' *Cretan Women,* and various phases of this complicated story were covered; but the banquet was its most famous event. Among the Romans this story was easily the most popular for tragedy. Four tragedies entitled *Atreus* and perhaps seven entitled *Thyestes* are known to have been written. These included plays by the masters Ennius and Accius, but most famous of all was the *Thyestes* of Lucius Varius Rufus, the intimate friend of Vergil and Horace, which Quintilian thought comparable to any Greek tragedy.

Only fragments of a few of these Greek and Latin plays have been preserved, however, and they furnish little of interest in connection with Seneca's play. One point is noteworthy: in some versions Thyestes returned of his own accord. Hence Atreus might well be afraid of him and thus be driven to crime. In Seneca, however, Atreus invites the return in order to obtain his vengeance. In any treatment the banquet must have been gory and dreadful.

The *Thyestes,* a model play of revenge, has exerted more influence on English drama than any other play of Seneca.

DISCUSSION.—In form the prelude between Tantalus and the Fury is somewhat reminiscent of various scenes in Greek tragedy, such as the prelude of the *Alcestis* or that of the *Trojan Women* and the scene between Iris and Lyssa in the *Heracles* of Euripides. In content, however, this scene is typically Senecan. The Fury lays grim stress on crime's passing from one generation to another in this house, and her words foreshadow every remarkable event and every dreadful future crime in the whole saga; but her most vivid prediction is reserved for the coming feast of Thyestes. After this it is small wonder that the ghost of Tantalus prefers his Hell.

The first choral song completes the saga by dwelling upon the past atrocities of Pelops and Tantalus and Tantalus' punishment in the underworld. Thus this lyric is bound to the previous scene. Cessation of the house's perpetual crime is the theme of the chorus' prayer.

Atreus now comes on to flagellate himself to fury and revenge. The efforts of his subaltern to deter him bring out his determination and the viciousness of tyranny—a favorite theme with Seneca—and again the inevitable progression from crime to greater crime. Finally, Atreus forms his plan: Thyestes will be lured into his clutches by his own desire for revenge. The prospect of return to power and escape from poverty will overcome all scruples if not of the father at least of his sons!

The chorus, who have apparently not been present during this scene, note the renewed harmony of the house. The main theme of their lyric, however, is the Stoic principle that the true king is he who has no fear and who rules his own soul—a theme that has real significance for the subsequent episode.

True to the prediction of Atreus, Thyestes does return. But he seems to have no desire to harm Atreus. His extreme reluctance to entrust himself to his brother and his desire to go back to the simple life of the free exile give him the Stoic virtue of which the chorus have just sung. Like them, Thyestes preaches against the life of the tyrant. The palace and the customs which he describes are those of the Palatine and the Roman emperors, especially Nero (455-67). Thyestes as a Stoic philosopher is hardly consistent with his actual return or with the motives predicted by Atreus; but this characterization does facilitate an excellent scene of irony when his son pleads with Thyestes to trust Atreus and restore them to wealth and power. Such a retiring Thyestes, furthermore, causes Atreus by contrast to appear all the more monstrous.

Irony plays a still more important role in the reunion of the two brothers, neither of whom can restrain his hatred without a great effort, as we observe in their grim asides. The innocent children of Thyestes are given as pledges of his faith, and Atreus in his last line promises to offer the destined victims to the gods! This last is reminiscent of Electra's similarly appalling line as she receives Clytemnestra in Euripides' play (1141).

The irony continues as the chorus celebrate the strength of family ties and the wonder of concord after war. But, as an introduction to the peripety, their lyric ends on the mutability of fortune. Afterward, the Messenger enters to give a gruesome description of this palace and a harrowing account of the "sacrifice." The chorus respond with a description of the turning aside of the sun and the apparently imminent destruction of the world—a strange motive in classical poetry, but a favorite one with Seneca.

Like Aeschylus' Clytemnestra after the murder of Agamemnon, Atreus appears to gloat over his deed. An interior scene, a rarity in Roman tragedy, now reveals the lonely Thyestes trying to drown his years of grief in the joys of the banquet. But strange misgivings rise up to choke his pleasure. Throughout he sings his lines in lyric anapests. The effect of this eerie scene is very powerful.

Atreus comes up to mock Thyestes and finally presents the heads of his sons for the ghastly climax of the play. The one defense of Atreus is that moderation should be shown in crime and not in revenge. Thus again the theme of perpetuation of crime is emphasized, and the play ends with Thyestes' resigned prediction of vengeance.

8. Agamemnon

The story of the **Agamemnon** is a continuation of that of the **Thyestes.** Like the **Agamemnon** of Aeschylus, this play deals mainly with the return and murder of Agamemnon. Many other Greek and early Roman tragedies dramatized the fate of the house of Atreus, however, and Seneca seems to have been influenced by some of these. Noteworthy points of difference from Aeschylus are found in the introduction of the ghost of Thyestes for the prologue and the escape of Orestes at the end of the play. Besides suggesting the larger framework of the action, these innovations stress the perpetuation of crime in this royal house. The central section of Seneca's play is given over to the messenger's speech and to Cassandra. The first brings out the destruction of the sacrilegious Greeks by the storm, the second the destruction of the victor himself by his wife and her paramour. The play lacks a central figure; but again Seneca shows little interest in character. The action progresses naturally, and there is more dramatic dialogue than usually in Seneca.

A few words from this play (line 730) are scratched on a wall in Pompeii, and it is not impossible that the play was produced in one of the two theaters there. But Seneca had sojourned at Pompeii in his youth and visited there later in life; it was the home of his great friend Lucilius.

DISCUSSION.—As the **Thyestes** opens with the ghost of Tantalus, so the **Agamemnon** opens with the ghost of Thyestes, and this ghost like that one would prefer its place in Hell to this palace of dreadful crimes. The whole series is again recounted, and the coming slaughter of Agamemnon is foretold. Finally the ghost encourages his wavering son Aegisthus, though later in the play no reference is made to the ghost and Aegisthus seems never to have heard it.

Clytemnestra's wavering, the ominous admonitions of the Nurse, and the bickerings with Aegisthus—all these have distinct dramatic possibilities. They suggest a new and interesting approach to this old material. Properly they belong to a treatment which makes Clytemnestra a very ordinary human being caught in the trap of adultery and forced to murder her husband. Seneca's primary interest seems to lie not in a study of her character but in the moral theme that one crime must inevitably lead to another and that any woman caught in this situation must act in similar fashion. The alternative for Clytemnestra here, as Atreus claims in the **Thyestes** (203), also, is to kill or be killed. When Aegisthus enters, Clytemnestra plays the foil for him as the Nurse has earlier done for her in order that the inevitability of this crime may be further emphasized with rhetorical point and cogency. Any emphasis on her vacillation would be wholly pointless in view of her minor role in the remainder of the play; and the question whether her sudden change is genuine or pretended, long debated among critics, is not, therefore, of any real importance.

Disregard for character, however, has involved Seneca in certain inconsistencies. Aegisthus is craven and base. He can plausibly become extremely cruel to Electra after the murder. But his Stoic readiness to commit suicide (304-5)

certainly does not seem consistent with such a character. Clytemnestra's talk of saving her children from a mad step-mother (198-99), furthermore, seems ridiculous in the light of her later desire to put Orestes and Electra out of the way.

At the mid-point of the play, the rhetorical fury of the messenger's storm is unleashed and threatens to blow the dramatic action quite away. Aeschylus had the natural elements run their course in some twenty lines; but Seneca, challenged also by Vergil's famous storm in the first book of the *Aeneid* and by many another such tour de force, adds a hundred to this score.

Cassandra's scenes are effective, and the use of a second chorus of Trojan captives is noteworthy. Madness is realistically suggested by the speeches of Cassandra—German scholars' complaints of illogicality and their tamperings with the text are sufficient proof of this. In her repartee with Agamemnon, however, Cassandra is much too smart for Greek or modern taste. The king himself, on stage for only a few lines, plays a very minor role in the action. After he has gone into the palace, the chorus sing a long interlude on the labors of Hercules. Although, at the end, a reference to Hercules' taking Troy in ten days brings this into superficial connection with Agamemnon, this distant subject may have been chosen in order not to jeopardize the suspense at the climax of the play—a Euripidean technique.

After the murder Strophius appears "pat . . . like the catastrophe of the old comedy." Thus Orestes is spirited away, but Electra is left to the fury of Clytemnestra and Aegisthus. Forced by one crime to another, they are now utterly heartless villains. But Cassandra's final prediction, the last words of the play, is one of vengeance and more crime to come with the return of Orestes.

9. Hercules On Oeta

Like the earliest dithyrambic tragedy, perhaps, the **Hercules on Oeta** glorifies the passion of a divinity—the death and rebirth of Hercules. But the moral spirit of this play looks to the Christian future rather than to the Greek past. The triumph of this laboring Stoic over suffering and death, the feeling that the world should end with his destruction, and his epiphany to his mother—all this breathes a mystical allegory not unlike that of the story of Seneca's contemporary, Jesus of Nazareth. Hercules furnished the outstanding example of persecuted virtue in Greek legend. Long before the origin of formal Stoicism, he was the ideal Stoic hero. It is not surprising, then, that the Stoic Seneca reworked both of the plays on Hercules known to have been written by the leading Greek tragic poets. The very features which made Hercules a poor subject for Greek tragedy made him a splendid one for Seneca.

The shortcomings of the play are typically Senecan. One needs the devotion of a saint and the endurance of a martyr to bear up under the endless repetition of Hercules' toils. Every section of the play is too lengthy, and the whole is over two hundred verses longer than any other ancient drama. It has been called the most formless product having the pretense of art which has been preserved from ancient times. Indeed, its formlessness, like its change of scene and length, is almost Elizabethan. Still, the play, though as crude and rough as Hercules himself, has its virtues. The description of Hercules' death, however extravagant, is imaginative and powerful. One may recall the magnificent description of the death of Oedipus in Sophocles' *Oedipus at Colonus.* Hercules' epiphany, last of all, and the chorus' invocation of the new divinity furnish a glorious finale.

SOURCES.—The main source of the play is doubtless Sophocles' *Trachiniae,* although plays on Hercules were written by minor Greek dramatists. The story was told also in other genres, and the influence of Ovid seems to be undeniable. He had treated the subject in his *Metamorphoses* (9. 134-272) and in his *Heroides* (9). So much of Seneca's play is original, however, that these dependencies are of little significance.

DISCUSSION.—The **Hercules on Oeta** opens apparently in Euboea. Hercules declares that he has fulfilled his mission on earth, and for his reward he now asks Jupiter to raise him to the stars. Other than this prayer, there is no indication, such as the oracle in Sophocles, that a crisis in his life has been reached. At the end of his monologue-prologue, the chorus of captives are driven off singing of their fallen city, of death, and of the might of Hercules. Iole follows with a monody which incidentally gives some exposition and thus prepares for the coming scene. This prelude fixes attention upon Hercules and also prepares for the sacrifice at which the poisoned robe will do its work.

The locale now apparently shifts from Euboea to Trachis. Deianira, "like a mother tigress," rages with jealous wrath against Iole and Hercules. Nothing that the Nurse can say consoles her. Seneca has made no effort to exalt the character of Deianira. His interest, as we should expect, lies rather in depicting her in violent emotional upheavals. Seneca also emphasizes the irony of Deianira's being able to cause the death of Hercules, a thing which all the monsters and Juno herself have so far failed to do. The Nurse, however, finally prevails upon her mistress to resort to the use of magic to regain the love of Hercules. Deianira then abandons any intention of harming Hercules and determines, as in Sophocles, to anoint a robe with the blood of Nessus.

After a lyric of Horatian praise of the simple life sung by the chorus of handmaidens, Deianira enters in great consternation. The idea that Nessus could wish Hercules no good has occurred to her, and she has observed the consuming effect of the blood upon the fleece. Hyllus appears and describes the destruction of his father. He does not, however, upbraid his mother, nor does she without a word retire—we might forgive her more readily if she did! Indeed her remorse now becomes as insanely violent as her jealous wrath has formerly been. Hyllus, of course, must play the foil and attempt to dissuade her from her lengthily avowed purpose of suicide. Her fate is left uncertain at the end of the act, when she rushes off and Hyllus follows to prevent her.

The choral song does not jeopardize this suspense, though it dwells on mortality and predicts the end of the world now that Hercules has been destroyed. Hercules upon his en-

trance continues this same theme and bemoans the irony of his dying at the hands of a mortal woman. The chorus express their sympathy in short verses. Alcmena, his mother, now appears to console him. In Sophocles, it will be remembered, the hero called for his mother but was told that she was not in Trachis (*Trachiniae* 1148-54). She is essentially an extraneous figure, but her wild grief nicely plays the foil for the Stoic heroism of Hercules and effectively motivates his final epiphany. At Hyllus' announcement of the innocence of Deianira, Hercules recognizes his fate. The theme of the irony of his downfall is now dropped. His mystical triumph over death begins.

After the chorus initiates the crescendo of Hercules' apotheosis, a Messenger enters to report the majestic end of the hero. Alcmena follows to bewail the small compass of the ashes of her colossal son. Even these ashes, however, will protect her and terrify kings. Her hymn of mourning is ended by the epiphany of her son. His virtue has again conquered death; the prayer of his first lines in the play has been answered.

Berthe Marti (essay date 1945)

SOURCE: "Seneca's Tragedies: A New Interpretation," in *Transactions and Proceedings of the American Philological Association,* Vol. LXXVI, 1945, pp. 216-45.

[*Below, Marti contends that modern critical disparagement of Seneca's plays is, in part, the result of inappropriate comparisons with Greek drama. She asserts that Seneca was not attempting to imitate the earlier models, but rather was trying to adapt the "technique of drama to the teaching of philosophy."*]

Perhaps no ancient writings have suffered more from the changing tastes of succeeding generations than Seneca's tragedies. Scaliger's extravagant praise of them, "Seneca . . . quem nullo Graecorum maiestate inferiorem existimo, cultu vero ac nitore etiam Euripide maiorem," is echoed by many of his contemporaries. Modern critics in general find themselves in agreement with Nisard's acid comments on Seneca's "tragédie de recette" and the ingredients of which it is composed. In both periods these extreme positions are due in part to a wrong estimate of Seneca's relation to Greek drama. In their almost complete ignorance of the tragedies of ancient Greece, the Elizabethans saw in his plays perfect examples of the dramatic technique of antiquity. To modern readers they appear as debased imitations of Greek drama. Recently, however, the Senecan tragedies have been reexamined in an attempt to arrive at a fairer estimate of their literary value. What in my opinion is lacking in most of these studies is an effort to determine Seneca's object in writing the plays, for while from a purely aesthetic point of view much in them deserves the most severe strictures, the critics who blame them for lacking the qualities of Euripides' or Sophocles' drama are guilty of one of the cardinal sins of criticism. The discussion of any literary work should start with an enquiry into the writer's aim and the measure of success he has attained in achieving his aim. Seneca repeatedly expresses his convictions as to the value and aim of literature. Life is too short, he says, to be wasted in such superfluous occupations as the study of philology, of dialectic, or the reading of the lyric poets (*Epistulae Morales* 49.5 ff.). Literature must be the interpreter of life and should teach justice, moral duty, abstinence and purity. Let the writer therefore give lessons in virtue, let him show by the example of Ulysses how to love one's country, one's wife, one's father, and how after shipwreck to sail on to honorable ends (*Epistulae Morales* 88, *passim*). Literature is to be judged from the quality of its ethical content; its one purpose is to teach. This is of course the orthodox Stoic doctrine, an echo of which is found in the *Praefatio* of the fifth book of Quintilian's *Institutio Oratoria*. There Quintilian criticizes the writers who hold that the sole duty of the orator is to instruct and who think that appeals to the emotions are to be avoided because all disturbance of the mind is a fault. These writers think, he says, that the attempt to charm is not only superfluous in a pleader but unworthy of a self-respecting man.

What then was Seneca's conception of the drama? Moses Hadas [in "The Roman Stamp of Seneca's Tragedies," *American Journal of Philology* 60 (1939)] assumes that Seneca, like most Roman playwrights, wrote tragedies for the sole purpose of entertaining a Roman audience used to spectacular and often violent shows and fond of virtuosity and rhetoric. But this is contrary to Seneca's idea of literature. To go to the theatre merely to be entertained by dramatic representations of mythological tales would be as frivolous a waste of time as to read the lyric poets. In the *De Brevitate Vitae* Seneca attacks the poets for "fostering human frailties by the tales in which they represent that Jupiter, under the enticement of the pleasures of a lover, doubled the length of the night. For what is it but to inflame our vices to inscribe the name of the gods as their sponsors, and to represent the excused indulgence of divinity as an example to our own weakness?" (16.5). "Veritatis simplex oratio est," he says (*Epistulae Morales* 49.12), quoting Euripides. Yet he must acknowledge the power of poetry. "The same words are listened to with less attention and affect us less when they are expressed in prose. When rhythm and regular metres are added and compress a lofty thought, this same idea is as if hurtled with a fuller fling." (*Epistulae Morales* 108.10). But poetry must have a moral purpose and, moreover, must be interpreted not as the scholar does when he deals only with the use and meaning of words, but as the philosopher who explains the ethical meaning and extracts the moral (*Epistulae Morales* 108.24 ff.). In this Seneca echoes the traditional theories of the Stoics, who even saw advantages in having the philosophers themselves use verse. "As our breath produces a louder sound when it passes through the long and narrow opening of the trumpet and escapes by a hole which widens at the end," Seneca quotes Cleanthes as stating, "even so the fettering rules of poetry clarify our meaning" (*Epistulae Morales* 108.10).

Just as poetry is more powerful than prose in rousing men, so the theatre could be a powerful inspiration: "Have you noticed how the theatre reechoes whenever any words are spoken whose truth we appreciate generally and confirm unanimously?" Seneca's frequent quotations from the dra-

matists show that he fully realised the didactic possibilities of drama. He also knew that the theatre with its mimes and dramatic recitations was more attractive to his contemporaries than any other genre:

> Privatum urbe tota sonat pulpitum. In hoc viri, in hoc feminae tripudiant. Mares inter se uxoresque contendunt uter det latus illis. Deinde sub persona cum diu trita frons est, transitur ad galeam: philosophiae nulla cura est.

> (*Quaestiones Naturales* 7.32)

While deploring this fact Seneca realised that drama, with its vivid representation of men struggling against destiny, might become a useful illustration of what he taught in the less popular **Moral Essays** and **Moral Epistles.** His aim always remained the teaching of philosophy, but since it was proving a bitter pill for his contemporaries to swallow, he used the dramatic form as sugarcoating, somewhat as Lucretius before him had used poetry to make Epicureanism more palatable. His readers would be interested in any new handling of the traditional themes of Greek drama. This would insure him large audiences for the public readings of the plays and wide circulation. Since drama wields such power of inspiration "how much more do you think this holds true when such things are uttered by a philosopher, when he introduces verses among his wholesome precepts, that he may thus make those verses sink more effectively into the mind of the novice?" (*Epistulae Morales* 108.9).

It is my purpose to show in this paper that Seneca did not intend to write plays after the manner of the Greek dramatists but that he adapted the technique of drama to the teaching of philosophy. For as Livy had observed of history that its great value consists in floodlighting the examples of the past by placing them for our instruction as if on a bright monument, so tragedy, dealing as it does with universals, with grave events and symbolic figures, might profitably be used as another vehicle to demonstrate the great ethical truths of Stoicism. In order to do so he did not simply translate Greek plays and adapt them to his purpose by stuffing them with Stoic *sententiae,* but instead composed philosophical propaganda-plays. He did not mean to have these pseudotragedies acted, for in his mind the individual plays were but parts of the whole series; he merely made use of the methods of the dramatists for the purpose of spreading his particular brand of eclectic Stoicism. In them he combined elements of the diatribe, satire and versified dialogue with those of drama, and he emphasised ethics and philosophy at the expense of plot and action. Thus his tragedies did not conform to the rules laid down by Aristotle, nor did Seneca intend them to. "Istae vero non sunt tragoediae," says Leo in the preface to his edition, "sed declamationes ad tragoediae amussim compositae et in actus deductae. . . . Itaque non comparabimus cum graecis has tragoedias ut artis opera, sed earum argumenta tantum et argumentorum tractationem." His characters remind T. S. Eliot of the "members of a minstrel troupe sitting in a semicircle, rising in turn each to do his 'number' or varying their recitations by a song or a little back-chat" [Introduction to **Seneca His Tenne Tragedies** (1927)]. Seneca's drama is something entirely different from the conventional imitations of the great Greek dramatists by his Roman predecessors.

This fact explains Quintilian's silence concerning Seneca's plays. While he quotes Seneca about the propriety of using a certain expression in tragedy (*Inst. Or.* 3.8.31), and states that Seneca had dealt with almost all the fields of knowledge (*ibid.* 10.1.128), he does not mention him in his catalogue of the Roman successors of the Greek playwrights. Yet he knew Seneca's *Medea* and quoted from that play. He included in his review of Roman tragedy Ovid's *Medea* and Varius' *Thyestes* but left out Seneca's *Medea* and his *Thyestes* as well as the remaining seven plays. The conclusion seems to me clear: Quintilian did not consider them real tragedies; his omission of Seneca's name from the review of the Roman dramatists was deliberate and justified. This omission has baffled many scholars and led some to argue against the authenticity of the plays, but the arguments against Seneca's authorship are far too slight to outweigh the manuscript evidence.

Ever since Leo's work on the text of Seneca's tragedies, editors have agreed that of the two recensions known as traditions A and E, E, represented by Codex Etruscus (Laurentianus 37, 13), should be the basis on which to establish the text of the plays. One of the differences between the two traditions is the inclusion in A of the *Octavia* and the different order in which the plays are given in A and E. Whether Seneca published his own edition of the tragedies or left them for his executor to edit, I am convinced that E has preserved the order planned by Seneca: *Hercules* [*Furens*], *Troades, Phoenissae, Medea, Phaedra, Oedipus, Agamennon* (sic), *Thyestes, Hercules* [*Oetaeus*]. I do not mean to imply that this is the order in which he wrote the plays, for this to my mind cannot be determined in the present state of our knowledge. But that he had a definite pattern in mind, that the nine plays form one whole and that Seneca intended them to be read in the order preserved by E can I think be proved.

Upon reading the titles of the plays in E, one fact is immediately obvious: they form a series, introduced and concluded by a play on Hercules, and within that frame the plays are arranged according to a deliberate order, the first two being named after the chorus (*Troades, Phoenissae*), the next two after the heroines (*Medea, Phaedra*), the next three after the heroes (*Oedipus, Agamemnon, Thyestes*). . . . The fact that in the first tragedy Seneca has represented the passion and in the last the apotheosis of the patron saint of Stoicism, Hercules, is an indication that the series forms a philosophical whole, and that Seneca intended it to be, like all his other works, a piece of neo-Stoic propaganda. It is my belief that Stoic readers would, upon seeing the titles of the plays, realise that in them dramatic treatment was to be given to the sins and passions which prevent the attainment of virtue and wisdom. Even a cursory reading would show them the principles underlying Seneca's choice of subject-matter and his arrangement of the plays. The first group (*Troades, Phoenissae*) seems to be primarily centered upon the religious problems of life, death and destiny. The two plays represent men and women who, in their rebellion against the injustice of their fate, question the goodness of Providence. The next group (*Medea, Phaedra*) is a study of character and emphasises the effect of strong emotions, specifically passionate love, upon the lives of a group of human beings. These two plays illustrate the most significant contribution of the Stoics to psychology, the analysis of the effect of emotional impulses upon the struggle between vice and virtue. They provide *exempla* for a Treatise of the Passions. The last group (*Agamemnon, Oedipus, Thyestes*) deals with ethics and is focussed primarily upon the problem of free choice in life, and of sin and retribution. This does not mean that Fate, Fortune and Destiny are not involved in all the plays or that the passions of the main characters are not an important element in every one of the plays. Seneca was haunted by the thought of death and its shadow is seen on almost every page he wrote, in verse as well as in prose. He was passionately interested in the problems of Justice and Providence, and also in the study of the perturbations and vices of human nature. These constant preoccupations of a philosophical mind form therefore the background of all the plays. Nevertheless each reading strengthens my conviction that Seneca systematically ordered the tragedies according to their principal theme and adopted an arrangement (religion, psychology, ethics) which is more akin to a Stoic treatise than to a set of plays. A German dissertation [Paul Schaefer, *De Philosophiae Annaeanae in Senecae Tragoediis Vestigiis* (1909)] provides a very useful compilation of parallel passages from the plays and the essays, and the comparison of these quotations shows the extraordinarily close similarity in thought and expression between the two sets of works. But the tragedies represent his most ambitious literary effort. Nowhere does he come to grips more earnestly with the supreme problems of philosophy, and he seems to have conceived his set of tragedies as a sort of glorified Essay on Man. He lacked the dramatic and poetic qualities which might have given them real life and power, but as illustrations of his thought and as symbols of his beliefs they are of the utmost interest.

Others have suggested before this that Seneca's aim in writing the plays was primarily philosophical or pedagogical. They did not, however, realise that each tragedy is but a part of one whole and that apparent variations in some of them from Seneca's eclectic Stoicism, deliberate contradictions and unsolved problems, are removed in the final conclusion. Thus they failed to see that the individual plays, being the constituent parts of one set, present only partial solutions to the problems they raise, and that Seneca's ultimate aim can only be judged from the total effect of all the tragedies.

The story of Hercules had been allegorised ever since the time of Socrates. . . . What Hercules meant to the neo-Stoics may be seen in the works of Seneca, Dio Chrysostom, Epictetus and others. Hercules has been called wise by the Stoics, says Seneca, because he was never subdued by hardships, because he despised pleasure and conquered all terrors (*Consolationes* 2.2.1). He conquered nothing for himself, but travelled over the whole world, an enemy of the wicked, a defender of the good, a peace-maker on land and sea (*De Beneficiis* 1.13.2-3). His fortune did not match his virtue, but he bore his fate with wisdom and courage, and when his work was done discovered how to become immortal. The manner of his death by fire added symbolic meaning to his labors, for the Stoics believed that Fire was the creative god who, at the end of each cycle, destroyed all things in the general conflagration. . . .

Although Seneca did not believe in an exaggerated use of the allegorical method (*Epistulae Morales* 88.5), he, like other Stoic teachers, attributed great moral value to the ancient myths and often pointed out their deep ethical meaning. No wonder, therefore, that he exploited the dramatic possibilities of the story of Hercules. No better symbol of man's struggle against fate and adversity could be found than the tale of Juno's unjust persecution of the hero, the subject of Seneca's first tragedy, no greater allegory of the triumph of man's soul than Hercules' final vindication, the victory and immortality he gained through the Stoic purification by fire. Juno, unable to crush the hero who "thrives on trouble, enjoys her wrath and turns her hate to his own credit" (*Hercules Furens* 33-35), drives him to madness and makes him kill his sons and wife during a fit of insanity. Though his hands are guilty he is of course innocent. The tone of this first play is one of unrelieved horror, of bitter indignation at the injustice of the gods. If we were to take this play as a separate unit we could not reconcile its mood of harsh pessimism with the fundamental optimism of the Stoic doctrine. But the nine plays form a set, and the *Hercules Oetaeus* is a necessary complement of the *Hercules Furens*. Only in this last tragedy does Seneca justify the divine power, when he shows the justification for the trials Hercules has undergone so serenely. This technique of posing problems in the tragedies to which only partial solutions are given, the complete answer being reserved for the concluding play, is reminiscent of Seneca's method of asking rhetorical questions in his prose works. There he writes abstractly about universal problems and after he has questioned the justice of the gods and their management of the world he gives his solution immediately. In the tragedies the problems become alive, and the sight of the apparently undeserved agonies of symbolic human beings forces the reader to ask himself questions. The final solution, through a skilful use of dramatic suspense, is only foreshadowed, until we come to the last play, where the reader is at last made to see clearly the purpose of the divine wisdom.

Let us now turn to the plays inserted between the two on Hercules. I have said that in the first group Seneca considers the problems of fate, life and death. In the *Troades* he has combined the plots of two of Euripides' most harrowing tragedies, the *Hecuba* and the *Trojan Women*. He has made of it what at first seems to be an indictment of Fate and Providence. The relentless persecution of Hecuba, Andromache and the other innocent captives outrages the reader's sense of justice. The gods seem as vindictive against them as Juno was in her hatred of the hero Hercules in the preceding play. Their fate condemns the women to be stripped of everything they hold dear; no glimmer of hope lightens the blackness of their mourning. In their utter destitution they question the beneficence of providence (981 ff.). Hecuba, who typifies their grim tragedy, has lost Troy

and Priam, Hector and a happy throng of children and grandchildren; she sees Cassandra, Andromache and her sorrowing comrades given by lot to the victors, and in the final disaster her only remaining daughter, Polyxena, is sacrificed to the shades of Achilles while her grandson, Astyanax, is hurled by the Greeks from a lofty watch-tower. It is clear that the main interest of the play is centered upon the scene in which the death of Polyxena and Astyanax is described. For the child and the maid have faced their fate boldly and bravely, undaunted in spirit and with a sternness worthy of the greatest Stoic heroes. In the midst of the wretched captives they alone are free, for death has brought them release.

The chorus expresses the traditional Stoic view (a view not consistently held by Seneca in all his prose works) that death is complete annihilation:

> post mortem nihil est ipsaque mors nihil,
> velocis spatii meta novissima . . .
> mors individua est, noxia corpori
> nec parcens animae . . .
> quaeris quo iaceas post obitum loco?
> quo non nata iacent.
>
> (397 ff.)

The theme that death alone brings release and freedom, that only the dead are secure, recurs throughout the play and is accompanied by another Stoic commonplace, that of the fickleness of Fortune and the danger inherent in high rank and earthly felicity. A passage of the *Quaestiones Naturales* (6.2.1-2) seems to me one of the best commentaries on the *Troades*. After discussing the calamities which overtake cities and the very earth as well as men, and the impermanence of all things including life, Seneca says that fear is folly when there is no escape, and that philosophy delivers the wise from terror. He adds that Vergil's words, una salus victis nullam sperare salutem, addressed to those overwhelmed with sudden captivity amid fire and foe, should be regarded as applying to the whole human race. Over and over in his prose works, Seneca teaches that life is small but the contempt of it is great (*Epistulae Morales* 32.3), that the Stoic considers all things which make men cry and groan as unimportant and not worth noticing (*Epistulae Morales* 13.4), for death is ever near to set the unfortunate free (*Epistulae Morales* 110.4) and deliver them from fear (*Epistulae Morales* 24.11). Since death must come to all "let courage be derived from our very despair" (*Quaestiones Morales* 2.59.5). What matters is the human spirit, which can only be known after it has grappled with fortune (*Epistulae Morales* 13.1: sic verus ille animus et in alienum non venturus arbitrium probatur).

Andromache recognises this spirit in her little son:

> quid retro fugis
> tutasque latebras spernis? agnosco indolem:
> pudet timere.
>
> (503 ff.)

She, fearing for the child, knows that the worst evil is to fear without hope (miserrimum est timere cum speres nihil,

425). She also knows that one who has lost everything is no longer vulnerable. There is dignity and noble Stoic resignation in her words:

> hic mihi malorum maximum fructum abstulit,
> nihil timere.
>
> (422)

The second play of this group, the **Phoenissae,** is so incomplete that it is difficult to make any certain statement about its purpose. The first fragment represents the wanderings of blind Oedipus and his daughter Antigone, the second the feud of his two sons and their mother's intercession. Both fragments are in the form of debates. In the first, Antigone, who is filled not only with filial devotion but also with Stoic wisdom, attempts to convince her father of three truths; first that only deliberate crimes can be called sinful and that men are not guilty who have sinned unconsciously:

> non es nec ulla pectus hoc culpa attigit.
> et hoc magis te, genitor, insontem voca,
> quod innocens es dis quoque invitis.
>
> (203 ff.)

The second truth she comes back to repeatedly. Death should not be sought as an escape from trouble, for only the coward yearns for it:

> resiste; tantis in malis vinci mori est . . .
>
> (79)

> quare ille mortem cupiat aut quare petat?
> utrumque timidi est; nemo contempsit mori
> qui concupivit.
>
> (196 ff.)

Thus Seneca, who in the first play had shown death as the deliverer, now clarifies his thought. There are two kinds of suicide, that resorted to by the weak who foolishly choose escape and defeat, and that wisely settled upon by the philosopher who has met and conquered his fate. In the third place, she shows him that only those who have thrown away life's blessings and trodden destiny underfoot are safe from the attacks of fate:

> cuius haut ultra mala
> exire possunt, in loco tuto est situs.
>
> (199 f.)

The theme of the second debate is more difficult to determine because the fragment breaks off just before the climax. But the trend of Jocasta's message to her sons seems to be similar to that of Antigone to Oedipus: where fate and fortune drive men they need not feel guilty for their actions, since guilt depends upon the possibility of choice. Her sons, however, are now planning deliberately to break the law of nature, and if they do they will have to pay the penalty:

> error invitos adhuc
> fecit nocentes, omne Fortunae fuit

> peccantis in nos crimen: hoc primum nefas
> inter scientes geritur.
>
> (451 ff.)

She adds that wealth and royal authority are nothing without peace and justice, and seems to be leading to some statement that will vindicate providence:

> ne metue. poenas et quidem solvet graves:
> regnabit. est haec poena . . .
>
> (645 f.)

> invisa nunquam imperia retinentur diu.
>
> (660)

The two fragments seem in their present form to have little in common, yet both contain discussions of the meaning of life, power and death; they emphasise at the same time man's subjection to fate and fortune and his independence from them. In both fragments two attitudes are represented in sharp opposition. Oedipus' wretched lamentations are contrasted with his daughter's sense of duty and with her serene acceptance of destiny. Eteocles' cynical reliance upon brutal force and the value he puts upon earthly sovereignty are opposed on the one hand by the weakness of his fearful and foolish brother and on the other by the prophetic wisdom of his mother.

These are clearly problem-plays written to force the reader to think about life and death, for like G. B. Shaw, Seneca used drama to preach and to prove his theses. The plots may have been borrowed from Euripides or others, but the technique is that of the Stoic teacher who has asked searching questions and so far has only hinted at the solution.

The second group of plays (**Medea, Phaedra**) form what might be called *exempla* for a treatise on the passions. Seneca's debt to the Middle Stoa, his adaptations of what he found in his predecessors as to the divisions of the soul and the relationship of the rational and the irrational, have frequently been studied. His psychological system is illustrated in these two tragedies. The highest wisdom, according to him, is the ability to distinguish clearly between good and evil (*Epistulae Morales* 71.7); virtue is the only good and consists in a true and steadfast judgment, "ab hoc enim impetus venient mentis, ab hoc omnis species, quae impetum movet, redigetur ad liquidum" (*ibid.* 32). Since man's soul is composed of a rational and an irrational part (*ibid.* 27) he progresses only by checking all impulses arising from the irrational part and by consistently following the guidance of reason. The Stoics never tired of discussing the effects of emotional impulses. "Ex perturbationibus autem primum morbi conficiuntur. . . . Hoc loco nimium operae consumitur a Stoicis," says Cicero (*Tusc.* 4.10). Seneca shows much penetration in his analyses of the first symptoms of passion: "Imbecillus est primo omnis adfectus. Deinde ipse se concitat et vires, dum procedit, parat; excluditur facilius quam expelliture . . . ergo intrantibus resistamus" (*Epistulae Morales* 116.3). Reason must remain aloof and uncontaminated in order to deny admission to the passions (*De Ira* 1.7.2), for it is easier to remove wrong impulses than to control them if you once permit them to get a start; they will increase along with their causes (*Epistulae Morales* 85.10 f.). The ideal condition is soberness, the state of a soul uncontaminated by emotions or perturbations. *Securitas* and *perpetua tranquillitas* (*Epistulae Morales* 92.3) are essential to a happy life and depend on a sound judgment and a firm will. While all passions are bad, Seneca considered anger the worst of all, "maxime ex omnibus taetrum ac rabidum" (*De Ira* 1.1.1). Now the passion of love which gives rise to the four sinful conditions described by the Stoics (fear, desire, grief, excitement) is, when spurned, likely to stir the most violent anger. I believe that Seneca chose Medea and Phaedra for the heroines of his psychological plays not only because they had been the prey of an overwhelming passion but also because, through the helplessness of their injured pride, they had become *exempla* of the most annihilating effects of anger. Seneca's description of anger in the beginning of the *De Ira* provides a very vivid commentary on the actions of the two women:

> Ceteris enim aliquid quieti placidique inest, hic totus concitatus et in impetu doloris est, armorum sanguinis suppliciorum minime humana furens cupiditate, dum alteri noceat sui neglegens, in ipsa irruens tela et ultionis secum ultorem tracturae avidus. Quidam itaque e sapientibus viris iram dixerunt brevem insaniam; aeque enim impotens sui est, decoris oblita, necessitudinum immemor, in quod coepit pertinax et intenta, rationi consiliisque praeclusa, vanis agitata causis, ad dispectum aequi verique inhabilis, ruinis simillima, quae super id quod oppressere franguntur.

No other two heroines of mythology could better have served as illustrations for this and other similar passages. Both act as if possessed by a fit of temporary madness, both are equally devoid of self-control and decency, both are eager for revenge and give no thought to their own safety provided they can hurt and drag down in the ruin that overwhelms them the man against whom their resentment is so violent. But there is a great difference between them. Phaedra's judgment is clear, she knows what is right but deliberately chooses evil. Medea, on the other hand, for all her physical strength (268), is weak, irrational, ignorant of wisdom, impulsive and completely blinded by her passion.

Medea's actions have always been motivated by her passions and are therefore all wicked, all harmful (trahere cum pereas libet, 428). In her self-pity she does not blame herself for any of the crimes committed because of her love but considers that the end amply justifies the means (241 ff.):

> iuvat, iuvat rapuisse fraternum caput; artus iuvat secuisse et arcano patrem spoliasse sacro, iuvat in exitium senis armasse natas (911 ff.).

From the beginning her one thought is vengeance; she utters a terrible curse against her faithless husband and vows destruction upon his new wife and her whole family. She plans "wild deeds, unheard of, horrible calamities, at which heaven and earth alike shall tremble . . . wounds, slaughter, death creeping from limb to limb" (45-48). She laughs and cries hysterically and her nurse compares her to a maenad raving at the coming of the god, showing the symptoms of

every passion, with madness marked upon her face (382 ff.): irae novimus veteris notas (394). The theme that her hatred is a frenzy and a fit of madness recurs at intervals throughout the play, and the chorus watching her exclaims:

> quonam cruenta maenas
> praeceps amore saevo
> rapitur? quod impotenti
> facinus parat furore? . . .
> frenare nescit iras
> Medea, non amores.

> (849 ff.)

Phaedra is a far more complex character and is more subtly drawn. She knows her passion to be a grave illness (100 ff.), but does not even wish to be well. The rational part of her soul sees clearly the wise and virtuous path: quae memoras scio vera esse, nutrix (177); but she has allowed passion to enter, and now, fully conscious of the wrongness of her choice, she moves on to her own ruin:

> sed furor cogit sequi
> peiora. vadit animus in praeceps sciens
> remeatque frustra sana consilia appetens.

> (178 ff.)

Since passion rules supreme what can reason do? (quid ratio possit? 184). Her nurse considers her mad (361), and she herself calls her infatuation *furor*. At the end of the play she confesses that she has been insane: quod ipsa demens pectore insano hauseram (1193). She is a terrible proof of what Seneca repeats so often in his prose works, that the time for drastic action is the moment when the first symptoms of a passion are felt: facilius est enim initia illorum prohibere quam impetum regere . . . facilius sustuleris illa quam rexeris (*Epistulae Morales* 85.9 f.). Once indulged in, her passion is like a fire which cannot be quenched (186 ff.).

During the first part of the play, Seneca uses the nurse as an exponent of his own philosophy and seems to have meant her to personify the rational part of Phaedra's soul. She insists upon the necessity of quickly putting out the fire before it is too late:

> nefanda casto pectore exturba ocius,
> extingue flammas neve te dirae spei
> praebe obsequentem. quisquis in primo obstitit
> pepulitque amorem, tutus ac victor fuit;
> qui blandiendo dulce nutrivit malum,
> sero recusat ferre quod subiit iugum.

> (130-135)

Cicero says that for the Stoics *honestum* constituted the *summum bonum* (*Off.* 3.11) and Seneca constantly repeats this: summum bonum est quod honestum est (*Epistulae Morales* 71.4). The nurse echoes this thought when she states: honesta primum est velle nec labi via (140), and she adds that even if Phaedra should escape punishment for her sins she could not escape from the judgement of her own conscience (162). The wise man, she says, must ever be ready to endure his fate; he is self-sufficient, for freedom is near at hand (139).

Later, when no rational argument can break the queen's resolve to die, the nurse yields in order to avoid that evil and approaches Hippolytus. From that moment the nurse's attitude changes completely, and Seneca means by this, I think, to show concretely and symbolically the contagion with which the irrational part of the soul can infect the rational part. The character of the nurse is considered one of Seneca's original creations; it seems to me that she serves to embody the conflict within Phaedra's soul and to show the deterioration of her judgement. As for Hippolytus, who at no point seems really alive, he is the mouthpiece of the Stoic philosopher advocating the simple, natural life, one of the commonplaces of the creed. . . .

The change from these two psychological plays is very abrupt, both in tone and treatment, when we take up the next group, the *Oedipus,* the *Agamemnon* and the *Thyestes.* As usual the opening speech of the first play sets the theme: quisquamne regno gaudet? (6). Oedipus has "happily escaped the sceptre of his father" (12) only to receive another from Chance and Fortune. He is now struck with a blind terror of what the Fates have in store for him, since he knows the curse which threatens him (cuncta expavesco meque non credo mihi, 27). The hero of all three plays is a king threatened with ruin or murder by an inherited curse and whose terrible punishment is represented in the course of the action. Three heroes who seem to be innocent appear to be led by a predetermined fate to ruin and self-destruction. Upon reading the plays, however, we see that predestination is by no means the only agent, that the heroes are actually responsible for their fate, since each one has made the wrong choice of life in order either to acquire or to preserve a royal throne. Thus ethical problems are handled in this group, and particularly that of retribution. It is also clear that there is a gradation in the heroes' responsibility, and equally a crescendo of horror in their suffering, from Oedipus' self-inflicted blindness to the murder of Agamemnon by his wife and finally to the unspeakable banquet of Thyestes.

The clue to Seneca's aim in this group is found, not in the Greek dramatists, but in a passage of Plato's *Republic* (618A-619C). Toward the end of his tale, Er the Armenian explains how the souls who are about to start another course of earthly existence are given their choice of lives:

> And after this again the prophet placed the patterns of lives before them on the ground, far more numerous than the assembly. They were of every variety, for there were lives of all kinds of animals and all sorts of human lives, for there were tyrannies among them, some uninterrupted till the end and others destroyed midway and issuing in penuries and exiles and beggaries. . . . When the prophet had thus spoken he said that the drawer of the first lot at once sprang to seize the greatest tyranny, and that in his folly and greed he chose it without sufficient examination, and failed to observe that it involved the fate of eating his own children, and other horrors, and that when he inspected it at leisure he beat his breast and bewailed his choice, not abiding by the forewarning of the prophet. For he did not blame himself for his woes, but fortune and the gods and anything except himself.

Plato in this passage describes a man's prenatal choice of the greatest kingship, . . . but this man's soul does not realise that his choice determines for him a life filled with evils and dooms him to eat his own children. Thus Plato by way of a myth attempts to reconcile Necessity with Free Will. Each individual is "free to choose the life unto which he shall be bound by Necessity . . . Virtue is her own mistress" (617E); once the choice is made it is irrevocable; "the blame is his who chooses, God is blameless" (*ibid.*).

This must have made a great impression upon Seneca, who had thought and written a great deal about Fate and freedom of choice: Fata nos ducunt et quantum cuique temporis restat prima nascentium hora disposuit. Causa pendet ex causa, privata ac publica longus ordo rerum trahit. . . . Quid est boni viri? Praebere se fato. . . . Irrevocabilis humana pariter ac divina cursus vehit. Ille ipse omnium conditor et rector scripsit quidem fata, sed sequitur; semper paret, semel iussit (*De Providentia*, 5.7-8). I suspect that this passage of the myth of Er, which not only deals with the great problems of predestination and retribution but also emphasises the dangers of the exalted position of kings (one of Seneca's favorite themes) may have inspired him to write his trilogy of the *Oedipus, Agamemnon* and *Thyestes.* For it seems obvious that Plato must be referring to a proto-type of Thyestes in his description of the incipient tyrant who condemns himself to eat his own children.

A chapter from Epictetus also throws light upon the Stoic ideas behind Seneca's three ethical tragedies. Epictetus contrasts our judgements on material things and ethical questions: "In a case where we wish to judge of weights we do not judge at haphazard; where we wish to judge what is straight and what is crooked we do not judge at haphazard; in short where it makes any difference to us to know the truth in the case, no one of us will do anything at haphazard. Yet where there is involved the first and only cause of acting aright or erring . . . I have nothing like a balance, nothing like a standard, but some sense-impression comes and immediately I go and act upon it" (Arr. 1.28.29 f.). He goes on to say that because of this lack of a standard measure of right and wrong many characters of tragedy have had to suffer evil. That is to say, what has caused Oedipus', Agamemnon's and Thyestes' downfall is that they made the wrong choice and valued the wrong thing. Instead of having a moral purpose in life, instead of pursuing what reason shows to be the highest good, they have been ambitious and have treasured a throne.

Oedipus, the hero of the first tragedy, is by far the weakest character. He is blind long before he has deprived himself of the use of his eyes. Moreover he is proud of his strength and wisdom and utters vain boasts of his victory over the sphinx (87-102). His pride in having solved the riddle would at the outset seem suspicious to the Stoics, who tended to distrust any claim of intellectual superiority. Where Sophocles had created a determined, stern and self-assured Oedipus, Seneca's is a weaker and smaller human being, who worries, hesitates and scolds. In Seneca his behavior is the very opposite of that of the Stoic sage; he is vain and impulsive, and because of his exalted position behaves like an autocrat and a tyrant. In his prologue, Sophocles stresses

Oedipus' wisdom, his paternal beneficence, his thoughtfulness toward his people. Seneca's prologue is a complaint of the danger of royalty and the recital of Oedipus' terrors, a clear statement of his feeling of insecurity. He has a premonition that he is the cause of the pestilence that is ruining Thebes ("Couldst thou hope that to crimes like thine a whole kingdom would be granted? I have made heaven pestilent" 35 f.). He is cast down with grief (75) and deplores the fact that he has not left the land sooner. Jocasta speaks the words of Stoicism, that courage in the face of adversity is manly and regal and that lamentations make woe heavier (81 ff.). Oedipus' answer reveals his real weakness: he is, he says, no coward and would gladly face war. But he is afraid of his destiny, not knowing that a wise man triumphs over his fate by willingly surrendering to it. He has physical but no moral courage (87 ff.; 206 ff.).

Both Sophocles and Seneca show him quick to anger. In the Greek play this anger is regal and dignified, but in Seneca it is impetuous and completely lacking in self-control. He is unjust to Tiresias, Creon and his own sons, not because he is wicked but because he lacks wisdom and feels insecure. Until the final catastrophe, when he is maddened with grief and bitterness, he shows in Sophocles' play the nobility and the bearing of a king. In Seneca's, his complaints against fortune are abject (786 ff. etc.), and one remembers Cicero's statement that distress must be avoided because it is loathsome, wretched, execrable (*Tusc.* 3.25). He lacks the spirit of Sophocles' hero, is instead pusillanimous, querulous and jealous of his own position, as the following utterances show: Hortaris etiam, sponte deponam ut mea tam gravia regna? (678); dubia pro certis solent timere reges (699); quisquis in culpa fuit dimissus odit, omne quod dubium est cadat (702); odia qui nimium timet regnare nescit; regna custodit metus (704).

Where Sophocles uses dramatic irony to represent the inevitable unfolding of the tragedy, without attempting to draw from it any ethical conclusion, Seneca points out the Stoic moral. For him, Oedipus may be the victim of a curse, but he has chosen his present exalted position without realising that he was thereby condemning himself. He is blind as well as weak, an *exemplum* of what the Stoics called foolishness, a ruler incessantly complaining of the instability of fortune, suspicious of the fate for which his own ignorance is responsible. The story of Oedipus was frequently used by the philosophers to illustrate discussions of predestination. Oenomaus the Cynic, discussing Chrysippus' statement that Laius could have refused to beget children, contended that Oedipus was free to choose whether or not he would murder his own father and that his decision depended on too many factors to make prediction possible. The stress on Oedipus' freedom of choice in such discussions is significant and may have been a commonplace of the Schools, in which case Seneca's intention in his tragedy would have been immediately clear to his readers.

Agamemnon is more obviously guilty and therefore more responsible than Oedipus, though he is equally unaware of the fact. He need not have sacrificed his own daughter and thereby earned his wife's hatred (158 ff., etc.) if he had not desired to be the king of kings, as he is constantly called in

the tragedy and if he had not had the ambition to lead "a thousand ships spreading sail together" (171). Moreover, he is a tyrant rather than a king, and the first chorus emphasizes the danger of his exalted position:

> ut praecipites regum casus
> Fortuna rotat. metui cupiunt
> metuique timent.
>
> (71 ff.)

We do not have to believe Aegisthus, who accuses him of tyranny, of being harsh to his allies, fierce by nature, with a pride swollen by prosperity (248 ff.). Agamemnon's own actions prove the right of this accusation. In his arrogance he has refused to let Apollo's priest ransom his daughter. When obliged to give her up, he has carried off Briseis, Achilles' captive maid, although he was warned against this by the very seer whom he had believed and obeyed when he was ordered to sacrifice his own daughter Iphigenia. He has made Cassandra, Apollo's bride, his mistress and brought her home, utterly disregarding his wife's pride and jealousy.

Here again Seneca intends to show that although Clytemnestra's crime is in no way justified, for she too will have to pay the penalty, Agamemnon by his actions, by his pride and ambition, has condemned himself to the death that awaits him at Mycenae. Though as the son of Atreus he was fated to perish at the hand of Thyestes' son, he is in spite of this predetermined necessity responsible for his own fate.

The manner in which Seneca has handled in this play a situation resulting partly from actions represented in the next and last play of the group reminds one of some of Seneca's more artificial rhetorical devices. By having Thyestes' ghost introduce the *Agamemnon,* he not only emphasises the connection between the two plays but, using the device of tragic irony, gives the reader the clue to the events which are to follow. Having thus clearly indicated Thyestes' guilt at this point, he is able in the next play to stress the wisdom and magnanimity Thyestes has acquired in exile after he has lost the power he had wickedly schemed to obtain.

Before I indicate how, to my mind, Thyestes fits in with this group of heroes who, in spite of appearances, are responsible for their fate, I must say a few words about a recent interpretation of the play. Olof Gigon has argued that Thyestes is not only an innocent man unjustly punished but represents Seneca's highest ideal of the Sage ["Bemerkungen zu Senecas Thyestes," *Ph.* 93 (1938-39)]. While this interpretation of Thyestes' character contradicts the conventional story of the two brothers, it is also contradicted by the text of Seneca's tragedy. For in spite of Gigon's comments many passages seem to me to show that Thyestes both realises and confesses his guilt. When his brother welcomes him home, he exclaims that now indeed is his case proved most wrong:

> diluere possem cuncta, nisi talis fores.
> sed fateor, Atreu, fateor, admisi omnia
> quae credidisti. pessimam causam meam

hodierna pietas fecit. est prorsus nocens
quicumque visus tam bono fratri est nocens . . .
ponatur omnis ira et ex animo tumor
erasus abeat. obsides fidei accipe
hos innocentes, frater.

(512-521)

When Thyestes complains of Atreus' revenge upon his sons and calls upon the gods (piorum praesides deos) Atreus taunts him with the retort, "quin coniugales?" Whereupon Thyestes answers with a clear admission of his former guilt: scelere quis pensat scelus? (1103).

Moreover, the reader has just finished the **Agamemnon**. There he has already seen, and this was deliberate on Seneca's part, the results of Thyestes' former ambition and the feud between the two brothers. He has watched Aegisthus, the offspring of Thyestes' incestuous union with his daughter, avenge him by murdering Agamemnon, Atreus' son. He has also read, and this is a passage which he could not easily forget, Thyestes' ghost loudly proclaiming himself more impious and more guilty than the great criminals who suffer torture in Tartarus: vincam Thyestes sceleribus cunctos meis (*Agamemnon* 25). Only his brother's crimes, he says, surpass his own.

Indeed, what seems to me remarkable about this play is that Thyestes has been made truly humble by the consciousness of his guilt. His suffering in exile has taught him much. He realises, as neither Oedipus nor Agamemnon do, that his wretchedness has been caused by his desire for power:

> clarus hic regni nitor
> fulgore non est quod oculos falso auferat;
> cum quod datur spectabis, et dantem aspice.
> modo inter illa, quae putant cuncti aspera,
> fortis fui laetusque; nunc contra in metus
> revolvor.

(414 ff.)

He explains to his sons that greatness attracts with false pretences, that fear is the lot of those in exalted positions, that crimes belong to the throne: immane regnum est posse sine regno pati (470). Seneca clearly intends to show that Thyestes' wisdom, his humility, his generosity have been acquired through suffering and exile, thus again foreshadowing the conclusion of the **Hercules Oetaeus**. Through suffering he has come to understand the cause of his crimes and to abhor them, and also to accept retribution. His only complaint is that innocent children should have been made to pay.

Epictetus often discusses the fatal effects of a mistake in judgement. Eteocles and Polynices, he says, were enemies because of their mistaken opinion that royal power is a good thing (*Encheir.* 31.4). "That which made Eteocles and Polynices what they were was nothing else but this—their judgement about a throne, and their judgement about exile, namely, that one was the greatest of evils, the other the greatest of goods" (Arr. *Epict.* 4.5.29). In this group of plays, Seneca shows that this is also true of Oedipus, Agamemnon and Thyestes. A seemingly endless chain of crimes seems to be the curse of the house of Tantalus, and the ghosts and furies of the play symbolise this. But Atreus, Thyestes and Agamemnon are all, through their characters and actions, the architects of their fate. Ambition is the worst counsellor; the only true sovereignty is the kingdom which each man bestows upon himself (*Thyestes* 389 ff.).

As **Hercules Furens** introduces the series so **Hercules Oetaeus** concludes it. The remark has often been made that the **Hercules Oetaeus** is filled with reminiscences and borrowings from the previous plays and this has been used by some as an argument against the authenticity of the play. Summers believed ["The Authorship of the *Hercules Oetaeus*," CR 19 (1905)] that the numerous parallel passages between this and the other tragedies were due to the fact that a rough draft of the **Hercules Oetaeus** was left by Seneca and was supplemented by an amplifier who sometimes wrote original lines, sometimes simply introduced a patchwork of tags from other plays. But if my interpretation of the tragedies is correct, the reason for these reminiscences and borrowings from the other plays is now obvious. Seneca has gathered together in the **Hercules Oetaeus** all the threads left loose in the preceding plays and has given us an epitome of the Stoics' creed and an abstract of their wisdom. Up to this point he has shown Fortune fickle and vengeful, "something halfway between blind chance and canny Nemesis" [C. W. Mendel, *Our Seneca* (1941)], attacking the great in preference to the humble. He has shown innocent victims paying for crimes they have not committed, men and women who think that happiness consists in the satisfaction of their desires, ambitions and passions. He has shown that the Fates are harsh and that the righteous are made to suffer. But since we cannot change them we must adjust to the eternal order of nature and bring ourselves into harmony with the divine will. In the **Hercules Oetaeus** as in the prose works, Seneca shows how man is to make this adjustment. He must rely upon himself alone and only take counsel of his rational soul. He must forever struggle on toward new victories over his lower self and over external obstacles until in death he finds deliverance and everlasting rest. As a Stoic, Seneca stresses individualism and self-confidence. Thus he provided the dramatic literature of Rome with the super-man, with new types of heroes and heroines who stand alone and "dwell on colder, lonelier heights than their Greek antecedents" [H. W. Wells, "Senecan Influence on Elizabethan Tragedy: A Re-estimation," *Shakespeare Association Bulletin* 19 (1944)].

First he takes up again some of the questions that had been left unanswered and the problems that were incompletely solved. A pathetic chorus of captive maidens is the exact replica of the **Troades,** but here, without any softening through pity, the chorus criticises the maidens' complaint according to the stern teaching of the school:

> quid regna tui clara parentis
> casusque tuos respicis amens?
> fugiat vultus fortuna prior.
> felix quisquis novit famulum
> regemque pati vultusque suos
> variare potest. rapuit vires
> pondusque malis casus animo

qui tulit aequo.

(225 ff.)

Moreover, Alcmena becomes the great symbol of all sorrowing mothers, grieving like Hecuba and Andromache, but for a loss greater than that of any woman. The parallel of Alcmena watching her divine son's passion and mourning by his pyre with Mary at the Cross has often been made and the passage in Seneca is so forceful that the comparison between the two situations is inescapable. That Alcmena is a symbol like the other characters in Seneca's plays, he has stressed by calling her an *exemplar* of bereaved mothers: matribus miseris adhuc exemplar ingens derat—Alcmene dabo (1852 f.). She is comforted by the knowledge that her son will live in his heroic deeds (1498 f.). She knows that he is not to be mourned, that he is invincible and that only cowards deserve our tears (1374-1376):

> virtute quisquis abstulit fatis iter;
> aeterna virtus Herculem fleri vetat.
> fortes vetant maerere, degeneres iubent.

(1834 ff.)

In Dejanira, Seneca has pictured a woman as passionate as Medea and Phaedra, and has almost duplicated in her case the tale of their mad fury and of their conflicts between love, jealousy and anger, and also the description of the physical symptoms of their passion. But she is made to realise that while in her blind passion she has sought to subdue Hercules, she has, through her impulsive actions, unwittingly brought about his death and her own destruction. More clearly even than in the two psychological plays Seneca stresses here the fatal results of unreasoning passions and lack of sound judgement. Ackermann [in "De Senecae Hercule Oetaeo," *Ph.* 10 (1907)] has pointed out so many parallels between this play and Seneca's prose works that it is useless to review them here. The tragedy is full of philosophical digressions, of considerations about law and order (1094) and about the general conflagration by which the final destruction of our present world will be accomplished (1110 ff.). There are also in this play striking correspondences with the tirades on kings and on the love of power in the group of the ethical plays. This is particularly true of a very long sermon by the chorus (583-690):

> tu quicumque es qui sceptra tenes,
> licet omne tua vulgus in aula
> centum pariter limina pulset;
> cum tot populis stipatus eas,
> in tot populis vix una fides . . .
> colit hic reges regumque lares,
> non ut presso vomere semper
> numquam cesset curvus arator
> vel mille secent arva coloni;
> solas optat quas ponat opes.
> colit hic reges, calcet ut omnes
> perdatque aliquos nullumque levet;
> tantum ut noceat, cupit esse potens.

(603-639)

Some lines in this song even seem to refer specifically to the plays of that group: "aurea miscet pocula sanguis" (657)

is probably an allusion to the banquet of Thyestes (satur est, capaci ducit argento merum, ne parce potu . . . mixtum suorum sanguinem genitor bibat, *Thyestes* 913 ff.). The contrast between the faithful wife of the poor man and the wealthy bride pursued by Erinys seems to be a reference to Clytemnestra or to Jocasta's tragic marriage. But the climax of the play is Hercules' self-imposed death by fire—the purification of the Stoics—and his apotheosis. Hercules has ever been seeking the skies, and now that his heroic struggle for virtue is to have its reward, the pessimism of some of the characters in the previous plays will be proved to have shown their foolish lack of faith. What Seneca said elsewhere of the wise man is true of Hercules: exemplar boni viri posuit, qualis quantusque esset ostendit (*Epistulae Morales* 93.8). He knows that his fate is now unfolding itself. His madness has been overcome, he has crushed kings and cruel tyrants and brought peace to the whole world (3-6). All the obstacles put in his way by Juno and the gods he has conquered without complaint:

> quidquid est iussum leve est,
> nec ulla nobis segnis illuxit dies.
> o quanta fudi monstra quae nullus mihi
> rex imperavit! institit virtus mihi
> Iunone peior.

(59 ff.)

Defiant and unafraid he has met his fate, and now faces his end with majestic calm (1746), for he knows that he has triumphed over life and death (1610 ff.; 1834 ff.): quanta pax habitum tulit (1685). Such is his assurance that none can mourn, not even Alcmena, "a mother almost equal to her son":

> haesere lacrimae, cecidit impulsus dolor
> nobis quoque ipsis, nemo periturum ingemit.
> iam flere pudor est; ipsa quam sexus iubet
> maerere, siccis haesit Alcmene genis
> stetitque nato paene iam similis parens.

(1686 ff.)

And now from the sky above Hercules declares his triumph:

> quidquid in nobis tui
> mortale fuerat, ignis evictus tulit;
> paterna caelo, pars data est flammis tua . . .
> virtus in astra tendit, in mortem timor.
> praesens ab astris, mater, Alcides cano . . .
> me iam decet subire caelestem plagam;
> inferna vici rursus Alcides loca.

(1966 ff.)

The conflicts are resolved. The chorus affirms that virtue and valor are borne to heaven and that the brave live on: iter ad superos gloria pandet. Those who are inspired by the example of his heroic life now pray to him for protection. Seneca's conclusion to the set of tragedies might appropriately be expressed in the words of a far greater poet:

> His servants he, with new acquist
> Of true experience, from this great event

With peace and consolation hath dismissed
And, calm of mind, all passion spent.

Denis Henry and B. Walker (essay date 1963)

SOURCE: "Seneca and the *Agamemnon*: Some Thoughts
on Tragic Doom," in *Classical Philology,* Vol. LVIII, No.
1, January, 1963, pp. 1-10.

*[Henry and Walker examine the "emotional and imagina-
tive content of the philosophical concepts and abstractions"
that Seneca treats in his plays, focusing particularly on
Agamemnon.]*

In 1927 T.S. Eliot wrote two essays on Seneca the dramatist, *Seneca in Elizabethan Translation* and *Shakespeare
and the Stoicism of Seneca.* In the first of these essays Mr.
Eliot's main purpose was to discuss the *Tenne Tragedies*
and their influence on Elizabethan drama; but he does also
provide as assessment of the Latin tragedies themselves.
The second essay is more limited in scope and in mainly
concerned with the attitudes adopted by tragic heroes on the
point of death; but like the previous essay it contains much
that is illuminating on the whole subject of Senecan drama.
It is surprising that the two have had so little effect on
subsequent critics. There is in fact still no full evaluative
criticism in English of any of Seneca's plays or of his drama as a whole.

Most editors and critics of Seneca since 1927, as before,
have endeavored to apply to the plays traditional dramatic
canons, derived more or less directly from Aristotle. They
have examined structure, plot, characterization and so on,
and measured the plays by their obvious deficiencies in
these departments. They have pointed out that where these
plays use the conventional machinery of Greek drama, they
do not use it well; that the structure is frequently clumsy,
the plot static, and characterization entirely artificial. There
is a greater degree of dramatic inaction than is normal in a
Greek tragedy; and there is an absence of climax, which
makes it easy to label the plays essentially undramatic.
Even if the general supposition that Seneca did not write his
plays for stage performance but for recitation be accepted,
such criticisms might seem damning to their chances of
being considered literary achievements at all.

Nor is this all. Such critics in considering Seneca's use of
the chorus find in it a stale revival of a Greek convention
already outworn. The chorus, they point out, is employed
more in imitation of Euripides than Aeschylus to provide
interludes or breaks in the dramatic inaction. It is destructive of what unity the plays may possess, fragmenting them
into a series of more or less disjointed tableaux.

The value of Mr. Eliot's work on Seneca was that he avoided using criteria of this kind and pointed in a direction that
should have led others at least to reconsider their dramatic
premises. There is one remark made by Eliot in the first
essay mentioned that might serve as a starting point for
critical discussion: "In the plays of Seneca, the drama is all
in the word, and the word has no further reality behind it."
This remark is made with the familiar decisiveness of Mr.

Title page of Thomas Newton's 1581 edition of Seneca's tragedies.

Eliot's famous generalizations, and the context in which it
is made does not at first fully clarify Mr. Eliot's meaning.
He is at the time contrasting Seneca's tragedies with those
of the Greek dramatists; in the Greek dramatists the tragic
idea, he seems to suggest, springs directly from a creative
experience in which moral concept and feeling are unified.
In describing a play of Aeschylus, for example, it is impossible to isolate *moral lessons* or to speak of a *drama of
ideas.* The artistic wholeness of an Aeschylean play is so
highly complex and realized in terms so physical that to
abstract from it a theme is impossible. Seneca's plays, on
the contrary, directly invite a critical treatment which includes consideration of moral and philosophical issues,
such issues being explicitly stated in the writing of the play.
For instance, where Euripides both in the *Hecuba* and
Phoenissae presents in vividly realized terms the sufferings
of women in war, Seneca uses the same incidents to indicate the idea of cosmic order and destruction: "tempus nos
avidum devorat et chaos" (*Troades* 400). Similarly one can
fairly say that Seneca's **Medea** and **Phaedra** are meditations on the theme of passion, and his **Thyestes** a play about
power, without distorting or reducing to banality the dramatic meaning of those plays. The **Oedipus** again may be
said to present a series of episodes and choruses illustrating
the idea of unnaturalness *natura versa est* (371). Clearly to

describe the plays of Sophocles and Euripides on these subjects in such abstract terms would be entirely inappropriate.

Mr. Eliot in the remark quoted seems to have been referring to this explicit mentioning of moral themes by Seneca and to have called it dramatic, but dramatic in a way different from the Greek dramatists. This difference he related closely to the tradition and context in which Seneca was writing. A preoccupation with moral themes and in particular with questions of practical morality is characteristic of Roman writers in general and especially of those who lived in the first century of the Empire, when the questions raised by Stoic and Epicurean philosophers were common currency among all the literate. The preoccupation with ethics and with ideas such as fatalism, human freedom, and so on, is not merely implied in the writers of this age; it is stated in explicit terms, often in the form of moral maxims or aphorisms, the Silver Age *sententiae*. Such maxims are frequent not only in philosophical and didactic writing where one would expect them, but in epic poetry, lyric, and drama, where one would not. They are very common in Horace, who can end an ode of personal grief with the general reflection: "sed levius fit patientia / quicquid corrigere est nefas" (*Carm.* 1. 24. 19-20), and Lucan's style is continually pointed by lines in the aphoristic manner: "servat multos fortuna nocentis / et tantum miseris irasci numina possunt" (*BC* 3. 448-49).

When such maxims appear in didactic writing of an aphoristic kind they serve to condense and summarize argument into an easily memorable phrase. They provide a succinct and bare record of stages reached in argument, pointing what has gone before, and they are essentially related to the section or paragraph preceding. In poetry and drama they do not normally have this integral place: they may be felicitous to adorn a passage and make it memorable, or perhaps more often they may be passed over as irrelevance or intrusion. Poetry uses the language of imagery; the apothegm or maxim uses terse and abstract language from which imagery is absent.

When the maxim appears in Greek tragedy, it usually stands out in marked contrast to the rest of the speech or scene in which it occurs. . . . At other times the plainness of the apothegm may be deliberately intended to startle the audience by its explicit statement of the moral situation underlying the dramatic action.

In Seneca's tragedies moral observations of this kind do not have the startling effect they may have in the Greek. There is no change in the texture of the language, and the static, often oracular, utterance causes no break in the dramatic action. The Senecan apothegm has the same appropriateness in the plays as in the *Moral Epistles* and other prose writings. The writing throughout whether in dialogue, narrative speeches, or choruses, is of a consistent texture using abstractions in preference to specific expression, and it presents human experience by the static analysis of states of mind. If Seneca's plays are examined in the traditional terms of dramatic criticism they can hardly be accepted as plays at all; and if the verse is read as dramatic poetry in the

traditional sense, it may well be dismissed as devitalized rhetoric. Yet there is a real vitality and immediacy of expression in Seneca and it is here that Mr. Eliot's judgment may be misleading. When he observed that "the drama is all in the word, and the word has no further reality behind it" he was referring, as we have said, to Seneca as contrasted with the Greek dramatists. Of them he goes on to say "Behind the drama of words is the drama of action, the timbre of voice and voice, the uplifted hand or tense muscle, and the particular emotion . . . the unity of concrete and abstract in philosophy, the unity of thought and feeling, action and speculation, in life." All this is, of course, absent from Seneca, and indeed from every Roman writer. But there is, we would suggest, another kind of reality behind the word in Seneca, the kind of reality which lies behind abstractions when an imaginative writer trained in rhetoric and philosophy expresses an experience in the language most meaningful to him.

The abstractions in Seneca are not merely scaffolding, but the essential fabric of the work. They are charged with significance in a way in which other dramatists have charged poetic imagery, or sometimes symbolic characters. Few critics have tried to study the emotional and imaginative content of the philosophic concepts and abstractions in the plays. And it is this approach which would, we feel, lead to a very different evaluation of them from the traditional one based on Aristotelian canons.

II

This view of Seneca the dramatist can be illustrated by reference to his *Agamemnon.* This is not the best and certainly not the worst of Seneca's plays; it provides a representative example of his very real merits as a writer together with some of his worst rhetorical vices. It bears in outline a close resemblance to the *Agamemnon* of Aeschylus, and the particular differences of treatment between the two dramatists throw light on Seneca's moral and philosophical preoccupations. The two plays have been compared in detail by Pratt, Marti, and others, and we are not here concerned with their similarities and differences except when they illuminate Seneca's work itself and his attempt to write a new kind of drama.

In her first appearance in Seneca's play Clytemnestra addresses herself in the traditional soliloquy that precedes the moment of decision. This is also the opening in the play of the dramatic dialogue, following the prologue by Thyestes and the first chorus. The opening is characteristically abrupt:

quid, segnis, anime, tuta consilia expetis?
quid flictuaris? clausa iam melior via est.
licuit pudicos coniugis quondam toros
et sceptra casta vidua tutari fide—
periere mores, ius, decus, pietas, fides,
et qui redire cum perit nescit pudor.
da frena et omnem prona nequitiam incita.
per scelera semper sceleribus tutum est iter.

[108-15]

Clytemnestra is here speaking in terms of moral judgment (*segnis anime*), and rebukes herself for hesitation and timidity in undertaking the murder of Agamemnon (*quid fluctuaris?*). The metaphor used here was long dead when Seneca wrote, as were the images in "clausa iam melior via est" and "da frena . . . incita." In none of these phrases is there imagery suggestive of life. The passage quoted contains two apothegms (*qui redire . . . nescit* and *per scelera . . . iter*) and these go in fact provide the most vigorous lines of the passage, apart from the remarkable "periere mores, ius, decus, pietas, fides." Seneca can here successfully carry off a string of abstractions because this is really the form of expression which is natural and congenial to him and it is weighted by the practice of the Roman literary tradition to which we have referred. They do not cause any break in the dramatic movement or failure in portrayal of character because the play itself contains no movement or characterization of the conventional kind. Clytemnestra's reference to her own indecisions, to the moral collapse which caused her unfaithfulness to her husband, are seen as curiously anonymous and remote.

A speech like this shows very clearly that the elements of Greek drama which Mr. Eliot points to as lying behind the words, "the drama of action . . . the particular emotion," hardly exist in Seneca. What actually happens is unimportant; action and thought remain distinct and sometimes even unrelated. Emotion is explored and exploited, but hardly ever particularized. Incident and character serve to illustrate a series of moral situations and moral issues.

The result of using incident and character in this illustrative way has a marked effect of fragmentation on both. In the passage quoted, the meditation of Clytemnestra remains divorced from any possible outcome in action. If the line "per scelera semper sceleribus tutum est iter" can be said to look forward at all, it does so in such vague and general terms that it cannot sharpen the reader's perception of what is to come or whet his dramatic anticipation. When after an interjection by the *nutrix* Clytemnestra continues to analyze her own state of mind and feeling:

> flammae medullas et cor exurunt meum,
> mixtus dolori subdidit stimulos timor,
> invidia pulsat pectus. . . .
>   . . . fluctibus variis agor
>   . . . . .
> ubi animus errat, optimum est casum sequi,
>
>   [132-44]

she is describing a psychological condition of herself which can have no release in action. The verse, though so generalized in expression and so staccato in its nervous movement from one physical manifestation of tension to another, has considerable intensity and passion. But it is a passion isolated from both past and future, and isolated too from any moral context. Just as in the opening speech Clytemnestra spoke of the simple disappearance of moral criteria, *periere mores,* so here the one positive moral control is *pudor* (138) which is described as "fessus . . . et devinctus et pessumdatus" (137). If it rebels, the effect of the rebellion is not to increase Clytemnestra's sense of sin and guilt

but merely to add to her purposeless drifting and agitation: "fluctibus variis agor . . . / . . . proinde omisi regimen e manibus meis" (138-41). The decision (if it can be called that) to follow fortune can in no sense be considered as a proper and effective plan to act.

One can make the point in another way by remarking the manner in which the incidents of the play are presented. Thyestes in the Prologue alludes to the past horrors of the House of Pelops. Like Clytemnestra he declares his intention to advance by crime, "vincam Thyestes sceleribus cunctos meis" (25), but no attempt is made in what follows to relate the action of the play to the working out of any demonic design by Thyestes or the *di inferi,* or indeed to regard the horrors of the present as influenced by the horrors of the past. They are rather the expression of a complete state of cosmic confusion the result of which is likely to be terrible, though not in a clearly patterned way. Thyestes' own statement of the existence of this confusion, "versa natura est retro" (34), is echoed again by Cassandra, "fata se vertunt retro" (758), just as Thyestes' reference to "sortis incertae *fides*" (38) is picked up and emphasized first by Clytemnestra, "periere mores, ius, decus, pietas, *fides*" (112), and then by Aegisthus, "non intrat umquam regium limen *fides*" (285). Clytemnestra even hopes that she can anchor *fides* by binding it to her allegiance, "opibus merebor ut *fidem* pretio obligem" (286). Aegisthus dispels the illusion, "pretio parata vincitur pretio *fides*" (287), and the confusion remains as before. In other words, the incidents of the play follow a meaningless and chaotic series without due sequence or causality.

In passages of dialogue such as this there is indeed no reason why particular remarks in the aphoristic style should be assigned to any one speaker rather than another. As we see in the interchange on *fides* between Clytemnestra and Aegisthus different characters adopt and re-echo not only the phrases and words but even the style of the other. Remarks in the aphoristic style are comments made on the general situation which in its confusion is the same for all. If "versa natura est retro," all the characters of the play experience it. If such remarks have no influence on the development of dramatic action, they equally contribute nothing to the realization of dramatic character. The dialogue between Clytemnestra and Aegisthus handles the idea of *fides* in an exploratory way, setting it in different contexts, presenting different implications and overtones. It has already been a key word in the dialogue between Clytemnestra and the *nutrix* and in the first chorus, "iura pudorque / et coniugii sacrata *fides* / fugiunt aulas" (79-81), and was in fact introduced as early as the Prologue in the phrase already referred to, *sortis incertae fides.* This first introduction of the *fides* theme follows closely on the striking pronouncement in which Thyestes states the main theme of the play:

> versa natura est retro.
> avo parentem, pro nefas, patri virum
> natis nepotes miscui—nocti diem.
>
>   [34-36]

Seneca is using abstractions much as Elizabethan or Jacobean dramatists used sensuous images in a thematic way which (to use the language of painting) establishes a play's color or tone values, not necessarily related to its content or structure. *Fides* and *retro* are motifs in the work in much the same way as "storm" and "jewel" are motifs in Shakespearean tragedy. The difference is that Seneca's motifs are almost invariably abstract terms of a kind customary in philosophical writing.

There are two places in this play where Seneca seems to be trying to develop dramatic incident in a conventionally dramatic way. The results are far from successful and merge into the general atmosphere of confusion. The first is in the "messenger" speech of Eurybates narrating the fate of the Greek expeditionary force after the capture of Troy, which heralds the arrival of Agamemnon. He recounts the departure of the fleet from Troy in verse which in contrast to much of the writing of this play is simple, effective, and orderly:

> hinc aura primo lenis impellit rates
> adlapsa velis; unda vix actu levi
> tranquilla Zephyri mollis adflatu tremit,
> splendetque classe pelagus et pariter latet
>
> [431-34]

This has a clarity and dramatic vigor similar to that of many such speeches in Greek tragedy. The description is particular and vivid:

> fususque transtris miles aut terras procul
> quantum recedunt vela fugientes notat,
>
> . . . . .
>
> et iam quod unum pervicax acies videt.
> Iliacus atra fumus apparet nota.
>
> [444-59]

There is, it would seem, for the moment a progressing series of events leading to a climax. But what starts as a true dramatic narrative soon changes into a rhetorical *mise-en-scène* in which the storm becomes not one event in a sequence but a manifestation of cosmic confusion:

> mundum revelli sedibus totum suis
> ipsosque rupto crederes caelo deos
> decidere et atrum rebus induci chaos.
>
> (485-87)

The progress of the fleet has ceased to matter; the scale of the event has been enlarged to portray a battle of the elements. What in the early part of the speech has been style becomes mannerism and the figure of Ajax contending against shipwreck and thunderbolt is inflated to absurdity:

> (fulmen) transit Aiacem et ratem
> ratisque partem secum et Aiacem tulit.
> nil ille motus, ardua ut cautes salo
> ambustus extat, dirimit insanum mare
> fluctusque rumpit pectore et navem manu
> conplexus in se traxit.
>
> [537-42]

This passage has nervous energy enough, but the kind of energy which has shown itself effective in describing the tension of inner mental states is in narrative productive of incoherence and exaggeration.

The second place where narrative is similarly attempted is where Cassandra has a vision of the murder of Agamemnon then taking place within the palace. This is intended as the climax of the play, the death of Agamemnon signifying the complete reversal of the mood of triumphant return by the conqueror of Troy. The conqueror is conquered and Cassandra is doomed to suffer the same fate as her compatriots who died at Troy. The speech of Cassandra narrating the murder is uncertain and fitful from the start. The opening lines attempt to heighten the tension of expectation for the event, already roused by the preceding atmosphere of foreboding suspense:

> res agitur intus magna, par annis decem.
> eheu, quid hoc est? anime, consurge et cape
> pretium furoris. . . .
>
> . . . . .
>
> imago visus dubia non fallit meos.
> spectemus.
>
> [867-75]

This has the spurious quality of the introducer of a peep show. The main current of narrative, however, beginning at line 875, has the clarity and vigor of Eurybates' account so far as the words in 885 *venere fata.* From here on the detail becomes exaggerated and confused in the same way as before, and the final impression is of disorder and chaos.

One cannot help thinking that Seneca introduced these narrative passages into his tragedies mainly because he felt they were indispensable to tragedy as a recognized literary form. They have to be read as pieces of occasional writing detached from the rest of the play and alien to it in style and often in feeling. They are set pieces like "the rugged Pyrrhus . . . " and they have only an external connection with the scenes of dialogue and the choruses which present the real themes and emotional content of the play. They illustrate by their bizarre qualities the impossibility of regarding Seneca as any kind of successor to the Greek dramatists. As Mr. Eliot says in *Seneca in Elizabethan Translation,* his way of thinking and feeling is one congenial not to the Greek tradition but to the "natural public temper" of the Roman mind.

It is in dialogue that the peculiar nature of Seneca's dramatic conception can best be seen. One can start by making the point that here there is subtle variation in pace and texture, a variation that emerges in performance and reading aloud. One can say too that the characters of the plays are used as mouthpieces for a series of moral attitudes. But a more detailed analysis is needed if these two observations are to be linked to a general understanding of Senecan drama.

The scenes introducing Aegisthus provide a good example of his manner in dialogue. In Seneca's **Agamemnon** Aegisthus makes a brief appearance in the closing scene of the play. He has already appeared in an early scene in discussion with Clytemnestra. Here he plays the role of the unscrupulous usurper and in this he is playing out the destined part of his family:

> sceleris infandi artifex
> per scelera natus, nomen ambiguum suis,
> idem sororis natus et patris nepos?
>
> [983-85]

These lines are spoken by Electra, and Aegisthus makes no reply to them except to threaten her with hideous punishment and the aphorism "rudis est tyrannus morte qui poenam exigit" (995). In his earlier more prolonged appearance at the time when Clytemnestra is hesitating whether to make a late return to virtue, "nam sera numquam est ad bonos mores via: / quem paenitet peccasse, paene est innocens" (242-43), she asks him "quid me rursus in praeceps agis?" (260). Aegisthus replies with a generalization on the nature of political power: "id esse regni maximum pignus putant / si quicquid aliis non licet solis licet" (271-72). The last of his aphoristic utterances is the paradoxical reply to Electra's "mortem aliquid ultra est?" "vita si cupias mori" (996), in which he is presenting another of the play's main themes, the desire for death as an end of pain and an assertion of human freedom, death as seen in the chorus assigned to the Trojan captives who enter with Cassandra:

> cum pateat malis
> effugium et miseros libera mors vocet
> portus aeterna placidus quiete.
>
> [590-92]

There is no particular appropriateness in any of these utterances to the character of Aegisthus. In the case of the exchange with Electra, the remark "vita si cupias mori" would be more suitable for Electra. But this kind of appropriateness is not important in the Senecan tragedy at all. Unlike the medieval Morality figures, the characters of Seneca are not spokesmen for a single idea or attitude throughout the play; their roles shift according to the movement of themes, and what really determines the shape of a dialogue is the development and interplay of ideas, not the encounter of personalities or symbolic figures. One can say that a formal conflict in a scene of dialogue is often a clash of two principles rather than of two persons, though these are not static and unemotional discussions like the dialogues traditionally contrived in philosophic writing for the exposition of opposing viewpoints.

It would be difficult to regard the clash of two principles presented by way of moral abstractions as dramatically exciting unless one was confronted with the actuality of Senecan drama. Seneca has indeed an extraordinary power, a power no doubt derived from the Roman literary tradition, to charge abstractions with feeling, whether he is writing dialogue or choruses. His habit is to introduce a personification in reply to some direct question or comment of an ordinary personal kind. The rejoinder has the effect of suddenly enlarging the situation's significance:

> AGAM. ne metue dominam famula. CASS. libertas adest.
> AGAM. secura vive, CASS. mihi mori est securitas,
>
> [796-97]

Where the abstractions *libertas* and *securitas* become invested with an unusual emotional content. The same is true of the closing line of the play:

> CLYT. furiosa, morere. CASS. veniet et vobis
> furor
>
> [1012]

where the personal utterance of Clytemnestra is enlarged into a remark of high emotional significance in the menacing abstract of *furor.*

The chorus also use abstractions in an elaborate way and with wide emotional range. The whole of the first chorus of the ***Agamemnon*** is a fine example, the quality of which can be seen in the lines:

> metui cupiunt
> metuique timent, non nox illis
> alma recessus praebet tutos,
> non curarum somnus domitor
> pectora solvit.
>
> [72-76]

Such writing is found in the *Odes* of Horace and even in Vergil ("si qua est caelo pietas, quae talia curet"). As Mr. Eliot suggests in a remark we have already quoted, it springs from a way of thinking and feeling congenial to the "natural public temper" of the Roman literary mind. The emotional experience is distanced and at the same time strengthened and dignified by its detachment from the personal and circumstantial; it in no way loses in intensity. The Latin tragedies of Seneca's forerunners and contemporaries being lost, it is impossible to estimate how much is due here to Seneca's own individuality and how much to the traditional style and tone of Roman dramatic writing.

What does seem to be peculiarly Senecan is the intensely frustrated melancholy and uncertainty that prevails in the plays, particularly in the choral odes:

> alia ex aliis cura fatigat
> vexatque animos nova tempestas
>
> . . . . .
>
> non curarum somnus domitor
> pectora solvit.
>
> [62-76]

Such feelings are very close to the characteristically annihilating gloom of the ***Moral Epistles*** and the form of death wish which is expressed again and again with a sort of wan intensity. In the ***Agamemnon*** and in all the ten tragedies the keenest feeling and the most powerful writing is found in the expression of negatives, despair, frustration, apprehension. These are the characteristic emotions in Seneca, accompanied by the desperate shoring of fragments against ruin which is the Stoic style of meeting disaster, the famous *Medea superest.*

What makes this sense of doom and frustation so inescapable throughout the plays is the imaginative experience that accompanies it—the vision of disintegration and moral chaos which occurs so continually and which can hardly be accounted for as simply part of a dramatic or literary convention. We have referred to Thyestes' prologue to the **Agamemnon.** Here "versa natura est retro" (34) merely condenses the significance of all the ideas and images of its fifty-six lines. Thyestes arises from Tartarus grotesquely uncertain whether to shun heaven or hell; the sight of Agamemnon's palace recalls a tangle of incestuous relationships and crimes which parodies the natural order of life—*hic epulis locus* (11). At this reference to the Thyestean banquet the ghost recoils and turns to the milder horrors of hell, the merited torments of Ixion, Sisyphus, and the rest. Like most of Seneca's prologues—Medea's invocation to Chaos and Oedipus' lament for the plague-stricken Thebes are the best examples—this speech strikes the emotional pitch for the succeeding scenes and brings forward all the themes and images which are to recur throughout the play: *opaca, profundo, incertus, inhorret, pavor, excutit.* All these words appear in the first five lines establishing a sense of fear, violence, and uncertainty. The first chorus repeats the same ideas and emotions, but in a more generalized way, providing a simplified discussion of their philosophical background; then in the first dialogue the emotions of the prologue are developed and explored, and a new important theme presented in Clytemnestra's "mors misera non est" (202).

These ideas of uncertainty and moral chaos do not spring from the events of the play, chaotic though these indeed are; there is no direct relationship, even when natural phenomena are thrown into confusion and this is interpreted as directly portentous.

These expressions of "moral reversal" carry conviction in themselves rather than in relation to the dramatic situation, but they do carry conviction. It is asserted as it is in the closing speeches of the **Agamemnon** that destructive and insane forces will prevail over any principle of justice and order in things. Senecan drama is a drama of moral values in reverse. In moral chaos the only recourse for a wise man is to die as his one means of retaining human dignity: "heu quam dulce malum mortalibus additum / vitae dirus amor" (589-90) and Cassandra's "mihi mori est securitas" (797). Wisdom is a contempt for death won by understanding this paradox.

III

This paper has attempted briefly to assess some of the qualities of a particular play as an example of Senecan drama. A full critical survey would enlarge understanding of the individual plays by a fuller account of his work as a whole; for the plays are constantly presenting in imaginative terms the themes treated in his prose writings. A theme like *mundum revelli* for example is an accepted topic of Stoic literature, and Seneca refers to it often enough in philosophic terms, relating it sometimes to the idea of moral reversal and decline from the Golden Age. Elsewhere Seneca writes directly, though inevitably with reserve, of his actual experiences of public life and his relationship with Nero. The connection between these personal experiences and the philosophical reflections is not made explicit. But clearly

ideas of a moral and even metaphysical kind did become heavily charged with emotion as the result of Seneca's extraordinary role in public and court life. The plays, ostensibly concerned with mythological material of the accepted kind, provided an opportunity for expressing this emotion and for distancing the ideas from actual circumstances and from personal elements. A full evaluative study of the plays would need to examine Seneca's poetic technique and the emotional content of the ideas which animate both plays and prose, expressing as they do a vision of disintegration and a conviction of tragic doom.

G. K. Hunter (essay date 1974)

SOURCE: "Seneca and English Tragedy," in *Seneca,* edited by C. D. N. Costa, Routledge & Kegan Paul Ltd., 1974, pp. 166-204.

[*In the following essay, Hunter cautions that Seneca's influence on Elizabethan drama was not a simple process, but rather a complex interplay between a multifaceted writer and a dynamic stage tradition.*]

The *Literaturwissenschaft* within which the origins or causes of Renaissance (or 'modern') tragedy have been sought is bound, by its method, to give importance to the tragedies of Seneca. The seminal surveys of Cloetta, Fischer and Creizenach adopted (inevitably enough) a chronological view of the development of a separate genre 'tragedy' [W. Cloetta: Beiträge zu Literaturgeschichte des Mittelalters und der Renaissance (1890); R. Fischer: *Die Kunstentwicklung der englischen Tragödie* (1898); W. Creizenach: *Geschichte des neueren Dramas* (1909)]. Cunliffe's article on early tragedy in the *Cambridge History of English Literature* (vol. v, 1910) spells out the pattern which emerged, with model simplicity:

> The history of renascence tragedy may be divided into three stages, not definitely limited, and not following in strict chronological succession, but distinct in the main: the study, imitation and production of Senecan tragedy; translation; the imitation of Greek and Latin tragedy in the vernacular.

To this pattern one ought to add, to complete the received critical picture, a geographical drift of influence from Italy, to France, to England, which made each subsequent country the inheritor not only of the prime cause, Seneca, but also of the subsequent sub-Senecan developments that happened on the way. Thus M. T. Herrick tells us that Seneca's 'vivid depiction of horrible deeds and black thoughts . . . fascinated the Italians, just as much as the sixteenth-century Italian tragedies of blood and lust and revenge fascinated French and English playwrights' (*Italian Tragedy in the Renaissance,* 1965).

H. B. Charlton's elaborate and deeply-researched essay on 'The Senecan Tradition in Renaissance Tragedy' (first published as the Introduction to vol. 1 of the Scottish Text Society edition of Sir William Alexander's *Poetical Works,* Edinburgh, 1921) is probably the prime example in English of the charting of these routes, and I shall use this as a model presentation of received attitudes. Charlton sees a powerful Italian influence on Elizabethan tragedy as well as a general Senecan influence. He also sees that the Italian imitators of Seneca made him more horrific and 'romantic' by combining his form with material from the *novelle,* and therefore brought him closer to Elizabethan taste. This means that, in Charlton's view, something called 'the Italian Seneca' is present in Elizabethan borrowings of horrific *novelle* materials. The logical flaw in the argument is perhaps too obvious to require much elaboration. The danger of charting the changes in 'Seneca' as he passes through Dolce or Corraro or Garnier and so reaches England is that elements genuinely Senecan (i.e. characteristically if not uniquely present in Seneca's plays) may cease to be present at all, while elements generally characteristic of late medieval and Renaissance taste (sententiousness, a gloomy sense of overpowering rule by fortune or fate in human affairs, a morbid interest in the limits of human suffering), or indeed characteristic of tragedy as a genre (horror, blood, desolation) come to be labelled 'Senecan' because Seneca also displays them and is thought responsible for the tradition (late medieval tragedy) in which they appear. The Senecan example may have provided the earliest formal model for European tragedy, but it could quickly become (in spite of this status) totally irrelevant to the day-by-day imagination of tragic playwrights.

The same flaw is manifestly present in the use of the chronological sequence: reading and producing Seneca, translation of Seneca, 'Senecan' plays in the vernacular. That these three things happened is abundantly clear, and undoubtedly they usually happened in the order indicated; but the third element in the sequence can only be said to be logically dependent on either the first or the second if the features called 'Senecan' are necessarily derived from the preceding stages of the reception of Seneca and from no other source. The *post hoc ergo propter hoc* argument, which has supported much chronological study and 'explanation' of European or English tragedy, is clearly not enough by itself to establish a detailed and inescapable proof that similar features appearing in some Elizabethan tragedies and some Senecan tragedies are in the former only because they are in the latter. And this is particularly the case when the features in question are available in other (and in some cases more immediate) sources. Thus stichomythia, ghosts, five-act structure, rhetorical speeches, a devotion to horror, a stress on the ineluctable quality of fate—these 'Senecan' features are equally available in England in vernacular comedy, the *Mirror for Magistrates,* Terence, Ovid, and the Miracle Plays. If we are to talk meaningfully about Seneca and English tragedy it can only be within an awareness of these alternative sources and with some sense of the strainers through which Seneca's plays had to pass if they were to be assimilated into the English scene.

The distinctions we have to make do not, however, concern only the Elizabethan scene. They also involve the multifaceted quality of Seneca himself. Critics have tended to speak of 'Senecan influence' as if a single and homogeneous quality was being transmitted. I will not dwell here on the problem of excluding from our sense of 'Seneca' the moral treatises that were (in Renaissance England at any rate) his primary source of fame. Even if we suppose that the plays were read in isolation from the treatises and the letters, we are still far from homogeneity. Out of the ten (or nine, or eight) plays in the canon, which are the central texts? When we speak of 'Seneca', do we refer to the doom-laden family histories of the Pelopidae (the **Thyestes** and the **Agamemnon**), or do we refer to the tales of passionate and sorrowful womanhood (**Phaedra** and **Medea**), or are we thinking of the comparatively open atmosphere of the **Hercules Furens,** in which paternal and wifely loyalties are not destroyed and where the father and the friend (Theseus) survive to comfort the hero? The **Troades** offers yet another model: of passive and undeserved suffering caught in the impersonal toils of war, while the **Oedipus** describes the defilement of even the hero in flight from defilement.

If we are to take as 'Senecan' only what is common to the whole body of plays we are left with a residue of pretty obvious features. There is a continuity of style of course, though what I. Scott-Kilvert has recently called 'Seneca's sharply distinct varieties of speech' ["Seneca or Scenario," *Arion* VII (1968)] is often overlooked; and to this I shall return. In formal terms there is the classically simple linear or progressive construction ('arguments . . . naked and casual', as Fulke Greville calls them in *Life of Sidney*), usually centred on the woes of the protagonist, showing an attempt to avoid fate or alleviate suffering, with the consequence that misery is only hastened and suffering deepened.

In these formal elements, Elizabethan publicly performed tragedy (the only kind of Elizabethan tragedy to have any aesthetic importance) is notably uninterested. However, in a rigorously progressivist theory the lack of interest may be explained as showing, not the presence of an alternative (Gothic) concept of unity, but the slowness of the Elizabethans to learn the one lesson that is possible. In Brander Matthews's *A Study of the Drama* (1910) we hear that:

> The development of English tragedy . . . out of the lax chronicle play, which was only a straggling panorama of the events of a reign, was due largely to the influence exerted by Seneca's tragedies, poor enough as plays, but vigorous in the stoical assertion of man's power over himself and of his right to control his own destiny.

It is difficult to see just what this is saying, but it may be thought to be trying to express a relationship between individual self-assertion and unity of action. If Shakespeare's *King John* is better than Bale's *King Johan* or the anonymous *Troublesome Reign of King John,* it may be implied that this is because Seneca had taught Elizabethan drama to centre action on a single dominant individual.

The trouble with such a theory is that Elizabethan drama shows a total reluctance to unify by other than the thematic interests which had appeared in *Damon and Pithias* (1564), *Cambyses* (?1561) and other pre-Senecan examples of the 'lax chronicle play'. The advance from these plays to the drama of Marlowe, Shakespeare and Webster is not an advance along a line of increasing 'unity of motive', but an advance to an increasingly subtle and brilliantly focused organization of thematic interests. The route to the drama of Scribe and Ibsen could have been shortened by an appropriate attention to the tragedies of Seneca, but quite another route was being followed by the major tragedies of the English Renaissance. Their aim is to crowd the stage and create complex and ironic evaluations. Person is set against person and group against group, so that the validity of alternative positions is allowed to appear. And in this respect (as in others) one must make the point that the formal differences which separate Elizabethan tragedies from Seneca's mark ethical distinctions. All Seneca's plays stress the malevolent power of fate to bring men beyond what they had thought of as the final limits of cruelty and injustice. In all (except the Hercules plays) the ending is shown without any alleviation of misery: either cruel tyranny is triumphant, or the martyr sinks into further degradation, or both happen together. Elizabethan tragedy's complex structure reflects a different attitude to fate. While allowing the cruelty of tragic destiny, it is also strongly assertive of the redeeming features of a tragic existence: the gratuitous loyalties, the constancy under pressure, the renewed faith. Its variety of moods allows the tragedy to be placed in a context of different and less shadowed lives.

T. S. Eliot has presented Othello, especially at the end of the play when he looks back over his life (*O sors dura!*), as Senecan ["Shakespeare and the Stoicism of Seneca," *Selected Essays* (1948)], but in fact Othello's position is totally unlike anything existing or possible in any of Seneca's plays. Othello does in a sense 'dramatize himself' (and so does the Medea of *Medea superest*), but vivid self-description seems to be an inescapable dramatist's device (surely Sophocles's Oedipus 'dramatizes himself', not to mention Ibsen's Hedda). The quality of Othello's end is derived from the awareness of a normal world existing in his own past and in other people's future, for whom he will be only a name (if that). The perspectives of the ordinary world are essential to Shakespearean tragedy; they are quite absent from Seneca.

The difference I have suggested here may be subsumed under the general rubric that Shakespeare's ethic is Christian, and Seneca's is not. But this distinction has not always been allowed the central importance it undoubtedly has to explain both the attraction of Seneca for the Elizabethans and the inevitability of their failure to be like him. It was often suggested in the late nineteenth and early twentieth centuries that, given the immeasurable superiority of Aeschylus and Sophocles to subsequent tragedies (according to the taste of the nineteenth and twentieth centuries), the Elizabethan drama would have been immeasurably benefited by imitating Sophocles instead of Seneca. The wish that the Elizabethans could have shared modern preferences shows a lack of historical perspective and an unpreparedness for the different (and shocking) revaluation that the past exacts from those attentive enough to it. The Greek drama (except for Euripides in some of his aspects) was necessarily inaccessible to the Elizabethans, not only because the possession of enough Greek to read it properly was rare (after all there were Latin translations), but principally because the Greek drama was embedded in a socioreligious matrix that a Christian writer could not afford not to despise.

It was Seneca's freedom from any real response to the numinous that made him particularly repellent to the nineteenth-century Romantics, for whom his bleak moralism seemed denatured and pedantic. It was his merely intellectual relationship to the 'leaden gods' (as Stephen Bateman called the Roman deities in 1577) that allowed the Renaissance to regard him as a proto-Christian, and enabled them to accept his views without changing their own. In a more credulous age this quality had been expressed by the forged correspondence between Seneca and St Paul, and also by the forged treatises then read as Seneca's, but now attributed to St Martin.

Erasmus was, of course, free of these pious frauds, but he reflects their legacy. As he says in his prefatory letter to his edition of Seneca, sent to the Bishop of Durham (*Opus Epistolarum*):

> Et Senecam tanti fecit divus Hieronymus, ut hunc unum ex omnibus ethnicis in Catalogo scriptorum illustrium recensuerit, non tam ob epistolas illas Pauli ad Senecam et Senecae ad Paulum (quas nec a Paulo nec a Seneca scriptas probe noverat . . .) quam quod hunc unum dignum iudicarit qui non Christianus a Christianis legeretur.

> (Indeed St Jerome made so much of Seneca that he included him as the only pagan in his Catalogue of famous authors, not so much on account of those letters of St Paul to Seneca and Seneca to St Paul (which he knew perfectly well to be by neither Seneca nor St Paul) but rather because he judged that he alone among non-Christians was fit to be read by Christians.)

In the new prefatory letter he addresses to the Bishop of Cracow in 1529, he repeats these sentiments and adds a rather crisp and memorable statement of Seneca's ambiguous position:

> Etenim si legas illum ut paganum, scripsit Christiane; si ut Christianum, scripsit paganice.

> (For if you read him thinking of him as a pagan, then he appears to have written like a Christian; but if you read him as a Christian then he appears to have written like a pagan.)

He also, in this later letter, explains why Jerome included Seneca in his *Catalogus sanctorum: non admodum probatae sanctitatis . . . [sed] ob religionis amorem* (not because of proven sanctity . . . [but] on account of his love for religion). In the *Institutio Principis Christiani* he praises Seneca as the most suitable to be read (*Opera Omnia*):

> Qui scriptis suis mire exstimulat et inflammat ad honesti studium, lectoris animum a sordidis curis in sublime subvehit, peculiariter ubique dedocens Tyrannidem.

> (Who in his writings marvellously incites us and stirs us up to a zeal for honest action, carrying the mind of the

reader into the the heights, far above the base concerns of men, especially where he is warning against tyranny.)

It was thus possible in the Renaissance to think of Seneca as a man wholly acceptable in his moral outlook, and to view the fables of his plays therefore as wholly defensible didactic structures. Dean Nowell defended the ***Phaedra*** because of its similarity to the story of Potiphar's wife in the Holy Scripture. Indeed the primitive and horrific moral compulsions of the Old Testament provided a natural field for 'Christian Seneca'. Buchanan's *Jephthes* and Jean de la Taille's *Saul le Furieux,* Velo's *Tamar* and Bishop Watson's *Absalom* all reduce Biblical history to quasi-Senecan fable. But the fables of Seneca's plays could be defended at a rather simpler moral level. Philip Mel-anchthon (*Corpus Reformatorum,*) took out of the ***Thyestes:*** 'O how much evil does ambition breed':

> Proinde spectaculum exemplum damus utile;
> Nam cernere licebit hac in tragoedia
> Nil esse peius ambitione, quae omnia
> Divina humana, iusque et fas vertere solet.

(We present this to the spectators therefore as a useful model; for you will be justified in finding from this tragedy that there is nothing worse than ambition, which commonly overturns all things human and divine, both human law and divine law.)

Below this rather superficial level, at which Seneca could be thought of as quasi-Christian, the problems of true imitation are (and were) more difficult to solve. The ethic of Seneca was, as a unifying factor in his plays, quite hostile to the ethic that is tolerable to a Christian community. The most memorable statement of this incompatibility comes, fortunately enough, from the period of our principal concern and from a 'Senecan' dramatist, Fulke Greville. Greville in his life of Sir Philip Sidney describes his own tragedies and makes in the course of his description a distinction which is curiously overlooked when Elizabethan Senecan imitation is discussed, for it should be central to any such discussion. He speaks first of ancient tragedies which 'exemplify the disastrous miseries of man's life, where Order, Laws, Doctrine and Authority are unable to protect Innocency from the exorbitant wickedness of power, and so out of that melancholic vision stir horror, or murmur against Divine Providence'. On the other hand, modern tragedies 'point out God's revenging aspect upon every particular sin, to the despair or confusion of mortality'. The central distinction is, as Greville sees it, that the ancient (and he means Senecan) world was, because its gods were unjust, a world of total injustice. On the other hand, the Christian world shows man unable to face up to the justice of God, but hunted down in terms of particular sins, not overall corruption.

The point is not that the innocent do not perish in modern tragedy: Lavinia, Cordelia, and young Macduff perish just as surely as Hippolytus and the children of Thyestes and Medea. But the massacre of those innocents is part of a larger catastrophic movement which is eventually moral: the universe in casting out the particular evil also casts out

the good. In Seneca's tragedies the evil are regularly left in manic possession of what their wickedness has achieved: Atreus with his brother (who now incorporates his nephews) in his gloating power, Nero disposing of his relatives, Medea carried off in her magic car, Aegisthus and Clytemnestra in possession of Argos. The impotent chorus can only generalize from these instances that man's lot is indeed hard and (as Greville says) 'murmur against Divine Providence'.

Even a play as concerned to avoid explicit Christianity as Shakespeare's *Titus Andronicus* suggests in the end that justice can return to the world with comfort to the good as well as punishment to the wicked, and decent behaviour all round:

> Some loving friends convey the emperor hence
> And give him burial in his father's grave.
> My father and Lavinia shall forthwith
> Be closed in our household's monument.
> As for that ravenous tiger, Tamora. . . .

> [Then afterwards, to order well the state,
> That like events may ne'er it ruinate.]

Greville's distinction is one that is particularly important when we deal with that strain of Elizabethan tragedy concerned with revenge—a strain often thought to be particularly dependent on Seneca—though often this means no more than that there is horror in both. Shakespeare and other revenge dramatists do, of course, show deeds of horror and violent states of criminal irresponsibility, and in this are like Seneca (and Ovid and the martyrologies). But there is an essential difference. Reuben Brower speaks well of 'the amorality of Seneca's ***Agamemnon,*** where the heroine joyously gives way to crime' and where—for all the detachment and highmindedness of the choral odes—there is no assurance of a mind or a society outside the criminal mind' (*Hero and Saint,* 1971). But when Brower speaks of Titus Andronicus joining 'the happy criminal society of Seneca's Clytemnestra or Medea or Aaron, Tamora and her sons', one must regretfully part company with him.

When Seneca's slaves of passion are taken over by inhuman or anti-human emotions they are released from human responsibility, and in this sense 'happy' has its own ghastly appropriateness; they become the vessels or instruments of the *furor* which is personified by the *Furiae* we meet in the infernal prologues. When Medea, contemplating her final crime, begins to relent, the *Antiqua Erynis* snatches her unwilling hand, and forces her into the scream: *Ira, qua ducis, sequor* (Where wrath leads I follow) (953). She is sucked into an infernal and maddening vision (958-68):

> Quonam ista tendit turba Furiarum impotens?
> . . . quem trabe infesta petit
> Megaera? cuius umbra dispersis venit
> incerta membris? frater est, poenas petit.
> dabimus, sed omnes fige luminibus faces,
> lania, perure, pectus en Furiis patet.
> Discedere a me, frater, ultrices deas
> manesque ad imos ire securas iube.

(Whither goes that mob of Furies, powerless to
   restrain itself?
. . . Who does Megaera search for, waving her torch?
What dubious ghost, limbs torn apart, comes forth?
It is my brother; he seeks revenge. He will have it.
But first set all your torches in my eye-sockets,
Tear in pieces, set on fire. Lo, my heart receives the
   Furies.
Now, brother, you may order the revenging
   goddesses to leave me
and return satisfied to the deep-buried dead.)

What we seem to be given here is a passage of infernal
possession, such as Lady Macbeth talks about, but does not
display. It is impossible to know just how subjective or how
objective Seneca intended *Erynis* or *Megaera* to be, but
clearly we are not dealing only with a fluctuation of inner
mood. A more objective description of human processes
seems to be involved: reason has struggled with *furor* and
lost, and thereafter the inner resource of the individual is
empty and the infernal passions take its place; as Phaedra
remarks (184-5):

> Quid ratio possit? vicit ac regnat furor
> potensque tota mente dominatur deus.

> (What can reason do? *Furor* has conquered and reigns
> over me. The powerful god controls the whole of my
> mind.)

The Elizabethan model of the human state is more complex
than this, and the more complex form of the Elizabethan
play reflects it. Revenge as a passion, perhaps as *the* passion, stalks the Elizabethan stage; but in the form of what
Greville calls a 'particular sin', as an isolated madness, not
as the objective and possessive power of the *ultrices deae.*
The *Ultrix Deus* of the Elizabethan world ('Vengeance is
mine, saith the Lord, I will repay') is, of course, quite different: not the abrogator of rational order, but its guarantor.
Providence, even if only in the form of 'God's revenging
aspect', is never wholly withdrawn from the Elizabethan
scene, where potential grace is a condition of being alive.
Revengers are absorbed into the horror of their own obsessed imaginings, but they continue to exist inside a world
where justice is remembered as a value. Indeed a central
point about revenge on the Elizabethan stage is that it is a
perverted form of justice.

Of course, the most famous Elizabethan remark about revenge has always told us so: 'Revenge is a kind of wild
Justice', says Bacon, where 'wild' (as the imagery following seems to show) means 'fit for the wilderness, run to
seed, like a briar'. The madness of Titus Andronicus is a
withdrawal into the dream of perfect justice, over which
Astraea and not the *ultrices deae* presides as deity. He is the
martyr of a world from which the true strain of justice has
vanished, in which only the briar is left. Much of his madness turns on the search for justice (IV.iii.4f.):

> *Terras Astraea reliquit.*
> Be you remembered, Marcus: she's gone, she's fled.

He sends his family to spread nets, to dig into the earth for
justice, but he is told that only her 'wild' brother is available (IV.iii.38-40):

> Pluto sends you word,
> If you will have Revenge from hell, you shall.
> Marry, for Justice, she is so employed . . .

And in the end his sanity snaps and he grasps at the perverted justice of the 'wilderness of tigers' where he lives. If
Seneca is present in the Terean banquet of the final act it is
as a kind of antimasque to the central ethic of the play.
Tamora and her sons come to Titus's house to playact for
his madness the simplifying possession of Revenge, the
'dread Fury' of Seneca's plays. But Titus and the play accept these simplifications only at a level of make-believe
beyond that of the actual play-world (V.ii.141f.):

> I knew them all . . .
> And will o'er-reach them in their own devices.

He is content (like Hieronimo in *The Spanish Tragedy*) to
join their play of revenge, but outside the play he knows
well enough what justice is, what its cruxes and problems
are (V.iii.34-6):

> My lord the Emperor, resolve me this:
> Was it well done of rash Virginius
> To slay his daughter?

The play ends, not with the 'happy' murderer enjoying his
infernal reward and proving (like Medea) that *nullos esse,
qua veheris, deos* (wherever you go there will be no gods),
but with the brief madness of revenge atoned for in the face
of true justice by an expiatory death.

The revenge play of the Elizabethans would have been
wholly unacceptable if Titus, or Hieronimo, or Hoffman, or
Hamlet had been rewarded for their revenges, as Atreus or
Clytemnestra or Medea are. Even if we take an extreme
case—that most gloatingly horrific and smugly immoral of
scenes, in which Antonio murders the little Julio (Marston,
Antonio's Revenge, III.i)—we are in a moral world directly
opposite to that of Seneca. The difficulties of taste here are
often attributed to a surfeit of Seneca, and the quotation
from ***Thyestes*** 151f. (Atreus rejoices in his capture of
Thyestes and his children) shows that the corresponding
episode was in Marston's mind. In fact, however, the tastelessness of the scene belongs to a quite un-Senecan branch
of tastelessness. It sentimentalizes the child in a way that is
foreign to the Roman. Julio says (III.i.145-9):

> Brother Antonio are you here, i' faith?
> Why do you frown? Indeed my sister said
> That I should call you brother, that she did,
> When you were married to her. Buss me; good truth,
> I love you better than my father.

Antonio welcomes Julio into his embrace with ironies
which recall Atreus, but his motivations are quite distinct (it
is indeed difficult to speak at all of Atreus's motivations).
He apostrophizes heaven and justice, and declares his devo-

tion to a mad purism of justice which will unambiguously separate guilt and innocence (III.i.164-6):

> O that I knew which joint, which side, which limb,
> Were father all and had no mother in't.
> That I might rip it, vein by vein,
> In bleeding rases.

Once again revenge is presented as a monstrous mutation of justice, isolating and maddening, in a world still ruled by 'God's revenging aspect upon every particular sin'.

The Senecan ethic was, by a curious paradox, most tolerable when the subject-matter was not the intrigues and passions of individuals but the dynastic quarrels of the modern political world. Greville speaks of these as if somewhere between ancient and modern tragic practices, and reflecting his own interest to 'trace out the high ways of ambitious governors, and to show in the practice that the more audacity, advantage and good success such sovereignties have, the more they hasten to their own desolation and ruin'. Of course the Elizabethan audience did not suppose politics was eventually free of the revenging hand of God, but knowledge of recent history (e.g. the Wars of the Roses) and the Chronicles of those events, showed men that a time-scale longer than any single life was likely to operate before divine justice was seen to be fulfilled. And there was also the awareness that Machiavelli and others had suggested that the political world operated apart from God's providence, and was therefore open to Seneca's interpretation. Shakespeare's *Richard III* deals with a doomed dynasty like those of Argos or Thebes, where the pressure of the past justifies the abrogation of normal standards in the present; but the play is eventually a complex image of a whole world under moral siege, not a linear development of crime and possession. Richard has specific political aims, and a specific social context within which these aims have to be achieved; Atreus has neither.

The wailing queens in Act IV, scene iv, of *Richard III* have often been thought to derive from the wailing ladies of the *Troades*; and so they may, as Clarence's dream seems to derive from Virgil. In both cases a hint of classical material may have triggered off the development of a highly stylized exercise in rhetoric, meant no doubt in its solemn and witty formalism to recall a classical mode (Ovid in particular), but reflecting little or nothing of the meaning of any original. The queens create a joint interpretation of what history means: their repetitive stanzas reflect their repetitive destinies, and the extent to which history can be reduced to royal fate, and fate distilled into formal rhetoric. They create a patch of sombre colour, set against other patches, other interpretations, and beyond all interpretations lies the quite un-Senecan truth of Richmond's virtue and divine right to found the Tudor line.

The ghosts who throng to Richard's or Richmond's tents in Act V of *Richard III* indicate the supernatural world as the guarantor of justice, not its opposite; and in this they are typical of the Elizabethan supernatural. The ghosts who appear in Elizabethan plays may come from heaven or hell, but their interest is not (like Seneca's) in degrading and destroying humanity, but in achieving the satisfaction of justice seen to be done. It is the hunger for justice that drives them to appear and to demand action, whether to Baldwin, the author of the *Mirror for Magistrates,* who gives them satisfaction by telling their sad stories, or later to sons who will destroy their murderers. The ghosts in the *Mirror for Magistrates* offer a clear link between the dream-visions of hell that medieval literature shows and the 'filthy whining ghost / Lapt in some foul sheet or a leather pilch / . . . screaming like a pig half-stick'd / . . . Vindicta! Revenge, Revenge!' who provides a stock image of Elizabethan revenge tragedy. The prose links of the *Mirror* carry the burden of evoking the supernatural occasion, and relating the 'history' told to the moral pressures of the individual's timeless fate:

> I waxed drowsy and began indeed to slumber. But my imagination still prosecuting this tragical matter brought me such a fantasy: methought there stood before us a tall man's body full of fresh wounds, but lacking a head . . . And when through the ghastfulness of this piteous spectacle I waxed afeared and turned away my face methought there came a shrieking voice out of the wesand pipe of the headless body, saying as followeth . . .
>
> (Prose 12)

> And therefore imagine, Baldwin, that you see him all to be mangled, with blue wounds, lying pale and wan all naked upon the cold stones in Paul's Church . . .
>
> (Prose 4)

> I will take upon me the personage of the last who, full of wounds, miserably mangled, with a pale countenance and grisly look, may make his moan to Baldwin as followeth . . .
>
> (Prose 1)

The quality of the ghost is thus evoked in terms of description rather than narrative or drama (and I shall return to this point later); the narrator himself is made the principal agent of the pattern which leads from these violent disruptions of silence to the final silence of the conclusion, when all that is required for resolution has been said. The process is strongly reminiscent of a confession and absolution. The ghost is finally satisfied (or exorcized) by having his personal history fitted into an exemplary framework. As James I of Scotland remarks when he begins his tale:

> If for examples' sake thou write thy book,
> I charge thee, Baldwin, thou forget me not.

The fully dramatized ghosts of later drama live, of course, in a world of multiple personal relations, but their motivation is like that of the *Mirror* ghosts and unlike that of Seneca, in that they seek (and achieve) a personal and fully human satisfaction: seeing the criminal destroyed, the usurper brought low. The *furor* which rages unchecked through Seneca's world, the boundless horror and destruction that *Umbra Tantali* is forced to promote: these are held in Elizabethan tragedy within the dimension of a personal or political displacement of the natural equilibrium which justice holds. The Elizabethan playhouse ghosts may begin their reaction to this displacement with screams of 'Revenge, revenge' or *'Vindicta'* (phrases not in the vocabulary of Seneca's ghosts) but end with expressions of family or social stability. Thus Old Andrugio in *Antonio's Revenge* watches the final action from 'betwixt the music houses' and departs saying:

> 'Tis done; and now my soul shall sleep in rest.
> Sons that revenge their father's blood are blest.

At the end of *Locrine* the ghost of Corineus takes his stand to 'stay and see revenge'. This is satisfied, and then Até (the chorus) can pronounce an absolution on the turmoil:

> Lo, here the end of lawless treachery,
> Of usurpation and ambitious pride,
> And they that for their private amours dare
> Turmoil our land, and set their broils abroach
> Let them be warned by these premises.

At the end of Kyd's *The Spanish Tragedy* the ghost of Andrea seems to praise murder with equal enthusiasm whether the victims be innocent or guilty. But justice is assured for the afterlife, where

> . . . will I beg at lovely Proserpine
> That by the virtue of her princely doom
> I may consort my friends in pleasing sort
> And on my foes work just and sharp revenge.

And this is the note on which the whole play ends, with Revenge promising a final absolute of punishment:

> For here though death hath end their misery,
> I'll there begin their endless tragedy.

In its distribution of the cast into eternally separated sheep and goats this conclusion is more reminiscent of the Last Judgment sequence in the Mystery Cycles than of Seneca.

The chronological basis of literary history has, in the view propounded here, led scholars to overestimate the force of transmission into an alien culture. The superficial quasi-Christianity of Seneca's morals should not blind us to the real hostility of received English dramatic patterns to the nature of his plays. This is especially important if we concentrate on the popular and public drama of the Elizabethans, putting to one side the plays written for readers or for one specific performance before a noble patron. The force of this distinction is often overlooked.

The Senecan tragedies of the Italian Cinquecento all seem to derive from specific or private production. In this they are like tragedies in England before the opening of the public theatres in 1576, like *Gorboduc* of 1561, or Gascoigne's *Jocasta* of 1566 (from Dolce), like *Gismond of Salerne* of 1567-8, or the Latin tragedies of the universities, such as Legge's *Richardus Tertius* (1573) or Alabaster's *Roxana* of 1592 (from Groto's *La Dalida*), or the later 'closet' (unacted) plays of aristocratic amateurs, the Countess of Pembroke's *Antonius,* Sir William Alexander's *Darius,* Fulke Greville's *Alaham,* etc., written in this way, no

doubt, in reaction to the 'vulgar' form of the acted drama. As Greville says: 'be it known it was no part of my purpose to write for them against whom so many good and great spirits have already written'.

This whole strain of English tragedy is manifestly close to its Italian and French counterparts, and nearer to Seneca than the popular form. The chronological model would however go further and suggest that the aristocratic plays of the 'sixties should be regarded not only as precursors but also as progenitors of the popular tragedies of the 'eighties and 'nineties, so that Seneca operates on the popular drama at two removes, as well as directly, but with crucial effectiveness. From this point of view there is a continuum of tragedy in England, running unbroken from 1561—from *Gorboduc, Jocasta,* Hughes's *The Misfortunes of Arthur,* through *The Spanish Tragedy, Locrine, Hamlet, The Revenger's Tragedy* and so to Shirley's *The Cardinal*—to 1641. Fansler has put this view succinctly: 'One thing that bound all Elizabethan tragedies together, from *Gorboduc* to *The Traitor* and *The Cardinal,* was the influence of Seneca' [H.E. Fansler, *The Evolution of Technic in Elizabethan Tragedy* (1914)]. It seems doubtful, however, if the Inns-of-Court private tragedies in fact led directly to or provided the primary stimulus for the public tragedies. David Bevington [in his *From 'Mankind' to Marlowe* (1962)] has documented the connection between the forms of popular repertory entertainment and those of Marlowe. University men writing for professional actors and a paying public had to take note of the popular interest in a crowded stage, a wide variety of passions, a Christian ethic, a patriotic enthusiasm, a joking immediacy of theatrical contact. Seneca, Groto, Thomas Hughes, and the Countess of Pembroke could provide little guidance to deal with such demands, less indeed than the popular strolling theatricals of the English countryside. If Seneca were to be a powerful influence on the tragedy of the English public he would have, it seems, to make a fresh impact. His forms and his outlook could not be carried over, passively, from the private tragedies of the preceding decades.

H. B. Charlton, with his sights fixed eventually on Sir William Alexander, takes the Senecanism of the popular drama to be already proven by others, but the very brevity of his reference to its Senecan inheritance is convenient. He takes Nashe's famous attack on a dramatist (who may be Kyd) as representative of the methods of a school of popular tragedians, who

> busy themselves with the endeavours of art, that could scarcely Latinize their neck-verse if they should have need; yet English Seneca read by candle-light yields many good sentences, as *Blood is a beggar* and so forth; and if you entreat him fair in a frosty morning he will afford you whole Hamlets, I should say handfuls, of tragical speeches, But O grief! *Tempus edax rerum.* What's that will last always? The sea exhaled by drops will in continuance be dry, and Seneca, let blood line by line and page by page, at length must needs die to our stage; which makes his famished followers . . . to intermeddle with Italian translations. Wherein how poorly they have plodded . . . let all indifferent gentlemen that have travelled in that tongue discern by their twopenny pamphlets.

Charlton takes Nashe's description of popular tragedians' methods quite literally: 'Seneca . . . was their great store-house of tragic material'. However, a quite literal reading of the passage seems impossible: Nashe's contempt is more clear than his argument. The opening gibe (in the section I have quoted) is aimed at those who cannot read Latin and have to read blood-thirsty Senecan *sententiae* in translation. Unfortunately for literalism, no English line 'blood is a beggar' is known, neither from the 1581 nor other translation of Seneca, nor does the line appear in any extant English play. It may be answered that Nashe is talking in particular about a perished play, the so-called *Ur-Hamlet,* and that this play must have had all the characteristics he lists. But it is obviously dangerous to explain a whole movement in terms of a perished and indeed hypothetical play.

What other plays of the supposed movement show these characteristics? The usual answer is, 'Kyd's *The Spanish Tragedy*'. If *The Spanish Tragedy* fitted Nashe's description, then much of the case would be proved, since it was the most popular tragedy of the early period and exercised a profound influence on subsequent plays like *Titus Andronicus, Antonio's Revenge, Hamlet,* Chettle's *Hoffman,* and others. However, *The Spanish Tragedy* seems to contain not a single line derived from the 1581 translation of Seneca. It has some Senecan lines in Latin and some original lines in Latin, which implies (I take it) some knowledge of that language. And there are no 'tragical speeches' taken out of Seneca in this play. We may wish to continue to believe, however, that Nashe's points, though not true literally, have a general truth, in that Kyd's play is Senecan in its general cast. The evidence for this is hard to find unless we take 'Senecan' to mean things not found in Seneca, or found in many places. In this context 'Senecan' is sometimes, of course, taken to mean 'having a unified structure', the assumption being that *The Spanish Tragedy* is more unified than its predecessors (*Cambyses, Horestes, Apius and Virginia*) and that this improvement must be due to Seneca. In fact, *The Spanish Tragedy* is far from having what has been ascribed to it: 'unity of action, and . . . also unity of motive, for it all centres round revenge' [Legouis and Cazamian, *History of English Literature* (1937)]. Revenge as a motive, or a psychological propellant to action, only appears half-way through the play. *The Spanish Tragedy* is unified, far more effectively than the preceding plays, it is true; but not by motive; rather by the impersonal but pervasive idea of justice, which appears not only in the Hieronimo story, but also in the ghostly chorus, in the Portuguese episode, and the episodes of Pedringano and Bazulto. And in this mode of organization there is no influence of Seneca.

It is also true that *The Spanish Tragedy* has, in its interludes, a ghost (together with a Morality Personification); but this ghost has the usual non-Senecan characteristics I have described above. It may be said, on the other hand, that the ghost here is a *protatica persona* like the ghosts of Tantalus and Thyestes. And this is true. But the purpose of his eruption from hell and the atmosphere he brings into the play are quite distinct from anything in Seneca. Kyd's hell is a place of love and justice:

> Proserpine began to smile
> And begged that only she might give my doom.
> Pluto was pleased, and sealed it with a kiss.

Seneca's ghosts are given a causal relationship to all that follows: they cause the mortal characters to act as they do. The ghost of Andrea in *The Spanish Tragedy* is, however, only a spectator and commentator. It might be thought that his companion Revenge is more like a Senecan *Furia* 'causing' revenge to triumph in the play. In fact, however, the revenge that takes place is wholly determined by the natural emotions of the characters: Revenge is given no direct relationship to Hieronimo, the hero and revenger. The revenge that Andrea returns to see and that Revenge is sent to show him, in the manner of a dream, 'through the gates of horn', is in fact quite peripheral to the main dramatic action. The ghost of Andrea is puzzled by what is going on (II.vi.2-3):

> I looked that Balthazar should have been slain
> But 'tis my friend Horatio that is slain.

And the ghost's puzzlement is meant to represent, I take it, a natural if simple-minded reaction. Kyd creates, in short, a gap between the supernatural concern in the play, and the more central matter, the individual lives, which exhibit that unexplained capacity to make valid choices which is essential to a Christian view of the world and to modern drama. It is not any Senecan machinery, but this power to show emotion turning into action by the mysterious alchemy of free personal choice that gives *The Spanish Tragedy* and *Hamlet* and *Titus Andronicus* their grip on the audience. The tension between an external set of expectations and an internal set of compulsions ('God's revenging aspect' and 'particular sin') throws the weight of the play on the character of the protagonist in a manner wholly unclassical. Far from being the channel of Senecan influence into Elizabethan popular drama, *The Spanish Tragedy,* in this view of it, forged, in parallel to Marlowe, a dramatic vision of humanity to which Seneca's plays could offer only peripheral decoration.

It may be thought that a description of Seneca's relationship to English drama in terms of his dramatic structures and effects on the one hand and his ethical positions on the other, is too limited. It may be felt, in particular, that more important than any of these is his literary style. The recent Penguin translation of five plays tells us that 'in the effectiveness of the spoken word was all that mattered in Seneca's conception of drama'. Certainly the style of Seneca's plays was a point that few English critics of the Renaissance failed to mention:

> the stately style of Senec sage
> ('H.C. to the Reader' before Studley's
> *Agamemnon,* 1566)

> . . . grace and majesty of style
> (Preface to Heywood's *Thyestes,* 1560)

> . . . endight / with wondrous wit and regal style
> (Preface to Heywood's *Thyestes*)

. . . penned with a peerless sublimity and loftiness of style

> (Newton's Preface to *Seneca His Ten Tragedies,* 1581)

. . . stately speeches and well-sounding phrases, climbing to the height of Seneca his style

> (Sidney, *Apology for Poetry,* 1595)

Seneca's tragedies, Plautus' comedies, Virgil's Georgics and Warrior, of the Latins, for the stateliness of the matter and style are most honoured

> (L. Humphrey, *The Nobles,* 1563)

Albeit he borrowed the argument of his tragedies from the Grecians, yet the spirit, loftiness of sound and majesty of style is merely his own

> (H. Peacham, *The Complete Gentleman,* 1622).

The terms in which the style is praised remain remarkably constant: high, majestic, regal, lofty, stately; all these seem to be pointing to a single aesthetic category, the sublime.

This categorization tells us about the critics' admiration; it is less helpful in giving us a comparative description of the mode of Seneca's poetry. Seneca's prose style has been described with great exactitude (e.g. succinctly and conveniently in W. C. Summers's edition of *Select Letters*), but it is not clear if his verse belongs to the same class. Certainly some of the features of 'Senecan' prose rhetoric appear also in the poetry. The taste for sharp, compressed and weighty utterance is important here also, especially of course in stichomythia. But we should not forget that Quintilian speaks of Seneca's *ingenium facile et copiosum.* The style of the plays can veer quickly from sharp desiccated 'points' (*harena sine calce*) to flowing and hyperbolic eloquence, as in the following reply of the blinded Oedipus to Jocasta's attempted comfort (*Oedipus* 1012-18):

> Quis frui tenebris vetat?
> quis reddit oculos? matris, en matris sonus!
> perdidimus operam. Congredi fas amplius
> haut est. nefandos dividat vastum mare
> dirimatque tellus abdita et quisquis sub hoc
> in alia versus sidera ac solem avium
> dependet orbis alterum ex nobis ferat.

(Who forbids me to enjoy the darkness? Who returns me my eyes? Look, my mother, the voice of my mother! The good work is thrown away! It is God's law that we should meet no more. Let the vast ocean divide the guilty, let the spaces of the earth yawn between us, bearing away one of us to whatever world hangs beneath this one, looking only at other stars and at a truant sun.)

We do not know how the Elizabethans responded to these polarities of style or how their conception of the sublime depended on one or another pole. We do know, however, that they had a sustained taste for tricksy and conceited writers—Ovid and Lucan as well as Seneca—and that 'height of style' was closely associated in their minds with

daring conceits and sustained rhetorical structures. The natures of the Latin and the English languages hardly permit any carry-over of actual details of style, but the Neo-Latin plays of the period show their authors as happy to reproduce Seneca's range of rhetorical effects. Indeed even so considerable a Grecian as George Buchanan shows the extent to which Greek drama was seen through the rhetorical lenses of Seneca's style: translating *Alcestis* 488 . . . , he sharpens its rhetoric into a typically Senecan glitter: *Caeso redibis rege, vel caesus cades.*

The 1560-81 translators into English, however, have command of a rhetorical mode which would seem to be directly opposite to Seneca's. They are totally incapable of sharpness or compression; the hobnailed violence of their vocabulary is without self-conscious capacity for variation. To the modern ear, long inured to standards of the 'natural', the 'elegant', the 'easy', the 'conversational', the excesses and obviousness of Seneca's rhetoric may seem like that of his translators. But the sophistication (even decadence) of his repetitive cleverness seems outside the range of their language.

There is one modern frame of reference, however, which may be responsible for creating a greater disparity between Seneca's rhetoric and that of his 1560-81 translators than was seen to be the case in Elizabethan times, and it may be that in this case the modern frame distorts the picture.

Reading Seneca's plays as plays, and thinking of plays as immediate experiences, sharply focused, tensely direct in their confrontations and in the close-up attention they demand, we inevitably find their style grotesquely unreal in its simplified exaggeration and stridency, like posters seen at very short range. In the sixteenth century it was possible to think of a 'tragedy' anywhere along a range of considerable amplitude, stretching from the immediacy of theatrical tragedy to the dreamy and distancing vagueness of late medieval narrative tragedy. We have already noticed the descriptive bias of the *Mirror for Magistrates.* The Elizabethan translators of Seneca (belonging to the same intellectual group as Baldwin) impose a similar bias towards centralizing the narrator and distancing the action behind narrative and description. Jasper Heywood's preface to his translation of the ***Troades*** sets that work inside the framework of medieval and chivalric narrative of the 'matter of Troy':

> The ruins twain of Troy, the cause of each,
> The glittering helms, in field the banners spread,
> Achilles' ires and Hector's fights they teach,
> There may the gests of many a knight be read:
> Patroclus, Pyrrhus, Ajax, Diomed.

Heywood's versified Preface to ***Thyestes*** turns this work into the dream-vision of a request to write, in parallel fashion, to the *Mirror for Magistrates:*

> Then dreamed I thus, that by my side
>   methought I saw one stand
> That down to ground in scarlet gown
>   was dight, and in his hand

A book he bare: and on his head
  of bayes a garland green.
Full grave he was, well stepped in years
  and comly to be seen.
     . . . . .
Good sir (quod I) I you beseech
  (since that ye seem to me
By your attire some worthy wight)
  it may your pleasure be
To tell me what and whence you are.
     . . . . .
Spain was (quod he) my native soil:
  a man of worthy fame
Sometime I was in former age,
  and Seneca my name.

Heywood's addition of a final scene at the end of the *Thyestes* has a similar function. It gives narrative expansion to the pressures of the play, takes away the stark finality of the confrontation between Atreus and Thyestes with which Seneca ends. In this added scene Thyestes exclaims against his fate, forecasts his exile (in lines imitated from the end of the *Oedipus*) and suggests the eventual operation of justice:

Ye scape not fro me so, ye gods,
  still after you I go,
And vengeance ask on wicked wight
  your thunderbolt to throw.

The 'now-read-on' extension of the *Agamemnon* in Studley's translation has a similar effect. The particularity of the single play is absorbed into, and softened by, the longer perspectives of destiny.

The supply of a context or framework of this kind has the effect of making Seneca much closer to Ovid than he seems to be in our modern response to the tragedies. *The Metamorphoses* exhibits the same combination of smug horror and epigrammatic passion that revolts us in Seneca. But those characteristics do not seem to dominate Ovid's telling of his stories. In the tale of Tereus and Procne in Book VI of *The Metamorphoses* (very close in matter to the *Thyestes*) the tragic speeches of the principals are held within a mediating framework of author's narrative and description, and (even more) in the larger perspective of things remote, legendary and exemplary. Seneca's plays may be more like this than their genre suggests; for they are not in any real sense 'imitations of action'. They are comments on the mental states which would be appropriate to action; the interaction they contain is wholly static and sets static positions against one another. At the end of a typical Senecan exchange between *tyrannus* and *satelles,* or *regina* and *nutrix,* the dialogue is not led to a conclusion. A decision is simply taken to move to the next stage of the fable, a decision that could have been taken at any point in the dialogue.

In these terms Seneca's plays are unlike the modern conception of drama, and the style of the Elizabethan translations may be more appropriate than appears at first sight. Moreover, the assumption that Seneca's plays were like

narrative tragedies is not one that is confined to the early translators who wrote before the English theatre existed. As late as 1599 Thomas Storer in his *Life and Death of Thomas Wolsey* invokes Seneca as the patron of this *Mirror for Magistrates* image of a tragic fall:

Now write, Melpomene, my tragic moan
Call Nero's learned master, he will aid
Thy failing quill with what himself once said:
  Never did Fortune greater instance give
  In what frail state proud magistrates do live.

Samuel Daniel's *Complaint of Rosamond* (1592) shows how the rhetoric of these *Mirror*-type ghosts has advanced towards dramatic sharpness:

Out of the horror of infernal deeps
My poor afflicted ghost comes here to plain it.

But though this is sharper than the 1560-81 translators of Seneca, the basis of the rhetoric is still narrative, as is the relationship of the author to his material:

Then write (quoth she) the ruin of my youth,
Report the downfall of my slippery state,
Of all my life reveal the simple truth
To teach to others what I learnt too late.

Seneca is not himself, of course, a figure in his own plays (though he quickly figures in his disciple's *Octavia*), but the mode of his rhetoric seems designed to remind us that this is a particular way of telling facts widely known, where the mode of narration or description is at the centre of interest rather than the facts narrated. When Hecuba tells us at the beginning of the *Troades* of the murder of Priam she says that when Pyrrhus drew out his sword, *ensis senili siccus e iugulo redit* (the sword comes out of the old man's throat still dry). A little later she remarks that: *Priamus et flamma indiget / ardente Troia* (Though Troy is burning Priam lacks a funeral pyre). We seem to be asked to applaud the teller rather than wonder at the tale.

When we turn to the rhetoric of the popular Elizabethan drama, the 'real' drama, we find a very different deployment of rhetoric, for which Seneca can be little except a source of occasional *sententiae*. Kyd's *The Spanish Tragedy* is again a useful text to display the actual differences between Seneca and the so-called Senecan drama. The most famous of the many passionately rhetorical arias in *The Spanish Tragedy* is the speech of Hieronimo when he discovers his son hanging in his orchard (II.v.1-33):

What outcries pluck me from my naked bed
And chill my throbbing heart with trembling fear,
Which never danger yet could daunt before?
Who calls Hieronimo? speak, here I am.
I did not slumber, therefore 'twas no dream.
No, no, it was some woman cried for help,
And here within this garden did she cry,
And in this garden must I rescue her.
But stay, what murd'rous spectacle is this?
A man hanged up, and all the murderers gone,

And in my bower, to lay the guilt on me.
This place was made for pleasure, not for death.

He cuts him down.

These garments that he wears I oft have seen—
Alas, it is Horatio my sweet son,
O, no, but he that whilom was my son.
O was it thou that call'dst me from my bed?
O speak, if any spark of life remain.
I am thy father. Who hath slain my son?
What savage monster, not of human kind,
Hath here been glutted with thy harmless blood,
And left thy bloody corpse dishonoured here
For me amidst these dark and deathful shades
To drown thee with an ocean of my tears?
O heavens, why made you night to cover sin?
By day this deed of darkness had not been.
O earth, why didst thou not in time devour
The vild profaner of this sacred bower?
O poor Horatio, what hadst thou misdone
To lose thy life ere life was new begun?
O wicked butcher, whatsoe'er thou wert,
How could thou strangle virtue and desert?
Ay me, most wretched, that have lost my joy
In losing my Horatio my sweet boy.

These lines are specifically designed to make vivid and moving a spectacle visually presented (or imagined) on the stage. A man enters before us; he tells us where he has been and what his state of mind is. He makes a direct appeal to identification. We too have been wakened by night-noises and felt our scalps tingle. Here is no Senecan *nuntius* informing us that his veins freeze to remember a mythological horror for which he is a witness; but instead we have the principal person of the play asking us to participate in his mimesis. Seneca's rhetoric is used to distance from us the highly-charged events described, and continuously resolves them into wit and abstraction. Hieronimo's soliloquy, on the other hand, keeps him close beside us as step-by-step we proceed through the process of discovery, even though by tragic irony we already know what it is he is going to find. He addresses us directly, not simply as an audience, but as if he might expect an answer. To whom is the opening question proposed? Is he addressing himself or us? Are we involved or not? The theatrical situation feeds on these tensions: we are caught in a guilty complicity with the action.

The movement of Hieronimo's speech mimics the movement of circling round and identifying not only the situation but the subject of the situation. Is the call real or imaginary? 'I must find out, I am not a coward, I will name myself. It was not imaginary, it must have been real. It was here and it was to me the call came. I must act.' At the moment of resolve the image of horror is revealed, though still not understood. Kyd skilfully allows a momentary pause on the agonizing brink of recognition, a technique more regular in comedy. Here a powerful effect of pathos is built up by the contrast between what Hieronimo still thinks and what we know, reinforced by the contrast between the bower (and the love-scene we have seen in it) and the present horror.

The actual recognition has been delayed till line fourteen, and a series of relationships have been established between us and Hieronimo, and with the place and the object, the body of Horatio. The triple anaphora on 'O' marks the climax of the speech and a return to the opening question, addressed now to a specific answerer, with specific self-definition, 'I am thy father', and a specifically appropriate context, 'these dark and deathful shades'. The remainder of the speech is a circuit of anguished rhetorical questions based on the male *pieta* pose of father and son, aimed (as it were) at the world of values standing behind the audience: 'O heavens . . . O earth . . . O poor Horatio . . . O wicked butcher', and so returning to himself, the only answerer as the only speaker.

The situation of this speech (the discovery of a horror) is paralleled in Seneca, but the mode of its rhetoric is wholly unlike Seneca's. A line like 'O heavens, why made you night to cover sin?' could well have come from Seneca, but the method by which it makes its effect here is un-Senecan. In the **Thyestes,** after the death of Thyestes's children, an unnatural darkness settles over the earth. But this darkness is not conveyed to us as anyone's idea of darkness. The fourth chorus asks: *cur, Phoebe, tuos rapis aspectus?* (Why, O sun, do you hide your face from us?). But the idea of darkness is immediately developed as a general theme. The questions or answers proposed do not reflect on the minds of those speaking. The darkness of Hieronimo's garden acquires importance because we see Hieronimo coming to feel it is important: it is part of the world he creates for us out of the experience he undergoes.

Seneca's characters often describe their own feelings, or their position between alternative feelings. Medea describes the alternation in her mind between guilt and love, her rage for revenge and her desire for peace. But none of this is presented as feeling whose growth we have shared with the character, so that the more extreme moments of rhetoric are backed by a shared humanity. The classical technique of Seneca's plots means that the roots of character are in the distant past, in the habits of ancestors or the crimes of history. Medea presents her emotions as if she were the *nuntius* of her own situation. When we hear (943-4) *ira pietatem fugat / iramque pietas* (wrath chases away affection and affection, wrath), we seem to be hearing about the general qualities *ira* and *pietas* rather than participating in the psychological battle between them. In so far as they have a personal context it is one which requires us to enlarge *ira* to include all the acts of violence that Medea's history has encompassed, and *pietas* to stretch from her own family *pietas* in Colchis to that involving her children by Jason. The individual moment strains always to a generalization that (unlike the generalizations of Elizabethan dramatic rhetoric) lacks any personal, here-and-now dimension in the emotions we see and share with the common humanity of the presented character.

I have suggested that, below the level of cultural generality, the points of contact between Seneca and the public drama of the English Renaissance were small in number, distorted by great (though sometimes obscured) differences of outlook and expectation, and seldom wholly separable from other exemplars of similar taste. But Seneca remained, in spite of all this, an ancient, and praise of his morals and his style could not easily be evaded in an age hungry both for opportunities to reconcile the morality of Christian art with that of classical antiquity, and for models of power and sophistication in language. And this is as true in the England of the seventeenth century as in that of the sixteenth. In some senses the seventeenth century may be said to have increased Seneca's reputation, not only in the neo-Stoic movement associated with the names of Lipsius and Du Vair, Bacon and Feltham, but (in English at any rate) in an increasing sophistication and concision in the use of the language. When Drayton (in his epistle to Reynolds) speaks of 'strong Seneca' he is making the appropriate stylistic connection between Seneca's mode and the 'strong lines' of the Metaphysical poets and the sinewy prose of the early seventeenth century, which we know to exist in terms of the mode of thought and general moral outlook of the period.

It would seem to be no accident that the best English translation of the most translated passage of Seneca (the end of the second chorus of the *Thyestes*) should be the work of Andrew Marvell. The middle of the seventeenth century saw a second wave of English translations of the plays, the first since the 'sixties of the preceding century. Three of the plays (*Medea, Phaedra* and *Troades,* the three tragedies centred on female figures) were translated by Sir Edward Sherburn; the *Medea* being printed separately in 1648, the *Troades* in 1679, and all three issued together in 1701. It is a pity that the supposed historical significance of the 1581 volume has caused it to be twice reissued, when Sherburn's much more competent and readable work remains unknown. In addition, Edmund Prestwich translated the *Phaedra* in 1651. The *Troades,* translated by Samuel Pordage, was printed in 1660; and in 1674 came *Thyestes,* translated by John Wright. These remained the last translations of Seneca's plays till the historical interests of this century caused scholars to turn to them again.

With the fading of the Baroque the last connection between the taste of Seneca and that of any possible modern literature was broken. For, though the seventeenth century offered a more sophisticated response to Seneca's style and to the quality of his moral sensibility, the mode of his plays grew less and less acceptable, even to critics. Increasingly the English drama came to judge dramatic rhetoric by standards appropriate to real speech, and think of construction in terms of a fluent *liaison des scènes.*

It is predictable perhaps that Thomas Rymer, as an avowed enemy to non-realistic drama, should despise Seneca:

> It was then a strange imagination in . . . Seneca, to think his dry Morals and a tedious strain of sentences might do feats or have any wonderful operation in the drama.

Dryden says in the *Essay of Dramatic Poesy* that Seneca had the gift to make vulgar things sound lofty:

> One would think, *unlock the door,* was a thing as vulgar as could be spoken; and yet Seneca could make it sound high and lofty in his Latin: *Reserate clausos regii postes laris.*

In the context of the defence of rhyme in the Essay, this is clearly an admired gift, but the occasions when it needs to be exercised are allowed to be very few.

And Dryden's defence of rhyme and other 'heroick' appurtenances of tragedy is in any case clearly something of a paradox in the drama of his times. Even in the preface to his own and Lee's *furibund Oedipus* he says much the same thing as Rymer:

> Seneca on the other side, as if there were no such thing as nature to be minded in a play, is always running after pompous expressions, pointed sentences and philosophical notions, more proper for the study than the stage.

The pomposity of Seneca's style offended the canons of naturalness and ease which were to become increasingly the overriding requirements of both stage and study. Theobald in his *Double Falsehood* (1727), alleged to be based on an old play, was still Baroque enough to enjoy (presumably) and paraphrase a typical Senecan conceit (*Hercules Furens* 84): *Quaeris Alcidae parem? / Nemo est nisi ipse* (You are looking for the equal of Hercules? He has no equal except himself) as 'None but thyself can be thy parallel'. Pope seized on the conceit as typical of Theobald's bad taste and inserted the 'marvellous line' into *The Dunciad* (three-book version), III.271.

The final appearance of Seneca in *The Dunciad* marks very well what happened to his plays in the period of the Enlightenment. After this it clearly needed a complete shift of priorities to bring Seneca's plays back into anything like favour. Today we may be on the edge of some such shift. In 1968 London had what is probably its first ever public presentation of a Seneca play: *Oedipus,* in a translation or rather adaptation by Ted Hughes, produced by Peter Brook with Sir John Gielgud in the title role. Hughes writes (perhaps with memories of Camus's *La Peste*) of a world disintegrated by the Theban plague into separate moments of pain and incomprehension. His style is without sentence-structure, a series of vividly particular phrases expressing separate emotional and sensory responses, the connections unstated, and perhaps unimagined. By this technique the desperateness of man's state is brilliantly exposed; but it is a long way from the dignity and lucidity of Seneca's *senarii.* The 'Senecan style' is certainly one which reduces the power of connective—'shattered eloquence' is Dryden's fine phrase for it (in his *Life of Plutarch*)—but his contraction of meaning from large gestures of interpretation, to the privacy and limitation of individual integrity is not a retreat into incoherence and meaninglessness. The taste that lay behind this production goes back to the crazy theatrical theorist Antonin Artaud, who in 1932 was praising Seneca as a model for what he called 'The Theatre of Cruelty'. Writing to Jean Paulhan on 16 December 1932, he says (*Œuvres Complètes*):

> Je suis en train de lire Sénèque . . . Quoi qu'il en soit celui-ci me paraît le plus grand auteur tragique de l'histoire, un initié aux Secrets et qui mieux qu' Eschyle a su les faire passer dans les mots. Je pleure en lisant

son théâtre d'inspiré, j'y sens sous le verbe des syllabes crépiter de la plus atroce manière le bouillonnement transparent des forces du chaos . . . une fois guéri j'ai l'intention d'organiser des . . . lectures publiques où je lirai des Tragédies de Sénèque, et tous les commandtaires possibles du Théâtre de la Cruauté seront convoqués. On ne peut mieux trouver d'example écrit de ce qu'on peut entendre par cruauté au théâtre que dans toutes les Tragédies de Sénèque, mais surtout dans Atrée et Thyeste . . . Dans Sénèque les forces primordiales font entendre leur écho dans la vibration spasmodique des mots.

In these terms Seneca is treasured largely because his plays are an affront to the bourgeois sensibilities of traditional theatregoers. The violence, the *bouillonnement transparent des forces du chaos,* assault and disturb, force the spectators to admit the power of the frightening, the unknown, the disgusting. Artaud planned a version of **Thyestes** (*Le Supplice de Tantale*), but this seems not to have survived. The Ted Hughes version of **Oedipus,** however, shows the same ideals, in its intensification and increased particularity of horror and its avoidance or reduction of both morality and wit, the qualities which were earlier thought of central importance to an appreciation of Seneca the dramatist.

Denis Henry and Elisabeth Henry (essay date 1985)

SOURCE: "The Evil Will," in *The Mask of Power: Seneca's Tragedies and Imperial Rome,* Bolchazy-Carducci Publishers, 1985, pp. 56-74.

[*In the essay below, the critics scrutinize the actions of Seneca's protagonists inorder to demonstrate that the characters willfully choose their courses of action.*]

1. Choices

When Seneca's bad men and women originate independent action, it is by conscious choice and with often self-regarding awareness:

> Accingere, anime. . . .
>   scelus occupandum est.
>
> Be armed for battle, my soul. . . .
>   We must make the crime our own.
> *(Agamemnon* 192-3).

Clytemnestra is addressing a part of herself, her *animus;* perhaps 'heart' or even better 'will' is nearer to what the Latin term stands for, though 'soul' sounds more natural in English. (Studley piles up alternative equivalents:

> Now heart be bold, take corage good, of stomacke now be stout. . . .

and when *animus* appears elsewhere in this scene he uses 'soule' and 'my mynde' also.) She is trying to nerve herself for a moment of decision which is agonising and bewilder-

ing, the decision to kill her husband; she recoils and plunges into despair and shame, then cries out with rage, denounces herself for delaying, reverts again to denouncing herself for disloyalty. In the scene following the address to her *animus,* she vacillates in dialogue with her Nurse and then in dialogue with Aegisthus. What is never in doubt, in all these embittered exchanges, is the nature of her proposed deed of revenge.

The *scelus* (crime) of 193 defines her killing of Agamemnon as a criminal act, and it remains so, clearly, through all her fluctuations of purpose. *Culpa* and *peccare* (wrong-doing, sin) reiterate this judgment (307). Clytemnestra is again the speaker at this point. Having chosen this criminal course, she goes on to claim that it brings with it the possibility of exacting a kind of *fides,* a loyalty to guilt which submits itself to the values imposed by the wealthy criminal:

> CLY: Delicta novit nemo nisi *fidus* mea.
> AEG: Non intrat umquam regium limen *fides.*
> CLY: Opibus merebor, ut *fidem* pretio obligem.
>
> CLY: Only a loyal man is acquainted with my crimes.
> AEG: No loyalty ever enters across a royal threshold.
> CLY: Through my wealth I shall earn the right to
>   hold fast loyalty by payment.
>
> (284-6)

The moral word *merebor* suggests that Clytemnestra's morality will be of her own making and the loyalty she can exact all the more to be prized. As Atreus says (**Thyestes** 211-2), "Even a lowly man can often win truthful praises; false ones are given only to the powerful." She ignores the reply of Aegisthus, which casts doubt on this claim of hers:

> pretio parata vincitur pretio *fides.*
>
> The loyalty gained by payment is overcome by
>   payment.

Clytemnestra makes no answer on this point, but veers away once more to reject Aegisthus and the idea of murder; then almost at once she turns back to accept Aegisthus after all as partner in the wrongdoing she decides to choose. Their united plan will, she says, "disentangle the doubtful and threatening state of things".

From this moment Clytemnestra assumes a role of guiding intelligence, arranges religious rites for Agamemnon's return, comments appropriately on the long report of the shipwreck, and stands aside while Cassandra and the Trojan prisoners express their frantic despair. Cassandra and later Electra are seen in states of *furor* and only the last line of the play suggests that this dementia will also finally envelop Clytemnestra herself and her partner:

> CLY: at ista poenas capite persolvet suo
> captiva coniunx, regii paelex tori.
> rahite, ut sequatur coniugem ereptum mihi.
>
> CAS: ne trahite, vestros ipsa praecedam gradus.

perferre prima nuntium Phrygibus meis
propero: repletum ratibus eversis mare,
captas Mycenas, mille ductorem ducum,
ut paria fata Troicis lueret malis,
perisse dono feminae: stupro, dolo.
nihil moramur, rapite, quin grates ago.
iam, iam iuvat vixisse post Troiam, iuvat.

CLY: furiosa, morere.

CAS: veniet et vobis furor.

CLY: But that woman shall pay the penalty with
her own life—the prisoner—bride, the harlot
of the royal bed. Drag her away, to follow the
  husband
snatched from me.

CAS: Do not drag me, I will go myself, before
your steps. I am hurrying to be the first to
bring the news to my own Phrygians: news
that the sea is filled with overturned
hulls, Mycenae is captured, and the leader
of the thousand leaders has perished, to
fulfil a destiny that equals the suffering
of Troy: perished by a woman's gift,
by adultery and deceit. We are not
delaying you: carry me off, I thank you even.
Now, now there is joy in having outlived Troy.
  There
 is joy.

CLY: Frenzied woman, die now.

CAS: On you too shall come frenzy.
                                    (1004-12)

The figure of Clytemnestra is a paradigm for Senecan villainy. There is hesitation, or at least analysis, before the
decision to act as personal anger or malevolence has
prompted. Then a deliberate choice is made, and the agent
of evil claims to be rationally in control. Events show that
this is a delusion; the force of *furor* which has been unleashed destroys the villain as well as his victims.

This is the pattern of action which provides the main structural line in six of our ten Imperial plays, and it is found as
an important element in some scenes in two more of them.
Phoenissae is too fragmentary for comment in this respect,
and the one complete play which has no example of evil
choice is *Oedipus.* With these exceptions, the action of
every play, or at least of some part of it, hinges on the
action of a man or woman who chooses, with knowledge,
to follow a passionate impulse which prompts to crime.

Clytemnestra's impulse was to avenge her sacrificed daughter and her own injured pride. Tarrant believes that Seneca
wished to make Agamemnon's infidelities the chief motive
for Clytemnestra's hatred, and her bitter words to Cassandra seem to bear this out, but early in the play her first
thought is of Iphigeneia's cruel death and her own humiliation:

I, Tyndaris, heaven's offspring, brought forth
a life to be sacrificed for the Greek fleet's
purification.

                                    (162-3)

What arises continually in her mind (the word again is
animus) is the scene of the girl's slaughter, with her father
standing by the altar where Iphigeneia has been sent for on
the pretext of betrothal to Achilles.

Similar motives impel Atreus in *Thyestes.* The wrongs done
to him by his brother in the past include treacherous seizure
of their father's throne, seduction of Atreus' wife, and the
theft of the golden ram which was the talisman of power for
the house of Pelops. Atreus' first speech in the play expresses self-reproach for his delay in taking vengeance for
these actions. His vengeance will, as he repeatedly says,
take the form of crimes more sinful than those he is avenging.

Vengeance enters into the motives of the ruthless killers in
Troades also. Here there are two characters who choose to
commit acts of extermination instead of exercising restraint
in conquest: Pyrrhus and Ulysses. Ulysses acts for fear of
harm the child Astyanax may do to the Greeks if he lives
to grow up and take vengeance for the doom of Troy: instead of risking this, Ulysses orders the child to be thrown
from the battlements. Some compunction restrains him for
a brief moment, but he suppresses this as weakness and
chooses clearly recognised atrocity:

now call up your skill, my heart (*animus*), your
deception, your guile. . . .

                                    (613)

Pyrrhus chooses to kill the virgin Polyxena as an offering
to his father Achilles, himself killed by Polyxena's brother
Hector; the motive is again one of vengeance and also the
glorification of Pyrrhus' own family.

Like Clytemnestra, the three women who choose to unleash
violence in *Medea, Phaedra,* and *Hercules Oetaeus* all
have motives of injured pride, but in these plays there are
no previous acts of violence to be avenged. In Medea's
case, and Deianira's, there are strong motives of sexual
jealousy also, and in Phaedra's the impulse of passionate
desire for Hippolytus. The Nero of *Octavia* is also moved
by desire for Poppaea, and also by the need to assert his
own authority by discarding the wife who was his predecessor Claudius' daughter. Like Clytemnestra and Atreus, he
chooses an act of murder as a means of imposing his own
morality:

and horrible 'tis a Prince to be constraynd.
            (*Octavia* 582. tr. Thomas Nuce, 1566)

The original here makes the issue more starkly a moral one:

principem cogi *nefas*

for a ruler to be constrained is sin.

A depiction of the death of Seneca. Print after a painting by Peter Paul Rubens.

Hercules Furens presents the victory of the evil will in a more complex way than any other tragedy. In this play Hercules kills Lycus because he was wronged by him during his absence in Hades. He also has valid grievances against Eurystheus, which he thinks he is satisfying by his slaughter of Megara and their children, during his fit of insanity. In this case, *furor* overtakes the hero even before he begins to put his intention of vengeance into practice.

This play is unique in presenting Furor through the figure of a goddess, to whom Hercules had long been subjected, through his obligation to carry out the twelve Labours imposed by her favourite Eurystheus. As in Virgil, Juno expresses unalloyed Furor, and a hatred of the hero; but unlike Aeneas, Hercules himself is drawn under the power of Furor, being tempted into self-delusion by the opportunities Juno offers him to take the monster-killing role.

Hercules is by far the most complex of Senecan characters, and he alone fails to realise what is the choice he is making when he embarks on his course of violence. (The decisive choice in his case was made before the time of the play's action, when he adopted the role of monster-killer. The only choice actually made during the play is the refusal to purify himself after the killing of Lycus: but this, like the insane slaughter of his family which follows, marks a further stage in a progressive disintegration already far advanced.)

A part from Hercules, the 'villains' in Imperial tragedy act *sciens volens,* with full knowledge and intention. Seneca emphasises this clear awareness many times. He was evidently at pains to confute the Socratic view that no man knowingly chooses to sin.

When Phaedra determines to pursue Hippolytus at all costs, she claims that she is helpless under the force of the *furor* that assails her; but she does not claim ignorance, indeed she insists repeatedly that she knows what is happening. In reply to the long speech from the Nurse, setting out all the moral and practical obstacles to adulterous love, Phaedra says that she knows all this already:

> quae memoras *scio*
> vera esse, nutrix, sed furor cogit sequi
> peiora, vadit animus in praeceps *sciens.* . . .

> What you say is true, Nurse, I
> know: but passion drives (me) to follow the worse
> course of action. My will is moving knowingly
> headlong. . . .
>
> (177-9)

The view of human action that is implied in this speech was not, of course, new in Seneca's time. He is presenting Phaedra in terms very close to those used by Euripides, in his *Medea* . . . :

> but I am overcome by evil things (or, suffering).
> I understand what evil acts I am about to commit;
> but passion is stronger than my consideration.
> (Eur. *Med.* 1077-9)

The language here could not be more straightforward; Euripides makes Medea's clear sighted acts a kind of choice not allowed for in Socratic-Platonist theory.

The Romans did habitually allow for this open-eyed choice of evil. Ovid's Medea describes herself much as Euripides' did (though at a different point in her history):

> aliudque cupido,
> meus aliud suadet. video meliora proboque,
> deteriora sequor.

> and desire prompts one way, intelligence
> another. I see what is better, and approve it;
> I follow what is worse.
> (Ov. *Met.* VII. 19-21)

The long speech which follows examines all the moral and pragmatic arguments to be set against the passionate impulse driving Medea towards Jason, and there is legal as well as moral language in it: supposing I betray my father to help Jason, she says, and then he sails away and marries someone else, am I—Medea—to be left to face the *poena* (legal penalty)? She tells herself to look at the magnitude of her sin (*nefas*), and avoid the charge (*crimen*) that will follow if she gives way to her passion. It is all set out before her in reckonable terms. Similarly for the Senecan villain there is almost always an opportunity to weigh the moral implications of his acts, and at least a theoretical possibility of an act of will in the direction of either passion or reason.

Sciens volens, sciens prudens, these are Roman formulas for the state of purposeful awareness needed either for legal culpability or for valid performance of religious ritual; it is because Medea has this awareness that she can be called *nocens* (guilty) in Seneca (280) (and also perhaps because of this she can successfully call on Hecate and the agents of magic). The same judgment is made in Phaedra's case; she claims that she was *innocens* until she was changed by her passion for Hippolytus (668-9). After this she speaks of herself (as does the Nurse) as guilty, of her love as crime; there is repeated use of legal language from the moment when Phaedra moves with full knowledge into the state of consenting guilt.

Hippolytus describes himself as *nocens* when he realises Phaedra's desire for him; "I am guilty, I have deserved to die; I have pleased my stepmother" (683-4). The guilt which he has acquired is more like a taint or infection than a criminal responsibility. He is *nocens* (in his own eyes) as the sky is *nocens* in *Oedipus* (36); it passes on harm to others while receiving it from a deliberately willing source. Oedipus himself is called *nocens* (1044), because his actions have brought evil upon Thebes although he did not choose to do them. But Jocasta rejects the idea of guilt in his case:

> fati ista culpa est; nemo fit fato nocens.

> that fault is destiny's; no one is made guilty
> by destiny.
>
> (1019)

Hippolytus and Oedipus are *nocentes* in the literal participial sense of 'causing injury'. They are not criminally guilty as Medea, Phaedra, and Atreus are, and because of this difference they do not, like those of evil will, enter into the guilty world of phantasmagoric *furor*.

Before the Senecan villain makes his decisive choice of evil, there is almost always a scene of hesitation when reason prompts him to pause, and does so through the mouth of a human spokesman who warns or advises restraint, but is rejected. Herington called these scenes "The Defeat of Reason by Passion" and identified such scenes as the Second Movement in his scheme of a Senecan tragedy. In five out of our ten Imperial plays, this human spokesman of Reason is the heroine's Nurse, which accounts for the label *Nutrixszene* given to this kind of dialogue by some German critics. The *Nutrixszene* is the prototype of all the confidante-scenes of European drama, and so has acquired an archetypal status which it may not essentially deserve. A Nutrix is plausible only when the villain is a woman; male sinners may be dissuaded by the women of their family (Jocasta takes this role, rather faintly, in both *Oedipus* and *Phoenissae,* and in the latter play Antigone also attempts to draw her father towards moderation). A male servant can also take the Nutrix-role, as the Satelles does in *Thyestes*; his scene with Atreus fits exactly into the Herington pattern. In *Troades* the representative of reason is himself a man of power, the Greek commander Agamemnon; his age and heavy responsibility in the war just ended fit him to speak for prudent experience. Again, in [*Hercules Furens*] the repentant Hercules, tempted to suicide, is dissuaded by his father Amphitryon. *Octavia* has no less than four spokesmen of reason; two of these are Nutrices, addressing their two mistresses Poppaea and Octavia; the two others are men, Seneca himself as Nero's tutor, and the Praefectus, commander of the Praetorian Guard.

Whatever the sex and status of the spokesman of Reason, he speaks with a feebly ineffectual voice in all the plays. The scene in *Phaedra* exemplifies them all. Phaedra addresses her Nurse:

> Unreason drives me into evil.
> I walk upon the brink with open eyes;
> Wise counsel calls, but I cannot turn back
> To hear it. When a sailor tries to drive
> His laden vessel counter to the tides,
> His toil is all in vain, his helpless ship
> Swims at the mercy of the current. Reason?
> What good can reason do?
>
> (178-84, tr. Watling)

The Nurse's reply to this speech attempts to show what good reason can do, and proves that it is not much. The voice which reason is allowed in all the plays proves to be far less powerful than the force of passion. Phaedra says that her passion is "driving her into evil". Like Medea's *dolor*, Atreus' *ira,* and the turmoil of emotions which sways Clytemnestra, the *furor* which assails Phaedra has the nature of an independent agent. This is why she can compare it to a natural force, the current which sweeps away sailor and ship in spite of the warning voice heard only on the

shore. The Nurse reasons in conventional style about the misleading tendencies of mythology and the value of self-control. There is no sense of direct experience to vivify the platitudes. From this exchange the dialogue moves on to the question whether seduction of Hippolytus would be practicable or not. The Nurse maintains that it would not, until Phaedra threatens to kill herself. Before this threat, moral and pragmatic objections alike vanish, and *furor* now directs both Phaedra and the Nurse.

This surrender of the human being to *furor* is not a single act producing a permanent new state of mind. The disruption of order in the soul that such surrender produces is progressive. *Furor cogit me sequi peiora,* Phaedra says, "frenzy drives me to follow the worse course of action": worse than other possible actions, or worse than before? The acts which Phaedra commits are progressively more criminal and the situation (for every character in the play) progressively more disastrous. As in *Macbeth*—the most profoundly Senecan of English plays—one evil action leads inescapably to another more evil still. Phaedra first attempts seduction, by persuasion and enticement and by the power of Hecate; then she brings the false charge of rape against Hippolytus and so causes his violent death and Theseus' despair. What uncontrollably springs from the original evil choice is (in Herington's phrase) an "explosion of evil" far more widespread and more horrifying than what was originally intended.

The deliberate choice of evil, considered in reckonable terms, operates like the use of magic by Medea; the forces it has released are soon out of control. When Phaedra said "frenzy drives me to follow what is worse", she seemed to be shrinking from a progression forced upon her; later she has abandoned herself to madness and exults in the idea of pursuing Hippolytus everywhere, with powers that sound superhuman:

> . . . yet knowing,
> I cannot help myself. Even through fire,
> Through raging seas, through rivers in full flood,
> Over the mountain heights, I shall pursue you.
> No matter where you go, I shall go with you,
> Mad for your love.
>
> (699-702, tr. Watling)

At a later point she declares she will follow the dead Hippolytus to the river Styx and the lake of Tartarus. The first sin has thus become merely the first step towards a state of megalomanic delusion.

The "explosion of evil" (the phrase is Herington's) is similarly seen in *Agamemnon,* where Clytemnestra's murder of Agamemnon leads her on to kill Cassandra also and to inflict banishment and torment upon her own daughter Electra; the forces of madness thus released will at last (Cassandra says) envelop Clytemnestra and her lover also. From the first Clytemnestra has been seeking "a greater sin" to satisfy her need for vengeance. "Greater" here (124) means "greater than anything known before", since she compares her imagined crime with "what any divelish trayterous dame durst do in working woe", as Studley says, and specifically with the vengeance of Medea.

In the same play, Thyestes' ghost appears as Prologue and recapitulates the crime of his family. He relates how he has been outdone in wickedness by his brother Atreus, although until then he had been the supreme criminal. The special achievement of both these brothers consisted in the unnaturalness of their crimes:

> Thyestes I in driery deedes will far surmount the rest,
> Yet to my Brother yelde I, (though I gorgde my
>   bloudy brest)
> And stuffed have my pampred paunche even with my
>   chyldren three,
> That crammed lye within my Rybs and have theyr
>   Tombe in mee,
> The bowels of my swallowed Babes, devoured up I
>   have,
> Nor fickle Fortune mee alone the Father doth
>   deprave,
> But enterprysing greater guilte than that is put in ure,
> To file my Daughters bawdy Bed, my lust shee doth
>   alure.
> To speak these words I do not spare, I wrought the
>   haynous deede,
> That therefore I through all my stocke might parent
>   still proceede. . . .

Studley is accurate here; Thyestes speaks in first person active verbs, emphasising the clear intention of his crimes:

> non pavidus *hausi* dicta, sed *cepi* nefas.
> ergo *ut* per omnis liberos *irem* parens. . . .
>
>   (31-2)

Like Atreus in *Thyestes,* the ghost here speaks with pride as well as horror of the upheaval in nature that his deliberate acts have caused. It is because of this deliberate plunge into chaos that he now finds himself in Hades. The world of the dead in this Prologue is characterised by frustration rather than terror. The scenes of torment chosen from the traditional Hades-picture are those which show interminable self-defeating effort and the reversal of natural processes: the punishments of Ixion, Sisyphus, Tityus, and above all of Tantalus, the speaker's own grandfather. Hades is seen as the sphere of disorder, to which those who have overturned the laws of nature must be banished. Thyestes' ghost describes this realm with horror, but also with a craving to return there. His exclamation *libet reverti,* "I want to go back there", is not merely a rhetorical flourish but a demonstration of his inner perversion which makes the world of chaos and frustration a congenial home to him. The same effect is produced in the opening speech of *Thyestes,* where the Ghost is Thyestes' ancestor Tantalus, who again speaks of the torments of Sisyphus and Tityus as examples of perverted nature, now familiar and even reassuring to him. Tantalus expects his descendants to meet some even more grotesque and unimaginable punishment, from which he recoils:

> harsh judge of shadows   whoever you are
> you who allot new punishments to the dead

> if anything can be added to my suffering which
>   would make
> even the guardian of my terrible prison tremble and
>   the sad
> river of Acheron recoil   some fear which might
>   cause
> even me to shudder   seek it
> now from my stock a multitude is coming to surpass
>   its ancestry
> to make me innocent   to dare the undared
> in the unholy region of hell   whatever space is
>   empty
> I and my family will fill it.
>
>   (*Thyestes* 13-22, tr. Elder)

The ghost-prologues in the two plays which deal with the blighted family of Tantalus are especially fitting for these scenes of escalating evil that follow. In these plays the escalation seems to spring in part from an inherited pre-disposition to sin. The Tantalids act under a compulsion to find their destiny and their satisfaction in devising new forms of evil. This theme is a major one in *Agamemnon* as well as in *Thyestes,* because although the decisive choice of evil in this play is Clytemnestra's, her lover Aegisthus is more than a passive partner, and when Clytemnestra falters he will rest his claim to share in directing action on his identity as Thyestes' son. Because he is the child of Thyestes' deliberate incest which "mingled day with night", the murder of Agamemnon can be seen as his *causa natalis,* the moment for which he was born (*Agamemnon* 48). His father's ghost addresses him:

> iam scelera prope sunt, iam dolus, caedes, cruor—
> parantur epulae. causa natalis tui,
> Aegisthe, venit.

> now the crimes are near, now craft and murder
> and blood. The banquet is being prepared. The reason
> for your birth approaches, Aegisthus. . . .
>
>   (47-9)

The feast now being prepared is ostensibly the celebration welcoming Agamemnon's return (though Studley took it to be a birthday party for Aegisthus). But the gloating anticipation of the Ghost inevitably recalls the banquet of human meat which in a similar sense had offered fruition to Atreus. The memory has already been evoked for the audience earlier in the Ghost's speech, as he looks about him and recognises the earthly home of his ancestors:

> hic epulis locus

> this was the scene of banqueting
>
>   (11)

The note of eagerness in the two Ghost-prologues, as new forms and degrees of horror are awaited, is matched by the perpetrators themselves when the moment of choice has come. Just as Hercules in his madness sees Giants to be destroyed and imagines a *greater* struggle awaiting him (*maius mihi* bellum . . . , 997), so Seneca's Medea is continually looking for a greater crime (*maius* scelus, 933, where she is describing her own nature). The scene of Medea's approach to the *ultimum scelus* of murdering her own children is the fullest presentation of the soul's movement—after the initial choice of wrong doing—towards a progressive series of evil actions which demand total surrender to *furor*. Her long speech (893-977) shows her moving from a sense of triumph at the destruction of Jason's bride and her palace to a contemptuous dismissal of this and all her previous acts; they were childish in comparison with the unknown atrocity she has already chosen (*nescio quid ferox / decrevit animus intus*, 917-8).

This speech of decision—or perhaps of recognition of what was already decided in Medea's first moment of choice—is prompted by the Nurse's advice to flee from the land where she has destroyed the royal house; Medea dismisses this advice, with an outburst of self-regarding passion:

> *egone* ut *recedam*? si *profugissem* prius,
> ad hoc *redirem*. nuptias *specto* novas,
> quid, anime, cessas? . . .
>
> Shall I withdraw? I? if I had fled before,
> I would return for this. I see the new marriage.
> Why do you hesitate, my heart. . . . ?
>
> (893-5)

After this urgent series of first-person verbs, Medea begins a long dialogue with herself. She first summons her will, to follow up her successful onslaught on Jason's interests by devising some unprecendented further act of punishment for him (*poenarum genus haut usitatum*, 898-9). To allow her will to operate, *fas* and *pudor* must go. Instead, she says, she needs *ira* and *dolor* to bring her to a mature strength. So far her *furor* has been childish, but now she claims to be the true Medea:

> Medea nunc sum; crevit ingenium malis.
>
> I am Medea now; my nature has grown through
>   wrongdoing (suffering?)
>
> (910)

Her approach to the *ultimum scelus* of child-murder is agitated, even appalled, as *pietas* returns to resist the *dolor* that drives her on. These abstractions are engaged in conflict which she describes visually like a spectator of a single combat: "rage puts my devotion (*pietas*) to flight—then devotion my rage—O yield, my resentment! . . . " This section of the speech (926-53) is impassioned and (allowing for the Roman rhetorician's use of abstractions) naturalistic; it is the prototype of all the soliloquies in European drama (and opera) which show the heroine, or hero, driven by successive conflicting impulses to act or not act at a moment when action also means irrevocable inward change. This is the voice we hear in Corneille's *Médée*, unmistakably; but also it is Hamlet's "About, my brain!" and even the Beatrice of *Much Ado* when she cries "maiden pride, adieu".

What is Senecan at such a moment is the speaker's projection of impulses and assumption of an observer's role, so that when the choice of action/inaction is made she can describe and judge herself by new standards whose responsibility is not hers alone. Medea's dementia leads to a vision of a throng of Furies, together with the mutilated ghost of her murdered brother, who seeks revenge. She offers him "this hand that drew the sword" (that cut him in pieces) and makes this hand the instrument of his vengeance. She can then call on her will to act, as if it were not part of herself. The phrase used is the terse *hoc age*, a phrase both colloquial and ritual—"get on with it", or "make this offering." With these words she kills the first of her children, and calls on the people to witness and applaud her crime.

In the Atreus of ***Thyestes*** the will to commit escalating crimes is more whole-hearted, with no vacillation. Atreus, as we have seen, claims the power to go "beyond the bounds of human custom" and to make his own morality. He has already attained this liberated state when he first appears in the play. His scene with the Satelles who here takes the Nutrix-role (176-335) presents him as untouched by any scruple or argument. He can say *age, anime*, prompting himself to action, at the beginning, not the end, of the scene; there is none of the hesitation which Medea found in her *animus*. The long dialogue includes moral and practical considerations raised by the Satelles in terms which must seem weighty to the audience, but for Atreus they do not exist.

Thyestes has been disliked, or ridiculed, more than any other play of Seneca, partly because of the gruesome theme of the cannibal meal, but chiefly because the figure of Atreus can so easily be burlesqued, and the whole tragedy dismissed as Grand Guignol. But Atreus—who fathered Richard III and Iago—is certainly presented to us as a serious study in megalomania (and in recent years has been considered more seriously as such). To take Atreus as the supremely evil man, the psychopath rejoicing in a novel form of killing, was not an original dramatic idea in Seneca's time. No Greek *Thyestes* survives, and we know earlier Latin versions only in the briefest fragments; but a line from Accius, preserved in quotation by Cicero, expresses the authentic glee of Atreus as Seneca also portrayed him:

> *maior* mihi moles, *maius* miscendumst malum.
>
> (Cic. *Tusc. Disp.* IV, 77)

As Studley did not translate fragments of Republican tragedy, the gloating alliteration must be diminished into bare prose:

> for me there is a greater task, a greater evil to be stirred
> up.

Seneca took this figure of perverted ambition and—starting at a later point than with Medea and Phaedra—presented a portrait of progressively disintegrating personality under impulsion from the evil force he has welcomed into his house to replace human love and duty:

> Excede, Pietas, si modo in nostra domo
> umquam fuisti, dira Furiarum cohors
> discorsque Erinys veniat et geminas faces

Megaera quatiens: non satis magno meum
ardet furore pectus, impleri iuvat
maiore monstro.

Depart, Pietas, if ever you were in our house
at all. Grim battalion of Furies, and Erinys
goddess of strife, may come, and Megaera,
brandishing her twin torches. My heart
does not blaze with frenzy great enough;
it is my pleasure to be filled with a
greater horror.

(249-54)

These Furies are a multiplication of the Fury who appeared in the Prologue, driving on the ghost of Tantalus to bring evil and madness into his children's house. The Fury's whole purpose was to make wrath grow into new forms of crime and to spread confusion ever wider. The length of the speech given to the Fury's expression of this purpose (23-67) allows this idea to be developed in precise and horrifying detail:

Let loose the Furies on your impious house,
Let evil vie with evil, sword with sword;
Let anger be unchecked, repentance dumb.
Spurred by insensate rage, let fathers' hate
Live on, and the long heritage of sin
Descend to their posterity. Leave none
The respite for remorse; let crimes be born
Ever anew and, in their punishment,
Each single sin give birth to more than one. . . .
Vengeance shall think no way forbidden her;
Brother shall flee from brother, sire from son,
And son from sire; children shall die in shames
More shameful than their birth; revengeful wives
Shall menace husbands, armies sail to war
In lands across the sea, and every soil
Be soaked with blood; the might of men of battle
In all the mortal world shall be brought down
By Lust triumphant. In this house of sin
Brothers' adultery with brothers' wives
Shall be the least of sins; all law, all faith,
All honour shall be dead. Nor shall the heavens
Be unaffected by your evil deeds;
What right have stars to twinkle in the sky?
Why need their lights still ornament the world?
Let night be black, let there be no more day. . . .

(tr. Walting)

It is to this universal chaos that Atreus gives consent and welcome when he invites the Furies into his house, and the Fury of the Prologue is allowed to make this long prediction primarily so that the audience may know what his assenting will has chosen. The access of such chaos is not possible without human consent. The force of chaos is like Wrath in Seneca's *de Ira*; a *voluntarium animi vitium,* a spiritual evil dependent on willed choice. Anger, says Seneca, ventures no kind of action except with the consent of the will.

The majority of those who make the choice of destruction and disorder in Seneca's plays are monarchs (in the case of

Hercules Furens, a goddess). These are the characters who have power to make their choice effective; and they also have the power to choose what means they will use for conflict or revenge. Their choices are real ones, and they know what is to follow, for themselves as well as for their victims: "Why are you not mad yet?" Juno says to herself as she plans to send madness on Hercules (*Hercules Furens* 109).

Why do these Senecan autocrats deliberately plunge into insanity? The theme is not new, if we leave out the word 'deliberately'; Plato speaks of the soul of a tyrant rocked by frenzy and pain as he goes on his irrevocable course; but the Platonic sinner does not anticipate and relish his wickedness as Atreus does. These tyrants of the Imperial stage must be considered for themselves.

2. The Soul of a Tyrant

To find that all Seneca's deliberate wrongdoers are monarchs may seem unsurprising; most characters in ancient tragedy are monarchs, or at any rate nobles with royal or even divine ancestry. No ancient writer ever attempted to present a humbly-born character as the central figure in a tragedy. It may seem then that Seneca's plots are simply standard Greek ones, and that he deals with kings because the Greek dramatists dealt with kings. But there are important differences.

Greek tragedies usually had plots about ill-fated dynasties: "a few families", Aristotle observed, "for example those of Alcmaeon, Oedipus, Orestes . . . who were destined to experience, or to commit, terrifying acts." These families were of course likely to be royal ones. However, Aristotle does not suggest that royalty or power is a pre-requisite for the agent in tragedy. Rather it is "great reputation and good fortune", and goodness (though not perfection) of character, that makes the Aristotelian hero capable of tragic action. Although some degree of eminence was needed to make possible the *peripeteia,* the reversal of fortune, this reversal need not be brought about by actions or circumstances relating to the protagonist's autocracy. Some tragic plots depend entirely on the central character's royal power; any *Agamemnon* or *Oedipus* must do so. Other Greek plays (*Philoctetes* and *Ion* are two examples) are not concerned with royal power at all. Seneca chose, from all the range of Greek tragic plots, those which turn on the protagonist's role as autocrat; his plays are all stories of kings, or queens, whose acts were possible only because they were kings or queens.

Seneca's protagonists are royal, then, and also they are bad; they do not correspond at all to the Aristotelian tragic hero who is deservedly honoured and fails in his flawed goodness to an end that inspires awe. The end of every Senecan play inspires fear, but only a minority (*Troades, Octavia,* perhaps *Phaedra*) can evoke pity, the second element in the Aristotelian response. The irrelevance of Aristotelian criticism to Seneca's plays is apparent here, as in many other ways. The reason for his use of monarchical power as a central theme is not to be found in any unquestioning following of Greek models.

One subject on which Seneca took an attitude independent of Greek traditional ideas was precisely the question of how far the poor or socially unacceptable might be thought to live valuable or worthy lives. He considered with serious attention the often platitudinous praises of the detached ascetic life, and looked on voluntary poverty as an aid to tranquility. It must be said (and his enemies did not neglect to say it) that while publishing these reflections he continued to be one of the richest men in the world. But his view of poverty, and of slavery, was by Greek standards unusual, even slightly perverse. Many passages in the prose works make it clear that he was well aware of moral realities in a poor or humble person's life which could be as complex and intense as they were for the rich. For him, as for few other pagans, there might be a sense of awe at a poor man's end. Yet his plays remain tales of ill-fated dynasties: wealthy and conspicuous men and women, destined to experience, or commit, terrifying acts. Wealthy, conspicuous, and (what Aristotle did not add) possessed of absolute power.

This preoccupation with power and its misuse in Seneca's plays was by no means an imposed part of Greek tragic convention, but it had long been familiar elsewhere. Bloodthirsty tyrants appear more frequently in Greek rhetorical literature than on the Greek stage, and the rhetors could draw on a long philosophic tradition for the link between autocratic power and vice. If wrongdoing is the result of human choice (whether open-eyed or not), the choices of those who have power to make evil purposes into actuality must bring more momentous and more dramatic consequences than the injurious impulses of ordinary men. The rich and powerful, choosing wrongdoing, might work much greater havoc than others could do. Also, philosophers would say, for them the evil choice was far more likely. The temptations of great men to sins of the Stoic canon—wrath, envy, fear, and all kinds of emotional indulgence—had been a constant theme for both philosophers and satirists for at least three centuries before Seneca; and the social harm which could spread from corrupt and cruel men in power had been powerfully stated in the last years of the republic by writers as different as Sallust and Cicero.

Seneca's evil autocrats belong to this line of social-ethical comment, the tradition of rhetoric and satire, rather than to the tradition of the Greek theatre. What he has added to the moral pronouncements of Sallust and Horace (and what could not have been added in satire or in prose) is the insistence on the cosmic dimension which he believed inseparable from the world of human action.

Because Kings—or Emperors—held a position in the social order which was analagous to that of the Sun in the cosmos, Seneca would say their acts of aggrandisement and cruelty must evoke analogous disruption in the heavens, such as the darkening of the Sun in *Thyestes.* When beggars die there are no comets seen; or if there are, they are shooting from their course not for the beggar's death but for the brutality of the despot who killed him.

Brutality, making oneself a beast, is the image which Seneca uses at the climax of his essay *On Mercy*, addressed to the young Emperor Nero as a guide to government rather than a literary exercise in moral philosophy. The Imperial ruler holds the place of a god in human society, Seneca says at the beginning of this work; he should act like a god rather than as a man. A cruel ruler has taken on the nature of an animal; men might as well live under lions or bears. Similarly, when Atreus in *Thyestes* spoke of crossing the boundary of human custom, his actions led to the claim that he trod the ways of heaven, a king of kings, highest of gods:

> aequalis astris gradior . . . o me caelitum
>   excelsissimum,
> regum atque regem! vota transcendi mea.

> nowe equall with the Starres I go . . . now chiefe of
>   goddes in highest place I stand,
> and king of kinges. I have my wish, and more than I
>   could thinke.

(885, 911-2, tr. Heywood)

But at this point in the play the audience has already heard the Messenger describing Atreus' slaughter of Thyestes' sons:

> silva iubatus qualis Armenia leo
> in caede multa victor armento incubat
> —cruore rictus madidus et pulsa fame
> non point iras: hinc et hinc tauros premens
> vitulis minatur dente iam lasso piger—
> non aliter Atreus saevit atque ira tumet,
> ferrumque gemina perfusum caede tenens
> oblitus in quem fureret, infesta manu
> exegit ultra corpus. . . .

>   like a long-maned lion in the Armenian
> forests, victorious in all the slaughter as he swoops
> on a herd of cattle—his jaws dripping with blood,
> and hunger quelled, he does not let his rage
> abate; he drives the bulls this way and that,
> threatening the calves when he grows slow, with
> weary bite. So Atreus rages and swells in
> wrath, grasping his sword that is steeped in
> double slaughter; forgetting who was the
> object of his frenzy, he strikes with deadly hand
> right through the body. . . .

(732-40)

This simile repeats the comparison of Atreus to a savage beast, already made earlier in the scene when the Messenger describes him "like a tigress" (707-16). The second simile however takes the brutalising of Atreus much further than the first—not simply in terms of detailed atrocity but in his total loss of rationality. The tigress in the first simile is going to kill to satisfy hunger. She moves about, observing her prey, deciding which of two steers she should attack first. Atreus at this stage is similarly deciding which of the two boys should be his first victim:

> it makes no difference; yet he hesitates, and it
> gives him pleasure to set his savage crime in order.

(715-6)

The pleasure of setting things in order—*ordinare*—might well be appropriate for a king, or for the divinity which Atreus soon claims to be attaining. The note (not the word) is heard again in Clytemnestra's claim that she and Aegisthus can by their *consilia* "disentangle the doubtful and threatening state of things" (*Agamemnon* 308-9). These words occur at a comparable point in *Agamemnon* to the moment when Atreus begins to "set his crimes in order"; the preliminary hesitations, or analyses, are over, and the tyrant is committed to the crime he plans and can begin to determine its details. At this point Atreus believes he is in control of everything and experiences a sense of superhuman elevation. Similarly Clytemnestra has become confident and imperious. To others she becomes a figure of savage terror, with her grim expression and bloodstained hands (897, 947-50). In her own eyes she remains the authoritative mother and queen. Cassandra prophesies, in the last words of the play, that frenzy will take hold of the two criminals in the end; their sense of being in control is a delusion. In the same way Medea, when her vengeance is planned, experiences a sense of power and authority restored to her (982-4) and with the words "it is well, it is all done" (1019) soars in her chariot towards the heavens. But again the last line of the play is spoken by another, one who has been injured; far from apotheosis, Medea the Sun's descendant will find that in the heaven to which she goes there are no gods:

> testare nullos esse qua veheris deos.

> bear witness that no gods exist where you travel.

As in the repeated examples of hideous cruelties recounted in *On Anger*, Seneca presents in these scenes examples (and they might well serve also as *exempla* in the Stoic sense, as exemplifications of moral lessons) of men who sought to become more than men, and ended by becoming less.

On Mercy, written some years later than *On Anger*, returns to the theme of cruelty as an abrogation of human nature. "None of the virtues is more appropriate for a man (than mercy), since none is more human. . . ." "Cruelty is an evil alien to the human. . . ." But for the monarch, Seneca repeatedly insists here, mercy is not only appropriate but positively glorious, since his power to inflict injury is so great. "Every house that mercy enters she will render fortunate and tranquil, but in a palace she is more rare and so more wonderful. For what is more remarkable than for the man whose anger nothing withstands, whose oppressive sentence meets with consent even from those who perish by it, whom no one will interrupt, indeed no one even entreat if he is moved to passion—for this man to lay a hand upon himself and use his power for better and gentler ends as he reflects, 'Anyone can break the law by murder; only I by saving life?'. . . Only wild animals—and not even the nobler beasts—worry and mangle their fallen victims. . . . To save life is peculiar to exalted fortune, which should never be admired more than when it has power like that of the gods, by whose kindness we are all—both good and bad—brought forth into the light. Let a ruler then put upon himself the spirit of the gods. . . ."

No other Senecan discourse has a more personal note than *On Mercy*; its didactic purpose is not general or abstract but specific and practical. Seneca here writes with the aim (we do not know whether he wrote with much hope) of influencing the young Nero to adopt policies of government based on humanitarian principles of the widest application. *Mansuetudo,* a civilised mildness, is the keynote of this treatise, as of Seneca's own policies while largely in control of Nero's administration. Nero was seventeen when he became Emperor, and had been Seneca's pupil from the age of twelve.

Nero was not the first Emperor personally known to Seneca, who had lived in Rome since his boyhood, when he left Spain to be educated in the capital. Though his entry into political life apparently did not begin until he was nearly forty, Seneca was well known in Rome before then; Suetonius says the Emperor Caligula thought him too successful (as a speaker) to be trusted. Whether Claudius had any personal interest or not in Seneca is unknown; the malice towards Claudius in the *Apocolocyntosis* suggests that (as Tacitus says people generally believed) there were motives for animosity. Claudius ordered banishment rather than death as the punishment when Seneca was tried before the Senate and found guilty of adultery with the Emperor's niece Julia Livilla; but this may have been in response to a plea from her sister, Agrippina. Eight years later, Agrippina—now the Emperor's wife—intervened to gain Seneca's recall from his exile in Corsica, to undertake the education of her son.

So at the age of about fifty Seneca moved into the Imperial household as tutor to the future Emperor; he also (thanks to Agrippina) held the office of praetor. Tacitus' account of this move makes it clear that his services in the palace were not to be concerned purely with academic instruction. Agrippina probably hoped to gain credit by recalling a prominent intellectual from exile; if so, he must go on being prominent in the intellectual world, and preferably beyond it; she would also value his intelligence as an aid to policy, and no doubt believed that gratitude to herself would lead him to put his *consilia* at her service in the struggle for power.

Seneca then wrote speeches for Nero as well as giving him formal lessons in (we assume) rhetoric and philosophy. He also exercised a strong influence on public affairs (*princeps potentia,* "foremost in power" is Pliny the Elder's description of him). Since (like Afranius Burrus, commander of the praetorians) he had entered the household as Agrippina's protégé, he would clearly be expected to act as her *satelles,* always supplying advice in his patron's interest, as Atreus expects his *satelles* to do in *Thyestes.* But when Nero became Emperor, power shifted away from his mother, and it was Nero, not Agrippina, who then called on Seneca to be available as his *satelles,* for guidance on all sorts of occasions. These had at times disturbing and even ludicrous elements, which reach their extreme in Tacitus' account of Nero's turning to Seneca for advice when he attempted to murder Agrippina in 59 A.D. The ingenious scheme to kill her by drowning in a boat built to collapse had failed; Nero was panic-stricken. "She might arm her slaves, or stir up the army; she might make her way to the Senate and the people, charging him with the shipwreck, her wound, the murders of her friends; what support was there for him? unless Burrus and Seneca could do something. He had aroused them and demanded their attendance at once; whether they had any knowledge already is uncertain. So both were silent for some time, in case it might be futile to try dissuading him; or perhaps they believed that things had gone so far that unless Agrippina were frustrated, Nero must perish. Eventually Seneca took the initiative, to the extent of looking at Burrus and asking him whether the troops should be ordered to kill her. . . . "

Nero's letter to the Senate, reporting Agrippina's death and recounting the offences which made it a providential release for Rome, was (Tacitus says) known to have been Seneca's composition. No one believed that the shipwreck had been accidental. But the letter did more harm to Seneca, who by such a composition had merely incriminated himself, than to Nero, whose monstrous inhumanity (*immanitas*) went beyond all criticism.

We are forced at many points to depend on Tacitus' account of Seneca's conduct and motives during these years. This account is ambivalent, and the portrait often seems deliberately colourless. Ambivalent but not fumbling; the writing here is too forceful to leave our judgment of Seneca uninfluenced, even if we think we are allowing for animosity. There is no such ambiguity in the Tacitean portrait of Nero. Tacitus does not qualify assertions of Nero's atrocities and vulgarities (as he habitually does if there is any room for doubt in recording discreditable actions), and there are no gaps between motive and action such as those which make the portrait of Tiberius a riddle. Nero in the *Annals* is vicious from the first; with his act of matricide he becomes a man of evil will.

The role of Seneca in his encounters with Nero in the *Annals* is an ineffectual one at every point; he is like the Nurses and Attendants in Senecan tragedy who are usually platitudinous mouthpieces of a Reason which cannot be translated into action.

Seneca wrote *On Mercy* probably in the first or second year of Nero's reign. The work is traditional in form, a didactic pamphlet which could offer a model for such literary compositions, but clearly also expressing recommendations of practical relevance to the new Emperor's policy-making. It must, however, have been clear to Seneca (he had taught Nero for five or six years) that there was little prospect of holding his pupil's serious attention by such exhortation, now that he had actually gained imperial power. After the three extraordinary Emperors who preceded him—Tiberius, Caligula, Claudius—Nero was subject to the pressure of example and social expectations of such an abnormal kind that only a man of very exceptional integrity and clarity of mind could have resisted them. The portrait in Tacitus agrees with all other sources in making it clear that Nero had no such capacity.

For Seneca, the autocrat of evil will was not a theoretical construct from academic philosophy; he had known more

than one such ruler even before his close association with Nero. There are no means of dating any of the plays precisely, but some at least must have been written before Nero became Emperor. Tacitus says that in the years after Agrippina's murder Seneca began to write more poetry than before; but does *carmina* refer to tragedies? It is hard to believe that Jocasta's death in *Oedipus,* with a sword replacing Sophocles' noose, and the cry "strike at my teeming womb" echoing Agrippina's, did not take its form and expression from the actuality Seneca had known under Nero. But the figure of the autocrat deliberately sinning had been in Seneca's mind much earlier than this; Sejanus takes this role in the *Consolation to Marcia,* generally dated to Caligula's reign, even before Seneca's years of exile. It is clear, however, that the idea of the evil tyrant became more and more insistently present to him, in the treatise *On Anger* for example (and the composition of these three Books seems to have been spread over several years; the most horrifying accounts of tyrannical cruelty are found in the Third Book, written probably after his recall to Rome from exile).

When Seneca came to write *On Mercy,* he was developing themes and using images which he had found significant to him over a period of many years, and already handled many times in prose and in the plays. The plan of the treatise is set out in positive terms; the praises of mercy, as exemplified in Nero himself, *humanissimus Nero,* at the opening of his reign, an examination of this virtue, and a discussion of how the human soul may be led to goodness. The portrayal of mercy's opposite, the inhuman vice of cruelty, takes a more prominent place in the work than this plan would lead us to expect. There is a strong note of warning, as much as encouragement.

Whether or not Seneca had already written *Thyestes,* he had seen the death of Britannicus within months of Nero's accession; Nero on this occasion, seeing his adoptive brother convulsed by poison at a palace meal, "lay back unconcernedly and remarked that this often happened to epileptics. . . . Agrippina realised that her last support was gone. And here was Nero murdering a relation." The detachment, even satisfaction, with which Nero saw Britannicus die, was not far from the spirit of Atreus "setting things in order". And when Nero, only four years later, proceeded to murder his mother and then his wife, he did so with every sign of deliberate choice. This massacre of relatives was not carried out in a hallucinatory fit, like that of Hercules, or even in a moment of intense passion overmastering reason and human feeling, like Medea's. Nero destroyed Britannicus, Agrippina, and Octavia because they continually irritated and frustrated him, and he did so after considering, and toying with various schemes, for a long time; there was a willed choice. This was very much like Atreus making his pronouncement.

> excede, Pietas, si modo in nostra domo
> umquam fuisti. . . .

> begone, family devotion, if ever you were in
>   my house at all. . . .
>   (*Thyestes* 249-50)

Pietas, after all, was one of the "private goods", like holiness and integrity, which Atreus declared were not for kings. In his words, "kings may go which way they please".

Guiding a monarch towards virtue was thus likely to be an exceptionally difficult task. If Seneca took this task very seriously, it was not because Agrippina had appointed him to do so, but because positive guidance for troubled men— even monarchs—was a prime duty of a philosopher according to the Stoic ethics. Philosophy was seen both as a form of psychotherapy and as a guide to political action; it should thus benefit both individuals and society. There was also, of course, the motive of self-preservation; a monarch's tutor could be murdered as easily as his relatives, especially if the moralist's own life had not been irreproachable.

To restore order to Nero's troubled soul was not within Seneca's power, and he must have known that the immediate realities of government were not likely to be much influenced by anything he might say about Mercy. One hope remained for the philosophic writer, the only hope when he was constrained to social impotence:

> With what thought does the wise man retire into leisure? In the knowledge that there also he will be doing something that will benefit posterity. Our school at any rate is ready to say that both Zeno and Chrysippus accomplished greater things than if they had led armies, held public office, and framed laws. The laws they framed were not for one state only, but for the whole human race. Why, therefore, should such leisure as this not be fitting for the good man, who by means of it *may govern the ages to come (futura saecula ordinet)* and speak, not to the ears of the few, but to the ears of all men of all nations, both those who now are and those who shall be?
>
> [*De Otio* VI.4]

Setting future ages in order might be an intelligible motive for the writing of treatises on such universal moral themes as Mercy, Steadfastness, or Tranquillity of Soul. It would not seem necessary, or consistent, for a philosopher inspired by this purpose to write plays. It is because the two genres of Seneca's work appear so alien to each other that for centuries they were thought to be the work of two different men. Any adequate account of his philosophic purposes must find room for the tragedies too. And the man of evil will (both those whom Seneca knew and those yet to come) were not to be set in order by any exercise of philosophic eloquence.

Anna Lydia Motto and John R. Clark (essay date 1988)

SOURCE: "Art and Ethics in the Drama: Senecan 'Pseudo-tragedy' Reconsidered," in *Senecan Tragedy*, Adolf M. Hakkert, 1988, pp. 43-65.

[Motto and Clark study the literary merits of the seven plays that can be ascribed to Seneca with certainty. They postulate that an over-emphasis on the importance of his philosophical writings to his drama impedes appreciation and understanding of the plays.]

Perhaps the major stumbling-block to an understanding and appreciation of Seneca's theater is the fact that Seneca was a philosopher. For many, that fact virtually constitutes an insurmountable obstacle and blinding light. As a result, too many critics argue that Seneca wrote his tragedies to expound his philosophic doctrines. They postulate—what has ever been in some quarters suspected—that the plays by the Stoic Philosopher are fundamentally Stoical. One critic [Berthe Marti, "Seneca's Tragedies: A New Interpretation," *Transactions and Proceedings of the American Philological Association* 76 (1945)] has gone so far as to propose that these "philosophical propaganda-plays" constitute indeed a single "set" of tragedies which should be studied in the sequence and order they occupy in the Codex Etruscus, beginning and concluding with a Hercules play [*Hercules Furens, Troades, Phoenissae, Medea, Phaedra, Oedipus, Agamemnon, Thyestes, Hercules Oeaeus*]. Thus the plays must be read altogether, *en masse,* as a single "Stoic treatise" which may be designated "as a sort of glorified Essay on Man." There are, she believes, unrelieved horrors and gloom, uncontrolled passions, and an evil fate operative throughout the series—until the reader comes at last to the final play, the *Oetaeus,* where Stoic virtue is finally rewarded.

This critic's overall hypothesis has been largely discounted for a number of very good reasons. We have absolutely no evidence nor inkling that Seneca himself "arranged" the ordering of his plays; indeed, we have no information about their original "publication" whatsoever. Again, we have not one iota of evidence that would lend credence to the suggestion that the ordering of the Codex Etruscus is to be preferred to the ordering of A or any other recensions. In addition, the *Phoenissae* is admittedly an incomplete fragment, and many critics question the authorship of the *Hercules Oetaeus.* Finally, until the era of Proust, no one had encountered the nonalogical structure; a Greek audience had enough to do to sustain its attention-span when faced with the performance of a trilogy (together with a satyr-play); a nine-headed monster would have overwhelmed it. Whatever one might say to the contrary, it was never Seneca's practice to keep his readers suspended for some five hundred pages before granting them respite — and enlightenment. As Jonathan Swift once remarked [in *A Tale of a Tub*], "Going *too* long is a Cause of Abortion as effectual, tho' not so frequent, as *Going too* short. . . . " If Seneca were as eager to inculcate philosophical doctrine as this critic appears to believe, his astonishingly outstretched sequence of plays would contribute mightily to the loss of instruction entirely. No; such a critic's conjectures simply have not been able to pass muster because they are so free-wheeling and insubstantial. C.D.N. Costa, for example, [in his *Seneca* (1974)] finds such a theory "most unlikely"; "it needs a good deal of special pleading to infer Stoic teaching from all the plays. . . . "

Although such a conjectural thesis has been, in large measure, shunted aside, it is important to come to terms with a beguiling and rather widely-held opinion concerning the presence of overt Stoicism in the Philosopher's drama and with the popularly received notion that there is or ought to be explicit didacticism and moral teaching in works of literature, particularly the drama. We are told, for example, that Seneca's plays constitute "a piece of neo-Stoic propaganda," and are primarily dedicated to "the teaching of philosophy"; hence, this critic believes that the Senecan plays are "pseudotragedies," utilizing dramatic form as deceptive "sugar-coating." Accordingly, "from a purely aesthetic point of view much in [these plays] deserves the most severe strictures." Needless to say, the very term "pseudotragedy" is pejorative, suggesting the synthetic, the counterfeit, and the second rate. Such a critic's emphasis upon Stoicism stems from the "effort to determine Seneca's object in writing the plays . . ."; we might suggest that such criticism is guilty of "The Intentional Fallacy." For we can never predicate an author's intentions with certainty, and when we then proceed to locate the effects of that postulated intention in his writings, our argument becomes hopelessly circular; such criticism, as Wimsatt observes [in *The Verbal Icon: Studies in the Meaning of Poetry* (1958)], " . . . begins by trying to derive the standard of criticism from the psychological *causes* of the poem and ends in biography and relativism."

It is also interesting to note that so many modern critics endorse a kind of unwritten "law of literary specialization": a philosopher cannot write plays, etc. Rigidly applied, this criterion would prevent a Caesar from writing memoirs or plays, a Plato from writing poetry, any poet from writing criticism, any doctor, lawyer, or priest from writing fiction.

Indeed, for many a critic, it is the philosophical content in Senecan drama that counts and that saves his plays from total condemnation. Hopefully, the reader at this point will be seriously dismayed to observe how congenially such criticism sacrifices "mere aesthetic" in works of art in favor of solid moral teaching. Certainly, as in all great literature, Seneca's plays abound in deep thought and in psychological understanding of human nature, but one can hardly argue that he employed the tragic genre primarily to impart philosophic concepts.

To be sure, the whole question of literature's "utility" and "moral purpose" has been a recurrent and vexing problem in literary criticism for two thousand years. The exertions and requirements of moralizers never diminish, and many a theorist becomes frankly ambivalent. Thus W. K. Wimsatt, Jr. insists that he tends to side with those who would separate art from morality; yet later he admits that, for him, the greatest poetry will *not* be immoral or indifferent, but "morally right" ["Poetry and Morals: A Relation Reargued," *Thought* 23 (1948)]. Perhaps such ambivalence cannot ever be eliminated. . . .

In general, then, over the centuries moralism and didacticism in literary criticism have tended to prevail. We might well answer critics' "discovery" that Seneca is philosophizing and moralizing in his dramas by reminding them that Sophoclean or Aeschylean or Euripidean drama is all too frequently comprehended in precisely the same instructional light.

Indeed, most dramatists in some sense employ ideas in their plays, and this is particularly true of the ancient Greek playwrights. William Arrowsmith, for example, [in "A Greek Theatre of Ideas," *Ideas in the Drama: Selected Papers from the English Institute*, ed. John Gassner (1964)] has argued that both Aeschylus and Sophocles use their contemporary cultural situation "as framing dramatic ideas" in their plays, and he goes on to urge that Euripides especially was the experimentalist who literally creates a theater of ideas. There was something of a hue and cry when Eric Bentley's *The Playwright as Thinker* first appeared in 1946, but Bentley has stood by his general thesis: that the major dramatists of the modern era (Wagner, Ibsen, Strindberg, Shaw) have fostered ideas in their dramas.

Yet the difficulties with a predominant didacticism should become apparent. Far too frequently, for instance, in such a climate, the literary work is yanked and pulled and distorted by *allegorizing*, in order to force it to yield up its acceptable modicum of lesson and message. At its most silly, such message-mongering leads a critic like Thomas Rymer to discern two "morals" in Shakespeare's *Othello* [in his *A Short View of Tragedy* (1692)]:

> . . . a caution to maidens of quality how, without their parents' consent, they run away with blackamoors . . . [and] a warning to all good wives that they look well to their linen.

Still more importantly, a regnant moral didacticism is tempted to become "militant," demanding that religious and philosophical instruction in the literary work be made pikestaff clear and overt. At its worst, such criticism is recurrently moved to advocate censorship (necessitating just as repeatedly that authors counter with their *Areopagiticas*). Such rigid moralizing criticism commences by doubting whether good poetry can ever be written by "bad" men. Where it cannot censure, it attempts to prescribe what sort of literature is "acceptable." Over the years, for example, this practice led to the development of the concept of "poetic justice" in the drama of the seventeenth and eighteenth centuries—that doctrine which called overtly (as at the tacked-on conclusion of the Book of Job) for the onstage punishment of vice and the remuneration of rectitude (and may be perceived in the curious pabulum of Richard Steele's sentimental plays or in Richardson's novel, *Pamela, or Virtue Rewarded* [1740]). By such a standard, only a limited number of "cheerful" plots would be admissible. Tragedy would be virtually ham-strung (unless the protagonist be vicious); satire would prove unruly (refusing in tone, word, and deed to "suffer fools gladly"); and comedy would only be permitted to trifle and jest at the expense of the morally reprehensible. Lest these reflections seem extreme and at any rate unnecessary in our own enlightened era, let us remind the reader of the frequency with which Tennessee Williams has been chastized for dwelling so frequently in his dramas upon the unsavory and the depressing, and recollect as well Kenneth Tynan's strictures of Eugene Ionesco's plays for failing to be "affirmative." Such ethical vigilantes are ever upon the alert. Furthermore, it has become commonplace in recent years for the occasional moralist to raise his voice against our own period's literature for celebrating decadence, violence, pornography, obscenity, and vice—the most recent instance being Mr. John Gardner's *On Moral Fiction* (1978).

The truth of the matter is that we cannot, even if we wanted to, prescribe what we will accept as suitable to world literature. In the epic, in the novel, in much poetry, and especially in the drama—in all of these fictional modes the author simply is not present *in propria persona*. Nor will normative literary conventions allow him to break in upon the scene. . . .

Hence, an author may well brilliantly express action and character in literary works of art, but he cannot express himself; he cannot express his morality or his philosophy. We obtain only a hint of these latter by the breadth, the particularity, the assurance, and the intensity of his creativity. We cannot be certain of the discursive meaning of Seneca's plays (we cannot be certain of such meaning of any plays—and debates over interpretations of *Hamlet* and the *Oedipus Tyrannos* are relevant here), but we can indeed be certain of the force and intensity of much of Seneca's achievement—the gloomy atmosphere of the *Oedipus,* the furious ragings of a Medea, an Atreus, or a Juno, the witty asperity of a Megara's rejoinders to the tyrant Lycus, the frustrated clairvoyance of a Cassandra, the desperate sufferings of the mother Andromache, the poisoned physical torments of a Hercules, the insane loves of a Phaedra. We cannot in all honesty label these works "pseudotragedies" or thank our stars that they are without aesthetic interest—lest with the art we toss out the artifact, and there be nothing left!

If we set aside hypotheses about instruction and philosophizing for a time and examine squarely into Seneca's plays, we ought to discern those features that lend them psychic power and dramatic force. For one thing, his plays are austere etchings and rich mood-pieces, as Herington has observed [C. J. Herington, "Senecan Tragedy," *Arion* 5 (1966)]. Herington stresses in Seneca a tone of "almost religious fervor" and a "terrible moral sensitivity" realized by the playwright's "concrete, pictorial imagination" and brilliant painter's eye for "fantasy." Prescient choruses keen and brood, and grotesque images recur with a fatal insistence. Such features lend an intensity to scenes of suffering, as Regenbogen has particularly remarked and astutely explored [Otto Regenbogen, *Schmerz und Tod in den Tragödien Senecas* (1927)]. Further, of course, such settings and distorting scenes suggest the nightmarish, almost hallucinatory visions that bespeak a lurid and perceptive psychological presentation—a presentation enhanced by his characters' soliloquies, dramatic laments, and "self-apostrophes."

To add to this psychiatric milieu, characters speak with stichomythic and almost shotgun tenseness and unreal clarity, as violent emotions build. Moreover, scenes tend to be isolated, blocked off, separate—even disjunct. Jo-Ann Shelton [in "Problems of Time in Seneca's *Hercules Furens* and *Thyestes*," *CSCA* 8 (1975)] speaks of temporal repetitions in the *Hercules Furens* and the *Thyestes* and of the playwright's presentation of "simultaneous events linearly"; but what is achieved is a staccato effect in the dreamlike tracing

not of clock but of psychic time. For example, in the *Thyestes* when Tantalus curses the House of Atreus, characters in the play are *already infected,* and subsequently edged and jarred and caromed onward into a mainstream of emotional fever pitch and taut melodramatic posturing and performance. Needless to say, such a psychological theater of extremity and cruelty was particularly attractive to Elizabethans and Jacobeans. As Michael Higgins notes [in "The Development of the 'Senecal' Man: Chapman's *Bussy D'Ambois* and Some Precursors," *RES* 23 (1947)]:

> . . . the Stoic revival of the sixteenth and seventeenth centuries was a symptom of a general dissolution of established beliefs and institutions. This atmosphere of chaos, of moral and intellectual disintegration, is reflected in the tragedies of the Jacobean era.

Seneca's theater clearly reflected crises of a mass urban society and of the rising dictatorships of first-century Rome. The Neronian world of chaos, foreboding, fantasy, and the grotesque are perhaps best exemplified in his *Oedipus.* Moreover, such characteristics are again in the twentieth century a particularly relevant dramatic form of art.

Seneca's influential, psychologically charged, and violently emotional theater is hardly tragic or cathartic in the traditional Aristotelian sense—characters in his plays are too frenzied and furious in their violence and obsessions; and a suppurating flux of evil prevails. As the Chorus in the *Phaedra* gloomily intones:

> res humanas ordine nullo
> Fortuna regit sparsitque manu
> munera caeca, peiora fovens;
> vincit sanctos dira libido,
> fraus sublimi regnat in aula.
>
> (978-82)
>
> (Fortune in disarray governs human affairs
> and blindly scatters her gifts,
> favoring the foul;
> dreadful lust conquers blameless men,
> fraud in the lofty palace prevails.)

Nor is *Fortuna* even so innocently blind; for spirits like Tantalus and deities like Juno actually intrude in behalf of savagery and mayhem. But, most importantly, despite all of the fury and destruction, Senecan drama is pervaded by a large and persistent irony. Vice triumphs—but is never gratified. Phaedra's revenge, after all, includes her own destruction and the slaughter of her beloved Hippolytus. Medea's righting of the balance betwixt herself and Jason includes the murder of her own children; her final claim that she has been restored to chastity and innocence is perceived as being outrageously and pathetically deluded. Atreus, for all of his towering fury, continues frustrated and insecure even at the moment of his most horrible victory over Thyestes: his jealousy, suspicion, and ire are pitched at such an extremity that they can never be satisfied or allayed. Similarly, in a broad historical sense, Clytemnestra's and Aegisthus' vengeance upon Agamemnon is but the helpless accomplishment of recompense to Cassandra and the dead of Troy; and, to be sure, the play concludes with no resolution or pause in the train of crimes and reprisals, and the mad Cassandra has the last prophetic word with Agamemnon's assassins: *"Veniet et vobis furor"* (1012)—upon the destroyers shall mad destruction be yet to descend. Even beyond the human realm, the spirits of Thyestes and Achilles, the shade of Tantalus, cry for cruelty and vengeance. Even the deity Juno is rabidly incensed. Whether among humans, among spirits, or among the gods themselves, Senecan theater merely presents a brutal *ethos* of continual slaughter. His pervasive, secular irony attests to the ignobility of gods and heroes alike that borders upon—nay, that topples over into—insanity. Ultimately, such characters stand revealed as puppets in the universe, for their freedom and self-realization and self-expression has been totally lost to mania and passion.

It is erroneous to argue that Seneca composed such intense, original, and powerful dramatic visions merely to inculcate philosophic thought. Yet, to be sure, such thought abounds in his plays. Needless to say, all major literary works that have been presumably admired are replete with intellectual content. A true classic is remembered for its distinction in content as well as in form. It is virtually impossible to insist that Seneca wrote these tragedies merely to formulate a syllogism or a maxim. He is rather endowing us with a poetic, creative, new tragic invention—one that envisions a livid, ruinous world where evil characters rant and rave, perpetrating the destruction of themselves and of others. His brilliantly darkened world-picture can hardly be reduced or construed as torts and orts of instruction for little Marcuses and Juliuses. Rather he has created for us an unreasoning universe, a second world closely set beside our own, a nightmare neighborhood where passion and frenzy are forever in fullest flower. If he touches us profoundly, it is because his neighborhood, after all, is dangerously near to our own. Such is his gift to us of a genuine literature.

"What?" we might question: "Seneca a maker of 'literature'?" It is quite true that Seneca, in his philosophical writings, appears to give pure literature a second-row seat. The Stoics naturally placed philosophy above the other "arts"; thus Seneca claims philosophy is the only art that investigates good and evil and contributes to the perfection of the soul. Yet we know of his impressive familiarity with Ovid, Homer, and Vergil from the great number of times he mentions or quotes from them. As he makes clear in one passage, it is not so much that he ignores literature, as that he approaches it—not as the philologist or the grammarian—but as the philosopher; his chief concern is how to live and how to die, how to obtain strength to practice virtue, to strive for intellectual perfections, and to be borne, as it were, aloft toward the gods. Seneca knew that outstanding literary achievement, whatever its genre, guaranteed for the writer immortal glory. At one point he quotes from Vergil:

Optima quaeque dies miseris mortalibus aevi prima figut.

(For wretched mortals, the best days of life are the first to flee.)

[*Georgics*]

Overcome with emotion and response to the poet's painful insight, Seneca observes:

Clamat ecce maximus uates et uelut diuino ore instinctus salutare carmen canit.

(Behold the greatest bard exclaims and as if inspired with divine words sings a salutary song.)

[*On the Happy Life*]

In his studies, Seneca regularly honors the great minds of every genre, the grand geniuses of every age:

. . . sed cum optimo quoque sum; ad illos, in quocumque loco, in quocumque saeculo fuerunt, animum meum mitto.

(. . . but I am with all the best; to them, in whatever place, in whatever century they have been, I send my own soul.)

[*Epistuale Morales* 62.2]

And he, like them, escaped the oblivion of time, not only through his philosophic Letters and Dialogues but through his Tragedies as well.

Dana Gioia   (essay date 1993-94)

SOURCE: "Seneca and European Tragedy" and "Seneca & the Idea of Lyric Tragedy," in *The New Criterion,* Vol. XII, Nos. 4 and 5, December, 1993 and January, 1994, pp. 16-25, pp. 29-38.

[*In the first section of the following two-part essay, Gioia analyzes Seneca's contribution to the formal aspects of Elizabethan drama, including the five-act structure, the introduction of essential secondary characters, and the presentation of the ghost figure. In the second part Gioia characterizes Seneca as "the creator of a new theatrical genre—lyric tragedy."*]

In 1543 Giambattista Giraldi Cinthio, the influential Italian playwright, critic, and writer of *novelle* (from whom Shakespeare borrowed the plots of *Othello* and *Measure for Measure*), judiciously summarized the Renaissance view of Seneca's dramas: "In almost all his tragedies he surpassed (in as far as I can judge) all the Greeks who ever wrote—in wisdom, in gravity, in decorum, in majesty, and in memorable aphorism."

Renaissance criticism often employs vague and platitudinous language, but Cinthio's terms of praise are refreshingly exact. He asserts Seneca's pre-eminence among classical tragedians in five specific areas—*wisdom* (the moral truth and importance of what is presented), *gravity* (the integrity of tragic tone and vision), *decorum* (the appropriate consistency of language, character, action, and idea), *majesty* (the ability to create the imposing and sublime), and *memorable aphorism* (Cinthio's Italian term is *sentenze* in the Elizabethan sense of *sentences*—insightful and quotable maxims). Needless to say, none of Cinthio's evaluative categories enjoys much critical currency today (though whether their absence represents our age's gain remains an open question). Indeed Cinthio himself has been largely forgotten except by Renaissance scholars. And yet his perspective on Seneca remains illuminating because he was no academic antiquarian. He was a visionary artist-intellectual engaged in an imaginative enterprise beyond the scope and ambition of most writers—to re-create one of the central European literary genres, tragic theater, after a hiatus of nearly fifteen hundred years. Though Cinthio and his Italian contemporaries failed to compose enduring masterpieces, they decisively shaped the renascence of European tragedy that culminated in Shakespeare, Corneille, and Racine, a tradition they consciously grounded in Seneca.

Today Cinthio's high opinion appears perverse and ill-informed. Seneca the tragedian is a forgotten author. The plays are never performed, rarely discussed, and hardly read, except by specialists. To ascertain how low Seneca now stands in critical esteem requires no great scholarly effort. A cursory examination of a few dozen histories of theater or comprehensive dramatic anthologies will reveal the little there is to know. If Seneca is mentioned at all in these general surveys, he is never presented as an author whose plays have enduring intrinsic worth. He usually appears in a few sentences about his historical influence on Renaissance tragedy. Among the many critical volumes that discuss the history or theory of tragedy, I have yet to find one that affords Seneca serious, extended coverage. Nor have I found a general anthology of drama that reprints one of Seneca's tragedies. Even collections of classical drama or poetry rarely represent him. In part Seneca's decline reflects the broader devaluation of Roman literature over the last two centuries, but contemporary critics and scholars have seemed especially eager to jettison him wholesale from the classical canon. Bernard Knox's *Norton Book of Classical Literature* (1993), for example, finds no space in its 866 pages for a single line of Seneca's verse or prose. (Knox also excludes Seneca's eminent fellow Iberians, Martial and Lucan—crypto-Hispanaphobia?) Although Seneca has had some champions among modern classicists—notably John Fitch, Moses Hadas, and Frederick Ahl—he remains a marginal figure, even among specialists. Elsewhere Seneca *tragicus* is less a dramatist than a footnote.

On those rare occasions when Seneca's plays are discussed outside of the classics department, one finds a standard set of indictments. Herbert J. Muller's *The Spirit of Tragedy* (1956) presents the conventional view of his dramatic *oeuvre:* "Almost all readers today are struck by how crude his drama is, and how invincibly abominable his taste. It is hard to understand why for centuries Western critics and poets had so high an admiration of Seneca, installing his plays among the classics."

Muller's study, which is exceptional in affording Seneca a few pages (and unique in devoting an entire paragraph to discussing an actual text, the ***Oedipus***), presents the material in a chapter on "Greek Tragedy" under the subtitle "Epilogue: The Decline to Seneca." Subtitle tells all. The Roman drama, Muller asserts, is "an unconscious caricature of Greek tragedy." Muller gets so excited in condemning Seneca that the complaints come out pell-mell. If one liberally paraphrases and organizes his objections, we can list the standard legal charges leveled against the ancient Iberian:

> 1. *Seneca is derivative and decadent:* He borrows the formal conventions of Greek tragedy without capturing its essential spirit. His use of devices like the chorus no longer has dramatic meaning.

> 2. *Seneca is rhetorical rather than dramatic:* His plays are full of oratorical declamation and aphoristic repartee rather than the economic unfolding of dramatic action. His verse is marred, to quote another critic, by "aphoristic obscurities and far-fetched allusions."

> 3. *Seneca's sensibility is lurid and violent:* Seneca's chief innovation on his Greek models was to make them more graphic in their violence. Killings occur onstage. Characters describe gruesome offstage events in dramatic set pieces.

> 4. *Seneca is technically incompetent as a dramatist:* His plays lack "economy, purity, symmetry, appropriateness of any sort." He is "indifferent to form." The plays are shapeless displays of rhetoric and terror.

> 5. *Seneca's vision is ultimately not tragic, just horrifying:* Seneca (and, according to Muller, all Romans) lacked "a tragic sense of life." There is no catharsis in Seneca, no pity and awe—just horror.

Muller's charges may sound excessive to anyone familiar with Seneca's long-standing (if now long-vanished) popularity and influence on European literature. But to the average student of literature, the condemnation probably comes as good news. As David Slavitt has remarked, "We live in a busy time with many distractions and pressures, and it is a relief to be told that we may skip these plays." Muller's charges, moreover, merely echo the Romantic assessment of Seneca. In his lectures on drama, August Wilhelm von Schlegel declared Seneca's tragedies "beyond all description bombastic and frigid, utterly devoid of nature in character and action, full of the most revolting violations of propriety." Hegel referred to them as "dramatic failures." Nietzsche, a classicist by training, mentioned them not at all in his many discussion of tragedy. By the beginning of the twentieth century Seneca had ceased to exist for both critics and readers as a living presence in the tradition of European tragedy. Meanwhile for classical scholars he became more interesting as a set of textual problems to unravel than as an artist deserving advocacy. Discriminating literary critics were properly concerned, to use George Steiner's terms from *The Death of Tragedy,* with "the genius of Greek tragedy" and not "its inferior Latin version."

Giraldi Cinthio was not alone in admiring Seneca. For over fifteen hundred years no classical author except Virgil enjoyed more esteem. Along with Cicero, Horace, and Ovid, Seneca was an indispensable author. The early Church Fathers, eager to save the best classical literature, found him greatly to their liking largely for the same reasons Cinthio celebrated a millennium later—his moral seriousness, decorous style, imaginative sweep, and exceptionally quotable *sententiae.* The Iberian's Stoic philosophy neatly corresponded to the austere puritanism of early Christianity. Stern Tertullian affectionately called him "our Seneca." St. Jerome went even further. He suggested that Seneca deserved sainthood—an unusual honor, to say the least, for the pagan who had tutored the Emperor Nero. Seneca's work, especially his essays and epistles, became part of medieval Catholic culture.

As long as Latin remained the central language in European learning, Seneca occupied an eminent position in literature. Erasmus produced the first critical edition of his work. Calvin's first publication was a commentary on *De Clementia.* Montaigne listed Seneca and Plutarch as his favorite reading, and he quotes the Iberian more than any author except Plato. Scaliger preferred him to Euripides. Dante and Chaucer praised his skillful rhetoric and stoic morality. In an epistle, Petrarch declared him an ideal spiritual companion. Queen Elizabeth I admired his "wholesome advisings." Meanwhile her subject Ben Jonson inscribed Seneca's motto "tanquam explorator" ("as an explorer") on the title page of his books. Jonson was not the only explorer inspired by the philosopher poet. In the margins of the family copy of Seneca's tragedies Christopher Columbus's son Ferdinand wrote that his father has fulfilled the poet's prophesy that a later age would find a land beyond Thule, the boundary of the Roman known world.

If the Middle Ages prized Seneca the philosopher, the Renaissance found transforming inspiration in the dramatist. Seneca stands—without any serious rival—as the most important influence on Renaissance tragedy, not only in English but also in Italian, French, and Spanish. He was, first of all, the only classical tragedian whom most writers could savor in the original. The early Renaissance barely knew Greek literature and even then mainly in Latin translation. Seneca, however, was avidly studied and performed in grammar schools, seminaries, legal academies, and universities. Seneca's stoic tragedies, full of stirring rhetoric and striking *sententiae,* were a schoolmaster's dream (just as their violent plots and noble sentiments were surely a schoolboy's delight). At the Rotherham School near Sheffield, weekly lessons in Shakespeare's time consisted of two afternoons of Horace and two afternoons of Seneca's tragedies, which the students translated into English. There was no more engrossing way to perfect a student's Latin than by reading, memorizing, and reciting the plays of Seneca, Plautus, and Terence. Latin drama also served a ceremonial and financial function; schools presented plays as public entertainments for their patrons. Seneca was performed at the Inns of Court, Oxford, and Cambridge. Continental Jesuit schools organized performances to attract and recruit young intellectuals to their order.

In his native Spain, Seneca (and Cinthio's Senecan adaptations) became the classical models with which dramatists like Juan de la Cueva and Cristóbal de Virtués tried to discipline the vital but unruly popular theater. If the Iberian's example of intensifying drama through classical form

and compression proved only intermittently influential, the stunning sensationalism of his plots made a lasting impression. His latter-day countrymen outdid him in devising spectacular revenges, horrifying ghosts, inspiring declamations, and lurid pageants of seduction, rape, incest, and murder. Miguel de Cervantes displayed more restraint in his classical tragedy, *El Cerco de Numancia* ("The Siege of Numantia," c. 1580), but he, too, used Seneca as a model.

Less rooted in the economics of popular theater than the Spanish stage, French drama quickly assimilated the formal principles of classical tragedy. The French knew some Greek tragedy from the Latin translations of Erasmus and others, but in France, too, Seneca provided the most accessible model. French theater observed the classical unities of time, place, and action as well as the restrictions against comedy and low diction longer than any other tradition. For better and worse, Seneca remained a model for French tragedy from early plays like La Péruse's *Médée* (1553), a direct adaptation of Seneca's *Medea,* to neoclassical masterpieces like Pierre Corneille's *Médée* (1635) and Jean Racine's *Andromaque* (1667) and *Phèdre* (1677). As George Saintsbury observed, Seneca's influence pervaded French tragic theater, "from Jodelle, through Garnier and Montchrestien and even Hardy, through Corneille and Racine and Voltaire, leaving his traces even on Victor Hugo."

The sheer volume of Renaissance translations, adaptations, and imitations attests to Seneca's pre-eminent popularity. He was the first classical poet to be translated *in toto* into English. The Jesuit Jasper Heywood, who called Seneca "the flowre of all writers," published his free adaptation of *Troas* in 1559, followed by increasingly more faithful versions of *Thyestes* (1560) and *Hercules Furens* (1561). Other eager Elizabethan translators soon followed. By 1581 Thomas Newton was able to collect Seneca's *Tenne Tragedies* in one volume. (At that time only one Greek tragedy was available in English, a 1566 version of Euripides' *Phoenissae* translated from an Italian Senecan adaptation and retitled *Jocasta;* it remained the only Greek translation until the next century.) Seneca's plays became the model for both the traditions of English tragedy—the courtly dramas of Samuel Daniel and Fulke Greville, sponsored by the learned Countess of Pembroke, and the popular theater of Thomas Kyd and Christopher Marlowe. *Gorboduc* (1562), the first blank-verse tragedy, imitated Seneca, but it was Kyd's *The Spanish Tragedy* (c. 1585) that first made the Senecan conventions come alive in English.

It would be difficult to overstate the influence of Seneca on Elizabethan tragedy. English dramatists absorbed him from every side—directly from the Latin, from French and Italian adaptations, and from Newton's popular *Tenne Tragedies.* Thomas Nash, like most learned Elizabethans, deplored writers who could not read the Latin classics in the original and "feed on nought but the crummes that fal from the translators trencher," but in 1589 even he recognized the inspirational impact these translations had on his contemporaries: " . . . yet English *Seneca* read by candle light yeeldes manie good sentences . . . and if you intreate him faire in a frostie morning, he will affoord you whole *Hamlets,* I should say handfulls of tragical speeches."

Seneca provided the formal pattern for Elizabethan tragedy. He gave Tudor playwrights their five-act structure to frame the dramatic action with a beginning, middle, and end (rather than the episodic form of most medieval drama). He introduced a cast of helpful secondary characters to keep the narrative moving: the messenger to report important (and usually violent) offstage events; the female confidante to elicit private thoughts from the heroine; the loyal friend or servant to listen to and advise the hero; as well as a decidely un-Athenian version of a chorus that moralizes on events but never participates in them. Seneca also introduced the catalyzing figure of the ghost who returns from death to provoke revenge. The classical stature of Seneca's tragedies also gave the Elizabethans permission to use violent and sensational plots featuring murder, suicide, adultery, incest, trickery, insanity, and vengeance. All of these attributes came together in the most influential Seneca contribution to English drama—the revenge tragedy. Modeled mostly on Seneca's *Thyestes,* these "tragedies of blood" combined violence, intrigue, and constant psychological tension. Is it any wonder they became the most popular genre of the Elizabethan stage? Senecan revenge tragedy gave shape not only to Kyd's crowd-pleasing *Spanish Tragedy* and Tourneur's adorably lurid *Revenger's Tragedy* but also to Shakespeare's innovative psychological drama, *Hamlet.*

Seneca's other contribution to English tragedy was magnificent language. He showed playwrights the lofty alternatives to the drab verse of earlier drama. In style as in subject matter, Seneca is the poet of extremes. His verse is never better than when at its most expansive or its most concise. His extended, emotional speeches in which the language and the passions build to explosive levels dazzled the word-drunk Elizabethans. If Seneca's dramatic orations with their sonorous allusions, musical syntax, and dizzy rhetorical turns encouraged hurricanes of theatrical bombast, they also demonstrated how mixing the techniques of poetry and oratory could create dramatic verse of powerful eloquence. To understand how Seneca's great speeches sound in Latin, an English-speaker need go no further than Marlowe, who patterned his dramatic verse after Seneca's high tragic style:

> If all the pens that ever poets held
> Had fed the feeling of their masters' thoughts,
> And every sweetness that inspired their hearts,
> Their minds, and muses on admired themes;
> If all the heavenly quintessence they still
> From their immortal flowers of poesy,
> Wherein, as in a mirror, we perceive
> The highest reaches of a human wit;
> If these had made one poem's period,
> And all combined in beauty's worthiness,
> Yet should there hover in their restless heads
> One thought, one grace, one wonder, at the least,
> Which into words no virtue can digest.

This passage from *Tamburlaine the Great* displays the lush, declamatory, hyperbolic language of Senecan drama. The characters in tragedy do not lead quotidian lives. They suffer the extremities of ambition, lust, horror, pain, and remorse, and they require speech capable of carrying their extraordinary burdens. The syntax is often overtly rhetori-

cal, as when Marlowe piles one hypothetical phrase on another, and the phrasing is often pointed, as in the calculated and balanced alliterations in key lines, but the total effect is poetic.

Renaissance playwrights also learned the theatrical impact of brevity from Seneca. Ingenious one-liners are not a conspicuous feature of folk drama; striking aphorism, however, is the trademark of Seneca's theatrical language. Lapidary *sententiae* end major speeches, announce turning points in soliloquies, and add edge to important conversations. Seneca also handled the traditional Greek technique of *stichomythia* (verse dialogue in which characters trade one-line repartees) with unsurpassed brilliance. Seneca has had many detractors, but no one has ever questioned his genius for aphorism.

It is no accident that the *sententia* is a characteristic Roman form. Latin is the ideal medium for epigram. Since it is an inflected language where the endings of words signal their grammatical functions, most prepositions and auxiliary verbs are unnecessary. It also lacks articles. Consequently, Latin can say something in about half the words required in English. Word order is also almost entirely flexible, so a poet can freely arrange the language to achieve the maximum musical and semantic effect.

Seneca's fellow Iberian Martial became the greatest epigrammatic poet in European literature, but Seneca had little interest in the epigram as an independent literary form. In both his verse and prose he used it as a means of punctuating and intensifying longer works. His prose is celebrated for its quotable maxims:

> There is no great genius without some touch of madness.

> It is not the man who has too little, but the man who craves more, that is poor.

> The best ideas are common property.

> What nature requires is obtainable, and within easy reach. It's for the superfluous we sweat.

His verse epigrams, however, show even greater compression. Seneca carefully matches his syntax to his meter, making the aphoristic sentence fit exactly into a single line of verse (a trick far less common in Latin poetry than an English-speaker would imagine). His pointed lines have the brevity, clarity, balance, and polish characteristic of the form.

> *Curae leves locuntur, ingentes stupent.*
> [Light griefs speak easily, the great ones are struck dumb.]

> *Prima quae vitam dedit hora, carpit.*
> [The first hour that gave life also began to take it away.]

> *Per scelera semper sceleribus tutum est iter.*
> [The safe journey through crimes is always by more crimes.]

The careful shaping and compression of speech into formal patterns exercised immense influence on European dramatic poets. In England, both Seneca's expansive and epigrammatic styles helped determine the development of blank verse. In his 1927 essay "Seneca in Elizabethan Translation," which remains the most profound modern defense of the tragedian (and the last time a major English-language writer discussed Seneca at any length), Eliot observed: "The art of dramatic language . . . is as near to oratory as to ordinary speech or to other poetry. If the Elizabethans distorted and travestied Seneca in some ways . . . they also learned from him the essentials of declaimed verse."

Ironically, it was only in Italy, where the Senecan revival had begun, that no tragic theater emerged comparable to the traditions of England, France, and Spain. Today the influential Italian playwrights of the mid-sixteenth century like Cinthio and Ludovico Dolce survive mainly as figures of literary history. The failure of Renaissance Italy to develop a national theater has fascinated critics, and many complex theories have been offered in explanation. Surely near the heart of the problem, however, lurks Seneca.

Italian tragedy was the creation of self-conscious intellectuals cut off from a viable tradition of popular theater. They tried to re-create classical tragedy for a sophisticated audience of nobles, courties, and intelligentsia. Choosing Seneca as a model, however, they began to exploit the stylized and lyric elements of drama at the expense of its narrative and realistic features. From the beginning Cinthio and Dolce used *intermedi* (music, madrigals, and choruses performed between the acts). Within fifty years Italian artists had developed the ritual and lyric potentials of the Senecan aesthetic to their logical end—opera. In 1597 the first opera, *Dafne,* was produced by three members of the Florentine *camerata,* a coterie of poets, musicians, aristocrats, and intellectuals. By 1607, when Claudio Monteverdi staged his *Orfeo,* opera had fond its first genius. His final work, *L'incornazione di Poppea* ("The Coronation of Poppea," 1642), became opera's first incontestable masterpiece. Not coincidentally it tells the same story as the pseudo-Senecan play *Octavia,* and Seneca himself is one of the major characters. If opera eventually became Italy's true tragic theater, the new art form owed as much to Seneca as to its professed model, Greek tragedy. Indeed, the dark masterpieces of Italian Romantic lyric tragedy by Donizetti, Bellini, and Verdi not only share a common dramatic aesthetic with Seneca, they also provide the best analogy for a modern audience as to how Roman tragedy achieves its emotional effects. Three centuries after Cinthio's death his dream of re-creating the grave majesty of Seneca's tragedies had become a reality—not in the theaters of Italy but in its opera houses.

. . . . .

[Seneca's plays] do not fit comfortably into either the dominant ancient or modern traditions of European tragedy. Classical scholars, who are trained to compare ancient texts with their sources and parallels, habitually evaluate Seneca retrospectively in relation to earlier Greek drama. This method implicitly overemphasizes the conservative elements in Seneca's dramas and ignores the revisionary na-

ture of his aesthetic. As Moses Hadas observed, "If we choose to call Seneca's plays Greek tragedies, we must pronounce them debased." Judged by the Aristotelian aesthetic of tragedy as a public, narrative genre, Seneca's plays hardly make sense. His asymmetrical expositions, lyric digressions, subjective psychology, scene-stealing ancillary characters, and spectacular violence mock Athenian taste and decorum. Likewise Seneca's plays make little dramatic sense judged by the assumptions of realist drama, especially the works of Henrik Ibsen, who invented the most influential form of modern prose tragedy. Judged as realist drama, Seneca's plays appear bombastic, lurid, schematic, and dramatically inert. They rely too exclusively on the power of speech to portray human action, rather than presenting the action itself. Their characteristic eloquence often misses the elusive truths that slip between and behind words. His sensational plots explore emotional extremes at the expense of understanding the pathos of the ordinary. Seneca is no more satisfactory as Eugene O'Neill than as Euripides.

Neither aesthetic, however, seems intrinsically appropriate to the author of ***Hercules Furens, Phaedra,*** and ***Thyestes.*** Seneca's concept of tragedy is neither narrative nor sociological; it is lyric and poetic. If he is to be understood as a dramatist, he must be seen as an innovator, the creator of a new theatrical genre—lyric tragedy. While the new genre was historically rooted in the Athenian tradition, by selectively emphasizing and exploring certain features of the original form, it developed into a distinctive type of tragic theater. Seneca's highly allusive style, which incorporates a myriad of elements large and small from earlier Greek and Roman writers, has blinded many critics to the sheer novelty of his artistic aims. In this sense Seneca resembled modernist poets like Pound, Eliot, Montale, Radnoti, and Mandelstam; he was meticulously attentive to the tradition he had transformed.

Lyric poetry presents the sensibilities of a speaker at a particular moment often in a specific place and time. It seeks to capture with compelling exactitude a single, intensely unified experience. The lyric mode is subjective, heightened, and emotional. Originally sung, lyric poetry still aspires to the conditions of music. One might characterize lyric tragedy, therefore, as a form of spoken drama that aspires to the conditions of opera. While it presents a story (because lyric tragedy no less than opera needs narrative structure to provide cohesion), the plot is primarily a means to the genre's real artistic end—the vivid depiction and amplification of its characters' subjective experience. The purpose of plotting, therefore, is not to create narrative suspense but to lead the spectator through a sequence of extended lyric moments that combine into a powerfully expressive total design.

Seneca builds his tragedies around a series of arresting, emotional, lyric moments—verbal arias, duets, and choruses—designed to move the audience to a heightened emotional state. If one reads Seneca looking primarily for the story, one will inevitably be disappointed. His tragedies are well-plotted, but Seneca rarely explores the expressive possibilities of narrative. His central artistic concern is to convey the most extreme states of human suffering. Eliot was correct, therefore, in asserting that "'plot' in the sense in which we find plot in *The Spanish Tragedy* does not exist for Seneca." Slyly, Eliot went on to observe:

> He took a story perfectly well known to everybody, and interested his auditors entirely by his embellishments of description and narrative and by smartness and pungency of dialogue; suspense and surprise attached solely to verbal effect.

One might push Eliot's insight even further to reach the essence of Senecan tragedy. Perhaps Seneca's particular genius lay in understanding that the only way he could charge the familiar tragic plots with their original cathartic intensity—especially to a Roman audience inured to violence and injustice whether in the Coliseum or the imperial court—was by putting his auditors inside his character's sensibility. Seneca was not concerned with creating "suspense or surprise"; he wanted pity and terror. He willingly traded narrative complexity, symmetry, and momentum for the opportunity to achieve imaginative force and immediacy. Seneca has been rightly praised for the psychological complexity of his protagonists. His Hercules, Phaedra, Thyestes, Medea, and Oedipus are not flat stereotypes; their personalities contain the virtues, weaknesses, and contradictory impulses that Aristotle demanded for the complex character of the tragic protagonist. Seneca, however, puts this deep psychology to unusual ends; he is less interested in how his characters act in tragic circumstances than in how they feel. What inspires him both as dramatist and as poet is imagining what it is like to experience unbearable levels of pain and passion.

The subjectivity of Senecan lyric tragedy leads to a structural idiosyncrasy in the plays. The most important connections between scenes are not always logical or narrative but imagistic and emotional. Lyric poetry often works most effectively by talking around a subject rather than addressing it directly. Seneca's originality as a dramatist was to incorporate elaborately crafted scenes that are tangential to a play's plot but central to its subtext. Juno's dazzling soliloquy in **Hercules Furens** is largely superfluous to the narrative. Likewise Theseus's extensive descriptions of the underworld could have been compressed into a single speech. What Seneca accomplishes by expanding these episodes is to submerge his audience in the psychic environment of the play. Juno's uncontrollable rage sets the tense emotional tone of the story; her fear of Hercules ironically prefigures the terror others will feel during his murderous rampage. When she describes his vainglorious conquest of the underworld, her palpable horror suggests the terrible consequences of his profanation of death's mysteries. Theseus's own obsession with the darkness and emptiness of Hell implies Hercules' unrecognized vulnerability to its destructive effects. No one can escape the primal forces he has unleashed by opening the gates of Hell. Juno's and Theseus's powerful set pieces saturate the audience with the images, ideas, and sensations needed to understand the play's horrifying climax. As Seneca demonstrates, there are other ways than narrative to foreshadow tragic events and establish dramatic irony.

One also sees the essentially lyric nature of Seneca's trag-

edy in his use of the chorus. Greek tragedy began as a series of choral songs and dances. Thespis reportedly created drama by introducing a single actor impersonating a mythic or legendary character who conversed with the chorus. Aeschylus, Sophocles, and Euripides added more actors and elaborated the narrative elements, but the role of the chorus remained primary to Greek tragedy. Even in Euripides, it remained onstage during the entire drama and represented the public nature of the genre. Seneca has frequently been criticized for denying his chorus any meaningful role in the action. If Seneca's plays were fully staged—and there is much debate on the issue of how they were performed—then the chorus appears frequently to disappear into the wings. It rarely speaks except during the elaborate choral odes between each act. While Seneca denies the chorus a dramatic role, he gives it a central function in the lyric structure of his plays. His long choral odes explore, amplify, and supplement the mood of the plays. They frame the dramatic scenes around them in poetic terms. These odes show Seneca's largely unrecognized gift as a lyric poet. The final chorus from **Oedipus,** to choose one example out of many, opens with rare elegance and power:

> Fatis agimur; cedite fatis.
> non sollicitae possunt curae
> mutare rati stamina fusi.
> quidquid patimur mortale genus,
> quidquid facimus venit ex alto,
> servatque suae decreta colus
> Lachesis nulla revoluta manu.
> omnia secto tramite vadunt
> primusque dies dedit extremum.

One need not know Latin to appreciate the overt musicality of these lines. Sounds echo across and between lines. The language is stately and epigrammatically exact (most lines have only four carefully chosen and arranged words). To catch the flavor of the passage a Latinless reader might profit from looking at more than one translation. E. F. Watling conveys the majestic tone of the original, while Rachel Hadas emulates its lapidary compression:

> Fate guides us; let Fate have her way.
> No anxious thought of ours can change
> The pattern of the web of destiny.
> All that we do, all that is done to us,
> Mortals on earth, comes from a power above.
> Lachesis measures out the portions
> Spun from her distaff, and no other hand
> Can turn the spindle back.
> All creatures move on their appointed paths;
> In their beginning is their end.
>
> (Watling)

> By fate propelled, to fate we yield.
> No fussy gestures set us free.
> It is decreed, our human doom,
> all from above. Lachesis' laws
> (tightly she grasps them) point one way.
> Through narrow channels our lives move:
> our first day singles out our last.
>
> (Hadas)

Seneca's transformation of the chorus into an entirely lyric and meditative device also highlights a fundamental difference between his conception of drama and the modern ideal. Despite his occasional employment of spectacle—Hercules' entry dragging Cerberus, Medea's exit in a chariot drawn by the flying dragons, or Atreus uncovering a platter to reveal the heads of Thyestes' sons—the dramatic action in Seneca's plays is over-whelmingly located in the language. Just as the bel canto tragedies of Donizetti and Bellini assumed the human voice's ability to convey everything essential to the drama, lyric tragedy rests on the assumption that poetic speech can articulate everything necessary to create tragic theater. Needless to say, contemporary theater no longer assumes the clarifying power of speech—whether in poetry or prose—as the central dynamic of drama. If anything unites the divergent aesthetics of Samuel Beckett, Edward Albee, Joe Orton, David Mamet, Caryl Churchill, and Harold Pinter, it is a belief in the deceptions of speech and the expressive power of the inarticulate.

Can it be sheer coincidence, however, that it was those ages that understood and appreciated Seneca's aesthetic that produced the most enduring verse tragedies since the Greeks? When Seneca's reputation stood at its highest in England, France, Spain, and Italy, those traditions created the finest poetic drama in their histories. Can it also be mere chance that, as Seneca fell out of favor in Western Europe, poetic tragedy became a marginal theatrical genre? (Eastern Europe, never entirely part of Latin culture, followed a different course of development.) This is not the same as saying that Seneca's presence or absence had these effects on drama, only that a culture's ability to hear and understand how Seneca's plays worked reflected a broader faculty to marry poetry and serious drama. An unqualified conviction that tragedy requires the intensification of poetic speech is not only the tenet that separates Seneca from contemporary drama; it is also the belief that divides Marlowe, Shakespeare, and Racine from Büchner, Ibsen, and O'Neill.

Seneca's tragedies represent the ultimate development of poetic drama. While they outwardly fulfill the narrative requirements of theater, the effects they pursue are intrinsically poetic. Lyric tragedy balances on the border between what Aristotle called the "imitated human action" of drama and the purely verbal representation of poetry. If one were to push Seneca's aesthetic one step farther, the dramatic structure would disintegrate, and one would be left with the dramatic poetic sequence, like Tennyson's *Maud,* Hardy's *The Dynasts,* or Pound's *Homage to Sextus Propertius.*

Judged by their proper standards, the lyric tragedies of Seneca are considerable achievements. His much abused *Thyestes,* the most violent and gruesome play in the Western canon, is a dark and disturbing masterpiece. It was not only for its sensational plot that this play became one of the most influential tragedies ever written. Its feverish emotion and poetic energy make it an overwhelming experience to read. The sexually charged *Phaedra* and razor-edged *Medea,* which Eliot considered Seneca's best plays, are equally compelling. *Hercules Furens,* which Eliot raided for both "Marina" and *The Waste Land,* is Seneca's most innovative tragedy Alternately violent, visionary, phantas-

magoric, and poetic, it demonstrates the imaginative possibilities of lyric tragedy. The often splendid *Hercules Oetaeus* is less successful in dramatic terms, but with its great length, large cast, and double chorus, it shows the Senecan lyric form pushing beyond the limits of theatrical tragedy. *Hercules Oetaeus* is an unacknowledged ancestor of both dramatic poems like Goethe's *Faust* and romantic grand operas like Berlioz's Virgilian *Les Troyens.* Seneca's *Oedipus* will always suffer in comparison to Sophocles' masterpiece, but read on its own terms, it is a potent poetic drama and may illustrate most vividly the existential bleakness of Seneca's vision.

In Sophocles' *Oedipus the King* the final scenes lay the groundwork for a new social order. Although Oedipus's individual suffering remains primary, it is depicted in a civic context. Creon is already implicitly in charge. As he leads the blinded Oedipus away, the promise of health and prosperity returns to Thebes. In Seneca's *Oedipus,* however, the dramatic focus remains mercilessly on the suffering king; he has no comforters. In Sophocles, Oedipus blinds himself out of shame; he cannot bear to see his children or face his father in the underworld. Seneca's Oedipus puts out his eyes because death would be too easy; he wants to protract his agony and make his suffering commensurate with his sins. When Seneca's Oedipus staggers out of Thebes, alone and unconsoled, he may grimly take his curse with him, but the author offers no hint that his suffering will redeem the city.

Seneca's tragic vision admits no escape from evil, no defense against the mindless brutality of fate. The gods may witness human suffering, but they do nothing to prevent or amelioriate it. There is no welcome *deus ex machina.* When divinities intervene, they come like raging Juno in *Hercules Furens* or avenging Venus and Neptune in *Phaedra.* The supernatural world is represented by vindictive spirits and hellish demigods, as in the opening of *Thyestes,* where a demonic Fury drives the ghost of Tantalus out of Hell to provoke his grandson Atreus to unspeakable revenge. The eternal realm is less likely to endow the mortal world with grace than to pollute it with madness and evil. Hercules may have escaped physically from the underworld in *Hercules Furens,* but its forbidden knowledge has infected his spirit in ways he will not understand until too late. The end of *Thyestes* may be the bleakest conclusion in all tragedy. Atreus has killed and dismembered his nephews and tricked his brother Thyestes into publicly eating his own children at a banquet. Evil is joyfully triumphant. The innocent have been viciously destroyed. The hero has no shred of dignity left, only shame, horror, and defeat. And yet Seneca has kept the reader fixed and fascinated during the terrifying spectacle. He has managed the difficult but essential feat of magic theater—to lure the audience to the edge of the abyss to watch a fellow human's sudden fall to destruction, to make them feel the injustice and agony of the doomed without ever wanting to turn away.

A genius for tragic drama is the rarest literary talent. In the history of European theater from the beginning of Athenian drama in 535 B.C. (when Pisistratus established the first public competition in tragedy) to the advent of Realism, only a few writers have managed to create enduring bodies of work in the genre. After naming the supreme masters of tragedy—Aeschylus, Sophocles, Euripides, Shakespeare, Corneille, and Racine—whom else can we list without sensing a significant falling-off in ambition, intensity, or quality? Goethe's *Faust* may be a masterpiece but it is no tragedy, and his other plays lack the dark intensity that characterizes the tragic mode. The once influential tragedies of Alfieri, Voltaire, Hugo, and Grillparzer now seem like elegant but dusty museum pieces. The best plays of Marlowe, Ford, and Webster remain vivid but also remind one of how uneven the rest of their work is. There are individual tragedies that stand on the higher levels of the genre—Schiller's *Maria Stuart*, Büchner's *Woyzeck*, Marlowe's *Edward II*, Pushkin's *Boris Godunov*, Musset's *Lorenzaccio*, and Milton's *Samson Agonistes*—but their authors (with the possible exception of Schiller) did not create total dramatic oeuvres equal to these isolated masterpieces. Perhaps a few tragedians like Büchner and Marlowe possessed a commensurate, native genius for the form, but they had no time to develop. Sophocles lived to be ninety and wrote until the end; Büchner died of typhus at twenty-three, and Marlowe was killed in a travern brawl at twenty-nine, an age at which Shakespeare was still a journeyman dramatist. Had they lived they might have immensely enriched the canon of tragedy, but such is the difficulty of the genre that even their truncated careers stand out.

The tradition of tragedy is a jagged, discontinuous line. The gaps and failures represent its problematic character more truthfully than its rare and often isolated triumphs. An extraordinary number of Europe's greatest writers struggled unsuccessfully with the form. In nineteenth-century England alone Byron, Wordsworth, Coleridge, Keats, Shelley, Landor, Hunt, Browning, Arnold, Tennyson, and Swinburne attempted to revive tragic theater. But the genre not only requires a double genius in poetry and theater, it also demands a fierce dialectical imagination that can face the unjust and irrational mockery of fate without flinching. If few authors possess the mandatory gifts, fewer ages permit the necessary vision.

It is against this small and fitful tradition that Seneca's work must ultimately be judged. He does not stand with the handful of tragedy's supreme masters. He lacks the genius for dramatic narrative of Shakespeare and Sophocles. He rarely achieves the perfect imaginative balance and compression of Racine. He lacks the innate theatricality of Euripides. And yet, once his plays are understood on their own terms, his dark, lyric tragedies can hold their own against the rest of the tradition. Seneca's plays display poetic integrity, psychological depth, linguistic force, and unsurpassed emotional intensity. The sheer originality of Seneca's concept of tragedy and the frenetic energy of his dramatic execution give his plays extraordinary impact. No dramatist has ever portrayed a darker vision of human existence. No tragedians except Shakespeare and Sophocles exerted a stronger influence on posterity. Seneca's plays were the matrix from which the Renaissance gave birth to modern tragedy. If his reputation has long been in decline, it is time to ask how much of that falling off reflected not only a general disparagement of all Latin literature but also a distrust of poetry itself as a dramatic medium. Readers

willing to approach Seneca without preconceptions will find a profound and original tragic poet. "Time discovers truth," he once wrote. Perhaps our time will rediscover him.

FURTHER READING

OVERVIEWS AND GENERAL STUDIES

Binns, J.W. "Seneca and Neo-Latin Tragedy in England." In *Seneca*, edited by C. D. N. Costa, pp. 205-34. London: Routledge & Kegan Paul, 1974.
  Looks at three Renaissance plays written in Latin—William Alabaster's *Roxana*, Matthew Gwinne's *Nero*, and the anonymous *Perfidus Hetruscus*—which he believes offer a novel perspective on Seneca's influence on Elizabethan theater.

Bishop, J. David. *Seneca's Daggered Stylus: Political Code in the Tragedies*. Königstein: Verlag Anton Hain, 1985, 468 p.
  Analyzes the "rhetorical undercurrent" in Seneca's plays.

Braden, Gordon. "The Rhetoric and Psychology of Power in the Dramas of Seneca." *Arion* 9, No. 1 (Spring 1970): 5-41.
  Explores the relationship between characterization and language in Seneca's plays.

———. *Renaissance Tragedy and the Senecan Tradition: Anger's Privilege*. New Haven, Conn.: Yale University Press, 1985, 260 p.
  Discusses the style of Seneca's tragedies.

Butler, Harold Edgeworth. "Drama: Seneca." In his *Post-Augustan Poetry: From Seneca to Juvenal*, pp. 31-78. 1922. Reprint. Freeport, N.Y.: Books for Libraries Press, 1969.
  A survey of Seneca's life and works, judging his influence a positive one in drama but a negative one in rhetoric.

Canter, Howard Vernon. *Rhetorical Elements in the Tragedies of Seneca*. Urbana: The University of Illinois Press, 1925, 185 p.
  Explores various types of rhetorical figures and techniques in Seneca's plays, in the context of the "rhetorical interests" of his age.

Charlton, H. B. *The Senecan Tradition in Renaissance Tragedy*. Manchester: Manchester University Press, 1946, 205 p.
  Compares Seneca's and Euripides' tragedies and traces the influence of Seneca in the drama of Italy, France, and England.

Cunliffe, John W. *The Influence of Seneca on Elizabethan Tragedy*. 1893. Reprint. Hamden, Conn.: Archon Books, 1965, 155 p.
  Investigates the themes and characters of Seneca's plays and assesses his contributions to Renaissance drama.

Curley, Thomas F., III. *The Nature of Senecan Drama*. Rome: Edizioni dell'Ateneo, 1986, 229 p.
  Concludes that Seneca's plays are "non-Stoic" and that

"they exhibit a self-conscious preoccupation with the nature of the theater."

Hadas, Moses. "Seneca." In his *A History of Latin Literature*, pp. 243-59. New York: Columbia University Press, 1952.
Important survey of Seneca's dramatic and philosophical works.

Herrington, C. J. "Senecan Tragedy." *Arion* V, No. 4 (Winter 1986): 422-71.
Overview of Seneca's plays, which Herrington finds to be "actable."

Holland, Francis. *Seneca*. New York: Longmans, Green, and Co., 1920, 205 p.
A respected biography of Seneca.

Kiefer, Frederick. "Seneca Speaks in English: What the Elizabethan Translators Wrought." *Comparative Literature Studies* XV, No. 4 (December 1978): 372-87.
Asserts that Seneca's Elizabethan translators stressed the role of fortune and just retribution in the tragedies because they "were led to accentuate those themes in the plays which had become part of their own tragic vision."

Lloyd-Evans, Gareth. "Shakespeare, Seneca, and the Kingdom of Violence." In *Roman Drama*, edited by T. A. Dorey and Donald R. Dudley, pp. 123-59. New York: Basic Books, 1965.
Studies how Shakespeare transformed his Senecan sources, making "tractable much that is dramatically and theatrically intractable."

Lucas, F. L. *Seneca and Elizabethan Tragedy*. Cambridge: Cambridge at the University Press, 1922, 136 p.
Critical biography outlining the traditions on which Seneca's work was based and those which, in turn, his plays influenced.

Mendell, Clarence W. *Our Seneca*. 1941. Reprint. Hamden, Conn.: Archon Books, 1968, 285 p.
Examines the dramatic technique and philosophical content of Seneca's plays in an effort to demonstrate the playwright's influence on early European drama.

Miller, Frank Justus. Introduction to *Seneca, Volume VIII: Tragedies I*, translated by Frank Justus Miller, pp. vii-xii. Cambridge, Mass.: Harvard University Press, 1979.
Stresses the historical importance of Seneca's dramas. This survey was first published in 1917.

Pratt, Norman T. *Seneca's Dramas*. Durham: University of North Carolina Press, 1983, 229 p.
Argues that Seneca's drama fuses several philosophic viewpoints of the author's time: "Stoic psychology and ethic with Roman pathos and the preparedness for death characteristic of Seneca's century."

Schlegel, Augustus William. "Lecture XV: Roman Theatre." In his *Course of Lectures on Dramatic Art and Literature*, edited by A. J. W. Morrison, translated by John Black, pp. 200-12. 1846. Reprint by AMS Press, 1965.
Evaluation of Seneca by one of the pre-eminent Romantic critics. Schlegel disparages Seneca's dramas, censuring his "display of bombast, which distorts everything great into nonsense."

Sørensen, Villy. *Seneca: The Humanist at the Court of Nero*, translated by W. Glyn Jones. Canongate Publishing Ltd., 1984, 352 p.
Focuses on several of the tragedies, asserting that Seneca was "more interested in the psychological motives of his characters" than Aeschylus was.

Watling, E. F. Introduction to *Seneca: "Thyestes," "Phaedra," "The Trojan Women," "Oedipus," with "Octavia,"* translated by E. F. Watling, pp. 7-39. Harmondsworth: Penguin Books, 1966.
Describes Roman culture in Seneca's time and suggests ways of approaching Seneca's works today.

MAD HERCULES

Henry, Denis, and Walker, B. "The Futility of Action: A Study of Seneca's *Hercules Furens*." *Classical Philology* LX, No. 1 (January 1965): 11-22.
Concludes that, while all Seneca's plays contain the idea of life as a preparation for death, the theme is most strongly stated in *Mad Hercules*.

Shelton, Jo-Ann. *Seneca's "Hercules Furens": Theme, Structure and Style*. Göttingen: Vandenhoeck & Ruprecht, 1978, 95 p.
Examines the play for evidence of Seneca's originality as an interpreter of myth.

THE TROJAN WOMEN

Fantham, Elaine. *Seneca's "Troades."* Princeton, N.J.: Princeton University Press, 1982, 412 p.
Provides, in addition to a translation of the text, commentary, background on Seneca and his times, and discussion of his literary progenitors and peers.

MEDEA

Henry, Denis, and Walker, B. "Loss of Identity: *Medea Superest?*: A Study of Seneca's *Medea*." *Classical Philology* LXII (July 1967): 169-81.
A comparison of Seneca's *Medea* with that of Euripides.

Lawall, Gilbert. "Seneca's *Medea*: The Elusive Triumph of Civilization." In *Arktouros: Hellenic Studies Presented to Bernard M. W. Knox on the Occasion of His 65th Birthday*, edited by Glen W. Bowersock, Walter Burkert, and Michael C. J. Putnam, pp. 419-26. Berlin: Walter de Gruyter, 1979.
Develops the idea that *Medea* "is an exploration of the clash between raw, untamed nature and man's attempt to impose political and technological control over his world."

PHAEDRA

Henry, Denis, and Walker, B. "Phantasmagoria and Idyll: An

Element of Seneca's *Phaedra.*" *Greece & Rome* XIII (April 1966): 223-39.

> States that despite being Seneca's best-known play, *Phaedra* has "suffered from inadequate or misdirected critical attention," largely because of comparisons to the *Hippolytus* of Euripides or concentration on Seneca's elaborate rhetoric.

Segal, Charles. *Language and Desire in Seneca's "Phaedra."* Princeton, N.J.: Princeton University Press, 1986, 240 p.

> Psychological interpretation of the play, integrating such elements as imagery and symbolism, character, and structure. Segal also explores the theme of the Golden Age and the relationship between language and the unconscious.

THYESTES

Poe, Joe Park. "An Analysis of Seneca's *Thyestes.*" *Transactions and Proceedings of the American Philological Association* 100 (1969): 355-76.

> Detailed examination of *Thyestes*, proposing that the main theme of the play is the "natural human impulse to violence and ultimately to self-destruction."

> **Additional coverage of Seneca's life and career is contained in the following source published by Gale Research:** *Classical and Medieval Literature Criticism*, **Vol. 6.**

Sam Shepard
1943-

Born Samuel Shepard Rogers.

INTRODUCTION

Emerging from the off-off-Broadway theater community in the 1960s, Shepard has been acclaimed as the premier American dramatist of his generation, particularly for his explorations of American myths and archetypes. Shepard's works are marked by a highly theatrical presentation emphasizing forceful language and visual imagery, and they commonly possess enigmatic structures that can be interpreted on both mythic and realistic levels. Thematically, his work often confronts the cultural identity of the United States, utilizing cowboy trappings and Western locales to dramatize the influence and corruption of the American frontier. Shepard has also been concerned with the dynamics of the American family, portraying the irresistible yet sometimes destructive force that relatives wield over one another.

BIOGRAPHICAL INFORMATION

Shepard was born in Fort Sheridan, Illinois. His father was in the Army Air Corps, and after World War II the family shuttled between various military bases before settling in Duarte, California. Shepard has described his family life as chaotic; his father was an alcoholic, and he and Shepard eventually clashed in violent confrontations. In the early 1960s Shepard left home, eventually migrating to New York City in 1963. "I was very lucky to have arrived in New York at that time," Shepard has stated, "because the whole off-off-Broadway theatre was just starting." By his own admission, he "hardly knew anything about the theatre" at that time, but his work soon became a staple of New York's experimental theaters. In addition to writing plays, he was a member of the rock band The Holy Modal Rounders in the late 1960s. His interest in music partially motivated his move to England in 1971, as he hoped to join a rock band in London. Although this plan never materialized, Shepard settled in the London area where he assumed the role of stage director for some of his plays. After returning to the United States in 1974, film acting became a new field of interest for Shepard. His movie credits include the films *Days of Heaven, Frances, The Right Stuff* (for which he received an Oscar nomination), and the film adaptation of his own play *Fool for Love.* With this exposure, Shepard attracted much media interest, attention that increased in the early 1980s when he divorced his wife to begin a relationship with film star Jessica Lange. For a time Shepard the movie star threatened to overshadow Shepard the playwright, but he continued to produce plays on a regular basis through the mid-1980s, often serving as the

stage director for the initial presentations. Following the staging of *A Lie of the Mind* in 1985, Shepard's output as a playwright has slowed, although he continues to be involved in feature film projects as an actor, screenwriter, and director.

MAJOR WORKS

Shepard's work is marked by a distinct style change that occurred roughly midway through his career. His early one-act plays are abstract and absurdist explorations that are often compared to the drama of Samuel Beckett and Harold Pinter. These works eschew traditional plotting and characterization in favor of linguistic pyrotechnics, minimal story lines, and striking imagery. One of his trademark devices in these initial works are explosive and lengthy soliloquies—often referred to as "arias" by critics. *The Rock Garden,* one of Shepard's earliest works, offers a case in point. The play culminates in a verbal outburst by a teenager who details his sexual techniques to his dumbstruck father. Shepard's characterization in the early plays is also unusual. Avoiding conventional dictates regarding the creation of consistent and believable figures, Shepard often imbues his characters with cartoon-like qualities and also employs startling behavioral transformations. As Shepard has explained, he created characters that were "constantly unidentifiable, shifting through the actor, so that the actor could play anything, and the audience was never expected to identify with the character." Such an approach tends to emphasize the theatrical quality of the event itself as much as the story that is being presented, and Shepard exploits this situation by creating highly provocative images to command the audience's attention. In *Operation Sidewinder* a giant computer rattlesnake becomes a central figure, and the play ends in a prolonged burst of machine gun fire; *Cowboy Mouth* features a "rock-and-roll Jesus" that literally bursts from the shell of "Lobsterman" to conclude the play with a game of Russian roulette. Shepard's interest in rock music and other elements of popular culture runs through a number of the early works, as evidenced by *The Tooth of Crime,* a two-act play that employs musical numbers and, as a program note for the London premiere described it, an "invented language" that draws on youth and gangster slang, among other sources.

In the mid-1970s, Shepard's work turned more toward realism, employing plot lines that have more structure and characters that are developed to a greater degree than in his early plays. The major Shepard works from the late 1970s and early 1980s use this approach to examine family relationships and, by extension, America as a whole. The family in *Buried Child* is confronted with destructive aspects of its past when a long-absent grandson returns to the family farm. Within this straightforward framework, however, Shepard invokes a mythic level of meaning, employing symbolic elements that have led to a number of interpretations. A similar process takes place in *True West,* where a seemingly realistic tale of feuding brothers incorporates less-realistic character transformations, resulting in a play that considers a number of themes, including the contrast between Western myths and the region's contemporary reality and the lingering influence of an absent father. As *True West* illustrates, Shepard has tended to feature male characters in his plays and to emphasize the relationships between fathers and sons or between male siblings. In both *Fool for Love* and *A Lie of the Mind,* however, he focuses on female characters to a greater degree and treats the subject of male-female relations. Both plays involve obsessive love relationships, and the latter play investigates the consequences of extreme violence—a man beating his wife until she is brain damaged—as no previous Shepard play has done.

CRITICAL RECEPTION

Overall, Shepard's work has received largely enthusiastic reviews, although critics have sometimes had difficulty articulating the merits of his unconventional methods. His initial plays were often dismissed as being bad imitations of the works of earlier absurdist playwrights, and detractors complained about the obscure nature of his work. Others have since championed Shepard's plays, however, recognizing them as part of the postmodern departure from traditional literary modes. Works such as *The Tooth of Crime* and *Cowboy Mouth* have been commended for imaginative-

ly employing elements of popular culture and for critiquing the American fixation on fame and celebrity. Likewise, the nonrealistic elements of Shepard's dramas have been acclaimed for focusing attention on the act of performing and on the audience's role in the artistic process. His later works have also been generally well-regarded, but for somewhat different reasons. Their greater emphasis on content rather than form has led to wider popularity, but it has also prompted complaints that Shepard is repeating the same ideas rather than exploring new themes. The preponderance of masculine characters and archetypes in his work has led some critics to question his ability and desire to consider female characters in depth. Despite these reservations, reviewers have frequently granted Shepard a pivotal role in contemporary American theater, applauding his ability to create accessible dramas while pioneering nontraditional techniques. As Jack Kroll has stated, Shepard's work has "overturned theatrical conventions and created a new kind of drama filled with violence, lyricism and an intensely American compound of comic and tragic power."

PRINCIPAL WORKS

PLAYS

Cowboys　　1964

The Rock Garden　　1964

Up to Thursday　　1965

Dog　　1965

Rocking Chair　　1965

Chicago　　1965

Icarus's Mother　　1965

4-H Club　　1965

Fourteen Hundred Thousand　　1966

Red Cross　　1966

Melodrama Play　　1966

La Turista　　1967

Cowboys #2　　1967

Forensic and the Navigators　　1967

Shaved Splits　　1969

Holy Ghostly　　1970

Operation Sidewinder　　1970

The Unseen Hand　　1970

Mad Dog Blues　　1971

Cowboy Mouth　[with Patti Smith]　　1971

Back Bog Beast Bait　　1971

The Tooth of Crime　　1972

Blue Bitch　　1973

Nightwalk [with Megan Terry and Jean-Claude van Itallie]　　1973

Geography of a Horse Dreamer　　1974

Little Ocean　　1974

Action　　1975

Killer's Head　　1975

Angel City　　1976

Inacoma　　1976

The Sad Lament of Pecos Bill on the Eve of Killing His Wife　　1976

Suicide in B Flat   1976
Curse of the Starving Class   1977
Buried Child   1978
Savage/Love [with Joseph Chaikin]   1978
Seduced   1978
Tongues [with Joseph Chaikin]   1978
True West   1980
Jackson's Dance [with Jacques Levy]   1980
Superstitions   1981
Fool for Love   1983
A Lie of the Mind   1985
True Dylan   1987
States of Shock   1991
Simpatico   1994

OTHER MAJOR WORKS

Me and My Brother [with Robert Frank]   (screenplay)
   1969
Zabriskie Point [with Michelangelo Antonioni, Tonino
   Guerra, Fred Graham, and Clare Peploe]   (screenplay)
   1970
Ringaleevio [with Murray Mednick]   (screenplay)   1971
Hawk Moon (short stories, poems, and monologues)   1973
Rolling Thunder Logbook (journal)   1977
Jacaranda (text for dance and drama)   1979
Motel Chronicles (poems, prose, and monologues)   1982
Paris, Texas [with L. M. Kit Carson]   (screenplay)   1984
Fool for Love [adapted from Shepard's play]   (screenplay)
   1985
The War in Heaven [with Joseph Chaikin]   (radio play)
   1985
Far North (screenplay)   1988
Letters and Texts 1972-1984 [with Joseph Chaikin]   (non-
   fiction)   1989
Silent Tongue (screenplay)   1993

AUTHOR COMMENTARY

Metaphors, Mad Dogs and Old Time Cowboys (1974)

SOURCE: An interview with the editors and Kenneth
Chubb, in *Theatre Quarterly,* Vol. IV, No. 15, August-
October, 1974, pp. 3-16.

[*In the following interview, Shepard discusses his background, his early experiences as a dramatist, and a number
of specific plays.*]

[Theatre Quarterly]: *Born 5 November 1943 at Fort Sheridan, Illinois, say my notes. . . .*

[Shepard]: They weren't kidding, it was a real fort, where
army mothers had their babies. My father was in Italy then,
I think, and we moved around, oh, to Rapid City, South
Dakota, to Utah, to Florida—then to the Mariana Islands in
the South Pacific, where we lived on Guam. There were
three of us children.

Do you remember much about living on Guam?

I remember the tin-roofed huts that we lived in, because it
used to rain there a lot, and the rain would make this incredible sound on the tin roof. Also there were a lot of Japanese
on the island, who had been forced back into living in the
caves, and they would come down and steal clothes off the
clothes-lines, and food and stuff. All the women were issued with army Lugers, and I remember my mother shooting at them. At that time everyone referred to oriental people or to Philippino people as gooks, and it wasn't until the
Vietnam War that I realized that gook was a derogatory
term—it had just been part of the army jargon, all the kids
called them gooks too.

You were in Guam until your father left the army?

Yeah, then we went to live with my aunt in South Pasadena,
California—she somehow had some money through my
mother's family, so we had a place to stay. But then we
found a house of our own in South Pasadena, and I started
going to high school.

What were your parents doing then?

My dad was still trying to get his degree, after the interruptions of the army, and he had to work for his Bachelors by
going to night school. But my mother already had this
qualification for teaching kids, so they were working it out
with jobs. He was very strict, my father, very aware of the
need for discipline, so-called, very into studying and all that
kind of stuff. I couldn't stand it—the whole thing of writing
in notebooks, it was really like being jailed.

But you did share your father's liking for music?

Yes, he used to listen to Dixieland music while he was
studying, and he had this band—it wasn't really professional, more of a hobby, though they got paid for it. But he was
a drummer, and that's how I learned to play, just banging
on his set of drums. And then I started getting better than
him.

What was the town like?

Oh, one of these white, middle-class, insulated communities—not all that rich, but very proud of the municipal
swimming plunge and the ice-skating rink, and all that
small-town-America-type stuff.

Did you have many friends?

Yeah, I did. I had one good friend, Ernie Ernshaw—the
first guy I started smoking cigarettes with. Later he joined
the navy, and I went back to see him about ten years afterwards, and he'd turned into this Hollywood slick-guy with
tight pants and a big fancy hair-do. It was fantastic.

But you left South Pasadena—when you were how old?

About 11 or 12, something like that. We moved to this
avocado ranch, it was a real nice place actually. It was like

a little greenhouse that had been converted into a house, and it had livestock and horses and chickens and stuff like that. Plus about 65 avocado trees.

You worked on the farm?

Yeah. You can't depend on the rain in California like you do here [London], so we had to rig up an irrigation system which had to be operated every day. And we had this little Wisconsin tractor with a spring-tooth harrow and a disc, and I made some money driving that for other people in the neighbourhood—there were a lot of citrus groves.

Did you like the change from small-town life?

I really liked being in contact with animals and the whole agricultural thing, but it was a bit of a shock leaving the friends I'd made. It was a funny community, divided into three very distinct social groups. There were the very wealthy people, who had ranches up in the mountains with white-faced Hereford cattle roaming around, and swimming-pools and Cadillacs. And then you'd get these very straight middle-class communities, people who sold encyclopedias and stuff like that. It was the first place where I understood what it meant to be born on the wrong side of the tracks, because the railroad tracks cut right down through the middle of this place: and below the tracks were the blacks and Mexicans.

Did this create tensions in school?

Oh yeah, there were a lot of anxieties. There were these Mexican guys who used to have tattoos and stuff, and I remember the incredible terror of looking into their eyes for even a flash of a second, because without knowing anything previously about the racial thing, just by looking at these guys you knew that you didn't have anything to do with them, and they didn't have anything to do with you. And that they wanted it to stay that way.

Were you a 97-pound weakling or a tough-guy?

I had a few fist-fights but I wouldn't say that I was a tough guy. I didn't grow until I was about 17 or 18, though, I was about five foot six.

Popular?

I found that the friends I had were these sort of strange guys. There was one guy who was from British Columbia—the one I wrote about in *Tooth of Crime.* He'd just come down from Canada, and he looked exactly like Elvis Presley. He had this incredible black hair-do and flash clothes, which nobody wore in school except for a few Mexicans—the white kids all wore Ivy League button-down numbers and loafers. So he was immediately ostracized, but he turned out to be a brilliant student—he didn't read any books, just got straight A grades. I got to be really good friends with him. And there were a couple of computer freaks, who were working at this aeronautics plant where they built computers for nose-cones. One guy used to bring in paper bags full of amphetamine and benzedrine from

Mexico. I swear to god, those pills—if you took two of them, you were just flying. And these guys would work in the plant on amphetamine, and steal all these parts and sell them. The pay was really good too, and they got something like triple the money if they worked overtime, so they'd buy these incredible cars and go out stealing and looting . . . all on benzedrine and amphetamine.

Were they older than you, these guys?

Yes, everybody was older than me, because I was born in November, so I was always one year younger than everybody in my class.

But you really just wanted to leave high school as soon as you could?

Oh yeah, everybody did. I was thinking that I wanted to be a veterinarian. And I had a chance actually to manage a sheep ranch, but I didn't take it. I wanted to do something like that, working with animals. I even had the grand champion yearling ram at the Los Angeles County Fair one year. I did. It was a great ram.

Quite a break from this very pastoral sort of prospect, when you decided to go to New York?

Yeah. At that time the whole beat generation was the big influence. It was just before the time of acid and the big dope freakout, which was then still very much under cover. We talked about Ferlinghetti and Corso and Kerouac and all those guys, and jazz . . .

But you weren't writing yourself?

No. I mean, I tried poetry and stuff, but it was pretty bad. But I went to New York with this guy Charles, who was a painter, and really just liked that whole idea of being independent, of being able to do something on your own. I tried to get into the acting scene in New York, though I really very soon dropped out of that. We were living on the Lower East Side, and there were these jazz musicians, Danny Richmond who played drums, and I got into this really exciting music scene. The world I was living in was the most interesting thing to me, and I thought the best thing I could do maybe would be to write about it, so I started writing plays.

Why plays, rather than novels or poetry?

I always liked the idea that plays happened in three dimensions, that here was something that came to life in space rather than in a book. I never liked books, or read very much.

Did you write anything before you started getting performed?

Well, I'd written one very bad play in California—a sort of Tennessee Williams imitation, about some girl who got raped in a barn and her father getting mad at her or something . . . I forget. But the first play I wrote in New York was *Cowboys.*

Cowboys, why cowboys? Cowboys figure largely in lots of your plays. . . .

Cowboys are really interesting to me—these guys, most of them really young, about 16 or 17, who decided they didn't want to have anything to do with the East Coast, with that way of life, and took on this immense country, and didn't have any real rules. Just moving cattle, from Texas to Kansas City, from the North to the South, or wherever it was.

Why **Cowboys No. 2,** *not just another title?*

Well, I wrote the original **Cowboys,** and then I rewrote it and called it *No. 2,* that's all. The original is lost now—but, anyway, it got done at St. Mark's. And that just happened because Charles and me used to run around the streets playing cowboys in New York. We'd both had the experience of growing up in California, in that special kind of environment, and between the two of us there was a kind of camaraderie, in the midst of all these people who were into going to work and riding the buses. In about 1963, anyway—five years or so later it all suddenly broke down.

Had you had much to do with live theatre?

I hardly knew anything about the theatre. I remember once in California I went to this guy's house who was called a beatnik by everybody in the school because he had a beard and he wore sandals. And we were listening to some jazz or something and he sort of shuffled over to me and threw this book on my lap and said, why don't you dig this, you know. I started reading this play he gave me, and it was like nothing I'd ever read before—it was *Waiting for Godot.* And I thought, what's this guy talking about, what is this? And I read it with a very keen interest, but I didn't know anything about what it *was.* I didn't really have any references for the theatre, except for the few plays that I'd acted in. But in a way I think that was better for me, because I didn't have any idea about how to shape an action into what is seen—so the so-called originality of the early work just comes from ignorance. I just didn't know.

You were writing very prolifically around those early years.

Yeah, there was nothing else to do.

So what were you doing for money?

I was working at a place called the Village Gate, which is a big night-club. Charles had a job there as a waiter, and he got me a job there too, and later I found out that all the waiters there were either actors or directors or painters or something like that who were out of work. It was a nice place to work because I got to see like the *cream* of American jazz, night-after-night for free. Plus I got paid for working there.

It was at night-time so you were free during the day?

Right. I worked three nights a week, and got about 50 bucks a week for doing hardly anything, except cleaning up dishes and bringing Nina Simone ice, you know. It was fantastic.

All those early plays give the impression that once you'd got the habit you couldn't stop. . . .

Yeah, I used to write very fast, I mean I wrote **Chicago** in one day. The stuff would just come out, and I wasn't really trying to shape it or make it into any big thing.

You wrote without any sort of planning?

Yeah. I would have like a picture, and just start from there. A picture of a guy in a bathtub, or of two guys on stage with a sign blinking—you know, things like that.

How important was it to you when your plays started to get performed?

It was frightening at first. I can remember defending myself against it mostly. I was really young for one thing, about 19, and I was very uptight about making a whole public thing out of something that you do privately. And I was strongly influenced by Charles—he was very into not selling-out, and keeping himself within his own sphere of reference. I felt that by having the play become public, it was almost like giving it away or something. I was really hard to get along with in those days, actually. I would always bitch a lot during rehearsals and break things up. . . .

How did **Cowboys** *first come to get on stage?*

The head-waiter at the Village Gate was a guy named Ralph Cook, and he had been given this church, called St. Mark's in the Bowery, and he started a theatre there called Theatre Genesis. He said he was looking for new plays to do, and I said I had one. He came up and he read this play, and two of the waiters at the Village Gate were the actors in it. So it was sort of the Village Gate company. Well, Jerry Talmer from the *Post* came, and all these guys said it was a bunch of shit, imitated Beckett or something like that. I was ready to pack it in and go back to California. Then Michael Smith from *Village Voice* came up with this rave review [October 22, 1967], and people started coming to see it.

Did these early plays change much, between writing and the public performance?

The writing didn't change, I never changed the words. That's even true now, but, depending on the people you have, the performance changes. I was very lucky to have arrived in New York at that time, though, because the whole off-off-Broadway theatre was just starting—like Ellen Stewart with her little cafe, and Joe Chino, and the Judson Poets Theatre and all these places. It was just a lucky accident really that I arrived at the same time as that was all starting. This was before they had all become famous, of course—like Ellen just had this little loft, served hot chocolate and coffee, did these plays.

So how much money did you make from those early plays—not very much?

No money. There wasn't any money at all, until the grants started coming in from Ford and Rockefeller and all these places that were supporting the theatres because of the publicity they started getting. Then they began paying the actors and playwrights—but it wasn't much, 100 dollars for five weeks' work or something.

How much did it matter to you that critics like Michael Smith started writing approvingly about your plays?

Well, it changes everything you know, from being something that you do in quite a private way to something that you do publicly. Because no matter how much you don't like the critics, or you don't want them to pass judgement on what you're doing, the fact that they're there reflects the fact that a play's being done in public. It means that you steadily become aware of people going to see your plays—of audiences. Not just critics, but people.

Did you feel part of this developing off-off-Broadway 'movement'?

Not in anything to do with stagecraft so much as in the ingredients that go into a play. . . . On the Lower East Side there *was* a special sort of culture developing. You were so close to the people who were going to the plays, there was really no difference between you and them—your own experience was their experience, so that you began to develop that consciousness of what was happening. . . . I mean nobody knew what *was* happening, but there was a sense that something was going on. People were arriving from Texas and Arkansas in the middle of New York City, and a community was being established. It was a very exciting time.

Did you begin to think of playwriting as your real job?

Well, I never thought of it as my job, because it was something that made me feel more relaxed, whereas I always thought of jobs as something that made you feel less alive—you know, the thing of working ten hours a day cleaning horseshit out of a stable.

Did the second play, **Rock Garden,** *also emerge from your experience of New York?*

Rock Garden is about leaving my mom and dad. It happens in two scenes. In the first scene the mother is lying in bed ill while the son is sitting in a chair, and she is talking about this special sort of cookie that she makes, which is marshmallow on salt crackers melted under the oven. It's called angels on horseback, and she has a monologue about it. And then the father arrives in the second scene. The boy doesn't say anything, he's just sitting in this chair, and the father starts to talk about painting the fence around the house, and there's a monologue about that in the course of which the boy keeps dropping asleep and falling off his chair. Finally the boy has a monologue about orgasm that goes on for a couple of pages and ends in him coming all over the place, and then the father falls off the chair. The father also talks about this rock garden, which is his obsession, a garden where he collects all these rocks from different sojourns to the desert.

The orgasm scene was the one used in **Oh Calcutta!** *wasn't it?*

Yes—that production was pretty bad, and the play hasn't been done much in its entirety. Theatre Genesis did the first production, but I don't think it's been seen in England.

Then came **Up to Thursday***?*

Yes. **Up to Thursday** was a bad exercise in absurdity, I guess. This kid is sleeping in an American flag, he's only wearing a jockstrap or something, and there's four people on stage who keep shifting their legs and talking. I can't remember it very well—it's only been done once. It was a terrible play, really. It was the first commercial production I'd done, and it was put on with a bunch of other plays, in this off-off-Broadway-moves-off-Broadway kind of bill.

What about **Dog** *and* **Rocking Chair***?*

Dog was about a black guy—which later I found out it was uncool for a white to write about in America. It was about a black guy on a park bench, a sort of *Zoo Story*-type play. I don't even remember **Rocking Chair,** except it was about somebody in a rocking-chair.

How do you feel about those early plays now—a bit vague, it seems!

Yeah, the thing is, I find it hard to remain with a certain attachment to things that I wrote. I've heard that a lot of writers make reams of notes before they even go into the thing, but with me I write plays before I go into something else. I may like write six one-act plays before I get to another kind of a play, and each play may be a sort of evolution to something else. I always feel like leaving those behind rather than hanging on to them.

You say the texts don't change much in rehearsal—do you revise much while you're writing?

I hate to rewrite, but I can see the importance of it, mainly because of what it means for an actor to actually meet the task of doing this thing on stage. Just from directing **Geography of a Horse-Dreamer** myself, I've found I think I'm often too flippant about what I write—it's too easy to dash something off and say, okay, now act it: because when it comes down to the flesh-and-blood thing of making it work, it's a different world. I think that's where rewriting comes in—if it seems that the angle that the actor has to come at is too impossible or too difficult.

So it's revision of the mechanics rather than of the language . . . ?

It may be that there's a hole somewhere that needs to be blocked. Something missing.

Are you concerned at all about how accessible your plays are going to be to an audience? I'm thinking of how you described earlier the common background of experience you shared in those early New York years. But now, obviously, you're going to be writing for wider audiences, who don't necessarily share any similarities of background. How far are you, or aren't you, concerned to give them a way in?

It depends on whether you're writing in social terms, or whether the things that you're taking on can cut through that somehow. You always *start* with some sort of social terms, because of being white, or living in England, or whatever the conditions are, but hopefully it can then cut into something that everybody has some touch with—otherwise it just remains a kind of *cosy* accessibility.

Isn't there a change, too, between the exclusive emphasis on private worlds in the very early plays, and the almost political sense of an outside threat in **Icarus's Mother**?

People talk about political consciousness as though it were a thing that you could decide in your head—that you can shift your ways of thinking and suddenly you have political consciousness. But I found that, especially in America, it came from the emotional context that you were moving in. I mean, people in New York are cutting themselves down everyday of the week—from the inside, you know, but the conditions come from the outside. Junk, heroin and all that stuff is a social condition and it's also an emotional response to the society they're living in. . . . But I don't have any political theories, if that's what you mean.

Around the time we're talking of in the States, it was the peak of the anti-Bomb movement in England—were you caught up in anything like that?

I was in a few Civil Rights marches and stuff like that—but it's different. When you see that on the news it's one thing, but when you're in it it's a different thing, it's a whole different thing.

Can you say something about how **Icarus's Mother** *germinated?*

I was in Wisconsin, in Milwaukee, and for the Fourth of July we have this celebration—fireworks and all that kind of stuff—and I was in this sort of park with these people, with this display going on. You begin to have a feeling of this historical thing being played out in contemporary terms—I didn't even know what the Fourth of July meant, really, but here was this celebration taking place, with explosions. One of the weird things about being in America now, though I haven't been there much lately, is that you don't have any connection with the past, with what history means: so you can be there celebrating the Fourth of July, but all you know is that things are exploding in the sky. And then you've got this emotional thing that goes a long way back, which creates a certain kind of chaos, a kind of terror, you don't know what the fuck's going on. It's really hard to grab the whole of the experience.

And that's the circling aeroplane—Icarus's mother . . . ?

There's a vague kind of terror going on, the people not really knowing what is happening. . . .

How 'real' is the image in **4-H Club** *of those four guys in a kitchen killing rats?*

Well, there's a big rat problem in New York, but maybe some of the people who talk about poverty and so on never had a rat in their house. And it's different when you have a rat in your house—doesn't all come down to talk.

Had you experienced that kind of poverty?

Yeah, in New York, sure—unless you have a million dollars lots of people experience that in New York. . . .

About your next play, **Fourteen Hundred Thousand**—*I get the feeling that it changes direction two-thirds of the way through—there's this play about building a bookshelf, and this other play about a linear city. . . .*

Yeah, I had a long talk with an architect before I wrote that play, and stuck that into it. I was very interested in the idea of the linear city, because it struck me as being a strong visual conception as opposed to radial cities—the idea of having a whole country, especially like America, with these lines cutting across them. . . .

It makes a tremendous climax but it seems like the climax to another play somehow. . . .

Yeah, right.

To go back to what you were saying earlier about your plays developing from images, from mental pictures—was this a case of the image as it were switching half way through? And how should the switch work theatrically?

When you talk about images, an image can be seen without looking at anything—you can see something in your head, or you can see something on stage, or you can see things that don't appear on stage, you know. The fantastic thing about theatre is that it can make something be seen that's invisible, and that's where my interest in theatre is—that you can be watching this thing happening with actors and costumes and light and set and language, and even plot, and something emerges from beyond that, and that's the image part that I'm looking for, that's the sort of added dimension.

Does **Fourteen Hundred Thousand** *maybe represent a kind of watershed between those early plays, which were largely concerned with simple . . . well, not really simple, but single images, and the plays after this, which start to get very much more complex—and maybe the characters too start moving from the ordinary towards the extraordinary . . . ?*

They're the *same* people, but the situations are different. What I was interested in was, like, you see somebody, and you have an impression of that person from seeing them—the way they talk and behave—but underneath many, many different possibilities could be going on. And the possibilities that I brought out, like in *Icarus,* could have taken a completely different direction. It's not as though you started out with a character who suddenly developed into another character—it's the same character, who's enlivened by animals, or demons, or whatever's inside of him. Everybody's like that. . . .

But I still feel that the plays get more complex—perhaps

that the early plays are images, the later plays are more like metaphors—creating not one segment of a society through a fairly direct image, but finding another way of representing it—say in **The Tooth of Crime**. . . .

To me, that's the only thing I can do, because . . . first of all, I don't know what this world is. I mean, look at it. Like when you look at Ted Heath and Harold Wilson giving their opinions and trying to sell people on their programmes. If you showed those two guys on the stage it would be as boring as watching them on television—it wouldn't have any other dimension to it. Satire is another thing, but there's very few people can do it really well—Jules Feiffer, but even he has to create another world to show something about this one. . . .

Well, can we try another tack—clearly the early plays, from what you said about them, have their origins in your own childhood and adolescent world, and you're writing about that world. What are you harking back to, where do the images come from, for the later plays?

Well, they come from all kinds of things, they come from the country, they come from that particular part of the country, they come from that particular sort of temporary society that you find in Southern California, where nothing is permanent, where everything could be knocked down and it wouldn't be missed, and the feel of impermanence that comes from that—that you don't belong to any particular culture. I mean it wasn't until I came to England that I found out what it means to be an American. Nothing really makes sense when you're there, but the more distant you are from it, the more the implications of what you grew up with start to emerge.

Is there a point at which you stopped writing plays about Southern California, say, and started writing plays about New York?

Yeah, but it's very hard to talk about, because . . . obviously, if you were writing in Jamaica, you'd be writing under a different influence, or even if a man wanted to write about the Industrial Revolution in England but went to South Africa to do it, he'd be writing under those conditions. He'd have to take on the conditions of where he's writing, he can't escape that.

But all these things are accumulative, aren't they? You really haven't lost any of the early influences, you've simply put influences on. I mean, **Geography of a Horse Dreamer** *is about dog-racing in London, which is very much your immediate experience, and yet there's something very reminiscent in all your later work of the early plays. Is that the way the plays are building, complicating themselves as they go on, and maybe becoming more interesting the more complicated they get?*

Well, I don't know if they're more complicated, they're *different,* because, yes, you accumulate the experience of having written all those other plays, so they're all in you somewhere. But sometimes it gets in the way—you sit down and you find yourself writing the same play, which is a drag. Terrible feeling when you suddenly find yourself doing the same thing over and over again. . . .

How conscious are you of length when you write—do you write a short play consciously, or a long play, or does it just make its own length?

Oh yeah, it makes its own length. The term full-length to me doesn't make any sense, because people call a two-act or a three-act play, or a play with a certain number of pages, a full-length play, but I think it's ridiculous, because . . . well, Beckett wrote *Come and Go* and it's five pages long but it's full-length, whereas some of O'Neill's. . . . No, people are always making distinctions about full-length plays, and I think it's really a shame that it's gotten into that kind of groove.

Well, I was going to ask, and perhaps I'll ask it anyway—it seems to me that quite apart from one being an early play and one being a later play, a great deal more conscious craftsmanship, or shaping, would have to go into writing say **Tooth of Crime** *than say* **Chicago.**

No I don't think so. Your craftsmanship always comes from some interior thing, it's not something you can stick onto the play to make it have a style or a form—it has to come out of what's making the play, what's motivating the play. It's not the size of it, it's the quality of it. I guess it's just a matter of terms really, but to me *Tooth of Crime* performs a different quality than *Chicago* does. Put another way, it's playing for different stakes. You can play for the high stakes or the low stakes, or you can play for a compromise in between: maybe *Geography* was playing for more modest stakes than *Tooth of Crime.* But what makes a play is how true it is to the stakes that you defined at the beginning.

But how do you define them—how did you know, say, that **Tooth of Crime** *was going to play for high stakes?*

It's an interesting thing that happened with that play, because I wrote it in London—it's been called an American play, right, but it was written in the middle of Shepherds Bush, and for about a month before that I was struggling to write this other play called *The Tooth of Crime,* which was a three-act epic number in a jail . . . and at the end it was a complete piece of shit, so I put it in the sink and burnt it, and then an hour later I started to write this one that's been performed. So, no, it's not so easy to say what it is when you sit down and write a play. You can sit down and say, now I know all the ingredients that are going to go into this and I'm shooting for something very big, and then you begin to write, and it may work out or it may not. The next time you may sit down, and say, I don't have an idea in my head, and yet something incredible may come out, you know. It has to do with the conditions at the time you sit down and write.

Fair enough. So say **Chicago** *starts with the idea, the image, of a bloke in a bath-tub—what does something like* **Tooth of Crime** *start with—what did it start with?*

It started with language—it started with hearing a certain sound which is coming from the voice of this character,

Hoss. And also this sort of black figure appearing on stage with this throne, and the whole kind of world that he was involved in, came from this voice—I don't mean it was any weird psychological voice in the air thing, but that it was a very real kind of sound that I heard, and I started to write the play from there. It just accumulated force as I wrote it.

We've rather jumped to this very American play written in Shepherds Bush: can you say something about your reasons for coming to London from New York?

Well, when I first got to New York it was wide open, you were like a kid in a fun park, but then as it developed, as more and more elements came into it, things got more and more insane—you know, the difference between living in New York and working in New York became wider and wider, so that you were doing this thing called *theatre* in these little places and you were bringing your so-called experience to it, and then going back and living in this kind of tight, insular, protective way, where you were defending yourself. And also I was into a lot of drugs then—it became very difficult you know, everything seemed to be sort of shattering. I didn't feel like going back to California, so I thought I'd come here—really to get into music, you know. I was in a band in New York, and I'd heard that this was the rock'n'roll centre of the world—so I came here with that kind of idea. London was notorious for its rock'n'roll bands, and my favourite bands are The Who, groups like that, so I had this fantasy that I'd come over here and somehow fall into a rock'n'roll band. It didn't work. . . .

In spite of the fact that people were already saying that you were the darling of off-Broadway, you wanted to get into something else?

I really wanted to find another kind of thing over here. I much prefer playing music really to theatre, but it's hard to find the right situation.

Yet music doesn't seem to have played a large part in many of your plays, has it? People talk about there being a musical structure to your plays, which I'm sure is intuitive, and there have been a couple of plays which have had music connected with them—the one where it's most integral is **Mad Dog Blues.** *But certainly in* **The Tooth of Crime,** *though it may have been the production I saw rather than anything else, the music seemed rather superficially connected. . . .*

It depends what you mean by music. I think music's really important, especially in plays and theatre—it adds a whole different kind of perspective, it immediately brings the audience to terms with an emotional reality. Because nothing communicates emotions better than music, not even the greatest play in the world. But it's not a question of just putting music in plays. First of all there may be some plays that don't require music, like *Geography of a Horse Dreamer*—I've used music from records, but there wasn't any opportunity really for songs or anything like that.

But there was lots of room for it in **Tooth of Crime,** *and yet it wasn't really used integrally?*

Yeah, I know what you're saying. I wanted the music in **Tooth of Crime** so that you could step out of the play for a minute, every time a song comes, and be brought to an emotional comment on what's been taking place in the play. When you go back to the play you go back to the spoken word, then when a song comes again, it takes you out of it just a little bit. I wanted the music to be used as a kind of sounding-board for the play, you know. At the Open Space, I worked with the band that did the music, Blunderpuss, and it was never right—they're a really good band, but *because* they're a band, that already has an identity of its own, you're starting with the type of music that they can perform, that they've been used to performing, and the most you can get is a good compromise. The only way to do it really is to gather musicians together independently who can get along with each other and know how to play and create the music from scratch. That's what we'll do in the Royal Court production, so hopefully the music will be a little truer to the way it was written.

You say you think music can potentially affect an audience much more strongly than even the best playwright's words. . . . ?

Oh, yeah.

How do you feel about the vogue for so-called rock operas?

I haven't ever seen a good rock opera. But I don't think that the music in theatre necessarily has to take on a rock'n'roll idiom—it could be any kind of music. What I think is that music, no matter what its structure, has a very powerful emotional influence, it can't help but have that—it's in the nature of music, it's when you can play a note and there's response immediately—you don't have to build up to it through seven scenes.

Can you think of a play or a production which has achieved the impact you're talking about?

With music? Brecht's plays. Plays like *Mahagonny*. He's my favourite playwright, Brecht. If you look at *Jungle of the Cities*, it's a play—a bout, between these two characters, taken in a completely open-ended way, the bout is never defined as being anything but metaphysical.

Do you think the music works in Brecht in the way he wanted it to work, as a means of distancing?

I never saw a production that he did, and I've seen very few good Brecht productions. It's very hard to do.

What effect would you like a play of yours—one that you really felt totally happy with, play and production—to have on an audience?

Well, it depends on the play, but hopefully it would be something that would transform the emotions of the people watching. People come into the theatre in very different circumstances, expecting something to happen, and then hopefully when they walk out of the theatre the chemistry's changed. What specifically that is depends on the

Shepard and coauthor Patti Smith performing their play Cowboy Mouth, *1971.*

material of the play, because every play's different.

I find it rather surprising when you say things like that, that you haven't written a play that has required an environmental situation—some sort of a situation in which the audience comes in to the play, or comes into a space that the play has taken over. . . .

There's a whole myth about environmental theatre as it's being practised now in New York. The myth is that in order for the audience to be actively participating in the event that they're watching they have to be physically sloshed into something, which isn't true at all. An audience can sit in chairs and be watching something in front of them, and can be actively participating in the thing that's confronting them, you know. And it doesn't necessarily mean that if an audience walks into the building and people are swinging from the rafters and spaghetti's thrown all over them, or whatever the environment might be, that their participation in the play is going to be any closer. In fact it might very well be less so, because of the defences that are put up as soon as that happens.

Can one relate that to Dick Schechner's production of **Tooth of Crime***?*

Well, I think he's lost. I think he's lost in a certain area of experimentation which is valid for him. He feels that he wants to experiment with the environment of theatre, which is okay, I've nothing against it. Except when you write a play it sets up certain assumptions about the context in which it's to be performed, and in that play they had nothing to do with what Schechner set up in the theatre. You can take that or leave it. It can be okay—the playwright isn't a holy man, you know. Except I'd rather that the experimentation took place with something that left itself open to that—a play that from the start defines its context as undefinable, so that you can fuck around with it if you want to.

Do you visualize a particular type of performance space when you're writing—proscenium arch, open stage conditions, or whatever?

Yes, sometimes I see a play in a particular theatre, in a particular place—like I used to for Theatre Genesis, because I was so familiar with that environment. . . .

Has it proved important that those plays should go on being done in that sort of theatre?

It's important in terms of the size of the play—in other words the number of characters. For one thing you feel that if you have too many people involved in a production it can only be done in very special financial circumstances—you can only have it done in Lincoln Center, for instance, which turns out to be a disaster, and from there on it can't really be performed in colleges or anything like that because it's too expensive. It's important to take into consideration the general environment the play's going to hit. It's more important to have a five-character play or less that can be done in a close, non-financial situation than it is to have a circus.

Have you seen many amateur and student productions of your plays? Do you think they work with amateurs and students?

Yeah, sure. Again it depends on the play, some plays work very well with amateurs.

I was thinking, almost by analogy with Brecht, that maybe amateurs and students, not approaching your work with actorish preconceptions, might find a better style on occasions.

Well there's a certain excitement goes on with that kind of thing, because you know it's not being performed in this kind of blown-up way, it's not being performed for an anonymous audience—it's being done very specifically for people everybody knows.

How specifically do you conceive a play being staged when you're actually writing it?

This experience with **Horse Dreamer** opened my eyes to all the possibilities of productions, because I've been very opinionated about productions before. [Shepard had recently directed **Geography of a Horse Dreamer** at the Royal Court Theatre.]

You've not found yourself getting on with your directors?

Very rarely have I got on with them, except for a few instances.

You take an active part in rehearsals nonetheless? Where you can?

Sometimes—it depends on the situation, it depends who you're working with. I like to take part in rehearsals, it's just very delicate, you have to watch out, it's easy to say the wrong things to the actors.

Was **Horse Dreamer** *the first play of your own you've directed?*

Yeah, first time I ever did it. I much prefer working in England, though, because the actors I've found are much better equipped to do things. . . .

Technically?

No, not only technically, but in other ways, like these guys

I've gotten in **Horse Dreamer,** who are fantastic—the best actors I've ever worked with, they're really great. In New York you're lucky if you find anybody. Everybody's acting, and doing some lifestyle sort of thing at the same time, sort of mixing their lifestyles with their acting, so it's very hard to get the same dedication.

In terms of your future relationship with directors have you learned anything from directing **Horse Dreamer***?*

Well, I've learned that it's very important to have patience, and that things can't be rushed. I've learned that the rehearsal process is actually a process. The reason it takes three or four or five or six weeks is because it actually needs that amount of time to evolve. Whereas I used to think that a production was a miracle act, that actors very suddenly came to the play and it was realized in a matter of days. But that's not true, it takes a great deal of time, and in the production at the Court now, they're still finding things, still working on things and bringing new things to it.

Do you think you've found that a particular kind of rehearsal process suits your plays—from reading to blocking to working, or whatever?

When I first went into this thing, because I didn't have any experience I called up several different directors that I knew and said, could you fill me in on the details? And some of them told me some very interesting things about the way they worked, the sort of process, but I found none of it held true for this particular experience. It's very like writing— you can't have any set kind of preconceptions about what it's going to be. You can *say* first week we're going to read it, second week we're going to block it, third week we're going to churn it out, but it doesn't make any difference, because when you get to the actual thing it makes its own rules.

So how did the rules work out?

The rules came from the actors. Because they were so good and they've had so much experience, it wasn't me making absolute decisions, though I saw things that they were doing and pointed them out, and then tried to mould a little bit from what they were doing.

There is a problem it seems to me, insofar as there are styles of playing on the one hand, and there are very clear literary things happening in the writing on the other, and sometimes the two don't quite go together. Did you find that at all with **Geography of a Horse Dreamer***?*

That play is different because it's more structured, it's more straightforward in its plot and that kind of thing. I think what you're talking about does come into a play like **Icarus's Mother,** though, which is really a bitch to produce. It's very difficult for actors to do—being physically there on stage and having monologues that run for a page and a half—to bridge that gap between the language and the physical acting of the play. Is that what you're talking about?

Yes—do you think you're getting closer to bridging that gap now?

Yeah. One of the things I've found is that it's too much to expect an actor to do a vocal aria, standing there in the middle of the stage and have the thing work in space, without actually having him physically involved in what he's talking about. The speeches have been shaved quite considerably since the early plays, I don't go in for long speeches any more.

Although there are some quite beautiful and very long speeches in **The Unseen Hand.**

Yeah, right. But even so, even that is difficult, like I said.

But the first speech, for example, where Blue is on stage by himself. . . .

He's got something to do, he's working with the car, and he's on the highway. . . . The imagery comes out of the situation. It also does in the earlier plays, except that there the characters are physically marooned by their speaking, which makes it hard.

What do you think about the criticism that's been made of **Geography of a Horse Dreamer,** *that it doesn't contain the intensity of language of* **Tooth of Crime** *or* **The Unseen Hand***?*

Well, I can see how people would be disappointed if they found that the language filled them out more, gave them more of a thing to spring from, but it's just not right for this play. It's not a play that's investigating a whole complicated language scheme. I was using language from Raymond Chandler, from Dashiell Hammett—from the 'thirties, which to me is a beautiful kind of language, and very idiomatic of a period in America which was really strong.

Is this something you can turn on without thinking—a particular idiom, whether it's of rock music or Dashiell Hammett—or do you have to think yourself into it?

You have to make an adjustment, you have to sort of click into something: a trigger is set off, and then you're able to do it. . . .

Why the combination of the dog-racing theme and the Raymond Chandler style? They're pretty disparate elements, aren't they?

Not really, no, they both have to do with crime and the underworld. Raymond Chandler actually visited London a lot—he dug London. He never got involved in dog-racing, but I think the kind of working-class people here who go to dog-racing talk in the English version of what that American idiom is.

How did you get involved in the dog-racing scene—what was the fascination?

Well, I loved horse-racing before, I really used to like the horse-track, we lived right near one. But it's very expensive, as far as actually getting involved in it. Then when I

came here I found dog-racing is the second biggest spectator sport in England, you've got twelve tracks or something, and suddenly it was like all your romantic childhood dreams come true—only with dogs. So I thought, shit, this is great, and I got involved in it. It's really a sort of romantic impulse, you know. Being around the track, punters and all that kind of stuff—I like that world.

Do you consider yourself a romantic?

What does that mean?

Well, you've been talking about things being romantic, in that they obviously have a primarily emotional pull. . . .

Like for instance Wyoming. . . . Yes, just in that a thing pulls me in a certain way. In that sense I'm a romantic.

And in the sense that you don't pre-structure your plays?

Yeah, but I wouldn't say that that was necessarily romantic. I like poetry a lot, I like the impulse that makes poetry happen, the feeling that language can occur out of an emotional context. I mean, it's not any specific poetry, it's just that I think that theatre especially has a lot of room for that.

Is there maybe something romantic about your preoccupation with death, too?

Death? The idea of dying and being reborn is really an interesting one, you know. It's always there at the back of my head.

In a religious, or metaphysical, or philosophical way, or what?

In real terms, what it means to die and be born again. I mean, you can call it religious if you want. It's something I've wanted somehow to get into, but I've never really found how to make it work in the plays.

Were you raised in a religion?

Yes, I was, but that's not necessarily where it's coming from—I was raised as an Episcopalian. . . . But that was another kind of prison to get out of, you know. There's nothing worse than listening to a lot of people mumbling, and outside the sun is shining. . . . But you have this personality, and somehow feel locked into it, jailed by all of your cultural influences and your psychological ones from your family, and all that. And somehow I feel that that isn't the whole of it, you know, that there's another possibility.

You still feel yourself escaping from those influences?

You can't escape, that's the whole thing, you can't. You finally find yourself in a situation where, like, that's the way it is—you can't get out of it. But there is always that impulse towards another kind of world, something that doesn't necessarily confine you in that way. Like I've got a name, I speak English, I have gestures, wear a certain kind of clothes . . . but once upon a time I didn't have all that shit.

Do you have any ideas about the way you're going as a dramatist?

I wish I did. I don't know. I'd like to try a whole different way of writing now, which is very stark and not so flashy and not full of a lot of mythic figures and everything, and try to scrape it down to the bone as much as possible.

But not realism?

Well, it could be called realism, but not the kind of realism where husbands and wives squabble and that kind of stuff.

Are you keen to direct your own plays again, or to consider directing somebody else's?

Yeah, without having a great deal of time to think about it first, though I wouldn't want to plunge right into another one. But that's a whole area of possibilities—where you begin to find out what it really means to write a play. That it isn't a piece of paper, it's something that's really happening in real life. And the more you find out about it the more you can grow as a writer. I'm very interested in the kind of chemistry that goes on with directing, finding the right language to use with the actors, finding the way an actor works. Every single actor in **Horse Dreamer** worked in a completely different way, and it took a couple of weeks to find that out. I was saying the same things to everybody, and then I began to find that you have to talk differently to each actor—something you say to one guy doesn't mean a thing to the next guy.

Is it important what people, professional critics or others, say about your plays?

Well, it would be silly to say that I'm immune to it, because it affects you in one way or another. But with this particular play I'm not particularly concerned about the press criticism, because it's been such a strong experience. For three weeks you've been working with people, going through this very intricate process, and you arrive at this thing, and then it's judged by people who've never seen anything until that moment. So whatever they say about it, whether they like it or don't like it, whether it's constructive criticism or not, it doesn't have anything to do with that process that went on. I mean, that's what's important to me, and that's really the life of the play.

Anything else in England that has really turned you on, like dog-racing?

I like pubs and football a lot. There's nothing like pubs in America. And Guinness, I like Guinness.

Any of those going to be dramatically productive?

Football . . . yeah, football very well might.

Visualization, Language and the Inner Library (1977)

SOURCE: *The Drama Review,* Vol. 21, No. 4, December, 1977, pp. 49-58.

[*In the following essay, Shepard details the processes and principles that figure in the creation of his plays.*]

I feel a lot of reluctance in attempting to describe any part of a process which, by its truest nature, holds an unending mystery. At the same time I'm hoping that by trying to formulate some of this territory I can make certain things clearer to myself.

I've always felt that the term "experimental" in regard to theatre forms has been twisted by the intellectual community surrounding the artist to the extent that now even the artist has lost track of its original essence. In other words, a search for "new forms" doesn't seem to be exactly where it's at.

There comes a point where the exterior gyrations are no longer the most interesting aspect of what you're practicing, and brand-new exploration starts to take root. For example: In the writing of a particular character where does the character take shape? In my experience the character is visualized, he appears out of nowhere in three dimensions and speaks. He doesn't speak to me because I'm not in the play. I'm watching it. He speaks to something or someone else, or even to himself, or even to no one.

I'm talking now about an open-ended structure where anything could happen as opposed to a carefully planned and regurgitated event which, for me, has always been as painful as pissing nickels. There are writers who work this way successfully, and I admire them and all that, but I don't see the point exactly. The reason I began writing plays was the hope of extending the sensation of *play* (as in "kid") on into adult life. If "play" becomes "labor," why play?

Anyway, to veer back to visualization—right here is where the experiment starts. With the very first impulse to see something happen on a stage. Any stage. This impulse is mistakenly called an idea by those who have never experienced it. I can't even count how many times I've heard the line, "Where did the idea for this play come from?" I never can answer it because it seems totally back-assward. Ideas emerge from plays—not the other way around.

I don't mean to make this sound like a magic act or a mystical experience. It has nothing to do with hallucination or drugs or meditation. These things may all have an influence on the general picture, but they aren't the picture itself. The picture is moving in the mind and being allowed to move more and more freely as you follow it. The following of it is the writing part. In other words, I'm taking notes in as much detail as possible on an event that's happening somewhere inside me. The extent to which I can actually follow the picture and not intervene with my own two-cents worth is where inspiration and craftsmanship hold their real meaning. If I find myself pushing the character in a certain direction, it's almost always a sure sign that I've fallen back on technique and lost the real thread of the thing.

This isn't to say that it's possible to write on nothing but a wave of inspired vision. There has to be some kind of common ground between the accumulated knowledge of what you know how to do (because you've done it before) and the completely foreign country that always demands a new expression. I've never written a play that didn't require both ends of the stick.

Another part of this that interests me is: How is this inner visualizing different from ordinary daydreaming or ordinary nightdreaming? The difference seems to lie in the idea of a "watcher" being engaged while writing, whereas ordinarily this watcher is absent. I'm driving a truck and daydreaming about myself in Mexico, but, in this case, I'm not really seeing the dream that's taking place. If I start to see it, then it might become a play.

Now, another thing comes into focus. It must be true that we're continuously taking in images of experience from the outside world through our senses, even when we're not aware of it. How else could whole scenes from our past which we thought we'd long forgotten suddenly spring up in living technicolor? These tastes from our life must then be stored away somewhere in some kind of inner library. So this must mean that if I could be truly resourceful, I could draw on this library at any given moment for the exact information I needed. Not only that, but the information is then given back to me as a living sensation. From this point of view, I'm diving back into the actual experience of having been there and writing from it as though it's happening now.

This is very similar to the method-acting technique called "recall." It's a good description—I'm recalling the thing itself. The similarity between the actor's art and the playwright's is a lot closer than most people suspect. In fact the playwright is the only actor who gets to play all the parts. The danger of this method from the actor's point of view is that he becomes lost in the dream and forgets about the audience. The same holds true for the writer, but the writer doesn't really realize where he became lost until he sees an audience nodding out through what he'd thought were his most blazing passages.

This brings me down to words. Words as tools of imagery in motion. I have a feeling that the cultural environment one is raised in predetermines a rhythmical relationship to the use of words. In this sense, I can't be anything other than an American writer.

I noticed though, after living in England for three straight years, that certain subtle changes occurred in this rhythmic construction. In order to accommodate these new configurations in the way a sentence would overblow itself (as is the English tendency), I found myself adding English characters to my plays. *Geography of a Horse Dreamer* was written in London, and there's only one truly American character in the play.

Still, the power of words for me isn't so much in the delineation of a character's social circumstances as it is in the capacity to evoke visions in the eye of the audience. Amer-ican Indian poetry (in its simplest translation) is a prime example. The roots of this poetry stem from a religious belief in the word itself. Like "crow." Like "hawk." Words as living incantations and not as symbols. Taken in this way, the organization of living, breathing words as they hit the air between the actor and the audience actually possesses the power to change our chemistry. Still, the critical assessment of this kind of event is almost always relegated to the categories of symbolism or "surrealism" or some other accepted niche. In other words, it's removed from the living and dedicated to the dead.

I seem to have come around now to the ear as opposed to the eye, but actually they work in conjunction with each other. They seem to be joined in moments of heightened perception. I hear the phrase a lot that this or that writer has a "great ear for language." What this usually means is that the writer has an openness to people's use of language in the outside world and then this is recorded and reproduced exactly as it's heard. This is no doubt a great gift, but it seems to fall way short of our overall capacity to listen. If I only hear the sounds that people make, how much sound am I leaving out? Words, at best, can only give a partial glimpse into the total world of sensate experience, but how much of that total world am I letting myself in for when I approach writing?

The structure of any art form immediately implies limitation. I'm narrowing down my field of vision. I'm agreeing to work within certain boundaries. So I have to be very careful how those boundaries are defined at the outset. Language, then, seems to be the only ingredient in this plan that retains the potential of making leaps into the unknown. There's only so much I can do with appearances. Change the costume, add a new character, change the light, bring in objects, shift the set, but language is always hovering right in there, ready to move faster and more effectively than all the rest of it put together. It's like pulling out a .38 when someone faces you with a knife.

Language can explode from the tiniest impulse. If I'm right inside the character in the moment, I can catch what he smells, sees, feels and touches. In a sudden flash, he opens his eyes, and the words follow. In these lightning-like eruptions words are not thought, they're felt. They cut through space and make perfect sense without having to hesitate for the "meaning."

From time to time I've practiced Jack Kerouac's discovery of jazz-sketching with words. Following the exact same principles as a musician does when he's jamming. After periods of this kind of practice, I begin to get the haunting sense that something in me writes but it's not necessarily me. At least it's not the "me" that takes credit for it. This identical experience happened to me once when I was playing drums with The Holy Modal Rounders, and it scared the shit out of me. Peter Stampfel, the fiddle player explained it as being visited by the Holy Ghost, which sounded reasonable enough at the time.

What I'm trying to get at here is that the real quest of a writer is to penetrate into another world. A world behind the form. The contradiction is that as soon as that world opens up, I tend to run the other way. It's scary because I can't answer to it from what I know.

Now, here's the big rub—it's generally accepted in the scholarly world that a playwright deals with *"ideas."* That idea in itself has been inherited by us as though it were originally written in granite from above and nobody, but nobody, better mess with it. The problem for me with this concept is that its adherents are almost always referring to ideas which speak only to the mind and leave out completely the body, the emotions and all the rest of it.

Myth speaks to everything at once, especially the emotions. By myth I mean a sense of mystery and not necessarily a traditional formula. A character for me is a composite of different mysteries. He's an unknown quantity. If he wasn't, it would be like coloring in the numbered spaces. I see an old man by a broken car in the middle of nowhere and those simple elements right away set up associations and yearnings to pursue what he's doing there.

The character of Crow in *Tooth of Crime* came from a yearning toward violence. A totally lethal human with no way or reason for tracing how he got that way. He just appeared. He spit words that became his weapons. He doesn't "mean" anything. He's simply following his most savage instincts. He speaks in an unheard-of tongue. He needed a victim, so I gave him one. He devoured him just like he was supposed to. When you're writing inside of a character like this, you aren't pausing every ten seconds to figure out what it all means. If you do, you lose the whole shot, because the character isn't going to hang around waiting for you. He's moving.

I write fast because that's the way it happens with me. Sometimes long stretches happen in between where I don't write for weeks. But when I start, I don't stop. Writing is born from a need. A deep burn. If there's no need, there's no writing.

I don't mean to give the impression from all this that a playwright isn't responsible toward the audience. He is. But which audience? An imagined one or a real one? The only real audience he has at the moment of writing is himself. Only later does the other audience come into it. At that point he begins to see the correspondence or lack of it between his own "watching" and the watching of others.

I used to be dead set against rewriting on any level. My attitude was that if the play had faults, those faults were part and parcel of the original process, and that any attempt to correct them was cheating. Like a sculptor sneaking out in the night with his chisel and chipping little pieces off his work or gluing them back on.

After a while this rigid "holy-art" concept began to crumble. It was no longer a case of "correction," as though what I was involved with was some kind of definitive term paper. I began to see that the living outcome (the production) always demanded a different kind of attention than the written form that it sprang from. The spoken word, no matter how you cut it, is different than the written word. It happens in a different space, under different circumstances and demands a different set of laws.

Action is the only play I've written where I spoke each line out loud to myself before I put it down on paper. To me that play still comes the closest to sounding on stage exactly like it was written. This method doesn't work for every play, though, since it necessarily sets up a slower tempo. It just happened to be the right approach for that particular piece.

La Turista was the first play I ever rewrote, under the urging of Jacques Levy, who directed it. We were in the second week of rehearsals at the American Place Theatre when I walked in with a brand-new second act. It's a tribute to Wynn Handman that he allowed this kind of procedure to take place. That was the first taste I got of regarding theatre as an ongoing process. I could feel the whole evolution of that play from a tiny sweltering hotel in the Yucatan, half wasted with the trots, to a full-blown production in New York City. Most of the writing in that piece was hatched from a semidelirious state of severe dysentery. What the Mexicans call "La Turista" or "Montezuma's Revenge." In that state any writing I could manage seemed valid, no matter how incoherent it might seem to an outside eye. Once it hit the stage in rehearsals and I was back to a fairly healthy physical condition, the whole thing seemed filled with an overriding self-pity. The new second act came more from desperation than anything else.

I think immediate environments tend to play a much heavier role on my writing than I'm aware of most of the time. That is, the physical place I'm in at the time of sitting down to the machine. In New York I could write any time in any place. It didn't matter what was happening in the streets below or the apartment above. I just wrote. The funny thing is that I can remember the exact place and time of every play. Even the people I was with. It's almost as though the plays were a kind of chronicle I was keeping on myself.

It seems that the more you write, the harder it gets, because you're not so easily fooled by yourself anymore. I can still sit down and whip off a play like I used to, but it doesn't have the same meaning now as it did when I was nineteen. Even so, writing becomes more and more interesting as you go along, and it starts to open up some of its secrets. One thing I'm sure of, though. That I'll never get to the bottom of it.

OVERVIEWS AND GENERAL STUDIES

Michael Smith (review date 22 October 1964)

SOURCE: A review of *Cowboys* and *The Rock Garden,* in *The Village Voice,* Vol. X, No. 1, October 22, 1964, p. 13.

[*Smith is a critic, stage director, and theater director, whose books include* Eight Plays from Off-Off Broadway

(1966) and More Plays from Off-Off Broadway (1972). A drama critic for the Village Voice from 1959 to 1974, Smith wrote the following review of Shepard's first produced plays, becoming an influential supporter of the author's early work.]

I know it sounds pretentious and unprepossessing—Theatre Genesis at St. Mark's Church in-the-Bouwerie, dedicated to the new playwright—but they have actually found a new playwright, which is more than you can often say for Broadway or Off-Broadway. The playwright's name is Sam Shepard, and I know nothing about him except that he has written a pair of provocative and genuinely original plays. They will be given their final weekend of performances this Friday, through Sunday at 8.30.

The plays are difficult to categorize, and I'm not sure it would be valuable to try. Shepard is still feeling his way working with an intuitive approach to language and dramatic structure and moving into an area between ritual and naturalism, where character transcends psychology, fantasy breaks down literalism, and the patterns of ordinariness have their own lives. His is a gestalt theatre which evokes the existence behind behavior. Shepard clearly is aware of previous work in this mode, mostly by Europeans, but his voice is distinctly American and his own.

SURROUNDED BY INDIANS

The first play, *Cowboys,* presents two young men attempting to deny the external world and live in terms of specific small remembered physical realities and various simple heroic myths. Their basic mood is exhaustion bordering on despair, but from it they rouse themselves into bursts of wild energy, alternately joyous and desperate, in which they impersonate Wild West heroes surrounded by marauding Indians and relish in memory the sensate details of breakfast, among many things. The play's prime virtue is the author's self-trust; language and form have a questing air of spontaneity which is perfectly appropriate to the content. The language is vital and engaging, and the characters are not the less convincing for being stranded in no-space. The play also has flaws: occasional flashes of defensiveness and second-hand hostility toward convention, and insufficient attachment to the level of fact, a conclusion which is too vague and too easy. One comes away feeling that the playwright has kept some of his secrets, perhaps kept them from himself, but at least he has secrets to keep.

The Rock Garden is a more schematic play. A boy serves without comment a demanding, nagging, boring bed-ridden woman; then in a separate scene he sits passively, falling asleep while listening to a beer-drinking man make inane and endless plans for building rock gardens. One marvels at the boy's self-containment, his not needing to fight back, until his focus finally is revealed in a single quiet, specific speech about sex which ends the play. The writing is beautifully controlled and conveys the overpowering boredom of the situation without being boring for a moment.

ATTENTION TO SPECIFICS

The production of *Cowboys* is excellent. Robert F. Lyons and Kevin O'Connor are the two actors, and they animate the writing with extraordinary energy and attention to specifics. The play is done on a bare stage as it should be, and it has been directed with subtlety and precision by Ralph Cook. *The Rock Garden* is not so convincingly staged. Its physical setting attempts realism with inadequate means, and there is room for further exploration of the two talkative characters. Stephanie Gordon as the nagging woman fails to define a tone early enough and leaves us thinking we are watching dull naturalism until the play's structure takes over, and Kevin O'Connor as the planning man stays on the same note too long and resorts to somewhat excessive mugging. However, the central figure of the play, although he has the fewest lines, is the boy, who is played with exact understatement by Lee Kissman. He manages some remarkably precise physical acting and oversteps all the dangers in the final speech. Again the work of director Cook is unusually responsive to the play's intent.

Theatre Genesis intends to continue finding and producing the work of new playwrights. Already we have reason to be grateful, and the project deserves all the encouragement we can give it.

Michael Bloom (essay date 1981)

SOURCE: "Visions of the End: The Early Plays," in *American Dreams: The Imagination of Sam Shepard,* edited by Bonnie Marranca, Performing Arts Journal Publications, 1981, pp. 72-8.

[*A director and critic, Bloom addresses Shepard's initial work, arguing that the early plays are a form of "gestalt theatre" that conveys the consciousness of America in the 1960s.*]

Even without being there, one can easily imagine that the first audiences to see Sam Shepard's early one-acts must have been shocked by their strange and novel theatricality. Although by 1964 off-off-Broadway audiences had already been exposed to the European avant-garde as well as to such Americans as Joel Oppenheimer, Al Carmines, and Leonard Melfi, nothing could have prepared them for Shepard's spare, cool, yet explosive short plays; specifically, for a central character in *Chicago* who spent most of the play in a bathtub situated on an otherwise bare stage, and two characters who used a tablecloth and barbecue to send smoke signals to an airplane in *Icarus's Mother.* Even within their contexts these occurrences seemed, to many, to be deliberately mysterious and arbitrary, and Shepard was attacked for being a theatrical provocateur, producing effect for its own sake. But as understanding of non-realistic work has increased and as myth and a transformation of realism have clarified Shepard's intentions, the early one-acts have become more resonant and intelligible.

From *The Rock Garden* through *Red Cross* (1964-68) and beyond, Shepard's one-acts are plotless, without obvious subject matter, and lacking in the complete individuation of character and place. An early director and critic of Shepard, Michael Smith, describes the playwright's early method as "a gestalt theatre which evokes the existence behind behavior." But getting to the meaning of these plays means going beyond this excellent capsule description to the question of the *quality* of the existence behind the behavior, to the *type* of consciousness Shepard chose to dramatize.

The Rock Garden, Shepard's first extant script, conforms nicely to Smith's notion of a "gestalt theatre." Lacking any narrative at all, the play describes in a kind of triptych portrait a single condition of sensation—the utter tedium and boredom of a typical American family situation. In the silent, opening "panel," a Boy and a Girl (probably brother and sister) exchange glances and sip glasses of milk until finally, out of boredom, the Girl drops her glass and spills the milk. The two other panels that follow this comic "blackout" scene elaborate on the same condition. In the second panel a Woman (apparently the children's mother) chatters on about her father, who led an absurdly sedentary existence:

> Sometimes he just stayed in the attic. He'd stay up there for days and never come down . . . He knew a lot of people. They'd stop by to see him but he was always in the attic. I always wondered why they kept coming back.

From time to time she tells the Boy how much he resembles her father, and after each comparison she orders him to fetch her a glass of water or a blanket. Gradually it becomes clear that on some level of consciousness the Woman has been using the memory to suppress the Boy, continuing the static, vapid existence that characterized her father's life. In response to this threat the Boy—who begins the scene in his underwear—covers himself by gradually putting on all his clothes. The scene ends when the Boy hurriedly exits and the Man, dressed only in his underwear, takes the Boy's place opposite the Woman.

With the juxtaposition of similar images—the Boy and the Man dressed in underwear and seated identically—Shepard symbolizes the Man's impotence, the Boy's future, and the continuity of generations in a sterile, empty family. Because it foregoes strong dramatic actions, juxtaposing simple, banal activities to express a single condition or gestalt, this oblique, deliberately static method is the perfect formal equivalent to the family's emptiness.

In the final panel of this family portrait the Man explains to the Boy the enjoyment he gets from working his garden. But instead of living, growing plants, the Man's idea of a garden is an arrangement of rocks. As the Man rambles on, mindlessly praising the rock garden, the Boy continually falls off his chair out of boredom. Finally, in a stunning non-sequitur, the Boy breaks through the malaise by launching into a catalogue of his sexual techniques with women (real or imagined), at the end of which, for a very different reason, the Man falls off his chair. Although it is an obvious shock effect, the Boy's search for what Norman

Mailer would have called "an orgasm more apocalyptic than the one that preceded it" is an appropriately desperate effort to transcend a stifling, barren, inert existence. In poetic terms the image of the Boy's ejaculation—his foundation of life—is in perfect antimony to the image of the lifeless rock garden.

If the playwright's technique was strange and unfamiliar, his vision was, in retrospect, poetically consistent, incisive, and sensually alive. In his later "family plays," most notably *Buried Child,* Shepard extends the simple gestalt of *The Rock Garden,* elaborating the petrified nuclear family into a national metaphor.

Chicago, the next extant play, confirmed Shepard's radically pessimistic vision of contemporary reality. Moving beyond the stifling pressures of the family, *Chicago* dramatized the feelings of anomie that threaten all existence in the nuclear age. Although there is more of a narrative here than in the previous play, the intent once again was not to tell a story but to project images that would provoke a visceral awareness of the dislocation and disorientation of contemporary existence.

The layered reality of *Chicago* is far more complicated than that of *The Rock Garden* because its surface action is so playful and casual. In fact most of the play consists of Stu's game-playing, by himself and with his mate, Joy. His fantasies give the play a lazy, improvised quality that neatly belies the underlying tension. But as Joy prepares to leave, an obsessive fear creeps into Stu's musings. Sitting in a bathtub that he imagines to be a boat, he daydreams about a fisherman and his potential catch, focusing on the fish's frozen moment of indecision.

> You're pretty hungry but you're not sure. So you take your time. You're down there moving slowly around this worm, taking your time. And they're up there drinking split pea soup and grinning and pointing at the moon and the pier and all the trees. You're both hung up.

As this imagery of suspension begins to infiltrate Stu's humorous facade, the expression of dislocation intensifies. Gradually the play's single controlling image takes effect. The disorientation contained in the presence of the bathtub—a real object—on an empty stage rather than in a bathroom setting reflects Stu's condition. He is an inert object stranded between two realities, his fantasies and the world outside himself, trapped by an overwhelming fear of activity. As Joy's vacation is enacted expressionistically, Stu imagines her vacation to be the prelude to a mass suicide. Pushing these fantasies to excess, Shepard means to overwhelm the audience with the existential fear that, in our alienating environment, makes even simple activities difficult.

In retrospect *Chicago* seems both too general and overly ambitious. Stu's *angst,* transmitted directly rather than dramatized through conflicting characters, lacks specific causes and a context connected to the rest of the world. Nor is the situation complex enough to express Stu's existential fear of global disaster. Without the context of violence and potential catastrophe that threatened so much of the 1960s, Stu's hallucinations can appear to be the paranoia of an eccentric.

And yet it is exactly this kind of surface behavior, composed mostly of games and fantasies, that Shepard uses so successfully to structure nearly all of the succeeding one-acts. The sheer quantity of these games and fantasies reflects on the emptiness, boredom, and alienation of modern existence. But the most useful aspect of the fantasy/game behavior is, to quote Smith again, as a means of revealing "the existence behind behavior"—the repressed fears and struggles in an "age of genocide."

In *Icarus's Mother* the vision of a traumatic existence is elaborated more fully and more seriously than in the earlier plays. The vision of **The Rock Garden** is limited to the nuclear family, just as the vision of **Chicago** derives only from the rather eccentric fantasies of a single character. But the world of Shepard's third play is wider and more universal. The skywriting plane and the fireworks display are significant as touchstones of a world outside the characters' inner lives. This external world is not articulated in a fully realistic way; it envelops the characters atmospherically. Nevertheless, by setting the characters off against an external reality, Shepard begins to show us a more substantial dramatic vision. Not only is there a sense of the outside world in this play; there is also a pervasive fear that transmits a powerful gestalt to the audience.

Frank, Bill, Howard, and Jill argue with Pat (over whether she should take a walk by herself) as if their lives depended on the outcome. Just as Stu created his own story about Joy's vacation, so these five characters make up different tales about the skywriting pilot in order to "possess" him and thus to have their own way. Using bogus scientific jargon, Howard goes to extraordinary lengths to scare Pat into staying with the group. Underneath the gamesmanship is a desperate need to hold sway over another person. The play gradually reveals that what is at stake for these people runs far deeper than winning an argument. It is exactly this mysterious disparity between the fantastical nature of the stories and the desperation with which they are used that conveys the characters' tenuous grip on an uneasy world.

When the others finally go walking, leaving Bill and Howard alone, it becomes fully evident that a monumental but unspecified fear is at work beneath the power struggles. For an unexplained reason, Bill and Howard become desperate in their need to send smoke signals to the pilot. When they are interrupted they carefully hide their actions from the others, making up lies to get them to leave. When one of their lies—that the plane has crashed—later turns out to be true, they are left virtually paralyzed by the loss of the pilot, the one bit of reality they had been clinging to. In describing the horrors of the crash, Frank has also evoked their vision of the end of the world.

The fear of that possibility is of course the informing psychological principle of *Icarus's Mother.* Even at the play's end we still do not know why the pilot was so important to Bill and Howard. But we do sense the fear that informed the

desperate power struggles and the intense need to communicate with the pilot. Instead of unraveling a plot, the play elaborates a gestalt conditioned by the threat of an apocalypse. In *Chicago* that fear was contained entirely in Stu's fantasies. But in *Icarus's Mother* the fact that the plane actually crashes gives credence and significance to the characters' fears. For the first time in Shepard's writing, a real context is provided for the characters, a context which includes explicit resonances of American life, namely the technological failure at what must be a Fourth of July celebration.

In the early plays Shepard does manage to convey the experience—the consciousness—of existence. Instead of dramatizing events, social forces, or heroic actions, he transmits an immediate visceral sensation of contemporary reality. Focusing in on the minutiae of behavior, he records a picture of a nervous obsessive world where feelings of rootlessness and alienation predominate. Yet even within his obsessive, microscopic vision, the actions and images resonate with the experience of contemporary American life. The behavior of these plays, though universally recognizable, is especially characteristic of America in the middle of this century: the conforming to boring social rituals, the obeisance to work, the obsessive game-playing, and of course the emotional repression. When Shepard went on to write **La Turista, Operation Sidewinder,** and **Mad Dog Blues,** it became obvious that his primary interests were the myths and archetypal figures of America; but the focus on America, though not yet full blown, is clearly evident in the early plays.

With its vision of the apocalypse, *Icarus's Mother* is a model for many of Shepard's later one-acts, especially **Fourteen Hundred Thousand** and **Red Cross.** In the former, the giant bookcase that has a life of its own but no function is a hilarious symbol of a society gone out of control. Determined to have a bookcase even though she has no books to fill it, Donna bullies Tom into finishing their project. Similar to the struggles in the earlier plays, this one also takes on a vehemence far too excessive for the issue at hand. But it is Ed who is especially prone to fears of isolation and death. When he tries to abandon their project, Tom and Donna frighten him into staying, telling a story of a catastrophic snowstorm that will bury him in his country house. In an about-face to their obsession with building the bookcase, the characters dismantle the entire stage set in a symbolic enactment of an apocalypse.

But instead of having a cleansing effect, the end of their former world makes way for an even more object-oriented world—the infinite linear city described by Mom and Pop. **Fourteen Hundred Thousand** illuminates the threat of doom in a more specific way by connecting it with the materialistic and technological obsessions of modern society. Unfortunately, the symbolic apocalypse seems imposed by the playwright because the struggle over the bookcase is not allowed to play itself out. Nor is the linear city proposed by Mom and Pop ever linked to that initial struggle. We are bombarded with an array of ideas and concepts that remain unconnected dramatically, making the play an unwieldy theatrical experience.

Red Cross, on the other hand, is a far more subtle evocation of apocalyptic anxiety. Here there are no plane crashes, no tales of mass suicides, no giant self-propelled objects; the threat to Jim, his case of "crabs," seems almost laughably harmless. Yet Jim mysteriously keeps the problem from Carol, even after she complains of tingling sensations, and he refuses to let the Maid change the bedsheets. In order to divert her attention, he gives her a swimming lesson, an imaginary event that is the highlight of the play's comic surface.

But the Maid begins to believe that she is in danger of drowning; the lesson reveals the insecurity beneath Jim's need to dominate the Maid. When Carol returns with the realization that she is literally being eaten alive by bugs, she unleashes a terror that Jim had been trying to suppress. What had seemed like a minor annoyance now becomes a plague that encompasses an almost cosmic fear. In the rarefied world of this three character play, set in a perfectly white box, the trickle of blood down Jim's face signifies the advent of a horror that has the dimension of an apocalypse.

Even without specific references, *Red Cross* can be seen as an allegory for America's collective behavior in the 1960s. When Carol demands an answer about the blood on Jim's face, his dodging makes clear that the catastrophe has been brought on largely by his failure to confront the problem.

Faced with a society that suppressed the awareness of danger, Shepard, like many other writers, turned to apocalypse as the only way to describe the turmoil of American life in the 1960s. Since Biblical times apocalypse has meant, among other things, social chaos, fruitlessness, war, and world-wide disaster. Writing the early plays when his country was mired in a foreign war, and racial and generational conflicts threatened to destroy the fabric of American life, Shepard justifiably presented pessimistic visions of impending doom. What we see in the one-acts as a "coolness"—an absence of beliefs, affective actions, and strong relationships—actually belies the feeling of betrayal, the grief about America that surfaces completely in the bitterness and hunger for peace in *Operation Sidewinder.*

Since the prophet's words to a majority that is largely indifferent to their own crises must invoke a non-rational basis of authority (for rationality, overtaken by sophists, can no longer provide the means for reform), it is easy to see why the apocalyptic flourished in the hands of a 1960s playwright. In an address at Columbia University in 1960 entitled "Apocalypse: The Place of Mystery in the Life of the Mind," Norman O. Brown set the tone for a decade by calling for an end to the reliance on Mind and an embracing of the blessed madness of the Dionysian spirit. As with much of the writing of this time, Shepard's work is itself an attack on the objective, rational apprehension of knowledge. The apocalyptic proceeds by dreams, visions, and hallucinations. Given the anti-rationalist method of the apocalyptic vision, it is clear why realism, with its rational, objective vision of reality, held no interest for Shepard in the early part of his career.

In these short plays where character and relationship are minimal, there is nonetheless a developing vision of external reality. Shepard's introduction to a later play, *The Unseen Hand,* describes a reality that is remarkably similar to that of all the plays prior to it:

> Everybody's caught up in a fractured world that they can't even see. What's happening to them is unfathomable but they have a suspicion. Something unseen is working on them. Using them. They have no power and all the time they believe they're controlling the situation.

What is crucial in the remark is not only the very exact description of the characters' behavior throughout the one-acts but also the delineation of a reality—the "fractured world"—that is external to the characters. Although Shepard was interested more often than not in expressing his characters' strange inner reality, each succeeding play does more to validate their fears. With the relatively ordinary behavior of *Red Cross,* we can feel that these characters are not eccentric but are in touch with a very real danger. Even though we may only glimpse the horror, by the end of this series of plays we realize that the "something unseen" is the advent of the apocalypse and that it is the key to Shepard's vision of reality rather than merely a figment of the character's imaginations.

In *Forensic and the Navigators* and *The Holy Ghostly* Shepard theatricalizes the apocalypse, as colored smoke and gas consume the theatre at the end of both plays. In *Operation Sidewinder* Shepard finally articulates the entire myth of the apocalypse, presenting on stage not only the destruction of modern civilization but also its regeneration. Looking back from that play and remembering the historical context, the one-acts appear as single shock effects, images of breakdown under the pressures of modern American society, brief visions of the end.

With its prophesy of regeneration, *Operation Sidewinder* can be seen as the appropriate conclusion to a series of plays which, although depicting a universal condition, also possesses an important and distinctive vision of American life. In Shepard's work, "gestalt theatre" does not mean bombarding spectators with sensations so as to produce a like condition in the audience; rather it comes to mean using the sensations to provoke a visceral awareness of the potential chaos that lurks beneath the contemporary scene.

Richard Gilman (essay date 1981)

SOURCE: An introduction to *Sam Shepard: Seven Plays,* Bantam Books, 1981, pp. ix-xxv.

[*Gilman is an American critic, editor, and educator whose books include* The Confusion of Realms *(1969) and* The Making of Modern Drama *(1974). In the following essay, he outlines biographical and cultural influences on Shepard's work and finds that the search for identity is a central theme in the author's plays.*]

Dust jacket for the 1986 edition of The Unseen Hand and Other Plays.

Not many critics would dispute the proposition that Sam Shepard is our most interesting and exciting American playwright.

Fewer, however, can articulate just where the interest and excitement lie. There is an extraordinarily limited and homogeneous vocabulary of critical writing about Shepard, a thin lexicon of both praise and detraction. Over and over one sees his work described as "powerful"—"brutally" or "grimly" or "oddly" powerful, but muscular beyond question. Again and again one hears him called "surrealist" or "gothic" or, a bit more infrequently, a "mythic realist" (the most colorful appelation I've seen, affixed to Shepard by our most rococo reviewer, is the "bucking bronco" of American theater.) To his dectractors he is always "obscure," usually "willfully" so, and always "undisciplined." But even some of his enemies acknowledge his "theatrical magic," always with that phrase, and admirers and some enemies alike point to his plays' "richness of texture," always in those words.

The same sort of ready-made language can be found in discussions of Shepard's themes or motifs. Nearly everyone is agreed that the great majority of his plays deal with one or more of these matters: the death (or betrayal) of the American dream; the decay of our national myths; the growing mechanization of our lives; the search for roots; the travail of the family. (The trouble is, this cluster of related notions would apply to a good many other American writers as well.)

Most critics find it hard clearly to extract even these ideas from Shepard's plays, many of which are in fact extraordinarily resistant to thematic exegesis. Shepard's most ardent enthusiasts have got round the problem by arguing that he isn't (or wasn't; there's been a significant change in his latest plays, which I'll take up later) talking *about* anything but rather *making* something, a familiar notion in avantgarde circles and, as far as it goes, a correct one. They point out that his genius lies not in ideas or thought but in the making of images; he speaks more to the eye, or to the ear (in terms of expressive sound, though not necessarily in terms of immediate sense), than to the mind.

I don't fully accept this argument, though I see its virtues, and I do share in some of the prevailing uncertainties. I don't mean that I'm uncertain about the value of Shepard's work, but I find the question of "themes" troubling, primarily because I detect a confusion in *him* about them. But the real difficulty I share with many critics isn't so much deciding what the work is as knowing how to write about what it is. How to wield a critical vocabulary that won't be composed of clichés and stock phrases, how to devise a strategy of discourse to deal usefully with this dramatist who slips out of all the categories?

I hold Shepard before me as the subject of this essay. There he is, changing his skin as though by an annual molting; seeming, and often being, disorderly, sometimes to the point of chaos; obeying—until recently at any rate—no fixed or familiar principles of dramatic construction; borrowing, like an exultant magpie, from every source in or out of the theater; being frequently obscure, though never, I think, "willfully" so.

If there's a more nearly perfect exemplar of a cultural education gained ("absorbed" is a better word) in the fifties than Sam Shepard, I can't imagine who it might be. I first saw him at the Open Theater in 1965, a James Dean-like youth with an un-Dean-like intellectual glint in his eyes. Even after I'd overcome my initial dismay at such easy and untutored confidence, it took me a while to see that there wasn't any reason he couldn't be a playwright or anything else. For the fifties, out of which he came, or sidled, was the era in which two things started to happen of great importance to our subsequent culture. One was that the distance between "high" and "low" in art began to be obliterated, and the other was that the itch for "expression," for hurling the self's words against anonymity and silence, began to beat down the belief in the necessity for formal training, apprenticeship and growth, that had always been held in regard to drama or any art.

Shepard is much more than the product of these developments, but they do infect or, from another judgment, animate him in profound ways. He was born in Illinois but grew up in Southern California, and that vivid, disastrous milieu has been the psychic and imaginative ground of all his plays, whatever their literal geography might be. He has said that he lived in a "car culture for the young" and that the Southern California towns held a "kind of junk magic." In a few autobiographical fragments and elliptical interviews he tells of a life resembling that in the movie *American Graffiti,* only tougher, shrewder, more seeded with intimations of catastrophe in the midst of swagger.

Shepard seems to have come out of no literary or theatrical tradition at all but precisely from the breakdown or absence—on the level of art if not of commerce—of all such traditions in America. Such a thing is never a clean, absolute stride away from the ruins; fragments of tradition, bits of history, cling to every razed site and to one's shoes. But in his case one does see a movement with very little cultural time at its back, or only the thinnest slice of the immediate past, a *willed* movement, it might be said, for one sometimes suspects Shepard of wanting to be thought *sui generis,* a self-creation. That he must, for example, have been influenced by Jack Gelber's 1959 play *The Connection,* by some of Ronald Tavel's work, by certain aspects of Pinter and, more recently, by Edward Bond, as well as by elements of what we call theatrical "absurdity," are things he has never mentioned.

What we do know is that in a sense he's a writer in spite of himself. In 1971 he said that "I don't want to be a playwright, I want to be a rock and roll star . . . I got into writing plays because I had nothing else to do. So I started writing to keep from going off the deep end." Naturally, there's much disingenuousness in this, something tactical, but it oughtn't to be disbelieved entirely. Shepard's plays sometimes do give off a whiff of reluctance to being plays, a hint of dissatisfaction with the form. And his recent incarnation as a film actor increases our sense that he's had something else, or something additional, in mind all along.

For what was true for him when he started (as it was true for the general culture in its youthful sectors), was that a mode of expression existed more compelling, more seductive and more in affinity with the outburst of the personal than writing in the old high formal sense. In light of Shepard's rock ambitions, listen to him on the genre. It made, he said (without punctuation) "movies theater books painting and art go out the window none of it stands a chance against the Who the Stones and Old Yardbirds Credence Traffic the Velvet Underground Janis and Jimi . . . "

Nevertheless Shepard did pluck drama from outside the window and became a writer. But the influence of rock is major and pervasive, if most direct in his early plays. It can be seen in the plays' songs, of course, but also, more subtly, in a new kind of stage language, contemporary in a harsh, jumpy way, edging, as both rock lyrics and rock talk do, between psuedo-professional argot and a personal tone of cocksure assertion. It is almost hermetic at times, but one can always detect a type of savage complaint and a belligerent longing. Thematically, rock, or rather the legendary status of its star performers, provided the direct subject of *Suicide in bFlat* and *The Tooth of Crime.*

But rock isn't the only musical style Shepard employs. A whole range of other genres can be found: modern jazz, blues, country and western and folk music of several kinds. Shepard has always claimed, or others have on his behalf, that these musical elements are as important to many of his plays as their speech, and that the same thing is true for his decors. Indeed it's difficult to imagine much of his work without its music, by which I mean that it's not an embellishment or a strategic device, in the manner of Brecht, to interrupt the flow of a sequential narrative, but an integral part of the plays' devising of new consciousness.

Shepard's physical materials and perspectives come largely from developments in the graphic arts and dance during his adolescence and early career. He has said that Jackson Pollack was important to him, but what seems more active in his sensibility are emanations from the "happenings" phase of painting and sculpture, collage in the manner of Johns and Rauschenberg, and the mixed-media experiments of the latter artist with John Cage and others. His sets reveal all these influences at two extremes: their occasional starkness, a bare space in which lighting is the chief or only emotive or "placing" factor, and their frequent stress on dirt, *dreck*—the kitchen of *4-H Club,* "littered with paper, cans, and various trash," or the set for *The Unseen Hand,* composed of an "old '51 Chevrolet convertible, bashed and dented, no tires . . . garbage, tin cans, cardboard boxes, coca-cola bottles and other junk."

More generally, in regard to subject and reference, to iconography, we can observe a far-flung network of influences, interests and obsessions that have gone into the making of Shepard's work. The most substantial of these are the car or "road" culture of his youth, science-fiction, Hollywood Westerns and the myth of the West in general, and television in its pop or junk aspects. Besides these Shepard himself has mentioned "vaudeville, circuses . . . trance dances, faith healing ceremonials . . . medicine shows," to which we might add telepathic states, hallucinatory experiences (drug-induced or not), magic and witchcraft.

Eclectic as all this seems, something binds it together, and this is that nearly everything I've mentioned is to one degree or another an interest or engagement of the pop and counter cultures that had their beginnings in the fifties. When we reflect on what these movements or climates have left us—their presence is still felt in the form of a corpse not quite grown cold—a set of major impulses immediately emerges: a stance against authority and tradition, anti-elitism, the assertion of the untaught self in impatience and sometimes mockery.

But one sees in it all too—something most pertinent to a rumination on Shepard's plays—another and more subtle configuration: a world of discards and throwaways, of a *nostalgie de boue* appeased by landscapes filled with detritus and interiors strewn with debris, of floating images, unfinished acts, discontinuity and dissonance, abruptnesses and illogicalities; an impatience with time for proceeding instead of existing all at once, like space; and with space for having limits, fixed contours and finality.

This in large part is Shepard's theatrical world. I said that his plays emerged far more from new movements outside the theater than from within it, but what really happened can't be that clear. If he's never acknowledged any debt to the so-called Absurdists, or to any other playwrights for that matter, whether or not he learned directly from them scarcely matters. He learned alongside them, so to speak, or in their wake, in the same atmosphere of rejection of linear construction, cause and effect sequences, logical procedures, coherent or consistent characters, and the tying of language to explicit meanings that distinguished the new drama from its predecessors.

Except for its final phrases, a note to the actors preceding the text of *Angel City* might have been written by almost any avant-garde playwright of recent years, and in fact goes back in its central notion to Strindberg's revolutionary preface to *Miss Julie.* "The term 'character'," Shepard wrote, "could be thought of in a different way when working on this play. Instead of the idea of a 'whole character' with logical motives behind his behavior which the actor submerges himself into, he should consider instead a fractured whole with bits and pieces of characters flying off the central theme. Collage construction, jazz improvisation. Music or painting in space."

What distinguished Shepard's plays from most others in the new American repertoire was their greater vivacity and elasticity, even more their far greater impurity, the presence in them of so many energies and actions not previously thought properly dramatic. More than any other American playwright of the sixties, he broke down the fixed definitions of the dramatic. But doing this brought risks. He has said he wants to create "total" theater, and this ambition is both the spur to his triumphs and the clue to his delinquencies. For total theater, where everything is present at once, can result in a canceling-out, a murk and confusion.

If the American theater was ready for Shepard's wayward gifts, it was because it was ready for anything in the emptiness in which it then existed. In the late fifties and early sixties our theater was just beginning to catch up with developments in arts like painting and dance, and with the revolutionary changes in drama that had taken place in France with Beckett and Ionesco and, more modestly, in England with the early Pinter. Albee's first plays, Gelber's *Connection* and the work of the Living Theater were all signs and artifacts of a stirring here that was to result a couple of years later in the burgeoning of off and off-off Broadway. A major aspect of this was the creation of experimental, insurrectionary groups like the Open Theater, the Performance Group and others.

Shepard's first plays to be staged were done in New York in late 1964, and it's no accident that a few months later he appeared at the door of the Open Theater, for that body of actors, directors and writers was one of the centers of the upheaval.

This isn't the place for an extended discussion of Shepard's debt to the Open Theater, nor are the intellectual transactions between them entirely clear. What can be said is that Shepard learned something important about "transforma-tions," one of the group's main lines of exploration into both the psychology of the actor and the relationship between acting and formal texts. Briefly, a transformation exercise was an improvised scene—a birthday party, survivors in a lifeboat, etc.—in which after a while, and suddenly, the actors were asked to switch immediately to a new scene and therefore to wholly new characters. Among the aims (which were never wholly clear) were increased flexibility, insight into theatrical or acting clichés and more unified ensemble playing.

Shepard carried the idea of transformations much farther than the group had by actually writing them into his texts, in plays like *Angel City, Back Bog Beast Bait* and *The Tooth of Crime,* where characters become wholly different in abrupt movements within the course of the work, or speak suddenly as someone else, while the scene may remain the same. Besides this, Shepard has maintained a connection to the Open Theater's Joseph Chaikin . . .

More than that of any important playwright I know, Shepard's work resists division into periods, stages of growth or development. The only exceptions to this, once more, are the latest plays, which do seem to constitute a rough phase. Unlike the serial way in which we arrange most writers' work in our minds, the body of Shepard's writing seems present to us all at once, lying rudely sprawled across our consciousness, connected in all its parts less by organic adhesion than by a distinctive ebb and flow of obsession. Shepard doesn't move from theme to theme or image to image in the separate plays; he doesn't conquer a dramatic territory and move on, doesn't extend his grasp or refine it. What he does from play to play is lunge forward, move sideways, double back, circle round, throw in this or that, adopt a voice then drop it, pick it up again.

Most of his plays seem like fragments, chunks of various sizes thrown out from some mother lode of urgent and heterogeneous imagination in which he has scrabbled with pick, shovel, gunbutt and hands. The reason so many of them seem incomplete is that they lack the clear boundaries as artifact, the internal order, the progress toward a denouement (of some kind: a crystallization, a summarizing image, a poise in the mind) and the consistency of tone and procedure that ordinarily characterize good drama, even most avant-garde drama of the postwar time.

Many of his plays seem partial, capricious, arbitrarily brought to an end and highly unstable. They spill over, they leak. They change, chameleon-like, in self-protection as we look at them. This is a source of the difficulty one has in writing about them, as it's also a source of their originality. Another difficulty is that we tend to look at all plays for their single "meanings" or ruling ideas but find this elusive in Shepard and find, moreover, his plays coalescing, merging into one another in our minds. Rather than always trying to keep them separate, trying by direct plunges into their respective depths to find clear meanings tucked away like kernels within gorgeous ragged husks, I think we ought to accept, at least provisionally, their volatility and interdependence; they constitute a series of facets of a single continuing act of imagination.

Beyond this, and as an aspect of it, we have to see Shepard's work as existing in an especially intricate and disorderly relationship with life outside the theater. Such a relationship obviously is true of any drama, but in Shepard's case it shows itself as a rambunctious reciprocity in which the theatrical, as a mode of behavior, takes a special wayward urgency from life, while the living—spontaneous, unorganized and unpredictable—keeps breaking into the artificial, composed world of the stage.

There is a remark of John Cage's that's especially pertinent here: "Theater exists all around us and it is the purpose of formal theater to remind us that this is so." Much of Shepard's energy and inventiveness are given (undeliberately, of course; as part of the action of being an artist) to this kind of reminder; his theater is as much about theater as about the "real" world. Above all, it's about performing, and here the relations between art and life become particularly close.

There are indeed themes in his work—sociological, political, etc.—but the plays aren't demonstrations or enactments of them; they exist as dispositions, pressures, points of inquiry. And if there's any overriding vision it's this: our lives are theatrical, but it's a besieged, partly deracinated theater we act in. We want, as though in a theater, to be *seen* (the Greek root of "theater": a place for *seeing*), but there are great obstacles to this desire.

If it's not useful to search for the specific meanings of all Shepard's plays, then their general meaning or significance (or perhaps simply what these plays cause in our minds, what Henry James called the "thinkable" actions of drama) is something else. I want to start on the way toward that by contemplating the surfaces of this ungainly body of drama, and what more immediate data are there than Shepard's titles?

Most of his titles float, bob up and down from the plays on shorter or longer strings. They appear as aggressions, put-ons or parodies, but almost never as traditional titles in some direct or logical connection to the works. They seem crazily theatrical in themselves; they scare you or break you up before the curtain has even risen: *Dog; Killer's Head; 4-H Club; The Holy Ghostly; Cowboy Mouth; Shaved Splits; Fourteen Hundred Thousand; Back Bog Beast Bait; The Tooth of Crime; Blue Bitch; Action; The Mad Dog Blues; Angel City; Geography of a Horse Dreamer; Operation Sidewinder; Curse of the Starving Class; Forensic and the Navigators; Icarus's Mother.*

I don't know if it has been pointed out how these titles resemble the names of rock groups, or pieces of graffiti or certain writings on tee-shirts. They don't denote finished, discrete dramas as much as a continuing action, a calling of attention; they're less identifications than announcements.

This is also true of his characters' names, which are like knives, road-signs or trade-marks. There are some prosaic ones—Ed, Frank, Jill, Becky, Stu—but with these we think Shepard is playing a joke. The real names are and ought to be: Cherry and Geez and Wong; Shooter and Jeep; Shadow;

Beaujo and Santee; Forensic; Galactic Jack; Dr. Vector; Tympani; Hoss and Crow; Salem and Kent; Kosmo and Yahoodi; Miss Scoons; Sloe Gin Martin and Booger Montgomery; Gris Gris; Ice; Blood; Blade; Dukie; Dude. There are very few last names, for like the titles they're less identifiers than assertions.

It's as if these characters had named themselves or gone behind the playwright's back to get named by some master of hype, some poet of the juke-box. They're like movie starlets and a type of star—Rock, Tab, Tuesday; they're like rock personalities, even bands. Their names seek to confer one or another quality on their persons, soliciting us to read them as dangerous or alluring or zany—in any case as original. This is a function of nicknames or pseudonyms at any time, but in Shepard they're the names first given; his characters start with a flight from anonymity.

Some of them smack of science fiction, others of pop sensibility. They're partly japes, sly mockeries of staid naming in theater and life. But most of them aren't just tactical but move in our minds like signals from a particular human and geographical environment, one that vibrates simultaneously with sadness and violence, eccentricity, loneliness and self-assertion, bravado and the pathos of rootless existence. The "real" place is California and the Southwest; the site in our minds is American toughness and despair, danger and isolation. I think of rodeo riders, poker dealers, motorcycle gangs, bar hostesses, gangsters' sidekicks, hotrodders and drifters, killers on the plains, electric guitarists in roadhouses. And I think of the stars who would wear such epithet-like names if they didn't have to use reasonable ones.

In laying such emphasis on these names I naturally don't mean to suggest they can bear a weight of interpretation of the plays, only that they can help us toward the dramatic center. For if something like a "quest for identity" is central to Shepard's vision, as I think it is, then names, first clues to identity or its lack, are greatly instructive.

Now "quest for identity" is a flaccid term in popular psychology and perfunctory cultural criticism, and it has of course to do with the question of "who am I?" But is this a useful or even a true question, especially in the theater? Can we ever, in life, know who we are except in a formal, abstract way, as the result, say, of a Cartesian inquiry, a religious definition or membership in a human category? Might not the true questions in putting forth the self, certainly in the theater but also in life with its theatrical hunger, be "who do I seem to be?" and "what am I taken for?" And might not the quest for identity really be the quest for a *role*?

I intend nothing pejorative by this, nothing having to do with "role-playing" as a neurotic maneuver; but rather that we either take our places in a drama and discover ourselves as we act, or we remain unknown (as some indeed choose to do). In the reciprocal glances of the actors we all are, in our cues to dialogue, the perpetual agons and denouements that we participate in with others, identities are found, discarded, altered but above all *seen.* Not to be able to act, to be turned away from the audition, is the true painful condition of anonymity. But to try to act too much, to wish to star, the culmination and hypertrophy of the common desire, is a ripeness for disaster.

I think Shepard's shamanistic or totemistic names are the initial signs of his art's fundamental impulse. The selves behind the names, the characters, are avid to be but above all to be *seen* to be. I know this can be said in one way or another of the substance of all formal theater. Jarry once said that a playwright wants to "unleash" his characters on a stage, and Robbe-Grillet said of Beckett's Didi and Gogo that they have to "ad lib for their very lives." To write plays is to invent characters to live more visibly and perilously than oneself.

But what is remarkable about Shepard's plays is the way they display the new raw unstable anguish and wit that marks the self seeking itself now, and that they display with such half-demented, half-lyrical force the things that oppose this quest, its exacerbated American circumstances, which Shepard's own new raw questing sensibility has made its scene, obsession and poetry.

I believe that all Shepard's themes or motifs can be subsumed, even if loosely and with jagged projections everywhere, by this perspective. Consider the question of "roots," so stark or shadowy in his plays. To have roots is to have continuity and so a basis on which to act (a step to a step), to act in both senses of the word. Not to have roots is to risk acting on air. This is why I think the facts of Shepard's literal and cultural background are important. He couldn't have come from the East or North or at another time. In the West rootlessness is far more widespread and for many almost the condition of life. But at the same time the West, particularly California, is the place where, most acutely, visible success, gestures of self, personality, fame are means, conscious or not, of making up for or disguising the lack of roots.

Isn't it also the place—as a metaphor beyond its kleig lights and therapies and bronzed bodies—where energy and anguish, talent and emptiness, the hope of a name and the corruption of a self are the matings from which come a special piercing sense of dismay, which may be one thing we mean by the destruction of the "American Dream"?

"Identity" and "roots" merge as themes in Shepard. For if the American Dream means anything more than its purely physical and economic implications, it means the hope and promise of identity, of a "role" in the sense I indicated before. Inseparable from this is the hope of flexibility, of suppleness in the distribution of roles—the opportunities of being seen—such as was largely absent from the more fixed and closed European world. In turn this promise, sometimes fullfilled, is met with the ironic condition of rootlessness, lack of continuity and ground. The effect of this in Shepard's theater is either to crush or literally deracinate—tear the mind from *its* roots—the seeking self or to hyperbolize it into flamboyance, violence, or the ultimate madness, the fever for what we call "stardom."

The very "rootlessness" of Shepard's theater, its springing

so largely from a condition outside the continuity of the stage, is a source of the difficulty we have with it, as it is also a source of its dazzling disturbances. But inside his theater, within its own continuousness, a tragi-comic drama of names and selves unfolds. I think of the frantic efforts of so many of his characters to make themselves felt, often by violence (or cartoon violence—blows without injuries, bullets without deaths: dream or make-believe, something filmed), of the great strand in his work of the ego run wild, of the craving for altered states of being and the power to transcend physical or moral or psychic limitations—and the very alterations and transcendences of this kind carried out in the plays: the transformations, the splitting of characters, the masks, the roles within roles, the mingling of legendary figures with invented ones. And I think of the "turns," the numbers, the oratorios and arias, and especially the monologues or soliloquies that aren't simply contributions to the plot but outcries of characters craving to be known.

The monologues take many forms. One is a kind of technical disquisition, such as Jeez's on deer-skinning in *Shaved Splits* or Howard's on flying in *Icarus's Mother*. They may be prosaic or bizarre but they have the effect of claiming for the speaker an individuality based on some sort of detailed knowledge. More often the monologue is simply a "story," matter-of-fact or exotic, which may or may not contribute to the plot, but which always serves to distinguish the speaker as a voice, as someone with *something* to tell.

Occasionally such a monologue will contain within itself a crystallization or recapitulation of the play itself and of Shepard's angle of vision. A speech of this kind is Shooter's in *Action* about the risks and necessities of acting:

> . . . You go outside. The world's quiet. White. Everything resounding. Not a sound of a motor. Not a light. You see into the house. You see the candles. You watch the people. You can see what it's like inside. The candles draw you. You get a cold feeling being outside. Separated. You have an idea that being inside it's cosier. Friendlier. Warmth. People. Conversation. Everyone using a language. Then you go inside. It's a shock. It's not like how you expected. You lose what you had outside. You forget that there even is an outside. The inside is all you know. You hunt for a way of being with everyone. A way of finding how to behave. You find out what's expected of you. You act yourself out.

Another is Miss Scoons on the dream of stardom, in *Angel City*:

> I look at the screen and I am the screen . . . I look at the movie and I am the movie. I am the star . . . For days I am the star and I'm not me. I'm me being the star. I look at my life when I come down . . . and I hate my life when I come down. I hate my life not being a movie. I hate my life not being a star. I hate being myself in my life which isn't movie and never will be. I hate having to eat. Having to work. Having to sleep. Having to go to the bathroom. Having to get from one place to another with no potential. Having to live in this body which isn't a star's body and all the time knowing that stars exist . . .

The monologues are most often tight, staccato, gathering a strange cumulative eloquence. In their varied voices they reveal as nothing else does Shepard's marvelous ear, not for actual speech but for the imagined possibilities of utterance as invention, as victory over silence.

Everything I've been discussing converges in **The Tooth of Crime,** which I think is Shepard's greatest achievement, the one play which is most nearly invulnerable to charges of occlusion or arbitrary procedures, the one that rests most self-containedly, that seems whole, inevitable, *ended.* It contains his chief imaginative ideas and obsessions at their highest point of eloquence and most sinewy connection to one another. It exhibits his theatrical inventiveness at its most brilliant yet most uncapricious and coherent, and it reveals most powerfully his sense of the reciprocities of art and life. A splendid violent artifact, it broods on and wrestles with the quest not simply to be known but to be known inexhaustibly, magically, cosmically: the exaltation and tragedy of fame.

For this drama of confrontation between a rock "king" and his challenger, Shepard calls on an astonishing range of sources. The chief plot action, the eventual "shoot-out," is borrowed of course from Western movies and legends. But the play is more than its narrative; or rather, the true narrative, the tale of consciousness, is of the vivacity and anguish of the swollen name, the self propelled into a beleaguered exemplary condition in which the general need is fullfilled for some selves and names to be transfigured so that others may at least elbow into their light. The mobile levels of discourse, the amazing variety of textures serve to proffer and sustain a painful, refulgent myth, itself drawn from a public mythology, that greed for and apotheosis of *status* that began to gather intensity some years ago and rages without let-up now, so that we meet its vocabulary everywhere: "We"; "Us"; "Superstar"; "King of the Hill"; "Number One."

On a bare stage with its only prop an "evil-looking black chair," or throne, Shepard composes a drama whose main impulsions are the rage for competing, the savage jostling for the top that strangely implies there isn't enough fame to go round; and the dehumanization induced by celebrity, which converts true actions into poses, frozen stances. Hoss, the menaced king, says at one point that he'd be "O.K." if he " . . . had a self. Something to fall back on in a moment of doubt or terror or even surprise." And when Crow, his rival, who has been talking in a murderous insider's jargon, speaks normally once, Hoss says: "Why'd you slip just then? Why'd you suddenly talk like a person?"

The contest employs various "languages," some actual, others invented or mythical, to display the half-real, half-imagined ways we define ourselves by vying. The gunfighter metaphor is central, but there's also car talk, where you top through rare makes and horsepower, and a range of images from sports. Shepard brilliantly places the event in a deadly sci-fi world where computers determine rankings and an interplanetary commission guards the rules or "codes." Against this Hoss, who retains something of the older humanness, speaks of a time when "we were warriors" not

incarnate appetites, and when there was a correlation between style and being. In a greatly revealing speech he indicates the new distance between authenticity and appearance: "Just help me into the style. I'll develop my own image. I'm an original man, a one and only. I just need some help."

In the play's climactic moments Hoss makes a last effort to re-establish his rule over the new soulless domain where nothing is valued except the deified name. He describes himself as a "true killer," who "can't do anything false," who's "true to his heart . . . his voice . . . pitiless, indifferent and riding a state of grace." Upon which he breaks down and cries over and over "It ain't me!" The last word is Crow's, the victor: "Didn't answer to no name but loser. All that power goin' backwards . . . Now the power shifts and sits until a bigger wind blows." The power, the force of ego turned ruthless and mechanical, will reign in a world without grace or true light; only the blinding sterile "stars" remain in their pitiless hierarchy.

In his last three plays Shepard has withdrawn noticeably from the extravagant situations, the complex wild voices and general unruliness of the earlier work. His themes, so elusive before, seem clearer now, if not pellucidly so, his vision dwells more on actual society. Physical or economic circumstances play more of a part than before.

I said before that one has to go beyond the economic implications of the "American Dream," but you do start there. Having money is both a form of and a means to identity; it lets you act. More than that, money makes itself felt in America as a chief agency of the distortion of the human theater; it forces people into roles and out of them, and by its presence or absence it dictates the chief values of our dramas. The very pursuit of it, beyond sustenance, flattens out selves, converts them into instances of success or failure, makes the play we're in single-minded and soulless. Still, as Freud once said, money isn't a primal need of the psyche, and it isn't one for Shepard's characters.

In **Curse of the Starving Class** the family is poor but not hopelessly so; their material need isn't so much the question as the instigation to enact a deeper need. They're starving but not really physically. The set is a kitchen, images of food and eating abound, but the weight isn't on physical hunger as a motif and nothing indicates this better than the incident when to a depleted larder Weston brings an enormous number of artichokes. The absurdity of this is evident, but what it reveals is the way food operates as a metaphor for a quest and not its aim.

What they're really starved for is selfhood, distinctiveness, satisfying roles. On any level they refuse to be of the starving *class.* As Emma insists, they're different from those who are starving as a function of their *status,* their definition, which is obscurity. They struggle to emerge, be seen by others, escape from being members of a class, a category.

The "curse" is the dark side of the American Dream and is manifested in its victims partly through standardization, and the quantification of values imposed by lawyers, developers, ad-men, and the like (the "zombies . . . they've moved in on us like a creeping disease," Wesley says) and partly by the very distortions of the craving for selfhood that results in ill-fated measures to achieve it. Apart from Wesley the members of the family come to disastrous ends or these impend; only he, the quiet, somewhat deadened, unambitious one, has the right, if uncolorful, idea. He wants to remain on the seedy place, extend such roots as there are. He will settle for that role, that tiniest of bit parts.

In *Buried Child* the family to which the son, Vincent, returns is also poor, or marginal, but this isn't their *dramatic* condition. Vincent discovers that they don't know him, that in fact they're locked together in unknowingness, in a fixity of objectless rage and spiritual lameness. A struggle ensues between what we might call principles of movement and arrest. After fleeing the maimed scene, Vincent comes back to take over: "I've got to carry on the line. I've got to see to it that things keep rolling." The father, the incarnation of discontinuity, shouts that there's no past to propel a future. In the face of a photo from his youth, he insists: "That isn't me! That never was me! This is me. This is it. The whole shootin' match . . . "

The mysterious field behind the house that everyone knows to be arid nevertheless produces vegetables in abundance. The fantastic field is a metaphor for fecundity, of course, and at the same time works as a hope of future life against the bitter, hidden truth which emerges at the end in the form of the murdered, "buried" child. The childhood buried in the adult who has refused the connection and so the continuity? An image of the secret life of families, burying the issue of their lovelessness? I don't think the symbol or metaphor is susceptible of neat interpretation. But it remains, as does the play with all its loose ends and occasionally unconvincing events—Vincent's violent change near the end, for example—strong and echoing in the mind.

In its straightforwardness and sparseness of action *True West,* Shepard's newest play, is surely the least typical of all his works. Its protagonists, two brothers who somewhat resemble Lenny and Teddy in Pinter's *Homecoming* (as the play itself also resembles Pinter in its portentous pauses and mysterious references) clash over their respective roles. Lee, the drifter and man of the desert, envies Austin, the successful screenwriter and takes over his position by selling a producer on an "authentic" Western, one, that's to say, drawn entirely from his own matter of fact and therefore non-artistic, uninvented experience.

Austin, not an artist but a contriver of entertainment, nevertheless represents the imagination against Lee's literalness. Their battle shifts its ground until Austin, in the face of Lee's claim that his story reveals the 'true' West, retorts that "there's no such thing as the West anymore. It's a dead issue!" The myths are used up. Still, his own identity has been found within his work of manipulating popular myths and he finds himself draining away under the pressure of Lee's ruthless "realism." The play ends with Austin's murderous attack on his brother, a last desperate attempt to preserve a self.

A last word on *Tongues* and *Savage/Love* . . . Both are more theater pieces than plays. They're the outcome of Shepard's and Chaikin's experiments with a dramatic form stripped of accessories, of plot elements and physical action, reduced to essentials of sound and utterance. When they rise, as they sometimes do, to a point of mysterious and resilient lyricism, they reach us as reminders at least of Shepard's wide and far from exhausted gifts.

I suspect he'll astonish us again.

Sheila Rabillard   (essay date 1987)

SOURCE: "Sam Shepard: Theatrical Power and American Dreams," in *Modern Drama,* Vol. XXX, No. 1, March, 1987, pp. 58-71.

[*In the following essay, Rabillard notes the marked difference between Shepard's abstract early plays and his more realistic later work. The critic finds, however, that both styles are explorations of theatricality that exert a powerful hold on audiences and draw attention to the dramatic act.*]

The plays of Sam Shepard present some peculiar difficulties. There appears to be a wide split between the early and the later works, one that Shepard himself acknowledges. In an interview published in 1974 [in *Theatre Quarterly* IV, No. 15 (August-October 1974)], he announced that he was now trying for less flash and fewer mythic figures; in 1980 he told Robert Coe [in *New York Times Magazine,* (23 November)] that, although he had thought character a "corny idea," he was now becoming interested in it "on a big scale"; *True West* (1980), he told one interviewer [as recorded by Ellen Oumano in *Sam Shepard: The Life and Work of an American Dreamer* (1986)], was the first of his plays he could watch, night after night, without embarrassment. This division is reflected in the response to Shepard which is in itself problematic: the plays before *Curse of the Starving Class* (1977), especially when they first appeared, were generally received with a good deal of bafflement even from the directors who presented them; the later plays have enjoyed much wider acceptance, but some of the popular response seems to be directed not so much to the plays themselves as to a clichéd patina enveloping Shepard and the dissolution of the American Dream. The second, and related, difficulty lies in the power Shepard exercises over an audience, a power that may well make the spectator uneasy. For the early plays can strike one as somehow meretricious, mere show-biz, a collection of *coups de théâtre* floating untethered by character, plot, or theme; while the later plays, with their apparently more conventional and realistic anchoring, hold the spectator with a force that one can scarcely attribute to themes so readily reducible to cliché. How does Shepard take his audience so violently? Is one merely being "taken"?

In a sense the plays, both early and later, are undeniably sequences of spectacular theatrical effects: violent confrontations between characters; sudden and bizarre transformations in the roles characters play; striking gestures and images that compel attention without yielding to interpretation. The audience is drawn and held—but not meretriciously. I propose that Sam Shepard's dramas can be regarded as, in some essential respects, explorations of theatricality. With the help of analytical categories outlined in Anne Ubersfeld's *Lire le Théâtre,* it is possible to examine how Shepard uses or disqualifies certain semiotic practices. Such an analysis, I suggest, provides a way of describing the sources of Shepard's power over his audience and reveals some vital connections between the earlier plays and the later, at first glance more realistic and illusionistic, works.

A collection of earlier plays, *Five Plays by Sam Shepard* (1967), includes introductory notes by directors who, for the most part, failed to create successful Shepard productions. Their complaints are instructive: "When I read [*Icarus's Mother* (1965)], I couldn't tell the characters apart—and Sam said he doesn't think about characters." "It's always hard to tell what, if anything, Sam's plays are 'about'." One director records that he made the staging of *Fourteen Hundred Thousand* (1966) more dynamic, made its opening scenes more realistic, and, as the characters approached stasis in the later scenes, used the actors expressionistically. Shepard, who was observing, declared his efforts "unacceptable." What these directors [Michael Smith and Sydney Schubert Walter, respectively] found unproduceable in Shepard is precisely what I argue is most theatrical. Here it is that he strips away elements traditional to realistic drama—psychologically detailed character, developed themes, shapely and consistently-moving plots—in order to concentrate upon the bare bones that remain and to explore the nature of the theatrical event.

Shepard's plays defy easy categorization, but the attempt to apply a familiar taxonomy may help to clarify their character. The early plays are, in some sense, abstract, yet they seem neither expressionist nor symbolist. They have none of the symbolist aura of mystery—there is too much of the comic in them, and most symbolic readings so far offered seem too restrictive for the disorderly life of dramas such as *Chicago* (1965), or *Red Cross* (1966). Nor do these plays focus, expressionistically, on a mind's experience—although one does encounter in *The Mad Dog Blues* (1971), and perhaps in *True West,* the consciousnesses of two characters alternately shaping the world of the play. Shepard may come closest to theatre of cruelty, for he does shock the spectator, yet an overwhelming emotional experience is not the centre of Shepard's drama. It may be significant in this regard that Shepard disliked Richard Schechner's production of *The Tooth of Crime,* and distanced himself from Schechner's assault upon the audience, remarking [as quoted by Oumano] that the spectator doesn't have to be "physically sloshed into something" to be participating. Shepard seems, thus, to allow the spectator a certain amount of observational distance from the performance. Shepard's early plays are abstract in the sense that (while inevitably composed of elements bearing culturally coded "messages") they seem to convey no overall "message." But they move beyond mere emotional experience into exploration of structures peculiar to dramatic performance, particularly those of theatrical speech.

It seems unnecessary to argue that Shepard's early plays break with psychological realism although, as I have mentioned, a number of actors, directors, and audiences who first confronted them had difficulty abandoning realistic expectations to meet their demands. However, by examining Shepard's rents in the tissue of realistic illusion, one can observe the nature of the abstraction he achieves, and the effect that it has on his audience. In more traditional, psychologically realistic drama the spectator looks not only for what the play as a whole means, but also for what the characters mean by what they say and do. Shepard makes both kinds of response difficult in a play such as *Icarus's Mother.* Bill, Howard, Jill, Pat, and Frank, the characters, are given first names only; their formal relations to one another, ties of blood, marriage, or friendship, are never disclosed. As the one-act play opens, they are outdoors, near a beach, where they appear to have just recently finished a picnic, and are waiting for fireworks to begin. (Is it the Fourth of July? We are not told.) A jet plane appears overhead, and the various characters respond to it differently—Howard and Bill react aggressively, as if it were an intruder, the women Jill and Pat become giggly and beckon it down, signalling sexual invitations. The pilot writes the message "$E = MC^2$" in the sky. Howard and Bill send up smoke signals from a blanket flapped over their barbeque fire. Are they, too, calling the pilot down? Perhaps they are, for next they tell the women that the plane has crashed and exploded and, when Jill and Pat run to the beach to view the debris, they witness instead the crash which only now takes place. One can gather from this plot summary that in this early play characters simply do things to one another; there is no apparent reason why Howard and Bill are aggressive, but Frank not, nor why Howard and Bill should lie to the women (if indeed they are lying, and not predicting or commanding the plane's fall).

Hence the spectator is not distracted from the present events on the stage by any explanatory motivation; Shepard thus reveals a skeletal structure of power, in which words function as power tools. To put it another way, the words spoken by the characters in the play are the bearers of power, rather than of meaning. Without a developed context they convey virtually nothing about the character's thoughts or feelings and can scarcely be interpreted (are statements seriously intended? jocular? speculative?) by spectator or by actor. One director of the early plays found that the only way to proceed was to instruct the actors not to look for meaning in words and actions but simply to perform them. "The actors were thereby able to abandon . . . what was 'natural' or 'organic' for the character and to show instead a strong image of what the character was doing" [Jacques Levy, in *Five Plays by Sam Shepard*]. In this presentational, anti-realistic style, words simply sound on the stage and produce an effect on their hearers—both spectators and listening characters. Near the opening of *Icarus's Mother,* for example, the characters gang up on Pat, who wants to go for a walk, and batter her into immobility with descriptions of the mishaps she will suffer if she goes. What the characters say is what they do to each other. Indeed, the function of words is indicated when Howard and Bill's description of the jet's crash seems almost to cause it. This quality of the speech in Shepard's drama has been remarked upon,

Shepard as Eddie in the 1985 film adaptation of Fool for Love.

especially in reference to **The Tooth of Crime** where words are clearly weapons. Shepard himself [in an essay in *The Drama Review* 21, No. 4 (December 1977)] has said that the character Crow "just appeared. He spit words that became his weapons. He doesn't 'mean' anything." In other plays, Shepard's characters combat one another in an analogous fashion, not by adopting competing verbal styles, as in **Tooth,** but by creating conflicting scenarios. In a sense, of course, words are characters' means of acting upon one another in any play, but Shepard exposes this function of theatrical language to us by removing virtually any other.

Shepard's paring away focuses attention on another aspect of the theatrical play of power as well—the power that commands the spectator's view. Since no clear, unitary, conscious themes draw the spectator's attention—the play has been variously interpreted as a political drama of aggression and external threat, a depiction of nuclear disaster, the flight of Icarus from his mother, a giant, explosive sexual climax—one's gaze is forced upon what happens on the stage, and one's mind cannot veer away to elaborate a private interpretation. The eternal present of the theatrical event is heightened, too, for, with no sense of detailed character psychology, and no realistic plot drawing a chain of causes and effects, the viewer is not tempted to construct in

imagination probable pasts and futures. We are in the present moment of the performance.

At a still more essential level, certain functions of theatrical discourse come to the fore: first, what Anne Ubersfeld calls the dramatic text's fundamental trait, the conative function whose mode is imperative. Ubersfeld adapts her terms from Jakobson; theatrical discourse is conative when it commands: characters may command one another to do something, of course, but the written text of the play's dialogue (just as much as the stage directions) commands that the dialogue be *said* on the stage, and indirectly conditions visual and auditory signs. Seemingly emptied of content, the text of **Icarus's Mother** becomes a series of orders for the presentation of what is to be seen and heard on stage. Every line of the text instructs, "speak me." The spectator is made aware of the author commanding, in different senses, his characters and his actors, and hence dictating the stimuli the spectator experiences. Second, Shepard frequently reduces the dialogue of **Icarus's Mother** to its phatic function. The phatic, according to Ubersfeld (who again draws upon Jakobson), is that function of discourse that says "I am speaking to you, do you hear me?" Taken to the extreme, as in certain Beckett dialogues, theatrical discourse can be entirely phatic. One can think of exchanges in *Waiting for Godot* with no "content"; they simply maintain or demand contact. . . . Similarly, as conversations in Shepard's play seem to be about nothing, their only content becomes the very act of communication and the conditions of its exercise:

PAT. It's skywriting.

HOWARD. No, it's not skywriting. It's just a trail. A gas trail.

PAT. I thought it was.

FRANK. It's gas.

BILL. I don't like it. I don't like the looks of it from here. It's distracting.

FRANK. It's a vapor trail. All jets do it.

BILL. I don't like the way he's making it. I mean a semicircle thing like that. In a moon shape.

JILL. I like it.

BILL. If he knows what he's doing, that means he could be signaling or something.

FRANK. Jets don't signal.

PAT. It's gas, Bill.

The phatic functioning of language between characters is perhaps its most obvious level of operation: witness the number of critics who have remarked upon the way in which Shepard's protagonists put on performances intended to force an opposing character into the role of receptive audience. Coe comments, for example, on the ferocity of the struggle between Hoss and Crow in *The Tooth of Crime* [Robert Coe, in an essay in *American Dreams: The Imagination of Sam Shepard,* ed. by Bonnie Marranca (1981)]; and others have noticed the interesting reversal in *Red Cross* when the maid, at first an almost literally captive audience for Jim's rantings, succeeds in making him listen to her fantasy. In Shepard's hands, however, drama stripped to its essentials reveals that language in the theatre performs a complex web of phatic functions. One further aspect of the phatic is suggested by Kenneth Chubb's report [in *Theatre Quarterly* 4 (1974)] of the acting style he discovered was most suited to a number of the early plays, including *Icarus's Mother*: the actors should admit, both as characters and as actors, that they are playing roles, and thus "play" the audience as a comedian or a singer does; especially in *The Tooth of Crime,* they should do a "turn" like that of a musical star—"deliver" to the audience. In other words, the appropriate acting style Chubb found is one that emphasizes the phatic function of the words spoken by character and by actor—the appeal "listen to me," "hear me perform."

As Shepard's "contentless" play sensitizes the spectator to the phatic functioning of the discourse, he realizes that not only does character say to character, in effect, "I speak to you, do you hear me?" but also actor says this to audience,

actor to actor, and perhaps in some sense author to audience. In Ubersfeld's words, the phatic function makes the spectator aware of the conditions of communication and of his own presence as an auditor in the theatre. One might add that it makes him feel his participation in a kind of verbal exercise of power. In isolating and heightening certain elements of the theatrical event, Shepard discloses to the spectator structures of theatrical discourse and invites him to become aware of exercises of power: not only the author's power to command what is shown and spoken on stage, but the phatic functioning of language by which an auditor—actor, character, the spectator in the auditorium—is held. Jacques Levy, one of the more successful directors of Shepard's early work, asserts [in *Five Plays*] that Shepard is "more interested in doing something to his audience than in saying something to them," but Shepard does more: he makes them conscious of what is being done to them and of their role in a theatrical event.

In the later Shepard, as many critics have noted, there appear to be more realistic characterization, more accessible and coherent plotting, even rather boldly drawn Big American Themes: decay and alienation in family and society; the son's struggle to escape a poisoned heritage; the artist's isolation in a commercial culture; the self-made man and the horrors of solipsism; dreams—or nightmares—of wealth, freedom, the frontier; and so on. Here is Richard Gilman, for instance, commenting on Shepard in 1981 [in the introduction to *Sam Shepard: Seven Plays* (1981)]:

> Shepard has withdrawn noticeably from the extravagant situations, the complex wild voices and general unruliness of the earlier work. His themes, so elusive before, seem clearer now, if not pellucidly so, and his vision dwells more on actual society. Physical or economic circumstances play more of a part than before.

But these critics would not, I think, want to argue that Shepard has turned to a realistic exploration of psychological, social, or political themes. Shepard employs the trappings of kitchen-sink realism only to dispel its illusion the more effectively. Gilman goes on to say that Shepard's drama, above all, is about performing. These plays are equally theatre about theatre.

The themes a spectator may derive from these later Shepard plays seem strangely over-scale and blatant in part because Shepard suggests them by means of signs already culturally and theatrically coded. In *Fool for Love* (1983), for example, or *True West* (1980), we encounter a cowboy loner; in *Seduced* (1976) a Howard Hughes figure; *Buried Child* (1978) presents another mysterious loner, Tilden, as well as Vince, a young man driving the roads of America seeking his origins and identity. *Curse of the Starving Class* (1977) deals with the threatened loss of the old homestead. This is theatre constructed from the stuff of Hollywood. Further, the later plays frequently acknowledge their own theatricality—recognizing the audience's presence, for example—and emphasize the tools of the stage. At the climax of *Buried Child,* Vince narrates his attempt at flight in a long speech delivered to the audience, facing front. Often, Shepard draws attention to the physical properties of the stage by having a character bring some startling prop on to what is usually a rather bare set: Wesley of *Curse of the Starving Class* deposits a lamb in the middle of the kitchen; Tilden keeps carrying huge piles of vegetables into the living room in *Buried Child*; the protagonist of *Seduced* arranges and rearranges two potted plants, the only living objects in his otherwise sterile environment, like an extremely nervous set designer. As these props are frequently organic, or even alive, they have the further effect of emphasizing the unreality of the set. While a lamb or carrot on stage fulfils an iconic function, it does not represent in the way that a structure of canvas and lath stands for a wall, nor is it able to act being itself, as an actor can.

Ubersfeld notes that the text of a play is "troué"—much has to be supplied by the actors, the directors, and the imagination of the audience. Shepard's dramas are more than usually "holey"; coincidences and improbabilities are unexplained, vital pieces of information are not provided. Both grandmother and grandson in *Buried Child* disappear for mysteriously long periods of time. The carrots and the corn Tilden brings in come, he claims, from the back yard, but his mother insists that nothing has grown there for years. Does "The Countess" in *Fool for Love* really exist? How did she track down her cowboy lover, and why should she want to destroy his truck and horses? Further, realism is often deliberately flouted in staging, dialogue, and incident. The clearest example here is *Fool for Love,* in which the stage directions instruct that the supposed headlights that shine through the motel window should not look like real headlights, and drums should be attached to the doors of the set so that when they are slammed they will boom unnaturally. The "holes" and the breaches of realism further Shepard's exploration of theatricality by making the spectator aware of his place in the auditorium, of his efforts to interpret.

In a number of Shepard's plays the past—which might be expected to supply the audience with the origins and meaning of the conflicts they view—is itself the subject of dispute. Was the buried child in the play of that name Tilden's or Dodge's? Was the dead son Ansel a basketball hero as his mother claims? In *Fool for Love,* Eddie and May tell conflicting stories of their parents and of their own past relationship, both to each other and to May's "date." Far from providing the spectator with the motivations of the characters on stage before him, the past becomes shifting and multiple—a fiction created by the characters in conflict with one another. This undecidable past not only disturbs conventions of realism, but reminds the spectator of the functioning of language in the theatre: though the present can be represented in part by objectivities (in Ingarden's terms) which the audience perceives—decor, actors, gestures, and so forth—the past must be represented exclusively through the characters' dialogue [Roman Ingarden, *The Literary Work of Act* (1973)]. To be sure, the past is represented linguistically in narrative fiction as well; but in the case of a novel, there is no peculiar contrast between the means of representing past and present.

As in the earlier plays, thus, Shepard's characters seem to exist in a vivid present only. Shepard does not allow the

audience to explore, in imagination, motivations, causes and past influences, with any satisfaction or confidence. Characters' behaviour seems inexplicable, obsessive, or perhaps merely conventionalized. In *Buried Child,* Vince seeks because he is a seeker. His girlfriend Shelly, expostulating with him and trying to understand, exists almost solely for the purpose of pointing up his want of comprehensible motive. Eddie and May simply come together in *Fool for Love*'s motel room with a simultaneous attraction and repulsion whose violence is not really explained at all by the fact of their semi-incestuous blood tie. Likewise the fierce competition between the two brothers and between father and son in *Buried Child* is a given. One scarcely needs to add that it is a recurrent motif in Shepard's work.

Shepard employs equally non-realistic transformations of character—absolute reversals of action, or peculiar transferences of behaviour from one character to another. In *Curse of the Starving Class,* Wesley assumes his father's patterns of action when he puts on his parent's clothing while, at the same time, the father Weston abruptly casts off his former drunkenness as if his son had somehow taken on his demon. Vince inherits his grandfather's house and possessions in *Buried Child* and is possessed by the madness and misery of the family that had lived there. Such transitions are so abrupt, indeed, that they seem almost analogous to the startling role shifts in earlier plays like *Cowboys #2* (1967), *The Mad Dog Blues* (1971), and *Action* (1974), where Shepard appears to be recalling the transformation exercises he observed during his contacts with the Open Theater.

Realistic motivations are thus peeled away; but while the later plays clearly defy readings based upon psychological realism, neither do they yield themselves to wholly satisfactory symbolic interpretations—the results of such an approach tend toward clichéd statements of theme that seem inadequate to one's experience of the plays. *Curse of the Starving Class* might serve as a paradigm: it disturbs the audience with a peculiarly unresolved clash of disparate elements. The realistic story of a farm family's financial and emotional struggles never merges with an underlying narrative of a tainted heritage, and when the dialogue seems to rise toward myth and symbol, in the tale of the cat and the eagle, Shepard has evaded proposed interpretations with the dismissive statement that his source for the beasts' struggle was a comic book [reported by Oumano]. For the spectator weighing multiple interpretive possibilities, events on stage become, more and more, simply things performed—what the playwright has ordered to be said and done, through the words of his text. Words spoken, while they are still pseudo-statements of the characters, resound with their conative function; they demand their own utterance.

When Shepard breaks open the illusion of realism he exposes theatrical language in its phatic function as well. In these later plays, the phatic is made particularly prominent by the recurrent intrusion into the dialogue of a verbal device that links the recent drama with Shepard's earlier and more abstract work: "arias," extended speeches, sometimes almost two pages long, usually narrative. The precursors of these extended narrative "arias" are the jazz-like riffs of plays such as *The Tooth of Crime.* And there, in the earlier play, their phatic function is patently clear: Hoss and Crow alternately give vent to long extravaganzas of verbal display in competition for the top of the charts, for the most listeners to their songs. (I am considering the musical aspect of their competition; there are, of course, suggestions of a criminal struggle for gang territory as well.) Some of the more recent "arias" are addressed to other characters on stage: Dodge recites his will in the presence of Bradley, Vince, and Shelly in *Buried Child*; Halie in the same play narrates the loss of her son, Ansel, as she descends the staircase into the living-room where Dodge and Tilden are sitting. Wesley, in *Curse of the Starving Class,* rehearses, while his mother cooks, an account of being awakened in the night by his father's drunken return. In such instances, the extraordinary length of the speeches reveals their phatic purpose—the character's need to hold the ears of his listeners. And, frequently, the other characters on stage give little satisfaction on this count. At the close of Wesley's lyrical recital, for example, his mother ignores his speech completely and begins to talk about the onset of menarche as if she were addressing her daughter Emma, although she is now alone in the kitchen; moreover, she commences apparently in the middle of a lengthy explanation as though she had already begun her own "aria," silently, while Wesley was still speaking. As so often in Shepard's world, there is need to demand a hearing.

At the same time as these speeches attempt to exert power over characters on stage, they are also making demands on the audience's attention. Every word spoken on stage, of course, asks to be heard, and an actor is always speaking in part as actor attuned to the audience's attention at the same time as he speaks as character. But in these cases the peculiar unbroken length of the speech underlines its phatic function. Shepard emphasizes the actor's (and the author's) attempt to establish contact when he directs that Vince's narrative of his drive should be delivered not to Shelly, who has asked where he has been, but "facing front." Some of Shepard's "arias" do not even pretend to be directed to another character—for example, Weston in *Curse of the Starving Class* narrates the battle of the eagle and the cat, according to the stage directions, to the lamb penned in the kitchen. Wesley overhears the close of the speech and asks how the battle turned out, but is told he has heard the story already—it is not being recited for him. In fact, it seems to be recited for Weston himself; turned in upon itself; thus, the speech suggests the nature of the hunger behind the need to be heard. Even if the auditor is oneself, there is some satisfaction in speaking to a listening ear. Ingarden has suggested that when one speaks, one ripens one's thoughts and becomes more conscious of them in the hearing; this self-influencing of the speaker by his act of expression allows him to catch hold of, and make real, aspects of himself that slip away, incomplete, in the silent life of thought. It is, of course, even more sustaining and affirming of the self if one's speech, and the thought developing in it, are understood and accepted by another person.

Finally, in certain of Shepard's plays the need expressed by this recurrent verbal device is played out on a larger, thematic scale. The familiar competition between two men

closely tied by blood takes shape in *True West* as a contest, in part, to seize the ear of a movie executive with a truer narrative of the manly west. And the film-business characters of *Angel City* (1976) pursue the dream of holding an audience literally spell-bound, entranced. Both dramas, since they deal with script writing, hint that Shepard is slyly aware of the artist's own phatic use of language and his particular hunger to compel an auditor.

By all of these means, then, the spectator is made aware of the stage, made aware of his attention fixed upon what is said and done in the present instant, made aware of the complex structures of power, the conative and phatic functioning of theatrical discourse. The earlier plays, thus, are not mere appeals to the senses, nor are the Big American Themes of the cowboys and seekers of the later plays in any simple sense the real source of Shepard's power. At the centre of Shepard's dramas, throughout his career, is an exploration of theatricality. It is an exploration that grows progressively richer and even thematically suggestive as Shepard moves away from the more abstract examination of theatrical event and brings into his plays evocative images from the American cultural landscape.

In the context of the American icons Shepard imports into the later plays, his stress upon the phatic and conative functions of theatrical discourse becomes a revelation of an American phenomenon: this is the culture of theatricality, where all speech is for the sake of its power to command attention and words are thus a tool of violent dominance. The truth of which Shepard's non-illusionistic drama reminds us—that we are in the theatre—takes on an added significance. As Ubersfeld says, the theatre of realism causes a "dénégation," for it creates an illusion of "real life" but is, of course, unreal. When theatricality announces itself, however, one accepts that it tells the truth. ("*Je suis le théâtre, alors sur ce point la dénégation se renverse; puisqu'il est bien vrai que nous sommes au théâtre.*") This is a phenomenon in which, we realize, we participate as we sit in the theatre submitting to demands that we listen, gazing at spectacular displays that command, "look at me." In Sam Shepard's theatre we play the role of victims subject to that violent American theatricality and at the same time play the audience with the power to feed or deny the all-pervading hunger to be seen, to be heard.

Shepard's most recent play, *A Lie of the Mind* (1986), provides an uncomfortable test case for this hypothesis. It is difficult to argue that, with this play, narrative interest and psychologically realistic characterization are disturbed so as to focus attention on the structures and language of performance. To be sure, there is an almost unrealistic extremity of violence in the play and, as in previous Shepard dramas, an intrusive object to disrupt the decorum of the set—a deer carcase. In the New York production of the play directed by Shepard himself, live country music played as overture and during two intermissions set a tone of cheatin', hurtin', and drinkin', and by suggesting stereotypical roles added a degree of abstraction to the drama. In comparison to previous plays, however, *A Lie of the Mind* allows much more of its realistic illusion to remain intact.

If there is an exploration of theatricality here it lies in this play's novel focus on women. With some warrant, actress Joyce Aaron [in an essay in *American Dreams*] once complained that her friend Shepard had written no good female roles. Shepard is recorded as telling an interviewer [Michiko Kakutani, in the *New York Times* (29 January 1987)] that there was "more mystery to relationships between men." In *A Lie of the Mind,* however, particularly in the character of Beth, Shepard creates much richer women's roles than ever before. The depiction of Beth's painful and partial recovery from brain damage surely draws some of its strength from two experiences Shepard has already dealt with in print: Joyce Aaron's regression to inarticulacy during a bad drug trip, and his mother-in-law's mutilated existence after brain surgery. Through the women's roles, he examines the difference—and the threat—of female theatricality.

Under Shepard's direction, *A Lie of the Mind*'s women characters have a stage presence different from the men's. Much of the play's humour comes from the women's lines, because they are self-regarding in a way that the men are not; they act as their own audiences, and see themselves as they are seen. Lorraine, for example, retreats to bed in her son Jake's room exactly as he has done earlier in the play. She too curls up in a foetal position under the suspended model airplane. But she is aware of the incongruity of her rounded form under the blankets juxtaposed with the memory of his angular anguish. She is distraught, she wants very much to retreat from the world, but she cannot remain long in this position she can see looks ridiculous. Meg, Beth's mother, also observes herself from the audience's viewpoint. She knows her requests to the menfolk to track less dirt and refrain from swearing in the house fall on deaf ears, and she plays the ditherer, ineffectual and ignored, with a rueful touch of self-mockery. In this role, the actress Louise Latham laughed at her character, but without ever breaking out of character; for Meg continually observes herself, and the actress thus earned a great many laughs from self-mocking cues to the audience. At least when the women hold the stage, the spectators at this play are not the victims of a violent comandeering of attention, but sharers in the women's self-regarding gaze. The men, in contrast, played their roles with no trace of self-mockery.

There are some curious implications, not only in the sexually differentiated performance styles, but also in the plot of *A Lie of the Mind.* While here, as in other plays, man may strive to hold an audience, affirming himself by performing and controlling, woman perceives herself as others see her and defines herself in those terms. Even for herself an object, her performing entails an entirely different kind of dependence upon an audience. What does it mean, then, when the character Beth plays a loose woman in a local theatrical performance? The logic of the plot shows that, perceived as a tramp, she is one. This shift in identity is what her husband Jake fears, and what drives him to beat her with passionate brutality. And, brain-damaged by his jealous assault, she enters a childlike state; in this condition her affections are completely indiscriminate, and she cuddles happily with Jake's brother in lieu of him. Under Shepard's direction, Beth dresses in the gaudiest clothes she can find in the final scene, with a tellingly ambivalent effect:

she looks equally like a child playing dress-up and like a hooker. This is not, in short, an *Othello* play but almost *Othello* inside-out; the dangerousness of woman's performance is confirmed—the curious alliance between what she appears to others and what she is. *A Lie of the Mind* may indicate the direction Shepard's writing will take in the future; in all of the plays that precede it, however, Shepard exposes the violence of male, rather than the dangers of female, theatricality.

In Shepard's hands, then, theatrical performance penetrates the thematic. Indeed, Shepard reveals the desolateness of a theatrical culture—the desperate acting in a "theatre of indifference" that the critic John Berger [in an essay in *The Sense of Sight,* ed. by Lloyd Spencer (1985)] describes as the condition of modern urban society. Shepard's reduction of the functions of language to their performative essentials—words used merely to demand attention or compel compliance—reflects the decay of the fabric of society. The flesh-and-blood actor on stage assumes the role of a Shepard character, but the character performs like an actor before an audience, speaking lines not so much because he intends what they mean, as in order to have his performance regarded, his presence and power felt. Shepard anatomizes a profound need for audience. His exploration of theatricality moves beyond the superficial exhibitionism of popular American culture, beyond the violence of male performance, to suggest the deeper anxieties of modern western society.

According to Berger, most public life in the city has only the coherence of a theatre in which living caricatures—not of character, but of performance—strive for an audience.

> The indifference is between spectator and performer . . . The experience of every performer—that's to say everyone—has led him to believe that, as soon as he begins, the audience will leave, the theatre will empty. Equally, the experience of every spectator has led him to expect that the performance of another will be irrelevant and indifferent to his own personal situation.
>
> Performing in the theater of indifference inevitably leads to assuming and cultivating exaggerated expressions . . . The most usual final appeal to the departing audience is violence. This may be in words (swearing, threats, shouts), in grimaces, or in action. Some crimes which take place are the theatre's purest expression.

Shepard employs none of the socialist analysis that underpins Berger's description; he begins with the nature of theatrical performance and by exploring its structures and heightening the audience's sensitivity to them allows the spectator to experience, in Berger's words, the way in which exaggeration and violence become habitual, and the violence that lies in the *address* of the performer's exaggeration *to* an audience. Nor does Shepard contrast, as Berger does, the theatre of indifference of modern urban society with traditional European village life where the drama, though no less artificial, is one in which "both the principal protagonists and the audience have a common interest." Shepard may betray a certain longing for a time and place in the "true west" when men could be partners—but, as in

Cowboys #2, it seems to belong now solely to the realm of play. Shepard presents not a rural/urban division of experience, but a national condition, a world in which "only one thing can defeat indifference: a star performance."

THE TOOTH OF CRIME

PRODUCTION REVIEWS

Robert Cushman (review date September 1972)

SOURCE: A review of *The Tooth of Crime,* in *Plays and Players,* Vol. 19, No. 228, September, 1972, pp. 49-50.

[The Tooth of Crime *was first produced at London's Open Space Theatre in 1972. In the following review of that performance, Cushman criticizes the play as being a simplistic story of dueling musicians.*]

I must begin, like everybody else, by quoting the programme note, though since it was prefaced by the injunction 'NB' I am perhaps only doing my duty: 'A good deal of this play has been written in an "invented language" derived from contemporary American idioms such as sports vernacular, underworld slang and musicians' jargon.' The warning was pasted onto the programme on a separate slip and was presumably the product of last-minute alarm. It proved in the end to be a source of consolation as well as apprehension since however hip the Open Space audience might consider itself to be, it was hardly to be blamed for failing to grasp three unfamiliar argots simultaneously.

Statistics should show that in the first act of Sam Shepard's play the three were given about equal representation. This meant that when the text was not obscure it was—not ambiguous; amtriguous, I suppose. There is this character called Hoss, and he was a successful sportsman/criminal/rock musician—by turns and in ascending order of likelihood. The options were kept cleverly open, the dialogue veering whenever it seemed possible to settle for a single solution. Hoss might of course have been plain versatile; as putative boss-man of Las Vegas he surely needed to be. He was at any rate about to have his supremacy challenged, his throne (he really had one) usurped.

Shakespearean usage comes easy at the Open Space these days. Launched on this parenthesis I may as well point out that Hoss slumped on his throne (with his girl sat down before him holding a knife in each hand) looked remarkably like Macbeth, and that his young opponent was got up like a tattered avenging Hamlet, whose arrival at court, surveying the territory in silent contemptuous confidence like a rooster about to take over the barnyard, provided a generally muddy evening with the first of two crystal moments.

In the second half the scene begins to contract. We settle for Hoss as a singer—a country singer when you really get down to his roots—and for Crow, his rival, as the new loose rocker who is to unseat him, and who predictably ends up in full possession of all the glory that once was Hoss: mansion, retinue and girl, all of them ready to desert him in favour of the next contender.

The battle of song between Hoss and Crow is fairly diverting, and the referee has the sense to stop the fight before boredom supervenes (we had been promised a daunting number of rounds). But the defeat of one pop-style by another—is that all there is? And if the moral is that those who live by style shall perish by it, it rebounds onto the play itself. Baffled by the dialogue, we could only laugh in relief each time a familiar name floated by. In this play Mr Shepard is as much the prisoner of his language as Christopher Fry ever was.

But I promised you another magic moment. When Hoss is sprawling on the ropes he has—I think—a memory of his past and what he remembers is a girl he once seduced, undressing her while she made desperate small talk and pretended not to notice. Petronella Ford plays both the girl defending her virtue and Hoss's hand, stripping her of it, and she is stunning in both roles. She has, to be sure, considerable assistance from the text; the scene has built-in suspense (how much is she going to take off?) and commands our grateful attention by its use of simple English. It does not appear to have much to do with the rest of the play but that is maybe no great handicap either.

Miss Ford in this scene is blonde and beautiful; for the rest of the evening she is dark and generates more nervous tension than is strictly necessary, a quality she shares with most of the other actors. The production (by Charles Marowitz and Walter Donohue) has what is known as a brooding power, but has it to the exclusion of very much else. It looks good, and up to a point it sounds good, but the cast are generally reduced to playing atmosphere rather than character. David Schofield as Crow does better than most; he has the appropriate untouchable cool, and—alone in the cast—he brings some flair to the rock numbers which punctuate the action. Malcolm Storry as Hoss puts up a very good fight, and for light relief I commend Anthony Milner, and John Grillo who gives his mad European scientist—familiar but welcome.

Edith Oliver (review date 17 March 1973)

SOURCE: "Fractured Tooth," in *The New Yorker,* Vol. XLIV, No. 4, March 17, 1973, pp. 92, 94.

[*Oliver began her career as an actor, writer, and producer and joined the* New Yorker *in 1948, becoming one of the magazine's theater critics in 1961. Here she praises Shepard's writing in* The Tooth of Crime, *despite the unusual staging the play received in a series of New York performances.*]

Sam Shepard, at around thirty, is one of the three or four most gifted playwrights alive. His *The Tooth of Crime* is so strong and vivid and funny that it is not entirely overwhelmed—although it is surely scrambled—by its production at the Performing Garage. The play, like Mr. Shepard's wonderful *The Unseen Hand,* of several years ago, is a

Mike Pratt as Hoss and Christopher Malcolm as Cheyenne in a 1974 production of The Tooth of Crime *at the Royal Court Theatre.*

which, as presented, defies synopsis anyway. The story is told in small scenes and songs and dances and—as was also true of *The Unseen Hand*—in language as vigorous and humorous and audacious as the imagination behind it. One of the joys is seeing the playwright slip in and out of parody and toss clichés into the air without ever losing his balance. He is indeed an original, but it might be pointed out that the qualities that make him so valuable are the enduring ones— good writing, wit, dramatic invention, and the ability to create characters. The second act is better, or perhaps just clearer and more concentrated, than the first. The fight between Hoss and Crow is almost entirely verbal; the men never touch each other as they try to dominate each other with their contrasting images and rhythms. Old Hoss chants of "country music from Chicago, King Oliver, New Orleans, cat house, professor," and the lethal, gelid Crow matches him with "fix, stereo, and"—in comic up-and-down pitch—"forty-five, seventy-eight, thirty-three." (These quotes may not be exact, and the order in each instance is mine.) After the fight is over, Crow tries, in the funniest scene of all, to give Hoss lessons in his "style" in return for Hoss's turf.

Under Richard Schechner's direction, the production is, as is usual at his Performing Garage, "environmental." The playing area is the whole floor, and the action moves all over it, and onto ladders and staircases and wooden structures of various kinds. The members of the audience almost have to move with it, getting as close to the actors as they can, sitting (legs dangling) or standing or running around on the rafters above. Considerable scampering is called for. Even so, it is impossible to get all the words all the time. I enjoyed the show, scene by scene, and I was also impressed with the acting (my heart used to sink every time anyone had to speak at the Garage), but to further disperse, by direction, a script as disjointed as this one seems a poor decision. I'd like to see it again, under less creative circumstances. Spalding Gray and Timothy Shelton are excellent as Hoss and Crow, respectively, and I also admired James Griffiths' performance, and his drumming and singing, as Hoss's sidekick, Cheyenne. Joan Mac Intosh, very good as Hoss's girl, does a splendidly silly vaudeville turn in which she fights for her honor against her own grabbing, importunate right arm, concealed in a man's sleeve and glove. Jerry Rojo was responsible for the effective, though superfluous, "environment," and James Clayburgh was responsible for the effective lighting.

CRITICAL COMMENTARY

Bruce W. Powe (essay date 1981)

SOURCE: "*The Tooth of Crime:* Sam Shepard's Way with Music," in *Modern Drama,* Vol. XXIV, No. 1, March, 1981, pp. 13-25.

[*In the following excerpt, Powe discusses Shepard's use of music in* The Tooth of Crime *and the influence of rock music on some of the playwright's other works.*]

The Tooth of Crime is, at present, [Shepard's] ultimate rock 'n' roll play: "A Play with Music . . ." that articulates

comedy with science-fiction trimmings. It is about an aging and garrulous fellow of the Old West called Hoss, whose control of his territory is threatened by a "new" man, an icy, impersonal, taciturn young fellow called Crow. The play is also about the nature of fantasy (Mr. Shepard may be the first dramatist since Pirandello to bring us news on the subject of illusion and reality) and about power and feeling and the end of romance, and in the Old West Shepard has found the perfect setting for his ideas. *The Tooth of Crime* could be considered an allegory, I suppose, but let's not. It is surely a satire. Most of Act I is taken up with the anticipation of Crow's arrival and with preparations for it; most of Act II is taken up with a fight between him and Hoss, which ends with Hoss's overthrow. So much for the plot, a vision of stars, styles and death. It is his *Star Wars:* a brilliant combination of western movie clichés, gangland rituals, organized sports, science fiction—in the future there will be no war, but there will be rock 'n' roll—and the star system in the pop world. (Interestingly, the whole last act of *The Tooth of Crime* is curiously reminiscent of an obscure western of the early seventies called *A Gunfight,* with Kirk Douglas and Johnny Cash. In that film, two gunfighters are convinced to give one last fight before a paying audience. Whether consciously or not, the film's producers created a striking image of the battle for public notice between film stars and pop musicians: who will be the new hero? the ultimate gunslinger by whom all aspiring "cowboys" must judge themselves?) In this play, Shepard creates a texture of language and music that echoes these distinctly American traditions and concerns by using songs, slang, profanity, quotations from rock hits, and words themselves as music. The form is surreal, yet anchored in a realistic frame, the rock music scene.

Like *Angel City, Mad Dog Blues, 4-H Club, Killer's Head,* and *Cowboys #2, The Tooth of Crime* begins with a stage that is bare, except for one evil-looking black chair. Also, very characteristically, this play starts with music, low strains from a hidden band. Shepard's plays frequently open with off-stage music playing: *Seduced* starts with Randy Newman's plaintive "Sail Away"; *Suicide in B Flat,* with a jazz piano sounding; *Angel City,* with a portentous tympany. Here the music is specifically employed to establish an ominous mood; it is a warm-up, an overture. Then Hoss enters. He is an Elvis Presley type; but like Elvis in his later years, he is past his prime. He has become isolated and protected: a star, unreal and manufactured.

Hoss starts the production with a song, "The Way Things Are." The song illuminates the underlying theme of the play, which is, as it turns out, one of Shepard's major concerns:

> You may think every picture you see is a true history
> of the way things used to be or the way things are
> While you're ridin' in your radio or walkin' through
> the late show ain't it a drag to
> know you just don't know
> you just don't know
>
> So here's another illusion to add to your confusion
> Of the way things are

Illusions, "to add to your confusion": illusions are deceptions, mocking images, often fantastic, as if in a dream. Is that the way things are? Confused, and phantasmagoric, and potentially dangerous:

> So here's another sleep-walkin' dream
> A livin' talkin' show of the way things seem

"the way things seem": a reference, perhaps, to the theatrical experience itself: the apprehension of a reality that is, paradoxically, artificial. It is, as Hoss sings, both a "sleep-walkin' dream" and "a livin' talkin' show."

> I used to believe in rhythm and blues

> Always wore my blue suede shoes
> Now everything I do goes down in doubt.

Allusions to rhythm and blues and old Elvis hits—"Blue Suede Shoes"—establish both a mythical and a contemporary reference; the present has its live traditions. Elvis and the fifties, early rock 'n' roll, blue suede shoes: how many suggestions of clothing and hair styles are embedded in those lines!

Thus, the song is a prelude. Shepard is informing us from the beginning that *The Tooth of Crime* is going to be set in a dream structure. It will not be logical or realistic; it will have the surrealism of a dream, the violence of surprise, the playfulness of one adept with illusion. The lyrics are also an admonition to the audience to watch out, to catch what happens when what "seems to be" is pushed to extremes.

But why a song to say this? Music communicates, emotionally and sensually, before it is rationally understood. It does not mediate; it is not reflective; it expresses and absorbs instantaneously. (Schopenhauer, in a famous comment on music in *The World as Will and Idea* [1888], says: "This is why the effect of music is more powerful and penetrating than the other arts, for they speak only of shadows, while it speaks of the thing itself.") Shepard himself speaks of this effect in a *Theatre Quarterly* interview [*Theatre Quarterly* 4, No. 15 (August-October 1974)]: "I think music's really important, especially in plays and theatre—it adds a whole different kind of perspective, it immediately brings the audience to terms with an emotional reality. Because nothing communicates emotions better than music, not even the greatest play in the world." This statement makes one realize that unlike many modern writers, Shepard is committed to expressing deep feelings. What occurs in the theatre, then, is the instant establishment of "a common note" ("an emotional reality") shared by the performer, the play, and the audience.

Shepard continues: "What I think is that music, no matter what its structure, has a very powerful emotional influence, it can't help but have that—it's in the nature of music, it's when you can play a note and there's a response immediately—you don't have to build up to it through seven scenes." But he also says: "I wanted the music in *The Tooth of Crime* so that you could step out of the play for a minute, every time a song comes, and be brought to an emotional comment on what's been taking place in the play." As in Brecht's plays ("He's my favorite playwright . . . ," Shepard says), the songs can serve as a counterpoint to the dialogue and the break-up of the narrative flow, providing interludes. Unlike Brecht's intentions, though, Shepard's are visceral rather than intellectual, moody rather than political. The loud volume and tempo affect listeners—whether they want to be touched or not. The raw energy of rock can engender excitement: it literally *resounds.*

The use of music in Shepard's plays, then, has several primary functions. First, it communicates the emotional perspective of either a character or situation, or the thematic centre of a work; it establishes mood and tone. Second, it initiates a kind of communion, a community of involved listeners; and, since rock 'n' roll is *rape,* seduction through the release of energy and rhythm, it increases tension in a volatile scene. Third, through their lyrics, the songs provide another comment on some action or situation in the work and hence yet another link with the audience.

In *The Tooth of Crime,* the songs function in all these ways. Hoss begins the show with a tune that initiates us into the play's aims and themes—it is a "sleep-walkin' dream"—and illuminates something about himself. Hoss is an old rocker; he is becoming passé; but he is equally a part of the fantasy, a superstar. At the end of Act One, Crow, Hoss's nemesis, sings "Poison":

> Ever since I was good
>
> I wanted to be—evil
> Ever since I went bad
> I wanted to be—badder
>
> Ever since I was dead
> I wanted to be—born like a maniac
> And now that I got all that I wished
> I don't see me ever goin' back
> At the moment the angel grew in me
> I started to strangle her oh so tenderly

This is like a Rolling Stones put-on; and, not surprisingly, in Act Two we are told that Crow resembles the Stones' Keith Richard. The song suggests the pseudo-satanic image of the punk, a raunchy, playful rock "evil" based on a street-tough aesthetic ("Have sympathy for the devil," as the Stones used to sing). "Poison" communicates who and what Crow is, and his threat to Hoss. And because rock 'n' roll is played loud and fast, on gleaming electric instruments under intense spotlights, emphasizing physical intensity and stressing—in the music—a repeated beat that can practically mesmerize an audience, elements of a visual spectacle and aural force are also introduced. This is purely a stage effect and impossible to perceive in the text. However, the rock 'n' roll sound and light show is a "sensational" part of the live impact.

This effect is achieved even more elaborately in the earlier *Operation Sidewinder,* where Shepard's employment of rock 'n' roll, as a bridge between scenes, as a commentary on the action, as an explosive method of establishing feelings, brings out other ironic and comic dimensions of a scene. The music was performed in the first production by an authentic country rock band, The Holy Modal Rounders (who, incidentally, did some of the music for the film *Easy Rider*). Though some of the songs were not written by Shepard, he assimilates all of them into the play's structure. At the end of Scene One, for example, after Honey has been caught by the rattlesnake-computer, and it wraps around her in a frankly sexual embrace—the snake itself, of course, being a sexual image—this song is heard:

> DO IT GIRL
>
> Everytime I see you wanna do it girl
> Right out in the street I wanna do it girl
> In front of everybody wanna do it girl

> I'm losing my control I feel it in my soul
> I wanna do it I wanna do it
> I wanna do it, do it, do it, do it,
> do it, do it, do it, do it, do it

This is obviously an absurd and hilarious comment on the snake's embrace. The use of rock clichés and orgasmic repetition (as in an old Presley number)—"do it, do it"—reinforces the comical effect.

At the end of *Operation Sidewinder,* in the *Close Encounters of the Third Kind* sequence, Shepard combines Hopi Indian chants, the electronic rhythms of the snake and the unseen flying saucer, and the staccato chatter of machine guns, in a fantastic display that integrates science fiction, the music of the spheres, and ritual transformation. All of this is whirled together in a light show reminiscent of the acid rock concerts at Bill Graham's Fillmore in the sixties. The impact of music, voices, and light is of a non-verbal apocalypse. ("Everywhere that language ceases, I meet with the musical," Kierkegaard writes in his chapter on Mozart in *Either/Or.*) Here the effect is also of a large-scale assemblage of elements and allusions culled from a variety of sources, combined to create a simultaneity of events.

Against this effect may be set *Cowboy Mouth* (or "Who's Afraid of Janis Joplin?"), which uses music as a deliberately frenetic and inarticulate counterpoint to the profane, slangy clichés and monosyllables that Cavale and Slim speak with nearly random abandon. "Have No Fear" is played *"loud . . . with a lot of feedback"*; it is "mean, shitkickin' rock-and-roll":

> Have no fear
>
> The worst is here
> The worst has come
> So don't run
> Let it come
> Let it go
> Let it rock and roll
> The worst has come.

"Have No Fear" is as debased and violent as Cavale and Slim have become. The numbing volume, the dumb lyrics, the screeching feedback (feedback is reverberation) are expressions of aggression, hostility, and fear. It is the music in *Cowboy Mouth*—which is about the myth of a super-rock-star-saviour—which underlies the anger and the absurdity of such a situation. The play depicts two characters in a surreal nightmare, and the music enhances the frantic mood and helps as well to accelerate the crude accents of tension that build to the outbreak of violence at the play's end. The image of the Lobster-Man turned rock saviour playing Russian roulette is an ominous image of the American star system as suicide, which prefigures the threats of annihilation in *The Tooth of Crime* and *Suicide in B Flat.* Roulette is nihilism—the trivialization of life to the point of a game, the testing of individual endurance through murderous chance—and the fast-talking blues played over this gesture reinforces the energy and near despair, "the close to the edge" feelings, that the principals feel.

In its original off-off-Broadway production, *Cowboy Mouth* featured one genuine rock star—Patti Smith. Her music is up-tempo, hard rock 'n' roll, very theatrical; the intensity of her live performance, the extremity it achieves in execution, is part of her musical strategy. The more apparently spontaneous it is, the more "electric" the effect. And Shepard's collaboration with her in *Cowboy Mouth* looks forward to the duel in *The Tooth of Crime,* in the battle of the two stars, the rock *Götterdämmerung.* Shepard appears to have learned a great deal from rock 'n' roll stars, in fact, about how to stage an "event"—which differs from a "happening" in that the former is planned for specific effects, whereas the latter is unstructured and cannot be repeated. Most rock acts try to achieve both; the spontaneity of, say, The Who—one of the best live bands—is always achieved within the organized limits of a definite production, with planned songs, laser shows, routines of physical gestures. The unexpected is encouraged; but it has to fit. This rock "event," which is, in every way, a creation or manipulation of the performer's *presence,* relates to Shepard's thematic concern with the effect of heroism, the mythic dimensions of a bold character, the potential within a tumultuous individual. As he writes of Bob Dylan in the *Rolling Thunder Logbook* [1978]:

> This is Dylan's true magic. Leave aside his lyrical genius for a second and just watch this transformation of energy which he carries. Only a few minutes ago the place was deadly thick with tension and embarrassment, and now he's blown the top right off it. He's infused the room with a high feeling of life-giving excitement. It's not the kind of energy that drives people off the deep end but the kind that brings courage and hope and above all brings life pounding into the foreground. If he can do it here . . . then it's no wonder he can rock the nation.

Obviously, this is precisely the flip side of the destructiveness in *Cowboy Mouth,* but it accurately illuminates the dynamic situations in *The Tooth of Crime.* The notion of a performer offering "life-giving excitement" is central to Shepard's theatricality. Thus, his use of electric music—the songs are always amplified—as a formal device is highly involving (communal), immediate and sensual. The rock beat itself often becomes analogous to the electrified sensibilities of Cavale and Slim, and of Hoss and Crow in *The Tooth of Crime.* But, importantly, as Shepard surely knows, at a rock concert there are no passive audiences: the listeners *feed back,* clap, yell, yelp, and dance, adding to the charge of the occasion. The whole atmosphere can become, potentially, one of "joining together."

We should also note that rock 'n' roll is the music of the spoken word, of idiomatic speech; rock 'n' roll comes closer to the way we speak than any other form of music. Listen to Bob Dylan's "Desolation Row" or the Rolling Stones' "Sympathy for the Devil," and hear how a vigorously colloquial speech is employed in the singing. As such, then, the dynamic range of the vocals are severely limited. But this again is an attempt to locate the music in an intimate, identifiable realm between audience and performer, the instantly understandable communication of that which is *commonly* apprehended. So, for example, in Round I in *The*

Tooth of Crime, in the duel itself, Shepard invests the language with musical qualities—that is, the diction, allusions, colloquialisms, and rhythms are attuned to sound, to the rock beat—making it, in a sense, unaccompanied rock talk:

> CROW. Pants down. The moon show. Ass out the window. Belt lash. Whip lash. Slide lash to the kid with a lisp. The dumb kid. The loser. The runt. The mutt. The shame kid. Kid on his belly. Belly to the blacktop. Slide on the rooftop. Slide through the parkin' lot. Slide kid. Shame kid. Slide. Slide.

The repetition of words and sounds, of perfect and imperfect rhymes, makes the passage formulaic, like a song. Traditional motifs of the rock loser, "The runt," "The shame kid," are intoned; variations on sounds, in "Ass," "lash," "runt," "mutt," "top," "lot," are stressed. The syntax—though there are no full sentences here—is expressive; the diction is orally associative; the rushing rhythm, the accelerando, is accented at the end by the alliterative "Slide kid. Shame kid. Slide. Slide."

One observes, too, the use of colloquialisms and jargon—hard, cutting words that exist in the characters' mouths like savage, affective things. Characters hurtle the words as if they were notes from a sax or a guitar; they project them, perform them. Employed in this way, words are *dangerous.* They have power precisely because they are alive as sound. Thus, the complex relationship between music and the spoken word, rhythm and pacing, performing and acting and being, is explored in this exchange.

Obviously, all this is quite different from the integration of songs into the play's structure. As Shepard's stage direction before the duel tells us:

> They [Hoss and CROW] *begin their assaults just talking the words in rhythmic patterns, sometimes going with the music, sometimes counterpointing it. As the round progresses, the music builds with drums and piano coming in, maybe a rhythm guitar, too. Their voices build so that sometimes they sing the words or shout. The words remain as intelligible as possible, like a sort of talking opera.*

Shepard is conscious, then, of how words can be arranged dynamically, orchestrated to form both a pounding, alliterative tension and a discordant duet.

Hoss responds to Crow's greaseball chatter by quoting what are in fact the origins of rock 'n' roll, the Carl ("Blue Suede Shoes") Perkins type of rockabilly:

> Never catch me with beer in my hand. Never caught me with my pecker out. Never get caught. Never once. Never, never. Fast on the hoof. Fast on the roof.

Again the repetition enforces tempo, the short staccato sentences augment the rhythmic thrust; the unadorned diction recalls old country song lyrics; the images conjure bars, teenagers, and the American Midwest.

Later in Round I, we find an even more graphic example of language as music:

> CROW. Coughin' in the corner. Dyin' from pneumonia. Can't play after dinner. Lonely in a bedroom. Dyin' for attention. Starts to hit the small time. Knockin' over pay phones. Rollin' over Beethoven. Rockin' pneumonia. Beboppin' to the Fat Man. Drivin' to the small talk. Gotta make his big mark. Take a crack at the teacher. Find him in the can can. There he's doin' time time. Losin' like a wino. Got losin' on his mind. Got losin' all the time.

In a collage of song titles, from Chuck Berry—"Roll over Beethoven"—to Little Richard, in a string of adolescent clichés—"Lonely in a bedroom. Dyin' for attention"—repeated words, as in a chorus—"Got losin' on his mind"—and images evoking *Rebel Without a Cause,* these lines fall naturally into the specifically measured fragments of a melody:

> Rollin' over Beethoven / Rockin' pneumonia / Beboppin' to the Fat Man / Drivin' to the small talk /

This is composed virtually in 4/4 time (all rock 'n' roll is counted in common time, with the second and fourth beats accented), up-tempo, rushing, in that "poetry of Speed" [as Patti Smith puts it in her poem, "Sam Shepard 9 Random years [7 + 2]," published in Shepard's *Angel City, Curse of the Starving Class and Other Plays* (1976)]. Also, it is highly compact speech, held together by the tension of the character's delivery. Behind these lines is the articulation and the associative verbal drive of a personality who has discovered his rhythm, his beat, his idiom, what Crow refers to as "the walk." These "walk" references that surface throughout Act Two are significant because they suggest a visual counterpoint for the beat. Crow imitates Hoss's walk, his "gait," his beat, which is representative of style, direction, motion, force. He talks of finding a new pattern of walking as a mode of being: "Now try out yer walk"; "Start movin' to a different drummer man." Crow looks for the dominant cadence, the key to a form of personal expression (a different "walk" of life). His speech is cast in the evocative strain of rock talk; his whole physical movement is integral to what he says and how his words move. "The walk" is, then, suggestive of the use of language as an instrument, as a reflection of being.

This emphasis on vocal stylistics, on the motion of words, on delivery (performance), enhances the understanding that language for Shepard is, when manipulated orally, resonant, near musical, a definite force.

In the *Rolling Thunder Logbook,* a chronicle of his fascination with music and musicians, Shepard describes music's connotative powers: "One thing that gets me about Dylan's songs is how they conjure up images, whole scenes that are being played out in full color as you listen." And earlier: "One thing for sure is that you never doubt it [a Dylan song] when it hits you. You recognize something going on in your chest cavity that wasn't going on before."

Shepard's use of music, then, is centred primarily in this application of it as expression, as an affective agent to incite and inspire, as another means of theatrical presentation—that is, to intensify the proceedings with sound—and as a lyrical counterpoint. But it is worth remembering that his use of music is only one part of the total form that he creates, that the presence of music is a part of the unfolding of his often ritualistic examinations of myths and images. A revealing comment can be found in Kenneth Chubb's article ["Fruitful Difficulties of Directing Shepard," in *Theatre Quarterly* 4, No. 15 (August-October 1974)], in which Shepard is quoted as saying: "I'm interested in exploring the writing of plays through attitudes derived from other forms such as music, painting, sculpture, film, etc., all the time keeping in mind that I'm writing for the theatre."

The attitudes derived from "music, painting, sculpture, film, . . . " in the three-dimensional arrangement of the stage, combine with cowboys and gangsters, rock and rock stars, science fiction, realism, hopped-up hipsters, artists, and families, in a pop art pastiche. And because there is a non-intellectualized, intuitive, and subjective aspect to this pattern—one must be "inside" the work, feeling it, following it, willing to let it go in whatever direction it chooses—a sense of enthralling possibility, of audience involvement, seems to be constantly breaking out. Music is integral to this; music is always "now," "here," direct, touching. So Shepard relies heavily on music in those plays which deal explicitly with energy and expression to create mood, propel the story, design a sensational sound and light show, and not only to reflect a response to the electronic present, but to articulate its dynamic reality. As he writes in *Suicide in B Flat*:

> NILES. Did you listen or just watch?
>
> PETRONE. What do you mean?
>
> NILES. Did you listen to the music?
>
> PETRONE. Yeah. Sure.
>
> NILES. What did it say?
>
> PETRONE. What?
>
> NILES. What did the music say? Did you hear it?
>
> PETRONE. Yes. It wasn't words. I mean it wasn't words like we're talking now.

To see and hear Shepard's plays in all their dazzling theatricality is to recognize a young playwright shaping his language and form and music to express contemporary images and voices. And learning to see and hear Shepard's work is like learning to see and hear "now."

Leonard Mustazza (essay date 1989)

SOURCE: "'In the Old Style': The Tragic Vision in Sam Shepard's *The Tooth of Crime*," in *Text and Performance Quarterly,* Vol. 9, No. 4, October, 1989, pp. 277-85.

[Mustazza is an educator and critic. In the following essay, he outlines the similarities between The Tooth of Crime and traditional tragedies such as Shakespeare's Richard II.]

Most commentators on Sam Shepard's **The Tooth of Crime** (1972) have understandably focussed their attention on the play's strikingly original concept and its unique use of language, music, and spectacle. By the same token, however, another important feature of the play, a more familiar informing principle, has gone largely unnoticed and therefore unexplicated—namely, the classic tragic lines that lie beneath a novel surface. Only two critics have noticed this subtle conception, and both have commented very briefly. Florence Falk [in an essay in *American Dreams: The Imagination of Sam Shepard,* ed. by Bonnie Marranca, 1981] has argued that " . . . the *de cassibus* [*sic*] theme, mirrored in the simultaneous fall of the old order and the rise of the new, is as classically rendered as any Elizabethan tragedy." Lynda Hart [in *Sam Shepard's Metaphorical Stages,* 1987] has observed that " . . . Shepard broadens the basis of his hero's quest by posing a metaphysical conflict in a classical mythic form," the culmination of that conflict being " . . . a classical agon, a sacred combat between the Old King and the new." Because their interests lie in other matters relating to the play, neither Falk nor Hart explores in detail the critical consequences of those observations. The fact is that, for all its flash and fury—its use of rock music to establish mood and context, its evocation of bankrupt American myths past (cowboys, gangsters), present (rock superstars), and futuristic (cosmic warriors)—**Tooth** bears the marks of earlier conceptions of tragedy, and its powerful emotional impact depends largely upon Shepard's fusion of old and new.

The older conception of tragedy, as reflected in both classical Greek and Renaissance tragedy, contains three main themes, according to Northrop Frye, Sheridan Baker, and George Perkins in an essay in *The Harper Handbook to Literature,* 1985: 1) the theme of isolation, in which a hero, a character greater than ordinary human size, becomes separated from the community; 2) the hero's gradual understanding of his human limitations; and 3) a violation and reestablishment of a political order. Each of these standard themes is evident in Shepard's rock drama and, to effect the fusion of old and new, of classical conception and contemporary milieu, Shepard relies almost exclusively upon his protagonist. Hoss, for all his stylistic idiosyncrasy, is the most conventional of Shepard's central characters. In most of his plays, Shepard's conception of character conforms in one way or another with the description he includes in the "Note to the Actors" prefacing *Angel City.* "Instead of the idea of a 'whole character' with logical motives behind his behavior which the actor submerges himself into," Shepard writes there, "he should consider instead a fractured whole with bits and pieces of character flying off the central theme." This approach to character, clearly applied in other Shepard plays such as **Buried Child, True West,** and, of course, *Angel City* itself, is not in evidence in **Tooth.** Rather, Hoss is no less coherent a character than, say, Sophocles' Oedipus or Shakespeare's Richard II, and, in fact, he is conceived by the playwright and perceived by the audience in much the same way that these other characters are.

Like them, he is a man of larger-than-life proportions, a "king" who, through a combination of ill fate and flawed judgment, becomes isolated, learns his own limitations, and suffers a catastrophic fall. And, as in these Sophoclean and Shakespearean tragic visions, the hero's demise is meant to be seen not as the working out of poetic justice for his flaws, though, like Oedipus and Richard, he is flawed, but as pitiable, owing to our recognition of his sympathetic qualities, his humanity, his suffering out of all proportion to his misjudgments. In the following paragraphs, I shall consider the ways in which **The Tooth of Crime** reflects this conventional tragic outlook which Shepard deftly combines with his unique vision of "monarchy" in our time.

At the beginning of the play, Hoss walks out onto a stage that is [as is stated in the play's stage directions] bare "except for an evil-looking black chair with silver studs and a very high back, something like an Egyptian Pharaoh's throne," and sings a song that both evokes mood and prefigures theme. Entitled "The Way Things Are," the song suggests the illusory nature of things, notably art: "While you're ridin' in your radio or walkin' through the late show ain't it a drag to know you just don't know / you just don't know." Bruce Powe [in *Modern Drama* 24 (March 1981)] contends that this opening is meant to inform us that the play " . . . is going to be set in a dream structure. It will not be logical or realistic; it will have the surrealism of a dream, the violence of surprise, the playfulness of one adept with illusion." The problem with this interpretation is that it is not borne out by the play. Apart from the futuristic setting of the plot, a fairly superficial matter, nothing dream-like or surreal occurs here. Rather, the fundamental situation is all too realistic, concerned as it is with the protagonist's doubts about life and self. Despite his invitation to the song's auditor to agree that life and art are often illusory, Hoss is concerned here not with the experiences of others but with his own doubts and perceptions:

> I used to believe in rhythm and blues
> Always wore my blue suede shoes
> Now everything I do goes down in doubt
> But sometimes in the blackest night I can see a little
>   light
> That's the only thing that keeps me rockin'—keeps
>   me rockin'
>
> So here's another fantasy
> About the way things seem to be to me.

If we attend carefully to the movement of this opening song, we see the subtle transition from the second person ("While you're ridin' in your radio . . . ") to the first ("Now everything I do goes down in doubt"), from the generalized ("the way things are") to the specific ("the way things seem to be to me").

This movement towards the self is appropriate, for we learn before long that Hoss's real fear concerns his own ability to maintain supremacy in his musical field, to hold on to his monarchical status as symbolized by the silver-studded black throne that remains fittingly empty throughout the first act. To address that doubt, he will spend the first act meeting individually with a variety of characters in his retinue, each of whom tries to ease his doubts and to correct his excesses, his impatience with the "game," his desire to go "against the code," the "code" being the rules of conduct established by music-industry executives, critics, disk jockeys, and others. Interestingly, however, while we recognize Hoss's emotional excesses, what Charles Bachman [in *Modern Drama* 19 (December 1976)] has called his " . . . hip version of hubris before the fall," we must also note that each of the characters with whom he contends also serves as a foil, enabling us to sympathize with the protagonist as we recognize his admirable qualities.

The most important such characters in this scheme are, not surprisingly, those closest to the "king," Becky and Cheyenne. Unlike those who serve Hoss's occasional needs—Star-Man, his astrological advisor; Galactic Jack, the disk jockey; and Doc, who gives him drugs—Becky and Cheyenne are permanent members of the monarchical household, people who have been with Hoss from the beginning, trusted friends. As such, their principal function is, they seem to believe, to protect Hoss from himself, from his own restlessness and ennui, from his desire to return to life and art outside the code. In this " . . . parable of a generation of outsiders turned insiders" [as the play was described by Vivian Patraka and Mark Siegel in *Sam Shepard* (1985)], they represent the comfortable status quo, those who have learned to place commerce above art, protected fame above risk. Indeed, so much do they value their material acquisitions and status as near-celebrities that in the end they will place these priorities even above the "king" whom they purport to serve.

Of the two, Becky is the more assertive and power-hungry. When Hoss complains that the code is too restrictive, that fame is proving to be too insular, and that it is not in his nature to conform to the degree expected of him, she responds with a repudiation of "nature" as a value system:

> That's what we saved you from, your nature. Maybe you forgot that. When we first landed you, you were a complete beast of nature. A sideways killer. Then we molded and shaped you and sharpened you down to perfection because we saw in you a true genius killer. A killer to end them all. A killer's killer.

The distinction Becky draws here between nature and nurture, the distinction between natural talent and disciplined art, seems reasonable, and we are even led perhaps to side with her position in this debate, just as Hoss himself does for a while. "She's right!" he asserts after she leaves. "She's right goddamnit. . . . I can't chicken out of it now. This is my last chance. I'm gettin' old. I can't do a Lee Marvin in the late sixties."

This facile answer, however, will not serve for very long, particularly when Hoss learns that the "safety" Becky and Cheyenne counsel is illusory, that threats to his safety are present not only externally from competitors bent on unseating the "king" but also from within, from the artistic self that no longer believes in its own legitimacy. This lesson is impressed upon him even more forcefully when he learns of the suicide of Little Willard, another superstar with whom he has planned to join forces. Shocked by the news, he asks why a man of Willard's status, a star "in the top ten and risin'," would do such a thing, but one senses that the question is merely rhetorical, that he knows precisely why the East-Coast mirror-image of his own celebrity in the West would want to drop out of a game in which he is squeezed between an insular, restrictive code on the one hand and the threat posed by Gypsy usurpers on the other. Indeed, Willard's suicide turns out to be a foreshadowing of Hoss's own self-determined fate.

The shocking realization that comes to Hoss at this point effects a profound change in his attitudes and, accordingly, in our perceptions of him. No longer the completely self-centered and uncontrolled character we meet at the beginning of the play, Hoss grows progressively more introspective and analytical, assessing not only the faults that he himself possesses but also the flawed system in which the artist is forced to operate. Cut off from his community (both the community from which he originates and his current fans) and doubting his own restless nature whence his art derives, Hoss struggles to understand the new "self" that his celebrity has forged. Such is the threat from within. From without, moreover, he is threatened by vicious individuals appropriately named "Gypsies." Divorced from tradition, the Gypsies represent nothing beyond themselves—violent, unruly marauders who have nothing to offer except flashes of pure style. As Robert Coe has suggested [in an essay in *American Dreams*], Shepard operates in this play under the assumption that rock is about violence with its own codes and standards of behavior, and "*Tooth* applies the realization that if denied a living historical base, a continuity of myth, past and present, then such violence is empty, and ultimately self-destructive." Likewise, in a recent interview [with Kevin Sessums in *Interview* 18 (September, 1988)], Shepard was asked whether he thought the violence found in *Tooth,* among other plays of his, was in any way redemptive. His response was quite interesting: "No. I think violence is absolutely hopeless. *It's the main source of tragedy*" (emphasis added). Although in a more restricted sense, this is precisely the conclusion that Hoss reaches, that violence and tragedy are intimately bound. Hence, when he asserts that the Gypsies' form of "art" is little more than "crime," when he says that "These are gonna be the last days of honor," his allegiance to an artistic code invests him with a moral stature, an authority that transforms him into a foil and a victim. Ultimately, this change in his attitude toward himself and his respect for the musical past effect in the audience a sympathetic reaction that moves us along towards a recognition of Hoss as tragic figure.

This rather sudden attitudinal transformation in the protagonist from self-consumed whiner to victim is curiously reminiscent of the character-reversal technique that Shakespeare employs in *Richard II*, a history play which the playwright dubbed a "tragedy." There, too, we begin with a king who is concerned primarily with self and who, through the eventual loss of his kingdom, comes to certain realizations about the shifting nature of rule in his own times. Resembling in a general way the situation in *Tooth,* Shakespeare's tragic history is about a transitional period in the monarchy, a time when the old idea of the divine right of kings is about to give way to Machiavellian politics, thus making it necessary for a king to be sure of his own power base and not rest complacent in his hereditary tenure. Just prior to his forced abdication, Richard, in a puny threat to Northumberland, deludes himself for a moment with a belief in the old order:

> Yet know, my master, God omnipotent
> Is mustering in his clouds on our behalf
> Armies of pestilence, and they shall strike
> Your children yet unborn and unbegot
> That lift your vassal hands against my head,
> And threat the glory of my precious crown.

And yet, his abdication just moments later reveals the impotence of the old conception of monarchy and the real threat posed by those who know how to use power. From this point on, we begin to hear a new Richard, one who is concerned less with himself now and more with England's future, which he predicts will be far less stable as powerful men continually contend with one another for dominance.

In *Tooth,* likewise, Shepard locates the action in a transitional period from one order to another. Hoss, like Richard II, has little understanding of the new breed of would-be kings, no notion that the old rules, which involved, among other things, a knowledge of and appreciation for the musical past, are meaningless to the usurpers, for whom only style is important. Hoss's time is, as Coe suggests, a period of " . . . bizarre cultural obsolescence," and Hoss's failure to understand and accept that fact makes him both a victim and a hero, a man bound to suffer and one who serves as a foil to the moral and cultural emptiness of his challengers. This paradoxical view of character is most evident when, near the end of the first act, Hoss reveals two "selves." Having complained to Becky that he has no self, which he defines as "something to fall back on in a moment of doubt or terror or even surprise," he then divides his mind, so to speak, engaging in an inner debate with the old—the reassuring and realistic voice of his father—and the new—the person he is and dislikes so much:

> (*old*) O.K. You're not so bad off. It's good to change. Good to feel your blood pump. (*himself*) But where to? Where am I going? (*old*) It don't matter. The road's what counts. Just look at the road. Don't worry about where it's goin'. (*himself*) I feel so trapped. . . . They're all countin' on me. The bookies, the agents, the Keepers. . . . I even affect the stocks and bonds. (*old*) You're just a man, Hoss. Just a man. (*himself*) Yeah, maybe you're right. I'm just a man.

Contrary to what Hoss asserts elsewhere, his recollection of his father's traditional wisdom and his admission of his own humanity indicate that he does have a self "to fall back on in a moment of doubt or terror." He calls upon that self here, even though, as is always the case in tragedy, the strength he summons to his aid comes too late to save him. Two of the conventional tragic themes noted by Frye, Baker, and Perkins here become evident—Hoss's isolation and his confrontation with his own humanity. His self-admission that "I'm just a man" represents a marked change from his earlier infatuation with and worry over the self, and this change prompts the reader or viewer to find Hoss sympathetic. The third thematic ingredient of tragedy, the overturning of order, will come soon, with the arrival of Crow, and when he tells himself at the end of the first act, "Tomorrow you live or die," referring to his inevitable duel with the usurper, the remark is bound to evoke tragic foreboding and pity for the lone king.

Accordingly, the first view of the usurper in Act Two confirms our pity and admiration for Hoss (a measure of how far Shepard has taken us since the beginning of the play), and deepens the sense of imminent catastrophe. Contemptuously moving about the stage, the arrogant Crow finally and symbolically settles himself on Hoss's throne and "chews gum at the audience," a gesture that cannot fail to elicit a visceral and negative response. For his part, however, Hoss seems to be oddly calm when he meets Crow, as if they were colleagues rather than competitors. Indeed, Hoss is remarkably forthcoming and honest, claiming to be tired, offering him a drink, complaining that Crow's neologisms are beyond him ("Can't you back the language up, man. I'm too old to follow the flash"), and admitting that he had Crow all wrong, that he can learn something from Crow's flash and polish. It is not until he notices that Crow can imitate Hoss's own style, if he likes, that Hoss begins to suspect the real threat that the outsider poses. Herbert Blau [in *Modern Drama,* 27 (December 1984)] has correctly observed that Hoss here shows himself to be old-fashioned. "The trouble with Hoss," Blau goes on, "is that he partially identifies with Crow, weakening the venom he needs to do him in. . . . Hoss makes a fatal mistake; he gives Crow a human face not unlike his own." Even though Hoss will suspect this error in judgment before the actual duel, it is already too late. He has revealed more about himself to Crow than he should have.

In his article **"Language, Visualization and the Inner Library"** [in *The Drama Review* 27 (December 1977)], Shepard comments on the genesis and meaning of Crow:

> The character Crow in *Tooth of Crime* came from a yearning toward violence. A totally lethal human with no way or reason for tracing how he got that way. He just appeared. He spit words that became his weapons. He doesn't "mean" anything. He is simply following his most savage instincts.

Most commentators would agree with Shepard's own assessment of character, particularly on the question of language. Sheila Rabillard [in *Modern Drama* 30 (March 1987)], for instance, has argued that Shepard uses words as "power tools" in this play, that " . . . words spoken by the characters in the play are the bearers of power rather than of meaning." Leonard Wilcox [in *Modern Drama* 30 (December 1987)], moreover, notes that the characters' host of styles and ideolects results in " . . . a destabilization of discourse and a decentering play of language in which every signified is commutable, every signifier 'free floating'." I agree with both of these commentators, and yet I think that, ultimately, language cannot fail to "mean" something specific even when it functions symbolically, and that Crow is far more in control of himself and his words than Shepard suggests in the quotation above. Hoss himself realizes as much when, noting that Crow uses some fairly conventional phrasing in one of his retorts, he says, "There! Why'd you slip just then? Why'd you suddenly talk like a person? You're into a wider scope than I thought. You're playin' my time Gypsy but it ain't gonna work." Claiming to "sense an internal smokin' at the seam," or a loss of self-control in Hoss, Crow confronts Hoss with a truth the current king will not acknowledge: "Time warps don't shift the purpose, just the style." The "meaning" of these lines is clear and conventional in the literary context of an agon, and the degree of self-awareness and control that Crow shows here is remarkable. Contrary to Shepard's argument that Crow is lethal because he operates on the level of savage instinct, one must conclude that Crow, like all other successful usurpers, is lethal because he is very much aware and in control, however much his emphasis on style may appear to belie those qualities.

Moreover, style and self are not discrete qualities for Crow as they are for Hoss. The latter is adept at manipulating a variety of styles because he is aware of his predecessors, of tradition, just as a good king is a student of history, understanding the strengths and the mistakes of those who occupied the throne before him. We see and admire this informed talent of his both before the duel, when Hoss easily adopts the voices of a Western cowboy and a 1920s gangster, and during the prize-fight-style agon itself, when he mimics the speech of "an ancient delta blues singer," warning Crow, "You could use a little cow flop on yer shoes, boy." We admire Hoss's reproach of the arrogant younger man's apparent ignorance of musical traditions. And yet, paradoxically, Shepard goes on to turn that admiration we feel for the traditionalist into pity for the dying king. Hoss surely stands on the shoulders of the giants who preceded him, but Crow merely sees that position as a higher place from which to fall.

Several critics of *Tooth* have commented on the connection Shepard draws here between style and self or identity. Bonnie Marranca in *American Dreams* has argued that "*Tooth* is about making up language and using it to manipulate reality" and that "for any character to imitate someone else and transform his way of speaking (that is, his way of thinking) is to give up his identity." Likewise, Leonard Wilcox maintains that the play " . . . suggests that self and language are integrally connected." Commenting on Crow's language, Charles Bachman notes, "His style is all he is—and thus he has seemingly solved the age-old problems of security, repression, piety, justice and personal identity. . . . The new savior is indeed enviable and/or pitiable depending on one's mood and psychological set." And Ron Mottram [in *Inner Landscapes: The Theatre of Sam Shepard* (1984)] observes that Crow, unlike Hoss, cannot (or will not) switch voices to summon up the past " . . . because he believes that the one he projects is not a voice at all but is his true self. He believes in the mask he has created." I would like to add to these assessments the fact that Crow's inseparable style and self also make for a kind of painful honesty that Hoss, for all his talent and understanding, can-

not withstand. We see this cutting honesty most clearly when Crow delivers the verbal thrust that finally unseats the king:

> Can't get it sideways walkin' the dog. Tries trainin' his voice to sound like a frog. Sound like a Dylan, sound like a Jagger, sound like an earthquake all over the Fender. . . . Can't get it together for all of his tryin'. Can't get it together for fear that he's dyin'. Fear that he's crackin' busted in two. . . . Busted and dyin' and cryin' for more. Busted and bleedin' all over the floor. All bleedin' and wasted and tryin' to score.

His ridicule of Hoss's stylistic posturing, his correct assessment of Hoss's insecurities, his accurate prediction of Hoss's imminent professional demise, and his unwitting foretelling of Hoss's death—all of these things conspire to bring down the "monarchy" in a single blow. Hoss may kill the ref-messenger for delivering the bad news, but he quickly accepts the new reality as it presents itself, begging Crow to teach him the latest style, giving up his turf, and finally killing himself.

With that final gesture, Shepard moves us emotionally yet again—away from the world of *realpolitik* and back into the world of tragedy. For all his excesses and insecurities, for all his egotism and misguided beliefs, the "king" was an admirable man, a man who, in Robert Coe's words, " . . . has earned his style, and in Shepard's view, this makes him an original—which is to say an innocent as well as a victim. . . . " Coe goes on to suggest that Shepard's allegiances in the end are with Hoss, though he identifies with both Hoss and Crow. Herbert Blau sees a similar identification on the part of the playwright, though he concludes that "Shepard doesn't choose one over the other." Both critics may be right on the question of identification, but I think that Shepard does take sides in the end, as seen through the panegyrics to the fallen "hero" that the victor delivers. "Perfect, Leathers. Perfect," Crow apostrophizes to the dead body of Hoss. "A genius mark. I gotta hand it to ya'. It took ya' long enough but you slid right home." And when Becky traitorously switches sides, flattering the new king and asking whether the struggle was hard, Crow openly praises that which he earlier disparaged and emulates the stylistic clarity that the earlier belittled: "Yeah. He was pretty tough. Went out in the old style. Clung right up to the drop."

"Went out in the old style": that statement serves as a fitting assessment not only of Hoss's final refusal to forgo his identity but also of the play itself. For all its dramatic and linguistic pyrotechnics, for all its stylistic and thematic shifts, *The Tooth of Crime* is a conventionally conceived play about the tragic fall of a modern king. Lynda Hart has argued that "[t]he mythic undertones in the play do not succeed in elevating Hoss to archetypal proportions" and that "Hoss's destiny . . . seems to fulfill a particular pattern rather than represent a universal condition." She is right, but then again neither are most well-known agons of this sort "archetypal." Again, Shakespeare's *The Tragedy of Richard II* is a prime example. Like that Shakespearean work, Shepard's *Tooth* is concerned not with establishing archetypes but with projecting tragic and noble visions of humanity—humanity bound by situation, imprisoned by self and society, and struggling to remain free and intact. It is about the "crime" perpetrated by our very humanity—our ambitions, our insecurities, our doubts, our existential pains. It is also about time and its effects on ourselves and the world. "I wasted time, and now doth Time waste me," Richard II complains near the end of his life. So does Hoss lament the passage of time, and so, for that matter, does Crow finally, boasting that "this is my time" but admitting that the power he now holds "sits till a bigger wind blows." In Shepard's unique manipulation of these familiar themes lies the play's emotional force.

Shepard on how his approach to characterization changed in the mid-1970s:

I wouldn't call it a development, . . . though it's some kind of evolution. It has to do with moving inside the character. Originally, I was fascinated by form, by exteriors—starting from the outside and going in, with the idea that character is something shifting and that it can shift from one person to another. You had different attitudes drifting in and out from actors who are part of the ensemble. So in the past, it was the overall tone of the piece I was interested in rather than in characters as individuals. That sort of played itself out, and for a while I didn't know where to go from there. But then I started to delve into character and it came about pretty naturally.

Sam Shepard, quoted by Michiko Kakutani, in The New York Times, *29 January 1984, p. 26.*

BURIED CHILD

PRODUCTION REVIEWS

Harold Clurman (review date 2 December 1978)

SOURCE: A review of *Buried Child*, in *The Nation*, New York, Vol. 227, No. 19, December 2, 1978, pp. 621-22.

[Buried Child *was presented in New York City at the Theatre for the New City in November, 1978, and went on to receive the Pulitzer Prize for Drama in 1979. Clurman, a highly regarded director, educator, and author, and the drama critic for the* Nation *from 1953 to 1980, wrote the following review of* Buried Child, *praising the improvisational energy of the play and the "quintessentially American" nature of Shepard's work.*]

The 35-year-old Sam Shepard is an oddly significant writer. He is prolific to a fault, but that may be due to the nature of his talent. The only one of his plays to have achieved a "major" production in the neighborhood of Broadway is *Operation Sidewinder* (Lincoln Center, 1970). His first full-length play, *La Turista,* was presented, without benefit of wide press coverage, at the American Place Theatre in 1967. Last year Joseph Papp offered Shepard's *The Curse of the Starving Class* at the Public Theatre. Though fully conscious of its shortcomings, I nominated it at the New

York Drama Critics Circle as the "best play of the season." For the rest, Shepard is almost wholly an Off and off-Off Broadway playwright, just as he is an "off West End" playwright in England. He is definitely not "commercial."

He, nonetheless, is quintessentially American. Our theatre is New York oriented; Shepard's plays have a country or grass-roots twang. They are very close to the poorer folk who live on the land outside the big cities. He is a man of the "road," that barely charted but wide-spread territory which we pass through on trains or cars between the main stops. To define him a little more narrowly, one may say that his plays are related to largely unwritten or more or less buried permanent American "myths," a kind of itinerant, hobo, open field mystique. Metropolitan civilization has all but obliterated its every trace, yet it exists deep in our soil, where "soil" is still to be found. Indeed the tradition is so American that it has become alien.

Shepard's latest play to be seen here is *Buried Child,* recently at the Theatre for the New City, a nine-year-old organization previously located at the Westbeth complex on Bank St. and "dedicated to the discovery of new playwrights and relevant new writing." *Buried Child* is in the vein of *The Curse of the Starving Class* in that it deals with a family (this one somewhere in the Middle West) that lives on the fringes of everything. That makes them seem more rather than less crazy. Though the "story" of *Buried Child* is relatively clear, to make it intelligible one must take most of its details as metaphor or symbol, though these too are hardly exact. They do, however, convey a feeling—like some Woody Guthrie type of chant—of Shepard's sense of America.

It is a land gone to seed, its roots sunk deep in the neglected earth, still alive but rotting. It cannot or will not remember its past, which harbors criminal elements. Its older women live in a dream world, only faintly connected to reality. Its younger women turn away from its madness because they are confused, frightened and disheartened by it. The older men do not contemplate a future, wish to shut it out, even refuse to admit its possibility. They want to cut off further growth, wipe it out, having killed its most recently born child as illegitimate, while the older offspring are either crippled or gone bats.

A grandson, unable to establish a sound relationship with his elders, has freed himself from them by leaving them for years. On his return, his grandfather and one brother pretend not to recognize him and his loony father is indifferent to him. As a result, he becomes violently aggressive: he will take over his grandparents' property and run it like a brutal dictator. This property (the country) has been held to be unproductive but is still fertile because "the sun shines on it."

None of this, I repeat, is literal; all is implicit in the extravagant, sometimes bewildering, narrative data. What strikes the ear and eye is comic, occasionally hilarious behavior and speech at which one laughs while remaining slightly puzzled and dismayed (if not resentful), and perhaps indefinably saddened. Yet there is a swing to it all, a vagrant freedom, a tattered song. Something is coming to an end, yet on the other side of disaster there is hope. From the bottom there is nowhere to go but up.

Shepard writes so much and with such dangerous facility because he is an improviser, a tramp-like bard who doesn't concern himself with total coherence or immediate lucidity. I must confess that several of his plays have baffled me, and I may have misinterpreted some of them, but I am convinced that he is not only a genuinely gifted but a meaningful writer.

The performance, directed by Robert Woodruff of San Francisco (Shepard is also a Californian), and the acting are both commensurate with the script. The production cost $2,000: the actors receive a pittance. Two utterly worthless musicals now on Broadway cost more than $1 million each.

William A. Raidy (review date February 1979)

SOURCE: A review of *Buried Child,* in *Plays and Players,* Vol. 26, No. 6, February, 1979, pp. 36-7.

[*In this review Raidy expresses reservations about the obscurity of* Buried Child, *yet praises Shepard's imagination and declares the play an "enormously stimulating" experience.*]

Abundant, but now empty, America, presented in almost surreal terms, is the central theme of Sam Shepard's *Buried Child,* which is certainly an effective companion piece to his unfunny cartoon of last year, *Curse of the Starving Class.* The Theatre for the New City production, recently presented off-off Broadway, is now at the Theatre deLys and it is an enormously stimulating one.

Earlier plays of Shepard, such as *The Unseen Hand,* and some of his cowboy mock epics, poke fun at an America saddled with a myth that has become a joke. *Buried Child* digs a bit deeper, probing the disintegration of the American family, overfed and spiritually under-nourished and indifferent to one another's needs. Like *Curse, Buried Child* is written in almost cartoon-like pen strokes. It is a surreal glance into a fun house mirror and its distortions are more grotesque than they are 'fun'.

The scene of this new drama, splendidly directed by Robert Woodruff, is the American wasteland, a decimated farm where skeletons of bygone abundance and optimism haunt the landscape. We meet Mom and Pop living in chaos with two idiot sons, who seem to be deranged as well as mentally deficient. While Pop, surrounded by a drug store full of pills and a bottle of whisky secreted away, seems at death's door, Mom is bustling with energy, deliberately oblivious to the decay around her. In the midst of what seems to be almost lunatic behaviour, there is a 'homecoming', not quite in the Pinter grain.

The son of one of the sons arrives with his girl friend for an unexpected reunion. The girl, expecting 'all turkey dinner and apple pie' Norman Rockwell America, is numbed by the characters who inhabit the ramshackle homestead.

As for the grandson, he is unrecognized by the family he hopes to embrace, complaining 'How could they not recognize me? I'm their son'. While 'the family' turns its back to the new generation, it holds a dark secret in its bosom. Dodge, the old grandpa now almost determinedly senile, murdered his wife's child, fathered by someone else, and buried it in a field in back of the homestead. Suddenly an unexpected harvest of corn and other vegetables, almost as if in the sacrificial tradition of Frazer's 'Golden Bough', springs up where no seed has been planted in decades. 'Nothing's ever been wrong here', says a member of the family as they clutch the lie closer.

Shepard often overreaches in *Buried Child* as he condemns America, built on pioneer spirit and hoked-up legends, with his grotesque figures who have inherited this once energetic land. His surrealism, intertwined with anthropological symbolism of fecundity and sacrifice, sometimes obscures his message of America's desecration and self-delusion. But *Buried Child,* for all its enigma, is a powerful reflection, no matter how 'funny' the mirror, of the dilemma of present day America. Somewhere, Shepard seems to be telling us that the new generation, whether it wishes to turn its back or not, is heir to the whole rotten carcass—maggots and all.

Buried Child, with its bizarre excursions into and out of 'reality', is beautifully acted, no easy task in a play like this. Richard Hamilton, as the dying old man, raving away in his dirty old baseball cap, is remarkable and so is Jacqueline Brookes, as his determined, 'everything's all right' wife. Tom Noonan and Jay Sanders as the zombie-like sons both give finely etched characterizations.

Buried Child is one of Sam Shepard's most interesting plays and so far it is certainly the most stimulating, noteworthy off-Broadway presentation of the season. Shepard reaffirms his position as one of America's most adventurous and imaginative playwrights.

CRITICAL COMMENTARY

Doris Auerbach (essay date 1982)

SOURCE: *"Buried Child,"* in *Sam Shepard, Arthur Kopit, and the Off Broadway Theatre,* Twayne Publishers, 1982, pp. 53-61.

[*In the following essay, Auerbach, an educator and critic, offers an interpretation of* Buried Child, *stressing the play's discouraging message of lost American promise, yet also noting a sense of hope at the conclusion of the drama.*]

THE THEME RESTATED

One of Shepard's recurring themes is the decay of the American family, which can readily be seen as a synonym for the nonviability of today's American society. The playwright sounded this theme very early in his career in the one-act play *Rock Garden,* which he still considers among the best of his one-act plays. He treats the theme more fully in *Curse of the Starving Class,* which marks the next stage of development that culminates in Shepard's definitive treatment of the American family in *Buried Child.* The family plays are among the few of Shepard's works that dispense with music. *Buried Child,* the play that brought him the 1979 Pulitzer Prize for drama, is mockingly described by its author [in an article by Michael Vermeulen in *Esquire,* February 1980] as a "typical Pulitzer Prize winning play." While he denies having written the play for that purpose, he nevertheless admits that, "If I was gonna write a play that would win the Pulitzer Prize, I think it would have been that play." Couching the problems of America in the metaphor of the breakdown of the American family, *Buried Child* makes them more accessible and understandable to the audience. It brought this "epitaph for the American family as an institution" [as Shepard described the play to Vermeulen] an Off Broadway run that was a record for a Shepard play. It was a work that could have easily been moved to Broadway and, bolstered by the publicity connected to the prize, have had a respectable number of performances. Shepard, however, balked at this [in an unpublished letter to Doris Auerbach dated 7 December, 1979]:

> . . . my reservations about Broadway go beyond the "Commercialism" stigma. I really believe the theatre experience is an experience of intimacy, a personal transaction between actors and audience. As the audience increases in size, the intimacy is reduced and becomes absorbed in a kind of mass psychology. Reactions sweep through the audience overtaking the individual and causing him to believe they're his own reactions. Sometimes this sensation may even be thrilling but it often has little to do with, and even robs the person of his own response.

Buried Child, like the majority of Shepard's plays, takes place in the most ordinary of backgrounds, a shabby rural living room. Here Shepard sets out to expose not Pinter's "weasel under the cocktail table" but the child buried in the backyard—the decaying corpse of the American dream. The atmosphere in the family is stifling, repressive, sterile, and noncaring, for the essential element of love is missing. The action is played against a background of archaic, primeval power struggles. It portrays a savage world expressing exclusive patriarchal values of violence and dominance.

The American dream of bountiful Eden, the poetic image of the land, seems no longer fulfillable in an industrial, mechanized, computerized, and dehumanizing society. Shepard suggests the possibility of returning to an America that was once strong, held promises, and nourished its people. This return, however, is possible only when America's reality is confronted without the veil of Norman Rockwell sentimentality, when the crimes of the past are acknowledged and atoned for, and the young can be enlisted to accept their responsibility for the recreation of the dream. From that point on *Buried Child* is the perfect post-Vietnam play, which exhorts the young to turn away from the drop-out world of drugs and cults and the narcissistic concern with "me."

THE MYTHIC WORLD

Shepard has always been noted for his propensity for myth-making. The myths he utilized in *Buried Child* go far back into archaic times to give substance to the struggle of the father to keep his son from gaining power. Dodge, the father who has always "dodged" responsibility for his sons, is the archetypal threatening father whose infanticidal impulse still haunts man's subconscious. The love-denying father ("You think just because people propagate they have to love their offsprings") projects his violence to the mother: "You never saw a bitch eat her puppies?"

The only paternal attribute that Dodge exults in is the macho one of potency: "You know how many kids I've spawned?" But even Dodge senses that this kind of procreation is death rather than life oriented, a murder of the once fecund American tradition. "There's not a living soul behind me. Not a one." He fears his sons, for the prophecy cannot be denied, fate cannot be averted. As Cronus feared death at the hands of his progeny, as Laius tried to escape the prophesied meeting with Oedipus at the crossroad, Dodge is terrified of losing control: "They'll steal your bottle! They'll cut your hair! They'll murder your children."

Ironically, the sons of Dodge are portrayed as impotent against him, and the only children who have been murdered have been killed by him alone. Dodge's three sons are a mockery. Tilden is described as "profoundly burned out and displaced," a walking wounded terribly injured in battle, yet carrying within him memories of a once fruitful land. He is a man whose troubles are explained as: "He got mixed up." Tilden's belief in the fertile paradise that once was and can be again is constantly concretized before the audiences's eyes by the seemingly never ending supplies of corn and carrots that are dumped on stage by him.

Bradley, the second son, is the personification of the ultimate male castration fear. He has a wooden leg that is taken from him by Shelly and Vince, making his helplessness a symbol of impotence. In his hands he carries the instrument of his castration, the scissors with which he threatens and terrorizes Dodge. The impotent son is unable to replace his father; able only to make the father as impotent as he is by cutting off his hair. Dodge, like a modern-day Samson, has lost his power and potency to the now castrating figure of the son. Bradley, who mocks Tilden, and Vince, who ultimately mocks Bradley, are acting out the primeval, brutal Cain and Abel conflict of brotherhood. The castrated, crippled Bradley has all the cruelty of the deeply threatened and all the self-delusion of the powerless: "There was a time, when I had to take that tone of voice from pretty near everyone. Him for one! Him and that half-brain that just ran outa here. They don't talk to me like that now." Bradley deceives himself that he has power, but his words are belied by his action on stage. His sterility is shown by the ultimate act of violent and cruel powerlessness—his fellatio rape of Shelly at the end of the second act.

The third son, Ansel, has been dead for years before the play begins. Halie, the mother, fantasizes him into an avenging hero. "He would have seen we were repaid." The irony is obvious. What should he have repaid his parents for? What do you repay a family that mutilates and kills its offspring?

Into this claustrophobic family enter the two outsiders, Vince (the conqueror) and Shelly. Vince is the archetypal questing hero searching for "his heritage." Vince, the son without a mother, is impelled to carry out his destiny. "Vince has this thing about his family now," says Shelly. He is the personification of the unconscious male womb creation myth, doomed forever to search for the unknowable mother. Neither Dodge nor Tilden acknowledges Vince. To his plea, "I'm their son," Dodge answers, "You're no son of mine. I've had sons in my time and you're not one of them."

"Have I committed an unpardonable offense?" Vince cries out. Tilden, his supposed father, recognizes only a glimpse of him: "I thought I recognized something about him—I thought I saw a face inside the face." Was that face the face of innocence betrayed? The face of an American eager for adventure, for the fulfillment of the dream, the face of the child before it was killed?

The crime of which Vince is guilty is his denial of the caring and nurturing tradition in favor of the violent tradition personified by Dodge. He is Dodge's true son. His long monologue at the end of the third act, his "aria" (Shepard becomes operatic at times) describing his meeting with his daemon, clarifies this:

> I could see myself in the windshield. My face. My eyes. I studied everything about it. As though I was looking at another man. As though I could see his whole face behind him. Like a mummy's face. I saw him dead and alive at the same time. In the same breath. . . . And then his face changed. His face became his father's face. Same bones. Same eyes . . . and his father changed to his grandfather's face. And it went on like that. Changing. Clear on back to faces I'd never seen before but still recognized. . . .

THE BETRAYAL OF THE DREAM

The alienation that the betrayal of the American dream brings is shown by changing Vince's speech from the first to the third person in the middle of the monologue. Vince will never be able to make the earth and the dream fruitful again, for he has accepted the world of power, domination, and violence. This son, cut off forever from the world of the mother, has been fated to usurp the equally sterile reign of Dodge. When Vince reenters the stage in the third act in a drunken rage, breaking empty bottles, he orchestrates his alliance to the violent world of Dodge by the singing of the Marine Hymn. Dodge understands that Vince will replace him. "Maybe I should come in and usurp your territory," Vince announces. Dodge accedes to him. "The house goes to my Grandson Vince." Vince, however, is death, not life, directed. While expounding his plans for making the farm fruitful again, he continues to torture Bradley. When Brad-

ley finally crawls off stage, Vince pulls the blanket away from him and throws it around his own shoulders, just as Bradley had taken the same blanket from Dodge. It shows an endless progression from one violent man to another, dooming us to sterility and death. When the minister suggests that Vince go to Halie and comfort her, he only answers: "My grandmother? There's no one else in the house." It was his last chance to act humanely and humanly. That chance refused, Vince lies down on the couch in the same position we saw Dodge in at the play's opening. The stage direction reads, "His body is in the same relationship to Dodge's," who lies dead on the stage covered with Halie's roses "that almost cover up the stench of sin."

Only one character consistently believes in the land's fruitfulness, Tilden (the tiller of the soil), who appears in the play as the fool purified by suffering. He is the only one who does not try to repress the sins that have been committed and sees the vegetables growing in the backyard that has lain fallow for years. Dodge had planted the corn, but he can neither see nor harvest it. He failed to give it nurturance as he failed to nuture his sons. He never responded to their needs as Tilden plaintively says, "You shoulda worried about me then . . . I was lonely."

Even to Tilden the sudden fecundity of the earth is puzzling. "It's a mystery to me," he says. The only one who can see what Tilden sees is Halie at the end of the play: "Tilden was right about the corn you know. I've never seen such corn. Have you taken a look at it lately? Tall as a man already. This early in the year. Carrots too. Potatoes. Peas. It's like a paradise out there, Dodge—a miracle." Both Halie and Tilden allude clearly to the religious nature of this event. This is a play that makes the meaninglessness of conventional Christianity clear throughout. This is not the religion that can bring about the miracle of a renewed American dream. The minister, Dewis, is drunken, slyly lecherous and profoundly cynical ("God only hears what he wants to") and completely bankrupt spiritually: "I don't know what to do. I don't know what my position is. I just came in for some tea." He neither understands Halie's need for belief nor her realization that we cannot live without it: "We can't not believe in something. We can't stop believing. We just end up dying if we stop. Just end up dead."

Dewis's Christianity is one of meaningless platitudes that instead of facing and resolving problems, covers them up: "These are good people. All righteous people." His spiritual impotence is parallelled by Bradley's physical one. Bradley too wants to pretend all is well: "Nothing is wrong here! Nothing has ever been wrong! Everything's the way it's supposed to be. Nothing ever happened that's bad! Everything is allright here! We're all good people!"

Dodge needs no sentimentalities to cover up his complete lack of belief as he tells Shelly: "Full of faith. Hope. Faith and hope, You're all alike. If it's not God then it's man. If it's not a man then it's a woman. If it's not a woman then it's the land or the future of some kind. Some kind of future." He not only lacks faith in the possibility of transcendence but in humanity as well. "There's nothing a man can't do. You dream it up and he can do it. Anything."

Man, as exemplified by Dodge, is capable of any evil, and there is no reason to believe it will ever be different. "Now you think everything is gonna be different. Just 'cause the sun comes out," he mocks Shelly. The emptiness of this kind of religion is echoed by the meaninglessness of our culture. This is always in front of the audience's eyes in the form of the large TV set which never transmits a picture. The sound is never on, and no one ever seems to watch it but Dodge, who stares at its visionless screen. The jargon of advertisement comes between Halie's memories of youth and her articulation of the present. Her words are couched in travel advertisement words, "flaming sun, flamingos, bougainvilleas, palm trees," and her recollections peopled with travel poster images, "everything was dancing with life. Everyone was dressed to the nines." The recollections are merely remembered ads. She cannot even recall where they took place.

Shelly is the true outsider in this house of "rustic creepiness that verges into visionary madness among these characters who seem to be by Hyronimus Bosch superimposed on Grant Wood" [Harold Clurman, in the *Nation* (2 December 1978)]. Her question, "What's happened to this family anyhow?" sounds the theme of the play. She is frustrated in trying to make any sense of the strange menage. "There isn't any reason here! I can't find any reason for anything."

Dodge senses Shelly's threat to his authority instantly. She is the only innocent and untainted among them. She is the one who unknowingly will force the secret, so long repressed, out into the open. Shelly understands the threat that the buried secret holds for her and the terror that lies behind the cliché of "turkey dinner and apple pie. Her instinct for self-preservation is strong: "I'm fuckin' terrified. I wanna go." The longer she stays, however, the greater becomes her despair at the betrayal of the American dream she shared. This is heightened by her realization that the family has become strangers in their own house, that they no longer correspond to the images and beliefs she has been taught: "For every name, I had an image. I really believed when I walked in through that door that the people who lived here would turn out to be the same people in my imagination. But I don't recognize any of you." Shelly, however, is a survivor. She knows that she is powerless against Dodge and submits to his insulting sexual slurs. She calms him, puts him off his guard by assuming a seemingly nonthreatening domestic role: "I'll stay and cut the carrots and I'll cook the carrots and I'll do whatever I have to do to survive." She sits on stage cutting large carrots, ironically emasculating him while he continues his sexual banter. Her rabbit coat, that both Tilden and Bradley want, provides the only warmth on stage throughout the play. They long for it like for the promise of love that has been so long denied.

Shelly will not be deterred from searching for reason and sense by Dodge's warning, "It's much better not to know anything." Tilden understands the uselessness of pretense; understands that repression and silence can produce only death. Dodge refuses to face the sins that were committed: "I don't want to talk about anything. I don't want to talk about troubles or what happened fifty years ago or thirty years ago. . . . " Tilden warns him that silence will produce only death: "Well, you gotta talk or you'll die." He senses that the answers lie in the past, in traditions that were once viable but have been debased and perverted, traditions that have now turned the land and its inhabitants toward death not life. The answer cannot lie in Dodge's senseless, unfeeling and unreflected action: "There's nothing to figure out. You just forge ahead."

A PROMISE FOR THE FUTURE

Yet even Dodge knows that the emptiness of his present, the disasters that befell his three sons, are connected to the child he had killed: "My flesh and blood is buried in the backyard." Yet he continues to try to convince Tilden into believing that it all happened before he was born. Tilden, confused and burned out as he may be, will not forget: "I had a son once but we buried him." He can still remember before he was "grown up," the days of innocence, the day before the unspeakable crime was committed. Tilden cannot forget. The memory of his child may have burned him out, but it still enables him to be the only one who sees the possibility of the land. The one who nurtured the child is the one who will make the earth fruitful again: "He'd walk all night out in the pasture with it. Talkin' to it. Singing to it. Used to hear him singing to it." But Tilden could not protect the child from Dodge. "Little baby. Dodge killed it." Tilden continues to mourn the child: "He [Dodge] is the only one who knows where it's buried. The only one. Like a secret treasure. Won't tell any of us. Won't tell me or mother. . . . "

This is the only time in the play that Tilden refers to Halie as mother—his mother and also the mother of his child. The mother who was unable to protect the true son, the savior. Like Eve, Halie bore the child in pain. It was Tilden's child that "begged to be born" and that wanted to live, that would deny the heritage of Dodge's violence. It was the child that "wanted to be believed in." Tilden is the image of the caring man who has returned to the world of the mother and has turned his back upon his father. Dodge commits infanticide for his patriarchal power was threatened: "Couldn't allow a thing like that to grow up in the middle of our lives." The existence of the child promised a new world order which would have ended patriarchy's violent hegemony. This child had to be conceived through incest. How else are new races founded—with whom did Adam's son mate but with Eve?

But Dodge could not destroy the promise of the child. As Halie describes it: "You just gotta wait till it pops up out of the ground. Tiny little shoot. Tiny little white shoot all hairy and fragile. Strong though. Strong enough to break the earth even. It's a miracle. . . . "

The play ends like a miracle play with the symbol of the resurrection. The child is taken from the tomb, tended by its father and carried up, not to the patriarchal figure who lies dead on stage before us, but to the mother who is waiting above. ***Buried Child*** leaves the audience with hope for a revitalized America, for one that nourishes its children and holds the promise of the American dream once again.

Thomas Nash (essay date 1983)

SOURCE: "Sam Shepard's *Buried Child:* The Ironic Use of Folklore," in *Modern Drama,* Vol. XXVI, No. 4, December, 1983, pp. 486-91.

[In the essay below, Nash finds that Shepard utilizes elements of traditional folklore in Buried Child, *creating "a modern version of the central theme of Western mythology, the death and rebirth of the Corn King."]*

Although Sam Shepard's **Buried Child** won the 1979 Pulitzer Prize for drama, this eerie and provocative story continues to baffle critics and audiences alike—at least those who have not done their homework in folklore and anthropology. **Buried Child,** like the famous Shirley Jackson short story "The Lottery," borrows heavily from the images and motifs found in Sir James Frazer's *The Golden Bough.* Those who do not see the hand of the anthropologist in Shepard's play—and there are surprisingly many who write review columns—have called **Buried Child** "an American gothic comedy" or "a poor impression of a play by Pinter or Albee." Directors are also not immune from confusion, sometimes interpreting as comedy several scenes of the play which are clearly intended as ritual. In fact, **Buried Child** is a serious statement that pulls at the very bone and marrow, its plot a modern version of the central theme of Western mythology, the death and rebirth of the Corn King.

What bothers and even mortifies so many viewers is Shepard's style. Like Jackson, who angered thousands of readers when "The Lottery" first appeared in a 1948 edition of *The New Yorker,* Shepard begins his story in the manner of realism. His realistically drawn characters bicker, argue, and insult one another, establishing the recognizable beacons of a domestic conflict. However, in the course of plot development, the influence of folklore and mythology becomes more forceful, so that the realism of the early scenes fades like twilight; in the final scenes, Shepard's characters, like Jackson's, move in the dusky light of ritual. Both authors employ what Northrop Frye [in *Anatomy of Criticism* (1967)] calls the *ironic mode,* a style that "begins in realism and dispassionate observation. But as it does so, it moves steadily towards myth, and dim outlines of sacrificial rituals and dying gods begin to reappear in it." Both authors, Jackson and Shepard, conclude their works with the revelation of murders that are tied to the growth of corn. In "The Lottery," Old Man Warner obliquely justifies the approaching ritual sacrifice of a community member when he recites the ancient proverb "Lottery in June, corn be heavy soon." In **Buried Child,** the dramatist ties the regeneration of the long fallow cornfields to the resurrection of the young boy who was buried between the rows some forty years ago, having been murdered by Dodge, the family patriarch. Jackson's story ends with the festive stoning of Tessie Hutchinson as homeopathic insurance of fertile fields; Shepard's play concludes with the ritual return of the buried child, come to life to claim his inheritance and to preside benignly over the scene of his murderer's death.

The initial curtain of **Buried Child** reveals an old man watching television in a decrepit farmhouse in Middle America. Dodge, a man in his seventies, sits like Eliot's Gerontion, awaiting death as a release from the boredom of a hollow life. Occasionally he swigs at a bottle of whiskey hidden in the lumpy folds of his couch. As Halie, his wife, nags and pontificates from the top of the stairs, we discover that an incessant rain has been falling in the untilled fields. A significant rain, it washes the marrow from the bones of the buried child, fertilizing the long neglected cornfields, preparing the land for a miraculous rebirth.

Dodge has fathered three sons. Tilden, the eldest, once an all-American football player, is now a half-wit, reduced by the Fall of this House of Oedipus to the mentality of a child. As the play begins, he is plodding through the fields, picking the suddenly emergent corn. Bradley, the second son, has designs on his father's property; but he also has been reduced to a grotesque, having lost a leg in a chain-saw accident some years earlier. The youngest son, Ansel, is dead, killed in his motel room on the night of his honeymoon, after having married unwisely into a family with connections to the Mob. The youngest son, as we are constantly reminded by Halie, "was a hero," and he "would've stopped him!" In folklore, it is a recognized rule of narrative that the third son is the heroic one. Therefore, as the folkloric roots of the drama become more evident, it is clear that a kind of "heroic vacuum" paralyzes the family, a void that will soon be filled, however.

Like the House of Oedipus, the family of Dodge and Halie is cursed by the combined acts of *overrating* and *underrating* blood relations, to use Claude Lévi-Strauss's terms [from "The Structural Study of Myth," in *Myth: A Symposium,* edited by A. Sebeok (1958)]. Dodge explains the origins of the curse to the one character who has the least right to know—Shelly, a stranger:

> Halie had this kid. This baby boy. She had it. I let her have it on her own. All the other boys I had had the best doctors, best nurses, everything. This one I let her have by herself. This one hurt real bad. Almost killed her, but she had it anyway. It lived, see. It lived. It wanted to grow up in this family. It wanted to be just like us. It wanted to be a part of us. It wanted to pretend that I was its father. She wanted me to believe in it. Even when everyone around us knew. Everyone. All our boys knew. Tilden knew. . . . Tilden was the one who knew. Better than any of us. He'd walk for miles with that kid in his arms. Halie let him take it. All night sometimes. He'd walk all night out there in the pasture with it. Talkin' to it. Singin' to it. Used to hear him singing to it. He'd make up stories. He'd tell that kid all kinds a' stories. Even when he knew it couldn't understand him. . . . We couldn't let a thing like that continue. We couldn't allow that to grow up right in the middle of our lives. It made everything we'd accomplished look like it was nothin'. Everything was cancelled out by this one mistake. This one weakness.

In this initial scene of conflict, the family's dark secret reveals an *overrating* of blood relations: Tilden's incest and the subsequent birth of the unwanted child. The secret also reveals the *underrating* of blood ties: the infanticide that Dodge later confesses. As Lévi-Strauss says in "The Structural Study of Myth," this polarization can be resolved only by the introduction of a third element that subsumes the antithetical properties of the first two. Vince, the grandson of Dodge and Halie, is the mediating element; he is also a character whose entry into the drama marks the beginning of the mythic theme.

The first of the three acts of **Buried Child** establishes the naturalistic setting that Vince will invade in the second act. In the early moments of the play, Dodge awaits death in a costume of khaki clothes, his body draped in colors that symbolically represent the withering of his body and soul. He and Halie recall their domestic troubles, their losses, their tragedies; Tilden then enters with arms full of corn and is accused of stealing from the neighbors' fields; Bradley, thumping in on his wooden leg, arrives to give his father a vicious haircut. Throughout, the gloom of impending death casts a long shadow; a destructive emptiness pervades the scene.

When Vince, the grandson, finally arrives, the drama assumes a different character, a remoteness and communality that accompany the ritual of the killing of the Corn Spirit— the Old Man of the European Harvest, as Frazer describes him. At first, Dodge and the other family members do not recognize Vince; he is an intruder into a home where no one has the will to throw him out. And yet, Tilden offers some clue to the boy's identity. He says, "I thought I recognized him. I thought I recognized something about him. . . . I thought I saw a face inside his face." The face, of course, is his son's. Yet Vince remains unrecognized because he is the reincarnation of the buried child, now returned to claim his patrimony, a return signaled by the sudden and startling growth of corn in the fields. However, Vince is also the lost brother Ansel and, in fact, the spirit of all the children born to Dodge's ancestry. And Vince himself recognizes his multifarious identities. In Act III, after having tried to escape the madness of the farmhouse scene by getting drunk and driving west, he returns to explain a vision that visited him on his journey:

> . . . last night. . . . I could see myself in the windshield. My face. My eyes. I studied my face. Studied everything about it. As though I was looking at another man. As though I could see his whole race behind him. Like a mummy's face. I saw him dead and alive at the same time. In the same breath. In the windshield, I watched him breathe as though he was frozen in time. And every breath marked him. Marked him forever without him knowing. And then his face changed. His face became his father's face. Same bones. Same eyes. Same nose. Same breath. And his father's face changed to his Grandfather's face. And it went on like that. Changing. Clear on back to faces I'd never seen before but still recognized. Still recognized the bones underneath. The eyes. The breath. The mouth. I followed my family clear into Iowa. Every last one. Straight into the Corn Belt and further. Straight back as far as they'd take me.

Gradually, as Act III unfolds, the play reveals its ritual quality and its roots in folk drama. For instance, when Vince returns from his drunken travels into the night, he enters the house—drunk and boisterous—by cutting his way through a locked screen door. Now he is recognized by

all. Clearly, Shepard has used his dramatic moment as a *symbolic rebirth,* calculated to correspond to the exact moment when Tilden, alone in the rain, must be pulling the decayed corpse of the buried child from the mud of the cornfields. Ironically, in the next moment Dodge, who has previously ignored the boy, announces that his house and property will be given to Vince.

The ritual atmosphere of this rebirth scene is reinforced in several ways. First, Dodge's testament and Vince's reawakening are presided over by the ineffectual figure of Father Dewis, slightly drunk, who has returned from town with Halie. Second, when Halie stumbles into the assembly, she carries a single rose, which she drops between the legs of Dodge, who is lying on the floor. The moment is given more meaning when we recall early events in the play. In Act I, while Dodge sleeps on the couch, he is visited by his sons Tilden and Bradley. Tilden, after shucking an entire basket of corn, spreads the husks gravely over the body of his father, suggesting Dodge's symbolic role as the Corn King in the winter of his life. Bradley, as though to emphasize the impotence of the dying patriarch, sneaks up on Dodge and gives him a vicious haircut, leaving bloody scars and lacerations across the old man's scalp. Halie's rose apparently signifies the figurative castration and imminent death of the old man, coming especially as it does during the moment of Vince's rebirth. Finally, having allowed Vince to fill the "heroic vacuum" in the family, Dodge announces his own impending death and asks for a burial suitable for the dying Corn King:

> The house goes to my Grandson, Vincent. All the furnishings, accoutrements and paraphernalia therein. Everything tacked to the walls or otherwise resting under this roof. My tools—namely my band saw, my skill saw, my drill press, my chain saw, my lathe, my electric sander, all go to my eldest son, Tilden. That is, if he ever shows up again. My shed and gasoline powered equipment, namely my tractor, my dozer, my hand tiller plus all the attachments and riggings for the above mentioned machinery, namely my spring tooth harrow, my deep plows, my disk plows, my automatic fertilizing equipment, my reaper, my swathe, my seeder, my John Deere Harvester, my post hole digger, my jackhammer, my lathe. . . . Did I mention my lathe? I already mentioned my lathe—my Bennie Goodman records, my harnesses, my bits, my halters, my brace, my rough rasp, my forge, my welding equipment, my shoeing nails, my levels and bevels, my milking stool—no, not my milking stool—my hammers and chisels, my hinges, my cattle gates, my barbed wire, self-tapping augers, my horse hair ropes and all related materials are to be pushed into a gigantic heap and set ablaze in the very center of my fields. When the blaze is at its highest, preferably on a cold, windless night, my body is to be pitched into the middle of it and burned till nothing remains but ash.

In *The Golden Bough,* Frazer explains the special reasons why agrarian dwellers use fire to consume the body of any figure who represents the spirit of vegetation: "light and heat are necessary for vegetable growth; and, on the principle of sympathetic magic, by subjecting the personal representative of vegetation to their influence, you secure a supply of these necessaries for trees and crops. In other words, by burning the spirit of vegetation in a fire which represents the sun, you make sure that, for the time being at least, vegetation shall have plenty of sun." Dodge, after his symbolic burial under a blanket of cornhusks, and after his symbolic castration under the attack of Bradley's clippers, now seeks the proper end for a Corn King too enfeebled by age and impotent to continue his rule: the ceremonial pyre.

As if by an act of will, Dodge dies, his head dropping to his chest. Few of the family members notice, however, for the house's lights have dimmed, revealing the hulking figure of Tilden, who appears framed in the smoky light of a distant doorway. Very slowly he comes forward, bearing a small burden through the dark halls. Dramatically, as Tilden reaches the center of the stage, the harsher light from Halie's upstairs room illuminates him. Raised to eye level, Tilden's burden is the tattered corpse of a small child, its bones wrapped in muddy, rotten cloth. As Tilden climbs the lighted stairs, Halie's voice intrudes from above. Ironically, she addresses Dodge, now lying dead, in terms rich with ambiguity:

> Good hard rain. Takes everything straight down deep to the roots. The rest takes care of itself. You can't force a thing to grow. You can't interfere with it. It's all hidden. It's all unseen. You just gotta wait til it pops up out of the ground. Tiny little shoot. Tiny little white shoot. All hairy and fragile. Strong though. Strong enough to break the earth even. It's a miracle, Dodge. I've never seen a crop like this in my whole life. Maybe it's the sun. Maybe that's it. Maybe it's the sun.

The play has come full circle. *Buried Child* achieves what Lévi-Strauss describes happening in the course of the relation of a myth: binary opposites are reconciled by a third, mediating element. In fact, the polar opposites of Shepard's play—the overrating and underrating of blood relations—are the same ones used by Lévi-Strauss to describe the structure of the Oedipus myth. The blood ties of family were overrated in Tilden's incest with Halie; they were underrated in the infanticide that became the family secret. In the end, Vince's rebirth reconciles these antitheses. The Corn Spirit has died, ending his tenure in the symbolic lick of the flames, but he lives again in the person of the new king.

As in "The Lottery," the debts to tradition and to folklore are not apparent until the final scene of epiphany, even though a symbolic level of meaning has been emerging since the first act. *Buried Child,* like the Jackson story of similar tone, moves from realism to ritual in a manner that can clearly be called "ironic," for here, behind the seemingly trivial squabbles and musings of a typical Midwestern family, are the shadows of sacrificial rites and the shades of dying gods.

FOOL FOR LOVE

PRODUCTION REVIEWS

Walter Kerr (review date 5 June 1983)

SOURCE: "Where Has Sam Shepard Led His Audience?," in *The New York Times,* June 5, 1983, pp. 3, 16.

[Fool for Love *was first presented at Magic Theatre in San Francisco in February 1983, with Shepard serving as the play's director, and this production later played the Circle Repertory Theatre in New York City. In the following review of one of the New York performances, Kerr criticizes Shepard as a "cult dramatist" whose work, despite its skilled presentation, addresses only a select audience and a limited range of topics.*]

During the more than 20 years that Sam Shepard has been writing for the theater he has gradually acquired what is called a cult audience. What is a cult audience? It is a band of faithful playgoers whose tastes are identical or at least strongly similar to one another's and who respond well, as a group, to the rather private and deliberately enigmatic signals being sent from the stage. This is indeed an audience and it is capable of some enlargement as devotees pass the word along to friends of like mind. A prolific writer—and Sam Shepard is certainly that, turning out new work yearly—may find productions of his plays on the increase, especially in regional theaters. He may also find his playing-time being extended here and there, while one or another of his pieces may come up with a prize, sometimes a prestigious one. And I suspect that he may, in passing and not really by calculation, make a reasonably good living as a professional dramatist.

For all that, a cult dramatist seems to be a man facing a cutoff point. It's not often that he hooks into the much larger—indeed the unlimited—general audience, the audience that embraces all comers and all tastes, provoking them into a universalized response. Either he doesn't care to make his imagery clear and newly illuminating to this across-the-board gathering, or he doesn't know how to. Either way, his tendency is to stick to his bailiwick and keep on doing what he's been doing, even if this forces him into repeating doleful banalities about our estrangement from the good earth (shades of Walter Brennan, running dirt through his fingers!) or about the regretable disappearance of the frontiers of the West (which surely disappeared sometime before Mr. Shepard arrived on the scene to regret them). But doing retreads, with variations, for the very same people who saw the earlier samples, has got to be a dangerous habit for a dramatist to indulge. By resting contentedly at the cutoff point, he brings his own development to a standstill.

Fool for Love, which the Circle Rep has brought from Mr. Shepard's own Magic Theater of San Francisco, is an excellent case in point because it is performed with such absolute authority. The staging is precise, confident and reliable, having been done by Mr. Shepard himself. The performing, alternating between snakelike quiet and near-volcanic uproar, is skilled at every temperature. The lighting and sound effects, designed by Kurt Landisman and Ardyss L. Golden, are spectacular enough to suggest that the Jedi have returned to this particular motel room on the edge of the Mojave Desert (and promptly checked out again, revolted by the setting's Nausea Green paint-job). Physically and mechanically, the production knows what it is about.

I wish we did. I don't say that to be flippant, or to pretend to a confusion caused by the author's carelessness. I say it because Mr. Shepard does not *want* us—ever—to be certain of what his door-slamming dance of rage is meant to signify. The first lines spoken during the evening inform us that no matter what we see happen, no matter what we hear happen, we dare not assume that we can believe any of it. To explain:

In the nearly naked room—the rear windows give on utter blackness, the orange-yellow doors at either side perfectly complement the hideousness of the walls—there are two people. One, a disheveled young woman named May, sits limply on the edge of a wrought-iron bed, bare feet askew and hands crossed as helplessly as a discarded rag doll's. The other, a going-to-seed rodeo "stunt man" (the phrase may also have sexual connotations, I'm not sure), is fiddling with his leather holster and trying to stir up a conversation. The two have had an off-and-on affair, made up of passion and scorn in about equal parts, for 15 years (or since their chance meeting in high school), but before we can learn as much there is a slight stir at downstage Left and a half-bearded, well-bloated old boy in a rocking chair is speaking from the space beyond the proscenium (or Out of Frame, as it were).

"You're supposed to be a fantasist, aren't you?" he asks the young man, Eddie, before instructing him to look at a picture on the wall. There is no picture on the wall, though Eddie agrees that he sees one. The old fellow, after a swig of handy Jim Bean, remarks that he is himself married to Barbara Mandrell, carefully adding the phrase, "in my mind." Thus we are warned. What follows may exist only in the characters' minds; we have no way of knowing whether the action, the dialogue, or the people are true or false. The point is made again at play's end, creating a kind of sandwich of uncertainty.

Inside the sandwich, there is only one noticeable reference to the possibility that a strong whiff of reality might wipe the slate clean. In her first burst of violence, May screams that she knows Eddie has come back only to erase her or have her erased. Do we take this to mean that she knows she is part of someone else's fantasy and can easily be scrubbed? Or is she just engaging in mobsters'-moll talk, and not very good mobsters'-moll talk at that? Our question, if asked, is never answered, for after a short time spent in the bathroom she reenters with both her hair and her courage all pulled together. She is easily Eddie's equal now, and as she sensually strides into the center of the play there is no further suggestion that she is in imminent danger of disappearing.

Ed Harris as Eddie and Kathy Baker as May in a 1983 production of Fool for Love *at the Magic Theatre, San Francisco.*

The center of the play includes, to begin with, a long silent sexual stalking that ends in a cobra-like wrap-around; I suppose that this must be considered generic stage business by now and that Harold Pinter can no longer claim copyright on it. This is preceded, interrupted, and followed by a habit both lovers have of slamming *something* against the green wall: their hands, their backs, their buttocks, a lariat, a purse and heaven knows what I may have missed. Tired of abusing the wall (how does designer Andy Stacklin keep the set standing under the assault?), they open both doors just to have the pleasure of whapping them back into place with enough force to jar their hinges and our teeth.

These are of course not realistic uses of the premises. Mayhap they are meant to serve as dramatic punctuation, as establishing beats in an overall rhythm. Since they do not vary from slam to slam or in any way seem to influence the bitter contest going on, I am afraid we must call them arbitrary and simply one more sampling of Mr. Shepard's fondness for disconnective, dislocating "effect."

As in all of the author's plays, there are many such. Here the noisiest and most threatening had to do with what is happening to Eddie's truck and horse-trailer, parked outside. May stands in the doorway, seeing (or inventing) a woman who waits for Eddie in a Mercedes Benz. Suddenly there is a great revving of motors, a shrill squeal of skidding tires, a blacking out of the motel room lights so that only the careering headlights in the yard can be seen flashing giddily across the windowpanes. The crash and clatter on the outside is echoed by a frantic chase inside, with Eddie winding up the victor, protectively (?) astride his love. Later on, the presence of a third party is promised ("He's just an ordinary date," "Hell, I'm going to turn him into a fig"). Arriving, the newcomer makes a running leap to land on Eddie's back while May, with a taste for acrobatics, leaps onto *his* back.

If the entertainment's percussive "effects" have no real effect on the long-standing resentments of the temporarily caged couple, neither do they have any bearing on the gradual revelation that Eddie and May are children of the same father, the untroubled old fellow who is sometimes Out of Frame and sometimes In. The subject of incest is now heatedly discussed. It is not, however, the cause of the pair's automated flareups. These are reflexes, dating back to a time when the two were no more than ignorant adolescents and they are not going to be modified by questions of consanguinity now. Particularly when the whole tale may not be true.

When all that is happening in a play may not be happening, and when the people to whom it is happening may simply not exist, difficulties do arise. The now-you-see-it-now-you-don't treatment of the characters, for instance, must be so skittish and indefinite that it tends to deny them the chance to *be* anybody. The evening flirts with a fundamental boredom because of a strong sense that, under the make-up, there is nobody there. And if we are to call into question the reality of personality as well as of event, Pirandello-style, then we surely need a richer use of language to hold us spellbound while all secrets are kept. I do not hear that in a line like May's "Fifteen years I've been a yoyo for you." The production, then, is firm and energetic. The play I must leave to the cult.

With this afterthought. Surprisingly, the cult itself is divided in an odd but unmistakable way. At every Shepard play I have seen, a portion of the audience—a minority, perhaps, but a determined one—has treated the work as comedy, forcing giggles and titters regularly as though in support of their man. Another portion treats the work before it with entire sobriety. People whose opinions I respect are to be found in both camps: some audibly amused, some almost grim in their fixed attentiveness. I find *that* disconnecting. I can understand a cult, its causes and perhaps its consequences. What I cannot quite understand is a split cult, re-subdivided.

William Kleb (review date Summer-Fall 1983)

SOURCE: "Sam Shepard's Free-for-All: *Fool for Love* at the Magic Theatre," in *Theater,* Vol. XIV, No. 3, Summer-Fall, 1983, pp. 77-82.

[*In the following excerpt, Kleb discusses Shepard's thematic treatment of fantasy and reality in* Fool for Love *and*

also points out several "troubling" factors regarding Shepard's "attitude towards gender, sexuality and sexual role definition."]

Fool for Love, Sam Shepard's new play, lasts one hour and forty minutes. There is no intermission. As directed by Shepard himself in a world premiere at the Magic Theatre in San Francisco, the effect is relentless, explosive, exhausting—and troubling. The playwright/director and his four actors seem determined to generate enough energy to blast themselves and the audience out of the cramped confines of the Magic Theatre's tiny, 99-seat proscenium house. The performance is passionate; the play, on the most immediate level, is about passion. . . .

Fool for Love, . . . comes across as a kind of psycho-sexual free-for-all, or nightmare, and Shepard's production magnifies and intensifies the violence of its action and imagery. The set is a tight, Skinnerian box of a room, empty except for the bed, off-center, and a formica-topped table with two chrome dinette chairs pushed into the corner down left. The floor is bare; the walls are blank. Two canary yellow doors, right and left, lead to the bathroom and the parking lot. In the back wall, a narrow, aluminum-framed window with green plastic curtains opens out onto the night; a street lamp throws a sharp, blue-white rectangle against one wall. The side walls angle sharply inward, towards the back, creating a forced perspective that increases the sense of claustrophobia and isolation. At times, the room looks bleakly realistic; at others, austere and abstract. Within it, the actors seem huge, as if projected, larger than life, against the blank green walls. Because of the size of the theatre, we see them close up, and the harsh, flat lighting emphasizes their raw physicality. This is underscored by the two actors Shepard has cast as Eddy and May—Ed Harris and Kathy Baker. Both exude a kind of rank, over-ripe sexuality and Shepard directs them at full-throttle, emphasizing movement and contact. They throw themselves around the room like wrestlers and they use the walls like the ropes of a fight ring. The slamming of bodies and fists is punctuated by the slamming of doors; Shepard has even amplified the latter with reverberating microphones in the jambs.

But what, if anything, does all this sound and fury signify? Such a production does not lend itself to critical reflection, at least not in transit. When the dust clears, however, it becomes apparent that *Fool for Love* does have an intention beyond simply providing an experience of "passionate intensity." Shepard himself hinted as much in an interview before the opening in which he said that his new play would have something to do with the relationship between "realism" and "fantasism"—not surprisingly, of course, since this has been a central theme in his work from the beginning. *Fool for Love* not only slips and slides between various levels of reality; it sets up "realism" and "fantasism" as contradictory approaches to experience and generates a conflict between them—one which, finally, implies value judgements both in its development and its resolution. When the Old Man first speaks to Eddy, he actually calls him a "fantasist," and obviously this is the side Eddy represents: he has just had a love affair with a countess who gets her picture on the cover of fashion magazines; he wants to take May to a farm in Wyoming where they'll raise chickens and vegetables; he makes his living as a rodeo cowboy and stuntman, the ultimate modern-day illusionist. Martin, on the other hand, is Shepard's stand-in for "realism"—he's brave, clean, considerate; he has a responsible job at the high school; he doesn't know any "stories" and won't make any up because that would be "lyin'." Clearly, the fight is fixed. Eddy may be living in a dream world, but he is also sexy, funny and tough; not only that, he's an artist—a performer and storyteller of wit and imagination. He has sexual and creative power; he's a force. Martin, to be blunt, is a wimp; he's unattractive, meek, earthbound, not-quite-there. The choice, of course, is May's and the out-come is never in doubt. Despite her struggle to live in the real world (she has a new job as a cook, she wants to be a "regular citizen," and she's going to the movies with Martin), when Eddy's around, she can't. She hates his "country dream" ("What's up in Wyoming, Marlboro Men?"), she wants to kill his countess, and she knees him viciously in the groin to prove, presumably, that even stunt men get the blues. But she's also obsessively attracted to him and to everything he represents: his absurd posturing with a lasso turns her on; she refuses to go away with him, then packs her bag when he's out of the room. His presence infuriates yet mesmerizes her. There's no escape; again and again he pulls her to him, then, like the Old Man, disappears.

This conflict, May's dilemma, is the thematic center of Shepard's play and it is clearly restated at the climax. May has introduced Eddy to Martin as her "cousin," but when she goes into the bathroom to get ready to leave, Eddy tells Martin that May is really his half-sister: "I never even knew I had a sister until it was too late . . . by the time I found out, we'd already, you know, fooled around." Eddy's intention is clear; he wants to shock Martin and frighten him off. Martin, however, is skeptical, so Eddy tells the story of how he and May first met. Actually, he doesn't just tell it, he stages it, forcing Martin to join him in acting it out. Together they walk around and around the bed as Eddy tells how, one night when he was a boy, he went with the Old Man through muddy fields, past a huge drive-in movie screen with Spencer Tracy on it talking silently to a woman in red, on to a liquor store, then finally to a small, white suburban house with red awnings where the Old Man was greeted passionately by a woman with red hair. At this point, Eddy's tone shifts, his performance stops, and he stands motionless, ignoring Martin now, staring intently at the Old Man as he continues his tale:

> And then through the doorway, behind them both, I see this girl. She just appears. She's just standing there, staring at me and I'm staring back at her and we can't take our eyes off each other. It was like we knew each other from somewhere but we couldn't place where. But the second we saw each other, that very second, we knew we'd never stop being in love.

Just at that moment, May reappears, framed by the door and the red bathroom walls behind her. She's furious. "None of that's true, Martin," she says, and at first it seems as though she's denying everything, even that she and Eddy are relat-

ed. Then it becomes clear that she is only attacking Eddy's *version* of the story, the *way* he has told it. When he tries to continue, she insists on telling it herself, "exactly the way it happened, without any little tricks added onto it." Predictably, May's version seems radically different. She tells it directly to Eddy with a kind of fierce intensity, and she tells it from her mother's point of view as well as her own. Obsessed by love for the Old Man, May's mother searched for him from town to town until she finally tracked him down; two weeks later he disappeared. By then, May and Eddy were going to school together, and they were in love; their love became so strong that it made them both physically sick; May's mother knew what was wrong, but she couldn't keep them apart. Finally she appealed to Eddy's mother who, apparently, had not known of the Old Man's "split" love; stunned, Eddy's mother shot herself.

Actually, the details of these two stories do not contradict each other in any significant way; the difference is in the manner in which each is told, the point of view and the emphasis. In short, May refuses to romanticize the past, to theatricalize it; in particular, she refuses to distort or ignore the tragic outcome for Eddy's mother; she insists: "Didn't she Eddy? Blew her brains right out." At first Eddy just stares at her in silence, but the Old Man challenges May immediately on this point. He denies the suicide ever happened, and the implication is that Eddy has denied it, too, in the past. So crucial is this question that it draws the Old Man off his platform and actually into the room where he confronts Eddy and demands that he defend him—"face her eyeball to eyeball." Instead, Eddy simply says "It was your shotgun. Same one we used to duck hunt with. Browning." Then, as the Old Man rails in disbelief, Eddy and May move silently toward each other, center stage, embrace and kiss. The moment seems less a reconciliation than a capitulation and it takes place against the background of Eddy's exploding truck, screaming horses, and the flash of the countess's headlights. Eddy, presumably, has accepted May's "reality" but he has also suckered her in, again. After a moment, he pulls back; he has to go outside; he'll be right back—in "a second." May stares after him; she knows "he's gone." As Martin watches, May slowly packs her bag and walks out into the night, alone. In short, for May, there can be no escape, no resolution: she exemplifies (and *Fool for Love* dramatizes) the Old Romantic Agony. She is trapped, like Keats's "wretched wight," between two symbolic worlds—Reality (concrete, secure, stable, but also bleak, sordid, empty, dead) and Fantasy (dangerous, insubstantial, unreliable, self-destructive, but passionate, exciting, full of life.)

This analysis is complicated by two factors in particular, both troubling—gender and the fact of May and Eddy's kinship. Questioning May about Martin early in the play, Eddy asks if he's a "guy" or a "man." Being a "guy," it turns out, means being like Eddy; being a "man" means being Martin. One, of course, is identified with "fantasism," the other, with "realism," and perhaps this is simply Shepard's way of making an ironic comment on the kind of maleness Eddy represents (and on his snide condescension towards Martin). But if, in Shepard's scheme, the deck is clearly stacked in favor of "fantasism," so, too, it seems that we are meant to prefer and admire the kind of maleness Eddy represents. This is confirmed not only by May's attraction to Eddy, but by her inability to free herself *from him, and by her willingness to participate in her own objectification for* him. Shortly after the play begins, May changes clothes, presumably for her date with Martin. Logically, she would do this in the bathroom; clearly this is her "space," as we can see through the open door (it is stuffed with her clothes, hanging and in piles), while there is nothing of her in the outer room but the suitcase under the bed. Still, she changes on the stage, in front of Eddy, stripping to her black bra and panties, putting on pantyhose, high heels and a scarlet wrap-around dress. Her nakedness in this all-but-empty space, next to the un-made bed, is less startling than the bright red dress she puts on. The symbolic value of the color red is explicitly stressed by Shepard throughout the play, from May's red toe nails, to the red walls of her bathroom, to the repetition of the color red in the story Eddy tells at the end. It connotes female sexuality, or more precisely, the objectification of male sexual fantasy—the romantic (erotic) picture in the mind.

Shepard's use of incest is equally disturbing. Even today, when we know that the incest taboo is not and never was "universal," especially as it pertains to half-brothers and half-sisters, the act itself still carries such emotional power and weight that we immediately assume it must have a central thematic role in any work that features it. In *Fool for Love,* this is not the case. Initially we learn of the blood-bond between Eddy and May only by inference. When the Old Man first addresses them, separately, he does not actually say that he is the father of either; nor does he directly refer to their kinship to each other. Then when he does speak to them as brother and sister, it is only to deny that he recognizes them as *his:* "You could be anybody's." For their part, May and Eddy seem to ignore the matter almost entirely, at least when they're alone. May calls Eddy "guilty" at one point (without saying why), Eddy refers enigmatically to their "pact," and there are one or two other comments which seem to vibrate ambiguously in light of the Old Man's (delayed and oblique) revelations. Without these, however (or without his presence), such comments would be virtually meaningless. In short, for the first two-thirds of his play, Shepard keeps the incestuous aspect of May and Eddy's relationship mysteriously in the background, or, in light of the Old Man's physical position on stage, literally at the edge of the action. After Martin's arrival, of course, the matter is brought to the fore, but then the dramatic focus (or question) shifts immediately from *what* has occurred between the two of them to a conflict (in which the Old Man takes part) over *how* it occurred—the manner in which it is remembered and perceived. From being mysteriously suppressed, the incestuous nature of May and Eddy's relationship seems, at the climax of *Fool for Love,* almost to be irrelevant.

This interpretation is reinforced by the moral attitude towards incest which runs throughout Shepard's play. Brother-sister incest is, in fact, the most common type encountered in history and literature, and *Fool for Love* evokes a number of intriguing echoes (e.g., Amnon's passion for Tamar, *2 Sam.,* 13). However, while the overheated intensity of May and Eddy's love is typical (especially in its love-hate emphasis), what sets the lovers apart from the vast majority of their literary and dramatic siblings is the lack of any real sense of guilt or shame. Martin, of course, is shocked when he learns the truth, but for the others, incest is a matter of moral indifference. May and Eddy are tormented by their love but not because it is incestuous, while the Old Man (who personifies the mental or spiritual presence of the Father) raises the issue only at the end and only in self-defense; until the final confrontation, their sexual encounters only seem to amuse him.

Nevertheless is it possible that *Fool for Love* is a kind of moral parable, with incest as the key to its meaning, despite the moral "blindness" or lack of "recognition" of its main characters. May and Eddy might feel guiltless simply because there has been no firm social context for their actions, no *social* consequences. Eddy lives on the road and out of a trailer; May is trying to settle down but the bleak motel room in which she lives indicates that she is as much a transient in the world as Eddy. Indeed, it might be argued that their fragmented, rootless, barren and violent lives symbolize what happens when the incest taboo is violated, while the condition for their act (or sin) could even be said to stem (a favorite theme in Shepard) from the breakdown of a paternalistic nuclear family (the Old Man has two families and abandons both when he is exposed).

On the other hand, the explosive contour of May and Eddy's love seems actually shaped not by the fact of their kinship but by genetic inheritance. Like the Old Man, Eddy cannot be satisfied by one woman no matter how intense the bond between them; his "love," too, is "split," not between two women but between one and many. Like her mother, May is the victim of an obsessive passion for one man, and she makes it quite clear in her story that this is a sickness that was passed directly from mother to daughter. Strangely, then, in *Fool for Love,* genetic transmission seems to have operated strictly along the lines of gender. Eddy has inherited his character from the Old Man, while May's owes nothing to him at all; she is entirely her mother's child. Again, their kinship seems to be essentially beside the point: they could have had *different* fathers; their mismatched temperaments would have been the same.

Thus, in *Fool for Love,* incest has little or no real function in the development of the central conflict of the play, and it is a matter of moral indifference not only to the characters but, here, to the playwright as well. It seems to have been included simply for its metaphoric value, as a particularly potent symbol for the intensity of the bond that exists between Eddy and May. Indeed, throughout his work, Shepard insists on the blood-bond as a powerful, primal connective force. Theoretically, its natural erotic component is purged by daily association within the context of normal family life; the result is sexual indifference or aversion (the root, some think, of the incest taboo). If such a process does not occur (when, for example, a brother and sister are raised separately), the forces of kinship and sexuality may operate together (even, Shepard seems to believe, when the lovers are not aware that they are related). As a result, the relationship is doubly primed, tapped in at once to the two most powerful sources of emotional attraction. Shepard even seems to suggest that this connection is so intense that the two are practically one person. If so, the composite ego they represent is indeed depressing—dominated by a masculine component defined as a sexually obsessed, self-involved, self-dramatizing "cowboy," with a repressed feminine component seen exclusively in sexual terms (a kind of "scarlet woman"), perpetually in revolt yet, at the same time, participating willingly in her own enslavement and victimization.

These thoughts, framed in retrospect to be sure, may yet account for some of the discomfort and uneasiness one *feels* while experiencing *Fool for Love.* The production is a *tour de force,* and with it Shepard proves himself, again, to be a consummate director of Shepard. In his hands, the actors are totally convincing; the play is vivid, often very funny, and occasionally quite moving. It is also probably Shepard's best piece of writing since *Curse of the Starving Class*—blessedly free from the mythic pseudo-profundities of *Buried Child* and the conceptual self-consciousness of *True West.* In spirit, it recaptures some of the messy, adolescent energy of "early" work like *The Unseen Hand, La Turista, Cowboy Mouth,* or even *The Tooth of Crime.* Nevertheless, the exhaustion and exhilaration one feels at the end of *Fool for Love* is also laced with irritation and distaste. Never before have the more troubling and questionable aspects of Shepard's vision (especially his attitude towards gender, sexuality and sexual role definition) been so nakedly, so passionately exposed. The experience "suckers" us in; *thinking* about it makes us wonder, and (like May), in part at least, resist.

David J. Derose (review date March 1984)

SOURCE: A review of *Fool for Love,* in *Theatre Journal,* Vol. 36, No. 1, March, 1984, pp. 100-01.

[*In the following review of the San Francisco premiere of* Fool for Love *in 1983, Derose emphasizes the strength of Shepard's direction and finds that the play, while employing elements of realism, also contains "dreamlike" components that are reminiscent of Shepard's earlier work.*]

The premiere of Sam Shepard's *Fool for Love* at the Magic Theatre in San Francisco serves to dispel the myth that Shepard's work has turned irrevocably toward realism. Yet this premiere production, directed by the author, fuels another myth: that of Shepard's condemned American West. A violent, Western-American family, of the same breed as Shepard's accursed "starving class," is once again at the center of this play. But unlike his other recent plays, *Fool for Love* is a return to the more self-consciously theatrical and dreamlike stage imagery of Shepard's earlier work. Realism is mixed with ritual in a tightly-knit plot where past and present, truth and illusion, clash with irresistible force.

The play, set in a dusty motel on the Mojave desert, revolves around Eddie and May, a pair of on again-off again lovers rehashing the worn-out differences of their sporadic

Will Marchetti as the Old Man and Kathy Baker as May in the Magic Theatre production of Fool for Love, *1983.*

fifteen year romance. Eddie is a veteran rodeo bronc buster sporting worn-out boots, faded jeans, and a wide leather belt with an impressive silver buckle. May has the look of an off-duty small town hooker; in her faded denim prairie skirt and V-neck T-shirt, she alternates between complete exhaustion and explosive bobcat anger. The conflict between these two characters is quickly established: Eddie has only just returned after a long and passionate affair with a mysterious countess. May does not wish to become once again the victim of Eddie's macho, romantic delusions, nor of his hopeless infidelity. Her own wish is to free herself of Eddie; she tells him that she has a new life and a boyfriend, Martin, who appears later in the play. But May is inexplicably tied to Eddie, as he is to her, in a consuming love/hate relationship, the incestuous nature of which the author only gradually reveals in the inevitable tragic style of a Sophocles.

In *Fool for Love,* Shepard deals with subject matter which at first appears mundane, almost stereotypical. But appearances are recurrently misleading with Shepard, who often uses stage realism to lull audiences into a false sense of security so that the theatrical destruction of that apparent reality will be all the more effective. In *Fool for Love,* the split between surface reality and a greater metaphysical significance is explicit from the opening moments of the play, for present on stage at all times is an old man in a rocking chair who, with his bottle of sour-mash close at hand, watches the action from an alcove in a downstage corner of the set. He is present at this meeting between Eddie and May, but not really part of it. Or, he is part of it, but not really present. Like a ghostly witness to a ceremonial family rite, his presence takes the play clearly out of the realm of realism, framing the lovers' reunion in a dreamlike, theatrical setting. The nature of his relationship to Eddie and May—he is the common father of these incestuous half-siblings—slowly unfolds as the shared past of the three is carefully revealed. But Shepard wisely refuses to explain rationally or qualify the old man's presence, and so creates his richest theatrical image since the surreal *Angel City* or *Suicide in B-Flat.*

Shepard builds to a powerful climax through the dramatic use of one of his most characteristic techniques: story-telling. In earlier plays, Shepard's narrative monologues have often taken the form of a pause in the action—what Shepard termed jazz-like improvisation—adding little or nothing to the dramatic development of the play. However, the stories told by Eddie and May, leading to *Fool for Love*'s climax, are neatly integrated into the play's action, building tension, collecting information from the past, and revealing to the old man the fatal fruit of his bigamous and incestuous family tree.

The staging of *Fool for Love* proves the value, in Shepard's case, of the playwright directing his own work. Shepard has a distinct flair for the irrational, the surreal, and the physically explosive which makes his "realistic" plays burst with chilling dramatic energy. *Fool for Love*'s motel-room set, by Andy Stacklin, is bare-walled and raked up and in toward the rear in a forced, expressionistic perspective, creating a deep, empty chamber with all the hospitality of a holding cell. The actors creep around the edges of the set, flattening themselves against walls, throwing themselves into corners, and crawling along the floorboards like inmates of a padded cell or trapped animals in a cage. Shepard has placed microphones behind the walls and doors so that each slamming of a door, each pounding of a wall, each elbow, knee, and fist is amplified and broadcast through speakers beneath the audience.

Among Shepard's other trademarks is his ingenious use of functional props, such as food cooking or mechanical devices operating on stage. In *Fool for Love,* physical business is used to add discomforting immediacy, as well as humor, to the action. When Eddie enters with a rifle in his hands, Shepard veterans squirm in their seats. Although it never goes off, the rifle's strong physical presence, its stature as more than just an inoperative stage prop, is always felt. Actor Ed Harris, as Eddie, makes equally effective use of his spurs, or "hooks" as he calls them; kicking his way around the room, he slaps a coiled rope noisily against the walls, finally lassoing and hog-tying an empty chair. Like so many of Shepard's western men, Eddie has the undaunted desire and uncanny ability to make everyone else in the room uncomfortable in his presence. His little annoying habits, like pulling on Martin's retractable key-chain, make for some of the most memorable comic business in the play.

Shepard's physical staging, his use of the room as a huge drum off of which characters bounce their emotions, the dangerous presence of guns, ropes, and spurs, are all master strokes of playwrighting and direction. Shepard's script encourages a bigger-than-life style, and this premiere production supplies it. In addition, the old man's presence turns a realistic confrontation between incestuous siblings into a disturbing, nightmarish stage image that totters the line between reality and fantasy. Jacques Levy once said of Shepard's work: "Sam is more interested in *doing* something to audiences than in saying something to them." *Fool for Love* certainly falls within the boundaries of that intention.

CRITICAL COMMENTARY

Lynda Hart (essay date 1989)

SOURCE: "Sam Shepard's Spectacle of Impossible Heterosexuality: *Fool for Love,*" in *Feminist Rereadings of Modern American Drama,* edited by June Schlueter, Fairleigh Dickinson University Press, 1989, pp. 213-26.

[*Hart is the author of* Sam Shepard's Metaphorical Stages *(1987) and the editor of* Making a Spectacle: Feminist Essays on Contemporary Women's Theatre *(1988). In the following excerpt she criticizes Shepard's portrayal of May, the female lead in* Fool for Love, *noting May's subservience to the male protagonist Eddie. Hart also finds that Shepard upholds the authority of the patriarchal father in the play and that* Fool for Love *turns more on the relationship between a father and son than between a man and a woman.*]

Fool for Love was the first of Shepard's plays that addressed the question of heterosexual "love" as a central theme. In 1981, Marranca pointed out that Shepard seemed to have no interest in relationships between men and women: "He writes as if he is unaware of what has been happening between men and women in the last decade. . . . his female characters are much less independent and intelligent than many of those created by [his literary] forefathers a hundred years ago" [Bonnie Marranca, in the Introduction to *American Dreams: The Imagination of Sam Shepard,* ed. by Bonnie Marranca (1981)]. Shepard says [as quoted by Michiko Kakutani in *New York Times* (29 January 1984)] that he had always believed that there is "more mystery to relationships between men." Just before he wrote *Fool for Love,* he decided that he could find "the *same* mystery between men and women" (emphasis mine). *Fool for Love,* then, became his first conscious effort to create a fully autonomous female character, one who could "remain absolutely true to herself." A year later, Shepard [as quoted by Stephen Fay in *Vogue* (February 1985)] described the "true relationship" between men and women as "terrible and *impossible*" (emphasis mine). Taking Shepard literally, the relationship between men and women is *impossible,* and men and women relate in the *same* way that men relate to men. Is he saying that the relationship between the opposite sexes is thinly disguised male homoeroticism? That men and women's relationships are really veiled male relationships? *Fool for Love* is the play that purports to realize a fully developed relationship between a man and a woman. My reading of the play supports Shepard's contention that heterosexual relationship is impossible; I take the man at his word.

Fool for Love has not been Shepard's greatest critical success despite winning an Obie award. It puzzled critics like Walter Kerr, who saw it as evidence of Shepard's growing reputation as a "cult dramatist" who played to a coterie audience [*New York Times* (5 June 1983)]. But *Fool for Love* is essentially a realistic play, like the domestic trilogy that preceded it: the characters are searching for an identity that is gradually revealed through dialogue and action; a character (Martin) functions as an outsider who facilitates exposition; dialogue alternates between concealment and revelation; recognition scenes uncover a secret that explains the main characters' problems. Although Shepard bends and stretches these conventions, they are recognizable structural patterns in the play. The one distinctive deviance from this realistic pattern is the father's presence outside the onstage illusion—an anti-illusionistic device that Shepard does not use in his earlier realistic plays. Although gender conflict and heterosexual relationship appear to be the play's central concerns, paternal control and manipulation frames the play and determines its onstage action. Unlike the family trilogy, in which the father was either realistically absent (*True West*) or center stage (*Buried Child* and *Curse of the Starving Class*), the father in *Fool for Love* moves in and out of the narrative, physically as he crosses the proscenium boundary and psychologically as he invades and is erased from his children's memories. He is thus both omnipresent (like Pirandello's absent author) and missing. The father in the drama is then like the father in his children's narrative as they remember his pervasive and controlling influence in their lives that was characterized by a series of appearances and disappearances.

Although May and Eddie did not meet each other until they were teenagers, their experiences coincided as children of the same man who alternately cohabited with their respective mothers. Because the old man fathered each of them with different mothers, they are half-sister and brother; thus, incest is their fearful secret, the bond that holds them together and the shame that tears them apart. Eddie has "inherited" his father's proclivity for disappearance. As we find out in the first scenes, for fifteen years he has left May many times and returned to her. His most recent disappearance was taken to have a fling with an enigmatic "countess." As the play opens, May is sitting limply on the bed, Eddie is working resin into a leather bucking strap, and the old man watches them from his rocking chair outside the frame. Shepard's play enacts the sad spectacle of patriarchy's determination of sexual difference that prescribes the dominance of one sex over the other and the father's control over the narrative.

May and Eddie are exemplary characterizations of Luce Irigaray's "obsessive" and "hysteric" [in her *Speculum of the Other Woman,* trans. Gillian C. Gill (1985)]. Eddie, "the 'obsessive' . . . who wants and demands and repeats, and

turns around and around in his original desire, which he claims to master in order, finally, to establish his omnipotence," and May "the 'hysteric' . . . who drifts aimlessly, wanting nothing, no longer knowing her own mind or desire, acting 'as if' or 'as you like it,' her body the only reminder of what has been. . . . " The structure of *Fool for Love* plays out the inevitability of their imposed roles— "the game seems to have got off to a bad start. At best, a mournful pleasure seems in store. Sadly repetitive, painstakingly, or infinitely fragmenting things, rambling on with pauses only for explosions." This description from Irigaray's close rereading of Freud's "Femininity" is taken from a section she calls "mimesis imposed." Shepard's play reproduces that imposition through re-presentation.

The scenario is pornographic: Eddie, like the pornographer, is obsessed, "chained and enslaved, not to a real woman, nor to a body, but to the past and his image of the past, which he must recreate again and again" [as Susan Griffin states in *Pornography and Silence* (1981)]. Eddie's primary relationship is not with May but with the past and its representative—the father. He shares with his father a desire that constructs reality in his own image, and that image is Woman. "Take a look at that picture on the wall over there," the old man says to his son as he points at an empty picture frame in which he sees a photograph of Barbara Mandrell, his wife "in [his] mind." "That's realism," he insists. Eddie and the old man share an understanding on this point, for Eddie, like his father, is a "fantasist." May is as absent as the image of Barbara Mandrell. Eddie constructs the reality of their relationship even in the face of her denial of his claims. "It's all a fantasy," she tells him, "you got me confused with somebody else," "you're gonna' erase me," she says. Walter Kerr finds May's remarks incomprehensible, but for women who have been silenced, colonized, and eradicated from history, May's remarks are straightforward.

From Eddie's dominant perspective, May's history is made up of fragments of his desire. She is his fetish. As evidence of his love for her, he hangs his head and confesses: "I missed you. I did. I missed you more than anything I ever missed in my whole life. I kept thinkin' about you the whole time I was driving. Kept seeing you. Sometimes just a part of you . . . your neck kept coming up for some reason. I kept crying about your neck." Eddie constantly wields a lasso, a less than incidental action when we consider his choice of an eroticized part of May, and he strokes and fondles a twelve-gauge shotgun. His masturbatory pleasure depends on May's presence to be subjected to his controlling look, his specularization of her, a gaze that he insists she return to validate him: "May, look. May? I'm not goin' anywhere. See? I'm right here. I'm not gone. Look."

Thus within the onstage narrative, May and Eddie's relationship is clearly "terrible," a history of violence, abandonment, and possessiveness in which May has been the object of his obsessive desire. He has pursued her across country and has come to claim her again as the dramatic action of *Fool for Love* begins: "I was comin' back to get you," "I'm takin' you back"—such is Eddie's project. May is trapped in the motel room; on the one occasion that she tries to escape, Eddie carries her back as she kicks and screams. At one point in the action, May circles the room crying and hugging the walls, finally sinking to her knees and crawling on the floor, much like the creeping and crawling woman in Charlotte Perkins Gilman's *The Yellow Wallpaper,* who is also reduced to these circumstances by a man who claims to be protecting and rescuing her.

Eddie can come and go from the claustrophobic set; his mobility is also emphasized in his frequent reminders of the distance he has traveled to pursue her. May, on the other hand, is immobilized; she is limp and inert when we first see her. She is alienated from her body as Shepard's telling stage direction suggests—"*face staring at floor*"—and as a recent critic [William Herman, in *Understanding Contemporary American Drama* (1987)] unselfconsciously described—"the first stage image features her body." May is, in Jurij Lotman's typological description of the "mythical text" [in *Poetics Today* 1, Nos. 1-2 (1979)], "a function of this space" whereas Eddie is the "mythical subject":

> Characters can be divided into those who are mobile, who enjoy freedom with regard to plot-space, who can change their place in the structure of the artistic world and cross the frontier, . . . and those who are immobile, who represent, in fact, a function of this space.

De Lauretis's commentary on Lotman's mythical text is supported in Shepard's representation: "As he [the mythical subject] crosses the boundary and 'penetrates' the other space, the mythical subject is constructed as human being and as male; he is the active principle of culture, the establisher of distinction, the creator of differences. Female is what is not susceptible to transformation . . ." [Teresa De Lauretis, *Technologies of Gender* (1987)]. As much as May has tried to free herself from Eddie, he always returns, and she always succumbs to his desire. Although she insists that he leave, when he attempts to do so, she becomes "hysterical," hangs onto his legs, and pleads with him to stay. Thus Shepard renders the female subject remaining "absolutely true to herself."

So far, we have seen how Shepard's play supports his assertion that the relationship between men and women is "terrible." But *Fool for Love* goes further to assert that their heterosexual union is "impossible," that it is the "same" as men's relationships with men, i.e., (hommo)erotic. [Hart states in a footnote that this spelling is used to emphasize "*male* sexuality," punning on the French word "homme," man]. As I stated previously, the distinguishing feature of *Fool for Love* is the placement of the father. In the earlier family plays, Shepard represented the father as controlling the son's destiny. Wesley in *Curse of the Starving Class,* Vince in *Buried Child,* and Lee and Austin in *True West* all succumb to their father's authority by *becoming* them. Despite the internal narrative of resistance to the father's power, Wesley dons his father's filthy, discarded clothing until by the end of the play his mother is unable to distinguish between her son and her husband; Vince returns to the family home and violently usurps Dodge, the patriarch, who claims Vince as his true son and heir; Lee and Austin gradually partake of their absent father's charac-

teristics until they are both versions of him. In these three plays, the father exists within the internal narrative of the play.

In *Fool for Love,* however, Shepard places the father outside the action by initially confining him to a black-curtained space outside the proscenium. But this apparent banishment of the father only serves to foreground his (author)ity. As the dialogue moves toward recognition of the source of Eddie and May's conflict, we learn that their shared paternity is as much or more at issue than Eddie's infidelities. We can see in Eddie's actions an "inherited" repetition of his father's history. But his fundamental claim to May's love is their link with the father: "you know we're connected, May. We'll always be connected. That was decided a long time ago." Although the old man resists acknowledging his paternity, "You could be anybody's. Probably are. I can't even remember the original circumstances," May and Eddie fully recognize him as their mutual father. Thus, their incestuous affair does not preclude their union but establishes its inevitability. The father's power is inexorable. Paternity determines the possibility of the couple's relationship and renders it inescapable.

The project of *Fool for Love* is the abandonment of the father, a project that fails. Shepard does not keep the father outside the boundaries of the onstage narrative; he brings him onstage to demand that his story be told. When May and Eddie relate their respective versions of their history for the first time, they are incongruent. But they merge when May fills in the "detail" about Eddie's mother's suicide. "Eddie's mother blew her brains out. Didn't she, Eddie?" she asks. At this moment the father crosses the platform onto the stage and protests: "Stand up! Get on yer feet now goddamn it! I wanna' hear the male side a' this thing. You gotta' represent me now. Speak on my behalf. There's no one to speak for me now." Eddie breaks his allegiance with his father by corroborating May's story with the crucial detail: "It was your shotgun." Eddie and May then meet each other's gaze. Fixed on each other, they move slowly toward each other and unite in an embrace that shuts out the father's warnings: "Keep away from her! You two can't come together! You gotta hold up my end a' this deal. I got nobody now! Nobody! You can't betray me! You gotta' represent me now! You're my son!" Although the father's demands are ignored momentarily by his son, his authority is recuperated by Eddie's final action—he disappears again into the desert, under the pretext of rounding up his horses that the Countess has set loose. "He's gone," May repeats, "he's gone." The patriarch has the last words in the play. Pointing again to the empty space on the wall, he says: "Ya' see that picture over there? Ya' know who that is? That's the woman of my dreams. That's who that is. And she's mine. She's all mine. Forever."

Onstage or offstage, externally or internally, the Father's vision of reality retains its authority. May and Eddie's relationship is indeed impossible. Under their father's control because of the social reality of their incestuous "love," they are bound by the Law of the Father, the patriarchal prescription for antagonism and asymmetry through the construction of gender difference. Sexuality in the play is located in

May's body (emphasized when we watch her change clothes onstage, transforming [as stated in Shepard's stage directions] from her "former tough drabness" into a "very sexy woman," a male property. Most critics agree that Shepard's family and gender conflict plays represent the demise of the family and thus the breakdown or degeneration of a social order; what they usually fail to see is that the plays exhibit a power struggle for the *maintenance* of the social order that is crumbling and that struggle is between fathers and sons, with the latter overthrowing the father only to assume his position and reinstate the old order. The sign of this struggle is violence, which is both a subject of the plays and the structural principle that activates them. Shepard is aware that violence as a subject and social reality holds special appeal for him as he reveals in an interview [with Kakutani in *New York Times*]: "There's something about American violence that to me is very touching. In full force it's very ugly, but there's also something very moving about it, because it has to do with humiliation. There's some hidden, deeply rooted thing in the Anglo male American that has to do with inferiority, that has to do with not being a man, and always, continually having to act out some idea of manhood that invariably is violent."

Shepard is indeed "touched" by violence. His plays represent the fantasy of a writer who is deeply committed to a "rhetoric of violence" and a violent rhetoric. Violence pervades the social constructs in his plays and is embodied in their discursive practices, both of which, as De Lauretis demonstrates [in *Technologies of Gender*], are "engendered in representation." Shepard's return to realism was not a casual choice nor simply the selection of one structural principle over another. His realism perpetuates the power structures of the patriarchy and presents them as natural and inevitable no matter how deplorable they may seem to be. *Fool for Love* is as much an Oedipal narrative as any of the previous family plays, perhaps even more so because in this play Shepard attempts to account for the place of Woman in the narrative and demonstrates her vacancy. May's body becomes a space, [as De Lauretis puts it] "a territory in which the battle is waged." "The story of Oedipus weaves the inscription of violence (and family violence, at that) into the representation of gender."

Thus, although Shepard tries to create female subjectivity in his plays, he merely returns to the struggle between men; the "mystery between men and women" in his plays is indeed "the *same*" as the mystery between men. For the feminist spectator, there is not much mystery. . . . Shepard shares the role of "fantasist" with his father and son characters. His plays continue and perpetuate the story of male desire, (hommo) sexual desire and power. Hence his popularity, his honorary status as a mythic spokesman for America, and his penetration into the psyche of the American mind is no mystery for the feminist spectator who knows that the maintenance of the patriarchy is the collective vision of our culture's majority.

Shepard's attempt in *Fool for Love* to represent a heterosexual encounter turns out to be only his male characters' encounters with their imaginary others, "lies of their minds," monologues masked as dialogue. The rule of the Father (Phallus) renders all possibility of relation between the sexes impossible, as Shepard's controlling patriarch exemplifies. Ironically, the playwright who is portrayed as an aggressive heterosexual is fully committed to representing the same tired story of his fathers (which is the story of hommo-sexuality disguised as heterosexuality). Shepard may have succeeded in creating a female character who can announce her fear of being erased, but she has already been erased by the playwright's representation. *Fool for Love* is, at best, a tale of the "mournful pleasure" of failed heterosexuality.

FURTHER READING

AUTHOR COMMENTARY

Cott, Jonathan. "The *Rolling Stone* Interview: Sam Shepard." *Rolling Stone* (18 December 1986): 166-68, 170, 172, 198, 200.

> Interview that touches on various subjects, including Shepard's views on music and his play *A Lie of the Mind*.

Shepard, Sam. "American Experimental Theatre: Then and Now." *Performing Arts Journal* 11, No. 2 (Fall 1977): 13-14.
> Shepard's reflections on experimental theater.

OVERVIEWS AND GENERAL STUDIES

Bachman, Charles R. "Defusion of Menace in the Plays of Sam Shepard." *Modern Drama* XIX, No. 4 (December 1976): 405-15.

> Analyzes Shepard's use of menacing situations in his drama but finds that these circumstances seldom result in "believably terrifying violence."

Carroll, Dennis. "Sam Shepard's Plays: The Filmic Cut and 'Switchback'." *Modern Drama* XXVIII, No. 1 (March 1985): 125-38.
> Analyzes Shepard's use of cinematic techniques in his dramas concluding that they are used "to depict a profound schism of both identity and vision" within his characters.

Davis, Richard A. "'Get up outa' Your Homemade Beds': The Plays of Sam Shepard." *Players* 47, No. 1 (October-November 1971): 12-19.
> Synopsis and analysis of several of Shepard's plays, including *Icarus's Mother*, *Red Cross*, *Chicago*, and *Operation Sidewinder*.

Erben, Rudolf. "Women and Other Men in Sam Shepard's Plays." *Studies in American Drama, 1945-Present* 2 (1987): 29-41.
> Asserts that women and "other men" are the "antagonists of Shepard's drama, the agents behind the major changes in American life to which the heroes cannot adjust."

Hamill, Pete. "The New American Hero." *New York* (5 December 1983): 75-102.
    Biographical feature on Shepard that concentrates on his work as a film actor.

Hart, Lynda. "Sam Shepard's Pornographic Visions." *Studies in the Literary Imagination* XXI, No. 2 (Fall 1988): 69-82.
    Argues that Shepard's female characters in *Fool for Love, A Lie of the Mind*, and the film screenplay *Paris, Texas* are pornographic representations that condone violence against women.

King, Kimball, ed. *Sam Shepard: A Casebook.* New York: Garland Publishing, 1988, 176 p.
    A collection of essays that address various aspects of Shepard's work, covering plays from throughout his career.

Kramer, Mimi. "In Search of the Good Shepard." *The New Criterion* 2, No. 2 (October 1983): 51-7.
    Questions the favorable reviews that Shepard's work has received, while conceding that Shepard is able "to use the form of the theater to artistic advantage."

Kroll, Jack, with Constance Guthrie and Janet Huck. "Who's That Tall, Dark Stranger?" *Newsweek* (11 November 1985): 68-74.
    Biographical feature on Shepard that covers his playwriting career and his work as a film actor.

Luedtke, Luther S. "From Fission to Fusion: Sam Shepard's Nuclear Families." *New Essays on American Drama*, edited by Gilbert Debusscher and Henry I. Schvey, pp. 143-66. Amsterdam: Rodopi, 1989.
    Traces Shepard's "'chronicle' of the self in nine family dramas."

Marranca, Bonnie, ed. *American Dreams: The Imagination of Sam Shepard.* New York: Performing Arts Journal Publications, 1981, 223 p.
    Presents a broad selection of criticism and other writings on Shepard, as well as interviews with, and essays by, the playwright.

Mazzocco, Robert. "Heading for the Last Roundup." *New York Review of Books* XXXII, No. 8 (May 1985): 21-7.
    Overview of Shepard's life and work that regards him as an "embattled realist" often concerned with folkloric aspects of the American experience.

Mottram, Ron. *Inner Landscapes: The Theatre of Sam Shepard.* Columbia: University of Missouri Press, 1984.
    Offers a critical overview of Shepard's career and an interpretive reading of his plays.

Oumano, Ellen. *Sam Shepard: The Life and Work of an American Dreamer.* New York: St. Martin's, 1986.
    Biographical study of Shepard's career.

Patraka, Vivian M., and Mark Siegel. *Sam Shepard,* Number 69 of the *Boise State University Western Writers Series.* Boise, Idaho: Boise State University, 1985.
    Concise overview of Shepard's work.

Tucker, Martin. *Sam Shepard.* New York: Continuum Publishing Company, 1992, 179 p.
    A critical study of Shepard's career through 1991, with consideration of important biographical events.

Weales, Gerald. "American Theater Watch, 1978-1979." *Georgia Review* XXXIII, No. 3 (Fall 1979): 569-81.
    Reviews a number of Shepard plays, including *Buried Child, Seduced,* and *Jacaranda.*

THE TOOTH OF CRIME

Burgess, John. Review of *The Tooth of Crime. Plays and Players* 21, No. 10 (July 1974): 36, 38.
    Finds that Shepard's play is inappropriate for the "adventure story" presentation it received at the Royal Court Theatre in 1974.

Kauffmann, Stanley. Review of *The Tooth of Crime. New Republic* 168, No. 12 (24 March 1973): 22, 33.
    Criticizes Shepard's self-indulgence in creating a play that is "just one long, long metaphor."

Wilcox, Leonard. "Modernism vs. Postmodernism: Shepard's *The Tooth of Crime* and Discourses of Popular Culture." *Modern Drama* XXX, No. 4 (December 1987): 560-73.
    Analyzes the principal characters in the play and concludes that Shepard expresses a postmodern sensibility.

BURIED CHILD

Orbison, Tucker. "Authorization and Subversion of Myth in Shepard's *Buried Child.*" *Modern Drama* XXXVII, No. 3 (Fall 1994): 509-20.
    Argues that Shepard's use of myth in the play presents a situation where "the natural world is renewed, the human world is not."

Shea, Laura. "The Sacrificial Crisis in Sam Shepard's *Buried Child.*" *Theatre Annual* XLIV (1989-1990): 1-9.
    Argues that the death of the child is a "sacrifice intended to end the disintegration of the family."

Simon, John. "Theater Chronicle." *Hudson Review* XXXII, No. 1 (Spring 1979): 85-8.
    Praises the symbolism in *Buried Child,* declaring that it "plays absorbingly, disturbingly, and finally overpoweringly."

FOOL FOR LOVE

Feingold, Michael. "Fool's Gold." *Village Voice* (7 June 1983): 81-2.
    Praises the "richness and excitement" of *Fool for Love* and compliments Shepard's stage direction.

Simon, John. "Soft Centers." *New York* 17, No. 24 (13 June 1983): 76-7.
    Faults Shepard as both author and director of *Fool for Love,* asserting that the play fails to make a conclusive statement.

OTHER PLAYS

Brustein, Robert. "The Shepard Enigma." *New Republic* 194, No. 4 (27 January 1986): 25-6, 28.

> Negative review of *A Lie of the Mind* that faults the excessive length of the play and a lack of the "fantastic and demonic" elements that Shepard typically features.

Holden, Stephen. "Laying Odds on America's Soul." *New York Times* (15 November 1994): B1, B4.

> Review of *Simpatico* that finds the play "symbolically provocative" but faults the "languid style" of Shepard's direction.

Kleb, William. Review of *True West. Theater* 12, No. 1 (Fall-Winter 1980): 65-71.

> Detailed and largely positive review that outlines the various thematic elements in the play.

Additional coverage of Shepard's life and career is contained in the following sources published by Gale Research: *Authors & Artists for Young Adults,* Vol. 1; *Contemporary Authors,* Vols. 69-72; *Contemporary Authors Bibliographical Series,* Vol. 3; *Contemporary Authors New Revision Series,* Vol. 22; *Contemporary Literary Criticism,* Vols. 4, 6, 17, 34, 41, 44; *Dictionary of Literary Biography,* Vol. 7; and *Major 20th-Century Writers.*

Paul Zindel
1936-

INTRODUCTION

Zindel is an award-winning playwright who received a Pulitzer prize, Obie Award, and New York Drama Critics Circle Award for *The Effect of Gamma Rays on Man-in-the-Moon Marigolds.* In many of his plays Zindel depicts troubled characters based on people from his own life, most notably his mother. Though he is also a celebrated novelist for young adults, Zindel considers himself foremost a dramatist, commenting that, "A person is born with a disposition for one type of expression. For me, it was playwriting."

BIOGRAPHICAL INFORMATION

Zindel and his sister were raised by their eccentric mother, whose husband abandoned the family while Zindel was a young boy. Her occupations included real estate broker, collie breeder, and caregiver for the terminally ill—a line of work that Zindel later depicted as the career of some of his characters. Due to his mother's nomadic nature, Zindel spent most of his childhood changing residences on Staten Island. He therefore found it difficult to maintain friendships and sought enjoyment in his imagination. A creative youth, he became involved in school plays as a writer and an actor. At the age of fifteen he contracted tuberculosis and was institutionalized at a sanatorium for more than a year. When he returned to school upon his recovery, Zindel wrote a drama about an ill pianist. Although he retained an interest in theater and composed another play in college, Zindel obtained a degree in chemistry and taught the subject for almost ten years. He continued to pen theatrical pieces, however, and he eventually produced *The Effects of Gamma Rays on Man-in-the-Moon Marigolds.* The success of that drama prompted the author to retire from teaching and focus on writing plays and, subsequently, screenplays and young adult novels.

MAJOR WORKS

Most of Zindel's plays portray tormented women, a characteristic that has led to comparisons with the works of Tennessee Williams. In three of his major dramatic pieces, *The Effect of Gamma Rays on Man-in-the-Moon Marigolds, And Miss Reardon Drinks a Little,* and *Amulets against the Dragon Forces,* Zindel delves into the relationship between domineering mothers and their sensitive children. *Marigolds* features a widowed mother of two daughters who cares for a disabled elderly woman boarder. Each of the characters is psychologically damaged; however, one daughter, Tillie, overcomes her afflictions. The lives of the four women are reflected in Tillie's high school experiment to determine the effect of gamma rays on marigolds: resulting blighted flowers symbolize the mother Beatrice, her elder daughter Ruth, and Nanny the boarder, while the

marigolds that develop rare double blooms represent Tillie. *Miss Reardon* portrays the breakdown of a relationship among three sisters who were mentally abused by their mother. *Amulets* focuses on the unfortunate life of a teenaged boy who has been shuffled among homes by his mother, whose career is providing at-home care for terminally ill patients.

CRITICAL RECEPTION

Critics were impressed with *The Effect of Gamma Rays on Man-in-the-Moon Marigolds.* Clive Barnes "warmly recommended" the 1970 off-Broadway show, calling it the "best of the season so far," and Edith Oliver described the drama as a "touching and often funny play." Walter Kerr even praised Zindel as "one of our most promising new writers." However, the playwright's following theatrical pieces disappointed the hopeful critics. *And Miss Reardon Drinks a Little* and *Amulets against the Dragon Forces* both garnered mixed reviews. The former received praise for its honest portraiture but was faulted for describing instead of developing the action. The latter was lauded for its compassion but was criticized for an ambivalent tone and unbelievable action. Following *Amulets,* Zindel stated that he would pursue new themes and characters in subsequent works, commenting, "I know that the heavens are temporary and I have to move on. I'll now be going after the next paradise."

PRINCIPAL WORKS

PLAYS

The Effect of Gamma Rays on Man-in-the-Moon Marigolds 1964
And Miss Reardon Drinks a Little 1967
The Secret Affairs of Mildred Wild 1972
Ladies at the Alamo 1975
Amulets against the Dragon Forces 1989

OTHER MAJOR WORKS

The Pigman (young adult novel) 1968
My Darling, My Hamburger (young adult novel) 1969
I Never Loved Your Mind (young adult novel) 1970
Pardon Me, You're Stepping on My Eyeball (young adult novel) 1976
Confessions of a Teenage Baboon (young adult novel) 1977
The Pigman's Legacy (young adult novel) 1980
Maria's Lovers [with Gerard Brach, Andrei Konchalovsky, and Marjorie David] (screenplay) 1985
Runaway Train [with Djordje Milicevic and Edward Bunker] (screenplay) 1985
The Pigman and Me (young adult novel) 1992

AUTHOR COMMENTARY

The Theater Is Born within Us (1970)

SOURCE: *The New York Times,* 26 July 1970, pp. 1, 3.

[*Here, in the course of arguing that drama is a form of expression inherent in humankind, Zindel recollects events in his own life that demonstrate an innate affinity for the theater.*]

I am told I am born a playwright at a time when the Theater is dying. Somehow I think if my "birth" were better understood, it would show that the Theater is breathing quite autonomously and will continue to do so until the last man on earth raises a pistol and blasts his head off (an occasion I am quite devoted to helping avoid).

I have come to this conclusion about theatrical respiration via what may be a unique path! I evolved into a writer of plays by never having gone near a theater until I was in my twenties. The fact that I had written two plays by that time makes me believe that the seeds of theater are born inside of us.

My first set: Staten Island—a weird place to be born of a Woman Scorned who annually changed residences as though to make certain I would not miss a single square foot of its soil. Staten Island—in my childhood an exotic sampling of other lands: South Beach was Sicily; Stapleton was Killarney; Silver Lake was Alexandria; Tottenville was The Congo. I have not the least doubt I would have emerged staggeringly polylingual if that Woman Scorned had been a mixer. And each town offered a lush new backdrop: St. George—a buzzing city, hordes rushing on and off the five-cent ferry; Oakwood—a wooded backyard, pheasant families parading beneath hanging fat apples; Travis—a mad tiny airport, weekend pilots in Piper Cubs who circled above their lovers' homes and tossed bottles of Chanel No. 5 affixed to midget parachutes. And a mulberry tree. It was a time when Kilbasi, pepperoni and knockwurst were the relentless culinary dividers of this little island in New York Bay.

By the time I was 10 I had gone nowhere but had seen the world.

My first actors: I remember a love of marionettes—nautical, laughing, demoniacal. Some I fashioned myself. One—a grotesque sailor—was given to me for my second birthday. I recall cardboard boxes housing cycloramas, crepe-paper palm trees back-lighted by flash-light batteries with bulbs attached by twisted paper clips. The aquariums—two gallons, five gallons, 20 gallons. I sat for hours looking in at guppies hunting their young through forests of elodea. An insectarium, incredible centipedes, plump red ants—a sinister black spider unearthed in the backyard of the Travis home where I lived for my fifth Easter. I remember a terrarium, green silent stalks as magical to me as any bug, fish or puppet. Then there was the crippled boy who cried "Shazaam" to become Captain Marvel—and Wonder Woman with her transparent lasso and magic girdle. And there was the terrifying world at the Empire Theater where Batman and friend were nearly murdered each Saturday morning.

What a great love I had of microcosms, of peering at other worlds framed and separate from me.

My first performances: One day I tired of eavesdropping on the world and decided to enter it.

At last, a part!

I was 11 years old and selected to be one of the comic characters to make up the entourage for a "Tom Thumb Wedding" to be held at the Dickinson Methodist Church. For those who have never heard of a "Tom Thumb Wedding," it is an esoteric celebration in which children who do not know what they are doing march down an aisle in a mock ceremony while their parents stand in pews and grin a lot. I believe only Sigmund Freud would know what the hell they are grinning at. Anyway, some woman with a heightened sense of character assassination designated me to portray B. O. Plenty and carry a Sparkle doll. This was my first clue that as a child I physically resembled a rather tall chicken with a thyroid condition. I was so hurt and angry at the casting I silently prayed during the wedding for the cute little boy and girl playing Tom and his bride to mature into dwarfs. I waited two years to be offered another part. Finally, it came. I was Santa Claus in the seventh-grade Christmas extravaganza at P.S. 26. Needless to say, I did not receive plaudits for my performance as a *bewhiskered* chicken with a thyroid condition.

In the eighth grade I considered that perhaps I was trying in the wrong way to enter into the real world, so I launched my career as a vocalist. I sang "Till the End of Time" and "I'm Looking Over a Four Leaf Clover" a capella for my eighth-grade shop class. I am afraid both the location and the selections were ill-chosen, and if the teacher had not been in the room, chisels and hacksaws would have gone flying through the air. And I suppose my final gesture toward being an active participant in this world was when I volunteered at the Ritz Theater to be swung around at 180 rpms by a roller-skating acrobat who supplemented the flick.

My first script: By high school I decided that even if I could not succeed in the real world, perhaps my appointed role in life was to help other people succeed. I do not quite know how, but some of my classmates got the impression I had a strange sense of humor: *macabre,* I believe, was the summoned term. A group of the student officers asked me to help create a hilarious assembly sketch which would help sell G.O. cards. I gave them a version of *The Monkey's Paw*, which has a final moment when a corpse, having been buried for six months, returns home. This is not especially the meat from which comedies are carved. My only other script contribution was an idea for a Senior Day sketch in which, as Dean Martin sang "When the Moon Hits Your Eye Like a Big Pizza Pie," some mozzarella masochist got it in the face.

Then I got T.B. and was whisked off to a sanatorium at Lake Kushaqua, New York, where once again the world became something I could look at only through a frame.

Big deal, Paul Zindel—15 years old, tubercular, drab, love-less and desperate.

My first original: A year and a half of feeding humming-birds from vials of sugar water goes by and I return, cured and shy, to my high school and there write a play for a contest sponsored by the American Cancer Society. The plot: a pianist recovers from a dread disease and goes on to win tumultuous applause at Carnegie Hall for pounding out "The Warsaw Concerto." For this literary achievement I was awarded a Parker pen.

Leap with me now through a sprinkling of events during the next decade. (Please do not weary or lose sight of what I am after—to prove to you the Theater is as alive and as eternal as man.)

The events are:

1) I am studying chemistry at Wagner College. Now it is test tubes and retorts I am peeking into. I have become an atomic voyeur.

2) An English professor mounts a verse drama about the rise of Staten Island from the Jurassic Period through the Industrial Revolution. It is performed in the college auditorium and it seems to run for seven and a half hours, occupying a cast of thousands and a singing group the size of the Tabernacle Choir, which spasmodically screams "Hallelujah! Hallelujah!"

3) It is my last year in college and I write my second play, **Dimensions of Peacocks,** the title being my subtle way of expressing a fascination with the psychiatric term dementia praecox—which has nothing to do with the theme. It is the story of a misunderstood youth whose mother is a visiting nurse with a penchant for stealing monogrammed linen napkins from her patients by stuffing them down her bra.

4) Lillian Hellman theatrically baptizes me with my first real play; *Toys in the Attic*, in 1959. I behold for the first time Maureen Stapleton, unbelievably incandescent, a priestess of human laughter and pain. I remember thinking I had at last found what would be my religion, my cathedral.

5) And at this point I cannot stop my typewriter from spilling out the experience which exploded my consciousness in a way that protects me from being a *dumb* playwright. It was early one summer evening about 10 years ago. I was walking through Greenwich Village with a friend I had reason to believe possessed psychic powers. He has since gone mad. But on that evening he made me pause at an alley between two apartment houses. He told me he felt something strange was going to happen in that spot, although he did not know what or when. I did not pay much attention to his remark and we went on our way to see *The American Dream* at the Cherry Lane Theater. It was two hours later that we were back out on the street when suddenly my friend began to run. He cried out:

"Something's going on in the alley!"

The alley was several blocks away but I ran with him anyway, thinking it was just a lot of nonsense. When we reached the alley, we saw 20 or more people hanging out their windows yelling, throwing money—coins and dollar bills—down to an old woman hovering over a row of garbage pails. She was stuffing the garbage into her mouth and ignoring the money as it fell around her. That incident haunted me. Shortly after I met Edward Albee and told him about it and how much it disturbed me. I could not understand why the woman had not picked up the money to buy food.

"She was doing penance," he told me quietly, simply.

Cut to the present: Paul Zindel *succeeding.* Still drab, loveless and desperate; quite a bit more conscious. But on with it. What about the great invincibility I claim for the Theater?

It's like this:

Zindel at age fifteen with fellow patients at Stony Wold Tuberculosis Sanatorium, Lake Kushagua, New York.

No human being particularly loves the microcosm to which he is born. His life is a wandering from one sphere to another, each equally filled with imperfection. But it is a part of the human spirit for man to stalk a perfect world, a world he can control. In that is the primordial thrust which demands that Theater exist. The uniqueness of the Theater is that it is the ultimate companion of reality. If one can cause a moment to happen on the stage, it is quite possible that one can make it happen in reality. The Theater is the least illusionary phenomenon in the world. Other mediums can cut, fade, lip-sync, overlap, dissolve, but a moment must be truer, more real on the stage.

Because Theater demands greater honesty, people now wonder if it is dying. It just happens that little honesty can emerge at this particular time of chaos in our world because nobody knows what the hell is going on. No wonder no one's writing anything terribly honest. Frauds succeed right and left in television and the movies because there are more guiles, more hiding places for their dishonesty. Unhappily, at this moment even our theaters are laced with transient fakers—special effects personnel who are determined to lure the public by being cruder, lewder and nuder.

Another point: Sometimes the audience overtakes certain aspects of its Theater. At the moment, the lives of the audiences are often far more theatrical and dramatic than what is available to them on the stage. The public has stolen the greasepaint and raped the wardrobe mistress. Histrionics have taken to the streets—braying, battling and bludgeoning. Our country has taken on the accoutrements of theater. But no one can kill Theater. It can become dormant for a period of time, but Theater is so inextricably a voice, a device for survival, that man will rediscover it within himself time and time again. Thank God, the theatrical drought cannot ever last for too long a time. Man eventually tires of dishonesty and crawls off alone, perhaps in a dark place, to commune with his instinct once more. His dream is of a brilliant world, a universe too colossal and golden for him alone to create in totality, and so he marks out a space in the sand. Into it he places actors, and to those actors he gives words. Move for me. Dance for me, he whispers. Here in this place I will glimpse what paradise can be.

An interview with Zindel (1977)

SOURCE: "An Interview with Paul Zindel," by Paul Janeczko, in *English Journal,* Vol. 66, No. 7, October, 1977, pp. 20-1.

[*Janeczko is an American educator and editor of works for young adults. Below, Zindel discusses with Janeczko his development as an author and offers advice to new writers.*]

[Janeczko]: *What is the difference between Paul Zindel, author of successful books for young people, and Paul Zindel, author of successful plays?*

[Zindel]: The difference mainly is in the audience. A writer must make a decision about which audience he is writing for. Sometimes he writes for himself. Sometimes he writes for a particular type of adult audience. He may write for what's called a four-to-eight group, or maybe for an eight-to-twelve-year-old. And sometimes he writes for the young adult section, usually twelve and up. Some people don't recognize any difference, and feel that their work just transcends all the ages. However, I have recognized through ten years of teaching that there is a type of student who could be called the young adult literature consumer. That reader has special needs which must be met, and the writer must keep in mind that he is directing every word and title of his book toward that reader. If, at any time, he strays from it by wanting to become suddenly profound in a mature manner or to present a point of view that might be better suited for a group of teachers, then he is violating the audience that he's selected. So the main difference is that in one case I've decided to write for an adult theatre-going audience, which incidentally is in such transition at the moment I'm not sure how one defines what *that* is. And in the other case I'm writing for what I think is a more exact reader, one that I have a better definition of, which is the teenage audience.

Do you feel, therefore, that you "owe" different things to different audiences?

I find it not so much owing as. . . . No, the main thing that a writer owes is actually . . . it's kind of an automatic decision by the writer. It's predestined by his neurosis, by his compulsion to write, which makes him a writer to begin with. I'm talking about the true writer, not someone who becomes a writer through technique and artifice, or to make money, but the true writer who really just writes because he has to. Chances are he is living out and exploring many ideas and fantasies that he missed out on as a child or during his youth, so that compulsion causes him to create the fantasy world. No matter which audience he selects, he's usually satisfying himself. The question is, how does one satisfy oneself? Then you can do it, I think, on every age level because basically the process is problem solving for an author. When I begin to write, you see, I write because I'm solving a problem for myself. The writing of the story acts in much the same way that a dream functions, bringing one as close as one can come to a solution to the problem that's posed. By completing the work of fiction, an answer is arrived at, one that can be reached through a picture book for children or by writing as though you were

writing for Einstein. One of the tricks of fiction writers is to pick a specific person as their audience which gives them a little clue as to whom they are aiming their material at.

Were you a reader as an adolescent?

No. I came from a home that never read books. We had no books in the house. We had no desire to have books in the house, and I find that kids are very much a product of their homes. That old-fashioned saying is quite true, and so we had no politics. We had no books, no theatre. We had none of those things.

You were a chemistry teacher for ten years. How did you get from being a teacher of high school chemistry to a Pulitzer Prize winning playwright?

Well, like most people who select a career, sometimes they select the wrong one. But if they remain flexible, if they are not fixed, and if their ears are attuned to the critics in the wind, whether it's your family and your friends, or your audience, your co-workers, or any influences like that, you begin to find out what you should be doing. I found after ten years of teaching that my writing was beginning to gain a wider audience than my teaching was. About that time I went on a leave of absence to Houston on a grant to work on the production of *Gamma Rays*. Anyway, when I returned, I returned to a classroom in which most of the students were on drugs, particularly the audience I write for in my mind. I write for the people who don't like to read, as a rule. I found that the academic students, the ones from better homes and gardens, so to speak, were able to enjoy a whole range of material. Some were even able to enjoy Shakespeare! But as a rule, that left out an enormous body of students. I found even the subject of chemistry becoming too sophisticated and leaving behind a whole lot of kids, and even those from better homes and gardens weren't able to catch on to the new chemistry. And they had no need for it. They had need for other, more immediate bodies of information.

What is your work schedule like? Your writing schedule?

I find that first I have to have an idea for a work. There is a whole period of time in which I'm working on the idea, the situation, the characters, and seeing if there's something about the project that is going to be worth my living with for six months to a year of writing. If it isn't worth it, then I dismiss it and go on. But once I've decided that it's worthwhile, and thought about, over a period of months, a character and situation and problem that I want to solve for myself and the structure of it; once I've done a considerable amount of research by checking other achievements in the genre I want to work, things that exist that are closest to what I'm aiming for; once I've digested all that and still believe it's something that I want to work on, then it's rather easy. Then I begin to write and I spend about a month working on the outline. Now, if it's been an inspired first draft, the rewrites will be minimal and I can do them in a month or two. My last book was not an inspired first draft. In fact, the first draft, I think, was not an uninspired one, but rather it was overinspired. It broke my rule of forgetting my audience, and it did what most writers do or most authors do as soon as they become independent enough, as soon as they have enough money. They begin to express themselves more and more openly and sometimes they remove the cover of fiction and things become so enlarged that they no longer have that poetic cover, that artistic cover, and they translate themselves into rather vulgar indulgent expressions. That happened on my last book. It required a complete rewrite, and so it took me a full year to really work on it and do the rewrite.

What is your day-to-day routine like?

I am definitely a morning person. I like to work between eight and noon. Three hours is plenty and I'm exhausted by that time. I think it makes me more accessible to my dreams and the problem solving that goes on in dreams. Many things are solved in dreams and I like to be as close to that dream as possible.

What advice would you give young people who are interested in writing?

I think the major advice is not to be discouraged, because if they're interested in writing that means that they're in touch with the need to write and I don't see any quick success for young people in writing. I think it requires a certain amount of maturation. I think there's a certain amount of age that's necessary before you learn how to translate your own impulses into more universal terms. How to master the craft of writing fiction? I can't imagine myself as a teenager being able to comprehend some of the needs of structure. I think for young people interested in writing they must simply *do*. They must sit down and write as much as they can about whatever they feel they should. They should know the various types of writing they could do, and they should try all of them. Try the short story, the novel, the drama, the poem, and try to discover which one they feel most comfortable in. They should also explore books on structure as much as possible. They should take writing courses. They should take creative writing courses in high school. They should sign up for summer courses in creative writing if there's a writer's conference around. They should expose themselves to reading real writers, professional writers. If a kid is in high school and knows that he wants to write and that he enjoys writing, there is no question in my mind that he will become a successful writer.

How does Paul Zindel see the world?

The way I see my world is reflected in what I write. I find the way I see the world constantly undergoes transition. This is part of a maturation process, part of the experiences that go on. But again very seriously I feel there's a type of biological clock that allows certain insights into the world and into life, and those change. The fearlessness that teenagers have about death is no longer a fearlessness that I have. When I look at most of my work I see the word "pathos" ringing out, which was once diagnosed as my style of seeing things—things exaggerated. In that exaggeration I am able to see the world exaggerated as a place of home which, in a sense, can be the dream of the nonexist-

ence of death. Through pathos I can see the world as one of the most hilarious and comic places that there can be to live. Then, by the use of pathos again, I can look at another element and see the world as quite ghastly, see it through very morbid eyes and find everything threatening and dangerous. So there's a great complexity of these feelings. These themes have been repeated in my work. So in a sense, what I'm telling you is self-analysis which really is not as valuable as a person with a more objective viewpoint, the critic, the reader who follows my works, who can look at them and see the themes which are repeated over and over again and that in a sense tell what the author's true vision of the world is. So what I think of the world really is reflected through my books. It's in transition and like the motion of being keys on a piano: I just play different ones at different times, but what I do learn now, and what I'm concerned about now, is how to maintain the most sensible level of happiness and fulfillment for myself, while at the same time trying to satisfy the demands of society which are to bring innovation to civilization, to institutions, to make contributions which make the world a better place to live. So that really I try to satisfy both. I see the world as a problem solving situation, and the solution of those problems through fiction seems to be the adventure that I've chosen for myself.

OVERVIEWS AND GENERAL STUDIES

Jack Jacob Forman (essay date 1988)

SOURCE: "Women in Distress: The Plays of Paul Zindel," in *Presenting Paul Zindel,* Twayne Publishers, 1988, pp. 41-9.

[*In the following excerpt, Forman comments on the autobiographical elements and depiction of women in Zindel's plays, often comparing the characterizations in his dramas to those in his young adult novels.*]

Just after Zindel was released from the tuberculosis sanatorium where he had spent eighteen months recuperating from the disease, the seventeen-year-old high school senior submitted a play to a contest sponsored by the American Cancer Society. He won a silver ballpoint pen as a prize, and ever since, he has been interested in creating drama. Many Americans, in fact, know him not as the author of young adult novels but as the Pulitzer Prize—winning playwright of *The Effect Of Gamma Rays on Man-in-the-Moon Marigolds*. Zindel himself believes that his major literary talent and interests lie in writing for the stage.

Examining his plays in the context of his young adult novels shows both some striking similarities to his stories for teenagers and some revealing differences. Unlike his novels, the plays were written for an adult audience, and they contain mostly adult characters. (One exception is *Gamma Rays*'s portrayal of teenagers Tillie and Ruth, whose characterizations ultimately led to Harper & Row's invitation to

Zindel to write young adult novels.) Whereas the young adult stories depict troubled adolescents resolving their problems, Zindel's plays are mostly about neurotic women who are unable to overcome their crippling obsessions and depressions. These women in distress bear a close resemblance to the neurotic mothers of the author's young adult novels.

Zindel's dramatic characterizations have been influenced by Tennessee Williams's plays about fragile and loveless women. Like Williams, Zindel seems to believe that the vulnerability inherent in his female characters can lead to the development of sensitivity and imagination. The teenage heroines in his young adult novels—such as Edna in *Pardon Me* and Lorraine in the two *Pigman* books—clearly demonstrate this. But whereas readers of Williams's plays feel pity and regret for his emotionally battered tragic women, readers of Zindel's plays are likely to feel contempt for his exaggerated female characters. Williams's characters are truly tragic because they are not equal to the world's demands; Zindel's women appear to be perversely crazy, destroying the lives of those around them as well as their own.

Zindel has written six published plays, three unpublished plays, and several teleplays and screenplays. *Dimensions of Peacocks*, about a visiting nurse and her confused son, was written under the tutelage of Edward Albee while Zindel was at Wagner College, and it was performed in New York City in 1959. Two other plays—*Euthanasia and the Endless Hearts* and *A Dream of Swallows*—were written and performed in New York during Zindel's first years as a high school teacher in the early 1960s. None of the three plays was critically well received, and all closed soon after their initial performances.

Zindel was not taken seriously as a playwright until he wrote *The Effect of Gamma Rays on Man-in-the-Moon Marigolds* in 1963. But success did not come immediately. *Gamma Rays* first played in Houston for six weeks in 1965. It took five years and many revisions before it was produced in New York and won the 1971 Pulitzer Prize.

The Effect of Gamma Rays on Man-in-the-Moon Marigolds has to be one of the strangest titles ever given to a play. Zindel got the idea for it from one of his high school students who responded to an ad in a comic book for marigold seeds exposed to gamma rays. Clive Barnes of the *New York Times* thought it was "one of the most discouraging titles yet devised by man" [*New York Times,* 8 April 1970]. Discouraging or not, the eccentricity of the title prepares the reader to expect the unusual. A bitter and cynical Beatrice Hunsdorfer lives with her teenage daughters, Ruth and Tillie. Her entire income is derived from her caring for Nanny, an elderly deaf mute abandoned by her daughter. Both Tillie and Ruth, although conditioned by Beatrice to be dependent on her and to accept her frequent outbursts of frustration and anger, struggle to forge an identity for themselves. Ruth, however, is directionless and easily intimidated; she very often is overcome with seizures brought on by her mother's verbal abuse. (Zindel remembers that when his older sister, Betty, was twelve years old, she had chronic

Zindel at the Marilyn Monroe Theatre, located in Los Angeles and part of the Lee Strasberg Institute, 1982.

convulsions.) Ruth's only interest is a rabbit given to her sister by a high school science teacher—a pet that Beatrice repeatedly threatens to kill. But Tillie, although shy and withdrawn, clings to the rabbit and concentrates her energies on a science project involving marigold seeds exposed to radiation. The results of her experiment show that some seeds die, some live on normally, and others survive in a mutated state (with double flowers and enlarged stems, for example). Tillie is happily surprised when her project wins a competition.

Beatrice, however, cannot bear either Tillie's success or her own failures. She kills Tillie's rabbit and then bitterly tells her daughter, "I hate the world." Ruth fares no better; she succumbs to a seizure after learning of the slaughter of the one thing she loved. But Tillie is redeemed by her success. "My experiment," she exclaims in exultation, "has made me feel important—every atom in me, in everybody, has come from the sun—from places beyond our dreams."

By ending with Tillie's affirmation of life, Zindel tells his readers and himself that it is possible not only to survive but also to overcome maternal "toxic radiation." This is a theme Zindel has dealt with over and over again in his novels for teenagers. He projects on Tillie—as he does on Maggie, Lauri, and Edna—many traits he had as a teenager (shyness, vulnerability, resolve, curiosity, quest for self-identity) and pits her against a mother who seems to be a combination of Marsh's drunken, schizoid mother and Chris's overbearing mother. Beatrice Hunsdorfer is called "Betty the Loon" early in the play, and although alcohol was not a problem for Zindel's own mother (whose name, it will be recalled, was also Beatrice), the author admits that Tillie and Ruth's mother is his own parent "in nightmarish exaggeration" ["Prizewinning Marigolds," *Time,* 17 May 1971].

Another similarity between Zindel's young adult novels and this play is the cosmic resolution of the worldly conflicts in each work. Tillie's exultant exclamation recalls the conclusion of *Pardon Me*: "At last there were the stars set in their place." Chris ends *Confessions of a Teenage Baboon* with a comparable statement: "I began to look past the moon, past all the great satellites of Jupiter, and dream upon the stars." Even in Zindel's adult novel, *When a Darkness Falls*, he reaches for the cosmic in the aftermath of the devastating tragedy depicted in the novel and says that Marjorie Krenner, the wife of Jack Krenner, the pathological killer who has just been shot to death by the police, "would look beyond to the distant horizon, to the first signs that soon dawn would be there." In the play and the novels, Zindel uses science—represented by the physical order of the universe—as a metaphor for security and hope, and as a source of meaning and comfort for his unhappy characters. "I remember thinking," Zindel told a *Time* interviewer after winning the Pulitzer Prize, "that all carbon atoms on earth had to come from the sun. The idea of being linked to the universe by these atoms, which really don't die, gave me a feeling of meaning" [*Time,* 19 May 1987].

There is, however, very little meaning (or comfort, for that matter) in the confused and empty female lives dramatized in Zindel's short play *The Ladies Should Be in Bed*, a teleplay commissioned by National Educational Television after the author's successful NET production of *Gamma Rays*. It is based on Zindel's remembrance of the time when he was living in the Staten Island castle that inspired *The Pigman*. Next to the castle was a brightly lit large brick house with picture windows. Every week at an appointed time, he would see four women playing bridge at a table visible through the window. They also saw him watching them. What, Zindel kept thinking, were *they* thinking about him?

In the play, the four card-playing women gossip about others and berate and mock one another, all the while focusing their attention on a young man in an adjacent house that was formerly a convent. The man they gawk at stands naked in the window staring out at the trees and sky. In speculating about what is going on in the house, the four reveal their personalities and express their sexual attitudes, which run the gamut from repression to ostentation. At four o'clock every day, they notice that two boys and a girl meet with this mysterious exhibitionist. So involved are these women in their sexual neuroses that when one of them resolves to call the father of one of the boys and the mother of the girl to accuse their neighbor of endangering the morals of their children, the other three acquiesce in this

malicious prank and wait expectantly for the inevitable showdown (which never takes place). In the meantime, the four continue their abusive banter, until the aged and infirm mother of the hostess makes her way to the top of the stairs and shouts down to them: "Ladies should be in bed. The ladies should be in bed."

The life image of the young man in this play derived from Zindel's experience at the castle and his source for Lloyd Dipardi in *Confessions of a Teenage Baboon*—a character who befriended teenagers and raised dark suspicions among residents of the community. NET had commissioned the play but considered it "too ugly for television" and refused to air it, according to Zindel. In its stead, he submitted another teleplay he had written called *Let Me Hear You Whisper*. This is a short, didactic drama inspired by Zindel's reading on dolphin research. The play shows that he is as suspicious of the human use of science as he is trusting of the physical order of the universe. Portrayed in this touching drama is a commodity often missing from the lives of Zindel's adult literary characters—love. Here the love is between Helen, a science lab cleaning woman, and a dolphin about to be killed because the mammal will not cooperate in an experiment being conducted for military development. When Helen discovers the reason the scientists are trying to get the dolphin to communicate, she first tries to rescue the mammal. But the experimenters catch her in the act and fire her. Just at this point, the dolphin bleeps out the word L-O-V-E. Surprised and excited by this turn of events, the scientists try to convince Helen to stay on the job and work with them. Helen, however, wants no part of it and leaves. How much good this does the dolphin or how much it sets back the military experiment is unclear. But Zindel does succeed in casting a dark shadow on scientific experimentation—the same goal he had when in *Gamma Rays* he satirically depicted one of Tillie's competitors boiling a live cat and skinning it in order to understand the anatomy of the animal.

Zindel returns to his forsaken female characters in his second full-length play, *And Miss Reardon Drinks a Little*. "There is less unity here than in *Gamma Rays*," the author says of *Miss Reardon*, "but there is better, more dynamic writing." Although some critics disagreed with this self-appraisal, the play is probably Zindel's most biting, dramatic, and emotional portrayal of out-of-control women. Originally written as a one-act play in 1966, *Miss Reardon* was revised and enlarged several times before its New York performance in 1971.

The play concerns the three Reardon sisters—Ceil, Catherine, and Anna—each professionally involved in education. Their mother, who has died seven months before, left them with psychological scars. She made them suspicious and afraid of males—like Lorraine's mother in *The Pigman*. She bullied and dominated them until they had little self-esteem—like Chris's mother in *Confessions*. And her neurotic behavior warped their lives as Lloyd's eccentric and destructive mother warped his. Like Nanny, who was abandoned by her daughter in *Gamma Rays*, the Reardons' mother had been left to die alone by Catherine and Ceil. Only Anna had helped her, and now Anna is suffering a nervous breakdown from the emotional strain of watching her die. In addition, Anna has been recently suspended from her high school teaching job after trying to seduce one of her students. Throughout the play, she is pictured as hopelessly paranoic and dependent on Catherine for almost everything. A teacher at the same school as Anna, Catherine is a sharp-tongued alcoholic, deeply hurt by Ceil years before when her sister stole Catherine's only boyfriend. Ceil, a sweet-talking and two-faced school administrator, appears to be the only "success" in the family, but her veneer of respectability is shattered quickly by Catherine's pointed accusations.

A motley collection of recriminations tossed around by Catherine and Ceil (as well as by two irascible neighbors), the play ends in family disintegration. A guilty and deflated Ceil angrily walks out, Anna screams "I'm losing my mind," and Catherine tells Anna that "everyone's going crazy." In a token attempt at reconciliation, Catherine reaches out and touches Anna consolingly, but this seems little more than a gesture in the face of all the broken lives on and off the stage. The maternal toxic fallout in this play has left only mutated survivors.

Perhaps written as a comic antidote to the histrionics of *Miss Reardon*, Zindel's third full-length play, *The Secret Affairs of Mildred Wild*, is billed as a "comedy in three acts," but it reads more like a farce gone sour. Mildred Wild is a frustrated, alienated woman who lives with her diabetic husband, Roy, in the back of their small New York City candy store, from which they barely eke out a living. Roy's sister, Helen, pays the rent. Roy wears a wig to cover his bare skull (and empty head) and gorges on so much candy he is in a semicomatose state at one point. He is having an affair with their landlady, Bertha Gale. Mildred hides from reality by making herself up heavily and fantasizing in the style of Walter Mitty about classic films like *King Kong* and *Gone with the Wind*. When Mildred wins a potpourri of prizes on a television game show, her biggest dream seems to have come true: she is to be given a Hollywood screen test. But she soon finds that the screen test and most of the other prizes are as empty as the fantasy she has made of her life. Although disillusioned and defeated, Mildred and Roy at the end of the play come to their senses. He gives up his wig and she her cosmetics, thereby cutting the ties to their make-believe worlds. They decide to accept Helen's proposal that they take care of a vacant convent in return for being allowed to live there rent-free.

Like *Miss Reardon*, *Mildred Wild* abounds with insults exchanged among Mildred, Roy, and Helen, but the harshness of the barbs is offset by sight gags and more humor than appears in the earlier play. But despite the fact that Mildred and Roy come to terms with each other at the end of the play, Mildred is not much better off than the three hapless Reardon sisters.

Ladies at the Alamo, Zindel's most recent play, was performed in New York City in 1975. Probably the strongest female character in any of Zindel's plays appears here in the person of Dede Cooper, "a gutsy, honest and striking" Texas woman who is the director of a newly built lavish theater complex. Many have speculated that the source of this character is Nina Vance, the director of the Alley Theatre in Houston, where Zindel was playwright-in-residence in 1967. But the author denies it, claiming that Nina Vance is "a refined, strong lady," whereas Dede is "a gruff, down-to-earth fighter."

Dede has just come from her mother's funeral, and she is immediately thrust into a power struggle with her benefactor, Joanne, who claims that under Dede's management the theater is losing money. Although threatening to fire her, Joanne instead brings in Dede's old nemesis to help run the company—a woman named Shirley who was once an Academy Award nominee and is now recovering from a nervous breakdown. The theater troupe that Dede directs includes a loud-mouthed, theatrical, and alcoholic actress named Bella and an ineffectual and overweight actress named Beatrice (again!), whose nickname is "Suits" because she wears pantsuits. With the help of her friend Bella, Dede fights back and undermines Shirley's credibility by proving she is a sexual eccentric and a lesbian. She then verbally browbeats Joanne into submission, emerging a clear victor.

Confronted with a conspiracy to embarrass her for the way she runs the theater, Dede relies on her strong instinct for survival, digging up dirt on her adversaries to take attention away from her own mistakes. Nevertheless, she is preoccupied as the play ends not with the fruits of victory but with guilt-ridden memories of her mother—which connects her to the Zindel lineage of female characters. And the other women in the play reflect the Hunsdorfer-Reardon pattern: alcoholic, hypocritical, schizophrenic, sexually repressed, and bizarre.

Not only do Zindel's female dramatic personalities resemble many of the parental authority figures in his young adult novels; they also repeat some unusual behavior. Mildred Wild's sister-in-law, Helen, for instance, compulsively steals from the sanatorium in which she works, and Fleur Stein—the Reardons' odd neighbor—steals sugar, salt, and paper napkins from the teachers' lunchroom. Such work-related petty thievery is also the hallmark of the decadence of many of Zindel's female characters in his stories for teenagers (for example, Yvette in *I Never Loved Your Mind* and Chris's mother, Helen, in *Confessions of a Teenage Baboon*). Similarly, Fleur Stein and Chris's mother both manifest a strange reluctance to use bathrooms in homes other than their own and have a propensity for urinating in milk bottles—an eccentricity that plays an important role in Zindel's *When a Darkness Falls*.

The author also employs some of the same literary devices in his plays that he has used in his young adult novels. For example, he names characters to reflect their role in the play. Beatrice Hunsdorfer is a contemporary Hun in her domineering control over her daughters. Mildred Wild is always fantasizing and seldom grounded in reality. Mr. Fridge is a coldhearted assistant to the scientist, Dr. Crocus, who acts like a morally lower form of life than the dolphin he is exploiting in *Let Me Hear You Whisper*.

Zindel's plays exaggerate and embellish the themes, styles, and characters that appear in his young adult novels. Why this is so probably can be traced to Zindel's own observation that the main difference between his plays and his novels is his audience. When he writes for teenagers, he is adhering to a set of guidelines; he is teaching and learning lessons, and he is more controlled in his writing. His main goal is to keep teenage readers turning the pages. Zindel seems to have less control in his plays, relying on sharp-sounding insults and argumentative banter as a substitute for communication between his characters and using melodrama to resolve conflicts. The problem-solving teenagers of **The Pigman** and **Pardon Me** almost never come on stage in his plays. Instead, Zindel spotlights the adults who cause the problems for these enterprising teenagers, but they are drawn in "nightmarish exaggeration" and they seldom end up as better people. These irredeemable and forsaken adults do not seem capable of absorbing the lessons of life that Zindel's adolescent heroes and heroines—and the author himself—have learned in his young adult novels.

THE EFFECT OF GAMMA RAYS ON MAN-IN-THE-MOON MARIGOLDS

PRODUCTION REVIEWS

Clive Barnes (review date 8 April 1970)

SOURCE: "'Gamma Rays on Marigolds'," in *The New York Times,* 8 April 1970, p. 32.

[*An English-born American drama and dance critic whose commentary has appeared regularly in* New York Times *and* New York Post, *Barnes has been called "the first, second, and third most powerful critic in New York." In the following review, he encourages theater-goers to attend the 1970 off-Broadway production of* The Effect of Gamma Rays on Man-in-the-Moon Marigolds. *Addressing the analogy between the marigolds and the depicted family, Barnes observes: "We are all the product of our environment, all the product of our particular 'gamma rays,' but some survive and some are destroyed."*]

Off Broadway is at last warming up again. At the weekend we had the engaging *Dear Janet Rosenberg, Dear Mr. Kooning*, and now I can also most warmly recommend a new domestic drama that arrived last night at the Mercer-O'Casey Theater. It is a new play by Paul Zindel and it is one of the best of the season so far.

It has, I must admit, one of the most discouraging titles yet devised by man. It is called **The Effect of Gamma Rays on Man-in-the-Moon Marigolds**, which sounds as if Arthur Kopit might have taken up science fiction. Yet curiously enough you realize at the end of the play that the title is valid—valid but stupid.

The play is about a mother bringing up two daughters. The mother is an acid-tongued slut, wears a dressing gown all day, smokes too much, doesn't approve of housework and drinks whisky from a tooth mug. She scrapes up a living by giving home to a human wreck whose relations are prepared to pay money for the privilege of not having to look after her. Her house is the last stop before the graveyard.

Her name is Beatrice, and at first you think she is all bad. She stands in the way of her daughters' schooling, she attacks life itself without offering any alternative to it. And yet she is a victim.

Her older daughter, Ruth, is also a victim. She has already had one mental seizure and she is even now narrowly balanced. And the second daughter? She, Tillie, is vague—an indeterminate girl, loves her white angora rabbit and is interested in science.

A high school science teacher encourages the young girl—encourages her to the point of an experiment with the effect of atomic energy, gamma rays on marigold seeds. The results are either interesting mutants or genetic disasters. Most are disasters.

Mr. Zindel, who writes alarmingly well, contrasts the fate of the poor marigolds with the fate of this tortured family. We are all the product of our environment, all the product of our particular "gamma-rays," but some survive and some are destroyed.

Marigolds, if Mr. Zindel will forgive the contraction, is precisely one of those plays that seems easy enough to write, even though the history of dramatic literature unnoticeably rides upon the fossil-remains of so many writers who have tried to write them. This is the kind of true-life melodrama that fascinates Arthur Miller, and rather like Mr. Miller it is extremely successful. My heart was held by it. And, unlike most of its genre, the ending is unusually satisfying.

Melvin Bernhardt's staging is unemphatic and most successfully naturalistic. You really become involved with these people—sad that Beatrice and Ruth are bitterly unsalvageable, glad that Tillie—the new and tentative mutant—is going to survive. I admired also the squalid and cluttered setting provided by Fred Voepel, the cleverly apt costumes by Sara Brook, and the impeccable acting of the cast.

Sada Thompson's Beatrice, embittered, beleaguered, cynical and yet, despite herself, supremely pitiable, is among the best things in the current New York theater. Pamela Payton-Wright's Tillie is a delicate portrayal of shadings for circumstances, and Amy Levitt's abrasive yet poignant Ruth is another performance to remember. Also there is Judith Lowry, silent yet eloquent, as Nanny, Beatrice's geriatric boarder, insensate yet poignant. See this play—it has a compassion that is all to its own.

Sada Thompson (center) as Beatrice, Amy Levitt as Ruth, and Pamela Payton-Wright as Tillie in the 1970 off-Broadway production of The Effect of Gamma Rays on Man-in-the-Moon Marigolds.

Edith Oliver (review date 18 April 1970)

SOURCE: "Why the Lady Is a Tramp," in *The New Yorker,* Vol. XLVI, No. 9, 18 April 1970, pp. 82, 87-8.

[Oliver began her career as an actress and television writer and producer. She joined the New Yorker *in 1948, becoming its off-Broadway theater critic in 1961. Here, she regards Beatrice as the central figure in* The Effect of Gamma Rays on Man-in-the-Moon Marigolds.*]*

The title *The Effect of Gamma Rays on Man-in-the-Moon Marigolds* is a false clue to a touching and often funny play that, whatever its faults, is not nonsensical or verbose or pretentious or way-out flashy. Actually, it is a rather old-fashioned domestic drama (old-fashioned is no insult from me) in that it is about people—and interesting ones at that—whose behavior, while outlandish at times, is made as comprehensible as anybody's behavior ever can be made. The play, which was written by Paul Zindel and opened last week at the Mercer-O'Casey, is more than anything else the study of a woman. Her name is Beatrice Hunsdorfer, and she has been all but destroyed by a life that so far has consisted of one disappointment after another. With all her expectations crushed but with plenty of energy left, much of it spent on wreaking a kind of petty vengeance on everybody around her, she is as much a victim of her own nature as she is of circumstance. There is, however, nothing bleak or whiny about Mrs. H. She is the fierce, embittered, wise-

cracking mother of two young daughters. One of them, Ruth, is a highly strung, rather bratty girl subject to convulsions, and the other, Matilda, is an awkward, dim-looking but not dim, science prodigy. It is Matilda's gamma-ray experiment with marigolds at the local high school that gives the play its bumpy title, eventually wins her a prize, and, indirectly, almost finishes off her mother and sister and the rickety life they have built.

The plot is the least of it. The character of Mrs. H. is all, or nearly all. We learn that the only man she ever loved was her father, that her husband never amounted to anything and left her penniless in the horrible mess of a house where the action takes place, that she considers her daughters millstones around her neck (or she says she does; she is capable of sudden, remorseful tenderness and pride), and that there is no one on earth that she hates as much as she hates herself. She makes fifty dollars a week ("I'd be better off as a cabdriver") by providing minimum care for a decrepit old woman boarder. She is very intelligent. She is also, wandering around in a shabby bathrobe with a cigarette in one hand and a glass of whiskey in the other, a holy terror, and she is so convincingly played by Sada Thompson that it is all but impossible to separate the role from the actress. The first and by far the better of the two acts is a series of vignettes and conversations: Mrs. H., all offhand iron courtesy and cutting explanations, talking on the telephone to a science teacher who is looking for Matilda; the girl herself, clutching her pet rabbit, listening to the conversation in frozen apprehension; Mrs. H. berating her daughter for not doing the housework ("This house is going to ferment"); Mrs. H., behind a glittery smile, raining down insults on her poor old boarder, who is as deaf as she is feeble; Mrs. H., impulsive and loving, soothing her edgy Ruth, who has had a nightmare. The second act, in which events and crises take over, and in which incidents are given more significance than they appear to warrant, seems artificial, and even melodramatic, after the first one, but the play stands up pretty well, all the same. The performances, under Melvin Bernhardt's direction, are all that any dramatist could wish for. Pamela Payton-Wright is the shy, inspired Matilda, Amy Levitt is Ruth, and Judith Lowry is the tottery paying guest. Sara Brook designed the good costumes, and the good set is by Fred Voelpel.

Walter Kerr (review date 19 April 1970)

SOURCE: "Everything's Coming Up Marigolds . . . ," in *The New York Times,* 19 April 1970, pp. 1, 3.

[*Kerr is an American essayist, playwright, and Pulitzer Prize-winning drama critic. Throughout his career, he has written theater reviews for such publications as* Commonweal, *the* New York Herald Tribune *, and the* New York Times. *Below, he recounts the memorable aspects of* The Effect of Gamma Rays on Man-in-the-Moon Marigolds *and probes the desperate lives of the characters.*]

Whenever I think of Paul Zindel's *The Effect of Gamma Rays on Man-in-the-Moon Marigolds,* I am going to think of three things, not one of them the title (the title, by the way, makes perfect sense and you will remember it readily once you have seen the play). The first is the sound, the sheer weighted sound, of a load of old newspapers being dumped from a balcony landing. Sada Thompson, slatternly mother of two and savior of none, is at her house-cleaning again, which means that she is picking up the accumulated refuse of her life and hurling it to another, though no better, spot. The bundle comes down like a dead heart; the force of the drop is shattering. And familiar. You seem to have heard it before.

The second memory that keeps coming back is the tactile, naked terror with which Miss Thompson, at midnight during a thunderstorm, brushes a prying flashlight away from her face. Her older daughter has long ago had a breakdown, for very good reasons, and is now desperately fearful of lightning; Miss Thompson has crawled out of bed to console her, a motherly duty she is perfectly willing to perform. But in the dark the daughter has discovered a flashlight, and she is using it to find the face that will reassure her. Suddenly, to Miss Thompson, the probing, isolating, totally revealing finger of light becomes a spider seeking out the seams of failure in her face; without warning she is flailing at it, attacking it as though the truth itself were something to be killed.

The moment continues, but in another vein altogether, arriving at one of the most evocative conjunctions of per-

forming, staging and writing that we have had in the theater, on Broadway or off, in some years past. Miss Thompson must suppress her own terrors to help ease those of her daughter. To do it she passes from her sharp alarm and irritation to making girlish funny faces, conjuring up the child she once was and the way—perhaps—she once made her father laugh.

From that she passes to telling stories of her father, of his vegetable wagon that she sometimes rode through the streets, of the rhythmic cries he made to advertise his wares, of the singsong warmth that so long ago promised her a golden life. As she talks, the daughter becomes calm, pleased, half-drugged with delight, so much so that at last the two of them are musically whispering "apples—pears—cuc*um*bers!" into the night while the flashlight swings as lazily as the clapper of an old bell. The image is morose and singularly charming; it is also essential to the cruel body of the play.

The third thing I'll remember is the play's ending, a coming-together of harshness and hope that exactly summarizes, without preachment of any sort, the meanings Mr. Zindel wishes his compressed and honest little play to carry. The brief lyricism of the wagon-bell-at-midnight passage is necessary if we are to endure, and understand, the venom that overtakes Miss Thompson in her relationship with a younger daughter.

This daughter, played plainly and plaintively and very well indeed by Pamela Payton-Wright, is as bright as she is rumpled. We first meet her alone, idly stroking a pet rabbit, staring at her hand, mouthing thoughts to herself about what the universe has had to go through—the tongues of fire, the explosions of suns—to produce her own five fingers. A knobby-kneed schoolchild with thin blond hair and a dress that bunches up in the back, she has a gift for scientific speculation; she is, at the moment, engaged in growing and studying marigolds that have been exposed to radiation, and she may just possibly win a competition her teacher has urged her to enter at school. Precisely because she is intelligent, because others are interested in her, because some sort of future may open itself to her, her mother cannot abide her. "I hate the world," Miss Thompson seethes as she stares at all the dreams that have emptied out before her. No one else is going to find it fascinating. Miss Payton-Wright is not even going to go to school all that often.

When a teacher phones to ask why the child is not at school, Miss Thompson descends a cluttered staircase in a shapeless robe—toweling with the nap all gone—that contains both her despair and her cigarettes. She snatches up the ringing instrument with such brisk indifference that you know she can only parody conversation, never truly enter it. Her eyes are wide, darting, expectant: they expect insult. Her body moves restlessly beneath the robe: it is a fencer's body, wary of attack and ready for evasion or assault. The woman is ordinary, recognizable; and half-mad.

On the phone, she is four or five persons at once. She is a plain bully: she will keep her daughter home when she pleases. She is a plausible, painful flirt. The teacher will either respond to her coy gestures or get himself classified a fag. She is all motherly concern: she cares so much for her children's studies that she "provides them with 75-watt light bulbs right there at their desks." Her eyes search the room for the nonexistent desks as she prattles on: the room is almost nothing but empty cartons and sagging bureaus; she sees the desks.

She sees, when she wishes, the carfree creature she might have become; she was, after all, elected "Best Dancer of the Class of 19-bootle-de-doo." (No one alive could manage this fey cop-out as well as Miss Thompson.) She sees the husband who first got a divorce and then a coronary. ("He deserved it," she parenthesizes, swiftly, meanly.) She sees her older daughter, tight sweater unbuttoned enticingly, turning into a fierce repetition of herself. She sees where they all are now, all except the gifted one. Their only source of income is a "$50-a-week corpse," an abandoned crone for whom they care, without caring. She sees "zero" wrapping its arms around her, and she repeats the word in a run-on babble that sounds like steam bubbling up from a lava bed. She is greedy, cynical, jealous, clever, irresponsible, vicious and lost.

In the play's last sequence, we are permitted to hear the schoolgirl's shy, halting, but determined brief lecture on the effects of radiation. Displaying her flowers in the high school contest—some of them blighted, some richer through mutation, all the product of those first exploding suns—she voices, tremulously, but insistently, her own stubborn confidence that "man will someday thank God for the strange and beautiful energy of the atom."

That is half of the final stage image. The other half is of Miss Thompson, near-mindless now, endlessly folding napkins for a tearoom she will never open, face-to-face with the half-paralyzed crone, aware of the presence of that other, older, sick and sensual daughter.

The play is thus framed. The mother is the wrong and right mother for these children, as the children are wrong and right sisters to each other. They all hurt one another simply by existing; the damage can never be repaired. But they constitute the situation as given, the human mutations thrown off; there is no dodging the gamma rays, there is only disaster for some and double-blooms for some others.

The ending doens't press the point. It just expands to it, and bitterly—but gently—leaves the matter there. The play itself is one of the lucky blooms; it survives, and is beautiful. With it, Mr. Zindel becomes one of our most promising new writers. In it, Sada Thompson calls clear attention—perhaps more emphatically than ever before—to the fact that she is one of the American theater's finest actresses.

CRITICAL COMMENTARY

Thomas P. Adler (essay date 1987)

SOURCE: "The Idea of Progress," in *Mirror on the Stage: The Pulitzer Plays as an Approach to American Drama,* Purdue University Press, 1987, pp. 127-41.

[*In the following excerpt, Adler notes flaws in* The Effect of Gamma Rays on Man-in-the-Moon Marigolds *and comments on the themes of the play.*]

For critics to call ***The Effects of Gamma Rays on Man-in-the-Moon Marigolds***, Paul Zindel's Off-Broadway work and the 1971 prize winner, "honest" or "engaging" creates the impression that here is a work which pretends to be nothing other than what it is: a stark if overly familiar family-problem play about life's ability to sustain itself against great odds—doing for a particular family something of what Wilder does for the universal family of man in [*The Skin of Our Teeth*]. Zindel, though, appears to have pretensions to something more, attempting to impart additional weight to his basically simple characterization and content through overblown stage trickery. Originally produced at Houston's Alley Theatre, ***Effects*** too obviously recalls Williams's *Glass Menagerie* in its character configurations and stylistic techniques: both concern a mother, who lives mostly on dreams, and two children, one healthy, the other not; both households lack a father, through either death or desertion; in both, a gentleman from the outside world helps, or thinks he helps, one of the children. The stylistic similarities are even more pronounced: in both, the stage setting, while essentially realistic—an apartment in St. Louis, a vegetable store in New York—is used in a nonillusionistic fashion, particularly as regards lighting and music. In *Menagerie*, the nonrealistic elements, including the images and legends flashed on a screen, are integral to the play as "memory" occurring in Tom's mind. In *Marigolds*, however, such devices as recorded voice-overs (sometimes used pretentiously as when a character's voice reverberates electronically) and blackouts and spotlighting of characters (equivalent to cinematic fade-outs and close-ups) seem superimposed upon a fragile content that cannot support them, as if the form could supply a weightiness the content does not itself merit. Zindel seems interested in the techniques in and for themselves, simply as a means of avoiding straight realism.

Furthermore, perhaps because Zindel usually writes novels for adolescents, the abundant symbolism in ***Marigolds*** frequently lacks subtlety. The mother, Beatrice, for example, to assuage her guilt over having sent her own father off to a sanatorium, cares for the senile Nanny who, with her "smile from a soul half-departed" and her "shuffling motion that reminds one of a ticking clock," serves as a walking personification of death and of how affluent Americans (her daughter is "Miss Career Woman") mistreat their aged parents. More compellingly, the once orderly vegetable store now symbolically reflects the clutter and refuse of Beatrice's psychic and emotional life. With her motto "just yesterday," Beatrice lives on reminiscences of things *past*— a word prominently displayed on a placard at the high school science exhibit—on would-have-beens and should-have-beens. All her life she has romantically dreamed and schemed, yet she has seldom carried through on her plans, some of them, like turning the run-down store into a neighborhood tea shop, slightly outrageous. Like Willy Loman [in Aruthur Miller's *Death of a Salesman*], Beatrice tends to blame something outside herself for her failure, though she accurately assesses the way that a competitive, success-

Sada Thompson and Judith Lowry as Nanny in a scene from The
Effect of Gamma Rays on Man-in-the-Moon Marigolds.

oriented society attempts to force everyone into a predetermined mold, decrying the lack of tolerance and the level-
ling down to sameness and mediocrity that, paradoxically,
is a part of the American system: "If you're just a little bit
different in this world, they try to kill you off." Difference
may threaten the status quo and not be easily handled or
accommodated, yet Zindel argues not only that some differences are beneficial but that variation rather than sameness
is essential for there to be progress.

Although Zindel's exposition leaves some past events an-
noyingly obscure, it seems to have been criticism by the
father she idolized that began Beatrice's descent into a
present condition she characterizes as "half-life" and
"zero." One day she hitched up the horses and rode through
the streets selling fruit, to be met by her father's stern re-
buke; ever since, she has dreamed of riding a shiny wagon
pulled by white horses, only to see the forbidding figure of
her father look on disapprovingly. She married badly,
merely to please her father, but then no man could live up
to her dream. After she took her father off to the hospital,
she had the horses "taken care of"—a cycle of failure, guilt,
and still more failure.

The cycle of parent destroying child continues in Beatrice's
erratic relationship with her daughters, shifting suddenly
between compassion and bitterness—in much the way that
the pet rabbit is alternately loved and then hurt. Beatrice's
older daughter, the mentally disturbed Ruth who was trau-
matized by contact with death and violence, tells tales,
craves the attention of men by flaunting her sexuality, and
appears just as destructive and vindictive as her mother;
when she cannot have what she desires, she ruins it for
everyone else. The younger Tillie, in her awkwardness and
unprettiness and firm grasp on reality, stands as Ruth's
opposite and a living denial that one need be determined by
heredity and environment. Tillie discovers a much-needed
father figure in her high school teacher (unfortunately
named Mr. Goodman), who introduces her to the word
atom, which she comes to love. The notion that everything
in the universe, herself included, is somehow connected
with every other thing from the moment of creation en-
thralls her; it provides a fixed point of reference and a feeling of importance. For her science project, she exposes
marigold seeds to radiation, which need not produce sterility and may even yield a positive effect: while those that
receive little radiation are normal and those exposed to
excessive radiation (like Beatrice and Ruth) are killed or
dwarfed, those subject to only moderate radiation produce
mutations, some of which (like Tillie, who has experienced
very detrimental influences but has emerged relatively un-
scathed) are good and wonderful things. Against all odds,
Tillie not only survives but actually thrives.

Finally, though, Zindel's optimism does not grow organically from the play. Some might argue that Tillie's (and the
playwright's) optimism, because it is won with so much
difficulty and is so at variance with the adverse and negative atmosphere from which she arises, is therefore all the
more impressive and no more facile or unwarranted than
Wilder's. The widely divergent perspectives of the two
writers, however, militate against this: where Wilder discerns a pattern of ultimate success after repeated failures
over the entire sweep of human history, Zindel ties his faith
and hope to a specific—and atypical rather than representative—household that he then proposes as symbolic and
universally applicable. Though Zindel seems to find little
difficulty in asserting this optimism, an audience might
have a considerably harder time assenting to it.

Jeffrey B. Loomis (essay date 1991)

SOURCE: "Female Freedoms, Dantesque Dreams, and Paul
Zindel's Anti-Sexist *The Effect of Gamma Rays on Man-in-
the-Moon Marigolds,*" in *Studies in American Drama,
1945-Present,* Vol. 6, 1991, pp. 123-33.

[*In the essay below, Loomis extols the anti-sexist message
of* The Effect of Gamma Rays on Man-in-the-Moon Marigolds *and points out the correlation between Zindel's play
and Dante's* Divine Comedy.]

Already preparing a bridge to such a recent male feminist
play as Robert Harling's *Steel Magnolias.* Paul Zindel, in
The Effect of Gamma Rays on Man-in-the-Moon Mari-

golds, gave us, two full decades ago, a strong indictment of sexism. In Zindel's revisionary Dantesque play, the frumpy housewife Beatrice Hunsdorfer may look like an illusion-frustrated female transplanted into a Northern urban landscape from the barren Mississippi River towns of Tennessee Williams. Beatrice's tantrum in Act Two, turning her house into a chaos, may seem fully explained when she declares "I hate the world"; she thus appears at first no more positive a rebel than Kopit's Madame Rosepettle, in *Oh Dad, Poor Dad, Mamma's Hung You In The Closet And I'm Feeling So Sad.* But Beatrice's rebellion does not seek merely to hiss venom toward dominant patriarchs, in the manner adopted by La Rosepettle, and she surely does not demonstrate strength (like Williams's Serafina Delle Rose and Maggie Pollitt) only while working out an alliance with males on whom she remains dependent. If Beatrice is like a Williams character, the model seems Big Mama. Like that Mississippi matriarch by the end of her play, Beatrice fully intends to create a freer, more dignified life for herself and the children she loves—including, in her case, a highly intelligent daughter, Tillie, who, if she fully grasps her evident educational opportunities, might eventually live a life of considerable success.

Whatever the superficial resemblances one might remark between *Gamma Rays* and Williams's *Glass Menagerie,* the "hopeful" philosophy apparent in Zindel seems a radical departure from Tennessee Williams. Williams's most famous heroines, in *Menagerie* and *Streetcar,* remain, for all their vividness of personality, resolutely trapped in all the illusions imposed on them by patriarchal culture. His heroines surely often enough prove sexually liberated—but still, frequently, remain encaged. Perhaps the ideal Williams heroine is one of calm spiritual liberation—a person like Hannah in *Iguana.* Yet Hannah, despite her spiritual liberty, remains economically starving; Big Mama is more amply fed, but only because she inherited a wealthy man's estate. Even though Hannah and other Williams heroines might become, like Big Mama, capable businesspersons, few even dare think of seeking economic self-determination, as Zindel's Beatrice finally does.

Gamma Rays may ultimately appear too much a product of late Sixties social optimism; Zindel does not seem aware of how harshly even educated Tillies must struggle for independence. Yet the main power of this play still remains its long-unrecognized anti-sexist vision. That vision makes it clearly a historically prophetic work; it is not, as multiple critics have narrowly claimed, a mere tired echo of earlier writers.

Gamma Rays ends with the rhapsodic teenage scientist Tillie Hunsdorfer declaring that

> . . . [T]he effect of gamma rays on man-in-the-moon marigolds has made me curious about *the sun and the stars,* for the universe itself must be like a world of great atoms—and I want to know more about it. But most important, I suppose, my experiment has made me feel important—every atom in me, in everybody, has come *from the sun*—from places *beyond our dreams.* The atoms of our hands, the atoms of *our hearts. . .* (emphasis mine).

Surely, whether consciously or not, these lines—like Tillie's earlier response to a wondrous atomic cloud-chamber—call to mind both the imagery and the visionary fervor which conclude Dante's *Paradiso:*

> . . . [L]ike to a wheel whose circle nothing jars,
> Already on my desire and will prevailed
> The Love that moves the sun and the others stars.

Zindel's play—if by accident, nonetheless with uncanny regularity—demonstrates remarkable affinity with Dante's *Divine Comedy.* The clearest hint of such affinity is Zindel's choice of the two main characters' names: Beatrice and Matilda. Obviously, Beatrice Hunsdorfer does share the name of Dante's central female character, although she markedly differs from her namesake, the medieval icon of spiritually quiescent splendor. Tillie Huns-dorfer, the incipient teenage intellectual, bears more direct resemblance to the Dantesque character she recalls. Matilda of Tuscany, the likely historical model for the character Matelda whom readers meet at the height of Purgatory near Dante's Beatrice, was "a wise and powerful woman, . . . splendid, illustrious . . . surpassing all others in her brilliance, . . . educated, [with] a large collection of books. . . . "

At least in Tillie Hunsdorfer, then, Zindel has a character who closely recalls an analogous character in Dante's great poem. It is, of course, Tillie who voices this play's most Dantesque sentiments; she shares Dante's belief that all earthly atoms are connected with originating stars of Love; that they were, as she speculates, "formed from a tongue of fire [the Holy Spirit?] that screamed through the heavens until there was our sun."

But the Dantesque affinities of Zindel's text do not cease with Beatrice's name and Tillie's name and personality. Zindel's earliest stage directions in the play set the action in "a room of wood," "once a vegetable store." The mention of "wood" and "vegetation," and, most of all, the note that this place was once "a point of debarkation for a horse-drawn wagon to bring its wares to a small town," all summon to my mind Dante's *selva oscura,* the "dark wood" which serves, in *Inferno* 1, as Dante's own "point of debarkation" for a pilgrimage toward the starry multifoliate rose of Paradise. According to Dante, he completed the visionary journey which young Matilda Hunsdorfer hopes, in her lifetime, to share.

But Matilda's mother Beatrice seems long ago to have lost any chance for a meaningful pilgrimage through life. Even as a child, she thought herself proven unworthy to take over her father's vegetable business—to sit atop its wagon, as if clothed in the radiant garb of Dante's own edenic chariot-rider Beatrice, and be a woman recognized (independently of any male mate) for her talents. She might, given other life-circumstances than those she knew, have imitated Dante's successful pilgrimage. But—because her father truly was not, as she mistakenly still wants to believe, one who "made up for all other men in this whole world"—she encountered in him her primal "bogey man." He made her think that she, as a woman, was inferior to all men, that she could not care for his vegetable business either before or after his death, that she needed instead to "marry . . . [and] be taken care of." As a result, by the time of the play's scenes Beatrice has become a perpetual "widow of confusion," much as Dante began (but only began) the *Commedia* as one whose "way was lost."

Like Dante, too, Beatrice Hunsdorfer has dream-visions. But her visions do not foresee an attainable future bliss; they recall, instead, a "nightmare" of past denial. Her dreams, also like Dante's, contain ghosts of lost loved ones. Yet Dante's lost Beatrice still beckons ahead of him; she there pledges to teach him "nobility, . . . virtue, . . . the Redeemed Life," his soul's "ordained end." By contrast, Beatrice Hunsdorfer's lost earthly father, as a ghost, continues to deny her the self-esteem he first refused her long ago:

> And while he was sleeping, I got the horses hitched up and went riding around the block waving to everyone. . . . I had more nerve than a bear when I was a kid. Let me tell you it takes nerve to sit up on that wagon every day yelling "Apples!" . . .
>
> . . . . .
>
> Did he find out? He came running down the street after me and started spanking me right on top of the wagon—not hard—but it was embarrassing—and I had one of those penny marshmallow ships in the back pocket of my overalls, and it got all squished. And you better believe I never did it again. . . .
>
> Let me tell you about my nightmare that used to come back and back: Well, I'm on Papa's wagon, but it's newer and shinier, and it's being pulled by beautiful white horses, not dirty workhorses—these are like circus horses with long manes and tinsel—and the wagon is blue, shiny blue. And it's full—filled with yellow apples and grapes and green squash.
>
> . . . . .
>
> Huge bells swinging on a gold braid [are] strung across the back of the wagon, and they're going DONG, DONG . . . DONG, DONG. And I'm yelling "APPLES! PEARS! CUCUM . . . BERS!"
>
> . . . . .
>
> And then I turn down our street and all the noise stops. This long street, with all the doors of the houses shut and everything crowded next to each other, and there's not a soul around. And then I start getting afraid that the vegetables are going to spoil . . . and that nobody's going to buy anything, and I feel as though I shouldn't be on the wagon, and I keep trying to call out.
>
> But there isn't a sound. Not a single sound. Then I turn my head and look at the house across the street. I see an upstairs window, and a pair of hands pull the curtains slowly apart. I see the face of my father and my heart stands still. . . .
>
> Ruth . . . take the light out of my eyes.

Convinced by her sexist father that she had no gifts for managing her own meaningful career—"afraid that [if guarded only by her] the vegetables would spoil . . . and

. . . nobody . . . [would] buy anything"—Beatrice has ever since been trapped in her own everyday earthly Inferno: on a "long street," "everything crowded," "not a soul around." Although she is like Zindel's own mother in her concocting "charmingly frantic scheme[s] . . . to get rich quick," she is, not surprisingly, highly jealous of her invalid boarder Nanny's daughter, "Miss Career Woman of the Year." She also envies her own daughters, refusing to admit that they have gifts which could lead them to careers even semi-professional. She can't believe that her daughter Ruth can even use a typewriter; at one point, she proclaims that Tillie should forget about her scientific ambitions and instead go to work in a dime store.

And Tillie might have been behind that dime store sales counter the next week had she not suddenly become a finalist in her high school's Science Fair. Her science teacher Mr. Goodman—himself typically sexist, at least in his shock that "he never saw a girl do anything like that before"—was convinced of her promise. As a slightly inattentive Ruth reports to her mother, Mr. Goodman said that Tillie "was going to be another Madame Pasteur."

So Tillie is spared the dime store, and Beatrice as her mother seems simultaneously spared her sense of being a complete "zero," "the original half-life!" Once it reaches her consciousness that Tillie has achieved what Ruth calls "an honor," Beatrice can declare, as she embraces her brainy child, an expletive which almost briefly approaches a creedal statement of faith: "Oh, my God. . . . " And, as she tells Ruth in the next act, "Somewhere in the back of this turtle-sized brain of mine I feel just a little proud! Jesus Christ!"

Indeed, it does not seem altogether fanciful to suggest that Act Two of *Gamma Rays* becomes (although not at all in a traditional Dantesque manner) Beatrice Hunsdorfer's encounter with a personal purgatory. As Act One ends, the school principal Mr. Berg (translation from the German: "Mr. [Purgatorial?] Mountain") invites Beatrice to the Science Fair competition ceremonies. At the opening of the play's second act she has dressed for that event in a feathery costume, leading Ruth to quote some gossip from one of her mother's childhood companions: "[Mama's] idea of getting dressed up is to put on all the feathers in the world and go as a bird. Always trying to get somewhere, like a great big bird." Has Beatrice always frustratingly hoped that an eagle would lift her, as it lifted Dante, up to higher purgatorial crests?

Beatrice, after all, recalls her own youth as being something like Tillie's youth now. She might have advanced toward a better life had she not been intimidated (as Tillie herself is not) by others' disparagings. As Ruth tells Tillie, Beatrice as a girl "was just like you and everybody thought she was a big weirdo"; "First they had Betty the Loon, and now they've got Tillie the Loon."

Unfortunately, the selfish Ruth who utters these words eventually comes close to ruining her mother's chances for any sort of purgatorial experience. In brattish rage because she herself is being asked to skip the Science Fair and replace her mother as guardian of Nanny the Boarder, Ruth screeches "Goodnight, Betty the Loon" at a Beatrice who is finally escaping, if still somewhat timidly, her fear of the outside world in order to attend Tillie's school ceremonies. Ruth's vicious ploy does gain her what she wants: Beatrice now immediately returns (or so it seems) to the agoraphobic terror of life which has for so long characterized her; she "helplessly" sends Ruth off with the Science Fair paraphernalia that she herself was to carry, and she then "breaks into tears that shudder her body, and the lights go down on her pathetic form."

Yet Act One had already prepared the way for Beatrice's doing something (in an earthly purgatory) with the insights which her memories (like Dante's in non-earthly Inferno) were giving her. She said then that she had "almost forgot[ten] about everything [she] was supposed to be." Still, Zindel built irony into such of her statements as "Me and cobalt-60! Two of the biggest half-lifes you ever saw!" Zindel's stage-directions soon afterwards told us that Beatrice was forming "mushroom cloud" smoke rings with her cigarettes; thus, her "half-life," like that of cobalt-60, always perhaps could, in its "mushroom cloud" explosion, hold positive mutation within it.

And, in the last scenes of *Gamma Rays*, Beatrice does lunge after such positive mutation. She tears newspapers off from the house's windows, then rearranges tables and places tablecloths and napkins on them. She calls Nanny's daughter, ordering her to take the old boarder away. Sitting down, guffawing over that conquest, and hitting her daughter's pet rabbit cage with her foot, she decides to chloroform the creature—which is, in Hugh Hefner's America, not only a children's pet, but an unfortunate symbol of female suppression.

No mere self-centered cruelty leads Beatrice to these behaviors. She is striving to make meaningful mutation occur in her (and in her daughters') life. Thus, when the girls start to express a fear that she may truly have killed their bunny, she doesn't directly respond to them. She matter-of-factly pronounces broader concerns: "Nanny goes tomorrow. First thing tomorrow"; "I don't know what it's going to be. Maybe a tea shop. Maybe not."

So long trapped in a hellish rut because not daring to lead a business-woman's produce-wagon off from "a point of debarkation," pilgrim Beatrice now seeks to redirect her life. For her, "hat[ing] the world" has not meant a spiritual leap beyond that world, in the manner of Dante's original Beatrice. She has, instead, made a ramshackle earthbound leap into self-assertion. And yet a certain level of spiritual other-centeredness has allied itself with that self-assertion. Even though she will force her daughters to "work in the [tea-shop] kitchen," she will not any longer seek to deny them an education for future self-determination. They will have "regular hours" in the business, but those hours will be scheduled "after school." She will no longer live so much in the shadow of her father that she tries to limit others in the way he limited her.

In introductory comments to the *Gamma Rays* script, which are really an unofficial dedication of the play to his

mother, Zindel makes it clear that he considered that woman a beautiful mutation: someone who had at least striven, in her limited way, to become like the liberated modern mom he described in a short children's piece written for *Ms.* in 1976:

> . . . She says "Absolutely not," when I want to drive the car, and "Have a good time," when I tell her I'm running away to Miami. She doesn't want me to know when we don't have enough money. . . . If I see her crying she says, "It's just something in my eye." She tells me secrets like she's lonely. When I tell her I miss my father she hugs me and says he misses me too. I love my mother. I really do.

("**I Love My Mother**")

Zindel has given us enough information to show his own mother's clear resemblances to Beatrice Hunsdorfer. One thus chuckles at his jocose offhand comment: "I suspect [the play] is autobiographical." Besides, autobiography may extend past the characterization of Beatrice to a character (unseen onstage) who may in some ways markedly suggest Paul Zindel himself: Mr. Goodman, Tillie's high school chemistry teacher.

Zindel taught high school chemistry for ten years and only left Staten Island, where he had taught, after the Pulitzer Prize award for *Gamma Rays.* Despite that fact, one of course would not claim that he deliberately insults himself when he has Beatrice at first describe Mr. Goodman as a "delightful and handsome young man" but then refer to him, a few minutes later, as "a Hebrew hermaphrodite." After all, the "hermaphrodite" reference is not ultimately intended as a physical description—at least not in the play's thematic undertext. A statement which at first seems only to exemplify Beatrice's crude-mouthed bitterness more importantly helps introduce the play's revisionist Hebrew theology, viewing all humankind as androgynous.

Zindel's anti-sexist thoughts of 1970 might be challenged now by such radical feminists as Mary Daly. She considers "androgyny" to be "a vacuous term," "expressing pseudo-wholeness" as an example of one of those "false universalisms (e.g., humanism, people's liberation) . . . which Spinsters must leap over, . . . must span" in order to affirm their own "intuition of integrity" [*Gyn/Ecology: The Metaethics of Radical Feminism* (1978)]. And, it is true, Zindel's androgyny still has a patriarchal sound; his anti-sexist thesis emphasizes the pun "Adam"/"atom," and he thus does recall for us the name of the first legendary Hebrew patriarch. Still, even Daly would grant "deceptive" but hard-to-avoid concepts of androgyny some relative value in progress to a non-sexist world. And others would remain more encouraged than she by Zindel's androgynous creed.

That creed is voiced throughout a play which has appeared to invite regular misreading. For instance, despite her obvious affection for the character's gutsy energy, Edith Oliver claims that Beatrice "is as much a victim of her own nature as she is of circumstance" [*New Yorker,* 18 April 1970]. Yet, given Zindel's pointed indictment of her father's sexism, why should we be assigning Beatrice herself with a heavy load of blame? Adler does perceive, without explaining why, that Beatrice's father caused her psychological problems. And yet he, too, does not seem at all to sense that this is a feminist play; he does not discuss it in his mildly feminist chapter "Nora's American Cousins," and he indeed rates Beatrice's plan to open a tea-shop as "slightly outrageous."

I do not believe for a moment, as Adler implies and as Brustein shouts, that **Gamma Rays** simply clones the illusion-ridden mother-daughter encaging atmosphere of *The Glass Menagerie* [Thomas P. Adler, *Mirror on the Stage: The Pulitzer Plays as an Approach to American Drama* (1987); Robert Brustein, *The Culture Watch: Essays on Theatre and Society, 1969-1974* (1975)]. Jack Kroll approaches closer to the truth about the play when he says that "The calculus of love, jealous vengefulness, remorse, flaring hatred, and desperate reconciliation[,] among these three people fighting for spiritual life, is the point and merit of Zindel's affecting play" [*Newsweek,* 27 April 1970]. And Harold Clurman, that ever-trustworthy sage, adds that "In **Gamma Rays** . . . a real person [he means Tillie, but I think Beatrice also fits the description] flowers from the compost of abject defeat and hysteria" [*Nation,* 15 March 1971].

In the play's very opening monologue, Tillie expresses indomitable faith in human androgynous potential as she tells of how Mr. Goodman, in chemistry class, helped her sense that in adamic atoms of origin all human beings are equal:

> He told me to look at my hand, for a part of it came from a star that exploded too long ago to imagine. This part of me was formed from a tongue of fire that screamed through the heavens until there was our sun.
>
> . . . . .
>
> . . . When there was life, perhaps this part of me got lost in a fern that was crushed and covered until it was coal. And then it was a diamond as beautiful as the star from which it had first come.
>
> . . . . .
>
> And he called this bit of me an atom. And when he wrote the word, I fell in love with it.
>
> Atom.
>
> Atom.
>
> What a beautiful word.

For all its potential Dantesque echoes, Zindel's beautiful play finally shines with the ameliorative twentieth-century hope of an original, deeply sensitive, and highly enlightened modern good man. Paul Zindel, that man, is distant from the norm, even in our own age, as he rebuffs the patriarchal sexism which was not absent even from Dante's enlightened Renaissance Christianity. Neither Beatrice Hunsdorfer nor Paul Zindel wants to idealize only "GOODY-GOODY GIRLS" like Dante's Beatrice Portinari dei Bardi. Both believe, or at least want to believe by their play's conclu-

sion, that, by "hat[ing] the world" which limits women to roles as men's slaves (or even sacred muses), they may recreate that world—in Zindel's words, "bring innovation to civilization, to institutions, . . . make contributions . . . [toward a] world which is a better place to live" [interview with Paul Janeczko, *English Journal* 66, No. 7 (October 1977)]. Zindel's revised Genesis myth (perhaps his own creatively revisionist response to the very different Garden of Eden scenes which culminate Dante's *Purga-torio*) suggests how hard a non-sexist world is to create, and even to define. But such a world—in which we would recreate the meaning of "Adam" by finding our common personhood as "atom"—still seems to him a necessary earthly paradise, one always meant to be.

AND MISS REARDON DRINKS A LITTLE

PRODUCTION REVIEWS

Brendan Gill (review date 6 March 1971)

SOURCE: "Shopworn," in *The New Yorker,* Vol. XLVII, No. 3, 6 March 1971, pp. 67-8.

[*Here, Gill assesses* And Miss Reardon Drinks a Little *as "so shopworn in form, so flyblown in content, that one would suppose it had been written several decades ago by a bookish hermit thoroughly out of touch with the theatrical innovations of even his day."*]

Having been radically overpraised last year for a not very robust pastiche of early Tennessee Williams called *The Effect of Gamma Rays on Man-in-the-Moon Marigolds*, Paul Zindel now risks being underdamned for his **And Miss Reardon Drinks a Little**, at the Morosco. The risk springs from a sorry fact about reviewing: to keep from being seen to have loved an earlier work not wisely but too well, reviewers encountering a later work that they don't like at all tend to mask their dislike and let the playwright sink by controlled stages, like a barge in canal locks, to his proper level, thus augmenting their reputations in the course of diminishing his. It is a practice related, in a reversed, mirror image, to what is known in Wall Street as "averaging," and I am sorry that Mr. Zindel should have to become a victim of it. Since he has written a much worse play this time than his erstwhile admirers can afford to admit, they bring up all the usual cant phrases of indirect apology for their previous praise, beginning with "Mr. Zindel can write, but . . . " And what evidence of his ability to write do they adduce from the present play? None whatever. They are thinking nervously of what they said about his *other* play, and they are assuming that few people will go back and check up on the quality of writing manifested in that work. A serious playwright must not be dealt with gently in order to preserve the self-esteem of a handful of journalists; much more is at

Estelle Parsons, Julie Harris, and Nancy Marchand in the 1971 Broadway production of And Miss Reardon Drinks a Little.

stake here than "averaging," and if Mr. Zindel is to survive as an artist we owe it to him to say, with concern, that *And Miss Reardon Drinks a Little* has put his professional life in jeopardy.

Miss Reardon—I am not going to bother using the whole title, which is scarcely less irritating in its pretentiousness than *The Effect of Gamma Rays, Etc.*—is a play so shopworn in form, so flyblown in content, that one would suppose it had been written several decades ago by a bookish hermit thoroughly out of touch with the theatrical innovations of even his day. The mysterious fact of the matter is that Mr. Zindel is a comparatively young man, of thirty-four, and his play appears, on the strength of at least one piece of internal evidence—the currently fashionable scatological language that he puts in the mouth of a middle-aged Irish Catholic woman schoolteacher—to have been composed within the last couple of years. Still, who would believe that in 1971 the curtain would rise on an apartment-house living room in which the first significant action consists of a doorbell ringing, someone emerging from an off-stage kitchen to answer the bell, and the visitor at the door proving to be the building superintendent's wife, fat and unlovely, introduced partly to make us laugh (with mala-propisms of a mind-numbing improbability) and partly to provide us with clues to the fact that something is desperately wrong with one of the occupants of the apartment? Step by step, through three conventionally carpentered acts, we are shown the plight of a family in whom we cannot

believe, since its members are literary constructions designed to support certain structural weights but incapable of evincing life. Everything that befalls the three Reardon sisters in the grim shadow of their dead mother bears the mark of fabrication. The single surprise of the evening is revealed when the curtain falls for the last time and we perceive that the poor playwright has had nothing to tell us; the dreary surface of his melodrama was all, and was intended to be all, and it plainly never struck him that it would not be enough.

Bad as the play is, it serves as the occasion for two or three fine performances. Estelle Parsons is especially resourceful as the bibulous Miss Reardon of the title, and Rae Allen, Bill Macy, and Nancy Marchand are admirable in roles made difficult by their papery thinness. Julie Harris has to play a Reardon sister who has gone mad; she does her best, but the taint of Ophelia is in the role, and Miss Harris has brought it out instead of concealing it. The casting of the three sisters is odd—as an amateur geneticist, I consider it the unlikeliest thing imaginable that Miss Parsons, Miss Harris, and Miss Marchand could be siblings. The director of *Miss Reardon* is Melvin Bernhardt, and the designer of the set is Fred Voelpel, who has fallen into the extraordinary aesthetic error of supposing that the way to convey the squalid tackiness of a middle-class apartment-house living room is to reproduce to the last detail the squalid tackiness of a middle-class apartment-house living room. I can tell you it was a horrible thing to have to stare at for three acts.

Harold Clurman (review date 15 March 1971)

SOURCE: A review of *And Miss Reardon Drinks a Little,* in *The Nation,* New York, Vol. 212, No. 11, 15 March 1971, pp. 347-48.

[*Clurman was a highly-regarded American director, educator, author, and drama critic for* The Nation *from 1953 to 1980. His writings include the acclaimed book of reminiscences* All People Are Famous (Instead of an Autobiography) *(1974). In the review below, he praises the performance of the cast and remarks on the caustic comedy of* And Miss Reardon Drinks a Little, *concluding that the play "is chiefly a display of bad manners and excruciating rudeness."*]

If Paul Zindel's new play **And Miss Reardon Drinks a Little** (Morosco Theatre) has any special point, it is that we are living in a society of nuts—which is no longer news. But though Zindel has sympathy or an affinity for the neglected and disturbed, he is more adept at depicting them than in drawing any conclusions about them—except perhaps that we ought not allow ourselves, through pity, to be overwhelmed by them. In his earlier and much better **The Effect of Gamma Rays on Man-in-the-Moon Marigolds**, a real person flowers from the compost of abject defeat and hysteria. In **Miss Reardon** there are only weeds.

The three Reardon sisters are public schoolteachers. Their father abandoned his home when they were children. Anna Reardon, the most fragile of the three, was consigned to the care of their increasingly ailing and neurotic mother, whose death terribly shocked the girl. The rugged but not so attractive Catherine Reardon lost her boyfriend to Ceil, the steadiest of the sisters and now a school superintendent. Of the two spinsters, Anna is quite mad and Catherine drinks; Ceil, married to Catherine's former swain, remains rigorously proper and adjusted to the circumstances of her tight circle.

Nothing much happens, except that Catherine, after having to take care of, really enslave herself to, the mentally ill Anna, finally decides to get rid of the burden by sending her sister to a hospital. These, then, are character studies, to which are added another teacher and her husband, who live in the same building as do the unfortunate Catherine and Anna. These neighbors, the Steins (the man is "in glass"), are people of the crummy middle class and more amusingly drawn than any of the others.

Though its atmosphere is sordid, the audience finds the play funny. There are loads of laughs, the reason for which—beyond Zindel's slickly expert writing—interests me. **Miss Reardon** is chiefly a display of bad manners and excruciating rudeness. The play abounds in taunts, and the well-turned elaborate insult evidently gratifies today's audience. We vent undisclosed frustrations and hostilities in jokes and mockery, which supposedly render our festering hate anodyne. The audience, moreover, compliments itself (and the author) by believing that it is observing "real people," and thus proving that it does not balk at the astringent.

I suspect the "reality" of Zindel's characters in this play, even if they are persons he has known in "real life," which is probably the case. They have become atrocious gags. Ugliness and cruelty are as much proper subjects for art as virtue, but they must be seen in the light of some larger vision. An artist's derision must not demean; it must reveal an ultimately fortifying sense of life, a generosity or enkindling energy of spirit. In this connection I recall Coleridge's aphorism about abrasive works of art, "There ought never to be more pain than is compatible with co-existing pleasure, and [we ought] to be amply repaid by thought."

Most of the pleasure in **And Miss Reardon Drinks a Little** is provided by the excellent cast. Julie Harris never fails to charm; she lends innocence to whatever she does, and Anna Reardon demands that grace to save her from ghoulishness. Estelle Parsons, as the bibulous sister, brings an honest and unvulgar earthiness to her part that is constantly endearing. Rae Allen and Bill Macy evince a straightforward simplicity in their acting of the absurdly gross Steins which dispels their noxious fumes and converts them into genuine comedy.

A word about the "scenery": it serves. But I have become impatient with "realistic" settings which are no more than that: they depress me.

John Simon (review date 15 March 1971)

SOURCE: "No Foundations, All the Way Down the Line," in *New York* Magazine, Vol. 4, No. 11, 15 March 1971, p. 57.

[*A Yugoslavian-born American film and drama critic, Simon has been both praised as a judicious reviewer and censured as a petty faultfinder. He believes that criticism should be subjective, and as Andrew Sinclair has observed: "He is as absolute and arrogant in his judgments as any dictator of culture, a rigidity that is his great strength and weakness." In the following review, he points out the shortcomings of* And Miss Reardon Drinks a Little *but offers a generally positive assessment of the production's acting ensemble.*]

The best thing to be said about **And Miss Reardon Drinks a Little** is that Paul Zindel wrote it well before his very charming **Marigolds.** I never trust a work whose title starts with "and": it always suggests that we are to assume something momentous but ineffable lurking in the empty space before that "and," and leaves us stranded in an inferno of inferences. I cannot trust a playwright who'll do that to me before his title, never mind his play, has even begun. Sure enough, the play proves a routine comedy with serious overtones, whose jokes often do not go over, and whose overtones have a tendency to go under. One is uncomfortably aware throughout that the young playwright has approached his mentors, Tennessee Williams and Arthur Miller, with slavish reverence. At times, I felt literally inundated by the two masters' used bathwater. Unfortunately, Zindel has thrown in the bathwater without the baby.

We have here the three Reardon sisters whose mother has just died. Two of them, Catherine and Anna, are spinster schoolmarms; the third, Ceil, stole Catherine's beau, married him lovelessly, and worked her way up to superintendent of schools. Anna, who had to nurse her agonizingly slowly dying mother, has gone batty, and, among other things, imagines she has rabies and refuses to eat meat or suffer furry objects to come near her; she has also had a scandalous affair with the most precocious and unwholesome of her high school students. The first and the last of these misfortunes she seems to have inherited from Blanche DuBois. The actual subject of the play is whether Anna should be confined to an institution (*Streetcar*), but the texture of it is sibling rivalry (*Death of a Salesman, The Price*). The main difficulty is that the material tends toward comedy, whither Zindel happily nudges it, whereas the impact and the implications are meant to be dramatic. Unlike Chekhov's three sisters, these three seem neither to have problems that mesh into a single, unified distress, nor are they each individually developed with sufficient fullness.

Much has been made by reviewers of the great ensemble acting. Well, Melvin Bernhardt has directed the show with tidiness verging on slickness, and there are some good performances. As the hard, grasping Ceil, Nancy Marchand overcomes both the sketchiness and the frozen stasis of the permanent interlocutor's part, and gives it gusts of genuineness and credibility without fudging either its ludicrous or its sour aspects. As a neighbor couple with rifts of their own, Bill Macy and Rae Allen manage to maintain a kind of absurd dignity in the midst of their repulsiveness that is totally right and captivating, and they make the last part of the second act, which they dominate, into a pleasant dip into meaningful, resonant comedy. Estelle Parsons, as Catherine or anything else, is always Estelle Parsons: though she does not enrich the part with any imaginative depth, she coasts trimly along its surfaces. Julie Harris, alas, is back to her forte of playing disturbed adolescents, neither becoming to nor believable at her age. Her emotional locus is again somewhere between bobby sox and booby hatch, and it is hard to accept her problem as a horribly dying mother rather than sheer arrested development.

Some sort of serious problem seems to have affected also the opening-night audience, which insisted on laughing uproariously at jokes like "Those were not Lebanons, Mrs. Pentrano, those were lesbians," often drowning out whatever punchline there was. We keep hearing about absence of audiences killing the theater; their presence, frequently, is not all that salutary either.

AMULETS AGAINST THE DRAGON FORCES

PRODUCTION REVIEWS
Frank Rich (review date 6 April 1989)

SOURCE: "Overcoming a Loveless Childhood," in *The New York Times*, 6 April 1989, p. C17.

[*Since 1977, Rich has been the chief cinema and television critic for* Time *magazine. He is also a contributor to* Ms., the New York Times, *and* Esquire. *In the following review of the 1989 Circle Repertory Company's production of* Amulets against the Dragon Force, *Rich comments on the anguish in the characters' lives and finds Zindel's plot and use of mythology overworked.*]

While most of François Truffaut's *Small Change* has receded in memory, I can't imagine forgetting the scene in which a baby tumbles from a high apartment-house window and survives. Truffaut made an indelible image out of profound questions that had defined his career from *The 400 Blows* and that never leave most of us: By what miracle do some children survive? What happens to those victims of cruel, lonely, loveless childhoods who do grow up but don't bounce back?

These questions also animate the far different work of Paul Zindel, whose breakthrough play of 1970, **The Effect of Gamma Rays on Man-in-the-Moon Marigolds**, told of two sisters trying to escape the suffocating grip of their bitter mother. Mr. Zindel's new play at the Circle Repertory Company, **Amulets Against the Dragon Forces**, returns to the same themes, a similar mother, another Staten Island household (of 1955) and, as the title indicates, some of the same overwriting. It's easy to mock Mr. Zindel's unshapely hothouse drama, whose occupants are variously afflicted by cancer, dipsomania, kleptomania, bisexual nymphomania and poetic excess. Then we see the child at center stage trying to ward off the horrors, the child too genuine to dismiss as fiction, and **Amulets** becomes gripping and disturbing despite its Gothic overkill.

The child is the teen-age Chris (Matt McGrath), who travels with his mother (Deborah Hedwall), an itinerant practical nurse, from house to house as she takes on live-in assignments with terminal patients. Chris was long ago abandoned by his father, who fled to St. Augustine, Fla. ("near the Ripley's Believe It or Not Museum"). Now the boy finds himself carrying his suitcase and shopping bags into a dingy household populated entirely by abandoned souls. The dying widow (Ruby Holbrook) in the care of Chris's mother is ignored by her son, a brutish, alcoholic longshoreman named Floyd (John Spencer). The middle-aged Floyd reserves most of his love and abuse for the young Harold (Loren Dean), a sweet hustler who had been abandoned by his own parents before finding his way into Floyd's bed.

Though they have not all been created with equal depth by Mr. Zindel, the characters are invariably fascinating—even the ravaged, nearly comatose patient who bites anyone who comes near her. But **Amulets** is primarily a Tennessee Williams-like standoff between the sensitive Chris and the bellicose Floyd, who will not rest until he has brutalized the vulnerabilities of everyone around him. Floyd not only hates women—his mother, Chris's mother, his discarded wife—but he also likes to fire up the local male roughnecks by inviting them over for booze and whores.

The struggle between the frail Chris and the destructive

Floyd would seem no contest. Chris has no defenses—only a collection of carved figures, his amulets, that provides him with a fantasy world of escapist storytelling. Floyd has ready fists and an abusive tongue poised to spill anyone's most shameful secrets. But as the compassionate Mr. Zindel avoided simple moral judgments with the mother in *Marigold*, so he does with Floyd: we can still find the abused child who was father to the vicious man. In Mr. Spencer's volatile performance, the longshoreman is alternately a "slobbering, horrendous freak" and an articulate student of human nature, with equally devastating results.

As nakedly acted by the brave and talented Mr. McGrath, Chris is an open wound, almost painful to watch. A gawky, delicate misfit with an epicene voice, he tries to head off rejection by chattily advertising his own precociousness. The only teacher who ever thought the boy anything but "completely deranged" had decided that he was a writer. Chris clings to this diagnosis even though the teacher, a Shakespeare scholar, herself suffered a nervous breakdown after being ridiculed by students.

In this teacher's class, Chris learned that "everyone loved action and suspense." Mr. Zindel, a popular author of fiction for adolescents, knows the same lesson, but he piles on too much florid action in *Amulets*: Do we need a smashed chandelier, a gay love triangle, a sudden financial windfall *and* an orgy? None of these events are underplayed by the director, B. Rodney Marriott, or are left unaccompanied by Norman L. Berman's creepy incidental score. One must also quarrel with the overworked mythology of Chris's amulets, with the psychoanalytical symmetry of the parent-child relationships and with the unlikely Act II exchange of confessional monologues (however well written) between Floyd and Chris's mom, who otherwise hate each other.

Ms. Hedwall, despite some uneasiness with her lines, becomes rending in that scene, the starchy mother's one chance to reveal how she went from being one women's-magazine cliché (the model 1950's housewife) to another ("the desperate divorcée") without ever finding the woman she might have been. Mr. Dean's lost boy of the streets also commands attention—with his ethereal ingenuousness, if not with his mumbling.

But Chris is the child crashing toward earth in Mr. Zindel's play, and it is for him that the playwright holds out the blind hope denied the others. As the pitiful Mr. McGrath cries into a phone, begging his dismissive father in vain for love, it's hard to imagine how he can possibly grow up intact. "It's all in the timing" is Floyd's explanation of how Chris might yet survive the same dragon forces that maimed him, and who knows? It's not without wisdom that Mr. Zindel situates the searing drama of childhood, like Chris's absent father, in the mysterious, macabre neighborhood of Ripley's Believe It or Not.

Clive Barnes (review date 7 April 1989)

SOURCE: "Troubled Times for a Teen," in *New York Post,* 7 April 1989.

[*Here, Barnes discusses the various themes in* Amulets Against the Dragon Forces.]

Paul Zindel is one of those unfortunate playwrights best-known for his first play—*The Effect of Gamma Rays on Man-in-the-Moon Marigolds*, an unnerving and sensitive study of survival through a stricken childhood in a dysfunctional family.

Now, in his newest play, *Amulets Against the Dragon Forces* at the Circle Repertory Company, Zindel has returned to similar themes of adolescence, alienation and survival.

It has the same quality of compassion of *Moon Marigolds*, although perhaps it now less convincingly pulls those threads of memory strands that 20 years ago gave the earlier play its resonances of Tennessee Williams and hints of a grand maturity.

The beleagured protagonist of *Amulets* (Zindel has not lost his taste for provocatively teasing titles) is a young boy, Chris (Matt McGrath).

He is dominated by an overbearing and over-protective divorced mother (Deborah Hedwell), who is a trained nurse making her living by moving into the homes of the terminally ill.

It is thus that he finds himself in a new and bizarre household, ruled by a brutally boozy, homosexual longshoreman, Floyd (John Spencer).

This new play, which is suffused with an atmosphere redolent of the overdrawn gothic horrors of old Hollywood movies in their 'B' picture mode, is, however, not simply about survival.

Even more, it concerns itself with the fight for identity—an identity a human being can live with, an identity that can protect one against the dragon-forces of life's uncertainties.

Chris, abandoned by life and his father, benevolently bullied by his disturbed mother, uses his carved puppets (not quite a glass menagerie!) as amulets against misfortune.

Now he is being briefly thrown into Floyd's hating world of alcholism and drifter-sex—a world crazily inhabited by Floyd's mother (Ruby Holbrook), a vicious near-corpse biting any male unwise enough to come near her, Chris' own mother, a kleptomaniac dreaming of a house of her own, and Harold (Loren Dean), a young hustler, who has become Floyd's houseboy and general factotum.

Both Floyd and Chris' mother, with a parallelism rather too cutely neat, made an early mistake; Floyd in not recognizing his homosexuality soon enough, before he was washed away in booze, guilt and self-hatred, and the mother in not overlooking the marital trangressions of her former husband.

Chris himself, longing for the father who first deserted him

Matt McGrath and John Spencer in the 1989 off-Broadway production of Amulets Against the Dragon Forces.

and now rejects him, already has homosexual leanings. When little more than a child, he was picked up, while cruising, by a drunk, marauding Floyd, who has now forgotten the incident.

At the end—having been warned by Floyd that "timing is everything"—he rushes off to the future, presumably to face the consequences of what appears to be his sexual nature.

The play is overwritten and overwrought, at times dangerously fringing self-parody. Yet beneath its pretentiousness there lies a commonplace honesty that is probably not all that commonplace.

The staging by B. Rodney Marriott was as appropriately heavy-handed as the writing, but the acting proved generally excellent. What good actors we have nowadays!

As Chris, McGrath, who may be remembered from his appearance in the Circle Rep's last play, *Dalton's Back*, is altogether admirable, weak, reed-like, pathetic, yet with a kind of tenacity that lets one believe in his survival.

Spencer, as the coarse Floyd, is also excellent, horrifically convincing as an aging bully-boy with faint intimations of a now lost gentler, kinder self.

Hedwell has a brusque Ortonesque authority as the nurse/mother, while Dean, in the one truly sympathetic role in the play as the good-natured hustler who befriends Chris, reveals a sweetness that even survives the play's intentionally pervasive nastiness.

Amulets Against the Dragon Forces has the air of a work written to enable its author to get something off his chest and perhaps clear the decks for a different future. One hopes so.

Laurie Winer (review date 12 April 1989)

SOURCE: "Power of Innocence," in *The Wall Street Journal*, 12 April 1989.

[*In the following review, Winer compares Zindel's depiction of Chris Boyd in* Amulets Against the Dragon Forces *to J. D. Salinger's portrait of Holden Caulfield in* The Catcher in the Rye.]

Like J.D. Salinger, Paul Zindel cannot forget the turbulent years of adolescence. The author of a series of popular novels for young adults, Mr. Zindel writes vividly of teenagers who overcome loneliness by finding friendship, love and adventure. For the young characters who inhabit the darker worlds of Mr. Zindel's drama, however, salvation is often a much trickier proposition.

The titles of the plays (for instance, *The Effect of Gamma Rays on Man-in-the-Moon Marigolds*) suggest unequal opposing forces that do battle, and they refer specifically to that most unequal war between a vengeful adult and a trust-

ing child. But Mr. Zindel's teen-age protagonists are not necessarily destined to repeat the pattern of emotional cruelty inflicted on them by grownup guardians. His new play, *Amulets Against the Dragon Forces*, at Circle Repertory, illuminates the miracle by which the weaker force, the child, finds the courage to hold on to his own sweetness and his ability to love. And in this impassioned new work, Mr. Zindel gives us a teen-age protagonist who is as original, believable and decent as Salinger's Holden Caulfield.

The year is 1955 and young Chris Boyd (Matt McGrath) has become inured to living in other people's homes. His pragmatic mother (Deborah Hedwall), made shrewd and suspicious from an acrimonious divorce, nurses terminally ill patients while stealing canned foods from their families' pantries. Her newest charge is a mean old woman named Mrs. Depardi who wants to die in her Staten Island home, now headed by her surly middle-aged son, Floyd (John Spencer). Or maybe Mrs. Depardi just wants to have one last chance to torture Floyd, a shipyard worker who clearly could have been more than what he is—an alcoholic exploiter of young men, one of whom, Harold (Loren Dean), lives in the house as a domestic and sexual servant.

Bright and geeky, Chris hopes to make friends by dispensing ingratiatingly energetic remarks on anything that happens in the Depardi household. "I don't know much about herbs but I understand that they're really crucial to exotic cooking!" he tells Harold, who's preparing a shopping list. To Floyd: "You've got a lot of psychological literature for a shipyard worker; very riveting!" But despite his desperate need to be liked, Chris *is* likable. His endless anecdotes and observations reveal a keen appreciation for the absurd and a love of fun, even in the most depressing circumstances.

With an inherited gift for wounding children, Floyd soon singles out Chris as an especially vulnerable target. Chris makes it easy; he's trusting and good-natured. After Floyd, momentarily disarmed by the boy's lack of guile, admits that he no longer dreams, the youngster in turn shares his secret world. It's a universe peopled by talismanical papiermache dolls that he makes and whose lives he enacts on a dark blue cloth, which he calls The Zone Unknown. There's something particularly heartbreaking about the doll that represents Chris himself—it carries two suitcases and wears an oversized coat just as he does. When Chris shows Floyd the dolls, Floyd is momentarily struck dumb. But inevitably, as if it's coded into his genes, Floyd must try to destroy what's loving in Chris, just as it was destroyed in him during his own childhood.

Staged with assurance by director E. Rodney Marriott, *Amulets* is superbly acted by two Circle Rep regulars, Mr. McGrath and Mr. Spencer. They make fascinating adversaries. Mr. Spencer's flat delivery and threateningly sexual gait spell the lie of his character's disinguous shows of concern. Using a realistically screechy adolescent voice, Mr. McGrath delicately and powerfully etches the extraordinary potential in a boy who could be just another lost cause. Making a striking New York stage debut, Loren Dean is touching as another deserving young kid who has even less going for him than Chris; his Harold, a '50s greaser who Floyd found hustling on the streets, probably won't find his own way out of the maze.

Although Mr. Zindel is sometimes accused of overwriting, he strips his language down to essentials in the play's crucial confrontations. When Chris tells Floyd, "I don't want to be ashamed and angry like you," and an almost comatose Floyd responds, "Maybe you won't," the redemptive power of innocence asserts itself in these simple words.

John Simon (review date 17 April 1989)

SOURCE: "Myself when Young, Twice," in *New York* Magazine, Vol. 22, No. 16, 17 April 1989, pp. 80-1.

[*Here, Simon approves of the production of* Amulets against the Dragon Forces, *praising Zindel's use of dialogue.*]

Paul Zindel's *Amulets Against the Dragon Forces* is not up to the author's best previous dramatic work or down to his worst, but it is one of those confessions many a writer must get off his chest, and, happily, it is of some interest to the rest of us. Yes, it is a hysterical play; yes, it churns away almost without respite; but it is also recognizably a play, and its characters are recognizably people. Nowadays, that is something.

Mrs. Boyd is a nurse who usually attends persons dying in their own homes. A divorced mother, she moves in with her patients and brings along her teenage son. The boy, Chris, has had a rough time of it, but finds consolation in carving figurines out of balsa wood and making them act out stories he tells himself. Right now, the house is that of Floyd Dipardi, a book-reading shipyard worker, who hates but tries to do right by his moribund mother and lives with a young ex-hustler, Harold. But he also enjoys throwing noisy poolside orgies with young boys—a practice that doesn't endear him to his Staten Island neighbors in this year of 1955.

Chris yearns to visit his father in Florida and would take along Harold, with whom he has become fast friends and who needs to get away from Floyd. Mrs. Boyd, on bad terms with her ex, doesn't want Chris to go; but, then, she is on bad terms with Floyd, too, and tries to get away from the Dipardis herself. It is an untenable situation for everyone, not least for the dying Mrs. D. And so the Dipardi home becomes a gladiatorial arena, a battleground for orgiasts and anti-orgiasts, from which Chris tries to wrest what peace he can. And then there are all sorts of revelations.

Zindel writes juicy dialogue, simple yet idiosyncratic. "That whole place is infected with contradictions" or, about Floyd, who drinks incessantly, "He's got to have a liver the size of a goose," which allows you to speculate pleasantly on whether that means as big as a goose liver or as big as the whole honking fowl. Or Chris about a teacher: "She was the only one who told me I wasn't deranged; I was just a writer." There are many good little things about *Amulets*, including the nascent affection between Floyd and Mrs.

Boyd, even if it isn't entirely believable. But what is rather disturbingly missing is what happens in the house when people are just doing mundane things such as eating. Where are the firm platforms from which all these fireworks can take off?

The acting is mostly good. Despite a mannerism involving running the end of one sentence into the next and coming to a full stop a few words into that sentence, Deborah Hedwall is a believable nurse, bitter divorcée, overprotective mother, and jangling-nerved human being. As Chris, Matt McGrath gives us another of his headlong-hurtling, affable yet insecure, nerdy yet endearing adolescents to whom all hearts go out. As Harold, Loren Dean would not imperil his performance were he to speak a bit more audibly. Best of all, though, is John Spencer, whose Floyd is as troubled as he is troubling—you never know whether he calls for laughter or shudders—and whose acting elucidates this difficult part without overexplaining it.

David Potts's set, in which three rooms are always visible and two others, thanks to diaphanous walls, appear periodically, keeps every facet of this revolving, shimmering globe of a play in full view; Walker Hicklin's costumes are suitably inconspicuous, and Dennis Parichy's lighting doesn't miss a trick. And who wouldn't forgive the work's periodic cutesiness when this can lead to the likes of "Even I know it was Carmen Miranda who single-handedly destroyed a vast section of American manhood"?

CRITICAL COMMENTARY

Gerard Raymond (essay date 1989)

SOURCE: "The Effects of Staten Island on a Pulitzer Prize-Winning Playwright," in *Theater Week,* Vol. 2, No. 37, 24 April 1989, pp. 16-21.

[*In the following excerpt, Raymond examines Zindel's life and literary career and highlights the autobiographical details in* Amulets against the Dragon Forces.]

"I was really born to be a playwright," says Paul Zindel. Like Chris, the 16-year-old protagonist of *Amulets Against the Dragon Forces*, his new play which recently opened at Circle Rep, the young Zindel would make up stories using marionettes and statuettes. During his lonely childhood on Staten Island in the '40s, and as a mature playwright, author and screenwriter today, he realized "the thing that keeps me alive is storytelling. That's how I problem-solve. When I looked back, I was happy to see I was making a little stage on which I was doing everything that a playwright would be doing. Here was somebody who was trying to create his own heaven, which is what happens each time when you begin a play."

Zindel has worked a long time to seek this particular heaven. Some of the characters and events in *Amulets Against the Dragon Forces* were first encountered in his young adult novel, *Confessions of a Teenage Baboon* in 1977; an earlier version of the play, *A Destiny on Half Moon Street* (also known as *The Party Begins at Midnight*) was first produced at Florida's Coconut Grove Playhouse in 1983. In each of these several incarnations, the story remained distinctly autobiographical.

Zindel's mother Beatrice is the inspiration for many of the central characters in his books and plays. A domineering woman, she was abandoned by her husband, a New York policeman, when Zindel was two years old. *The Effect of Gamma Rays on Man-in-the-Moon Marigolds*, produced in 1971, immortalized Beatrice as the cynical and bitter Beatrice "Betty the Loon" Hunsdorfer, who vents her frustrations and unhappiness on her two teenage daughters. In *Amulets*, the young boy's mother, Mrs. Boyd, is a practical nurse who, like Beatrice, travels from place to place looking after the terminally ill. Mrs. Boyd cannot forgive her husband, also a policeman, for the infidelities which led to their divorce.

Like the young Zindel, the boy Chris sorely feels the lack of a father—a piece of his life that can never be replaced. "When I grew up," Zindel says, "I was the outsider. I was the only kid whose family was divorced." Today, divorce carries less of a stigma. Now 53, he feels that time (and the changes it brings about in its passage) is the most important element in his play, set in 1955. "When I look back, exploring elements of myself and look at what I sometimes call the inspirational homonculi of these characters, one of the tragedies is that time has determined who they are, what they do, and how they feel. For me, the biggest tragedy has to do with time affecting the ability to love and be intimate. Time creates the fashion of how we love and our sexual behavior."

Such changing fashions have affected the plot of *Amulets*. In *Confessions of a Teenage Baboon*, the character of Mr. Dipardi, the shipyard worker who hires Mrs. Boyd to nurse his dying mother, is a hard-drinking man who likes the company of teenagers. He rehabilitates a street kid named Harold and attempts to be a father to Chris. In the play, Harold is a street hustler whom Dipardi has picked up and taken under his wing. A homosexual suggestion in the novel has been made explicit in the play.

"I knew that I would eventually want to deal with these themes for an adult audience," he says. "There was, probably, a great amount of personal fear tied into this. I was not ready to face whatever I had to face in myself in order to write that way. Here's where time and the changing fashion of sexuality can be a friend. I can now talk about my own dimensions of homosexuality, and because I insist on my own dimensions of heterosexuality [Zindel has been married for the past 15 years and is the father of two teenagers], it lets me go back and look at this in a way that is comfortable and exciting for me. Hopefully, it brings a truth not only to me, which would not be enough to write a play about, but transcends that into some sort of lesson learned for the viewer as well. I hope there is something universal about this little boy going through this labyrinth, this rite of passage and connections with these people. The last line of the play is, 'It's all in the timing m'boy.' If I was born now, I'd have fewer hang-ups in the sexual areas than I did."

Amulets deals with young boys hustling on Stuyvesant and Hyatt Streets on Staten Island circa 1955. "This is something I wanted to write about, because there was a sexual behavior, a sexual culture, on Staten Island which I had never seen before on stage. On Staten Island every Friday or Saturday night men and women would go to a bar; as the evening went on, some of the men got women and took them out in cars or whatever—they didn't usually go home, everything was done outside—and then whoever was left over, people just made do. There was no conversation about it the next day, whether you went home with a sailor or with someone's father, it just was taken for granted. Now the difference in my play is that Harold is staying a little bit too long with Dipardi—he's cooking for him, and when you do that, that's against tradition."

Judging from Zindel's stories, Staten Island, which Chris describes in *Confessions* as "a sort of geographical version of a detached retina," must be one of the most eccentric corners of the earth. In *Amulets* Chris declares that "if Margaret Mead had first come to Staten Island, she wouldn't have had to spend all those years studying the bizarre behavior of pygmies in Borneo," adding that he spent 30 years there. "It was a big piece of my life and therefore it was what I knew."

In college, Zindel attended a conference at which playwright Edward Albee spoke. After taking a course with Albee, who became his mentor, he wrote his first play, *Dimensions of Peacocks*, in 1959. It was the precursor of the story which grew into *Confessions of a Teenage Baboon* and *Amulets Against the Dragon Forces*. He wrote two more plays before *Gamma Rays* was written in 1962. In the interim, he had a much publicized falling-out with Albee. "This is first time I have really understood it," Zindel remarks, "because it has now happened to me with other young writers who came into my life. What happens is that a young writer selects a mentor. You want to be like that person. You want to love that person. Your mentor is God; Edward Albee was the God of the Universe at that time. But when you become educated and insightful and more informed you find that your God was created from other ashes—he didn't leap full-blown. And so, when I read Eugene Ionesco's *Jacques ou la soumission*, I saw where *The American Dream* [Albee's 1961 play] came from. And then you find that you can't be like anybody else; you have to look for your own fingerprints, your own signature, and then you grow up."

The Effect of Gamma Rays on Man-in-the-Moon Marigolds, the play that would give Zindel his own identity, was eventually produced by the Alley Theater in Houston in 1965. On the strength of it he received a Ford Foundation grant to become playwright-in-residence at the Alley Theater. He spent a year there, taking a sabbatical from teaching, and learned the nuts and bolts of playwriting.

A television version of *Gamma Rays* in 1966 led to a new development in Zindel's career: Charlotte Zolotow, a children's book editor at Harper and Row, was struck by the two teenage sisters in the show and suggested to Zindel that he work in the field of young adult fiction. "Writing about teenage protagonists suited me," he says, citing Noel Coward's admonition that one should pop out of a different hole every time. Zindel's first novel, *The Pigman*, was published in 1968 and was an instant success. When *My Darling, My Hamburger* came out the following year, he became a leading author in a rapidly growing young adult market.

Zindel drew on his experience as a teacher, along with his Staten Island background, for his teenage novels. Now that he has quit teaching, he misses the fresh supply of material his students provided. "You miss out on the imagery and the energy that they have. I don't miss out on their slang because I never used it. Slang only lasts two or three years. So I create my own form of language by using hyperbole and bathos, which gives the effect of slang, but which isn't." With his most recent young adult novel, *A Begonia for Miss Applebaum* (1988), Zindel says his son and daughter, aged 14 and 12, "are just reaching the age when their material is now starting to affect my writings."

Zindel considers himself primarily a playwright but found the young adult genre a convenient means to try out the stories he had to tell. "In a sense it was something that Tennessee Williams did in his short stories. Working in another form lets you initially live with themes in the plot in the form of a beginning sketch." He points out that if he only had the theater as a means to tell stories—and "I must tell stories; that's how I stay sane"—he might have starved.

The fate of *Gamma Rays* demonstrates the risks of having a single profession. "Brooks Atkinson flew down to see the play when it opened in Houston in 1965. He wrote a review in the *Times* stating that my play was elliptical. That was the nicest thing he said about it. In 1970, the play opened [with Sada Thompson] in New York with one sentence added to it, no other change, and it won the Pulitzer Prize."

His next play, *And Miss Reardon Drinks a Little*, which was produced on Broadway in 1971 with Julie Harris, Estelle Parsons, and Nancy Marchand, was classified as a hit by *Variety*. Since then, Zindel has not had comparable success in New York; such works as *The Secret Affairs of Mildred Wild* and *Ladies at the Alamo* had disappointing runs. In the mid-70s he went to Hollywood, where, among other things, he wrote the screenplay for the expensive and disastrous film of the Broadway musical *Mame* starring Lucille Ball. Among his other screenplays are two for director Andrei Konchalovsky, *Maria's Lovers* (1984) and *Runaway Train* (1985), and the 1985 television adaptation of *Alice in Wonderland*. Although the money was good in California, Zindel claims he was "damaged" in the process: "Films are so collaborative, and you can no longer approach your work from a central truth of yourself. You have to also consider the truths of the producer, the star, and the director. After your first draft, you end up becoming a stenographer. This process is very destructive." Three years ago, Zindel returned to New York, having realized that "you have to use money to support talent. Now I only write those things that I want to write, that I am directly connected to."

The most personal of Zindel's works has an off-the-wall aspect so outrageous that it can only be true. In *Confessions* the novel, Chris tells the reader: "One of the first things I learned about Life: it's not always like you read about in your local newspaper. It's more like what you read in the *National Enquirer*." Zindel agrees. "I found that to be absolutely true. You always think the person at the next table is normal. All you have to do is visit other people, let them talk for a little while and you discover how unique they are and the strange things they do in their houses. It's unbelievable." In *Amulets* a dying old woman viciously bites people who try to help her; a mother makes her 16-year-old son urinate in a milk bottle. Zindel acknowledges the "outrageous audacity" of his stories. In this play, "all the elements are true. Some things may have come from other parts of the world, or I have found images somewhere else, but as I coalesce them into these characters, the concentration of truth is disturbing."

With *Amulets Against the Dragon Forces* Zindel feels he has finished the story that he has carried around for 30 years "in the very best way I could." Having finally perfected a heaven, he can now put it to rest. "As a mature writer I know that the heavens are temporary and I have to move on. I'll now be going after the next paradise." Will his new paradise also be located on Staten Island? Zindel will not disclose anything about the new play he is now working on, but he confirms that *Amulets* marks the last time Staten Island will be featured in his work. "The people I now have to write about don't live there." Has he worked through all the permutations of Beatrice? "Yes, this is the last time you will see Beatrice in action!"

FURTHER READING

OVERVIEWS AND GENERAL STUDIES

Forman, Jack Jacob. *Presenting Paul Zindel.* Boston: Twayne, 1988, 121 p.

> Discusses various aspects of Zindel's writings and provides a selective primary and secondary bibliography.

THE EFFECT OF GAMMA RAYS ON MAN-IN-THE-MOON MARIGOLDS

Barnes, Clive. "'Marigolds' in Bloom Again." *New York Post* (15 March 1978).

> Lauds *The Effect of Gamma Rays on Man-in-the-Moon Marigolds* as a "beautifully crafted piece . . . like hollow Wedgewood or solid Ming." However, Barnes describes shortcomings in the Broadway show, citing problems with the directing and setting.

Eder, Richard. "'Marigolds' with Shelley Winters." *The New York Times* (15 March 1978).

> Assesses the Broadway staging of *The Effect of Gamma Rays on Man-in-the-Moon Marigolds.* Eder judges some of the acting flawed and finds the 1978 performance antiquated.

Flatley, Guy. ". . . And Gamma Rays Did It!" *The New York Times* (19 April 1970): 1, 5.

    Comments on the success of the 1970 off-Broadway staging of *The Effect of Gamma Rays on Man-in-the-Moon Marigolds.* Flatley presents an in-depth interview with Zindel, exploring the playwright's biography, insights about life, and motivations behind his plays.

Greer, Germaine. Review of *The Effect of Gamma Rays on Man-in-the-Moon Marigolds. Plays and Players* 20, No. 232 (January 1973): 44.

    Rebukes many of the critics' assessments of the 1972 London presentation of the play, calling it "misunderstood." Greer maintains that the drama is "about women and the family written not from the aesthetic or the ethical point of view, but from the underside."

Hewes, Henry. "The Half-Life." *Saturday Review* (2 May 1970): 12.

    Praises Sada Thompson's portrayal of Beatrice in the off-Broadway production of *The Effect of Gamma Rays on Man-in-the-Moon Marigolds* as "probably the finest performance of the current theater season." Hewes summarizes the drama's action, focusing on Beatrice's deteriorating life.

Kalem, T. E. "Prizewinning *Marigolds.*" *Time* 97, No. 20 (17 May 1971): 66, 69.

    Commemorates Zindel's receipt of the Pulitzer prize and shares the playwright's reaction to the honor.

Leonard, William Torbert. "*The Effect of Gamma Rays on Man-in-the-Moon Marigolds.*" In *Theatre: Stage to Screen to Television,* Vol. I, pp. 537-39. Metuchen, N.J.: The Scarecrow Press, 1981.

    Provides an overview of the stage, film, and television productions of *The Effect of Gamma Rays on Man-in-the-Moon Marigolds.*

AND MISS REARDON DRINKS A LITTLE

Barnes, Clive. "Reardon Sisters Arrive." *The New York Times* (26 February 1971): 29.

    Offers a mixed appraisal of the 1971 production of *And Miss Reardon Drinks a Little,* highlighting the "excellent" cast.

Watt, Douglas. "Miss Reardon Drinks a Little—So Would You in This Layout." *Daily News* (26 February 1971).

    Reviews the 1971 production of *And Miss Reardon Drinks a Little,* judging it "very funny" and commending the actors' performances. Watt also admires the roles Zindel creates for women.

Watts, Richard. "'Miss Reardon' at Morosco." *New York Post* (26 February 1971).

    Recognizes the merit of the cast in the 1971 staging of *And Miss Reardon Drinks a Little* but describes the play as a "startlingly aimless drama."

Additional coverage of Zindel's life and career is contained in the following sources published by Gale Research: *Authors and Artists for Young Adults,* Vol. 2; *Children's Literature Review,* Vol. 3; *Contemporary Authors,* Vols. 73-6; *Contemporary Authors New Revision Series,* Vol. 31; *Contemporary Literary Criticism,* Vols. 6, 26; *Dictionary of Literary Biography,* Vols. 7, 52; *DISCovering Authors; Major Authors and Illustrators for Children and Young Adults; Major 20th-Century Writers;* and *Something about the Author,* Vols. 16, 58.

CUMULATIVE INDEXES

How to Use This Index

The main references

Calvino, Italo
1923-1985.....CLC 5, 8, 11, 22, 33, 39,
73; SSC 3

list all author entries in the following Gale Literary Criticism series:

BLC = *Black Literature Criticism*
CLC = *Contemporary Literary Criticism*
CLR = *Children's Literature Review*
CMLC = *Classical and Medieval Literature Criticism*
DA = *DISCovering Authors*
DC = *Drama Criticism*
HLC = *Hispanic Literature Criticism*
LC = *Literature Criticism from 1400 to 1800*
NCLC = *Nineteenth-Century Literature Criticism*
PC = *Poetry Criticism*
SSC = *Short Story Criticism*
TCLC = *Twentieth-Century Literary Criticism*
WLC = *World Literature Criticism, 1500 to the Present*

The cross-references

See also CANR 23; CA 85-88;
obituary CA 116

list all author entries in the following Gale biographical and literary sources:

AAYA = *Authors & Artists for Young Adults*
AITN = *Authors in the News*
BEST = *Bestsellers*
BW = *Black Writers*
CA = *Contemporary Authors*
CAAS = *Contemporary Authors Autobiography Series*
CABS = *Contemporary Authors Bibliographical Series*
CANR = *Contemporary Authors New Revision Series*
CAP = *Contemporary Authors Permanent Series*
CDALB = *Concise Dictionary of American Literary Biography*
CDBLB = *Concise Dictionary of British Literary Biography*
DLB = *Dictionary of Literary Biography*
DLBD = *Dictionary of Literary Biography Documentary Series*
DLBY = *Dictionary of Literary Biography Yearbook*
HW = *Hispanic Writers*
JRDA = *Junior DISCovering Authors*
MAICYA = *Major Authors and Illustrators for Children and Young Adults*
MTCW = *Major 20th-Century Writers*
NNAL = *Native North American Literature*
SAAS = *Something about the Author Autobiography Series*
SATA = *Something about the Author*
YABC = *Yesterday's Authors of Books for Children*

Literary Criticism Series
Cumulative Author Index

Abasiyanik, Sait Faik 1906-1954
See Sait Faik
See also CA 123

Abbey, Edward 1927-1989...... **CLC 36, 59**
See also CA 45-48; 128; CANR 2, 41

Abbott, Lee K(ittredge) 1947-...... **CLC 48**
See also CA 124; DLB 130

Abe, Kobo 1924-1993..... **CLC 8, 22, 53, 81**
See also CA 65-68; 140; CANR 24; MTCW

Abelard, Peter c. 1079-c. 1142 ... **CMLC 11**
See also DLB 115

Abell, Kjeld 1901-1961........... **CLC 15**
See also CA 111

Abish, Walter 1931-.............. **CLC 22**
See also CA 101; CANR 37; DLB 130

Abrahams, Peter (Henry) 1919- ..... **CLC 4**
See also BW 1; CA 57-60; CANR 26;
DLB 117; MTCW

Abrams, M(eyer) H(oward) 1912-... **CLC 24**
See also CA 57-60; CANR 13, 33; DLB 67

Abse, Dannie 1923-............ **CLC 7, 29**
See also CA 53-56; CAAS 1; CANR 4, 46;
DLB 27

Achebe, (Albert) Chinua(lumogu)
1930- ..... **CLC 1, 3, 5, 7, 11, 26, 51, 75;**
BLC; DA; WLC
See also BW 2; CA 1-4R; CANR 6, 26;
CLR 20; DLB 117; MAICYA; MTCW;
SATA 38, 40

Acker, Kathy 1948- .... **CLC 45**
See also CA 117; 122

Ackroyd, Peter 1949-.......... **CLC 34, 52**
See also CA 123; 127

Acorn, Milton 1923-.............. **CLC 15**
See also CA 103; DLB 53

Adamov, Arthur 1908-1970 ...... **CLC 4, 25**
See also CA 17-18; 25-28R; CAP 2; MTCW

Adams, Alice (Boyd) 1926- ... **CLC 6, 13, 46**
See also CA 81-84; CANR 26; DLBY 86;
MTCW

Adams, Andy 1859-1935......... **TCLC 56**
See also YABC 1

Adams, Douglas (Noel) 1952- ... **CLC 27, 60**
See also AAYA 4; BEST 89:3; CA 106;
CANR 34; DLBY 83; JRDA

Adams, Francis 1862-1893....... **NCLC 33**

Adams, Henry (Brooks)
1838-1918 .... **TCLC 4, 52; DA**
See also CA 104; 133; DLB 12, 47

Adams, Richard (George)
1920- .... **CLC 4, 5, 18**
See also AITN 1, 2; CA 49-52; CANR 3,
35; CLR 20; JRDA; MAICYA; MTCW;
SATA 7, 69

Adamson, Joy(-Friederike Victoria)
1910-1980 .... **CLC 17**
See also CA 69-72; 93-96; CANR 22;
MTCW; SATA 11; SATA-Obit 22

Adcock, Fleur 1934-.............. **CLC 41**
See also CA 25-28R; CANR 11, 34;
DLB 40

Addams, Charles (Samuel)
1912-1988 .... **CLC 30**
See also CA 61-64; 126; CANR 12

Addison, Joseph 1672-1719 .... **LC 18**
See also CDBLB 1660-1789; DLB 101

Adler, C(arole) S(chwerdtfeger)
1932- .... **CLC 35**
See also AAYA 4; CA 89-92; CANR 19,
40; JRDA; MAICYA; SAAS 15;
SATA 26, 63

Adler, Renata 1938-............ **CLC 8, 31**
See also CA 49-52; CANR 5, 22; MTCW

Ady, Endre 1877-1919 .... **TCLC 11**
See also CA 107

Aeschylus
525B.C.-456B.C........ **CMLC 11; DA**

Afton, Effie
See Harper, Frances Ellen Watkins

Agapida, Fray Antonio
See Irving, Washington

Agee, James (Rufus)
1909-1955 .... **TCLC 1, 19**
See also AITN 1; CA 108;
CDALB 1941-1968; DLB 2, 26

Aghill, Gordon
See Silverberg, Robert

Agnon, S(hmuel) Y(osef Halevi)
1888-1970 .... **CLC 4, 8, 14**
See also CA 17-18; 25-28R; CAP 2; MTCW

Agrippa von Nettesheim, Henry Cornelius
1486-1535 .... **LC 27**

Aherne, Owen
See Cassill, R(onald) V(erlin)

Ai 1947-................... **CLC 4, 14, 69**
See also CA 85-88; CAAS 13; DLB 120

Aickman, Robert (Fordyce)
1914-1981 .... **CLC 57**
See also CA 5-8R; CANR 3

Aiken, Conrad (Potter)
1889-1973 ... **CLC 1, 3, 5, 10, 52; SSC 9**
See also CA 5-8R; 45-48; CANR 4;
CDALB 1929-1941; DLB 9, 45, 102;
MTCW; SATA 3, 30

Aiken, Joan (Delano) 1924-........ **CLC 35**
See also AAYA 1; CA 9-12R; CANR 4, 23,
34; CLR 1, 19; JRDA; MAICYA;
MTCW; SAAS 1; SATA 2, 30, 73

Ainsworth, William Harrison
1805-1882 .... **NCLC 13**
See also DLB 21; SATA 24

Aitmatov, Chingiz (Torekulovich)
1928-...................... **CLC 71**
See also CA 103; CANR 38; MTCW;
SATA 56

Akers, Floyd
See Baum, L(yman) Frank

Akhmadulina, Bella Akhatovna
1937-...................... **CLC 53**
See also CA 65-68

Akhmatova, Anna
1888-1966 .... **CLC 11, 25, 64; PC 2**
See also CA 19-20; 25-28R; CANR 35;
CAP 1; MTCW

Aksakov, Sergei Timofeyvich
1791-1859 .... **NCLC 2**

Aksenov, Vassily .... **CLC 22**
See also Aksyonov, Vassily (Pavlovich)

Aksyonov, Vassily (Pavlovich)
1932-...................... **CLC 37**
See also Aksenov, Vassily
See also CA 53-56; CANR 12

Akutagawa Ryunosuke
1892-1927 .... **TCLC 16**
See also CA 117

Alain 1868-1951 .... **TCLC 41**

Alain-Fournier .... **TCLC 6**
See also Fournier, Henri Alban
See also DLB 65

Alarcon, Pedro Antonio de
1833-1891 .... **NCLC 1**

Alas (y Urena), Leopoldo (Enrique Garcia)
1852-1901 .... **TCLC 29**
See also CA 113; 131; HW

Albee, Edward (Franklin III)
1928-...... **CLC 1, 2, 3, 5, 9, 11, 13, 25,**
53; DA; WLC
See also AITN 1; CA 5-8R; CABS 3;
CANR 8; CDALB 1941-1968; DLB 7;
MTCW

Alberti, Rafael 1902- .... **CLC 7**
See also CA 85-88; DLB 108

Alcala-Galiano, Juan Valera y
See Valera y Alcala-Galiano, Juan

Alcott, Amos Bronson 1799-1888 .. **NCLC 1**
See also DLB 1

Alcott, Louisa May
1832-1888 .... **NCLC 6; DA; WLC**
See also CDALB 1865-1917; CLR 1;
DLB 1, 42, 79; JRDA; MAICYA;
YABC 1

Aldanov, M. A.
See Aldanov, Mark (Alexandrovich)

Aldanov, Mark (Alexandrovich)
1886(?)-1957 .... **TCLC 23**
See also CA 118

Aldington, Richard 1892-1962...... **CLC 49**
See also CA 85-88; CANR 45; DLB 20, 36,
100

Aldiss, Brian W(ilson)
1925- .... **CLC 5, 14, 40**
See also CA 5-8R; CAAS 2; CANR 5, 28;
DLB 14; MTCW; SATA 34

Alegria, Claribel 1924-........... **CLC 75**
See also CA 131; CAAS 15; DLB 145; HW

Alegria, Fernando 1918-.......... **CLC 57**
See also CA 9-12R; CANR 5, 32; HW

Aleichem, Sholom .... **TCLC 1, 35**
See also Rabinovitch, Sholem

Aleixandre, Vicente 1898-1984 ... **CLC 9, 36**
See also CA 85-88; 114; CANR 26;
DLB 108; HW; MTCW

Alepoudelis, Odysseus
See Elytis, Odysseus

Aleshkovsky, Joseph 1929-
See Aleshkovsky, Yuz
See also CA 121; 128

Aleshkovsky, Yuz .... **CLC 44**
See also Aleshkovsky, Joseph

Alexander, Lloyd (Chudley) 1924- **CLC 35**
See also AAYA 1; CA 1-4R; CANR 1, 24,
38; CLR 1, 5; DLB 52; JRDA; MAICYA;
MTCW; SAAS 19; SATA 3, 49

Alfau, Felipe 1902-.............. **CLC 66**
See also CA 137

Alger, Horatio, Jr. 1832-1899..... **NCLC 8**
See also DLB 42; SATA 16

Algren, Nelson 1909-1981 .... **CLC 4, 10, 33**
See also CA 13-16R; 103; CANR 20;
CDALB 1941-1968; DLB 9; DLBY 81,
82; MTCW

Ali, Ahmed 1910- .... **CLC 69**
See also CA 25-28R; CANR 15, 34

Alighieri, Dante 1265-1321 .... **CMLC 3**

Allan, John B.
See Westlake, Donald E(dwin)

Allen, Edward 1948-.............. **CLC 59**

Allen, Paula Gunn 1939-......... **CLC 84**
See also CA 112; 143; NNAL

Allen, Roland
See Ayckbourn, Alan

Allen, Sarah A.
See Hopkins, Pauline Elizabeth

Allen, Woody 1935-........... **CLC 16, 52**
See also AAYA 10; CA 33-36R; CANR 27,
38; DLB 44; MTCW

Allende, Isabel 1942-.... **CLC 39, 57; HLC**
See also CA 125; 130; DLB 145; HW;
MTCW

Alleyn, Ellen
See Rossetti, Christina (Georgina)

Allingham, Margery (Louise)
1904-1966 .... **CLC 19**
See also CA 5-8R; 25-28R; CANR 4;
DLB 77; MTCW

Allingham, William 1824-1889 ... **NCLC 25**
See also DLB 35

Allison, Dorothy E. 1949-........ **CLC 78**
See also CA 140

Allston, Washington 1779-1843.... **NCLC 2**
See also DLB 1

Almedingen, E. M. .... **CLC 12**
See also Almedingen, Martha Edith von
See also SATA 3

Almedingen, Martha Edith von 1898-1971
See Almedingen, E. M.
See also CA 1-4R; CANR 1

Almqvist, Carl Jonas Love
1793-1866 .... **NCLC 42**

Alonso, Damaso 1898-1990 .... **CLC 14**
See also CA 110; 131; 130; DLB 108; HW

Alov
See Gogol, Nikolai (Vasilyevich)

Alta 1942-...................... **CLC 19**
See also CA 57-60

Alter, Robert B(ernard) 1935-...... **CLC 34**
See also CA 49-52; CANR 1

Alther, Lisa 1944-.............. **CLC 7, 41**
See also CA 65-68; CANR 12, 30; MTCW

Altman, Robert 1925-............. **CLC 16**
See also CA 73-76; CANR 43

Alvarez, A(lfred) 1929-.......... **CLC 5, 13**
See also CA 1-4R; CANR 3, 33; DLB 14,
40

Alvarez, Alejandro Rodriguez 1903-1965
See Casona, Alejandro
See also CA 131; 93-96; HW

Amado, Jorge 1912-..... **CLC 13, 40; HLC**
See also CA 77-80; CANR 35; DLB 113;
MTCW

Ambler, Eric 1909-............ **CLC 4, 6, 9**
See also CA 9-12R; CANR 7, 38; DLB 77;
MTCW

Amichai, Yehuda 1924- ...... **CLC 9, 22, 57**
See also CA 85-88; CANR 46; MTCW

Amiel, Henri Frederic 1821-1881 .. **NCLC 4**

Amis, Kingsley (William)
1922-.. **CLC 1, 2, 3, 5, 8, 13, 40, 44; DA**
See also AITN 2; CA 9-12R; CANR 8, 28;
CDBLB 1945-1960; DLB 15, 27, 100, 139;
MTCW

Amis, Martin (Louis)
1949-................ **CLC 4, 9, 38, 62**
See also BEST 90:3; CA 65-68; CANR 8,
27; DLB 14

Ammons, A(rchie) R(andolph)
1926-....... **CLC 2, 3, 5, 8, 9, 25, 57**
See also AITN 1; CA 9-12R; CANR 6, 36;
DLB 5; MTCW

Amo, Tauraatua i
See Adams, Henry (Brooks)

Anand, Mulk Raj 1905-........... **CLC 23**
See also CA 65-68; CANR 32; MTCW

Anatol
See Schnitzler, Arthur

Anaya, Rudolfo A(lfonso)
1937-................. **CLC 23; HLC**
See also CA 45-48; CAAS 4; CANR 1, 32;
DLB 82; HW 1; MTCW

Andersen, Hans Christian
1805-1875 .. **NCLC 7; DA; SSC 6; WLC**
See also CLR 6; MAICYA; YABC 1

Anderson, C. Farley
See Mencken, H(enry) L(ouis); Nathan,
George Jean

Anderson, Jessica (Margaret) Queale
.... **CLC 37**
See also CA 9-12R; CANR 4

Anderson, Jon (Victor) 1940- .... **CLC 9**
See also CA 25-28R; CANR 20

Anderson, Lindsay (Gordon)
1923-...................... **CLC 20**
See also CA 125; 128

Anderson, Maxwell 1888-1959 ..... **TCLC 2**
See also CA 105; DLB 7

Anderson, Poul (William) 1926-.... **CLC 15**
See also AAYA 5; CA 1-4R; CAAS 2;
CANR 2, 15, 34; DLB 8; MTCW;
SATA 39

Anderson, Robert (Woodruff)
1917-...................... **CLC 23**
See also AITN 1; CA 21-24R; CANR 32;
DLB 7

Anderson, Sherwood
1876-1941 .... **TCLC 1, 10, 24; DA;
SSC 1; WLC**
See also CA 104; 121; CDALB 1917-1929;
DLB 4, 9, 86; DLBD 1; MTCW

Andouard
See Giraudoux, (Hippolyte) Jean

Andrade, Carlos Drummond de ...... **CLC 18**
See also Drummond de Andrade, Carlos

Andrade, Mario de 1893-1945..... **TCLC 43**

Andreas-Salome, Lou 1861-1937... **TCLC 56**
See also DLB 66

Andrewes, Lancelot 1555-1626 .... **LC 5**

Andrews, Cicily Fairfield
See West, Rebecca

Andrews, Elton V.
See Pohl, Frederik

Andreyev, Leonid (Nikolaevich)
1871-1919 .... **TCLC 3**
See also CA 104

Andric, Ivo 1892-1975 .... **CLC 8**
See also CA 81-84; 57-60; CANR 43;
DLB 147; MTCW

Angelique, Pierre
See Bataille, Georges

Angell, Roger 1920-.............. **CLC 26**
See also CA 57-60; CANR 13, 44

Angelou, Maya
1928-.... **CLC 12, 35, 64, 77; BLC; DA**
See also AAYA 7; BW 2; CA 65-68;
CANR 19, 42; DLB 38; MTCW;
SATA 49

Annensky, Innokenty Fyodorovich
1856-1909 .... **TCLC 14**
See also CA 110

Anon, Charles Robert
See Pessoa, Fernando (Antonio Nogueira)

Anouilh, Jean (Marie Lucien Pierre)
1910-1987 ...... **CLC 1, 3, 8, 13, 40, 50**
See also CA 17-20R; 123; CANR 32;
MTCW

Anthony, Florence
See Ai

Anthony, John
See Ciardi, John (Anthony)

Anthony, Peter
See Shaffer, Anthony (Joshua); Shaffer, Peter (Levin)

Anthony, Piers 1934- . . . . **CLC 35**
See also AAYA 11; CA 21-24R; CANR 28; DLB 8; MTCW

Antoine, Marc
See Proust, (Valentin-Louis-George-Eugene-) Marcel

Antoninus, Brother
See Everson, William (Oliver)

Antonioni, Michelangelo 1912- . . . . . **CLC 20**
See also CA 73-76; CANR 45

Antschel, Paul 1920-1970
See Celan, Paul
See also CA 85-88; CANR 33; MTCW

Anwar, Chairil 1922-1949 . . . . **TCLC 22**
See also CA 121

Apollinaire, Guillaume . . **TCLC 3, 8, 51; PC 7**
See also Kostrowitzki, Wilhelm Apollinaris de

Appelfeld, Aharon 1932- . . . . **CLC 23, 47**
See also CA 112; 133

Apple, Max (Isaac) 1941- . . . . **CLC 9, 33**
See also CA 81-84; CANR 19; DLB 130

Appleman, Philip (Dean) 1926- . . . . . **CLC 51**
See also CA 13-16R; CAAS 18; CANR 6, 29

Appleton, Lawrence
See Lovecraft, H(oward) P(hillips)

Apteryx
See Eliot, T(homas) S(tearns)

Apuleius, (Lucius Madaurensis)
125(?)-175(?) . . . . **CMLC 1**

Aquin, Hubert 1929-1977 . . . . **CLC 15**
See also CA 105; DLB 53

Aragon, Louis 1897-1982 . . . . **CLC 3, 22**
See also CA 69-72; 108; CANR 28; DLB 72; MTCW

Arany, Janos 1817-1882 . . . . **NCLC 34**

Arbuthnot, John 1667-1735 . . . . **LC 1**
See also DLB 101

Archer, Herbert Winslow
See Mencken, H(enry) L(ouis)

Archer, Jeffrey (Howard) 1940- . . . . **CLC 28**
See also BEST 89:3; CA 77-80; CANR 22

Archer, Jules 1915- . . . . **CLC 12**
See also CA 9-12R; CANR 6; SAAS 5; SATA 4

Archer, Lee
See Ellison, Harlan (Jay)

Arden, John 1930- . . . . **CLC 6, 13, 15**
See also CA 13-16R; CAAS 4; CANR 31; DLB 13; MTCW

Arenas, Reinaldo
1943-1990 . . . . **CLC 41; HLC**
See also CA 124; 128; 133; DLB 145; HW

Arendt, Hannah 1906-1975 . . . . **CLC 66**
See also CA 17-20R; 61-64; CANR 26; MTCW

Aretino, Pietro 1492-1556 . . . . **LC 12**

Arghezi, Tudor . . . . **CLC 80**
See also Theodorescu, Ion N.

Arguedas, Jose Maria
1911-1969 . . . . **CLC 10, 18**
See also CA 89-92; DLB 113; HW

Argueta, Manlio 1936- . . . . **CLC 31**
See also CA 131; DLB 145; HW

Ariosto, Ludovico 1474-1533 . . . . **LC 6**

Aristides
See Epstein, Joseph

Aristophanes
450B.C.-385B.C. . . . . **CMLC 4; DA; DC 2**

Arlt, Roberto (Godofredo Christophersen)
1900-1942 . . . . **TCLC 29; HLC**
See also CA 123; 131; HW

Armah, Ayi Kwei 1939- . . . . **CLC 5, 33; BLC**
See also BW 1; CA 61-64; CANR 21; DLB 117; MTCW

Armatrading, Joan 1950- . . . . **CLC 17**
See also CA 114

Arnette, Robert
See Silverberg, Robert

Arnim, Achim von (Ludwig Joachim von Arnim) 1781-1831 . . . . **NCLC 5**
See also DLB 90

Arnim, Bettina von 1785-1859 . . . . **NCLC 38**
See also DLB 90

Arnold, Matthew
1822-1888 . . . . . **NCLC 6, 29; DA; PC 5; WLC**
See also CDBLB 1832-1890; DLB 32, 57

Arnold, Thomas 1795-1842 . . . . . . **NCLC 18**
See also DLB 55

Arnow, Harriette (Louisa) Simpson
1908-1986 . . . . **CLC 2, 7, 18**
See also CA 9-12R; 118; CANR 14; DLB 6; MTCW; SATA 42; SATA-Obit 47

Arp, Hans
See Arp, Jean

Arp, Jean 1887-1966 . . . . **CLC 5**
See also CA 81-84; 25-28R; CANR 42

Arrabal
See Arrabal, Fernando

Arrabal, Fernando 1932- . . . **CLC 2, 9, 18, 58**
See also CA 9-12R; CANR 15

Arrick, Fran . . . . **CLC 30**

Artaud, Antonin 1896-1948 . . . . . **TCLC 3, 36**
See also CA 104

Arthur, Ruth M(abel) 1905-1979 . . . . **CLC 12**
See also CA 9-12R; 85-88; CANR 4; SATA 7, 26

Artsybashev, Mikhail (Petrovich)
1878-1927 . . . . **TCLC 31**

Arundel, Honor (Morfydd)
1919-1973 . . . . **CLC 17**
See also CA 21-22; 41-44R; CAP 2; CLR 35; SATA 4; SATA-Obit 24

Asch, Sholem 1880-1957 . . . . **TCLC 3**
See also CA 105

Ash, Shalom
See Asch, Sholem

Ashbery, John (Lawrence)
1927- . . . . . . **CLC 2, 3, 4, 6, 9, 13, 15, 25, 41, 77**
See also CA 5-8R; CANR 9, 37; DLB 5; DLBY 81; MTCW

Ashdown, Clifford
See Freeman, R(ichard) Austin

Ashe, Gordon
See Creasey, John

Ashton-Warner, Sylvia (Constance)
1908-1984 . . . . **CLC 19**
See also CA 69-72; 112; CANR 29; MTCW

Asimov, Isaac
1920-1992 . . . . . . **CLC 1, 3, 9, 19, 26, 76**
See also AAYA 13; BEST 90:2; CA 1-4R; 137; CANR 2, 19, 36; CLR 12; DLB 8; DLBY 92; JRDA; MAICYA; MTCW; SATA 1, 26, 74

Astley, Thea (Beatrice May)
1925- . . . . **CLC 41**
See also CA 65-68; CANR 11, 43

Aston, James
See White, T(erence) H(anbury)

Asturias, Miguel Angel
1899-1974 . . . . **CLC 3, 8, 13; HLC**
See also CA 25-28; 49-52; CANR 32; CAP 2; DLB 113; HW; MTCW

Atares, Carlos Saura
See Saura (Atares), Carlos

Atheling, William
See Pound, Ezra (Weston Loomis)

Atheling, William, Jr.
See Blish, James (Benjamin)

Atherton, Gertrude (Franklin Horn)
1857-1948 . . . . **TCLC 2**
See also CA 104; DLB 9, 78

Atherton, Lucius
See Masters, Edgar Lee

Atkins, Jack
See Harris, Mark

Atticus
See Fleming, Ian (Lancaster)

Atwood, Margaret (Eleanor)
1939- . . . . . **CLC 2, 3, 4, 8, 13, 15, 25, 44, 84; DA; PC 8; SSC 2; WLC**
See also AAYA 12; BEST 89:2; CA 49-52; CANR 3, 24, 33; DLB 53; MTCW; SATA 50

Aubigny, Pierre d'
See Mencken, H(enry) L(ouis)

Aubin, Penelope 1685-1731(?) . . . . **LC 9**
See also DLB 39

Auchincloss, Louis (Stanton)
1917- . . . . **CLC 4, 6, 9, 18, 45**
See also CA 1-4R; CANR 6, 29; DLB 2; DLBY 80; MTCW

Auden, W(ystan) H(ugh)
1907-1973 . . . . . . **CLC 1, 2, 3, 4, 6, 9, 11, 14, 43; DA; PC 1; WLC**
See also CA 9-12R; 45-48; CDBLB 1914-1945; DLB 10, 20; MTCW

Audiberti, Jacques 1900-1965 . . . . . . **CLC 38**
See also CA 25-28R

Audubon, John James
1785-1851 . . . . **NCLC 47**

Auel, Jean M(arie) 1936- . . . . **CLC 31**
See also AAYA 7; BEST 90:4; CA 103; CANR 21

Auerbach, Erich 1892-1957 . . . . **TCLC 43**
See also CA 118

Augier, Emile 1820-1889 . . . . **NCLC 31**

August, John
See De Voto, Bernard (Augustine)

Augustine, St. 354-430 . . . . **CMLC 6**

Aurelius
See Bourne, Randolph S(illiman)

Austen, Jane
1775-1817 . . . . **NCLC 1, 13, 19, 33; DA;**
                                                        WLC
See also CDBLB 1789-1832; DLB 116

Auster, Paul 1947- . . . . **CLC 47**
See also CA 69-72; CANR 23

Austin, Frank
See Faust, Frederick (Schiller)

Austin, Mary (Hunter)
1868-1934 . . . . **TCLC 25**
See also CA 109; DLB 9, 78

Autran Dourado, Waldomiro
See Dourado, (Waldomiro Freitas) Autran

Averroes 1126-1198 . . . . **CMLC 7**
See also DLB 115

Avison, Margaret 1918- . . . . **CLC 2, 4**
See also CA 17-20R; DLB 53; MTCW

Axton, David
See Koontz, Dean R(ay)

Ayckbourn, Alan
1939- . . . . **CLC 5, 8, 18, 33, 74**
See also CA 21-24R; CANR 31; DLB 13;
MTCW

Aydy, Catherine
See Tennant, Emma (Christina)

Ayme, Marcel (Andre) 1902-1967 . . . **CLC 11**
See also CA 89-92; CLR 25; DLB 72

Ayrton, Michael 1921-1975 . . . . **CLC 7**
See also CA 5-8R; 61-64; CANR 9, 21

Azorin . . . . **CLC 11**
See also Martinez Ruiz, Jose

Azuela, Mariano
1873-1952 . . . . **TCLC 3; HLC**
See also CA 104; 131; HW; MTCW

Baastad, Babbis Friis
See Friis-Baastad, Babbis Ellinor

Bab
See Gilbert, W(illiam) S(chwenck)

Babbis, Eleanor
See Friis-Baastad, Babbis Ellinor

Babel, Isaak (Emmanuilovich)
1894-1941(?) . . . . . . **TCLC 2, 13; SSC 16**
See also CA 104

Babits, Mihaly 1883-1941 . . . . **TCLC 14**
See also CA 114

Babur 1483-1530 . . . . **LC 18**

Bacchelli, Riccardo 1891-1985 . . . . . **CLC 19**
See also CA 29-32R; 117

Bach, Richard (David) 1936- . . . . **CLC 14**
See also AITN 1; BEST 89:2; CA 9-12R;
CANR 18; MTCW; SATA 13

Bachman, Richard
See King, Stephen (Edwin)

Bachmann, Ingeborg 1926-1973 . . . . . **CLC 69**
See also CA 93-96; 45-48; DLB 85

Bacon, Francis 1561-1626 . . . . **LC 18**
See also CDBLB Before 1660

Bacon, Roger 1214(?)-1292 . . . . . . **CMLC 14**
See also DLB 115

Bacovia, George . . . . **TCLC 24**
See also Vasiliu, Gheorghe

Badanes, Jerome 1937- . . . . **CLC 59**

Bagehot, Walter 1826-1877 . . . . . . **NCLC 10**
See also DLB 55

Bagnold, Enid 1889-1981 . . . . **CLC 25**
See also CA 5-8R; 103; CANR 5, 40;
DLB 13; MAICYA; SATA 1, 25

Bagrjana, Elisaveta
See Belcheva, Elisaveta

Bagryana, Elisaveta
See Belcheva, Elisaveta
See also DLB 147

Bailey, Paul 1937- . . . . **CLC 45**
See also CA 21-24R; CANR 16; DLB 14

Baillie, Joanna 1762-1851 . . . . **NCLC 2**
See also DLB 93

Bainbridge, Beryl (Margaret)
1933- . . . . **CLC 4, 5, 8, 10, 14, 18, 22, 62**
See also CA 21-24R; CANR 24; DLB 14;
MTCW

Baker, Elliott 1922- . . . . **CLC 8**
See also CA 45-48; CANR 2

Baker, Nicholson 1957- . . . . **CLC 61**
See also CA 135

Baker, Ray Stannard 1870-1946 . . . **TCLC 47**
See also CA 118

Baker, Russell (Wayne) 1925- . . . . . . **CLC 31**
See also BEST 89:4; CA 57-60; CANR 11,
41; MTCW

Bakhtin, M.
See Bakhtin, Mikhail Mikhailovich

Bakhtin, M. M.
See Bakhtin, Mikhail Mikhailovich

Bakhtin, Mikhail
See Bakhtin, Mikhail Mikhailovich

Bakhtin, Mikhail Mikhailovich
1895-1975 . . . . **CLC 83**
See also CA 128; 113

Bakshi, Ralph 1938(?)- . . . . **CLC 26**
See also CA 112; 138

Bakunin, Mikhail (Alexandrovich)
1814-1876 . . . . **NCLC 25**

Baldwin, James (Arthur)
1924-1987 . . . . . . **CLC 1, 2, 3, 4, 5, 8, 13,**
                    15, 17, 42, 50, 67; BLC; DA; DC 1;
                                                  SSC 10; WLC
See also AAYA 4; BW 1; CA 1-4R; 124;
CABS 1; CANR 3, 24;
CDALB 1941-1968; DLB 2, 7, 33;
DLBY 87; MTCW; SATA 9;
SATA-Obit 54

Ballard, J(ames) G(raham)
1930- . . . . **CLC 3, 6, 14, 36; SSC 1**
See also AAYA 3; CA 5-8R; CANR 15, 39;
DLB 14; MTCW

Balmont, Konstantin (Dmitriyevich)
1867-1943 . . . . **TCLC 11**
See also CA 109

Balzac, Honore de
1799-1850 . . . . **NCLC 5, 35; DA; SSC 5;**
                                                        WLC
See also DLB 119

Bambara, Toni Cade
1939- . . . . **CLC 19; BLC; DA**
See also AAYA 5; BW 2; CA 29-32R;
CANR 24; DLB 38; MTCW

Bamdad, A.
See Shamlu, Ahmad

Banat, D. R.
See Bradbury, Ray (Douglas)

Bancroft, Laura
See Baum, L(yman) Frank

Banim, John 1798-1842 . . . . **NCLC 13**
See also DLB 116

Banim, Michael 1796-1874 . . . . . . **NCLC 13**

Banks, Iain
See Banks, Iain M(enzies)

Banks, Iain M(enzies) 1954- . . . . **CLC 34**
See also CA 123; 128

Banks, Lynne Reid . . . . **CLC 23**
See also Reid Banks, Lynne
See also AAYA 6

Banks, Russell 1940- . . . . **CLC 37, 72**
See also CA 65-68; CAAS 15; CANR 19;
DLB 130

Banville, John 1945- . . . . **CLC 46**
See also CA 117; 128; DLB 14

Banville, Theodore (Faullain) de
1832-1891 . . . . **NCLC 9**

Baraka, Amiri
1934- . . . . **CLC 1, 2, 3, 5, 10, 14, 33;**
                                                  BLC; DA; PC 4
See also Jones, LeRoi
See also BW 2; CA 21-24R; CABS 3;
CANR 27, 38; CDALB 1941-1968;
DLB 5, 7, 16, 38; DLBD 8; MTCW

Barbellion, W. N. P. . . . . **TCLC 24**
See also Cummings, Bruce F(rederick)

Barbera, Jack (Vincent) 1945- . . . . . . **CLC 44**
See also CA 110; CANR 45

Barbey d'Aurevilly, Jules Amedee
1808-1889 . . . . **NCLC 1; SSC 17**
See also DLB 119

Barbusse, Henri 1873-1935 . . . . **TCLC 5**
See also CA 105; DLB 65

Barclay, Bill
See Moorcock, Michael (John)

Barclay, William Ewert
See Moorcock, Michael (John)

Barea, Arturo 1897-1957 . . . . **TCLC 14**
See also CA 111

Barfoot, Joan 1946- . . . . **CLC 18**
See also CA 105

Baring, Maurice 1874-1945 . . . . **TCLC 8**
See also CA 105; DLB 34

Barker, Clive 1952- . . . . **CLC 52**
See also AAYA 10; BEST 90:3; CA 121;
129; MTCW

Barker, George Granville
1913-1991 . . . . **CLC 8, 48**
See also CA 9-12R; 135; CANR 7, 38;
DLB 20; MTCW

Barker, Harley Granville
See Granville-Barker, Harley
See also DLB 10

Barker, Howard 1946-............ **CLC 37**
See also CA 102; DLB 13

Barker, Pat 1943-.............. **CLC 32**
See also CA 117; 122

Barlow, Joel 1754-1812........ **NCLC 23**
See also DLB 37

Barnard, Mary (Ethel) 1909-....... **CLC 48**
See also CA 21-22; CAP 2

Barnes, Djuna
1892-1982 ... **CLC 3, 4, 8, 11, 29; SSC 3**
See also CA 9-12R; 107; CANR 16; DLB 4,
9, 45; MTCW

Barnes, Julian 1946-............. **CLC 42**
See also CA 102; CANR 19; DLBY 93

Barnes, Peter 1931-............ **CLC 5, 56**
See also CA 65-68; CAAS 12; CANR 33,
34; DLB 13; MTCW

Baroja (y Nessi), Pio
1872-1956 .... **TCLC 8; HLC**
See also CA 104

Baron, David
See Pinter, Harold

Baron Corvo
See Rolfe, Frederick (William Serafino
Austin Lewis Mary)

Barondess, Sue K(aufman)
1926-1977 .... **CLC 8**
See also Kaufman, Sue
See also CA 1-4R; 69-72; CANR 1

Baron de Teive
See Pessoa, Fernando (Antonio Nogueira)

Barres, Maurice 1862-1923....... **TCLC 47**
See also DLB 123

Barreto, Afonso Henrique de Lima
See Lima Barreto, Afonso Henrique de

Barrett, (Roger) Syd 1946- .... **CLC 35**

Barrett, William (Christopher)
1913-1992 .... **CLC 27**
See also CA 13-16R; 139; CANR 11

Barrie, J(ames) M(atthew)
1860-1937 .... **TCLC 2**
See also CA 104; 136; CDBLB 1890-1914;
CLR 16; DLB 10, 141; MAICYA;
YABC 1

Barrington, Michael
See Moorcock, Michael (John)

Barrol, Grady
See Bograd, Larry

Barry, Mike
See Malzberg, Barry N(athaniel)

Barry, Philip 1896-1949......... **TCLC 11**
See also CA 109; DLB 7

Bart, Andre Schwarz
See Schwarz-Bart, Andre

Barth, John (Simmons)
1930- ...... **CLC 1, 2, 3, 5, 7, 9, 10, 14,
27, 51; SSC 10**
See also AITN 1, 2; CA 1-4R; CABS 1;
CANR 5, 23; DLB 2; MTCW

Barthelme, Donald
1931-1989 ...... **CLC 1, 2, 3, 5, 6, 8, 13,
23, 46, 59; SSC 2**
See also CA 21-24R; 129; CANR 20;
DLB 2; DLBY 80, 89; MTCW; SATA 7;
SATA-Obit 62

Barthelme, Frederick 1943-....... **CLC 36**
See also CA 114; 122; DLBY 85

Barthes, Roland (Gerard)
1915-1980 .... **CLC 24, 83**
See also CA 130; 97-100; MTCW

Barzun, Jacques (Martin) 1907- .... **CLC 51**
See also CA 61-64; CANR 22

Bashevis, Isaac
See Singer, Isaac Bashevis

Bashkirtseff, Marie 1859-1884 ... **NCLC 27**

Basho
See Matsuo Basho

Bass, Kingsley B., Jr.
See Bullins, Ed

Bass, Rick 1958-................. **CLC 79**
See also CA 126

Bassani, Giorgio 1916-............ **CLC 9**
See also CA 65-68; CANR 33; DLB 128;
MTCW

Bastos, Augusto (Antonio) Roa
See Roa Bastos, Augusto (Antonio)

Bataille, Georges 1897-1962 .... **CLC 29**
See also CA 101; 89-92

Bates, H(erbert) E(rnest)
1905-1974 .... **CLC 46; SSC 10**
See also CA 93-96; 45-48; CANR 34;
MTCW

Bauchart
See Camus, Albert

Baudelaire, Charles
1821-1867 ..... **NCLC 6, 29; DA; PC 1;
WLC**

Baudrillard, Jean 1929-.......... **CLC 60**

Baum, L(yman) Frank 1856-1919 ... **TCLC 7**
See also CA 108; 133; CLR 15; DLB 22;
JRDA; MAICYA; MTCW; SATA 18

Baum, Louis F.
See Baum, L(yman) Frank

Baumbach, Jonathan 1933- ...... **CLC 6, 23**
See also CA 13-16R; CAAS 5; CANR 12;
DLBY 80; MTCW

Bausch, Richard (Carl) 1945- ...... **CLC 51**
See also CA 101; CAAS 14; CANR 43;
DLB 130

Baxter, Charles 1947-......... **CLC 45, 78**
See also CA 57-60; CANR 40; DLB 130

Baxter, George Owen
See Faust, Frederick (Schiller)

Baxter, James K(eir) 1926-1972 .... **CLC 14**
See also CA 77-80

Baxter, John
See Hunt, E(verette) Howard, Jr.

Bayer, Sylvia
See Glassco, John

Baynton, Barbara 1857-1929..... **TCLC 57**

Beagle, Peter S(oyer) 1939-......... **CLC 7**
See also CA 9-12R; CANR 4; DLBY 80;
SATA 60

Bean, Normal
See Burroughs, Edgar Rice

Beard, Charles A(ustin)
1874-1948 .... **TCLC 15**
See also CA 115; DLB 17; SATA 18

Beardsley, Aubrey 1872-1898 ..... **NCLC 6**

Beattie, Ann
1947- .... **CLC 8, 13, 18, 40, 63; SSC 11**
See also BEST 90:2; CA 81-84; DLBY 82;
MTCW

Beattie, James 1735-1803 .... **NCLC 25**
See also DLB 109

Beauchamp, Kathleen Mansfield 1888-1923
See Mansfield, Katherine
See also CA 104; 134; DA

Beaumarchais, Pierre-Augustin Caron de
1732-1799 .... **DC 4**

Beauvoir, Simone (Lucie Ernestine Marie
Bertrand) de
1908-1986 .... **CLC 1, 2, 4, 8, 14, 31, 44,
50, 71; DA; WLC**
See also CA 9-12R; 118; CANR 28;
DLB 72; DLBY 86; MTCW

Becker, Jurek 1937-............ **CLC 7, 19**
See also CA 85-88; DLB 75

Becker, Walter 1950-............. **CLC 26**

Beckett, Samuel (Barclay)
1906-1989 ...... **CLC 1, 2, 3, 4, 6, 9, 10,
11, 14, 18, 29, 57, 59, 83; DA; SSC 16;
WLC**
See also CA 5-8R; 130; CANR 33;
CDBLB 1945-1960; DLB 13, 15;
DLBY 90; MTCW

Beckford, William 1760-1844 .... **NCLC 16**
See also DLB 39

Beckman, Gunnel 1910-........... **CLC 26**
See also CA 33-36R; CANR 15; CLR 25;
MAICYA; SAAS 9; SATA 6

Becque, Henri 1837-1899......... **NCLC 3**

Beddoes, Thomas Lovell
1803-1849 .... **NCLC 3**
See also DLB 96

Bedford, Donald F.
See Fearing, Kenneth (Flexner)

Beecher, Catharine Esther
1800-1878 .... **NCLC 30**
See also DLB 1

Beecher, John 1904-1980.......... **CLC 6**
See also AITN 1; CA 5-8R; 105; CANR 8

Beer, Johann 1655-1700............. **LC 5**

Beer, Patricia 1924-.............. **CLC 58**
See also CA 61-64; CANR 13, 46; DLB 40

Beerbohm, Henry Maximilian
1872-1956 .... **TCLC 1, 24**
See also CA 104; DLB 34, 100

Beerbohm, Max
See Beerbohm, Henry Maximilian

Begiebing, Robert J(ohn) 1946-..... **CLC 70**
See also CA 122; CANR 40

Behan, Brendan
1923-1964 .... **CLC 1, 8, 11, 15, 79**
See also CA 73-76; CANR 33;
CDBLB 1945-1960; DLB 13; MTCW

Behn, Aphra
1640(?)-1689 .... **LC 1; DA; DC 4; WLC**
See also DLB 39, 80, 131

Behrman, S(amuel) N(athaniel)
1893-1973 .... **CLC 40**
See also CA 13-16; 45-48; CAP 1; DLB 7,
44

Belasco, David 1853-1931 . . . . **TCLC 3**
See also CA 104; DLB 7

Belcheva, Elisaveta 1893- . . . . **CLC 10**
See also Bagryana, Elisaveta

Beldone, Phil "Cheech"
See Ellison, Harlan (Jay)

Beleno
See Azuela, Mariano

Belinski, Vissarion Grigoryevich
1811-1848 . . . . **NCLC 5**

Belitt, Ben 1911- . . . . **CLC 22**
See also CA 13-16R; CAAS 4; CANR 7;
DLB 5

Bell, James Madison
1826-1902 . . . . **TCLC 43; BLC**
See also BW 1; CA 122; 124; DLB 50

Bell, Madison (Smartt) 1957- . . . . . . **CLC 41**
See also CA 111; CANR 28

Bell, Marvin (Hartley) 1937- . . . . . **CLC 8, 31**
See also CA 21-24R; CAAS 14; DLB 5;
MTCW

Bell, W. L. D.
See Mencken, H(enry) L(ouis)

Bellamy, Atwood C.
See Mencken, H(enry) L(ouis)

Bellamy, Edward 1850-1898 . . . . . . **NCLC 4**
See also DLB 12

Bellin, Edward J.
See Kuttner, Henry

Belloc, (Joseph) Hilaire (Pierre)
1870-1953 . . . . **TCLC 7, 18**
See also CA 106; DLB 19, 100, 141;
YABC 1

Belloc, Joseph Peter Rene Hilaire
See Belloc, (Joseph) Hilaire (Pierre)

Belloc, Joseph Pierre Hilaire
See Belloc, (Joseph) Hilaire (Pierre)

Belloc, M. A.
See Lowndes, Marie Adelaide (Belloc)

Bellow, Saul
1915- . . . . . . **CLC 1, 2, 3, 6, 8, 10, 13, 15,
25, 33, 34, 63, 79; DA; SSC 14; WLC**
See also AITN 2; BEST 89:3; CA 5-8R;
CABS 1; CANR 29; CDALB 1941-1968;
DLB 2, 28; DLBD 3; DLBY 82; MTCW

Bely, Andrey . . . . **TCLC 7; PC 11**
See also Bugayev, Boris Nikolayevich

Benary, Margot
See Benary-Isbert, Margot

Benary-Isbert, Margot 1889-1979 . . . **CLC 12**
See also CA 5-8R; 89-92; CANR 4;
CLR 12; MAICYA; SATA 2;
SATA-Obit 21

Benavente (y Martinez), Jacinto
1866-1954 . . . . **TCLC 3**
See also CA 106; 131; HW; MTCW

Benchley, Peter (Bradford)
1940- . . . . **CLC 4, 8**
See also AAYA 14; AITN 2; CA 17-20R;
CANR 12, 35; MTCW; SATA 3

Benchley, Robert (Charles)
1889-1945 . . . . **TCLC 1, 55**
See also CA 105; DLB 11

Benedikt, Michael 1935- . . . . **CLC 4, 14**
See also CA 13-16R; CANR 7; DLB 5

Benet, Juan 1927- . . . . **CLC 28**
See also CA 143

Benet, Stephen Vincent
1898-1943 . . . . **TCLC 7; SSC 10**
See also CA 104; DLB 4, 48, 102; YABC 1

Benet, William Rose 1886-1950 . . . **TCLC 28**
See also CA 118; DLB 45

Benford, Gregory (Albert) 1941- . . . . **CLC 52**
See also CA 69-72; CANR 12, 24;
DLBY 82

Bengtsson, Frans (Gunnar)
1894-1954 . . . . **TCLC 48**

Benjamin, David
See Slavitt, David R(ytman)

Benjamin, Lois
See Gould, Lois

Benjamin, Walter 1892-1940 . . . . . **TCLC 39**

Benn, Gottfried 1886-1956 . . . . **TCLC 3**
See also CA 106; DLB 56

Bennett, Alan 1934- . . . . **CLC 45, 77**
See also CA 103; CANR 35; MTCW

Bennett, (Enoch) Arnold
1867-1931 . . . . **TCLC 5, 20**
See also CA 106; CDBLB 1890-1914;
DLB 10, 34, 98

Bennett, Elizabeth
See Mitchell, Margaret (Munnerlyn)

Bennett, George Harold 1930-
See Bennett, Hal
See also BW 1; CA 97-100

Bennett, Hal . . . . **CLC 5**
See also Bennett, George Harold
See also DLB 33

Bennett, Jay 1912- . . . . **CLC 35**
See also AAYA 10; CA 69-72; CANR 11,
42; JRDA; SAAS 4; SATA 27, 41

Bennett, Louise (Simone)
1919- . . . . **CLC 28; BLC**
See also BW 2; DLB 117

Benson, E(dward) F(rederic)
1867-1940 . . . . **TCLC 27**
See also CA 114; DLB 135

Benson, Jackson J. 1930- . . . . **CLC 34**
See also CA 25-28R; DLB 111

Benson, Sally 1900-1972 . . . . **CLC 17**
See also CA 19-20; 37-40R; CAP 1;
SATA 1, 35; SATA-Obit 27

Benson, Stella 1892-1933 . . . . **TCLC 17**
See also CA 117; DLB 36

Bentham, Jeremy 1748-1832 . . . . . **NCLC 38**
See also DLB 107

Bentley, E(dmund) C(lerihew)
1875-1956 . . . . **TCLC 12**
See also CA 108; DLB 70

Bentley, Eric (Russell) 1916- . . . . . . **CLC 24**
See also CA 5-8R; CANR 6

Beranger, Pierre Jean de
1780-1857 . . . . **NCLC 34**

Berger, Colonel
See Malraux, (Georges-)Andre

Berger, John (Peter) 1926- . . . . . **CLC 2, 19**
See also CA 81-84; DLB 14

Berger, Melvin H. 1927- . . . . **CLC 12**
See also CA 5-8R; CANR 4; CLR 32;
SAAS 2; SATA 5

Berger, Thomas (Louis)
1924- . . . . **CLC 3, 5, 8, 11, 18, 38**
See also CA 1-4R; CANR 5, 28; DLB 2;
DLBY 80; MTCW

Bergman, (Ernst) Ingmar
1918- . . . . **CLC 16, 72**
See also CA 81-84; CANR 33

Bergson, Henri 1859-1941 . . . . **TCLC 32**

Bergstein, Eleanor 1938- . . . . **CLC 4**
See also CA 53-56; CANR 5

Berkoff, Steven 1937- . . . . **CLC 56**
See also CA 104

Bermant, Chaim (Icyk) 1929- . . . . . . **CLC 40**
See also CA 57-60; CANR 6, 31

Bern, Victoria
See Fisher, M(ary) F(rances) K(ennedy)

Bernanos, (Paul Louis) Georges
1888-1948 . . . . **TCLC 3**
See also CA 104; 130; DLB 72

Bernard, April 1956- . . . . **CLC 59**
See also CA 131

Berne, Victoria
See Fisher, M(ary) F(rances) K(ennedy)

Bernhard, Thomas
1931-1989 . . . . **CLC 3, 32, 61**
See also CA 85-88; 127; CANR 32;
DLB 85, 124; MTCW

Berriault, Gina 1926- . . . . **CLC 54**
See also CA 116; 129; DLB 130

Berrigan, Daniel 1921- . . . . **CLC 4**
See also CA 33-36R; CAAS 1; CANR 11,
43; DLB 5

Berrigan, Edmund Joseph Michael, Jr.
1934-1983
See Berrigan, Ted
See also CA 61-64; 110; CANR 14

Berrigan, Ted . . . . **CLC 37**
See also Berrigan, Edmund Joseph Michael,
Jr.
See also DLB 5

Berry, Charles Edward Anderson 1931-
See Berry, Chuck
See also CA 115

Berry, Chuck . . . . **CLC 17**
See also Berry, Charles Edward Anderson

Berry, Jonas
See Ashbery, John (Lawrence)

Berry, Wendell (Erdman)
1934- . . . . **CLC 4, 6, 8, 27, 46**
See also AITN 1; CA 73-76; DLB 5, 6

Berryman, John
1914-1972 . . . . . . **CLC 1, 2, 3, 4, 6, 8, 10,
13, 25, 62**
See also CA 13-16; 33-36R; CABS 2;
CANR 35; CAP 1; CDALB 1941-1968;
DLB 48; MTCW

Bertolucci, Bernardo 1940- . . . . **CLC 16**
See also CA 106

Bertrand, Aloysius 1807-1841 . . . . **NCLC 31**

Bertran de Born c. 1140-1215 . . . . . **CMLC 5**

Besant, Annie (Wood) 1847-1933 . . . **TCLC 9**
See also CA 105

Bessie, Alvah 1904-1985 . . . . **CLC 23**
See also CA 5-8R; 116; CANR 2; DLB 26

Bethlen, T. D.
See Silverberg, Robert

Beti, Mongo . . . . **CLC 27; BLC**
See also Biyidi, Alexandre

Betjeman, John
1906-1984 . . . . **CLC 2, 6, 10, 34, 43**
See also CA 9-12R; 112; CANR 33;
CDBLB 1945-1960; DLB 20; DLBY 84;
MTCW

Bettelheim, Bruno 1903-1990 . . . . . . **CLC 79**
See also CA 81-84; 131; CANR 23; MTCW

Betti, Ugo 1892-1953 . . . . **TCLC 5**
See also CA 104

Betts, Doris (Waugh) 1932-. . . . **CLC 3, 6, 28**
See also CA 13-16R; CANR 9; DLBY 82

Bevan, Alistair
See Roberts, Keith (John Kingston)

Bialik, Chaim Nachman
1873-1934 . . . . **TCLC 25**

Bickerstaff, Isaac
See Swift, Jonathan

Bidart, Frank 1939- . . . . **CLC 33**
See also CA 140

Bienek, Horst 1930-. . . . . **CLC 7, 11**
See also CA 73-76; DLB 75

Bierce, Ambrose (Gwinett)
1842-1914(?) . . . . . . **TCLC 1, 7, 44; DA;**
SSC 9; WLC
See also CA 104; 139; CDALB 1865-1917;
DLB 11, 12, 23, 71, 74

Billings, Josh
See Shaw, Henry Wheeler

Billington, (Lady) Rachel (Mary)
1942- . . . . **CLC 43**
See also AITN 2; CA 33-36R; CANR 44

Binyon, T(imothy) J(ohn) 1936- . . . . **CLC 34**
See also CA 111; CANR 28

Bioy Casares, Adolfo
1914- . . . . . . **CLC 4, 8, 13; HLC; SSC 17**
See also CA 29-32R; CANR 19, 43;
DLB 113; HW; MTCW

Bird, Cordwainer
See Ellison, Harlan (Jay)

Bird, Robert Montgomery
1806-1854 . . . . **NCLC 1**

Birney, (Alfred) Earle
1904- . . . . **CLC 1, 4, 6, 11**
See also CA 1-4R; CANR 5, 20; DLB 88;
MTCW

Bishop, Elizabeth
1911-1979 . . . . . **CLC 1, 4, 9, 13, 15, 32;**
DA; PC 3
See also CA 5-8R; 89-92; CABS 2;
CANR 26; CDALB 1968-1988; DLB 5;
MTCW; SATA-Obit 24

Bishop, John 1935-. . . . . **CLC 10**
See also CA 105

Bissett, Bill 1939-. . . . . **CLC 18**
See also CA 69-72; CAAS 19; CANR 15;
DLB 53; MTCW

Bitov, Andrei (Georgievich) 1937-. . . **CLC 57**
See also CA 142

Biyidi, Alexandre 1932-
See Beti, Mongo
See also BW 1; CA 114; 124; MTCW

Bjarme, Brynjolf
See Ibsen, Henrik (Johan)

Bjornson, Bjornstjerne (Martinius)
1832-1910 . . . . **TCLC 7, 37**
See also CA 104

Black, Robert
See Holdstock, Robert P.

Blackburn, Paul 1926-1971 . . . . . . **CLC 9, 43**
See also CA 81-84; 33-36R; CANR 34;
DLB 16; DLBY 81

Black Elk 1863-1950 . . . . **TCLC 33**
See also CA 144; NNAL

Black Hobart
See Sanders, (James) Ed(ward)

Blacklin, Malcolm
See Chambers, Aidan

Blackmore, R(ichard) D(oddridge)
1825-1900 . . . . **TCLC 27**
See also CA 120; DLB 18

Blackmur, R(ichard) P(almer)
1904-1965 . . . . **CLC 2, 24**
See also CA 11-12; 25-28R; CAP 1; DLB 63

Black Tarantula, The
See Acker, Kathy

Blackwood, Algernon (Henry)
1869-1951 . . . . **TCLC 5**
See also CA 105

Blackwood, Caroline 1931- . . . . **CLC 6, 9**
See also CA 85-88; CANR 32; DLB 14;
MTCW

Blade, Alexander
See Hamilton, Edmond; Silverberg, Robert

Blaga, Lucian 1895-1961 . . . . **CLC 75**

Blair, Eric (Arthur) 1903-1950
See Orwell, George
See also CA 104; 132; DA; MTCW;
SATA 29

Blais, Marie-Claire
1939- . . . . **CLC 2, 4, 6, 13, 22**
See also CA 21-24R; CAAS 4; CANR 38;
DLB 53; MTCW

Blaise, Clark 1940-. . . . . **CLC 29**
See also AITN 2; CA 53-56; CAAS 3;
CANR 5; DLB 53

Blake, Nicholas
See Day Lewis, C(ecil)
See also DLB 77

Blake, William
1757-1827 . . . . . **NCLC 13, 37; DA; WLC**
See also CDBLB 1789-1832; DLB 93;
MAICYA; SATA 30

Blasco Ibanez, Vicente
1867-1928 . . . . **TCLC 12**
See also CA 110; 131; HW; MTCW

Blatty, William Peter 1928-. . . . . **CLC 2**
See also CA 5-8R; CANR 9

Bleeck, Oliver
See Thomas, Ross (Elmore)

Blessing, Lee 1949-. . . . . **CLC 54**

Blish, James (Benjamin)
1921-1975 . . . . **CLC 14**
See also CA 1-4R; 57-60; CANR 3; DLB 8;
MTCW; SATA 66

Bliss, Reginald
See Wells, H(erbert) G(eorge)

Blixen, Karen (Christentze Dinesen)
1885-1962
See Dinesen, Isak
See also CA 25-28; CANR 22; CAP 2;
MTCW; SATA 44

Bloch, Robert (Albert) 1917-. . . . . . . **CLC 33**
See also CA 5-8R; CAAS 20; CANR 5;
DLB 44; SATA 12

Blok, Alexander (Alexandrovich)
1880-1921 . . . . **TCLC 5**
See also CA 104

Blom, Jan
See Breytenbach, Breyten

Bloom, Harold 1930- . . . . **CLC 24**
See also CA 13-16R; CANR 39; DLB 67

Bloomfield, Aurelius
See Bourne, Randolph S(illiman)

Blount, Roy (Alton), Jr. 1941- . . . . . **CLC 38**
See also CA 53-56; CANR 10, 28; MTCW

Bloy, Leon 1846-1917. . . . . **TCLC 22**
See also CA 121; DLB 123

Blume, Judy (Sussman) 1938-. . . **CLC 12, 30**
See also AAYA 3; CA 29-32R; CANR 13,
37; CLR 2, 15; DLB 52; JRDA;
MAICYA; MTCW; SATA 2, 31, 79

Blunden, Edmund (Charles)
1896-1974 . . . . **CLC 2, 56**
See also CA 17-18; 45-48; CAP 2; DLB 20,
100; MTCW

Bly, Robert (Elwood)
1926-. . . . . **CLC 1, 2, 5, 10, 15, 38**
See also CA 5-8R; CANR 41; DLB 5;
MTCW

Boas, Franz 1858-1942. . . . . **TCLC 56**
See also CA 115

Bobette
See Simenon, Georges (Jacques Christian)

Boccaccio, Giovanni
1313-1375 . . . . **CMLC 13; SSC 10**

Bochco, Steven 1943-. . . . . **CLC 35**
See also AAYA 11; CA 124; 138

Bodenheim, Maxwell 1892-1954 . . . **TCLC 44**
See also CA 110; DLB 9, 45

Bodker, Cecil 1927- . . . . **CLC 21**
See also CA 73-76; CANR 13, 44; CLR 23;
MAICYA; SATA 14

Boell, Heinrich (Theodor)
1917-1985 . . . . **CLC 2, 3, 6, 9, 11, 15, 27,**
32, 72; DA; WLC
See also CA 21-24R; 116; CANR 24;
DLB 69; DLBY 85

Boerne, Alfred
See Doeblin, Alfred

Bogan, Louise 1897-1970. . . . . **CLC 4, 39, 46**
See also CA 73-76; 25-28R; CANR 33;
DLB 45; MTCW

Brathwaite, Edward (Kamau)
1930- . . . . **CLC 11**
See also BW 2; CA 25-28R; CANR 11, 26;
DLB 125

Brautigan, Richard (Gary)
1935-1984 . . . . **CLC 1, 3, 5, 9, 12, 34, 42**
See also CA 53-56; 113; CANR 34; DLB 2,
5; DLBY 80, 84; MTCW; SATA 56

Braverman, Kate 1950- . . . . **CLC 67**
See also CA 89-92

Brecht, Bertolt
1898-1956 . . . . . . **TCLC 1, 6, 13, 35; DA;**
DC 3; WLC
See also CA 104; 133; DLB 56, 124; MTCW

Brecht, Eugen Berthold Friedrich
See Brecht, Bertolt

Bremer, Fredrika 1801-1865 . . . . . **NCLC 11**

Brennan, Christopher John
1870-1932 . . . . **TCLC 17**
See also CA 117

Brennan, Maeve 1917- . . . . **CLC 5**
See also CA 81-84

Brentano, Clemens (Maria)
1778-1842 . . . . **NCLC 1**
See also DLB 90

Brent of Bin Bin
See Franklin, (Stella Maraia Sarah) Miles

Brenton, Howard 1942- . . . . **CLC 31**
See also CA 69-72; CANR 33; DLB 13;
MTCW

Breslin, James 1930-
See Breslin, Jimmy
See also CA 73-76; CANR 31; MTCW

Breslin, Jimmy . . . . **CLC 4, 43**
See also Breslin, James
See also AITN 1

Bresson, Robert 1907- . . . . **CLC 16**
See also CA 110

Breton, Andre 1896-1966 . . . **CLC 2, 9, 15, 54**
See also CA 19-20; 25-28R; CANR 40;
CAP 2; DLB 65; MTCW

Breytenbach, Breyten 1939(?)- . . **CLC 23, 37**
See also CA 113; 129

Bridgers, Sue Ellen 1942- . . . . **CLC 26**
See also AAYA 8; CA 65-68; CANR 11,
36; CLR 18; DLB 52; JRDA; MAICYA;
SAAS 1; SATA 22

Bridges, Robert (Seymour)
1844-1930 . . . . **TCLC 1**
See also CA 104; CDBLB 1890-1914;
DLB 19, 98

Bridie, James. . . . . **TCLC 3**
See also Mavor, Osborne Henry
See also DLB 10

Brin, David 1950- . . . . **CLC 34**
See also CA 102; CANR 24; SATA 65

Brink, Andre (Philippus)
1935- . . . . **CLC 18, 36**
See also CA 104; CANR 39; MTCW

Brinsmead, H(esba) F(ay) 1922- . . . . **CLC 21**
See also CA 21-24R; CANR 10; MAICYA;
SAAS 5; SATA 18, 78

Brittain, Vera (Mary)
1893(?)-1970 . . . . **CLC 23**
See also CA 13-16; 25-28R; CAP 1; MTCW

Broch, Hermann 1886-1951 . . . . . . **TCLC 20**
See also CA 117; DLB 85, 124

Brock, Rose
See Hansen, Joseph

Brodkey, Harold 1930- . . . . **CLC 56**
See also CA 111; DLB 130

Brodsky, Iosif Alexandrovich 1940-
See Brodsky, Joseph
See also AITN 1; CA 41-44R; CANR 37;
MTCW

Brodsky, Joseph . . **CLC 4, 6, 13, 36, 50; PC 9**
See also Brodsky, Iosif Alexandrovich

Brodsky, Michael Mark 1948- . . . . . **CLC 19**
See also CA 102; CANR 18, 41

Bromell, Henry 1947- . . . . **CLC 5**
See also CA 53-56; CANR 9

Bromfield, Louis (Brucker)
1896-1956 . . . . **TCLC 11**
See also CA 107; DLB 4, 9, 86

Broner, E(sther) M(asserman)
1930- . . . . **CLC 19**
See also CA 17-20R; CANR 8, 25; DLB 28

Bronk, William 1918- . . . . **CLC 10**
See also CA 89-92; CANR 23

Bronstein, Lev Davidovich
See Trotsky, Leon

Bronte, Anne 1820-1849. . . . . **NCLC 4**
See also DLB 21

Bronte, Charlotte
1816-1855 . . . **NCLC 3, 8, 33; DA; WLC**
See also CDBLB 1832-1890; DLB 21

Bronte, (Jane) Emily
1818-1848 . . . . **NCLC 16, 35; DA; PC 8;**
WLC
See also CDBLB 1832-1890; DLB 21, 32

Brooke, Frances 1724-1789 . . . . **LC 6**
See also DLB 39, 99

Brooke, Henry 1703(?)-1783 . . . . **LC 1**
See also DLB 39

Brooke, Rupert (Chawner)
1887-1915 . . . . **TCLC 2, 7; DA; WLC**
See also CA 104; 132; CDBLB 1914-1945;
DLB 19; MTCW

Brooke-Haven, P.
See Wodehouse, P(elham) G(renville)

Brooke-Rose, Christine 1926- . . . . . . **CLC 40**
See also CA 13-16R; DLB 14

Brookner, Anita 1928- . . . . . . **CLC 32, 34, 51**
See also CA 114; 120; CANR 37; DLBY 87;
MTCW

Brooks, Cleanth 1906-1994 . . . . **CLC 24**
See also CA 17-20R; 145; CANR 33, 35;
DLB 63; MTCW

Brooks, George
See Baum, L(yman) Frank

Brooks, Gwendolyn
1917- . . . . . . **CLC 1, 2, 4, 5, 15, 49; BLC;**
DA; PC 7; WLC
See also AITN 1; BW 2; CA 1-4R;
CANR 1, 27; CDALB 1941-1968;
CLR 27; DLB 5, 76; MTCW; SATA 6

Brooks, Mel. . . . . **CLC 12**
See also Kaminsky, Melvin
See also AAYA 13; DLB 26

Brooks, Peter 1938- . . . . **CLC 34**
See also CA 45-48; CANR 1

Brooks, Van Wyck 1886-1963 . . . . . . **CLC 29**
See also CA 1-4R; CANR 6; DLB 45, 63,
103

Brophy, Brigid (Antonia)
1929- . . . . **CLC 6, 11, 29**
See also CA 5-8R; CAAS 4; CANR 25;
DLB 14; MTCW

Brosman, Catharine Savage 1934-. . . . **CLC 9**
See also CA 61-64; CANR 21, 46

Brother Antoninus
See Everson, William (Oliver)

Broughton, T(homas) Alan 1936- . . . **CLC 19**
See also CA 45-48; CANR 2, 23

Broumas, Olga 1949- . . . . **CLC 10, 73**
See also CA 85-88; CANR 20

Brown, Charles Brockden
1771-1810 . . . . **NCLC 22**
See also CDALB 1640-1865; DLB 37, 59,
73

Brown, Christy 1932-1981 . . . . **CLC 63**
See also CA 105; 104; DLB 14

Brown, Claude 1937- . . . . **CLC 30; BLC**
See also AAYA 7; BW 1; CA 73-76

Brown, Dee (Alexander) 1908- . . **CLC 18, 47**
See also CA 13-16R; CAAS 6; CANR 11,
45; DLBY 80; MTCW; SATA 5

Brown, George
See Wertmueller, Lina

Brown, George Douglas
1869-1902 . . . . **TCLC 28**

Brown, George Mackay 1921-. . . . **CLC 5, 48**
See also CA 21-24R; CAAS 6; CANR 12,
37; DLB 14, 27, 139; MTCW; SATA 35

Brown, (William) Larry 1951-. . . . . . **CLC 73**
See also CA 130; 134

Brown, Moses
See Barrett, William (Christopher)

Brown, Rita Mae 1944- . . . . . **CLC 18, 43, 79**
See also CA 45-48; CANR 2, 11, 35;
MTCW

Brown, Roderick (Langmere) Haig-
See Haig-Brown, Roderick (Langmere)

Brown, Rosellen 1939- . . . . **CLC 32**
See also CA 77-80; CAAS 10; CANR 14, 44

Brown, Sterling Allen
1901-1989 . . . . **CLC 1, 23, 59; BLC**
See also BW 1; CA 85-88; 127; CANR 26;
DLB 48, 51, 63; MTCW

Brown, Will
See Ainsworth, William Harrison

Brown, William Wells
1813-1884 . . . . **NCLC 2; BLC; DC 1**
See also DLB 3, 50

Browne, (Clyde) Jackson 1948(?)-. . . **CLC 21**
See also CA 120

Browning, Elizabeth Barrett
1806-1861 . . . . . **NCLC 1, 16; DA; PC 6;**
WLC
See also CDBLB 1832-1890; DLB 32

Browning, Robert
1812-1889 . . . . **NCLC 19; DA; PC 2**
See also CDBLB 1832-1890; DLB 32;
YABC 1

Browning, Tod 1882-1962 . . . . **CLC 16**
See also CA 141; 117

Bruccoli, Matthew J(oseph) 1931- . . **CLC 34**
See also CA 9-12R; CANR 7; DLB 103

Bruce, Lenny . . . . **CLC 21**
See also Schneider, Leonard Alfred

Bruin, John
See Brutus, Dennis

Brulard, Henri
See Stendhal

Brulls, Christian
See Simenon, Georges (Jacques Christian)

Brunner, John (Kilian Houston)
1934- . . . . **CLC 8, 10**
See also CA 1-4R; CAAS 8; CANR 2, 37;
MTCW

Bruno, Giordano 1548-1600 . . . . **LC 27**

Brutus, Dennis 1924- . . . . **CLC 43; BLC**
See also BW 2; CA 49-52; CAAS 14;
CANR 2, 27, 42; DLB 117

Bryan, C(ourtlandt) D(ixon) B(arnes)
1936- . . . . **CLC 29**
See also CA 73-76; CANR 13

Bryan, Michael
See Moore, Brian

Bryant, William Cullen
1794-1878 . . . . **NCLC 6, 46; DA**
See also CDALB 1640-1865; DLB 3, 43, 59

Bryusov, Valery Yakovlevich
1873-1924 . . . . **TCLC 10**
See also CA 107

Buchan, John 1875-1940 . . . . **TCLC 41**
See also CA 108; 145; DLB 34, 70; YABC 2

Buchanan, George 1506-1582 . . . . **LC 4**

Buchheim, Lothar-Guenther 1918- . . . **CLC 6**
See also CA 85-88

Buchner, (Karl) Georg
1813-1837 . . . . **NCLC 26**

Buchwald, Art(hur) 1925- . . . . **CLC 33**
See also AITN 1; CA 5-8R; CANR 21;
MTCW; SATA 10

Buck, Pearl S(ydenstricker)
1892-1973 . . . . **CLC 7, 11, 18; DA**
See also AITN 1; CA 1-4R; 41-44R;
CANR 1, 34; DLB 9, 102; MTCW;
SATA 1, 25

Buckler, Ernest 1908-1984 . . . . **CLC 13**
See also CA 11-12; 114; CAP 1; DLB 68;
SATA 47

Buckley, Vincent (Thomas)
1925-1988 . . . . **CLC 57**
See also CA 101

Buckley, William F(rank), Jr.
1925- . . . . **CLC 7, 18, 37**
See also AITN 1; CA 1-4R; CANR 1, 24;
DLB 137; DLBY 80; MTCW

Buechner, (Carl) Frederick
1926- . . . . **CLC 2, 4, 6, 9**
See also CA 13-16R; CANR 11, 39;
DLBY 80; MTCW

Buell, John (Edward) 1927- . . . . **CLC 10**
See also CA 1-4R; DLB 53

Buero Vallejo, Antonio 1916- . . . **CLC 15, 46**
See also CA 106; CANR 24; HW; MTCW

Bufalino, Gesualdo 1920(?)- . . . . **CLC 74**

Bugayev, Boris Nikolayevich 1880-1934
See Bely, Andrey
See also CA 104

Bukowski, Charles
1920-1994 . . . . **CLC 2, 5, 9, 41, 82**
See also CA 17-20R; 144; CANR 40;
DLB 5, 130; MTCW

Bulgakov, Mikhail (Afanas'evich)
1891-1940 . . . . **TCLC 2, 16**
See also CA 105

Bulgya, Alexander Alexandrovich
1901-1956 . . . . **TCLC 53**
See also Fadeyev, Alexander
See also CA 117

Bullins, Ed 1935- . . . . **CLC 1, 5, 7; BLC**
See also BW 2; CA 49-52; CAAS 16;
CANR 24, 46; DLB 7, 38; MTCW

Bulwer-Lytton, Edward (George Earle Lytton)
1803-1873 . . . . **NCLC 1, 45**
See also DLB 21

Bunin, Ivan Alexeyevich
1870-1953 . . . . **TCLC 6; SSC 5**
See also CA 104

Bunting, Basil 1900-1985 . . . . **CLC 10, 39, 47**
See also CA 53-56; 115; CANR 7; DLB 20

Bunuel, Luis 1900-1983 . . **CLC 16, 80; HLC**
See also CA 101; 110; CANR 32; HW

Bunyan, John 1628-1688 . . **LC 4; DA; WLC**
See also CDBLB 1660-1789; DLB 39

Burford, Eleanor
See Hibbert, Eleanor Alice Burford

Burgess, Anthony
. **CLC 1, 2, 4, 5, 8, 10, 13, 15, 22, 40, 62, 81**
See also Wilson, John (Anthony) Burgess
See also AITN 1; CDBLB 1960 to Present;
DLB 14

Burke, Edmund
1729(?)-1797 . . . . **LC 7; DA; WLC**
See also DLB 104

Burke, Kenneth (Duva)
1897-1993 . . . . **CLC 2, 24**
See also CA 5-8R; 143; CANR 39; DLB 45,
63; MTCW

Burke, Leda
See Garnett, David

Burke, Ralph
See Silverberg, Robert

Burney, Fanny 1752-1840 . . . . **NCLC 12**
See also DLB 39

Burns, Robert
1759-1796 . . . . . . **LC 3; DA; PC 6; WLC**
See also CDBLB 1789-1832; DLB 109

Burns, Tex
See L'Amour, Louis (Dearborn)

Burnshaw, Stanley 1906- . . . . . **CLC 3, 13, 44**
See also CA 9-12R; DLB 48

Burr, Anne 1937- . . . . **CLC 6**
See also CA 25-28R

Burroughs, Edgar Rice
1875-1950 . . . . **TCLC 2, 32**
See also AAYA 11; CA 104; 132; DLB 8;
MTCW; SATA 41

Burroughs, William S(eward)
1914- . . . . **CLC 1, 2, 5, 15, 22, 42, 75;
DA; WLC**
See also AITN 2; CA 9-12R; CANR 20;
DLB 2, 8, 16; DLBY 81; MTCW

Burton, Richard F. 1821-1890 . . . . **NCLC 42**
See also DLB 55

Busch, Frederick 1941- . . . **CLC 7, 10, 18, 47**
See also CA 33-36R; CAAS 1; CANR 45;
DLB 6

Bush, Ronald 1946- . . . . **CLC 34**
See also CA 136

Bustos, F(rancisco)
See Borges, Jorge Luis

Bustos Domecq, H(onorio)
See Bioy Casares, Adolfo; Borges, Jorge
Luis

Butler, Octavia E(stelle) 1947- . . . . . **CLC 38**
See also BW 2; CA 73-76; CANR 12, 24,
38; DLB 33; MTCW

Butler, Robert Olen (Jr.) 1945- . . . . . **CLC 81**
See also CA 112

Butler, Samuel 1612-1680 . . . . **LC 16**
See also DLB 101, 126

Butler, Samuel
1835-1902 . . . . . . **TCLC 1, 33; DA; WLC**
See also CA 143; CDBLB 1890-1914;
DLB 18, 57

Butler, Walter C.
See Faust, Frederick (Schiller)

Butor, Michel (Marie Francois)
1926- . . . . **CLC 1, 3, 8, 11, 15**
See also CA 9-12R; CANR 33; DLB 83;
MTCW

Buzo, Alexander (John) 1944- . . . . . . **CLC 61**
See also CA 97-100; CANR 17, 39

Buzzati, Dino 1906-1972 . . . . **CLC 36**
See also CA 33-36R

Byars, Betsy (Cromer) 1928- . . . . **CLC 35**
See also CA 33-36R; CANR 18, 36; CLR 1,
16; DLB 52; JRDA; MAICYA; MTCW;
SAAS 1; SATA 4, 46

Byatt, A(ntonia) S(usan Drabble)
1936- . . . . **CLC 19, 65**
See also CA 13-16R; CANR 13, 33;
DLB 14; MTCW

Byrne, David 1952- . . . . **CLC 26**
See also CA 127

Byrne, John Keyes 1926-
See Leonard, Hugh
See also CA 102

Byron, George Gordon (Noel)
1788-1824 . . . . . . **NCLC 2, 12; DA; WLC**
See also CDBLB 1789-1832; DLB 96, 110

C. 3. 3.
See Wilde, Oscar (Fingal O'Flahertie Wills)

Caballero, Fernan 1796-1877 . . . . . **NCLC 10**

Cabell, James Branch 1879-1958 . . . **TCLC 6**
See also CA 105; DLB 9, 78

Cable, George Washington
    1844-1925 . . . . **TCLC 4; SSC 4**
    See also CA 104; DLB 12, 74

Cabral de Melo Neto, Joao 1920-. . . **CLC 76**

Cabrera Infante, G(uillermo)
    1929- . . . . **CLC 5, 25, 45; HLC**
    See also CA 85-88; CANR 29; DLB 113;
    HW; MTCW

Cade, Toni
    See Bambara, Toni Cade

Cadmus and Harmonia
    See Buchan, John

Caedmon fl. 658-680. . . . . **CMLC 7**
    See also DLB 146

Caeiro, Alberto
    See Pessoa, Fernando (Antonio Nogueira)

Cage, John (Milton, Jr.) 1912- . . . . . **CLC 41**
    See also CA 13-16R; CANR 9

Cain, G.
    See Cabrera Infante, G(uillermo)

Cain, Guillermo
    See Cabrera Infante, G(uillermo)

Cain, James M(allahan)
    1892-1977 . . . . **CLC 3, 11, 28**
    See also AITN 1; CA 17-20R; 73-76;
    CANR 8, 34; MTCW

Caine, Mark
    See Raphael, Frederic (Michael)

Calasso, Roberto 1941- . . . . **CLC 81**
    See also CA 143

Calderon de la Barca, Pedro
    1600-1681 . . . . **LC 23; DC 3**

Caldwell, Erskine (Preston)
    1903-1987 . . . . **CLC 1, 8, 14, 50, 60**
    See also AITN 1; CA 1-4R; 121; CAAS 1;
    CANR 2, 33; DLB 9, 86; MTCW

Caldwell, (Janet Miriam) Taylor (Holland)
    1900-1985 . . . . **CLC 2, 28, 39**
    See also CA 5-8R; 116; CANR 5

Calhoun, John Caldwell
    1782-1850 . . . . **NCLC 15**
    See also DLB 3

Calisher, Hortense
    1911- . . . . **CLC 2, 4, 8, 38; SSC 15**
    See also CA 1-4R; CANR 1, 22; DLB 2;
    MTCW

Callaghan, Morley Edward
    1903-1990 . . . . **CLC 3, 14, 41, 65**
    See also CA 9-12R; 132; CANR 33;
    DLB 68; MTCW

Calvino, Italo
    1923-1985 . . . . . **CLC 5, 8, 11, 22, 33, 39,**
                         73; SSC 3
    See also CA 85-88; 116; CANR 23; MTCW

Cameron, Carey 1952- . . . . **CLC 59**
    See also CA 135

Cameron, Peter 1959-. . . . . **CLC 44**
    See also CA 125

Campana, Dino 1885-1932. . . . . . . **TCLC 20**
    See also CA 117; DLB 114

Campbell, John W(ood, Jr.)
    1910-1971 . . . . **CLC 32**
    See also CA 21-22; 29-32R; CANR 34;
    CAP 2; DLB 8; MTCW

Campbell, Joseph 1904-1987 . . . . . . **CLC 69**
    See also AAYA 3; BEST 89:2; CA 1-4R;
    124; CANR 3, 28; MTCW

Campbell, Maria 1940-. . . . . **CLC 85**
    See also CA 102; NNAL

Campbell, (John) Ramsey 1946- . . . . **CLC 42**
    See also CA 57-60; CANR 7

Campbell, (Ignatius) Roy (Dunnachie)
    1901-1957 . . . . **TCLC 5**
    See also CA 104; DLB 20

Campbell, Thomas 1777-1844 . . . . **NCLC 19**
    See also DLB 93; 144

Campbell, Wilfred . . . . **TCLC 9**
    See also Campbell, William

Campbell, William 1858(?)-1918
    See Campbell, Wilfred
    See also CA 106; DLB 92

Campos, Alvaro de
    See Pessoa, Fernando (Antonio Nogueira)

Camus, Albert
    1913-1960 . . . . **CLC 1, 2, 4, 9, 11, 14, 32,**
             63, 69; DA; DC 2; SSC 9; WLC
    See also CA 89-92; DLB 72; MTCW

Canby, Vincent 1924-. . . . . **CLC 13**
    See also CA 81-84

Cancale
    See Desnos, Robert

Canetti, Elias 1905- . . . . . . **CLC 3, 14, 25, 75**
    See also CA 21-24R; CANR 23; DLB 85,
    124; MTCW

Canin, Ethan 1960-. . . . . **CLC 55**
    See also CA 131; 135

Cannon, Curt
    See Hunter, Evan

Cape, Judith
    See Page, P(atricia) K(athleen)

Capek, Karel
    1890-1938 . . . . . **TCLC 6, 37; DA; DC 1;**
                             WLC
    See also CA 104; 140

Capote, Truman
    1924-1984 . . . . . . **CLC 1, 3, 8, 13, 19, 34,**
              38, 58; DA; SSC 2; WLC
    See also CA 5-8R; 113; CANR 18;
    CDALB 1941-1968; DLB 2; DLBY 80,
    84; MTCW

Capra, Frank 1897-1991. . . . . **CLC 16**
    See also CA 61-64; 135

Caputo, Philip 1941-. . . . . **CLC 32**
    See also CA 73-76; CANR 40

Card, Orson Scott 1951- . . . . **CLC 44, 47, 50**
    See also AAYA 11; CA 102; CANR 27;
    MTCW

Cardenal (Martinez), Ernesto
    1925- . . . . **CLC 31; HLC**
    See also CA 49-52; CANR 2, 32; HW;
    MTCW

Carducci, Giosue 1835-1907. . . . . . **TCLC 32**

Carew, Thomas 1595(?)-1640. . . . . . . **LC 13**
    See also DLB 126

Carey, Ernestine Gilbreth 1908- . . . . **CLC 17**
    See also CA 5-8R; SATA 2

Carey, Peter 1943-. . . . . **CLC 40, 55**
    See also CA 123; 127; MTCW

Carleton, William 1794-1869. . . . . . . **NCLC 3**

Carlisle, Henry (Coffin) 1926-. . . . . . **CLC 33**
    See also CA 13-16R; CANR 15

Carlsen, Chris
    See Holdstock, Robert P.

Carlson, Ron(ald F.) 1947-. . . . . **CLC 54**
    See also CA 105; CANR 27

Carlyle, Thomas 1795-1881 . . **NCLC 22; DA**
    See also CDBLB 1789-1832; DLB 55; 144

Carman, (William) Bliss
    1861-1929 . . . . **TCLC 7**
    See also CA 104; DLB 92

Carnegie, Dale 1888-1955 . . . . **TCLC 53**

Carossa, Hans 1878-1956. . . . . **TCLC 48**
    See also DLB 66

Carpenter, Don(ald Richard)
    1931- . . . . **CLC 41**
    See also CA 45-48; CANR 1

Carpentier (y Valmont), Alejo
    1904-1980 . . . . **CLC 8, 11, 38; HLC**
    See also CA 65-68; 97-100; CANR 11;
    DLB 113; HW

Carr, Emily 1871-1945. . . . . **TCLC 32**
    See also DLB 68

Carr, John Dickson 1906-1977 . . . . . . **CLC 3**
    See also CA 49-52; 69-72; CANR 3, 33;
    MTCW

Carr, Philippa
    See Hibbert, Eleanor Alice Burford

Carr, Virginia Spencer 1929-. . . . . . . **CLC 34**
    See also CA 61-64; DLB 111

Carrier, Roch 1937- . . . . **CLC 13, 78**
    See also CA 130; DLB 53

Carroll, James P. 1943(?)-. . . . . **CLC 38**
    See also CA 81-84

Carroll, Jim 1951- . . . . **CLC 35**
    See also CA 45-48; CANR 42

Carroll, Lewis . . . . **NCLC 2; WLC**
    See also Dodgson, Charles Lutwidge
    See also CDBLB 1832-1890; CLR 2, 18;
    DLB 18; JRDA

Carroll, Paul Vincent 1900-1968. . . . **CLC 10**
    See also CA 9-12R; 25-28R; DLB 10

Carruth, Hayden
    1921- . . . . . . **CLC 4, 7, 10, 18, 84; PC 10**
    See also CA 9-12R; CANR 4, 38; DLB 5;
    MTCW; SATA 47

Carson, Rachel Louise 1907-1964. . . **CLC 71**
    See also CA 77-80; CANR 35; MTCW;
    SATA 23

Carter, Angela (Olive)
    1940-1992 . . . . . . **CLC 5, 41, 76; SSC 13**
    See also CA 53-56; 136; CANR 12, 36;
    DLB 14; MTCW; SATA 66;
    SATA-Obit 70

Carter, Nick
    See Smith, Martin Cruz

Carver, Raymond
    1938-1988 . . . **CLC 22, 36, 53, 55; SSC 8**
    See also CA 33-36R; 126; CANR 17, 34;
    DLB 130; DLBY 84, 88; MTCW

Cary, (Arthur) Joyce (Lunel)
1888-1957 . . . . **TCLC 1, 29**
See also CA 104; CDBLB 1914-1945;
DLB 15, 100

Casanova de Seingalt, Giovanni Jacopo
1725-1798 . . . . **LC 13**

Casares, Adolfo Bioy
See Bioy Casares, Adolfo

Casely-Hayford, J(oseph) E(phraim)
1866-1930 . . . . **TCLC 24; BLC**
See also BW 2; CA 123

Casey, John (Dudley) 1939- . . . . **CLC 59**
See also BEST 90:2; CA 69-72; CANR 23

Casey, Michael 1947- . . . . **CLC 2**
See also CA 65-68; DLB 5

Casey, Patrick
See Thurman, Wallace (Henry)

Casey, Warren (Peter) 1935-1988 . . . **CLC 12**
See also CA 101; 127

Casona, Alejandro . . . . **CLC 49**
See also Alvarez, Alejandro Rodriguez

Cassavetes, John 1929-1989 . . . . **CLC 20**
See also CA 85-88; 127

Cassill, R(onald) V(erlin) 1919- . . . **CLC 4, 23**
See also CA 9-12R; CAAS 1; CANR 7, 45;
DLB 6

Cassity, (Allen) Turner 1929- . . . . **CLC 6, 42**
See also CA 17-20R; CAAS 8; CANR 11;
DLB 105

Castaneda, Carlos 1931(?)- . . . . **CLC 12**
See also CA 25-28R; CANR 32; HW;
MTCW

Castedo, Elena 1937- . . . . **CLC 65**
See also CA 132

Castedo-Ellerman, Elena
See Castedo, Elena

Castellanos, Rosario
1925-1974 . . . . **CLC 66; HLC**
See also CA 131; 53-56; DLB 113; HW

Castelvetro, Lodovico 1505-1571 . . . . . **LC 12**

Castiglione, Baldassare 1478-1529 . . . **LC 12**

Castle, Robert
See Hamilton, Edmond

Castro, Guillen de 1569-1631 . . . . **LC 19**

Castro, Rosalia de 1837-1885 . . . . . **NCLC 3**

Cather, Willa
See Cather, Willa Sibert

Cather, Willa Sibert
1873-1947 . . . . **TCLC 1, 11, 31; DA;**
SSC 2; WLC
See also CA 104; 128; CDALB 1865-1917;
DLB 9, 54, 78; DLBD 1; MTCW;
SATA 30

Catton, (Charles) Bruce
1899-1978 . . . . **CLC 35**
See also AITN 1; CA 5-8R; 81-84;
CANR 7; DLB 17; SATA 2;
SATA-Obit 24

Cauldwell, Frank
See King, Francis (Henry)

Caunitz, William J. 1933- . . . . **CLC 34**
See also BEST 89:3; CA 125; 130

Causley, Charles (Stanley) 1917- . . . . . **CLC 7**
See also CA 9-12R; CANR 5, 35; CLR 30;
DLB 27; MTCW; SATA 3, 66

Caute, David 1936- . . . . **CLC 29**
See also CA 1-4R; CAAS 4; CANR 1, 33;
DLB 14

Cavafy, C(onstantine) P(eter) . . . . . . **TCLC 2, 7**
See also Kavafis, Konstantinos Petrou

Cavallo, Evelyn
See Spark, Muriel (Sarah)

Cavanna, Betty . . . . **CLC 12**
See also Harrison, Elizabeth Cavanna
See also JRDA; MAICYA; SAAS 4;
SATA 1, 30

Caxton, William 1421(?)-1491(?) . . . . . **LC 17**

Cayrol, Jean 1911- . . . . **CLC 11**
See also CA 89-92; DLB 83

Cela, Camilo Jose
1916- . . . . **CLC 4, 13, 59; HLC**
See also BEST 90:2; CA 21-24R; CAAS 10;
CANR 21, 32; DLBY 89; HW; MTCW

Celan, Paul . . . . . . **CLC 10, 19, 53, 82; PC 10**
See also Antschel, Paul
See also DLB 69

Celine, Louis-Ferdinand
. . . . **CLC 1, 3, 4, 7, 9, 15, 47**
See also Destouches, Louis-Ferdinand
See also DLB 72

Cellini, Benvenuto 1500-1571 . . . . **LC 7**

Cendrars, Blaise
See Sauser-Hall, Frederic

Cernuda (y Bidon), Luis
1902-1963 . . . . **CLC 54**
See also CA 131; 89-92; DLB 134; HW

Cervantes (Saavedra), Miguel de
1547-1616 . . . . . **LC 6, 23; DA; SSC 12;**
WLC

Cesaire, Aime (Fernand)
1913- . . . . **CLC 19, 32; BLC**
See also BW 2; CA 65-68; CANR 24, 43;
MTCW

Chabon, Michael 1965(?)- . . . . **CLC 55**
See also CA 139

Chabrol, Claude 1930- . . . . **CLC 16**
See also CA 110

Challans, Mary 1905-1983
See Renault, Mary
See also CA 81-84; 111; SATA 23;
SATA-Obit 36

Challis, George
See Faust, Frederick (Schiller)

Chambers, Aidan 1934- . . . . **CLC 35**
See also CA 25-28R; CANR 12, 31; JRDA;
MAICYA; SAAS 12; SATA 1, 69

Chambers, James 1948-
See Cliff, Jimmy
See also CA 124

Chambers, Jessie
See Lawrence, D(avid) H(erbert Richards)

Chambers, Robert W. 1865-1933 . . . **TCLC 41**

Chandler, Raymond (Thornton)
1888-1959 . . . . **TCLC 1, 7**
See also CA 104; 129; CDALB 1929-1941;
DLBD 6; MTCW

Chang, Jung 1952- . . . . **CLC 71**
See also CA 142

Channing, William Ellery
1780-1842 . . . . **NCLC 17**
See also DLB 1, 59

Chaplin, Charles Spencer
1889-1977 . . . . **CLC 16**
See also Chaplin, Charlie
See also CA 81-84; 73-76

Chaplin, Charlie
See Chaplin, Charles Spencer
See also DLB 44

Chapman, George 1559(?)-1634 . . . . . . **LC 22**
See also DLB 62, 121

Chapman, Graham 1941-1989 . . . . . . **CLC 21**
See also Monty Python
See also CA 116; 129; CANR 35

Chapman, John Jay 1862-1933 . . . . . **TCLC 7**
See also CA 104

Chapman, Walker
See Silverberg, Robert

Chappell, Fred (Davis) 1936- . . . . **CLC 40, 78**
See also CA 5-8R; CAAS 4; CANR 8, 33;
DLB 6, 105

Char, Rene(-Emile)
1907-1988 . . . . **CLC 9, 11, 14, 55**
See also CA 13-16R; 124; CANR 32;
MTCW

Charby, Jay
See Ellison, Harlan (Jay)

Chardin, Pierre Teilhard de
See Teilhard de Chardin, (Marie Joseph)
Pierre

Charles I 1600-1649 . . . . **LC 13**

Charyn, Jerome 1937- . . . . **CLC 5, 8, 18**
See also CA 5-8R; CAAS 1; CANR 7;
DLBY 83; MTCW

Chase, Mary (Coyle) 1907-1981 . . . . . . **DC 1**
See also CA 77-80; 105; SATA 17;
SATA-Obit 29

Chase, Mary Ellen 1887-1973 . . . . **CLC 2**
See also CA 13-16; 41-44R; CAP 1;
SATA 10

Chase, Nicholas
See Hyde, Anthony

Chateaubriand, Francois Rene de
1768-1848 . . . . **NCLC 3**
See also DLB 119

Chatterje, Sarat Chandra 1876-1936(?)
See Chatterji, Saratchandra
See also CA 109

Chatterji, Bankim Chandra
1838-1894 . . . . **NCLC 19**

Chatterji, Saratchandra . . . . **TCLC 13**
See also Chatterje, Sarat Chandra

Chatterton, Thomas 1752-1770 . . . . **LC 3**
See also DLB 109

Chatwin, (Charles) Bruce
1940-1989 . . . . **CLC 28, 57, 59**
See also AAYA 4; BEST 90:1; CA 85-88;
127

Chaucer, Daniel
See Ford, Ford Madox

Chaucer, Geoffrey
1340(?)-1400 . . . . **LC 17; DA**
See also CDBLB Before 1660; DLB 146

Chaviaras, Strates 1935-
See Haviaras, Stratis
See also CA 105

Chayefsky, Paddy . . . . **CLC 23**
See also Chayefsky, Sidney
See also DLB 7, 44; DLBY 81

Chayefsky, Sidney 1923-1981
See Chayefsky, Paddy
See also CA 9-12R; 104; CANR 18

Chedid, Andree 1920- . . . . **CLC 47**
See also CA 145

Cheever, John
1912-1982 . . . . . . **CLC 3, 7, 8, 11, 15, 25,
64; DA; SSC 1; WLC**
See also CA 5-8R; 106; CABS 1; CANR 5,
27; CDALB 1941-1968; DLB 2, 102;
DLBY 80, 82; MTCW

Cheever, Susan 1943- . . . . **CLC 18, 48**
See also CA 103; CANR 27; DLBY 82

Chekhonte, Antosha
See Chekhov, Anton (Pavlovich)

Chekhov, Anton (Pavlovich)
1860-1904 . . . . . **TCLC 3, 10, 31, 55; DA;
SSC 2; WLC**
See also CA 104; 124

Chernyshevsky, Nikolay Gavrilovich
1828-1889 . . . . **NCLC 1**

Cherry, Carolyn Janice 1942-
See Cherryh, C. J.
See also CA 65-68; CANR 10

Cherryh, C. J. . . . . **CLC 35**
See also Cherry, Carolyn Janice
See also DLBY 80

Chesnutt, Charles W(addell)
1858-1932 . . . . **TCLC 5, 39; BLC; SSC 7**
See also BW 1; CA 106; 125; DLB 12, 50,
78; MTCW

Chester, Alfred 1929(?)-1971 . . . . **CLC 49**
See also CA 33-36R; DLB 130

Chesterton, G(ilbert) K(eith)
1874-1936 . . . . **TCLC 1, 6; SSC 1**
See also CA 104; 132; CDBLB 1914-1945;
DLB 10, 19, 34, 70, 98; MTCW;
SATA 27

Chiang Pin-chin 1904-1986
See Ding Ling
See also CA 118

Ch'ien Chung-shu 1910- . . . . **CLC 22**
See also CA 130; MTCW

Child, L. Maria
See Child, Lydia Maria

Child, Lydia Maria 1802-1880 . . . . **NCLC 6**
See also DLB 1, 74; SATA 67

Child, Mrs.
See Child, Lydia Maria

Child, Philip 1898-1978 . . . . **CLC 19, 68**
See also CA 13-14; CAP 1; SATA 47

Childress, Alice
1920- . . . . **CLC 12, 15; BLC; DC 4**
See also AAYA 8; BW 2; CA 45-48;
CANR 3, 27; CLR 14; DLB 7, 38; JRDA;
MAICYA; MTCW; SATA 7, 48

Chislett, (Margaret) Anne 1943- . . . . **CLC 34**

Chitty, Thomas Willes 1926- . . . . **CLC 11**
See also Hinde, Thomas
See also CA 5-8R

Chomette, Rene Lucien 1898-1981
See Clair, Rene
See also CA 103

Chopin, Kate . . . . **TCLC 5, 14; DA; SSC 8**
See also Chopin, Katherine
See also CDALB 1865-1917; DLB 12, 78

Chopin, Katherine 1851-1904
See Chopin, Kate
See also CA 104; 122

Chretien de Troyes
c. 12th cent. - . . . . **CMLC 10**

Christie
See Ichikawa, Kon

Christie, Agatha (Mary Clarissa)
1890-1976 . . . . . . **CLC 1, 6, 8, 12, 39, 48**
See also AAYA 9; AITN 1, 2; CA 17-20R;
61-64; CANR 10, 37; CDBLB 1914-1945;
DLB 13, 77; MTCW; SATA 36

Christie, (Ann) Philippa
See Pearce, Philippa
See also CA 5-8R; CANR 4

Christine de Pizan 1365(?)-1431(?) . . . . **LC 9**

Chubb, Elmer
See Masters, Edgar Lee

Chulkov, Mikhail Dmitrievich
1743-1792 . . . . **LC 2**

Churchill, Caryl 1938- . . . **CLC 31, 55; DC 5**
See also CA 102: CANR 22; DLB 13;
MTCW

Churchill, Charles 1731-1764 . . . . **LC 3**
See also DLB 109

Chute, Carolyn 1947- . . . . **CLC 39**
See also CA 123

Ciardi, John (Anthony)
1916-1986 . . . . **CLC 10, 40, 44**
See also CA 5-8R; 118; CAAS 2; CANR 5,
33; CLR 19; DLB 5; DLBY 86;
MAICYA; MTCW; SATA 1, 65;
SATA-Obit 46

Cicero, Marcus Tullius
106B.C.-43B.C. . . . . **CMLC 3**

Cimino, Michael 1943- . . . . **CLC 16**
See also CA 105

Cioran, E(mil) M. 1911- . . . . **CLC 64**
See also CA 25-28R

Cisneros, Sandra 1954- . . . . . . **CLC 69; HLC**
See also AAYA 9; CA 131; DLB 122; HW

Clair, Rene . . . . **CLC 20**
See also Chomette, Rene Lucien

Clampitt, Amy 1920- . . . . **CLC 32**
See also CA 110; CANR 29; DLB 105

Clancy, Thomas L., Jr. 1947-
See Clancy, Tom
See also CA 125; 131; MTCW

Clancy, Tom . . . . **CLC 45**
See also Clancy, Thomas L., Jr.
See also AAYA 9; BEST 89:1, 90:1

Clare, John 1793-1864 . . . . **NCLC 9**
See also DLB 55, 96

Clarin
See Alas (y Urena), Leopoldo (Enrique
Garcia)

Clark, Al C.
See Goines, Donald

Clark, (Robert) Brian 1932- . . . . **CLC 29**
See also CA 41-44R

Clark, Curt
See Westlake, Donald E(dwin)

Clark, Eleanor 1913- . . . . **CLC 5, 19**
See also CA 9-12R; CANR 41; DLB 6

Clark, J. P.
See Clark, John Pepper
See also DLB 117

Clark, John Pepper
1935- . . . . **CLC 38; BLC; DC 5**
See also Clark, J. P.
See also BW 1; CA 65-68; CANR 16

Clark, M. R.
See Clark, Mavis Thorpe

Clark, Mavis Thorpe 1909- . . . . **CLC 12**
See also CA 57-60; CANR 8, 37; CLR 30;
MAICYA; SAAS 5; SATA 8, 74

Clark, Walter Van Tilburg
1909-1971 . . . . **CLC 28**
See also CA 9-12R; 33-36R; DLB 9;
SATA 8

Clarke, Arthur C(harles)
1917- . . . . . . **CLC 1, 4, 13, 18, 35; SSC 3**
See also AAYA 4; CA 1-4R; CANR 2, 28;
JRDA; MAICYA; MTCW; SATA 13, 70

Clarke, Austin 1896-1974 . . . . **CLC 6, 9**
See also CA 29-32; 49-52; CAP 2; DLB 10,
20

Clarke, Austin C(hesterfield)
1934- . . . . **CLC 8, 53; BLC**
See also BW 1; CA 25-28R; CAAS 16;
CANR 14, 32; DLB 53, 125

Clarke, Gillian 1937- . . . . **CLC 61**
See also CA 106; DLB 40

Clarke, Marcus (Andrew Hislop)
1846-1881 . . . . **NCLC 19**

Clarke, Shirley 1925- . . . . **CLC 16**

Clash, The
See Headon, (Nicky) Topper; Jones, Mick;
Simonon, Paul; Strummer, Joe

Claudel, Paul (Louis Charles Marie)
1868-1955 . . . . **TCLC 2, 10**
See also CA 104

Clavell, James (duMaresq)
1925- . . . . **CLC 6, 25**
See also CA 25-28R; CANR 26; MTCW

Cleaver, (Leroy) Eldridge
1935- . . . . **CLC 30; BLC**
See also BW 1; CA 21-24R; CANR 16

Cleese, John (Marwood) 1939- . . . . . **CLC 21**
See also Monty Python
See also CA 112; 116; CANR 35; MTCW

Cleishbotham, Jebediah
See Scott, Walter

Cleland, John 1710-1789 . . . . **LC 2**
See also DLB 39

Coppard, A(lfred) E(dgar)
    1878-1957 . . . . **TCLC 5**
    See also CA 114; YABC 1

Coppee, Francois 1842-1908 . . . . . . **TCLC 25**

Coppola, Francis Ford 1939- . . . . **CLC 16**
    See also CA 77-80; CANR 40; DLB 44

Corbiere, Tristan 1845-1875 . . . . . **NCLC 43**

Corcoran, Barbara 1911- . . . . **CLC 17**
    See also AAYA 14; CA 21-24R; CAAS 2;
    CANR 11, 28; DLB 52; JRDA; SATA 3,
    77

Cordelier, Maurice
    See Giraudoux, (Hippolyte) Jean

Corelli, Marie 1855-1924 . . . . **TCLC 51**
    See also Mackay, Mary
    See also DLB 34

Corman, Cid . . . . **CLC 9**
    See also Corman, Sidney
    See also CAAS 2; DLB 5

Corman, Sidney 1924-
    See Corman, Cid
    See also CA 85-88; CANR 44

Cormier, Robert (Edmund)
    1925- . . . . **CLC 12, 30; DA**
    See also AAYA 3; CA 1-4R; CANR 5, 23;
    CDALB 1968-1988; CLR 12; DLB 52;
    JRDA; MAICYA; MTCW; SATA 10, 45

Corn, Alfred (DeWitt III) 1943- . . . . **CLC 33**
    See also CA 104; CANR 44; DLB 120;
    DLBY 80

Cornwell, David (John Moore)
    1931- . . . . **CLC 9, 15**
    See also le Carre, John
    See also CA 5-8R; CANR 13, 33; MTCW

Corso, (Nunzio) Gregory 1930- . . . **CLC 1, 11**
    See also CA 5-8R; CANR 41; DLB 5, 16;
    MTCW

Cortazar, Julio
    1914-1984 . . . . . . **CLC 2, 3, 5, 10, 13, 15,**
                        33, 34; HLC; SSC 7
    See also CA 21-24R; CANR 12, 32;
    DLB 113; HW; MTCW

Corwin, Cecil
    See Kornbluth, C(yril) M.

Cosic, Dobrica 1921- . . . . **CLC 14**
    See also CA 122; 138

Costain, Thomas B(ertram)
    1885-1965 . . . . **CLC 30**
    See also CA 5-8R; 25-28R; DLB 9

Costantini, Humberto
    1924(?)-1987 . . . . **CLC 49**
    See also CA 131; 122; HW

Costello, Elvis 1955- . . . . **CLC 21**

Cotter, Joseph Seamon Sr.
    1861-1949 . . . . **TCLC 28; BLC**
    See also BW 1; CA 124; DLB 50

Couch, Arthur Thomas Quiller
    See Quiller-Couch, Arthur Thomas

Coulton, James
    See Hansen, Joseph

Couperus, Louis (Marie Anne)
    1863-1923 . . . . **TCLC 15**
    See also CA 115

Coupland, Douglas 1961- . . . . **CLC 85**
    See also CA 142

Court, Wesli
    See Turco, Lewis (Putnam)

Courtenay, Bryce 1933- . . . . **CLC 59**
    See also CA 138

Courtney, Robert
    See Ellison, Harlan (Jay)

Cousteau, Jacques-Yves 1910- . . . . . . **CLC 30**
    See also CA 65-68; CANR 15; MTCW;
    SATA 38

Coward, Noel (Peirce)
    1899-1973 . . . . **CLC 1, 9, 29, 51**
    See also AITN 1; CA 17-18; 41-44R;
    CANR 35; CAP 2; CDBLB 1914-1945;
    DLB 10; MTCW

Cowley, Malcolm 1898-1989 . . . . **CLC 39**
    See also CA 5-8R; 128; CANR 3; DLB 4,
    48; DLBY 81, 89; MTCW

Cowper, William 1731-1800 . . . . . . **NCLC 8**
    See also DLB 104, 109

Cox, William Trevor 1928- . . . **CLC 9, 14, 71**
    See Trevor, William
    See also CA 9-12R; CANR 4, 37; DLB 14;
    MTCW

Cozzens, James Gould
    1903-1978 . . . . **CLC 1, 4, 11**
    See also CA 9-12R; 81-84; CANR 19;
    CDALB 1941-1968; DLB 9; DLBD 2;
    DLBY 84; MTCW

Crabbe, George 1754-1832 . . . . . . **NCLC 26**
    See also DLB 93

Craig, A. A.
    See Anderson, Poul (William)

Craik, Dinah Maria (Mulock)
    1826-1887 . . . . **NCLC 38**
    See also DLB 35; MAICYA; SATA 34

Cram, Ralph Adams 1863-1942 . . . . **TCLC 45**

Crane, (Harold) Hart
    1899-1932 . . . . **TCLC 2, 5; DA; PC 3;**
                        WLC
    See also CA 104; 127; CDALB 1917-1929;
    DLB 4, 48; MTCW

Crane, R(onald) S(almon)
    1886-1967 . . . . **CLC 27**
    See also CA 85-88; DLB 63

Crane, Stephen (Townley)
    1871-1900 . . . . **TCLC 11, 17, 32; DA;**
                        SSC 7; WLC
    See also CA 109; 140; CDALB 1865-1917;
    DLB 12, 54, 78; YABC 2

Crase, Douglas 1944- . . . . **CLC 58**
    See also CA 106

Crashaw, Richard 1612(?)-1649 . . . . . . **LC 24**
    See also DLB 126

Craven, Margaret 1901-1980 . . . . **CLC 17**
    See also CA 103

Crawford, F(rancis) Marion
    1854-1909 . . . . **TCLC 10**
    See also CA 107; DLB 71

Crawford, Isabella Valancy
    1850-1887 . . . . **NCLC 12**
    See also DLB 92

Crayon, Geoffrey
    See Irving, Washington

Creasey, John 1908-1973 . . . . **CLC 11**
    See also CA 5-8R; 41-44R; CANR 8;
    DLB 77; MTCW

Crebillon, Claude Prosper Jolyot de (fils)
    1707-1777 . . . . **LC 1**

Credo
    See Creasey, John

Creeley, Robert (White)
    1926- . . . . . **CLC 1, 2, 4, 8, 11, 15, 36, 78**
    See also CA 1-4R; CAAS 10; CANR 23, 43;
    DLB 5, 16; MTCW

Crews, Harry (Eugene)
    1935- . . . . **CLC 6, 23, 49**
    See also AITN 1; CA 25-28R; CANR 20;
    DLB 6, 143; MTCW

Crichton, (John) Michael
    1942- . . . . **CLC 2, 6, 54**
    See also AAYA 10; AITN 2; CA 25-28R;
    CANR 13, 40; DLBY 81; JRDA;
    MTCW; SATA 9

Crispin, Edmund . . . . **CLC 22**
    See also Montgomery, (Robert) Bruce
    See also DLB 87

Cristofer, Michael 1945(?)- . . . . **CLC 28**
    See also CA 110; DLB 7

Croce, Benedetto 1866-1952 . . . . . . **TCLC 37**
    See also CA 120

Crockett, David 1786-1836 . . . . **NCLC 8**
    See also DLB 3, 11

Crockett, Davy
    See Crockett, David

Crofts, Freeman Wills
    1879-1957 . . . . **TCLC 55**
    See also CA 115; DLB 77

Croker, John Wilson 1780-1857 . . **NCLC 10**
    See also DLB 110

Crommelynck, Fernand 1885-1970 . . **CLC 75**
    See also CA 89-92

Cronin, A(rchibald) J(oseph)
    1896-1981 . . . . **CLC 32**
    See also CA 1-4R; 102; CANR 5; SATA 47;
    SATA-Obit 25

Cross, Amanda
    See Heilbrun, Carolyn G(old)

Crothers, Rachel 1878(?)-1958 . . . . . **TCLC 19**
    See also CA 113; DLB 7

Croves, Hal
    See Traven, B.

Crowfield, Christopher
    See Stowe, Harriet (Elizabeth) Beecher

Crowley, Aleister . . . . **TCLC 7**
    See also Crowley, Edward Alexander

Crowley, Edward Alexander 1875-1947
    See Crowley, Aleister
    See also CA 104

Crowley, John 1942- . . . . **CLC 57**
    See also CA 61-64; CANR 43; DLBY 82;
    SATA 65

Crud
    See Crumb, R(obert)

Crumarums
    See Crumb, R(obert)

Crumb, R(obert) 1943- . . . . **CLC 17**
    See also CA 106

Dickey, James (Lafayette)
1923- .... CLC 1, 2, 4, 7, 10, 15, 47
See also AITN 1, 2; CA 9-12R; CABS 2;
CANR 10; CDALB 1968-1988; DLB 5;
DLBD 7; DLBY 82, 93; MTCW

Dickey, William 1928-1994 ..... CLC 3, 28
See also CA 9-12R; 145; CANR 24; DLB 5

Dickinson, Charles 1951-......... CLC 49
See also CA 128

Dickinson, Emily (Elizabeth)
1830-1886 .. NCLC 21; DA; PC 1; WLC
See also CDALB 1865-1917; DLB 1;
SATA 29

Dickinson, Peter (Malcolm)
1927- .... CLC 12, 35
See also AAYA 9; CA 41-44R; CANR 31;
CLR 29; DLB 87; JRDA; MAICYA;
SATA 5, 62

Dickson, Carr
See Carr, John Dickson

Dickson, Carter
See Carr, John Dickson

Diderot, Denis 1713-1784 .... LC 26

Didion, Joan 1934-..... CLC 1, 3, 8, 14, 32
See also AITN 1; CA 5-8R; CANR 14;
CDALB 1968-1988; DLB 2; DLBY 81,
86; MTCW

Dietrich, Robert
See Hunt, E(verette) Howard, Jr.

Dillard, Annie 1945-........... CLC 9, 60
See also AAYA 6; CA 49-52; CANR 3, 43;
DLBY 80; MTCW; SATA 10

Dillard, R(ichard) H(enry) W(ilde)
1937- .... CLC 5
See also CA 21-24R; CAAS 7; CANR 10;
DLB 5

Dillon, Eilis 1920-............... CLC 17
See also CA 9-12R; CAAS 3; CANR 4, 38;
CLR 26; MAICYA; SATA 2, 74

Dimont, Penelope
See Mortimer, Penelope (Ruth)

Dinesen, Isak........... CLC 10, 29; SSC 7
See also Blixen, Karen (Christentze
Dinesen)

Ding Ling........................ CLC 68
See also Chiang Pin-chin

Disch, Thomas M(ichael) 1940-... CLC 7, 36
See also CA 21-24R; CAAS 4; CANR 17,
36; CLR 18; DLB 8; MAICYA; MTCW;
SAAS 15; SATA 54

Disch, Tom
See Disch, Thomas M(ichael)

d'Isly, Georges
See Simenon, Georges (Jacques Christian)

Disraeli, Benjamin 1804-1881 .. NCLC 2, 39
See also DLB 21, 55

Ditcum, Steve
See Crumb, R(obert)

Dixon, Paige
See Corcoran, Barbara

Dixon, Stephen 1936-..... CLC 52; SSC 16
See also CA 89-92; CANR 17, 40; DLB 130

Dobell, Sydney Thompson
1824-1874 .... NCLC 43
See also DLB 32

Doblin, Alfred .... TCLC 13
See also Doeblin, Alfred

Dobrolyubov, Nikolai Alexandrovich
1836-1861 .... NCLC 5

Dobyns, Stephen 1941-.......... CLC 37
See also CA 45-48; CANR 2, 18

Doctorow, E(dgar) L(aurence)
1931- ..... CLC 6, 11, 15, 18, 37, 44, 65
See also AITN 2; BEST 89:3; CA 45-48;
CANR 2, 33; CDALB 1968-1988; DLB 2,
28; DLBY 80; MTCW

Dodgson, Charles Lutwidge 1832-1898
See Carroll, Lewis
See also CLR 2; DA; MAICYA; YABC 2

Dodson, Owen (Vincent)
1914-1983 .... CLC 79; BLC
See also BW 1; CA 65-68; 110; CANR 24;
DLB 76

Doeblin, Alfred 1878-1957....... TCLC 13
See also Doblin, Alfred
See also CA 110; 141; DLB 66

Doerr, Harriet 1910- .... CLC 34
See also CA 117; 122

Domecq, H(onorio) Bustos
See Bioy Casares, Adolfo; Borges, Jorge
Luis

Domini, Rey
See Lorde, Audre (Geraldine)

Dominique
See Proust, (Valentin-Louis-George-Eugene-)
Marcel

Don, A
See Stephen, Leslie

Donaldson, Stephen R. 1947-...... CLC 46
See also CA 89-92; CANR 13

Donleavy, J(ames) P(atrick)
1926- .... CLC 1, 4, 6, 10, 45
See also AITN 2; CA 9-12R; CANR 24;
DLB 6; MTCW

Donne, John
1572-1631 .... LC 10, 24; DA; PC 1
See also CDBLB Before 1660; DLB 121

Donnell, David 1939(?)-........... CLC 34

Donoso (Yanez), Jose
1924- .... CLC 4, 8, 11, 32; HLC
See also CA 81-84; CANR 32; DLB 113;
HW; MTCW

Donovan, John 1928-1992 .... CLC 35
See also CA 97-100; 137; CLR 3;
MAICYA; SATA 29

Don Roberto
See Cunninghame Graham, R(obert)
B(ontine)

Doolittle, Hilda
1886-1961 ..... CLC 3, 8, 14, 31, 34, 73;
DA; PC 5; WLC
See also H. D.
See also CA 97-100; CANR 35; DLB 4, 45;
MTCW

Dorfman, Ariel 1942-..... CLC 48, 77; HLC
See also CA 124; 130; HW

Dorn, Edward (Merton) 1929-... CLC 10, 18
See also CA 93-96; CANR 42; DLB 5

Dorsan, Luc
See Simenon, Georges (Jacques Christian)

Dorsange, Jean
See Simenon, Georges (Jacques Christian)

Dos Passos, John (Roderigo)
1896-1970 ...... CLC 1, 4, 8, 11, 15, 25,
34, 82; DA; WLC
See also CA 1-4R; 29-32R; CANR 3;
CDALB 1929-1941; DLB 4, 9; DLBD 1;
MTCW

Dossage, Jean
See Simenon, Georges (Jacques Christian)

Dostoevsky, Fedor Mikhailovich
1821-1881 ...... NCLC 2, 7, 21, 33, 43;
DA; SSC 2; WLC

Doughty, Charles M(ontagu)
1843-1926 .... TCLC 27
See also CA 115; DLB 19, 57

Douglas, Ellen .... CLC 73
See also Haxton, Josephine Ayres;
Williamson, Ellen Douglas

Douglas, Gavin 1475(?)-1522........ LC 20

Douglas, Keith 1920-1944 .... TCLC 40
See also DLB 27

Douglas, Leonard
See Bradbury, Ray (Douglas)

Douglas, Michael
See Crichton, (John) Michael

Douglass, Frederick
1817(?)-1895 .... NCLC 7; BLC; DA;
WLC
See also CDALB 1640-1865; DLB 1, 43, 50,
79; SATA 29

Dourado, (Waldomiro Freitas) Autran
1926- .... CLC 23, 60
See also CA 25-28R; CANR 34

Dourado, Waldomiro Autran
See Dourado, (Waldomiro Freitas) Autran

Dove, Rita (Frances)
1952- .... CLC 50, 81; PC 6
See also BW 2; CA 109; CAAS 19;
CANR 27, 42; DLB 120

Dowell, Coleman 1925-1985........ CLC 60
See also CA 25-28R; 117; CANR 10;
DLB 130

Dowson, Ernest Christopher
1867-1900 .... TCLC 4
See also CA 105; DLB 19, 135

Doyle, A. Conan
See Doyle, Arthur Conan

Doyle, Arthur Conan
1859-1930 .... TCLC 7; DA; SSC 12;
WLC
See also AAYA 14; CA 104; 122;
CDBLB 1890-1914; DLB 18, 70; MTCW;
SATA 24

Doyle, Conan
See Doyle, Arthur Conan

Doyle, John
See Graves, Robert (von Ranke)

Doyle, Roddy 1958(?)-............ CLC 81
See also AAYA 14; CA 143

Doyle, Sir A. Conan
See Doyle, Arthur Conan

Doyle, Sir Arthur Conan
See Doyle, Arthur Conan

Engel, Marian 1933-1985. . . . . **CLC 36**
See also CA 25-28R; CANR 12; DLB 53

Engelhardt, Frederick
See Hubbard, L(afayette) Ron(ald)

Enright, D(ennis) J(oseph)
1920- . . . . **CLC 4, 8, 31**
See also CA 1-4R; CANR 1, 42; DLB 27;
SATA 25

Enzensberger, Hans Magnus
1929- . . . . **CLC 43**
See also CA 116; 119

Ephron, Nora 1941- . . . . **CLC 17, 31**
See also AITN 2; CA 65-68; CANR 12, 39

Epsilon
See Betjeman, John

Epstein, Daniel Mark 1948- . . . . **CLC 7**
See also CA 49-52; CANR 2

Epstein, Jacob 1956- . . . . **CLC 19**
See also CA 114

Epstein, Joseph 1937- . . . . **CLC 39**
See also CA 112; 119

Epstein, Leslie 1938- . . . . **CLC 27**
See also CA 73-76; CAAS 12; CANR 23

Equiano, Olaudah
1745(?)-1797 . . . . **LC 16; BLC**
See also DLB 37, 50

Erasmus, Desiderius 1469(?)-1536. . . . **LC 16**

Erdman, Paul E(mil) 1932- . . . . **CLC 25**
See also AITN 1; CA 61-64; CANR 13, 43

Erdrich, Louise 1954- . . . . **CLC 39, 54**
See also AAYA 10; BEST 89:1; CA 114;
CANR 41; MTCW; NNAL

Erenburg, Ilya (Grigoryevich)
See Ehrenburg, Ilya (Grigoryevich)

Erickson, Stephen Michael 1950-
See Erickson, Steve
See also CA 129

Erickson, Steve . . . . **CLC 64**
See also Erickson, Stephen Michael

Ericson, Walter
See Fast, Howard (Melvin)

Eriksson, Buntel
See Bergman, (Ernst) Ingmar

Eschenbach, Wolfram von
See Wolfram von Eschenbach

Eseki, Bruno
See Mphahlele, Ezekiel

Esenin, Sergei (Alexandrovich)
1895-1925 . . . . **TCLC 4**
See also CA 104

Eshleman, Clayton 1935- . . . . **CLC 7**
See also CA 33-36R; CAAS 6; DLB 5

Espriella, Don Manuel Alvarez
See Southey, Robert

Espriu, Salvador 1913-1985 . . . . **CLC 9**
See also CA 115; DLB 134

Espronceda, Jose de 1808-1842 . . . **NCLC 39**

Esse, James
See Stephens, James

Esterbrook, Tom
See Hubbard, L(afayette) Ron(ald)

Estleman, Loren D. 1952- . . . . **CLC 48**
See also CA 85-88; CANR 27; MTCW

Eugenides, Jeffrey 1960(?)- . . . . **CLC 81**
See also CA 144

Euripides c. 485B.C.-406B.C. . . . . **DC 4**
See also DA

Evan, Evin
See Faust, Frederick (Schiller)

Evans, Evan
See Faust, Frederick (Schiller)

Evans, Marian
See Eliot, George

Evans, Mary Ann
See Eliot, George

Evarts, Esther
See Benson, Sally

Everett, Percival L. 1956- . . . . **CLC 57**
See also BW 2; CA 129

Everson, R(onald) G(ilmour)
1903- . . . . **CLC 27**
See also CA 17-20R; DLB 88

Everson, William (Oliver)
1912-1994 . . . . **CLC 1, 5, 14**
See also CA 9-12R; 145; CANR 20; DLB 5,
16; MTCW

Evtushenko, Evgenii Aleksandrovich
See Yevtushenko, Yevgeny (Alexandrovich)

Ewart, Gavin (Buchanan)
1916- . . . . **CLC 13, 46**
See also CA 89-92; CANR 17, 46; DLB 40;
MTCW

Ewers, Hanns Heinz 1871-1943 . . . **TCLC 12**
See also CA 109

Ewing, Frederick R.
See Sturgeon, Theodore (Hamilton)

Exley, Frederick (Earl)
1929-1992 . . . . **CLC 6, 11**
See also AITN 2; CA 81-84; 138; DLB 143;
DLBY 81

Eynhardt, Guillermo
See Quiroga, Horacio (Sylvestre)

Ezekiel, Nissim 1924- . . . . **CLC 61**
See also CA 61-64

Ezekiel, Tish O'Dowd 1943- . . . . **CLC 34**
See also CA 129

Fadeyev, A.
See Bulgya, Alexander Alexandrovich

Fadeyev, Alexander . . . . **TCLC 53**
See also Bulgya, Alexander Alexandrovich

Fagen, Donald 1948- . . . . **CLC 26**

Fainzilberg, Ilya Arnoldovich 1897-1937
See Ilf, Ilya
See also CA 120

Fair, Ronald L. 1932- . . . . **CLC 18**
See also BW 1; CA 69-72; CANR 25;
DLB 33

Fairbairns, Zoe (Ann) 1948- . . . . **CLC 32**
See also CA 103; CANR 21

Falco, Gian
See Papini, Giovanni

Falconer, James
See Kirkup, James

Falconer, Kenneth
See Kornbluth, C(yril) M.

Falkland, Samuel
See Heijermans, Herman

Fallaci, Oriana 1930- . . . . **CLC 11**
See also CA 77-80; CANR 15; MTCW

Faludy, George 1913- . . . . **CLC 42**
See also CA 21-24R

Faludy, Gyoergy
See Faludy, George

Fanon, Frantz 1925-1961 . . . . . **CLC 74; BLC**
See also BW 1; CA 116; 89-92

Fanshawe, Ann 1625-1680 . . . . **LC 11**

Fante, John (Thomas) 1911-1983 . . . **CLC 60**
See also CA 69-72; 109; CANR 23;
DLB 130; DLBY 83

Farah, Nuruddin 1945- . . . . **CLC 53; BLC**
See also BW 2; CA 106; DLB 125

Fargue, Leon-Paul 1876(?)-1947 . . . **TCLC 11**
See also CA 109

Farigoule, Louis
See Romains, Jules

Farina, Richard 1936(?)-1966 . . . . **CLC 9**
See also CA 81-84; 25-28R

Farley, Walter (Lorimer)
1915-1989 . . . . **CLC 17**
See also CA 17-20R; CANR 8, 29; DLB 22;
JRDA; MAICYA; SATA 2, 43

Farmer, Philip Jose 1918- . . . . **CLC 1, 19**
See also CA 1-4R; CANR 4, 35; DLB 8;
MTCW

Farquhar, George 1677-1707 . . . . **LC 21**
See also DLB 84

Farrell, J(ames) G(ordon)
1935-1979 . . . . **CLC 6**
See also CA 73-76; 89-92; CANR 36;
DLB 14; MTCW

Farrell, James T(homas)
1904-1979 . . . . **CLC 1, 4, 8, 11, 66**
See also CA 5-8R; 89-92; CANR 9; DLB 4,
9, 86; DLBD 2; MTCW

Farren, Richard J.
See Betjeman, John

Farren, Richard M.
See Betjeman, John

Fassbinder, Rainer Werner
1946-1982 . . . . **CLC 20**
See also CA 93-96; 106; CANR 31

Fast, Howard (Melvin) 1914- . . . . . . **CLC 23**
See also CA 1-4R; CAAS 18; CANR 1, 33;
DLB 9; SATA 7

Faulcon, Robert
See Holdstock, Robert P.

Faulkner, William (Cuthbert)
1897-1962 . . . . . **CLC 1, 3, 6, 8, 9, 11, 14,
18, 28, 52, 68; DA; SSC 1; WLC**
See also AAYA 7; CA 81-84; CANR 33;
CDALB 1929-1941; DLB 9, 11, 44, 102;
DLBD 2; DLBY 86; MTCW

Fauset, Jessie Redmon
1884(?)-1961 . . . . **CLC 19, 54; BLC**
See also BW 1; CA 109; DLB 51

Faust, Frederick (Schiller)
1892-1944(?) . . . . **TCLC 49**
See also CA 108

Faust, Irvin 1924-................. **CLC 8**
See also CA 33-36R; CANR 28; DLB 2, 28;
DLBY 80

Fawkes, Guy
See Benchley, Robert (Charles)

Fearing, Kenneth (Flexner)
1902-1961 .... **CLC 51**
See also CA 93-96; DLB 9

Fecamps, Elise
See Creasey, John

Federman, Raymond 1928- ...... **CLC 6, 47**
See also CA 17-20R; CAAS 8; CANR 10,
43; DLBY 80

Federspiel, J(uerg) F. 1931-........ **CLC 42**

Feiffer, Jules (Ralph) 1929-.... **CLC 2, 8, 64**
See also AAYA 3; CA 17-20R; CANR 30;
DLB 7, 44; MTCW; SATA 8, 61

Feige, Hermann Albert Otto Maximilian
See Traven, B.

Feinberg, David B. 1956-.......... **CLC 59**
See also CA 135

Feinstein, Elaine 1930-........... **CLC 36**
See also CA 69-72; CAAS 1; CANR 31;
DLB 14, 40; MTCW

Feldman, Irving (Mordecai) 1928-.... **CLC 7**
See also CA 1-4R; CANR 1

Fellini, Federico 1920-1993 ..... **CLC 16, 85**
See also CA 65-68; 143; CANR 33

Felsen, Henry Gregor 1916- .... **CLC 17**
See also CA 1-4R; CANR 1; SAAS 2;
SATA 1

Fenton, James Martin 1949-....... **CLC 32**
See also CA 102; DLB 40

Ferber, Edna 1887-1968........... **CLC 18**
See also AITN 1; CA 5-8R; 25-28R; DLB 9,
28, 86; MTCW; SATA 7

Ferguson, Helen
See Kavan, Anna

Ferguson, Samuel 1810-1886..... **NCLC 33**
See also DLB 32

Ferling, Lawrence
See Ferlinghetti, Lawrence (Monsanto)

Ferlinghetti, Lawrence (Monsanto)
1919(?)-........ **CLC 2, 6, 10, 27; PC 1**
See also CA 5-8R; CANR 3, 41;
CDALB 1941-1968; DLB 5, 16; MTCW

Fernandez, Vicente Garcia Huidobro
See Huidobro Fernandez, Vicente Garcia

Ferrer, Gabriel (Francisco Victor) Miro
See Miro (Ferrer), Gabriel (Francisco
Victor)

Ferrier, Susan (Edmonstone)
1782-1854 .... **NCLC 8**
See also DLB 116

Ferrigno, Robert 1948(?)-.......... **CLC 65**
See also CA 140

Feuchtwanger, Lion 1884-1958 ..... **TCLC 3**
See also CA 104; DLB 66

Feuillet, Octave 1821-1890 ...... **NCLC 45**

Feydeau, Georges (Leon Jules Marie)
1862-1921 .... **TCLC 22**
See also CA 113

Ficino, Marsilio 1433-1499 .... **LC 12**

Fiedeler, Hans
See Doeblin, Alfred

Fiedler, Leslie A(aron)
1917-................. **CLC 4, 13, 24**
See also CA 9-12R; CANR 7; DLB 28, 67;
MTCW

Field, Andrew 1938-.............. **CLC 44**
See also CA 97-100; CANR 25

Field, Eugene 1850-1895 .... **NCLC 3**
See also DLB 23, 42, 140; MAICYA;
SATA 16

Field, Gans T.
See Wellman, Manly Wade

Field, Michael .... **TCLC 43**

Field, Peter
See Hobson, Laura Z(ametkin)

Fielding, Henry
1707-1754 .... **LC 1; DA; WLC**
See also CDBLB 1660-1789; DLB 39, 84,
101

Fielding, Sarah 1710-1768 .... **LC 1**
See also DLB 39

Fierstein, Harvey (Forbes) 1954- ... **CLC 33**
See also CA 123; 129

Figes, Eva 1932-................. **CLC 31**
See also CA 53-56; CANR 4, 44; DLB 14

Finch, Robert (Duer Claydon)
1900-...................... **CLC 18**
See also CA 57-60; CANR 9, 24; DLB 88

Findley, Timothy 1930-........... **CLC 27**
See also CA 25-28R; CANR 12, 42;
DLB 53

Fink, William
See Mencken, H(enry) L(ouis)

Firbank, Louis 1942-
See Reed, Lou
See also CA 117

Firbank, (Arthur Annesley) Ronald
1886-1926 .... **TCLC 1**
See also CA 104; DLB 36

Fisher, M(ary) F(rances) K(ennedy)
1908-1992 .... **CLC 76**
See also CA 77-80; 138; CANR 44

Fisher, Roy 1930-................. **CLC 25**
See also CA 81-84; CAAS 10; CANR 16;
DLB 40

Fisher, Rudolph
1897-1934 .... **TCLC 11; BLC**
See also BW 1; CA 107; 124; DLB 51, 102

Fisher, Vardis (Alvero) 1895-1968.... **CLC 7**
See also CA 5-8R; 25-28R; DLB 9

Fiske, Tarleton
See Bloch, Robert (Albert)

Fitch, Clarke
See Sinclair, Upton (Beall)

Fitch, John IV
See Cormier, Robert (Edmund)

Fitzgerald, Captain Hugh
See Baum, L(yman) Frank

FitzGerald, Edward 1809-1883 .... **NCLC 9**
See also DLB 32

Fitzgerald, F(rancis) Scott (Key)
1896-1940 ...... **TCLC 1, 6, 14, 28, 55;**
DA; SSC 6; WLC
See also AITN 1; CA 110; 123;
CDALB 1917-1929; DLB 4, 9, 86;
DLBD 1; DLBY 81; MTCW

Fitzgerald, Penelope 1916-... **CLC 19, 51, 61**
See also CA 85-88; CAAS 10; DLB 14

Fitzgerald, Robert (Stuart)
1910-1985 .... **CLC 39**
See also CA 1-4R; 114; CANR 1; DLBY 80

FitzGerald, Robert D(avid)
1902-1987 .... **CLC 19**
See also CA 17-20R

Fitzgerald, Zelda (Sayre)
1900-1948 .... **TCLC 52**
See also CA 117; 126; DLBY 84

Flanagan, Thomas (James Bonner)
1923-..................... **CLC 25, 52**
See also CA 108; DLBY 80; MTCW

Flaubert, Gustave
1821-1880 .... **NCLC 2, 10, 19; DA;**
SSC 11; WLC
See also DLB 119

Flecker, (Herman) James Elroy
1884-1915 .... **TCLC 43**
See also CA 109; DLB 10, 19

Fleming, Ian (Lancaster)
1908-1964 .... **CLC 3, 30**
See also CA 5-8R; CDBLB 1945-1960;
DLB 87; MTCW; SATA 9

Fleming, Thomas (James) 1927- .... **CLC 37**
See also CA 5-8R; CANR 10; SATA 8

Fletcher, John Gould 1886-1950... **TCLC 35**
See also CA 107; DLB 4, 45

Fleur, Paul
See Pohl, Frederik

Flooglebuckle, Al
See Spiegelman, Art

Flying Officer X
See Bates, H(erbert) E(rnest)

Fo, Dario 1926-................. **CLC 32**
See also CA 116; 128; MTCW

Fogarty, Jonathan Titulescu Esq.
See Farrell, James T(homas)

Folke, Will
See Bloch, Robert (Albert)

Follett, Ken(neth Martin) 1949- .... **CLC 18**
See also AAYA 6; BEST 89:4; CA 81-84;
CANR 13, 33; DLB 87; DLBY 81;
MTCW

Fontane, Theodor 1819-1898 ..... **NCLC 26**
See also DLB 129

Foote, Horton 1916-.............. **CLC 51**
See also CA 73-76; CANR 34; DLB 26

Foote, Shelby 1916- .... **CLC 75**
See also CA 5-8R; CANR 3, 45; DLB 2, 17

Forbes, Esther 1891-1967.......... **CLC 12**
See also CA 13-14; 25-28R; CAP 1;
CLR 27; DLB 22; JRDA; MAICYA;
SATA 2

Forche, Carolyn (Louise)
1950- .... **CLC 25, 83; PC 10**
See also CA 109; 117; DLB 5

Ford, Elbur
See Hibbert, Eleanor Alice Burford

Ford, Ford Madox
1873-1939 . . . . **TCLC 1, 15, 39, 57**
See also CA 104; 132; CDBLB 1914-1945;
DLB 34, 98; MTCW

Ford, John 1895-1973. . . . . **CLC 16**
See also CA 45-48

Ford, Richard 1944- . . . . **CLC 46**
See also CA 69-72; CANR 11

Ford, Webster
See Masters, Edgar Lee

Foreman, Richard 1937-. . . . . **CLC 50**
See also CA 65-68; CANR 32

Forester, C(ecil) S(cott)
1899-1966 . . . . **CLC 35**
See also CA 73-76; 25-28R; SATA 13

Forez
See Mauriac, Francois (Charles)

Forman, James Douglas 1932-. . . . . **CLC 21**
See also CA 9-12R; CANR 4, 19, 42;
JRDA; MAICYA; SATA 8, 70

Fornes, Maria Irene 1930-. . . . . . **CLC 39, 61**
See also CA 25-28R; CANR 28; DLB 7;
HW; MTCW

Forrest, Leon 1937- . . . . **CLC 4**
See also BW 2; CA 89-92; CAAS 7;
CANR 25; DLB 33

Forster, E(dward) M(organ)
1879-1970 . . . . . **CLC 1, 2, 3, 4, 9, 10, 13,**
15, 22, 45, 77; DA; WLC
See also AAYA 2; CA 13-14; 25-28R;
CANR 45; CAP 1; CDBLB 1914-1945;
DLB 34, 98; DLBD 10; MTCW;
SATA 57

Forster, John 1812-1876 . . . . **NCLC 11**
See also DLB 144

Forsyth, Frederick 1938-. . . . . . **CLC 2, 5, 36**
See also BEST 89:4; CA 85-88; CANR 38;
DLB 87; MTCW

Forten, Charlotte L. . . . . **TCLC 16; BLC**
See also Grimke, Charlotte L(ottie) Forten
See also DLB 50

Foscolo, Ugo 1778-1827. . . . . **NCLC 8**

Fosse, Bob . . . . **CLC 20**
See also Fosse, Robert Louis

Fosse, Robert Louis 1927-1987
See Fosse, Bob
See also CA 110; 123

Foster, Stephen Collins
1826-1864 . . . . **NCLC 26**

Foucault, Michel
1926-1984 . . . . **CLC 31, 34, 69**
See also CA 105; 113; CANR 34; MTCW

Fouque, Friedrich (Heinrich Karl) de la Motte
1777-1843 . . . . **NCLC 2**
See also DLB 90

Fournier, Henri Alban 1886-1914
See Alain-Fournier
See also CA 104

Fournier, Pierre 1916-. . . . . **CLC 11**
See also Gascar, Pierre
See also CA 89-92; CANR 16, 40

Fowles, John
1926- . . . . **CLC 1, 2, 3, 4, 6, 9, 10, 15, 33**
See also CA 5-8R; CANR 25; CDBLB 1960
to Present; DLB 14, 139; MTCW;
SATA 22

Fox, Paula 1923-. . . . . **CLC 2, 8**
See also AAYA 3; CA 73-76; CANR 20,
36; CLR 1; DLB 52; JRDA; MAICYA;
MTCW; SATA 17, 60

Fox, William Price (Jr.) 1926- . . . . . **CLC 22**
See also CA 17-20R; CAAS 19; CANR 11;
DLB 2; DLBY 81

Foxe, John 1516(?)-1587 . . . . **LC 14**

Frame, Janet . . . . **CLC 2, 3, 6, 22, 66**
See also Clutha, Janet Paterson Frame

France, Anatole. . . . . **TCLC 9**
See also Thibault, Jacques Anatole Francois
See also DLB 123

Francis, Claude 19(?)- . . . . **CLC 50**

Francis, Dick 1920- . . . . **CLC 2, 22, 42**
See also AAYA 5; BEST 89:3; CA 5-8R;
CANR 9, 42; CDBLB 1960 to Present;
DLB 87; MTCW

Francis, Robert (Churchill)
1901-1987 . . . . **CLC 15**
See also CA 1-4R; 123; CANR 1

Frank, Anne(lies Marie)
1929-1945 . . . . **TCLC 17; DA; WLC**
See also AAYA 12; CA 113; 133; MTCW;
SATA 42

Frank, Elizabeth 1945-. . . . . **CLC 39**
See also CA 121; 126

Franklin, Benjamin
See Hasek, Jaroslav (Matej Frantisek)

Franklin, Benjamin 1706-1790. . . **LC 25; DA**
See also CDALB 1640-1865; DLB 24, 43,
73

Franklin, (Stella Maraia Sarah) Miles
1879-1954 . . . . **TCLC 7**
See also CA 104

Fraser, (Lady) Antonia (Pakenham)
1932- . . . . **CLC 32**
See also CA 85-88; CANR 44; MTCW;
SATA 32

Fraser, George MacDonald 1925-. . . . **CLC 7**
See also CA 45-48; CANR 2

Fraser, Sylvia 1935-. . . . . **CLC 64**
See also CA 45-48; CANR 1, 16

Frayn, Michael 1933-. . . . . . **CLC 3, 7, 31, 47**
See also CA 5-8R; CANR 30; DLB 13, 14;
MTCW

Fraze, Candida (Merrill) 1945-. . . . . **CLC 50**
See also CA 126

Frazer, J(ames) G(eorge)
1854-1941 . . . . **TCLC 32**
See also CA 118

Frazer, Robert Caine
See Creasey, John

Frazer, Sir James George
See Frazer, J(ames) G(eorge)

Frazier, Ian 1951-. . . . . **CLC 46**
See also CA 130

Frederic, Harold 1856-1898. . . . . . **NCLC 10**
See also DLB 12, 23

Frederick, John
See Faust, Frederick (Schiller)

Frederick the Great 1712-1786 . . . . . . **LC 14**

Fredro, Aleksander 1793-1876. . . . . **NCLC 8**

Freeling, Nicolas 1927- . . . . **CLC 38**
See also CA 49-52; CAAS 12; CANR 1, 17;
DLB 87

Freeman, Douglas Southall
1886-1953 . . . . **TCLC 11**
See also CA 109; DLB 17

Freeman, Judith 1946-. . . . . **CLC 55**

Freeman, Mary Eleanor Wilkins
1852-1930 . . . . **TCLC 9; SSC 1**
See also CA 106; DLB 12, 78

Freeman, R(ichard) Austin
1862-1943 . . . . **TCLC 21**
See also CA 113; DLB 70

French, Marilyn 1929-. . . . . . **CLC 10, 18, 60**
See also CA 69-72; CANR 3, 31; MTCW

French, Paul
See Asimov, Isaac

Freneau, Philip Morin 1752-1832. . **NCLC 1**
See also DLB 37, 43

Freud, Sigmund 1856-1939 . . . . **TCLC 52**
See also CA 115; 133; MTCW

Friedan, Betty (Naomi) 1921-. . . . . . . **CLC 74**
See also CA 65-68; CANR 18, 45; MTCW

Friedman, B(ernard) H(arper)
1926- . . . . **CLC 7**
See also CA 1-4R; CANR 3

Friedman, Bruce Jay 1930-. . . . **CLC 3, 5, 56**
See also CA 9-12R; CANR 25; DLB 2, 28

Friel, Brian 1929-. . . . . **CLC 5, 42, 59**
See also CA 21-24R; CANR 33; DLB 13;
MTCW

Friis-Baastad, Babbis Ellinor
1921-1970 . . . . **CLC 12**
See also CA 17-20R; 134; SATA 7

Frisch, Max (Rudolf)
1911-1991 . . . . . **CLC 3, 9, 14, 18, 32, 44**
See also CA 85-88; 134; CANR 32;
DLB 69, 124; MTCW

Fromentin, Eugene (Samuel Auguste)
1820-1876 . . . . **NCLC 10**
See also DLB 123

Frost, Frederick
See Faust, Frederick (Schiller)

Frost, Robert (Lee)
1874-1963 . . . . **CLC 1, 3, 4, 9, 10, 13, 15,**
26, 34, 44; DA; PC 1; WLC
See also CA 89-92; CANR 33;
CDALB 1917-1929; DLB 54; DLBD 7;
MTCW; SATA 14

Froude, James Anthony
1818-1894 . . . . **NCLC 43**
See also DLB 18, 57, 144

Froy, Herald
See Waterhouse, Keith (Spencer)

Fry, Christopher 1907-. . . . . . . **CLC 2, 10, 14**
See also CA 17-20R; CANR 9, 30; DLB 13;
MTCW; SATA 66

Frye, (Herman) Northrop
1912-1991 . . . . CLC 24, 70
See also CA 5-8R; 133; CANR 8, 37;
DLB 67, 68; MTCW

Fuchs, Daniel 1909-1993 . . . . CLC 8, 22
See also CA 81-84; 142; CAAS 5;
CANR 40; DLB 9, 26, 28; DLBY 93

Fuchs, Daniel 1934- . . . . CLC 34
See also CA 37-40R; CANR 14

Fuentes, Carlos
1928- . . . . . . CLC 3, 8, 10, 13, 22, 41, 60;
DA; HLC; WLC
See also AAYA 4; AITN 2; CA 69-72;
CANR 10, 32; DLB 113; HW; MTCW

Fuentes, Gregorio Lopez y
See Lopez y Fuentes, Gregorio

Fugard, (Harold) Athol
1932- . . . . CLC 5, 9, 14, 25, 40, 80; DC 3
See also CA 85-88; CANR 32; MTCW

Fugard, Sheila 1932- . . . . CLC 48
See also CA 125

Fuller, Charles (H., Jr.)
1939- . . . . CLC 25; BLC; DC 1
See also BW 2; CA 108; 112; DLB 38;
MTCW

Fuller, John (Leopold) 1937- . . . . CLC 62
See also CA 21-24R; CANR 9, 44; DLB 40

Fuller, Margaret . . . . NCLC 5
See also Ossoli, Sarah Margaret (Fuller
marchesa d')

Fuller, Roy (Broadbent)
1912-1991 . . . . CLC 4, 28
See also CA 5-8R; 135; CAAS 10; DLB 15,
20

Fulton, Alice 1952- . . . . CLC 52
See also CA 116

Furphy, Joseph 1843-1912 . . . . TCLC 25

Fussell, Paul 1924- . . . . CLC 74
See also BEST 90:1; CA 17-20R; CANR 8,
21, 35; MTCW

Futabatei, Shimei 1864-1909 . . . . . TCLC 44

Futrelle, Jacques 1875-1912 . . . . . . TCLC 19
See also CA 113

Gaboriau, Emile 1835-1873 . . . . . . NCLC 14

Gadda, Carlo Emilio 1893-1973 . . . . CLC 11
See also CA 89-92

Gaddis, William
1922- . . . . CLC 1, 3, 6, 8, 10, 19, 43
See also CA 17-20R; CANR 21; DLB 2;
MTCW

Gaines, Ernest J(ames)
1933- . . . . CLC 3, 11, 18; BLC
See also AITN 1; BW 2; CA 9-12R;
CANR 6, 24, 42; CDALB 1968-1988;
DLB 2, 33; DLBY 80; MTCW

Gaitskill, Mary 1954- . . . . CLC 69
See also CA 128

Galdos, Benito Perez
See Perez Galdos, Benito

Gale, Zona 1874-1938 . . . . TCLC 7
See also CA 105; DLB 9, 78

Galeano, Eduardo (Hughes) 1940- . . . CLC 72
See also CA 29-32R; CANR 13, 32; HW

Galiano, Juan Valera y Alcala
See Valera y Alcala-Galiano, Juan

Gallagher, Tess 1943- . . . . CLC 18, 63; PC 9
See also CA 106; DLB 120

Gallant, Mavis
1922- . . . . CLC 7, 18, 38; SSC 5
See also CA 69-72; CANR 29; DLB 53;
MTCW

Gallant, Roy A(rthur) 1924- . . . . CLC 17
See also CA 5-8R; CANR 4, 29; CLR 30;
MAICYA; SATA 4, 68

Gallico, Paul (William) 1897-1976 . . . CLC 2
See also AITN 1; CA 5-8R; 69-72;
CANR 23; DLB 9; MAICYA; SATA 13

Gallup, Ralph
See Whitemore, Hugh (John)

Galsworthy, John
1867-1933 . . . . TCLC 1, 45; DA; WLC 2
See also CA 104; 141; CDBLB 1890-1914;
DLB 10, 34, 98

Galt, John 1779-1839 . . . . NCLC 1
See also DLB 99, 116

Galvin, James 1951- . . . . CLC 38
See also CA 108; CANR 26

Gamboa, Federico 1864-1939 . . . . . . TCLC 36

Gann, Ernest Kellogg 1910-1991 . . . . CLC 23
See also AITN 1; CA 1-4R; 136; CANR 1

Garcia, Cristina 1958- . . . . CLC 76
See also CA 141

Garcia Lorca, Federico
1898-1936 . . . . TCLC 1, 7, 49; DA;
DC 2; HLC; PC 3; WLC
See also CA 104; 131; DLB 108; HW;
MTCW

Garcia Marquez, Gabriel (Jose)
1928- . . . . CLC 2, 3, 8, 10, 15, 27, 47, 55,
68; DA; HLC; SSC 8; WLC
See also AAYA 3; BEST 89:1, 90:4;
CA 33-36R; CANR 10, 28; DLB 113;
HW; MTCW

Gard, Janice
See Latham, Jean Lee

Gard, Roger Martin du
See Martin du Gard, Roger

Gardam, Jane 1928- . . . . CLC 43
See also CA 49-52; CANR 2, 18, 33;
CLR 12; DLB 14; MAICYA; MTCW;
SAAS 9; SATA 28, 39, 76

Gardner, Herb . . . . CLC 44

Gardner, John (Champlin), Jr.
1933-1982 . . . . . CLC 2, 3, 5, 7, 8, 10, 18,
28, 34; SSC 7
See also AITN 1; CA 65-68; 107;
CANR 33; DLB 2; DLBY 82; MTCW;
SATA 40; SATA-Obit 31

Gardner, John (Edmund) 1926- . . . . . CLC 30
See also CA 103; CANR 15; MTCW

Gardner, Noel
See Kuttner, Henry

Gardons, S. S.
See Snodgrass, W(illiam) D(e Witt)

Garfield, Leon 1921- . . . . CLC 12
See also AAYA 8; CA 17-20R; CANR 38,
41; CLR 21; JRDA; MAICYA; SATA 1,
32, 76

Garland, (Hannibal) Hamlin
1860-1940 . . . . TCLC 3
See also CA 104; DLB 12, 71, 78

Garneau, (Hector de) Saint-Denys
1912-1943 . . . . TCLC 13
See also CA 111; DLB 88

Garner, Alan 1934- . . . . CLC 17
See also CA 73-76; CANR 15; CLR 20;
MAICYA; MTCW; SATA 18, 69

Garner, Hugh 1913-1979 . . . . CLC 13
See also CA 69-72; CANR 31; DLB 68

Garnett, David 1892-1981 . . . . CLC 3
See also CA 5-8R; 103; CANR 17; DLB 34

Garos, Stephanie
See Katz, Steve

Garrett, George (Palmer)
1929- . . . . CLC 3, 11, 51
See also CA 1-4R; CAAS 5; CANR 1, 42;
DLB 2, 5, 130; DLBY 83

Garrick, David 1717-1779 . . . . LC 15
See also DLB 84

Garrigue, Jean 1914-1972 . . . . CLC 2, 8
See also CA 5-8R; 37-40R; CANR 20

Garrison, Frederick
See Sinclair, Upton (Beall)

Garth, Will
See Hamilton, Edmond; Kuttner, Henry

Garvey, Marcus (Moziah, Jr.)
1887-1940 . . . . TCLC 41; BLC
See also BW 1; CA 120; 124

Gary, Romain . . . . CLC 25
See also Kacew, Romain
See also DLB 83

Gascar, Pierre . . . . CLC 11
See also Fournier, Pierre

Gascoyne, David (Emery) 1916- . . . . CLC 45
See also CA 65-68; CANR 10, 28; DLB 20;
MTCW

Gaskell, Elizabeth Cleghorn
1810-1865 . . . . NCLC 5
See also CDBLB 1832-1890; DLB 21, 144

Gass, William H(oward)
1924- . . . CLC 1, 2, 8, 11, 15, 39; SSC 12
See also CA 17-20R; CANR 30; DLB 2;
MTCW

Gasset, Jose Ortega y
See Ortega y Gasset, Jose

Gates, Henry Louis, Jr. 1950- . . . . . . CLC 65
See also BW 2; CA 109; CANR 25; DLB 67

Gautier, Theophile 1811-1872 . . . . . NCLC 1
See also DLB 119

Gawsworth, John
See Bates, H(erbert) E(rnest)

Gaye, Marvin (Penze) 1939-1984 . . . CLC 26
See also CA 112

Gebler, Carlo (Ernest) 1954- . . . . CLC 39
See also CA 119; 133

Gee, Maggie (Mary) 1948- . . . . CLC 57
See also CA 130

Gee, Maurice (Gough) 1931- . . . . CLC 29
See also CA 97-100; SATA 46

Gelbart, Larry (Simon) 1923- . . . CLC 21, 61
See also CA 73-76; CANR 45

Gelber, Jack 1932-........ CLC **1, 6, 14, 79**
See also CA 1-4R; CANR 2; DLB 7

Gellhorn, Martha (Ellis) 1908- .. CLC **14, 60**
See also CA 77-80; CANR 44; DLBY 82

Genet, Jean
1910-1986 ... CLC **1, 2, 5, 10, 14, 44, 46**
See also CA 13-16R; CANR 18; DLB 72;
DLBY 86; MTCW

Gent, Peter 1942-.............. CLC **29**
See also AITN 1; CA 89-92; DLBY 82

Gentlewoman in New England, A
See Bradstreet, Anne

Gentlewoman in Those Parts, A
See Bradstreet, Anne

George, Jean Craighead 1919-...... CLC **35**
See also AAYA 8; CA 5-8R; CANR 25;
CLR 1; DLB 52; JRDA; MAICYA;
SATA 2, 68

George, Stefan (Anton)
1868-1933 .... TCLC **2, 14**
See also CA 104

Georges, Georges Martin
See Simenon, Georges (Jacques Christian)

Gerhardi, William Alexander
See Gerhardie, William Alexander

Gerhardie, William Alexander
1895-1977 .... CLC **5**
See also CA 25-28R; 73-76; CANR 18;
DLB 36

Gerstler, Amy 1956-.............. CLC **70**

Gertler, T. .... CLC **34**
See also CA 116; 121

Ghalib 1797-1869 .... NCLC **39**

Ghelderode, Michel de
1898-1962 .... CLC **6, 11**
See also CA 85-88; CANR 40

Ghiselin, Brewster 1903-.......... CLC **23**
See also CA 13-16R; CAAS 10; CANR 13

Ghose, Zulfikar 1935-............. CLC **42**
See also CA 65-68

Ghosh, Amitav 1956-............. CLC **44**

Giacosa, Giuseppe 1847-1906 ...... TCLC **7**
See also CA 104

Gibb, Lee
See Waterhouse, Keith (Spencer)

Gibbon, Lewis Grassic .... TCLC **4**
See also Mitchell, James Leslie

Gibbons, Kaye 1960- .... CLC **50**

Gibran, Kahlil
1883-1931 .... TCLC **1, 9; PC 9**
See also CA 104

Gibson, William 1914-........ CLC **23; DA**
See also CA 9-12R; CANR 9, 42; DLB 7;
SATA 66

Gibson, William (Ford) 1948- ... CLC **39, 63**
See also AAYA 12; CA 126; 133

Gide, Andre (Paul Guillaume)
1869-1951 .... TCLC **5, 12, 36; DA;
SSC 13; WLC**
See also CA 104; 124; DLB 65; MTCW

Gifford, Barry (Colby) 1946-...... CLC **34**
See also CA 65-68; CANR 9, 30, 40

Gilbert, W(illiam) S(chwenck)
1836-1911 .... TCLC **3**
See also CA 104; SATA 36

Gilbreth, Frank B., Jr. 1911-...... CLC **17**
See also CA 9-12R; SATA 2

Gilchrist, Ellen 1935-.. CLC **34, 48; SSC 14**
See also CA 113; 116; CANR 41; DLB 130;
MTCW

Giles, Molly 1942- .... CLC **39**
See also CA 126

Gill, Patrick
See Creasey, John

Gilliam, Terry (Vance) 1940-...... CLC **21**
See also Monty Python
See also CA 108; 113; CANR 35

Gillian, Jerry
See Gilliam, Terry (Vance)

Gilliatt, Penelope (Ann Douglass)
1932-1993 .... CLC **2, 10, 13, 53**
See also AITN 2; CA 13-16R; 141; DLB 14

Gilman, Charlotte (Anna) Perkins (Stetson)
1860-1935 .... TCLC **9, 37; SSC 13**
See also CA 106

Gilmour, David 1949-............. CLC **35**
See also CA 138

Gilpin, William 1724-1804....... NCLC **30**

Gilray, J. D.
See Mencken, H(enry) L(ouis)

Gilroy, Frank D(aniel) 1925-....... CLC **2**
See also CA 81-84; CANR 32; DLB 7

Ginsberg, Allen
1926- ...... CLC **1, 2, 3, 4, 6, 13, 36, 69;
DA; PC 4; WLC 3**
See also AITN 1; CA 1-4R; CANR 2, 41;
CDALB 1941-1968; DLB 5, 16; MTCW

Ginzburg, Natalia
1916-1991 .... CLC **5, 11, 54, 70**
See also CA 85-88; 135; CANR 33; MTCW

Giono, Jean 1895-1970......... CLC **4, 11**
See also CA 45-48; 29-32R; CANR 2, 35;
DLB 72; MTCW

Giovanni, Nikki
1943- .... CLC **2, 4, 19, 64; BLC; DA**
See also AITN 1; BW 2; CA 29-32R;
CAAS 6; CANR 18, 41; CLR 6; DLB 5,
41; MAICYA; MTCW; SATA 24

Giovene, Andrea 1904-............. CLC **7**
See also CA 85-88

Gippius, Zinaida (Nikolayevna) 1869-1945
See Hippius, Zinaida
See also CA 106

Giraudoux, (Hippolyte) Jean
1882-1944 .... TCLC **2, 7**
See also CA 104; DLB 65

Gironella, Jose Maria 1917- .... CLC **11**
See also CA 101

Gissing, George (Robert)
1857-1903 .... TCLC **3, 24, 47**
See also CA 105; DLB 18, 135

Giurlani, Aldo
See Palazzeschi, Aldo

Gladkov, Fyodor (Vasilyevich)
1883-1958 .... TCLC **27**

Glanville, Brian (Lester) 1931-...... CLC **6**
See also CA 5-8R; CAAS 9; CANR 3;
DLB 15, 139; SATA 42

Glasgow, Ellen (Anderson Gholson)
1873(?)-1945 .... TCLC **2, 7**
See also CA 104; DLB 9, 12

Glaspell, Susan (Keating)
1882(?)-1948 .... TCLC **55**
See also CA 110; DLB 7, 9, 78; YABC 2

Glassco, John 1909-1981 .... CLC **9**
See also CA 13-16R; 102; CANR 15;
DLB 68

Glasscock, Amnesia
See Steinbeck, John (Ernst)

Glasser, Ronald J. 1940(?)-........ CLC **37**

Glassman, Joyce
See Johnson, Joyce

Glendinning, Victoria 1937-........ CLC **50**
See also CA 120; 127

Glissant, Edouard 1928-........ CLC **10, 68**

Gloag, Julian 1930- .... CLC **40**
See also AITN 1; CA 65-68; CANR 10

Glowacki, Aleksander
See Prus, Boleslaw

Glueck, Louise (Elisabeth)
1943-............ CLC **7, 22, 44, 81**
See also CA 33-36R; CANR 40; DLB 5

Gobineau, Joseph Arthur (Comte) de
1816-1882 .... NCLC **17**
See also DLB 123

Godard, Jean-Luc 1930-.......... CLC **20**
See also CA 93-96

Godden, (Margaret) Rumer 1907-... CLC **53**
See also AAYA 6; CA 5-8R; CANR 4, 27,
36; CLR 20; MAICYA; SAAS 12;
SATA 3, 36

Godoy Alcayaga, Lucila 1889-1957
See Mistral, Gabriela
See also BW 2; CA 104; 131; HW; MTCW

Godwin, Gail (Kathleen)
1937-............ CLC **5, 8, 22, 31, 69**
See also CA 29-32R; CANR 15, 43; DLB 6;
MTCW

Godwin, William 1756-1836...... NCLC **14**
See also CDBLB 1789-1832; DLB 39, 104,
142

Goethe, Johann Wolfgang von
1749-1832 .... NCLC **4, 22, 34; DA;
PC 5; WLC 3**
See also DLB 94

Gogarty, Oliver St. John
1878-1957 .... TCLC **15**
See also CA 109; DLB 15, 19

Gogol, Nikolai (Vasilyevich)
1809-1852 .... NCLC **5, 15, 31; DA;
DC 1; SSC 4; WLC**

Goines, Donald
1937(?)-1974 .... CLC **80; BLC**
See also AITN 1; BW 1; CA 124; 114;
DLB 33

Gold, Herbert 1924-...... CLC **4, 7, 14, 42**
See also CA 9-12R; CANR 17, 45; DLB 2;
DLBY 81

Goldbarth, Albert 1948-........ CLC **5, 38**
See also CA 53-56; CANR 6, 40; DLB 120

Goldberg, Anatol 1910-1982 .... **CLC 34**
See also CA 131; 117

Goldemberg, Isaac 1945- .... **CLC 52**
See also CA 69-72; CAAS 12; CANR 11,
32; HW

Golding, William (Gerald)
1911-1993 .... **CLC 1, 2, 3, 8, 10, 17, 27,**
58, 81; DA; WLC
See also AAYA 5; CA 5-8R; 141;
CANR 13, 33; CDBLB 1945-1960;
DLB 15, 100; MTCW

Goldman, Emma 1869-1940 ...... **TCLC 13**
See also CA 110

Goldman, Francisco 1955- .... **CLC 76**

Goldman, William (W.) 1931- .... **CLC 1, 48**
See also CA 9-12R; CANR 29; DLB 44

Goldmann, Lucien 1913-1970 ...... **CLC 24**
See also CA 25-28; CAP 2

Goldoni, Carlo 1707-1793 .... **LC 4**

Goldsberry, Steven 1949- .... **CLC 34**
See also CA 131

Goldsmith, Oliver
1728-1774 .... **LC 2; DA; WLC**
See also CDBLB 1660-1789; DLB 39, 89,
104, 109, 142; SATA 26

Goldsmith, Peter
See Priestley, J(ohn) B(oynton)

Gombrowicz, Witold
1904-1969 .... **CLC 4, 7, 11, 49**
See also CA 19-20; 25-28R; CAP 2

Gomez de la Serna, Ramon
1888-1963 .... **CLC 9**
See also CA 116; HW

Goncharov, Ivan Alexandrovich
1812-1891 .... **NCLC 1**

Goncourt, Edmond (Louis Antoine Huot) de
1822-1896 .... **NCLC 7**
See also DLB 123

Goncourt, Jules (Alfred Huot) de
1830-1870 .... **NCLC 7**
See also DLB 123

Gontier, Fernande 19(?)- .... **CLC 50**

Goodman, Paul 1911-1972 .... **CLC 1, 2, 4, 7**
See also CA 19-20; 37-40R; CANR 34;
CAP 2; DLB 130; MTCW

Gordimer, Nadine
1923- .... **CLC 3, 5, 7, 10, 18, 33, 51, 70;**
DA; SSC 17
See also CA 5-8R; CANR 3, 28; MTCW

Gordon, Adam Lindsay
1833-1870 .... **NCLC 21**

Gordon, Caroline
1895-1981 ... **CLC 6, 13, 29, 83; SSC 15**
See also CA 11-12; 103; CANR 36; CAP 1;
DLB 4, 9, 102; DLBY 81; MTCW

Gordon, Charles William 1860-1937
See Connor, Ralph
See also CA 109

Gordon, Mary (Catherine)
1949- .... **CLC 13, 22**
See also CA 102; CANR 44; DLB 6;
DLBY 81; MTCW

Gordon, Sol 1923- .... **CLC 26**
See also CA 53-56; CANR 4; SATA 11

Gordone, Charles 1925- .... **CLC 1, 4**
See also BW 1; CA 93-96; DLB 7; MTCW

Gorenko, Anna Andreevna
See Akhmatova, Anna

Gorky, Maxim .... **TCLC 8; WLC**
See also Peshkov, Alexei Maximovich

Goryan, Sirak
See Saroyan, William

Gosse, Edmund (William)
1849-1928 .... **TCLC 28**
See also CA 117; DLB 57, 144

Gotlieb, Phyllis Fay (Bloom)
1926- .... **CLC 18**
See also CA 13-16R; CANR 7; DLB 88

Gottesman, S. D.
See Kornbluth, C(yril) M.; Pohl, Frederik

Gottfried von Strassburg
fl. c. 1210- .... **CMLC 10**
See also DLB 138

Gould, Lois .... **CLC 4, 10**
See also CA 77-80; CANR 29; MTCW

Gourmont, Remy de 1858-1915 .... **TCLC 17**
See also CA 109

Govier, Katherine 1948- .... **CLC 51**
See also CA 101; CANR 18, 40

Goyen, (Charles) William
1915-1983 .... **CLC 5, 8, 14, 40**
See also AITN 2; CA 5-8R; 110; CANR 6;
DLB 2; DLBY 83

Goytisolo, Juan
1931- .... **CLC 5, 10, 23; HLC**
See also CA 85-88; CANR 32; HW; MTCW

Gozzano, Guido 1883-1916 .... **PC 10**
See also DLB 114

Gozzi, (Conte) Carlo 1720-1806 .. **NCLC 23**

Grabbe, Christian Dietrich
1801-1836 .... **NCLC 2**
See also DLB 133

Grace, Patricia 1937- .... **CLC 56**

Gracian y Morales, Baltasar
1601-1658 .... **LC 15**

Gracq, Julien .... **CLC 11, 48**
See also Poirier, Louis
See also DLB 83

Grade, Chaim 1910-1982 .... **CLC 10**
See also CA 93-96; 107

Graduate of Oxford, A
See Ruskin, John

Graham, John
See Phillips, David Graham

Graham, Jorie 1951- .... **CLC 48**
See also CA 111; DLB 120

Graham, R(obert) B(ontine) Cunninghame
See Cunninghame Graham, R(obert)
B(ontine)
See also DLB 98, 135

Graham, Robert
See Haldeman, Joe (William)

Graham, Tom
See Lewis, (Harry) Sinclair

Graham, W(illiam) S(ydney)
1918-1986 .... **CLC 29**
See also CA 73-76; 118; DLB 20

Graham, Winston (Mawdsley)
1910- .... **CLC 23**
See also CA 49-52; CANR 2, 22, 45;
DLB 77

Grant, Skeeter
See Spiegelman, Art

Granville-Barker, Harley
1877-1946 .... **TCLC 2**
See also Barker, Harley Granville
See also CA 104

Grass, Guenter (Wilhelm)
1927- ..... **CLC 1, 2, 4, 6, 11, 15, 22, 32,**
49; DA; WLC
See also CA 13-16R; CANR 20; DLB 75,
124; MTCW

Gratton, Thomas
See Hulme, T(homas) E(rnest)

Grau, Shirley Ann
1929- .... **CLC 4, 9; SSC 15**
See also CA 89-92; CANR 22; DLB 2;
MTCW

Gravel, Fern
See Hall, James Norman

Graver, Elizabeth 1964- .... **CLC 70**
See also CA 135

Graves, Richard Perceval 1945- .... **CLC 44**
See also CA 65-68; CANR 9, 26

Graves, Robert (von Ranke)
1895-1985 ...... **CLC 1, 2, 6, 11, 39, 44,**
45; PC 6
See also CA 5-8R; 117; CANR 5, 36;
CDBLB 1914-1945; DLB 20, 100;
DLBY 85; MTCW; SATA 45

Gray, Alasdair 1934- .... **CLC 41**
See also CA 126; MTCW

Gray, Amlin 1946- .... **CLC 29**
See also CA 138

Gray, Francine du Plessix 1930- .... **CLC 22**
See also BEST 90:3; CA 61-64; CAAS 2;
CANR 11, 33; MTCW

Gray, John (Henry) 1866-1934 .... **TCLC 19**
See also CA 119

Gray, Simon (James Holliday)
1936- .... **CLC 9, 14, 36**
See also AITN 1; CA 21-24R; CAAS 3;
CANR 32; DLB 13; MTCW

Gray, Spalding 1941- .... **CLC 49**
See also CA 128

Gray, Thomas
1716-1771 ...... **LC 4; DA; PC 2; WLC**
See also CDBLB 1660-1789; DLB 109

Grayson, David
See Baker, Ray Stannard

Grayson, Richard (A.) 1951- .... **CLC 38**
See also CA 85-88; CANR 14, 31

Greeley, Andrew M(oran) 1928- .... **CLC 28**
See also CA 5-8R; CAAS 7; CANR 7, 43;
MTCW

Green, Brian
See Card, Orson Scott

Green, Hannah
See Greenberg, Joanne (Goldenberg)

Green, Hannah .... **CLC 3**
See also CA 73-76

Harrison, Elizabeth Cavanna 1909-
See Cavanna, Betty
See also CA 9-12R; CANR 6, 27

Harrison, Harry (Max) 1925- . . . . . . **CLC 42**
See also CA 1-4R; CANR 5, 21; DLB 8;
SATA 4

Harrison, James (Thomas)
1937- . . . . **CLC 6, 14, 33, 66**
See also CA 13-16R; CANR 8; DLBY 82

Harrison, Jim
See Harrison, James (Thomas)

Harrison, Kathryn 1961- . . . . **CLC 70**
See also CA 144

Harrison, Tony 1937- . . . . **CLC 43**
See also CA 65-68; CANR 44; DLB 40;
MTCW

Harriss, Will(ard Irvin) 1922- . . . . . . **CLC 34**
See also CA 111

Harson, Sley
See Ellison, Harlan (Jay)

Hart, Ellis
See Ellison, Harlan (Jay)

Hart, Josephine 1942(?)- . . . . **CLC 70**
See also CA 138

Hart, Moss 1904-1961 . . . . **CLC 66**
See also CA 109; 89-92; DLB 7

Harte, (Francis) Bret(t)
1836(?)-1902 . . . . **TCLC 1, 25; DA;
SSC 8; WLC**
See also CA 104; 140; CDALB 1865-1917;
DLB 12, 64, 74, 79; SATA 26

Hartley, L(eslie) P(oles)
1895-1972 . . . . **CLC 2, 22**
See also CA 45-48; 37-40R; CANR 33;
DLB 15, 139; MTCW

Hartman, Geoffrey H. 1929- . . . . **CLC 27**
See also CA 117; 125; DLB 67

Haruf, Kent 19(?)- . . . . **CLC 34**

Harwood, Ronald 1934- . . . . **CLC 32**
See also CA 1-4R; CANR 4; DLB 13

Hasek, Jaroslav (Matej Frantisek)
1883-1923 . . . . **TCLC 4**
See also CA 104; 129; MTCW

Hass, Robert 1941- . . . . **CLC 18, 39**
See also CA 111; CANR 30; DLB 105

Hastings, Hudson
See Kuttner, Henry

Hastings, Selina . . . . **CLC 44**

Hatteras, Amelia
See Mencken, H(enry) L(ouis)

Hatteras, Owen . . . . **TCLC 18**
See also Mencken, H(enry) L(ouis); Nathan,
George Jean

Hauptmann, Gerhart (Johann Robert)
1862-1946 . . . . **TCLC 4**
See also CA 104; DLB 66, 118

Havel, Vaclav 1936- . . . . **CLC 25, 58, 65**
See also CA 104; CANR 36; MTCW

Haviaras, Stratis . . . . **CLC 33**
See also Chaviaras, Strates

Hawes, Stephen 1475(?)-1523(?) . . . . . **LC 17**

Hawkes, John (Clendennin Burne, Jr.)
1925- . . . . . . **CLC 1, 2, 3, 4, 7, 9, 14, 15,
27, 49**
See also CA 1-4R; CANR 2; DLB 2, 7;
DLBY 80; MTCW

Hawking, S. W.
See Hawking, Stephen W(illiam)

Hawking, Stephen W(illiam)
1942- . . . . **CLC 63**
See also AAYA 13; BEST 89:1; CA 126;
129

Hawthorne, Julian 1846-1934 . . . . . **TCLC 25**

Hawthorne, Nathaniel
1804-1864 . . . . . . **NCLC 39; DA; SSC 3;
WLC**
See also CDALB 1640-1865; DLB 1, 74;
YABC 2

Haxton, Josephine Ayres 1921-
See Douglas, Ellen
See also CA 115; CANR 41

Hayaseca y Eizaguirre, Jorge
See Echegaray (y Eizaguirre), Jose (Maria
Waldo)

Hayashi Fumiko 1904-1951 . . . . **TCLC 27**

Haycraft, Anna
See Ellis, Alice Thomas
See also CA 122

Hayden, Robert E(arl)
1913-1980 . . . . . . **CLC 5, 9, 14, 37; BLC;
DA; PC 6**
See also BW 1; CA 69-72; 97-100; CABS 2;
CANR 24; CDALB 1941-1968; DLB 5,
76; MTCW; SATA 19; SATA-Obit 26

Hayford, J(oseph) E(phraim) Casely
See Casely-Hayford, J(oseph) E(phraim)

Hayman, Ronald 1932- . . . . **CLC 44**
See also CA 25-28R; CANR 18

Haywood, Eliza (Fowler)
1693(?)-1756 . . . . **LC 1**

Hazlitt, William 1778-1830 . . . . . . **NCLC 29**
See also DLB 110

Hazzard, Shirley 1931- . . . . **CLC 18**
See also CA 9-12R; CANR 4; DLBY 82;
MTCW

Head, Bessie 1937-1986 . . . **CLC 25, 67; BLC**
See also BW 2; CA 29-32R; 119; CANR 25;
DLB 117; MTCW

Headon, (Nicky) Topper 1956(?)- . . . **CLC 30**

Heaney, Seamus (Justin)
1939- . . . . **CLC 5, 7, 14, 25, 37, 74**
See also CA 85-88; CANR 25;
CDBLB 1960 to Present; DLB 40;
MTCW

Hearn, (Patricio) Lafcadio (Tessima Carlos)
1850-1904 . . . . **TCLC 9**
See also CA 105; DLB 12, 78

Hearne, Vicki 1946- . . . . **CLC 56**
See also CA 139

Hearon, Shelby 1931- . . . . **CLC 63**
See also AITN 2; CA 25-28R; CANR 18

Heat-Moon, William Least . . . . **CLC 29**
See also Trogdon, William (Lewis)
See also AAYA 9

Hebbel, Friedrich 1813-1863 . . . . . **NCLC 43**
See also DLB 129

Hebert, Anne 1916- . . . . **CLC 4, 13, 29**
See also CA 85-88; DLB 68; MTCW

Hecht, Anthony (Evan)
1923- . . . . **CLC 8, 13, 19**
See also CA 9-12R; CANR 6; DLB 5

Hecht, Ben 1894-1964 . . . . **CLC 8**
See also CA 85-88; DLB 7, 9, 25, 26, 28, 86

Hedayat, Sadeq 1903-1951 . . . . **TCLC 21**
See also CA 120

Hegel, Georg Wilhelm Friedrich
1770-1831 . . . . **NCLC 46**
See also DLB 90

Heidegger, Martin 1889-1976 . . . . . . **CLC 24**
See also CA 81-84; 65-68; CANR 34;
MTCW

Heidenstam, (Carl Gustaf) Verner von
1859-1940 . . . . **TCLC 5**
See also CA 104

Heifner, Jack 1946- . . . . **CLC 11**
See also CA 105

Heijermans, Herman 1864-1924 . . . **TCLC 24**
See also CA 123

Heilbrun, Carolyn G(old) 1926- . . . . . **CLC 25**
See also CA 45-48; CANR 1, 28

Heine, Heinrich 1797-1856 . . . . **NCLC 4**
See also DLB 90

Heinemann, Larry (Curtiss) 1944- . . **CLC 50**
See also CA 110; CANR 31; DLBD 9

Heiney, Donald (William) 1921-1993
See Harris, MacDonald
See also CA 1-4R; 142; CANR 3

Heinlein, Robert A(nson)
1907-1988 . . . . . . **CLC 1, 3, 8, 14, 26, 55**
See also CA 1-4R; 125; CANR 1, 20;
DLB 8; JRDA; MAICYA; MTCW;
SATA 9, 69; SATA-Obit 56

Helforth, John
See Doolittle, Hilda

Hellenhofferu, Vojtech Kapristian z
See Hasek, Jaroslav (Matej Frantisek)

Heller, Joseph
1923- . . . . **CLC 1, 3, 5, 8, 11, 36, 63; DA;
WLC**
See also AITN 1; CA 5-8R; CABS 1;
CANR 8, 42; DLB 2, 28; DLBY 80;
MTCW

Hellman, Lillian (Florence)
1906-1984 . . . . . . **CLC 2, 4, 8, 14, 18, 34,
44, 52; DC 1**
See also AITN 1, 2; CA 13-16R; 112;
CANR 33; DLB 7; DLBY 84; MTCW

Helprin, Mark 1947- . . . . . **CLC 7, 10, 22, 32**
See also CA 81-84; DLBY 85; MTCW

Helvetius, Claude-Adrien
1715-1771 . . . . **LC 26**

Helyar, Jane Penelope Josephine 1933-
See Poole, Josephine
See also CA 21-24R; CANR 10, 26

Hemans, Felicia 1793-1835 . . . . . . **NCLC 29**
See also DLB 96

Hemingway, Ernest (Miller)
1899-1961 .... **CLC 1, 3, 6, 8, 10, 13, 19, 30, 34, 39, 41, 44, 50, 61, 80; DA; SSC 1; WLC**
See also CA 77-80; CANR 34;
CDALB 1917-1929; DLB 4, 9, 102;
DLBD 1; DLBY 81, 87; MTCW

Hempel, Amy 1951- .... **CLC 39**
See also CA 118; 137

Henderson, F. C.
See Mencken, H(enry) L(ouis)

Henderson, Sylvia
See Ashton-Warner, Sylvia (Constance)

Henley, Beth .... **CLC 23**
See also Henley, Elizabeth Becker
See also CABS 3; DLBY 86

Henley, Elizabeth Becker 1952-
See Henley, Beth
See also CA 107; CANR 32; MTCW

Henley, William Ernest
1849-1903 .... **TCLC 8**
See also CA 105; DLB 19

Hennissart, Martha
See Lathen, Emma
See also CA 85-88

Henry, O. .... **TCLC 1, 19; SSC 5; WLC**
See also Porter, William Sydney

Henry, Patrick 1736- .... **LC 25**
See also CA 145

Henryson, Robert 1430(?)-1506(?).... **LC 20**
See also DLB 146

Henry VIII 1491-1547 .... **LC 10**

Henschke, Alfred
See Klabund

Hentoff, Nat(han Irving) 1925- ..... **CLC 26**
See also AAYA 4; CA 1-4R; CAAS 6;
CANR 5, 25; CLR 1; JRDA; MAICYA;
SATA 27, 42, 69

Heppenstall, (John) Rayner
1911-1981 .... **CLC 10**
See also CA 1-4R; 103; CANR 29

Herbert, Frank (Patrick)
1920-1986 ...... **CLC 12, 23, 35, 44, 85**
See also CA 53-56; 118; CANR 5, 43;
DLB 8; MTCW; SATA 9, 37;
SATA-Obit 47

Herbert, George 1593-1633 .... **LC 24; PC 4**
See also CDBLB Before 1660; DLB 126

Herbert, Zbigniew 1924- .... **CLC 9, 43**
See also CA 89-92; CANR 36; MTCW

Herbst, Josephine (Frey)
1897-1969 .... **CLC 34**
See also CA 5-8R; 25-28R; DLB 9

Hergesheimer, Joseph
1880-1954 .... **TCLC 11**
See also CA 109; DLB 102, 9

Herlihy, James Leo 1927-1993 ...... **CLC 6**
See also CA 1-4R; 143; CANR 2

Hermogenes fl. c. 175- .... **CMLC 6**

Hernandez, Jose 1834-1886 ...... **NCLC 17**

Herrick, Robert
1591-1674 .... **LC 13; DA; PC 9**
See also DLB 126

Herring, Guilles
See Somerville, Edith

Herriot, James 1916- .... **CLC 12**
See also Wight, James Alfred
See also AAYA 1; CANR 40

Herrmann, Dorothy 1941- .... **CLC 44**
See also CA 107

Herrmann, Taffy
See Herrmann, Dorothy

Hersey, John (Richard)
1914-1993 ...... **CLC 1, 2, 7, 9, 40, 81**
See also CA 17-20R; 140; CANR 33;
DLB 6; MTCW; SATA 25;
SATA-Obit 76

Herzen, Aleksandr Ivanovich
1812-1870 .... **NCLC 10**

Herzl, Theodor 1860-1904 .... **TCLC 36**

Herzog, Werner 1942- .... **CLC 16**
See also CA 89-92

Hesiod c. 8th cent. B.C.- .... **CMLC 5**

Hesse, Hermann
1877-1962 .... **CLC 1, 2, 3, 6, 11, 17, 25, 69; DA; SSC 9; WLC**
See also CA 17-18; CAP 2; DLB 66;
MTCW; SATA 50

Hewes, Cady
See De Voto, Bernard (Augustine)

Heyen, William 1940- .... **CLC 13, 18**
See also CA 33-36R; CAAS 9; DLB 5

Heyerdahl, Thor 1914- .... **CLC 26**
See also CA 5-8R; CANR 5, 22; MTCW;
SATA 2, 52

Heym, Georg (Theodor Franz Arthur)
1887-1912 .... **TCLC 9**
See also CA 106

Heym, Stefan 1913- .... **CLC 41**
See also CA 9-12R; CANR 4; DLB 69

Heyse, Paul (Johann Ludwig von)
1830-1914 .... **TCLC 8**
See also CA 104; DLB 129

Hibbert, Eleanor Alice Burford
1906-1993 .... **CLC 7**
See also BEST 90:4; CA 17-20R; 140;
CANR 9, 28; SATA 2; SATA-Obit 74

Higgins, George V(incent)
1939- .... **CLC 4, 7, 10, 18**
See also CA 77-80; CAAS 5; CANR 17;
DLB 2; DLBY 81; MTCW

Higginson, Thomas Wentworth
1823-1911 .... **TCLC 36**
See also DLB 1, 64

Highet, Helen
See MacInnes, Helen (Clark)

Highsmith, (Mary) Patricia
1921- .... **CLC 2, 4, 14, 42**
See also CA 1-4R; CANR 1, 20; MTCW

Highwater, Jamake (Mamake)
1942(?)- .... **CLC 12**
See also AAYA 7; CA 65-68; CAAS 7;
CANR 10, 34; CLR 17; DLB 52;
DLBY 85; JRDA; MAICYA; SATA 30, 32, 69

Hijuelos, Oscar 1951- ...... **CLC 65; HLC**
See also BEST 90:1; CA 123; DLB 145; HW

Hikmet, Nazim 1902(?)-1963....... **CLC 40**
See also CA 141; 93-96

Hildesheimer, Wolfgang
1916-1991 .... **CLC 49**
See also CA 101; 135; DLB 69, 124

Hill, Geoffrey (William)
1932- .... **CLC 5, 8, 18, 45**
See also CA 81-84; CANR 21;
CDBLB 1960 to Present; DLB 40;
MTCW

Hill, George Roy 1921- .... **CLC 26**
See also CA 110; 122

Hill, John
See Koontz, Dean R(ay)

Hill, Susan (Elizabeth) 1942- .... **CLC 4**
See also CA 33-36R; CANR 29; DLB 14, 139; MTCW

Hillerman, Tony 1925- .... **CLC 62**
See also AAYA 6; BEST 89:1; CA 29-32R;
CANR 21, 42; SATA 6

Hillesum, Etty 1914-1943 .... **TCLC 49**
See also CA 137

Hilliard, Noel (Harvey) 1929- ...... **CLC 15**
See also CA 9-12R; CANR 7

Hillis, Rick 1956- .... **CLC 66**
See also CA 134

Hilton, James 1900-1954........ **TCLC 21**
See also CA 108; DLB 34, 77; SATA 34

Himes, Chester (Bomar)
1909-1984 .... **CLC 2, 4, 7, 18, 58; BLC**
See also BW 2; CA 25-28R; 114; CANR 22;
DLB 2, 76, 143; MTCW

Hinde, Thomas .... **CLC 6, 11**
See also Chitty, Thomas Willes

Hindin, Nathan
See Bloch, Robert (Albert)

Hine, (William) Daryl 1936- .... **CLC 15**
See also CA 1-4R; CAAS 15; CANR 1, 20;
DLB 60

Hinkson, Katharine Tynan
See Tynan, Katharine

Hinton, S(usan) E(loise)
1950- .... **CLC 30; DA**
See also AAYA 2; CA 81-84; CANR 32;
CLR 3, 23; JRDA; MAICYA; MTCW;
SATA 19, 58

Hippius, Zinaida .... **TCLC 9**
See also Gippius, Zinaida (Nikolayevna)

Hiraoka, Kimitake 1925-1970
See Mishima, Yukio
See also CA 97-100; 29-32R; MTCW

Hirsch, E(ric) D(onald), Jr. 1928- ... **CLC 79**
See also CA 25-28R; CANR 27; DLB 67;
MTCW

Hirsch, Edward 1950- .... **CLC 31, 50**
See also CA 104; CANR 20, 42; DLB 120

Hitchcock, Alfred (Joseph)
1899-1980 .... **CLC 16**
See also CA 97-100; SATA 27;
SATA-Obit 24

Hitler, Adolf 1889-1945......... **TCLC 53**
See also CA 117

Hoagland, Edward 1932- .... **CLC 28**
See also CA 1-4R; CANR 2, 31; DLB 6;
SATA 51

Hoban, Russell (Conwell) 1925- . . **CLC 7, 25**
See also CA 5-8R; CANR 23, 37; CLR 3;
DLB 52; MAICYA; MTCW; SATA 1,
40, 78

Hobbs, Perry
See Blackmur, R(ichard) P(almer)

Hobson, Laura Z(ametkin)
1900-1986 . . . . **CLC 7, 25**
See also CA 17-20R; 118; DLB 28;
SATA 52

Hochhuth, Rolf 1931- . . . . **CLC 4, 11, 18**
See also CA 5-8R; CANR 33; DLB 124;
MTCW

Hochman, Sandra 1936- . . . . **CLC 3, 8**
See also CA 5-8R; DLB 5

Hochwaelder, Fritz 1911-1986 . . . . . . **CLC 36**
See also CA 29-32R; 120; CANR 42;
MTCW

Hochwalder, Fritz
See Hochwaelder, Fritz

Hocking, Mary (Eunice) 1921- . . . . . **CLC 13**
See also CA 101; CANR 18, 40

Hodgins, Jack 1938- . . . . **CLC 23**
See also CA 93-96; DLB 60

Hodgson, William Hope
1877(?)-1918 . . . . **TCLC 13**
See also CA 111; DLB 70

Hoffman, Alice 1952- . . . . **CLC 51**
See also CA 77-80; CANR 34; MTCW

Hoffman, Daniel (Gerard)
1923- . . . . **CLC 6, 13, 23**
See also CA 1-4R; CANR 4; DLB 5

Hoffman, Stanley 1944- . . . . **CLC 5**
See also CA 77-80

Hoffman, William M(oses) 1939- . . . **CLC 40**
See also CA 57-60; CANR 11

Hoffmann, E(rnst) T(heodor) A(madeus)
1776-1822 . . . . **NCLC 2; SSC 13**
See also DLB 90; SATA 27

Hofmann, Gert 1931- . . . . **CLC 54**
See also CA 128

Hofmannsthal, Hugo von
1874-1929 . . . . **TCLC 11; DC 4**
See also CA 106; DLB 81, 118

Hogan, Linda 1947- . . . . **CLC 73**
See also CA 120; CANR 45; NNAL

Hogarth, Charles
See Creasey, John

Hogg, James 1770-1835 . . . . **NCLC 4**
See also DLB 93, 116

Holbach, Paul Henri Thiry Baron
1723-1789 . . . . **LC 14**

Holberg, Ludvig 1684-1754 . . . . **LC 6**

Holden, Ursula 1921- . . . . **CLC 18**
See also CA 101; CAAS 8; CANR 22

Holderlin, (Johann Christian) Friedrich
1770-1843 . . . . **NCLC 16; PC 4**

Holdstock, Robert
See Holdstock, Robert P.

Holdstock, Robert P. 1948- . . . . **CLC 39**
See also CA 131

Holland, Isabelle 1920- . . . . **CLC 21**
See also AAYA 11; CA 21-24R; CANR 10,
25; JRDA; MAICYA; SATA 8, 70

Holland, Marcus
See Caldwell, (Janet Miriam) Taylor
(Holland)

Hollander, John 1929- . . . . . . **CLC 2, 5, 8, 14**
See also CA 1-4R; CANR 1; DLB 5;
SATA 13

Hollander, Paul
See Silverberg, Robert

Holleran, Andrew 1943(?)- . . . . **CLC 38**
See also CA 144

Hollinghurst, Alan 1954- . . . . **CLC 55**
See also CA 114

Hollis, Jim
See Summers, Hollis (Spurgeon, Jr.)

Holmes, John
See Souster, (Holmes) Raymond

Holmes, John Clellon 1926-1988 . . . . **CLC 56**
See also CA 9-12R; 125; CANR 4; DLB 16

Holmes, Oliver Wendell
1809-1894 . . . . **NCLC 14**
See also CDALB 1640-1865; DLB 1;
SATA 34

Holmes, Raymond
See Souster, (Holmes) Raymond

Holt, Victoria
See Hibbert, Eleanor Alice Burford

Holub, Miroslav 1923- . . . . **CLC 4**
See also CA 21-24R; CANR 10

Homer c. 8th cent. B.C.- . . . . . **CMLC 1; DA**

Honig, Edwin 1919- . . . . **CLC 33**
See also CA 5-8R; CAAS 8; CANR 4, 45;
DLB 5

Hood, Hugh (John Blagdon)
1928- . . . . **CLC 15, 28**
See also CA 49-52; CAAS 17; CANR 1, 33;
DLB 53

Hood, Thomas 1799-1845 . . . . **NCLC 16**
See also DLB 96

Hooker, (Peter) Jeremy 1941- . . . . . . **CLC 43**
See also CA 77-80; CANR 22; DLB 40

Hope, A(lec) D(erwent) 1907- . . . . **CLC 3, 51**
See also CA 21-24R; CANR 33; MTCW

Hope, Brian
See Creasey, John

Hope, Christopher (David Tully)
1944- . . . . **CLC 52**
See also CA 106; SATA 62

Hopkins, Gerard Manley
1844-1889 . . . . **NCLC 17; DA; WLC**
See also CDBLB 1890-1914; DLB 35, 57

Hopkins, John (Richard) 1931- . . . . . . **CLC 4**
See also CA 85-88

Hopkins, Pauline Elizabeth
1859-1930 . . . . **TCLC 28; BLC**
See also BW 2; CA 141; DLB 50

Hopkinson, Francis 1737-1791 . . . . . **LC 25**
See also DLB 31

Hopley-Woolrich, Cornell George 1903-1968
See Woolrich, Cornell
See also CA 13-14; CAP 1

Horatio
See Proust, (Valentin-Louis-George-Eugene-)
Marcel

Horgan, Paul 1903- . . . . **CLC 9, 53**
See also CA 13-16R; CANR 9, 35;
DLB 102; DLBY 85; MTCW; SATA 13

Horn, Peter
See Kuttner, Henry

Hornem, Horace Esq.
See Byron, George Gordon (Noel)

Horovitz, Israel 1939- . . . . **CLC 56**
See also CA 33-36R; DLB 7

Horvath, Odon von
See Horvath, Oedoen von
See also DLB 85, 124

Horvath, Oedoen von 1901-1938 . . . **TCLC 45**
See also Horvath, Odon von
See also CA 118

Horwitz, Julius 1920-1986 . . . . **CLC 14**
See also CA 9-12R; 119; CANR 12

Hospital, Janette Turner 1942- . . . . . **CLC 42**
See also CA 108

Hostos, E. M. de
See Hostos (y Bonilla), Eugenio Maria de

Hostos, Eugenio M. de
See Hostos (y Bonilla), Eugenio Maria de

Hostos, Eugenio Maria
See Hostos (y Bonilla), Eugenio Maria de

Hostos (y Bonilla), Eugenio Maria de
1839-1903 . . . . **TCLC 24**
See also CA 123; 131; HW

Houdini
See Lovecraft, H(oward) P(hillips)

Hougan, Carolyn 1943- . . . . **CLC 34**
See also CA 139

Household, Geoffrey (Edward West)
1900-1988 . . . . **CLC 11**
See also CA 77-80; 126; DLB 87; SATA 14;
SATA-Obit 59

Housman, A(lfred) E(dward)
1859-1936 . . . . . . **TCLC 1, 10; DA; PC 2**
See also CA 104; 125; DLB 19; MTCW

Housman, Laurence 1865-1959 . . . . . **TCLC 7**
See also CA 106; DLB 10; SATA 25

Howard, Elizabeth Jane 1923- . . . **CLC 7, 29**
See also CA 5-8R; CANR 8

Howard, Maureen 1930- . . . . . **CLC 5, 14, 46**
See also CA 53-56; CANR 31; DLBY 83;
MTCW

Howard, Richard 1929- . . . . . . **CLC 7, 10, 47**
See also AITN 1; CA 85-88; CANR 25;
DLB 5

Howard, Robert Ervin 1906-1936 . . . **TCLC 8**
See also CA 105

Howard, Warren F.
See Pohl, Frederik

Howe, Fanny 1940- . . . . **CLC 47**
See also CA 117; SATA 52

Howe, Irving 1920-1993 . . . . **CLC 85**
See also CA 9-12R; 141; CANR 21;
DLB 67; MTCW

Howe, Julia Ward 1819-1910 . . . . . **TCLC 21**
See also CA 117; DLB 1

Howe, Susan 1937- . . . . **CLC 72**
See also DLB 120

Howe, Tina 1937- . . . . **CLC 48**
See also CA 109

Iron, Ralph
See Schreiner, Olive (Emilie Albertina)

Irving, John (Winslow)
1942- . . . . **CLC 13, 23, 38**
See also AAYA 8; BEST 89:3; CA 25-28R;
CANR 28; DLB 6; DLBY 82; MTCW

Irving, Washington
1783-1859 . . . . **NCLC 2, 19; DA; SSC 2;**
WLC
See also CDALB 1640-1865; DLB 3, 11, 30,
59, 73, 74; YABC 2

Irwin, P. K.
See Page, P(atricia) K(athleen)

Isaacs, Susan 1943- . . . . **CLC 32**
See also BEST 89:1; CA 89-92; CANR 20,
41; MTCW

Isherwood, Christopher (William Bradshaw)
1904-1986 . . . . **CLC 1, 9, 11, 14, 44**
See also CA 13-16R; 117; CANR 35;
DLB 15; DLBY 86; MTCW

Ishiguro, Kazuo 1954- . . . . . . **CLC 27, 56, 59**
See also BEST 90:2; CA 120; MTCW

Ishikawa Takuboku
1886(?)-1912 . . . . **TCLC 15; PC 10**
See also CA 113

Iskander, Fazil 1929- . . . . **CLC 47**
See also CA 102

Ivan IV 1530-1584 . . . . **LC 17**

Ivanov, Vyacheslav Ivanovich
1866-1949 . . . . **TCLC 33**
See also CA 122

Ivask, Ivar Vidrik 1927-1992. . . . . . . **CLC 14**
See also CA 37-40R; 139; CANR 24

Jackson, Daniel
See Wingrove, David (John)

Jackson, Jesse 1908-1983 . . . . **CLC 12**
See also BW 1; CA 25-28R; 109; CANR 27;
CLR 28; MAICYA; SATA 2, 29;
SATA-Obit 48

Jackson, Laura (Riding) 1901-1991
See Riding, Laura
See also CA 65-68; 135; CANR 28; DLB 48

Jackson, Sam
See Trumbo, Dalton

Jackson, Sara
See Wingrove, David (John)

Jackson, Shirley
1919-1965 . . . . . **CLC 11, 60; DA; SSC 9;**
WLC
See also AAYA 9; CA 1-4R; 25-28R;
CANR 4; CDALB 1941-1968; DLB 6;
SATA 2

Jacob, (Cyprien-)Max 1876-1944 . . . **TCLC 6**
See also CA 104

Jacobs, Jim 1942-. . . . . **CLC 12**
See also CA 97-100

Jacobs, W(illiam) W(ymark)
1863-1943 . . . . **TCLC 22**
See also CA 121; DLB 135

Jacobsen, Jens Peter 1847-1885 . . **NCLC 34**

Jacobsen, Josephine 1908-. . . . . **CLC 48**
See also CA 33-36R; CAAS 18; CANR 23

Jacobson, Dan 1929- . . . . **CLC 4, 14**
See also CA 1-4R; CANR 2, 25; DLB 14;
MTCW

Jacqueline
See Carpentier (y Valmont), Alejo

Jagger, Mick 1944-. . . . . **CLC 17**

Jakes, John (William) 1932- . . . . **CLC 29**
See also BEST 89:4; CA 57-60; CANR 10,
43; DLBY 83; MTCW; SATA 62

James, Andrew
See Kirkup, James

James, C(yril) L(ionel) R(obert)
1901-1989 . . . . **CLC 33**
See also BW 2; CA 117; 125; 128; DLB 125;
MTCW

James, Daniel (Lewis) 1911-1988
See Santiago, Danny
See also CA 125

James, Dynely
See Mayne, William (James Carter)

James, Henry
1843-1916 . . . . . **TCLC 2, 11, 24, 40, 47;**
DA; SSC 8; WLC
See also CA 104; 132; CDALB 1865-1917;
DLB 12, 71, 74; MTCW

James, M. R.
See James, Montague (Rhodes)

James, Montague (Rhodes)
1862-1936 . . . . **TCLC 6; SSC 16**
See also CA 104

James, P. D. . . . . **CLC 18, 46**
See also White, Phyllis Dorothy James
See also BEST 90:2; CDBLB 1960 to
Present; DLB 87

James, Philip
See Moorcock, Michael (John)

James, William 1842-1910. . . . . **TCLC 15, 32**
See also CA 109

James I 1394-1437 . . . . **LC 20**

Jameson, Anna 1794-1860 . . . . **NCLC 43**
See also DLB 99

Jami, Nur al-Din 'Abd al-Rahman
1414-1492 . . . . **LC 9**

Jandl, Ernst 1925- . . . . **CLC 34**

Janowitz, Tama 1957- . . . . **CLC 43**
See also CA 106

Jarrell, Randall
1914-1965 . . . . **CLC 1, 2, 6, 9, 13, 49**
See also CA 5-8R; 25-28R; CABS 2;
CANR 6, 34; CDALB 1941-1968; CLR 6;
DLB 48, 52; MAICYA; MTCW; SATA 7

Jarry, Alfred 1873-1907. . . . . . . **TCLC 2, 14**
See also CA 104

Jarvis, E. K.
See Bloch, Robert (Albert); Ellison, Harlan
(Jay); Silverberg, Robert

Jeake, Samuel, Jr.
See Aiken, Conrad (Potter)

Jean Paul 1763-1825 . . . . **NCLC 7**

Jefferies, (John) Richard
1848-1887 . . . . **NCLC 47**
See also DLB 98, 141; SATA 16

Jeffers, (John) Robinson
1887-1962 . . . . **CLC 2, 3, 11, 15, 54; DA;**
WLC
See also CA 85-88; CANR 35;
CDALB 1917-1929; DLB 45; MTCW

Jefferson, Janet
See Mencken, H(enry) L(ouis)

Jefferson, Thomas 1743-1826 . . . . **NCLC 11**
See also CDALB 1640-1865; DLB 31

Jeffrey, Francis 1773-1850. . . . . . **NCLC 33**
See also DLB 107

Jelakowitch, Ivan
See Heijermans, Herman

Jellicoe, (Patricia) Ann 1927- . . . . . . **CLC 27**
See also CA 85-88; DLB 13

Jen, Gish . . . . **CLC 70**
See also Jen, Lillian

Jen, Lillian 1956(?)-
See Jen, Gish
See also CA 135

Jenkins, (John) Robin 1912- . . . . **CLC 52**
See also CA 1-4R; CANR 1; DLB 14

Jennings, Elizabeth (Joan)
1926- . . . . **CLC 5, 14**
See also CA 61-64; CAAS 5; CANR 8, 39;
DLB 27; MTCW; SATA 66

Jennings, Waylon 1937-. . . . . **CLC 21**

Jensen, Johannes V. 1873-1950. . . . **TCLC 41**

Jensen, Laura (Linnea) 1948- . . . . . . **CLC 37**
See also CA 103

Jerome, Jerome K(lapka)
1859-1927 . . . . **TCLC 23**
See also CA 119; DLB 10, 34, 135

Jerrold, Douglas William
1803-1857 . . . . **NCLC 2**

Jewett, (Theodora) Sarah Orne
1849-1909 . . . . **TCLC 1, 22; SSC 6**
See also CA 108; 127; DLB 12, 74;
SATA 15

Jewsbury, Geraldine (Endsor)
1812-1880 . . . . **NCLC 22**
See also DLB 21

Jhabvala, Ruth Prawer
1927- . . . . **CLC 4, 8, 29**
See also CA 1-4R; CANR 2, 29; DLB 139;
MTCW

Jiles, Paulette 1943-. . . . . **CLC 13, 58**
See also CA 101

Jimenez (Mantecon), Juan Ramon
1881-1958 . . . . **TCLC 4; HLC; PC 7**
See also CA 104; 131; DLB 134; HW;
MTCW

Jimenez, Ramon
See Jimenez (Mantecon), Juan Ramon

Jimenez Mantecon, Juan
See Jimenez (Mantecon), Juan Ramon

Joel, Billy . . . . **CLC 26**
See also Joel, William Martin

Joel, William Martin 1949-
See Joel, Billy
See also CA 108

John of the Cross, St. 1542-1591 . . . . **LC 18**

Johnson, B(ryan) S(tanley William)
1933-1973 . . . . **CLC 6, 9**
See also CA 9-12R; 53-56; CANR 9;
DLB 14, 40

Johnson, Benj. F. of Boo
See Riley, James Whitcomb

Killens, John Oliver 1916-1987..... CLC 10
   See also BW 2; CA 77-80; 123; CAAS 2;
   CANR 26; DLB 33

Killigrew, Anne 1660-1685.......... LC 4
   See also DLB 131

Kim
   See Simenon, Georges (Jacques Christian)

Kincaid, Jamaica 1949- ... CLC 43, 68; BLC
   See also AAYA 13; BW 2; CA 125

King, Francis (Henry) 1923-..... CLC 8, 53
   See also CA 1-4R; CANR 1, 33; DLB 15,
   139; MTCW

King, Martin Luther, Jr.
   1929-1968 .... CLC 83; BLC; DA
   See also BW 2; CA 25-28; CANR 27, 44;
   CAP 2; MTCW; SATA 14

King, Stephen (Edwin)
   1947-...... CLC 12, 26, 37, 61; SSC 17
   See also AAYA 1; BEST 90:1; CA 61-64;
   CANR 1, 30; DLB 143; DLBY 80;
   JRDA; MTCW; SATA 9, 55

King, Steve
   See King, Stephen (Edwin)

Kingman, Lee.................... CLC 17
   See also Natti, (Mary) Lee
   See also SAAS 3; SATA 1, 67

Kingsley, Charles 1819-1875 ..... NCLC 35
   See also DLB 21, 32; YABC 2

Kingsley, Sidney 1906-........... CLC 44
   See also CA 85-88; DLB 7

Kingsolver, Barbara 1955-...... CLC 55, 81
   See also CA 129; 134

Kingston, Maxine (Ting Ting) Hong
   1940-................ CLC 12, 19, 58
   See also AAYA 8; CA 69-72; CANR 13,
   38; DLBY 80; MTCW; SATA 53

Kinnell, Galway
   1927-.......... CLC 1, 2, 3, 5, 13, 29
   See also CA 9-12R; CANR 10, 34; DLB 5;
   DLBY 87; MTCW

Kinsella, Thomas 1928-......... CLC 4, 19
   See also CA 17-20R; CANR 15; DLB 27;
   MTCW

Kinsella, W(illiam) P(atrick)
   1935-................... CLC 27, 43
   See also AAYA 7; CA 97-100; CAAS 7;
   CANR 21, 35; MTCW

Kipling, (Joseph) Rudyard
   1865-1936 ...... TCLC 8, 17; DA; PC 3;
                                  SSC 5; WLC
   See also CA 105; 120; CANR 33;
   CDBLB 1890-1914; DLB 19, 34, 141;
   MAICYA; MTCW; YABC 2

Kirkup, James 1918- .... CLC 1
   See also CA 1-4R; CAAS 4; CANR 2;
   DLB 27; SATA 12

Kirkwood, James 1930(?)-1989 ...... CLC 9
   See also AITN 2; CA 1-4R; 128; CANR 6,
   40

Kis, Danilo 1935-1989 .... CLC 57
   See also CA 109; 118; 129; MTCW

Kivi, Aleksis 1834-1872 .... NCLC 30

Kizer, Carolyn (Ashley)
   1925- .... CLC 15, 39, 80
   See also CA 65-68; CAAS 5; CANR 24;
   DLB 5

Klabund 1890-1928............. TCLC 44
   See also DLB 66

Klappert, Peter 1942-............ CLC 57
   See also CA 33-36R; DLB 5

Klein, A(braham) M(oses)
   1909-1972 .... CLC 19
   See also CA 101; 37-40R; DLB 68

Klein, Norma 1938-1989 .... CLC 30
   See also AAYA 2; CA 41-44R; 128;
   CANR 15, 37; CLR 2, 19; JRDA;
   MAICYA; SAAS 1; SATA 7, 57

Klein, T(heodore) E(ibon) D(onald)
   1947-..................... CLC 34
   See also CA 119; CANR 44

Kleist, Heinrich von
   1777-1811 .... NCLC 2, 37
   See also DLB 90

Klima, Ivan 1931-............... CLC 56
   See also CA 25-28R; CANR 17

Klimentov, Andrei Platonovich 1899-1951
   See Platonov, Andrei
   See also CA 108

Klinger, Friedrich Maximilian von
   1752-1831 .... NCLC 1
   See also DLB 94

Klopstock, Friedrich Gottlieb
   1724-1803 .... NCLC 11
   See also DLB 97

Knebel, Fletcher 1911-1993 .... CLC 14
   See also AITN 1; CA 1-4R; 140; CAAS 3;
   CANR 1, 36; SATA 36; SATA-Obit 75

Knickerbocker, Diedrich
   See Irving, Washington

Knight, Etheridge
   1931-1991 .... CLC 40; BLC
   See also BW 1; CA 21-24R; 133; CANR 23;
   DLB 41

Knight, Sarah Kemble 1666-1727 ..... LC 7
   See also DLB 24

Knister, Raymond 1899-1932...... TCLC 56
   See also DLB 68

Knowles, John
   1926- .... CLC 1, 4, 10, 26; DA
   See also AAYA 10; CA 17-20R; CANR 40;
   CDALB 1968-1988; DLB 6; MTCW;
   SATA 8

Knox, Calvin M.
   See Silverberg, Robert

Knye, Cassandra
   See Disch, Thomas M(ichael)

Koch, C(hristopher) J(ohn) 1932- ... CLC 42
   See also CA 127

Koch, Christopher
   See Koch, C(hristopher) J(ohn)

Koch, Kenneth 1925-....... CLC 5, 8, 44
   See also CA 1-4R; CANR 6, 36; DLB 5;
   SATA 65

Kochanowski, Jan 1530-1584....... LC 10

Kock, Charles Paul de
   1794-1871 .... NCLC 16

Koda Shigeyuki 1867-1947
   See Rohan, Koda
   See also CA 121

Koestler, Arthur
   1905-1983 .... CLC 1, 3, 6, 8, 15, 33
   See also CA 1-4R; 109; CANR 1, 33;
   CDBLB 1945-1960; DLBY 83; MTCW

Kogawa, Joy Nozomi 1935-........ CLC 78
   See also CA 101; CANR 19

Kohout, Pavel 1928-.............. CLC 13
   See also CA 45-48; CANR 3

Koizumi, Yakumo
   See Hearn, (Patricio) Lafcadio (Tessima
   Carlos)

Kolmar, Gertrud 1894-1943...... TCLC 40

Konrad, George
   See Konrad, Gyoergy

Konrad, Gyoergy 1933- ...... CLC 4, 10, 73
   See also CA 85-88

Konwicki, Tadeusz 1926-..... CLC 8, 28, 54
   See also CA 101; CAAS 9; CANR 39;
   MTCW

Koontz, Dean R(ay) 1945-......... CLC 78
   See also AAYA 9; BEST 89:3, 90:2;
   CA 108; CANR 19, 36; MTCW

Kopit, Arthur (Lee) 1937- .... CLC 1, 18, 33
   See also AITN 1; CA 81-84; CABS 3;
   DLB 7; MTCW

Kops, Bernard 1926-.............. CLC 4
   See also CA 5-8R; DLB 13

Kornbluth, C(yril) M. 1923-1958.... TCLC 8
   See also CA 105; DLB 8

Korolenko, V. G.
   See Korolenko, Vladimir Galaktionovich

Korolenko, Vladimir
   See Korolenko, Vladimir Galaktionovich

Korolenko, Vladimir G.
   See Korolenko, Vladimir Galaktionovich

Korolenko, Vladimir Galaktionovich
   1853-1921 .... TCLC 22
   See also CA 121

Kosinski, Jerzy (Nikodem)
   1933-1991 .... CLC 1, 2, 3, 6, 10, 15, 53,
                                              70
   See also CA 17-20R; 134; CANR 9, 46;
   DLB 2; DLBY 82; MTCW

Kostelanetz, Richard (Cory) 1940- .. CLC 28
   See also CA 13-16R; CAAS 8; CANR 38

Kostrowitzki, Wilhelm Apollinaris de
   1880-1918
   See Apollinaire, Guillaume
   See also CA 104

Kotlowitz, Robert 1924-............ CLC 4
   See also CA 33-36R; CANR 36

Kotzebue, August (Friedrich Ferdinand) von
   1761-1819 .... NCLC 25
   See also DLB 94

Kotzwinkle, William 1938- ... CLC 5, 14, 35
   See also CA 45-48; CANR 3, 44; CLR 6;
   MAICYA; SATA 24, 70

Kozol, Jonathan 1936-............ CLC 17
   See also CA 61-64; CANR 16, 45

Kozoll, Michael 1940(?)- .... CLC 35

Kramer, Kathryn 19(?)- .... CLC 34

Kramer, Larry 1935- .... **CLC 42**
See also CA 124; 126

Krasicki, Ignacy 1735-1801 .... **NCLC 8**

Krasinski, Zygmunt 1812-1859 .... **NCLC 4**

Kraus, Karl 1874-1936 .... **TCLC 5**
See also CA 104; DLB 118

Kreve (Mickevicius), Vincas
1882-1954 .... **TCLC 27**

Kristeva, Julia 1941- .... **CLC 77**

Kristofferson, Kris 1936- .... **CLC 26**
See also CA 104

Krizanc, John 1956- .... **CLC 57**

Krleza, Miroslav 1893-1981 .... **CLC 8**
See also CA 97-100; 105; DLB 147

Kroetsch, Robert 1927- ...... **CLC 5, 23, 57**
See also CA 17-20R; CANR 8, 38; DLB 53;
MTCW

Kroetz, Franz
See Kroetz, Franz Xaver

Kroetz, Franz Xaver 1946- .... **CLC 41**
See also CA 130

Kroker, Arthur 1945- .... **CLC 77**

Kropotkin, Peter (Aleksieevich)
1842-1921 .... **TCLC 36**
See also CA 119

Krotkov, Yuri 1917- .... **CLC 19**
See also CA 102

Krumb
See Crumb, R(obert)

Krumgold, Joseph (Quincy)
1908-1980 .... **CLC 12**
See also CA 9-12R; 101; CANR 7;
MAICYA; SATA 1, 48; SATA-Obit 23

Krumwitz
See Crumb, R(obert)

Krutch, Joseph Wood 1893-1970 .... **CLC 24**
See also CA 1-4R; 25-28R; CANR 4;
DLB 63

Krutzch, Gus
See Eliot, T(homas) S(tearns)

Krylov, Ivan Andreevich
1768(?)-1844 .... **NCLC 1**

Kubin, Alfred 1877-1959 .... **TCLC 23**
See also CA 112; DLB 81

Kubrick, Stanley 1928- .... **CLC 16**
See also CA 81-84; CANR 33; DLB 26

Kumin, Maxine (Winokur)
1925- .... **CLC 5, 13, 28**
See also AITN 2; CA 1-4R; CAAS 8;
CANR 1, 21; DLB 5; MTCW; SATA 12

Kundera, Milan
1929- .... **CLC 4, 9, 19, 32, 68**
See also AAYA 2; CA 85-88; CANR 19;
MTCW

Kunene, Mazisi (Raymond) 1930- ... **CLC 85**
See also BW 1; CA 125; DLB 117

Kunitz, Stanley (Jasspon)
1905- .... **CLC 6, 11, 14**
See also CA 41-44R; CANR 26; DLB 48;
MTCW

Kunze, Reiner 1933- .... **CLC 10**
See also CA 93-96; DLB 75

Kuprin, Aleksandr Ivanovich
1870-1938 .... **TCLC 5**
See also CA 104

Kureishi, Hanif 1954(?)-.......... **CLC 64**
See also CA 139

Kurosawa, Akira 1910-............ **CLC 16**
See also AAYA 11; CA 101; CANR 46

Kushner, Tony 1957(?)- .... **CLC 81**
See also CA 144

Kuttner, Henry 1915-1958 .... **TCLC 10**
See also CA 107; DLB 8

Kuzma, Greg 1944-............... **CLC 7**
See also CA 33-36R

Kuzmin, Mikhail 1872(?)-1936 .... **TCLC 40**

Kyd, Thomas 1558-1594 ...... **LC 22; DC 3**
See also DLB 62

Kyprianos, Iossif
See Samarakis, Antonis

La Bruyere, Jean de 1645-1696 ...... **LC 17**

Lacan, Jacques (Marie Emile)
1901-1981 .... **CLC 75**
See also CA 121; 104

Laclos, Pierre Ambroise Francois Choderlos
de 1741-1803 .... **NCLC 4**

Lacolere, Francois
See Aragon, Louis

La Colere, Francois
See Aragon, Louis

La Deshabilleuse
See Simenon, Georges (Jacques Christian)

Lady Gregory
See Gregory, Isabella Augusta (Persse)

Lady of Quality, A
See Bagnold, Enid

La Fayette, Marie (Madelaine Pioche de la
Vergne Comtes 1634-1693 .... **LC 2**

Lafayette, Rene
See Hubbard, L(afayette) Ron(ald)

Laforgue, Jules 1860-1887 .... **NCLC 5**

Lagerkvist, Paer (Fabian)
1891-1974 .... **CLC 7, 10, 13, 54**
See also Lagerkvist, Par
See also CA 85-88; 49-52; MTCW

Lagerkvist, Par
See Lagerkvist, Paer (Fabian)
See also SSC 12

Lagerloef, Selma (Ottiliana Lovisa)
1858-1940 .... **TCLC 4, 36**
See also Lagerlof, Selma (Ottiliana Lovisa)
See also CA 108; SATA 15

Lagerlof, Selma (Ottiliana Lovisa)
See Lagerloef, Selma (Ottiliana Lovisa)
See also CLR 7; SATA 15

La Guma, (Justin) Alex(ander)
1925-1985 .... **CLC 19**
See also BW 1; CA 49-52; 118; CANR 25;
DLB 117; MTCW

Laidlaw, A. K.
See Grieve, C(hristopher) M(urray)

Lainez, Manuel Mujica
See Mujica Lainez, Manuel
See also HW

Lamartine, Alphonse (Marie Louis Prat) de
1790-1869 .... **NCLC 11**

Lamb, Charles
1775-1834 .... **NCLC 10; DA; WLC**
See also CDBLB 1789-1832; DLB 93, 107;
SATA 17

Lamb, Lady Caroline 1785-1828 .. **NCLC 38**
See also DLB 116

Lamming, George (William)
1927- .... **CLC 2, 4, 66; BLC**
See also BW 2; CA 85-88; CANR 26;
DLB 125; MTCW

L'Amour, Louis (Dearborn)
1908-1988 .... **CLC 25, 55**
See also AITN 2; BEST 89:2; CA 1-4R;
125; CANR 3, 25, 40; DLBY 80; MTCW

Lampedusa, Giuseppe (Tomasi) di ... **TCLC 13**
See also Tomasi di Lampedusa, Giuseppe

Lampman, Archibald 1861-1899 .. **NCLC 25**
See also DLB 92

Lancaster, Bruce 1896-1963 .... **CLC 36**
See also CA 9-10; CAP 1; SATA 9

Landau, Mark Alexandrovich
See Aldanov, Mark (Alexandrovich)

Landau-Aldanov, Mark Alexandrovich
See Aldanov, Mark (Alexandrovich)

Landis, John 1950- .... **CLC 26**
See also CA 112; 122

Landolfi, Tommaso 1908-1979 ... **CLC 11, 49**
See also CA 127; 117

Landon, Letitia Elizabeth
1802-1838 .... **NCLC 15**
See also DLB 96

Landor, Walter Savage
1775-1864 .... **NCLC 14**
See also DLB 93, 107

Landwirth, Heinz 1927-
See Lind, Jakov
See also CA 9-12R; CANR 7

Lane, Patrick 1939- .... **CLC 25**
See also CA 97-100; DLB 53

Lang, Andrew 1844-1912 .... **TCLC 16**
See also CA 114; 137; DLB 98, 141;
MAICYA; SATA 16

Lang, Fritz 1890-1976 .... **CLC 20**
See also CA 77-80; 69-72; CANR 30

Lange, John
See Crichton, (John) Michael

Langer, Elinor 1939- .... **CLC 34**
See also CA 121

Langland, William
1330(?)-1400(?) .... **LC 19; DA**
See also DLB 146

Langstaff, Launcelot
See Irving, Washington

Lanier, Sidney 1842-1881 .... **NCLC 6**
See also DLB 64; MAICYA; SATA 18

Lanyer, Aemilia 1569-1645 .... **LC 10**

Lao Tzu .... **CMLC 7**

Lapine, James (Elliot) 1949- .... **CLC 39**
See also CA 123; 130

Larbaud, Valery (Nicolas)
1881-1957 .... **TCLC 9**
See also CA 106

Lardner, Ring
See Lardner, Ring(gold) W(ilmer)

Lardner, Ring W., Jr.
See Lardner, Ring(gold) W(ilmer)

Lardner, Ring(gold) W(ilmer)
1885-1933 . . . . **TCLC 2, 14**
See also CA 104; 131; CDALB 1917-1929;
DLB 11, 25, 86; MTCW

Laredo, Betty
See Codrescu, Andrei

Larkin, Maia
See Wojciechowska, Maia (Teresa)

Larkin, Philip (Arthur)
1922-1985 . . . . **CLC 3, 5, 8, 9, 13, 18, 33,**
39, 64
See also CA 5-8R; 117; CANR 24;
CDBLB 1960 to Present; DLB 27;
MTCW

Larra (y Sanchez de Castro), Mariano Jose de
1809-1837 . . . . **NCLC 17**

Larsen, Eric 1941- . . . . **CLC 55**
See also CA 132

Larsen, Nella 1891-1964 . . . . . **CLC 37; BLC**
See also BW 1; CA 125; DLB 51

Larson, Charles R(aymond) 1938-. . . **CLC 31**
See also CA 53-56; CANR 4

Lasker-Schueler, Else 1869-1945 . . **TCLC 57**
See also DLB 66, 124

Latham, Jean Lee 1902-. . . . . **CLC 12**
See also AITN 1; CA 5-8R; CANR 7;
MAICYA; SATA 2, 68

Latham, Mavis
See Clark, Mavis Thorpe

Lathen, Emma . . . . **CLC 2**
See also Hennissart, Martha; Latsis, Mary
J(ane)

Lathrop, Francis
See Leiber, Fritz (Reuter, Jr.)

Latsis, Mary J(ane)
See Lathen, Emma
See also CA 85-88

Lattimore, Richmond (Alexander)
1906-1984 . . . . **CLC 3**
See also CA 1-4R; 112; CANR 1

Laughlin, James 1914-. . . . . **CLC 49**
See also CA 21-24R; CANR 9; DLB 48

Laurence, (Jean) Margaret (Wemyss)
1926-1987 . . **CLC 3, 6, 13, 50, 62; SSC 7**
See also CA 5-8R; 121; CANR 33; DLB 53;
MTCW; SATA-Obit 50

Laurent, Antoine 1952- . . . . **CLC 50**

Lauscher, Hermann
See Hesse, Hermann

Lautreamont, Comte de
1846-1870 . . . . **NCLC 12; SSC 14**

Laverty, Donald
See Blish, James (Benjamin)

Lavin, Mary 1912- . . . . . . **CLC 4, 18; SSC 4**
See also CA 9-12R; CANR 33; DLB 15;
MTCW

Lavond, Paul Dennis
See Kornbluth, C(yril) M.; Pohl, Frederik

Lawler, Raymond Evenor 1922- . . . . **CLC 58**
See also CA 103

Lawrence, D(avid) H(erbert Richards)
1885-1930 . . . . . . **TCLC 2, 9, 16, 33, 48;**
DA; SSC 4; WLC
See also CA 104; 121; CDBLB 1914-1945;
DLB 10, 19, 36, 98; MTCW

Lawrence, T(homas) E(dward)
1888-1935 . . . . **TCLC 18**
See also Dale, Colin
See also CA 115

Lawrence of Arabia
See Lawrence, T(homas) E(dward)

Lawson, Henry (Archibald Hertzberg)
1867-1922 . . . . **TCLC 27**
See also CA 120

Lawton, Dennis
See Faust, Frederick (Schiller)

Laxness, Halldor . . . . **CLC 25**
See also Gudjonsson, Halldor Kiljan

Layamon fl. c. 1200-. . . . . **CMLC 10**
See also DLB 146

Laye, Camara 1928-1980 . . . **CLC 4, 38; BLC**
See also BW 1; CA 85-88; 97-100;
CANR 25; MTCW

Layton, Irving (Peter) 1912- . . . . . **CLC 2, 15**
See also CA 1-4R; CANR 2, 33, 43;
DLB 88; MTCW

Lazarus, Emma 1849-1887. . . . . **NCLC 8**

Lazarus, Felix
See Cable, George Washington

Lazarus, Henry
See Slavitt, David R(ytman)

Lea, Joan
See Neufeld, John (Arthur)

Leacock, Stephen (Butler)
1869-1944 . . . . **TCLC 2**
See also CA 104; 141; DLB 92

Lear, Edward 1812-1888 . . . . **NCLC 3**
See also CLR 1; DLB 32; MAICYA;
SATA 18

Lear, Norman (Milton) 1922-·. . . . . . **CLC 12**
See also CA 73-76

Leavis, F(rank) R(aymond)
1895-1978 . . . . **CLC 24**
See also CA 21-24R; 77-80; CANR 44;
MTCW

Leavitt, David 1961-. . . . . **CLC 34**
See also CA 116; 122; DLB 130

Leblanc, Maurice (Marie Emile)
1864-1941 . . . . **TCLC 49**
See also CA 110

Lebowitz, Fran(ces Ann)
1951(?)-. . . . . **CLC 11, 36**
See also CA 81-84; CANR 14; MTCW

Lebrecht, Peter
See Tieck, (Johann) Ludwig

le Carre, John . . . . **CLC 3, 5, 9, 15, 28**
See also Cornwell, David (John Moore)
See also BEST 89:4; CDBLB 1960 to
Present; DLB 87

Le Clezio, J(ean) M(arie) G(ustave)
1940- . . . . **CLC 31**
See also CA 116; 128; DLB 83

Leconte de Lisle, Charles-Marie-Rene
1818-1894 . . . . **NCLC 29**

Le Coq, Monsieur
See Simenon, Georges (Jacques Christian)

Leduc, Violette 1907-1972. . . . . **CLC 22**
See also CA 13-14; 33-36R; CAP 1

Ledwidge, Francis 1887(?)-1917 . . . **TCLC 23**
See also CA 123; DLB 20

Lee, Andrea 1953- . . . . **CLC 36; BLC**
See also BW 1; CA 125

Lee, Andrew
See Auchincloss, Louis (Stanton)

Lee, Don L. . . . . **CLC 2**
See also Madhubuti, Haki R.

Lee, George W(ashington)
1894-1976 . . . . **CLC 52; BLC**
See also BW 1; CA 125; DLB 51

Lee, (Nelle) Harper
1926- . . . . **CLC 12, 60; DA; WLC**
See also AAYA 13; CA 13-16R;
CDALB 1941-1968; DLB 6; MTCW;
SATA 11

Lee, Julian
See Latham, Jean Lee

Lee, Larry
See Lee, Lawrence

Lee, Lawrence 1941-1990. . . . . **CLC 34**
See also CA 131; CANR 43

Lee, Manfred B(ennington)
1905-1971 . . . . **CLC 11**
See also Queen, Ellery
See also CA 1-4R; 29-32R; CANR 2;
DLB 137

Lee, Stan 1922-. . . . . **CLC 17**
See also AAYA 5; CA 108; 111

Lee, Tanith 1947-. . . . . **CLC 46**
See also CA 37-40R; SATA 8

Lee, Vernon . . . . **TCLC 5**
See also Paget, Violet
See also DLB 57

Lee, William
See Burroughs, William S(eward)

Lee, Willy
See Burroughs, William S(eward)

Lee-Hamilton, Eugene (Jacob)
1845-1907 . . . . **TCLC 22**
See also CA 117

Leet, Judith 1935- . . . . **CLC 11**

Le Fanu, Joseph Sheridan
1814-1873 . . . . **NCLC 9; SSC 14**
See also DLB 21, 70

Leffland, Ella 1931- . . . . **CLC 19**
See also CA 29-32R; CANR 35; DLBY 84;
SATA 65

Leger, Alexis
See Leger, (Marie-Rene Auguste) Alexis
Saint-Leger

Leger, (Marie-Rene Auguste) Alexis
Saint-Leger 1887-1975. . . . . . . **CLC 11**
See also Perse, St.-John
See also CA 13-16R; 61-64; CANR 43;
MTCW

Leger, Saintleger
See Leger, (Marie-Rene Auguste) Alexis
Saint-Leger

Lucas, Craig 1951- . . . . **CLC 64**
See also CA 137

Lucas, George 1944- . . . . **CLC 16**
See also AAYA 1; CA 77-80; CANR 30;
SATA 56

Lucas, Hans
See Godard, Jean-Luc

Lucas, Victoria
See Plath, Sylvia

Ludlam, Charles 1943-1987 . . . . . **CLC 46, 50**
See also CA 85-88; 122

Ludlum, Robert 1927- . . . . **CLC 22, 43**
See also AAYA 10; BEST 89:1, 90:3;
CA 33-36R; CANR 25, 41; DLBY 82;
MTCW

Ludwig, Ken. . . . . **CLC 60**

Ludwig, Otto 1813-1865. . . . . **NCLC 4**
See also DLB 129

Lugones, Leopoldo 1874-1938 . . . . . **TCLC 15**
See also CA 116; 131; HW

Lu Hsun 1881-1936 . . . . **TCLC 3**

Lukacs, George . . . . **CLC 24**
See also Lukacs, Gyorgy (Szegeny von)

Lukacs, Gyorgy (Szegeny von) 1885-1971
See Lukacs, George
See also CA 101; 29-32R

Luke, Peter (Ambrose Cyprian)
1919- . . . . **CLC 38**
See also CA 81-84; DLB 13

Lunar, Dennis
See Mungo, Raymond

Lurie, Alison 1926- . . . . **CLC 4, 5, 18, 39**
See also CA 1-4R; CANR 2, 17; DLB 2;
MTCW; SATA 46

Lustig, Arnost 1926- . . . . **CLC 56**
See also AAYA 3; CA 69-72; SATA 56

Luther, Martin 1483-1546 . . . . **LC 9**

Luzi, Mario 1914- . . . . **CLC 13**
See also CA 61-64; CANR 9; DLB 128

Lynch, B. Suarez
See Bioy Casares, Adolfo; Borges, Jorge
Luis

Lynch, David (K.) 1946- . . . . **CLC 66**
See also CA 124; 129

Lynch, James
See Andreyev, Leonid (Nikolaevich)

Lynch Davis, B.
See Bioy Casares, Adolfo; Borges, Jorge
Luis

Lyndsay, Sir David 1490-1555 . . . . . . **LC 20**

Lynn, Kenneth S(chuyler) 1923- . . . . **CLC 50**
See also CA 1-4R; CANR 3, 27

Lynx
See West, Rebecca

Lyons, Marcus
See Blish, James (Benjamin)

Lyre, Pinchbeck
See Sassoon, Siegfried (Lorraine)

Lytle, Andrew (Nelson) 1902- . . . . . . **CLC 22**
See also CA 9-12R; DLB 6

Lyttelton, George 1709-1773 . . . . **LC 10**

Maas, Peter 1929- . . . . **CLC 29**
See also CA 93-96

Macaulay, Rose 1881-1958 . . . . . **TCLC 7, 44**
See also CA 104; DLB 36

Macaulay, Thomas Babington
1800-1859 . . . . **NCLC 42**
See also CDBLB 1832-1890; DLB 32, 55

MacBeth, George (Mann)
1932-1992 . . . . **CLC 2, 5, 9**
See also CA 25-28R; 136; DLB 40; MTCW;
SATA 4; SATA-Obit 70

MacCaig, Norman (Alexander)
1910- . . . . **CLC 36**
See also CA 9-12R; CANR 3, 34; DLB 27

MacCarthy, (Sir Charles Otto) Desmond
1877-1952 . . . . **TCLC 36**

MacDiarmid, Hugh
. . . . **CLC 2, 4, 11, 19, 63; PC 9**
See also Grieve, C(hristopher) M(urray)
See also CDBLB 1945-1960; DLB 20

MacDonald, Anson
See Heinlein, Robert A(nson)

Macdonald, Cynthia 1928- . . . . . . **CLC 13, 19**
See also CA 49-52; CANR 4, 44; DLB 105

MacDonald, George 1824-1905 . . . . . **TCLC 9**
See also CA 106; 137; DLB 18; MAICYA;
SATA 33

Macdonald, John
See Millar, Kenneth

MacDonald, John D(ann)
1916-1986 . . . . **CLC 3, 27, 44**
See also CA 1-4R; 121; CANR 1, 19;
DLB 8; DLBY 86; MTCW

Macdonald, John Ross
See Millar, Kenneth

Macdonald, Ross . . . . . **CLC 1, 2, 3, 14, 34, 41**
See also Millar, Kenneth
See also DLBD 6

MacDougal, John
See Blish, James (Benjamin)

MacEwen, Gwendolyn (Margaret)
1941-1987 . . . . **CLC 13, 55**
See also CA 9-12R; 124; CANR 7, 22;
DLB 53; SATA 50; SATA-Obit 55

Macha, Karel Hynek 1810-1846 . . **NCLC 46**

Machado (y Ruiz), Antonio
1875-1939 . . . . **TCLC 3**
See also CA 104; DLB 108

Machado de Assis, Joaquim Maria
1839-1908 . . . . **TCLC 10; BLC**
See also CA 107

Machen, Arthur. . . . . **TCLC 4**
See also Jones, Arthur Llewellyn
See also DLB 36

Machiavelli, Niccolo 1469-1527 . . **LC 8; DA**

MacInnes, Colin 1914-1976 . . . . . . **CLC 4, 23**
See also CA 69-72; 65-68; CANR 21;
DLB 14; MTCW

MacInnes, Helen (Clark)
1907-1985 . . . . **CLC 27, 39**
See also CA 1-4R; 117; CANR 1, 28;
DLB 87; MTCW; SATA 22;
SATA-Obit 44

Mackay, Mary 1855-1924
See Corelli, Marie
See also CA 118

Mackenzie, Compton (Edward Montague)
1883-1972 . . . . **CLC 18**
See also CA 21-22; 37-40R; CAP 2;
DLB 34, 100

Mackenzie, Henry 1745-1831 . . . . **NCLC 41**
See also DLB 39

Mackintosh, Elizabeth 1896(?)-1952
See Tey, Josephine
See also CA 110

MacLaren, James
See Grieve, C(hristopher) M(urray)

Mac Laverty, Bernard 1942- . . . . **CLC 31**
See also CA 116; 118; CANR 43

MacLean, Alistair (Stuart)
1922-1987 . . . . **CLC 3, 13, 50, 63**
See also CA 57-60; 121; CANR 28; MTCW;
SATA 23; SATA-Obit 50

Maclean, Norman (Fitzroy)
1902-1990 . . . . **CLC 78; SSC 13**
See also CA 102; 132

MacLeish, Archibald
1892-1982 . . . . **CLC 3, 8, 14, 68**
See also CA 9-12R; 106; CANR 33; DLB 4,
7, 45; DLBY 82; MTCW

MacLennan, (John) Hugh
1907-1990 . . . . **CLC 2, 14**
See also CA 5-8R; 142; CANR 33; DLB 68;
MTCW

MacLeod, Alistair 1936- . . . . **CLC 56**
See also CA 123; DLB 60

MacNeice, (Frederick) Louis
1907-1963 . . . . **CLC 1, 4, 10, 53**
See also CA 85-88; DLB 10, 20; MTCW

MacNeill, Dand
See Fraser, George MacDonald

Macpherson, (Jean) Jay 1931- . . . . . . **CLC 14**
See also CA 5-8R; DLB 53

MacShane, Frank 1927- . . . . **CLC 39**
See also CA 9-12R; CANR 3, 33; DLB 111

Macumber, Mari
See Sandoz, Mari(e Susette)

Madach, Imre 1823-1864 . . . . **NCLC 19**

Madden, (Jerry) David 1933- . . . . **CLC 5, 15**
See also CA 1-4R; CAAS 3; CANR 4, 45;
DLB 6; MTCW

Maddern, Al(an)
See Ellison, Harlan (Jay)

Madhubuti, Haki R.
1942- . . . . **CLC 6, 73; BLC; PC 5**
See also Lee, Don L.
See also BW 2; CA 73-76; CANR 24;
DLB 5, 41; DLBD 8

Maepenn, Hugh
See Kuttner, Henry

Maepenn, K. H.
See Kuttner, Henry

Maeterlinck, Maurice 1862-1949 . . . **TCLC 3**
See also CA 104; 136; SATA 66

Maginn, William 1794-1842 . . . . . . **NCLC 8**
See also DLB 110

Mahapatra, Jayanta 1928- . . . . **CLC 33**
See also CA 73-76; CAAS 9; CANR 15, 33

Mahfouz, Naguib (Abdel Aziz Al-Sabilgi)
1911(?)-
See Mahfuz, Najib
See also BEST 89:2; CA 128; MTCW

Mahfuz, Najib . . . . CLC 52, 55
See also Mahfouz, Naguib (Abdel Aziz
Al-Sabilgi)
See also DLBY 88

Mahon, Derek 1941- . . . . CLC 27
See also CA 113; 128; DLB 40

Mailer, Norman
1923- . . . . . . CLC 1, 2, 3, 4, 5, 8, 11, 14,
28, 39, 74; DA
See also AITN 2; CA 9-12R; CABS 1;
CANR 28; CDALB 1968-1988; DLB 2,
16, 28; DLBD 3; DLBY 80, 83; MTCW

Maillet, Antonine 1929- . . . . CLC 54
See also CA 115; 120; CANR 46; DLB 60

Mais, Roger 1905-1955 . . . . TCLC 8
See also BW 1; CA 105; 124; DLB 125;
MTCW

Maistre, Joseph de 1753-1821 . . . . NCLC 37

Maitland, Sara (Louise) 1950- . . . . . . CLC 49
See also CA 69-72; CANR 13

Major, Clarence
1936- . . . . CLC 3, 19, 48; BLC
See also BW 2; CA 21-24R; CAAS 6;
CANR 13, 25; DLB 33

Major, Kevin (Gerald) 1949- . . . . CLC 26
See also CA 97-100; CANR 21, 38;
CLR 11; DLB 60; JRDA; MAICYA;
SATA 32

Maki, James
See Ozu, Yasujiro

Malabaila, Damiano
See Levi, Primo

Malamud, Bernard
1914-1986 . . . . . . CLC 1, 2, 3, 5, 8, 9, 11,
18, 27, 44, 78, 85; DA; SSC 15; WLC
See also CA 5-8R; 118; CABS 1; CANR 28;
CDALB 1941-1968; DLB 2, 28;
DLBY 80, 86; MTCW

Malaparte, Curzio 1898-1957 . . . . . TCLC 52

Malcolm, Dan
See Silverberg, Robert

Malcolm X . . . . CLC 82; BLC
See also Little, Malcolm

Malherbe, Francois de 1555-1628 . . . . . LC 5

Mallarme, Stephane
1842-1898 . . . . NCLC 4, 41; PC 4

Mallet-Joris, Francoise 1930- . . . . . . CLC 11
See also CA 65-68; CANR 17; DLB 83

Malley, Ern
See McAuley, James Phillip

Mallowan, Agatha Christie
See Christie, Agatha (Mary Clarissa)

Maloff, Saul 1922- . . . . CLC 5
See also CA 33-36R

Malone, Louis
See MacNeice, (Frederick) Louis

Malone, Michael (Christopher)
1942- . . . . CLC 43
See also CA 77-80; CANR 14, 32

Malory, (Sir) Thomas
1410(?)-1471(?) . . . . LC 11; DA
See also CDBLB Before 1660; DLB 146;
SATA 33, 59

Malouf, (George Joseph) David
1934- . . . . CLC 28
See also CA 124

Malraux, (Georges-)Andre
1901-1976 . . . . . . CLC 1, 4, 9, 13, 15, 57
See also CA 21-22; 69-72; CANR 34;
CAP 2; DLB 72; MTCW

Malzberg, Barry N(athaniel) 1939- . . . CLC 7
See also CA 61-64; CAAS 4; CANR 16;
DLB 8

Mamet, David (Alan)
1947- . . . . CLC 9, 15, 34, 46; DC 4
See also AAYA 3; CA 81-84; CABS 3;
CANR 15, 41; DLB 7; MTCW

Mamoulian, Rouben (Zachary)
1897-1987 . . . . CLC 16
See also CA 25-28R; 124

Mandelstam, Osip (Emilievich)
1891(?)-1938(?) . . . . TCLC 2, 6
See also CA 104

Mander, (Mary) Jane 1877-1949 . . . TCLC 31

Mandiargues, Andre Pieyre de . . . . . . CLC 41
See also Pieyre de Mandiargues, Andre
See also DLB 83

Mandrake, Ethel Belle
See Thurman, Wallace (Henry)

Mangan, James Clarence
1803-1849 . . . . NCLC 27

Maniere, J.-E.
See Giraudoux, (Hippolyte) Jean

Manley, (Mary) Delariviere
1672(?)-1724 . . . . LC 1
See also DLB 39, 80

Mann, Abel
See Creasey, John

Mann, (Luiz) Heinrich 1871-1950 . . . TCLC 9
See also CA 106; DLB 66

Mann, (Paul) Thomas
1875-1955 . . . . TCLC 2, 8, 14, 21, 35, 44;
DA; SSC 5; WLC
See also CA 104; 128; DLB 66; MTCW

Manning, David
See Faust, Frederick (Schiller)

Manning, Frederic 1887(?)-1935 . . . TCLC 25
See also CA 124

Manning, Olivia 1915-1980 . . . . . . CLC 5, 19
See also CA 5-8R; 101; CANR 29; MTCW

Mano, D. Keith 1942- . . . . CLC 2, 10
See also CA 25-28R; CAAS 6; CANR 26;
DLB 6

Mansfield, Katherine
. . . . TCLC 2, 8, 39; SSC 9; WLC
See also Beauchamp, Kathleen Mansfield

Manso, Peter 1940- . . . . CLC 39
See also CA 29-32R; CANR 44

Mantecon, Juan Jimenez
See Jimenez (Mantecon), Juan Ramon

Manton, Peter
See Creasey, John

Man Without a Spleen, A
See Chekhov, Anton (Pavlovich)

Manzoni, Alessandro 1785-1873 . . NCLC 29

Mapu, Abraham (ben Jekutiel)
1808-1867 . . . . NCLC 18

Mara, Sally
See Queneau, Raymond

Marat, Jean Paul 1743-1793 . . . . LC 10

Marcel, Gabriel Honore
1889-1973 . . . . CLC 15
See also CA 102; 45-48; MTCW

Marchbanks, Samuel
See Davies, (William) Robertson

Marchi, Giacomo
See Bassani, Giorgio

Margulies, Donald . . . . CLC 76

Marie de France c. 12th cent. - . . . . CMLC 8

Marie de l'Incarnation 1599-1672 . . . . LC 10

Mariner, Scott
See Pohl, Frederik

Marinetti, Filippo Tommaso
1876-1944 . . . . TCLC 10
See also CA 107; DLB 114

Marivaux, Pierre Carlet de Chamblain de
1688-1763 . . . . LC 4

Markandaya, Kamala . . . . CLC 8, 38
See also Taylor, Kamala (Purnaiya)

Markfield, Wallace 1926- . . . . CLC 8
See also CA 69-72; CAAS 3; DLB 2, 28

Markham, Edwin 1852-1940 . . . . . . TCLC 47
See also DLB 54

Markham, Robert
See Amis, Kingsley (William)

Marks, J
See Highwater, Jamake (Mamake)

Marks-Highwater, J
See Highwater, Jamake (Mamake)

Markson, David M(errill) 1927- . . . . CLC 67
See also CA 49-52; CANR 1

Marley, Bob . . . . CLC 17
See also Marley, Robert Nesta

Marley, Robert Nesta 1945-1981
See Marley, Bob
See also CA 107; 103

Marlowe, Christopher
1564-1593 . . . . . LC 22; DA; DC 1; WLC
See also CDBLB Before 1660; DLB 62

Marmontel, Jean-Francois
1723-1799 . . . . LC 2

Marquand, John P(hillips)
1893-1960 . . . . CLC 2, 10
See also CA 85-88; DLB 9, 102

Marquez, Gabriel (Jose) Garcia
See Garcia Marquez, Gabriel (Jose)

Marquis, Don(ald Robert Perry)
1878-1937 . . . . TCLC 7
See also CA 104; DLB 11, 25

Marric, J. J.
See Creasey, John

Marrow, Bernard
See Moore, Brian

Marryat, Frederick   1792-1848 .... **NCLC 3**
See also DLB 21

Marsden, James
See Creasey, John

Marsh, (Edith) Ngaio
1899-1982 .... **CLC 7, 53**
See also CA 9-12R; CANR 6; DLB 77;
MTCW

Marshall, Garry   1934- .... **CLC 17**
See also AAYA 3; CA 111; SATA 60

Marshall, Paule
1929- .... **CLC 27, 72; BLC; SSC 3**
See also BW 2; CA 77-80; CANR 25;
DLB 33; MTCW

Marsten, Richard
See Hunter, Evan

Martha, Henry
See Harris, Mark

Martial   c. 40-c. 104 .... **PC 10**

Martin, Ken
See Hubbard, L(afayette) Ron(ald)

Martin, Richard
See Creasey, John

Martin, Steve   1945- .... **CLC 30**
See also CA 97-100; CANR 30; MTCW

Martin, Violet Florence
1862-1915 .... **TCLC 51**

Martin, Webber
See Silverberg, Robert

Martindale, Patrick Victor
See White, Patrick (Victor Martindale)

Martin du Gard, Roger
1881-1958 .... **TCLC 24**
See also CA 118; DLB 65

Martineau, Harriet   1802-1876.... **NCLC 26**
See also DLB 21, 55; YABC 2

Martines, Julia
See O'Faolain, Julia

Martinez, Jacinto Benavente y
See Benavente (y Martinez), Jacinto

Martinez Ruiz, Jose   1873-1967
See Azorin; Ruiz, Jose Martinez
See also CA 93-96; HW

Martinez Sierra, Gregorio
1881-1947 .... **TCLC 6**
See also CA 115

Martinez Sierra, Maria (de la O'LeJarraga)
1874-1974 .... **TCLC 6**
See also CA 115

Martinsen, Martin
See Follett, Ken(neth Martin)

Martinson, Harry (Edmund)
1904-1978 .... **CLC 14**
See also CA 77-80; CANR 34

Marut, Ret
See Traven, B.

Marut, Robert
See Traven, B.

Marvell, Andrew
1621-1678 ..... **LC 4; DA; PC 10; WLC**
See also CDBLB 1660-1789; DLB 131

Marx, Karl (Heinrich)
1818-1883 .... **NCLC 17**
See also DLB 129

Masaoka Shiki .... **TCLC 18**
See also Masaoka Tsunenori

Masaoka Tsunenori   1867-1902
See Masaoka Shiki
See also CA 117

Masefield, John (Edward)
1878-1967 .... **CLC 11, 47**
See also CA 19-20; 25-28R; CANR 33;
CAP 2; CDBLB 1890-1914; DLB 10, 19;
MTCW; SATA 19

Maso, Carole   19(?)- .... **CLC 44**

Mason, Bobbie Ann
1940- .... **CLC 28, 43, 82; SSC 4**
See also AAYA 5; CA 53-56; CANR 11,
31; DLBY 87; MTCW

Mason, Ernst
See Pohl, Frederik

Mason, Lee W.
See Malzberg, Barry N(athaniel)

Mason, Nick   1945- .... **CLC 35**

Mason, Tally
See Derleth, August (William)

Mass, William
See Gibson, William

Masters, Edgar Lee
1868-1950 ...... **TCLC 2, 25; DA; PC 1**
See also CA 104; 133; CDALB 1865-1917;
DLB 54; MTCW

Masters, Hilary   1928- .... **CLC 48**
See also CA 25-28R; CANR 13

Mastrosimone, William   19(?)- ...... **CLC 36**

Mathe, Albert
See Camus, Albert

Matheson, Richard Burton   1926- ... **CLC 37**
See also CA 97-100; DLB 8, 44

Mathews, Harry   1930- .... **CLC 6, 52**
See also CA 21-24R; CAAS 6; CANR 18,
40

Mathews, John Joseph   1894-1979... **CLC 84**
See also CA 19-20; 142; CANR 45; CAP 2;
NNAL

Mathias, Roland (Glyn)   1915- ...... **CLC 45**
See also CA 97-100; CANR 19, 41; DLB 27

Matsuo Basho   1644-1694........... **PC 3**

Mattheson, Rodney
See Creasey, John

Matthews, Greg   1949- .... **CLC 45**
See also CA 135

Matthews, William   1942- .... **CLC 40**
See also CA 29-32R; CAAS 18; CANR 12;
DLB 5

Matthias, John (Edward)   1941- ...... **CLC 9**
See also CA 33-36R

Matthiessen, Peter
1927- .... **CLC 5, 7, 11, 32, 64**
See also AAYA 6; BEST 90:4; CA 9-12R;
CANR 21; DLB 6; MTCW; SATA 27

Maturin, Charles Robert
1780(?)-1824 .... **NCLC 6**

Matute (Ausejo), Ana Maria
1925- .... **CLC 11**
See also CA 89-92; MTCW

Maugham, W. S.
See Maugham, W(illiam) Somerset

Maugham, W(illiam) Somerset
1874-1965 ...... **CLC 1, 11, 15, 67; DA;**
SSC 8; WLC
See also CA 5-8R; 25-28R; CANR 40;
CDBLB 1914-1945; DLB 10, 36, 77, 100;
MTCW; SATA 54

Maugham, William Somerset
See Maugham, W(illiam) Somerset

Maupassant, (Henri Rene Albert) Guy de
1850-1893 .... **NCLC 1, 42; DA; SSC 1;**
WLC
See also DLB 123

Maurhut, Richard
See Traven, B.

Mauriac, Claude   1914- .... **CLC 9**
See also CA 89-92; DLB 83

Mauriac, Francois (Charles)
1885-1970 .... **CLC 4, 9, 56**
See also CA 25-28; CAP 2; DLB 65;
MTCW

Mavor, Osborne Henry   1888-1951
See Bridie, James
See also CA 104

Maxwell, William (Keepers, Jr.)
1908- .... **CLC 19**
See also CA 93-96; DLBY 80

May, Elaine   1932- .... **CLC 16**
See also CA 124; 142; DLB 44

Mayakovski, Vladimir (Vladimirovich)
1893-1930 .... **TCLC 4, 18**
See also CA 104

Mayhew, Henry   1812-1887 ...... **NCLC 31**
See also DLB 18, 55

Maynard, Joyce   1953- .... **CLC 23**
See also CA 111; 129

Mayne, William (James Carter)
1928- .... **CLC 12**
See also CA 9-12R; CANR 37; CLR 25;
JRDA; MAICYA; SAAS 11; SATA 6, 68

Mayo, Jim
See L'Amour, Louis (Dearborn)

Maysles, Albert   1926- .... **CLC 16**
See also CA 29-32R

Maysles, David   1932- .... **CLC 16**

Mazer, Norma Fox   1931- .... **CLC 26**
See also AAYA 5; CA 69-72; CANR 12,
32; CLR 23; JRDA; MAICYA; SAAS 1;
SATA 24, 67

Mazzini, Guiseppe   1805-1872 .... **NCLC 34**

McAuley, James Phillip
1917-1976 .... **CLC 45**
See also CA 97-100

McBain, Ed
See Hunter, Evan

McBrien, William Augustine
1930- .... **CLC 44**
See also CA 107

McCaffrey, Anne (Inez)   1926- ...... **CLC 17**
See also AAYA 6; AITN 2; BEST 89:2;
CA 25-28R; CANR 15, 35; DLB 8;
JRDA; MAICYA; MTCW; SAAS 11;
SATA 8, 70

McCann, Arthur
See Campbell, John W(ood, Jr.)

Merritt, E. B.
See Waddington, Miriam

Merton, Thomas
1915-1968 . . **CLC 1, 3, 11, 34, 83; PC 10**
See also CA 5-8R; 25-28R; CANR 22;
DLB 48; DLBY 81; MTCW

Merwin, W(illiam) S(tanley)
1927- . . . . . . **CLC 1, 2, 3, 5, 8, 13, 18, 45**
See also CA 13-16R; CANR 15; DLB 5;
MTCW

Metcalf, John 1938- . . . . **CLC 37**
See also CA 113; DLB 60

Metcalf, Suzanne
See Baum, L(yman) Frank

Mew, Charlotte (Mary)
1870-1928 . . . . **TCLC 8**
See also CA 105; DLB 19, 135

Mewshaw, Michael 1943- . . . . **CLC 9**
See also CA 53-56; CANR 7; DLBY 80

Meyer, June
See Jordan, June

Meyer, Lynn
See Slavitt, David R(ytman)

Meyer-Meyrink, Gustav 1868-1932
See Meyrink, Gustav
See also CA 117

Meyers, Jeffrey 1939- . . . . **CLC 39**
See also CA 73-76; DLB 111

Meynell, Alice (Christina Gertrude Thompson)
1847-1922 . . . . **TCLC 6**
See also CA 104; DLB 19, 98

Meyrink, Gustav . . . . **TCLC 21**
See also Meyer-Meyrink, Gustav
See also DLB 81

Michaels, Leonard
1933- . . . . **CLC 6, 25; SSC 16**
See also CA 61-64; CANR 21; DLB 130;
MTCW

Michaux, Henri 1899-1984 . . . . . . **CLC 8, 19**
See also CA 85-88; 114

Michelangelo 1475-1564 . . . . **LC 12**

Michelet, Jules 1798-1874 . . . . . . **NCLC 31**

Michener, James A(lbert)
1907(?)- . . . . **CLC 1, 5, 11, 29, 60**
See also AITN 1; BEST 90:1; CA 5-8R;
CANR 21, 45; DLB 6; MTCW

Mickiewicz, Adam 1798-1855 . . . . . **NCLC 3**

Middleton, Christopher 1926- . . . . . . **CLC 13**
See also CA 13-16R; CANR 29; DLB 40

Middleton, Richard (Barham)
1882-1911 . . . . **TCLC 56**

Middleton, Stanley 1919- . . . . **CLC 7, 38**
See also CA 25-28R; CANR 21, 46;
DLB 14

Middleton, Thomas 1580-1627 . . . . **DC 5**
See also DLB 58

Migueis, Jose Rodrigues 1901- . . . . . **CLC 10**

Mikszath, Kalman 1847-1910 . . . . . **TCLC 31**

Miles, Josephine
1911-1985 . . . . **CLC 1, 2, 14, 34, 39**
See also CA 1-4R; 116; CANR 2; DLB 48

Militant
See Sandburg, Carl (August)

Mill, John Stuart 1806-1873 . . . . . **NCLC 11**
See also CDBLB 1832-1890; DLB 55

Millar, Kenneth 1915-1983 . . . . **CLC 14**
See also Macdonald, Ross
See also CA 9-12R; 110; CANR 16; DLB 2;
DLBD 6; DLBY 83; MTCW

Millay, E. Vincent
See Millay, Edna St. Vincent

Millay, Edna St. Vincent
1892-1950 . . . . . . **TCLC 4, 49; DA; PC 6**
See also CA 104; 130; CDALB 1917-1929;
DLB 45; MTCW

Miller, Arthur
1915- . . . . **CLC 1, 2, 6, 10, 15, 26, 47, 78;**
DA; DC 1; WLC
See also AITN 1; CA 1-4R; CABS 3;
CANR 2, 30; CDALB 1941-1968; DLB 7;
MTCW

Miller, Henry (Valentine)
1891-1980 . . . . **CLC 1, 2, 4, 9, 14, 43, 84;**
DA; WLC
See also CA 9-12R; 97-100; CANR 33;
CDALB 1929-1941; DLB 4, 9; DLBY 80;
MTCW

Miller, Jason 1939(?)- . . . . **CLC 2**
See also AITN 1; CA 73-76; DLB 7

Miller, Sue 1943- . . . . **CLC 44**
See also BEST 90:3; CA 139; DLB 143

Miller, Walter M(ichael, Jr.)
1923- . . . . **CLC 4, 30**
See also CA 85-88; DLB 8

Millett, Kate 1934- . . . . **CLC 67**
See also AITN 1; CA 73-76; CANR 32;
MTCW

Millhauser, Steven 1943- . . . . **CLC 21, 54**
See also CA 110; 111; DLB 2

Millin, Sarah Gertrude 1889-1968 . . **CLC 49**
See also CA 102; 93-96

Milne, A(lan) A(lexander)
1882-1956 . . . . **TCLC 6**
See also CA 104; 133; CLR 1, 26; DLB 10,
77, 100; MAICYA; MTCW; YABC 1

Milner, Ron(ald) 1938- . . . . **CLC 56; BLC**
See also AITN 1; BW 1; CA 73-76;
CANR 24; DLB 38; MTCW

Milosz, Czeslaw
1911- . . . **CLC 5, 11, 22, 31, 56, 82; PC 8**
See also CA 81-84; CANR 23; MTCW

Milton, John 1608-1674 . . . **LC 9; DA; WLC**
See also CDBLB 1660-1789; DLB 131

Minehaha, Cornelius
See Wedekind, (Benjamin) Frank(lin)

Miner, Valerie 1947- . . . . **CLC 40**
See also CA 97-100

Minimo, Duca
See D'Annunzio, Gabriele

Minot, Susan 1956- . . . . **CLC 44**
See also CA 134

Minus, Ed 1938- . . . . **CLC 39**

Miranda, Javier
See Bioy Casares, Adolfo

Mirbeau, Octave 1848-1917 . . . . . . **TCLC 55**
See also DLB 123

Miro (Ferrer), Gabriel (Francisco Victor)
1879-1930 . . . . **TCLC 5**
See also CA 104

Mishima, Yukio
. . . . **CLC 2, 4, 6, 9, 27; DC 1; SSC 4**
See also Hiraoka, Kimitake

Mistral, Frederic 1830-1914 . . . . . . **TCLC 51**
See also CA 122

Mistral, Gabriela . . . . **TCLC 2; HLC**
See also Godoy Alcayaga, Lucila

Mistry, Rohinton 1952- . . . . **CLC 71**
See also CA 141

Mitchell, Clyde
See Ellison, Harlan (Jay); Silverberg, Robert

Mitchell, James Leslie 1901-1935
See Gibbon, Lewis Grassic
See also CA 104; DLB 15

Mitchell, Joni 1943- . . . . **CLC 12**
See also CA 112

Mitchell, Margaret (Munnerlyn)
1900-1949 . . . . **TCLC 11**
See also CA 109; 125; DLB 9; MTCW

Mitchell, Peggy
See Mitchell, Margaret (Munnerlyn)

Mitchell, S(ilas) Weir 1829-1914 . . **TCLC 36**

Mitchell, W(illiam) O(rmond)
1914- . . . . **CLC 25**
See also CA 77-80; CANR 15, 43; DLB 88

Mitford, Mary Russell 1787-1855 . . **NCLC 4**
See also DLB 110, 116

Mitford, Nancy 1904-1973 . . . . **CLC 44**
See also CA 9-12R

Miyamoto, Yuriko 1899-1951 . . . . . **TCLC 37**

Mo, Timothy (Peter) 1950(?)- . . . . . . **CLC 46**
See also CA 117; MTCW

Modarressi, Taghi (M.) 1931- . . . . . . **CLC 44**
See also CA 121; 134

Modiano, Patrick (Jean) 1945- . . . . . **CLC 18**
See also CA 85-88; CANR 17, 40; DLB 83

Moerck, Paal
See Roelvaag, O(le) E(dvart)

Mofolo, Thomas (Mokopu)
1875(?)-1948 . . . . **TCLC 22; BLC**
See also CA 121

Mohr, Nicholasa 1935- . . . . . . **CLC 12; HLC**
See also AAYA 8; CA 49-52; CANR 1, 32;
CLR 22; DLB 145; HW; JRDA; SAAS 8;
SATA 8

Mojtabai, A(nn) G(race)
1938- . . . . **CLC 5, 9, 15, 29**
See also CA 85-88

Moliere 1622-1673 . . . . **LC 10; DA; WLC**

Molin, Charles
See Mayne, William (James Carter)

Molnar, Ferenc 1878-1952 . . . . **TCLC 20**
See also CA 109

Momaday, N(avarre) Scott
1934- . . . . **CLC 2, 19, 85; DA**
See also AAYA 11; CA 25-28R; CANR 14,
34; DLB 143; MTCW; NNAL; SATA 30,
48

Monette, Paul 1945- . . . . **CLC 82**
See also CA 139

Monroe, Harriet 1860-1936 . . . . **TCLC 12**
See also CA 109; DLB 54, 91

Monroe, Lyle
See Heinlein, Robert A(nson)

Montagu, Elizabeth 1917- . . . . **NCLC 7**
See also CA 9-12R

Montagu, Mary (Pierrepont) Wortley
1689-1762 . . . . **LC 9**
See also DLB 95, 101

Montagu, W. H.
See Coleridge, Samuel Taylor

Montague, John (Patrick)
1929- . . . . **CLC 13, 46**
See also CA 9-12R; CANR 9; DLB 40;
MTCW

Montaigne, Michel (Eyquem) de
1533-1592 . . . . **LC 8; DA; WLC**

Montale, Eugenio 1896-1981 . . . **CLC 7, 9, 18**
See also CA 17-20R; 104; CANR 30;
DLB 114; MTCW

Montesquieu, Charles-Louis de Secondat
1689-1755 . . . . **LC 7**

Montgomery, (Robert) Bruce 1921-1978
See Crispin, Edmund
See also CA 104

Montgomery, L(ucy) M(aud)
1874-1942 . . . . **TCLC 51**
See also AAYA 12; CA 108; 137; CLR 8;
DLB 92; JRDA; MAICYA; YABC 1

Montgomery, Marion H., Jr. 1925- . . **CLC 7**
See also AITN 1; CA 1-4R; CANR 3;
DLB 6

Montgomery, Max
See Davenport, Guy (Mattison, Jr.)

Montherlant, Henry (Milon) de
1896-1972 . . . . **CLC 8, 19**
See also CA 85-88; 37-40R; DLB 72;
MTCW

Monty Python
See Chapman, Graham; Cleese, John
(Marwood); Gilliam, Terry (Vance); Idle,
Eric; Jones, Terence Graham Parry; Palin,
Michael (Edward)
See also AAYA 7

Moodie, Susanna (Strickland)
1803-1885 . . . . **NCLC 14**
See also DLB 99

Mooney, Edward 1951-
See Mooney, Ted
See also CA 130

Mooney, Ted . . . . **CLC 25**
See also Mooney, Edward

Moorcock, Michael (John)
1939- . . . . **CLC 5, 27, 58**
See also CA 45-48; CAAS 5; CANR 2, 17,
38; DLB 14; MTCW

Moore, Brian
1921- . . . . **CLC 1, 3, 5, 7, 8, 19, 32**
See also CA 1-4R; CANR 1, 25, 42; MTCW

Moore, Edward
See Muir, Edwin

Moore, George Augustus
1852-1933 . . . . **TCLC 7**
See also CA 104; DLB 10, 18, 57, 135

Moore, Lorrie . . . . **CLC 39, 45, 68**
See also Moore, Marie Lorena

Moore, Marianne (Craig)
1887-1972 . . . . **CLC 1, 2, 4, 8, 10, 13, 19,
47; DA; PC 4**
See also CA 1-4R; 33-36R; CANR 3;
CDALB 1929-1941; DLB 45; DLBD 7;
MTCW; SATA 20

Moore, Marie Lorena 1957-
See Moore, Lorrie
See also CA 116; CANR 39

Moore, Thomas 1779-1852 . . . . **NCLC 6**
See also DLB 96, 144

Morand, Paul 1888-1976 . . . . **CLC 41**
See also CA 69-72; DLB 65

Morante, Elsa 1918-1985 . . . . **CLC 8, 47**
See also CA 85-88; 117; CANR 35; MTCW

Moravia, Alberto . . . . . . **CLC 2, 7, 11, 27, 46**
See also Pincherle, Alberto

More, Hannah 1745-1833 . . . . **NCLC 27**
See also DLB 107, 109, 116

More, Henry 1614-1687 . . . . **LC 9**
See also DLB 126

More, Sir Thomas 1478-1535 . . . . **LC 10**

Moreas, Jean . . . . **TCLC 18**
See also Papadiamantopoulos, Johannes

Morgan, Berry 1919- . . . . **CLC 6**
See also CA 49-52; DLB 6

Morgan, Claire
See Highsmith, (Mary) Patricia

Morgan, Edwin (George) 1920- . . . . . **CLC 31**
See also CA 5-8R; CANR 3, 43; DLB 27

Morgan, (George) Frederick
1922- . . . . **CLC 23**
See also CA 17-20R; CANR 21

Morgan, Harriet
See Mencken, H(enry) L(ouis)

Morgan, Jane
See Cooper, James Fenimore

Morgan, Janet 1945- . . . . **CLC 39**
See also CA 65-68

Morgan, Lady 1776(?)-1859 . . . . . . **NCLC 29**
See also DLB 116

Morgan, Robin 1941- . . . . **CLC 2**
See also CA 69-72; CANR 29; MTCW

Morgan, Scott
See Kuttner, Henry

Morgan, Seth 1949(?)-1990 . . . . **CLC 65**
See also CA 132

Morgenstern, Christian
1871-1914 . . . . **TCLC 8**
See also CA 105

Morgenstern, S.
See Goldman, William (W.)

Moricz, Zsigmond 1879-1942 . . . . . **TCLC 33**

Morike, Eduard (Friedrich)
1804-1875 . . . . **NCLC 10**
See also DLB 133

Mori Ogai . . . . **TCLC 14**
See also Mori Rintaro

Mori Rintaro 1862-1922
See Mori Ogai
See also CA 110

Moritz, Karl Philipp 1756-1793 . . . . . . **LC 2**
See also DLB 94

Morland, Peter Henry
See Faust, Frederick (Schiller)

Morren, Theophil
See Hofmannsthal, Hugo von

Morris, Bill 1952- . . . . **CLC 76**

Morris, Julian
See West, Morris L(anglo)

Morris, Steveland Judkins 1950(?)-
See Wonder, Stevie
See also CA 111

Morris, William 1834-1896 . . . . **NCLC 4**
See also CDBLB 1832-1890; DLB 18, 35, 57

Morris, Wright 1910- . . . **CLC 1, 3, 7, 18, 37**
See also CA 9-12R; CANR 21; DLB 2;
DLBY 81; MTCW

Morrison, Chloe Anthony Wofford
See Morrison, Toni

Morrison, James Douglas 1943-1971
See Morrison, Jim
See also CA 73-76; CANR 40

Morrison, Jim . . . . **CLC 17**
See also Morrison, James Douglas

Morrison, Toni
1931- . . **CLC 4, 10, 22, 55, 81; BLC; DA**
See also AAYA 1; BW 2; CA 29-32R;
CANR 27, 42; CDALB 1968-1988;
DLB 6, 33, 143; DLBY 81; MTCW;
SATA 57

Morrison, Van 1945- . . . . **CLC 21**
See also CA 116

Mortimer, John (Clifford)
1923- . . . . **CLC 28, 43**
See also CA 13-16R; CANR 21;
CDBLB 1960 to Present; DLB 13;
MTCW

Mortimer, Penelope (Ruth) 1918- . . . . **CLC 5**
See also CA 57-60; CANR 45

Morton, Anthony
See Creasey, John

Mosher, Howard Frank 1943- . . . . . . **CLC 62**
See also CA 139

Mosley, Nicholas 1923- . . . . **CLC 43, 70**
See also CA 69-72; CANR 41; DLB 14

Moss, Howard
1922-1987 . . . . **CLC 7, 14, 45, 50**
See also CA 1-4R; 123; CANR 1, 44;
DLB 5

Mossgiel, Rab
See Burns, Robert

Motion, Andrew 1952- . . . . **CLC 47**
See also DLB 40

Motley, Willard (Francis)
1909-1965 . . . . **CLC 18**
See also BW 1; CA 117; 106; DLB 76, 143

Motoori, Norinaga 1730-1801 . . . . **NCLC 45**

Mott, Michael (Charles Alston)
1930- . . . . **CLC 15, 34**
See also CA 5-8R; CAAS 7; CANR 7, 29

Mowat, Farley (McGill) 1921- . . . . . **CLC 26**
See also AAYA 1; CA 1-4R; CANR 4, 24,
42; CLR 20; DLB 68; JRDA; MAICYA;
MTCW; SATA 3, 55

Moyers, Bill 1934- . . . . **CLC 74**
See also AITN 2; CA 61-64; CANR 31

Mphahlele, Es'kia
See Mphahlele, Ezekiel
See also DLB 125

Mphahlele, Ezekiel 1919-. . . . . **CLC 25; BLC**
See also Mphahlele, Es'kia
See also BW 2; CA 81-84; CANR 26

Mqhayi, S(amuel) E(dward) K(rune Loliwe)
1875-1945 . . . . **TCLC 25; BLC**

Mr. Martin
See Burroughs, William S(eward)

Mrozek, Slawomir 1930- . . . . **CLC 3, 13**
See also CA 13-16R; CAAS 10; CANR 29;
MTCW

Mrs. Belloc-Lowndes
See Lowndes, Marie Adelaide (Belloc)

Mtwa, Percy (?)-. . . . . **CLC 47**

Mueller, Lisel 1924-. . . . . **CLC 13, 51**
See also CA 93-96; DLB 105

Muir, Edwin 1887-1959 . . . . **TCLC 2**
See also CA 104; DLB 20, 100

Muir, John 1838-1914 . . . . **TCLC 28**

Mujica Lainez, Manuel
1910-1984 . . . . **CLC 31**
See also Lainez, Manuel Mujica
See also CA 81-84; 112; CANR 32; HW

Mukherjee, Bharati 1940-. . . . . **CLC 53**
See also BEST 89:2; CA 107; CANR 45;
DLB 60; MTCW

Muldoon, Paul 1951- . . . . **CLC 32, 72**
See also CA 113; 129; DLB 40

Mulisch, Harry 1927-. . . . . **CLC 42**
See also CA 9-12R; CANR 6, 26

Mull, Martin 1943-. . . . . **CLC 17**
See also CA 105

Mulock, Dinah Maria
See Craik, Dinah Maria (Mulock)

Munford, Robert 1737(?)-1783 . . . . **LC 5**
See also DLB 31

Mungo, Raymond 1946-. . . . . **CLC 72**
See also CA 49-52; CANR 2

Munro, Alice
1931- . . . . **CLC 6, 10, 19, 50; SSC 3**
See also AITN 2; CA 33-36R; CANR 33;
DLB 53; MTCW; SATA 29

Munro, H(ector) H(ugh) 1870-1916
See Saki
See also CA 104; 130; CDBLB 1890-1914;
DA; DLB 34; MTCW; WLC

Murasaki, Lady. . . . . **CMLC 1**

Murdoch, (Jean) Iris
1919- . . . . . . **CLC 1, 2, 3, 4, 6, 8, 11, 15,
22, 31, 51**
See also CA 13-16R; CANR 8, 43;
CDBLB 1960 to Present; DLB 14;
MTCW

Murnau, Friedrich Wilhelm
See Plumpe, Friedrich Wilhelm

Murphy, Richard 1927-. . . . . **CLC 41**
See also CA 29-32R; DLB 40

Murphy, Sylvia 1937-. . . . . **CLC 34**
See also CA 121

Murphy, Thomas (Bernard) 1935-. . . **CLC 51**
See also CA 101

Murray, Albert L. 1916- . . . . **CLC 73**
See also BW 2; CA 49-52; CANR 26;
DLB 38

Murray, Les(lie) A(llan) 1938- . . . . . **CLC 40**
See also CA 21-24R; CANR 11, 27

Murry, J. Middleton
See Murry, John Middleton

Murry, John Middleton
1889-1957 . . . . **TCLC 16**
See also CA 118

Musgrave, Susan 1951- . . . . **CLC 13, 54**
See also CA 69-72; CANR 45

Musil, Robert (Edler von)
1880-1942 . . . . **TCLC 12**
See also CA 109; DLB 81, 124

Musset, (Louis Charles) Alfred de
1810-1857 . . . . **NCLC 7**

My Brother's Brother
See Chekhov, Anton (Pavlovich)

Myers, Walter Dean 1937- . . . **CLC 35; BLC**
See also AAYA 4; BW 2; CA 33-36R;
CANR 20, 42; CLR 4, 16, 35; DLB 33;
JRDA; MAICYA; SAAS 2; SATA 27, 41,
71

Myers, Walter M.
See Myers, Walter Dean

Myles, Symon
See Follett, Ken(neth Martin)

Nabokov, Vladimir (Vladimirovich)
1899-1977 . . . . . **CLC 1, 2, 3, 6, 8, 11, 15,
23, 44, 46, 64; DA; SSC 11; WLC**
See also CA 5-8R; 69-72; CANR 20;
CDALB 1941-1968; DLB 2; DLBD 3;
DLBY 80, 91; MTCW

Nagai Kafu. . . . . **TCLC 51**
See also Nagai Sokichi

Nagai Sokichi 1879-1959
See Nagai Kafu
See also CA 117

Nagy, Laszlo 1925-1978. . . . . **CLC 7**
See also CA 129; 112

Naipaul, Shiva(dhar Srinivasa)
1945-1985 . . . . **CLC 32, 39**
See also CA 110; 112; 116; CANR 33;
DLBY 85; MTCW

Naipaul, V(idiadhar) S(urajprasad)
1932- . . . . **CLC 4, 7, 9, 13, 18, 37**
See also CA 1-4R; CANR 1, 33;
CDBLB 1960 to Present; DLB 125;
DLBY 85; MTCW

Nakos, Lilika 1899(?)-. . . . . **CLC 29**

Narayan, R(asipuram) K(rishnaswami)
1906- . . . . **CLC 7, 28, 47**
See also CA 81-84; CANR 33; MTCW;
SATA 62

Nash, (Frediric) Ogden 1902-1971 . . **CLC 23**
See also CA 13-14; 29-32R; CANR 34;
CAP 1; DLB 11; MAICYA; MTCW;
SATA 2, 46

Nathan, Daniel
See Dannay, Frederic

Nathan, George Jean 1882-1958 . . . **TCLC 18**
See also Hatteras, Owen
See also CA 114; DLB 137

Natsume, Kinnosuke 1867-1916
See Natsume, Soseki
See also CA 104

Natsume, Soseki . . . . **TCLC 2, 10**
See also Natsume, Kinnosuke

Natti, (Mary) Lee 1919-
See Kingman, Lee
See also CA 5-8R; CANR 2

Naylor, Gloria
1950- . . . . **CLC 28, 52; BLC; DA**
See also AAYA 6; BW 2; CA 107;
CANR 27; MTCW

Neihardt, John Gneisenau
1881-1973 . . . . **CLC 32**
See also CA 13-14; CAP 1; DLB 9, 54

Nekrasov, Nikolai Alekseevich
1821-1878 . . . . **NCLC 11**

Nelligan, Emile 1879-1941. . . . . . . **TCLC 14**
See also CA 114; DLB 92

Nelson, Willie 1933-. . . . . **CLC 17**
See also CA 107

Nemerov, Howard (Stanley)
1920-1991 . . . . **CLC 2, 6, 9, 36**
See also CA 1-4R; 134; CABS 2; CANR 1,
27; DLB 6; DLBY 83; MTCW

Neruda, Pablo
1904-1973 . . . . . **CLC 1, 2, 5, 7, 9, 28, 62;
DA; HLC; PC 4; WLC**
See also CA 19-20; 45-48; CAP 2; HW;
MTCW

Nerval, Gerard de 1808-1855. . . . . . **NCLC 1**

Nervo, (Jose) Amado (Ruiz de)
1870-1919 . . . . **TCLC 11**
See also CA 109; 131; HW

Nessi, Pio Baroja y
See Baroja (y Nessi), Pio

Nestroy, Johann 1801-1862. . . . . . . **NCLC 42**
See also DLB 133

Neufeld, John (Arthur) 1938- . . . . . . **CLC 17**
See also AAYA 11; CA 25-28R; CANR 11,
37; MAICYA; SAAS 3; SATA 6

Neville, Emily Cheney 1919-. . . . . . . **CLC 12**
See also CA 5-8R; CANR 3, 37; JRDA;
MAICYA; SAAS 2; SATA 1

Newbound, Bernard Slade 1930-
See Slade, Bernard
See also CA 81-84

Newby, P(ercy) H(oward)
1918-. **CLC 2, 13**
See also CA 5-8R; CANR 32; DLB 15;
MTCW

Newlove, Donald 1928- . . . . **CLC 6**
See also CA 29-32R; CANR 25

Newlove, John (Herbert) 1938-. . . . . **CLC 14**
See also CA 21-24R; CANR 9, 25

Newman, Charles 1938-. . . . . **CLC 2, 8**
See also CA 21-24R

Newman, Edwin (Harold) 1919- . . . . **CLC 14**
See also AITN 1; CA 69-72; CANR 5

Newman, John Henry
1801-1890 . . . . **NCLC 38**
See also DLB 18, 32, 55

O'Donnell, Lawrence
See Kuttner, Henry

O'Donovan, Michael John
1903-1966 .... CLC 14
See also O'Connor, Frank
See also CA 93-96

Oe, Kenzaburo 1935- .... CLC 10, 36
See also CA 97-100; CANR 36; MTCW

O'Faolain, Julia 1932- .... CLC 6, 19, 47
See also CA 81-84; CAAS 2; CANR 12;
DLB 14; MTCW

O'Faolain, Sean
1900-1991 .... CLC 1, 7, 14, 32, 70;
SSC 13
See also CA 61-64; 134; CANR 12;
DLB 15; MTCW

O'Flaherty, Liam
1896-1984 .... CLC 5, 34; SSC 6
See also CA 101; 113; CANR 35; DLB 36;
DLBY 84; MTCW

Ogilvy, Gavin
See Barrie, J(ames) M(atthew)

O'Grady, Standish James
1846-1928 .... TCLC 5
See also CA 104

O'Grady, Timothy 1951- .... CLC 59
See also CA 138

O'Hara, Frank
1926-1966 .... CLC 2, 5, 13, 78
See also CA 9-12R; 25-28R; CANR 33;
DLB 5, 16; MTCW

O'Hara, John (Henry)
1905-1970 .... CLC 1, 2, 3, 6, 11, 42;
SSC 15
See also CA 5-8R; 25-28R; CANR 31;
CDALB 1929-1941; DLB 9, 86; DLBD 2;
MTCW

O Hehir, Diana 1922- .... CLC 41
See also CA 93-96

Okigbo, Christopher (Ifenayichukwu)
1932-1967 ..... CLC 25, 84; BLC; PC 7
See also BW 1; CA 77-80; DLB 125;
MTCW

Olds, Sharon 1942- .... CLC 32, 39, 85
See also CA 101; CANR 18, 41; DLB 120

Oldstyle, Jonathan
See Irving, Washington

Olesha, Yuri (Karlovich)
1899-1960 .... CLC 8
See also CA 85-88

Oliphant, Laurence
1829(?)-1888 .... NCLC 47
See also DLB 18

Oliphant, Margaret (Oliphant Wilson)
1828-1897 .... NCLC 11
See also DLB 18

Oliver, Mary 1935- .... CLC 19, 34
See also CA 21-24R; CANR 9, 43; DLB 5

Olivier, Laurence (Kerr)
1907-1989 .... CLC 20
See also CA 111; 129

Olsen, Tillie
1913- .... CLC 4, 13; DA; SSC 11
See also CA 1-4R; CANR 1, 43; DLB 28;
DLBY 80; MTCW

Olson, Charles (John)
1910-1970 ..... CLC 1, 2, 5, 6, 9, 11, 29
See also CA 13-16; 25-28R; CABS 2;
CANR 35; CAP 1; DLB 5, 16; MTCW

Olson, Toby 1937- .... CLC 28
See also CA 65-68; CANR 9, 31

Olyesha, Yuri
See Olesha, Yuri (Karlovich)

Ondaatje, (Philip) Michael
1943- .... CLC 14, 29, 51, 76
See also CA 77-80; CANR 42; DLB 60

Oneal, Elizabeth 1934-
See Oneal, Zibby
See also CA 106; CANR 28; MAICYA;
SATA 30

Oneal, Zibby .... CLC 30
See also Oneal, Elizabeth
See also AAYA 5; CLR 13; JRDA

O'Neill, Eugene (Gladstone)
1888-1953 ...... TCLC 1, 6, 27, 49; DA;
WLC
See also AITN 1; CA 110; 132;
CDALB 1929-1941; DLB 7; MTCW

Onetti, Juan Carlos 1909-1994 ... CLC 7, 10
See also CA 85-88; 145; CANR 32;
DLB 113; HW; MTCW

O Nuallain, Brian 1911-1966
See O'Brien, Flann
See also CA 21-22; 25-28R; CAP 2

Oppen, George 1908-1984 .... CLC 7, 13, 34
See also CA 13-16R; 113; CANR 8; DLB 5

Oppenheim, E(dward) Phillips
1866-1946 .... TCLC 45
See also CA 111; DLB 70

Orlovitz, Gil 1918-1973 .... CLC 22
See also CA 77-80; 45-48; DLB 2, 5

Orris
See Ingelow, Jean

Ortega y Gasset, Jose
1883-1955 .... TCLC 9; HLC
See also CA 106; 130; HW; MTCW

Ortiz, Simon J(oseph) 1941- .... CLC 45
See also CA 134; DLB 120; NNAL

Orton, Joe .... CLC 4, 13, 43; DC 3
See also Orton, John Kingsley
See also CDBLB 1960 to Present; DLB 13

Orton, John Kingsley 1933-1967
See Orton, Joe
See also CA 85-88; CANR 35; MTCW

Orwell, George
.... TCLC 2, 6, 15, 31, 51; WLC
See also Blair, Eric (Arthur)
See also CDBLB 1945-1960; DLB 15, 98

Osborne, David
See Silverberg, Robert

Osborne, George
See Silverberg, Robert

Osborne, John (James)
1929- .... CLC 1, 2, 5, 11, 45; DA; WLC
See also CA 13-16R; CANR 21;
CDBLB 1945-1960; DLB 13; MTCW

Osborne, Lawrence 1958- .... CLC 50

Oshima, Nagisa 1932- .... CLC 20
See also CA 116; 121

Oskison, John Milton
1874-1947 .... TCLC 35
See also CA 144; NNAL

Ossoli, Sarah Margaret (Fuller marchesa d')
1810-1850
See Fuller, Margaret
See also SATA 25

Ostrovsky, Alexander
1823-1886 .... NCLC 30

Otero, Blas de 1916-1979 .... CLC 11
See also CA 89-92; DLB 134

Otto, Whitney 1955- .... CLC 70
See also CA 140

Ouida .... TCLC 43
See also De La Ramee, (Marie) Louise
See also DLB 18

Ousmane, Sembene 1923- .... CLC 66; BLC
See also BW 1; CA 117; 125; MTCW

Ovid 43B.C.-18(?) .... CMLC 7; PC 2

Owen, Hugh
See Faust, Frederick (Schiller)

Owen, Wilfred (Edward Salter)
1893-1918 ...... TCLC 5, 27; DA; WLC
See also CA 104; 141; CDBLB 1914-1945;
DLB 20

Owens, Rochelle 1936- .... CLC 8
See also CA 17-20R; CAAS 2; CANR 39

Oz, Amos 1939- ... CLC 5, 8, 11, 27, 33, 54
See also CA 53-56; CANR 27; MTCW

Ozick, Cynthia
1928- .... CLC 3, 7, 28, 62; SSC 15
See also BEST 90:1; CA 17-20R; CANR 23;
DLB 28; DLBY 82; MTCW

Ozu, Yasujiro 1903-1963 .... CLC 16
See also CA 112

Pacheco, C.
See Pessoa, Fernando (Antonio Nogueira)

Pa Chin .... CLC 18
See also Li Fei-kan

Pack, Robert 1929- .... CLC 13
See also CA 1-4R; CANR 3, 44; DLB 5

Padgett, Lewis
See Kuttner, Henry

Padilla (Lorenzo), Heberto 1932- ... CLC 38
See also AITN 1; CA 123; 131; HW

Page, Jimmy 1944- .... CLC 12

Page, Louise 1955- .... CLC 40
See also CA 140

Page, P(atricia) K(athleen)
1916- .... CLC 7, 18
See also CA 53-56; CANR 4, 22; DLB 68;
MTCW

Paget, Violet 1856-1935
See Lee, Vernon
See also CA 104

Paget-Lowe, Henry
See Lovecraft, H(oward) P(hillips)

Paglia, Camille (Anna) 1947- .... CLC 68
See also CA 140

Paige, Richard
See Koontz, Dean R(ay)

Pakenham, Antonia
See Fraser, (Lady) Antonia (Pakenham)

Palamas, Kostes 1859-1943 . . . . **TCLC 5**
See also CA 105

Palazzeschi, Aldo 1885-1974 . . . . **CLC 11**
See also CA 89-92; 53-56; DLB 114

Paley, Grace 1922- . . . . **CLC 4, 6, 37; SSC 8**
See also CA 25-28R; CANR 13, 46;
DLB 28; MTCW

Palin, Michael (Edward) 1943- . . . . . **CLC 21**
See also Monty Python
See also CA 107; CANR 35; SATA 67

Palliser, Charles 1947- . . . . **CLC 65**
See also CA 136

Palma, Ricardo 1833-1919 . . . . **TCLC 29**

Pancake, Breece Dexter 1952-1979
See Pancake, Breece D'J
See also CA 123; 109

Pancake, Breece D'J . . . . **CLC 29**
See also Pancake, Breece Dexter
See also DLB 130

Panko, Rudy
See Gogol, Nikolai (Vasilyevich)

Papadiamantis, Alexandros
1851-1911 . . . . **TCLC 29**

Papadiamantopoulos, Johannes 1856-1910
See Moreas, Jean
See also CA 117

Papini, Giovanni 1881-1956 . . . . **TCLC 22**
See also CA 121

Paracelsus 1493-1541 . . . . **LC 14**

Parasol, Peter
See Stevens, Wallace

Parfenie, Maria
See Codrescu, Andrei

Parini, Jay (Lee) 1948- . . . . **CLC 54**
See also CA 97-100; CAAS 16; CANR 32

Park, Jordan
See Kornbluth, C(yril) M.; Pohl, Frederik

Parker, Bert
See Ellison, Harlan (Jay)

Parker, Dorothy (Rothschild)
1893-1967 . . . . **CLC 15, 68; SSC 2**
See also CA 19-20; 25-28R; CAP 2;
DLB 11, 45, 86; MTCW

Parker, Robert B(rown) 1932- . . . . . . **CLC 27**
See also BEST 89:4; CA 49-52; CANR 1,
26; MTCW

Parkin, Frank 1940- . . . . **CLC 43**

Parkman, Francis, Jr.
1823-1893 . . . . **NCLC 12**
See also DLB 1, 30

Parks, Gordon (Alexander Buchanan)
1912- . . . . **CLC 1, 16; BLC**
See also AITN 2; BW 2; CA 41-44R;
CANR 26; DLB 33; SATA 8

Parnell, Thomas 1679-1718 . . . . **LC 3**
See also DLB 94

Parra, Nicanor 1914- . . . . **CLC 2; HLC**
See also CA 85-88; CANR 32; HW; MTCW

Parrish, Mary Frances
See Fisher, M(ary) F(rances) K(ennedy)

Parson
See Coleridge, Samuel Taylor

Parson Lot
See Kingsley, Charles

Partridge, Anthony
See Oppenheim, E(dward) Phillips

Pascoli, Giovanni 1855-1912 . . . . . **TCLC 45**

Pasolini, Pier Paolo
1922-1975 . . . . **CLC 20, 37**
See also CA 93-96; 61-64; DLB 128;
MTCW

Pasquini
See Silone, Ignazio

Pastan, Linda (Olenik) 1932- . . . . . . **CLC 27**
See also CA 61-64; CANR 18, 40; DLB 5

Pasternak, Boris (Leonidovich)
1890-1960 . . . . . . **CLC 7, 10, 18, 63; DA;
PC 6; WLC**
See also CA 127; 116; MTCW

Patchen, Kenneth 1911-1972 . . . **CLC 1, 2, 18**
See also CA 1-4R; 33-36R; CANR 3, 35;
DLB 16, 48; MTCW

Pater, Walter (Horatio)
1839-1894 . . . . **NCLC 7**
See also CDBLB 1832-1890; DLB 57

Paterson, A(ndrew) B(arton)
1864-1941 . . . . **TCLC 32**

Paterson, Katherine (Womeldorf)
1932- . . . . **CLC 12, 30**
See also AAYA 1; CA 21-24R; CANR 28;
CLR 7; DLB 52; JRDA; MAICYA;
MTCW; SATA 13, 53

Patmore, Coventry Kersey Dighton
1823-1896 . . . . **NCLC 9**
See also DLB 35, 98

Paton, Alan (Stewart)
1903-1988 . . . . . . **CLC 4, 10, 25, 55; DA;
WLC**
See also CA 13-16; 125; CANR 22; CAP 1;
MTCW; SATA 11; SATA-Obit 56

Paton Walsh, Gillian 1937-
See Walsh, Jill Paton
See also CANR 38; JRDA; MAICYA;
SAAS 3; SATA 4, 72

Paulding, James Kirke 1778-1860 . . **NCLC 2**
See also DLB 3, 59, 74

Paulin, Thomas Neilson 1949-
See Paulin, Tom
See also CA 123; 128

Paulin, Tom . . . . **CLC 37**
See also Paulin, Thomas Neilson
See also DLB 40

Paustovsky, Konstantin (Georgievich)
1892-1968 . . . . **CLC 40**
See also CA 93-96; 25-28R

Pavese, Cesare 1908-1950 . . . . **TCLC 3**
See also CA 104; DLB 128

Pavic, Milorad 1929- . . . . **CLC 60**
See also CA 136

Payne, Alan
See Jakes, John (William)

Paz, Gil
See Lugones, Leopoldo

Paz, Octavio
1914- . . . . **CLC 3, 4, 6, 10, 19, 51, 65;
DA; HLC; PC 1; WLC**
See also CA 73-76; CANR 32; DLBY 90;
HW; MTCW

Peacock, Molly 1947- . . . . **CLC 60**
See also CA 103; DLB 120

Peacock, Thomas Love
1785-1866 . . . . **NCLC 22**
See also DLB 96, 116

Peake, Mervyn 1911-1968 . . . . **CLC 7, 54**
See also CA 5-8R; 25-28R; CANR 3;
DLB 15; MTCW; SATA 23

Pearce, Philippa . . . . **CLC 21**
See also Christie, (Ann) Philippa
See also CLR 9; MAICYA; SATA 1, 67

Pearl, Eric
See Elman, Richard

Pearson, T(homas) R(eid) 1956- . . . . **CLC 39**
See also CA 120; 130

Peck, Dale 1968(?)- . . . . **CLC 81**

Peck, John 1941- . . . . **CLC 3**
See also CA 49-52; CANR 3

Peck, Richard (Wayne) 1934- . . . . . . **CLC 21**
See also AAYA 1; CA 85-88; CANR 19,
38; CLR 15; JRDA; MAICYA; SAAS 2;
SATA 18, 55

Peck, Robert Newton 1928- . . . . **CLC 17; DA**
See also AAYA 3; CA 81-84; CANR 31;
JRDA; MAICYA; SAAS 1; SATA 21, 62

Peckinpah, (David) Sam(uel)
1925-1984 . . . . **CLC 20**
See also CA 109; 114

Pedersen, Knut 1859-1952
See Hamsun, Knut
See also CA 104; 119; MTCW

Peeslake, Gaffer
See Durrell, Lawrence (George)

Peguy, Charles Pierre
1873-1914 . . . . **TCLC 10**
See also CA 107

Pena, Ramon del Valle y
See Valle-Inclan, Ramon (Maria) del

Pendennis, Arthur Esquir
See Thackeray, William Makepeace

Penn, William 1644-1718 . . . . **LC 25**
See also DLB 24

Pepys, Samuel
1633-1703 . . . . **LC 11; DA; WLC**
See also CDBLB 1660-1789; DLB 101

Percy, Walker
1916-1990 . . . . **CLC 2, 3, 6, 8, 14, 18, 47,
65**
See also CA 1-4R; 131; CANR 1, 23;
DLB 2; DLBY 80, 90; MTCW

Perec, Georges 1936-1982 . . . . **CLC 56**
See also CA 141; DLB 83

Pereda (y Sanchez de Porrua), Jose Maria de
1833-1906 . . . . **TCLC 16**
See also CA 117

Pereda y Porrua, Jose Maria de
See Pereda (y Sanchez de Porrua), Jose
Maria de

Peregoy, George Weems
See Mencken, H(enry) L(ouis)

Perelman, S(idney) J(oseph)
1904-1979 . . . **CLC 3, 5, 9, 15, 23, 44, 49**
See also AITN 1, 2; CA 73-76; 89-92;
CANR 18; DLB 11, 44; MTCW

Peret, Benjamin 1899-1959 . . . . **TCLC 20**
See also CA 117

Peretz, Isaac Loeb 1851(?)-1915 . . . **TCLC 16**
See also CA 109

Peretz, Yitzkhok Leibush
See Peretz, Isaac Loeb

Perez Galdos, Benito 1843-1920 . . . **TCLC 27**
See also CA 125; HW

Perrault, Charles 1628-1703 . . . . **LC 2**
See also MAICYA; SATA 25

Perry, Brighton
See Sherwood, Robert E(mmet)

Perse, St.-John . . . . **CLC 4, 11, 46**
See also Leger, (Marie-Rene Auguste) Alexis
Saint-Leger

Peseenz, Tulio F.
See Lopez y Fuentes, Gregorio

Pesetsky, Bette 1932- . . . . **CLC 28**
See also CA 133; DLB 130

Peshkov, Alexei Maximovich 1868-1936
See Gorky, Maxim
See also CA 105; 141; DA

Pessoa, Fernando (Antonio Nogueira)
1888-1935 . . . . **TCLC 27; HLC**
See also CA 125

Peterkin, Julia Mood 1880-1961 . . . . **CLC 31**
See also CA 102; DLB 9

Peters, Joan K. 1945- . . . . **CLC 39**

Peters, Robert L(ouis) 1924- . . . . **CLC 7**
See also CA 13-16R; CAAS 8; DLB 105

Petofi, Sandor 1823-1849 . . . . **NCLC 21**

Petrakis, Harry Mark 1923- . . . . **CLC 3**
See also CA 9-12R; CANR 4, 30

Petrarch 1304-1374 . . . . **PC 8**

Petrov, Evgeny . . . . **TCLC 21**
See also Kataev, Evgeny Petrovich

Petry, Ann (Lane) 1908- . . . . . . **CLC 1, 7, 18**
See also BW 1; CA 5-8R; CAAS 6;
CANR 4, 46; CLR 12; DLB 76; JRDA;
MAICYA; MTCW; SATA 5

Petursson, Halligrimur 1614-1674 . . . . **LC 8**

Philipson, Morris H. 1926- . . . . **CLC 53**
See also CA 1-4R; CANR 4

Phillips, David Graham
1867-1911 . . . . **TCLC 44**
See also CA 108; DLB 9, 12

Phillips, Jack
See Sandburg, Carl (August)

Phillips, Jayne Anne
1952- . . . . **CLC 15, 33; SSC 16**
See also CA 101; CANR 24; DLBY 80;
MTCW

Phillips, Richard
See Dick, Philip K(indred)

Phillips, Robert (Schaeffer) 1938- . . . **CLC 28**
See also CA 17-20R; CAAS 13; CANR 8;
DLB 105

Phillips, Ward
See Lovecraft, H(oward) P(hillips)

Piccolo, Lucio 1901-1969 . . . . **CLC 13**
See also CA 97-100; DLB 114

Pickthall, Marjorie L(owry) C(hristie)
1883-1922 . . . . **TCLC 21**
See also CA 107; DLB 92

Pico della Mirandola, Giovanni
1463-1494 . . . . **LC 15**

Piercy, Marge
1936- . . . . **CLC 3, 6, 14, 18, 27, 62**
See also CA 21-24R; CAAS 1; CANR 13,
43; DLB 120; MTCW

Piers, Robert
See Anthony, Piers

Pieyre de Mandiargues, Andre 1909-1991
See Mandiargues, Andre Pieyre de
See also CA 103; 136; CANR 22

Pilnyak, Boris . . . . **TCLC 23**
See also Vogau, Boris Andreyevich

Pincherle, Alberto 1907-1990 . . . **CLC 11, 18**
See also Moravia, Alberto
See also CA 25-28R; 132; CANR 33;
MTCW

Pinckney, Darryl 1953- . . . . **CLC 76**
See also BW 2; CA 143

Pindar 518B.C.-446B.C. . . . . **CMLC 12**

Pineda, Cecile 1942- . . . . **CLC 39**
See also CA 118

Pinero, Arthur Wing 1855-1934 . . . **TCLC 32**
See also CA 110; DLB 10

Pinero, Miguel (Antonio Gomez)
1946-1988 . . . . **CLC 4, 55**
See also CA 61-64; 125; CANR 29; HW

Pinget, Robert 1919- . . . . **CLC 7, 13, 37**
See also CA 85-88; DLB 83

Pink Floyd
See Barrett, (Roger) Syd; Gilmour, David;
Mason, Nick; Waters, Roger; Wright,
Rick

Pinkney, Edward 1802-1828 . . . . . **NCLC 31**

Pinkwater, Daniel Manus 1941- . . . . **CLC 35**
See also Pinkwater, Manus
See also AAYA 1; CA 29-32R; CANR 12,
38; CLR 4; JRDA; MAICYA; SAAS 3;
SATA 46, 76

Pinkwater, Manus
See Pinkwater, Daniel Manus
See also SATA 8

Pinsky, Robert 1940- . . . . **CLC 9, 19, 38**
See also CA 29-32R; CAAS 4; DLBY 82

Pinta, Harold
See Pinter, Harold

Pinter, Harold
1930- . . . . . **CLC 1, 3, 6, 9, 11, 15, 27, 58,
73; DA; WLC**
See also CA 5-8R; CANR 33; CDBLB 1960
to Present; DLB 13; MTCW

Pirandello, Luigi
1867-1936 . . . . . **TCLC 4, 29; DA; DC 5;
WLC**
See also CA 104

Pirsig, Robert M(aynard)
1928- . . . . **CLC 4, 6, 73**
See also CA 53-56; CANR 42; MTCW;
SATA 39

Pisarev, Dmitry Ivanovich
1840-1868 . . . . **NCLC 25**

Pix, Mary (Griffith) 1666-1709 . . . . . . **LC 8**
See also DLB 80

Pixerecourt, Guilbert de
1773-1844 . . . . **NCLC 39**

Plaidy, Jean
See Hibbert, Eleanor Alice Burford

Planche, James Robinson
1796-1880 . . . . **NCLC 42**

Plant, Robert 1948- . . . . **CLC 12**

Plante, David (Robert)
1940- . . . . **CLC 7, 23, 38**
See also CA 37-40R; CANR 12, 36;
DLBY 83; MTCW

Plath, Sylvia
1932-1963 . . . . . **CLC 1, 2, 3, 5, 9, 11, 14,
17, 50, 51, 62; DA; PC 1; WLC**
See also AAYA 13; CA 19-20; CANR 34;
CAP 2; CDALB 1941-1968; DLB 5, 6;
MTCW

Plato 428(?)B.C.-348(?)B.C. . . . . **CMLC 8; DA**

Platonov, Andrei . . . . **TCLC 14**
See also Klimentov, Andrei Platonovich

Platt, Kin 1911- . . . . **CLC 26**
See also AAYA 11; CA 17-20R; CANR 11;
JRDA; SAAS 17; SATA 21

Plick et Plock
See Simenon, Georges (Jacques Christian)

Plimpton, George (Ames) 1927- . . . . . **CLC 36**
See also AITN 1; CA 21-24R; CANR 32;
MTCW; SATA 10

Plomer, William Charles Franklin
1903-1973 . . . . **CLC 4, 8**
See also CA 21-22; CANR 34; CAP 2;
DLB 20; MTCW; SATA 24

Plowman, Piers
See Kavanagh, Patrick (Joseph)

Plum, J.
See Wodehouse, P(elham) G(renville)

Plumly, Stanley (Ross) 1939- . . . . . . **CLC 33**
See also CA 108; 110; DLB 5

Plumpe, Friedrich Wilhelm
1888-1931 . . . . **TCLC 53**
See also CA 112

Poe, Edgar Allan
1809-1849 . . . . . **NCLC 1, 16; DA; PC 1;
SSC 1; WLC**
See also AAYA 14; CDALB 1640-1865;
DLB 3, 59, 73, 74; SATA 23

Poet of Titchfield Street, The
See Pound, Ezra (Weston Loomis)

Pohl, Frederik 1919- . . . . **CLC 18**
See also CA 61-64; CAAS 1; CANR 11, 37;
DLB 8; MTCW; SATA 24

Poirier, Louis 1910-
See Gracq, Julien
See also CA 122; 126

Poitier, Sidney 1927- . . . . **CLC 26**
See also BW 1; CA 117

Polanski, Roman 1933- . . . . **CLC 16**
See also CA 77-80

Poliakoff, Stephen 1952- . . . . **CLC 38**
See also CA 106; DLB 13

Police, The
See Copeland, Stewart (Armstrong);
Summers, Andrew James; Sumner,
Gordon Matthew

Pollitt, Katha 1949- .... **CLC 28**
See also CA 120; 122; MTCW

Pollock, (Mary) Sharon 1936- ...... **CLC 50**
See also CA 141; DLB 60

Pomerance, Bernard 1940- .... **CLC 13**
See also CA 101

Ponge, Francis (Jean Gaston Alfred)
1899-1988 .... **CLC 6, 18**
See also CA 85-88; 126; CANR 40

Pontoppidan, Henrik 1857-1943 ... **TCLC 29**

Poole, Josephine .... **CLC 17**
See also Helyar, Jane Penelope Josephine
See also SAAS 2; SATA 5

Popa, Vasko 1922- .... **CLC 19**
See also CA 112

Pope, Alexander
1688-1744 .... **LC 3; DA; WLC**
See also CDBLB 1660-1789; DLB 95, 101

Porter, Connie (Rose) 1959(?)- ..... **CLC 70**
See also BW 2; CA 142

Porter, Gene(va Grace) Stratton
1863(?)-1924 .... **TCLC 21**
See also CA 112

Porter, Katherine Anne
1890-1980 ...... **CLC 1, 3, 7, 10, 13, 15,
27; DA; SSC 4**
See also AITN 2; CA 1-4R; 101; CANR 1;
DLB 4, 9, 102; DLBD 12; DLBY 80;
MTCW; SATA 39; SATA-Obit 23

Porter, Peter (Neville Frederick)
1929- .... **CLC 5, 13, 33**
See also CA 85-88; DLB 40

Porter, William Sydney 1862-1910
See Henry, O.
See also CA 104; 131; CDALB 1865-1917;
DA; DLB 12, 78, 79; MTCW; YABC 2

Portillo (y Pacheco), Jose Lopez
See Lopez Portillo (y Pacheco), Jose

Post, Melville Davisson
1869-1930 .... **TCLC 39**
See also CA 110

Potok, Chaim 1929- .... **CLC 2, 7, 14, 26**
See also AITN 1, 2; CA 17-20R; CANR 19,
35; DLB 28; MTCW; SATA 33

Potter, Beatrice
See Webb, (Martha) Beatrice (Potter)
See also MAICYA

Potter, Dennis (Christopher George)
1935-1994 .... **CLC 58**
See also CA 107; 145; CANR 33; MTCW

Pound, Ezra (Weston Loomis)
1885-1972 ..... **CLC 1, 2, 3, 4, 5, 7, 10,
13, 18, 34, 48, 50; DA; PC 4; WLC**
See also CA 5-8R; 37-40R; CANR 40;
CDALB 1917-1929; DLB 4, 45, 63;
MTCW

Povod, Reinaldo 1959- .... **CLC 44**
See also CA 136

Powell, Anthony (Dymoke)
1905- .... **CLC 1, 3, 7, 9, 10, 31**
See also CA 1-4R; CANR 1, 32;
CDBLB 1945-1960; DLB 15; MTCW

Powell, Dawn 1897-1965 .... **CLC 66**
See also CA 5-8R

Powell, Padgett 1952- .... **CLC 34**
See also CA 126

Powers, J(ames) F(arl)
1917- .... **CLC 1, 4, 8, 57; SSC 4**
See also CA 1-4R; CANR 2; DLB 130;
MTCW

Powers, John J(ames) 1945-
See Powers, John R.
See also CA 69-72

Powers, John R. .... **CLC 66**
See also Powers, John J(ames)

Pownall, David 1938- .... **CLC 10**
See also CA 89-92; CAAS 18; DLB 14

Powys, John Cowper
1872-1963 .... **CLC 7, 9, 15, 46**
See also CA 85-88; DLB 15; MTCW

Powys, T(heodore) F(rancis)
1875-1953 .... **TCLC 9**
See also CA 106; DLB 36

Prager, Emily 1952- .... **CLC 56**

Pratt, E(dwin) J(ohn)
1883(?)-1964 .... **CLC 19**
See also CA 141; 93-96; DLB 92

Premchand .... **TCLC 21**
See also Srivastava, Dhanpat Rai

Preussler, Otfried 1923- .... **CLC 17**
See also CA 77-80; SATA 24

Prevert, Jacques (Henri Marie)
1900-1977 .... **CLC 15**
See also CA 77-80; 69-72; CANR 29;
MTCW; SATA-Obit 30

Prevost, Abbe (Antoine Francois)
1697-1763 .... **LC 1**

Price, (Edward) Reynolds
1933- .... **CLC 3, 6, 13, 43, 50, 63**
See also CA 1-4R; CANR 1, 37; DLB 2

Price, Richard 1949- .... **CLC 6, 12**
See also CA 49-52; CANR 3; DLBY 81

Prichard, Katharine Susannah
1883-1969 .... **CLC 46**
See also CA 11-12; CANR 33; CAP 1;
MTCW; SATA 66

Priestley, J(ohn) B(oynton)
1894-1984 .... **CLC 2, 5, 9, 34**
See also CA 9-12R; 113; CANR 33;
CDBLB 1914-1945; DLB 10, 34, 77, 100,
139; DLBY 84; MTCW

Prince 1958(?)- .... **CLC 35**

Prince, F(rank) T(empleton) 1912- .. **CLC 22**
See also CA 101; CANR 43; DLB 20

Prince Kropotkin
See Kropotkin, Peter (Aleksieevich)

Prior, Matthew 1664-1721 .... **LC 4**
See also DLB 95

Pritchard, William H(arrison)
1932- .... **CLC 34**
See also CA 65-68; CANR 23; DLB 111

Pritchett, V(ictor) S(awdon)
1900- .... **CLC 5, 13, 15, 41; SSC 14**
See also CA 61-64; CANR 31; DLB 15,
139; MTCW

Private 19022
See Manning, Frederic

Probst, Mark 1925- .... **CLC 59**
See also CA 130

Prokosch, Frederic 1908-1989.... **CLC 4, 48**
See also CA 73-76; 128; DLB 48

Prophet, The
See Dreiser, Theodore (Herman Albert)

Prose, Francine 1947- .... **CLC 45**
See also CA 109; 112; CANR 46

Proudhon
See Cunha, Euclides (Rodrigues Pimenta) da

Proulx, E. Annie 1935- .... **CLC 81**

**Proust, (Valentin-Louis-George-Eugene-)
Marcel**
1871-1922 ... **TCLC 7, 13, 33; DA; WLC**
See also CA 104; 120; DLB 65; MTCW

Prowler, Harley
See Masters, Edgar Lee

Prus, Boleslaw 1845-1912 .... **TCLC 48**

Pryor, Richard (Franklin Lenox Thomas)
1940- .... **CLC 26**
See also CA 122

Przybyszewski, Stanislaw
1868-1927 .... **TCLC 36**
See also DLB 66

Pteleon
See Grieve, C(hristopher) M(urray)

Puckett, Lute
See Masters, Edgar Lee

Puig, Manuel
1932-1990 ... **CLC 3, 5, 10, 28, 65; HLC**
See also CA 45-48; CANR 2, 32; DLB 113;
HW; MTCW

Purdy, Al(fred Wellington)
1918- .... **CLC 3, 6, 14, 50**
See also CA 81-84; CAAS 17; CANR 42;
DLB 88

Purdy, James (Amos)
1923- .... **CLC 2, 4, 10, 28, 52**
See also CA 33-36R; CAAS 1; CANR 19;
DLB 2; MTCW

Pure, Simon
See Swinnerton, Frank Arthur

Pushkin, Alexander (Sergeyevich)
1799-1837 .... **NCLC 3, 27; DA; PC 10;
WLC**
See also SATA 61

P'u Sung-ling 1640-1715 .... **LC 3**

Putnam, Arthur Lee
See Alger, Horatio, Jr.

Puzo, Mario 1920- .... **CLC 1, 2, 6, 36**
See also CA 65-68; CANR 4, 42; DLB 6;
MTCW

Pym, Barbara (Mary Crampton)
1913-1980 .... **CLC 13, 19, 37**
See also CA 13-14; 97-100; CANR 13, 34;
CAP 1; DLB 14; DLBY 87; MTCW

Pynchon, Thomas (Ruggles, Jr.)
    1937- . . . . . CLC 2, 3, 6, 9, 11, 18, 33, 62,
                    72; DA; SSC 14; WLC
    See also BEST 90:2; CA 17-20R; CANR 22,
    46; DLB 2; MTCW

Qian Zhongshu
    See Ch'ien Chung-shu

Qroll
    See Dagerman, Stig (Halvard)

Quarrington, Paul (Lewis) 1953- . . . . CLC 65
    See also CA 129

Quasimodo, Salvatore 1901-1968 . . . CLC 10
    See also CA 13-16; 25-28R; CAP 1;
    DLB 114; MTCW

Queen, Ellery . . . . CLC 3, 11
    See also Dannay, Frederic; Davidson,
    Avram; Lee, Manfred B(ennington);
    Sturgeon, Theodore (Hamilton); Vance,
    John Holbrook

Queen, Ellery, Jr.
    See Dannay, Frederic; Lee, Manfred
    B(ennington)

Queneau, Raymond
    1903-1976 . . . . CLC 2, 5, 10, 42
    See also CA 77-80; 69-72; CANR 32;
    DLB 72; MTCW

Quevedo, Francisco de 1580-1645 . . . . LC 23

Quiller-Couch, Arthur Thomas
    1863-1944 . . . . TCLC 53
    See also CA 118; DLB 135

Quin, Ann (Marie) 1936-1973 . . . . . . CLC 6
    See also CA 9-12R; 45-48; DLB 14

Quinn, Martin
    See Smith, Martin Cruz

Quinn, Simon
    See Smith, Martin Cruz

Quiroga, Horacio (Sylvestre)
    1878-1937 . . . . TCLC 20; HLC
    See also CA 117; 131; HW; MTCW

Quoirez, Francoise 1935- . . . . CLC 9
    See also Sagan, Francoise
    See also CA 49-52; CANR 6, 39; MTCW

Raabe, Wilhelm 1831-1910 . . . . TCLC 45
    See also DLB 129

Rabe, David (William) 1940- . . . CLC 4, 8, 33
    See also CA 85-88; CABS 3; DLB 7

Rabelais, Francois
    1483-1553 . . . . LC 5; DA; WLC

Rabinovitch, Sholem 1859-1916
    See Aleichem, Sholom
    See also CA 104

Radcliffe, Ann (Ward) 1764-1823 . . NCLC 6
    See also DLB 39

Radiguet, Raymond 1903-1923 . . . . TCLC 29
    See also DLB 65

Radnoti, Miklos 1909-1944 . . . . TCLC 16
    See also CA 118

Rado, James 1939- . . . . CLC 17
    See also CA 105

Radvanyi, Netty 1900-1983
    See Seghers, Anna
    See also CA 85-88; 110

Rae, Ben
    See Griffiths, Trevor

Raeburn, John (Hay) 1941- . . . . CLC 34
    See also CA 57-60

Ragni, Gerome 1942-1991 . . . . CLC 17
    See also CA 105; 134

Rahv, Philip 1908-1973 . . . . CLC 24
    See also Greenberg, Ivan
    See also DLB 137

Raine, Craig 1944- . . . . CLC 32
    See also CA 108; CANR 29; DLB 40

Raine, Kathleen (Jessie) 1908- . . . CLC 7, 45
    See also CA 85-88; CANR 46; DLB 20;
    MTCW

Rainis, Janis 1865-1929 . . . . TCLC 29

Rakosi, Carl . . . . CLC 47
    See also Rawley, Callman
    See also CAAS 5

Raleigh, Richard
    See Lovecraft, H(oward) P(hillips)

Rallentando, H. P.
    See Sayers, Dorothy L(eigh)

Ramal, Walter
    See de la Mare, Walter (John)

Ramon, Juan
    See Jimenez (Mantecon), Juan Ramon

Ramos, Graciliano 1892-1953 . . . . . TCLC 32

Rampersad, Arnold 1941- . . . . CLC 44
    See also BW 2; CA 127; 133; DLB 111

Rampling, Anne
    See Rice, Anne

Ramuz, Charles-Ferdinand
    1878-1947 . . . . TCLC 33

Rand, Ayn
    1905-1982 . . . . . . CLC 3, 30, 44, 79; DA;
                        WLC
    See also AAYA 10; CA 13-16R; 105;
    CANR 27; MTCW

Randall, Dudley (Felker)
    1914- . . . . CLC 1; BLC
    See also BW 1; CA 25-28R; CANR 23;
    DLB 41

Randall, Robert
    See Silverberg, Robert

Ranger, Ken
    See Creasey, John

Ransom, John Crowe
    1888-1974 . . . . CLC 2, 4, 5, 11, 24
    See also CA 5-8R; 49-52; CANR 6, 34;
    DLB 45, 63; MTCW

Rao, Raja 1909- . . . . CLC 25, 56
    See also CA 73-76; MTCW

Raphael, Frederic (Michael)
    1931- . . . . CLC 2, 14
    See also CA 1-4R; CANR 1; DLB 14

Ratcliffe, James P.
    See Mencken, H(enry) L(ouis)

Rathbone, Julian 1935- . . . . CLC 41
    See also CA 101; CANR 34

Rattigan, Terence (Mervyn)
    1911-1977 . . . . CLC 7
    See also CA 85-88; 73-76;
    CDBLB 1945-1960; DLB 13; MTCW

Ratushinskaya, Irina 1954- . . . . CLC 54
    See also CA 129

Raven, Simon (Arthur Noel)
    1927- . . . . CLC 14
    See also CA 81-84

Rawley, Callman 1903-
    See Rakosi, Carl
    See also CA 21-24R; CANR 12, 32

Rawlings, Marjorie Kinnan
    1896-1953 . . . . TCLC 4
    See also CA 104; 137; DLB 9, 22, 102;
    JRDA; MAICYA; YABC 1

Ray, Satyajit 1921-1992 . . . . CLC 16, 76
    See also CA 114; 137

Read, Herbert Edward 1893-1968 . . . . CLC 4
    See also CA 85-88; 25-28R; DLB 20

Read, Piers Paul 1941- . . . . . . CLC 4, 10, 25
    See also CA 21-24R; CANR 38; DLB 14;
    SATA 21

Reade, Charles 1814-1884 . . . . NCLC 2
    See also DLB 21

Reade, Hamish
    See Gray, Simon (James Holliday)

Reading, Peter 1946- . . . . CLC 47
    See also CA 103; CANR 46; DLB 40

Reaney, James 1926- . . . . CLC 13
    See also CA 41-44R; CAAS 15; CANR 42;
    DLB 68; SATA 43

Rebreanu, Liviu 1885-1944 . . . . TCLC 28

Rechy, John (Francisco)
    1934- . . . . CLC 1, 7, 14, 18; HLC
    See also CA 5-8R; CAAS 4; CANR 6, 32;
    DLB 122; DLBY 82; HW

Redcam, Tom 1870-1933 . . . . TCLC 25

Reddin, Keith . . . . CLC 67

Redgrove, Peter (William)
    1932- . . . . CLC 6, 41
    See also CA 1-4R; CANR 3, 39; DLB 40

Redmon, Anne . . . . CLC 22
    See also Nightingale, Anne Redmon
    See also DLBY 86

Reed, Eliot
    See Ambler, Eric

Reed, Ishmael
    1938- . . . CLC 2, 3, 5, 6, 13, 32, 60; BLC
    See also BW 2; CA 21-24R; CANR 25;
    DLB 2, 5, 33; DLBD 8; MTCW

Reed, John (Silas) 1887-1920 . . . . . . TCLC 9
    See also CA 106

Reed, Lou . . . . CLC 21
    See also Firbank, Louis

Reeve, Clara 1729-1807 . . . . NCLC 19
    See also DLB 39

Reich, Wilhelm 1897-1957 . . . . TCLC 57

Reid, Christopher (John) 1949- . . . . . CLC 33
    See also CA 140; DLB 40

Reid, Desmond
    See Moorcock, Michael (John)

Reid Banks, Lynne 1929-
    See Banks, Lynne Reid
    See also CA 1-4R; CANR 6, 22, 38;
    CLR 24; JRDA; MAICYA; SATA 22, 75

Reilly, William K.
    See Creasey, John

Roberts, Kate 1891-1985 .... **CLC 15**
See also CA 107; 116

Roberts, Keith (John Kingston)
1935- .... **CLC 14**
See also CA 25-28R; CANR 46

Roberts, Kenneth (Lewis)
1885-1957 .... **TCLC 23**
See also CA 109; DLB 9

Roberts, Michele (B.) 1949-....... **CLC 48**
See also CA 115

Robertson, Ellis
See Ellison, Harlan (Jay); Silverberg, Robert

Robertson, Thomas William
1829-1871 .... **NCLC 35**

Robinson, Edwin Arlington
1869-1935 .... **TCLC 5; DA; PC 1**
See also CA 104; 133; CDALB 1865-1917;
DLB 54; MTCW

Robinson, Henry Crabb
1775-1867 .... **NCLC 15**
See also DLB 107

Robinson, Jill 1936-.............. **CLC 10**
See also CA 102

Robinson, Kim Stanley 1952- ...... **CLC 34**
See also CA 126

Robinson, Lloyd
See Silverberg, Robert

Robinson, Marilynne 1944-........ **CLC 25**
See also CA 116

Robinson, Smokey................. **CLC 21**
See also Robinson, William, Jr.

Robinson, William, Jr. 1940-
See Robinson, Smokey
See also CA 116

Robison, Mary 1949-............. **CLC 42**
See also CA 113; 116; DLB 130

Rod, Edouard 1857-1910 .... **TCLC 52**

Roddenberry, Eugene Wesley 1921-1991
See Roddenberry, Gene
See also CA 110; 135; CANR 37; SATA 45;
SATA-Obit 69

Roddenberry, Gene .... **CLC 17**
See also Roddenberry, Eugene Wesley
See also AAYA 5; SATA-Obit 69

Rodgers, Mary 1931-............. **CLC 12**
See also CA 49-52; CANR 8; CLR 20;
JRDA; MAICYA; SATA 8

Rodgers, W(illiam) R(obert)
1909-1969 .... **CLC 7**
See also CA 85-88; DLB 20

Rodman, Eric
See Silverberg, Robert

Rodman, Howard 1920(?)-1985 ..... **CLC 65**
See also CA 118

Rodman, Maia
See Wojciechowska, Maia (Teresa)

Rodriguez, Claudio 1934-......... **CLC 10**
See also DLB 134

Roelvaag, O(le) E(dvart)
1876-1931 .... **TCLC 17**
See also CA 117; DLB 9

Roethke, Theodore (Huebner)
1908-1963 ...... **CLC 1, 3, 8, 11, 19, 46**
See also CA 81-84; CABS 2;
CDALB 1941-1968; DLB 5; MTCW

Rogers, Thomas Hunton 1927- ..... **CLC 57**
See also CA 89-92

Rogers, Will(iam Penn Adair)
1879-1935 .... **TCLC 8**
See also CA 105; 144; DLB 11; NNAL

Rogin, Gilbert 1929-.............. **CLC 18**
See also CA 65-68; CANR 15

Rohan, Koda .... **TCLC 22**
See also Koda Shigeyuki

Rohmer, Eric..................... **CLC 16**
See also Scherer, Jean-Marie Maurice

Rohmer, Sax .... **TCLC 28**
See also Ward, Arthur Henry Sarsfield
See also DLB 70

Roiphe, Anne (Richardson)
1935- .... **CLC 3, 9**
See also CA 89-92; CANR 45; DLBY 80

Rojas, Fernando de 1465-1541 ..... **LC 23**

**Rolfe, Frederick (William Serafino Austin
Lewis Mary)** 1860-1913..... **TCLC 12**
See also CA 107; DLB 34

Rolland, Romain 1866-1944....... **TCLC 23**
See also CA 118; DLB 65

Rolvaag, O(le) E(dvart)
See Roelvaag, O(le) E(dvart)

Romain Arnaud, Saint
See Aragon, Louis

Romains, Jules 1885-1972 .... **CLC 7**
See also CA 85-88; CANR 34; DLB 65;
MTCW

Romero, Jose Ruben 1890-1952 ... **TCLC 14**
See also CA 114; 131; HW

Ronsard, Pierre de
1524-1585 .... **LC 6; PC 11**

Rooke, Leon 1934-............. **CLC 25, 34**
See also CA 25-28R; CANR 23

Roper, William 1498-1578......... **LC 10**

Roquelaure, A. N.
See Rice, Anne

Rosa, Joao Guimaraes 1908-1967 ... **CLC 23**
See also CA 89-92; DLB 113

Rose, Wendy 1948-.............. **CLC 85**
See also CA 53-56; CANR 5; NNAL;
SATA 12

Rosen, Richard (Dean) 1949-....... **CLC 39**
See also CA 77-80

Rosenberg, Isaac 1890-1918....... **TCLC 12**
See also CA 107; DLB 20

Rosenblatt, Joe .... **CLC 15**
See also Rosenblatt, Joseph

Rosenblatt, Joseph 1933-
See Rosenblatt, Joe
See also CA 89-92

Rosenfeld, Samuel 1896-1963
See Tzara, Tristan
See also CA 89-92

Rosenthal, M(acha) L(ouis) 1917-... **CLC 28**
See also CA 1-4R; CAAS 6; CANR 4;
DLB 5; SATA 59

Ross, Barnaby
See Dannay, Frederic

Ross, Bernard L.
See Follett, Ken(neth Martin)

Ross, J. H.
See Lawrence, T(homas) E(dward)

Ross, Martin
See Martin, Violet Florence
See also DLB 135

Ross, (James) Sinclair 1908-....... **CLC 13**
See also CA 73-76; DLB 88

Rossetti, Christina (Georgina)
1830-1894 ... **NCLC 2; DA; PC 7; WLC**
See also DLB 35; MAICYA; SATA 20

Rossetti, Dante Gabriel
1828-1882 .... **NCLC 4; DA; WLC**
See also CDBLB 1832-1890; DLB 35

Rossner, Judith (Perelman)
1935- .... **CLC 6, 9, 29**
See also AITN 2; BEST 90:3; CA 17-20R;
CANR 18; DLB 6; MTCW

Rostand, Edmond (Eugene Alexis)
1868-1918 .... **TCLC 6, 37; DA**
See also CA 104; 126; MTCW

Roth, Henry 1906-........... **CLC 2, 6, 11**
See also CA 11-12; CANR 38; CAP 1;
DLB 28; MTCW

Roth, Joseph 1894-1939......... **TCLC 33**
See also DLB 85

Roth, Philip (Milton)
1933-...... **CLC 1, 2, 3, 4, 6, 9, 15, 22,
31, 47, 66; DA; WLC**
See also BEST 90:3; CA 1-4R; CANR 1, 22,
36; CDALB 1968-1988; DLB 2, 28;
DLBY 82; MTCW

Rothenberg, Jerome 1931-....... **CLC 6, 57**
See also CA 45-48; CANR 1; DLB 5

Roumain, Jacques (Jean Baptiste)
1907-1944 .... **TCLC 19; BLC**
See also BW 1; CA 117; 125

Rourke, Constance (Mayfield)
1885-1941 .... **TCLC 12**
See also CA 107; YABC 1

Rousseau, Jean-Baptiste 1671-1741 ... **LC 9**

Rousseau, Jean-Jacques
1712-1778 .... **LC 14; DA; WLC**

Roussel, Raymond 1877-1933 ..... **TCLC 20**
See also CA 117

Rovit, Earl (Herbert) 1927-........ **CLC 7**
See also CA 5-8R; CANR 12

Rowe, Nicholas 1674-1718.......... **LC 8**
See also DLB 84

Rowley, Ames Dorrance
See Lovecraft, H(oward) P(hillips)

Rowson, Susanna Haswell
1762(?)-1824 .... **NCLC 5**
See also DLB 37

Roy, Gabrielle 1909-1983....... **CLC 10, 14**
See also CA 53-56; 110; CANR 5; DLB 68;
MTCW

Rozewicz, Tadeusz 1921-........ **CLC 9, 23**
See also CA 108; CANR 36; MTCW

Sansom, William 1912-1976...... CLC 2, 6
See also CA 5-8R; 65-68; CANR 42;
DLB 139; MTCW

Santayana, George 1863-1952..... TCLC 40
See also CA 115; DLB 54, 71

Santiago, Danny .... CLC 33
See also James, Daniel (Lewis); James,
Daniel (Lewis)
See also DLB 122

Santmyer, Helen Hoover
1895-1986 .... CLC 33
See also CA 1-4R; 118; CANR 15, 33;
DLBY 84; MTCW

Santos, Bienvenido N(uqui) 1911-... CLC 22
See also CA 101; CANR 19, 46

Sapper .... TCLC 44
See also McNeile, Herman Cyril

Sappho fl. 6th cent. B.C.-.... CMLC 3; PC 5

Sarduy, Severo 1937-1993......... CLC 6
See also CA 89-92; 142; DLB 113; HW

Sargeson, Frank 1903-1982....... CLC 31
See also CA 25-28R; 106; CANR 38

Sarmiento, Felix Ruben Garcia
See Dario, Ruben

Saroyan, William
1908-1981 ..... CLC 1, 8, 10, 29, 34, 56;
DA; WLC
See also CA 5-8R; 103; CANR 30; DLB 7,
9, 86; DLBY 81; MTCW; SATA 23;
SATA-Obit 24

Sarraute, Nathalie
1900- .... CLC 1, 2, 4, 8, 10, 31, 80
See also CA 9-12R; CANR 23; DLB 83;
MTCW

Sarton, (Eleanor) May
1912- .... CLC 4, 14, 49
See also CA 1-4R; CANR 1, 34; DLB 48;
DLBY 81; MTCW; SATA 36

Sartre, Jean-Paul
1905-1980 .... CLC 1, 4, 7, 9, 13, 18, 24,
44, 50, 52; DA; DC 3; WLC
See also CA 9-12R; 97-100; CANR 21;
DLB 72; MTCW

Sassoon, Siegfried (Lorraine)
1886-1967 .... CLC 36
See also CA 104; 25-28R; CANR 36;
DLB 20; MTCW

Satterfield, Charles
See Pohl, Frederik

Saul, John (W. III) 1942- .... CLC 46
See also AAYA 10; BEST 90:4; CA 81-84;
CANR 16, 40

Saunders, Caleb
See Heinlein, Robert A(nson)

Saura (Atares), Carlos 1932-....... CLC 20
See also CA 114; 131; HW

Sauser-Hall, Frederic 1887-1961.... CLC 18
See also CA 102; 93-96; CANR 36; MTCW

Saussure, Ferdinand de
1857-1913 .... TCLC 49

Savage, Catharine
See Brosman, Catharine Savage

Savage, Thomas 1915- .... CLC 40
See also CA 126; 132; CAAS 15

Savan, Glenn 19(?)- .... CLC 50

Sayers, Dorothy L(eigh)
1893-1957 .... TCLC 2, 15
See also CA 104; 119; CDBLB 1914-1945;
DLB 10, 36, 77, 100; MTCW

Sayers, Valerie 1952-............ CLC 50
See also CA 134

Sayles, John (Thomas)
1950- .... CLC 7, 10, 14
See also CA 57-60; CANR 41; DLB 44

Scammell, Michael .... CLC 34

Scannell, Vernon 1922- .... CLC 49
See also CA 5-8R; CANR 8, 24; DLB 27;
SATA 59

Scarlett, Susan
See Streatfeild, (Mary) Noel

Schaeffer, Susan Fromberg
1941- .... CLC 6, 11, 22
See also CA 49-52; CANR 18; DLB 28;
MTCW; SATA 22

Schary, Jill
See Robinson, Jill

Schell, Jonathan 1943-........... CLC 35
See also CA 73-76; CANR 12

Schelling, Friedrich Wilhelm Joseph von
1775-1854 .... NCLC 30
See also DLB 90

Schendel, Arthur van 1874-1946 ... TCLC 56

Scherer, Jean-Marie Maurice 1920-
See Rohmer, Eric
See also CA 110

Schevill, James (Erwin) 1920-...... CLC 7
See also CA 5-8R; CAAS 12

Schiller, Friedrich 1759-1805 .... NCLC 39
See also DLB 94

Schisgal, Murray (Joseph) 1926-..... CLC 6
See also CA 21-24R

Schlee, Ann 1934-................ CLC 35
See also CA 101; CANR 29; SATA 36, 44

Schlegel, August Wilhelm von
1767-1845 .... NCLC 15
See also DLB 94

Schlegel, Friedrich 1772-1829 .... NCLC 45
See also DLB 90

Schlegel, Johann Elias (von)
1719(?)-1749 .... LC 5

Schlesinger, Arthur M(eier), Jr.
1917- .... CLC 84
See also AITN 1; CA 1-4R; CANR 1, 28;
DLB 17; MTCW; SATA 61

Schmidt, Arno (Otto) 1914-1979 .... CLC 56
See also CA 128; 109; DLB 69

Schmitz, Aron Hector 1861-1928
See Svevo, Italo
See also CA 104; 122; MTCW

Schnackenberg, Gjertrud 1953-..... CLC 40
See also CA 116; DLB 120

Schneider, Leonard Alfred 1925-1966
See Bruce, Lenny
See also CA 89-92

Schnitzler, Arthur
1862-1931 .... TCLC 4; SSC 15
See also CA 104; DLB 81, 118

Schor, Sandra (M.) 1932(?)-1990 ... CLC 65
See also CA 132

Schorer, Mark 1908-1977 .... CLC 9
See also CA 5-8R; 73-76; CANR 7;
DLB 103

Schrader, Paul (Joseph) 1946-...... CLC 26
See also CA 37-40R; CANR 41; DLB 44

Schreiner, Olive (Emilie Albertina)
1855-1920 .... TCLC 9
See also CA 105; DLB 18

Schulberg, Budd (Wilson)
1914- .... CLC 7, 48
See also CA 25-28R; CANR 19; DLB 6, 26,
28; DLBY 81

Schulz, Bruno
1892-1942 .... TCLC 5, 51; SSC 13
See also CA 115; 123

Schulz, Charles M(onroe) 1922-.... CLC 12
See also CA 9-12R; CANR 6; SATA 10

Schumacher, E(rnst) F(riedrich)
1911-1977 .... CLC 80
See also CA 81-84; 73-76; CANR 34

Schuyler, James Marcus
1923-1991 .... CLC 5, 23
See also CA 101; 134; DLB 5

Schwartz, Delmore (David)
1913-1966 ...... CLC 2, 4, 10, 45; PC 8
See also CA 17-18; 25-28R; CANR 35;
CAP 2; DLB 28, 48; MTCW

Schwartz, Ernst
See Ozu, Yasujiro

Schwartz, John Burnham 1965- .... CLC 59
See also CA 132

Schwartz, Lynne Sharon 1939-..... CLC 31
See also CA 103; CANR 44

Schwartz, Muriel A.
See Eliot, T(homas) S(tearns)

Schwarz-Bart, Andre 1928-....... CLC 2, 4
See also CA 89-92

Schwarz-Bart, Simone 1938-........ CLC 7
See also BW 2; CA 97-100

Schwob, (Mayer Andre) Marcel
1867-1905 .... TCLC 20
See also CA 117; DLB 123

Sciascia, Leonardo
1921-1989 .... CLC 8, 9, 41
See also CA 85-88; 130; CANR 35; MTCW

Scoppettone, Sandra 1936-........ CLC 26
See also AAYA 11; CA 5-8R; CANR 41;
SATA 9

Scorsese, Martin 1942- .... CLC 20
See also CA 110; 114; CANR 46

Scotland, Jay
See Jakes, John (William)

Scott, Duncan Campbell
1862-1947 .... TCLC 6
See also CA 104; DLB 92

Scott, Evelyn 1893-1963.......... CLC 43
See also CA 104; 112; DLB 9, 48

Scott, F(rancis) R(eginald)
1899-1985 .... CLC 22
See also CA 101; 114; DLB 88

Scott, Frank
See Scott, F(rancis) R(eginald)

Scott, Joanna 1960- .... CLC 50
See also CA 126

Shelley, Mary Wollstonecraft (Godwin)
    1797-1851 . . . . **NCLC 14; DA; WLC**
    See also CDBLB 1789-1832; DLB 110, 116;
    SATA 29

Shelley, Percy Bysshe
    1792-1822 . . . . **NCLC 18; DA; WLC**
    See also CDBLB 1789-1832; DLB 96, 110

Shepard, Jim   1956- . . . . **CLC 36**
    See also CA 137

Shepard, Lucius   1947- . . . . **CLC 34**
    See also CA 128; 141

Shepard, Sam
    1943- . . . . **CLC 4, 6, 17, 34, 41, 44; DC 5**
    See also AAYA 1; CA 69-72; CABS 3;
    CANR 22; DLB 7; MTCW

Shepherd, Michael
    See Ludlum, Robert

Sherburne, Zoa (Morin)   1912- . . . . . . **CLC 30**
    See also AAYA 13; CA 1-4R; CANR 3, 37;
    MAICYA; SAAS 18; SATA 3

Sheridan, Frances   1724-1766 . . . . **LC 7**
    See also DLB 39, 84

Sheridan, Richard Brinsley
    1751-1816 . . . **NCLC 5; DA; DC 1; WLC**
    See also CDBLB 1660-1789; DLB 89

Sherman, Jonathan Marc . . . . **CLC 55**

Sherman, Martin   1941(?)- . . . . **CLC 19**
    See also CA 116; 123

Sherwin, Judith Johnson   1936- . . . **CLC 7, 15**
    See also CA 25-28R; CANR 34

Sherwood, Frances   1940- . . . . **CLC 81**

Sherwood, Robert E(mmet)
    1896-1955 . . . . **TCLC 3**
    See also CA 104; DLB 7, 26

Shestov, Lev   1866-1938 . . . . **TCLC 56**

Shiel, M(atthew) P(hipps)
    1865-1947 . . . . **TCLC 8**
    See also CA 106

Shiga, Naoya   1883-1971 . . . . **CLC 33**
    See also CA 101; 33-36R

Shilts, Randy   1951-1994 . . . . **CLC 85**
    See also CA 115; 127; 144; CANR 45

Shimazaki Haruki   1872-1943
    See Shimazaki Toson
    See also CA 105; 134

Shimazaki Toson . . . . **TCLC 5**
    See also Shimazaki Haruki

Sholokhov, Mikhail (Aleksandrovich)
    1905-1984 . . . . **CLC 7, 15**
    See also CA 101; 112; MTCW;
    SATA-Obit 36

Shone, Patric
    See Hanley, James

Shreve, Susan Richards   1939- . . . . . . **CLC 23**
    See also CA 49-52; CAAS 5; CANR 5, 38;
    MAICYA; SATA 41, 46

Shue, Larry   1946-1985 . . . . **CLC 52**
    See also CA 145; 117

Shu-Jen, Chou   1881-1936
    See Hsun, Lu
    See also CA 104

Shulman, Alix Kates   1932- . . . . . . **CLC 2, 10**
    See also CA 29-32R; CANR 43; SATA 7

Shuster, Joe   1914- . . . . **CLC 21**

Shute, Nevil . . . . **CLC 30**
    See also Norway, Nevil Shute

Shuttle, Penelope (Diane)   1947- . . . . . **CLC 7**
    See also CA 93-96; CANR 39; DLB 14, 40

Sidney, Mary   1561-1621 . . . . **LC 19**

Sidney, Sir Philip   1554-1586 . . . . **LC 19; DA**
    See also CDBLB Before 1660

Siegel, Jerome   1914- . . . . **CLC 21**
    See also CA 116

Siegel, Jerry
    See Siegel, Jerome

Sienkiewicz, Henryk (Adam Alexander Pius)
    1846-1916 . . . . **TCLC 3**
    See also CA 104; 134

Sierra, Gregorio Martinez
    See Martinez Sierra, Gregorio

Sierra, Maria (de la O'LeJarraga) Martinez
    See Martinez Sierra, Maria (de la
    O'LeJarraga)

Sigal, Clancy   1926- . . . . **CLC 7**
    See also CA 1-4R

Sigourney, Lydia Howard (Huntley)
    1791-1865 . . . . **NCLC 21**
    See also DLB 1, 42, 73

Siguenza y Gongora, Carlos de
    1645-1700 . . . . **LC 8**

Sigurjonsson, Johann   1880-1919 . . . **TCLC 27**

Sikelianos, Angelos   1884-1951 . . . . **TCLC 39**

Silkin, Jon   1930- . . . . **CLC 2, 6, 43**
    See also CA 5-8R; CAAS 5; DLB 27

Silko, Leslie (Marmon)
    1948- . . . . **CLC 23, 74; DA**
    See also AAYA 14; CA 115; 122;
    CANR 45; DLB 143; NNAL

Sillanpaa, Frans Eemil   1888-1964 . . . **CLC 19**
    See also CA 129; 93-96; MTCW

Sillitoe, Alan
    1928- . . . . **CLC 1, 3, 6, 10, 19, 57**
    See also AITN 1; CA 9-12R; CAAS 2;
    CANR 8, 26; CDBLB 1960 to Present;
    DLB 14, 139; MTCW; SATA 61

Silone, Ignazio   1900-1978 . . . . **CLC 4**
    See also CA 25-28; 81-84; CANR 34;
    CAP 2; MTCW

Silver, Joan Micklin   1935- . . . . **CLC 20**
    See also CA 114; 121

Silver, Nicholas
    See Faust, Frederick (Schiller)

Silverberg, Robert   1935- . . . . **CLC 7**
    See also CA 1-4R; CAAS 3; CANR 1, 20,
    36; DLB 8; MAICYA; MTCW; SATA 13

Silverstein, Alvin   1933- . . . . **CLC 17**
    See also CA 49-52; CANR 2; CLR 25;
    JRDA; MAICYA; SATA 8, 69

Silverstein, Virginia B(arbara Opshelor)
    1937- . . . . **CLC 17**
    See also CA 49-52; CANR 2; CLR 25;
    JRDA; MAICYA; SATA 8, 69

Sim, Georges
    See Simenon, Georges (Jacques Christian)

Simak, Clifford D(onald)
    1904-1988 . . . . **CLC 1, 55**
    See also CA 1-4R; 125; CANR 1, 35;
    DLB 8; MTCW; SATA-Obit 56

Simenon, Georges (Jacques Christian)
    1903-1989 . . . . **CLC 1, 2, 3, 8, 18, 47**
    See also CA 85-88; 129; CANR 35;
    DLB 72; DLBY 89; MTCW

Simic, Charles   1938- . . . **CLC 6, 9, 22, 49, 68**
    See also CA 29-32R; CAAS 4; CANR 12,
    33; DLB 105

Simmons, Charles (Paul)   1924- . . . . . **CLC 57**
    See also CA 89-92

Simmons, Dan   1948- . . . . **CLC 44**
    See also CA 138

Simmons, James (Stewart Alexander)
    1933- . . . . **CLC 43**
    See also CA 105; DLB 40

Simms, William Gilmore
    1806-1870 . . . . **NCLC 3**
    See also DLB 3, 30, 59, 73

Simon, Carly   1945- . . . . **CLC 26**
    See also CA 105

Simon, Claude   1913- . . . . **CLC 4, 9, 15, 39**
    See also CA 89-92; CANR 33; DLB 83;
    MTCW

Simon, (Marvin) Neil
    1927- . . . . **CLC 6, 11, 31, 39, 70**
    See also AITN 1; CA 21-24R; CANR 26;
    DLB 7; MTCW

Simon, Paul   1942(?)- . . . . **CLC 17**
    See also CA 116

Simonon, Paul   1956(?)- . . . . **CLC 30**

Simpson, Harriette
    See Arnow, Harriette (Louisa) Simpson

Simpson, Louis (Aston Marantz)
    1923- . . . . **CLC 4, 7, 9, 32**
    See also CA 1-4R; CAAS 4; CANR 1;
    DLB 5; MTCW

Simpson, Mona (Elizabeth)   1957- . . . **CLC 44**
    See also CA 122; 135

Simpson, N(orman) F(rederick)
    1919- . . . . **CLC 29**
    See also CA 13-16R; DLB 13

Sinclair, Andrew (Annandale)
    1935- . . . . **CLC 2, 14**
    See also CA 9-12R; CAAS 5; CANR 14, 38;
    DLB 14; MTCW

Sinclair, Emil
    See Hesse, Hermann

Sinclair, Iain   1943- . . . . **CLC 76**
    See also CA 132

Sinclair, Iain MacGregor
    See Sinclair, Iain

Sinclair, Mary Amelia St. Clair   1865(?)-1946
    See Sinclair, May
    See also CA 104

Sinclair, May . . . . **TCLC 3, 11**
    See also Sinclair, Mary Amelia St. Clair
    See also DLB 36, 135

Sinclair, Upton (Beall)
    1878-1968 . . . . . . **CLC 1, 11, 15, 63; DA;
                                                    WLC**
    See also CA 5-8R; 25-28R; CANR 7;
    CDALB 1929-1941; DLB 9; MTCW;
    SATA 9

Singer, Isaac
    See Singer, Isaac Bashevis

Sorrentino, Gilbert
1929- . . . . **CLC 3, 7, 14, 22, 40**
See also CA 77-80; CANR 14, 33; DLB 5;
DLBY 80

Soto, Gary 1952-. . . . . . . **CLC 32, 80; HLC**
See also AAYA 10; CA 119; 125; DLB 82;
HW; JRDA

Soupault, Philippe 1897-1990 . . . . . . **CLC 68**
See also CA 116; 131

Souster, (Holmes) Raymond
1921- . . . . **CLC 5, 14**
See also CA 13-16R; CAAS 14; CANR 13,
29; DLB 88; SATA 63

Southern, Terry 1926- . . . . **CLC 7**
See also CA 1-4R; CANR 1; DLB 2

Southey, Robert 1774-1843 . . . . **NCLC 8**
See also DLB 93, 107, 142; SATA 54

Southworth, Emma Dorothy Eliza Nevitte
1819-1899 . . . . **NCLC 26**

Souza, Ernest
See Scott, Evelyn

Soyinka, Wole
1934- . . . . **CLC 3, 5, 14, 36, 44; BLC;
DA; DC 2; WLC**
See also BW 2; CA 13-16R; CANR 27, 39;
DLB 125; MTCW

Spackman, W(illiam) M(ode)
1905-1990 . . . . **CLC 46**
See also CA 81-84; 132

Spacks, Barry 1931-. . . . . **CLC 14**
See also CA 29-32R; CANR 33; DLB 105

Spanidou, Irini 1946- . . . . **CLC 44**

Spark, Muriel (Sarah)
1918- . . . . **CLC 2, 3, 5, 8, 13, 18, 40;
SSC 10**
See also CA 5-8R; CANR 12, 36;
CDBLB 1945-1960; DLB 15, 139; MTCW

Spaulding, Douglas
See Bradbury, Ray (Douglas)

Spaulding, Leonard
See Bradbury, Ray (Douglas)

Spence, J. A. D.
See Eliot, T(homas) S(tearns)

Spencer, Elizabeth 1921- . . . . **CLC 22**
See also CA 13-16R; CANR 32; DLB 6;
MTCW; SATA 14

Spencer, Leonard G.
See Silverberg, Robert

Spencer, Scott 1945-. . . . . **CLC 30**
See also CA 113; DLBY 86

Spender, Stephen (Harold)
1909- . . . . **CLC 1, 2, 5, 10, 41**
See also CA 9-12R; CANR 31;
CDBLB 1945-1960; DLB 20; MTCW

Spengler, Oswald (Arnold Gottfried)
1880-1936 . . . . **TCLC 25**
See also CA 118

Spenser, Edmund
1552(?)-1599 . . . . **LC 5; DA; PC 8; WLC**
See also CDBLB Before 1660

Spicer, Jack 1925-1965 . . . . . . **CLC 8, 18, 72**
See also CA 85-88; DLB 5, 16

Spiegelman, Art 1948- . . . . **CLC 76**
See also AAYA 10; CA 125; CANR 41

Spielberg, Peter 1929- . . . . **CLC 6**
See also CA 5-8R; CANR 4; DLBY 81

Spielberg, Steven 1947- . . . . **CLC 20**
See also AAYA 8; CA 77-80; CANR 32;
SATA 32

Spillane, Frank Morrison 1918-
See Spillane, Mickey
See also CA 25-28R; CANR 28; MTCW;
SATA 66

Spillane, Mickey . . . . **CLC 3, 13**
See also Spillane, Frank Morrison

Spinoza, Benedictus de 1632-1677 . . . . **LC 9**

Spinrad, Norman (Richard) 1940-. . . **CLC 46**
See also CA 37-40R; CAAS 19; CANR 20;
DLB 8

Spitteler, Carl (Friedrich Georg)
1845-1924 . . . . **TCLC 12**
See also CA 109; DLB 129

Spivack, Kathleen (Romola Drucker)
1938- . . . . **CLC 6**
See also CA 49-52

Spoto, Donald 1941-. . . . . **CLC 39**
See also CA 65-68; CANR 11

Springsteen, Bruce (F.) 1949- . . . . . . **CLC 17**
See also CA 111

Spurling, Hilary 1940-. . . . . **CLC 34**
See also CA 104; CANR 25

Squires, (James) Radcliffe
1917-1993 . . . . **CLC 51**
See also CA 1-4R; 140; CANR 6, 21

Srivastava, Dhanpat Rai 1880(?)-1936
See Premchand
See also CA 118

Stacy, Donald
See Pohl, Frederik

Stael, Germaine de
See Stael-Holstein, Anne Louise Germaine
Necker Baronn
See also DLB 119

Stael-Holstein, Anne Louise Germaine Necker
Baronn 1766-1817 . . . . **NCLC 3**
See also Stael, Germaine de

Stafford, Jean 1915-1979 . . . **CLC 4, 7, 19, 68**
See also CA 1-4R; 85-88; CANR 3; DLB 2;
MTCW; SATA-Obit 22

Stafford, William (Edgar)
1914-1993 . . . . **CLC 4, 7, 29**
See also CA 5-8R; 142; CAAS 3; CANR 5,
22; DLB 5

Staines, Trevor
See Brunner, John (Kilian Houston)

Stairs, Gordon
See Austin, Mary (Hunter)

Stannard, Martin 1947-. . . . . **CLC 44**
See also CA 142

Stanton, Maura 1946- . . . . **CLC 9**
See also CA 89-92; CANR 15; DLB 120

Stanton, Schuyler
See Baum, L(yman) Frank

Stapledon, (William) Olaf
1886-1950 . . . . **TCLC 22**
See also CA 111; DLB 15

Starbuck, George (Edwin) 1931-. . . . **CLC 53**
See also CA 21-24R; CANR 23

Stark, Richard
See Westlake, Donald E(dwin)

Staunton, Schuyler
See Baum, L(yman) Frank

Stead, Christina (Ellen)
1902-1983 . . . . **CLC 2, 5, 8, 32, 80**
See also CA 13-16R; 109; CANR 33, 40;
MTCW

Stead, William Thomas
1849-1912 . . . . **TCLC 48**

Steele, Richard 1672-1729 . . . . **LC 18**
See also CDBLB 1660-1789; DLB 84, 101

Steele, Timothy (Reid) 1948-. . . . . . . **CLC 45**
See also CA 93-96; CANR 16; DLB 120

Steffens, (Joseph) Lincoln
1866-1936 . . . . **TCLC 20**
See also CA 117

Stegner, Wallace (Earle)
1909-1993 . . . . **CLC 9, 49, 81**
See also AITN 1; BEST 90:3; CA 1-4R;
141; CAAS 9; CANR 1, 21, 46; DLB 9;
DLBY 93; MTCW

Stein, Gertrude
1874-1946 . . . . . . **TCLC 1, 6, 28, 48; DA;
WLC**
See also CA 104; 132; CDALB 1917-1929;
DLB 4, 54, 86; MTCW

Steinbeck, John (Ernst)
1902-1968 . . . . . . **CLC 1, 5, 9, 13, 21, 34,
45, 75; DA; SSC 11; WLC**
See also AAYA 12; CA 1-4R; 25-28R;
CANR 1, 35; CDALB 1929-1941; DLB 7,
9; DLBD 2; MTCW; SATA 9

Steinem, Gloria 1934-. . . . . **CLC 63**
See also CA 53-56; CANR 28; MTCW

Steiner, George 1929-. . . . . **CLC 24**
See also CA 73-76; CANR 31; DLB 67;
MTCW; SATA 62

Steiner, K. Leslie
See Delany, Samuel R(ay, Jr.)

Steiner, Rudolf 1861-1925 . . . . **TCLC 13**
See also CA 107

Stendhal
1783-1842 . . . . . **NCLC 23, 46; DA; WLC**
See also DLB 119

Stephen, Leslie 1832-1904 . . . . **TCLC 23**
See also CA 123; DLB 57, 144

Stephen, Sir Leslie
See Stephen, Leslie

Stephen, Virginia
See Woolf, (Adeline) Virginia

Stephens, James 1882(?)-1950. . . . . . . **TCLC 4**
See also CA 104; DLB 19

Stephens, Reed
See Donaldson, Stephen R.

Steptoe, Lydia
See Barnes, Djuna

Sterchi, Beat 1949-. . . . . **CLC 65**

Sterling, Brett
See Bradbury, Ray (Douglas); Hamilton,
Edmond

Sterling, Bruce 1954-. . . . . **CLC 72**
See also CA 119; CANR 44

Sterling, George 1869-1926 . . . . TCLC 20
See also CA 117; DLB 54

Stern, Gerald 1925- . . . . CLC 40
See also CA 81-84; CANR 28; DLB 105

Stern, Richard (Gustave) 1928- . . . CLC 4, 39
See also CA 1-4R; CANR 1, 25; DLBY 87

Sternberg, Josef von 1894-1969 . . . . . CLC 20
See also CA 81-84

Sterne, Laurence
1713-1768 . . . . LC 2; DA; WLC
See also CDBLB 1660-1789; DLB 39

Sternheim, (William Adolf) Carl
1878-1942 . . . . TCLC 8
See also CA 105; DLB 56, 118

Stevens, Mark 1951- . . . . CLC 34
See also CA 122

Stevens, Wallace
1879-1955 . . . . TCLC 3, 12, 45; DA;
PC 6; WLC
See also CA 104; 124; CDALB 1929-1941;
DLB 54; MTCW

Stevenson, Anne (Katharine)
1933- . . . . CLC 7, 33
See also CA 17-20R; CAAS 9; CANR 9, 33;
DLB 40; MTCW

Stevenson, Robert Louis (Balfour)
1850-1894 . . . . NCLC 5, 14; DA;
SSC 11; WLC
See also CDBLB 1890-1914; CLR 10, 11;
DLB 18, 57, 141; JRDA; MAICYA;
YABC 2

Stewart, J(ohn) I(nnes) M(ackintosh)
1906- . . . . CLC 7, 14, 32
See also CA 85-88; CAAS 3; MTCW

Stewart, Mary (Florence Elinor)
1916- . . . . CLC 7, 35
See also CA 1-4R; CANR 1; SATA 12

Stewart, Mary Rainbow
See Stewart, Mary (Florence Elinor)

Stifle, June
See Campbell, Maria

Stifter, Adalbert 1805-1868 . . . . . . NCLC 41
See also DLB 133

Still, James 1906- . . . . CLC 49
See also CA 65-68; CAAS 17; CANR 10,
26; DLB 9; SATA 29

Sting
See Sumner, Gordon Matthew

Stirling, Arthur
See Sinclair, Upton (Beall)

Stitt, Milan 1941- . . . . CLC 29
See also CA 69-72

Stockton, Francis Richard 1834-1902
See Stockton, Frank R.
See also CA 108; 137; MAICYA; SATA 44

Stockton, Frank R. . . . . TCLC 47
See also Stockton, Francis Richard
See also DLB 42, 74; SATA 32

Stoddard, Charles
See Kuttner, Henry

Stoker, Abraham 1847-1912
See Stoker, Bram
See also CA 105; DA; SATA 29

Stoker, Bram . . . . TCLC 8; WLC
See also Stoker, Abraham
See also CDBLB 1890-1914; DLB 36, 70

Stolz, Mary (Slattery) 1920- . . . . CLC 12
See also AAYA 8; AITN 1; CA 5-8R;
CANR 13, 41; JRDA; MAICYA;
SAAS 3; SATA 10, 71

Stone, Irving 1903-1989 . . . . CLC 7
See also AITN 1; CA 1-4R; 129; CAAS 3;
CANR 1, 23; MTCW; SATA 3;
SATA-Obit 64

Stone, Oliver 1946- . . . . CLC 73
See also CA 110

Stone, Robert (Anthony)
1937- . . . . CLC 5, 23, 42
See also CA 85-88; CANR 23; MTCW

Stone, Zachary
See Follett, Ken(neth Martin)

Stoppard, Tom
1937- . . . . . . CLC 1, 3, 4, 5, 8, 15, 29, 34,
63; DA; WLC
See also CA 81-84; CANR 39;
CDBLB 1960 to Present; DLB 13;
DLBY 85; MTCW

Storey, David (Malcolm)
1933- . . . . CLC 2, 4, 5, 8
See also CA 81-84; CANR 36; DLB 13, 14;
MTCW

Storm, Hyemeyohsts 1935- . . . . CLC 3
See also CA 81-84; CANR 45; NNAL

Storm, (Hans) Theodor (Woldsen)
1817-1888 . . . . NCLC 1

Storni, Alfonsina
1892-1938 . . . . TCLC 5; HLC
See also CA 104; 131; HW

Stout, Rex (Todhunter) 1886-1975 . . . CLC 3
See also AITN 2; CA 61-64

Stow, (Julian) Randolph 1935- . . CLC 23, 48
See also CA 13-16R; CANR 33; MTCW

Stowe, Harriet (Elizabeth) Beecher
1811-1896 . . . . NCLC 3; DA; WLC
See also CDALB 1865-1917; DLB 1, 12, 42,
74; JRDA; MAICYA; YABC 1

Strachey, (Giles) Lytton
1880-1932 . . . . TCLC 12
See also CA 110; DLBD 10

Strand, Mark 1934- . . . . . . CLC 6, 18, 41, 71
See also CA 21-24R; CANR 40; DLB 5;
SATA 41

Straub, Peter (Francis) 1943- . . . . . . CLC 28
See also BEST 89:1; CA 85-88; CANR 28;
DLBY 84; MTCW

Strauss, Botho 1944- . . . . CLC 22
See also DLB 124

Streatfeild, (Mary) Noel
1895(?)-1986 . . . . CLC 21
See also CA 81-84; 120; CANR 31;
CLR 17; MAICYA; SATA 20;
SATA-Obit 48

Stribling, T(homas) S(igismund)
1881-1965 . . . . CLC 23
See also CA 107; DLB 9

Strindberg, (Johan) August
1849-1912 . . . . . . TCLC 1, 8, 21, 47; DA;
WLC
See also CA 104; 135

Stringer, Arthur 1874-1950 . . . . . . TCLC 37
See also DLB 92

Stringer, David
See Roberts, Keith (John Kingston)

Strugatskii, Arkadii (Natanovich)
1925-1991 . . . . CLC 27
See also CA 106; 135

Strugatskii, Boris (Natanovich)
1933- . . . . CLC 27
See also CA 106

Strummer, Joe 1953(?)- . . . . CLC 30

Stuart, Don A.
See Campbell, John W(ood, Jr.)

Stuart, Ian
See MacLean, Alistair (Stuart)

Stuart, Jesse (Hilton)
1906-1984 . . . . CLC 1, 8, 11, 14, 34
See also CA 5-8R; 112; CANR 31; DLB 9,
48, 102; DLBY 84; SATA 2;
SATA-Obit 36

Sturgeon, Theodore (Hamilton)
1918-1985 . . . . CLC 22, 39
See also Queen, Ellery
See also CA 81-84; 116; CANR 32; DLB 8;
DLBY 85; MTCW

Sturges, Preston 1898-1959 . . . . TCLC 48
See also CA 114; DLB 26

Styron, William
1925- . . . . CLC 1, 3, 5, 11, 15, 60
See also BEST 90:4; CA 5-8R; CANR 6, 33;
CDALB 1968-1988; DLB 2, 143;
DLBY 80; MTCW

Suarez Lynch, B.
See Bioy Casares, Adolfo; Borges, Jorge
Luis

Su Chien 1884-1918
See Su Man-shu
See also CA 123

Sudermann, Hermann 1857-1928 . . TCLC 15
See also CA 107; DLB 118

Sue, Eugene 1804-1857 . . . . NCLC 1
See also DLB 119

Sueskind, Patrick 1949- . . . . CLC 44
See also Suskind, Patrick

Sukenick, Ronald 1932- . . . . . CLC 3, 4, 6, 48
See also CA 25-28R; CAAS 8; CANR 32;
DLBY 81

Suknaski, Andrew 1942- . . . . CLC 19
See also CA 101; DLB 53

Sullivan, Vernon
See Vian, Boris

Sully Prudhomme 1839-1907 . . . . . . TCLC 31

Su Man-shu . . . . TCLC 24
See also Su Chien

Summerforest, Ivy B.
See Kirkup, James

Summers, Andrew James 1942- . . . . . CLC 26

Summers, Andy
See Summers, Andrew James

Summers, Hollis (Spurgeon, Jr.)
1916- . . . . CLC 10
See also CA 5-8R; CANR 3; DLB 6

Summers, (Alphonsus Joseph-Mary Augustus)
   Montague 1880-1948 . . . . **TCLC 16**
   See also CA 118

Sumner, Gordon Matthew 1951- . . . . **CLC 26**

Surtees, Robert Smith
   1803-1864 . . . . **NCLC 14**
   See also DLB 21

Susann, Jacqueline 1921-1974 . . . . . . **CLC 3**
   See also AITN 1; CA 65-68; 53-56; MTCW

Suskind, Patrick
   See Sueskind, Patrick
   See also CA 145

Sutcliff, Rosemary 1920-1992 . . . . . . **CLC 26**
   See also AAYA 10; CA 5-8R; 139;
   CANR 37; CLR 1; JRDA; MAICYA;
   SATA 6, 44, 78; SATA-Obit 73

Sutro, Alfred 1863-1933 . . . . **TCLC 6**
   See also CA 105; DLB 10

Sutton, Henry
   See Slavitt, David R(ytman)

Svevo, Italo . . . . **TCLC 2, 35**
   See also Schmitz, Aron Hector

Swados, Elizabeth 1951- . . . . **CLC 12**
   See also CA 97-100

Swados, Harvey 1920-1972 . . . . **CLC 5**
   See also CA 5-8R; 37-40R; CANR 6;
   DLB 2

Swan, Gladys 1934- . . . . **CLC 69**
   See also CA 101; CANR 17, 39

Swarthout, Glendon (Fred)
   1918-1992 . . . . **CLC 35**
   See also CA 1-4R; 139; CANR 1; SATA 26

Sweet, Sarah C.
   See Jewett, (Theodora) Sarah Orne

Swenson, May
   1919-1989 . . . . **CLC 4, 14, 61; DA**
   See also CA 5-8R; 130; CANR 36; DLB 5;
   MTCW; SATA 15

Swift, Augustus
   See Lovecraft, H(oward) P(hillips)

Swift, Graham (Colin) 1949- . . . . **CLC 41**
   See also CA 117; 122

Swift, Jonathan
   1667-1745 . . . . . . **LC 1; DA; PC 9; WLC**
   See also CDBLB 1660-1789; DLB 39, 95,
   101; SATA 19

Swinburne, Algernon Charles
   1837-1909 . . . . . . **TCLC 8, 36; DA; WLC**
   See also CA 105; 140; CDBLB 1832-1890;
   DLB 35, 57

Swinfen, Ann . . . . **CLC 34**

Swinnerton, Frank Arthur
   1884-1982 . . . . **CLC 31**
   See also CA 108; DLB 34

Swithen, John
   See King, Stephen (Edwin)

Sylvia
   See Ashton-Warner, Sylvia (Constance)

Symmes, Robert Edward
   See Duncan, Robert (Edward)

Symonds, John Addington
   1840-1893 . . . . **NCLC 34**
   See also DLB 57, 144

Symons, Arthur 1865-1945 . . . . . . **TCLC 11**
   See also CA 107; DLB 19, 57

Symons, Julian (Gustave)
   1912- . . . . **CLC 2, 14, 32**
   See also CA 49-52; CAAS 3; CANR 3, 33;
   DLB 87; DLBY 92; MTCW

Synge, (Edmund) J(ohn) M(illington)
   1871-1909 . . . . **TCLC 6, 37; DC 2**
   See also CA 104; 141; CDBLB 1890-1914;
   DLB 10, 19

Syruc, J.
   See Milosz, Czeslaw

Szirtes, George 1948- . . . . **CLC 46**
   See also CA 109; CANR 27

Tabori, George 1914- . . . . **CLC 19**
   See also CA 49-52; CANR 4

Tagore, Rabindranath
   1861-1941 . . . . **TCLC 3, 53; PC 8**
   See also CA 104; 120; MTCW

Taine, Hippolyte Adolphe
   1828-1893 . . . . **NCLC 15**

Talese, Gay 1932- . . . . **CLC 37**
   See also AITN 1; CA 1-4R; CANR 9;
   MTCW

Tallent, Elizabeth (Ann) 1954- . . . . . **CLC 45**
   See also CA 117; DLB 130

Tally, Ted 1952- . . . . **CLC 42**
   See also CA 120; 124

Tamayo y Baus, Manuel
   1829-1898 . . . . **NCLC 1**

Tammsaare, A(nton) H(ansen)
   1878-1940 . . . . **TCLC 27**

Tan, Amy 1952- . . . . **CLC 59**
   See also AAYA 9; BEST 89:3; CA 136;
   SATA 75

Tandem, Felix
   See Spitteler, Carl (Friedrich Georg)

Tanizaki, Jun'ichiro
   1886-1965 . . . . **CLC 8, 14, 28**
   See also CA 93-96; 25-28R

Tanner, William
   See Amis, Kingsley (William)

Tao Lao
   See Storni, Alfonsina

Tarassoff, Lev
   See Troyat, Henri

Tarbell, Ida M(inerva)
   1857-1944 . . . . **TCLC 40**
   See also CA 122; DLB 47

Tarkington, (Newton) Booth
   1869-1946 . . . . **TCLC 9**
   See also CA 110; 143; DLB 9, 102;
   SATA 17

Tarkovsky, Andrei (Arsenyevich)
   1932-1986 . . . . **CLC 75**
   See also CA 127

Tartt, Donna 1964(?)- . . . . **CLC 76**
   See also CA 142

Tasso, Torquato 1544-1595 . . . . **LC 5**

Tate, (John Orley) Allen
   1899-1979 . . . . **CLC 2, 4, 6, 9, 11, 14, 24**
   See also CA 5-8R; 85-88; CANR 32;
   DLB 4, 45, 63; MTCW

Tate, Ellalice
   See Hibbert, Eleanor Alice Burford

Tate, James (Vincent) 1943- . . . **CLC 2, 6, 25**
   See also CA 21-24R; CANR 29; DLB 5

Tavel, Ronald 1940- . . . . **CLC 6**
   See also CA 21-24R; CANR 33

Taylor, Cecil Philip 1929-1981 . . . . . **CLC 27**
   See also CA 25-28R; 105

Taylor, Edward 1642(?)-1729 . . . . **LC 11; DA**
   See also DLB 24

Taylor, Eleanor Ross 1920- . . . . **CLC 5**
   See also CA 81-84

Taylor, Elizabeth 1912-1975 . . . **CLC 2, 4, 29**
   See also CA 13-16R; CANR 9; DLB 139;
   MTCW; SATA 13

Taylor, Henry (Splawn) 1942- . . . . . . **CLC 44**
   See also CA 33-36R; CAAS 7; CANR 31;
   DLB 5

Taylor, Kamala (Purnaiya) 1924-
   See Markandaya, Kamala
   See also CA 77-80

Taylor, Mildred D. . . . . **CLC 21**
   See also AAYA 10; BW 1; CA 85-88;
   CANR 25; CLR 9; DLB 52; JRDA;
   MAICYA; SAAS 5; SATA 15, 70

Taylor, Peter (Hillsman)
   1917- . . . . . . **CLC 1, 4, 18, 37, 44, 50, 71;**
                                            SSC 10
   See also CA 13-16R; CANR 9; DLBY 81;
   MTCW

Taylor, Robert Lewis 1912- . . . . **CLC 14**
   See also CA 1-4R; CANR 3; SATA 10

Tchekhov, Anton
   See Chekhov, Anton (Pavlovich)

Teasdale, Sara 1884-1933 . . . . **TCLC 4**
   See also CA 104; DLB 45; SATA 32

Tegner, Esaias 1782-1846 . . . . **NCLC 2**

Teilhard de Chardin, (Marie Joseph) Pierre
   1881-1955 . . . . **TCLC 9**
   See also CA 105

Temple, Ann
   See Mortimer, Penelope (Ruth)

Tennant, Emma (Christina)
   1937- . . . . **CLC 13, 52**
   See also CA 65-68; CAAS 9; CANR 10, 38;
   DLB 14

Tenneshaw, S. M.
   See Silverberg, Robert

Tennyson, Alfred
   1809-1892 . . **NCLC 30; DA; PC 6; WLC**
   See also CDBLB 1832-1890; DLB 32

Teran, Lisa St. Aubin de . . . . **CLC 36**
   See also St. Aubin de Teran, Lisa

Terence 195(?)B.C.-159B.C. . . . . . . **CMLC 14**

Teresa de Jesus, St. 1515-1582 . . . . . . **LC 18**

Terkel, Louis 1912-
   See Terkel, Studs
   See also CA 57-60; CANR 18, 45; MTCW

Terkel, Studs . . . . **CLC 38**
   See also Terkel, Louis
   See also AITN 1

Terry, C. V.
   See Slaughter, Frank G(ill)

Terry, Megan 1932-.............. **CLC 19**
See also CA 77-80; CABS 3; CANR 43;
DLB 7

Tertz, Abram
See Sinyavsky, Andrei (Donatevich)

Tesich, Steve 1943(?)-.......... **CLC 40, 69**
See also CA 105; DLBY 83

Teternikov, Fyodor Kuzmich 1863-1927
See Sologub, Fyodor
See also CA 104

Tevis, Walter 1928-1984 .... **CLC 42**
See also CA 113

Tey, Josephine................... **TCLC 14**
See also Mackintosh, Elizabeth
See also DLB 77

Thackeray, William Makepeace
1811-1863 .... **NCLC 5, 14, 22, 43; DA;
WLC**
See also CDBLB 1832-1890; DLB 21, 55;
SATA 23

Thakura, Ravindranatha
See Tagore, Rabindranath

Tharoor, Shashi 1956-........... **CLC 70**
See also CA 141

Thelwell, Michael Miles 1939-..... **CLC 22**
See also BW 2; CA 101

Theobald, Lewis, Jr.
See Lovecraft, H(oward) P(hillips)

Theodorescu, Ion N. 1880-1967
See Arghezi, Tudor
See also CA 116

Theriault, Yves 1915-1983........ **CLC 79**
See also CA 102; DLB 88

Theroux, Alexander (Louis)
1939-.................... **CLC 2, 25**
See also CA 85-88; CANR 20

Theroux, Paul (Edward)
1941-........ **CLC 5, 8, 11, 15, 28, 46**
See also BEST 89:4; CA 33-36R; CANR 20,
45; DLB 2; MTCW; SATA 44

Thesen, Sharon 1946-............. **CLC 56**

Thevenin, Denis
See Duhamel, Georges

Thibault, Jacques Anatole Francois
1844-1924
See France, Anatole
See also CA 106; 127; MTCW

Thiele, Colin (Milton) 1920- .... **CLC 17**
See also CA 29-32R; CANR 12, 28;
CLR 27; MAICYA; SAAS 2; SATA 14,
72

Thomas, Audrey (Callahan)
1935-................. **CLC 7, 13, 37**
See also AITN 2; CA 21-24R; CAAS 19;
CANR 36; DLB 60; MTCW

Thomas, D(onald) M(ichael)
1935-................. **CLC 13, 22, 31**
See also CA 61-64; CAAS 11; CANR 17,
45; CDBLB 1960 to Present; DLB 40;
MTCW

Thomas, Dylan (Marlais)
1914-1953 ... **TCLC 1, 8, 45; DA; PC 2;
SSC 3; WLC**
See also CA 104; 120; CDBLB 1945-1960;
DLB 13, 20, 139; MTCW; SATA 60

Thomas, (Philip) Edward
1878-1917 .... **TCLC 10**
See also CA 106; DLB 19

Thomas, Joyce Carol 1938-........ **CLC 35**
See also AAYA 12; BW 2; CA 113; 116;
CLR 19; DLB 33; JRDA; MAICYA;
MTCW; SAAS 7; SATA 40, 78

Thomas, Lewis 1913-1993 .... **CLC 35**
See also CA 85-88; 143; CANR 38; MTCW

Thomas, Paul
See Mann, (Paul) Thomas

Thomas, Piri 1928-.............. **CLC 17**
See also CA 73-76; HW

Thomas, R(onald) S(tuart)
1913-................. **CLC 6, 13, 48**
See also CA 89-92; CAAS 4; CANR 30;
CDBLB 1960 to Present; DLB 27;
MTCW

Thomas, Ross (Elmore) 1926-...... **CLC 39**
See also CA 33-36R; CANR 22

Thompson, Francis Clegg
See Mencken, H(enry) L(ouis)

Thompson, Francis Joseph
1859-1907 .... **TCLC 4**
See also CA 104; CDBLB 1890-1914;
DLB 19

Thompson, Hunter S(tockton)
1939-................. **CLC 9, 17, 40**
See also BEST 89:1; CA 17-20R; CANR 23,
46; MTCW

Thompson, James Myers
See Thompson, Jim (Myers)

Thompson, Jim (Myers)
1906-1977(?) .... **CLC 69**
See also CA 140

Thompson, Judith .... **CLC 39**

Thomson, James 1700-1748........ **LC 16**

Thomson, James 1834-1882...... **NCLC 18**

Thoreau, Henry David
1817-1862 ...... **NCLC 7, 21; DA; WLC**
See also CDALB 1640-1865; DLB 1

Thornton, Hall
See Silverberg, Robert

Thurber, James (Grover)
1894-1961 ... **CLC 5, 11, 25; DA; SSC 1**
See also CA 73-76; CANR 17, 39;
CDALB 1929-1941; DLB 4, 11, 22, 102;
MAICYA; MTCW; SATA 13

Thurman, Wallace (Henry)
1902-1934 .... **TCLC 6; BLC**
See also BW 1; CA 104; 124; DLB 51

Ticheburn, Cheviot
See Ainsworth, William Harrison

Tieck, (Johann) Ludwig
1773-1853 .... **NCLC 5, 46**
See also DLB 90

Tiger, Derry
See Ellison, Harlan (Jay)

Tilghman, Christopher 1948(?)-..... **CLC 65**

Tillinghast, Richard (Williford)
1940-..................... **CLC 29**
See also CA 29-32R; CANR 26

Timrod, Henry 1828-1867 .... **NCLC 25**
See also DLB 3

Tindall, Gillian 1938-.............. **CLC 7**
See also CA 21-24R; CANR 11

Tiptree, James, Jr. .... **CLC 48, 50**
See also Sheldon, Alice Hastings Bradley
See also DLB 8

Titmarsh, Michael Angelo
See Thackeray, William Makepeace

Tocqueville, Alexis (Charles Henri Maurice
Clerel Comte) 1805-1859..... **NCLC 7**

Tolkien, J(ohn) R(onald) R(euel)
1892-1973 .... **CLC 1, 2, 3, 8, 12, 38;
DA; WLC**
See also AAYA 10; AITN 1; CA 17-18;
45-48; CANR 36; CAP 2;
CDBLB 1914-1945; DLB 15; JRDA;
MAICYA; MTCW; SATA 2, 32;
SATA-Obit 24

Toller, Ernst 1893-1939.......... **TCLC 10**
See also CA 107; DLB 124

Tolson, M. B.
See Tolson, Melvin B(eaunorus)

Tolson, Melvin B(eaunorus)
1898(?)-1966 .... **CLC 36; BLC**
See also BW 1; CA 124; 89-92; DLB 48, 76

Tolstoi, Aleksei Nikolaevich
See Tolstoy, Alexey Nikolaevich

Tolstoy, Alexey Nikolaevich
1882-1945 .... **TCLC 18**
See also CA 107

Tolstoy, Count Leo
See Tolstoy, Leo (Nikolaevich)

Tolstoy, Leo (Nikolaevich)
1828-1910 ...... **TCLC 4, 11, 17, 28, 44;
DA; SSC 9; WLC**
See also CA 104; 123; SATA 26

Tomasi di Lampedusa, Giuseppe 1896-1957
See Lampedusa, Giuseppe (Tomasi) di
See also CA 111

Tomlin, Lily..................... **CLC 17**
See also Tomlin, Mary Jean

Tomlin, Mary Jean 1939(?)-
See Tomlin, Lily
See also CA 117

Tomlinson, (Alfred) Charles
1927-........... **CLC 2, 4, 6, 13, 45**
See also CA 5-8R; CANR 33; DLB 40

Tonson, Jacob
See Bennett, (Enoch) Arnold

Toole, John Kennedy
1937-1969 .... **CLC 19, 64**
See also CA 104; DLBY 81

Toomer, Jean
1894-1967 ...... **CLC 1, 4, 13, 22; BLC;
PC 7; SSC 1**
See also BW 1; CA 85-88;
CDALB 1917-1929; DLB 45, 51; MTCW

Torley, Luke
See Blish, James (Benjamin)

Tornimparte, Alessandra
See Ginzburg, Natalia

Torre, Raoul della
See Mencken, H(enry) L(ouis)

Torrey, E(dwin) Fuller 1937-....... **CLC 34**
See also CA 119

Torsvan, Ben Traven
See Traven, B.

Torsvan, Benno Traven
See Traven, B.

Torsvan, Berick Traven
See Traven, B.

Torsvan, Berwick Traven
See Traven, B.

Torsvan, Bruno Traven
See Traven, B.

Torsvan, Traven
See Traven, B.

Tournier, Michel (Edouard)
1924- .... **CLC 6, 23, 36**
See also CA 49-52; CANR 3, 36; DLB 83;
MTCW; SATA 23

Tournimparte, Alessandra
See Ginzburg, Natalia

Towers, Ivar
See Kornbluth, C(yril) M.

Townsend, Sue 1946- .... **CLC 61**
See also CA 119; 127; MTCW; SATA 48,
55

Townshend, Peter (Dennis Blandford)
1945- .... **CLC 17, 42**
See also CA 107

Tozzi, Federigo 1883-1920. ...... **TCLC 31**

Traill, Catharine Parr
1802-1899 .... **NCLC 31**
See also DLB 99

Trakl, Georg 1887-1914. .... **TCLC 5**
See also CA 104

Transtroemer, Tomas (Goesta)
1931- .... **CLC 52, 65**
See also CA 117; 129; CAAS 17

Transtromer, Tomas Gosta
See Transtroemer, Tomas (Goesta)

Traven, B. (?)-1969. .... **CLC 8, 11**
See also CA 19-20; 25-28R; CAP 2; DLB 9,
56; MTCW

Treitel, Jonathan 1959- .... **CLC 70**

Tremain, Rose 1943-. .... **CLC 42**
See also CA 97-100; CANR 44; DLB 14

Tremblay, Michel 1942-. .... **CLC 29**
See also CA 116; 128; DLB 60; MTCW

Trevanian. .... **CLC 29**
See also Whitaker, Rod(ney)

Trevor, Glen
See Hilton, James

Trevor, William
1928- .... **CLC 7, 9, 14, 25, 71**
See also Cox, William Trevor
See also DLB 14, 139

Trifonov, Yuri (Valentinovich)
1925-1981 .... **CLC 45**
See also CA 126; 103; MTCW

Trilling, Lionel 1905-1975 .... **CLC 9, 11, 24**
See also CA 9-12R; 61-64; CANR 10;
DLB 28, 63; MTCW

Trimball, W. H.
See Mencken, H(enry) L(ouis)

Tristan
See Gomez de la Serna, Ramon

Tristram
See Housman, A(lfred) E(dward)

Trogdon, William (Lewis) 1939-
See Heat-Moon, William Least
See also CA 115; 119

Trollope, Anthony
1815-1882 ...... **NCLC 6, 33; DA; WLC**
See also CDBLB 1832-1890; DLB 21, 57;
SATA 22

Trollope, Frances 1779-1863 ..... **NCLC 30**
See also DLB 21

Trotsky, Leon 1879-1940. .... **TCLC 22**
See also CA 118

Trotter (Cockburn), Catharine
1679-1749 .... **LC 8**
See also DLB 84

Trout, Kilgore
See Farmer, Philip Jose

Trow, George W. S. 1943-. .... **CLC 52**
See also CA 126

Troyat, Henri 1911-. .... **CLC 23**
See also CA 45-48; CANR 2, 33; MTCW

Trudeau, G(arretson) B(eekman) 1948-
See Trudeau, Garry B.
See also CA 81-84; CANR 31; SATA 35

Trudeau, Garry B.. .... **CLC 12**
See also Trudeau, G(arretson) B(eekman)
See also AAYA 10; AITN 2

Truffaut, Francois 1932-1984. ...... **CLC 20**
See also CA 81-84; 113; CANR 34

Trumbo, Dalton 1905-1976 .... **CLC 19**
See also CA 21-24R; 69-72; CANR 10;
DLB 26

Trumbull, John 1750-1831. ...... **NCLC 30**
See also DLB 31

Trundlett, Helen B.
See Eliot, T(homas) S(tearns)

Tryon, Thomas 1926-1991 .... **CLC 3, 11**
See also AITN 1; CA 29-32R; 135;
CANR 32; MTCW

Tryon, Tom
See Tryon, Thomas

Ts'ao Hsueh-ch'in 1715(?)-1763. ...... **LC 1**

Tsushima, Shuji 1909-1948
See Dazai, Osamu
See also CA 107

Tsvetaeva (Efron), Marina (Ivanovna)
1892-1941 .... **TCLC 7, 35**
See also CA 104; 128; MTCW

Tuck, Lily 1938-. .... **CLC 70**
See also CA 139

Tu Fu 712-770. .... **PC 9**

Tunis, John R(oberts) 1889-1975 ... **CLC 12**
See also CA 61-64; DLB 22; JRDA;
MAICYA; SATA 30, 37

Tuohy, Frank. .... **CLC 37**
See also Tuohy, John Francis
See also DLB 14, 139

Tuohy, John Francis 1925-
See Tuohy, Frank
See also CA 5-8R; CANR 3

Turco, Lewis (Putnam) 1934- ... **CLC 11, 63**
See also CA 13-16R; CANR 24; DLBY 84

Turgenev, Ivan
1818-1883 ...... **NCLC 21; DA; SSC 7;
WLC**

Turgot, Anne-Robert-Jacques
1727-1781 .... **LC 26**

Turner, Frederick 1943-. .... **CLC 48**
See also CA 73-76; CAAS 10; CANR 12,
30; DLB 40

Tutu, Desmond M(pilo)
1931-. .... **CLC 80; BLC**
See also BW 1; CA 125

Tutuola, Amos 1920- ... **CLC 5, 14, 29; BLC**
See also BW 2; CA 9-12R; CANR 27;
DLB 125; MTCW

Twain, Mark
... **TCLC 6, 12, 19, 36, 48; SSC 6; WLC**
See also Clemens, Samuel Langhorne
See also DLB 11, 12, 23, 64, 74

Tyler, Anne
1941- .... **CLC 7, 11, 18, 28, 44, 59**
See also BEST 89:1; CA 9-12R; CANR 11,
33; DLB 6, 143; DLBY 82; MTCW;
SATA 7

Tyler, Royall 1757-1826. .... **NCLC 3**
See also DLB 37

Tynan, Katharine 1861-1931 ...... **TCLC 3**
See also CA 104

Tyutchev, Fyodor 1803-1873 ..... **NCLC 34**

Tzara, Tristan. .... **CLC 47**
See also Rosenfeld, Samuel

Uhry, Alfred 1936-. .... **CLC 55**
See also CA 127; 133

Ulf, Haerved
See Strindberg, (Johan) August

Ulf, Harved
See Strindberg, (Johan) August

Ulibarri, Sabine R(eyes) 1919- ..... **CLC 83**
See also CA 131; DLB 82; HW

Unamuno (y Jugo), Miguel de
1864-1936 .... **TCLC 2, 9; HLC; SSC 11**
See also CA 104; 131; DLB 108; HW;
MTCW

Undercliffe, Errol
See Campbell, (John) Ramsey

Underwood, Miles
See Glassco, John

Undset, Sigrid
1882-1949 .... **TCLC 3; DA; WLC**
See also CA 104; 129; MTCW

Ungaretti, Giuseppe
1888-1970 .... **CLC 7, 11, 15**
See also CA 19-20; 25-28R; CAP 2;
DLB 114

Unger, Douglas 1952-. .... **CLC 34**
See also CA 130

Unsworth, Barry (Forster) 1930-. ... **CLC 76**
See also CA 25-28R; CANR 30

Updike, John (Hoyer)
1932- ...... **CLC 1, 2, 3, 5, 7, 9, 13, 15,
23, 34, 43, 70; DA; SSC 13; WLC**
See also CA 1-4R; CABS 1; CANR 4, 33;
CDALB 1968-1988; DLB 2, 5, 143;
DLBD 3; DLBY 80, 82; MTCW

Upshaw, Margaret Mitchell
See Mitchell, Margaret (Munnerlyn)

Voigt, Cynthia 1942- .... **CLC 30**
See also AAYA 3; CA 106; CANR 18, 37,
40; CLR 13; JRDA; MAICYA;
SATA 33, 48, 79

Voinovich, Vladimir (Nikolaevich)
1932- .... **CLC 10, 49**
See also CA 81-84; CAAS 12; CANR 33;
MTCW

Voloshinov, V. N.
See Bakhtin, Mikhail Mikhailovich

Voltaire
1694-1778 ... **LC 14; DA; SSC 12; WLC**

von Daeniken, Erich 1935- .... **CLC 30**
See also AITN 1; CA 37-40R; CANR 17,
44

von Daniken, Erich
See von Daeniken, Erich

von Heidenstam, (Carl Gustaf) Verner
See Heidenstam, (Carl Gustaf) Verner von

von Heyse, Paul (Johann Ludwig)
See Heyse, Paul (Johann Ludwig von)

von Hofmannsthal, Hugo
See Hofmannsthal, Hugo von

von Horvath, Odon
See Horvath, Oedoen von

von Horvath, Oedoen
See Horvath, Oedoen von

von Liliencron, (Friedrich Adolf Axel) Detlev
See Liliencron, (Friedrich Adolf Axel)
Detlev von

Vonnegut, Kurt, Jr.
1922- ...... **CLC 1, 2, 3, 4, 5, 8, 12, 22,
40, 60; DA; SSC 8; WLC**
See also AAYA 6; AITN 1; BEST 90:4;
CA 1-4R; CANR 1, 25;
CDALB 1968-1988; DLB 2, 8; DLBD 3;
DLBY 80; MTCW

Von Rachen, Kurt
See Hubbard, L(afayette) Ron(ald)

von Rezzori (d'Arezzo), Gregor
See Rezzori (d'Arezzo), Gregor von

von Sternberg, Josef
See Sternberg, Josef von

Vorster, Gordon 1924- .... **CLC 34**
See also CA 133

Vosce, Trudie
See Ozick, Cynthia

Voznesensky, Andrei (Andreievich)
1933- .... **CLC 1, 15, 57**
See also CA 89-92; CANR 37; MTCW

Waddington, Miriam 1917- .... **CLC 28**
See also CA 21-24R; CANR 12, 30;
DLB 68

Wagman, Fredrica 1937- .... **CLC 7**
See also CA 97-100

Wagner, Richard 1813-1883....... **NCLC 9**
See also DLB 129

Wagner-Martin, Linda 1936-....... **CLC 50**

Wagoner, David (Russell)
1926- .... **CLC 3, 5, 15**
See also CA 1-4R; CAAS 3; CANR 2;
DLB 5; SATA 14

Wah, Fred(erick James) 1939-...... **CLC 44**
See also CA 107; 141; DLB 60

Wahloo, Per 1926-1975 .... **CLC 7**
See also CA 61-64

Wahloo, Peter
See Wahloo, Per

Wain, John (Barrington)
1925-1994 .... **CLC 2, 11, 15, 46**
See also CA 5-8R; 145; CAAS 4; CANR 23;
CDBLB 1960 to Present; DLB 15, 27,
139; MTCW

Wajda, Andrzej 1926-............. **CLC 16**
See also CA 102

Wakefield, Dan 1932-............. **CLC 7**
See also CA 21-24R; CAAS 7

Wakoski, Diane
1937- .... **CLC 2, 4, 7, 9, 11, 40**
See also CA 13-16R; CAAS 1; CANR 9;
DLB 5

Wakoski-Sherbell, Diane
See Wakoski, Diane

Walcott, Derek (Alton)
1930- .... **CLC 2, 4, 9, 14, 25, 42, 67, 76;
BLC**
See also BW 2; CA 89-92; CANR 26;
DLB 117; DLBY 81; MTCW

Waldman, Anne 1945- .... **CLC 7**
See also CA 37-40R; CAAS 17; CANR 34;
DLB 16

Waldo, E. Hunter
See Sturgeon, Theodore (Hamilton)

Waldo, Edward Hamilton
See Sturgeon, Theodore (Hamilton)

Walker, Alice (Malsenior)
1944- .... **CLC 5, 6, 9, 19, 27, 46, 58;
BLC; DA; SSC 5**
See also AAYA 3; BEST 89:4; BW 2;
CA 37-40R; CANR 9, 27;
CDALB 1968-1988; DLB 6, 33, 143;
MTCW; SATA 31

Walker, David Harry 1911-1992.... **CLC 14**
See also CA 1-4R; 137; CANR 1; SATA 8;
SATA-Obit 71

Walker, Edward Joseph 1934-
See Walker, Ted
See also CA 21-24R; CANR 12, 28

Walker, George F. 1947-....... **CLC 44, 61**
See also CA 103; CANR 21, 43; DLB 60

Walker, Joseph A. 1935-.......... **CLC 19**
See also BW 1; CA 89-92; CANR 26;
DLB 38

Walker, Margaret (Abigail)
1915- .... **CLC 1, 6; BLC**
See also BW 2; CA 73-76; CANR 26;
DLB 76; MTCW

Walker, Ted...................... **CLC 13**
See also Walker, Edward Joseph
See also DLB 40

Wallace, David Foster 1962-....... **CLC 50**
See also CA 132

Wallace, Dexter
See Masters, Edgar Lee

Wallace, (Richard Horatio) Edgar
1875-1932 .... **TCLC 57**
See also CA 115; DLB 70

Wallace, Irving 1916-1990....... **CLC 7, 13**
See also AITN 1; CA 1-4R; 132; CAAS 1;
CANR 1, 27; MTCW

Wallant, Edward Lewis
1926-1962 .... **CLC 5, 10**
See also CA 1-4R; CANR 22; DLB 2, 28,
143; MTCW

Walpole, Horace 1717-1797......... **LC 2**
See also DLB 39, 104

Walpole, Hugh (Seymour)
1884-1941 .... **TCLC 5**
See also CA 104; DLB 34

Walser, Martin 1927-............. **CLC 27**
See also CA 57-60; CANR 8, 46; DLB 75,
124

Walser, Robert 1878-1956........ **TCLC 18**
See also CA 118; DLB 66

Walsh, Jill Paton.................. **CLC 35**
See also Paton Walsh, Gillian
See also AAYA 11; CLR 2; SAAS 3

Walter, Villiam Christian
See Andersen, Hans Christian

Wambaugh, Joseph (Aloysius, Jr.)
1937- .... **CLC 3, 18**
See also AITN 1; BEST 89:3; CA 33-36R;
CANR 42; DLB 6; DLBY 83; MTCW

Ward, Arthur Henry Sarsfield 1883-1959
See Rohmer, Sax
See also CA 108

Ward, Douglas Turner 1930-....... **CLC 19**
See also BW 1; CA 81-84; CANR 27;
DLB 7, 38

Ward, Mary Augusta
See Ward, Mrs. Humphry

Ward, Mrs. Humphry
1851-1920 .... **TCLC 55**
See also DLB 18

Ward, Peter
See Faust, Frederick (Schiller)

Warhol, Andy 1928(?)-1987........ **CLC 20**
See also AAYA 12; BEST 89:4; CA 89-92;
121; CANR 34

Warner, Francis (Robert le Plastrier)
1937- .... **CLC 14**
See also CA 53-56; CANR 11

Warner, Marina 1946-............ **CLC 59**
See also CA 65-68; CANR 21

Warner, Rex (Ernest) 1905-1986.... **CLC 45**
See also CA 89-92; 119; DLB 15

Warner, Susan (Bogert)
1819-1885 .... **NCLC 31**
See also DLB 3, 42

Warner, Sylvia (Constance) Ashton
See Ashton-Warner, Sylvia (Constance)

Warner, Sylvia Townsend
1893-1978 .... **CLC 7, 19**
See also CA 61-64; 77-80; CANR 16;
DLB 34, 139; MTCW

Warren, Mercy Otis 1728-1814... **NCLC 13**
See also DLB 31

Warren, Robert Penn
1905-1989 .... **CLC 1, 4, 6, 8, 10, 13, 18,**
39, 53, 59; DA; SSC 4; WLC
See also AITN 1; CA 13-16R; 129;
CANR 10; CDALB 1968-1988; DLB 2,
48; DLBY 80, 89; MTCW; SATA 46;
SATA-Obit 63

Warshofsky, Isaac
See Singer, Isaac Bashevis

Warton, Thomas 1728-1790 .... **LC 15**
See also DLB 104, 109

Waruk, Kona
See Harris, (Theodore) Wilson

Warung, Price 1855-1911 .... **TCLC 45**

Warwick, Jarvis
See Garner, Hugh

Washington, Alex
See Harris, Mark

Washington, Booker T(aliaferro)
1856-1915 .... **TCLC 10; BLC**
See also BW 1; CA 114; 125; SATA 28

Washington, George 1732-1799 ...... **LC 25**
See also DLB 31

Wassermann, (Karl) Jakob
1873-1934 .... **TCLC 6**
See also CA 104; DLB 66

Wasserstein, Wendy
1950- .... **CLC 32, 59; DC 4**
See also CA 121; 129; CABS 3

Waterhouse, Keith (Spencer)
1929- .... **CLC 47**
See also CA 5-8R; CANR 38; DLB 13, 15;
MTCW

Waters, Roger 1944- .... **CLC 35**

Watkins, Frances Ellen
See Harper, Frances Ellen Watkins

Watkins, Gerrold
See Malzberg, Barry N(athaniel)

Watkins, Paul 1964- .... **CLC 55**
See also CA 132

Watkins, Vernon Phillips
1906-1967 .... **CLC 43**
See also CA 9-10; 25-28R; CAP 1; DLB 20

Watson, Irving S.
See Mencken, H(enry) L(ouis)

Watson, John H.
See Farmer, Philip Jose

Watson, Richard F.
See Silverberg, Robert

Waugh, Auberon (Alexander) 1939- .. **CLC 7**
See also CA 45-48; CANR 6, 22; DLB 14

Waugh, Evelyn (Arthur St. John)
1903-1966 ...... **CLC 1, 3, 8, 13, 19, 27,**
44; DA; WLC
See also CA 85-88; 25-28R; CANR 22;
CDBLB 1914-1945; DLB 15; MTCW

Waugh, Harriet 1944- .... **CLC 6**
See also CA 85-88; CANR 22

Ways, C. R.
See Blount, Roy (Alton), Jr.

Waystaff, Simon
See Swift, Jonathan

Webb, (Martha) Beatrice (Potter)
1858-1943 .... **TCLC 22**
See also Potter, Beatrice
See also CA 117

Webb, Charles (Richard) 1939- ...... **CLC 7**
See also CA 25-28R

Webb, James H(enry), Jr. 1946- .... **CLC 22**
See also CA 81-84

Webb, Mary (Gladys Meredith)
1881-1927 .... **TCLC 24**
See also CA 123; DLB 34

Webb, Mrs. Sidney
See Webb, (Martha) Beatrice (Potter)

Webb, Phyllis 1927- .... **CLC 18**
See also CA 104; CANR 23; DLB 53

Webb, Sidney (James)
1859-1947 .... **TCLC 22**
See also CA 117

Webber, Andrew Lloyd .... **CLC 21**
See also Lloyd Webber, Andrew

Weber, Lenora Mattingly
1895-1971 .... **CLC 12**
See also CA 19-20; 29-32R; CAP 1;
SATA 2; SATA-Obit 26

Webster, John 1579(?)-1634(?) .... **DC 2**
See also CDBLB Before 1660; DA; DLB 58;
WLC

Webster, Noah 1758-1843 .... **NCLC 30**

Wedekind, (Benjamin) Frank(lin)
1864-1918 .... **TCLC 7**
See also CA 104; DLB 118

Weidman, Jerome 1913- .... **CLC 7**
See also AITN 2; CA 1-4R; CANR 1;
DLB 28

Weil, Simone (Adolphine)
1909-1943 .... **TCLC 23**
See also CA 117

Weinstein, Nathan
See West, Nathanael

Weinstein, Nathan von Wallenstein
See West, Nathanael

Weir, Peter (Lindsay) 1944- .... **CLC 20**
See also CA 113; 123

Weiss, Peter (Ulrich)
1916-1982 .... **CLC 3, 15, 51**
See also CA 45-48; 106; CANR 3; DLB 69,
124

Weiss, Theodore (Russell)
1916- .... **CLC 3, 8, 14**
See also CA 9-12R; CAAS 2; CANR 46;
DLB 5

Welch, (Maurice) Denton
1915-1948 .... **TCLC 22**
See also CA 121

Welch, James 1940- .... **CLC 6, 14, 52**
See also CA 85-88; CANR 42; NNAL

Weldon, Fay
1933- .... **CLC 6, 9, 11, 19, 36, 59**
See also CA 21-24R; CANR 16, 46;
CDBLB 1960 to Present; DLB 14;
MTCW

Wellek, Rene 1903- .... **CLC 28**
See also CA 5-8R; CAAS 7; CANR 8;
DLB 63

Weller, Michael 1942- .... **CLC 10, 53**
See also CA 85-88

Weller, Paul 1958- .... **CLC 26**

Wellershoff, Dieter 1925- .... **CLC 46**
See also CA 89-92; CANR 16, 37

Welles, (George) Orson
1915-1985 .... **CLC 20, 80**
See also CA 93-96; 117

Wellman, Mac 1945- .... **CLC 65**

Wellman, Manly Wade 1903-1986 .. **CLC 49**
See also CA 1-4R; 118; CANR 6, 16, 44;
SATA 6; SATA-Obit 47

Wells, Carolyn 1869(?)-1942 ...... **TCLC 35**
See also CA 113; DLB 11

Wells, H(erbert) G(eorge)
1866-1946 .... **TCLC 6, 12, 19; DA;**
SSC 6; WLC
See also CA 110; 121; CDBLB 1914-1945;
DLB 34, 70; MTCW; SATA 20

Wells, Rosemary 1943- .... **CLC 12**
See also AAYA 13; CA 85-88; CLR 16;
MAICYA; SAAS 1; SATA 18, 69

Welty, Eudora
1909- ...... **CLC 1, 2, 5, 14, 22, 33; DA;**
SSC 1; WLC
See also CA 9-12R; CABS 1; CANR 32;
CDALB 1941-1968; DLB 2, 102, 143;
DLBD 12; DLBY 87; MTCW

Wen I-to 1899-1946 .... **TCLC 28**

Wentworth, Robert
See Hamilton, Edmond

Werfel, Franz (V.) 1890-1945 ...... **TCLC 8**
See also CA 104; DLB 81, 124

Wergeland, Henrik Arnold
1808-1845 .... **NCLC 5**

Wersba, Barbara 1932- .... **CLC 30**
See also AAYA 2; CA 29-32R; CANR 16,
38; CLR 3; DLB 52; JRDA; MAICYA;
SAAS 2; SATA 1, 58

Wertmueller, Lina 1928- .... **CLC 16**
See also CA 97-100; CANR 39

Wescott, Glenway 1901-1987 .... **CLC 13**
See also CA 13-16R; 121; CANR 23;
DLB 4, 9, 102

Wesker, Arnold 1932- .... **CLC 3, 5, 42**
See also CA 1-4R; CAAS 7; CANR 1, 33;
CDBLB 1960 to Present; DLB 13;
MTCW

Wesley, Richard (Errol) 1945- .... **CLC 7**
See also BW 1; CA 57-60; CANR 27;
DLB 38

Wessel, Johan Herman 1742-1785 .... **LC 7**

West, Anthony (Panther)
1914-1987 .... **CLC 50**
See also CA 45-48; 124; CANR 3, 19;
DLB 15

West, C. P.
See Wodehouse, P(elham) G(renville)

West, (Mary) Jessamyn
1902-1984 .... **CLC 7, 17**
See also CA 9-12R; 112; CANR 27; DLB 6;
DLBY 84; MTCW; SATA-Obit 37

West, Morris L(anglo) 1916- ..... **CLC 6, 33**
See also CA 5-8R; CANR 24; MTCW

West, Nathanael
1903-1940 . . . . . **TCLC 1, 14, 44; SSC 16**
See also CA 104; 125; CDALB 1929-1941;
DLB 4, 9, 28; MTCW

West, Owen
See Koontz, Dean R(ay)

West, Paul 1930- . . . . **CLC 7, 14**
See also CA 13-16R; CAAS 7; CANR 22;
DLB 14

West, Rebecca 1892-1983 . . **CLC 7, 9, 31, 50**
See also CA 5-8R; 109; CANR 19; DLB 36;
DLBY 83; MTCW

Westall, Robert (Atkinson)
1929-1993 . . . . **CLC 17**
See also AAYA 12; CA 69-72; 141;
CANR 18; CLR 13; JRDA; MAICYA;
SAAS 2; SATA 23, 69; SATA-Obit 75

Westlake, Donald E(dwin)
1933- . . . . **CLC 7, 33**
See also CA 17-20R; CAAS 13; CANR 16,
44

Westmacott, Mary
See Christie, Agatha (Mary Clarissa)

Weston, Allen
See Norton, Andre

Wetcheek, J. L.
See Feuchtwanger, Lion

Wetering, Janwillem van de
See van de Wetering, Janwillem

Wetherell, Elizabeth
See Warner, Susan (Bogert)

Whalen, Philip 1923- . . . . **CLC 6, 29**
See also CA 9-12R; CANR 5, 39; DLB 16

Wharton, Edith (Newbold Jones)
1862-1937 . . . . . . **TCLC 3, 9, 27, 53; DA;
SSC 6; WLC**
See also CA 104; 132; CDALB 1865-1917;
DLB 4, 9, 12, 78; MTCW

Wharton, James
See Mencken, H(enry) L(ouis)

Wharton, William (a pseudonym)
. . . . **CLC 18, 37**
See also CA 93-96; DLBY 80

Wheatley (Peters), Phillis
1754(?)-1784 . . . . **LC 3; BLC; DA; PC 3;
WLC**
See also CDALB 1640-1865; DLB 31, 50

Wheelock, John Hall 1886-1978 . . . . **CLC 14**
See also CA 13-16R; 77-80; CANR 14;
DLB 45

White, E(lwyn) B(rooks)
1899-1985 . . . . **CLC 10, 34, 39**
See also AITN 2; CA 13-16R; 116;
CANR 16, 37; CLR 1, 21; DLB 11, 22;
MAICYA; MTCW; SATA 2, 29;
SATA-Obit 44

White, Edmund (Valentine III)
1940- . . . . **CLC 27**
See also AAYA 7; CA 45-48; CANR 3, 19,
36; MTCW

White, Patrick (Victor Martindale)
1912-1990 . . **CLC 3, 4, 5, 7, 9, 18, 65, 69**
See also CA 81-84; 132; CANR 43; MTCW

White, Phyllis Dorothy James 1920-
See James, P. D.
See also CA 21-24R; CANR 17, 43; MTCW

White, T(erence) H(anbury)
1906-1964 . . . . **CLC 30**
See also CA 73-76; CANR 37; JRDA;
MAICYA; SATA 12

White, Terence de Vere
1912-1994 . . . . **CLC 49**
See also CA 49-52; 145; CANR 3

White, Walter F(rancis)
1893-1955 . . . . **TCLC 15**
See also White, Walter
See also BW 1; CA 115; 124; DLB 51

White, William Hale 1831-1913
See Rutherford, Mark
See also CA 121

Whitehead, E(dward) A(nthony)
1933- . . . . **CLC 5**
See also CA 65-68

Whitemore, Hugh (John) 1936- . . . . . **CLC 37**
See also CA 132

Whitman, Sarah Helen (Power)
1803-1878 . . . . **NCLC 19**
See also DLB 1

Whitman, Walt(er)
1819-1892 . . . . . **NCLC 4, 31; DA; PC 3;
WLC**
See also CDALB 1640-1865; DLB 3, 64;
SATA 20

Whitney, Phyllis A(yame) 1903- . . . . **CLC 42**
See also AITN 2; BEST 90:3; CA 1-4R;
CANR 3, 25, 38; JRDA; MAICYA;
SATA 1, 30

Whittemore, (Edward) Reed (Jr.)
1919- . . . . **CLC 4**
See also CA 9-12R; CAAS 8; CANR 4;
DLB 5

Whittier, John Greenleaf
1807-1892 . . . . **NCLC 8**
See also CDALB 1640-1865; DLB 1

Whittlebot, Hernia
See Coward, Noel (Peirce)

Wicker, Thomas Grey 1926-
See Wicker, Tom
See also CA 65-68; CANR 21, 46

Wicker, Tom . . . . **CLC 7**
See also Wicker, Thomas Grey

Wideman, John Edgar
1941- . . . . **CLC 5, 34, 36, 67; BLC**
See also BW 2; CA 85-88; CANR 14, 42;
DLB 33, 143

Wiebe, Rudy (Henry) 1934- . . . **CLC 6, 11, 14**
See also CA 37-40R; CANR 42; DLB 60

Wieland, Christoph Martin
1733-1813 . . . . **NCLC 17**
See also DLB 97

Wiene, Robert 1881-1938 . . . . **TCLC 56**

Wieners, John 1934- . . . . **CLC 7**
See also CA 13-16R; DLB 16

Wiesel, Elie(zer)
1928- . . . . **CLC 3, 5, 11, 37; DA**
See also AAYA 7; AITN 1; CA 5-8R;
CAAS 4; CANR 8, 40; DLB 83;
DLBY 87; MTCW; SATA 56

Wiggins, Marianne 1947- . . . . **CLC 57**
See also BEST 89:3; CA 130

Wight, James Alfred 1916-
See Herriot, James
See also CA 77-80; SATA 44, 55

Wilbur, Richard (Purdy)
1921- . . . . **CLC 3, 6, 9, 14, 53; DA**
See also CA 1-4R; CABS 2; CANR 2, 29;
DLB 5; MTCW; SATA 9

Wild, Peter 1940- . . . . **CLC 14**
See also CA 37-40R; DLB 5

Wilde, Oscar (Fingal O'Flahertie Wills)
1854(?)-1900 . . . . **TCLC 1, 8, 23, 41; DA;
SSC 11; WLC**
See also CA 104; 119; CDBLB 1890-1914;
DLB 10, 19, 34, 57, 141; SATA 24

Wilder, Billy . . . . **CLC 20**
See also Wilder, Samuel
See also DLB 26

Wilder, Samuel 1906-
See Wilder, Billy
See also CA 89-92

Wilder, Thornton (Niven)
1897-1975 . . . . . . **CLC 1, 5, 6, 10, 15, 35,
82; DA; DC 1; WLC**
See also AITN 2; CA 13-16R; 61-64;
CANR 40; DLB 4, 7, 9; MTCW

Wilding, Michael 1942- . . . . **CLC 73**
See also CA 104; CANR 24

Wiley, Richard 1944- . . . . **CLC 44**
See also CA 121; 129

Wilhelm, Kate . . . . **CLC 7**
See also Wilhelm, Katie Gertrude
See also CAAS 5; DLB 8

Wilhelm, Katie Gertrude 1928-
See Wilhelm, Kate
See also CA 37-40R; CANR 17, 36; MTCW

Wilkins, Mary
See Freeman, Mary Eleanor Wilkins

Willard, Nancy 1936- . . . . **CLC 7, 37**
See also CA 89-92; CANR 10, 39; CLR 5;
DLB 5, 52; MAICYA; MTCW;
SATA 30, 37, 71

Williams, C(harles) K(enneth)
1936- . . . . **CLC 33, 56**
See also CA 37-40R; DLB 5

Williams, Charles
See Collier, James L(incoln)

Williams, Charles (Walter Stansby)
1886-1945 . . . . **TCLC 1, 11**
See also CA 104; DLB 100

Williams, (George) Emlyn
1905-1987 . . . . **CLC 15**
See also CA 104; 123; CANR 36; DLB 10,
77; MTCW

Williams, Hugo 1942- . . . . **CLC 42**
See also CA 17-20R; CANR 45; DLB 40

Williams, J. Walker
See Wodehouse, P(elham) G(renville)

Williams, John A(lfred)
1925- . . . . **CLC 5, 13; BLC**
See also BW 2; CA 53-56; CAAS 3;
CANR 6, 26; DLB 2, 33

Williams, Jonathan (Chamberlain)
1929- . . . . **CLC 13**
See also CA 9-12R; CAAS 12; CANR 8;
DLB 5

Wright, Charles Stevenson
1932- .... **CLC 49; BLC 3**
See also BW 1; CA 9-12R; CANR 26;
DLB 33

Wright, Jack R.
See Harris, Mark

Wright, James (Arlington)
1927-1980 .... **CLC 3, 5, 10, 28**
See also AITN 2; CA 49-52; 97-100;
CANR 4, 34; DLB 5; MTCW

Wright, Judith (Arandell)
1915- .... **CLC 11, 53**
See also CA 13-16R; CANR 31; MTCW;
SATA 14

Wright, L(aurali) R.   1939-........ **CLC 44**
See also CA 138

Wright, Richard (Nathaniel)
1908-1960 .... **CLC 1, 3, 4, 9, 14, 21, 48,
74; BLC; DA; SSC 2; WLC**
See also AAYA 5; BW 1; CA 108;
CDALB 1929-1941; DLB 76, 102;
DLBD 2; MTCW

Wright, Richard B(ruce)   1937- ...... **CLC 6**
See also CA 85-88; DLB 53

Wright, Rick   1945-............... **CLC 35**

Wright, Rowland
See Wells, Carolyn

Wright, Stephen Caldwell   1946- .... **CLC 33**
See also BW 2

Wright, Willard Huntington   1888-1939
See Van Dine, S. S.
See also CA 115

Wright, William   1930-............ **CLC 44**
See also CA 53-56; CANR 7, 23

Wu Ch'eng-en   1500(?)-1582(?)....... **LC 7**

Wu Ching-tzu   1701-1754 .... **LC 2**

Wurlitzer, Rudolph   1938(?)- ... **CLC 2, 4, 15**
See also CA 85-88

Wycherley, William   1641-1715 .... **LC 8, 21**
See also CDBLB 1660-1789; DLB 80

Wylie, Elinor (Morton Hoyt)
1885-1928 .... **TCLC 8**
See also CA 105; DLB 9, 45

Wylie, Philip (Gordon)   1902-1971... **CLC 43**
See also CA 21-22; 33-36R; CAP 2; DLB 9

Wyndham, John................... **CLC 19**
See also Harris, John (Wyndham Parkes
Lucas) Beynon

Wyss, Johann David Von
1743-1818 .... **NCLC 10**
See also JRDA; MAICYA; SATA 27, 29

Yakumo Koizumi
See Hearn, (Patricio) Lafcadio (Tessima
Carlos)

Yanez, Jose Donoso
See Donoso (Yanez), Jose

Yanovsky, Basile S.
See Yanovsky, V(assily) S(emenovich)

Yanovsky, V(assily) S(emenovich)
1906-1989 .... **CLC 2, 18**
See also CA 97-100; 129

Yates, Richard   1926-1992 ..... **CLC 7, 8, 23**
See also CA 5-8R; 139; CANR 10, 43;
DLB 2; DLBY 81, 92

Yeats, W. B.
See Yeats, William Butler

Yeats, William Butler
1865-1939 ..... **TCLC 1, 11, 18, 31; DA;
WLC**
See also CA 104; 127; CANR 45;
CDBLB 1890-1914; DLB 10, 19, 98;
MTCW

Yehoshua, A(braham) B.
1936- .... **CLC 13, 31**
See also CA 33-36R; CANR 43

Yep, Laurence Michael   1948- ...... **CLC 35**
See also AAYA 5; CA 49-52; CANR 1, 46;
CLR 3, 17; DLB 52; JRDA; MAICYA;
SATA 7, 69

Yerby, Frank G(arvin)
1916-1991 .... **CLC 1, 7, 22; BLC**
See also BW 1; CA 9-12R; 136; CANR 16;
DLB 76; MTCW

Yesenin, Sergei Alexandrovich
See Esenin, Sergei (Alexandrovich)

Yevtushenko, Yevgeny (Alexandrovich)
1933- .... **CLC 1, 3, 13, 26, 51**
See also CA 81-84; CANR 33; MTCW

Yezierska, Anzia   1885(?)-1970 ..... **CLC 46**
See also CA 126; 89-92; DLB 28; MTCW

Yglesias, Helen   1915-........... **CLC 7, 22**
See also CA 37-40R; CAAS 20; CANR 15;
MTCW

Yokomitsu Riichi   1898-1947 ...... **TCLC 47**

Yonge, Charlotte (Mary)
1823-1901 .... **TCLC 48**
See also CA 109; DLB 18; SATA 17

York, Jeremy
See Creasey, John

York, Simon
See Heinlein, Robert A(nson)

Yorke, Henry Vincent   1905-1974 ... **CLC 13**
See also Green, Henry
See also CA 85-88; 49-52

Yosano Akiko   1878-1942........... **PC 11**

Yoshimoto, Banana............... **CLC 84**
See also Yoshimoto, Mahoko

Yoshimoto, Mahoko   1964-
See Yoshimoto, Banana
See also CA 144

Young, Al(bert James)
1939- .... **CLC 19; BLC**
See also BW 2; CA 29-32R; CANR 26;
DLB 33

Young, Andrew (John)   1885-1971.... **CLC 5**
See also CA 5-8R; CANR 7, 29

Young, Collier
See Bloch, Robert (Albert)

Young, Edward   1683-1765........... **LC 3**
See also DLB 95

Young, Marguerite   1909-.......... **CLC 82**
See also CA 13-16; CAP 1

Young, Neil   1945-................ **CLC 17**
See also CA 110

Yourcenar, Marguerite
1903-1987 .... **CLC 19, 38, 50**
See also CA 69-72; CANR 23; DLB 72;
DLBY 88; MTCW

Yurick, Sol   1925-................. **CLC 6**
See also CA 13-16R; CANR 25

Zabolotskii, Nikolai Alekseevich
1903-1958 .... **TCLC 52**
See also CA 116

Zamiatin, Yevgenii
See Zamyatin, Evgeny Ivanovich

Zamyatin, Evgeny Ivanovich
1884-1937 .... **TCLC 8, 37**
See also CA 105

Zangwill, Israel   1864-1926........ **TCLC 16**
See also CA 109; DLB 10, 135

Zappa, Francis Vincent, Jr.   1940-1993
See Zappa, Frank
See also CA 108; 143

Zappa, Frank..................... **CLC 17**
See also Zappa, Francis Vincent, Jr.

Zaturenska, Marya   1902-1982.... **CLC 6, 11**
See also CA 13-16R; 105; CANR 22

Zelazny, Roger (Joseph)   1937- ..... **CLC 21**
See also AAYA 7; CA 21-24R; CANR 26;
DLB 8; MTCW; SATA 39, 57

Zhdanov, Andrei A(lexandrovich)
1896-1948 .... **TCLC 18**
See also CA 117

Zhukovsky, Vasily   1783-1852 .... **NCLC 35**

Ziegenhagen, Eric .... **CLC 55**

Zimmer, Jill Schary
See Robinson, Jill

Zimmerman, Robert
See Dylan, Bob

Zindel, Paul   1936- ... **CLC 6, 26; DA; DC 5**
See also AAYA 2; CA 73-76; CANR 31;
CLR 3; DLB 7, 52; JRDA; MAICYA;
MTCW; SATA 16, 58

Zinov'Ev, A. A.
See Zinoviev, Alexander (Aleksandrovich)

Zinoviev, Alexander (Aleksandrovich)
1922- .... **CLC 19**
See also CA 116; 133; CAAS 10

Zoilus
See Lovecraft, H(oward) P(hillips)

Zola, Emile (Edouard Charles Antoine)
1840-1902 ...... **TCLC 1, 6, 21, 41; DA;
WLC**
See also CA 104; 138; DLB 123

Zoline, Pamela   1941-............. **CLC 62**

Zorrilla y Moral, Jose   1817-1893.. **NCLC 6**

Zoshchenko, Mikhail (Mikhailovich)
1895-1958 .... **TCLC 15; SSC 15**
See also CA 115

Zuckmayer, Carl   1896-1977........ **CLC 18**
See also CA 69-72; DLB 56, 124

Zuk, Georges
See Skelton, Robin

Zukofsky, Louis
1904-1978 .... **CLC 1, 2, 4, 7, 11, 18;
PC 11**
See also CA 9-12R; 77-80; CANR 39;
DLB 5; MTCW

Zweig, Paul   1935-1984........ **CLC 34, 42**
See also CA 85-88; 113

Zweig, Stefan   1881-1942 .... **TCLC 17**
See also CA 112; DLB 81, 118

DC Cumulative Nationality Index

DC Cumulative Title Index

See *Heracles*

Hercules furens (*Furens; Furious Hercules; Mad Hercules*) (Seneca) **5**:270, 273, 276-79, 289-90, 295, 313, 315, 318, 321, 325, 327, 330, 332-34

Hercules oetaeus (*Hercules on Oeta; Oetaeus*) (Seneca) **5**:273, 275-76, 286-87, 289-90, 295, 303, 315, 325, 334

Hercules on Oeta (Seneca)
See *Hercules oetaeus*

Hero (Menander) **3**:355, 361, 382

A Hero Ain't Nothin but a Sandwich (Childress) **4**:67

Herr Puntila and His Servant Matti (Brecht)
See *Herr Puntila und sein Knecht Matti*

Herr Puntila und sein Knecht Matti (*Herr Puntila and His Servant Matti; Puntila*) (Brecht) **3**:31, 46, 53, 59, 70, 78

"He's That Dead Can Do No Hurt" (Synge) **2**:400

La hija del aire (*Daughter of the Air*) (Calderon de la Barca) **3**:95, 102

The Hind and the Panther (Dryden) **3**:162, 176, 179, 214

Hippeis (*The Knights*) (Aristophanes) **2**:5, 7, 9, 16, 18, 21, 23, 27, 35-6, 45, 47, 59-65, 67

Hippolytus (Euripides) **4**:97-9, 101-4, 107-10, 118, 121-22, 144-5, 157

His Rival's Valet (Scribe)
See *Le Valet de son rival*

Holcades (*The Merchant Ships*) (Aristophanes) **2**:41

The Holy Ghostly (Shepard) **5**:356, 360

Homegoing from the Theatre (Gogol)
See *Teatral'nyi raz'ezd posle predstavleniia novoi komedii*

L'homme révolté (*The Rebel*) (Camus) **2**:92, 94, 96, 100

The Honest Whore (Middleton) **5**:103

The Hospital at the Time of the Revolution (Churchill) **5**:34

The House of Bernarda Alba (Garcia Lorca)
See *La casa de Bernarda Alba*

A House with Two Doors Is Difficult to Guard (Calderon de la Barca)
See *Casa con dos puertas, mala es de guardar*

Les Huguenots (Scribe) **5**:246, 255

Huis clos (*No Exit*) (Sartre) **3**:434-37, 439-41, 445, 448-49, 452-64

Hymenaei (Jonson) **4**:249

Icarus's Mother (Shepard) **5**:344, 348, 353, 355, 360-61, 364-66

Ichneutai (*The Trackers*) (Sophocles) **1**:427

"Idanre" (Soyinka) **2**:365, 367

Les idées de Madame Aubray (Dumas) **1**:104, 107, 109, 113-17

Identical Twins (Churchill) **5**:7

If Five Years Pass (Garcia Lorca)
See *Así que pasen cinco años*

Igroki (*The Gamblers*) (Gogol) **1**:152, 156

"Ikeja, Friday, Four O'Clock" (Soyinka) **2**:366

I Love My Mother (Zindel) **5**:415

L'imaginaire: Psychologie phénoénologique de l'imagination (Sartre) **3**:437

L'imagination (*Imagination: A Psychological Critique*) (Sartre) **3**:437

Imagination: A Psychological Critique (Sartre)
See *L'imagination*

The Imbrians (Menander)
See *Gone to Imbros*

Im dickicht der städte (*In the Jungle of Cities; In the Swamp*) (Brecht) **3**:15-16, 18, 34, 60

Incident at Vichy (Miller) **1**:303

"In Defense of Equality of Men" (Hansberry) **2**:248

Les Independants (*The Independent Ones*) (Scribe) **5**:250

The Independent Ones (Scribe)
See *Les Independants*

The Indian Emperour; or, The Conquest of Mexico by the Spaniards, Being the Sequel of the Indian Queen (Dryden) **3**:182, 187-88, 192, 213

The Indian Queen (Dryden) **3**:160-61, 179, 181-82, 187-88, 192

I Never Loved Your Mind (Zindel) **5**:407

In Mourning for Himself (Menander) **3**:346

In One Act (Kennedy) **5**:92

The Insect Comedy (Capek)
See *Ze života hmyzu*

Insect Life (Capek)
See *Ze života hmyzu*

The Insect Play (Capek)
See *Ze života hmyzu*

Insects (Capek)
See *Ze života hmyzu*

Insect Story (Capek)
See *Ze života hmyzu*

The Inside of His Head (Miller)
See *Death of a Salesman*

"The Inspector General" (Gogol)
See *Révizor*

Inspired (Menander) **3**:346

The Interpreters (Soyinka) **2**:364-66, 378

In the Frame of Don Cristóbal (Garcia Lorca)
See *Retablillo de Don Cristóbal*

In the Jungle of Cities (Brecht)
See *Im dickicht der städte*

In the Shadow of the Glen (*The Shadow of the Glen*) (Synge) **2**:387-88, 392-93, 395, 400, 408, 415

In the Swamp (Brecht)
See *Im dickicht der städte*

"Intimacy" (Sartre) **3**:437

The Invention (Soyinka) **2**:366

The Invisible Brothers (Scribe)
See *Les frères invisibles*

In Wicklow, West Kerry and Connemara (Synge) **2**:415

Ion (Euripides) **4**:99, 102, 108, 113, 118, 121, 123

Iphigenia among the Tauri (Euripides)
See *Iphigenia at Tauris*

Iphigenia at Aulis (Euripides) **4**:97, 101-2, 111-2, 152

Iphigenia at Tauris (*Iphigenia among the Tauri*) (Euripides) **4**:102, 108, 118, 121, 124

The Island (Fugard) **3**:226-27, 234, 238, 246-49, 251-56

Isn't It Romantic (Wasserstein) **4**:346-50, 357-58, 360-61, 363-64

It Is So, if You Think So (Pirandello)
See *Così è (se vi pare)*

"I Useta Live in the World (But Then I Moved to Harlem)" (Shange) **3**:481

Japhet (Scribe) **5**:251, 253

Jealousy, the Greatest Monster of the World (Calderon de la Barca)
See *El mayor monstruo del mundo*

Jean Bête à la foire (Beaumarchais) **4**:6

Jedermann (*Everyman; Play of the Death of the Rich Man; Spiel vom Sterben des reichen Mannes*) (Hofmannsthal) **4**:165, 167, 170-2, 177, 179, 185-6

Jericho-Jim Crow (Hughes) **3**:275

The Jewess (Scribe)
See *La Juive*

The Jew of Malta (Marlowe)
See *The Famous Tragedy of the Rich Jew of Malta*

Jitney (Wilson) **2**:475

Joe Turner's Come and Gone (Wilson) **2**:473-76, 486-89

John Gabriel Borkman (Ibsen) **2**:276, 280-81, 284, 286, 299

Josephs Legende (Hofmannsthal) **4**:193

Joy to My Soul (Hughes) **3**:275

La Juive (*The Jewess*) (Scribe) **5**:255-56

Just a Little Simple (Childress) **4**:76

The Just Assassins (Camus)
See *Les justes*

Les justes (*The Assassins; The Just Assassins*) (Camus) **2**:78, 82-5, 92

Kantan (Mishima) **1**:354, 361, 363

"Kataku" (Mishima) **1**:353

Der kaukasische Kreidekreis (*The Caucasian Chalk Circle*) (Brecht) **3**:11-12, 19, 23, 26-7, 31, 35, 37, 43-44, 58-9, 75-8, 80-4

Kean (Sartre) **3**:445

Kedeia (Menander)
See *Samia*

Kejser og Galilaeer (*Emperor and Galilean*) (Ibsen) **2**:278, 289, 291, 329, 331

Killer's Head (Shepard) **5**:360, 372

Kindai nōgakushū (*Five Modern Nō Plays*) (Mishima) **1**:354, 358-72

The Kind Keeper; or, Mr. Limberham (*Mr. Limberham*) (Dryden) **3**:154, 166-71, 176, 188

Kingdom of Earth: The Seven Descents of Myrtle (*The Seven Descents of Myrtle*) (Williams) **4**:375-76

King Oedipus (Sophocles)
See *Oedipous Tyrannos*

Kjaerlighedens komedie (*Love's Comedy*) (Ibsen) **2**:284, 299, 319-20

Kleines Organon für das Theatre (*A Little Organum for the Theater; Small Organon*) (Brecht) **3**:20, 23, 28, 42, 46, 51, 65, 81

Das kleine Welttheater (*The Little Theater of the World*) (Hofmannsthal) **4**:172, 188

The Knights (Aristophanes)
See *Hippeis*

"Knowing the Human Condition" (Childress) **4**:75

Kolax (*The Flatterer*) (Menander) **3**:346

Kongi's Harvest (Soyinka) **2**:365-67

Kongs emnerne (*The Pretenders*) (Ibsen) **2**:289, 291, 329

Ladies at the Alamo (Zindel) **5**:407, 425

The Ladies' Battle; or, A Duel of Love (Scribe)
See *Bataille de dames; ou, Un duel en amour*

Ladies Lunching Together (Menander)
See *Synaristosai*

The Ladies Should Be in Bed (Zindel) **5**:406

The Lady Aoi (Mishima)
See *Aoi no ue*

The Lady from the Sea (Ibsen)
See *Fruen fra havet*

The Lady of Larkspur Lotion (Williams) **4**:371, 391

The Lady of the Camelias (Dumas)

Title Index

Title Index

Title Index